MOVIE STAR
CHRONICLES
A Visual History of the
World's Greatest Movie Stars

Ian Haydn Smith
Foreword by **David Gordon Green**

FIREFLY BOOKS

A FIREFLY BOOK

Published by Firefly Books Ltd. 2015

First printing

Publisher Cataloging-in-Publication Data (U.S.)

Smith, Ian Haydn, author
    Movie star chronicles : a visual history of the world's greatest 320 movie stars / Ian Haydn Smith. —First edition.
Includes index.
ISBN 978-1-77085-530-4 (pbk.)
1. Motion picture actors and actresses. t 2. Motion picture actors and actresses—Biography. I. Title.
PN1998.2.S65 2015 791.43092'2   C2015-900496-9

Library and Archives Canada Cataloguing in Publication

Smith, Ian Haydn.
Movie star chronicles : a visual history of the world's greatest 320 movie stars / Ian Haydn Smith.
[576] pages : color illustrations, photographs (some color) ; cm.
Includes index.
Summary: "This in-depth guide to 320 of the world's greatest stars, from the silent era to the blockbusters of today contains entries featuring an insightful critique of a star's career, supported by infographic timelines and stunning photographs. Twenty feature articles focus on popular trends in cinema, from western heroes to femme fatales and movie clowns."— from publisher.
ISBN-13: 978-1-77085-530-4 (pbk.)
1. I. Title.
791.43092/2 dc23   PN1998.2S5484 2015

Published in the United States by
Firefly Books (U.S.) Inc.
P.O. Box 1338, Ellicott Station
Buffalo, New York 14205

Published in Canada by
Firefly Books Ltd.
50 Staples Avenue, Unit1
Richmond Hill, Ontario L4B 0A7

Color reproduction by Portland Media Print Services Ltd.

Printed in China by Midas Printing International Ltd

This book was designed and produced by Quintessence Editions Ltd.
The Old Brewery
6 Blundell Street
London N7 9BH

Senior Editor: Elspeth Beidas
Designers: Isabel Eeles, Adam Hutchinson,
   Tom Howey, Dean Martin,
   Thomas Keenes
Editors: Fiona Plowman, Rebecca Gee
Editorial Assistants: Hannah Phillips,
   Ouassila Mebarek
Production Manager: Anna Pauletti
Editorial Director: Ruth Patrick
Publisher: Philip Cooper

MOVIE STAR
CHRONICLES

contents

foreword by david gordon green

In the world of movies, there is the inspiration of the screenplay, the atmosphere created by locations and the emotional navigation provided by music. But the definitive joy and defining moment of each cinematic journey is experiencing a story through actors' performances. The lives they've lived, the training they've had and the look in their eyes at any particular moment all play a part in what is captured by a camera, translated by editors and, finally, interpreted by an audience. From award-winning thespians to street performers, from child stars and rising talents to icons of yesteryear, audiences indulge in the pleasure of their performances, in which they employ the backdrop of the film like a canvas and utilize the collaborations with the film crew and their relationship to the camera in bringing these worlds to life. They take words on a page and inject them with pathos, tension, absurdity and wit. Sometimes they toss aside the script and from within — their guts and conviction — they inspire us with their improvisation.

My first experience as a film director was working with a cast of non-professional actors. They were mostly kids from a small town, without training or any defined process. I was relatively inexperienced myself in communicating with the cast and crew. I think that through this lack of proficiency and vocabulary I leaned on the personality and temperament of the performers as opposed to staying faithful to any script and stipulating they memorize every line. I remained open to their intuition and instincts, and let their characters evolve in the moment. These early exercises have remained with me as the foundation of my philosophy in working with actors. As the ambition of my projects has grown and the access to traditional and extremely capable actors has expanded, it's always the skill — the intuition and instinct — of those in front of the camera that feeds my interest the most and services the exploration of a character. The entire filmmaking process is an experiment and as a director at some point you have to sit back and acknowledge the importance of discovery in a performance and allow it to exist. Filmmakers often bring with them ideas and preconceptions, hoping there is some degree of control, but there is no creation of performance without compromise on our part. Sometimes we sit down formally with actors to rehearse and refine, in order to reach the very core — the DNA — of a character. Other times we let loose, roll film and freestyle our way through it. At the end of the day, it's the voice and gestures that result from these adventures that become the signature of our projects.

In today's culture, it's easy to glance at the headlines, with all the gossip and tabloid sensation, and become overwhelmed with the celebrity of stars who, at any given time, are the center of attention and in the public eye. I have watched from a close distance as fans try to capture a moment on their cameras or get an autograph from a movie star.

We want them to be a part of our lives. The characters they inhabit in films are a part of our lives and for some there is a desire to document any encounter with the person playing this or that character. It can be an odd experience, often funny, at the point where fact meets fiction. A movie hero that appears so tall on film is short in person. An on-screen villain is an off-screen gentleman. A comic mastermind is a lonely introvert with a different way of processing darkness. We presume to know who they are by the characters they've played — it's so easy fall for that mistake. It can sometimes be a beautiful disguise. These misconceptions also illustrate the enormous contribution of lighting, camera position and film editing as elements in this process. They are the technical resources that help create the mystique of the movie star.

Some actors are geniuses. Some actors are assholes. Some are gypsies while others are ghosts, pioneers or provocateurs. Some are dignified entertainers and others are irresponsible artists. The psychology is a complicated one. They are willing to stand trial in the critical eyes of movie-going audiences and a voracious media. To compound matters, we're living in an age where commercial success is frequently confused with credibility. A great actor may deserve to be a star but isn't — or might not want to be —and some stars are not great actors.

For me, being on a movie set is the most incredible feeling in the world. Designing an environment where actors have a place to expose themselves. Film sets are sacred temples, mindless toy stores and violent battlefields. They are infinite avenues of possibility based on the chemistry of those brave souls in front of the camera. Movies give us a method to capture these performances and replay them to share with others; time capsules of life and looks, words and wonder. Movie stars are the vessels through which our modern mythology is created. They embody who we are as a culture within this art form and this industry.

This volume offers an overview of stars past and present, reviewing what made them great and exploring audiences' continuing fascination with them. The nature of stardom shifts over time and with each generation. Today's leading man, femme fatale or comic is likely to change tomorrow, but as this volume makes clear, stars are here to stay.

introduction by ian haydn smith

What makes a star? Reality TV has been grasping at this question for years, offering up shows whose aim is to seek out and develop a new pop culture icon before our very eyes. If the *Got Talent* franchise aimed at identifying individuals or groups with the raw material to be forged into something unique, *The X Factor*, by its very name, suggested that even with talent, there has to be an extra ingredient that makes someone stand out from the crowd. Most winners from these series eventually fade back into the anonymity of everyday life after basking in the glow of fame — longer than Andy Warhol's 15 minutes, but hardly a career — highlighting that stardom can be a fickle beast.

To make a distinction, acting is a vocation, a career choice in which one's own life experiences, as well as empathy for the suffering, joy, pain, triumph and anguish of others, is brought to bear in the creation of a wholly — or mostly — fictitious being. Stardom is conferred on few, but not all, actors. And in its various forms, it is not always welcome. Stardom also stands in stark contrast to celebrity, which is a byproduct of fame, the bastion of the talentless or for some what remains when a star has waned.

There is a quality to an actor that makes them a star — an aura that surrounds them or something about their presence that makes it impossible for us to look away from them. (And not just on film. I was once in a second-hand bookshop on London's Charing Cross Road when Peter O'Toole walked in. Before seeing him, there was a sense that the atmosphere in the shop had changed. He wanted to know whether a copy of *Loitering with Intent* was in stock. The assistant, mystified as to why the actor was enquiring about the availability of the first volume of his own memoir, replied that there were no copies. O'Toole responded, with a wry smile, "Good. People should have to pay full price for it and not read someone else's bloody copy," and promptly walked out. The mood in the shop returned to one of subdued normality.)

Stars have always dominated cinema, too often at the expense of the many creative roles in a vastly populated industry. In the years before sound, people might not have known who D.W. Griffith, Abel Gance, Victor Sjöström, King Vidor or Giovanni Pastrone — some of the greatest directors of their day — were, but Charles Chaplin, Greta Garbo, Ruan Lingyu, Douglas Fairbanks, Mary Pickford and their peers were household names. Some change came with the rise of film criticism and the increased focus on the director as auteur. However, in the last 25 years, with agents increasing their power and the salary of the people they represent, the star once again burns brightly. And not just in Hollywood. Bollywood in India and Nollywood in Nigeria, as well as other national cinemas around the world, are dominated by stars. They not only play a significant role in our enjoyment of and emotional engagement with a film, but are also a key presence in the marketing campaign, whether it's their face appearing on huge billboards or appearances on chat shows around the globe. They are surrounded by an army of employees, from press and marketing through to managers, assistants, lawyers and those responsible for making them look good. Audiences' appetite for stars, or what the image of the star represents — from an idealized life through to the characters they play — is as voracious as it ever was.

Some stars bask in such fame. Tom Cruise has taken the responsibility of his stardom to an impressive professional level, always on hand at premieres to spend a few hours with the audiences who have queued up to see him. Others have a more truculent relationship with the fame that has accompanied their success as an actor. In Albert and David Maysles' 1966 documentary short *Meet Marlon Brando*, the star, who was meant to be promoting his new film *Morituri* (1965), eschews the conventions of the press junket, preferring instead to explore the nature of the unspoken agreement between studios and the media in promoting a film, as well as questioning his interviewers more than they are able to him. And yet, what shines through is the sheer magnetism of Brando — that thing that makes him so compelling a presence on the screen. As David Gordon Green points out in his preface to this book, not all great actors possess this quality, and no doubt some bad actors do. But a great star, one whose best work outlasts their lifetime, both personally and on the screen, is the one who has achieved the perfect symbiosis of talent and charisma.

Movie Star Chronicles is not an exhaustive encyclopedia of every star that has graced the screen. There have been too many to include in one volume. Instead, the book is a tapestry of stars past and present, whose profiles detail each actor's ascendancy, high points and career misfires, building into a wider portrait of those elements that help make a star. It highlights the vast spectrum of what constitutes a star, from the silent matinee idol to the turbulent youth, the charmer or femme fatale to the action hero or solitary outsider. And within these archetypes we see that extra element, unique to each individual but loved by their fans, that makes them so original — a major presence on the screen. An icon. A star.

how to use this book

color-coded character types

birth and death dates

acting awards won

name of star

key movies

key to the color-coding of movie genres

black award symbols denote acting awards won

award category

grey award symbols denote acting award nominations

color denotes movie genre

name of the movie's director

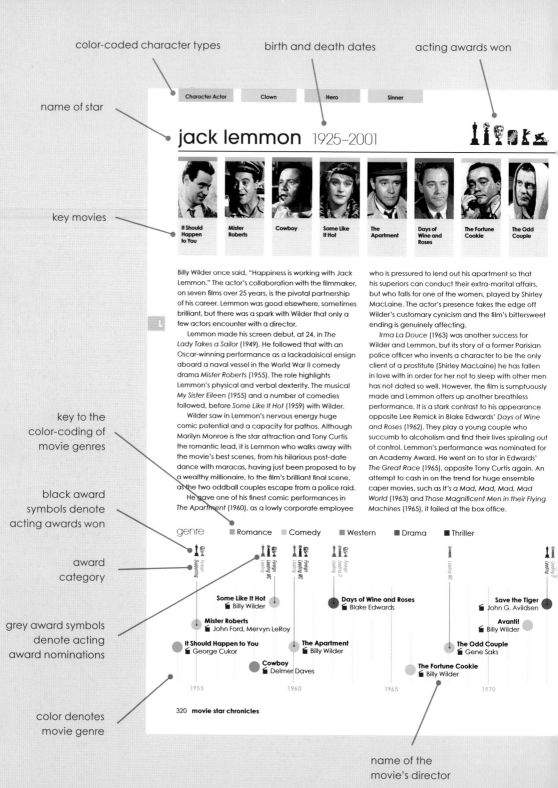

Character Actor   Clown   Hero   Sinner

jack lemmon 1925–2001

It Should Happen to You | Mister Roberts | Cowboy | Some Like It Hot | The Apartment | Days of Wine and Roses | The Fortune Cookie | The Odd Couple

Billy Wilder once said, "Happiness is working with Jack Lemmon." The actor's collaboration with the filmmaker, on seven films over 25 years, is the pivotal partnership of his career. Lemmon was good elsewhere, sometimes brilliant, but there was a spark with Wilder that only a few actors encounter with a director.

Lemmon made his screen debut, at 24, in *The Lady Takes a Sailor* (1949). He followed that with an Oscar-winning performance as a lackadaisical ensign aboard a naval vessel in the World War II comedy drama *Mister Roberts* (1955). The role highlights Lemmon's physical and verbal dexterity. The musical *My Sister Eileen* (1955) and a number of comedies followed, before *Some Like It Hot* (1959) with Wilder.

Wilder saw in Lemmon's nervous energy huge comic potential and a capacity for pathos. Although Marilyn Monroe is the star attraction and Tony Curtis the romantic lead, it is Lemmon who walks away with the movie's best scenes, from his hilarious post-date dance with maracas, having just been proposed to by a wealthy millionaire, to the film's brilliant final scene, as the two oddball couples escape from a police raid.

He gave one of his finest comic performances in *The Apartment* (1960), as a lowly corporate employee who is pressured to lend out his apartment so that his superiors can conduct their extra-marital affairs, but who falls for one of the women, played by Shirley MacLaine. The actor's presence takes the edge off Wilder's customary cynicism and the film's bittersweet ending is genuinely affecting.

Irma La Douce (1963) was another success for Wilder and Lemmon, but its story of a former Parisian police officer who invents a character to be the only client of a prostitute (Shirley MacLaine) he has fallen in love with in order for her not to sleep with other men has not dated so well. However, the film is sumptuously made and Lemmon offers up another breathless performance. It is a stark contrast to his appearance opposite Lee Remick in Blake Edwards' *Days of Wine and Roses* (1962). They play a young couple who succumb to alcoholism and find their lives spiraling out of control. Lemmon's performance was nominated for an Academy Award. He went on to star in Edwards' *The Great Race* (1965), opposite Tony Curtis again. An attempt to cash in on the trend for huge ensemble caper movies, such as *It's a Mad, Mad, Mad, Mad World* (1963) and *Those Magnificent Men in their Flying Machines* (1965), it failed at the box office.

genre   ■ Romance   ☐ Comedy   ■ Western   ■ Drama   ■ Thriller

Foreign / Supporting

Some Like It Hot
Billy Wilder

Mister Roberts
John Ford, Mervyn LeRoy

It Should Happen to You
George Cukor

Cowboy
Delmer Daves

Foreign / Leading MC / Leading

Foreign / Leading MC

Foreign / Leading D

Days of Wine and Roses
Blake Edwards

The Apartment
Billy Wilder

Leading MC

The Fortune Cookie
Billy Wilder

Leading D

Save the Tiger
John G. Avildsen

Avanti!
Billy Wilder

The Odd Couple
Gene Saks

1955   1960   1965   1970

320   **movie star chronicles**

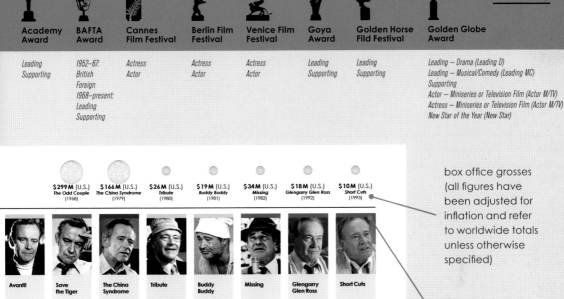

Academy Award	BAFTA Award	Cannes Film Festival	Berlin Film Festival	Venice Film Festival	Goya Award	Golden Horse Fild Festival	Golden Globe Award
Leading Supporting	1952–67: British Foreign 1968–present: Leading Supporting	Actress Actor	Actress Actor	Actress Actor	Leading Supporting	Leading Supporting	Leading – Drama (Leading D) Leading – Musical/Comedy (Leading MC) Supporting Actor – Miniseries or Television Film (Actor M/TV) Actress – Miniseries or Television Film (Actor M/TV) New Star of the Year (New Star)

box office grosses (all figures have been adjusted for inflation and refer to worldwide totals unless otherwise specified)

color denotes movie genre

Wilder's cynical view of the world is more present in *The Fortune Cookie* (1966), whose account of a sports cameraman's attempts to dupe his insurance company out of a huge indemnity has lost none of its satirical bite. Lemmon is hilarious as the injured man, while Walter Matthau is his straight-faced attorney, "Whiplash Willie" Gingrich. It was the first pairing of the two actors. Their most famous role together is as the bickering roommates in Neil Simon's *The Odd Couple* (1968). Lemmon would direct Matthau in the comedy drama *Kotch* (1971) and the pair would remain a fixture on the screen into the 1990s with the amiable *Grumpy Old Men* (1993) and its 1995 sequel. For Wilder, they starred opposite each other in *The Front Page* (1974), a fast-paced adaptation of Ben Hecht and Charles MacArthur's 1928 play. If it lacks the brilliance of *His Girl Friday* (1940), Lemmon and Matthau remain galvanizing as two journalists racing against time to help prevent an innocent man being executed. The pair also starred in Wilder's last film, *Buddy Buddy* (1981). It is hardly the director's best work, but Lemmon is paranoia personified as a man contemplating suicide after his wife has left him, only to become an accomplice to Matthau's assassin.

Lemmon also starred in Wilder's *Avanti!* (1972), as a businessman who travels to Italy to collect his deceased father's body. There, he discovers his father had been having an affair for years and embarks on a relationship with the dead lover's daughter. One of Wilder's gentlest films, Lemmon is a much calmer presence. It is a marked contrast to his Oscar-winning turn in *Save the Tiger* (1973), as an executive who finds himself heading toward a breakdown. A powerful performance, it presaged the more serious roles that would dominate his later years.

He is brilliant in *The China Syndrome* (1979), as an engineer at a nuclear power plant who locks himself in the control room to raise awareness of the dangers of this relatively new fuel. He won the Best Actor prize at Cannes for his performance in *Missing* (1982), playing a father searching for his son following the Chilean coup in 1973. He exudes desperation as a salesman in *Glengarry Glen Ross* (1992) and in his brief, single-scene appearance in *Short Cuts* (1993), he plays a man who tries and fails to make peace with his estranged son. The nervous energy remains, but it is imbued with incalculable sadness at the mistakes we make in life and our inability to undo them. **IHS**

contributor's initials

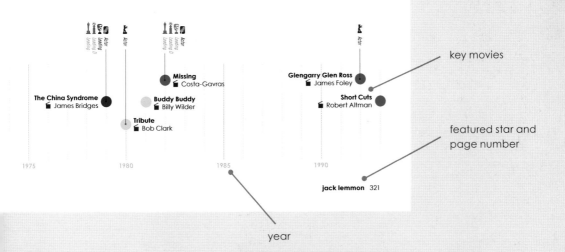

key movies

featured star and page number

year

subject of feature article

color denotes star/
character/movie
type

key stars

key to color
coding of star/
character/movie
types

year

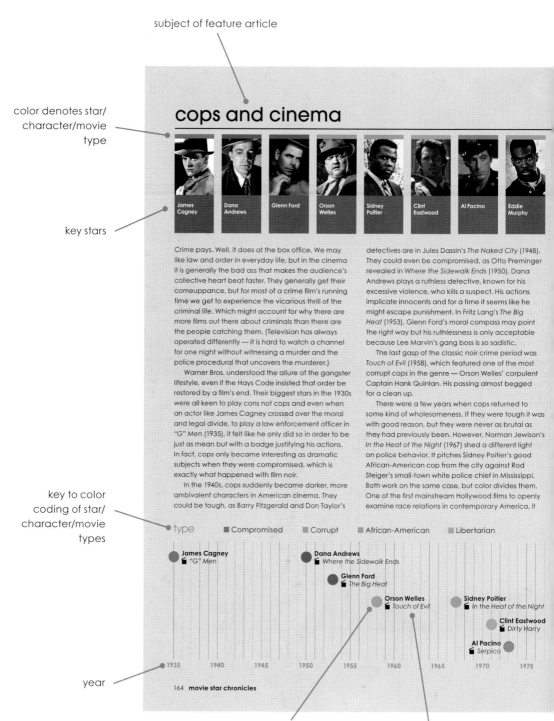

cops and cinema

James Cagney | Dana Andrews | Glenn Ford | Orson Welles | Sidney Poitier | Clint Eastwood | Al Pacino | Eddie Murphy

Crime pays. Well, it does at the box office. We may like law and order in everyday life, but in the cinema it is generally the bad ass that makes the audience's collective heart beat faster. They generally get their comeuppance, but for most of a crime film's running time we get to experience the vicarious thrill of the criminal life. Which might account for why there are more films out there about criminals than there are the people catching them. (Television has always operated differently — it is hard to watch a channel for one night without witnessing a murder and the police procedural that uncovers the murderer.)

Warner Bros. understood the allure of the gangster lifestyle, even if the Hays Code insisted that order be restored by a film's end. Their biggest stars in the 1930s were all keen to play cons not cops and even when an actor like James Cagney crossed over the moral and legal divide, to play a law enforcement officer in "G" Men (1935), it felt like he only did so in order to be just as mean but with a badge justifying his actions. In fact, cops only became interesting as dramatic subjects when they were compromised, which is exactly what happened with film noir.

In the 1940s, cops suddenly became darker, more ambivalent characters in American cinema. They could be tough, as Barry Fitzgerald and Don Taylor's

detectives are in Jules Dassin's The Naked City (1948). They could even be compromised, as Otto Preminger revealed in Where the Sidewalk Ends (1950). Dana Andrews plays a ruthless detective, known for his excessive violence, who kills a suspect. His actions implicate innocents and for a time it seems like he might escape punishment. In Fritz Lang's The Big Heat (1953), Glenn Ford's moral compass may point the right way but his ruthlessness is only acceptable because Lee Marvin's gang boss is so sadistic.

The last gasp of the classic noir crime period was Touch of Evil (1958), which featured one of the most corrupt cops in the genre — Orson Welles' corpulent Captain Hank Quinlan. His passing almost begged for a clean up.

There were a few years when cops returned to some kind of wholesomeness. If they were tough it was with good reason, but they were never as brutal as they had previously been. However, Norman Jewison's In the Heat of the Night (1967) shed a different light on police behavior. It pitches Sidney Poitier's good African-American cop from the city against Rod Steiger's small-town white police chief in Mississippi. Both work on the same case, but color divides them. One of the first mainstream Hollywood films to openly examine race relations in contemporary America, it

type ■ Compromised ■ Corrupt ■ African-American ■ Libertarian

James Cagney
🎞 "G" Men

Dana Andrews
🎞 Where the Sidewalk Ends

Glenn Ford
🎞 The Big Heat

Orson Welles
🎞 Touch of Evil

Sidney Poitier
🎞 In the Heat of the Night

Clint Eastwood
🎞 Dirty Harry

Al Pacino
🎞 Serpico

1935 1940 1945 1950 1955 1960 1965 1970 1975

color denotes
movie genre

name of the movie in
which the star appears

| Jamie Lee Curtis | Harvey Keitel | Morgan Freeman | Frances McDormand | Denzel Washington | Ray Liotta | Tommy Lee Jones | Samuel L. Jackson |

hinted at the complexity of the police representations that were to come in the 1970s.

If Clint Eastwood's iconic *Dirty Harry* (1971) offers up a portrait of a libertarian cop — one who believes in the innate nature of justice but eschews the limitations of the law in favor of his own moral code — then Al Pacino's *Serpico* (1973) gives us an unconventional cop who believes in rules but whose colleagues are all corrupt. Its director, Sidney Lumet, has done more than most filmmakers to explore the myriad aspects of police life.

If Sidney Poitier appeared to open the doors for African-Americans to play significant roles in films, cops were still mostly played by white actors in the 1970s — at least when it came to the main roles. Blaxploitation films featured the odd black cop, such as Yaphet Kotto in *Across 110th Street* (1972), but it was not until Eddie Murphy played Axel Foley in *Beverly Hills Cop* (1984) that a mainstream Hollywood film featured such a significant role for a black actor as a cop. A few years later, Danny Glover would share the screen with Mel Gibson in *Lethal Weapon* (1987), but in both cases the roles are comedic. Serious black cops are less common. There is Denzel Washington turning bad in some style for Antoine Fuqua's hard-hitting *Training Day* (2001) and Samuel L. Jackson's 20-year

veteran in Neil LaBute's incendiary *Lakeview Terrace* (2008) offering up a more complex representation. However, these are exceptions.

Women in cop films have also had to bear the brunt of supporting roles, although Kathryn Bigelow's *Blue Steel* (1989), starring Jamie Lee Curtis as a recent graduate pursued by Ron Silver's psychopath, was a welcome change to the norm. Also, Frances McDormand's Marge Gunderson in the Coen brothers' *Fargo* (1996) provided unquestionably one of the most memorable cops of the last two decades.

The corrupt cop still lingers, nonetheless. Washington's Alonzo Harris in *Training Day* takes some beating, while Ray Liotta is terrifying in *Narc* (2002). However, none come close to the levels of depravity demonstrated by Harvey Keitel's character in Abel Ferrara's brutal *Bad Lieutenant* (1992). The film is an assault on the senses as we witness the character's descent into hell, from which there is no redemption. Thankfully, we have the nobility of Morgan Freeman's Somerset in David Fincher's *Se7en* (1995) and Tommy Lee Jones' irascible but upstanding Sheriff Ed Tom Bell in *No Country for Old Men* (2007). Without them there would be law with no order. **IHS**

contributor's initials

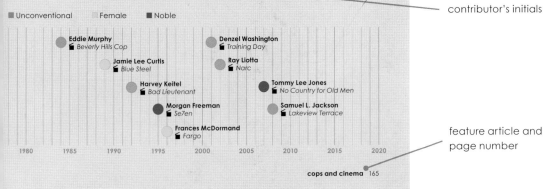

■ Unconventional ■ Female ■ Noble

Eddie Murphy
Beverly Hills Cop

Jamie Lee Curtis
Blue Steel

Harvey Keitel
Bad Lieutenant

Morgan Freeman
Se7en

Frances McDormand
Fargo

Denzel Washington
Training Day

Ray Liotta
Narc

Tommy Lee Jones
No Country for Old Men

Samuel L. Jackson
Lakeview Terrace

1980   1985   1990   1995   2000   2005   2010   2015   2020

feature article and page number

cops and cinema 165

A

amy adams 1974

Catch Me If You Can

Junebug

Enchanted

Doubt

The Fighter

The Master

American Hustle

Big Eyes

One of Hollywood's most versatile actors, Amy Adams made her screen debut in *Drop Dead Gorgeous* (1999). She followed this with occasional appearances in long-running television shows such as *Buffy the Vampire Slayer* (2000) and *The West Wing* (2002), as well as providing a number of voices for *King of the Hill* (2004). She seemed on the verge of a breakthrough as Leonardo DiCaprio's girlfriend in Steven Spielberg's *Catch Me If You Can* (2002), but it was not until *Junebug* (2005) that she gave the sense of having truly arrived. The role of Ashley, an unworldly and pregnant young wife, tapped into the wholesome and down-to-earth qualities that appear genuine and integral to Adams' persona. She attracted rave reviews for her portrayal of this beguilingly complex character, winning the Special Jury Prize at Sundance and receiving the first of her Academy Award nominations, for Best Supporting Actress.

Adams returned to television with a role in *The Office* (2005–06), before appearing in *Talladega Nights* (2006) with Will Ferrell. *Enchanted* (2007) found Adams drawing on her musical theater background and embracing the challenge of a Disney live action/animated adventure.

A supporting role in *Charlie Wilson's War* (2007) paired her with Philip Seymour Hoffman. *Doubt* (2008) saw her conflicted as a young nun caught between Hoffman's priest and Meryl Streep's bitter principal. In *The Fighter* (2010), her Boston-Irish barmaid was just as tough as Mark Wahlberg and the quiet center of David O. Russell's voluble film. She took a supporting role in *On the Road* (2012) and was arguably the most fascinating but least explored character in *The Master* (2012), playing opposite Hoffman for a final time. There, as in all her best work, Adams' complexity clouds an outer disposition that is sunny and bright.

In 2013 she reunited with David O. Russell on the 1970s-set crime caper *American Hustle*. Adams held her own opposite a strong cast, winning a Golden Globe and gaining another Oscar nomination. That same year, she offered up a subtle performance as Joaquin Phoenix's neighbor in *Her* and brought brassiness and intelligence to the role of Lois Lane in *Man of Steel*. Transparent in the best sense of the word, Adams' vulnerability is perhaps her greatest strength, nowhere more evident than in her portrayal of Margaret Keane in Tim Burton's *Big Eyes* (2014), for which she won a second Golden Globe. **MM**

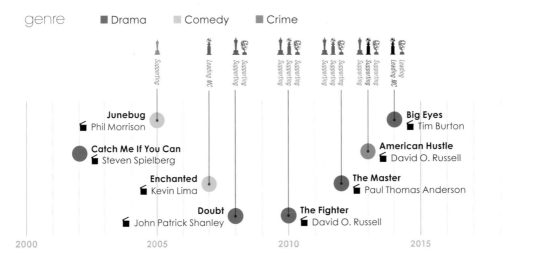

genre   ■ Drama   ■ Comedy   ■ Crime

Junebug
Phil Morrison

Catch Me If You Can
Steven Spielberg

Enchanted
Kevin Lima

Doubt
John Patrick Shanley

The Fighter
David O. Russell

The Master
Paul Thomas Anderson

American Hustle
David O. Russell

Big Eyes
Tim Burton

2000   2005   2010   2015   2020

isabelle adjani 1955

| The Story of Adèle H. | The Driver | Nosferatu the Vampyre | Possession | One Deadly Summer | Camille Claudel | La Reine Margot | Skirt Day |

Born near Paris in 1955, Isabelle Adjani has been a major presence in European cinema since her debut in *Le Petit Bougnat* (1970). Highly regarded in France, she holds the record for the most César Awards.

Adjani's first significant role was for François Truffaut in *The Story of Adèle H.* (1975), in which she starred as Adèle Hugo, a woman with a consuming but unrequited love for a dashing lieutenant. An Academy Award nomination for Best Actress was just reward for a mature and composed performance. In 1978 she answered a call from the United States to star alongside Ryan O'Neal and Bruce Dern in Walter Hill's *The Driver*. Influenced by the pared back existentialism of Jean-Pierre Melville, the film is a taut thriller in which Adjani must provide an alibi for a getaway driver who is being monitored by an obsessive cop.

A fluent German speaker, Adjani returned to European productions with the role of Lucy Harker in Werner Herzog's F.W. Murnau reconstruction, *Nosferatu the Vampyre* (1979). Heavily made up in ghostly white, she channels the spirit of silent cinema into her portrayal of a woman who sacrifices herself to Klaus Kinski's lovelorn count. Andrzej Zulawski's *Possession* (1981) — one of the most distinctive

European horror movies of all time — features arguably Adjani's strongest performance as an emotionally fragile woman who takes an inhuman lover.

Jean Becker's family drama *One Deadly Summer* (1983) offered further evidence of her ability to tackle emotionally complex roles, while Luc Besson's *Subway* (1985) was one of the most stylized and influential French films of the 1980s. A wounding U.S. studio experience with *Ishtar* (1987) was swiftly vanquished by the critically acclaimed *Camille Claudel* (1988), in which Adjani stars as the muse of the sculptor Rodin (Gérard Depardieu).

Based on a novel by Alexandre Dumas, *La Reine Margot* (1994) is a sumptuous spectacle set amid the events behind the Massacre of St. Bartholomew in 16th-century France. Adjani plays Margot, betrothed for political reasons to Henri of Navarre (Daniel Auteuil). Adventurous, exciting and erotic, the film is a triumph.

Adjani emerged from self-imposed exile for Jean-Paul Lilienfield's *Skirt Day* (2008). A less cerebral *The Class* (2008), Adjani is nonetheless a committed presence as a teacher at a violent school who finds a gun in one of her student's bags and decides to take the class hostage. **JW**

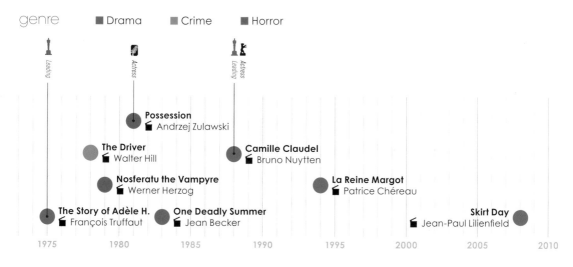

genre   ■ Drama   ■ Crime   ■ Horror

Leading   Actress   Actress / Leading

Possession
François Andrzej Zulawski

The Driver
Walter Hill

Camille Claudel
Bruno Nuytten

Nosferatu the Vampyre
Werner Herzog

La Reine Margot
Patrice Chéreau

The Story of Adèle H.
François Truffaut

One Deadly Summer
Jean Becker

Skirt Day
Jean-Paul Lilienfield

1975   1980   1985   1990   1995   2000   2005   2010

ben affleck 1972

Chasing
Amy

Good Will
Hunting

Armageddon

Changing
Lanes

Daredevil

Hollywood–
land

Argo

Gone Girl

Born in 1972 in California and raised in Massachusetts, Ben Affleck performed in a number of U.S. television series as a child. His big-screen break came in 1993, playing a school bully in Richard Linklater's cult hit *Dazed and Confused*. His first lead role was in director Kevin Smith's *Chasing Amy* (1997). Combining beefy good looks with a light comic touch that suited the movie's slacker sensibility, Affleck was charming as the love-struck hero. However, it was his involvement in another film that year that got the actor noticed. *Good Will Hunting* was a modestly budgeted drama about a working-class math prodigy that earned Affleck and his childhood friend Matt Damon an Oscar for their original screenplay. Also giving a supporting performance of easy-going charm, Affleck parlayed the film's success into his first major Hollywood role. Playing a maverick oil driller in the science-fiction disaster film *Armageddon* (1998), Affleck held his own alongside Bruce Willis and a plethora of visual effects. The film was a huge hit, cementing his A-list status.

However, the early 2000s brought mixed fortunes for the actor. His next film with director Michael Bay, *Pearl Harbor* (2001), severely tested audiences' patience. The action thriller *The Sum of All Fears* (2002) saw him on commanding form as the CIA agent Jack Ryan, albeit in a confused and not wholly satisfying film. In the road-rage drama *Changing Lanes* (2002) he gave a performance of unsettling, angry intensity. But Affleck's star began to wane, partly through the publicity surrounding his personal life and partly through a string of unimpressive roles in movies such as *Daredevil* (2003) and *Gigli* (2003).

It was in playing a performer whose fortunes had stalled that Affleck was able to revive his own career. As the former Superman actor George Reeves in the 2006 detective drama *Hollywoodland*, Affleck poignantly captured the turmoil of this tragic figure. However, it was his work behind the camera, as director of the acclaimed 2007 mystery film *Gone Baby Gone* (starring his brother Casey), that firmly re-established his status. Increasingly acclaimed for his directorial work, especially following his Oscar-winning political thriller *Argo* (2012), Affleck is once again hot property.

Affleck delivered his best performance yet as the husband of a missing woman clouded in suspicion in David Fincher's thriller *Gone Girl* (2014). It is a performance of masterly, jagged ambiguity and triumphantly reveals the depths underlying the breezy affability of Affleck's early roles. His star is set to shine even more brightly following his role as Batman in *Batman v. Superman: Dawn of Justice* (2016). **EL**

genre   ■ Romance   ■ Drama   ■ Sci-Fi   ■ Thriller   ■ Action   ■ Crime

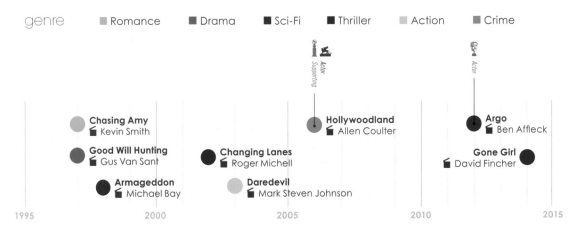

Actor
Supporting

Actor

Chasing Amy
Kevin Smith

Good Will Hunting
Gus Van Sant

Armageddon
Michael Bay

Changing Lanes
Roger Michell

Daredevil
Mark Steven Johnson

Hollywoodland
Allen Coulter

Argo
Ben Affleck

Gone Girl
David Fincher

1995   2000   2005   2010   2015

woody allen 1935

| Sleeper | Love and Death | Annie Hall | Manhattan | Stardust Memories | Hannah and Her Sisters | Husbands and Wives | Mighty Aphrodite |

Woody Allen began his career as a teenager, writing jokes for newspaper columnists before moving into television writing at the age of 19. He made his cinematic acting and writing debut with *What's New Pussycat?* (1965), but the bowdlerized result was a mess and he resolved to direct his own material.

Allen's work as an actor is difficult to separate from that as a writer-director, as his performances mostly come from his own features and are variations on his comedic identity as a fretful intellectual preoccupied by sex and death. A prolific filmmaker, he has directed a movie almost every year since 1966, and starred in many of them. His early films were comedies that relied on visual humor, one-liners and slapstick. These placed his on-screen persona into different scenarios, including a Latin American banana republic in *Bananas* (1971), the year 2173 in *Sleeper* (1973) and Napoleonic-era Russia in *Love and Death* (1975).

As Allen matured, his work became increasingly grounded and included dramatic elements, a shift signaled by *Annie Hall* (1977). This movie would be his biggest critical success and, out of 24 eventual Oscar nominations, would be the only one for which he was nominated for acting. He received similar acclaim for *Manhattan* (1979), but by *Stardust Memories* (1980) he appeared dissatisfied, playing a filmmaker uneasy with his success and tired of being funny.

During the next decade Allen diverged from his stock role, playing a social chameleon in *Zelig* (1983) and low-level talent agent in *Broadway Danny Rose* (1984). He appeared in fewer films as he focused on dramas and characters, although he gave one of his warmest performances in *Hannah and Her Sisters* (1986).

A widely publicized separation from Mia Farrow was prefigured by the events of *Husbands and Wives* (1992), and subsequently Allen made lighter films including *Mighty Aphrodite* (1995) and the musical *Everyone Says I Love You* (1996). In 1998, he starred in the animation *Antz*, but — his wonderful, self-parodic performance notwithstanding — he disliked voiceover acting.

As Allen aged he cast actors in parts he would have traditionally played himself, and after moving to Europe in 2003 only appeared in *Scoop* (2006) and *To Rome with Love* (2012), neither of which were standouts. His only other performance during this time was a bookshop-owner-turned-pimp in John Turturro's *Fading Gigolo* (2013), a late reminder of what a charming screen presence he can be. **JWA**

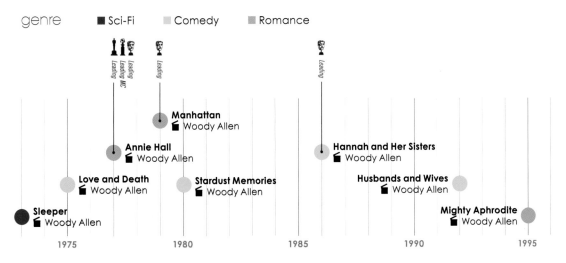

genre   ■ Sci-Fi   ■ Comedy   ■ Romance

Manhattan
Woody Allen

Annie Hall
Woody Allen

Love and Death
Woody Allen

Sleeper
Woody Allen

Stardust Memories
Woody Allen

Hannah and Her Sisters
Woody Allen

Husbands and Wives
Woody Allen

Mighty Aphrodite
Woody Allen

1975   1980   1985   1990   1995

julie andrews 1935

| Mary Poppins | The Americanization of Emily | The Sound of Music | Torn Curtain | 10 | Victor/ Victoria | Duet for One | The Princess Diaries |

Despite a seven-decade career, Julie Andrews is best known for her early roles. Born Julie Wells in Walton-on-Thames, England, in 1935, she later adopted her stepfather's surname. He and her mother were stage entertainers and quickly recognized her musical talent, having her trained as a soprano. She made her professional debut in London in 1947 and by 1954 she was on Broadway. In 1956 she created the role of Eliza Doolittle in *My Fair Lady*, but was replaced by Audrey Hepburn in the 1964 film version on the grounds that she was insufficiently famous.

Ironically, by the time *My Fair Lady* opened, this was no longer true: Andrews had made her big-screen debut in the title role of the lavish Disney musical adaptation of *Mary Poppins* (1964), a colossal hit that won her a Best Actress Oscar. She then made *The Americanization of Emily* (1964), playing a widow romanced by James Garner's U.S. Army lieutenant in wartime London. Next came the mega-blockbuster musical *The Sound of Music* (1965), in which she played the real-life Maria von Trapp.

Andrews sprinkled more box-office gold dust over *Hawaii* (1966), *Torn Curtain* (1966) and *Thoroughly Modern Millie* (1967), but her big-screen career then foundered with expensive flops *Star!* (1968) and *Darling Lili* (1970). She worked increasingly on television, with most of her cinematic incursions directed by her second husband Blake Edwards. In *The Tamarind Seed* (1974) her British civil servant romanced Soviet military attaché Omar Sharif, while in *10* (1979) she played Dudley Moore's long-suffering girlfriend. Bilious Hollywood satire *S.O.B.* (1981) was more notorious for her brief topless scene than anything else.

But *Victor/Victoria* (1982) was a triumph, a sharp, sassy musical comedy that cast her as a woman pretending to be a gay female impersonator. In *The Man Who Loved Women* (1983) she was a psychiatrist counseling womanizer Burt Reynolds while *Duet for One* (1986) cast her as an internationally renowned concert violinist coping with multiple sclerosis.

A decade later, she would undergo a real-life medical trauma when an operation permanently damaged her vocal cords, ending her singing career. Since then, she has mostly worked on television or as a voice artist, but has also made occasional big-screen appearances, notably a return to live-action Disney films with *The Princess Diaries* (2001) and its sequel three years later. **MBr**

genre   ■ Musical   ■ Comedy   ■ Thriller   ■ Romance   ■ Drama   ■ Family

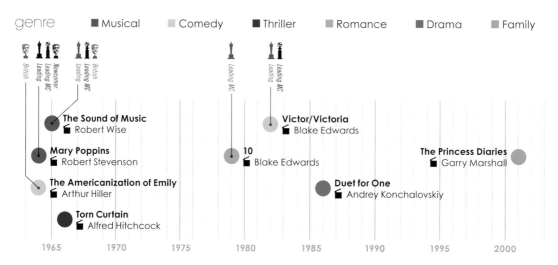

The Sound of Music
🎬 Robert Wise

Mary Poppins
🎬 Robert Stevenson

The Americanization of Emily
🎬 Arthur Hiller

Torn Curtain
🎬 Alfred Hitchcock

Victor/Victoria
🎬 Blake Edwards

10
🎬 Blake Edwards

Duet for One
🎬 Andrey Konchalovskiy

The Princess Diaries
🎬 Garry Marshall

1965   1970   1975   1980   1985   1990   1995   2000

tadanobu asano 1973

Fried Dragon Fish

Maborosi

Gohatto

Ichi the Killer

Last Life in the Universe

Zatoichi

Mongol

Thor

One of the most acclaimed Japanese actors of his generation, Tadanobu Asano has successfully balanced esoteric roles with appearances in mainstream domestic and international productions. Exuding a cooler-than-cool demeanor, he has been compared to both Johnny Depp and Toshiro Mifune.

Born Tadanobu Sato in a small town outside Yokohama in 1973, Asano's first screen appearance was at age 16 in the long-running TV series *Kinpachi-sensei* (1979–2011), which focused on the third year of a Japanese junior high school. The following year, he made his feature debut in the school drama *Swimming Upstream* (1990). However, he first made an impression with critics and audiences in Shunji Iwai's TV movie *Fried Dragon Fish* (1993). The actor's enigmatic screen presence was mined further by director Hirokazu Koreeda, who cast Asano as a man who inexplicably commits suicide in *Maborosi* (1995). The pair would reunite on *Distance* (2001), which attempted to grapple with a nation's shock following the Aum Shinrikyo's 1995 sarin attack on the Tokyo subway.

Before that, however, Asano appeared in Nagisa Oshima's powerful *Gohatto* (1999), which explored homosexuality in the Shinsengumi, the special police force created by the military government during Japan's Bakumatsu period in the 1860s. The film's star was Takeshi Kitano, who would cast Asano as the silent but deadly assassin in his immensely entertaining 2003 samurai adventure *Zatoichi*. In the same year, Asano starred in Kiyoshi Kurosawa's critically acclaimed drama *Bright Future* and played the lead in Taiwanese director Hou Hsiao-Hsien's *Café Lumière*.

Asano's cult status was assured thanks to his appearance in two distinctive films. Takashi Miike's *Ichi the Killer* (2001), based on Hideo Yamamoto's manga series, took cinematic violence to a new level, with Asano playing a Yakuza gang member battling both his rivals and a deranged killer. In Pen-Ek Ratanaruang's *Last Life in the Universe* (2003), Asano offers up a compelling portrait of a suicidal OCD librarian hiding out in Bangkok. Driven by mood and atmosphere, Pen-Ek's offbeat romance profits from the frisson that builds between the actor and his costar Sinitta Boonyasak. In 2006, Asano and Pen-Ek reunited for the director's crime thriller *Invisible Waves*.

Asano's international reputation has built up gradually, with appearances in the Marvel blockbuster *Thor* (2011) and its 2013 sequel. He brought much needed class to *Battleship* (2012), but could do nothing to save *47 Ronin* (2013). More impressive is Sergei Bodorov's *Mongol* (2007), about the rise to power of Genghis Khan. Asano is a riveting presence as the mighty leader in a film that the director intends to be the first part of a trilogy. In the meantime, Asano will appear in Martin Scorsese's long-in-gestation story of Jesuit priests in 17th-century Japan, *Silence* (2016). **IHS**

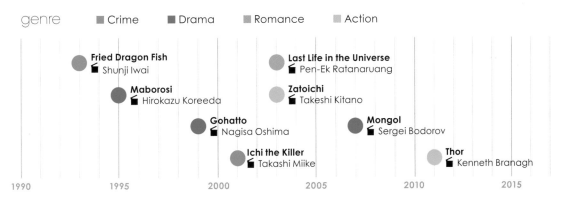

genre   ■ Crime   ■ Drama   ■ Romance   ■ Action

Fried Dragon Fish
Shunji Iwai

Maborosi
Hirokazu Koreeda

Gohatto
Nagisa Oshima

Ichi the Killer
Takashi Miike

Last Life in the Universe
Pen-Ek Ratanaruang

Zatoichi
Takeshi Kitano

Mongol
Sergei Bodorov

Thor
Kenneth Branagh

1990   1995   2000   2005   2010   2015

the musical star

Al Jolson

Maurice Chevalier

Ruby Keeler

Ginger Rogers & Fred Astaire

James Cagney

Judy Garland

Fred Astaire

Gene Kelly

The arrival of synchronous sound changed the course of cinema and introduced a new genre: the musical. It also produced a new kind of star. Al Jolson was the first, with *The Jazz Singer* (1927). Already a vaudeville celebrity, his sentimental approach in songs like "My Mammy" was a hit with audiences. His influence spread far and wide, with singers as diverse as Bing Crosby, Bob Dylan and David Bowie all citing him as an influence. Following his sound debut, Jolson remained popular throughout the 1930s and saw his star rise again after World War II with a series of dramatized biopics of his life.

The Jazz Singer may have been the first sound film, but *The Love Parade* (1929) is the first great musical. It made an international star out of Maurice Chevalier and gave Jeanette MacDonald her big break. Not only is it a smart comedy by German director Ernst Lubitsch, but it is also technically impressive. In one scene, two couples sing the same song from different locations. Lubitsch's solution to the problem of recording them both was to build two sound stages with an orchestra playing between them and film both performances simultaneously, intercutting the two sequences later in the editing suite.

The spirit of Lubitsch's ingenuity permeated the musicals of the 1930s. It also saw the appearance of some of its biggest stars. Ruby Keeler, who was married to Al Jolson from 1928 to 1940, made a splash in *42nd Street* (1933), opposite Dick Powell, whose fame in musical films would be eclipsed by his shift into darker noir territory in the 1940s. Keeler also starred in *Gold Diggers of 1933* (1933), *Footlight Parade* (1933), *Dames* (1934), opposite her husband in *Go into Your Dance* (1935) and *Colleen* (1936). She embodied a sweet innocence and reflected both the insecurity and aspiration of the United States in the 1930s.

Fred Astaire and Ginger Rogers remain the golden couple of the Hollywood musical. Although they started out as support players in *Flying Down to Rio* (1933), the chemistry between them was evident in the one number they performed together, "Carioca," dancing with their foreheads touching. At their best, in films such as *The Gay Divorcee* (1934), *Top Hat* (1935), *Follow the Fleet* (1936), *Swing Time* (1936) and *Shall We Dance* (1937), they elevated the dance musical to an art form. If *Top Hat* is their best all-round musical, then *Swing Time* is the finest showcase of their dance work, with "Never Gonna Dance" arguably being their greatest performance. Astaire was rare among stars of the era in taking a percentage of the box office and having complete artistic control over all choreography. Phenomenally successful with

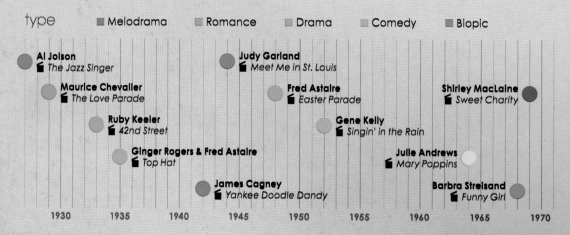

type ■ Melodrama ■ Romance ■ Drama ■ Comedy ■ Biopic

Al Jolson
The Jazz Singer

Judy Garland
Meet Me in St. Louis

Maurice Chevalier
The Love Parade

Fred Astaire
Easter Parade

Shirley MacLaine
Sweet Charity

Ruby Keeler
42nd Street

Gene Kelly
Singin' in the Rain

Ginger Rogers & Fred Astaire
Top Hat

Julie Andrews
Mary Poppins

James Cagney
Yankee Doodle Dandy

Barbra Streisand
Funny Girl

1930   1935   1940   1945   1950   1955   1960   1965   1970

| Julie Andrews | Barbra Streisand | Shirley MacLaine | Liza Minnelli | John Travolta & Olivia Newton-John | Nicole Kidman | Eminem | Idina Menzel |

audiences, the only film featuring either Astaire or Rogers that outperformed their work together was *Easter Parade* (1948), which Astaire was cast in only after Gene Kelly dropped out due to an injury.

James Cagney, best known for his gangster films, grew up in vaudeville and had performed the number "Shanghai Lil" in the climax of *Footlight Parade*. However, it was his energetic, Oscar-winning portrayal of showman George M. Cohan in *Yankee Doodle Dandy* (1942) that best demonstrated his talent. Two years later, Judy Garland, who had already become a star thanks to the Andy Hardy movies and *The Wizard of Oz* (1939), turned in one of her finest performances in *Meet Me in St. Louis* (1944), directed by Vincente Minnelli. Along with *A Star Is Born* (1954), *Meet Me in St. Louis* is a key Garland film in displaying her versatility, both as a singer and actress.

Gene Kelly had been a star of the musical film since the 1940s, but with *An American in Paris* (1951) and *Singin' in the Rain* (1952) he, like Astaire and Rogers, transformed the genre into something magical. Both films offer a commentary on art and love, and feature stunning performances by Kelly and their cast.

The mid-1950s marked the gradual decline of the Hollywood musical. Musicals were still made, but over time they became the exception and not the norm. The 1960s saw Julie Andrews dominate the decade with the box-office successes *Mary Poppins* (1964) and *The Sound of Music* (1965). Barbra Streisand also became a star with *Funny Girl* (1968), while Shirley MacLaine perfectly captured the naivety of a young girl adrift in New York in *Sweet Charity* (1969). That film marked the directorial debut of Bob Fosse, whose *Cabaret* (1972), which featured a riveting performance by Liza Minnelli, successfully looked back to the past — historically and musically — while offering something fresh and exciting. *Grease* (1978) meanwhile tapped into nostalgia for an earlier era and made John Travolta and Olivia Newton-John household names.

Since the late 1970s, musicals have come and gone but few featured a spellbinding central performance. Nicole Kidman is compelling and alluring as the doomed Satine in Baz Luhrmann's extravagant *Moulin Rouge!* (2001). However, the standout musical performance of the 2000s is arguably rapper Eminem's, in the absorbing dramatization of his break into MC-ing, *8 Mile* (2002). Yet, in terms of singing, Idina Menzel's performance in Disney's *Frozen* (2013) ranks alongside those of the finest stars of Hollywood's bygone years. **IHS**

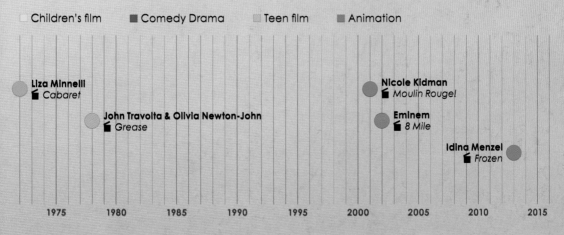

☐ Children's film ■ Comedy Drama ☐ Teen film ■ Animation

Liza Minnelli
Cabaret

John Travolta & Olivia Newton-John
Grease

Nicole Kidman
Moulin Rouge!

Eminem
8 Mile

Idina Menzel
Frozen

1975   1980   1985   1990   1995   2000   2005   2010   2015

fred astaire 1899–1987

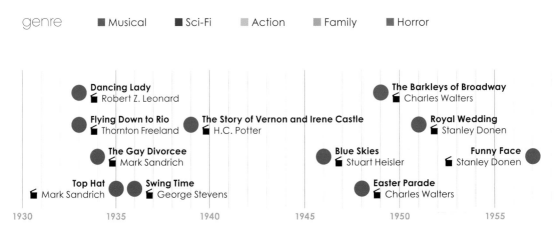

Dancing Lady

Flying Down to Rio

The Gay Divorcee

Top Hat

Swing Time

The Story of Vernon and Irene Castle

Blue Skies

Easter Parade

"Can't act. Slightly bald. Can dance a little." While the exact wording has been long debated, the studio report on Fred Astaire's first screen test, filed by an anonymous executive, remains famously ill-judged considering that he would go on to become one of the most popular movie stars in the world. Eschewing the camera-dependent, overpopulated approach of Busby Berkeley in favor of single-take performances of elegant solo or partnered dances, Astaire was a hugely influential figure in the depiction of dance on screen. He starred in 30 musicals between 1933 and 1957, his choreography mixing ballroom dancing, tap and ballet to deceptively effortless effect, before shifting into mainly dramatic roles toward the close of his career. Despite being best remembered for dancing, Astaire's singing was key to his work, and he performed the first filmed versions of dozens of songs that would subsequently become standards. A light comedian by nature, he was known for his relentless perfectionism and debonair appearance.

Born in Omaha, Nebraska, in 1899, Astaire started dancing at the age of 4, prompted by his ambitious mother to become the partner to his older sister Adele. The two would be dance partners for 27 years, forging a successful stage career on Broadway before Adele married and decided to step away from performing. The change necessitated a period of recalibration for Astaire that ultimately allowed him to play a greater range of roles. He made his screen debut as himself, dancing with Joan Crawford in *Dancing Lady* (1933), before taking a more substantial role opposite Ginger Rogers in *Flying Down to Rio* (1933).

Astaire starred with Rogers in eight further films over the following six years, including *The Gay Divorcee* (1934), *Roberta* (1935), *Top Hat* (1935), *Swing Time* (1936) and *Shall We Dance* (1937). Despite his wariness about being associated with a single partner again, the pairing was the most enduringly popular of his lengthy career and is the one with which both performers are inexorably linked. His only film made without Rogers during that time, dancing with an inexperienced Joan Fontaine in *A Damsel in Distress* (1937), was a commercial failure, but the pair's final two outings, *Carefree* (1938) and *The Story of Vernon and Irene Castle* (1939) did not fare much better and they made the mutual decision to move on.

Although Astaire's box-office appeal was less secure, he continued to create innovative dance sequences in several hits, starring with Rita Hayworth in *You'll Never Get Rich* (1941) and *You Were Never Lovelier* (1942), and Bing Crosby in *Holiday Inn* (1942) and *Blue Skies* (1946). An exception was Vincente

genre ■ Musical ■ Sci-Fi ■ Action ■ Family ■ Horror

Dancing Lady
Robert Z. Leonard

Flying Down to Rio
Thornton Freeland

The Gay Divorcee
Mark Sandrich

Top Hat
Mark Sandrich

Swing Time
George Stevens

The Story of Vernon and Irene Castle
H.C. Potter

The Barkleys of Broadway
Charles Walters

Royal Wedding
Stanley Donen

Blue Skies
Stuart Heisler

Easter Parade
Charles Walters

Funny Face
Stanley Donen

1930   1935   1940   1945   1950   1955

$557M (U.S.)
The Towering Inferno
(1974)

$61M (U.S.)
Ghost Story
(1981)

A

| The Barkleys of Broadway | Royal Wedding | Funny Face | On the Beach | Finian's Rainbow | The Towering Inferno | The Amazing Dobermans | Ghost Story |

Minnelli's flop *Yolanda and the Thief* (1945), in which his contribution to the choreography was minimal. The following year, Astaire announced his retirement, which only lasted until he was persuaded to replace an injured Gene Kelly in *Easter Parade* (1948). Kelly and Astaire were frequently compared throughout their lives, mainly due to being the preeminent dancers of the medium rather than because of overt similarities in their dancing styles. The two danced together in *Ziegfeld Follies* (1946) and the Kelly-directed *That's Entertainment, Part II* (1976), a revue and compilation film respectively.

Easter Parade became the biggest hit of Astaire's career. It was followed by a one-off reunion with Ginger Rogers in *The Barkleys of Broadway* (1949), hired after a troubled Judy Garland dropped out of the production. A year later he received an honorary Oscar for his achievements, presented by Rogers herself. During this time Astaire starred in *Royal Wedding* (1951) and *The Band Wagon* (1953), which was one of the defining MGM musicals and a highlight of his career. The popularity of the genre had started to wane significantly, however, as seen by the muted reception to films like *The Belle of New York* (1952) and *Daddy Long Legs* (1955). An ageing, recently bereaved Astaire had similarly lost interest, and after

starring in *Funny Face* (1957) opposite Audrey Hepburn and *Silk Stockings* (1957) with Cyd Charisse, he retired from film musicals for a second time. In the following years he made a quartet of popular musical specials for television, but mostly left dancing behind to focus on straight acting and other pursuits.

The next phase in Astaire's career began with his performance as a depressed racecar-driving scientist in the apocalyptic drama *On the Beach* (1959). Over the following two decades he appeared on screen infrequently, in films including *The Notorious Landlady* (1962), *Midas Run* (1969) and *The Amazing Dobermans* (1976). Other than his appearances in the *That's Entertainment* films, the only time he was coaxed back to a screen musical was to play an Irish rogue pursued by a leprechaun in Francis Ford Coppola's underrated early effort *Finian's Rainbow* (1968).

Almost 25 years after his honorary Oscar, Astaire received his first proper nomination for his role as a conman in *The Towering Inferno* (1974), perhaps the strongest of the glut of ensemble disaster films that were popular during the period. He made his last film appearance in *Ghost Story* (1981), a movie that would also provide final roles for Douglas Fairbanks, Jr. and Melvyn Douglas. After being an entertainer for 76 years, Astaire was finally willing to retire for good. **JW**

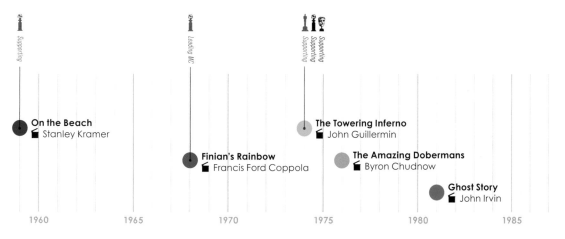

Supporting

On the Beach
Stanley Kramer

Leading MC

Finian's Rainbow
Francis Ford Coppola

Supporting
Supporting

The Towering Inferno
John Guillermin

The Amazing Dobermans
Byron Chudnow

Ghost Story
John Irvin

1960   1965   1970   1975   1980   1985

daniel auteuil 1950

| Manon des Sources | Romuald et Juliette | Un Coeur en Hiver | La Reine Margot | The Eighth Day | Small Cuts | Hidden | Marius |

On the face of it, Daniel Auteuil makes an unlikely movie star. Slightly built, with intriguingly lopsided features, he was 36 before he achieved fame as Ugolin in *Jean de Florette* and its sequel *Manon des Sources* (both 1986). Since then, Auteuil has consolidated his status as one of France's most popular and versatile actors.

Born in Algeria, the son of opera singers, Auteuil made his stage debut aged 4 as Madame Butterfly's son. He began acting professionally on stage in 1970, making his screen debut five years later. His early movies were mostly forgettable comedies, until the Marcel Pagnol-derived duo of *Florette* and *Manon* lifted him to stardom. Since then, he has explored a wide range of genres and roles, often playing conflicted characters. In *Romuald et Juliette* (1989) his company boss found himself dependent on the help of his Caribbean cleaning lady — and, to his even greater bewilderment, falling for her. He was a 19th-century master-criminal facing the guillotine in *Lacenaire* (1990), and at his most subtly agonized as a violin-maker unable to declare his passion to a beautiful violinist in *Un Coeur en Hiver* (1992).

My Favorite Season (1993) teamed him with Catherine Deneuve as siblings struggling to come to terms with their mother's imminent death; they played siblings again in the crime drama *Thieves* (1996). He was moving as the husband trying to save his marriage in *The Separation* (1994), and a misused husband of a different stamp, the cuckolded Henri of Navarre, in the historical bloodbath of *La Reine Margot* (1994). In *The Eighth Day* (1996) he played an unhappy salesman who develops a friendship with the resident of a mental asylum. Always intent on extending his range, he was a knife-thrower traveling across Europe with a suicidal young woman in *The Girl on the Bridge* (1999), went head-to-head with Depardieu as fellow-cops in the policier *36* (2004), and even played in English (rather uncomfortably) in *The Lost Son* (1999). Perhaps his finest role of this period was as a television pundit harboring undisclosed guilt in Michael Haneke's enigmatic *Hidden* (2005).

Recently, Auteuil has repaid his debt to Pagnol, as writer–director–star of *The Well-Digger's Daughter* (2011) and remakes of the early 1930s *Marseilles* trilogy (*Marius*, 2013; *Fanny*, 2013; *César*, 2015). Responses have been variable, but if the jury is still out on Auteuil as director, his status as one of France's foremost living actors seems assured. **PK**

genre ■ Drama ■ Comedy ■ Romance ■ Thriller

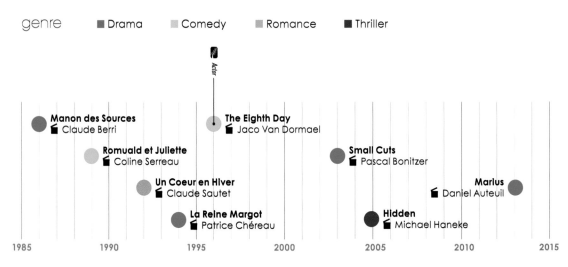

lauren bacall 1924–2014

To Have and Have Not | The Big Sleep | How to Marry a Millionaire | Written on the Wind | Murder on the Orient Express | The Shootist | The Mirror Has Two Faces | Dogville

Lauren Bacall's movie debut is one of the all-time greats: a 19-year-old ex-model sparring with one of Hollywood's veteran tough guys and flooring him with her seductive presence and sultry delivery. In Howard Hawks' maritime thriller *To Have and Have Not* (1944), Bacall threw not just the audience, but Humphrey Bogart, some 25 years her senior, for a loop; within a year they were married and she was a bona fide star.

Nicknamed "The Look," Bacall was born Betty Jean Perske in New York City, 1924. Hawks' wife spied her on a *Harper's Bazaar* magazine cover, they brought her to Hollywood, lowered her naturally high voice and the rest is history. Such was her sizzle with Bogart that their follow-up, detective mystery *The Big Sleep* (1946), was re-shot to add extra scenes of provocative banter. Two more Bogart thrillers followed — *Dark Passage* (1947) and *Key Largo* (1948) — but it was the first two that immortalized their screen chemistry.

Indeed, away from Bogart, Bacall lost much of her allure. Her femme fatale opposite Kirk Douglas in *Young Man With a Horn* (1950) felt contrived; and in hit comedy *How To Marry a Millionaire* (1953) she physically fades opposite Marilyn Monroe's effortless effervescence, her caustic one-liners coming off as catty, not witty. She is the lead in Douglas Sirk's subversive melodrama *Written on the Wind* (1956), but both she and Rock Hudson are overshadowed by their costars Robert Stack and Dorothy Malone.

After Bogart's death in 1957, Bacall largely retreated to theater, with several Broadway successes (and two Tony awards), only occasionally dipping back into movies. She played a conniving chief suspect in Sidney Lumet's all-star Agatha Christie adaptation *Murder on the Orient Express* (1974), and gave a touching performance as a starchy but sympathetic confidant to John Wayne's dying gunman in *The Shootist* (1976).

The 1980s and 1990s brought slim pickings, though she received her first Oscar nomination for Barbra Streisand's romance *The Mirror Has Two Faces* (1996), as the heroine's snippy mother. Deemed a likely winner and sentimental favorite, she surprisingly lost to Juliette Binoche. She braved Lars von Trier's chalk-drawn sets for *Dogville* (2003) and *Manderlay* (2005) and offered decent support in *Birth* (2004) and *The Walker* (2007). An Honorary Oscar in 2009 cemented her legendary status. She died, aged 89, in 2014. Bacall's place in movie history is secure, albeit more as an old-Hollywood star rather than a truly great actress. **LS**

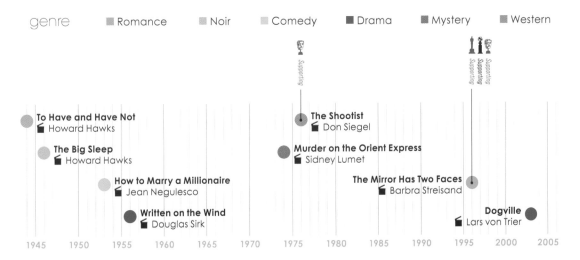

genre ■ Romance ■ Noir ■ Comedy ■ Drama ■ Mystery ■ Western

To Have and Have Not — Howard Hawks
The Big Sleep — Howard Hawks
How to Marry a Millionaire — Jean Negulesco
Written on the Wind — Douglas Sirk
The Shootist — Don Siegel
Murder on the Orient Express — Sidney Lumet
The Mirror Has Two Faces — Barbra Streisand
Dogville — Lars von Trier

1945 1950 1955 1960 1965 1970 1975 1980 1985 1990 1995 2000 2005

amitabh bachchan 1942

| Zanjeer | Namak Haraam | Sholay | Deewaar | Kabhie Kabhie | Amar Akbar Anthony | Don | Kaala Patthar |

The early 1970s were a time of transition in popular Hindi cinema, the industry today known as Bollywood. Rajesh Khanna was the reigning superstar and fed his audience a steady diet of hit after romantic hit. In 1971, he starred as a tragic hero in *Anand*. Playing his doctor and friend was a brooding young man named Amitabh Bachchan, who had had a quiet beginning in the industry and was at the time better known as the son of the renowned poet Harivansh Rai Bachchan. Khanna and Bachchan won the Filmfare Awards for Best Actor and Best Supporting Actor for their performances.

After the high of *Anand*, Bachchan appeared in a spate of flops until the writers Salim-Javed (Salim Khan and Javed Akhtar), arguably the last writers in Indian cinema to command fees equivalent to the stars they wrote vehicles for, recommended him to the director Prakash Mehra for his upcoming movie. It was a role that several stars, including Khanna, Raaj Kumar, Dharmendra and Dev Anand, had already turned down. Salim-Javed saw a raw intensity in the young man that others had not. That film, *Zanjeer* (1973), which saw Bachchan playing an honest cop traumatized by recurring nightmares who takes on a local gang boss, resonated with Indian audiences for the way it dealt with crime and corruption in daily life. The result was a smash hit and Bachchan's persona of the "Angry Young Man" who takes on the system was born.

The same year saw the release of Hrishikesh Mukherjee's *Namak Haraam* (1973), a tale of two friends turned foes, which was loosely inspired by *Becket* (1964). Khanna, who has more screen time, plays the sympathetic friend, while Bachchan took on the role of a scheming rich man. Audiences were tiring of Khanna's brand of love stories and embraced Bachchan's intensity. The actor duly won the Filmfare Best Supporting Actor Award again. *Abhimaan* (1973), an Indian version of *A Star Is Born* (1954), starred Jaya Bhaduri as the female lead alongside Bachchan, repeating their hit pairing from *Zanjeer*. Bachchan and Bhaduri married later that year.

The year 1975 was epochal for both Bachchan and Indian cinema. Yash Chopra directed the seminal *Deewaar*, a tale of two destitute brothers who grow up to become a cop and a gangster. Though Khanna was in the reckoning for the role of the gangster Vijay, Bachchan prevailed thanks to the insistence of Salim-Javed. The mother is an important figure in Indian cinema and Vijay's pain at not having her support because of his criminal ways, despite building an empire for her, manifests itself in a confrontation between him and his law-enforcing brother (Shashi Kapoor) that is hailed as one of the greatest ever in Indian cinema. Chopra and Salim-Javed would go on to further embellish Bachchan's bad boy persona in *Trishul* (1978) and *Kaala Patthar* (1979). The actor

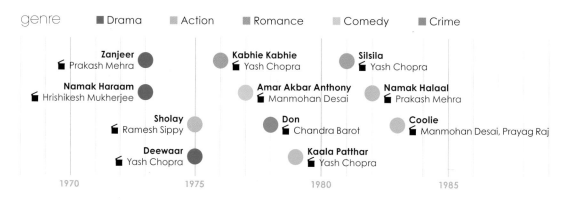

genre ■ Drama ■ Action ■ Romance □ Comedy ■ Crime

Zanjeer — Prakash Mehra	Kabhie Kabhie — Yash Chopra	Silsila — Yash Chopra
Namak Haraam — Hrishikesh Mukherjee	Amar Akbar Anthony — Manmohan Desai	Namak Halaal — Prakash Mehra
Sholay — Ramesh Sippy	Don — Chandra Barot	Coolie — Manmohan Desai, Prayag Raj
Deewaar — Yash Chopra	Kaala Patthar — Yash Chopra	

1970   1975   1980   1985

$6M
Mohabbatein
(2000)

$10M
Baghban
(2003)

$10M
Cheeni Kum
(2007)

B

Silsila

Namak
Halaal

Coolie

Agneepath

Mohabbatein

Baghban

Sarkar

Cheeni Kum

also costarred with Dharmendra in Ramesh Sippy's *Sholay* (1975), a curry western loosely based on Sergio Leone's spaghetti westerns, which would go on to become one of Indian cinema's biggest hits. Bachchan played a character, once again written by Salim-Javed, whose dry, sly and laconic wit further enhanced his screen image.

However, Bachchan's range was not just restricted to angry roles. Director Yash Chopra promoted the new superstar's romantic side in *Kabhie Kabhie* (1976) and, later on, in *Silsila* (1981). Manmohan Desai brought out Bachchan's gift for broad comedy in *Amar Akbar Anthony* (1977), while Prakash Mehra also gave Bachchan a landmark comedy role in *Namak Halaal* (1982).

Hit after hit followed and as India entered a new phase of life after Indira Gandhi's assassination in 1984, her son and Bachchan's great friend Rajiv Gandhi asked him to contest the Allahabad parliamentary seat in the general elections. Bachchan agreed and won with a large majority. However, during this hiatus from cinema he became implicated in a series of political scandals and for many his name was irrevocably tarnished. Bachchan quit politics, but the damage was done. His comeback film, *Shahenshah* (1988) had him play a bumbling cop by day and a vigilante by night. It was a moderate success. The actor pinned his

hopes on previously successful directors, such as Desai and Mehra, but they were past their prime and consequently Desai's *Gangaa Jamunaa Saraswathi* (1988) and *Toofan* (1989) and Mehra's *Jaadugar* (1989) were disasters. Bachchan was in his late forties now and, like many other Indian leading men, insisted on playing a far younger hero, even though audiences were embracing younger stars. *Agneepath* (1990) won him the first of his three Indian National Awards for Best Actor, but for the most part the 1990s were a forgettable decade, littered with poor film choices.

Reinvention came in the shape of television. With his salt-and-pepper bearded grey eminence persona, Bachchan hosted the inaugural season of *Kaun Banega Crorepati*, the Indian version of *Who Wants to be a Millionaire*. It was a ratings smash and Bachchan was back. *Mohabbatein* (2000) saw him transfer this image to cinema, playing a stern school headmaster. Again, it found an appreciative audience. He has maintained this persona ever since, dropping it only for *Paa* (2009), for which he won a National Award for his portrayal of a Progeria patient. Today, Bachchan remains a much-loved and avuncular figure — a ubiquitous presence on television, in the cinema and in countless commercials. But for the generation that grew up in the 1970s and 1980s, he will forever remain an "Angry Young Man" and the greatest superstar Hindi cinema has ever known. **NR**

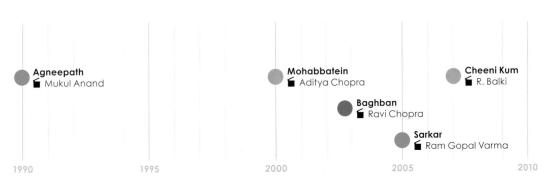

Agneepath
Mukul Anand

Mohabbatein
Aditya Chopra

Cheeni Kum
R. Balki

Baghban
Ravi Chopra

Sarkar
Ram Gopal Varma

1990   1995   2000   2005   2010

kevin bacon 1958

B

Friday
the 13th

Diner

Footloose

Criminal Law

Tremors

Flatliners

A Few Good
Men

The River
Wild

Kevin Bacon's career has been so prolific that it has spawned the game "Six Degrees of Kevin Bacon," which challenges players to show that any individual on Earth can be linked to the star via a maximum of six people. The Marvel blockbuster *Guardians of the Galaxy* (2014) went further in recognizing the star's role in popular culture. It features a scene in which the hero explains to an alien that the world he came from told of the legend of *Footloose* and a great hero called Kevin Bacon, who "teaches an entire city full of people with sticks up their butts that dancing, well, it's the greatest thing there is." It is an apt tribute to the actor's popularity. His career has consistently avoided stereotyping and he has often surprised with the depth and intelligence of his performances.

Bacon was born in Philadelphia in 1958. After a stint in theater, he took a small part in the anarchic frat house comedy *Animal House* (1978), followed by a key role in the classic slasher movie *Friday the 13th* (1980). He attracted praise for his performance in Barry Levinson's semi-autobiographical *Diner* (1982), but his commercial breakthrough came in 1984 with *Footloose*. Loosely based on the true story of a town in Oklahoma that banned music and dancing, the

film tells the story of an outsider, Ren McCormack, who arrives from Chicago to a small rural community. His exuberance and lust for life attracts the ire of the town's more conservative elements, led by John Lithgow's Reverend Moore. Bacon's energy and immense likability in the role found him a legion of fans, and the film and Bacon's performance are keystones of 1980s American cinema. He would bring the same raffish charm to one of his most entertaining films, *Tremors* (1990), a monster B-movie that sports a smart script and the perfect pairing of Bacon and Fred Ward, as two good-for-nothing wastrels battling a species of carnivore that travel beneath the earth.

Criminal Law (1988) gave Bacon his first villainous role, as a killer who initially outwits his lawyer (Gary Oldman). The actor has played several bad guys since, most notably the psycho who takes a family hostage in the action thriller *The River Wild* (1994), the sadistic guard who becomes the object of his victims' revenge in *Sleepers* (1996) and as a scientist driven mad after he experiments on himself in *Hollow Man* (2000). Most recently, he was devilishly wicked in the Marvel franchise re-boot *X-Men: First Class* (2011). He was wasted as a treacherous cop in *R.I.P.D.* (2013).

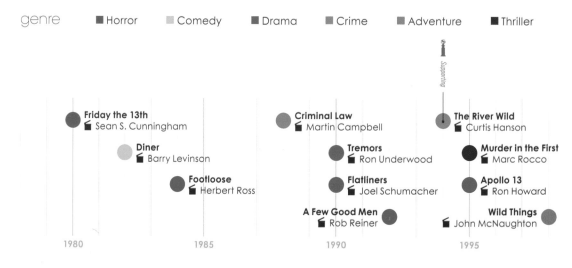

genre   ■ Horror   ■ Comedy   ■ Drama   ■ Crime   ■ Adventure   ■ Thriller

Supporting

Friday the 13th
🎬 Sean S. Cunningham

Criminal Law
🎬 Martin Campbell

The River Wild
🎬 Curtis Hanson

Diner
🎬 Barry Levinson

Tremors
🎬 Ron Underwood

Murder in the First
🎬 Marc Rocco

Footloose
🎬 Herbert Ross

Flatliners
🎬 Joel Schumacher

Apollo 13
🎬 Ron Howard

A Few Good Men
🎬 Rob Reiner

Wild Things
🎬 John McNaughton

1980   1985   1990   1995

$114 M (U.S.)
Friday the 13th
(1980)

$182 M (U.S.)
Footloose
(1984)

$111 M (U.S.)
Flatliners
(1990)

$410 M
A Few Good Men
(1992)

$151 M
The River Wild
(1994)

$552 M
Apollo 13
(1995)

$202 M
Mystic River
(2003)

$372 M
X-Men:
First Class
(2011)

Murder in
the First

Apollo 13

Wild Things

Stir of Echoes

Mystic River

The
Woodsman

Frost/Nixon

X-Men:
First Class

The heroic Ren McCormack notwithstanding, Bacon is most interesting playing characters that are neither lovable nor outright villains. In *Flatliners* (1990) he is a self-obsessed doctor whose racist past returns to haunt him. He is an unsettling presence in Oliver Stone's *JFK* (1991), an excellent foil to Tom Cruise's military lawyer in *A Few Good Men* (1992) and suitably slimy as the conniving cop who finds himself duped by lust in *Wild Things* (1998). He made much of his role as Jack Brennan in *Frost/Nixon* (2008), which reunited him with *Apollo 13* (1995) director Ron Howard. In that account of the ill-fated moon mission, Bacon plays astronaut Jack Swigert, a late replacement after Ken Mattingly (Gary Sinise) is exposed to measles and is removed from the team. The early scenes depict the tense relationship between Swigert and mission commander Jim Lovell (Tom Hanks). It is one of the drama's most fascinating elements, with Bacon's nuanced portrayal highlighting the awkwardness of an outsider joining a team that has proven itself as an effective unit. Likewise, his cop in Clint Eastwood's *Mystic River* (2003) is a fascinating and conflicted character, keen to ensure that the law is upheld, yet understanding the local code of honor that he has

lived with since his youth — a situation that eventually pits him against his childhood friend (Sean Penn).

More often a support player, when Bacon has been given a role equal to his talent, he has shown himself to be a versatile actor. *The Big Picture* (1989), Christopher Guest's gentle Hollywood satire, finds Bacon's recently graduated film student navigating the pitfalls of Hollywood studios. Though minor compared with Robert Altman's subsequent *The Player* (1992), Guest's film profits from the actor's genial performance. *Murder in the First* (1995) might be a conventional prison/courtroom drama, but Bacon compellingly captures the rage and desperation of a man wrongly imprisoned for murder. In *Stir of Echoes* (1999), Bacon excels as a blue-collar family man who discovers an ability to see the dead following a session under hypnosis. And in arguably the most impressive performance of his career, he plays a pedophile released from prison, returning to his hometown and a less than rapturous welcome, in *The Woodsman* (2004). A brave role, it is to the actor's credit that after so many years in the industry he is not only able to tackle such a challenging character, but also can bring so much humanity to it. **IHS**

■ Mystery　　■ Action

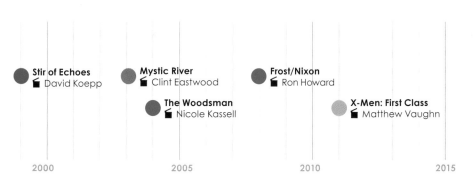

Stir of Echoes
David Koepp

Mystic River
Clint Eastwood

Frost/Nixon
Ron Howard

The Woodsman
Nicole Kassell

X-Men: First Class
Matthew Vaughn

2000　　　　　　　2005　　　　　　　2010　　　　　　　2015

christian bale 1974

| Empire of the Sun | Velvet Goldmine | American Psycho | The Machinist | Harsh Times | Batman Begins | The Fighter | American Hustle |

Since the age of 12 and his starring role as Jim in Steven Spielberg's *Empire of the Sun* (1987), Christian Bale has played characters that are often pushed to extremes. Jim is a case in point: with the intensity of his screen presence, Bale convincingly transports us through his journey from spoiled schoolboy to an emaciated witness of humanity's worst atrocities.

Born in Wales, Bale began his career on stage, followed by a couple of television roles before his big break in Spielberg's World War II epic. He followed it with a key role in Kenneth Branagh's *Henry V* (1989) and a series of minor but notable performances in *Little Women* (1994), *The Portrait of a Lady* (1996) and *The Secret Agent* (1996). In *Metroland* (1997), one of his few "ordinary" roles, he successfully conveys the fears of a man approaching middle age, while in *All the Little Animals* (1998) he plays an emotionally challenged man in an adaptation of Walker Hamilton's cult novel.

In Todd Haynes' *Velvet Goldmine* (1998), Bale is a journalist investigating the career of a 1970s rock star while coming to terms with his own sexuality. His major break came with the lead role in *American Psycho* (2000). Brilliantly capturing the narcissism of Patrick Bateman, an investment banker who believes he may be a serial killer, it was a controversial choice for the actor. He was only cast after a long line of high-profile

stars had previously been attached to the role, but it proved to be a watershed in Bale's career.

For the low-key sci-fi drama *The Machinist* (2004) Bale went on an extreme diet regime to convince as cadaverous neurotic insomniac Trevor Reznik. He did the same for Werner Herzog's *Rescue Dawn* (2006), based on the true story of a pilot who escaped from a Viet Kong prison, and his first collaboration with David O. Russell, *The Fighter* (2010). Bale excelled as Dicky Eklund, the livewire brother of champion boxer Micky Ward, earning an Academy Award for Best Supporting Actor. He would reunite with Russell for *American Hustle* (2013), playing a corpulent confidence trickster.

Bale is best known for his role as Bruce Wayne/Batman in Christopher Nolan's *Dark Knight* trilogy. The first entry, *Batman Begins* (2005), remains the most rounded, with Bale given the space to explore his character. The actor also collaborated with Nolan on the playful Victorian-era thriller *The Prestige* (2006).

Bale's most impressive performance to date is as deranged outsider Jim Luther Davis, in David Ayer's *Harsh Times* (2005). Whacked-out on speed, he lacks a moral compass and has a skewed view of justice. As terrifying as Luther is, Bale's performance allows us to sympathize with a man who is desperate to make a difference in a world he no longer understands. **IHS**

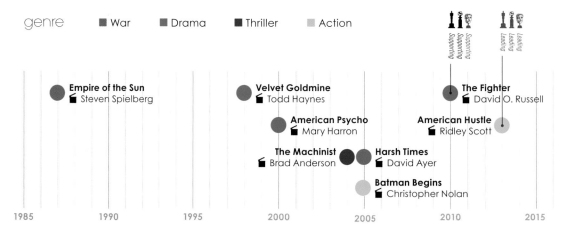

genre ■ War ■ Drama ■ Thriller ■ Action

Supporting / Supporting / Supporting

Leading / Leading / Leading

Empire of the Sun
Steven Spielberg

Velvet Goldmine
Todd Haynes

The Fighter
David O. Russell

American Psycho
Mary Harron

American Hustle
Ridley Scott

The Machinist
Brad Anderson

Harsh Times
David Ayer

Batman Begins
Christopher Nolan

1985 1990 1995 2000 2005 2010 2015

lucille ball 1911–89

Three Little Pigskins | **Follow the Fleet** | **Room Service** | **Five Came Back** | **Ziegfeld Follies** | **The Dark Corner** | **Lured** | **The Long, Long Trailer**

An actress with over 50 credited film roles to her name, Lucille Ball is nevertheless best remembered as the first superstar of U.S. television. The success of her small screen career stands in stark contrast to the multitude of film roles, often uncredited, that she had following her arrival in Hollywood. Undoubtedly talented, it was only with the explosion in popularity of the new medium in the late 1940s that Ball was able to find the perfect platform for her sassy humor and boundless energy.

Entering show business at the behest of her mother, more as a way to end her relationship with a local hoodlum nine years her senior, Ball was dispatched to New York, where she studied at the John Murray Anderson School for Dramatic Arts. She found work as a dancer, then a model, before departing for Hollywood in 1933. An uncredited appearance in *Roman Scandals* (1933) was followed by countless walk-on and minor roles throughout the 1930s, including the Three Stooges' short *Three Little Pigskins* (1934); the Astaire/Rogers vehicles *Roberta* (1935), *Top Hat* (1935) and *Follow the Fleet* (1936); opposite Rogers and Katharine Hepburn in *Stage Door* (1937); and with the Marx brothers in *Room Service* (1938).

At the same time, Ball branched out into theater, hoping that her appearance in Bartlett McCormack's *Hey Diddle Diddle* (1937) would lead to success on Broadway. However, the declining health of lead actor Conway Tearle resulted in delays and the production was canceled one week after it opened in Washington. In 1938, she took her first step into television, appearing in *The Wonder Show*. It is most notable now for beginning a 50-year professional partnership between Ball and the show announcer Gale Gordon.

A move to MGM in the early 1940s did little to help Ball's struggling career. She took over the title "Queen of the B's" from Fay Wray, starring in a string of low-key movies. She appeared in a few notable films later in the decade, particularly Henry Hathaway's *The Dark Corner* (1946), in which she plays the secretary of a private eye who has been framed for murder, and Douglas Sirk's *Lured* (1947), a London-set noir.

In 1948, Ball appeared on the CBS radio show "My Favorite Husband." It was a huge success and the studio asked her to develop it for television. She agreed, only on the proviso that she appear with her husband, Desi Arnaz, whom she met on the set of the 1940 comedy musical *Dance, Girl, Dance*. After initial concerns, the studio agreed and, in October 1951, *I Love Lucy* premiered. For the next three decades Ball would dominate the small screen — with the odd, moderately successful foray into cinema, in films such as *Yours, Mine, and Ours* (1968) and *Mame* (1974) — finding success and stardom in a way that she never fully managed to achieve in the cinema. **IHS**

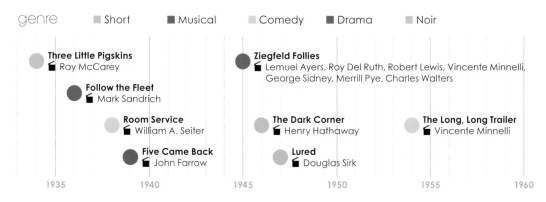

genre ■ Short ■ Musical ■ Comedy ■ Drama ■ Noir

Three Little Pigskins
Ray McCarey

Follow the Fleet
Mark Sandrich

Room Service
William A. Seiter

Five Came Back
John Farrow

Ziegfeld Follies
Lemuel Ayers, Roy Del Ruth, Robert Lewis, Vincente Minnelli, George Sidney, Merrill Pye, Charles Walters

The Dark Corner
Henry Hathaway

Lured
Douglas Sirk

The Long, Long Trailer
Vincente Minnelli

1935   1940   1945   1950   1955   1960

antonio banderas 1960

| Law of Desire | Tie Me Up! Tie Me Down! | Philadelphia | Desperado | Evita | The Mask of Zorro | Puss in Boots | The Skin I Live In |

Antonio Banderas has been one of Spain's biggest international stars since his Hollywood breakthrough in the mid-1990s. Unusually, however, it was appearing as himself in the 1991 documentary *Madonna: Truth or Dare* that helped launch his career stateside.

Born in Malaga in 1960, Banderas was working in a theater in Madrid when Pedro Almodóvar cast him in his camp comedy *Labyrinth of Passion* (1982). With classically handsome features that lend themselves to expressions of ardent intensity, the actor has the look of a matinee idol. It is an image that Hollywood made the most of when he was cast as the legendary outlaw and dashing swordsman in *The Mask of Zorro* (1998).

But Banderas also has a light comic touch that found a welcome home in Almodóvar's early films, most notably *Women on the Verge of a Nervous Breakdown* (1988). He has also shown a bold willingness to subvert the more macho aspects of his screen image. He played a young gay man in *Law of Desire* (1987), in which his male-on-male kiss with his costar was reported to be the first in Spanish cinema, and his first mainstream Hollywood role was as Tom Hanks' lover in the Oscar-winning *Philadelphia* (1993).

After his memorable turn as the disturbed kidnapper in Almodóvar's 1989 comedy *Tie Me Up! Tie Me Down!*, Banderas relocated to the United States. A relatively late learner of English, the actor has often been cast in Latino roles. He was commanding in the lavish 1996 musical *Evita*, which saw him reunited on screen with Madonna. He impressed as the taciturn Mexican action hero of Roberto Rodriguez's *Desperado* (1995), later reteaming with the director on the *Spy Kids* series (2001–03) and *Machete Kills* (2013). He even subverted his "Latin lover" image when voicing the role of a feline fencer in the *Shrek* sequels (2004–10) and their entertaining spin-off, *Puss in Boots* (2011).

More recently, Banderas has played supporting roles in a variety of films that include Woody Allen's *You Will Meet a Tall Dark Stranger* (2010), Steven Soderbergh's kick-ass *Haywire* (2011) and the more conventional actioner *The Expendables 3* (2014). The actor also found his way back to Almodóvar. His performance in *The Skin I Live In* (2011) is arguably his most memorable turn. Playing an obsessive surgeon with a dark secret, Banderas imbues the film with an elegant unease. **EL**

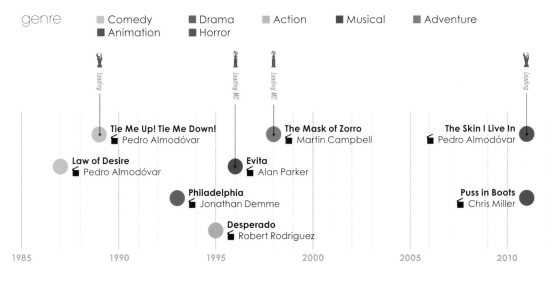

genre ■ Comedy ■ Drama ■ Action ■ Musical ■ Adventure
■ Animation ■ Horror

Leading

Tie Me Up! Tie Me Down!
Pedro Almodóvar

Law of Desire
Pedro Almodóvar

Philadelphia
Jonathan Demme

Leading MC

Leading MC

The Mask of Zorro
Martin Campbell

Evita
Alan Parker

Desperado
Robert Rodriguez

Leading

The Skin I Live In
Pedro Almodóvar

Puss in Boots
Chris Miller

1985 1990 1995 2000 2005 2010

javier bardem 1969

Jamón
Jamón

Live Flesh

Before Night
Falls

The Sea
Inside

No Country
for Old Men

Vicky
Cristina
Barcelona

Biutiful

Skyfall

Javier Ángel Encinas Bardem, born in 1969, comes from a long line of Spanish actors and filmmakers. As a youth he played for the Spanish national junior rugby team and his breakthrough role in Bigas Luna's raunchy comedy *Jamón Jamón* (1992) capitalized on this rugged physicality. The swaggering machismo of Bardem's would-be underwear model/bullfighter was overpowering; so much so that Luna hired the actor for his next film, *Golden Balls* (1993), in which he played a cocksure construction worker.

As an award-winning rising star, it was only a matter of time before Bardem worked with Spain's premier filmmaker, Pedro Almodóvar, acquitting himself well as a paralyzed cop-turned-Paralympic-basketball-player in romantic thriller *Live Flesh* (1997). His first foreign film soon followed, as gay Cuban poet and activist Reynaldo Areinas in *Before Night Falls* (2000), a role that won him a surprise Oscar nomination.

Despite a first English-language role in John Malkovich's crime thriller *The Dancer Upstairs* (2002), Bardem continued to focus on Spanish cinema. Notable performances included an unemployed shipyard worker in critics' favorite *Mondays in the Sun*

(2002), and *The Sea Inside*'s (2004) Ramon Sampedro, who campaigned in support of euthanasia following a diving accident that left him quadriplegic.

Then came the role that may well define Bardem's career. In the Coen brothers' gripping Cormac McCarthy adaptation *No Country for Old Men* (2007), Anton Chigurh is not just another hired killer — he is the embodiment of evil itself. Even with a ludicrous pageboy haircut, Bardem is genuinely chilling. He became the first Spanish actor to win an Oscar.

Confirming his versatility, Bardem was effortlessly charming and seductive as the painter who captivates three women in Woody Allen's *Vicky Cristina Barcelona* (2008). It reunited him with his *Jamón Jamón* costar Penélope Cruz and the couple married soon after. Bardem next gave a devastating performance as an impoverished and dying father in *Biutiful* (2010).

Now a global star, Bardem has appeared in several high-profile international films, notably as James Bond's gleefully sinister antagonist in *Skyfall* (2012). He played a sleazy underworld character in Ridley Scott's *The Counselor* (2013), a strange, quixotic role that underpins Bardem's willingness to push his range. **LS**

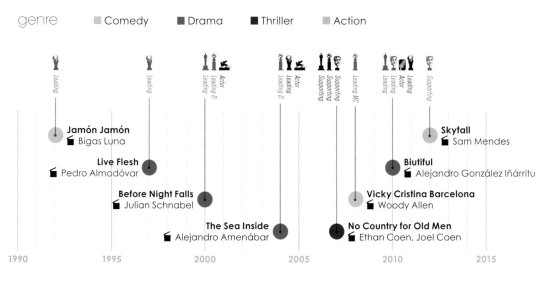

genre ■ Comedy ■ Drama ■ Thriller ■ Action

- Jamón Jamón — Bigas Luna (Leading)
- Live Flesh — Pedro Almodóvar (Leading)
- Before Night Falls — Julian Schnabel (Leading)
- The Sea Inside — Alejandro Amenábar (Actor, Leading D, Leading)
- No Country for Old Men — Ethan Coen, Joel Coen (Actor, Leading, Leading D)
- Vicky Cristina Barcelona — Woody Allen (Supporting, Supporting)
- Biutiful — Alejandro González Iñárritu (Leading MC, Leading, Actor, Leading)
- Skyfall — Sam Mendes (Supporting)

1990   1995   2000   2005   2010   2015

B

brigitte bardot 1934

| Doctor at Sea | Summer Manoeuvres | ...And God Created Woman | La Parisienne | Heaven Fell that Night | A Woman Like Satan | Testament of Orpheus | The Truth |

Brigitte Bardot was possibly more significant as a phenomenon than as an actress. The original "sex kitten" — her image created by Roger Vadim (her first husband and director of the film that made her famous), the press and the publicity machines — she came for some years to encapsulate what many people believed French cinema, and French actresses, were all about. The blond hair, the pout, and the lush and readily displayed curves provided an instant shorthand for cinematic va-va-voom. She herself came to loathe the image, longing to be taken seriously as an actress.

Born in Paris, daughter of a wealthy industrialist, she became a model before making her screen debut in 1952. She started out (as a brunette) in a range of negligible bit-parts, mostly in French-language films — though she did appear in the second installment of the anodyne British *Doctor* comedy series, *Doctor at Sea* (1955). She was appealingly tentative as an ingénue in René Clair's *Summer Manoeuvres* (1955), which would be her last supporting role. After that, starring roles started to come her way: *Naughty Girl* (1956), as the scatterbrained daughter of a Pigalle nightclub owner; *Mam'selle Striptease* (1956), as the author of a scandalous best-seller; *The Bride Is Too Beautiful* (1956), a comedy set in the fashion world. By now she was one of France's top stars, but as yet little known outside her native country.

And then came Vadim's *...And God Created Woman* (1956), the film that shot her to fame as the epitome of bikini-clad, Côte d'Azur youthful sexuality. The film attracted the attentions of the censor, and rumors were spread that the love scenes between Bardot and her costar, Jean-Louis Trintignant, were the real thing. When the movie opened in the United States, it broke box-office records for a French film. Wisely, Bardot turned down a seven-year contract with Warners, never making a Hollywood film.

Meanwhile, the international press leapt avidly on Bardot and her eventful love life. "Bardolatry" became a common term for the cult around her, and Simone de Beauvoir wrote a treatise, "Brigitte Bardot and the Lolita Syndrome." As de Beauvoir noticed, Bardot was often portrayed as the love interest of much older men, no doubt to appeal to her sizeable fan club of middle-aged males. In *La Parisienne* (1957), she was

genre   ■ Comedy   ■ Romance   ■ Drama   ■ Crime   ■ Horror   ■ Western

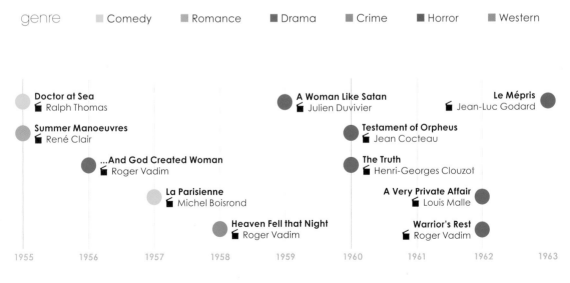

Doctor at Sea	Ralph Thomas
Summer Manoeuvres	René Clair
...And God Created Woman	Roger Vadim
La Parisienne	Michel Boisrond
Heaven Fell that Night	Roger Vadim
A Woman Like Satan	Julien Duvivier
Testament of Orpheus	Jean Cocteau
The Truth	Henri-Georges Clouzot
A Very Private Affair	Louis Malle
Warrior's Rest	Roger Vadim
Le Mépris	Jean-Luc Godard

1955   1956   1957   1958   1959   1960   1961   1962   1963

A Very
Private Affair

Warrior's
Rest

Le Mépris

Viva Maria!

Two Weeks in
September

Spirits of
the Dead

Shalako

The Legend
of Frenchie
King

teamed with Charles Boyer, and in Autant-Lara's *Love Is My Profession* (1958), her costar was Jean Gabin as a wealthy lawyer who falls for his seductive young client.

Rather improbably, she was a Resistance heroine in *Babette Goes to War* (1959), and briefly appeared as herself in Jean Cocteau's *Testament of Orpheus* (1960). Her first shot at being taken seriously as an actor was Henri-Georges Clouzot's courtroom drama *The Truth* (1960), in which she played a woman on trial for murder. Shooting was held up when she made an unsuccessful attempt at suicide. This incident partly inspired Louis Malle's *A Very Private Affair* (1962), costarring Marcello Mastroianni. Here Bardot played a version of herself, a movie star cracking under the pressures of fame.

She made another meretricious film for Vadim, *Warrior's Rest* (1962), and there were rumors that she was about to retire. Instead, she made her best film, *Le Mépris* (1963), adapted from a novel by Alberto Moravia and directed by Jean-Luc Godard. This was the closest Bardot came to making a mainstream movie and she was as good as she had ever been as a wife accompanying her screenwriter husband

(Michel Piccoli) to Cinecittà, and rejecting him in favor of a brash American producer (Jack Palance).

The film was a flop, however. Louis Malle's action-comedy western *Viva Maria!* (1965) did better, at least in France. She appeared for a few seconds in Godard's *Masculin Féminin* (1966) and played a model visiting London in the romance *Two Weeks in September* (1967). *Shalako* (1968) was a British western filmed in Spain, directed at the declining end of his career by Edward Dmytryk; both Bardot and her costar Sean Connery seemed ill at ease. For Malle again, she appeared in a segment of the Edgar Allan Poe triptych, *Spirits of the Dead* (1968).

By now, Bardot's box-office appeal was slipping. She made half a dozen more forgettable films, including *The Legend of Frenchie King* (1971) with Claudia Cardinale, and one final effort with Vadim, the lame *Don Juan, or If Don Juan Were a Woman* (1973), and then announced her retirement from acting. All attempts since to lure her out of retirement have failed. She lives mainly in the south of France and devotes herself to animal welfare causes through her Fondation Brigitte Bardot. **PK**

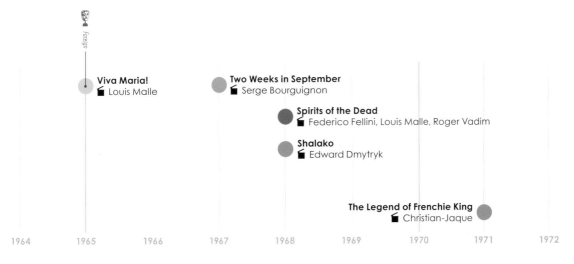

Foreign

Viva Maria!
Louis Malle

Two Weeks in September
Serge Bourguignon

Spirits of the Dead
Federico Fellini, Louis Malle, Roger Vadim

Shalako
Edward Dmytryk

The Legend of Frenchie King
Christian-Jaque

1964   1965   1966   1967   1968   1969   1970   1971   1972

sacha baron cohen 1971

Ali G Indahouse | Borat | Talladega Nights | Sweeney Todd: The Demon Barber of Fleet Street | Brüno | Hugo | The Dictator | Les Misérables

In 2013, Sacha Baron Cohen was given a Charlie Chaplin Britannia Award for Excellence in Comedy. It was presented to him by an 87-year-old woman in a wheelchair, one of Chaplin's last surviving costars. Moments later, Baron Cohen slipped, accidentally pushing the elderly woman off stage and killing her.

The prank was a fitting way for Baron Cohen to mark this recognition of his talent. Best known for his larger-than-life characters Ali G and Borat, he is a hugely gifted and smartly provocative comic performer.

Born in 1971, his big break came in 1998: creating and performing the character of Ali G, a hapless hip-hop fanatic from Staines, southern England, for the British satirical program The 11 O'Clock Show. In the guise of Ali G, Baron Cohen probed celebrities and politicians, creating discomfort for his interviewees with his boorish line of questioning. Baron Cohen would play Ali G in the 2002 movie Ali G Indahouse, a hit with UK audiences. While he gave a spirited performance, it lacked the improvised edge of the character's television appearances.

But in reprising another of his 11 O'Clock Show characters for the big screen in 2006, the blithely insensitive Kazakh reporter Borat, Baron Cohen was able to build on the guerrilla-style approach he had deployed so winningly on television. Directed by Larry Charles with documentary-like looseness, Borat: Cultural Learnings of America for Make Benefit Glorious Nation of Kazakhstan saw Baron Cohen immerse himself in the role of Borat for a trip across the United States, where he engaged with unsuspecting celebrities and members of the public. It was a riotously funny performance, but also a quick-thinking, astutely judged one: often his character's faux naivety reveals interviewees' attitudes that are as crass as his own.

The film's success turned Baron Cohen into a reluctant star, especially as his rising profile made it more difficult to continue his undercover pranksterism. The outrageous Austrian fashion reporter of Brüno (2009) and the Middle Eastern tyrant of The Dictator (2012) saw him go to increasing lengths to match the impact of Borat — to arguably diminishing returns.

Away from his own vehicles, Baron Cohen has shown himself to be a skilled actor, with notable cameos in the Will Ferrell vehicle Talladega Nights (2006) and Martin Scorsese's Hugo (2011), and accomplished singing roles in Sweeney Todd: The Demon Barber of Fleet Street (2007) and Les Misérables (2012). **EL**

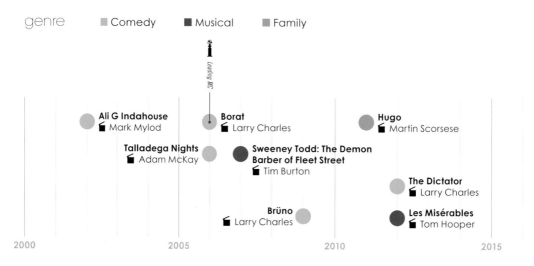

drew barrymore 1975

E.T. the Extra-Terrestrial   Firestarter   Guncrazy   Scream   The Wedding Singer   Charlie's Angels   Donnie Darko   Whip It

Few people have run the course of the child star-turned-rebellious youth, only to come out the other side and build a successful career, as fully as Drew Barrymore. Her offscreen antics, from substance abuse to nude photo-shoots, often threatened yet never fully destroyed her screen persona. Today, she is a popular actress and successful producer.

Born into Hollywood royalty — an acting dynasty that dates back to silent cinema — Barrymore's first feature role was playing William Hurt's daughter in Ken Russell's *Altered States* (1980). The 7-year-old was then cast into the limelight as one of the stars of *E.T. the Extra-Terrestrial* (1982). The innocence she displayed in Steven Spielberg's hugely successful adventure was channeled for markedly different results in the Stephen King adaptation *Firestarter* (1984). A few years of forgettable roles followed.

Poison Ivy (1992) may have played to Barrymore's then rebellious image, but *Guncrazy* (1992) revealed her potential. She was impressive in *Bad Girls* (1994), a revisionist western told from a female perspective, and the road movie *Boys on the Side* (1995), but was wasted in *Batman Forever* (1995). After a charming performance in Woody Allen's *Everyone Says I Love You* (1996), Barrymore sealed her cult status as the first victim in the brilliant opening sequence of Wes Craven's genre reboot, *Scream* (1996).

She scored one of her biggest successes opposite Adam Sandler in the romantic comedy *The Wedding Singer* (1998). Attempts to repeat the pair's success, with *50 First Dates* (2004) and *Blended* (2014) have attracted diminishing returns, but their first outing is a delight. Sandler tones down his idiot shtick, while Barrymore plays a blue-collar waitress to perfection. Her other successful comedy pairing was with Hugh Grant in the underrated *Music and Lyrics* (2007).

Charlie's Angels (2000) and its 2003 sequel were high-profile blockbuster successes for Barrymore's production company, Flower Films. She has since played a producing role in many of her films, including *Donnie Darko* (2001). She came to the rescue of Richard Kelly's beguiling feature debut and although she only has a cameo role as a schoolteacher, it remains one of her standout performances.

If Curtis Hanson's *Lucky You* (2007) lacked spark and *He's Just Not That Into You* (2009) meandered, *Grey Gardens* (2009) gave Barrymore one of her best roles. A dramatization of the acclaimed 1975 documentary, she received a Golden Globe for her performance as Little Edie. In the same year, she stepped into the director's chair for her feature debut, *Whip It* (2009), a smart comedy set in the world of the Texas women's roller derby and whose anarchic, playful spirit reflects Barrymore's own life and career. **IHS**

genre   ■ Family   ■ Thriller   ■ Crime   ■ Horror   ■ Romance   ■ Action
       ■ Mystery   ■ Drama

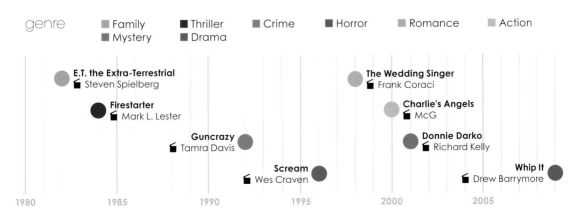

E.T. the Extra-Terrestrial — Steven Spielberg

The Wedding Singer — Frank Coraci

Firestarter — Mark L. Lester

Charlie's Angels — McG

Guncrazy — Tamra Davis

Donnie Darko — Richard Kelly

Scream — Wes Craven

Whip It — Drew Barrymore

1980   1985   1990   1995   2000   2005

emmanuelle béart 1963

| Manon des Sources | La Belle Noiseuse | Un Coeur en Hiver | Nelly and Mr. Arnaud | L'Enfer | Mission: Impossible | Time Regained | Elephant Juice |

An actress of striking beauty and piercing emotional power, Emmanuelle Béart won international prominence early on in her career with her performance in veteran director Claude Berri's *Manon des Sources* (1986). With her work for other established French directors like Jacques Rivette and Claude Sautet, she became associated with a style of arthouse cinema that might be thought of as characteristically French: intelligent, elegant and frequently underpinned with an erotic charge — qualities that also distinguish Béart's finest performances. She is often cast in dramas that explore romantic relationships in all their varied forms and throughout her work she has revealed, with subtlety and searching honesty, the enduring complexities of sexual desire. One of a handful of European actresses who enjoy an international profile, she continues to work mostly in France, where she is among the country's biggest stars.

Born in 1963 in the south of France, the teenage Béart acted in small parts in French television, but her breakthrough came when she was in her early twenties, in 1986's sweeping rural drama *Manon des Sources*. Set in 1930s Provence, the film features a major role for Béart as the young shepherdess Manon, who plots revenge against the villagers who alienated and exploited her late father. With her straw-blond hair and pellucid pale-blue eyes, Béart's is a startling

beauty that Berri's camera romanticizes — Manon's alluring looks are a significant feature of the plot. In a part with little dialogue, Béart brings an expressive physicality to a role that is all her own, and an attitude of fierce intensity that hints at her character's dark unspoken motivations.

There was a similar level of physicality to her performance in *La Belle Noiseuse* (1991). In director Jacques Rivette's absorbing drama, she plays a reluctant model under the demanding gaze of Michel Piccoli's ageing artist. Often manipulated into particular poses by Piccoli's firm hands, she is exposed and unguarded in the role, naked for much of the time. And as the power dynamic between artist and model shifts, with the young woman challenging the older man's creative processes, Béart's finely calibrated performance brilliantly conveys the sly emotional nuances of the script.

La Belle Noiseuse was one of the most critically acclaimed films of the year, further establishing Béart's reputation. The potent combination of sensuality and intelligence she displayed in this film was key to her next major role. In the drama *Un Coeur en Hiver* (1992) she plays Camille, a talented classical violinist who falls for a violin restorer, played by Daniel Auteuil. It is an exquisitely observed chamber piece and Béart's performance, which struggles to remain controlled as she realizes Auteuil's character

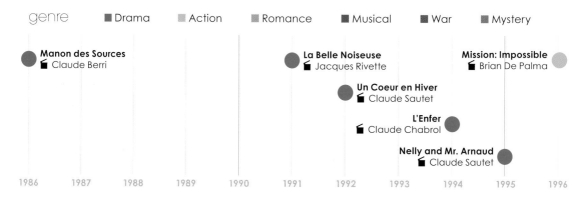

genre ■ Drama ■ Action ■ Romance ■ Musical ■ War ■ Mystery

Manon des Sources ⚑ Claude Berri
La Belle Noiseuse ⚑ Jacques Rivette
Mission: Impossible ⚑ Brian De Palma
Un Coeur en Hiver ⚑ Claude Sautet
L'Enfer ⚑ Claude Chabrol
Nelly and Mr. Arnaud ⚑ Claude Sautet

1986 1987 1988 1989 1990 1991 1992 1993 1994 1995 1996

| Les Destinées | 8 Women | La Répétition | Strayed | Nathalie... | The Story of Marie and Julien | Hell | The Witnesses |

is incapable of returning her love, is intimate, delicate and deeply moving. The part, for which Béart learned the violin, remains one of her finest performances. She reunited with Sautet for another resonant and restrained character study, *Nelly and Mr. Arnaud* (1995). In it, she plays a young Parisian with financial trouble who is in a loveless marriage, and develops a relationship with the older, affluent Mr. Arnaud (Michel Sarraut). Her typically subtle performance is perfectly attuned to the film's mood of haunting ambiguity.

By the mid-1990s, Béart was one of France's most prominent actresses and, like her contemporary Juliette Binoche, she attracted the attention of Hollywood. She lent glamour to the 1996 action film *Mission: Impossible*, was assured in the otherwise lackluster London-set romantic comedy *Elephant Juice* (1999), and gave a portrait of raw grief in her role as a mourning mother in the horror *Vinyan* (2008). But these English-language roles remain exceptions. "It opened a lot of doors," Béart has said of her *Mission: Impossible* role, "but I ran away from it."

France's director-centered, literary-minded, less commercially driven tradition of cinema has arguably offered more opportunity for her talent than she might have found elsewhere. Certainly, by the late 1990s she was a regular in some of France's most acclaimed dramas. In *Time Regained* (1999), Raoul Ruíz's sumptuous and dreamlike adaptation of the final

volume of Marcel Proust's *Remembrance of Things Past*, she gave a performance of poise and maturity as Gilberete, the woman with whom the narrator falls in love. And she was on commanding form in Olivier Assayas' period drama *Les Destinées* (2000), as the wife of a porcelain manufacturer, utterly compelling in a role that spanned three decades.

Béart also impressed in more contemporary roles, with such recent standouts as *Nathalie...* (2003), in which she played, with sly sensuality and a teasing sense of a provocation, a prostitute hired to seduce her client's husband, and *La Répétition* (2001), a psychological drama about the fractious relationship between a celebrated theatrical actress, played by Béart, and her friend from childhood. In 2003 she reunited with Rivette for *The Story of Marie and Julien*, playing a woman who returns to her older former lover, a delicate performance that enriches the film's enigmatic mood. And she collaborated with another esteemed European auteur, albeit posthumously, taking the lead role in *Hell* (2005), based on a script by the late, great Polish director Krzysztof Kieslowski.

Showing an aptitude for light comedy, she appeared in François Ozon's farcical *8 Women* (2001). The cast for this film was a roll call of France's most iconic actresses, including Catherine Deneuve, Isabelle Huppert and Fanny Ardent. It is a lineup in which Béart more than deserves her place. **EL**

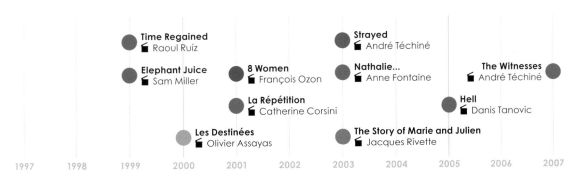

Time Regained
Raoul Ruíz

Elephant Juice
Sam Miller

8 Women
François Ozon

La Répétition
Catherine Corsini

Les Destinées
Olivier Assayas

Strayed
André Téchiné

Nathalie...
Anne Fontaine

The Story of Marie and Julien
Jacques Rivette

Hell
Danis Tanovic

The Witnesses
André Téchiné

| 1997 | 1998 | 1999 | 2000 | 2001 | 2002 | 2003 | 2004 | 2005 | 2006 | 2007 |

Manon des Sources
(1986)

La Belle Noiseuse
(1991)

Un Coeur en Hiver
(1992)

Mission: Impossible
(1996)

Les Destinées
(2000)

8 Women
(2001)

Nathalie...
(2003)

The Story of Marie and Julien
(2003)

Béart won a Best Supporting Actress César Award for her role in *Manon des Sources*, the sequel to *Jean de Florette* (1986). Shot together over a period of seven months, both films were highly successful.

Béart and Michel Piccolo in Jacques Rivette's *La Belle Noiseuse*.

Director Jacques Rivette with Béart on the set of *La Belle Noiseuse*, which cast the actress as the muse to Michel Piccolo's artist. Winner of the Palme d'Or prize at Cannes, the movie has a running time of four hours.

Béart and Andre Dussollier as a husband and wife in *Un Coeur en Hiver*, for which the actress spent 18 months learning to play the violin.

Mission: Impossible is one of Béart's few forays into Hollywood.

Set in the 1950s, *8 Women* is a murder-mystery comedy musical that revolves around an eccentric family of women and their employees. It won numerous plaudits for its all-star female cast.

Based on the novel of the same name by Jacques Chardonne, *Les Destinées* featured Béart as a young woman who falls in love with a married Protestant minister.

Béart said of her character in *Nathalie...* that "She wears a lot of make-up, but it is like a mask, something to protect her."

The Story of Marie and Julien reunited Béart with *La Belle Noiseuse* director Jacques Rivette. A supernatural love story, it starred the actress and Jerzy Radziwilowicz in the title roles.

warren beatty 1937

| Splendor in the Grass | Lilith | Mickey One | Bonnie and Clyde | McCabe & Mrs. Miller | The Parallax View | Shampoo | The Fortune |

Warren Beatty was born to be a star. Good looking and self-assured, his rise through the industry was faster than most. A star football player, he was encouraged to act following the success of his sister Shirley MacLaine. He spent a year at Northwestern University before leaving for New York, where he studied under Stella Adler.

Beatty's big break came when he was cast in *Splendor in the Grass* (1961), opposite Natalie Wood, with whom he would have the first in a series of high-profile affairs. Presaging the sexual revolution that would transform America in the late 1960s — and to which Beatty would become associated through his film work and offscreen antics — Elia Kazan's film was a hit and Beatty acclaimed by critics. He was nominated for Best Actor at the Golden Globes and received a New Star of the Year award.

A series of underwhelming features followed: *The Roman Spring of Mrs. Stone* (1961), opposite Vivien Leigh; *All Fall Down* (1962); Robert Rossen's *Lilith* (1964); *Promise Her Anything* (1965); the cult classic *Mickey One* (1965); and *Kaleidoscope* (1966). None of the films were able to capture the energy that Beatty displayed for Kazan. Looking at a failed career, Beatty took matters into his own hands. He began to build the reputation that would see him regarded as one of the most uncompromising figures in Hollywood.

On a visit to Paris, Beatty heard about a script for an American gangster film that François Truffaut had turned down. Returning to Hollywood, he bought the rights and convinced Arthur Penn to direct. After much deliberation, Faye Dunaway was cast and filming began on *Bonnie and Clyde* (1967). It transformed Beatty's career. With its potent cocktail of violence and anti-authoritarianism, *Bonnie and Clyde* heralded a new kind of Hollywood film, placing its producer-star at the vanguard of the movement.

After the forgettable *The Only Game in Town* (1970), Beatty starred opposite Julie Christie in Robert Altman's *McCabe & Mrs. Miller* (1971). One of Altman's best films, Beatty and Christie excel as the antihero and his opium-addicted business partner. Like *Bonnie and Clyde*, the film made the most of Beatty's rebel persona. As did *The Parallax View* (1974) and *Shampoo* (1975). Both films were concerned with the darker side of U.S. politics in the 1970s, but where Alan J. Pakula channeled it into one of the great conspiracy thrillers of the era, Hal Ashby's comedy drama, set in a Beverly

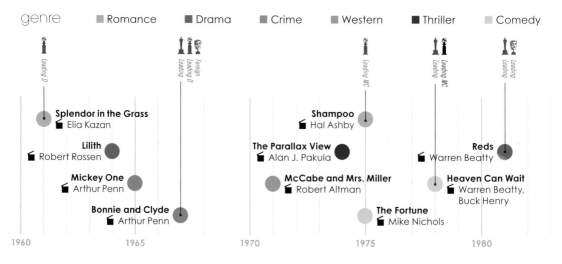

genre ■ Romance ■ Drama ■ Crime ■ Western ■ Thriller ■ Comedy

Splendor in the Grass
Elia Kazan

Lilith
Robert Rossen

Mickey One
Arthur Penn

Bonnie and Clyde
Arthur Penn

Shampoo
Hal Ashby

The Parallax View
Alan J. Pakula

McCabe and Mrs. Miller
Robert Altman

The Fortune
Mike Nichols

Reds
Warren Beatty

Heaven Can Wait
Warren Beatty, Buck Henry

1960   1965   1970   1975   1980

| $215M (U.S.) Shampoo (1975) | $293M (U.S.) Heaven Can Wait (1978) | $104M (U.S.) Reds (1981) | $30M (U.S.) Ishtar (1987) | $291M Dick Tracy (1990) | $84M (U.S.) Bugsy (1991) | $29M (U.S.) Love Affair (1994) | $42M Bulworth (1998) |

Heaven Can Wait | Reds | Ishtar | Dick Tracy | Bugsy | Love Affair | Bulworth | Town & Country

Hills hair salon, offers up a scathing satire set on the day Nixon first became president.

Beatty balanced charisma and intelligence with an air of bafflement at the way the world operates in the lead role of his first film as director, *Heaven Can Wait* (1978). A remake of *Here Comes Mr. Jordan* (1941), the updated film has Beatty playing Joe Pandleton, a football star who is prematurely plucked from Earth by an angel, only to return in various guises before settling on a millionaire whose wife and lover are planning a murder. The film succeeds thanks to the combination of Beatty's laid-back performance and Julie Christie's otherworldly charm, which contrast with the increasingly madcap antics of Diane Cannon and Charles Grodin's would-be killers. The film was a huge hit and Beatty was the first person to repeat Orson Welles' success with *Citizen Kane* (1941), when he was nominated for his roles as actor, director and producer at the Academy awards. He repeated the feat with his next film, *Reds* (1981).

Made at the height of Ronald Reagan's popularity, Beatty's account of the life of U.S. Communist John Reed and those he knew and loved, which included Eugene O'Neill (Jack Nicholson), Louise Bryant (Diane Keaton) and Emma Goldman (Maureen Stapleton), was a bold move for a mainstream Hollywood film. It is one of Beatty's finest performances, but the film will likely be remembered more for his daring in making such a provocative film at a time when America was veering further to the right.

After a six-year gap, Beatty starred alongside Dustin Hoffman and Isabelle Adjani in Elaine May's *Ishtar* (1987). Critically reviled and a disaster at the box office, the film deserves reappraisal. By contrast, the visually stunning *Dick Tracy* (1990), a critical and commercial success, now feels leaden. Far better is Barry Levinson's *Bugsy* (1991), about the life of the gangster who created Las Vegas. Beatty's compelling performance earned him his fourth Oscar nomination.

Beatty's work since has been varied. *Love Affair* (1994) is a hoary romance in which all involved should have known better. *Bulworth* (1998) is a brilliant, coruscating political satire, with the actor hilarious as a rapping senator. His most recent film, *Town & Country* (2001) was a misfire. Beatty has been working for some time on a drama about the later years of Howard Hughes. It will hopefully remind audiences of what a singular screen presence he can be. **IHS**

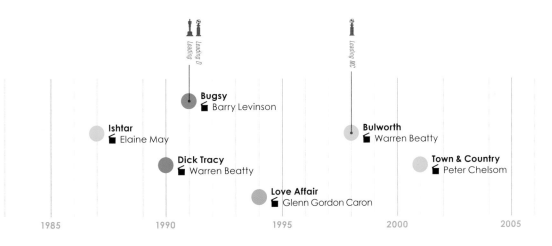

jean-paul belmondo 1933

Breathless   **Léon Morin, Priest**   **That Man from Rio**   **Pierrot le Fou**   **Mississippi Mermaid**   **Stavisky**   **Les Misérables**   **A Man and His Dog**

French actor Jean-Paul Belmondo's breakthrough role was in the 1960 film *Breathless*. Shot with freewheeling spontaneity on the streets of Paris, Jean-Luc Godard's debut helped usher in the French New Wave and Belmondo's portrayal of a petty criminal romantically involved with an American student fits perfectly with the movie's attitude of brash, pop-art provocation.

This sense of street-smart sophistication made Belmondo an icon of the French New Wave and he would reunite with Godard for *Une Femme est une Femme* (1961) and *Pierrot le Fou* (1965). The actor's work for the director was a glorious study in subversion, but it also resonated emotionally, especially in the poignant *Pierrot le Fou*.

Born in 1933, Belmondo had appeared in a handful of films prior to *Breathless*. In the same year as Godard's remarkable debut, he gave a memorable performance in Claude Sautet's taut crime drama *Classe Tous Risques* (1960), bringing tough-guy sensitivity to his role as a young crook. He also impressed in films that featured a less avowedly radical streak, including a collaboration with François Truffaut on the romantic comedy *Mississippi Mermaid* (1969), alongside Catherine Deneuve.

In Jean-Pierre Melville's *Léon Morin, Priest* (1961), Belmondo plays a young Catholic priest whose vows are challenged by Emmanuelle Riva's Communist widow. It was a performance of untypical introspection and quiet eroticism. The splashy James Bond spoof *That Man from Rio* (1964) saw the actor score a box-office hit with a more traditional action-adventure role and its success saw him steer toward more mainstream vehicles for the remainder of the 1960s and 1970s. However, he would occasionally return to more serious roles, such as his critically acclaimed performance in Alain Resnais' artful drama *Stavisky* (1974).

In the 1990s, Belmondo's work rate slowed, with the actor dividing his time between stage and screen. Still he continued to impress, most notably as Henri Fortin/Jean Valjean in Claude Lelouch's inventive take on Victor Hugo's *Les Misérables* (1995). In 2008 he interrupted a long absence from cinema (brought about by a stroke in 2001) with a performance of touching vulnerability in *A Man and His Dog*. **EL**

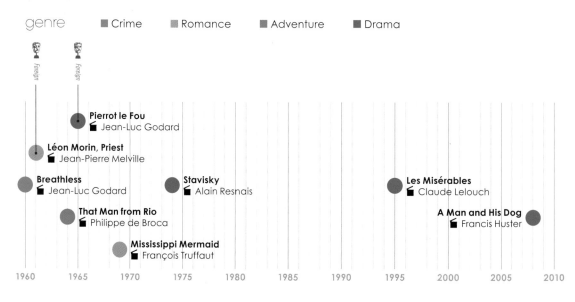

genre   ■ Crime   ■ Romance   ■ Adventure   ■ Drama

Pierrot le Fou — Jean-Luc Godard

Léon Morin, Priest — Jean-Pierre Melville

Breathless — Jean-Luc Godard

Stavisky — Alain Resnais

Les Misérables — Claude Lelouch

That Man from Rio — Philippe de Broca

A Man and His Dog — Francis Huster

Mississippi Mermaid — François Truffaut

1960   1965   1970   1975   1980   1985   1990   1995   2000   2005   2010

ingrid bergman 1915–82

| Intermezzo | Casablanca | Gaslight | Notorious | Journey to Italy | Anastasia | Murder on the Orient Express | Autumn Sonata |

One of the greatest stars of Hollywood's Golden Age, Ingrid Bergman was as comfortable working on films by European auteurs as she was on studio product. She brought a fearlessness to her performances that, at her best, radiated with passion and intelligence.

Born in Stockholm in 1915, Bergman became a star in her native Sweden before moving to Hollywood. She was the romantic obsession of a police inspector in her debut *Munkbrogreven* (1935), before taking the lead in *The Surf* (1935), *På solsidan* (1936) and *Intermezzo* (1936). The latter film proved so successful internationally that Hollywood remade it in 1939, keeping Bergman on. However, it was her appearance in the classic love story *Casablanca* (1942) that saw her star ascend.

Another remake, *Gaslight* (1944), followed. An equal to the British original, Bergman excels as the wife of a man who plans to kill her. It earned her the first of three Oscars. She followed it with three Hitchcock films: *Spellbound* (1945), *Notorious* (1946) and *Under Capricorn* (1949). *Notorious* is the best. An espionage thriller set mostly in Rio de Janeiro, Bergman and Cary Grant excel as two characters whose suspicion of each other gives way to desire.

Bergman's collaborations with Roberto Rossellini not only marked one of the high points in her career, but also almost destroyed her reputation in Hollywood when she left her husband for the Italian director. Of the five features they made together, *Stromboli* (1950) and *Journey to Italy* (1954) stand out. If the former is a powerful account of poverty, *Journey* is a withering study of a marriage in decline. As her own marriage to Rossellini was ending, Bergman starred in Jean Renoir's *Elena and Her Men* (1956), then returned to Hollywood to play the lead in *Anastasia* (1956), for which she received her second Academy Award.

If *Indiscreet* (1958) offered up little more than a slice of Hollywood froth, *The Inn of the Sixth Happiness* (1958) was an example of Hollywood taking liberties with a true story and Bergman's never quite grasping her character. The films were indicative of the gradual decline in good roles for the star. She received a third Oscar for a compelling cameo in Sidney Lumet's *Murder on the Orient Express* (1974), but her final great performance was in Ingmar Bergman's *Autumn Sonata* (1978). She plays a celebrated concert pianist who pays a visit to her estranged daughter. Playing opposite Liv Ullmann, Bergman excels as the matriarch. **IHS**

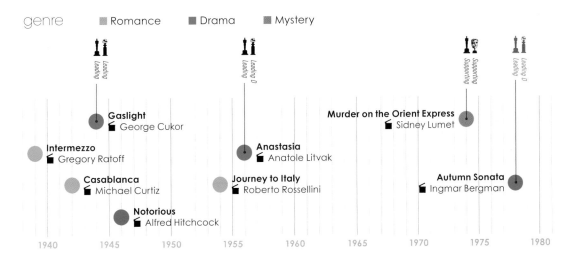

genre ■ Romance ■ Drama ■ Mystery

Gaslight — George Cukor

Intermezzo — Gregory Ratoff

Casablanca — Michael Curtis

Notorious — Alfred Hitchcock

Anastasia — Anatole Litvak

Journey to Italy — Roberto Rossellini

Murder on the Orient Express — Sidney Lumet

Autumn Sonata — Ingmar Bergman

1940 1945 1950 1955 1960 1965 1970 1975 1980

gael garcía bernal 1978

| Amores Perros | Y Tu Mamá También | The Motorcycle Diaries | Bad Education | The Science of Sleep | Even the Rain | No | Rosewater |

Enjoying phenomenal critical and commercial success, *Amores Perros* (2000) and *Y Tu Mamá También* (2001) drew the eyes of the world to the riches to be found in Mexican cinema. Significantly, both films featured the poster-boy looks and electrifying screen presence of Gael García Bernal.

Born in Guadalajara in 1978, the son of two liberal theater actors, Bernal learned his craft at London's Central School of Speech and Drama before moving back to Mexico for roles in television and shorts. With *Amores Perros*, a formally audacious portrait of contemporary Mexican society, the actor exploded onto the international stage. The charming, politically barbed road movie *Y Tu Mamá También* fanned the flames of Bernal's already growing fame. *El Crimen del Padre Amaro* (2002) may have been a more traditional piece of filmmaking but its narrative was incendiary, telling the tale of a recently ordained priest who becomes involved in a sexual relationship.

Resisting overtures to work in the United States, Bernal planned the next stage of his career with precision. Reprising the role of Ernesto "Che" Guevara from the TV movie *Fidel* (2002) for Walter Salles' hugely assured *The Motorcycle Diaries* (2004), the actor cemented his reputation with the lead in Pedro Almodóvar's cross-gender drama *Bad Education* (2004).

Bernal was suitably brooding as a vengeful son in the disturbing Gothic parable *The King* (2005), while in *The Science of Sleep* (2006) the actor displayed a skill for comedy, playing the shy and withdrawn Stephane whose fanciful and sometimes disturbing dream life constantly threatens to usurp his waking world.

Babel (2006) saw a re-pairing of Bernal with his *Amores Perros* director in a global tale of connected lives. Bernal's coolly received directorial debut, *Déficit* (2007) swiftly followed. *Blindness* (2008), *Rudo y Cursi* (2008) and Lukas Moodysson's *Mammoth* (2009) were flawed but interesting, while *The Limits of Control* saw Bernal working with Jim Jarmusch. Icíar Bollaín's *Even the Rain* (2010) was a major return to form. Shot in Bolivia the film looks at how indigenous peoples suffer in the face of corruption and privatization. *No* (2012), the tale of an advertising executive's attempts to defeat Pinochet in Chile's 1988 referendum, may well be Bernal's finest work to date. The actor's commitment to political issues continued with *Rosewater* (2014), an account of journalist Maziar Bahari's incarceration by the Iranian government on charges of espionage. **JW**

genre ■ Thriller ■ Drama ■ Adventure ■ Fantasy

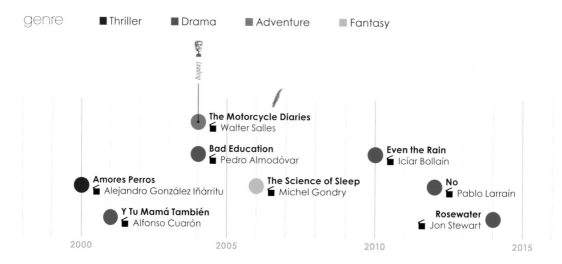

Leading

The Motorcycle Diaries
Walter Salles

Bad Education
Pedro Almodóvar

Even the Rain
Icíar Bollaín

Amores Perros
Alejandro González Iñárritu

The Science of Sleep
Michel Gondry

No
Pablo Larraín

Y Tu Mamá También
Alfonso Cuarón

Rosewater
Jon Stewart

2000   2005   2010   2015

halle berry 1966

| Jungle Fever | Boomerang | Bulworth | X-Men | Monster's Ball | Die Another Day | Things We Lost in the Fire | Cloud Atlas |

Born in Cleveland, Ohio, in 1966, Halle Maria Berry's first flush of fame came with her success in a number of beauty pageants, which prompted a brief career in modeling. In 1989, she moved to New York to pursue an acting career. However, it was a rocky start, which often found her living in sheltered accommodation. Her first television role was in the short-lived series *Living Dolls* (1989). Berry then moved to Los Angeles and, following a few minor television roles, she won a small part in Spike Lee's acclaimed *Jungle Fever* (1991). Her nuanced portrayal of a drug addict showed promise.

The next year, Berry was a captivating presence, opposite Eddie Murphy, in *Boomerang* (1992). Two noteworthy television appearances followed: *Queen* (1993), in which she played the illegitimate daughter of a slave and her white owner, and *Face of an Angel* (1999), which earned Berry a Golden Globe for her performance as Dorothy Dandridge, the first African-American actress to be nominated for an Oscar. She was impressive battling Jessica Lange in the child custody drama *Losing Isaiah* (1995), convincing as a panicked flight attendant in the action thriller *Executive Decision* (1996) and she excelled as the moral compass of Warren Beatty's political satire *Bulworth* (1998).

In 2000, Berry roared onto screens as Storm, the striking silver haired mutant with the power to control the weather, in the first of Marvel Comics' hit series of *X-Men* adaptations. Her brief stint as Catwoman in the 2004 misfire was lackluster, however.

Berry's finest moment to date is as Leticia Musgrove, the emotional heart of the masterful *Monster's Ball* (2001). The widow of a death row inmate who embarks on a relationship with one of the guards present at her husband's execution, Berry's portrayal of Leticia is palpable and tragic. She deservedly became the first African-American woman to win a Best Actress Oscar.

Berry's star grew brighter with her appearance in the otherwise forgettable Bond film *Die Another Day* (2002). In recent years, she has appeared in Susanne Bier's *Things We Lost in the Fire* (2007) as a woman dealing with her husband's untimely death, and played a stripper with multiple personality disorder in *Frankie and Alice* (2010). She also took on the challenging feat of multiple characters, across various time periods, in the sci-fi extravaganza *Cloud Atlas* (2012). In 2014 she launched her own production company, 606 Films, whose first project is the TV series *Extant* (2014–15), in which she stars. **MK**

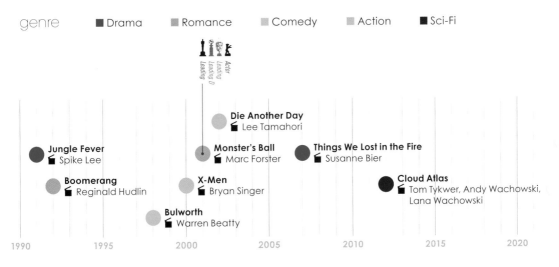

genre ■ Drama ■ Romance ■ Comedy ■ Action ■ Sci-Fi

Die Another Day
Lee Tamahori

Jungle Fever
Spike Lee

Monster's Ball
Marc Forster

Things We Lost in the Fire
Susanne Bier

Boomerang
Reginald Hudlin

X-Men
Bryan Singer

Cloud Atlas
Tom Tykwer, Andy Wachowski, Lana Wachowski

Bulworth
Warren Beatty

1990 | 1995 | 2000 | 2005 | 2010 | 2015 | 2020

juliette binoche 1964

| Rendez-vous | The Night Is Young | The Unbearable Lightness of Being | Les Amants du Pont-Neuf | Damage | Three Colors: Blue | The Horseman on the Roof | The English Patient |

From her emergence in the mid-1980s, Juliette Binoche has remained not only one of France's leading actresses, but also a truly international star, as evidenced by an enviable set of major film awards — an Oscar, Bafta and César, along with prizes from Cannes, Berlin and Venice, and three European Film Awards. Known for the fearlessness and commitment of her performances, as well as her fierce independence, the Parisian is that rarest of creatures, referred to by her compatriots with the definite article: La Binoche.

She was born in Paris in 1964, to a theater director father and drama teacher mother, and decided to become an actress in her teens. Giving early notice of that independent streak, she left drama school because she was unhappy with the curriculum, and shaped her own training — taking lessons with an acting coach and joining a touring theater company.

Her breakthrough in cinema came in 1985, first with a small role in Jean-Luc Godard's controversial retelling of the Virgin birth, Hail Mary, and later that year as a star of André Téchiné's Rendez-vous; her portrayal of a fledgling actress embroiled in a series of misbegotten relationships was both risqué and appealing, and heralded an exciting young performer.

She has stated that she "discovered the camera" while shooting the avant-garde crime thriller The Night Is Young (1986) with her then lover, Leos Carax. As the gamine point of a love triangle among thieves she certainly captivated the lens, while waiting more than 30 minutes before saying her first line.

Two years later, she was in another love triangle, and her first English-language film: Philip Kaufman's adaptation of Milan Kundera's The Unbearable Lightness of Being (1988). She was heartbreaking as Daniel Day-Lewis' more innocent lover, caught up in the Prague Spring. She then slept rough on the streets of Paris in preparation for her role as the homeless heroine in Carax's extravagant love story Les Amants du Pont-Neuf (1991). The film met with mixed reviews, as did her next English-language films, both released in 1992: Wuthering Heights, in which she played Cathy opposite Ralph Fiennes' Heathcliff, and Damage, as the icy object of Jeremy Irons' erotic obsession.

The young actress recovered from these minor setbacks superbly, giving one of cinema's definitive portrayals of grief in the sublime Three Colors: Blue (1993), and playing a romantic heroine in the energetic costume drama The Horseman on the Roof (1995).

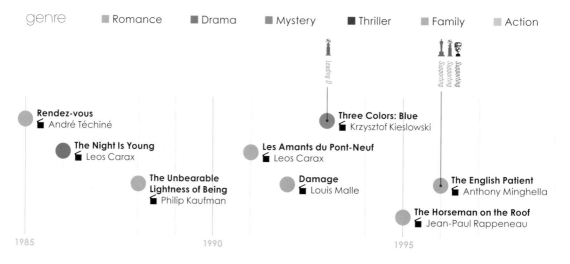

genre ■ Romance ■ Drama ■ Mystery ■ Thriller ■ Family ■ Action

Leading D

Supporting
Supporting
Supporting

Rendez-vous
André Téchiné

The Night Is Young
Leos Carax

The Unbearable Lightness of Being
Philip Kaufman

Three Colors: Blue
Krzysztof Kieslowski

Les Amants du Pont-Neuf
Leos Carax

Damage
Louis Malle

The English Patient
Anthony Minghella

The Horseman on the Roof
Jean-Paul Rappeneau

1985   1990   1995

$20 M (U.S.)	$13M (U.S.)	$2M (U.S.)	$350 M	$210 M	$20 M	$6 M	$529 M
The Unbearable Lightness of Being (1988)	*Damage* (1992)	*The Horseman on the Roof* (1995)	*The English Patient* (1996)	*Chocolat* (2000)	*Hidden* (2005)	*Certified Copy* (2010)	*Godzilla* (2014)

| Chocolat | The Widow of Saint-Pierre | Hidden | Flight of the Red Balloon | Certified Copy | Camille Claudel 1915 | Godzilla | Clouds of Sils Maria |

And then she experienced her biggest international success, in *The English Patient* (1996). Anthony Minghella's adaptation of Michael Ondaatje's World War II novel starred Fiennes and Kristin Scott Thomas as the ill-fated lovers, but the emotional bedrock of the film was provided by Binoche's nurse, who cares for Fiennes' stricken cartographer. She won one of the film's nine Oscars, for Best Supporting Actress.

Binoche famously passed on Spielberg's offer to appear in *Jurassic Park* (1993), and has worked sporadically in Hollywood without making a wholesale commitment to Los Angeles. She was the magical chocolatier who shakes up an uptight French village in *Chocolat* (2000), showed that she could let her hair down opposite Steve Carell in the formulaic romcom *Dan in Real Life* (2007), and finally got to act in a dinosaur movie, in *Godzilla* (2014).

But her focus, and her most adventurous work, has been elsewhere: she was sensational in Michael Haneke's grim treatise on multi-culturalism, *Code Unknown* (2000), and again with Daniel Auteuil in Haneke's chilling study of suppressed guilt and marital mistrust, *Hidden* (2005); gamely improvised throughout Hou Hsiao-Hsien's *Flight of the Red Balloon*

(2007); lended much-needed flesh and blood to *Certified Copy* (2010), Abbas Kiarostami's pretentious subversion of conventional romantic drama; and displayed tongue-in-cheek raunchiness in the back of a limousine in Cronenberg's *Cosmopolis* (2012).

She has a reputation for being proactive. Having made the polite family drama *Summer Hours* (2008) with Olivier Assayas, she felt she wanted more from the collaboration and challenged him to write a deeper female role. The result was *Clouds of Sils Maria* (2014), for which Binoche received rave reviews for her portrait of an actress forced to confront issues of age and continuing relevance. She also approached Bruno Dumont with the suggestion that they work together, despite the director's disinclination to use stars. Dumont's *Camille Claudel 1915* (2013), which charts the tragic sculptor's incarceration in a mental institution, showcased the actress' willingness to take risks — appearing alongside real psychiatric patients — and her ability to display the gamut of emotions, often within seconds of each other, with the utmost authenticity. It ranks with Julie in *Three Colors: Blue* as her greatest performance to date. As she entered her fifties, Binoche's own relevance was undiminished. **DM**

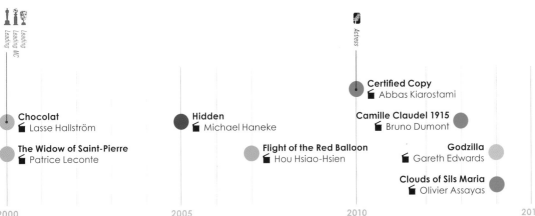

Leading
Leading MC
Leading

Actress

Chocolat
Lasse Hallström

The Widow of Saint-Pierre
Patrice Leconte

Hidden
Michael Haneke

Flight of the Red Balloon
Hou Hsiao-Hsien

Certified Copy
Abbas Kiarostami

Camille Claudel 1915
Bruno Dumont

Godzilla
Gareth Edwards

Clouds of Sils Maria
Olivier Assayas

2000   2005   2010   2015

The Unbearable
Lightness of Being
(1988)

Les Amants
du Pont-Neuf
(1991)

Three Colors: Blue
(1993)

Chocolat
(2000)

The English Patient
(1996)

Certified Copy
(2010)

Camille
Claudel 1915
(2013)

Clouds of
Sils Maria
(2014)

The Unbearable Lightness of Being featured Binoche as a waitress and photographer who falls in love with Daniel Day-Lewis' brain surgeon.

The Unbearable Lightness of Being is set during the events of the Prague Spring in 1968.

In *Les Amants du Pont-Neuf*, Binoche plays a painter driven to a life on the streets because of a failed relationship and a disease that is slowly destroying her sight.

In *Three Colors: Blue* Binoche gave a heart-rending portrayal of a woman whose family is killed in a car crash.

Binoche with Johnny Depp in *Chocolat*. Adapted from the novel by Joanne Harris, the movie tells the fairy tale-like story of a single mother who wins over the inhabitants of a French village with her healing chocolates.

Binoche with Naveen Andrews in *The English Patient*. The movie's director, Anthony Minghella, said of the star, "She has no skin, so tears and laughter are never very far away."

Certified Copy was the film debut of Binoche's costar, British opera singer William Shimell.

Binoche won the Best Actress award at Cannes for her role in *Certified Copy*. She plays a French antiques dealer whose name the audience never learns.

Camille Claudel 1915 depicts the life of the eponymous sculptor and lover of Auguste Rodin, who after suffering a breakdown was incarcerated in an asylum for the remaining 30 years of her life.

Clouds of Sils Maria director André Téchiné cowrote Binoche's breakthrough role in *Rendez-Vous* (1985).

Character Actor	Femme Fatale	Lover	Saint	Sinner

cate blanchett 1969

| Oscar and Lucinda | Elizabeth | The Lord of the Rings: The Fellowship of the Ring | The Aviator | Notes on a Scandal | I'm Not There | The Curious Case of Benjamin Button | Blue Jasmine |

Born in Melbourne in 1969, Cate Blanchett was a well-established stage actress when she made the transition to movies in 1997, appearing in *Paradise Road, Thank God He Met Lizzie* and Gillian Armstrong's adaptation of Peter Carey's novel *Oscar and Lucinda*. However, her international breakthrough was her stunning portrayal of Queen Elizabeth I in *Elizabeth* (1998), for which she received her first Oscar nomination. She would return to the character almost a decade later with the less successful *Elizabeth: The Golden Age* (2007).

Blanchett appeared in a number of movies over the next few years, but, aside from *The Talented Mr. Ripley* (1999), most of them were met with a muted critical response. However, she shone as the elf queen Galadriel in Peter Jackson's *The Lord of the Rings* trilogy (2001–03), and returned for its uneven prequel trilogy, *The Hobbit* (2012–14).

After costarring in Wes Anderson's underrated *The Life Aquatic with Steve Zissou* (2004), Blanchett won her first Oscar as Katharine Hepburn in *The Aviator* (2004), Martin Scorsese's biopic of Howard Hughes. The following year, she excelled in the Australian drama *Little Fish* (2005), as a recovering drug addict, while in Steven Soderbergh's World War II drama *The Good German* (2006), she was a spikey foil to George Clooney's journalist. The pair would reunite in the same era, in Clooney's *The Monuments Men* (2014).

Blanchett was impressive as a wounded tourist in *Babel* (2006) and the object of Judi Dench's obsession in *Notes on a Scandal* (2006). Perhaps her most notable performance of this period was as one of the six versions of Bob Dylan in Todd Haynes' experimental biopic *I'm Not There* (2007). Almost unrecognizable, Blanchett captures the musician's vulnerability as he controversially eschews acoustic folk in favor of an electric sound.

Blanchett reunited with her *Babel* costar Brad Pitt for *The Curious Case of Benjamin Button* (2008), an impressive technical achievement that was ultimately unsatisfying. Likewise, *Indiana Jones and the Kingdom of the Crystal Skull* (2008) proved a sequel too far for the Steven Spielberg-directed series.

One of Blanchett's most accomplished performances to date is as the troubled socialite protagonist of Woody Allen's comedy-drama *Blue Jasmine* (2013), creating sympathy for a woman whose behavior veers toward the abhorrent. The performance won her a second Oscar. **JWa**

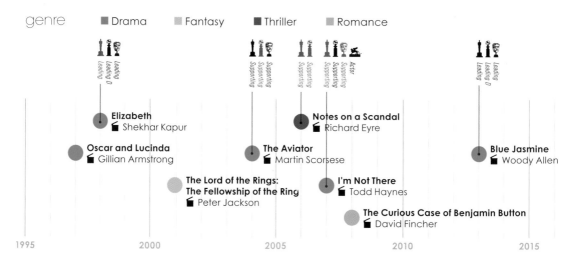

genre ■ Drama ■ Fantasy ■ Thriller ■ Romance

Elizabeth — Shekhar Kapur
Oscar and Lucinda — Gillian Armstrong
The Lord of the Rings: The Fellowship of the Ring — Peter Jackson
Notes on a Scandal — Richard Eyre
The Aviator — Martin Scorsese
I'm Not There — Todd Haynes
The Curious Case of Benjamin Button — David Fincher
Blue Jasmine — Woody Allen

1995 2000 2005 2010 2015

dirk bogarde 1921–99

| The Blue Lamp | Doctor in the House | Ill Met by Moonlight | A Tale of Two Cities | The Servant | Accident | The Damned | Death in Venice |

As Dirk Bogarde always readily admitted, he made a lot of terrible movies. In 1947, at the outset of his career, he signed a contract with the Rank Organisation, who proceeded to groom him as their new matinee idol and cast him in a long run of lightweight films. There was occasional relief from the dross: in Ealing's *The Blue Lamp* (1950) he was unexpectedly effective as the sneering young thug who guns down a policeman, and he played a criminal on the run who eluctantly takes a stray child under his wing in Charles Crichton's *Hunted* (1952). Often, though, he was badly miscast — as in *The Spanish Gardener* (1956), where he was wildly unconvincing as a Hispanic champion pelota player; as real-life man of action Patrick Leigh Fermor in Powell and Pressburger's misfiring *Ill Met by Moonlight* (1957); or as Sydney Carton in Ralph Thomas' ponderous take on *A Tale of Two Cities* (1958).

Bogarde also found himself trapped as the lead in Rank's money-spinning series of *Doctor* films (1954–63), which he came increasingly to loathe. Two of his most unsuitable assignments came in the abysmal *Song Without End* (1960), where he played Franz Liszt, and in the high-camp British western, *The Singer Not the Song* (1961), where he played a Mexican bandit.

But with *Victim* (1961), Bogarde broke away for good from matinee idol typecasting, playing older than his age — and bisexual — as an eminent barrister who speaks out against the legal oppression of homosexuals. It was a choice that would shatter his image and alienate most of his fan base. Bogarde welcomed this. It was, he wrote, "the wisest decision I ever made in my cinematic life." Though he never admitted he was gay, after *Victim* he felt able to accept roles that implicitly admitted it for him.

Bogarde made several films with his best director, Joseph Losey. *The Servant* (1963) turned a beady eye on the British class system, with Bogarde insinuatingly contemptuous as the valet undermining his feather-brained employer, while *Accident* (1967) scrutinizes the intellectual mind-games of two Oxford dons (Bogarde and Stanley Baker) as they compete for the charms of Jacqueline Sassard. Widening his scope yet further, he made two films with Luchino Visconti: in *The Damned* (1969) he was one of an upper-class German family crumbling under the impact of Nazism; and in *Death in Venice* (1971), he brought an effete dignity as a composer fatally fixated on a beautiful boy.

In his final film, *These Foolish Things* (1990), Bogarde played a dying Englishman resident in France, who reconciles with his estranged daughter. There was an elegiac gentleness to his performance that provided an ideal coda to his career. **PK**

genre ■ Crime ■ Comedy ■ War ■ Drama

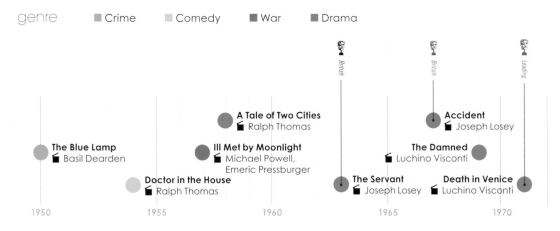

		A Tale of Two Cities	British	Accident — Leading
		🎗 Ralph Thomas		🎗 Joseph Losey
The Blue Lamp		Ill Met by Moonlight		The Damned
🎗 Basil Dearden		🎗 Michael Powell, Emeric Pressburger		🎗 Luchino Visconti
	Doctor in the House		The Servant	Death in Venice
	🎗 Ralph Thomas		🎗 Joseph Losey	🎗 Luchino Visconti
1950	1955	1960	1965	1970

humphrey bogart 1899–1957

| The Petrified Forest | Angels with Dirty Faces | The Roaring Twenties | The Maltese Falcon | High Sierra | Casablanca | To Have and Have Not | The Big Sleep |

Hollywood tough guy, romantic idol, comedy actor and star, Humphrey Bogart's talent was always greater than the image most audiences associated him with — that of the hardened criminal or antihero, who bristles against authority, always playing by his own rules. It reflected the actor's steeliness in real life, best exemplified by his stance against the House Un-American Activities Committee in the late 1940s.

A native New Yorker, Bogart was born in 1899. Rather than attend an Ivy League college after leaving school, as his parents wanted, he joined the navy. On his return, a friend found him a job as a stage manager and it was not long before he took to acting.

Bogart's first notable screen appearance was in *Up the River* (1930), which starred his friend and drinking buddy Spencer Tracy. However, his breakthrough came playing escaped murderer Duke Mantee in *The Petrified Forest* (1936), opposite Leslie Howard and Bette Davis. A box-office success, it raised the actor's profile.

Over the course of the 1930s, Bogart worked industriously, mostly on crime and gangster films. He brought depth to the roles he played and on certain films, such as *Marked Woman* (1937), appearing alongside Bette Davis again, and *Angels with Dirty Faces* (1938), featuring his first appearance opposite James Cagney, he proved to be a magnetic presence. Bogart starred with Cagney again in Raoul Walsh's epic gangster drama *The Roaring Twenties* (1939), giving a memorably malevolent turn. He reunited with Walsh for the noir *They Drive by Night* (1940). Appearing opposite George Raft, then the bigger star, Bogart proved himself a far more capable actor.

High Sierra (1941) was Bogart's last major performance as a gangster. Director Walsh initially opposed his being cast in the lead role of Roy Earle, still seeing him more as a supporting actor. However, Bogart assuaged any doubts with one of his finest performances, imbuing the gnarled, bitter character with feeling. He followed it with his stunning turn as Sam Spade in John Huston's *The Maltese Falcon* (1941). A year later, thanks to the machinations of uber-producer Hal B. Wallis, the actor finally broke through to the top echelon of Hollywood with *Casablanca* (1942). His casting was one of the film's many strokes of genius and Bogart threw himself into the role of Rick Blaine, the ex-gun-running owner of a popular bar in the exotic Moroccan city. Reeling in his tough guy image, Bogart's Rick is a smart, fast-talking chancer

genre ■ Crime ■ Mystery ■ Romance ■ Noir ■ Thriller ■ Adventure

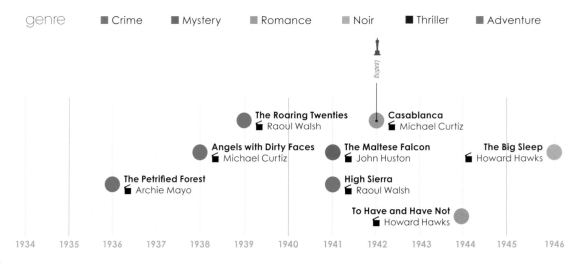

Leading

The Roaring Twenties
🎬 Raoul Walsh

Casablanca
🎬 Michael Curtiz

Angels with Dirty Faces
🎬 Michael Curtiz

The Maltese Falcon
🎬 John Huston

The Big Sleep
🎬 Howard Hawks

The Petrified Forest
🎬 Archie Mayo

High Sierra
🎬 Raoul Walsh

To Have and Have Not
🎬 Howard Hawks

1934 1935 1936 1937 1938 1939 1940 1941 1942 1943 1944 1945 1946

$41 M (U.S.)
Casablanca
(1942)

$189 M (U.S.)
The Caine Mutiny
(1954)

Dark Passage	The Treasure of the Sierra Madre	In a Lonely Place	The African Queen	The Caine Mutiny	Sabrina	We're No Angels	The Harder They Fall

whose heart was broken by the very woman that turns up in his bar asking for help. *Casablanca* features a fine support cast, but the film belongs to Bogart.

The star's encounter with Lauren Bacall on the set of *To Have and Have Not* (1944) is the stuff of Hollywood legend. Their on-screen relationship was incendiary, particularly in their next film, *The Big Sleep* (1946). William Faulkner, who cowrote the screenplay, admired Bogart's performance, acknowledging, "He has a sense of humor that contains that grating undertone of contempt." Bogart divorced his third wife after filming on *The Big Sleep* was completed and married Bacall a few months later.

Dark Passage (1947) was Bogart and Bacall's third feature together, although due to the story, of a man who undergoes transformative plastic surgery, he does not appear until later in the film. Like their final collaboration, *Key Largo* (1948), it lacks the power of *To Have and Have Not* and *The Big Sleep*.

Even by the standards of Bogart's previous films, *The Treasure of the Sierra Madre* (1948) is a bleak exploration of the heartlessness of men. Bogart plays one of three prospectors searching for gold in Mexico. Dobbs is Bogart's most ruthless character since

George Hally in *The Roaring Twenties*. However, he was outclassed by Walter Huston's Oscar-winning turn.

Nicholas Ray's *In a Lonely Place* (1950) remains one of the finest films made about Hollywood, with Bogart turning in one of his most complex performances as a hard-bitten, cynical screenwriter, who becomes a murder suspect. The film has grown in stature with time, but is still eclipsed by the popularity of *The African Queen* (1951). A knockabout drama centering on the relationship between Bogart's boat owner and Katharine Hepburn's missionary in Africa at the outbreak of World War I, it was a huge success and won the actor his only Academy Award.

Of his final roles, Bogart was impressive as a naval officer whose command of a ship is taken from him in *The Caine Mutiny* (1954). He also offered up his two finest comic performances, first in Billy Wilder's *Sabrina* (1954), playing a wealthy industrialist who falls for his driver's daughter, then as one of a trio of convicts who escape prison in *We're No Angels* (1955). His last film, *The Harder They Fall* (1956), is set in the boxing world where he plays a journalist caught up in a match-fixing scam. Like so many of his best roles, Bogart's character is a hardened shell with an honest heart. **IHS**

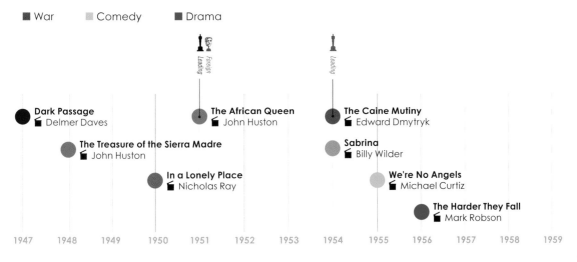

■ War   ■ Comedy   ■ Drama

Foreign
Leading

Leading

Dark Passage
🎬 Delmer Daves

The African Queen
🎬 John Huston

The Caine Mutiny
🎬 Edward Dmytryk

The Treasure of the Sierra Madre
🎬 John Huston

Sabrina
🎬 Billy Wilder

In a Lonely Place
🎬 Nicholas Ray

We're No Angels
🎬 Michael Curtiz

The Harder They Fall
🎬 Mark Robson

1947   1948   1949   1950   1951   1952   1953   1954   1955   1956   1957   1958   1959

marlon brando 1924–2004

| The Men | A Streetcar Named Desire | The Wild One | On the Waterfront | Guys and Dolls | The Fugitive Kind | One-Eyed Jacks | Reflections in a Golden Eye |

As Stanley Kowalski in the original 1947 stage production of *A Streetcar Named Desire*, Marlon Brando forever altered the landscape in American performance. Often cited as the leading exponent of Method acting — the system derived from the teachings of Russian actor and director Constantin Stanislavski and promulgated in America by acting teacher Lee Strasberg — what Brando had, or possessed, could not be schooled. Even though he had studied with acclaimed acting coach Stella Adler, the nature of Brando's gift was too large, too poetic and ultimately too mysterious to be attributed to any one movement. Playwright David Mamet was right to surmise that a talent like Brando would have succeeded anyway — regardless of the gurus who sought to claim his success a result of their expertise as opposed to his.

Born in Omaha, Nebraska, in 1924, Brando was educated at Shattuck Military Academy, where he was expelled for insubordination — though not before impressing in a school production. There had already been intimations as to where his future might lie: Brando's older sister had moved to New York to pursue an acting career; his mother had been a member of the Omaha Community Playhouse, where she had appeared onstage with Henry Fonda. After expulsion from Shattuck, Brando briefly returned home before joining his sister in New York, where he attended Erwin Piscator's Drama Workshop at the New School. It was here, in a class that included Rod Steiger and Shelley Winters, that Brando met Adler. On seeing Brando for the first time, she is reported to have said, "Who's the vagabond?" As first responses go, Adler's is remarkable in that it seemed to intuit what future audiences would feel — or a variation thereof — when Brando appeared on stage or on screen.

Brando made his screen debut with *The Men* (1950), as a returning war veteran and paraplegic. In what was considered unusual practice at the time, he spent weeks at a veterans' hospital in an attempt at understanding as well as verisimilitude. His performance was warmly reviewed, but the film was a disappointment at the box office. Still, Brando had made his mark. He followed with the movie version of *A Streetcar Named Desire* (1951), directed by Elia Kazan, the play's original director and Brando's most vital collaborator. A classic of its kind, Tennessee Williams' poetic masterpiece was always too florid

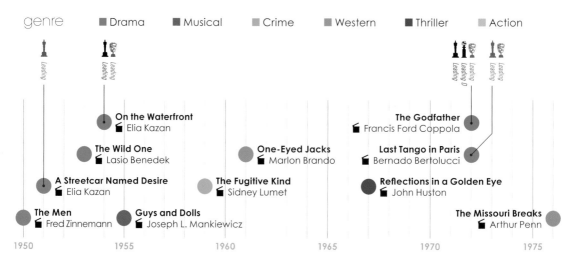

genre   ■ Drama   ■ Musical   ■ Crime   ■ Western   ■ Thriller   ■ Action

On the Waterfront
Elia Kazan

The Wild One
Lasio Benedek

A Streetcar Named Desire
Elia Kazan

The Men
Fred Zinnemann

Guys and Dolls
Joseph L. Mankiewicz

One-Eyed Jacks
Marlon Brando

The Fugitive Kind
Sidney Lumet

The Godfather
Francis Ford Coppola

Last Tango in Paris
Bernado Bertolucci

Reflections in a Golden Eye
John Huston

The Missouri Breaks
Arthur Penn

1950   1955   1960   1965   1970   1975

$1.4 BN	$205 M	$1.1 BN	$272 M (U.S.)	$7 M (U.S.)	$39 M (U.S.)	$152 M
The Godfather (1972)	Last Tango in Paris (1972)	Superman (1978)	Apocalypse Now (1979)	A Dry White Season (1989)	The Freshman (1990)	The Score (2001)

| The Godfather | Last Tango in Paris | The Missouri Breaks | Superman | Apocalypse Now | A Dry White Season | The Freshman | The Score |

for the screen. But Brando remains electric, and as the closest thing we have to a record of his famous Broadway performance, it should be cherished. *Viva Zapata!* (1952) and *Julius Caesar* (1953) saw Brando extend his range. *The Wild One* (1953) incited a stale rebellion, though its iconography remains potent.

In *On the Waterfront* (1954), Brando gave one of his greatest and most influential performances. As ex-fighter and longshoreman Terry Malloy, Brando exemplified the Method at its most poetic. Two scenes in particular are justifiably lauded: Brando at his most intuitively expressive, picking up Eva Marie Saint's glove and putting it on his hand; while his "contender" speech, in response to his brother's betrayal, remains one of the most moving and memorable scenes in cinema. Martin Scorsese and Robert De Niro would pay tribute to this scene in *Raging Bull* (1980), though they refrained from the emotion so evident in Brando's delivery. In hindsight, *On the Waterfront* can be seen as the culmination of Brando's genuine engagement with Hollywood and the precise moment he delivered on the promise of his Broadway arrival. After three successive Academy Award nominations (1952–54), he won Best Actor.

Brando himself became indifferent toward acting and fame. He made some poor choices, though he was still capable of a surprise like *Guys and Dolls* (1955). He directed himself in *One-Eyed Jacks* (1961) after firing Stanley Kubrick. But directors who fit the Kazan mould, and who had trained in theater and television, elicited the best from him — such as Sidney Lumet on *The Fugitive Kind* (1959) and Arthur Penn on *The Chase* (1966).

In the early 1970s, Brando made a spectacular comeback. *The Godfather* (1972) reaffirmed his status as America's greatest actor, forever linking him to the generation he had inspired — Al Pacino, James Caan and, by way of his young Vito Corleone in *The Godfather, Part II* (1974), Robert De Niro. *Last Tango in Paris* (1972) saw Brando at his most naked and personal before he withdrew altogether, aside from the occasional cameo or supporting role in films such as *The Missouri Breaks* (1976), *Superman* (1978), *A Dry White Season* (1989) and *The Freshman* (1990). His final film was *The Score* (2001), with De Niro and Edward Norton. But his last great film was *Apocalypse Now* (1979), where Brando's rogue colonel anticipated the actor's self-imposed exile from the profession he had done so much to redefine. **MM**

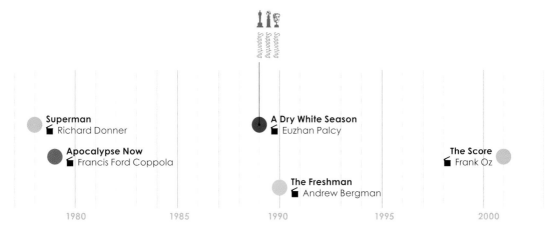

■ War   ■ Comedy

Supporting
Supporting
Supporting

Superman
🎬 Richard Donner

Apocalypse Now
🎬 Francis Ford Coppola

A Dry White Season
🎬 Euzhan Palcy

The Freshman
🎬 Andrew Bergman

The Score
🎬 Frank Oz

1980   1985   1990   1995   2000

The Men
(1950)

A Streetcar Named Desire
(1951)

On the Waterfront
(1954)

Guys and Dolls
(1955)

The Godfather
(1972)

Last Tango in Paris
(1972)

Apocalypse Now
(1979)

A Dry White Season
(1989)

Brando as the paraplegic solider Ken and Teresa Wright as his fiancee Ellen in *The Men*.

Despite his electrifying performance in *A Streetcar Named Desire*, Brando was the only one of the four cast members nominated for an acting Oscar who did not win one.

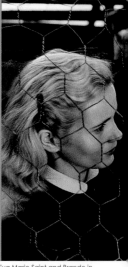

Brando and Vivien Leigh in *A Streetcar Named Desire*. Brando was initially rejected for the role of Stanley Kowalski in the Broadway production because he was considered too young and too handsome.

Eva Marie Saint and Brando in *On the Waterfront*.

In contrast to appearances on screen, Brandon and his costar Frank Sinatra did not get along. Tensions on set became so high that the pair eventually spoke to each other only through intermediaries.

Brando and director Francis Ford Coppola on the set of *The Godfather*.

Brando refused the Oscar he was awarded for his iconic role as Vito Corleone in **The Godfather**, and sent activist Sacheen Littlefeather to the ceremony in his place, to address the American Indian rights movement.

The explicit sexual content of **Last Tango in Paris** caused controversy worldwide upon its release.

Brando and Martin Sheen as Colonel Kurtz and Captain Willard in **Apocalypse Now**. Brando arrived late on set, having not read the script or the book it was based on. After arguing with director Francis Ford Coppola, an ad-lib style script was agreed upon.

Due to a recent weight gain, Brando stipulated that he be filmed mostly in shadows for **Apocalypse Now**.

Brando and Donald Sutherland in **A Dry White Season**, set in South Africa during apartheid.

rebels in cinema

Louise Brooks | Errol Flynn | Orson Welles | Marlon Brando | James Dean | Faye Dunaway & Warren Beatty | Dennis Hopper & Peter Fonda | Clint Eastwood

The rebel has been a key character in cinema since the 1950s, when a shift in cultural values raised questions about what constitutes morality. The archetypal rebel is Marlon Brando's biker Johnny in Laslo Benedek's *The Wild One* (1953). When asked "What are you rebelling against?" Johnny replies, nonchalantly as he picks a track on a jukebox (a key symbol of youthful rebellion in 1950s America), "Whadda you got?"

Rebellion need not exist on the fringes of contemporary society. Cinema has chronicled the lives of rebels of all periods; perhaps the earliest historical figure to get the Hollywood treatment was Spartacus. Robin Hood — a perennially popular rebel against the iniquities of the feudal system — has been portrayed on screen by Douglas Fairbanks, Errol Flynn, Richard Greene, Sean Connery, Kevin Costner and Russell Crowe. In Mexico, Robin Hood's equivalent is Zorro, whose love for the people and hatred of corrupt government produced no less mythic a character. A real-life Mexican, revolutionary Emiliano Zapata, was honored in Elia Kazan's *Viva Zapata!* (1952). The allure of Che Guevara, Salvatore Giuliano, T.E. Lawrence and John Reed inspired, respectively, Steven Soderbergh, Francesco Rosi, David Lean and Warren Beatty to direct biopics about them.

Some films depict rebels within the system, nowhere more than in the cop movie genre. The titular characters in *Dirty Harry* (1971), *Shaft* (1971) and *Bad Lieutenant* (1992 and 2009), as well as the rogue cops played by Takeshi Kitano, are mavericks who skirt the very edges of mainstream society. Their actions, justified by their own morality, may not be in the public interest, but they carry them out nonetheless.

In commerce, the rebel can soon become the institution, as witnessed in *Citizen Kane* (1941) and *There Will Be Blood* (2007). Orson Welles' Charles Foster Kane and Daniel Day-Lewis' Daniel Plainview are both keen to tear the status quo down in their respective worlds, but ultimately do little more than rewrite rules that, one day, someone else will attempt to destroy.

In civil society, the rebel may start out normal but become anti-social through force of circumstance. Thus Howard Beale (Peter Finch) in *Network* (1976) and Lester Burnham (Kevin Spacey) in *American Beauty* (1999) are close cousins to D-Fens (Michael Douglas) in *Falling Down* (1993) and Travis Bickle (Robert De Niro) in *Taxi Driver* (1976). The heroes of *Easy Rider* (1969) — played by Peter Fonda and Dennis Hopper — have been made outcasts by the terrible state of "normal" society in the United States of the late 1960s.

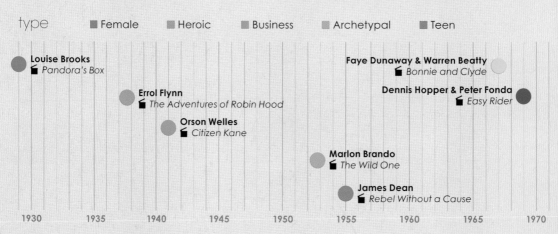

type   ■ Female   ■ Heroic   ■ Business   ■ Archetypal   ■ Teen

Louise Brooks
Pandora's Box

Errol Flynn
The Adventures of Robin Hood

Orson Welles
Citizen Kane

Marlon Brando
The Wild One

James Dean
Rebel Without a Cause

Faye Dunaway & Warren Beatty
Bonnie and Clyde

Dennis Hopper & Peter Fonda
Easy Rider

1930   1935   1940   1945   1950   1955   1960   1965   1970

| Robert De Niro | Matthew Broderick | Takeshi Kitano | Geena Davis & Susan Sarandon | Vincent Cassel | Kevin Spacey | Benicio Del Toro | Waad Mohammed |

Some rebels are forced into criminality; others are outlaws from the outset. The latter are often set in the past — *Butch Cassidy and the Sundance Kid* (1969), *The Wild Bunch* (1969), *Bonnie and Clyde* (1967) — but are critiques of contemporary mores. As such, they are no different to the antiheroes of *Breathless* (1960), *Le Samouraï* and *Point Blank* (both 1967), which are set in the time they were filmed.

Thus there is a cinematic distinction between hardened criminals and rebels such as Paul Newman's Lucas Jackson in *Cool Hand Luke* (1967); Vincent Cassel, Hubert Koundé and Saïd Taghmaoui's three young friends in *La Haine* (1995); Brad Pitt's Tyler Durden in *Fight Club* (1999); and the gangs in *The Warriors* (1979), who are all fighting for respect or for their rights.

A similar strand runs through movies about female rebels. Lulu (Louise Brooks) in *Pandora's Box* and *Diary of a Lost Girl* (both 1929) is a woman taking a stand against society's patriarchal values. More than 60 years later *Thelma & Louise* (1991) depicted Geena Davis and Susan Sarandon waging the same struggle against exploitation. Among a host of movie characters that respond rebelliously to gender imbalances are Varla (Tura Satana) in *Faster, Pussycat! Kill! Kill!* (1965), Jen (Ziyi Zhang) in *Crouching Tiger, Hidden Dragon* (2000), Phoolan Devi (Seema Biswas)

in *Bandit Queen* (1994) and the young heroine (Waad Mohammed) of *Wadjda* (2012).

The other common denominator of movie rebels is their youth. Ever since James Dean raged against his parents in *Rebel Without a Cause* (1955), children, teenagers and young adults have led the way to the barricades. School rebellion began with Jean Vigo's *Zero de Conduite* (1933) and continued through François Truffaut's *The 400 Blows* (1959), *The Blackboard Jungle* (1955), *If....* (1968), *Ferris Bueller's Day Off* (1986), *Heathers* (1988) and *Thirteen* (2003).

Dead End (1937), *Over the Edge* (1979), *Pixote* (1981), *Kids* (1995) and *Elephant* (2003) are prominent among the movies that focus on children who are invisible to the adult world. *Fish Tank* (2009), *The Outsiders* (1983), *Cruel Story of Youth* (1960) and, at the very extreme, *A Clockwork Orange* (1971) highlight the dangers of a society that neither understands nor takes care of its youth. *The Social Network* (2010) is a frat boy version of *Citizen Kane*. As with Welles' character, the "rebel" Mark Zuckerberg ultimately becomes the institution. Although this conclusion is in marked contrast to that of *Easy Rider*, one of the great moments of cinematic rebellion, they both seem to say that conformity comes to everyone; those who resist it are doomed to failure and may not survive. **IHS**

■ Lawless   ■ Anti Social   ■ Cop   ■ Criminal   ■ Historical

Clint Eastwood
Dirty Harry

Robert De Niro
Taxi Driver

Takeshi Kitano
Violent Cop

Matthew Broderick
Ferris Bueller's Day Off

Geena Davis & Susan Sarandon
Thelma & Louise

Vincent Cassel, Hubert Koundé & Saïd Taghmaoui
La Haine

Kevin Spacey
American Beauty

Benicio Del Toro
Che

Waad Mohammed
Wadjda

1975   1980   1985   1990   1995   2000   2005   2010

jeff bridges 1949

| The Last Picture Show | Fat City | Bad Company | Thunderbolt and Lightfoot | Heaven's Gate | Cutter's Way | TRON | Jagged Edge |

The son of Lloyd Bridges and younger brother of Beau, Jeff Bridges made his first screen appearance at the age of 2 in *The Company She Keeps* (1951). At 9, he appeared with his father and brother in the series *Sea Hunt* (1958–60). By the time of his first film, racial drama *Halls of Anger* (1970), he was a 20-year veteran of the entertainment industry.

Bridges' breakthrough performance came in Peter Bogdanovich's bittersweet study of lost innocence, *The Last Picture Show* (1971). He excels as a bored youth desperately looking for something to rebel against. Bogdanovich and the cast would reunite in 1990 for *Texasville*, set some 30 years after the original story.

In John Huston's *Fat City* (1972), he played Ernie, an upcoming boxer spotted by Stacy Keach's veteran. A downbeat tale of America's underbelly, Bridges' performance stands in stark contrast to his more wide-eyed earlier roles, as well as the characters he went on to play in Robert Benton's beautifully shot western, *Bad Company* (1972), and Michael Cimino's feature debut, *Thunderbolt and Lightfoot* (1974), in which he played a doomed young hustler learning from Clint Eastwood's more experienced criminal. He received Oscar nominations for both *Fat City* and *Thunderbolt*.

The commercially successful remake of *King Kong* (1976) might have dated badly, but along with Bob Rafaelson's *Stay Hungry* (1976), it showcased Bridges' effortless charm. That laid-back, easygoing persona is key to Bridges' attraction and has been used to impressive effect across a range of characters, from an embattled U.S. President in *The Contender* (2000) to a louche lounge pianist in *The Fabulous Baker Boys* (1989) or his wonderful, barely legible Rooster Cogburn in *True Grit* (2010). It is the central conceit of one of his most loved roles, the Dude — the dressing gown-wearing, pot-smoking hero of the Coen's comedy masterpiece *The Big Lebowski* (1998). A few films have subverted that image, none more convincingly than *Jagged Edge* (1985). Richard Marquand's erotic thriller works so well because it is Bridges playing the man who might have killed his wife. The audience is kept guessing until the film's nail-biting climax because it seems so incredible that this actor could ever possibly be a killer.

However, Bridges' irrepressible charm is not always enough to save a film. He is one of the key players in Michael Cimino's epic *Heaven's Gate* (1980). A notorious box-office failure, the film's reputation has

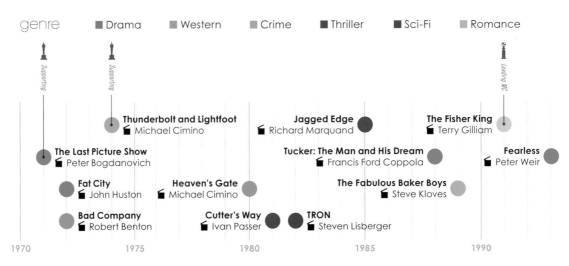

| $168M (U.S.) The Last Picture Show (1971) | $103M (U.S.) Thunderbolt and Lightfoot (1974) | $80M (U.S.) Tron (1982) | $88M (U.S.) Jagged Edge (1985) | $72M (U.S.) The Fisher King (1991) | $635M Iron Man (2008) | $52M Crazy Heart (2009) | $270M True Grit (2010) |

| Tucker: The Man and His Dream | The Fabulous Baker Boys | The Fisher King | Fearless | The Big Lebowski | Iron Man | Crazy Heart | True Grit |

improved with time, but unlike his costars Bridges still appears dwarfed by the magnitude of Cimino's enterprise. He is far better in *Cutter's Way* (1981), a noirish, post-Vietnam thriller about the souring of the American dream. John Heard grandstands in the title role, but it is Bridges who gives the film its heart. And in the entertaining *TRON* (1982), it is the actor's wry humor that prevents the children's sci-fi adventure from descending into silliness. However, as the 2010 sequel showed, it was an act he could not repeat.

Bridges excels at flawed characters. Not bad people, but imperfect ones. His alien in *Starman* (1984), the eponymous salesman in *Tucker: The Man and His Dream* (1988), the pianist in *The Fabulous Baker Boys* — gamely vying for Michelle Pfeiffer's affections with his actual brother Beau — and his radio DJ in Terry Gilliam's *The Fisher King* (1991) are all damaged in some way. In Gilliam's dazzling modern-day play on the Arthurian myth, Bridges is the calm to Robin Williams' psychologically disturbed turmoil, but as the film progresses, it is clear that Bridges' character is as much in need of healing. The actor reunited with Gilliam again on *Tideland* (2005), but the film lacked the emotional depth of their previous work.

American Heart (1992) saw Bridges play the alcoholic father to Edward Furlong's wayward son in a road movie whose convincing central performances are undermined by narrative contrivance. However, that film's flaws pale against George Sluizer's *The Vanishing* (1993). The director's own 1988 Dutch version remains one of the most unsettling modern horror films, while the remake pulls every punch and none of the cast convince. Bridges fared better in the genuinely unnerving *Arlington Road* (1999), about a man who suspects his neighbors are not quite the all-American family they make themselves out to be.

Among starrier appearances in films such as *Iron Man* (2008) and *The Men Who Stare at Goats* (2009), it is Bridges' quieter performances that make the greatest impression. In Peter Weir's powerful *Fearless* (1993), he offers up a moving study of a man traumatized following a plane crash. While in *Crazy Heart* (2009), for which he won an Oscar, the actor excels as a country singer down on his luck who is forced to reassess his life. Bridges' ability to draw us into ordinary worlds, or even make the extraordinary seem commonplace has made him one of the most beloved actors of the last 40 years. **IHS**

■ Comedy   ■ Action

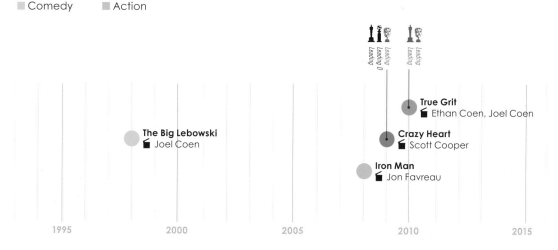

Leading | Leading 0 | Leading   Leading | Leading

True Grit
Ethan Coen, Joel Coen

The Big Lebowski
Joel Coen

Crazy Heart
Scott Cooper

Iron Man
Jon Favreau

1995   2000   2005   2010   2015

The Last Picture
Show
(1971)

Fat City
(1972)

Thunderbolt and
Lightfoot
(1974)

TRON
(1982)

The Fisher King
(1991)

The Big Lebowski
(1998)

Crazy Heart
(2009)

True Grit
(2010)

Timothy Bottoms and Bridges as high-school friends Sonny Crawford and Duane
Jackson in 1950s-set, coming-of-age tale *The Last Picture Show*.

Many of the fight scenes between Bridges and costar Stacy
Keach in *Fat City* were unstaged.

Clint Eastwood and Bridges as *Thunderbolt and Lightfoot*. Of his scenes in drag, Bridges
once said "It's mind blowing! ... you feel like you're looking at your sister!"

Critic Leonard Maltin's review of *Thunderbolt and Lightfoot*
declared that "Bridges steals the picture."

Inspired by the arcade game *Pong*, *TRON* is an important cinematic milestone as one of the first movies to make extensive use of
any form of computer animation.

Bridges and Robin Williams undertake an Arthurian quest for the Holy Grail in Terry Gilliam's fantastical *The Fisher King*.

Bridges in his iconic role as the Dude in *The Big Lebowski*, a part that the Coen brothers wrote specially for him.

Playing a musician in *Crazy Heart* came naturally to Bridges, who began writing and playing music as a teenager and put out his own album in 2000.

Bridges' performance as a down-and-out country music singer-songwriter in *Crazy Heart* won the actor his first Oscar.

True Grit saw Bridges play the role of Rooster Cogburn, for which John Wayne won an Oscar in 1969. Taking a completely different approach to the character, Bridges won praise for his performance.

charles bronson 1921–2003

| The Magnificent Seven | The Great Escape | The Dirty Dozen | Once Upon a Time in the West | The Mechanic | Mr. Majestyk | Death Wish | Hard Times |

Born Charles Buchinsky in 1921, Charles Bronson was the very definition of a late bloomer. Although he had starred in a number of high-profile films, it was not until his early fifties that he landed his most iconic role and, for better or worse, became the gun-toting vigilante antihero for which he will always be remembered.

Following his years of service in the U.S. Air Force during World War II, Bronson made his early film appearances under his family name Buchinsky. He featured in a variety of movies, including the Hepburn and Tracy comedy *Pat and Mike* (1952) and the Vincent Price horror picture *House of Wax* (1953).

In the mid-1950s, at the advice of his agent, the actor changed his surname to Bronson and, after a string of minor big-screen roles, found success with the television series *Man With a Camera* (1958–60), in which he played the lead. It was followed by a key role as the emotional center of John Sturges' classic ensemble western *The Magnificent Seven* (1960). Sturges cast Bronson again in his hit film *The Great Escape* (1963), in which the actor played a Polish prisoner of war known as "The Tunnel King." A few years, later he found further success in another World War II extravaganza, as one of a group of violent convicts being led into a potentially lethal military operation in Robert Aldrich's *The Dirty Dozen* (1967).

The following year Bronson uprooted to Europe, in search of more substantial parts than the

villainous supporting roles for which he had become associated, and landed iconic roles in films such as Sergio Leone's *Once Upon a Time in the West* (1968), in which he plays an angel of vengeance seeking out Henry Fonda's icy cold killer, and Terence Young's thriller *Cold Sweat* (1970).

Upon returning to the United States, Bronson appeared in Michael Winner's *The Mechanic* (1972) and the Elmore Leonard-penned actioner *Mr. Majestyk* (1974), but it was a later collaboration with Winner that remains his defining screen role, as Paul Kersey in the much-vilified smash hit *Death Wish* (1974). The role had apparently been written for Henry Fonda, who was appalled by Winner's story of a vigilante architect taking revenge for the murder of his wife and rape of his daughter by criminals. Despite receiving negative press, the morally bankrupt film proved a commercial success. Bronson would reprise the role for a string of sequels, to increasingly unpleasant effect.

With his reputation as an action man of few words firmly established, Bronson spent the rest of his career starring in a succession of violent, low-grade action films, which included *10 to Midnight* (1983), *The Evil That Men Do* (1984) and *Assassination* (1987). The films were loathed by critics but enjoyed by fans and Bronson continued working well into his seventies. In his later life he suffered from Alzheimer's, before passing away from pneumonia at age 81 in 2003. **MB**

genre   ■ Western   ■ Adventure   ■ War   ■ Thriller   ■ Action   ■ Drama

The Magnificent Seven
John Sturges

The Great Escape
John Sturges

The Dirty Dozen
Robert Aldrich

Once Upon a Time in the West
Sergio Leone

The Mechanic
Michael Winner

Mr. Majestyk
Richard Fleischer

Death Wish
Michael Winner

Hard Times
Walter Hill

1960   1965   1970   1975

louise brooks 1906–85

It's the Old
Army Game

Love 'Em and
Leave 'Em

A Girl in
Every Port

Beggars
of Life

The Canary
Murder Case

Pandora's
Box

Diary of
a Lost Girl

Miss Europe

One of the few silent film stars still familiar to the wider public (her lacquer-black bob has never gone out of fashion), Louise Brooks embodied the image and mores of late-1920s femininity on both sides of the Atlantic, a doubly impressive achievement given a comparatively brief screen career, and the fact that a third of her output is now lost and a further third (at least) is of negligible interest.

Born in Cherryvale, Kansas, in 1906, to emotionally distant parents, Brooks claimed that her molestation by a neighbor left her with a daringly open attitude (for the time) toward sexual experimentation. She became a dancer in her teens, achieving star billing with the Denishawn modern dance company by 1924, before becoming a featured Broadway attraction in 1925's *Ziegfeld Follies*. Talent-spotted by producer Walter Wanger, she signed a five-year Paramount contract and from 1925 played numerous, mostly comedic roles. The most outstanding of these were *It's the Old Army Game* (1926), opposite W.C. Fields; *Love 'Em and Leave 'Em* (1926), as the young flapper who ensnares her more conservative sister's beau; *A Girl in Every Port* (1928) for Howard Hawks, as the vamp who catches the eye of two sailors on shore leave; and her first part-talkie *Beggars of Life* (1928), as a country girl who goes on the run after killing her abusive stepfather.

Breaking her contract, she made her two best-known and best films in Germany, for G.W. Pabst.

Pandora's Box (1929) cast her as the definitive incarnation of playwright Frank Wedekind's iconic Lulu, driven by her sexuality to both the height of success and the most abject end. (Brooks was acutely aware of parallels with her own rollercoaster career and in 1982 published an anthology of her writing as *Lulu in Hollywood*.) In *Diary of a Lost Girl* (1929), she played a similarly rebellious spirit, this time dealing with illegitimate pregnancy, institutionalization and prostitution. The French film *Miss Europe* (1930) was billed as a musical comedy but had a darker edge characteristic of Pabst (producer and co-writer). Her typically understated screen presence was as magnetic as ever.

Given her career nosedive after her return to Hollywood, it is easy to assume that she simply struggled to adjust to talkies, although the jarring Bronx accent dubbed over her performance in *The Canary Murder Case* (1929) came about because she was in Germany when the film was converted to sound. She also had plenty of film-industry enemies thanks to her outspoken opposition to various professional and social codes. Her refusal to play the female lead in *The Public Enemy* (1931), opposite James Cagney, was considered the final straw. Disillusioned with the film business, she played only a handful of bit-parts thereafter, but reinvented herself in the 1950s as a witty and acerbic writer on film. She died in 1985. **MB**

genre   ■ Comedy   ■ Adventure   ■ Mystery   ■ Drama

It's the Old Army Game
🎬 A. Edward Sutherland

Love 'Em and Leave 'Em
🎬 Frank Tuttle

A Girl in Every Port
🎬 Howard Hawks

Beggars of Life
🎬 William A. Wellman

The Canary Murder Case
🎬 Malcolm St. Clair

Pandora's Box
🎬 Georg Wilhelm Pabst

Diary of a Lost Girl
🎬 Georg Wilhelm Pabst

Miss Europe
🎬 Augusto Genina

1923   1924   1925   1926   1927   1928   1929   1930   1931   1932   1933

daniel brühl 1978

The White Sound | **Good Bye, Lenin!** | **The Edukators** | **Salvador** | **The Countess** | **Inglourious Basterds** | **Rush** | **The Fifth Estate**

Daniel Brühl was born in Barcelona in 1978. With his Brazilian father and Spanish mother, Brühl moved to Cologne, Germany, as an infant. His first experience of acting was in the German soap opera *Forbidden* (1995).

Brühl's breakout performance in *Good Bye, Lenin!* (2003) catapulted the actor into the international spotlight and saw him win a number of awards. He plays a young man who goes to extraordinary lengths to convince his mother, fresh out of a coma, that the Berlin Wall is still standing to prevent her relapsing from shock. Brühl followed it with his first English-speaking role, opposite Maggie Smith and Judi Dench in *Ladies in Lavender* (2004), before returning to Berlin to star in *The Edukators* (2004), a smart satire about anti-capitalist activists.

Brühl speaks German, French, English, Portuguese, Spanish and Catalan, skills used to great effect in the affecting World War I drama, *Joyeux Noël* (2005), which recreated the legendary Christmas Day truce between German and allied troops. He next played the lead role in the critically acclaimed *Salvador* (2006), a Spanish drama telling the tragic story of Salvador Puig Antich, the last man executed by garrotte under the Franco dictatorship. A small role followed in *The Bourne Ultimatum* (2007), along with a starring role in German fantasy film, *Krabat and the Legend of the Satanic Mill* (2008). However, it was his outstanding performance as the insidious Frederik Zoller in Quentin Tarantino's World War II drama *Inglourious Basterds* (2009) that truly saw Brühl become a recognized international star.

Brühl starred in Julie Delpy's historical drama *The Countess* (2009), playing the infamous Elizabeth Báthory's lover István Thurzó. He also took a small role in Delpy's *2 Days in New York* (2012), played alongside John Malkovich in *In Transit* (2008) and opposite Clive Owen in the horror thriller *Intruders* (2011).

The actor played Wikileaks co-founder Daniel Berg opposite Benedict Cumberbatch's Julian Assange in *The Fifth Estate* (2013) and his international profile increased significantly with his exceptional portrait of Formula 1 driver Nikki Lauder in Ron Howard's thrilling *Rush* (2013). A brief cameo in *The Trip* (2014) led Brühl to collaborate with Michael Winterbottom on *The Face of an Angel* (2014), taking the role of a filmmaker investigating a murder in Italy. Winterbottom mines Brühl's mercurial talent to the hilt, and the actor offers one of his most complex performances to date. **CGD**

genre   ■ Drama   ■ Comedy   ■ War   ■ Action   ■ Thriller

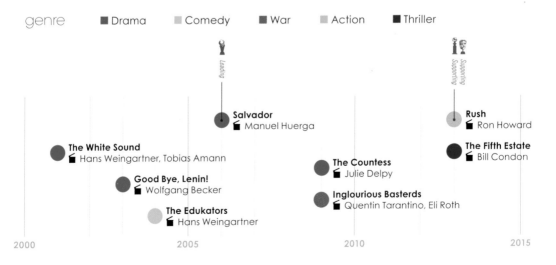

Leading

Supporting Supporting

Salvador
Manuel Huerga

Rush
Ron Howard

The White Sound
Hans Weingartner, Tobias Amann

The Fifth Estate
Bill Condon

Good Bye, Lenin!
Wolfgang Becker

The Countess
Julie Delpy

Inglourious Basterds
Quentin Tarantino, Eli Roth

The Edukators
Hans Weingartner

2000   2005   2010   2015

yul brynner 1920–85

| Port of New York | The King and I | The Ten Commandments | The Brothers Karamazov | Testament of Orpheus | The Magnificent Seven | The Light at the Edge of the World | Westworld |

Few Hollywood stars have looked as unique as Yul Brynner. He brought to the screen immense charisma and although he was often physically imposing, he could be warm and funny. He was as impressive a villain as he was a stoic hero.

Although he was born Yuliy Borisovich Bryner in 1920, in Vladivostok, the actor was known to present a more exotic account of his early life. He arrived in New York — via an upbringing in China and Paris — in 1940. Initially working for French radio, relaying propaganda programs back to Nazi-occupied Europe, he soon moved to theater and then, in 1949, starred as a drug kingpin in his first film, László Benedek's semi-documentary noir *Port of New York*. In 1951 he won the role of King Mongkut of Siam in the Rogers and Hammerstein stage musical *The King and I*, a part he would play on Broadway for 4,625 performances. When *The King and I* finally reached the screen in 1956, Brynner was awarded with an Oscar for his performance. In the same year, he was all moodiness and malevolence as Rameses in *The Ten Commandments* and an effective villain opposite Ingrid Bergman in *Anastasia*.

Richard Brooks' adaptation of Fyodor Dostoyevsky's *The Brothers Karamazov* (1958) is ponderous at best, with Brynner hampered from the outset by having Lee J. Cobb, William Shatner and Richard Baseheart as his siblings. Likewise, he is lost in Martin Ritt's *The Sound and the Fury* (1959), an insipid adaptation of William Faulkner's novel.

Brynner may not have looked the western hero, but as the leader of a gang of good-for-nothing gunslingers in *The Magnificent Seven* (1960), he became an icon of the genre. So much so that in *Westworld* (1973), Brynner's gunslinger channel's the earlier character's look — an all-black outfit — to menacing effect, transforming a hero into an unstoppable robotic killer.

If Brynner was miscast in too many films, at his best he was magnetic. A gifted photographer and guitarist, he looked at home in Jean Cocteau's *Testament of Orpheus* (1960). It is only a cameo appearance but it underpins the attraction of this curious, compelling star. But he will forever be associated with a king and cowboy — both good and bad — whose mischievous eyes hinted at benevolence and malice, often at the same time. **IHS**

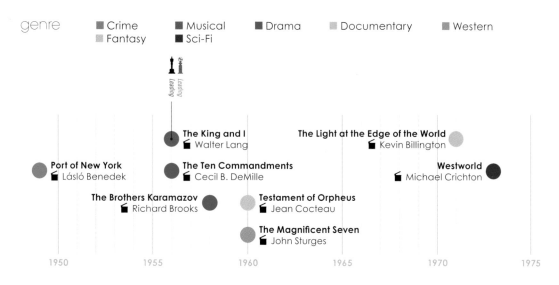

genre
- Crime
- Fantasy
- Musical
- Sci-Fi
- Drama
- Documentary
- Western

Leading

The King and I
 Walter Lang

The Light at the Edge of the World
 Kevin Billington

Port of New York
 Lásló Benedek

The Ten Commandments
 Cecil B. DeMille

Westworld
 Michael Crichton

The Brothers Karamazov
 Richard Brooks

Testament of Orpheus
 Jean Cocteau

The Magnificent Seven
 John Sturges

1950   1955   1960   1965   1970   1975

sandra bullock 1964

Speed

While You Were Sleeping

The Net

Miss Congeniality

Crash

The Blind Side

The Proposal

Gravity

With a handful of film and television performances under her belt, the turning point in Sandra Bullock's career came courtesy of a supporting role in the Sylvester Stallone blockbuster *Demolition Man* (1993). Having established her action woman credentials, Bullock landed a key role opposite Keanu Reeves in the bulldozing bus hit *Speed* (1994), bringing warmth and humor to Jan de Bont's lean thriller.

Bullock followed *Speed* with a string of hits, including the romance *While You Were Sleeping* (1995), the techno thriller *The Net* (1995) and courtroom drama *A Time To Kill* (1996). On her way to becoming one of the Hollywood's biggest stars, Bullock was paid $11 million to reprise her hit role in *Speed 2: Cruise Control* (1997), which, despite eager anticipation, was met with general disappointment and derision. Bullock apparently agreed to star in the action sequel in return for funding for her pet project *Hope Floats* (1998), a low-key romantic drama.

The beginning of the new millennium gave Bullock one of her biggest hits, and most loved roles, in the form of *Miss Congeniality* (2000). In addition to a producer credit, the film also showcased the actress' aptitude for comedy. However, it was followed by a number of years where Bullock did little more than tread water in a series of underwhelming movies

that included *Murder By Numbers* (2002), *Two Weeks Notice* (2002) and *Loverboy* (2005), although she was impressive as a wife on the verge of a breakdown in Paul Haggis' overwrought Oscar-winner *Crash* (2004).

Bullock reprised her *Miss Congeniality* role for the 2005 sequel, before reuniting with Keanu Reeves in the saccharine *The Lake House* (2006) and scoring another hit with the likeable rom-com *The Proposal* (2009).

It was Bullock's Oscar-winning performance in *The Blind Side* (2009) that saw her go from audience favorite to a bona fide critical darling. Based on the true story of a white family who took in a homeless African-American boy who went on to be a successful NFL player, Bullock brought compassion, intelligence and sassiness to the role of Leigh Anne Tuohy. With the exception of her Razzie-winning role in *All About Steve* (2009), recent years have seen her being taken more seriously as an actress, receiving another Oscar nomination for *Gravity* (2013). However, she has not altogether jettisoned comic roles, appearing opposite Melissa McCarthy in the broad comedy *The Heat* (2013) and supplying her voice to *Minions* (2015). *Our Brand Is in Crisis* (2015), in which she plays a political consultant who quotes famous people to drive home her arguments, finds Bullock balancing both elements of her screen persona. **MB**

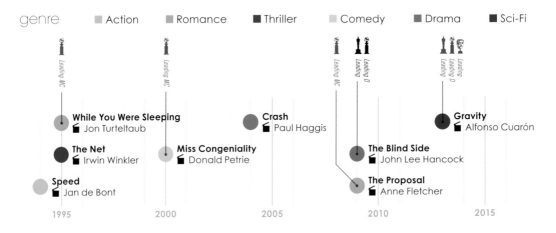

genre ■ Action ■ Romance ■ Thriller ▢ Comedy ■ Drama ■ Sci-Fi

While You Were Sleeping — Jon Turteltaub

The Net — Irwin Winkler

Speed — Jan de Bont

Miss Congeniality — Donald Petrie

Crash — Paul Haggis

The Blind Side — John Lee Hancock

The Proposal — Anne Fletcher

Gravity — Alfonso Cuarón

Leading MC / Leading MC / Leading MC / Leading D Leading / Leading D Leading

1995   2000   2005   2010   2015

richard burton 1925–84

| The Desert Rats | Look Back in Anger | Cleopatra | The Spy Who Came in from the Cold | Who's Afraid of Virginia Woolf? | Where Eagles Dare | Equus | Nineteen Eighty-Four |

A legendary stage actor, Richard Burton's film career is, at best, a mixed bag. However, if his finest performances are ultimately outnumbered by ones that financed a glamorous jet-setting lifestyle, they remain a testament to his incredible talent.

Born Richard Walter Jenkins in Wales, 1925, Burton took his stage name from the teacher who inspired him. A stint in the Royal Air Force enabled him to study at Oxford University, after which he took to the stage. On the recommendation of novelist Daphne Du Maurier, he was cast in Henry Koster's adaptation of *My Cousin Rachel* (1952), for which he received a Golden Globe.

Burton gave a riveting performance in the World War II drama *The Desert Rats* (1953), as an English officer leading an embattled unit on an offensive against Rommel. He would return to the same military campaign in Nicholas Ray's *Bitter Victory* (1957) and the inferior *Raid on Rommel* (1971). His most famous war film is *Where Eagles Dare* (1968), which remains one of the great "men on a mission" movies.

Burton reunited with Koster on the sumptuous biblical epic, *The Robe* (1953), for which he received his first Oscar nomination. The film's success led to a number of other spectacles, including *The Rains of Ranchipur* (1955), *Alexander the Great* (1956) and *Cleopatra* (1963), opposite Elizabeth Taylor, whom he also costarred with in the indulgent *The V.I.P.s* (1963). The films marked Burton's most successful period and the start of a high-profile love affair between the actor and Taylor. On film, their collaboration would peak with *Who's Afraid of Virginia Woolf?* (1966), playing a couple caught between loving and hating each other.

If the press highlighted the extravagance and luxury of Burton's life, his best roles were grittier fare. *Becket* (1964) was a raw period drama that detailed the fraught relationship between Henry II and the Archbishop of Canterbury, while *Look Back in Anger* (1959) channeled the rage of disconsolate youth. If *The Spy Who Came in From the Cold* (1965) was the opposite of James Bond in every way, *Villain* (1971) gave audiences an ugly face to gangster culture.

There were a few final good roles in Burton's film career. *Equus* (1977) found him on intense form, while his interrogator in *Nineteen Eighty-Four* (1984) remains chilling. In his diaries, Burton expressed dissatisfaction with acting. His heart lay in literature. But across his 40-odd films, there were moments of brilliance — a poetry to his performance that is equal to any art form. **IHS**

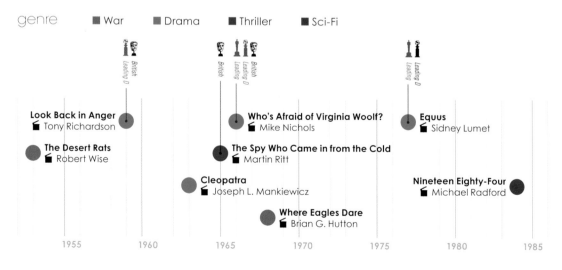

genre ■ War ■ Drama ■ Thriller ■ Sci-Fi

Look Back in Anger — Tony Richardson
The Desert Rats — Robert Wise
Who's Afraid of Virginia Woolf? — Mike Nichols
The Spy Who Came in from the Cold — Martin Ritt
Cleopatra — Joseph L. Mankiewicz
Where Eagles Dare — Brian G. Hutton
Equus — Sidney Lumet
Nineteen Eighty-Four — Michael Radford

British Leading D
British
Leading D
British Leading D
Leading D

1955   1960   1965   1970   1975   1980   1985

james caan 1940

| The Godfather | The Gambler | Funny Lady | A Bridge Too Far | Thief | Gardens of Stone | Misery | Honeymoon in Vegas |

Still probably best known for playing Sonny Corleone, in *The Godfather* (1972), James Caan was the studio's first choice to play Michael, the part that eventually went to Al Pacino. It now seems an unlikely proposition because the livewire Sonny was, in many ways, the role that defined Caan.

Born in New York in 1940, Caan worked in theater and television in the early 1960s, before landing supporting roles in studio pictures, often as a young face alongside established stars, such as the John Wayne and Robert Mitchum western *El Dorado* (1966). But it was in collaborating with filmmakers of his own generation that Caan achieved his breakthrough. Directed by Francis Ford Coppola and costarring Robert Duvall, *The Rain People* (1969) won Caan plaudits as a brain-damaged college football player.

Coppola went on to cast Caan in *The Godfather*, one of the landmark films of the so-called "New Hollywood" wave of the early 1970s. Along with Pacino and Robert De Niro, Caan was one of the leading New Hollywood actors, bringing to the screen a rare emotional rawness and aggressive physicality.

Over the next decade, Caan proved himself a fearless and committed performer. He is riveting as an ex-con looking for a hidden stash of money in Howard Zieff's *Slither* (1973) and surprisingly funny as a San Francisco detective in *Freebie and the Bean* (1974). He delivered an outstanding study in addiction and self-destruction as the title character of Karel Reisz's 1974 drama *The Gambler*, and would not find another character with such intensity until he took the lead in Michael Mann's cult crime drama *Thief* (1981).

Caan also worked in more mainstream pictures, notably as one of the all-star cast of World War II epic *A Bridge Too Far* (1977). He even impressed as Barbra Streisand's piano-playing costar in the 1975 musical *Funny Lady*, receiving a Golden Globe nomination.

After a break from Hollywood in the early 1980s, partly due to a cocaine addiction, Caan delivered a remarkable return to form in the 1987 drama *Gardens of Stone*. He enjoyed further success as a kidnapped novelist in *Misery* (1990), giving an unusually restrained performance that is among his best.

If Caan's recent roles haven't quite recaptured the intensity of his 1970s heyday, he remains busy and has shown himself adept at light comedy, notably in *Honeymoon in Vegas* (1992) and as a voice in *Cloudy with a Chance of Meatballs* (2009) and its sequel. **EL**

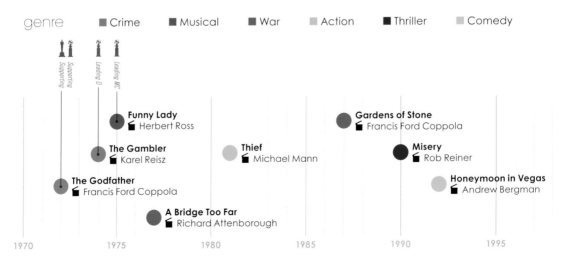

genre   ■ Crime   ■ Musical   ■ War   ■ Action   ■ Thriller   ■ Comedy

Supporting Supporting
Leading D
Leading MC

Funny Lady 🎬 Herbert Ross

Gardens of Stone 🎬 Francis Ford Coppola

The Gambler 🎬 Karel Reisz

Thief 🎬 Michael Mann

Misery 🎬 Rob Reiner

The Godfather 🎬 Francis Ford Coppola

Honeymoon in Vegas 🎬 Andrew Bergman

A Bridge Too Far 🎬 Richard Attenborough

1970   1975   1980   1985   1990   1995

nicolas cage 1964

| Peggy Sue Got Married | Raising Arizona | Wild at Heart | Leaving Las Vegas | The Rock | Face/Off | Adaptation | Bad Lieutenant: Port of Call — New Orleans |

Born Nicolas Coppola in 1964, Cage's name change was in part inspired by his determination to step out of the family shadow. Nevertheless, several of his early roles were for his uncle Francis Ford Coppola, most notably in *Peggy Sue Got Married* (1986). As the boyfriend/husband of time-traveling Kathleen Turner, Cage defied leading man conventions — and Turner's patience — with his nasal voice and exaggerated gestures. In the Coen brothers' comedy *Raising Arizona* (1987), Cage's hapless baby kidnapper was still cartoonlike yet somehow affectingly earnest, grounding the screwball antics. Those two roles, plus his tempestuous, one-handed baker in romantic comedy *Moonstruck* (1987) and his eating a live cockroach for *Vampire's Kiss* (1989), served notice that here was an actor unafraid of taking chances.

In David Lynch's lovers-on-the-run road movie *Wild at Heart* (1990), Cage was thrillingly wired as Sailor Ripley. The next few years, however, saw him focus more on sweet but slight romantic comedies, the best of which was *Honeymoon in Vegas* (1992).

Leaving Las Vegas (1995), by contrast, tells the story of an alcoholic screenwriter determined to drink himself to death and his relationship with a prostitute.

Cage's honest and delicate performance and tenderly unsentimental connection to costar Elisabeth Shue garnered the actor career-best reviews and numerous awards, including a Best Actor Oscar.

Almost perversely, Cage next embarked on a series of high-concept action movies, including producer Jerry Bruckheimer's *The Rock* (1996) and *Con Air* (1997) and, more intriguingly, John Woo's *Face/Off* (1997), in which Cage's master felon and John Travolta's cop literally switch faces.

Proving he could still do nuanced, understated work, his roles as twin screenwriters in Spike Jonze's meta-fictive hall-of-mirrors *Adaptation* (2002) were another career peak. Since then, Cage's gonzo work ethic has been hard to keep up with. For every decent outing — an OCD con artist in *Matchstick Men* (2003) or *Lord of War*'s (2005) amoral arms dealer — come several stinkers, none worse than the inept remake of *The Wicker Man* (2006). When paired with the right film or director, as in Werner Herzog's surreal *Bad Lieutenant: Port of Call — New Orleans* (2009), Cage's daring can still thrill. It will be fascinating to see how long he, audiences and Hollywood can afford his go-for-broke willingness to put himself on the line. **LS**

genre ■ Comedy ■ Thriller ■ Romance ■ Action ■ Crime

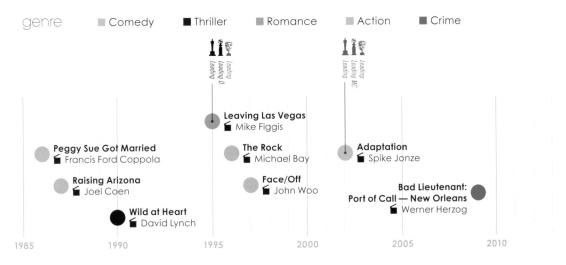

Leading
Leading
Leading D

Leading
Leading MC
Leading

Leaving Las Vegas
Mike Figgis

Peggy Sue Got Married
Francis Ford Coppola

Raising Arizona
Joel Coen

Wild at Heart
David Lynch

The Rock
Michael Bay

Face/Off
John Woo

Adaptation
Spike Jonze

Bad Lieutenant:
Port of Call — New Orleans
Werner Herzog

1985   1990   1995   2000   2005   2010

james cagney 1899–1986

The Public Enemy

Taxi!

Footlight Parade

A Midsummer Night's Dream

"G" Men

Angels with Dirty Faces

The Roaring Twenties

Yankee Doodle Dandy

One of the greatest stars of Hollywood's Golden Age, James Cagney left a searing impression on moviegoers with his early performances in a string of crime pictures. Introducing a new note of realism and tough-guy attitude to films like *The Public Enemy* (1931), Cagney's start in movies was sensational and lastingly influential. But he was also a performer of great range and quiet integrity. Admired by his peers and hugely popular with contemporary audiences, Cagney brought to the screen a dancer's virtuosity and seemingly effortless naturalism.

Born in Manhattan in 1899, Cagney had numerous jobs before landing a role in a chorus line on the New York stage, acquiring an unstinting work ethic that he would apply to his screen career. He spent 10 years on Broadway and in vaudeville, experience that Cagney would draw on to dazzling effect in his song-and-dance roles on screen. It also subtly informed his dramatic roles: Cagney moved with the grace and timing of a dancer, giving even his most naturalistic performances moments of exquisite choreography.

Given a brief contract with Warner Bros., Cagney made a memorable debut in the 1930 crime drama *Sinners' Holiday*. Playing a fast-talking young

bootlegger, he was utterly convincing, at once charming and cocky, and Warners made use of his street smarts in several more crime pictures.

His breakthrough came a year later, in *The Public Enemy*, playing a gangster in this rise-and-fall drama set against the backdrop of prohibition-era Chicago. A performance of compacted aggression and raw volatility, Cagney was abrasive and unsympathetic. He made no efforts to be likeable in the role, but he was fiercely charismatic and the film turned him into a star.

Cagney would repeatedly return to playing criminals and gangsters throughout his career, always impressing with a potent mix of menace and magnetism. Following the introduction of a new censorship code in the early 1930s, crime films became less brutal, but Cagney's impact rarely softened. He was Oscar-nominated as a New York gangster in the sweeping 1938 melodrama *Angels with Dirty Faces*, subverting his tough-guy image as a character who appeared to go to the electric chair as a coward. In Raoul Walsh's epic crime saga *The Roaring Twenties* (1939) Cagney was electrifying as a bootlegger, conveying his character's ruthless drive with commanding authority. And in Walsh's

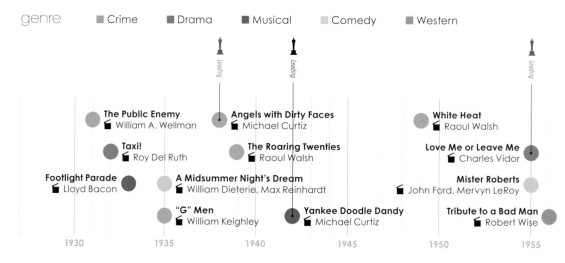

genre ■ Crime ■ Drama ■ Musical ■ Comedy ■ Western

The Public Enemy
William A. Wellman

Taxi!
Roy Del Ruth

Footlight Parade
Lloyd Bacon

Angels with Dirty Faces
Michael Curtiz

The Roaring Twenties
Raoul Walsh

A Midsummer Night's Dream
William Dieterle, Max Reinhardt

"G" Men
William Keighley

Yankee Doodle Dandy
Michael Curtiz

White Heat
Raoul Walsh

Love Me or Leave Me
Charles Vidor

Mister Roberts
John Ford, Mervyn LeRoy

Tribute to a Bad Man
Robert Wise

1930   1935   1940   1945   1950   1955

C

White Heat | Love Me or Leave Me | Mister Roberts | Tribute to a Bad Man | Man of a Thousand Faces | Shake Hands with the Devil | One, Two, Three | Ragtime

White Heat (1949), arguably the last of the great crime films of the era, he provided a layer of psychological complexity to his role as a paranoid, violent robber.

But Cagney also excelled in other parts and was proving his versatility even during the height of his fame in gangster pictures. He was compellingly incorruptible as an FBI agent in "*G*" *Men* (1935), a spirited Bottom in the all-star adaptation of *A Midsummer Night's Dream* (1935) and proved he could tap dance with finesse in the musical *Footlight Parade* (1933).

Footlight Parade was a prelude to one of Cagney's greatest performances: as song-and-dance entertainer George M. Cohan in the 1942 biopic *Yankee Doodle Dandy*. A stirringly patriotic effort released as the United States entered World War II, Cagney gave a richly detailed and powerfully poignant portrait of Cohan, from his early vaudeville days to his celebrated old age. But it was in the musical numbers that Cagney most impressed. His singing style brilliantly emulated Cohan's patter-like voice, and as a dancer he was a virtuoso. The role won him an Oscar for Best Actor.

After the war, Cagney's appearances became less frequent and his roles more varied. In *Love Me or Leave Me* (1955), he gave an unsettling performance as a shady admirer of singer Ruth Etting (played by Doris Day), earning an Oscar nomination. In *Mister Roberts* (1955), he was on characterful form as the veteran captain of a naval cargo ship, while in *Tribute to a Bad Man* (1956) he played a rancher with "hanging fever," driven to bring frontier justice to a group of horse rustlers. It was one of only a few westerns he starred in and was a standout late-career performance.

Cagney accepted fewer parts as he got older, but he remained a committed and ambitious performer. He was compelling as a hardline Irish Republican resisting British rule in the civil war drama *Shake Hands with the Devil* (1959). In a more gentle vein, he played silent film star Lon Chaney in the biopic *Man of a Thousand Faces* (1957), the title a telling reminder of Cagney's own versatility, which his "public enemy" persona sometimes overshadowed. And he was outstanding as a Coca Cola executive visiting Berlin in the uneven Cold War satire *One, Two, Three* (1961) — despite falling out with director Billy Wilder. Cagney retired soon after, but returned to the screen in 1981 for a cameo in *Ragtime*, as a powerful police commissioner in 1910s New York. It was a vivid swansong before his death in 1986. **EL**

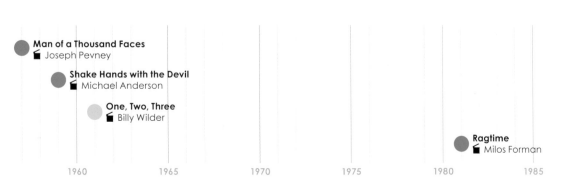

michael caine 1933

| Zulu | The Ipcress File | Alfie | Get Carter | The Man Who Would Be King | Educating Rita | Hannah and Her Sisters | Mona Lisa |

Born Maurice Joseph Mickelwhite in south London, 1933, Michael Caine took his screen name from the Humphrey Bogart drama *The Caine Mutiny* (1954). His breakthrough performance, playing Gonville Bromhead in *Zulu* (1964), came 10 years after his stage debut. The film was a huge success, with Caine perfectly cast opposite Stanley Baker's more earthy John Chard. However, it was as the bespectacled, culinary-minded spy Harry Palmer in *The Ipcress File* (1965) that Caine became a star. Unlike the globetrotting James Bond, Palmer was quintessentially British and his anti-authoritarian behavior, along with a relaxed attitude to sex, chimed with the times. The actor returned to Palmer on another two occasions, with *Funeral in Berlin* (1966) and *Billion Dollar Brain* (1967), though neither is as impressive.

Alfie (1966) is another key entry in Caine's filmography, his roguish charm played to the hilt in his portrayal of a promiscuous young man working his way through London's female population. *Gambit* (1966) and *The Italian Job* (1969) revealed his skill at comedy, but he was more impressive in André De Toth's *Play Dirty* (1969). A tougher role, it contrasted with his performances in the more conventional *Battle of Britain* (1969) and *Too Late the Hero* (1970), and looked forward to one of his defining roles, in *Get Carter* (1971).

A brutal tale of revenge in Britain's gangland, *Get Carter* redefined Caine's screen persona, offering up a ruthless, edgy side. It suited him. He appeared opposite Laurence Olivier in an adaptation of Anthony Schaffer's play *Sleuth* (1972), but a far better pairing was with Sean Connery in John Huston's version of Rudyard Kipling's *The Man Who Would Be King* (1975). Telling the story of two 19th-century adventurers seeking out their fortune in a region north of India, the actors spark off each other, taking viewers on a journey that begins as a knockabout comedy only to become an affecting study of hubris and loyalty.

Caine's output from this point on increased significantly. Some have criticized his willingness to appear in anything, with *Beyond the Poseidon Adventure* (1979), *Jaws: The Revenge* (1987) and *Bullseye!* (1990) offered up as examples. In his defense, Caine has said that acting is a job like any other and one needs to be in constant employment.

Littered among his body of work are films that reveal the breadth of Caine's range. He is convincing as a British agent whose son is kidnapped in *The Black*

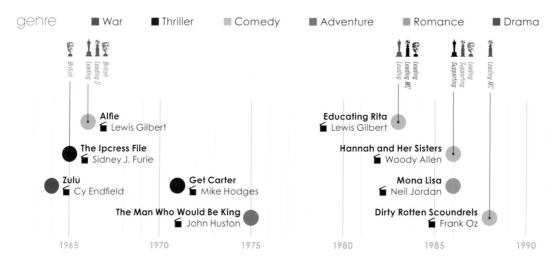

genre ■ War ■ Thriller ■ Comedy ■ Adventure ■ Romance ■ Drama

Alfie
Lewis Gilbert

The Ipcress File
Sidney J. Furie

Zulu
Cy Endfield

Get Carter
Mike Hodges

The Man Who Would Be King
John Huston

Educating Rita
Lewis Gilbert

Hannah and Her Sisters
Woody Allen

Mona Lisa
Neil Jordan

Dirty Rotten Scoundrels
Frank Oz

British
Leading D
British
Leading
Leading MC
Leading
Leading Supporting
Leading Supporting
Leading MC

1965   1970   1975   1980   1985   1990

| $34M (U.S.) Educating Rita (1983) | $85M (U.S.) Hannah and Her Sisters (1986) | $83M (U.S.) Dirty Rotten Scoundrels (1988) | $124M The Cider House Rules (1999) | $36M The Quiet American (2002) | $448M Batman Begins (2005) | $81M Children of Men (2006) | $664M Interstellar (2014) |

Dirty Rotten Scoundrels · Blood and Wine · The Cider House Rules · The Quiet American · Batman Begins · Children of Men · Harry Brown · Interstellar

Windmill (1974) and wonderfully duplicitous in Sidney Lumet's adaptation of Ira Levin's stage play *Deathtrap* (1982). In comedy, he is enjoyable opposite Ben Kingsley in the Sherlock Holmes spoof *Without a Clue* (1988) and Steve Martin in *Dirty Rotten Scoundrels* (1988), coldly calculating in the satirical *A Shock to the System* (1990) and a curmudgeonly Scrooge to a collection of lovable puppets in *The Muppet Christmas Carol* (1992). He is an imposing Colonel Steiner in *The Eagle Has Landed* (1976), impressive as the psychiatrist with a secret in *Dressed to Kill* (1980) and moving in *Little Voice* (1998).

Caine's drunk college lecturer in *Educating Rita* (1983) remains one of his most emotionally engaging roles and a far cry from his brilliant, terrifying London mobster, scrambling desperately to save his empire, in Neil Jordan's *Mona Lisa* (1986). He portrayed a cheating husband in Woody Allen's *Hannah and Her Sisters* (1986), for which he received his first Oscar. These outstanding roles were followed by a fallow creative period, with the exception of his gleefully perverse Lawrence Jamieson in *Dirty Rotten Scoundrels* (1988) — his raffish performance bettering David Niven's in the original, *Bedtime Story* (1964).

Caine's second Oscar for his performance in *The Cider House Rules* (1999) has seen the film lauded as his best of the 1990s, but he was better as an emphysemic safecracker planning a heist with Jack Nicholson's wine merchant in the moody *Blood and Wine* (1996). He brings an air of melancholy to the role, which is also present in his excellent portrayal of Thomas Fowler in Phillip Noyce's laudable adaptation of Graham Greene's *The Quiet American* (2002).

Caine's output over the last decade has been dominated by his work with Christopher Nolan. He has played Alfred the butler in the three *Batman* films, most notably in the first, *Batman Begins* (2005). He also took small roles in *The Prestige* (2006) and *Inception* (2010), and was one of the key characters in Nolan's space opera *Interstellar* (2014). In between, he played an elderly vigilante in *Harry Brown* (2009) and a duped millionaire in *Now You See Me* (2013). However, his best role in recent years is as a hippy in *Children of Men* (2006). In any other actor's hands it could have been a throwaway role. Caine invests it with pathos and wit, making Jasper the heart of the film. It is a trick the actor has performed on countless occasions and why he is such a commanding presence in any movie. **IHS**

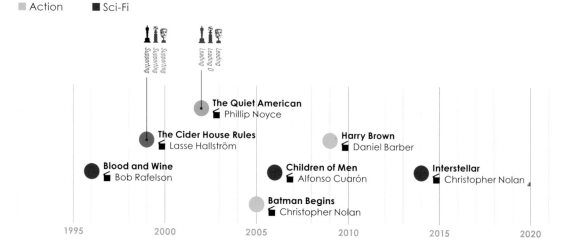

■ Action ■ Sci-Fi

The Quiet American
Phillip Noyce

The Cider House Rules
Lasse Hallström

Blood and Wine
Bob Rafelson

Children of Men
Alfonso Cuarón

Batman Begins
Christopher Nolan

Harry Brown
Daniel Barber

Interstellar
Christopher Nolan

1995   2000   2005   2010   2015   2020

Charmer Femme Fatale Lover Saint Sinner

claudia cardinale 1938

Big Deal on Madonna Street | Rocco and His Brothers | 8½ | The Leopard | The Pink Panther | The Professionals | Once Upon a Time in the West | Fitzcarraldo

Famous in Italy as a teenager, and an international star from her early twenties, Claudia Cardinale has consistently undermined expectations bestowed on someone who seemed physically destined for Brigitte Bardot-style sex kitten roles. Of Sicilian ancestry, she was born in Tunisia in 1938 and originally intended to become a teacher, but when she was filmed with her classmates in René Vautier's short *Anneaux d'Or* (1959) and it won a Berlin Film Festival prize, she became a local celebrity. She was reluctantly cast in the Tunisian film *Goha* (1958) opposite Omar Sharif and was later voted "the most beautiful girl in Italy" at the Venice Film Festival. Shortly afterward, she signed a seven-year contract with producer Franco Cristaldi, and made her Italian debut in a minor role in the comedy *Big Deal on Madonna Street* (1958). She was just 19. It was a huge hit and she graduated to the female lead of her very next film, *South Wind* (1959).

Cardinale filmed prolifically throughout the 1960s, alternating popular commercial hits with work for leading auteurs. Abel Gance's *Austerlitz* (1960) was fairly thankless, but Luchino Visconti's *Rocco and His Brothers* (1960), in which she played the fiancée of one of the siblings, was a small role in a great film. Her professional annus mirabilis was 1963, when she played the female lead in two of world cinema's major masterpieces, *The Leopard*, which reunited her with Visconti, and 8½, her only film with Federico Fellini. Startlingly beautiful in both, it is her pairing with Alain Delon in Visconti's film for which she will best be remembered — arguably the most beautiful couple in cinema. That same year she played Princess Dala, original recipient of the eponymous diamond in *The Pink Panther*.

Cardinale was now a major international star, regularly headlining big-budget films on both sides of the Atlantic. She appeared in numerous genres, but it was the westerns *The Professionals* (1966) and *Once Upon a Time in the West* (1968) that made the strongest impression. In particular, as the former prostitute Jill McBain — the only important female character in any of Sergio Leone's Italian westerns — her face was frequently framed in extreme close-up, expressing far more than any of her spoken dialogue.

From the 1970s, Cardinale mainly worked in French and Italian films, international highlights being the comedy adventure *Escape to Athena* (1979) and Werner Herzog's *Fitzcarraldo* (1982), in which she accompanied Klaus Kinski on his mad voyage to bring grand opera to the Peruvian Amazon. She continues acting in films, while also pursuing humanitarian activities as a UNESCO goodwill ambassador. **MBr**

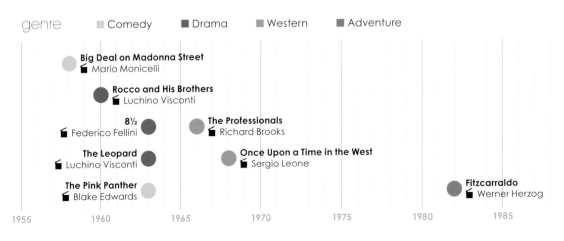

genre ■ Comedy ■ Drama ■ Western ■ Adventure

Big Deal on Madonna Street Mario Monicelli
Rocco and His Brothers Luchino Visconti
8½ Federico Fellini
The Leopard Luchino Visconti
The Pink Panther Blake Edwards
The Professionals Richard Brooks
Once Upon a Time in the West Sergio Leone
Fitzcarraldo Werner Herzog

1955 1960 1965 1970 1975 1980 1985

Clown   Hero   Villain

jim carrey 1962

| Ace Ventura: Pet Detective | The Mask | Dumb and Dumber | The Truman Show | Man on the Moon | Eternal Sunshine of the Spotless Mind | Lemony Snicket's A Series of Unfortunate Events | I Love You Philip Morris |

Born in Newmarket, Ontario, Canada, in 1962, Jim Carrey's early act specialized in impressions of famous stars. Despite a string of low-budget comedy films and television appearances throughout the 1980s, as well as small roles in *Peggy Sue Got Married* (1986) and *The Dead Pool* (1988), it was not until his meteoric rise in 1994 that his own star status was assured. First, he landed the leading role in *Ace Ventura: Pet Detective*, playing the eccentric detective with anarchic energy. It was followed by *The Mask* and *Dumb and Dumber*, which cemented his reputation for physical comedy.

Carrey returned to his star-making role in *Ace Ventura: When Nature Calls* (1995) and portrayed The Riddler in Joel Schumacher's wildly camp *Batman Forever* (1995). One of his earliest "serious" roles was in *The Cable Guy* (1996), in which Carrey channeled his manic persona into a man whose personality borders on the psychotic. *Liar Liar* (1997) followed. Like the later *Bruce Almighty* (2003) and *Yes Man* (2008), it profited from Carrey's ability to carry a slight premise.

In 1998, Carrey gained critical acclaim as a dramatic actor for his role in *The Truman Show*. The following year, he won further praise as comedian Andy Kaufman in Milos Forman's *Man on the Moon* (1999).

Carrey followed this period of critical success with a number of performances in financially successful features. He reunited with *Dumb and Dumber* directors the Farrelly brothers for the hilarious *Me, Myself & Irene* (2000) and played the unctuous antagonist in Ron Howard's respectful version of Dr. Seuss' *How The Grinch Stole Christmas* (2000).

Carrey excelled once again in a serious role in *Eternal Sunshine of the Spotless Mind* (2004). Michel Gondry's film benefits from the actor suppressing his comic instincts, allowing for one of his most naturalistic performances. Less demanding but attracting no less praise was Carrey's Count Olaf in *Lemony Snicket's A Series of Unfortunate Events* (2004).

I Love You Phillip Morris (2009) remains one of mainstream Hollywood's most outré explorations of a homosexual relationship and it is to Carrey's credit that he took what some might deem a risk in departing from his usual comedy role. It is also his most daring in recent years, compared with his cameos in *The Incredible Burt Wonderstone* (2013) and *Kick-Ass 2* (2013), the children's films *A Christmas Carol* (2009) and *Mr. Popper's Penguins* (2011), and the return of Lloyd Christmas in *Dumb and Dumber To* (2014). **CGD**

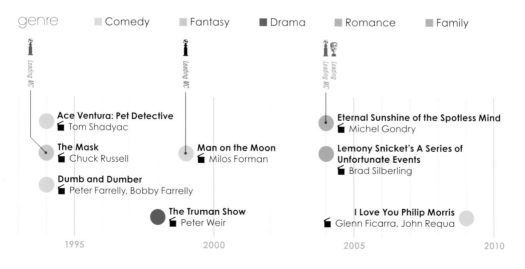

genre   Comedy   Fantasy   Drama   Romance   Family

Ace Ventura: Pet Detective Tom Shadyac

The Mask Chuck Russell

Dumb and Dumber Peter Farrelly, Bobby Farrelly

Man on the Moon Milos Forman

The Truman Show Peter Weir

Eternal Sunshine of the Spotless Mind Michel Gondry

Lemony Snicket's A Series of Unfortunate Events Brad Silberling

I Love You Philip Morris Glenn Ficarra, John Requa

1995   2000   2005   2010

john cassavetes 1929–89

Edge of the City

The Killers

The Dirty Dozen

Devil's Angels

Rosemary's Baby

Machine Gun McCain

Husbands

Capone

Born in New York in 1929, John Cassavetes graduated from the American Academy of Dramatic Arts and took small parts where he could find them. By 1956, he had begun teaching Method acting in his own workshop in Manhattan. An improvisation exercise inspired the idea for his writing and directorial movie debut, *Shadows* (1959). Unable to gain American distribution, Cassavetes found success in Europe, winning the Critics Award at the Venice Film Festival.

Cassavetes is best known today for his legacy as a pioneering filmmaker, but he also worked regularly as an actor, mainly to enable him to finance his own directorial efforts. It was his success as an actor that allowed Cassavetes to move to Los Angeles and finance, write, direct and star in *Faces* (1968), with his wife and muse Gena Rowlands. From 1970 to 1984, Cassavetes directed — and frequently acted in — a string of independent film classics: *Husbands* (1970), *Minnie and Moskowitz* (1971), *A Woman Under the Influence* (1974), *The Killing of a Chinese Bookie* (1976), *Opening Night* (1977), *Gloria* (1980) and *Love Streams* (1984). Raw in tone and eschewing mainstream

conventions of performance, Cassavetes' acting in his dramas could be brutal. However, there was also a tenderness, particularly noticeable in his final film.

Cassavetes' first significant role for another director was in Martin Ritt's feature debut, *Edge of the City* (1957), a tale of two New York longshoremen that also starred Sidney Poitier. It was notable for its interracial friendship, an idea that Cassavetes himself would touch on in *Shadows*. Don Siegel's *The Killers* (1964) was a significant breakthrough, with the actor excelling as a contract victim who makes no attempt to dissuade his assassins from killing him. *The Dirty Dozen* (1967) brought fame and both an Oscar and Golden Globe nomination for Best Supporting Actor. *Devil's Angels* (1967), a variation on *The Wild One* (1953) theme, proved a disappointing follow-up.

Far better was his performance as an actor who makes a pact with the devil in Roman Polanski's influential horror, *Rosemary's Baby* (1968). A leading role in *Machine Gun McCain* (1969), in which Cassavetes plays a violent criminal recently released from prison, is probably most notable for pitting the

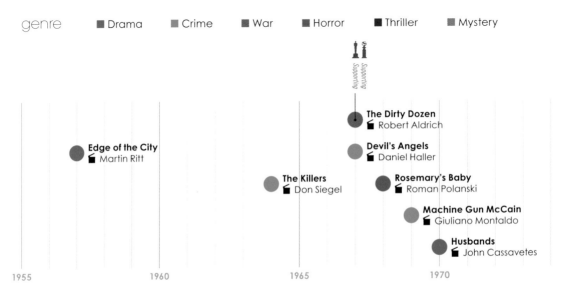

genre ■ Drama ■ Crime ■ War ■ Horror ■ Thriller ■ Mystery

Supporting

Edge of the City
Martin Ritt

The Dirty Dozen
Robert Aldrich

Devil's Angels
Daniel Haller

The Killers
Don Siegel

Rosemary's Baby
Roman Polanski

Machine Gun McCain
Giuliano Montaldo

Husbands
John Cassavetes

1955   1960   1965   1970

$18M (U.S.)
Brass Target
(1978)

$21M (U.S.)
Whose Life Is It Anyway?
(1981)

C

| Two-Minute Warning | Opening Night | The Fury | Brass Target | Whose Life Is It Anyway? | The Incubus | Marvin & Tige | Love Streams |

actor against Rowlands and Peter Falk, who would later form something of a repertory acting company.

Husbands (1970) is a classic of low-budget American filmmaking. A portrait of three middle-aged men who are thrown into crisis when one of their mutual friends dies, the camaraderie between Ben Gazzara, Peter Falk and Cassavetes is electrifying. Cassavetes and Gazzara also acted together in Steve Carver's *Capone* (1975), a conventional rise and fall narrative covering the life of gangster Al Capone. The unremarkable *Two-Minute Warning* (1976) features Cassavetes alongside Charlton Heston as two cops intent on stopping a psychotic sniper.

He took a smaller part in his own *Opening Night* (1977), a powerful look at a burned-out Broadway actress (Rowlands) as she embarks on a play written by an old friend. He is more prominent in Brian De Palma's schlocky horror *The Fury* (1978), a telekinesis-themed follow-up to the director's popular *Carrie* (1976). The actor later starred in another horror, *The Incubus* (1982), playing a doctor investigating a series of brutal murders in New England.

Brass Target (1978) is an average conspiracy drama that nevertheless features a committed performance from Cassavetes. He had better material to work with on John Badham's *Whose Life Is It Anyway?* (1981), which stars Richard Dreyfuss as a sculptor left paralyzed from the neck down after a car accident. Cassavetes plays a doctor supporting the man's plea for euthanasia. Far ahead of its time, the film's themes still reverberate.

Eric Watson's *Marvin & Tige* (1983) is one of the actor's best later performances. He stars as down-on-his-luck widower Marvin, who meets Tige, an 11-year-old boy distraught in the wake of his mother's death. Marvin develops a close bond with the youngster and decides to adopt him, but the authorities demur and a search for the boy's real-life father ensues. Cassavetes admirably keeps sentimentality at bay.

Love Streams (1984) came in the wake of a diagnosis of cirrhosis of the liver. The winner of the Golden Bear at Berlin, it is a characteristically uncompromising look at families and relationships, and a final, exemplary on-screen pairing of Cassavetes and Rowlands, as two people who have endured life's hurdles. **JW**

Capone
🎬 Steve Carver

Two-Minute Warning
🎬 Larry Peerce

Opening Night
🎬 John Cassavetes

The Fury
🎬 Brian De Palma

Brass Target
🎬 John Hough

Whose Life Is It Anyway?
🎬 John Badham

The Incubus
🎬 John Hough

Marvin & Tige
🎬 Eric Weston

Love Streams
🎬 John Cassavetes

1975   1980   1985   1990

vincent cassel 1966

| La Haine | The Apartment | Irréversible | Ocean's Twelve | Eastern Promises | Mesrine: Killer Instinct | Black Swan | Trance |

An intense actor with a distinctively expressive face, many of Vincent Cassel's most memorable characters exist on the precipice of violent action. Born in Paris in 1966, Cassel followed his actor father Jean-Pierre into the film industry with a role in *Café au lait* (1993). It was the feature debut of Mathieu Kassovitz, who would direct Cassel in his next film, the incendiary *La Haine* (1995). Cassel played Vinz, a young, strutting, confrontational tower of rage who, much like the film, was in thrall to American cinema. *La Haine* was an international arthouse hit and brought the actor immediate recognition for his magnetic performance.

Cassel went on to impress in the Hitchcockian *The Apartment* (1996), where he met his wife Monica Bellucci. He also starred in *The Pupil* (1996), the ultra-violent *Dobermann* (1997) and *As You Want Me* (1997), as well as appearing in the period dramas *Elizabeth* (1998) and *Joan of Arc* (1999). In 2000, he reunited with Kassovitz for grisly thriller *The Crimson Rivers*, before starring in Christophe Gans' cult action-horror *Brotherhood of the Wolf* (2001). He would reunite with Gans on the CG-infested *Beauty and the Beast* (2014).

Part of what makes Cassel so compelling as an actor is the way his characters can quickly shift between being attractive and repulsive. His skill at conveying unpredictable aggression has often led him toward dark roles: he played a volatile interloper in *Birthday Girl* (2001), an ex-con who seeks the help of his deaf boss in the engaging *Read My Lips* (2001), a man driven to brutality in the disturbing *Irréversible* (2002), a violent blackmailer in *Derailed* (2005) and a ferocious son in David Cronenberg's masterful *Eastern Promises* (2007). In considerably lighter fare, he also played a renowned cat burglar called the "Night Fox" in the lucrative but unnecessary sequels *Ocean's Twelve* (2004) and *Ocean's Thirteen* (2007).

The most mesmeric performance in Cassel's career to date is in the two-part crime epic comprised of *Mesrine: Killer Instinct* (2008) and *Mesrine: Public Enemy No. 1* (2008), tracing the rise and fall of the French gangster Jacques Mesrine. Embodying brute force and dangerous charisma, he won a best actor César for his work. Cassel then starred in the Brazilian drama *Adrift* (2009) and took a role as a disturbed therapist in the disappointing *Our Day Will Come* (2010).

One of his most popular recent roles is in Darren Aronofsky's feverish psychological thriller *Black Swan* (2010). As Natalie Portman's manipulative, hypercritical ballet director, Cassel conveys an amoral fickleness to his dancer that only serves to exacerbate her unmoored state of mind. Continuing a strong run of work, he was similarly excellent as a friar tempted by sin in *The Monk* (2011), the psychoanalyst Otto Gross preaching sexual anarchy in *A Dangerous Method* (2011) and a criminal gang leader trying to locate a stolen painting in *Trance* (2013). **JWa**

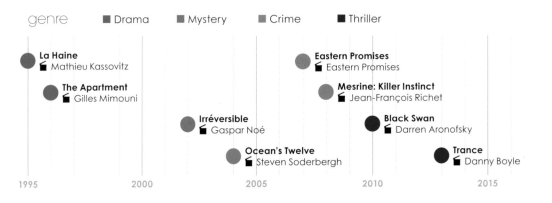

genre ■ Drama ■ Mystery ■ Crime ■ Thriller

La Haine — Mathieu Kassovitz
The Apartment — Gilles Mimouni
Irréversible — Gaspar Noé
Ocean's Twelve — Steven Soderbergh
Eastern Promises — Eastern Promises
Mesrine: Killer Instinct — Jean-François Richet
Black Swan — Darren Aronofsky
Trance — Danny Boyle

1995 2000 2005 2010 2015

jackie chan 1954

Snake in the Eagle's Shadow | Drunken Master | Project A | Police Story | Armour of God | Rumble in the Bronx | Rush Hour | Shanghai Noon

Jackie Chan became one of the world's biggest stars by consciously reviving the silent-comedy tradition of fusing laughs with fearsomely risk-taking acrobatics. Born in Hong Kong, he studied performance, acrobatics and martial arts at the China Drama Academy, and graduated just as Mao's Cultural Revolution decimated the Peking Opera tradition. He made his film debut aged 8, played his first lead role in the forgettable *Cub Tiger From Kwang Tung* (1973), but only became a regular leading man from 1976, initially under the tutelage of the late Bruce Lee's mentor Lo Wei, who unwisely attempted to market him as a successor.

Chan realized at the time that this was doomed to failure, because Lo sidelined his real strengths: a keen sense of fun allied to immaculate comic timing. These skills were finally exploited properly by director-choreographer Woo-ping Yuen in the uproarious *Snake in the Eagle's Shadow* (1978). It was not the first martial arts comedy, but along with the even more popular follow-up, *Drunken Master* (1978), they gave the genre commercial legs and established Chan's regular screen persona: a cheerfully good-natured buffoon who spends much time getting into trouble before being steered onto a more righteous path.

Between unsuccessful attempts at cracking the U.S. market with straight-faced thrillers like *Battle Creek Brawl* (1980) and *The Protector* (1985), Chan refined his comedic approach, directing many of his films himself. The much-loved period piratical romp *Project A* (1983) and cop thriller *Police Story* (1985) both feature him at his impressive physical peak. He survived a near-fatal accident on *Armour of God* (1987) with little slowing of his prodigious output.

Chan finally had a Stateside hit with *Rumble in the Bronx* (1995), and became a bona fide Hollywood star with thriller *Rush Hour* (1998), comedy western *Shanghai Noon* (2000) and their sequels, although rigorous insurance requirements and the encroachment of age forced him to rein in stunts that were considered de rigueur in his Hong Kong films. Partly because of this, he took on increasingly conventional dramatic roles post-millennium, playing an immigrant in *Shinjuku Incident* (2009) and the sole survivor of a massacre in *Little Big Soldier* (2010). In 2012, he announced that he was abandoning action roles altogether. But he remains a global star, one of the few Asian performers to have conquered the English-speaking world while also retaining his vast original fan base. **MB**

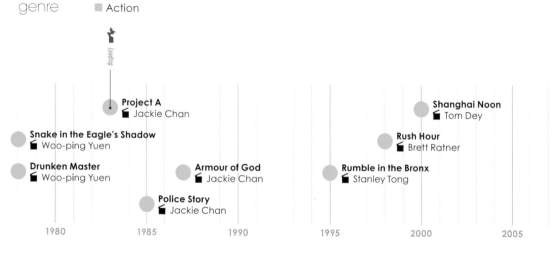

genre   ■ Action

Leading

Project A
🎬 Jackie Chan

Shanghai Noon
🎬 Tom Dey

Snake in the Eagle's Shadow
🎬 Woo-ping Yuen

Rush Hour
🎬 Brett Ratner

Drunken Master
🎬 Woo-ping Yuen

Armour of God
🎬 Jackie Chan

Rumble in the Bronx
🎬 Stanley Tong

Police Story
🎬 Jackie Chan

1980   1985   1990   1995   2000   2005

stars of the martial arts world

Kwan Tak-hing | **Toshiro Mifune** | **Shintaro Katsu** | **Cheng Pei Pei** | **Bruce Lee** | **Sonny Chiba** | **Ti Lung** | **Gordon Liu**

The martial arts genre surfaced within the first ten years of the invention of cinema. *The Battle of Dingjunshan* (1905) was directed by Ren Jingfeng and starred opera singer Tan Xinpei. A wuxia tale — a story of chivalrous combat — the film has since disappeared, but it was soon followed by a slew of other martial arts films.

The trend for martial arts on the big screen exploded in Shanghai during the 1920s and continued into the next decade, although the majority of film production by then had moved to Hong Kong. The first major star was Kwan Tak-hing. He is famous for playing folklore hero Wong Fei-hung in over 70 films, starting with *Story of Huang Feihong, Parts 1 & 2* (1949). However, he was not alone. Gordon Liu (*Challenge of the Masters*, 1976), Jackie Chan (*Drunken Master*, 1978) and Jet Li (*Once Upon a Time in China*, 1991) also played him in various tales of his adventures.

In the 1950s, the films of Akira Kurosawa began to gain international appeal and with them Toshiro Mifune became the most famous character with a sword. *Seven Samurai* (1954) featured him as the dogged upstart Kikuchiyo, but it was his lone swordsman role in *Yojimbo* (1961) and its follow-up *Sanjuro* (1962) that made him such an iconic figure. Around this time, Shintaro Katsu starred as Zatoichi,

the blind swordsman. His first film, *The Tale of Zatoichi* (1962), proved immensely popular with audiences, leading to a further 24 films between 1962 and 1973, as well as a final film in 1989 and a couple of television series. Takeshi Kitano resurrected the character for his stylish, eponymous 2003 feature.

The Shaw brothers ran the major studio producing martial arts films from the late 1950s. They produced over 1,000 films before their doors closed in the 1980s. Although viewed as a primarily commercial enterprise, they understood and appreciated the value of artistry in film. Nowhere more so than in the work of King Hu. His films are visually intoxicating action ballets. They also introduced the female action hero into the mix and none was more charismatic than Cheng Pei Pei. She balanced grace with savagery. Ang Lee paid homage to her and King Hu in the exquisite wuxia drama *Crouching Tiger, Hidden Dragon* (2000). The film also features Michelle Yeoh, a more recent female action star who has found success in U.S. and European action films as well as Asian martial arts spectaculars such as *The Heroic Trio* (1993).

Around the same time as King Hu's success, Bruce Lee broke through to the international mainstream, becoming the first global martial arts superstar. His

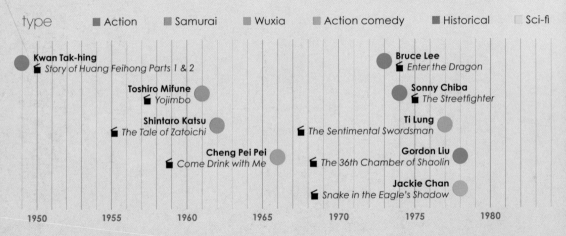

type   ■ Action   ■ Samurai   ■ Wuxia   ■ Action comedy   ■ Historical   □ Sci-fi

Kwan Tak-hing
🏴 *Story of Huang Feihong Parts 1 & 2*

Bruce Lee
🏴 *Enter the Dragon*

Toshiro Mifune
🏴 *Yojimbo*

Sonny Chiba
🏴 *The Streetfighter*

Shintaro Katsu
🏴 *The Tale of Zatoichi*

Ti Lung
🏴 *The Sentimental Swordsman*

Cheng Pei Pei
🏴 *Come Drink with Me*

Gordon Liu
🏴 *The 36th Chamber of Shaolin*

Jackie Chan
🏴 *Snake in the Eagle's Shadow*

1950   1955   1960   1965   1970   1975   1980

Jackie Chan | Jet Li | Jean-Claude Van Damme | Michelle Yeoh | Stephen Chow | Tony Jaa | Iko Uwais | Tony Leung

style was markedly different from what had come before. *Enter the Dragon* (1973) may not be great cinema, but it remains an incredible showcase for Lee's skills. At the same time, Sonny Chiba achieved international fame with the action thriller *The Streetfighter* (1974). It was the first film to receive an X-rating in the United States solely because of its violence. The success of the film prompted a number of sequels and a television spin-off, making Chiba a major figure on the martial arts scene.

The Shaw brothers also hit their stride in the 1970s. Thanks to the new generation of stars, there was a large fan base hungry for films and the studio were churning them out at an industrial rate. At their best, the movies they produced were thrilling entertainments. Gordon Liu became a star after the release of *The 36th Chamber of Shaolin* (1978), which told the story of San Te, a legendary disciple of the Shaolin discipline. In the same year, Jackie Chan rose to fame thanks to *Snake in the Eagle's Shadow* (1978). It was directed by the legendary choreographer Woo-ping Yuen, who went on to direct Chan in his next film, the phenomenally successful *Drunken Master* (1978), however, it was *Snake in the Eagle's Shadow* that played up the actor's ability to balance high jinks with comedy.

Like Jackie Chan, Jet Li started out in Chinese martial arts films, but has since crossed over to mainstream Hollywood. He is one of the most recent in a long list of Asian martial arts stars to perform in U.S. films, dating back to Bruce Lee in *Marlowe* (1969). One of the first appearances of martial arts in an American film was *Bad Day at Black Rock* (1955) and a move performed by Spencer Tracy's one-armed war veteran John J. Macreedy. Since then, non-Asian martial arts stars have come out of the competition circuit, as was the case with Chuck Norris and the "Muscle from Brussels," Jean-Claude Van Damme, whose best film, *Timecop* (1994) blends martial arts with an enjoyably silly sci-fi tale.

In recent years, Stephen Chow has taken Jackie Chan's penchant for action comedy to the extreme with the hilarious parodies *Shaolin Soccer* (2001) and *Kung Fu Hustle* (2004). Thai and Indonesian martial artists Tony Jaa and Iko Uwais have also wowed audiences with their own styles of combat in, respectively, *Ong-Bak* (2003) and The Raid (2011), and their subsequent sequels. While in Hong Kong, Wong Kar-wai brought artistry to the forefront once again with his meditative biopic of Bruce Lee's mentor Ip Man in *The Grandmaster* (2013). **IHS**

■ Romance ■ Comedy ■ Thriller ■ Kung Fu

Jet Li
🎬 *Once Upon a Time in China*

Jean-Claude Van Damme
🎬 *Timecop*

Michelle Yeoh
🎬 *Crouching Tiger, Hidden Dragon*

Tony Jaa
🎬 *Ong-Bak*

Stephen Chow
🎬 *Kung Fu Hustle*

Iko Uwais
🎬 *The Raid*

Tony Leung
🎬 *The Grandmaster*

1985 | 1990 | 1995 | 2000 | 2005 | 2010 | 2015 | 2020

charles chaplin 1889–1977

| Making a Living | Kid Auto Races at Venice | The Tramp | The Bank | The Pawnshop | The Immigrant | A Dog's Life | The Kid |

It took Charles Chaplin less than a year from his cinematic debut to become the world's foremost screen icon. On January 5, 1914, having joined Mack Sennett's Keystone Film Company, the young English vaudevillian appeared before a movie camera for the first time in *Making a Living*. By December, his shabby but oddly dandyish Tramp persona — derby hat, cane, too-tight jacket, baggy pants, outsize boots, toothbrush mustache — was known the world over.

He was born in south London, the son of struggling music-hall artistes. His professional stage career started at age 8, and at 18 he joined theater impresario Fred Karno's troupe, sailing with them to America in 1910. A success on the New York stage, he was invited to California by Sennett in 1913.

Such was his instant screen popularity that all but one of the 35 films he made in that first year of his screen career have survived. The Keystone films show him visibly learning on the job. In the earlier shorts he is mugging to camera, waving his arms about, falling down a lot. By the end of the year he has slowed the pace; the Tramp persona, first seen in his second film, *Kid Auto Races at Venice*, becomes a more rounded character, the mannerisms worked on and refined.

Chaplin soon took on directing duties as well; nearly half his Keystone films were directed by him.

Tillie's Punctured Romance (1914), his first feature, was directed by Sennett, but for the rest of his career, Chaplin would script and direct every one of his films. At the end of 1914, he quit for rival studio Essanay and a much larger salary. A year later, he moved again, this time to Mutual, on even more generous terms. By now he was probably the most famous man alive.

In these early films, Chaplin was not always the Tramp. Sometimes he played a dandy, a variant on a character from his vaudeville days. But always his delight in his own physical dexterity is evident. In *The Rink* (1916), he is a waiter who roller skates during his lunch hour; his skating virtuosity is impressive, but so is his manual dexterity mixing a cocktail. However, it was as the Tramp that he seemed happiest and most inventive. His work rate was slowing — he made 12 films in 1915, 10 in 1916, just four in 1917 — and the slapstick was becoming less formulaic, more inventive.

One A.M. (1916) was a solo tour de force: just Chaplin as a drunken swell, endlessly trying and failing to get himself to bed. *The Immigrant* (1917) added pathos: Chaplin and Edna Purviance (his on- and offscreen partner at this time) arriving in the United States on a steamer, labels hung around their necks. He moved studios again, this time to First National, where he made *A Dog's Life* (1918) — down-and-out,

genre ■ Short ■ Comedy ■ Romance

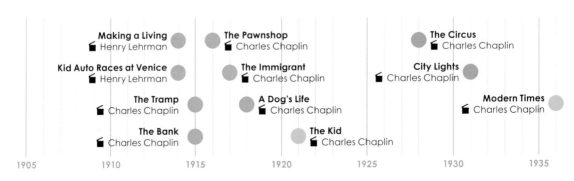

Making a Living Henry Lehrman	**The Pawnshop** Charles Chaplin		**The Circus** Charles Chaplin
Kid Auto Races at Venice Henry Lehrman	**The Immigrant** Charles Chaplin		**City Lights** Charles Chaplin
The Tramp Charles Chaplin	**A Dog's Life** Charles Chaplin		**Modern Times** Charles Chaplin
The Bank Charles Chaplin	**The Kid** Charles Chaplin		

| 1905 | 1910 | 1915 | 1920 | 1925 | 1930 | 1935 |

| The Circus | City Lights | Modern Times | The Great Dictator | Monsieur Verdoux | Limelight | A King in New York | A Countess from Hong Kong |

plus mongrel — and *Shoulder Arms* (1918), set in the trenches. In 1921, he directed his first feature, the six-reeler *The Kid*: streetsmart Chaplin battling poverty, bullies and cops, taking mini-me Jackie Coogan under his wing. First National had misgivings over the length, but it was hugely successful.

There were only a couple more shorts — *The Idle Class* (1921) and *Pay Day* (1922) — and the four-reel *The Pilgrim* (1923). An escaped convict, Charlie takes on the garb of a priest; his mimed sermon, the clash between David and Goliath, is a joy. He took two years to prepare his finest silent movie, *The Gold Rush* (1925); the heavy dose of pathos is balanced by inspired clowning — the "dance of the rolls" and the hut teetering on a precipice. *The Circus* (1928), his final silent, was plagued by production problems and feels bitty: some inspired set-pieces (Charlie disrupting a magic act; his tightrope walk hampered by monkeys) are strung together on a routine unrequited-love plot.

An instinctive mime, Chaplin resisted speech as long as he could. His first sound film, *City Lights* (1931), used a score (composed by Chaplin) and sound effects only. The sentimental relationship between Chaplin and the blind flower-girl is countered by the slapstick of the boozy millionaire who is bosom pals with Chaplin while drunk but does not know him when sober. *Modern Times* (1936) steals ideas from René Clair's *A Nous la Liberté* (1931), often improving on them, as when Chaplin gets caught in the cogs of the production line.

Given Hollywood's pre-war timidity with regard to Nazism, it took courage to satirize Hitler. In *The Great Dictator* (1940), his first real talkie, Chaplin took a double role: the megalomaniac Adenoid Hynkel and the Jewish barber who is mistaken for him. Some of the politics now seem simplistic, but his Hynkel — frothing at the mouth about Jews one minute, playing wistfully with a balloon-globe the next — still looks masterly.

But Chaplin's pro-USSR politics and his weakness for very young females were starting to erode his reputation. *Monsieur Verdoux* (1947) did not help. A black comedy about murder, based on a real-life serial wife-killer, it enshrines one of Chaplin's most subtle — if borderline misogynistic — performances. His Verdoux, fastidious and slightly camp, was a far cry from the Tramp. The film flopped and was widely reviled.

Limelight (1952), where he played an ageing clown, drew on his music-hall childhood. It felt over-nostalgic, but looked like a masterpiece beside his attempted satire on America, *A King in New York* (1957). Still worse was *A Countess from Hong Kong* (1967), with Chaplin in a tiny role as a ship's steward. The once-stratospheric career was unmistakably over. **PK**

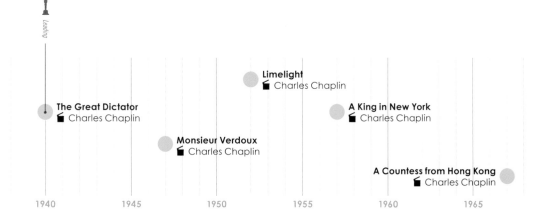

maggie cheung 1964

| As Tears Go By | Days of Being Wild | Song of the Exile | Center Stage | Irma Vep | In the Mood for Love | Hero | Clean |

In an interview with film historian Berenice Reynaud, Maggie Cheung describes how she creates a character: "I start with an image: her body language, how she would walk and talk. You have to be able to physically feel that person before you can get into her heart."

She was born in Hong Kong, but her family emigrated to the UK when she was 8. On holiday in Hong Kong when she was 18, Cheung was scouted by a modeling agency. She made her acting breakthrough in the romantic comedy *Prince Charming* (1984), followed by several Hong Kong romantic comedy and action films, such as Jackie Chan's *Police Story* (1985) and Johnnie To's comedy *Happy Ghost 3* (1986). However, it was starring opposite Andy Lau in Wong Kar-wai's feature debut *As Tears Go By* (1988) that Cheung would later credit as the beginning of her serious acting career.

Cheung starred in over 20 Hong Kong films over the next two years, including an impressive performance in Ann Hui's melodrama *Song of the Exile* (1990). International recognition also followed around this time, with her committed performance in Stanley Kwan's *Center Stage* (1991), playing the tragic Chinese actress Ruan Lingyu, winning several awards.

Cheung's first major international role was in Oliver Assayas' film-within-a-film, *Irma Vep* (1996). She plays herself, opposite Jean Pierre Leaud's director who has cast her as the famous villain in a remake of the 1915 serial *Les Vampires*. Cheung would marry Assaysas in 1998 and, despite their marriage ending in 2001, collaborated with him again in 2004 on *Clean*, for which she won the Best Actress award at Cannes.

It is the vision of Cheung in Wong's *In the Mood for Love* (2000) that lingers over her later career. A highly stylized and melancholy love story set in 1960s Hong Kong, Cheung is Mrs. Chan, the lonely wife of a philandering businessman who falls in love with her neighbor and husband to her spouse's partner, played by an equally heartbroken Tony Leung. Cheung's now legendary costumes, her movement and the style she exudes in the film added depth to a character of little dialogue and agency.

Cheung later starred in the wuxia blockbuster *Hero* (2002) as the warrior Flying Snow, once again cast opposite Leung in a doomed love affair. In 2007 Cheung won an award for outstanding contribution to Chinese cinema at the Shanghai International Film Festival. She has since retired from acting. **CMB**

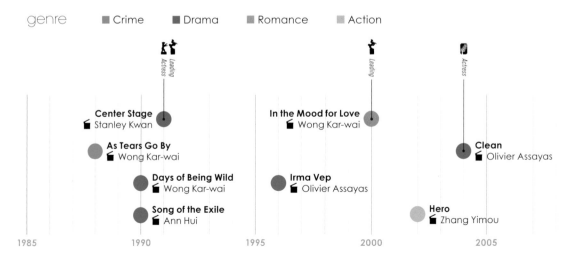

julie christie 1941

C

| Billy Liar | Darling | Far from the Madding Crowd | McCabe and Mrs. Miller | Don't Look Now | Afterglow | Finding Neverland | Away from Her |

For a period in the mid-1960s, Julie Christie was one of the most recognizable actresses in the world — an icon of London culture at its swinging height. But Christie's early fame has sometimes obscured her depth, subtlety and versatility as an actress.

Born in 1941 in India to British parents, Christie had worked on the London stage and British television before being cast in the film that made her name: *Billy Liar* (1963). John Schlesinger's comedy drama is a key film in the British New Wave. She played Liz, girlfriend to Tom Courtenay's eponymous daydreaming hero, offering a spark of optimism and possibility.

Christie's first starring role was in *Darling* (1965). Directed again by Schlesinger, she played a bored model who begins a string of affairs against the backdrop of London's vibrant cultural scene. Christie's award-winning performance is heartfelt and piercing.

Her profile continued to rise with a performance of romantic melancholy in David Lean's sweeping *Doctor Zhivago* (1965). In Schlesinger's lavish 1967 adaptation of *Far from the Madding Crowd* she was striking as the young heroine caught between three men, while in Joseph Losey's *The Go-Between* (1971), she is haunting as a woman torn between love and duty.

By the early 1970s, Christie was working increasingly in the United States. She made three films alongside Warren Beatty, with whom she had a long-term relationship; she was tough and compelling as the owner of a pioneer-town whorehouse in the revisionist western *McCabe and Mrs. Miller* (1971); and she displayed an adept light touch in the comedies *Shampoo* (1975) and *Heaven Can Wait* (1978).

Her standout performance of the decade was in the psychological horror *Don't Look Now* (1973), playing a grieving mother visiting Venice with her husband (Donald Sutherland). The movie was notorious for an explicit love scene, but what impresses now is Christie's naked emotional power.

Since returning to the UK in the late 1970s, Christie's career has been quieter and more varied, with forays into experimental projects such as Sally Potter's radical debut *The Gold Diggers* (1983), alongside supporting roles in prestige dramas like *Finding Neverland* (2004). In her rare lead roles, she remains commanding. She is wry and enigmatic in the romantic drama *Afterglow* (1997) and in *Away from Her* (2006) she is devastating as a woman struggling with Alzheimer's. **EL**

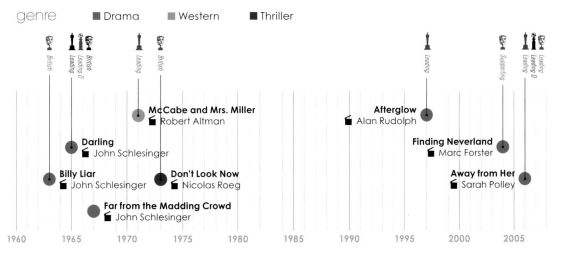

genre ■ Drama ■ Western ■ Thriller

British | British Leading D Leading | Leading | British | Leading | Supporting | Leading Leading D Leading

McCabe and Mrs. Miller
Robert Altman

Darling
John Schlesinger

Billy Liar
John Schlesinger

Don't Look Now
Nicolas Roeg

Far from the Madding Crowd
John Schlesinger

Afterglow
Alan Rudolph

Finding Neverland
Marc Forster

Away from Her
Sarah Polley

1960 | 1965 | 1970 | 1975 | 1980 | 1985 | 1990 | 1995 | 2000 | 2005

montgomery clift 1920–66

| Red River | The Heiress | A Place in the Sun | From Here to Eternity | I Confess | Suddenly, Last Summer | Judgment at Nuremberg | The Misfits |

One of the most tragic tales in Hollywood history, Montgomery Clift's time in the spotlight was defined by heady highs and crashing lows. However, the tragedies of his personal life should not overshadow his immense talent and his long-lasting impact over subsequent generations of actors.

Clift's striking screen debut was in Howard Hawks' acclaimed western *Red River* (1948). Next, the young actor appeared in *The Search* (1948), a performance that landed him with his first Academy Award nomination. Clift quickly followed this up with a role opposite Olivia de Havilland in the sumptuous *The Heiress* (1949), and the following year got his second Oscar nod for his turn in the glorious melodrama *A Place in the Sun* (1951), playing opposite Shelley Winters and his good friend Elizabeth Taylor. Clift's friendship with Taylor was one of several strong connections that the gay actor shared with women. He once said, "I love men in bed, but I really love women."

With the handsome star's career going from strength to strength, Clift won the lead role in Alfred Hitchcock's *I Confess* (1953). A more austere drama than other films by the director from this period, *I Confess* was met with ambivalence by audiences and

critics alike. However, Clift took one of the leads in the hugely popular *From Here to Eternity* (1953), for which he received yet another Oscar nomination. Sadly for Clift, this film would mark the end of the runaway success of his early years.

In 1956, while filming *Raintree County* (1957), Clift was involved in a car crash. He suffered a number of serious injuries, including a broken jaw and nose, fractured sinus and several serious lacerations to his face. When he returned to filming on *Raintree County*, his physical appearance had noticeably changed.

Following the accident, Clift became increasingly dependent on painkillers and alcohol. As a result, his career never truly recovered. He appeared in a series of films including *The Young Lions* (1958), *Suddenly, Last Summer* (1959) and *Wild River* (1960), but developed a reputation for erratic behavior and bouts of depression.

Clift starred opposite Marilyn Monroe and Clark Gable in the brilliant *The Misfits* (1961), a film that would prove fateful for all concerned. His performance in *Judgment at Nuremberg* (1961) saw him receive his final Oscar nomination. In 1966, he was found dead from a heart attack in his New York townhouse after a number of years in relative isolation. He was 45. **MB**

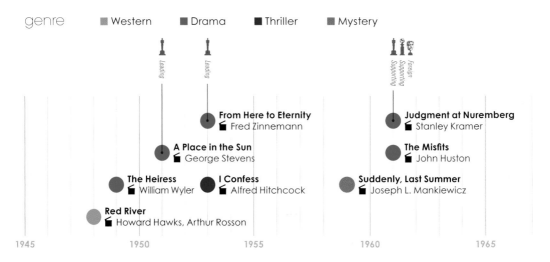

genre ■ Western ■ Drama ■ Thriller ■ Mystery

From Here to Eternity
🎬 Fred Zinnemann

Judgment at Nuremberg
🎬 Stanley Kramer

A Place in the Sun
🎬 George Stevens

The Misfits
🎬 John Huston

The Heiress
🎬 William Wyler

I Confess
🎬 Alfred Hitchcock

Suddenly, Last Summer
🎬 Joseph L. Mankiewicz

Red River
🎬 Howard Hawks, Arthur Rosson

1945   1950   1955   1960   1965

george clooney 1961

| From Dusk Till Dawn | Out of Sight | O Brother, Where Art Thou? | The Perfect Storm | Ocean's Eleven | Syriana | Michael Clayton | Gravity |

One of the most respected stars in Hollywood, George Clooney's classical good looks and commanding presence have often seen him compared to Gary Cooper and Clark Gable.

After a slew of forgettable film and television appearances, Clooney hit pay dirt at 33 with a leading role as Dr. Doug Ross in *E.R.* (1994–2009), which he left after five years in 1999. His first major film role was in Robert Rodriguez's *From Dusk Till Dawn* (1996). A crime caper-cum-horror movie, Clooney and Quentin Tarantino play two brothers fleeing the law who find themselves trapped in a bar run by vampires. The film's hokey premise notwithstanding, Clooney, with a razor-wire tattoo on his neck and cropped hair, is every bit the film star. The same cannot be said of him in the dull romantic comedy *One Fine Day* (1996), inert action thriller *The Peacemaker* (1997) or the superhero movie nadir that is *Batman & Robin* (1997).

What would have happened to Clooney's career had he not met Steven Soderbergh is anybody's guess, but their partnership marks the start of the actor's ascent through Hollywood. *Out of Sight* (1998) is a smart and sexy crime thriller, while *Ocean's Eleven* (2001) taps into the actor's charming screen persona.

(Two sequels followed, but neither emulated the easygoing pace of the first.) *Solaris* (2002) features one of Clooney's finest performances as a tortured psychologist whose waking life is haunted by his dreams. And if *The Good German* (2006) ultimately fails, it is an ambitious experiment.

Teaming up with the Coen brothers, Clooney channeled Clark Gable at his most knockabout in *O Brother, Where Art Thou?* (2000), a smart, zany take on the Odysseus myth. The bitter relationship comedy *Intolerable Cruelty* (2003) is less impressive, while *Burn After Reading* (2008) gave Clooney an earthier, cruder character to play. He also stars in their fictional account of Hollywood in the 1950s, *Hail Caesar!* (2016).

Clooney's best serious roles range from the physical, such as the stoic captain of a doomed fishing vessel in *The Perfect Storm* (2000) and an assassin on the run in *The American* (2010), to more cerebral characters, such as his deserved Oscar-winning performance in *Syriana* (2005) as a CIA operative caught up in Middle Eastern political games, a lawyer involved in a conspiracy in *Michael Clayton* (2007) and as the commanding officer of a doomed space shuttle in *Gravity* (2013). **IHS**

genre ■ Horror ■ Crime ■ Comedy ■ Action ■ Thriller ■ Sci-Fi

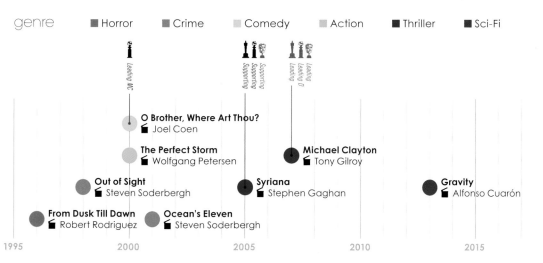

O Brother, Where Art Thou?
Joel Coen

The Perfect Storm
Wolfgang Petersen

Michael Clayton
Tony Gilroy

Out of Sight
Steven Soderbergh

Syriana
Stephen Gaghan

Gravity
Alfonso Cuarón

From Dusk Till Dawn
Robert Rodriguez

Ocean's Eleven
Steven Soderbergh

1995   2000   2005   2010   2015

stars from the small screen

Clint Eastwood · Dan Aykroyd · Bill Murray · Eddie Murphy · Morgan Freeman · Tom Hanks · Guy Pearce · Denzel Washington

The small screen has long been a breeding ground for big-screen talent, turning stand-up comedians into superstars, sitcom regulars into respected dramatic actors and soap stars into Oscar winners. The trend dates back to the western series *Rawhide* (1959–65) in which Clint Eastwood starred in 217 episodes. His first major part off the back of that series was Sergio Leone's *A Fistful of Dollars* (1964). As an actor, Eastwood soon became synonymous with the western, completing a trilogy with Leone. However, his biggest successes lay behind the camera and he now holds two Best Director Oscars for *Unforgiven* (1992) and *Million Dollar Baby* (2004).

Other bankable small-screen stars have not been as immediately fortunate. George Clooney was already a television heartthrob, mainly because of his performance as Doug Ross on *ER* (1994–2009). Yet his early attempts on the big screen were littered with missteps, from *One Fine Day* (1996) to *Batman & Robin* (1997), before his partnership with director Steven Soderbergh — *Out of Sight* (1998), *Ocean's Eleven* (2001), *Solaris* (2002) — paved the way to superstardom and an Oscar for *Syriana* (2005). Like Eastwood, Clooney has also successfully branched into directing and was nominated for Best Director Oscar for *Good Night, and Good Luck* (2005).

The list of Oscar regulars who began on television is a lengthy one. Morgan Freeman, the "voice of God" got his big break as the voice of the 1970s U.S. comedy series *The Electric Company* (1971–77). His move to film yielded three nominations — for *Street Smart* (1987), *Driving Miss Daisy* (1989) and *The Shawshank Redemption* (1994) — before he finally won for *Million Dollar Baby*. Tom Hanks was pegged for big things while on the short-lived series *Bosom Buddies* (1980–82), and a guest spot on *Happy Days* (1974–84) put him together with Ron Howard who, as a director, launched Hanks' film career with *Splash* (1984). Hanks went on to win Best Actor two years running, for *Philadelphia* (1993) and *Forrest Gump* (1994). Another double winner, Denzel Washington, who won for *Glory* (1989) and *Training Day* (2001), made his name as one of the few black characters on the medical series *St. Elsewhere* (1982–88). Washington was still a regular on the show when nominated for Best Actor for his portrayal of activist Steve Biko in *Cry Freedom* (1987).

More surprising is Catherine Zeta-Jones, who went from playing David Jason's daughter on *The Darling Buds of May* (1991–93) to winning an Oscar as bad girl Velma Kelly in *Chicago* (2002). And who would have imagined that *The Fresh Prince of Bel-Air* (1990–96), Will Smith, would go on to be nominated for Best Actor

type ■ Western ■ Sketch show ■ Children's ■ Sitcom ■ Soap

Dan Aykroyd
🎬 *The Blues Brothers*

Clint Eastwood
🎬 *A Fistful of Dollars*

Bill Murray
🎬 *Ghostbusters*

Eddie Murphy
🎬 *Beverly Hills Cop*

Morgan Freeman
🎬 *Driving Miss Daisy*

1965   1970   1975   1980   1985   1990

Will Smith | Russell Crowe | Catherine Zeta-Jones | Jamie Foxx | George Clooney | Jennifer Lawrence | Chris Hemsworth | Robert Downey Jr.

twice, for *Ali* (2001) and *The Pursuit of Happyness* (2006). Bradley Cooper exchanged playing support on *Alias* (2001–06) for three Oscar nominations in a row — for *Silver Linings Playbook* (2012), *American Hustle* (2013) and *American Sniper* (2014). Cooper's costar in the first two of that trio, Jennifer Lawrence, went from guest roles on shows such as *Cold Case* (2003–10), to Oscar nominee for *Winter's Bone* (2010) and winner of Best Actress for *Silver Linings Playbook*. Russell Crowe went all the way from Aussie soap *Neighbours* (1985–) to Best Actor for *Gladiator* (2000).

Neighbours has been an unusual early step on the ladder for many a star, also uncovering the talents of Guy Pearce — who impressed immediately alongside fellow alumnus Russell Crowe in *L.A. Confidential* (1997) — and went on to deliver intense performances in *Memento* (2000), *The Proposition* (2005) and *The Rover* (2014). Margot Robbie impressively traded Ramsay Street for *The Wolf of Wall Street* (2013), while Liam Hemsworth spent two years on the soap before breaking through in *The Hunger Games* (2012). His brother Chris left rival soap *Home and Away* (1988–) after four years, and went straight into *Star Trek* (2009) and superhero status in *Thor* (2011), *The Avengers* (2012), *Thor: The Dark World* (2013) and *Avengers: Age of Ultron* (2015).

American sketch comedy series have provided more conventional hotbeds for emerging talent. *Saturday Night Live* (1975–) has the best record, introducing 1980s comedy superstars Dan Aykroyd and John Belushi. The duo enjoyed huge success with *The Blues Brothers* (1980), reprising characters they had created on the show. Bill Murray joined the show in its second season and graduated to movies through *Caddyshack* (1980) and *Ghostbusters* (1984). He has since proved his worth as a dramatic actor with an Oscar-nominated turn in *Lost in Translation* (2003). Another key *SNL* graduate from the 1980s is Eddie Murphy, whose electric performance in *48 Hrs.* (1982) made him both a star and an action hero, a status further underlined by *Beverly Hills Cop* (1984). Other notable former cast members include Robert Downey Jr., Will Ferrell, Mike Myers, Tina Fey and Chris Rock.

The groundbreaking series *In Living Color* (1990–94) launched the careers of the Wayans family, including Keenan Ivory, Shawn, Marlon, Kim and Damon, all of whom starred in the Blaxploitation spoof *I'm Gonna Git You Sucka* (1988). It also launched the career of Jamie Foxx, who was quickly recognized as a serious talent, via roles in *Any Given Sunday* (1999) and *Ali*. Foxx was an Oscar nominee for *Collateral* (2004) and, in the same year, an Oscar winner for *Ray* (2004). **MG**

■ Medical drama   ■ Drama   ■ Detective

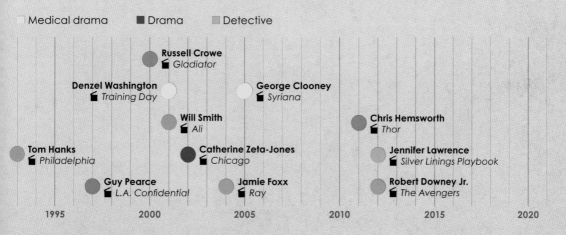

Russell Crowe — *Gladiator*

Denzel Washington — *Training Day*

George Clooney — *Syriana*

Will Smith — *Ali*

Chris Hemsworth — *Thor*

Tom Hanks — *Philadelphia*

Catherine Zeta-Jones — *Chicago*

Jennifer Lawrence — *Silver Linings Playbook*

Guy Pearce — *L.A. Confidential*

Jamie Foxx — *Ray*

Robert Downey Jr. — *The Avengers*

1995   2000   2005   2010   2015   2020

claudette colbert 1903–96

| It Happened One Night | Bluebeard's Eighth Wife | Drums Along the Mohawk | Midnight | Arise, My Love | The Palm Beach Story | The Egg and I | The Two Mrs. Grenvilles |

Claudette Colbert once said, "Audiences always sound like they're glad to see me, and I'm damned glad to see them." In a career spanning over 60 films the coquettish, French-born American actress was a hugely popular presence.

Born Emilie Claudette Chauchoin in 1903, her family moved to the United States when she was 3. Though trained as a stenographer, she felt the urge to act from an early age. Her Broadway debut in a 1923 production of *The Wild Westcotts* led to several years of theater work and minor film roles, which eventually brought her to the attention of studio bosses. Larger parts followed, including the vampish Poppaea in *The Sign of the Cross* (1932) and the titular role in *Cleopatra* (1934), both under the guidance of Cecil B. DeMille. However, it was Frank Capra's decision to cast her opposite heartthrob Clark Gable in *It Happened One Night* (1934) that ensured her stardom. The Oscar-winning role led to major parts in screwball comedies, including Ernst Lubitsch's *Bluebeard's Eighth Wife* (1938). Her easy charm in these roles endeared her to audiences.

Colbert was nevertheless impossible to typecast. Between the mid-1930s and 1950s she leavened meatier roles in period dramas such as *Drums Along the Mohawk* (1939), and Oscar-nominated performances in *Private Worlds* (1935) and *Since You Went Away* (1944), with a string of appearances in lighter fare such as the Billy Wilder-penned comedies *Midnight* (1939) and *Arise, My Love* (1940). Though light confections, there was a strong undercurrent of sophistication running through these films, and Colbert's sparkling presence would always add fizz to the comedy. Nowhere is this more apparent than Preston Sturges' *The Palm Beach Story* (1942).

By the mid-1950s, Colbert's star had waned. Her comedic style and old Hollywood glamour was no longer in vogue among younger audiences. As a result, she wisely reinvented herself as a star of television and appeared almost exclusively on the small screen, with a brief return to cinema with *Parrish* (1961). The remainder of her professional life involved television work and the theater. Her final screen appearance was in *The Two Mrs. Grenvilles* (1987), the critically acclaimed television movie of Dominick Dunne's bestselling family drama. She was awarded a Golden Globe for her portrayal of the domineering matriarch Alice Grenville. Colbert died in Barbados in 1996. **CP**

genre ■ Romance ■ Western ■ Comedy ■ Drama

Leading

It Happened One Night
Frank Capra

The Palm Beach Story
Preston Sturges

Bluebeard's Eighth Wife
Ernst Lubitsch

The Egg and I
Chester Erskine

Drums Along the Mohawk
John Ford

The Two Mrs. Grenvilles
John Erman

Midnight
Mitchell Leisen

Arise, My Love
Mitchell Leisen

Supporting M/TV

1935   1940   1945   1950   1980   1985   1990

Action Hero	Cop	Fighter	Hero	Saint

sean connery 1930

Dr. No

Marnie

The Hill

The Man Who Would Be King

The Name of the Rose

The Untouchables

Indiana Jones and the Last Crusade

The Hunt for Red October

If the definition of a star is to bring an imposing screen presence to every role, even if it means changing the characteristics of that role in order to play to their strengths, then Sean Connery is, without a doubt, a star.

Born into a working-class Scottish family in 1930, his first screen appearance was in *No Road Back* (1957), followed by *Hell Drivers* (1957). But it was as James Bond in *Dr. No* (1962) that Connery became a household name. *From Russia with Love* (1963), *Goldfinger* (1964), *Thunderball* (1965) and *You Only Live Twice* (1967) — arguably the finest run of films in the franchise — followed. He bowed out on the kitsch *Diamonds Are Forever* (1971), only to return in the *Thunderball* rehash *Never Say Never Again* (1983). In the best of the Bond films, Connery captured the charm and malevolence of Ian Fleming's antihero — a characteristic spotted by Alfred Hitchcock, who cast the actor as the bullying playboy who seduces the titular heroine of *Marnie* (1964). The role came at a time when Connery was keen to ensure that he could build a career beyond Bond. He stretched himself further with *The Hill* (1965). The first of five films for director Sidney Lumet, it gave Connery his most intense role to date. He was also impressive in Lumet's

The Anderson Tapes (1971), the unsettling police procedural *The Offence* (1972) and as one of the many luminaries in *Murder on the Orient Express* (1974). Only *Family Business* (1989) was a disappointment.

Connery's most acclaimed performances are not always his best. He won an Oscar for his portrayal of street cop Jimmy Malone in *The Untouchables* (1987), but his William of Baskerville in the previous year's *The Name of the Rose* (1986) is richer and no less compelling. He is excellent with Michael Caine as two rogue soldiers seeking riches in *The Man Who Would Be King* (1975), but his Robin Hood in Richard Lester's *Robin and Marian* (1976) deserves as much attention.

Of Connery's later work, *The Russia House* (1990) lacks energy, *The Rock* (1996) and *Entrapment* (1999) are enjoyably silly and he perhaps should have avoided *The Avengers* (1998) and *The League of Extraordinary Gentlemen* (2003). *The Hunt for Red October* (1990) is a perfect vehicle, honing in on what makes him so watchable. And if ever there was a need to prove how big a star Connery has been for most of his career, his cameo as Richard the Lionheart at the end of *Robin Hood: Prince of Thieves* (1991) sealed it: it takes a legend to play a legend. **IHS**

genre ■ Action ■ Thriller ■ War ■ Adventure ■ Mystery ■ Crime

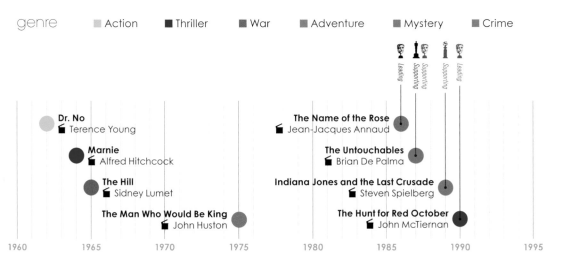

Dr. No — Terence Young
Marnie — Alfred Hitchcock
The Hill — Sidney Lumet
The Man Who Would Be King — John Huston
The Name of the Rose — Jean-Jacques Annaud
The Untouchables — Brian De Palma
Indiana Jones and the Last Crusade — Steven Spielberg
The Hunt for Red October — John McTiernan

Leading / Supporting / Supporting / Leading

1960   1965   1970   1975   1980   1985   1990   1995

gary cooper 1901–61

| The Virginian | Morocco | A Farewell to Arms | The Lives of a Bengal Lancer | Mr. Deeds Goes to Town | Desire | The Plainsman | Beau Geste |

With a career that spanned the end of the silent era to the majestic closing days of the U.S. studio system, Gary Cooper left a body of work that encapsulates the range and richness of Hollywood's Golden Age. Most closely associated with the western, he effortlessly embodied the solidly masculine, dependably stoic, quietly heroic values that are the genre's trademarks. He was one of Hollywood's most striking romantic leads, combining an imposing physicality with a lightly worn charisma. And he could convince as unimpeachably ordinary Joes, bringing to comedies a common touch that was a kind of grace.

Born in 1901 in Montana, Cooper was partly raised on a ranch, and the experience he gained there played into the image he would later project as a natural-born westerner. His ranching skills certainly won him his first break: having moved to Los Angeles, Cooper found a job as an extra and stunt rider on some of the low-budget silent westerns of the mid-1920s.

Switching to acting, Cooper rose quickly through the ranks; his breakthrough was a supporting role on the western The Winning of Barbara Worth (1926). But the actor soon revealed how at ease he was in other genres. Tall and classically handsome, with features that could switch from watchful intelligence to an almost feline sensuality, he was also soon matched with some of the leading female stars of the day.

Unlike many of his contemporaries, Cooper successfully made the transition to sound. In the western The Virginian (1929) he played a man of few words, but when he did speak his voice was deep and warm, delivered with an unforced naturalism. The laconic, unshowy, unshakeably honorable hero he played was typical of the roles that Cooper would return to throughout his career.

He could also be playful and sly, notably in his next major role, as a moody legionnaire alongside Marlene Dietrich in Josef von Sternberg's sumptuous romantic drama Morocco (1930). He would reunite with the actress six years later for the swoony comedy Desire (1936), Cooper's stolid American decency contrasting with Dietrich's wily exoticism.

Throughout the 1930s, Cooper established himself as a major box-office draw. Breezy adventure films like The Lives of a Bengal Lancer (1935) saw him display a commendable derring-do, a quality he would also flaunt in the stirring desert-based action drama Beau Geste (1939). He won plaudits for his more serious roles,

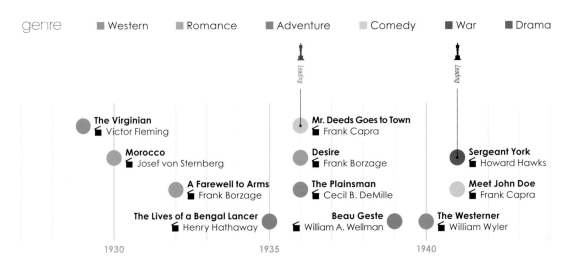

| The Westerner | Sergeant York | Meet John Doe | Along Came Jones | The Fountainhead | High Noon | Love in the Afternoon | Man of the West |

notably his intense and committed performance as the hero of Frank Borzage's sensous adaptation of Ernest Hemingway's *A Farewell to Arms* (1932). And, of course, he continued to maintain his reputation as one of the western's pre-eminent stars, taking the role of Wild Bill Hickock in *The Plainsman* (1936) for Cecil B. DeMille, and playing a cowboy wrongly accused of horse stealing in William Wyler's *The Westerner* (1940).

It was in a comedy, however, that Cooper gave one of his defining performances. Recognizing the actor's gift for conveying a plain-dealing, big-hearted kind of innocence, director Frank Capra cast him in *Mr. Deeds Goes to Town* (1936) as a small-town eccentric who runs up against big-business interests when he inherits a fortune. Cooper brought to life this gentle idealism with wit, courtly charm and surprising shrewdness. The film established him as an American everyman, a role he would inhabit again for Capra when he played a down-on-his-luck former baseball player whose good nature is exploited by scheming politicians in *Meet John Doe* (1941). Other directors responded to Cooper's incorruptible common touch, notably Howard Hawks, for whom the actor gave one of his finest performances, as a devoutly Christian small-town farmer turned reluctant military hero in the World War I drama *Sergeant York* (1941).

Cooper remained a star after World War II, with hits that included the comedy western *Along Came Jones* (1945). But while his folksy image struck a chord with the national mood of wartime patriotism, he sometimes struggled to adapt to the darker concerns of postwar American cinema. Critics were generally underwhelmed by his turn as the architect hero of King Vidor's lavish adaptation of Ayn Rand's *The Fountainhead* (1949). And in the romantic comedy *Love in the Afternoon* (1957) he was improbably paired with Audrey Hepburn, many years his junior.

Returning full circle to the genre that made his name, Cooper's greatest final performances were in westerns. Playing a sheriff who must stand alone against a gang of outlaws in *High Noon* (1952), he offered a masterly portrait of heroic integrity. And in 1958 he worked with Anthony Mann on a western that saw him bring an uneasy sense of ambiguity to his role as a reformed outlaw accidentally brought back in contact with his old gang. Made just three years before his death, the film's title could serve as Cooper's epitaph: *Man of the West*. **EL**

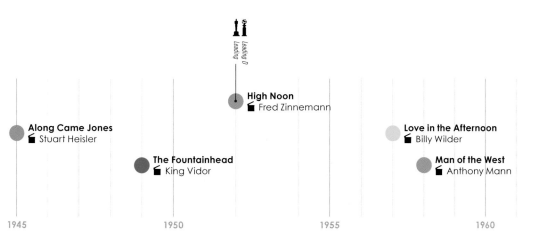

Leading Director
Leading

High Noon
Fred Zinnemann

Along Came Jones
Stuart Heisler

Love in the Afternoon
Billy Wilder

The Fountainhead
King Vidor

Man of the West
Anthony Mann

1945   1950   1955   1960

kevin costner 1955

| Silverado | No Way Out | The Untouchables | Field of Dreams | Dances with Wolves | Waterworld | Open Range | Man of Steel |

Over the course of three decades, Kevin Costner has perfected the role of the blue-collar everyman. As such, he was perfect as Clark Kent's father in *Man of Steel* (2013). Exuding decency and a sense of what is right, it was an archetypal role for the actor.

Costner started out as the dead friend that everyone talks about in *The Big Chill* (1983), but remained on the cutting-room floor. He showed promise in *American Flyers* (1985), but it was playing the rebellious Jake in *Silverado* (1985) that he caught audiences' attention. He followed it with the excellent thriller *No Way Out* (1987) and became a star as the noble lawman Elliot Ness in *The Untouchables* (1987).

Bull Durham (1988) and *Field of Dreams* (1989) followed. Both centered around baseball, the latter film is the more romantic, as a young farmer reconciles with his dead father by building a baseball field. *Bull Durham*, by contrast, is a hilarious locker-room account of a veteran pro training a rookie. Costner would continue the sports theme with the golf comedy *Tin Cup* (1996) and *For the Love of the Game* (1999), which takes the "baseball as life" metaphor a little too far.

Costner starred in his Oscar-winning directorial debut, *Dances with Wolves* (1990), playing a soldier who leaves the U.S. cavalry for life alone on the open plains before he befriends a Native American tribe. He is outclassed by Alan Rickman's villainous Sheriff in *Robin Hood: Prince of Thieves* (1991), but is excellent in Oliver Stone's conspiracy-laden *JFK* (1991). Neither he nor Whitney Houston deserved the sizeable audience that turned out for *The Bodyguard* (1992), but he redeemed himself as a likeable con-on-the-run in Clint Eastwood's *A Perfect World* (1993) and is a compelling incarnation of the legendary lawman in *Wyatt Earp* (1994). His other recent western, *Open Range* (2003), features one of his most enjoyable performances.

If the grand follies of *Waterworld* (1995) and the woeful *The Postman* (1997) still cast a shadow over Costner's more recent output, *Thirteen Days* (2000), *The Company Men* (2010) and football drama *Draft Day* (2014) highlight the strengths of the actor's screen persona. He may be edging toward Liam Neeson's action man territory with *3 Days to Kill* (2014), but Kevin Costner is at his best playing an everyday hero. **IHS**

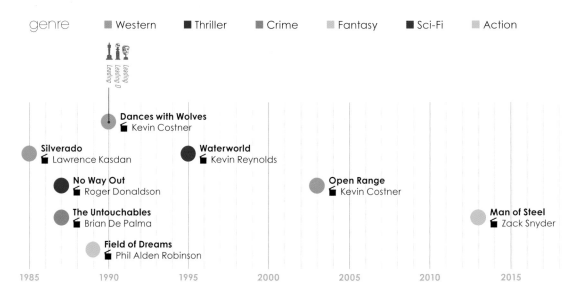

genre — ■ Western ■ Thriller ■ Crime ■ Fantasy ■ Sci-Fi ■ Action

Leading
Leading D
Leading

Dances with Wolves
Kevin Costner

Silverado
Lawrence Kasdan

Waterworld
Kevin Reynolds

No Way Out
Roger Donaldson

Open Range
Kevin Costner

The Untouchables
Brian De Palma

Man of Steel
Zack Snyder

Field of Dreams
Phil Alden Robinson

1985   1990   1995   2000   2005   2010   2015

marion cotillard 1975

| Taxi | Pretty Things | A Very Long Engagement | La Vie en Rose | Nine | Inception | Rust and Bone | Two Days, One Night |

C

Now seen as one of France's premier movie stars, Marion Cotillard worked solidly in films for over a decade before achieving international recognition. Born in Paris in 1975, her most notable early cinema role came as Lilly Bertineau in the frenetic action comedy *Taxi* (1998), a character she would reprise in *Taxi 2* (2000) and *Taxi 3* (2003). More substantial parts followed with *Furia* (1999) and *Lisa* (2001), while she had an early starring role as twins in *Pretty Things* (2001).

Firmly established and starring in films such as *A Private Affair* (2002) and *Love Me If You Dare* (2003), Cotillard made her Hollywood debut in Tim Burton's *Big Fish* (2003) before returning to France with a scene-stealing part alongside Audrey Tautou in *A Very Long Engagement* (2004). By 2005, she had become one of France's most prolific actresses, starring in *Cavalcade*, *Love Is in the Air*, *Mary*, *The Black Box*, *Edy* and *Burnt Out* that year alone. Roles in non-French films became more frequent, such as the Belgian comedy *Dikkenek* (2006) and Ridley Scott's misfiring *A Good Year* (2006).

The major breakthrough in Cotillard's career came with her portrayal of the tragic chanteuse Édith Piaf in *La Vie en Rose* (2007), capturing both the singer's deep passion and fame-enabled selfishness. Her

Oscar-winning performance led to a series of roles in major Hollywood productions, playing Johnny Depp's lover in *Public Enemies* (2009), Daniel Day-Lewis' wife in the musical *Nine* (2009) and Leonardo DiCaprio's spouse in *Inception* (2010). She excelled in all of these films, although it was a little disheartening to see her confined to playing the partner of the protagonist.

Cotillard joined the ensemble casts of *Little White Lies* (2010) and Steven Soderbergh's sober pandemic drama *Contagion* (2011). She took a small role as Picasso's mistress in Woody Allen's *Midnight in Paris* (2011) and reunited with *Inception* director Christopher Nolan for *The Dark Knight Rises* (2012).

One of her most accomplished performances was in the beautiful, harrowing *Rust and Bone* (2012). She plays Stéphanie, a former killer whale trainer putting her life back together after losing both legs. Working with complicated prosthetics, Cotillard's performance is both emotive and bracingly physical. Neither *The Immigrant* (2013) nor *Blood Ties* (2013) made much of an impact, but Cotillard was rightfully acclaimed for her restrained portrayal of a mother trying to escape redundancy in the Dardenne brothers' social-realist drama *Two Days, One Night* (2014). **JWa**

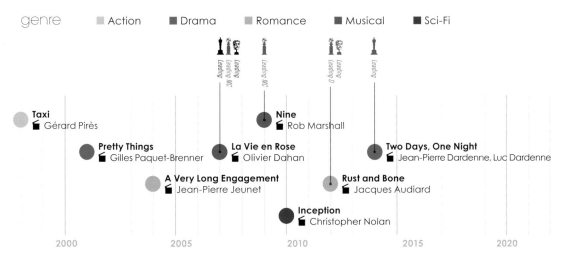

genre: Action, Drama, Romance, Musical, Sci-Fi

joseph cotten 1905-94

| Citizen Kane | The Magnificent Ambersons | Shadow of a Doubt | Duel in the Sun | Portrait of Jennie | The Third Man | Under Capricorn | Touch of Evil |

C

To all appearances, Joseph Cotten had the potential to become a major star. Intelligent, graceful, good-looking, with a mellifluous Southern-tinged voice, he brought to the screen a technique honed through a decade of stage experience. Yet somehow he never quite attained the topmost rank.

In 1936, Cotten joined Orson Welles' Federal Theater project, and it was Welles who gave him his screen debut, in *Citizen Kane* (1941). Also for Welles, he was the modern-minded intruder into the staid world of *The Magnificent Ambersons* (1942), ruefully realizing that he has brought about the ruin of the woman he loves. In *Journey Into Fear* (1942), he plays an engineer caught up in a series of Levantine shenanigans.

Alfred Hitchcock, always adept at drawing out the shadowy side of Hollywood leading men, skillfully exploited the darkness and disillusion behind Cotten's easy charm in *Shadow of a Doubt* (1943), where he played debonair Uncle Charlie with a sideline in murdering wealthy widows. In similar register he could have played the manipulative husband in the remake of *Gaslight* (1944), but was relegated to a support role as a helpful police officer. All too often in the next few years he was confined to romantic leads, squiring the

likes of Jennifer Jones in *Love Letters* (1945), *Duel in the Sun* (1946) and *Portrait of Jennie* (1948).

There was a return to form in *The Third Man* (1949), with Cotten the naive writer of westerns seeking his old pal Harry Lime (Welles) in war-shattered Vienna. Masking his innate intelligence, he played gullible quite convincingly. *Under Capricorn* (1949) was lesser Hitchcock, with Cotten uncomfortable as an Australian ex-convict. After that, it was back to romantic leads or support roles where he was rarely bad but never outstanding. Better material occasionally presented itself: he was an embezzling bank executive in *The Steel Trap* (1952) and played Marilyn Monroe's misused husband in *Niagara* (1953). In *Touch of Evil* (1958) he took an unbilled cameo for his old friend Welles.

Cotten visited his dark side again as an insidious schemer in *Hush … Hush, Sweet Charlotte* (1964) and as a neurotic, overprotective father in Richard Lester's psychedelic drama *Petulia* (1968). He was a murder victim in the sci-fi dystopia *Soylent Green* (1973) and played a brief cameo in *Heaven's Gate* (1980). Too often he appeared in films that were, at best, indifferent, and in roles that were dull shards in what might have been a glittering career. **PK**

genre ■ Drama ■ Thriller ■ Western ■ Fantasy ■ Noir

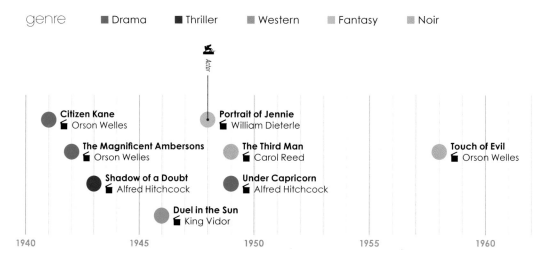

Actor

Citizen Kane
Orson Welles

Portrait of Jennie
William Dieterle

The Magnificent Ambersons
Orson Welles

The Third Man
Carol Reed

Touch of Evil
Orson Welles

Shadow of a Doubt
Alfred Hitchcock

Under Capricorn
Alfred Hitchcock

Duel in the Sun
King Vidor

1940   1945   1950   1955   1960

daniel craig 1968

| Love Is the Devil | Road to Perdition | Sylvia | Enduring Love | Layer Cake | Casino Royale | Cowboys and Aliens | The Girl with the Dragon Tattoo |

Like the five actors before him — and those who will follow — Daniel Craig's career is most closely associated with his stretch as the Secret Service agent James Bond. To focus solely on his most famous role, however, is to neglect the string of fine performances that led to it.

Born in Chester in 1968, Craig worked in television before capturing attention as Derek Jacobi's cat burglar lover in the Francis Bacon biopic *Love Is the Devil* (1998). A small part in *Elizabeth* (1998) followed, along with starring roles in a number of little-seen British films. Craig played Angelina Jolie's unscrupulous love interest in *Lara Croft: Tomb Raider* (2001), but wider recognition was slow coming until a key supporting part as Paul Newman's jealous son in the period gangster film *Road to Perdition* (2002).

Craig was cast as half of another tragic historical couple in *Sylvia* (2003), the story of the fractured relationship between Ted Hughes and Sylvia Plath. Along with *Enduring Love* (2004), it is one of his best performances. As drug dealer XXXX in *Layer Cake* (2004), Craig was better than the boorish film that surrounded him. However, it became an unexpected sleeper hit and led to his being cast as 007 in the James Bond reboot *Casino Royale* (2006).

With a physical performance that required him to bulk up significantly, Craig conveyed the sense of being the "blunt instrument" that Ian Fleming intended, even more than Sean Connery's near-definitive portrayal. It was the emotional dimension of his Bond, however, that most impressed: a tender scene where Craig comforted a distraught Eva Green was difficult to imagine coming from any of his predecessors. Craig starred again as 007 in *Quantum of Solace* (2008), the first direct sequel in the franchise, but the feature was a noisy disappointment.

After *Casino Royale* Craig had his pick of projects, but struggled to match its popularity. On paper, his choices were smart, being mostly acclaimed properties with potential for sequels and helmed by established filmmakers. However, *The Golden Compass* (2007), *Cowboys and Aliens* (2011), *The Adventures of Tintin* (2011) and *The Girl with the Dragon Tattoo* (2011) all underperformed. Craig fared better with his third Bond film, *Skyfall* (2012). Directed by *Road to Perdition*'s Sam Mendes, it was a critical and commercial highpoint for the series. But beyond that, Craig has yet to prove that he can find cinematic success without the aid of a tuxedo and a Walther PPK. **JWa**

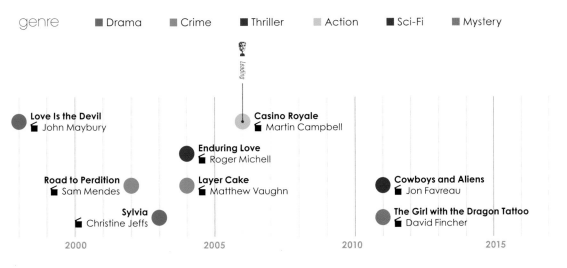

genre ■ Drama ■ Crime ■ Thriller ■ Action ■ Sci-Fi ■ Mystery

Leading

Love Is the Devil
🎬 John Maybury

Casino Royale
🎬 Martin Campbell

Enduring Love
🎬 Roger Michell

Road to Perdition
🎬 Sam Mendes

Layer Cake
🎬 Matthew Vaughn

Cowboys and Aliens
🎬 Jon Favreau

Sylvia
🎬 Christine Jeffs

The Girl with the Dragon Tattoo
🎬 David Fincher

2000   2005   2010   2015

joan crawford 1905–77

The Unknown

Grand Hotel

Sadie McKee

The Women

Mildred Pierce

Humoresque

Possessed

Daisy Kenyon

The subject of countless books, films and documentaries, the life and career of Joan Crawford is the stuff of Hollywood legend. But while it is impossible to ignore her diva reputation — the countless feuds and controversies — it should never overshadow the fact that she was, above all, a truly great movie star. When she was on top form, Joan Crawford could be a formidable screen presence.

Born Lucille Fay LeSueur in San Antonio, Texas, on March 23, 1905, Crawford started her professional career as a dancer before her move to film. She first appeared in *Lady of the Night* (1925), as Norma Shearer's body-double, followed by minor roles in a host of silent movies. Under instruction from MGM's publicity head Pete Smith, she changed her name to Joan Crawford before embarking on a campaign of self-promotion throughout Hollywood. The screenwriter Frederica Sagor Maas said of her ambition: "No one decided to make Joan Crawford a star. Joan Crawford became a star because Joan Crawford decided to become a star."

Following this Crawford landed significant roles in *Sally, Irene and Mary* (1925), Tod Browning's masterful horror *The Unknown* (1927) and the lighthearted comedy *Spring Fever* (1927). But while these roles helped raise her profile, it was her appearance in *Our Dancing Daughters* (1928) that proved to be the turning point in Crawford's career.

Crawford's first talkie was *Untamed* (1929) and over the next few years she made the successful transition from the silent to sound, appearing in a string of films that included *Possessed* (1931), *Grand Hotel* (1932), *Sadie McKee* (1934) and *Love on the Run* (1936). However, no sooner had Crawford found the success she so desperately craved, it appeared to be slipping out of her grasp. By the late-1930s, her popularity had started to wane and a number of her films, including *The Last of Mrs. Cheyney* (1937) and *The Bride Wore Red* (1937), failed at the box office.

Things went from bad to worse for Crawford when, in 1938, the *Independent Film Journal* included her on a list of actors deemed to be "box-office poison." Some success arrived with George Cukor's ensemble drama *The Women* (1939), but by this point it looked as though Crawford's fame was beyond salvaging.

As she entered the 1940s, there appeared little chance of Crawford's fortunes reversing. No longer offered roles that would boost her career, she found

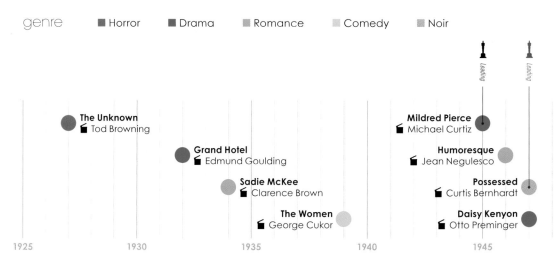

genre ■ Horror ■ Drama ■ Romance ■ Comedy ■ Noir

The Unknown
🎬 Tod Browning

Grand Hotel
🎬 Edmund Goulding

Sadie McKee
🎬 Clarence Brown

The Women
🎬 George Cukor

Mildred Pierce
🎬 Michael Curtiz

Humoresque
🎬 Jean Negulesco

Possessed
🎬 Curtis Bernhardt

Daisy Kenyon
🎬 Otto Preminger

1925   1930   1935   1940   1945

Flamingo Road

The Damned Don't Cry

Sudden Fear

Torch Song

Johnny Guitar

What Ever Happened to Baby Jane?

Strait-Jacket

Berserk

herself fighting a losing battle to win back the trust of the studio bosses. However, when Bette Davis turned down the titular role in Michael Curtiz's *Mildred Pierce* (1945), Crawford finally had a shot at a part she desperately wanted. Not only was the film a huge financial success, it won the star an Academy Award for Best Actress. Playing the middle-aged mother of an errant daughter, Crawford's performance displayed a depth and range hitherto rarely seen in her work.

Her career revived, Crawford experienced a renaissance in terms of performance. *Humoresque* (1946), *Possessed* (1947) — for which she received another Oscar nod — *Daisy Kenyon* (1947), *Flamingo Road* (1949) and *The Damned Don't Cry* (1950) were all critical and commercial hits. She received a further Oscar nomination for her work on *Sudden Fear* (1952) and appeared in the musical drama *Torch Song* (1953).

Already acclaimed for her ability to explore the darker aspects of her characters, Crawford excelled in Nicolas Ray's singular western *Johnny Guitar* (1954). Nonetheless, as the decade progressed Crawford's career once again began to fade. However, an encounter with Robert Aldrich, who directed her in the thriller *Autumn Leaves* (1956), paved the way

for one of the biggest hits of her career. The grand-guignol horror classic *What Ever Happened to Baby Jane?* (1962) saw Crawford cast opposite Bette Davis. The two had a notoriously turbulent history, having often vied for the same roles. Aldrich made the most of this and their performances, constantly competing to outdo each other, make for an explosive combination.

The next few years were not kind to Crawford, with roles in *Strait-Jacket* (1964) and *Berserk* (1967) — entertaining in their own way but a far cry from the A-list Hollywood movies she once starred in. Her final appearance was in the poorly received horror film *Trog* (1970). She died in May 1977 at the age of 72.

During her life, Crawford married three times, most famously to Douglas Fairbanks Jr. and then Alfred Steele, chairman of Pepsi-Cola. Following his death in 1959, Crawford joined Pepsi's board of directors and became a spokesperson for the company. She also adopted four children, one of whom, Christina, wrote a scathing memoir called *Mommie Dearest* (1978) in which she accused Crawford of tyrannical behavior and child abuse. The book was made into the infamous 1981 movie of the same name, starring a histrionic Faye Dunaway as Crawford. **MB**

■ Thriller   ■ Western

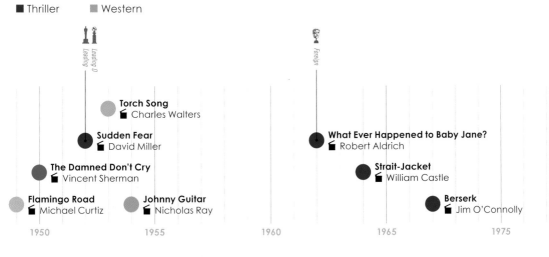

Leading D Leading

Foreign

Torch Song
🎬 Charles Walters

Sudden Fear
🎬 David Miller

The Damned Don't Cry
🎬 Vincent Sherman

Flamingo Road
🎬 Michael Curtiz

Johnny Guitar
🎬 Nicholas Ray

What Ever Happened to Baby Jane?
🎬 Robert Aldrich

Strait-Jacket
🎬 William Castle

Berserk
🎬 Jim O'Connolly

1950   1955   1960   1965   1975

bing crosby 1903–77

| Holiday Inn | Going My Way | The Bells of St. Mary's | Road to Bali | The Country Girl | White Christmas | High Society | Robin and the 7 Hoods |

Bing Crosby was the first superstar of the recording age. He began his film career in the early 1930s, with music spots and appearances in Mack Sennett two-reelers. His features from this period, mostly musical comedies such as 1933's *College Humor* and *Too Much Harmony* or the Raoul Walsh-directed *Going Hollywood* (1933), are known by few beyond his most ardent fans. *We're Not Dressing* (1934) is a highlight, if only for Carole Lombard's presence.

Road to Singapore (1940) was a breakout success and paved the way for Crosby's rise. The film works so well because of the combination of Crosby's talents as a singer and romantic lead, Bob Hope's knockabout humor and Dorothy Lamour's sultriness. It was the first of seven *Road to* films, of which *Morocco* (1942) is the best, with the quality of jokes and musical numbers superior to most other entries.

Holiday Inn (1942), opposite Fred Astaire, marked the first of Crosby's great film musicals. It is the first film to feature the song "White Christmas," made famous as the titular song of the popular 1954 musical that Crosby also starred in. Narratively, the two films are similar, although *Holiday Inn* veers more toward the dramatic. Though lesser known, *Holiday Inn* is better.

Crosby won an Oscar for his charming turn as Father Chuck O'Malley in *Going My Way* (1944), about a young priest replacing a veteran in a small parish. He was also nominated the next year, playing the same role, in *The Bells of St. Mary's* (1945). It was followed by his second and last pairing with Astaire on *Blue Skies* (1946), a musical comedy comprised of a series of vignettes about an enduring friendship.

The actor played the hero in the fantasy comedy *A Connecticut Yankee in King Arthur's Court* (1949) and starred in two of Frank Capra's weaker films, *Riding High* (1950), which unusally featured synchronous musical performances, and *Here Comes the Groom* (1951), which saw him nominated for a Golden Globe. He is far better, playing markedly against type, as the alcoholic has-been performer given one last chance at fame in *The Country Girl* (1954). Two of his best musicals followed in 1956: *Anything Goes* and *High Society* — the latter a far better collaboration with Frank Sinatra than the slight *Robin and the 7 Hoods* (1964). In 1974, he hosted the compilation film *That's Entertainment!*, which reminded audiences of Crosby's importance within the canon of the great American songbook and musical. **IHS**

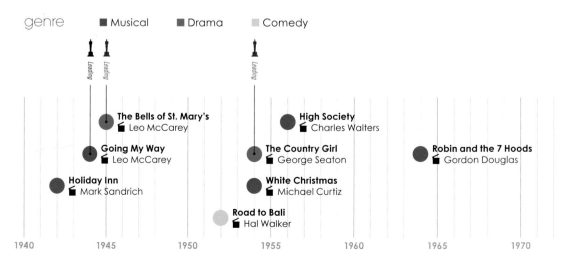

genre ■ Musical ■ Drama ▢ Comedy

The Bells of St. Mary's
Leo McCarey

Going My Way
Leo McCarey

Holiday Inn
Mark Sandrich

Road to Bali
Hal Walker

High Society
Charles Walters

The Country Girl
George Seaton

White Christmas
Michael Curtis

Robin and the 7 Hoods
Gordon Douglas

1940   1945   1950   1955   1960   1965   1970

russell crowe 1964

| Romper Stomper | L.A. Confidential | The Insider | Gladiator | A Beautiful Mind | Master and Commander: The Far Side of the World | American Gangster | Noah |

Born in Wellington, New Zealand, in 1964, Russell Crowe grew up in Australia and made his cinematic debut with *Blood Oath* (1990), although it did not travel much farther than his adopted country. His breakthrough came as a brutish yet charismatic neo-Nazi in *Romper Stomper* (1992).

Crowe then shifted his focus to the United States, playing android villain SID 6.7 opposite Denzel Washington in the ludicrous thriller *Virtuosity* (1995) and a gunslinger-turned-reverend in Sam Raimi's western *The Quick and the Dead* (1995). He received acclaim as Bud White in the 1950s-set crime film *L.A. Confidential* (1997), his clenched fist of a performance proving the standout among a superb ensemble cast.

Crowe would impress again as whistleblower Jeffrey Wigand in *The Insider* (1999), a role for which he gained considerable weight, shaved his hairline and was applied with ageing make-up. He received the first of three consecutive Best Actor Oscar nominations for the role, but his only win was for *Gladiator* (2000) as the Roman general Maximus Decimus Meridius.

Gladiator is Crowe's biggest commercial success and transformed him into a global star. He followed it up with the bland *Proof of Life* (2000) and a portrayal of schizophrenic mathematician John Nash in *A Beautiful Mind* (2001). However, he began to acquire a reputation for po-faced seriousness in the press. He fared better in his films, excelling as a captain in *Master and Commander: The Far Side of the World* (2003).

For the rest of the decade, Crowe continued to star in potentially strong films that produced mixed results, including *Cinderella Man* (2005), *3:10 to Yuma* (2007) and *State of Play* (2009). He reunited with his *Gladiator* director Ridley Scott on *A Good Year* (2006), *American Gangster* (2007), *Body of Lies* (2008) and *Robin Hood* (2010), but only *American Gangster* proved successful.

Crowe became more willing to take roles outside of his usual domain, and while some were failures, such as *Winter's Tale* (2014), the strategy occasionally worked. He appeared as the antagonist Javert in Tom Hooper's adaptation of the stage musical *Les Misérables* (2012), though his singing would be its least well-received element. And although Darren Aronofsky's ambitious biblical epic *Noah* (2014) divided audiences, the bombastic film featured one of his finest performances, as the eponymous hero. **JWa**

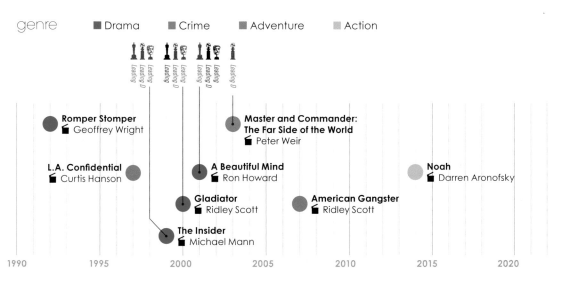

tom cruise 1962

Taps

Risky Business

Legend

Top Gun

The Color of Money

Rain Man

Born on the Fourth of July

The Firm

Sporting athletic looks and a wide smile, Tom Cruise has been a major international box-office attraction for over three decades. Every inch the committed movie star, from producing the films he appears in and performing his own stunts to indulging his fans at every premiere, he has become one of the most recognizable faces on the planet. The character arc that has dominated his work, like the name of the hotshot pilot he played in his star-making role in *Top Gun* (1986), is that of a maverick — an outsider who finally learns to play the game but retains enough independence to be seen as his own man.

Cruise appeared on screen for the first time at 19, in *Endless Love* (1981), but it was with his explosive performance as a deranged army cadet in *Taps* (1981) that he made a mark. He was a prominent gang member in Francis Ford Coppola's *The Outsiders* (1983), then a teenager joining friends on a road trip to Tijuana in the 1960s in *Losin' It* (1983) and an aspiring high school football player in *All the Right Moves* (1983), before he found major commercial success with *Risky Business* (1983). The first role to feature the

Cruise archetype, Joel is a chancer — popular, but with an element of the loner in him — who turns his vacationing parents' home into a brothel. The scene featuring him miming and dancing to Bob Seeger's "Old Time Rock & Roll" made him a star.

After Ridley Scott's visually dazzling but lackluster *Legend* (1985), with Cruise far too wimpy as the film's hero, Tony Scott launched the actor into the stratosphere with *Top Gun*. One of the defining U.S. movies of the 1980s — loud, brash and full of empty emotion — it was the perfect vehicle for Cruise. He would reunite with Tony Scott on *Days of Thunder* (1990), applying the same formula to the NASCAR circuit.

Although Cruise has developed his screen persona over the years, elements of these early roles are still prominent in most of his successes. Ethan Hunt, his character in the *Mission: Impossible* series is a classic Cruise role. From the outset, with Brian De Palma's consummately executed 1996 feature, Ethan is an outsider who learns that he must be a team player in order to succeed; he is distrustful of authority but loyal to those who stand by him. The tone of each entry in

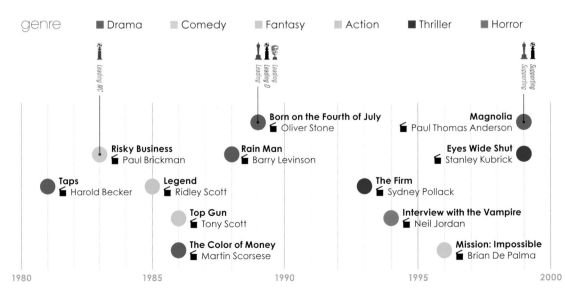

genre ■ Drama ■ Comedy ■ Fantasy ■ Action ■ Thriller ■ Horror

Leading MC

Leading
Leading D
Leading

Supporting
Supporting

Born on the Fourth of July
Oliver Stone

Magnolia
Paul Thomas Anderson

Risky Business
Paul Brickman

Rain Man
Barry Levinson

Eyes Wide Shut
Stanley Kubrick

Taps
Harold Becker

Legend
Ridley Scott

The Firm
Sydney Pollack

Top Gun
Tony Scott

Interview with the Vampire
Neil Jordan

The Color of Money
Martin Scorsese

Mission: Impossible
Brian De Palma

1980   1985   1990   1995   2000

Interview with the Vampire · Mission: Impossible · Magnolia · Eyes Wide Shut · Minority Report · Collateral · Tropic Thunder · Edge of Tomorrow

the franchise has changed, with J.J. Abrams' darker *Mission Impossible III* (2006) a high point, but like the roles he has played in Steven Spielberg's excellent sci-fi thriller *Minority Report* (2002), *The Last Samurai* (2003), *War of the Worlds* (2005), *Jack Reacher* (2012) and *Oblivion* (2013), the Cruise persona is ever present. Michael Mann made the most of it, transforming the actor into a cold-blooded hit man in *Collateral* (2004).

Scorsese also saw something fascinating in Cruise's profile when he cast him opposite Paul Newman in *The Color of Money* (1986). Cruise might be outclassed by the veteran star, but strutting around a pool table he revealed a playfulness, tinged with malice. It can be seen in the interview scene between his Frank T.J. Mackey and April Grace's journalist in *Magnolia* (1999). Cruise was also impressive opposite Dustin Hoffman in *Rain Man* (1988). He may have had the less showy role, but he excels as the selfish and self-interested Charlie Babbitt.

Acclaimed performances followed, as Ron Kovic in Oliver Stone's *Born on the Fourth of July* (1989), a military lawyer in *A Few Good Men* (1992) and an

attorney who realizes he is employed by the Mafia in Sydney Pollack's *The Firm* (1993). Stone's Vietnam-era drama gave Cruise his meatiest role to date and he plays the real-life war veteran with conviction. If *A Few Good Men* descends into a shouting match between the actor and Jack Nicholson, it is fun while it lasts, whereas Pollack brought Cruise's histrionics down a notch for a more controlled performance. As with the insecure husband in Stanley Kubrick's divisive *Eyes Wide Shut* (1999) and his senator in Robert Redford's *Lions for Lambs* (2007), a less frenetic Cruise often brings out a more nuanced performance. The odd outburst aside, it is what makes his characters in *Jerry Maguire* (1996) and *Magnolia* so compelling.

Now in his fifties, Cruise still convinces as an action star, as was proven by the entertaining *Edge of Tomorrow* (2014), his best non-franchise related action film of the last decade. And if his Stacee Jaxx in *Rock of Ages* (2012) was too much of a stretch for even the most ardent Cruise fan, his cameo as Les Grossman, the balding movie producer in *Tropic Thunder* (2008), was both a surprise and perverse delight. **IHS**

■ Sci-Fi ■ Crime

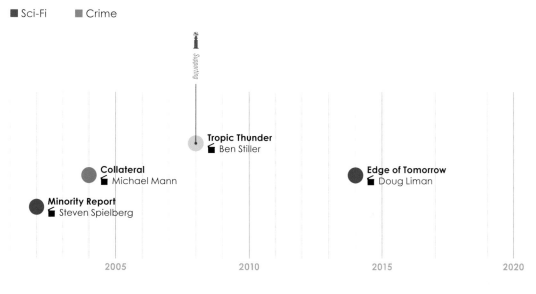

Supporting

Tropic Thunder
Ben Stiller

Collateral
Michael Mann

Minority Report
Steven Spielberg

Edge of Tomorrow
Doug Liman

2005   2010   2015   2020

penélope cruz 1974

| Jamón Jamón | Open Your Eyes | All About My Mother | All the Pretty Horses | Volver | Vicky Cristina Barcelona | Broken Embraces | Pirates of the Caribbean: On Stranger Tides |

Born in Madrid, Spain, in 1974, Penélope Cruz found fame early with her feature debut in Bigas Luna's *Jamón Jamón* (1992), a comedy drama in which she starred opposite her future husband Javier Bardem. In the same year she appeared in Fernando Trueba's Oscar-winning *Belle Époque*. However, it was as the girlfriend of a car crash victim in Alejandro Amenábar's thriller *Open Your Eyes* (1997), followed in the same year by a small role in Pedro Almodóvar's *Live Flesh*, that Cruz achieved international recognition.

Over the next few years, Cruz moved between Spanish and U.S. productions, taking a supporting role in another Almodóvar film, *All About My Mother* (1999), as well as parts in Stephen Frears' *The Hi-Lo Country* (1998) and Billy Bob Thornton's adaptation of Cormac McCarthy's *All the Pretty Horses* (2000). Other roles in U.S. films during this period included *Blow* (2001), *Captain Corelli's Mandolin* (2001), *Vanilla Sky* (2001), *Gothika* (2003) and *Sahara* (2005).

It was her role in Almodóvar's *Volver* (2006) that brought Cruz star status. In it she plays a woman who protects her young daughter while keeping her close-knit family of ageing matriarchs together, and trying to ignore the appearance of her mother's ghost.

Two years later, following a sensitive, nuanced performance in Isabelle Coixet's *Elegy*, an adaptation of Philip Roth's novel *The Dying Animal*, Cruz won the Best Supporting Actress Oscar for her portrayal of Javier Bardem's kooky girlfriend in Woody Allen's *Vicky Cristina Barcelona*.

Cruz's most complex performance to date is in Almodóvar's study of movies and obsession, *Broken Embraces* (2009). Their professional relationship was further cemented in his *I'm So Excited!* (2013), in which she plays an airport baggage handler.

Cruz received good reviews for her performance in *Nine* (2009), in which she played alongside Nicole Kidman, Marion Cottilard, Sophia Loren and leading man Daniel Day-Lewis, but bad ones for *Sex and the City 2* (2010), from which no one emerged unscathed. Her presence in *Pirates of the Caribbean: On Stranger Tides* (2011) made the film more bearable than it might otherwise have been. Cruz is one of the best elements of Woody Allen's *To Rome with Love* (2012) and although *The Counselor* (2013) looked like a promising project, the film is oblique to the point of obscurity. She went on from that to a reunion with Fernando Trueba in *La Reina de España* (2015). **IHS**

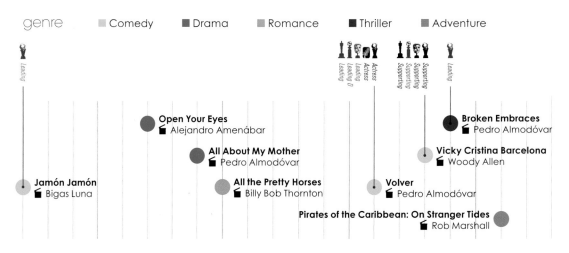

genre   ■ Comedy   ■ Drama   ■ Romance   ■ Thriller   ■ Adventure

Open Your Eyes
Alejandro Amenábar

All About My Mother
Pedro Almodóvar

Jamón Jamón
Bigas Luna

All the Pretty Horses
Billy Bob Thornton

Volver
Pedro Almodóvar

Broken Embraces
Pedro Almodóvar

Vicky Cristina Barcelona
Woody Allen

Pirates of the Caribbean: On Stranger Tides
Rob Marshall

benedict cumberbatch 1976

| Starter for Ten | War Horse | Tinker Tailor Soldier Spy | Star Trek Into Darkness | 12 Years a Slave | The Fifth Estate | The Hobbit: The Desolation of Smaug | The Imitation Game |

Early in his career, it appeared that Benedict Cumberbatch would be forever stranded playing unenlightened or unpleasant upper-class English supporting roles. Whether in modern stories such as *Starter For Ten* (2006) or in period pieces such as *Atonement* (2007), Cumberbatch's refined background and unconventional looks seemed to pigeonhole him. Then, in 2010, came the television sensation *Sherlock* (2010–16). Cumberbatch's revelatory 21st-century version of the sleuth reinvented the actor's screen career; an opportunity he immediately seized upon.

Larger supporting roles in prestige films were a good start: a noble army major leading a doomed World War I cavalry charge in Steven Spielberg's *War Horse* (2011); and a loyal lieutenant to Gary Oldman's Cold War spymaster in *Tinker Tailor Soldier Spy* (2011). Neither role was a stretch for his talents, but they showed him at ease in the highest cinematic circles.

Cumberbatch's luxurious baritone voice was a key component of his motion-capture performance in Peter Jackson's *Hobbit* instalment, *The Desolation of Smaug* (2013), embodying the sinuous arrogance and fearsome wrath of the eponymous dragon. He was fully visible on screen as another blockbuster villain:

genetically enhanced superhuman Khan in *Star Trek Into Darkness* (2013). The ruthless cunning, along with a newly bulked-up physique, created an antagonist actually too imposing for the film's blandness.

As part of the expert ensemble in Best Picture Oscar-winner *12 Years a Slave* (2013), Cumberbatch's plantation owner William Ford captures the unease in an archetypal "good" man of limited foresight and morality, whose inaction allows evil to flourish.

The innate intelligence Cumberbatch projects, used to such good effect in *Sherlock*, was employed again for a pair of biopics about two sharp-minded individuals. In *The Fifth Estate* (2013), Cumberbatch nailed WikiLeaks whistleblower Julian Assange's blend of techno-ingenuity and superciliousness, all in a flawless Australian accent. And as Alan Turing, World War II Enigma code-breaker and computing innovator in *The Imitation Game* (2014), he expertly showed both the haughty social ineptitude of a genius more comfortable in a world of equations, and the private pain of a man forced to hide his true sexuality.

Cumberbatch's upcoming projects and established heartthrob status suggest an ever-upward trajectory. Continued success seems almost elementary. **LS**

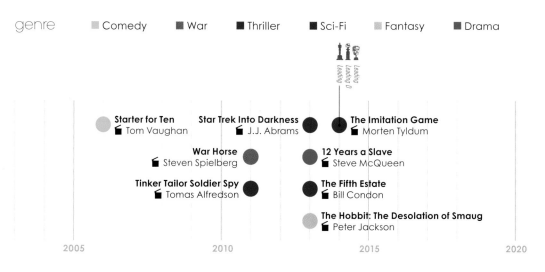

genre ■ Comedy ■ War ■ Thriller ■ Sci-Fi ■ Fantasy ■ Drama

Leading | Leading | Leading D

Starter for Ten — Tom Vaughan

Star Trek Into Darkness — J.J. Abrams

The Imitation Game — Morten Tyldum

War Horse — Steven Spielberg

12 Years a Slave — Steve McQueen

Tinker Tailor Soldier Spy — Tomas Alfredson

The Fifth Estate — Bill Condon

The Hobbit: The Desolation of Smaug — Peter Jackson

2005　2010　2015　2020

tony curtis 1925–2010

| Houdini | Sweet Smell of Success | The Defiant Ones | Some Like it Hot | Operation Petticoat | Spartacus | The Boston Strangler | Insignificance |

A star with matinee idol looks, but whose skills as an actor became apparent with his choice of riskier, less commercial fare, Tony Curtis was born Bernard Schwartz in Manhattan in 1925. After serving on a submarine during World War II, he attended City College of New York under the GI Bill before studying acting at The New School in Greenwich Village, alongside Walter Matthau and Rod Steiger.

Curtis arrived in Hollywood in 1948 and immediately caught the eye of an agent. He changed his name, but even though he was signed to Universal he still feared having to return home: "I was a million-to-one shot, the least likely to succeed. I wasn't low man on the totem pole, I was under the totem pole, in a sewer, tied to a sack." His first role was an uncredited appearance in Robert Siodmak's taut noir Criss Cross (1949), followed by roles in Winchester '73 (1950) and Meet Danny Wilson (1952), and a highly publicized marriage to star Janet Leigh.

Fame finally arrived with Houdini (1953), but his skill as an actor became apparent with his role as ruthless publicist Sidney Falco, opposite Burt Lancaster's vile columnist, in Alexander Mackendrick's Sweet Smell of Success (1957). It was followed by an Oscar-nominated performance in a key race-related film of the era, The Defiant Ones (1958), the hero opposite Kirk Douglas' raging warrior in The Vikings (1958) and, displaying impressive comic timing, as one half of a pair of jazz musicians on the run from the mob, along with Jack Lemmon, in Billy Wilder's Some Like it Hot (1959).

Following his brilliant impression of Cary Grant in Wilder's film, Curtis appeared opposite the star himself in Blake Edwards' Operation Petticoat (1959), one of the year's biggest hits. In 1960, Curtis returned to heavier drama with a pivotal role in Spartacus.

The 1960s saw Curtis' star start to wane in spite of standout performances as Ira Hayes, the Native American soldier who helped raise the U.S. flag on Iwo Jima in The Outsider (1961), and Albert DeSalvo in The Boston Strangler (1968). He achieved long-lasting popularity in his role opposite Roger Moore in the TV series The Persuaders! (1971–72), but thereafter he did little apart from an engaging appearance in Nicolas Roeg's Insignificance (1985). **IHS**

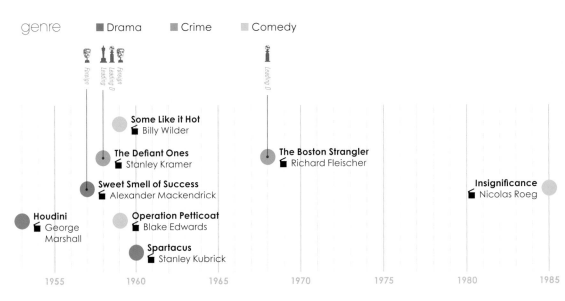

peter cushing 1913–94

| A Chump at Oxford | Hamlet | Nineteen Eighty-Four | The Curse of Frankenstein | Dracula | The Hound of the Baskervilles | Star Wars: Episode IV — A New Hope | House of the Long Shadows |

Few actors have been so universally liked as Peter Cushing. It is odd, then, that someone whom his close friend and frequent costar Christopher Lee would refer to as "the most generous and gentle of men," should be best known for his roles in horror films. However, he worked in film for 20 years before the genre came calling.

Born in 1913, Peter Wilton Cushing spent his formative years in the middle-class London suburb of Purley. After briefly following in his father's footsteps as a quantity surveyor, Cushing took up a scholarship at the Guildhall School of Music and Drama. He had a brief spell in theater before moving to Hollywood in 1939, where he appeared in several major productions, including *The Man in the Iron Mask* (1939), opposite matinee idol Louis Hayward, and the Laurel and Hardy vehicle *A Chump at Oxford* (1940). Despite his impressive resume, Cushing seemed destined to remain little more than a glorified extra, and so he returned to the UK in 1942.

It was there that he starred in his first major credited role, in Laurence Olivier's *Hamlet* (1948). However, it was the new medium of television that provided him with consistent work throughout most of the 1950s, including his BAFTA-winning role in the BBC's controversial production of George Orwell's utopian nightmare *Nineteen Eighty-Four* (1954). A few years later, he would embark on the role that changed the course of his career, playing the misguided scientist Baron Frankenstein in Hammer Films' *The Curse of Frankenstein* (1957). It made Cushing — along with Christopher Lee, who plays the Baron's monstrous creation — a star, and began an association with Hammer that dominated the remainder of his career. Despite working for numerous studios, it was his interpretations of characters like impassioned vampire hunter Van Helsing in *Dracula* (1958) and a tenacious Sherlock Holmes in *The Hound of the Baskervilles* (1959) for Hammer that defined his on-screen persona.

Devoted to his wife Helene, whom he married in 1943, it was her influence and encouragement that he credited for his success. Devastated by her premature death at the age of 65 in 1971, Cushing increased his workload, claiming that keeping busy was the only thing that stopped him dwelling on his loss. Gaunt and deceptively frail in appearance, he was perfect in roles where he appeared as mild mannered, grandfatherly figures, frequently hiding a darker, more sinister side. A number of late roles brought further fame, including the tyrannical Grand Moff Tarkin in *Star Wars: Episode IV — A New Hope* (1977) and Sebastian Grisbane, opposite fright stalwarts Lee, Vincent Price, John Carradine and Sheila Keith, in the comedy chiller *House of the Long Shadows* (1983). But it is his roles from the Golden Age of Hammer and British horror for which he is loved. **CP**

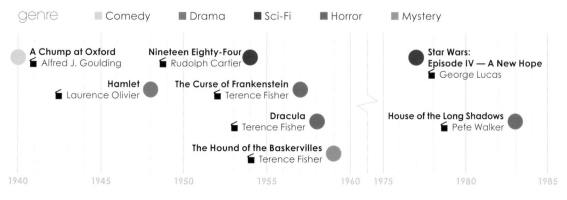

genre   ■ Comedy   ■ Drama   ■ Sci-Fi   ■ Horror   ■ Mystery

A Chump at Oxford
🎬 Alfred J. Goulding

Nineteen Eighty-Four
🎬 Rudolph Cartier

Star Wars: Episode IV — A New Hope
🎬 George Lucas

Hamlet
🎬 Laurence Olivier

The Curse of Frankenstein
🎬 Terence Fisher

Dracula
🎬 Terence Fisher

House of the Long Shadows
🎬 Pete Walker

The Hound of the Baskervilles
🎬 Terence Fisher

1940   1945   1950   1955   1960 1975   1980   1985

matt damon 1970

| Courage Under Fire | Good Will Hunting | The Rainmaker | Saving Private Ryan | The Talented Mr. Ripley | Ocean's Eleven | Gerry | The Bourne Identity |

Matt Damon ascended to the Hollywood A-list with a low-key thriller series that rejuvenated the action genre. He had appeared in major blockbusters, breakout indie features and Oscar-winning dramas, but *The Bourne Identity* (2002) transformed him from committed actor to bona fide star. He plays an amnesiac CIA operative who races against time to figure out who he is and why he is being hunted. With Paul Greengrass' superior sequels, *The Bourne Supremacy* (2004) and *The Bourne Ultimatum* (2007), Damon turned the action hero into a more believable character, which has since influenced the Daniel Craig Bond reboot and the Euro-thrillers starring the likes of Liam Neeson, Kevin Costner and Sean Penn.

A native of Boston, where he attended school with fellow actor Ben Affleck, Damon enrolled at Harvard while also appearing in *Mystic Pizza* (1988) and *School Ties* (1992). It was at the university that he developed an early version of the *Good Will Hunting* (1997) screenplay. He left before graduating to appear in *Geronimo: An American Legend* (1993), but it was his performance as an opiate-addicted soldier in the Gulf War drama *Courage Under Fire* (1996) that caught critics' attention. He held his own

alongside Danny DeVito in Francis Ford Coppola's *The Rainmaker* (1997) before scoring a huge success — and a shared Oscar with Affleck for Best Original Screenplay — with *Good Will Hunting*.

Damon is excellent as the eponymous soldier who does not want to be taken home by Tom Hanks' embattled unit in Steven Spielberg's *Saving Private Ryan* (1998), is wasted alongside Edward Norton in *Rounders* (1998), larks around with Ben Affleck in Kevin Smith's scabrously funny *Dogma* (1999) and offers up one of his most compelling performances as a cold killer in *The Talented Mr. Ripley* (1999). Billy Bob Thornton's disappointing Cormac McCarthy adaptation *All the Pretty Horses* (2000) failed to play to his strengths and his role in *Ocean's Eleven* (2001) — along with its two sequels — remains peripheral to the George Clooney and Brad Pitt double act. However, Gus Van Sant's *Gerry* (2002), alongside friend Casey Affleck, hinted at Damon's willingness to take on more challenging material. A road movie of sorts, influenced by European art house, Van Sant's near-wordless drama has the two actors roaming through a desert, increasingly desperate to make their way back to civilization.

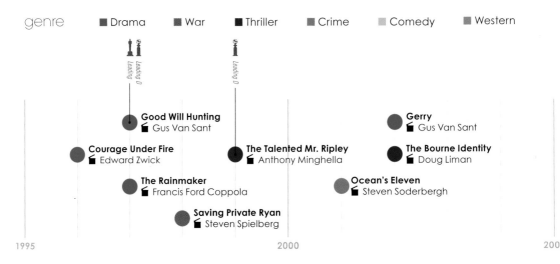

genre ■ Drama ■ War ■ Thriller ■ Crime ▪ Comedy ■ Western

Leading D / Leading

Leading D

Good Will Hunting
Gus Van Sant

Gerry
Gus Van Sant

Courage Under Fire
Edward Zwick

The Talented Mr. Ripley
Anthony Minghella

The Bourne Identity
Doug Liman

The Rainmaker
Francis Ford Coppola

Ocean's Eleven
Steven Soderbergh

Saving Private Ryan
Steven Spielberg

1995   2000   2005

$329M	$691M	$181M	$595M	$278M	$336M	$270M	$664M
Good Will Hunting (1997)	Saving Private Ryan (1998)	The Talented Mr. Ripley (1999)	Ocean's Eleven (2001)	The Bourne Identity (2002)	The Departed (2006)	True Grit (2010)	Interstellar (2014)

The Departed · The Good Shepherd · Invictus · The Informant! · True Grit · Margaret · Behind the Candelabra · Interstellar

The Bourne Identity followed, but rather than be typecast as another Hollywood action star, Damon starred alongside Greg Kinnear as a conjoined twin in the Farrelly brothers' Stuck on You (2003). He played another sibling in Terry Gilliam's disappointing The Brothers Grimm (2005) and impressed as a grieving financial analyst caught up in the murky world of the international oil trade in Syriana (2005). He had the least showy lead in Martin Scorsese's The Departed (2006), but is one of the film's strengths. He is solid in Robert De Niro's overly episodic The Good Shepherd (2006) and brought the first trilogy of the Bourne franchise to a thrilling close. He had a small cameo in Steven Soderbergh's ambitious Che: Part Two (2008), by which point he had replaced George Clooney as a key actor in the director's films. Soderbergh also directed Damon in one of his finest performances to date, as the confused government whistleblower Mark Whitacre in The Informant! (2009). With his voiceover constantly contradicting what we see on screen, the film is a riveting study in self-delusion, with Damon convincingly balancing the comedy of certain scenes with Whitacre's increasing mental instability. No less impressive is his François Pienaar, the captain of the South African rugby team that won their first World Cup following the collapse of the country's apartheid regime, in Invictus (2009). The first of two Clint Eastwood films starring Damon, it was followed by the insipid supernatural drama Hereafter (2010).

While Jeff Bridges dominated the Coens' True Grit (2010), Damon offered fine support as LaBoeuf, a Texas Ranger. The Philip K. Dick adaptation The Adjustment Bureau (2011) gave the actor a rare romantic lead, opposite Emily Blunt. Two fine support performances followed. Reunited with Soderbergh for Contagion (2011), Damon is the husband of a woman carrying an infectious disease, while in Margaret (2011) he played a teacher who has an affair with one of his pupils. He returned to starring roles in the entertaining We Bought a Zoo (2011) and Gus Van Sant's underwhelming eco-drama Promised Land (2012).

If The Zero Theorem (2013) and Elysium (2013) were disappointing, Damon's most recent collaboration with Soderbergh, Behind the Candelabra (2013) gave the actor one of his best roles, as the lover of Liberace. And an uncredited appearance at a pivotal moment in Christopher Nolan's epic space opera Interstellar (2014) reinforces Damon's status as a popular star. **IHS**

■ Sci-Fi

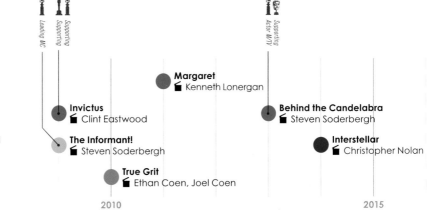

The Departed — Martin Scorsese

The Good Shepherd — Robert De Niro

Invictus — Clint Eastwood

The Informant! — Steven Soderbergh

True Grit — Ethan Coen, Joel Coen

Margaret — Kenneth Lonergan

Behind the Candelabra — Steven Soderbergh

Interstellar — Christopher Nolan

Leading MC · Supporting Supporting · Supporting Actor M/TV

2010 · 2015

bette davis 1908–89

| Of Human Bondage | Dangerous | Marked Woman | Jezebel | Dark Victory | The Private Lives of Elizabeth and Essex | The Letter | The Little Foxes |

Ruth Elizabeth Davis was born in Massachusetts, 1908. After her parents' divorce she moved with her mother and sister to New York City, where she got the acting bug. After working her way onto Broadway, a Hollywood talent scout invited her to screen test.

The studios were initially unsure what to do with Davis' unconventional beauty and versatility. Finally, in her 22nd screen role, came her breakthrough. In *Of Human Bondage* (1934), Davis played a desperate waitress who ruthlessly exploits the devotion of a well-to-do suitor. It was an unsympathetic role that scared off many actresses but, despite an overripe cockney accent, Davis' sheer intensity dominates the film. Many felt she should have won the Academy Award, and when she triumphed the following year, as a down-and-out actress seeking rehabilitation in *Dangerous* (1935), it was widely seen as compensation.

Although now successful, Davis still felt stymied by the quality of roles on offer. She fled to Britain to make two films, thus breaking her Warner Bros.

contract, then lost the dispute, being portrayed as arrogant and greedy. Chastened, almost broke but unrepentant, Davis returned to Hollywood — and began an incredible run of hits. Her portrayal of a scheming Southern belle in *Jezebel* (1938) won her a second Oscar, which made up for her missing out on playing Scarlett O'Hara in *Gone with the Wind* (1939). The sentimental hit *Dark Victory* (1939) allowed her to suffer nobly as a terminally ill socialite. She was able to show her range, shaving her hairline and eyebrows to play an ageing Elizabeth I opposite Errol Flynn in *The Private Lives of Elizabeth and Essex* (1939).

In *The Letter* (1940), her vengeful adulteress gets away with murdering her lover, but not from her own twisted desires. *The Great Lie* (1941) cast her more sympathetically, as a widow whose raises the child of her husband's lover. In *The Little Foxes* (1941) Davis was on stunning, nefarious form as a Southern aristocrat so determined to control the family business that she will watch her husband die without helping him. And

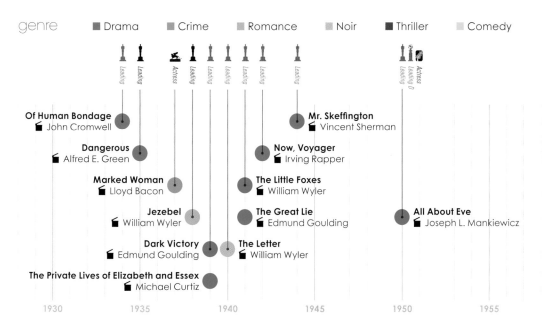

genre ■ Drama ■ Crime ■ Romance ■ Noir ■ Thriller ■ Comedy

Of Human Bondage — John Cromwell	**Mr. Skeffington** — Vincent Sherman
Dangerous — Alfred E. Green	**Now, Voyager** — Irving Rapper
Marked Woman — Lloyd Bacon	**The Little Foxes** — William Wyler
Jezebel — William Wyler	**The Great Lie** — Edmund Goulding
Dark Victory — Edmund Goulding	**The Letter** — William Wyler
The Private Lives of Elizabeth and Essex — Michael Curtiz	**All About Eve** — Joseph L. Mankiewicz

1930 1935 1940 1945 1950 1955

$1M (U.S.)
All About Eve
(1950)

$3M (U.S.)
The Whales of August
(1987)

The Great Lie

Now, Voyager

Mr. Skeffington

All About Eve

What Ever Happened to Baby Jane?

The Nanny

The Anniversary

The Whales of August

D

in *Now, Voyager* (1942), her fragile misfit undergoes psychotherapy and eventually finds love. These roles are merely the highlights of a period of intensive work and success, belying her difficult reputation. Her popularity was unparalleled, seeing her become both industry figurehead (Academy president) and the highest-paid woman in America.

While her private life was a mess, her career flourished, notably as Claude Rains' icy spouse in *Mr. Skeffington* (1944). Then, gradually, the hits dried up. Poor films and bad decisions did not help; by the end of the decade, she was deemed box-office poison. Then, some good fortune: she replaced the injured Claudette Colbert in Joseph Mankiewicz's *All About Eve* (1950), a savagely witty dissection of showbusiness and social climbing. Davis' role as feisty, insecure, ageing star Margo Channing was a perfect fit and provided a superb comeback.

Sadly, it did not last. Despite a couple of decent roles, including playing Elizabeth I again in *The Virgin Queen* (1955), the 1950s were a fallow period. Davis' fearsome character, no longer backed up by hit movies, counted against her. Arguably her last truly great role was as a deranged, former child star in *What Ever Happened to Baby Jane?* (1962). Cast opposite long-time nemesis Joan Crawford as two confined, feuding sisters, Davis, unnervingly caked in white make-up and relishing her deviancy, is a nightmarish vision in a camp-horror cult classic.

An attempt to recapture *Baby Jane*'s formula in *Hush … Hush, Sweet Charlotte* (1964) survived Crawford's controversial replacing, spawning another gothic hit. Davis continued to revel in her malevolent matriarchs with British horror *The Nanny* (1965) and black comedy *The Anniversary* (1968). Remaining roles were barely worthy of her reputation, with the exception of *The Whales of August* (1987), a touching tale of two elderly sisters, opposite fellow veteran Lillian Gish. Davis died of breast cancer in 1989, aged 81, leaving a legacy few stars could possibly match. **LS**

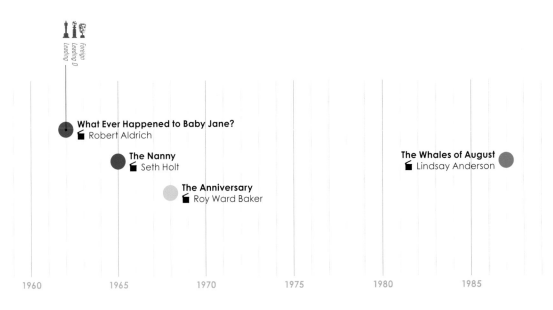

Foreign Leading D
Leading

What Ever Happened to Baby Jane?
Robert Aldrich

The Nanny
Seth Holt

The Anniversary
Roy Ward Baker

The Whales of August
Lindsay Anderson

1960   1965   1970   1975   1980   1985

ossie davis 1917–2005

The Cardinal   **The Hill**   **The Scalphunters**   **Slaves**   **Do the Right Thing**   **Get on the Bus**   **Bubba Ho-Tep**   **Proud**

Born in Georgia, in 1917, Raiford Chatman Davis experienced racism from an early age. He attended college, but left before graduating to take up acting. His stage debut was with Harlem's Rose McClendon Players. He served in World War II and on his return completed his studies, making his screen debut in 1950 in the Sidney Poitier film *No Way Out*.

In 1948, he married the actress Ruby Dee and over the course of the next six decades they were active in the Civil Rights movement. Davis delivered the eulogy at Malcolm X's funeral, with Ahmed Osman, part of which is read by the actor at the end of Spike Lee's 1992 biopic of the activist. His politics also informed his acting work. He appeared in films at a time when black actors were generally given little more than cursory minor parts. Inspired by Sidney Poitier, Davis chose to invest himself in every role, creating fully rounded, credible characters whenever he could.

He played a priest in Otto Preminger's *The Cardinal* (1963) and was then one of the imprisoned soldiers in Sidney Lumet's grueling *The Hill* (1965). He starred as one of several new inmates sharing a cell in a military prison in North Africa. A bullying officer uses his ethnicity as jibes against him, but what is notable in the film is the way the system ends up treating the men equally, no matter their color. He was nominated for an Oscar for his performance as a house slave in *The Scalphunters* (1968), who is promised freedom by Burt Lancaster's trapper if he helps recover stolen furs. And in 1969 he starred in the provocative *Slaves*.

Davis moved behind the camera in the 1970s, directing five films. However, his key roles on screen were in the films of Spike Lee. In particular, he is excellent as the local drunk in *Do the Right Thing* (1989), frequently admonished by Ruby Dee's upstanding citizen only for their roles to reverse as night falls and violence erupts. He also played one of the key roles in Lee's Million Man March drama *Get on the Bus* (1996).

In the black comedy *Bubba Ho-Tep* (2002), Davis is excellent as a nursing home resident who believes he is John F. Kennedy and joins with an elderly Elvis in a battle against an ancient mummy. And in his final film, *Proud* (2004), he is noble as a man looking back on the role he played in World War II, as a crewmember on the predominantly African-American-manned USS Mason. Although his career never achieved the heights of Poitier's, Davis' body of work is defined by the dignity with which he imbued his characters. **IHS**

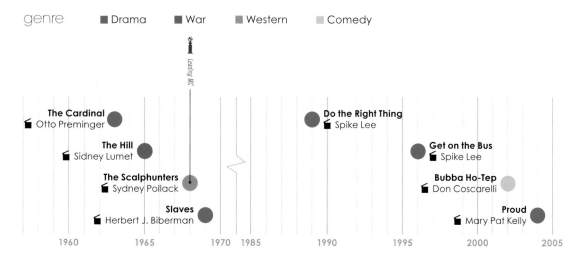

sammy davis jr. 1925–90

Porgy and Bess

Ocean's 11

Sergeants 3

Robin and the 7 Hoods

A Man Called Adam

Sweet Charity

The Cannonball Run

Tap

Born in Harlem, New York, in 1925, Sammy Davis Jr. was a legendary African-American singer, dancer and actor, and member of the celebrated "Rat Pack" with Dean Martin, Joey Bishop, Peter Lawford and "Chairman of the Board," Frank Sinatra.

From the age of 3, Davis Jr. performed in a vaudeville trio alongside his father and Will Mastin. He completed military service in World War II, countering the prejudice of servicemen with his incomparable talent and quick humor. He returned to the trio, but his skill as a singer was soon recognized by talent scouts, who signed him up for a number of solo albums.

His first major screen roles accompanied his entrance to the Rat Pack. In the heist movie *Ocean's 11* (1960), he played a member of Danny Ocean's (Frank Sinatra) crew of Las Vegas casino robbers. A perfunctory entertainment, it is now more famous for the antics that unfolded in Las Vegas after each day's shoot was done. Sinatra, Martin and Davis Jr. performed a series of gigs that have acquired the status of legend.

The Rat Pack then teamed up for *Sergeants 3* (1962). Davis Jr. played former slave Jonah Williams, a trumpet player dreaming of becoming a member of the U.S. Cavalry. *Robin and the 7 Hoods* (1964) followed. The group's lineup had changed, with Bing Crosby also making an appearance. No more distinguished than the previous two outings, the film relocated the story of Robin Hood to a mobster-ruled Chicago of the 1930s. As the 1960s progressed, Davis Jr. would appear in a number of films, often featuring cameos by other Rat Packers.

In 1966, Davis Jr. played jazz musician Adam Johnson in *A Man Called Adam*, capturing the tortured spirit of an artist attempting to tackle his demons and cope with a series of relationships. In particular, it allowed Davis to explore on screen the prejudice he had experienced in his life as a performer. Ably supported by Ossie Davis, Sinatra and Louis Armstrong, it is one of the actor's best films. He followed it with arguably his best musical performance, in Bob Fosse's *Sweet Charity* (1969). His charismatic preacher, Big Daddy, singing "Rhythm of Life," is one of the film's highlights.

Davis Jr.'s film career slowed in the 1970s. His music had become less fashionable, although he did score a surprise number one hit with "The Candy Man" in 1972. He was a frequent fixture on U.S. television, hosting his own talk show as well as appearing in the series *Mod Squad* (1969–70) and *Fantasy Island* (1983–84).

Davis Jr. and fellow Rat Pack members Frank Sinatra and Dean Martin made their final film appearances together in the Burt Reynolds action-comedy vehicle *The Cannonball Run* (1981) and its sequel (1984). Better is his final screen appearance, starring opposite fellow dancer Gregory Hines in *Tap* (1989). It is an exuberant epitaph to a unique individual. **CGD**

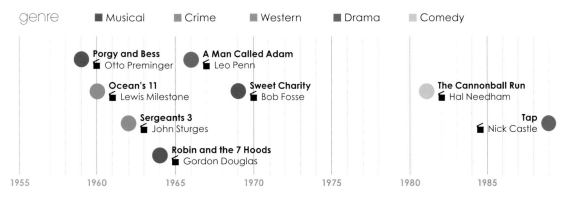

genre   ■ Musical   ■ Crime   ■ Western   ■ Drama   ■ Comedy

Porgy and Bess
Otto Preminger

A Man Called Adam
Leo Penn

Ocean's 11
Lewis Milestone

Sweet Charity
Bob Fosse

The Cannonball Run
Hal Needham

Sergeants 3
John Sturges

Tap
Nick Castle

Robin and the 7 Hoods
Gordon Douglas

1955   1960   1965   1970   1975   1980   1985

doris day 1924

| Romance on the High Seas | My Dream Is Yours | It's a Great Feeling | On Moonlight Bay | Calamity Jane | Young at Heart | Love Me or Leave Me | The Man Who Knew Too Much |

The quintessential "girl next door," Doris Day was one of the most popular actresses of the 1950s and 1960s. A talented singer and versatile performer, she became synonymous with a brand of lighthearted romantic comedies that traded on pastel-hued farce, mistaken identity and witty repartee.

Born in Cincinnati, Ohio, in 1924, Day was an in-demand big band vocalist who had also achieved success as a solo artist and radio performer before she moved into film. She made her screen debut as the star of Michael Curtiz's musical *Romance on the High Seas* (1948), replacing the pregnant Betty Hutton for whom the film had been designed as a star vehicle.

Following the film's release, Day starred in a series of minor musicals for Warner Bros. She reunited with Curtiz for *My Dream Is Yours* (1949), *Young Man with a Horn* (1950) and *I'll See You in My Dreams* (1951), while the rest of her output in this period was primarily directed by two other men: Roy Del Ruth in *The West Point Story* (1950) and *Starlift* (1951), and David Butler in *It's a Great Feeling* (1949), *Tea for Two* (1950), *Lullaby of Broadway* (1951), *April in Paris* (1952), *Calamity Jane* (1953) and *By the Light of the Silvery Moon* (1953), a sequel to Del Ruth's earlier film *On Moonlight Bay* (1951).

Aside from the occasional straight acting part, such as playing Ginger Rogers' sister in the thriller

Storm Warning (1951), Day's work during the early period of her career was confined almost entirely to musicals like *Lucky Me* (1954) and *Young at Heart* (1954), playing opposite Frank Sinatra. Rather than experiencing an immediate breakthrough, her star grew steadily. One of the most significant films in terms of her career progression was the biographical musical *Love Me or Leave Me* (1955), in which she played singer Ruth Etting, with James Cagney as her gangster husband. She depicted another singer in *The Man Who Knew Too Much* (1956), costarring with James Stewart in Alfred Hitcock's superior remake of his 1934 original suspense film. She also attempted a noir thriller, *Julie* (1956), but it was poorly received.

While her movie stardom ultimately eclipsed her first profession, Day remained a popular singer and continued to record music throughout her acting career and afterward, releasing 31 albums, the most recent in 2011. Given her early focus on musicals and the fact that she would also often sing in her non-musical work, it is unsurprising that her most famous songs came directly from films she starred in, such as "Embraceable You" from *Romance on the High Seas*, "Secret Love" from *Calamity Jane* and "Qué Será, Será" from *The Man Who Knew Too Much*, the latter two of which won Oscars for Best Original Song.

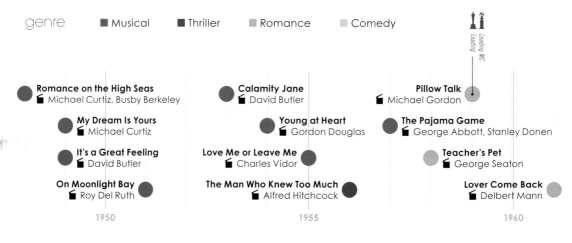

genre   ■ Musical   ■ Thriller   ■ Romance   ▢ Comedy

Leading
Leading MC

Romance on the High Seas
🎬 Michael Curtiz, Busby Berkeley

My Dream Is Yours
🎬 Michael Curtiz

It's a Great Feeling
🎬 David Butler

On Moonlight Bay
🎬 Roy Del Ruth

Calamity Jane
🎬 David Butler

Young at Heart
🎬 Gordon Douglas

Love Me or Leave Me
🎬 Charles Vidor

The Man Who Knew Too Much
🎬 Alfred Hitchcock

Pillow Talk
🎬 Michael Gordon

The Pajama Game
🎬 George Abbott, Stanley Donen

Teacher's Pet
🎬 George Seaton

Lover Come Back
🎬 Delbert Mann

1950 · 1955 · 1960

The Pajama Game	Teacher's Pet	Pillow Talk	Lover Come Back	That Touch of Mink	Send Me No Flowers	The Ballad of Josie	With Six You Get Eggroll

The Pajama Game (1957) marked the transition point between the musicals of the first decade of her career and the romantic comedies for which she would best be remembered. She appeared opposite Clark Gable in Teacher's Pet (1958), Richard Widmark in The Tunnel of Love (1958) and Jack Lemmon in It Happened to Jane (1959).

All of these efforts were dwarfed by the success of her most beloved film, Pillow Talk (1959), for which she received her first and only Oscar nomination. She plays Jan Morrow, an interior decorator feuding with playboy composer Brad Allen (Rock Hudson) and batting off the attentions of one of her clients (Tony Randall). While Day eventually developed a career-damaging — and unfair — reputation as the perpetual virgin, Jan Morrow, like the characters in most of her romantic comedies, is depicted as an independent, confident and successful career woman. Day, Hudson and Randall starred in two further films together, Lover Come Back (1961) and Send Me No Flowers (1964), although neither was as well received as Pillow Talk. Her pairing with Hudson in particular became emblematic of a specific form of breezy 1960s romantic comedy.

Day only strayed from musicals and comedies on one other occasion, starring in Midnight Lace (1960) as an heiress being stalked by a killer. She then returned to the format that audiences loved most, playing "America's Sweetheart" in the popular romantic comedies That Touch of Mink (1962), alongside Cary Grant, and a pair of films costarring James Garner, Move Over, Darling (1963) and The Thrill of It All (1963).

As the 1960s progressed, Day's wholesome image became increasingly unfashionable, and, following the poor response to the winsome Do Not Disturb (1965), her career took a downturn. Her persona sat uneasily next to the sexual and cultural revolution that was unfolding in the United States and the whole concept of a female icon was undergoing a radical transformation. A late exception was the western comedy The Ballad of Josie (1967), in which she plays a woman who sets up a suffrage movement. However, Day looks like she comes from another age when compared with Faye Dunaway's sexually ambiguous performance in the contemporary Bonnie and Clyde (1967).

After making With Six You Get Eggroll (1968), Day withdrew from cinema and moved into television, starring in her own, self-titled sitcom (1968–73). In later years, she retired from performing altogether, focusing instead on her work as an animal rights advocate. However, nearly half a century after her last film, Day is still the top female box-office star of all time. **JWa**

That Touch of Mink
🎬 Delbert Mann

The Ballad of Josie
🎬 Andrew V. McLaglen

Send Me No Flowers
🎬 Norman Jewison

With Six You Get Eggroll
🎬 Howard Morris

1965

1970

daniel day-lewis 1957

Gandhi — **The Bounty** — **My Beautiful Laundrette** — **A Room with a View** — **Stars and Bars** — **The Unbearable Lightness of Being** — **My Left Foot** — **The Last of the Mohicans**

Centuries ago, acting used to be considered something a little mystical, even arcane. No other modern actor has managed to maintain the aura of hushed wonder or the illusion of genuine alchemy than Daniel Michael Blake Day-Lewis, widely seen as the finest, most committed actor of his generation.

Born in London, 1957, to British poet laureate Cecil Day-Lewis and actress Jill Balcon, Day-Lewis' troubled teen years were partly soothed by pursuing acting. Early stage success led to a bit-part in the Oscar-winning *Gandhi* (1982), as a racist Afrikaans youth. He made a bigger impression in *The Bounty* (1984) as First Mate John Fryer, a steadfast sailor caught between Anthony Hopkins' ruthless Captain Bligh and Mel Gibson's rebellious Fletcher Christian.

The actor's next two films highlighted his enormous range. In state-of-the-Thatcher-nation *My Beautiful Laundrette* (1985), his working-class, ex-National Front, bleach-blond punk Johnny falls in love with a young Asian man; it is a world away from his role in the adaptation of E.M. Forster's *A Room with a View* (1985), as a stuffy, bespectacled upper-class Edwardian.

As the romantic lead in *The Unbearable Lightness of Being* (1988), adapted from Milan Kundera's novel, Day-Lewis' philandering surgeon dallies with both Juliette Binoche and Lena Olin amid the turbulent 1968 Prague Spring. Apparently Day-Lewis learned Czech, even though the film was shot in English — an early glimmer of the extreme Method acting that he would become legendary for with his next role.

My Left Foot (1989) is based on the life of cerebral palsy-afflicted Irish writer Christy Brown. Day-Lewis arrived for the first cast read-through in a wheelchair, communicating in Brown's barely intelligible speech; he then remained chair-bound and was fed for the entire shoot, as well as learning — as Brown did — to actually write with his left foot. But this was not mere slavish mimicry; it was a tour de force that won him, among other awards, his first Best Actor Oscar.

Concerns about his working practices were stoked in 1989 when Day-Lewis walked out mid-performance of *Hamlet* in London after seeing the ghost of his late father. Nevertheless, for *The Last of the Mohicans* (1992) he adopted the life of his 18th-century frontiersman character Hawkeye, living off the land and hunting wild animals. Whatever the methodology, he is entirely convincing as the hunter, a gracefully athletic, virile presence.

genre ■ Drama ■ Adventure ■ Comedy ■ Romance ■ Crime

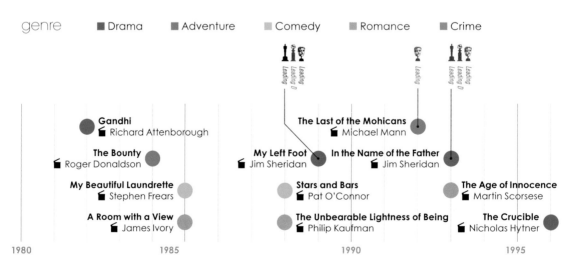

| Gandhi | The Last of the Mohicans |
| 🎬 Richard Attenborough | 🎬 Michael Mann |

The Bounty — 🎬 Roger Donaldson

My Left Foot — 🎬 Jim Sheridan — **In the Name of the Father** — 🎬 Jim Sheridan

My Beautiful Laundrette — 🎬 Stephen Frears

Stars and Bars — 🎬 Pat O'Connor

The Age of Innocence — 🎬 Martin Scorsese

A Room with a View — 🎬 James Ivory

The Unbearable Lightness of Being — 🎬 Philip Kaufman

The Crucible — 🎬 Nicholas Hytner

1980 — 1985 — 1990 — 1995

$129M (U.S.)	$46M (U.S.)	$127M (U.S.)	$108M	$53M (U.S.)	$255M	$87M	$284M
Gandhi (1982)	A Room with a View (1985)	The Last of the Mohicans (1992)	In the Name of the Father (1993)	The Age of Innocence (1993)	Gangs of New York (2002)	There Will Be Blood (2007)	Lincoln (2012)

In the Name of the Father | **The Age of Innocence** | **The Crucible** | **The Boxer** | **Gangs of New York** | **The Ballad of Jack and Rose** | **There Will Be Blood** | **Lincoln**

A relatively prolific period followed. In Martin Scorsese's Edith Wharton adaptation *The Age of Innocence* (1993), Day-Lewis vividly reveals the repressed torment of a lovestruck member of New York's elite class, thwarted by society's genteel emotional violence. And he is brutally convincing as the feckless Gerry Conlon, one of the falsely accused "Guildford Four" bombers, in *In the Name of the Father* (1993). He was noble and tortured in *The Crucible* (1996), based on Arthur Miller's play (he married Miller's daughter, novelist and filmmaker Rebecca, shortly afterward) and a convincing pugilist — no doubt due to his intensive 18-month training — in the otherwise unremarkable *The Boxer* (1997).

Now settled in Ireland with his wife and sons, Day-Lewis took a five-year hiatus that allegedly included a year as a cobbler in Italy. He returned to the screen for Scorsese's 19th-century epic *Gangs of New York* (2002), playing garrulous, one-eyed villain Bill "The Butcher" Cutting. It was scenery chewing of the highest order, and announced his return in some style. Though he next played a terminally-ill island-dweller caught in a fraught relationship with his daughter in his wife's *The Ballad of Jack and Rose* (2005), it is the subsequent, career-defining role for which Bill the Butcher seems the warm-up: oil man Daniel Plainview in Paul Thomas Anderson's *There Will Be Blood* (2007).

Plainview is the embodiment of rapacious capitalism, voracious and self-serving, whose greed becomes a sickness that drives away all love and compassion. With his guttural, John Huston-like voice, it is a grandstanding performance. Yet the fleeting moments when we glimpse the humanity that Plainview ultimately banishes are what really define the actor's astonishing achievement. Another Oscar was a given.

Seeing him next in the lightweight stage musical adaptation *Nine* (2009) was almost a relief. Steven Spielberg's *Lincoln* (2012), though, was another heavyweight role, portraying the President at the key moment of legislating against slavery. Day-Lewis avoided caricature, marrying the man's folksy charm and steely shrewdness. The result was another rapturous reception, Day-Lewis becoming the only person ever to win three Best Actor Oscars. That he remains so elusive and respected, yet, on his rare public appearances, so affable, only makes the recently knighted Day-Lewis even more mysterious; and the transformative power of his art ever more mesmeric. **LS**

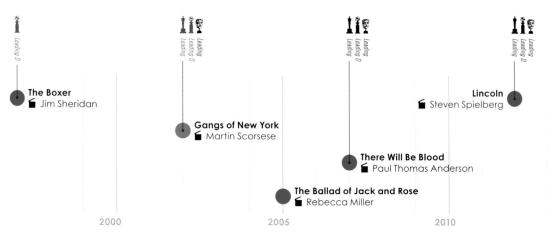

The Boxer
Jim Sheridan

Gangs of New York
Martin Scorsese

The Ballad of Jack and Rose
Rebecca Miller

There Will Be Blood
Paul Thomas Anderson

Lincoln
Steven Spielberg

2000   2005   2010

robert de niro 1943

Greetings	Mean Streets	The Godfather: Part II	Taxi Driver	New York, New York	The Deer Hunter	Raging Bull	The King of Comedy

An actor's actor and one of the most admired performers of his generation, both by his peers and audiences the world over, Robert De Niro's greatest roles are marked by their force, both in terms of psychology and physicality. Along with Al Pacino, he defined the New Hollywood of the 1970s.

Born in New York's Greenwich Village in 1943, De Niro is now most closely associated with Martin Scorsese, but his film career began with roles in Brian De Palma's *Greetings* (1968), *The Wedding Party* (1969) and *Hi, Mom!* (1970). Recognition first came with his incendiary performance as Johnny Boy in Scorsese's *Mean Streets* (1973), a role that fully realized his potential. A year before, De Niro had lost out to Pacino for the role of Michael Corleone in *The Godfather* (1972). As recompense, director Francis Ford Coppola cast De Niro as the young Vito Corleone in the flashback scenes of *The Godfather: Part II* (1974), It was for this role that De Niro won his first Oscar.

To the role of Travis Bickle in 1976's *Taxi Driver* De Niro brought an intensity that has rarely been equaled. The classic "You talkin' at me?" scene was improvised by the actor, who manages to make

Travis a compelling, even sympathetic character, in spite of his repugnance at times. Bernardo Bertolucci's *1900* and Elia Kazan's *The Last Tycoon* were released in the same year. Hardly either director's finest films, they did showcase De Niro's range. However, these performances pale in comparison to his volatile presence in Scorsese's *New York, New York* (1977) and his portrayal of Michael Vronsky, a man scarred by war and desperately trying to reconnect with civilian life, in *The Deer Hunter* (1978).

If Pacino is an actor who works from the inside out, De Niro operates in reverse, with physical transformation shaping his character's psyche. There is no better an example of this than his total immersion in the character and psyche of Jake LaMotta in Scorsese's *Raging Bull* (1980). De Niro worked out for the early scenes of LaMotta as a champion boxer, then withdrew for four months to northern Italy and France, where he binged on food in order to play the older, overweight LaMotta. Throughout, De Niro conveys every nuance of character in a landmark role that is rightly considered one of the greatest in cinema history.

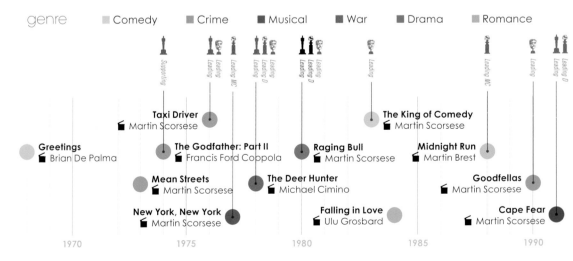

genre ■ Comedy ■ Crime ■ Musical ■ War ■ Drama ■ Romance

Greetings
Brian De Palma

Taxi Driver
Martin Scorsese

The Godfather: Part II
Francis Ford Coppola

Mean Streets
Martin Scorsese

New York, New York
Martin Scorsese

The Deer Hunter
Michael Cimino

Raging Bull
Martin Scorsese

Falling in Love
Ulu Grosbard

The King of Comedy
Martin Scorsese

Midnight Run
Martin Brest

Goodfellas
Martin Scorsese

Cape Fear
Martin Scorsese

1970	1975	1980	1985	1990

$228 M (U.S.)	$117M (U.S.)	$177M (U.S.)	$163M	$316M	$290M	$453M	$243M
The Godfather Part II (1974)	Taxi Driver (1976)	The Deer Hunter (1978)	Midnight Run (1988)	Cape Fear (1991)	Heat (1995)	Meet the Parents (2000)	Silver Linings Playbook (2012)

Falling in Love	Midnight Run	Goodfellas	Cape Fear	Heat	Jackie Brown	Meet the Parents	Silver Linings Playbook

After a solid performance opposite Robert Duvall in Ulu Grosbard's *True Confessions* (1981), De Niro returned to work with Scorsese as Rupert Pupkin in *The King of Comedy* (1983), purportedly the only role in which he cannot bear to watch himself. He followed it with starkly different roles, first as the melancholy "Noodles" in Sergio Leone's elegiac *Once Upon a Time in America* (1984) and as a married architect who falls for Meryl Streep's housewife in *Falling in Love* (1984).

Between entertaining cameos as a terrorist in *Brazil* (1985), Lucifer in *Angel Heart* (1987) and Al Capone in *The Untouchables* (1987), De Niro seemed to be uneasy as the slave trader seeking redemption in *The Mission* (1986) and was treading water as the Vietnam vet in *Jacknife* (1989). However, his bounty hunter in *Midnight Run* (1988) is a comedic delight and one of the star's warmest, most likeable performances.

In *Goodfellas* (1990), De Niro lets the antics of costars Ray Liotta and Joe Pesci take center stage, offering solid, convincing support. Two more collaborations with Scorsese followed, first as crazed killer Max Cady in the ultra-stylized *Cape Fear* (1991), then as a Las Vegas frontman for the mob in *Casino* (1995), delivering a nuanced character study. However, his most acclaimed performance from this period was as the skilled heist operator, playing a cat and mouse game with Al Pacino's cop in Michael Mann's epic crime drama *Heat* (1995). If Pacino played his role on an operatic scale, De Niro's characterization was in a quieter key and all the more rewarding for it. He is more sleazy but no less impressive as an ex-con drawn into a complex robbery in Quentin Tarantino's *Jackie Brown* (1997). That film is also notable for being the last of his great performances to date. He may be fine as the father who suspects Ben Stiller is not good enough for his daughter in *Meet the Parents* (2000) and its unnecessary sequels, but there has been a dearth of strong serious roles to showcase De Niro's considerable talent. If *The Adventures of Rocky & Bullwinkle* (2000) proved to be a creative nadir and *15 Minutes* (2001), *The Score* (2001), *Righteous Kill* (2008) and *The Family* (2013) all underwhelmed, *Limitless* (2011) offered up an impressive cameo. And in David O. Russell's *Silver Linings Playbook* (2012) and *American Hustle* (2013), audiences were treated to a brief reminder of just how compelling a screen presence De Niro can be. **IHS**

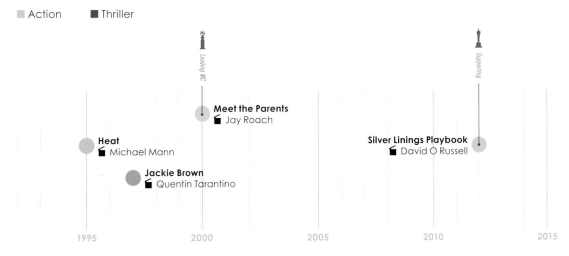

■ Action　　■ Thriller

Leading MC

Supporting

Meet the Parents
🎬 Jay Roach

Heat
🎬 Michael Mann

Jackie Brown
🎬 Quentin Tarantino

Silver Linings Playbook
🎬 David O Russell

1995	2000	2005	2010	2015

**New York,
New York**
(1977)

The Deer Hunter
(1978)

Raging Bull
(1980)

Mean Streets
(1973)

Taxi Driver
(1976)

Midnight Run
(1988)

Goodfellas
(1990)

Meet the Parents
(2000)

For his role as musician Jimmy Doyle in *New York, New York*, De Niro learned to play the saxophone.

De Niro as middleweight boxer Jake LaMotta at the height of his fame in *Raging Bull*. The actor gained 60 pounds (27 kg) to portray La Motta in his post-boxing years.

De Niro as Mike Vronsky in Michael Cimino's *The Deer Hunter*, which was shot entirely on location.

Offered his pick of supporting roles in *Mean Streets*, De Niro was advised by costar Harvey Keitel to take the role of Johnny Boy.

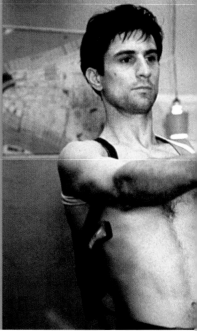

In preparation for his role in *Taxi Driver*, De Niro spent several weeks driving a cab around New York.

John Ashton with De Niro in **Midnight Run**. De Niro took the part after being rejected for the lead role in *Big* (1988), which eventually went to Tom Hanks.

Meryl Streep and De Niro in **The Deer Hunter**. The pair would reunite in 1984 for *Falling in Love* and in 1996 for *Marvin's Room*.

De Niro wises up young Christopher Serrone (L) and Joseph D'Onofrio in **Goodfellas**. De Niro's casting enabled Scorsese to secure the necessary funding for the movie.

De Niro's overprotective father tries an unusual form of bonding with his daughter's boyfriend (Ben Stiller) in **Meet the Parents**.

character actors vs. stars

Lon Chaney   Marie Dressler   Peter Lorre   Charles Laughton   Hattie McDaniel   Ernest Borgnine   Maggie Smith   Warren Oates

There is no avoiding the fact that "character actor" is both a peculiar designation — since surely all actors play characters — and a faintly insulting one, indicative as it is of a performer who lacks the obvious "good looks" required to play the lead. The term is clearly a functional one, however, having sustained itself throughout the history of cinema since the 1860s.

A true character actor is one of those slippery things that is hard to precisely define, but that you definitely recognize when you see one. Lon Chaney, Charles Laughton, Marie Dressler and Peter Lorre were all character actors; a random sampling from later cinematic history might draw in Warren Oates, Danny DeVito, Laurence Fishburne, Kathy Bates, Patricia Clarkson and William H. Macy. Successful character actors are more than simply hardworking, widely employed supporting players: they are particularly skilled, memorable or flamboyant supporting players, who sustain powerful face-recognition despite not necessarily scoring top billing.

While they might, at times, be cast in lead roles — like Laughton in *The Hunchback of Notre Dame* (1939), Ernest Borgnine in *Marty* (1955), Maggie Smith in *The Prime of Miss Jean Brodie* (1969) or Philip Seymour Hoffman in *Synecdoche, New York* (2008) — their

primary usefulness to casting directors will tend to be as providers of quirk, color or poignancy, rather than main narrative drive. Perhaps they possess a distinctive appearance — like Steve Buscemi, whose character in *Fargo* (1996) is persistently identified by the film's other personnel as "funny-looking" — or a specific idiosyncrasy, like Linda Hunt's small proportions or Morgan Freeman's rich voice.

The positioning of character actors as sideline attractions to the leading man and leading lady — although perhaps possessed of more charisma and humor — is an inheritance from theater. It might, indeed, be seen as a hangover from the 16th-century Italian *commedia dell'arte*, with its stock masked archetypes of virtuous lovers, eccentric servants and mean-spirited elders. This cast of characters was translated in the Victorian stage melodrama into six standbys: hero, heroine and villain, plus an elderly parent, a sidekick and a servant. Early cinema relied strongly on similar archetypes in whose portrayal particular performers specialized; and while big stars like Douglas Fairbanks, John Gilbert, Lillian Gish and Mary Pickford were steering the romantic narratives and the likes of Rudolf Valentino and Clara Bow inventing the sex symbol, the comedic, scary, disruptive or supportive secondary roles required

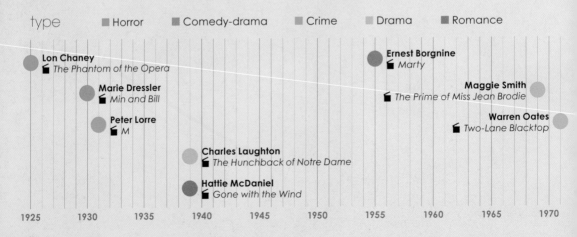

type   ■ Horror   ■ Comedy-drama   ■ Crime   ■ Drama   ■ Romance

Lon Chaney
🎬 *The Phantom of the Opera*

Marie Dressler
🎬 *Min and Bill*

Peter Lorre
🎬 *M*

Charles Laughton
🎬 *The Hunchback of Notre Dame*

Hattie McDaniel
🎬 *Gone with the Wind*

Ernest Borgnine
🎬 *Marty*

Maggie Smith
🎬 *The Prime of Miss Jean Brodie*

Warren Oates
🎬 *Two-Lane Blacktop*

1925   1930   1935   1940   1945   1950   1955   1960   1965   1970

Danny DeVito | Linda Hunt | Kathy Bates | Steve Buscemi | John Goodman | Peter Dinklage | Philip Seymour Hoffman | Gabourey Sidibe

forceful actors and actresses whose appeal was neither sentimental nor carnal. So emerged the likes of John Bunny, Oliver Hardy, W.C. Fields, Erich von Stroheim, Lionel Barrymore, Marie Dressler and Zasu Pitts — actors who embodied clowns and villains, romantic rivals and funny best friends, matriarchs and father figures. Although film narratives have arguably progressed beyond such reliance on stock characters, the expectation that a mainstream film will be peopled with certain archetypes is a tenacious one.

Nonetheless, to some extent, the identification of certain performers as "character actors" simply foregrounds the narrow range of physical types that mainstream film culture (and the majority of more marginal film culture) deems acceptably sexy and/or heroic. Linda Hunt, Warwick Davis and Peter Dinklage can expect to be considered character actors only on account of not clearing conventional height requirements for a bill-topping star; physically bulky performers from Roscoe Arbuckle, Oliver Hardy and Hattie McDaniel to John Goodman, Gabourey Sidibe and Melissa McCarthy have managed their careers in the knowledge that they are unlikely to come under consideration as action heroes or romantic leads. While debate might rumble on about whether it

would be acceptable for a black man to play James Bond, we may be reasonably sure that an overweight actor or one of restricted growth is never going to get the call. Similarly, for all the range of women that were considered to play Scarlett O'Hara in *Gone with the Wind* (1939), a certain level of beauty was a clear must, despite the fact that the first line of Margaret Mitchell's source novel is "Scarlett O'Hara was not beautiful." Katharine Hepburn was desperate for the part but she was reportedly rejected by producer David O. Selznick with the blunt assertion that he could not imagine Rhett Butler devoting 12 years to her seduction.

Hepburn, of course, was a star, but one of an unconventional and awkward stripe: doubts about her legitimacy as a leading lady dogged her early career, and she arguably found her stride playing "character" roles late into her career. Here is where character actors, although they live out most of their days at the periphery of the spotlight, can perhaps claim the last laugh. Since they do not have to match up to predominant standards of marketable attractiveness, they do not need to worry about it slipping away from them. In spite of Hollywood's cult of beauty, maybe "funny-looking" is the smartest thing to be. **HM**

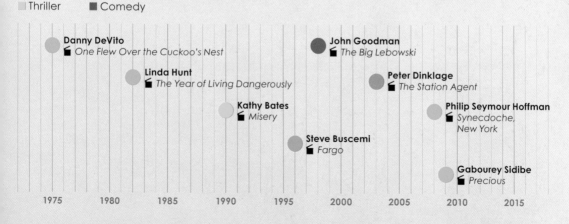

■ Thriller   ■ Comedy

Danny DeVito
🎬 *One Flew Over the Cuckoo's Nest*

John Goodman
🎬 *The Big Lebowski*

Linda Hunt
🎬 *The Year of Living Dangerously*

Peter Dinklage
🎬 *The Station Agent*

Kathy Bates
🎬 *Misery*

Philip Seymour Hoffman
🎬 *Synecdoche, New York*

Steve Buscemi
🎬 *Fargo*

Gabourey Sidibe
🎬 *Precious*

1975   1980   1985   1990   1995   2000   2005   2010   2015

james dean 1931–55

East of
Eden

Rebel
Without a
Cause

Giant

Given that James Dean had only three significant movie roles before his tragic death in 1955 at the age of 24, his impact on the industry and subsequent role in popular culture is nothing short of staggering. A young man who forever altered the landscape of Hollywood, Dean's legacy far outweighs his small body of work.

After a stint in television dramas and the odd commercial, Dean's first Hollywood film was the small role of a boxing trainer in the Dean Martin and Jerry Lewis comedy *Sailor Beware* (1952). He also had walk-on roles in Sam Fuller's *Fixed Bayonets!* (1951) and Douglas Sirk's *Has Anybody Seen My Gal?* (1952).

Soon after, Dean enrolled at the Actors' Studio, run by legendary teacher Lee Strasberg. It was here that he developed his distinctive style. Several more television roles came along in the early 1950s, but it was his role as an Arab houseboy in a 1954 theatrical production of André Gide's book *The Immoralist* (1902) that caught the attention of Hollywood.

He was cast in Elia Kazan's adaptation of John Steinbeck's *East of Eden* (1955). Although the original novel detailed the lives of two families over three generations, Kazan's film focused on the latter part of the story, which centers on the charismatic, willful character of Cal Trask. Dean's performance, which was largely improvised, is nothing short of revelatory. It would be the only film that featured him as star that Dean would see released in his lifetime.

If his portrayal of the errant Cal had pitched him as a pin-up for youthful disillusionment, it was his next film that confirmed him as the official voice of a lost generation. He lights up the screen as troubled teen Jim Stark in Nicolas Ray's extraordinary *Rebel Without a Cause* (1955). The film would become the actor's defining role and the only one for which he received top billing. A study of raging, tormented youth, *Rebel* was praised for its uncompromising portrayal of adolescent disenchantment. Once again, Dean was lauded for a raw, emotionally powerful performance.

Dean's final role was playing another rebellious character, Jett Rink, in George Steven's Texas oil epic, *Giant* (1956), proving to be a magnetic presence opposite Elizabeth Taylor and Rock Hudson. A more peripheral presence in *Giant* than his previous two films, Dean nonetheless captured Jett's feral qualities in the film's earlier scenes and his rapacious desire for wealth and power later on. Along with *East of Eden*, Dean received a posthumous Academy Award nomination for his performance in the film.

Dean was a car enthusiast and competitive racing driver. On September 30, 1955, shortly after he had completed filming on *Giant* and as he was making his way to a racing event, he was involved in a fatal car crash. His early death contributed to his legend, but his three incendiary performances cemented his star status. **MB**

genre   ■ Drama

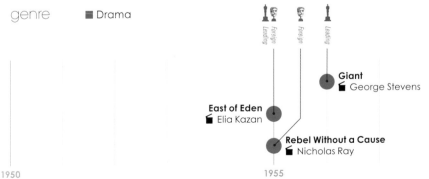

Giant
George Stevens

East of Eden
Elia Kazan

Rebel Without a Cause
Nicholas Ray

Foreign
Leading

Foreign

Leading

1950   1955   1960

benicio del toro 1967

| The Usual Suspects | Fear and Loathing in Las Vegas | Traffic | 21 Grams | The Hunted | Sin City | Che | The Wolfman |

Even in his most outlandish roles, Benicio Del Toro's soft-spoken delivery and unpredictable rhythms have made his characters seem authentic and believable. Born in San Juan, Puerto Rico, in 1967, his first screen appearances were as Duke the Dog-Faced Boy in *Big Top Pee-wee* (1988) and easily-dispatched Bond henchman Dario in *Licence To Kill* (1989). Supporting roles followed, notably as vindictive movie executive Kevin Spacey's assistant in *Swimming with Sharks* (1994).

Del Toro's breakthrough came when Spacey recommended him to play Fred Fenster, a flashy-dressing thief with a poor command of English, in Bryan Singer's taut thriller *The Usual Suspects* (1995). He subsequently pursued an eclectic range of supporting roles, including a gangster in *The Funeral* (1996), a baseball player in *The Fan* (1996) and the eponymous artist's roommate in *Basquiat* (1996). He was reliably the most compelling presence of each film.

His career accelerated after playing Hunter S. Thompson's lawyer Dr. Gonzo in Terry Gilliam's impressive adaptation of *Fear and Loathing in Las Vegas* (1998). In 2000 he played a Mexican police officer coping with drug cartels in Steven Soderbergh's ensemble drama *Traffic*, receiving an

Oscar for his thoughtful, understated performance, which was largely in Spanish. He was equally impressive as a mentally disabled Native American in *The Pledge* (2001) and an ex-convict struggling with his faith in *21 Grams* (2003). However, the dull thriller *The Hunted* (2003) did little for him or costar Tommy Lee Jones.

Del Toro joined another ensemble cast as Jackie Boy in Robert Rodriguez's neo-noir anthology *Sin City* (2005). Over the next few years he starred in a number of disappointments, including Susanne Bier's overblown melodrama *Things We Lost in the Fire* (2007).

Working once again with Soderbergh, Del Toro played the Argentine revolutionary Che Guevara in the biopic *Che* (2008), released in two parts. Del Toro has rarely been better, but the film did not find a large audience. The same fate befell the less impressive *The Wolfman* (2010). Del Toro has worked infrequently in recent years, appearing in Oliver Stone's woeful *Savages* (2012), as a Native American in *Jimmy P.* (2013), playing the infamous Pablo Escobar in *Escobar: Paradise Lost* (2014) and taking a cameo role in *Guardians of the Galaxy* (2014). He is also one of the many well-known faces to pop up in Paul Thomas Anderson's deliriously dense *Inherent Vice* (2014). **JWa**

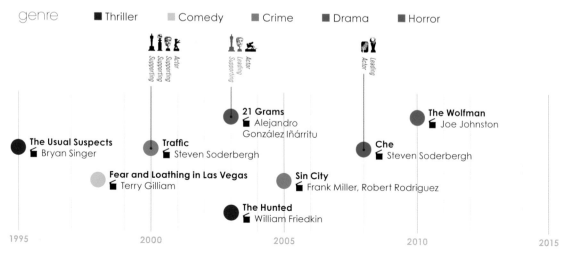

genre ■ Thriller ▨ Comedy ■ Crime ■ Drama ■ Horror

Actor Supporting / Supporting / Supporting

Actor Leading / Supporting

Leading Actor

21 Grams
Alejandro González Iñárritu

The Wolfman
Joe Johnston

The Usual Suspects
Bryan Singer

Traffic
Steven Soderbergh

Che
Steven Soderbergh

Fear and Loathing in Las Vegas
Terry Gilliam

Sin City
Frank Miller, Robert Rodriguez

The Hunted
William Friedkin

1995 2000 2005 2010 2015

alain delon 1935

Three Murderesses

Plein Soleil

Rocco and His Brothers

L'Eclisse

The Leopard

Le Samouraï

Spirits of the Dead

La Piscine

In his heyday during the 1960s and 1970s, Alain Delon was considered one of the most handsome actors in European cinema. But alongside his lean attractiveness was a formidable talent — his most fascinating characters were calculating and physically contained, driven by survival instincts.

Sociopaths, murderers and men on the wrong side of the law are not the only key roles in Delon's filmography, but they do stand out. Along with Jean-Paul Belmondo, he was one of Jean-Pierre Melville's favored performers, starring in a trilogy of the director's best thrillers. The collaboration began with *Le Samouraï* (1967), in which Delon played cool assassin Jef Costello, who finds himself pursued by the law. In *Le Cercle Rouge* (1970), he plays a soon-to-be ex-con whose hopes of going straight are dashed by a corrupt prison guard. His last collaboration with Melville, *The Cop* (1972), sees Delon play an equally elusive law enforcer.

It takes a small leap of the imagination to connect the distaste for authority coloring many of Delon's characters with the biographical facts of the man

himself. He left school at 14. Three years later, he enlisted in the French marines, but soon "got thrown out for being seasick," then marched with the regular, land-based army. Jail time and a dishonorable discharge rounded off his military career. He took various jobs to scrape by before a trip to Cannes with an actress friend changed the course of his life.

A talent scout for Hollywood executive David O. Selznick screen tested him, offering a Hollywood contract provided that he learned English. But Delon chose to stay in France and made his first film playing a hit man in *Send a Woman When the Devil Fails* (1957). A few minor films followed, but it was two breakthrough performances in 1960 that would assure his stardom.

Delon played the lead in René Clément's *Plein Soleil* (1960), as the sun-kissed sociopath Tom Ripley. In contrast to Anthony Minghella's 1999 version of Patricia Highsmith's novel *The Talented Mr. Ripley* (1955), in which the central character was a creepy outsider and there was a clear gay subtext, Clément's film portrays Tom as a golden charmer driven by lust

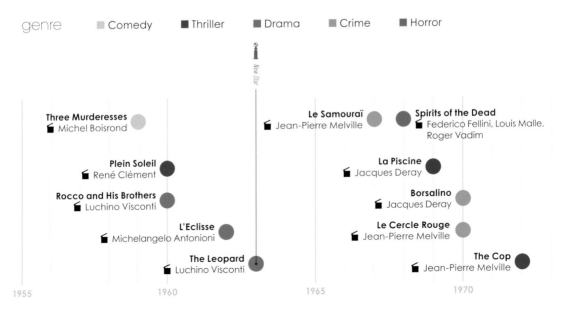

genre ■ Comedy ■ Thriller ■ Drama ■ Crime ■ Horror

New Star

Three Murderesses
Michel Boisrond

Plein Soleil
René Clément

Rocco and His Brothers
Luchino Visconti

L'Eclisse
Michelangelo Antonioni

The Leopard
Luchino Visconti

Le Samouraï
Jean-Pierre Melville

Spirits of the Dead
Federico Fellini, Louis Malle, Roger Vadim

La Piscine
Jacques Deray

Borsalino
Jacques Deray

Le Cercle Rouge
Jean-Pierre Melville

The Cop
Jean-Pierre Melville

1955   1960   1965   1970

Borsalino

Le Cercle Rouge

The Cop

Flic Story

Mr. Klein

Mort d'un Pourri

Notre Histoire

Nouvelle Vague

for Marge, the girlfriend of ill-mannered playboy Philippe. Delon's unsettlingly calm composure and astonishing good looks invited audiences to suspend rational judgment and to side with him.

Luchino Visconti saw something different when he cast Delon as the lead in *Rocco and His Brothers* (1960). The Italian director found in Delon an actor who could convincingly play an impassioned and loyal hero, trying to do right by his brothers as the noose of destiny tightens. Visconti focused on Delon's grace and youthful energy, as he would do again in *The Leopard* (1963), his lavish epic about a dying Sicilian dynasty.

Michelangelo Antonioni was another Italian director who saw potential in Delon, casting him as Monica Vitti's self-obsessed boyfriend in *L'Eclisse* (1962). Along with his role opposite Claudia Cardinale in *The Leopard*, Delon's appearance with Monica Vitti is one of the most beautiful pairings in cinema history.

Although an early film, *Three Murderesses* (1959), was well-received in the United States, Delon's appearances in English-language or international productions during the 1960s were less successful. René Clément's *Is Paris Burning?* (1966), detailing the liberation of Paris toward the end of World War II, is epic in scale but failed to win favor with audiences. The Algerian war drama *Lost Command* (1966) and *Texas Across the River* (1966) were not outright failures, but they failed to make the most of Delon's presence.

A better example of Delon's ability to light up the screen is Jacques Deray's *La Piscine* (1969). The director would cast him in a further eight films over the next two decades, long after the actor's star power had faded.

One of Delon's finest performances came in Joseph Losey's fascinating Holocaust drama, *Mr. Klein* (1976). However, it was not until 1984 that the French film academy recognized his talents with a César, for his portrayal of an alcoholic in *Notre Histoire* (1984).

Delon's last notable role was in Jean-Luc Godard's *Nouvelle Vague* (1990). Despite claiming in 1997 to have given up acting, Delon occasionally appears in films, such as *Asterix at the Olympic Games* (2008), in which he played Julius Caesar. **SMK**

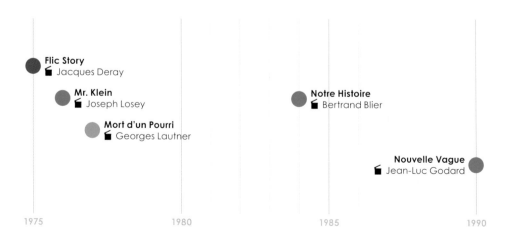

Flic Story
Jacques Deray

Mr. Klein
Joseph Losey

Mort d'un Pourri
Georges Lautner

Notre Histoire
Bertrand Blier

Nouvelle Vague
Jean-Luc Godard

1975　　　　　1980　　　　　1985　　　　　1990

D

julie delpy 1969

The Night
Is Young

Europa
Europa

Killing Zoe

Three
Colors:
White

Before
Sunrise

Before
Sunset

2 Days
in Paris

Before
Midnight

Born in 1969 in Paris, Julie Delpy's career is characterized by a fierce sense of independence and her effervescent presence, both on screen and off. Making her screen debut in Jean-Luc Godard's *Détective* (1985), Delpy announced her arrival as a luminous force in European cinema with a striking role in Leos Carax's *The Night Is Young* (1986). Holding her own against Denis Lavant and Juliette Binoche, she is excellent as Lise, the girlfriend of a card shark on the cusp of a life of crime. A more prominent role followed in *Europa Europa* (1990), Agnieszka Holland's wartime drama about a Jewish boy joining the Hitler Youth.

Delpy made a fine transition to English language features with Volker Schlöndorff's *Voyager* (1991). Adapted from the novel by Max Frisch, it is an existential tale of amour fou in which Delpy begins an ill-fated relationship with a taciturn older man, brilliantly played by Sam Shepard. Roger Avery's *Killing Zoe* (1993), a crime caper in which the titular Zoe (Delpy) finds herself embroiled in a bank robbery, has not aged so well.

The second part of Polish auteur Krzysztof Kieslowski's interconnecting *Three Colors* trilogy, *Three Colors: White* (1994), is a striking, blackly comic masterpiece. Delpy excels as the French wife of a Polish immigrant who files for divorce when he is unable to sexually consummate the union.

Delpy came to wider international attention with *Before Sunrise* (1995), initiating a fruitful collaboration with Richard Linklater. Appearing alongside Ethan Hawke as two students exploring Vienna who enjoy a night of passion, Delpy would return to her character Celine in the celebrated follow-up, *Before Sunset* (2004). A third film, *Before Midnight* (2013), revisits the couple, now married and struggling to cope with the realities of children and complicated former love lives. All three movies possess immense character, charm and insight.

2 Days in Paris (2007) saw Delpy taking up director duties for the first time. An affectionate and sharply observed culture clash tale in which Delpy brings her U.S. boyfriend (Adam Goldberg) to Paris to visit her parents — played by her real-life parents — it went on to spawn the similarly themed though less winning *2 Days in New York* (2012). Delpy's subsequent works as writer-actor-director have been patchier, though both the gothic *The Countess* (2009) and the more playful *Skylab* (2011) show her to be very much determined to exert control over her own career, having been critical of the patriarchal nature of the film industry. **JW**

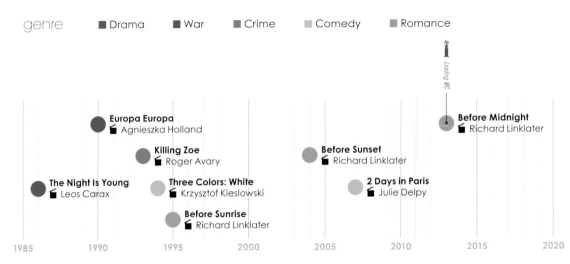

genre ■ Drama ■ War ■ Crime ▨ Comedy ■ Romance

Leading MC

Europa Europa
📽 Agnieszka Holland

Before Midnight
📽 Richard Linklater

Killing Zoe
📽 Roger Avary

Before Sunset
📽 Richard Linklater

The Night Is Young
📽 Leos Carax

Three Colors: White
📽 Krzysztof Kieslowski

2 Days in Paris
📽 Julie Delpy

Before Sunrise
📽 Richard Linklater

1985   1990   1995   2000   2005   2010   2015   2020

judi dench 1934

Goldeneye	Mrs. Brown	Shakespeare in Love	Chocolat	Iris	Notes on a Scandal	The Best Exotic Marigold Hotel	Philomena

In 1965 Judi Dench won a BAFTA for Most Promising Newcomer for her role as an overwhelmed mother in *Four in the Morning* (1965), and yet for the next two decades she was rarely seen on the big screen. Born in York in 1934, Dench had long been one of Britain's most significant theater actors before becoming one of the country's most beloved screen presences. Supporting roles in the Merchant-Ivory adaptation of E.M. Forster's *A Room with a View* (1985) and as Anthony Hopkins' wife in *84 Charing Cross Road* (1987) hinted at what was to come, but for some time film took a back seat to stage and television work.

Dench's introduction to international audiences arrived when she was cast as MI6 chief M in Martin Campbell's James Bond reboot *Goldeneye* (1995). She reprised the role six more times, but her most important contribution was in that first outing: denouncing 007 as "a sexist, misogynistic dinosaur," M's icy disdain was vital to the reinvention of Bond in a post-Cold War environment. Dench finally bowed out of the franchise with *Skyfall* (2012).

Dench was at her best in *Mrs. Brown* (1997), which explored the speculative romance between a grief-stricken Queen Victoria and her Scottish stable groom. She received the first of seven Oscar nominations for her performance. The following year, she won the Best Supporting Actress Oscar playing Elizabeth I in John Madden's in *Shakespeare in Love* (1998). Given that she was only in the film for eight delightfully tart minutes, the win was largely seen as recompense for her missing out for *Mrs. Brown*.

Dench was suddenly in demand, giving a series of acclaimed performances — as a diabetic chocolate-lover in *Chocolat* (2000), the novelist Iris Murdoch in *Iris* (2001) and excelling as a history teacher obsessed with colleague Cate Blanchett in *Notes on a Scandal* (2006). There were also some puzzling film choices, including the misfiring sci-fi sequel *The Chronicles of Riddick* (2004) and a role as Leonardo DiCaprio's mother in Clint Eastwood's biopic *J. Edgar* (2011). Dench had more luck when she reunited with John Madden for *The Best Exotic Marigold Hotel* (2012), a surprise international hit that prompted a 2015 sequel. Dench was also exceptional in *Philomena* (2013); where many of her most notable roles have relied upon conveying directness and a sharp intellect, it was a delight to see her play against type as a dotty, good-humored victim of injustice. **JWa**

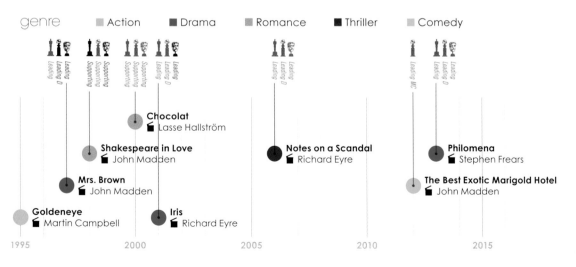

genre ■ Action ■ Drama ■ Romance ■ Thriller ■ Comedy

Chocolat
Lasse Hallström

Shakespeare in Love
John Madden

Notes on a Scandal
Richard Eyre

Philomena
Stephen Frears

Mrs. Brown
John Madden

The Best Exotic Marigold Hotel
John Madden

Goldeneye
Martin Campbell

Iris
Richard Eyre

1995   2000   2005   2010   2015

catherine deneuve 1943

The Umbrellas of Cherbourg

Repulsion

Belle de Jour

The Young Girls of Rochefort

Mississippi Mermaid

Tristana

The Last Metro

The Hunger

Born Catherine Fabienne Dorléac in Paris, 1943, Catherine Deneuve made her screen debut at the age of 14 in André Hunebelle's *The Twilight Girls* (1957). She found regular acting work in her late teens, most notably in Roger Vadim's *Vice and Virtue* (1963).

Success was brewing, but it was not until Jacques Demy's sublime, iridescently colorful musical *The Umbrellas of Cherbourg* (1964) that Deneuve found widespread recognition. The film won the coveted Palme d'Or at the 1964 Cannes Film Festival, while its star won the hearts of critics and moviegoers alike as a young girl who falls in love with a local car mechanic.

Following this breakthrough success, Deneuve began to craft an impressive filmography. In one of her most famous roles, she portrayed a young woman's descent into psychosis in Roman Polanski's claustrophobic, London-set masterpiece *Repulsion* (1965). She returned to an exploration of sexuality in Luis Buñuel's surrealist classic *Belle de Jour* (1967), playing a married housewife moonlighting as a prostitute. That

same year, she reunited with Demy for another vibrant musical, *The Young Girls of Rochefort* (1967).

Deneuve continued to work with some of the world's most respected filmmakers as the 1960s drew to a close. She was on stunning form as a mysterious mail-order bride in François Truffaut's beguiling *Mississippi Mermaid* (1969), after which she returned to Buñuel and Demy, for *Tristana* (1970) and *Once Upon a Time* (1970). Both showcased her versatility as an actress and penchant for diverse and distinctive roles.

In the early 1970s Deneuve worked with Jean-Pierre Melville on his final film *The Cop* (1972), with Demy again on *A Slightly Pregnant Man* (1973) and appeared in Robert Aldrich's *Hustle* (1975), playing a prostitute opposite Burt Reynolds' cop.

She was acclaimed for her performance in Truffaut's *The Last Metro* (1980), for which she won a César Award. Set during World War II, Deneuve plays the wife of a Jewish theater owner who strives to hide him from the Nazis while also keeping the struggling

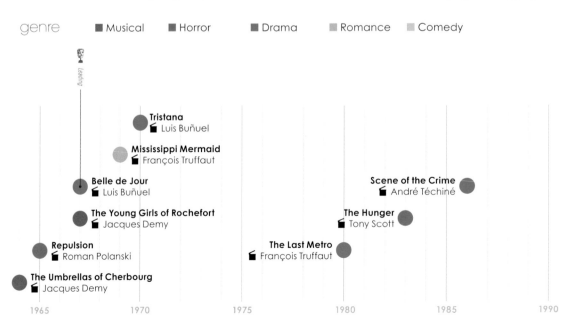

genre ■ Musical ■ Horror ■ Drama ■ Romance ■ Comedy

Tristana
Luis Buñuel

Mississippi Mermaid
François Truffaut

Belle de Jour
Luis Buñuel

Scene of the Crime
André Téchiné

The Young Girls of Rochefort
Jacques Demy

The Hunger
Tony Scott

Repulsion
Roman Polanski

The Last Metro
François Truffaut

The Umbrellas of Cherbourg
Jacques Demy

1965   1970   1975   1980   1985   1990

$9M (U.S.)	$14M	$9M	$1M	$55M	$56M	$8M	$25M
The Last Metro (1980)	The Hunger (1983)	Indochine (1992)	Place Vendôme (1998)	Dancer in the Dark (2000)	8 Women (2002)	A Christmas Tale (2008)	Potiche (2010)

Scene of the Crime | Indochine | Place Vendôme | Time Regained | Dancer in the Dark | 8 Women | A Christmas Tale | Potiche

theater company afloat. She starred as a centuries-old vampire in Tony Scott's stylized horror romp *The Hunger* (1983), but continued to favor European productions like André Téchiné's *Scene of the Crime* (1986) and François Dupeyron's *A Strange Place To Meet* (1988).

Deneuve's galvanizing performance in Régis Wargnier's historical epic *Indochine* (1992) not only saw her pick up a second César Award, but also receive her first Oscar nomination. She was sublime in *My Favorite Season* (1993) and *Thieves* (1993), both for Téchiné, and brought a magisterial presence to Nicole Garcia's elegant thriller *Place Vendôme* (1998). She was equally impressive in Leos Carax's eccentric *Pola X* (1999) and added class to Raúl Ruiz's beautiful Proust adaptation *Time Regained* (1999).

Deneuve's search for daring roles then led her to serial provocateur Lars von Trier, for his downbeat musical *Dancer in the Dark* (2000). The film was the second Deneuve musical to scoop the Palme d'Or at Cannes, although the film divided critical opinion.

With a revitalized taste for the musical genre, Deneuve joined the ensemble cast of the equally subversive, albeit much more upbeat, *8 Women* (2002), directed by François Ozon. The two would collaborate again on the gleefully kitsch and riotously funny *Potiche* (2010).

Entering a new century, Deneuve remained prolific. She is impressive in Arnaud Desplechin's *Kings and Queen* (2004) and mesmerizing as the dying matriarch in the director's subsequent *A Christmas Tale* (2008) — her 100th film role. She supplied the voice of Mom for Marjane Satrapi's animated hit *Persepolis* (2007) and joined the cast of Christophe Honoré's *Beloved* (2011). Recently, she has appeared in Emmanuelle Bercot's nuanced road movie *On My Way* (2013), played another matriarch in Benoît Jacquot's *3 Hearts* (2014) and reunited with Téchiné for the tender drama *In The Name of My Daughter* (2014). Showing no signs of slowing down and as dazzling, elegant and willing to challenge herself as ever, Deneuve is the quintessential star of French cinema. **MB**

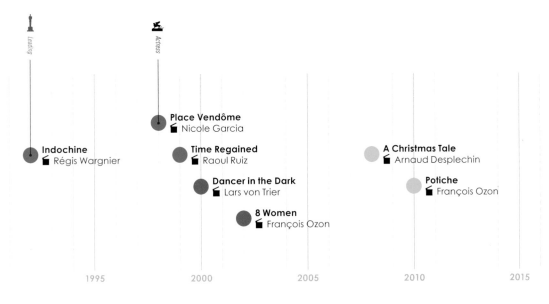

Indochine
Régis Wargnier

Place Vendôme
Nicole Garcia

Time Regained
Raoul Ruiz

Dancer in the Dark
Lars von Trier

8 Women
François Ozon

A Christmas Tale
Arnaud Desplechin

Potiche
François Ozon

1995   2000   2005   2010   2015

The Umbrellas of Cherbourg
(1964)

Repulsion
(1965)

Belle de Jour
(1967)

Mississippi Mermaid
(1969)

The Last Metro
(1980)

Indochine
(1992)

Time Regained
(1999)

Potiche
(2010)

In *The Umbrellas of Cherbourg* Deneuve plays a young girl who falls in love with a local car mechanic (Nino Castelnuovo), only to face the harsh realities of life.

The surreal *Belle de Jour*, in which Deneuve played a housewife who spends her afternoons as a prostitute, highlighted the hypocrisies of bourgeois life.

The performances of Deneuve and Jean-Paul Belmondo in *Mississippi Mermaid* were praised by critic Vincent Canby as being "played with marvelous style."

Deneuve and director Roman Polanski on the set of *Repulsion*, the first installment in Polanski's "Apartment Trilogy."

Deneuve with Jean Sorel, who plays her unsuspecting husband in *Belle de Jour*.

Deneuve and Gérard Depardieu both won César Awards for their roles in *The Last Metro*.

The Last Metro was the first pairing of Deneuve and Gérard Depardieu, an on-screen partnership that would be revisited in a further half a dozen films over two decades.

Set in French Indochina during the dying days of the colonial era, **Indochine** tells the story of Deneuve's French plantation owner and her adopted Vietnamese daughter.

Deneuve and Emmanuelle Béart in **Time Regained**, an adaptation of the final volume of Marcel Proust's masterpiece In Search of Lost Time (1913–27).

Potiche sees Deneuve play a trophy wife who takes over her husband's (Fabrice Luchini) business after a labor dispute.

gérard depardieu 1948

Going Places

1900

The Last Metro

Police

Jean de Florette

Under the Sun of Satan

Cyrano de Bergerac

Green Card

Gérard Depardieu is famed for excess, both in life and cinema. A prolific actor, he has appeared in more than 170 films over a career spanning nearly half a century, and is renowned for his energetic performances, robust charm and incendiary temper.

Born in Châteauroux in 1948, Depardieu had an eventful, impoverished upbringing before relocating to Paris to study performing. By the late 1960s, he had started to work on television, soon moving into film roles. His breakthrough was as the petty criminal Jean-Claude in the gauche comedy-drama *Going Places* (1974), which was one of that year's most commercially successful films in France and set a trend for Depardieu playing libidinous, roguish characters. The following year he received the first of 15 César nominations for Best Actor for his performance in *Seven Deaths by Prescription* (1975). He would only win the award twice, for *The Last Metro* (1980) and *Cyrano de Bergerac* (1990).

A significant early role saw him star opposite Robert De Niro in Bernardo Bertolucci's ambitious but flawed epic *1900* (1976). Depardieu had become a

fully fledged movie star by this point and appeared in a range of films that included Claude Miller's *This Sweet Sickness* (1977), Alain Resnais' *My American Uncle* (1980) and his first collaboration with Maurice Pialat, *Loulou* (1980). His performance as an actor and resistance member living under Nazi occupation in *The Last Metro* is perhaps his best known role from this period, and is one of director François Truffaut's most popular later films. The two worked together the following year on *The Woman Next Door* (1981), and 24 years later Depardieu reunited with his costar Catherine Deneuve for *Changing Times* (2004), the final scene of which references the ending of their earlier film.

Depardieu continued to attract acclaim in the early 1980s with a series of remarkable performances. He played the mysterious titular character in *The Return of Martin Guerre* (1982), the hero of the French Revolution in *Danton* (1983), a soldier in *Fort Saganne* (1984) and a cop obsessed with a drug dealer's girlfriend in *Police* (1985). The most internationally successful film during this time was the lush literary adaptation *Jean de Florette* (1986). Depardieu is

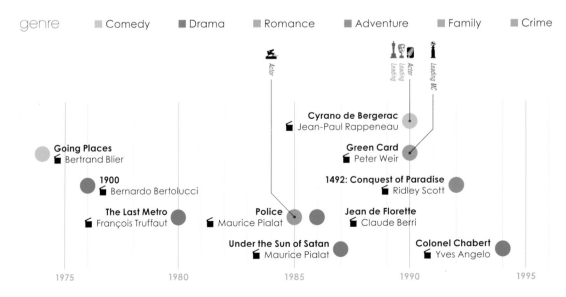

genre ■ Comedy ■ Drama ■ Romance ■ Adventure ■ Family ■ Crime

Cyrano de Bergerac
Jean-Paul Rappeneau

Going Places
Bertrand Blier

Green Card
Peter Weir

1900
Bernardo Bertolucci

1492: Conquest of Paradise
Ridley Scott

The Last Metro
François Truffaut

Police
Maurice Pialat

Jean de Florette
Claude Berri

Under the Sun of Satan
Maurice Pialat

Colonel Chabert
Yves Angelo

1975   1980   1985   1990   1995

1492: Conquest of Paradise

Colonel Chabert

The Man in the Iron Mask

Asterix & Obelix Take on Caesar

Mesrine: Killer Instinct

Potiche

Life of Pi

Welcome to New York

D

mesmerizing as a hunchbacked farmer whose life is destroyed by the avarice of his neighbors. Along with its companion film, *Manon des Sources* (1986), it was the most ambitious and costly French film project ever undertaken. Following it, Depardieu reunited with *Police* director Pialat for *Under the Sun of Satan* (1987), playing a zealous priest whose faith is severely tested.

Cyrano de Bergerac features arguably the defining role of Depardieu's career. He is revelatory as the outwardly brash but ultimately warm-hearted poet who is afraid to court the object of his love due to embarrassment over his substantial nose. It was the perfect role for the actor: like Cyrano, Depardieu has managed to be an oddly attractive presence despite his physical appearance. He was nominated for an Oscar for the film, which was an international arthouse hit. His increased recognition led to a sustained period of working in U.S. films, including *Green Card* (1990), *1492: Conquest of Paradise* (1992), *Unhook the Stars* (1996), *The Man in the Iron Mask* (1998) and *102 Dalmatians* (2000). He continued to work in France, however, most notably in the literary adaptations *Germinal* (1993) and *Colonel Chabert* (1994).

In 1999 Depardieu played the dim-witted, invincible Gaul Obelix in *Asterix & Obelix Take on Caesar*, a live-action version of René Goscinny and Albert Uderzo's long-running comic series. He returned to the character for three further features, each of which was the most expensive French film ever made at the time.

From the millennium onward Depardieu mostly acted in French productions. He is superb as the ageing idol in *The Singer* (2006), which he followed with cameos as Édith Piaf's first champion in *La Vie en Rose* (2007) and a crime boss in *Mesrine: Killer Instinct* (2008). He played a detective in Claude Chabrol's final film *Bellamy* (2009), an illiterate handyman in *My Afternoons with Margueritte* (2010) and a communist mayor in François Ozon's comedy *Potiche* (2010).

He took a small role in *Life of Pi* (2012), but the performance that towers over his recent work is his fictional version of disgraced politician Dominique Strauss-Kahn in Abel Ferrara's *Welcome to New York* (2014). Both repulsive and compelling, Depardieu is bold and uncompromising, a reminder of what a remarkable screen presence he can be. **JWa**

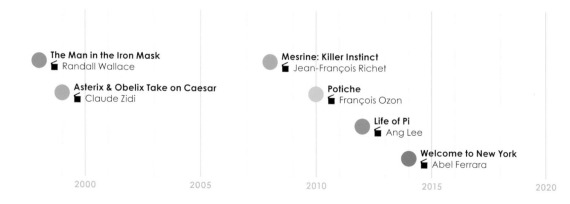

The Man in the Iron Mask
🎬 Randall Wallace

Asterix & Obelix Take on Caesar
🎬 Claude Zidi

Mesrine: Killer Instinct
🎬 Jean-François Richet

Potiche
🎬 François Ozon

Life of Pi
🎬 Ang Lee

Welcome to New York
🎬 Abel Ferrara

2000   2005   2010   2015   2020

johnny depp 1963

| Edward Scissorhands | Cry-Baby | What's Eating Gilbert Grape | Ed Wood | Dead Man | Fear and Loathing in Las Vegas | Pirates of the Caribbean: The Curse of the Black Pearl | Finding Neverland |

For someone blessed with the cheekbones, coolness and acting talent of Johnny Depp, leading man eminence was virtually guaranteed. Credit to Depp, then, for rejecting such bland commodification, constantly siding with eccentrics and outcasts. Eventual mainstream stardom seemed, if not accidental, then — initially — on his own terms.

Born in Kentucky, 1963, Depp quit school to follow his musical muse, before pursuing acting in LA. Minor roles in *A Nightmare on Elm Street* (1984) and *Platoon* (1986) led to teen worship on television show *21 Jump Street* (1987–90). But rather than cash in his new heartthrob status, Depp's next film confirmed his idiosyncratic nature: starring as the eponymous 1950s juvenile delinquent in John Waters' *Cry-Baby* (1990).

In Tim Burton's *Edward Scissorhands* (1990), Depp excelled as a scissor-fingered, punk-Goth, Frankensteinlike creation with a fragile, artistic soul. His next Burton collaboration, *Ed Wood* (1994) is another wonderful study in weird artistry. Depp brings an infectious, blissfully unaware joie de vivre to the 1950s B-moviemaker's wretched endeavors. Oddball outsiders remained the Depp-Burton specialty across eight further films together. Their double-act, however, evinced diminishing returns, notably a garish, visual effects-swollen *Alice in Wonderland* (2010).

Even without Burton, Depp chose similarly offbeat roles — a skilled silent clown in romance *Benny and Joon* (1993) and a sensitive soul struggling to hold his unconventional family together in *What's Eating Gilbert Grape* (1993). Jim Jarmusch's neo-western *Dead Man* (1995) was another triumph, Depp's William Blake watchful and haunted on his eerie, metaphysical odyssey. But he could also do extravagance — his thinly disguised Hunter S. Thompson in Terry Gilliam's hallucinatory *Fear and Loathing in Las Vegas* (1998) is a fevered, spindly presence.

In *Pirates of the Caribbean: The Curse of the Black Pearl* (2003), Depp plundered an entire movie, playing Captain Jack Sparrow as a roguish, slurring, Keith Richards-inspired dandy. Depp clearly loves the character, but appearing in three increasingly indulgent sequels, along with big-budget flops like *The Lone Ranger* (2013) and dopey sci-fi *Transcendence* (2014), lost the actor much of his megastar cool. After his lackluster performance in *Mortdecai* (2015), hopes are high for the actor's take on infamous gangster Whitey Bulger in the drama *Black Mass* (2015). **LS**

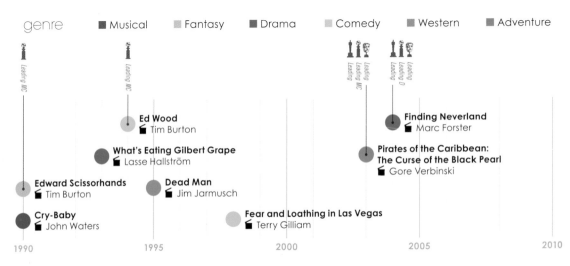

genre ■ Musical ■ Fantasy ■ Drama ■ Comedy ■ Western ■ Adventure

Ed Wood
Tim Burton

Finding Neverland
Marc Forster

What's Eating Gilbert Grape
Lasse Hallström

Pirates of the Caribbean: The Curse of the Black Pearl
Gore Verbinski

Edward Scissorhands
Tim Burton

Dead Man
Jim Jarmusch

Cry-Baby
John Waters

Fear and Loathing in Las Vegas
Terry Gilliam

1990   1995   2000   2005   2010

leonardo dicaprio 1974

D

What's
Eating Gilbert
Grape

Romeo +
Juliet

Titanic

The Beach

The Aviator

Revolutionary
Road

Inception

The Wolf of
Wall Street

Leonardo DiCaprio first attracted attention with his performance in *This Boy's Life* (1993). Later that year, he stunned audiences and critics with his breathtaking turn as a young man with severe developmental disabilities in *What's Eating Gilbert Grape* (1993). The performance earned him his first Oscar nomination, for Best Supporting Actor.

Appearances in cult films *The Quick and the Dead* (1995) and *The Basketball Diaries* (1995) brought the actor modest success, but it was two subsequent films that would take his fame to stratospheric heights. His on-screen chemistry with Claire Danes in *Romeo + Juliet* (1996), combined with director Baz Luhrmann's radical updating of Shakespeare's play, made the film an enormous hit. James Cameron's blockbusting *Titanic* (1997) required less of the actor but once again, he found a perfect partner in Kate Winslet. Although both films won him acclaim, it was overshadowed by his newfound status as a teenage heartthrob.

A small role in Woody Allen's *Celebrity* (1998) provided DiCaprio's "coming of age," while his performance in Danny Boyle's disappointing *The Beach* (2000) hinted at his willingness to challenge himself. He gave one of his best performances in Steven Spielberg's *Catch Me If You Can* (2002), capturing the charm and nervous energy of real-life con artist Frank Abagnale Jr. In the same year he worked with Martin Scorsese on the epic *Gangs Of New York* (2002), the first of many collaborations with the director. They reunited for *The Aviator* (2004) and *The Departed* (2006), the actor yet again impressing.

Now regarded as a respected "adult" actor, DiCaprio continued to take on weighty roles. *Blood Diamond* (2006) found him skirting the moral divide as a smuggler, while *Revolutionary Road* (2008) reunited him with Winslet in a moving adaptation of Richard Yates' novel. Over the next few years, he worked with Christopher Nolan on the mind-boggling sci-fi epic *Inception* (2010), Clint Eastwood on the misguided biopic of FBI head *J. Edgar* (2011) and Quentin Tarantino on *Django Unchained* (2012), turning in one of his finest performances, as a racist plantation owner.

DiCaprio played the titular character in Baz Luhrmann's adaptation of *The Great Gatsby* (2013), but fared better in *The Wolf of Wall Street* (2013), playing real-life financial crook Jordan Belfort. It is a gutsy portrayal, for which DiCaprio won almost unanimous universal acclaim. **MB**

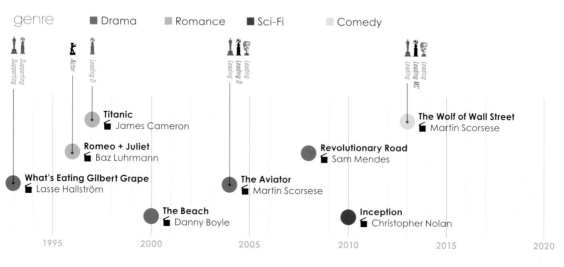

genre ■ Drama ■ Romance ■ Sci-Fi ■ Comedy

Supporting Supporting

Actor

Leading D

Leading Leading D

Leading Leading

Leading Leading MC

Leading

Titanic
James Cameron

The Wolf of Wall Street
Martin Scorsese

Romeo + Juliet
Baz Luhrmann

Revolutionary Road
Sam Mendes

What's Eating Gilbert Grape
Lasse Hallström

The Aviator
Martin Scorsese

The Beach
Danny Boyle

Inception
Christopher Nolan

1995   2000   2005   2010   2015   2020

marlene dietrich 1901–92

The Blue Angel

Morocco

Dishonored

Shanghai Express

Blonde Venus

The Scarlet Empress

The Devil Is a Woman

Knight Without Armour

"Age cannot wither her, nor custom stale her infinite sameness," wrote film historian David Shipman about Marlene Dietrich. A little unfair, perhaps, but he did have a point. Those ironically arched eyebrows, the hint of a self-mocking grin, the vampishly displayed legs, the Berlin cabaret accent — all too often, especially when faced with an indifferent script, Dietrich would fall back on her default performance. "I never ever took my career seriously," she once admitted, and it shows.

Given a good framework, she could be superb — running rings round Victor McLaglen in *Dishonored* (1931), wreathed in smoke and shadows in *Shanghai Express* (1932), huskily crooning "See What the Boys in the Back Room Will Have" in *Destry Rides Again* (1939). But with a shaky script and the wrong costar, the artifice starts to wear thin.

Born in Berlin, Dietrich made her screen debut in 1922 and had appeared in some 20 German films, to no great acclaim, before she met her Svengali and finest director, Josef von Sternberg. According to his own account, Sternberg saw something unique in this "modest little German hausfrau" and "instructed her,

presented her carefully, edited her charms, disguised her imperfections, and led her to crystallize a pictorial aphrodisiac," in the process creating one of cinema's most enduring (and sexually ambiguous) erotic icons.

The Blue Angel (1930), shot simultaneously in German and English, gave Dietrich the role that shot her to stardom, as nightclub singer Lola Lola, seducing and degrading respectable professor Emil Jannings. Clad in basque, black stockings and top hat, perched on a barstool and singing "Falling in Love Again," she had clearly found her true screen persona. The director and star would make six further movies together, of increasingly baroque extravagance.

Morocco (1930), her first Hollywood film, again playing a nightclub singer, stepped up her androgynous appeal by having her publicly kiss a woman on the lips. She was a spy in *Dishonored* and in *Shanghai Express* an international lady of pleasure, her eyes hooded and watchful, her face veiled, shadowed, nestling in furs or feathers. She was a nightclub artiste again in *Blonde Venus* (1932), unforgettably emerging from a gorilla suit; then came

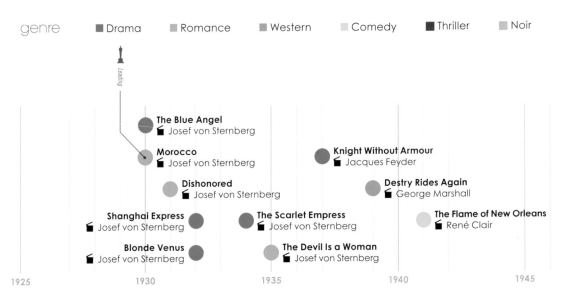

genre · ■ Drama · ■ Romance · ■ Western · □ Comedy · ■ Thriller · ■ Noir

The Blue Angel
📷 Josef von Sternberg

Morocco
📷 Josef von Sternberg

Dishonored
📷 Josef von Sternberg

Shanghai Express
📷 Josef von Sternberg

Blonde Venus
📷 Josef von Sternberg

The Scarlet Empress
📷 Josef von Sternberg

The Devil Is a Woman
📷 Josef von Sternberg

Knight Without Armour
📷 Jacques Feyder

Destry Rides Again
📷 George Marshall

The Flame of New Orleans
📷 René Clair

1925 · 1930 · 1935 · 1940 · 1945

$64M (U.S.)
Shanghai Express
(1932)

$18M (U.S.)
Touch of Evil
(1958)

| Destry Rides Again | The Flame of New Orleans | A Foreign Affair | Stage Fright | Rancho Notorious | Witness for the Prosecution | Touch of Evil | Judgment at Nuremberg |

the peak of the Sternberg films with her delirious turn as Catherine the Great in *The Scarlet Empress* (1934).

It flopped at the box office. *The Devil Is a Woman* (1935) did little better, and the partnership broke up. Together, Dietrich and Sternberg created something unique in cinema; apart neither of them ever did anything quite so exceptional. Even so, as a con-woman in *Desire* (1936) Dietrich proved she could play comedy, teasing a bemused Gary Cooper. But *The Garden of Allah* (1936) was pseudo-mystical nonsense, and the vapid *Knight without Armour* (1937) was feebler still.

Around this time, the Nazi government tried to tempt her back to act for the Reich; to her lasting credit, she turned them down flat. The spoof-western knockabout of *Destry* seemed to revive her career, but it was evident the studios had trouble knowing what to do with her. The South Sea drama *Seven Sinners* (1940) suggested there was precious little chemistry between her and John Wayne, and *The Spoilers* (1942) and *Pittsburgh* (1942) made it abundantly clear. René Clair cast her in his period romance *The Flame of New Orleans* (1941), but she seemed strangely ordinary. She had the worst casting of her career in *Golden Earrings* (1947), coated with boot polish to play a gypsy; but she was perfectly attuned to Billy Wilder's bittersweet humor in *A Foreign Affair* (1948).

Stage Fright (1950) was minor-league Hitchcock, though Dietrich contributed an enjoyably comic performance. Fritz Lang gave her one last good lead as the saloon queen in his final, masterly western, *Rancho Notorious* (1952). In *Witness for the Prosecution* (1957) Billy Wilder ill-advisedly took on an Agatha Christie courtroom drama, and Dietrich blew the plot apart with her attempt at a cockney accent. Her unbilled cameo in Orson Welles' late-noir *Touch of Evil* (1958) was brief but crucial, speaking corrupt sheriff Hank Quinlan's epitaph: "He was some kind of a man. What does it matter what you say about people?"

After this she largely abandoned the screen in favor of solo concert performances around the world, a career she apparently much preferred. "There is a lack of dignity to film stardom," she observed. "I never enjoyed working in a film." For all that, at her best she gave audiences a great deal of enjoyment. **PK**

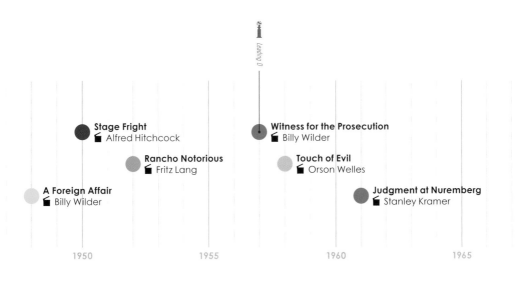

Leading 0

Stage Fright
Alfred Hitchcock

Rancho Notorious
Fritz Lang

A Foreign Affair
Billy Wilder

Witness for the Prosecution
Billy Wilder

Touch of Evil
Orson Welles

Judgment at Nuremberg
Stanley Kramer

1950   1955   1960   1965

The Blue Angel
(1930)

Morocco
(1930)

Shanghai Express
(1932)

The Scarlet Empress
(1934)

Knight Without Armour
(1937)

Destry Rides Again
(1939)

Rancho Notorious
(1952)

Witness for the Prosecution
(1957)

Dietrich as Lola Lola in **The Blue Angel**, the movie that brought her international fame. It was the start of one of the most productive pairings in cinematic history, between the actress and director Josef von Sternberg.

A studio portrait of Dietrich for **Morocco**, in the outfit in which her character scandalously kissed another woman.

Shanghai Express features Dietrich and Clive Brook as former lovers who are taken hostage by Chinese rebels seeking to overthrow the government.

Dietrich and **Morocco** costar Gary Cooper. The pair play a cabaret singer and a Legionnaire who fall in love.

As the Russian ruler Catherine the Great in **The Scarlet Empress**, Dietrich revels in sex and power.

Filmed in the UK, the expensive box-office failure **Knight Without Armour** is set against the backdrop of the Russian Revolution.

Dietrich's pairing with James Stewart in **Destry Rides Again** was one of her more successful on-screen partnerships.

In **Rancho Notorious** Dietrich plays a saloon chanteuse who oversees a combination horse ranch and criminal hideout called Chuck-a-Luck.

Dietrich and Tyrone Power in **Witness for the Prosecution**. This scene in which the actress' leg is shown was reportedly added into the script specifically for that purpose, and required 145 extras, 38 stunt men and $90,000 to film.

european stars in hollywood

Greta Garbo | Bela Lugosi | Peter Lorre | Ingrid Bergman | Sophia Loren | Max von Sydow | Alain Delon | Isabella Adjani

Film is a global art form, but if one word or one place, could sum up an entire industry, it is Hollywood. If U.S. cinema is not deemed the medium's artistic pinnacle among movie fans, it certainly maintained a cultural supremacy in 20th-century moviemaking. As a result, many of Europe's biggest stars have gone to grapple with Hollywood's "dream factory," with mixed results.

Perhaps the earliest transplanted success was Sweden's Greta Garbo. Imported by Louis B. Mayer who saw her in an early native hit, within three films, she became Hollywood's most enigmatic star and, even more impressively, survived the transition from silent movies to talkies. Indeed, her first sound film, *Anna Christie* (1930), was marketed with the tagline "Garbo talks!" Her strong accent added to her exotic allure rather than distancing her from audiences.

A decade later, her fellow countrywoman Ingrid Bergman also moved to the United States and was able to assimilate more successfully; in *Casablanca* (1942) she is the European damsel who causes Humphrey Bogart distress; but three years later, in Hitchcock's *Notorious* (1946) opposite Cary Grant, she is partly nationalized, her U.S. loyalty a central plot point. Both Bergman and her character pass the test.

Casablanca is a fascinating wider study of Europeans in Hollywood, given that three German actors all costar: Conrad Veidt, Paul Henreid and Peter Lorre. Lorre was the unforgettable child killer in Fritz Lang's *M* (1931), but with his unconventional looks and distinctive, sibilant voice, lead roles were inconceivable; instead he gave vivid support, most notably here and in *The Maltese Falcon* (1941). The tall and dashing Henreid, on the other hand, was granted romantic leads, famously lighting two cigarettes for himself and Bette Davis in *Now, Voyager* (1942). But most Europeans were restricted to supporting roles or villains, none more vividly than Hungarian Bela Lugosi, who never transcended his signature role as perhaps the screen's most iconic *Dracula* (1931).

After World War II, a flourishing Italian cinema enabled the stunning Sophia Loren to attract the attention of U.S. studios. Initially seen as a decorative beauty for light comedies like *Houseboat* (1958) with Cary Grant, she proved her dramatic credentials with her Oscar for *Two Women* (1960), the first by a performer in a foreign language.

Not every European star, though, saw Hollywood's appeal. Brigitte Bardot, France's "sex kitten" sensation showed scant interest in pursuing a Hollywood career. Likewise, Loren's male counterpart Marcello Mastroianni, seemed content to remain working for Federico Fellini and other high-profile Italian

type ■ Swedish ■ Hungarian ■ Italian/French ■ French ■ Austrian

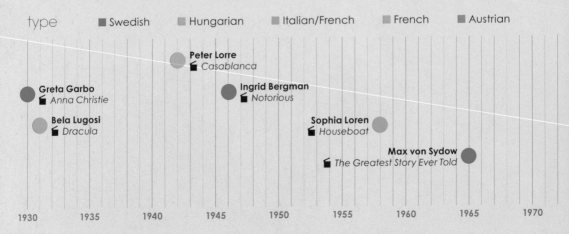

Peter Lorre
🎬 *Casablanca*

Greta Garbo
🎬 *Anna Christie*

Ingrid Bergman
🎬 *Notorious*

Bela Lugosi
🎬 *Dracula*

Sophia Loren
🎬 *Houseboat*

Max von Sydow
🎬 *The Greatest Story Ever Told*

1930 1935 1940 1945 1950 1955 1960 1965 1970

| Arnold Schwarze-negger | Gerard Dépardieu | Jean Reno | Antonio Banderas | Juliette Binoche | Javier Bardem | Marion Cotillard | Christoph Waltz |

directors. Perhaps one cannot blame them — French heartthrob Alain Delon could make gangster classic *Le Samouraï* (1967) in Europe. His U.S. equivalent: lackluster hit man thriller *Scorpio* (1973). Some were more fortunate. Max von Sydow's noble suffering for Ingmar Bergman presumably helped cast him as Jesus Christ in *The Greatest Story Ever Told* (1965) and later the title role, in horror blockbuster *The Exorcist* (1973).

From the 1970s onward, one sensed a greater ambivalence among European actors to "cross over." French stars like Isabelle Adjani (in stripped-down chase movie *The Driver*, 1978) or Gérard Depardieu (in rom-com *Green Card*, 1990) remained resolutely occasional guests in U.S. cinema. Ironically, the least talented actor of them all, became Hollywood's biggest foreign success. Arnold Schwarzenegger appeared stymied by his physique and impenetrable Teutonic accent; playing a killer cyborg in *The Terminator* (1984) seemed his limit. Yet Schwarzenegger's fan base widened so much that, by the time of *Total Recall* (1990), he could play an American everyman, despite that accent. In fact, post-Schwarzenegger, Hollywood seemed generally more receptive to foreign bodies. France's Jean Reno used Luc Besson's New York-set thriller *Leon* (1994) to springboard into mainstream films like *Mission:*

Impossible (1996). Spain's Antonio Banderas went from kinky Almodóvar dramas to action hero in *Desperado* (1995). Yet if these actors' popularity increased, their thespian skills were rarely challenged. In terms of acting credibility, actresses fared better. Juliette Binoche could pick and choose her English-language roles (winning an Oscar for *The English Patient*, 1996); and her compatriot Marion Cotillard, another Oscar-winner for Edith Piaf biopic *La Vie en Rose* (2007), is able to flit between European — and U.S. — arthouse and major films like Christopher Nolan's *Inception* (2010), where her nationality is not hugely significant.

Cotillard's male equivalent is arguably Spain's Javier Bardem, another actor comfortable with searing native dramas but whose chilling, Oscar-winning role in the Coen brothers' *No Country for Old Men* (2007) is as an avenging angel of death. Bardem's follow-up bad guy was *Skyfall*'s (2012) Bond villain; a mantle now taken on in *Spectre* (2015) by Austria's Christoph Waltz, an Oscar-winner himself for roles in Tarantino's *Inglourious Basterds* (2009) and *Django Unchained* (2012). European actors playing Bond villains is nothing new but casting actors of Bardem and Waltz's stature, it is Bond and thereby Hollywood which benefits most from this stronger European union. **LS**

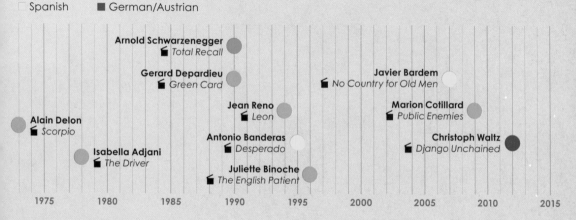

☐ Spanish   ■ German/Austrian

Arnold Schwarzenegger
Total Recall

Gerard Depardieu
Green Card

Javier Bardem
No Country for Old Men

Jean Reno
Leon

Marion Cotillard
Public Enemies

Alain Delon
Scorpio

Antonio Banderas
Desperado

Christoph Waltz
Django Unchained

Isabella Adjani
The Driver

Juliette Binoche
The English Patient

| 1975 | 1980 | 1985 | 1990 | 1995 | 2000 | 2005 | 2010 | 2015 |

divine 1945–88

Mondo
Trasho

Multiple
Maniacs

Pink
Flamingos

Female
Trouble

Tally Brown,
New York

Polyester

Lust in the
Dust

Hairspray

Despite his on-screen appearances being almost exclusively confined to the subversive cinema of cult filmmaker John Waters, drag queen Divine has become a household name, thanks to his anarchic humor, outrageous behavior and iconic sense of style.

Born in Baltimore in 1945, Harris Glenn Milstead began his acting career as one of the "Dreamlanders," the affectionate name given to John Waters' loyal troupe of regular contributors. He first appeared in the short films Roman Candles (1966) and Eat Your Makeup (1968), before graduating to underground feature films such as Mondo Trasho (1969) and Multiple Maniacs (1970). But it was in Waters' infamous Pink Flamingos (1972) that the cult of Divine was truly born, with his lead role as a criminal "filthmonger" forever cementing his place in trash cinema history.

Always more than a mere shock merchant, Divine continued to expand his acting range with subsequent collaborations with Waters, be it his riotous portrayal of tearaway delinquent Dawn Davenport on Female Trouble (1974) or his unexpectedly moving turn as downtrodden housewife Francine Fishpaw in comedic melodrama Polyester (1981), which gives us an idea of how a Douglas Sirk picture starring Divine might have looked. Divine also found time in between to make an appearance in prolific documentarian Rosa von Praunheim's Tally Brown, New York (1979).

Divine took a break from film in the early 1980s, instead devoting time to a moderately successful sideline in Hi-NRG club hits, and embarking on a world tour. His subsequent return to the screen was not for John Waters, but a leading role in Paul Bartel's Lust in the Dust (1985), which saw Divine reunited with his Polyester costar Tab Hunter. A bawdy Wild-West pastiche that was largely overlooked on its initial release, it has since gone on to achieve some cult notoriety.

Divine reteamed with Waters to make Hairspray (1988), which would prove to be both the director and star's breakthrough hit. Set in Baltimore in 1962 and telling the story of teenager Tracy Turnblad's (Ricki Lake) fight against racial inequality after landing a spot on a local television dance show, it was eventually adapted into a Broadway musical, which in turn was given a Hollywood makeover in 2007, albeit with a dragged up John Travolta taking Divine's role as Tracy's overbearing mother Edna. Sadly, Divine was not around to see the impact of the film. He tragically died in his sleep of heart failure just three weeks after the movie was released. He was 42.

The story of Divine's life and career has been well documented, both in print and on film, most notably in the documentaries Divine Trash (1998) and I Am Divine (2013), both of which paint affectionate tributes to the trailblazing icon. **MB**

genre   ■ Comedy   ■ Documentary

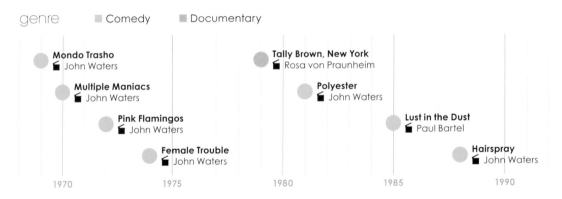

Mondo Trasho
John Waters

Multiple Maniacs
John Waters

Pink Flamingos
John Waters

Female Trouble
John Waters

Tally Brown, New York
Rosa von Praunheim

Polyester
John Waters

Lust in the Dust
Paul Bartel

Hairspray
John Waters

1970   1975   1980   1985   1990

kirk douglas 1916

The Strange Love of Martha Ivers

Champion

Ace in the Hole

The Bad and the Beautiful

Lust for Life

Paths of Glory

Spartacus

Lonely Are the Brave

In 1991, at the age of 75, Kirk Douglas was sole survivor of a helicopter crash that left him with a debilitating back injury. Four years later he suffered a stroke that impaired his speech. In 2004, aged 88, he starred in his last film (to date). For an actor who based his long career largely on playing tough, driven, unstoppable characters, such resilience seems apt.

Douglas was born Issur Danielovitch Demsky in New York, the son of Russian-Jewish immigrants, and acted in theater before wartime service in the U.S. Navy. Discharged, he made his screen debut as Barbara Stanwyck's alcoholic husband in *The Strange Love of Martha Ivers* (1946), then hit his groove as a double-crossing gang boss in the noir *Out of the Past* (1947). He had his first teaming with Burt Lancaster in *I Walk Alone* (1948) and played one of the possibly unfaithful husbands in *A Letter to Three Wives* (1949) before his first top-billing as a boxer in *Champion* (1949).

Billy Wilder's *Ace in the Hole* (1951), possibly the sourest movie ever to come out of Hollywood, was tailor-made for him. Douglas, at his most abrasive, played a reptilian reporter who happens across a man trapped in an underground crevice, and slows the rescue bid to make himself a bigger story.

He was a tough, unscrupulous cop in William Wyler's *Detective Story* (1951), and on best vulpine form for *The Bad and the Beautiful* (1952), as a ruthless, once all-powerful producer on the skids. His clenched intensity fitted him for Van Gogh in *Lust for Life* (1956), and he was well matched with Lancaster in *Gunfight at the O.K. Corral* (1957). One of his best roles was in *Paths of Glory* (1957); Douglas turned in a searing performance as the officer defending three French privates court martialled and shot as random scapegoats during World War I.

Suffering suited him. He had an eye torn out as leader of *The Vikings* (1958) and got crucified as the rebel slave *Spartacus* (1960). In the modern-day western *Lonely Are the Brave* (1962) he was a cowboy finally run over by a truckload of toilets. With Lancaster again he was one of a group of military top brass scheming to overthrow the president in *In Harm's Way* (1964), and *The Heroes of Telemark* (1965) found him as a Norwegian patriot fighting the German occupation.

Good roles tailed off after the mid-1960s, though he gave a relishable performance as a prisoner set on escaping in Joseph Mankiewicz's cynical western *There Was a Crooked Man...* (1970). But he never lacked for assignments, always remaining watchable. **PK**

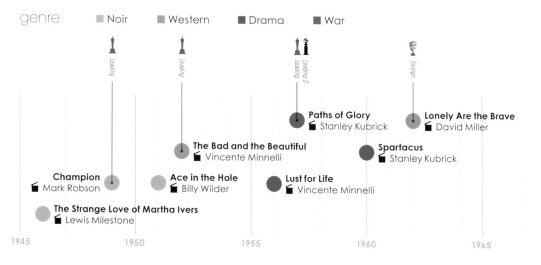

genre ■ Noir ■ Western ■ Drama ■ War

Paths of Glory
🎬 Stanley Kubrick

Lonely Are the Brave
🎬 David Miller

The Bad and the Beautiful
🎬 Vincente Minnelli

Spartacus
🎬 Stanley Kubrick

Champion
🎬 Mark Robson

Ace in the Hole
🎬 Billy Wilder

Lust for Life
🎬 Vincente Minnelli

The Strange Love of Martha Ivers
🎬 Lewis Milestone

1945   1950   1955   1960   1965

michael douglas 1944

| Coma | The China Syndrome | The Star Chamber | Romancing the Stone | Fatal Attraction | Wall Street | The War of the Roses | Basic Instinct |

The epitome of Hollywood royalty, Michael Douglas has taken on a variety of guises, from the scion of liberal Hollywood to a series of morally compromised characters, finally ending up, like his father Kirk, as an elder statesmen of the movie industry.

Douglas' key breakthrough was on the small screen. Although he had appeared in a few films it was as Inspector Steve Kellor, the enthusiastic young police officer in *The Streets of San Francisco* (1972–76), that he made his name. At the same time, he won an Oscar for co-producing *One Flew Over the Cuckoo's Nest* (1975). He would intermittently continue to produce films, half of which he has appeared in.

The actor's first major big-screen role was as the boyfriend of a doctor who believes there is a conspiracy to harm patients at the hospital they both work at, in *Coma* (1978). He followed it with *The China Syndrome* (1979), playing the television cameraman who follows Jane Fonda's journalist into the control room of a nuclear power station, which has been overtaken by Jack Lemmon's distraught engineer. Released just a few weeks before the Three Mile Island nuclear accident, the movie became the first of many controversial films Douglas has been attached to.

In *The Star Chamber* (1983), which features his first notable leading role, Douglas plays a crusading circuit judge who uncovers a vigilante kangaroo court set up by his colleagues. However, it was his turn as the dashing, self-centered, but wildly heroic Jack T. Colton in the enjoyable *Indiana Jones* rip-off *Romancing the Stone* (1984) that Douglas found fame with international audiences. Costar Kathleen Turner and close friend Danny DeVito returned for a sequel, *The Jewel of the Nile* (1985). There was a strong chemistry between the actors, which would see them reunite for the blackly comical divorce comedy *The War of the Roses* (1989). Directed by DeVito, it charts the relationship between Oliver and Barbara, from their first encounter to the eventual violence, albeit comical, that erupts when both refuse to leave the house they built together. Douglas, initially playing Oliver as a likeable rogue, is impressive as the pathetic, petty-minded divorcee. It was an extension of the two career-defining roles that not only brought him universal acclaim, but in many ways helped to define 1980s American cinema.

Dan Gallagher in *Fatal Attraction* (1987) and Gordon Gekko in *Wall Street* (1987) forever changed

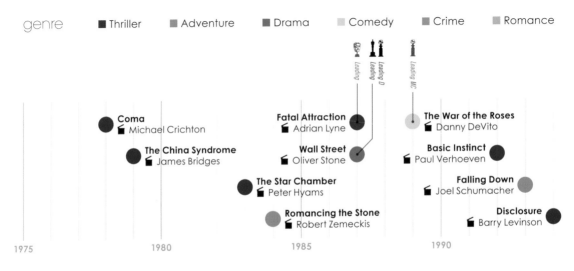

genre ■ Thriller ■ Adventure ■ Drama ■ Comedy ■ Crime ■ Romance

Coma Michael Crichton
The China Syndrome James Bridges
The Star Chamber Peter Hyams
Romancing the Stone Robert Zemeckis
Fatal Attraction Adrian Lyne
Wall Street Oliver Stone
The War of the Roses Danny DeVito
Basic Instinct Paul Verhoeven
Falling Down Joel Schumacher
Disclosure Barry Levinson

1975   1980   1985   1990

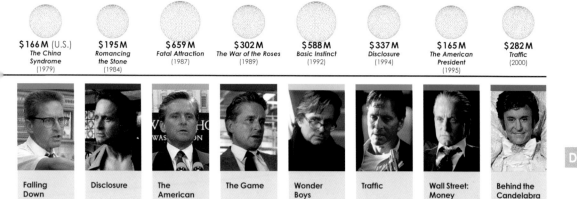

$166M (U.S.)	$195M	$659M	$302M	$588M	$337M	$165M	$282M
The China Syndrome (1979)	Romancing the Stone (1984)	Fatal Attraction (1987)	The War of the Roses (1989)	Basic Instinct (1992)	Disclosure (1994)	The American President (1995)	Traffic (2000)

Falling Down

Disclosure

The American President

The Game

Wonder Boys

Traffic

Wall Street: Money Never Sleeps

Behind the Candelabra

D

Douglas' screen persona. If Kirk had always been associated with darker roles, some critics had viewed his son as a lightweight. *Fatal Attraction* tapped into the shifting mores of Ronald Reagan's America, with the story of a happily married man who is tempted into an affair with Glen Close's psychotic vamp. If the film has not dated well, Douglas' performance as a man attempting to salvage his family life is impressive. He is even better as the pantomime villain of Oliver Stone's financial drama. A moral tale about greed and capitalism run wild, the film was embraced by the people it was meant to damn, but Douglas provides malevolent fun as the head of an empire that feeds off the hopes and dreams of blue collar Americans.

Basic Instinct (1992) provided Douglas with another controversial and memorable role, playing the sleazy cop drawn into the world of Sharon Stone's suspected killer. Its dubious gender politics notwithstanding, the film is a slick, visually striking thriller. *Disclosure* (1994) also explored gender relations in the workplace and Douglas once again portrays a character overtaken by his libido. He was better in *Falling Down* (1993), as an office worker driven to extreme measures by his inability to cope with life in the modern world.

By the time *The American President* (1995) was released, Douglas had not played played a straightforward good guy for some time. His role as an honest, incorruptible POTUS was a pleasant surprise and is a charming, witty turn. Likewise, his Nicholas Van Orten, the successful yet vexed corporate head in David Fincher's *The Game* (1997), offered another opportunity to play a — mostly — good guy.

In 2000, Douglas gave two of his best performances, as a drug tsar coming to terms with his own daughter's addiction in Steven Soderbergh's *Traffic* and as Grady Tripp, a university professor whose life is in free-fall, in Curtis Hanson's hilarious adaptation of Michael Chabon's *Wonder Boys*. The next 10 years are populated by smaller roles and a series of minor films, as well as the unnecessary sequel *Wall Street: Money Never Sleeps* (2010). More recently, there was a small cameo in Soderbergh's *Haywire* (2011) and the uneven *Last Vegas* (2013). However, Douglas' Liberace in Soderbergh's *Behind the Candelabra* (2013) is revelatory. Made after the actor was treated for cancer, it is an astonishing performance that places him alongside his father as a star with considerable range and depth. **IHS**

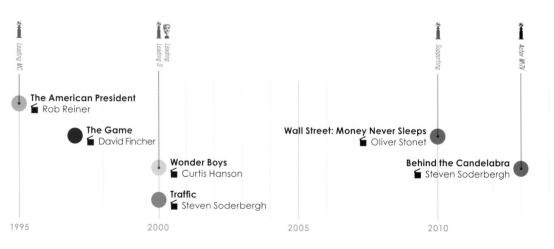

Leading MC

Leading
Leading D

Supporting

Actor MTV

The American President
Rob Reiner

The Game
David Fincher

Wonder Boys
Curtis Hanson

Traffic
Steven Soderbergh

Wall Street: Money Never Sleeps
Oliver Stonet

Behind the Candelabra
Steven Soderbergh

1995

2000

2005

2010

the star as superhero

| George Reeves | Christopher Reeves | Ray Wise | Michael Keaton | Billy Campbell | Brandon Lee | Hugh Jackman | Tobey Maguire |

Recently, superhero films have evolved into something akin to a postmodern mythology, with spandex-clad vigilantes morphing into the gods of contemporary society, displayed on the big screen with all their flaws and limitations erased. Like the Greek deities before them, their tales of heroism act to guide human behavior, teaching us right from wrong and allowing us to rise above the restrictions of our mortal form.

Superheroes rose to prominence during World War II, as evinced by novelist Michael Chabon's homage to the form, *The Amazing Adventures of Kavalier & Clay*. Born on the pages of comic books, these flamboyant soldiers of fortune were instantly adapted into radio and television plays. The first live-action superhero movie was *Superman and the Mole-Men* (1951) starring George Reeves. He was later played by Ben Affleck in *Hollywoodland* (2006) — a fictionalized account of Reeves' subsequent downfall.

The first major attempt at a respectable superhero — the 1966 movie version of the television series *Batman* does not quite count — was Richard Donner's *Superman* (1978). Its popularity sparked three sequels starring Christopher Reeve, although only *Superman II* (1980) remains watchable. Moreover, it exists in that rare category of sequels that are regarded as better

than the original, mostly thanks to Terence Stamp's enjoyably hammy portrayal of General Zod. It was not until Zac Snyder's somber *Man of Steel* (2013), starring Henry Cavill as the bulked-up superhero, that Krypton's most famous refugees faced each other again.

The 1980s were, for the most part, an arid period for decent superhero films, with Michael Crawford as *Condorman* (1981) and Tim Robbins probably wishing he never agreed to appear in *Howard the Duck* (1986). Only Wes Craven's *Swamp Thing* (1982) showed any understanding of the genre, balancing laughs with thrills and starring future *Twin Peaks* villain Ray Wise as the eponymous hero.

Tim Burton's brooding *Batman* (1989) was a huge improvement, taking the superhero movie down a new, darker direction. Starring Michael Keaton as the titular hero and Jack Nicholson as the Joker, Burton's gothic reimagining of the caped crusader was a phenomenal success. Keaton reprised the role once more with Burton, in *Batman Returns* (1992) before handing the reins over to Joel Schumacher and his stultifying, inane sequels.

The two Batman films that followed reflected a crisis in the form that would remain for the majority

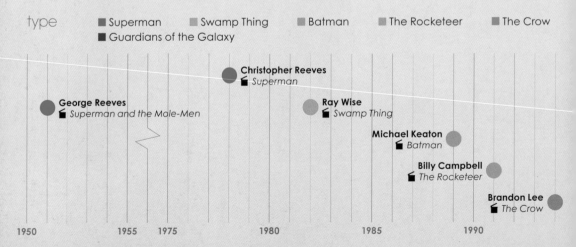

type ■ Superman ■ Swamp Thing ■ Batman ■ The Rocketeer ■ The Crow
■ Guardians of the Galaxy

Christopher Reeves
🏳 *Superman*

George Reeves
🏳 *Superman and the Mole-Men*

Ray Wise
🏳 *Swamp Thing*

Michael Keaton
🏳 *Batman*

Billy Campbell
🏳 *The Rocketeer*

Brandon Lee
🏳 *The Crow*

1950   1955   1975   1980   1985   1990

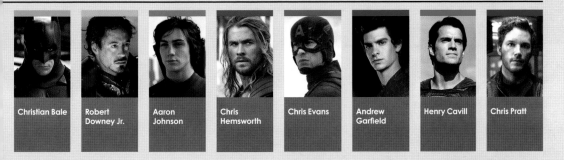

| Christian Bale | Robert Downey Jr. | Aaron Johnson | Chris Hemsworth | Chris Evans | Andrew Garfield | Henry Cavill | Chris Pratt |

of the 1990s. The woeful attempts to tackle *Captain America* (1990), *The Shadow* (1994), *Tank Girl* (1995) and *The Phantom* (1996) highlighted just how bad things were. However, there were moments of respite. *The Rocketeer* (1991) was a lovely homage to classical Hollywood, while Alex Proyas' *The Crow* (1994) gave us an unsettling apocalyptic world.

The modern-day superhero blockbuster began with Bryan Singer's *X-Men* (2000). Stage and screen heavyweights Ian McKellen and Patrick Stewart gave the film heft, while Hugh Jackman became a star, but there was also a fluidity to the drama that appealed to audiences. Sequels — including the excellent *X2* (2003) — and spin-offs followed and studios once again began to show interest in superheroes. Two years later, Sam Raimi's *Spider-Man* (2002), starring a young Tobey Maguire, became the first film to pass the $100 million mark in its opening weekend.

The genre is no longer home to B-list actors. Thanks to bigger budgets, the advancement of visual effects and studios throwing their weight behind each project, major stars now take on roles they would have balked at two decades ago. Hence character actor-turned-star Christian Bale's embracing the caped crusader in Chris Nolan's game-changing superhero movie, *Batman Begins* (2005), and its two sequels. However, it was one of Hollywood's most impressive comebacks that sent the notion of the superhero movie rocketing into the stratosphere.

Robert Downey Jr. not only recovered his star status with the hugely enjoyable *Iron Man* (2008), it launched Marvel as a major studio in its own right. The film also gave rise to one of the most successful franchises in Hollywood history — the *Avengers* series. Downey Jr. was soon followed by Chris Hemsworth in Kenneth Branagh's *Thor* (2011) and Chris Evans — formerly Human Torch in *Fantastic Four* (2005) and its 2007 sequel — in *Captain America: The First Avenger* (2011), with both attracting huge audiences. Then came the biggest hit to date, *The Avengers* (2012). Each strand looks set to continue, although the sequels so far have varied in quality.

Not to be outdone, the *X-Men* franchise continues, looking back and forth in time, while Batman, who appeared to hang up his cape in Nolan's *The Dark Knight Rises* (2012), returns in 2016 in *Batman v Superman: Dawn of Justice*. If all that sounds just a little too serious, we can thank *Guardians of the Galaxy* (2014) for proving that saving the universe does not mean you can't have fun. **PG**

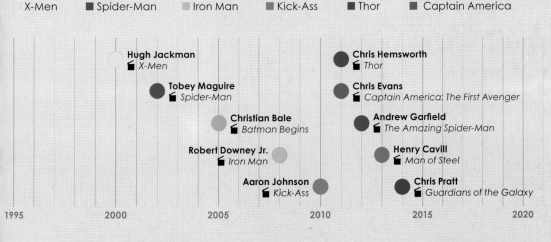

X-Men ■ Spider-Man Iron Man ■ Kick-Ass ■ Thor ■ Captain America

Hugh Jackman
X-Men

Tobey Maguire
Spider-Man

Christian Bale
Batman Begins

Robert Downey Jr.
Iron Man

Aaron Johnson
Kick-Ass

Chris Hemsworth
Thor

Chris Evans
Captain America: The First Avenger

Andrew Garfield
The Amazing Spider-Man

Henry Cavill
Man of Steel

Chris Pratt
Guardians of the Galaxy

1995   2000   2005   2010   2015   2020

robert downey jr. 1965

| Less Than Zero | Chaplin | Short Cuts | Natural Born Killers | Only You | Richard III | One Night Stand | Wonder Boys |

Robert Downey Jr.'s ascent from erratic talent to creative liability to a Marvel Comics franchise hero has been powered by his impressive comic sensibility and on-screen charm. His witty way with one-liners and a hearty helping of luck and friendship have made him one of Hollywood's highest-paid stars.

He was born into film, the son of underground filmmaker, Robert Downey Sr. His debut was in his father's *Pound* (1970), playing a puppy at the age of 5. His first substantial film role was as Julian in the adaptation of Bret Easton-Ellis' era-defining novel *Less Than Zero* (1987). A prophetic role for the actor, Downey Jr. has since likened the part to playing "the ghost of Christmas future," with Julian's destructive drug problem pre-dating Downey's own by a mere few years. It is one of his most haunting performances.

The actor's profile continued to grow, albeit with mixed results. Downey Jr. was the beating heart of the amiable fantasy comedy *Chances Are* (1989), but he was eclipsed by costar James Woods in *True Believer* (1989). In the mega-budget *Air America* (1990) he had equal billing with Mel Gibson, but the film crashed with critics and audiences. After appearing in the ensemble comedy *Soapdish* (1991), Downey Jr. played the titular role in Richard Attenborough's affectionate biopic *Chaplin* (1992). The actor's considerable effort in bringing the silent star to life was rewarded with an Oscar nomination for Best Actor.

More fine performances followed. He was at his narcissistic best in Robert Altman's *Short Cuts* (1993), while his self-obsessed television journalist in Oliver Stone's *Natural Born Killers* (1994) gave him one of his first over-the-top roles. However, as the actor's drug problems increased, his star began to wane.

He is magnetic as the love rat in James Toback's *Two Girls and a Guy* (1997) and offers a moving cameo as Wesley Snipes' HIV-positive dancer friend in Mike Figgis' *One Night Stand* (1997). However, he hit his creative nadir with *U.S. Marshals* (1998), his opinion of which is unequivocal: "I'd rather wake up in jail for a TB test than have to wake up another morning knowing I'm going to the set of *U.S. Marshals*."

He fared better as Michael Douglas' literary agent in *Wonder Boys* (2000), a role that channeled his

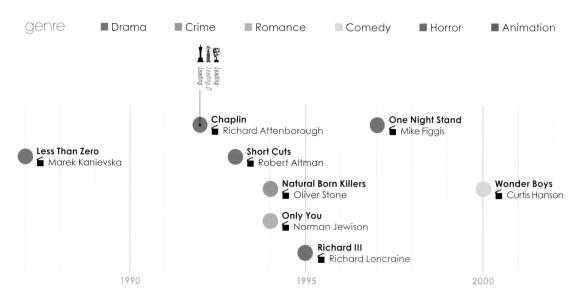

genre ■ Drama ■ Crime ■ Romance ☐ Comedy ■ Horror ■ Animation

Less Than Zero
Marek Kanievska

Chaplin
Richard Attenborough

Short Cuts
Robert Altman

Natural Born Killers
Oliver Stone

Only You
Norman Jewison

Richard III
Richard Loncraine

One Night Stand
Mike Figgis

Wonder Boys
Curtis Hanson

1990   1995   2000

$80M (U.S.)	$46M	$66M	$97M	$207M	$643M	$578M	$1.6BN
Natural Born Killers (1994)	Wonder Boys (2000)	Good Night, and Good Luck (2005)	Zodiac (2007)	Tropic Thunder (2008)	Iron Man (2008)	Sherlock Holmes (2009)	Avengers Assemble (2012)

Kiss Kiss Bang Bang

Good Night, and Good Luck

A Scanner Darkly

Zodiac

Tropic Thunder

Iron Man

Sherlock Holmes

Avengers Assemble

nervous energy. But further drug problems and jail time took him away from the screen and made him a liability for any studio. He enjoyed a brief comeback on the television show *Ally McBeal* (2000–02) before he was fired, again the result of his addiction.

By the time he had cleaned up, Downey Jr. had trouble finding work. It was his friend Mel Gibson who offered insurance against his appearance in *The Singing Detective* (2003). This time his recovery seemed permanent. It was accompanied by some of his best roles. He riffed off Val Kilmer, creating a strange, intoxicating chemistry in Shane Black's surreal murder mystery comedy *Kiss Kiss Bang Bang* (2005); he is amusing in Steven Soderbergh's section of *Eros* (2004); charming as Patricia Clarkson's secret partner in *Good Night, and Good Luck* (2005); and oddly compelling in Rotoscope form in Richard Linklater's *A Scanner Darkly* (2006). However, it was as the self-destructive crime reporter in David Fincher's serial killer procedural, *Zodiac* (2007), that Downey Jr. not only showed he was back for good, but also revealed new depths to his performance.

In *Iron Man* (2008), Jon Favreau saw in Downey Jr. the perfect actor to play the egotistical genius Tony Stark. It was inspired casting and the film's success assured the actor's star status. He gained muscle for *Iron Man 2* (2010), which lacked the first film's bite, before reuniting with Shane Black for the smart *Iron Man 3* (2013). Tony Stark is also the main draw of *Avengers Assemble* (2012) and leads the team of legendary superheroes in its sequel *Avengers: Age of Ultron* (2015).

In one of his most outrageous roles, Downey Jr. "blacked up" to play Kirk Lazarus, an Australian Method actor who adopts an extreme procedure in order to get into character in Ben Stiller's madcap parody of Vietnam war movies, *Tropic Thunder* (2008). Another franchise beckoned with the enjoyable big-budget revamp of Arthur Conan Doyle's detective *Sherlock Holmes* (2009) and its 2011 sequel.

Along with his ability to command enormous fees and with huge appeal to audiences of both sexes, he is one of the biggest stars in Hollywood. His is the perfect Hollywood story of the incendiary talent who almost lost everything, only to come back in style. **SMK**

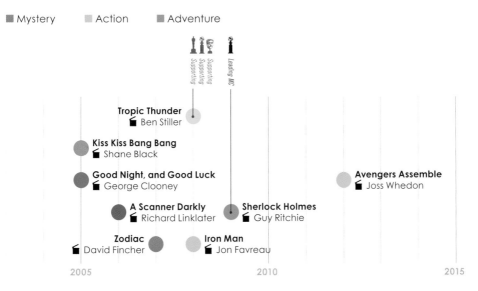

■ Mystery   ■ Action   ■ Adventure

Supporting
Supporting
Supporting

Leading MC

Tropic Thunder
Ben Stiller

Kiss Kiss Bang Bang
Shane Black

Good Night, and Good Luck
George Clooney

Avengers Assemble
Joss Whedon

A Scanner Darkly
Richard Linklater

Sherlock Holmes
Guy Ritchie

Zodiac
David Fincher

Iron Man
Jon Favreau

2005   2010   2015

richard dreyfuss 1947

| American Graffiti | Dillinger | The Apprenticeship of Duddy Kravitz | Jaws | Victory at Entebbe | The Goodbye Girl | Close Encounters of the Third Kind | Whose Life Is it Anyway? |

Richard Dreyfuss was one of the leading young actors of the 1970s. Associated with a run of films that brought to the screen a more adult, politically aware sense of realism, he was a key figure in the New Hollywood era. But while he headed up two of the decade's biggest hits, he was less a star than a character actor. A chameleon talent with a gift for comedy, Dreyfuss remains one of Hollywood's most assured actors.

The New York-born Dreyfuss was an experienced stage actor before he made his screen debut. Among his early roles was an uncredited appearance in *The Graduate* (1967). Compact in stature with a look of boyish enthusiasm, in 1973 he was cast as the tellingly named "Baby Face" Nelson in the Depression-era gangster drama *Dillinger*. And that same year, when the actor was in his early twenties, he impressed as the hero of George Lucas' 1962-set coming-of-age drama *American Graffiti*, evoking the guileless idealism of pre-Vietnam War teenage culture.

He was even more striking in the comedy-drama *The Apprenticeship of Duddy Kravitz* (1974), playing a restless young man from Montreal's Jewish community, on the hustle for ideas to make money. Canada's most commercially successful film at the time, it explored with unusual richness and sensitivity the Jewish immigrant experience. Dreyfuss was a revelation, bringing to the role a nervous energy and rough, unstoppable charm that got him noticed.

In his best performances from this era, Dreyfuss combined this jumpy charisma with an ordinary-Joe affability. In Steven Spielberg's spectacular 1975 breakthrough, *Jaws*, he was appealingly vulnerable as a marine scientist, lending the film an emotional credibility that is as key to its success as Spielberg's masterly control of suspense. Reuniting with the director for *Close Encounters of the Third Kind* (1977), Dreyfuss was compelling as a family man whose life is upended when he witnesses the flight of a UFO.

The success of Dreyfuss' collaborations with Spielberg established him as a major Hollywood player, a status confirmed by his appearance alongside such legendary actors as Burt Lancaster and Kirk Douglas in the true-life hostage drama *Victory at Entebbe* (1976). And he was warmly convincing in

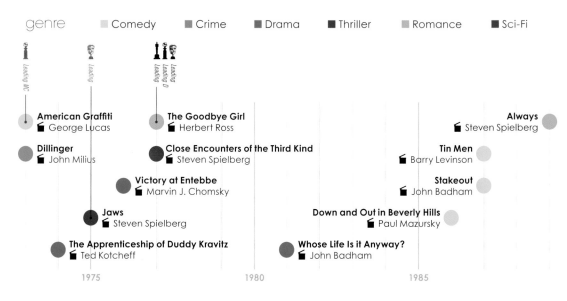

genre   ■ Comedy   ■ Crime   ■ Drama   ■ Thriller   ■ Romance   ■ Sci-Fi

Leading MC
Leading
Leading
Leading D
Leading

American Graffiti
George Lucas

Dillinger
John Milius

The Apprenticeship of Duddy Kravitz
Ted Kotcheff

Jaws
Steven Spielberg

The Goodbye Girl
Herbert Ross

Close Encounters of the Third Kind
Steven Spielberg

Victory at Entebbe
Marvin J. Chomsky

Whose Life Is it Anyway?
John Badham

Down and Out in Beverly Hills
Paul Mazursky

Always
Steven Spielberg

Tin Men
Barry Levinson

Stakeout
John Badham

1975   1980   1985

| $613M (U.S.)
American Graffiti
(1973) | $2BN
Jaws
(1975) | $1.2BN
Close Encounters
of the Third Kind
(1977) | $137M (U.S.)
Stakeout
(1987) | $142M
Always
(1989) | $165M
Mr. Holland's Opus
(1995) | $168M
The American
President
(1995) | $216M
RED
(2010) |

Down and Out in Beverly Hills — **Tin Men** — **Stakeout** — **Always** — **What About Bob?** — **Mr. Holland's Opus** — **The American President** — **RED**

a romantic role, as a struggling actor who falls for a recently jilted dancer in Neil Simon's 1977 comedy *The Goodbye Girl*, winning a Best Actor Oscar.

In the years that followed, however, he struggled to match his earlier success. Dreyfuss' intelligent, emotionally detailed approach to performance was arguably more suited to the character-led drama of the 1970s than the high-concept, effect-heavy fare the studios were focusing on in the early 1980s. His publicized addiction to cocaine did not help either.

But by the mid-1980s, Dreyfuss scored a significant comeback with the acclaimed comedy *Down and Out in Beverly Hills* (1986). He played a rich businessman who saves a penniless drifter from suicide, offering him a home in his family mansion. It is an immensely likeable performance, perfectly attuned to the film's atmosphere of breakneck satire. Aside from a muted reunion with Spielberg for the sentimental drama *Always* (1989), Dreyfuss spent the next few years focusing on modestly budgeted, character-driven, grown-up comedies: notably, *Tin Men* (1987), as an aluminum salesman whose rival is

Danny DeVito; and *Stakeout* (1987), a slick cop movie in which he was partnered with Emilio Estevez. A standout was *What About Bob?* (1991), in which he played a psychoanalyst pushed to the limits of his sanity by patient Bill Murray. Dreyfuss' exquisite comic timing is an exemplary foil to Murray's exuberance.

By the 1990s, Dreyfuss was largely seen in supporting roles, his lead performance in *Mr. Holland's Opus* (1995) being a notable exception. This Oscar-nominated account of one man's life work was a stirring reminder of Dreyfuss' own accomplishment, and if he has acquired a certain eminence as an actor, he also continues to take risks: building on his role as an untrustworthy political operator in *The American President* (1995), he gave a cutting impersonation of Dick Cheney in the George Bush biopic *W.* (2008).

In 2010 Dreyfuss starred in the action film *RED*. The cast was a roll call of some of the finest screen actors and stars of their generation, including Bruce Willis, Helen Mirren, Morgan Freeman and John Malkovich, an ensemble among which Dreyfuss has rightfully earned his place. **EL**

■ Action

Leading D
Leading

What About Bob?
🎬 Frank Oz

Mr. Holland's Opus
🎬 Stephen Herek

The American President
🎬 Rob Reiner

RED
🎬 Robert Schwentke

1990   1995   2000   2010

faye dunaway 1941

| Hurry Sundown | Bonnie and Clyde | The Thomas Crown Affair | Puzzle of a Downfall Child | Little Big Man | The Three Musketeers | Chinatown | The Towering Inferno |

Faye Dunaway rose to prominence during one of the strongest periods in American filmmaking. Renowned for playing cool, complex and forthright characters, her natural confidence meant she skipped ingénue roles and began her career seemingly fully formed.

Born in Bascome, Florida, in 1941, Dunaway's first role was a small part in *The Happening* (1967). Shortly afterward she appeared in Otto Preminger's *Hurry Sundown* (1967). She had signed a five-film contract with the director, but after the pair clashed during the troubled production she sued him to be released from it.

Later that year, Dunaway starred opposite Warren Beatty in *Bonnie and Clyde* (1967), Arthur Penn's crime drama about the infamous outlaws. An early film of the New Hollywood era, the movie became a milestone for its frank depiction of sex and violence, as well as for managing to be both hugely popular and critically acclaimed. The chemistry of the leads resonated with an emerging young audience, and Dunaway received one of the film's 10 Oscar nominations.

Dunaway next starred opposite another swaggering leading man in *The Thomas Crown Affair* (1968). Displaying her signature icy reserve, she plays an insurance investigator whose attempts to bring wealthy bank robber Steve McQueen to justice are complicated by their illicit affair. The film was a commercial success. Despite being directed by Vittorio De Sica, John Frankenheimer and Elia Kazan respectively, *A Place for Lovers* (1968), *The Extraordinary Seaman* (1969) and *The Arrangement* (1969) were creative and commercial failures. However, working again with Penn, she starred with Dustin Hoffman in the ambitious western *Little Big Man* (1970). A revisionist take on the genre, it struck a chord with critics and audiences, and was a runaway hit.

The same year she gave one of her best performances as an unstable fashion model in the little-seen *Puzzle of a Downfall Child* (1970). Other roles from this time include *The Deadly Trap* (1971), *"Doc"* (1971), *Oklahoma Crude* (1973) and Richard Lester's inventive retelling of *The Three Musketeers* (1973), plus its sequel, *The Four Musketeers* (1974).

In the superlative neo-noir *Chinatown* (1974), director Roman Polanski cast Dunaway in the crucial

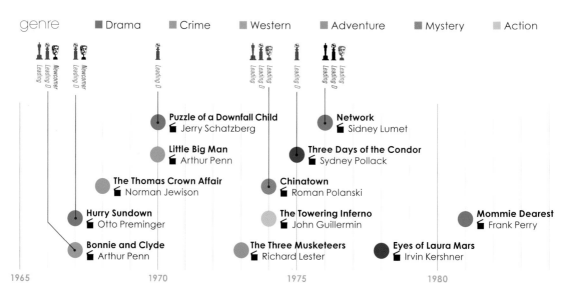

genre   ■ Drama   ■ Crime   ■ Western   ■ Adventure   ■ Mystery   ■ Action

Newcomer / Leading D / Leading
Newcomer / Leading D
Leading D
Leading D / Leading D / Leading
Leading D
Leading D / Leading D / Leading

Puzzle of a Downfall Child
Jerry Schatzberg

Network
Sidney Lumet

Little Big Man
Arthur Penn

Three Days of the Condor
Sydney Pollack

The Thomas Crown Affair
Norman Jewison

Chinatown
Roman Polanski

Hurry Sundown
Otto Preminger

The Towering Inferno
John Guillermin

Mommie Dearest
Frank Perry

Bonnie and Clyde
Arthur Penn

The Three Musketeers
Richard Lester

Eyes of Laura Mars
Irvin Kershner

1965   1970   1975   1980

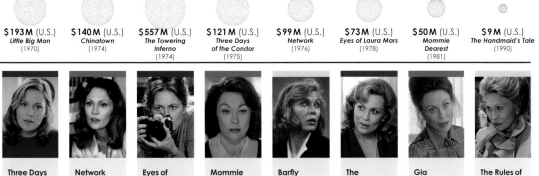

$193M (U.S.)	$140M (U.S.)	$557M (U.S.)	$121M (U.S.)	$99M (U.S.)	$73M (U.S.)	$50M (U.S.)	$9M (U.S.)
Little Big Man (1970)	*Chinatown* (1974)	*The Towering Inferno* (1974)	*Three Days of the Condor* (1975)	*Network* (1976)	*Eyes of Laura Mars* (1978)	*Mommie Dearest* (1981)	*The Handmaid's Tale* (1990)

Three Days of the Condor · **Network** · **Eyes of Laura Mars** · **Mommie Dearest** · **Barfly** · **The Handmaid's Tale** · **Gia** · **The Rules of Attraction**

role of Evelyn Mulwray, an apparent femme fatale harboring a dark secret. Like *Bonnie and Clyde*, *Chinatown* was set during the wild, impoverished 1930s, a period to which she seemed uniquely suited. The perfectly constructed film is one of the finest pictures of its era, the plot depending upon her layered, Oscar-nominated performance. As she had with Otto Preminger on *Hurry Sundown*, Dunaway fought with Polanski throughout, acquiring a reputation for being tough to work with that would hinder her efforts to find good material later in her career.

Dunaway's third major film in 1974 was as part of the all-star cast of *The Towering Inferno*, a massive hit that that chased the trend for ensemble disaster movies, although she did not have much to do in the film. More substantial roles followed as a woman kidnapped by on-the-run CIA analyst Robert Redford in *Three Days of the Condor* (1975) and as a brilliant, calculating, ratings-fixated television executive in the fine Sidney Lumet-directed satire *Network* (1976).

After winning a Best Actress Oscar for *Network*, Dunaway went on to star in *Voyage of the Damned* (1976), *Eyes of Laura Mars* (1978), slushy remake *The Champ* (1979) and *The First Deadly Sin* (1980). The latter two films were particularly poorly received, as was the most notorious film in her career, *Mommie Dearest* (1981), based on Christina Crawford's memoir of living with her actress mother Joan Crawford. Intended as a drama, Dunaway's oversized performance lent the film an unavoidable camp quality, turning it into an inadvertent comedy.

Mommie Dearest is commonly seen as the death knell in the actor's career. She struggled to find good parts over the next two decades, appearing in such dire efforts as *The Wicked Lady* (1983), *Supergirl* (1984), *The Gamble* (1988) and *Dunston Checks In* (1996). The scope and ambition of these films dwindled year by year, but scattered throughout were tantalizing reminders of her talent: as Mickey Rourke's alcoholic lover in *Barfly* (1987), a military leader's cruel wife in *The Handmaid's Tale* (1990), a tragic modeling agent in *Gia* (1998) and a pill-popping mother in *The Rules of Attraction* (2002). Unfortunately these roles became the exception rather than the rule. **JWa**

■ Thriller   ■ Comedy   ■ Sci-fi

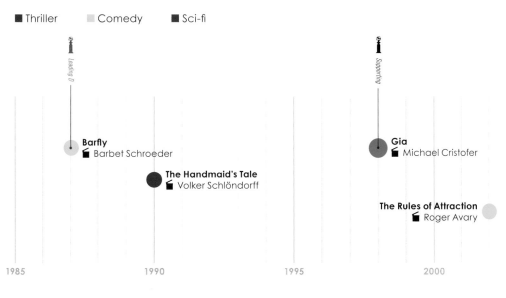

Leading D

Supporting

Barfly
Barbet Schroeder

The Handmaid's Tale
Volker Schlöndorff

Gia
Michael Cristofer

The Rules of Attraction
Roger Avary

1985 · 1990 · 1995 · 2000

cops and cinema

James Cagney | Dana Andrews | Glenn Ford | Orson Welles | Sidney Poitier | Clint Eastwood | Al Pacino | Eddie Murphy

Crime pays. Well, it does at the box office. We may like law and order in everyday life, but in the cinema it is generally the bad ass that makes the audience's collective heart beat faster. They generally get their comeuppance, but for most of a crime film's running time we get to experience the vicarious thrill of the criminal life. Which might account for why there are more films out there about criminals than there are the people catching them. (Television has always operated differently — it is hard to watch a channel for one night without witnessing a murder and the police procedural that uncovers the murderer.)

Warner Bros. understood the allure of the gangster lifestyle, even if the Hays Code insisted that order be restored by a film's end. Their biggest stars in the 1930s were all keen to play cons not cops and even when an actor like James Cagney crossed over the moral and legal divide, to play a law enforcement officer in "G" Men (1935), it felt like he only did so in order to be just as mean but with a badge justifying his actions. In fact, cops only became interesting as dramatic subjects when they were compromised, which is exactly what happened with film noir.

In the 1940s, cops suddenly became darker, more ambivalent characters in American cinema. They could be tough, as Barry Fitzgerald and Don Taylor's detectives are in Jules Dassin's The Naked City (1948). They could even be compromised, as Otto Preminger revealed in Where the Sidewalk Ends (1950). Dana Andrews plays a ruthless detective, known for his excessive violence, who kills a suspect. His actions implicate innocents and for a time it seems like he might escape punishment. In Fritz Lang's The Big Heat (1953), Glenn Ford's moral compass may point the right way but his ruthlessness is only acceptable because Lee Marvin's gang boss is so sadistic.

The last gasp of the classic noir crime period was Touch of Evil (1958), which featured one of the most corrupt cops in the genre — Orson Welles' corpulent Captain Hank Quinlan. His passing almost begged for a clean up.

There were a few years when cops returned to some kind of wholesomeness. If they were tough it was with good reason, but they were never as brutal as they had previously been. However, Norman Jewison's In the Heat of the Night (1967) shed a different light on police behavior. It pitches Sidney Poitier's good African-American cop from the city against Rod Steiger's small-town white police chief in Mississippi. Both work on the same case, but color divides them. One of the first mainstream Hollywood films to openly examine race relations in contemporary America, it

type ■ Compromised ■ Corrupt ■ African-American ■ Libertarian

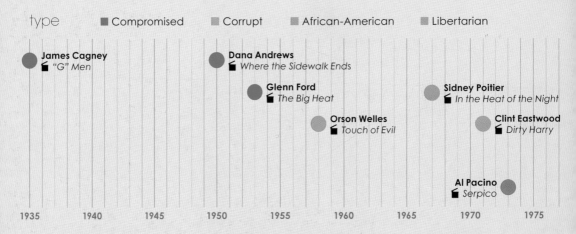

James Cagney
"G" Men

Dana Andrews
Where the Sidewalk Ends

Glenn Ford
The Big Heat

Orson Welles
Touch of Evil

Sidney Poitier
In the Heat of the Night

Clint Eastwood
Dirty Harry

Al Pacino
Serpico

1935   1940   1945   1950   1955   1960   1965   1970   1975

Jamie Lee Curtis | Harvey Keitel | Morgan Freeman | Frances McDormand | Denzel Washington | Ray Liotta | Tommy Lee Jones | Samuel L. Jackson

hinted at the complexity of the police representations that were to come in the 1970s.

If Clint Eastwood's iconic *Dirty Harry* (1971) offers up a portrait of a libertarian cop — one who believes in the innate nature of justice but eschews the limitations of the law in favor of his own moral code — then Al Pacino's *Serpico* (1973) gives us an unconventional cop who believes in rules but whose colleagues are all corrupt. Its director, Sidney Lumet, has done more than most filmmakers to explore the myriad aspects of police life.

If Sidney Poitier appeared to open the doors for African-Americans to play significant roles in films, cops were still mostly played by white actors in the 1970s — at least when it came to the main roles. Blaxploitation films featured the odd black cop, such as Yaphet Kotto in *Across 110th Street* (1972), but it was not until Eddie Murphy played Axel Foley in *Beverly Hills Cop* (1984) that a mainstream Hollywood film featured such a significant role for a black actor as a cop. A few years later, Danny Glover would share the screen with Mel Gibson in *Lethal Weapon* (1987), but in both cases the roles are comedic. Serious black cops are less common. There is Denzel Washington turning bad in some style for Antoine Fuqua's hard-hitting *Training Day* (2001) and Samuel L. Jackson's 20-year

veteran in Neil LaBute's incendiary *Lakeview Terrace* (2008) offering up a more complex representation. However, these are exceptions.

Women in cop films have also had to bear the brunt of supporting roles, although Kathryn Bigelow's *Blue Steel* (1989), starring Jamie Lee Curtis as a recent graduate pursued by Ron Silver's psychopath, was a welcome change to the norm. Also, Frances McDormand's Marge Gunderson in the Coen brothers' *Fargo* (1996) provided unquestionably one of the most memorable cops of the last two decades.

The corrupt cop still lingers, nonetheless. Washington's Alonzo Harris in *Training Day* takes some beating, while Ray Liotta is terrifying in *Narc* (2002). However, none come close to the levels of depravity demonstrated by Harvey Keitel's character in Abel Ferrara's brutal *Bad Lieutenant* (1992). The film is an assault on the senses as we witness the character's descent into hell, from which there is no redemption. Thankfully, we have the nobility of Morgan Freeman's Somerset in David Fincher's *Se7en* (1995) and Tommy Lee Jones' irascible but upstanding Sheriff Ed Tom Bell in *No Country for Old Men* (2007). Without them there would be law with no order. **IHS**

■ Unconventional □ Female ■ Noble

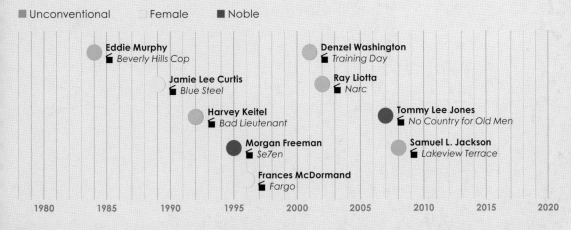

Eddie Murphy
■ *Beverly Hills Cop*

Jamie Lee Curtis
■ *Blue Steel*

Harvey Keitel
■ *Bad Lieutenant*

Morgan Freeman
■ *Se7en*

Frances McDormand
■ *Fargo*

Denzel Washington
■ *Training Day*

Ray Liotta
■ *Narc*

Tommy Lee Jones
■ *No Country for Old Men*

Samuel L. Jackson
■ *Lakeview Terrace*

1980   1985   1990   1995   2000   2005   2010   2015   2020

clint eastwood 1930

A Fistful of Dollars · **The Good, the Bad and the Ugly** · **Coogan's Bluff** · **Play Misty for Me** · **Dirty Harry** · **High Plains Drifter** · **The Outlaw Josey Wales** · **Escape from Alcatraz**

The word iconic has lost much of its power through overuse. In cinema, a star does not automatically deserve to have iconic status thrust upon them because they are a box-office success. In the western genre, there are countless heroes but arguably only two icons. John Wayne represents the old guard. And Clint Eastwood is the reactionary front. He transformed the western. For that reason, along with enduring star status, he is an icon.

Born in San Francisco, 1930, Eastwood's trademark acting style — a slightly stiff manner, narrow squint and rasping lines through his teeth — almost prevented him getting work. After a number of small movie roles, in 1958 he was cast as Rowdy Yates in the television series *Rawhide* (1959–65). A year before the series was canceled, he played the first of three roles for Italian director Sergio Leone. *A Fistful of Dollars* (1964) was a remake of Akira Kurosawa's *Yojimbo* (1961), itself an adaptation of Dashiell Hammett's 1929 novel *Red Harvest*. For Eastwood it was a chance to break away from the clean image he portrayed in *Rawhide* and for the genre as a whole it was a seismic shift, drawing a line under the conventional western, offering a less black-and-white view of the world where it is often difficult to discern between good and bad.

For a Few Dollars More (1965) broadened Leone's scope and gave Eastwood more space to develop the character of the man with no name. With *The Good, the Bad and the Ugly* (1966), the director and star's collaboration came to an end with an epic, bloody Civil War-era battle between three men for whom morality was of little concern. The three films were released in the United States over consecutive months in the spring of 1967. By the time the third part of the trilogy was screened, Eastwood was a star. *Hang 'Em High* (1968) offered another revisionist take on the western and was the first film to be co-produced by the star's own company, Malpaso Productions. It was a runaway success at the box office.

Coogan's Bluff (1968) is notable for being the first of five Eastwood films directed by Don Siegel who, along with Leone, would have a significant influence over the star's directorial style. It was also a smart way of introducing Eastwood as a contemporary hero to audiences. A western that happens to be mostly set in New York, the film features the actor as an Arizona sheriff who loses his quarry in the city and finds that his rural ways rub up against a city in the grip of cultural change. In the same year, he starred opposite Richard Burton in *Where Eagles Dare* (1968), doing little more than looking bemused.

genre ■ Western ■ Action ■ Thriller ■ Drama ■ Romance

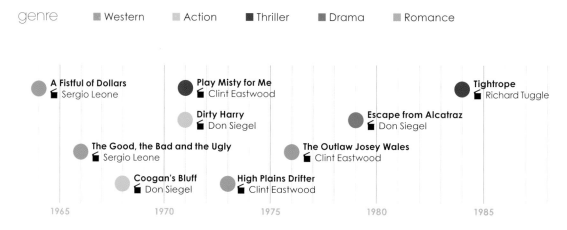

- **A Fistful of Dollars** — Sergio Leone
- **Play Misty for Me** — Clint Eastwood
- **Tightrope** — Richard Tuggle
- **Dirty Harry** — Don Siegel
- **Escape from Alcatraz** — Don Siegel
- **The Good, the Bad and the Ugly** — Sergio Leone
- **The Outlaw Josey Wales** — Clint Eastwood
- **Coogan's Bluff** — Don Siegel
- **High Plains Drifter** — Clint Eastwood

1965   1970   1975   1980   1985

| $176M (U.S.) The Good, the Bad and the Ugly (1966) | $208M (U.S.) Dirty Harry (1971) | $138M (U.S.) Escape from Alcatraz (1979) | $265M Unforgiven (1992) | $286M In the Line of Fire (1993) | $279M The Bridges of Madison County (1995) | $268M Million Dollar Baby (2004) | $293M Gran Torino (2008) |

| Tightrope | White Hunter Black Heart | Unforgiven | In the Line of Fire | The Bridges of Madison County | Absolute Power | Million Dollar Baby | Gran Torino |

He took on the first of his singing roles in the uneven *Paint Your Wagon* (1969) — he would convince more as the country singer in *Honkytonk Man* (1982) — then returned to Don Siegel, with a game Shirley MacLaine in tow, for *Two Mules for Sister Sarah* (1970). *Kelly's Heroes* (1970) offered up a psychedelic take on World War II.

Eastwood and Siegel's third film together, *The Beguiled* (1971), featured the actor's most interesting role to date. He plays a wounded Union soldier who is taken in and cared for by the headmistress of an all-girl's school, only to exploit their repressed sexuality. Like his stranger in *High Plains Drifter* (1973), compromised cop in *Tightrope* (1984) and the youthful version of himself that his character Bill Munny refers to in *Unforgiven* (1992), John McBurney allowed Eastwood to stretch his persona, taking it into a darker, morally ambivalent world. This time, however, audiences were not willing to follow him.

After his strong directorial debut, *Play Misty for Me* (1971), in which he played a radio DJ stalked by a violent woman he had a one night stand with, Eastwood played another career-defining role, Harry Callahan, a San Francisco homicide detective, in Don Siegel's *Dirty Harry* (1971). His laconic acting style suited the rogue cop, who breaks any rules to hunt down a serial killer. The film's politics may be divisive, but there is no denying the film's power. Four inferior sequels followed.

For the rest of the 1970s and 1980s, Eastwood played variations on his outsider character. Some films, such as *High Plains Drifter*, Michael Cimino's *Thunderbolt and Lightfoot* (1974), *The Outlaw Josey Wales* (1976) and *Escape from Alcatraz* (1979) — his last film with Siegel and an intense character study — are riveting, while others fail to engage.

White Hunter Black Heart (1990) marked a shift in gear. Eastwood's thinly veiled portrayal of director John Huston on location during the shooting of *The African Queen* (1951) is spirited and commanding. *Unforgiven* and *In the Line of Fire* (1993) are two of his best films, both playing with the audiences' familiarity with his screen persona. *The Bridges of Madison County* (1995) casts him in a convincing romantic light, while *Absolute Power* (1997) might meander narratively, but its pleasures lies in Eastwood's easygoing rapport with costars Laura Linney and Ed Harris. *Gran Torino* (2008) may not be Eastwood's final film as an actor but it should be. It feels like a swan song and a retort to the violent roles he played in his youth — an on-screen sign-off from one of the medium's bona fide stars. **IHS**

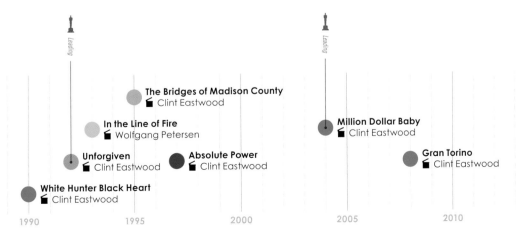

Leading

The Bridges of Madison County
Clint Eastwood

In the Line of Fire
Wolfgang Petersen

Unforgiven
Clint Eastwood

Absolute Power
Clint Eastwood

White Hunter Black Heart
Clint Eastwood

Leading

Million Dollar Baby
Clint Eastwood

Gran Torino
Clint Eastwood

| 1990 | 1995 | 2000 | 2005 | 2010 |

A Fistful of Dollars
(1964)

The Good, the Bad and the Ugly
(1966)

Coogan's Bluff
(1968)

Dirty Harry
(1971)

Escape from Alcatraz
(1979)

Unforgiven
(1992)

Million Dollar Baby
(2004)

Gran Torino
(2008)

Eastwood and Marianne Koch in *A Fistful of Dollars*, the first in the trilogy of spaghetti westerns that the actor made with Sergio Leone.

The Good, the Bad and the Ugly was Eastwood's final outing as the man with no name.

The famous Mexican standoff scene from *The Good, the Bad and the Ugly*, between Eli Wallach (the Ugly, left), Eastwood (the Good, center) and Lee Van Cleef (the Bad, right). Criticized for its depiction of violence upon its release, the movie is now hailed as one of the best westerns ever made.

Eastwood as the eponymous Arizona sheriff in *Coogan's Bluff*. Universal Studios offered him $1 million for the role, more than doubling his previous salary.

"You've got to ask yourself one question: do I feel lucky? Well do ya, punk?" — Eastwood as *Dirty Harry*.

ased on true events, *Escape from Alcatraz* starred Eastwood as one of three prisoners who attempt to break out of the infamous prison.

Morgan Freeman and Eastwood in ***Unforgiven***, which the actor also directed. He dedicated the picture to his mentors Don Siegel and Sergio Leone.

astwood coaches Hilary Swank in ***Million Dollar Baby***, for which e received his second Best Director Oscar.

Eastwood said of his racist character in ***Gran Torino*** that "If you don't play it all the way, then it becomes a Hollywood bailout. And if you're going to play this kind of guy, you've got to go all the way."

mia farrow 1945

| Rosemary's Baby | The Great Gatsby | Death on the Nile | Broadway Danny Rose | The Purple Rose of Cairo | Hannah and Her Sisters | Husbands and Wives | The Omen |

F

Mia Farrow's real life story shares some of the melodramatics of her breakthrough role in the U.S. soap *Peyton Place* (1964–66). Born in Los Angeles, 1945, her mother was film star Maureen O'Sullivan, her father the filmmaker John Farrow, and she married 50-year-old Frank Sinatra aged 21. He then famously served her divorce papers on the set of Roman Polanski's landmark *Rosemary's Baby* (1968), though it is doubtful Sinatra can claim credit for Farrow's unnerving performance. As the unwitting young bride sacrificed to birth the Devil's child, Farrow, with her short hair and elfin features, was widely acclaimed and looked ready to be a new type of screen star.

It was a promise largely unfulfilled, with the likes of barmy cult thriller *Secret Ceremony* (1968) and a failed attempt to visualize *The Great Gatsby* (1974). That Farrow's most successful 1970s work came as a chameleon-like murderess in all-star Agatha Christie whodunit *Death on the Nile* (1978), speaks volumes.

Then came one of the great actor-director partnerships, with Farrow appearing in all 12 movies her then-partner Woody Allen directed from 1982 to 1992. Highlights include her sassy, helium-voiced mobster's moll in *Broadway Danny Rose* (1984) and a

wistful 1930s movie lover in *The Purple Rose of Cairo* (1985), who starts a romance with a fictional character who literally walks out of the screen. A wonderful dissection of our desire to merge fantasy and reality, Farrow is heartbreaking.

In Allen's classic ensemble *Hannah and Her Sisters* (1986), Farrow shines as the seemingly most stable of a trio of New York sisters, who slowly reveals her own insecurities. As the sheltered housewife lead in fantasy *Alice* (1990), Farrow displayed her often overlooked comic skills, while her passive-aggressive shrew in *Husbands and Wives* (1992), completed during the hugely controversial and acrimonious Allen/Farrow split, seemed a window into their own strange relationship.

So toxic is the Allen/Farrow fallout, it appears to have sullied their remarkable collaboration by association. Moreover, despite the numerous Oscars bestowed on actresses in his films, Farrow scandalously received not a single nomination for any of her work with Allen. Largely withdrawing from acting, a rare return to horror as the sinister nanny Mrs. Blaylock in the remake of *The Omen* (2006) showed her capacity to chill, though Farrow now seems far more fulfilled focusing on her family and social activist causes. **LS**

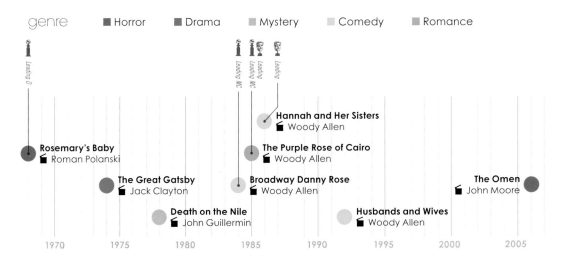

genre ■ Horror ■ Drama ■ Mystery ■ Comedy ■ Romance

Leading 0

Leading MC
Leading MC
Leading 0

Hannah and Her Sisters
Woody Allen

Rosemary's Baby
Roman Polanski

The Purple Rose of Cairo
Woody Allen

The Great Gatsby
Jack Clayton

Broadway Danny Rose
Woody Allen

The Omen
John Moore

Death on the Nile
John Guillermin

Husbands and Wives
Woody Allen

1970   1975   1980   1985   1990   1995   2000   2005

michael fassbender 1977

| Hunger | Fish Tank | Inglourious Basterds | Shame | A Dangerous Method | Prometheus | 12 Years a Slave | Frank |

F

It took 17 minutes for Michael Fassbender to prove that he was going to become a star. That is the length of the single unbroken shot that appears halfway through Steve McQueen's agonizing first feature *Hunger* (2008), in which Liam Cunningham's priest attempts to talk imprisoned IRA member Bobby Sands out of his hunger strike. Fassbender's performance in the scene — and throughout the rest of the film — was mesmeric.

Born in Heidelberg, Germany, in 1977, and raised in Ireland from the age of 2, Fassbender acted in stage and television roles for nearly a decade before *Hunger*. Following *Hunger*, he was an unsettling mix of charmer and predator in *Fish Tank* (2009), and received wider recognition for his brief but memorable role in Quentin Tarantino's gleefully violent World War II revenge-fantasy *Inglourious Basterds* (2009). His ascent slowed slightly with parts in the underrated *Centurion* (2010) and *Jonah Hex* (2010), a notorious flop.

By 2011, Fassbender had become one of the industry's most in-demand actors, playing four characters that year: a moody Mr. Rochester in Cary Fukunaga's atmospheric retelling of *Jane Eyre*; restrained as psychiatrist Carl Jung in *A Dangerous Method*; a young Magneto in the superhero franchise-starter *X-Men: First Class*; and as a sex addict in *Shame*, his second collaboration with McQueen. He excelled in all roles, but was particularly compelling in *Shame*.

Fassbender's work load was lighter the following year, only appearing in Steven Soderbergh's kinetic action movie *Haywire* (2012) and in Ridley Scott's long-awaited return to the Alien universe, *Prometheus* (2012). As a morally ambiguous android, David, Fassbender is the film's most intriguing character.

Fassbender reunited with McQueen again to play a vicious slave owner in *12 Years a Slave* (2013) and received an Oscar nomination for his performance. He cemented his rising star with a key role in Ridley Scott's *The Counselor* (2013), though it was met with a mixed critical response. If Fassbender is among his generation's most exciting actors then this is due to his daring choice of roles as much as his talent: from within a papier-mâché head he gave an unexpectedly moving performance as a talented, mentally fragile musician in the wonderfully offbeat *Frank* (2014). **JWa**

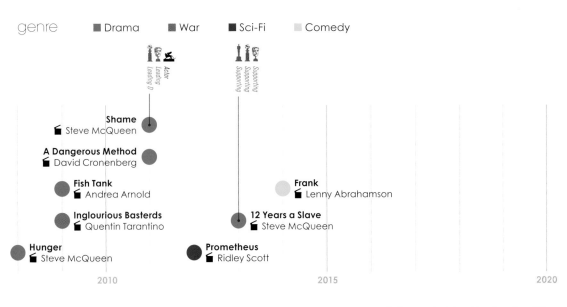

genre   ■ Drama   ■ War   ■ Sci-Fi   ■ Comedy

Shame
🎬 Steve McQueen

A Dangerous Method
🎬 David Cronenberg

Fish Tank
🎬 Andrea Arnold

Frank
🎬 Lenny Abrahamson

Inglourious Basterds
🎬 Quentin Tarantino

12 Years a Slave
🎬 Steve McQueen

Hunger
🎬 Steve McQueen

Prometheus
🎬 Ridley Scott

2010   2015   2020

ralph fiennes 1962

| The Baby of Mâcon | Schindler's List | Quiz Show | Strange Days | The English Patient | The End of the Affair | Sunshine | Spider |

In 1993, Steven Spielberg cast Ralph Fiennes in *Schindler's List*. Classically trained, Fiennes already had a few screen credits to his name. The year before, he had played Heathcliff opposite Juliette Binoche's Cathy in Peter Kosminsky's *Wuthering Heights*. He was also one of the leads in Peter Greenaway's controversial *The Baby of Mâcon* (1993). However, it was his unsettling performance as concentration-camp commandant Amon Goeth that gave the British actor his breakthrough role. His ferocious turn, capturing the barbarity of a man drunk on his own power, is an indelibly forceful performance that signaled the bold commitment Fiennes would bring to many roles in a screen career that has confirmed him as one of Britain's finest actors.

After being Oscar nominated for *Schindler's List*, Fiennes would show his versatility over the next few years. In Robert Redford's *Quiz Show* (1994) he played Charles Van Doren, who famously caused a scandal when he cheated on a primetime television game show. He followed it with another challenging role, playing a sleazy porn peddler caught up in a lethal situation in Kathryn Bigelow's visionary and controversial fin de siècle sci-fi thriller *Strange Days*

(1995), before returning to World War II in Anthony Minghella's lavish adaptation of Michael Ondaatje's *The English Patient* (1996). His performance in the film is exquisitely balanced between the rectitude expected of his class and times, and the great passion his affair with Kristin Scott Thomas' married heroine provokes. The intensity he brought to that role can also be seen in the entangled emotions that lie beneath his character's ostensibly contained reserve in Neil Jordan's *The End of the Affair* (1999). Drawing out the Catholic themes of Graham Greene's celebrated novel, Jordan elicits three extraordinary performances from Fiennes, Julianne Moore, as the woman his character loves, and Stephen Rea, as her husband.

If Gillian Armstrong's Peter Carey adaptation *Oscar and Lucinda* (1997) failed to light up the box office and the woeful *The Avengers* (1998) just failed, Istvan Szabo's *Sunshine* (1999) gave Fiennes three fascinating roles across three generations of Hungarian Jews, while his performance in his sister Martha's *Onegin* (1999) is beautifully nuanced. Other period dramas followed. James Ivory's *The White Countess* (2005) may have been lackluster, but Fiennes excelled as the bullying Duke of Devonshire, opposite Keira

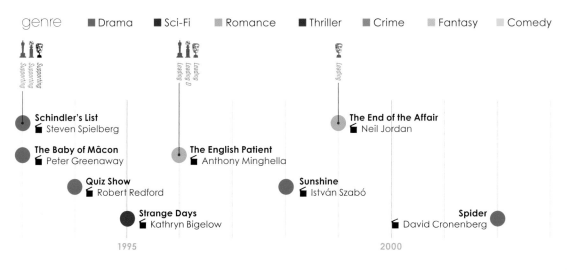

genre ■ Drama ■ Sci-Fi ■ Romance ■ Thriller ■ Crime ■ Fantasy ■ Comedy

Supporting
Supporting
Supporting

Leading
Leading 0
Leading

Leading

Schindler's List
🎬 Steven Spielberg

The End of the Affair
🎬 Neil Jordan

The Baby of Mâcon
🎬 Peter Greenaway

The English Patient
🎬 Anthony Minghella

Quiz Show
🎬 Robert Redford

Sunshine
🎬 István Szabó

Strange Days
🎬 Kathryn Bigelow

Spider
🎬 David Cronenberg

1995

2000

The Constant Gardener	The Duchess	The Reader	In Bruges	Harry Potter and the Deathly Hallows: Pt. 2	Coriolanus	The Invisible Woman	The Grand Budapest Hotel

Knightley, in *The Duchess* (2008). Likewise, his portrayal of Charles Dickens in *The Invisible Woman* (2013) — his second outing as director (his first was *Coriolanus* in 2011, in which he also starred) — is rich and complex.

Fiennes' characteristically English talent for hinting at what lies beneath a "proper" comportment was key to *The Constant Gardener* (2005). His performance as the quiet career diplomat, driven to confront his superiors over a conspiracy that caused the death of his wife, is one of his warmest, most poignant performances to date. No less impressive is his appearance in *The Reader* (2008), as a man haunted by his youthful encounter with a woman who turned out to be a prison guard in a concentration camp. Between these films he reunited with Kathryn Bigelow on the Oscar-winning *The Hurt Locker* (2008), offering up an impressive cameo as the head of a covert unit in the Iraqi desert.

In recent years, Fiennes has played key roles in a number of blockbuster franchises. He gradually gained more screen time as the dastardly Lord Voldemort in the *Harry Potter* series, imbuing the role with a depth that made the eventual face-off with Potter in *Harry Potter and the Deathly Hallows: Part 2* (2011) a spectacular climax to the popular series. He was an entertaining Hades in the otherwise unimpressive *Clash of the Titans* (2010) and its unnecessary 2012 sequel. And his initial appearance as a government pen pusher in *Skyfall* (2012) soon became something more substantial when he replaced Judi Dench's M at the end of the film, a role he continued in the series' next installment, *Spectre* (2015).

Another shift in the actor's screen persona is his growing repertory of comedy roles. He brought both a growling menace and a vicious humor to his cameo as the British gangster of Martin McDonagh's *In Bruges* (2008), while his lead performance as the fastidious, melancholy manager of Wes Anderson's *The Grand Budapest Hotel* (2014) is a masterclass in crisp, screwball comedy. It is no surprise, then, that Ethan and Joel Coen cast him in their riotous send-up of 1950s Hollywood, *Hail Caesar!* (2016).

Arguably the most remarkable performance of Fiennes' career so far is his turn as a glazed-looking schizophrenic who shuffles around the East End of 1950s London, mulling memories of bloody childhood, in David Cronenberg's *Spider* (2002). If Fiennes has yet to match the intensity and strangeness of that role, it is to his credit that he rarely ever plays safe. **EL**

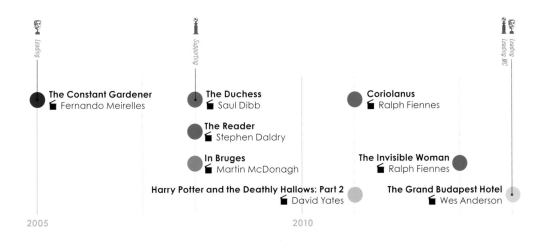

Leading

The Constant Gardener
🎬 Fernando Meirelles

Supporting

The Duchess
🎬 Saul Dibb

The Reader
🎬 Stephen Daldry

In Bruges
🎬 Martin McDonagh

Harry Potter and the Deathly Hallows: Part 2
🎬 David Yates

Coriolanus
🎬 Ralph Fiennes

The Invisible Woman
🎬 Ralph Fiennes

Leading
Leading MC

The Grand Budapest Hotel
🎬 Wes Anderson

2005　　　　　　　　　　　　　2010

colin firth 1960

| Another Country | A Month in the Country | The Hour of the Pig | Shakespeare in Love | Bridget Jones's Diary | Girl with a Pearl Earring | A Single Man | The King's Speech |

Although Colin Firth has been acting professionally since 1984, he first leapt (or splashed) to fame as the wet-shirted Mr. Darcy in the BBC's 1995 adaptation of *Pride and Prejudice*. Since then, Mr. Darcy has haunted him (he even played a character called Mark Darcy in the two *Bridget Jones* movies [2001 and 2004]), a fact he regards with resigned irony: "He is a figure that wont die ... I can't control him ... I've never resented it: if it wasn't for him I might be languishing."

Of course, his range is wider than that — he makes a good scowling villain (*Shakespeare in Love*, 1998), can deploy Wildean wit and elegance (*The Importance of Being Earnest*, 2002; *Dorian Gray*, 2009) and brings a light touch to farce (*St. Trinian's*, 2007). But the default set of his features suggests emotion held sternly in check. There was a smoldering intensity underlying his quiet portrayal of the painter Vermeer in *Girl with a Pearl Earring* (2003); and two of his finest performances to date came in Tom Ford's *A Single Man* (2009), as the bereaved gay Brit in California hiding an agony of grief behind his buttoned-up façade, and as the future King George VI in *The King's Speech* (2010), struggling with the twin handicaps of royal protocol and a speech impediment.

Firth's screen career got off to a good start, second-billed to Rupert Everett in the public school drama *Another Country* (1984), and he brought an elegiac vulnerability to his performance as the shellshocked World War I veteran in *A Month in the Country* (1987). If he seemed out of his depth in the title role of *Valmont* (1989), he did better as the sophisticated Parisian lawyer at once bemused and diverted by the rampant superstition of 15th-century provincial France in *The Hour of the Pig* (aka *The Advocate*, 1993).

Ensemble work suits him: he fitted in seamlessly to the multi-cast rom-com of *Love Actually* (2003) and gamely tried out as a song-and-dance man in the cheerful fluff of *Mamma Mia!* (2008). Underplaying is his strength, but it can leave him at the mercy of pedestrian scripts, as with *Gambit* (2012), a comedy-thriller remake scripted — in one of their less inspired moments — by the Coen brothers, or *The Railway Man* (2013), where he played an ex-POW.

Given a challenge, though, he can rise to it. *Kingsman: The Secret Service* (2015) finds him relishing the role of a suave, well-spoken spy with a knack for ultra-violence. Firth plays it with a nicely judged sense of (self) parody — a further extension to his range. **PK**

genre ■ Romance ■ Drama

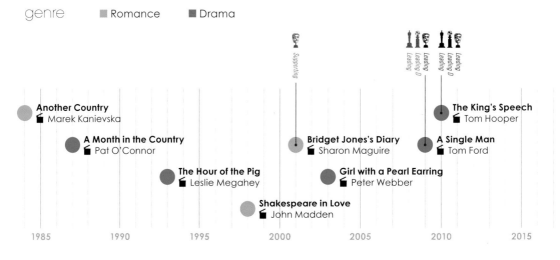

Supporting
Leading
Leading D
Leading
Leading
Leading D
Leading

Another Country
Marek Kanievska

A Month in the Country
Pat O'Connor

The Hour of the Pig
Leslie Megahey

Shakespeare in Love
John Madden

Bridget Jones's Diary
Sharon Maguire

Girl with a Pearl Earring
Peter Webber

A Single Man
Tom Ford

The King's Speech
Tom Hooper

1985   1990   1995   2000   2005   2010   2015

errol flynn 1909–59

Captain Blood

The Charge of the Light Brigade

The Adventures of Robin Hood

Four's a Crowd

The Sisters

The Private Lives of Elizabeth and Essex

Dodge City

The Sea Hawk

F

Born in Tasmania, Australia, Errol Flynn's good looks and natural athletic ability saw him cast as a heroic leading man in a number of swashbuckling Hollywood studio pictures throughout the 1930s and 1940s. Over the course of his career, Flynn gained a reputation as a hell-raiser and womanizer, often found at the center of drunken fistfights, melees and love affairs.

Flynn achieved stardom in Michael Curtiz's epic *Captain Blood* (1935), a tale of heroism on the high seas with the young actor relishing the opportunity to play such an alluring, daredevil matinee idol. It was the first of eight films Flynn would make with costar Olivia de Havilland and the start of a 12-feature partnership between the star and Curtiz.

Flynn built a reputation for dashing, swashbuckling heroes in films such as *The Charge of the Light Brigade* (1936) and *The Sea Hawk* (1940), but is best known for his engaging performance as the title character in *The Adventures of Robin Hood* (1938). If *Captain Blood* hinted at his potential, this hugely entertaining romp would forever seal Flynn's reputation as a derring-do hero with an eye for the ladies. The film was shot in glorious Technicolor, and his performance is as large as the vistas and set-pieces that Curtiz so expertly captures.

While Flynn quickly became typecast in action-adventure roles, he occasionally displayed some versatility as an actor, showing a skill for comedy in *Four's a Crowd* (1938), playing an ambitious newspaper editor, and high drama in *The Sisters* (1938), costarring with Bette Davis. He would appear opposite Davis again in *The Private Lives of Elizabeth and Essex* (1939), a lavish Hollywood production focusing on the relationship between Queen Elizabeth I and Robert Devereux, the second Earl of Essex. Relations on set between Flynn and Davies were reportedly tempestuous, with the pair quarrelling constantly.

Flynn was also impressive as a righteous man who puts on the Sheriff's badge to restore law and order in the notorious *Dodge City* (1939), as General Custer in *They Died with Their Boots On* (1941) and as a boxer in *Gentleman Jim* (1942), the latter two films directed by Raoul Walsh. However, as the 1940s wore on, Flynn's limitations as an actor were as noticeable as his off-screen antics. Films such as *The Adventures of Don Juan* (1948) lacked the luster of earlier swashbucklers and the material that best suited Flynn's skills no longer attracted audiences. In 1950 he was released from his contract with Warner Bros., a move that effectively ended his career as a Hollywood leading man. He continued to act until he died of a heart attack in 1959, aged just 50, but there were few performances of note. **CGD**

genre   ■ Adventure   ■ Romance   ■ Drama   ■ Western

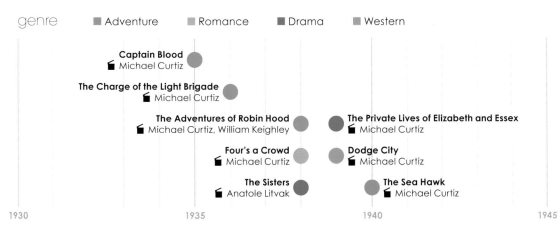

Captain Blood
Michael Curtiz

The Charge of the Light Brigade
Michael Curtiz

The Adventures of Robin Hood
Michael Curtiz, William Keighley

The Private Lives of Elizabeth and Essex
Michael Curtiz

Four's a Crowd
Michael Curtiz

Dodge City
Michael Curtiz

The Sisters
Anatole Litvak

The Sea Hawk
Michael Curtiz

1930   1935   1940   1945

acting dynasties

John Barrymore | Michael Redgrave | Henry Fonda | Ingrid Bergman | Kirk Douglas | Shirley MacLaine | Vanessa Redgrave | Warren Beatty

Working in the family business is perhaps a dying tradition in an era where the very notion of work and careers is so protean. Acting, however, continues to offer a fascinating look along a continuum, through the many successful thespians whose later generations have followed them into the profession.

The idea of an acting dynasty, like royal succession, suggests an almost God-given, even Darwinian lineage. That is certainly the implication with the Barrymores, America's first acting dynasty. Three siblings, Lionel, John and Ethel, although reigning on the stage, all found success on screen; Lionel most notably as villainous Mr. Potter in *It's a Wonderful Life* (1946), John in screwball classic *Twentieth Century* (1934) and Ethel, an Oscar-winner in *None But the Lonely Heart* (1944). The trio's only surviving film together is melodrama *Rasputin and the Empress* (1932), with Lionel as the eponymous scheming "Mad Monk" and Ethel as the vulnerable Czarina. John's son, John Drew, had limited acting success, but his daughter Drew fared better. A scene-stealing moppet in Steven Spielberg's *E.T. the Extra-Terrestrial* (1982), her troubled formative years eventually led to a more stable, highly likeable adult career, taking an active role in pushing popular, women-centric movies like the big-screen reboot of *Charlie's Angels* (2000).

Perhaps the British Barrymore equivalent would be the Redgraves. Michael Redgrave, whose debonair screen debut in Hitchcock classic *The Lady Vanishes* (1938) suggests an "English" Cary Grant, married fellow actor Rachel Kempson. Their children, son Corin and, especially, daughter Vanessa, became synonymous with British theater and film from the 1960s onward, when Vanessa's debut in *Morgan: A Suitable Case for Treatment* (1966) won her an Oscar nomination. She became one of the most acclaimed and respected actors of the last 50 years. Her daughters with director Tony Richardson, Natasha and Joely, also had some success, although Natasha sadly died in 2009.

It is interesting too, to see how the industry viewed family members in different eras. Henry Fonda was regularly cast as one of Hollywood's stoic, decent heroes, like man of the people Tom Joad in John Ford's adaptation of Steinbeck Dust Bowl novel *The Grapes of Wrath* (1940). Come the turbulent 1960s, his son Peter led the counterculture, cowriting and starring in the groundbreaking *Easy Rider* (1969), a film that sought to undermine everything his father's generation represented. And whereas offscreen, daughter Jane was seen as "the enemy," largely due to her Vietnam War opposition, her actual screen choices were less politically charged, if no less

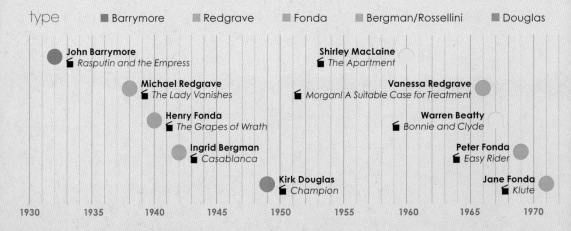

type ■ Barrymore ■ Redgrave ■ Fonda ■ Bergman/Rossellini ■ Douglas

John Barrymore
⚑ *Rasputin and the Empress*

Michael Redgrave
⚑ *The Lady Vanishes*

Henry Fonda
⚑ *The Grapes of Wrath*

Ingrid Bergman
⚑ *Casablanca*

Kirk Douglas
⚑ *Champion*

Shirley MacLaine
⚑ *The Apartment*

Vanessa Redgrave
⚑ *Morgan! A Suitable Case for Treatment*

Warren Beatty
⚑ *Bonnie and Clyde*

Peter Fonda
⚑ *Easy Rider*

Jane Fonda
⚑ *Klute*

1930   1935   1940   1945   1950   1955   1960   1965   1970

Peter Fonda | Jane Fonda | Isabella Rossellini | Michael Douglas | Laura Dern | Drew Barrymore | Maggie Gyllenhaal | Jake Gyllenhaal

emblematic of the New Hollywood, brilliant as the call girl in casually permissive thriller *Klute* (1971). Jane's son Troy Garity (*Sunshine*, 2007), and especially Peter's daughter Bridget (*Jackie Brown*, 1997), also briefly enjoyed success, although neither with work strong enough to capture the zeitgeist like their parents.

Contrast Kirk Douglas with his son Michael. Kirk, all clenched fury, was a very physical actor, whether hero, villain or both, like his ferocious boxer in *Champion* (1949). Michael mined similar antihero territory, but his characters tend to be more cerebral, like *Wall Street* (1987) villain Gordon Gekko. Ingrid Bergman was often cast as the unattainable object of desire, a rare, foreign enigma to bedazzle U.S. heroes like Humphrey Bogart in *Casablanca* (1942) or Cary Grant in *Notorious* (1946). There is an element of mutual noble suffering in their love affairs. Her daughter Isabella Rossellini was similarly exotic, but in David Lynch's *Blue Velvet* (1986), her suffering at psycho Dennis Hopper's hands makes her very much the victim. The hint of masochistic pleasure she derives from her deviant relationships is something that could never be shown so explicitly in her mother's era.

At least Fonda, Douglas and Bergman's offspring found their own success. The sons of some of the most iconic stars — Patrick Wayne, son of John, or Chris Mitchum and Lemmon, sons of Robert and Jack — have fallen short of the benchmarks set by their fathers. Thankfully we hear more of the success stories: Angelina Jolie (daughter of Jon Voight); Jamie Lee Curtis (daughter of Tony Curtis and Janet Leigh); Kiefer Sutherland (son of Donald); or Laura Dern, daughter of Bruce Dern and Dianne Ladd, whose *Rambling Rose* (1991), marked the first time mother and daughter were both Oscar-nominated for the same film.

Sometimes talent spreads within a generation rather than down through successive ones. Shirley MacLaine's sad-eyed kookiness was best captured in Billy Wilder's *The Apartment* (1960), as elevator operator Fran Kubelik. Her brother Warren seemed to be merely a pretty boy when he emerged in the following year's *Splendor in the Grass*, but six years later he produced and starred in a key American film of the decade, *Bonnie and Clyde* (1967).

MacLaine and Beatty went on to equally enduring careers. With other siblings, honors are not always so even: Jeff over Beau Bridges; Alec over Daniel, Stephen and William Baldwin. The best current example of siblings both succeeding are the Gyllenhaals, Maggie and Jake. Both have pursued challenging, ambitious work: notably Maggie in *Secretary* (2002) and Jake in *Brokeback Mountain* (2005). **LS**

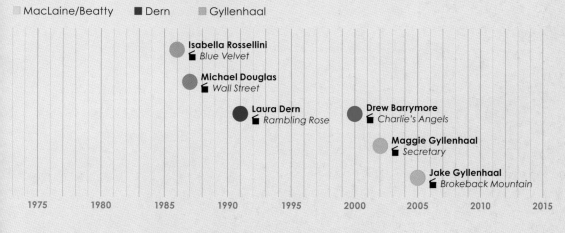

■ MacLaine/Beatty　■ Dern　■ Gyllenhaal

Isabella Rossellini *Blue Velvet*

Michael Douglas *Wall Street*

Laura Dern *Rambling Rose*

Drew Barrymore *Charlie's Angels*

Maggie Gyllenhaal *Secretary*

Jake Gyllenhaal *Brokeback Mountain*

1975　1980　1985　1990　1995　2000　2005　2010　2015

henry fonda 1905–82

The Farmer
Takes a Wife

You Only
Live Once

Jezebel

Young
Mr. Lincoln

The Grapes
of Wrath

The Lady
Eve

The Ox-Bow
Incident

My Darling
Clementine

There is nobility in many of Henry Fonda's most famous roles. Not the heroism of John Wayne or other western heroes, or the goodness of young James Stewart or the wisdom of his older screen persona. Fonda inhabited characters with a strong moral compass, aware that doing the right thing did not always align them with the popular choice or make them likeable. When he did play a bad character, the impact was incendiary.

He was born in Nebraska, 1905. In 1928, he joined the University Players in Falmouth, where he met James Stewart. The two boarded together while they appeared on Broadway and again in Hollywood. Fonda's first screen appearance was opposite Janet Gaynor in Victor Fleming's comedy *The Farmer Takes a Wife* (1935), followed quickly by King Vidor's remake of the D.W. Griffith classic *Way Down East* (1935). He was one of the leads in *The Trail of the Lonesome Pine* (1936), the first color film to be shot on location.

Fonda's first significant role was as an ex-convict wrongly charged with murder, who goes on the run with his wife in *You Only Live Once* (1937). Directed by Fritz Lang, the film was severely censored because of its violence, but is now considered a classic example of early film noir. He starred opposite Bette Davis in *Jezebel* (1938), as a man shamed by his fiancée's behavior at a ball but unwilling to give anyone the satisfaction of revealing it. He played the outlaw Frank James in *Jesse James*, one of the biggest hits of 1939, but is better, with his character given more depth, in Lang's 1940 sequel *The Return of Frank James*. In between, he was an honest man whose faith in the justice system is rocked when he wrongly faces the death penalty in *Let Us Live* (1939). It is a theme he would return to when Alfred Hitchcock cast him as Manny Balestrero, a musician picked up for a crime he could not have committed, in *The Wrong Man* (1956).

Ford played the titular role in *Young Mr. Lincoln* (1939). It is the archetype of a classic Fonda character: honest, willful and unafraid to speak his mind, but always fair. It was also the first of six features Fonda completed with John Ford. They worked together later that year on *Drums Along the Mohawk* (1939), with Fonda and Claudette Colbert playing 18th-century settlers who are struggling to survive on the

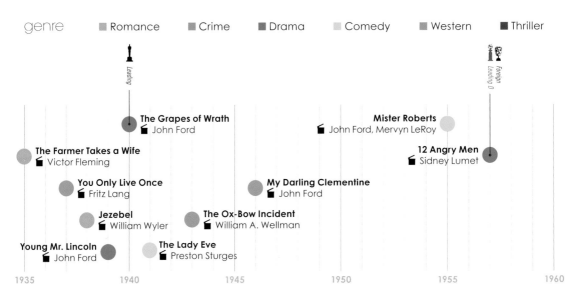

genre ■ Romance ■ Crime ■ Drama ■ Comedy ■ Western ■ Thriller

The Grapes of Wrath
John Ford

Mister Roberts
John Ford, Mervyn LeRoy

The Farmer Takes a Wife
Victor Fleming

12 Angry Men
Sidney Lumet

You Only Live Once
Fritz Lang

My Darling Clementine
John Ford

Jezebel
William Wyler

The Ox-Bow Incident
William A. Wellman

Young Mr. Lincoln
John Ford

The Lady Eve
Preston Sturges

1935   1940   1945   1950   1955   1960

| Mister Roberts | 12 Angry Men | Advise & Consent | Fail Safe | Once Upon a Time in the West | My Name Is Nobody | The Swarm | On Golden Pond |

F

American frontier. The actor is perfectly cast as Tom Joad in Ford's lyrical adaptation of John Steinbeck's *The Grapes of Wrath* (1940). Like his Wyatt Earp in *My Darling Clementine* (1946), Joad is a character who, when faced with seemingly insurmountable odds, always steers the right and honest course. The pair explored the nature of goodness and the power of redemption in *The Fugitive* (1947), their adaptation of Graham Greene's *The Power and the Glory* (1940). Fonda plays a priest in a Mexican town who escapes persecution but risks his life when he returns to carry out a charitable act. Surprisingly abstract for a mainstream Hollywood film, it is one of their best efforts. Fonda played against type in his last film for the director, *Fort Apache* (1948), as an egotistical commander of a U.S. Cavalry outpost. The pair did start to work together on the naval comedy *Mister Roberts* (1955), but ill health forced Ford to drop out.

William Wellman's *The Ox-Bow Incident* (1943) pits Fonda's rancher against a posse who mistakenly believe three cowboys are murderers. Unwilling to adhere to the law or rationalize their arguments,

they carry out their own form of justice. A damning indictment of mob mentality, its themes are echoed in one of Fonda's most famous dramas, *12 Angry Men* (1957). Produced by Fonda and directed by Sidney Lumet, the actor plays an architect serving out his jury service on the murder trial of a young Hispanic man and gradually reveals the prejudices of his peers.

Fonda's liberal politics are clear through his choice of roles in *Advise & Consent* (1962), *The Best Man* (1964) and *Fail Safe* (1964), and he is a strong presence in all. Sergio Leone understood how audiences would react to a truly evil incarnation of the actor when he cast him as Frank in *Once Upon a Time in the West* (1968). It is an inspired choice, not just for the actor's performance, but also for what he has represented. He is good in *Madigan* (1968) and *The Boston Strangler* (1968), fun in *My Name Is Nobody* (1973) and better than *The Swarm* (1978) deserves. He won an Oscar for *On Golden Pond* (1981), giving one of his best performances as an irascible old man who softens in the company of his grandson. That nobility is still there, strong and unwavering. **IHS**

■ Horror

Leading
Leading
Leading
Leading 0
Leading

Advise & Consent
🎬 Otto Preminger

On Golden Pond
🎬 Mark Rydell

Fail Safe
🎬 Sidney Lumet

The Swarm
🎬 Irwin Allen

Once Upon a Time in the West
🎬 Sergio Leone

My Name Is Nobody
🎬 Tonino Valerii

1965   1970   1975   1980   1985

jane fonda 1937

| Sunday in New York | Cat Ballou | Barefoot in the Park | They Shoot Horses, Don't They? | Barbarella | Klute | Tout Va Bien | Julia |

Few performers have been so defined by their contradictions as Jane Fonda: a socialist who has always dwelt in wealth and privilege; an activist for equality and a member of Hollywood's gilded elite; a feminist health and fitness guru who maintained her own sex appeal with recourse to the surgeon's knife. To some, her reputation will always be that of "Hanoi Jane," the "traitor" whose activism against the Vietnam War went as far as presenting anti-American broadcasts on Radio Hanoi and being photographed sitting on a North Vietnamese anti-aircraft gun. To others, Fonda is first and foremost a great screen beauty, and — thanks to her performance as the eponymous space siren in *Barbarella* (1968) — the quintessential 1960s sex kitten. And then there are those to whom she is simply one of the finest screen actors of all time: quick and winning in comedies; raw and risk-taking in dramas; always finely tuned to her material.

Fonda was born Lady Jayne Seymour Fonda in 1937, just as the career of her actor father Henry Fonda was heading for superstardom. His marriage to her mother, Frances Ford Brokaw, was a troubled one; Brokaw suffered mental health problems, and would kill herself when Jane was 12 years old. Despite this troubled early history, the young Jane found fame with a breezy, carefree image. The two *Vogue* covers she graced as a model in her early twenties show a wholesome girl who looks even younger than she is, while her early work on stage and screen tended to emphasize her girlish prettiness rather than the intensity she was busy honing in acting classes with Method guru Lee Strasberg.

Fonda reports in her autobiography that Joshua Logan, who directed her in her first film *Tall Story* (1960), told her that she was "too cute for drama." Sure enough, light roles would continue to dominate her output as she found greater recognition through the 1960s: the comedy western *Cat Ballou* (1965); the fluffy Neil Simon romcom *Barefoot in the Park* (1967); and the aforementioned *Barbarella*. However, the release of *They Shoot Horses, Don't They?* (1969) marked a

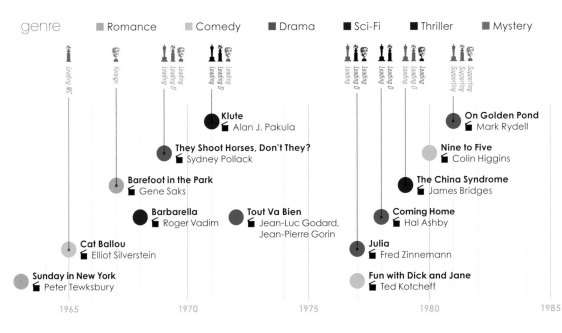

genre ■ Romance ■ Comedy ■ Drama ■ Sci-Fi ■ Thriller ■ Mystery

Klute
Alan J. Pakula

They Shoot Horses, Don't They?
Sydney Pollack

Barefoot in the Park
Gene Saks

Barbarella
Roger Vadim

Tout Va Bien
Jean-Luc Godard, Jean-Pierre Gorin

Cat Ballou
Elliot Silverstein

Sunday in New York
Peter Tewksbury

On Golden Pond
Mark Rydell

Nine to Five
Colin Higgins

The China Syndrome
James Bridges

Coming Home
Hal Ashby

Julia
Fred Zinnemann

Fun with Dick and Jane
Ted Kotcheff

1965　　　1970　　　1975　　　1980　　　1985

Fun with Dick and Jane	Coming Home	The China Syndrome	Nine to Five	On Golden Pond	The Morning After	Stanley & Iris	Monster-in-Law

significant change. As the beaten down and jaded Gloria, who attempts to withstand the privations of the Great Depression by participating in grueling dance marathons, she showed a new dramatic register, and was rewarded with her first Oscar nomination. Fonda missed out on a couple of surefire hits when she turned down both *Bonnie and Clyde* (1967) and *Rosemary's Baby* (1968), but she scored her first Best Actress Oscar for *Klute* (1971), as prostitute Bree Daniel, the key witness in a murder case.

Fonda also strove to expand her horizons beyond Hollywood, working with French New Wave legend Jean-Luc Godard on *Tout Va Bien* (1972) — a severe, self-deconstructing critique of industrial exploitation and artistic complacency. Though the film was unsuccessful, Fonda's shift into experimental, politicized European cinema reflected her broadening intellectual concerns — as well as the fact that her upfront opinions had cooled some of Hollywood's ardor for her. But despite the controversy surrounding her activism,

Fonda's time in the limelight was far from over. *Coming Home* (1978), which tackled the complexities of wartime loyalties by positioning Fonda as the wife of a deployed Marine (Bruce Dern) who dallies in his absence with a paraplegic veteran (Jon Voight), won her another Oscar. *Julia* (1977), in which she played the author Lillian Hellman, and James Bridges' nuclear thriller *The China Syndrome* (1979) brought further acclaim.

Her most celebrated 1980s films included the cheery feminist comedy *Nine to Five* (1980); *On Golden Pond* (1981), in which she and her father Henry enacted a close-to-the-bone version of their own fraught relationship; and *The Morning After* (1986), for which she was again Oscar-nominated. The 1990s saw Fonda retire from acting to concentrate on her hugely successful fitness videos, although she would return to both film and theater with supporting roles in the early 2000s. Fonda has since embraced Christianity, survived a bout of breast cancer and published two volumes of her autobiography. **HM**

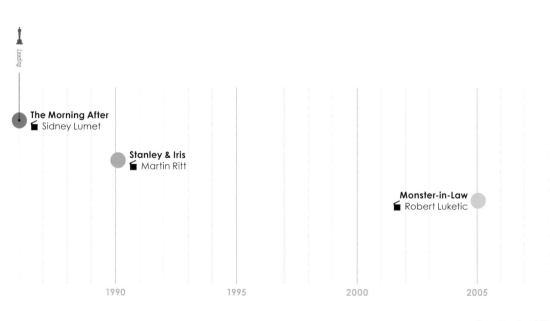

Leading

The Morning After
Sidney Lumet

Stanley & Iris
Martin Ritt

Monster-in-Law
Robert Luketic

1990   1995   2000   2005

joan fontaine 1917–2013

A Damsel in Distress

Gunga Din

The Women

Rebecca

Suspicion

The Constant Nymph

Jane Eyre

Letter from an Unknown Woman

Joan Fontaine was a movie star who refused to hide behind her fame. An outstanding golfer and Cordon Bleu chef who held a valid pilot's licence, she was nevertheless an actress with a truly fascinating career.

The younger sister of fellow star Olivia de Havilland, Fontaine was born Joan de Beauvoir de Havilland in Tokyo in 1917, but moved to California with her mother and sister when she was two. Her parents separated soon after, with Joan taking her step-father's name. The de Havilland sisters shared a tumultuous relationship, with paternal favoritism toward Olivia reportedly being the catalyst for a longstanding feud.

Fontaine's stage debut was in 1935, followed later that year by her screen debut opposite Joan Crawford, in George Cukor's *No More Ladies* (1935). Her next big chance would not come until 1937, starring alongside Fred Astaire in the musical *A Damsel in Distress*, but the film failed at the box office.

Fontaine's fortunes began to change when her performances in *Gunga Din* (1939) and *The Women* (1939) attracted favorable reviews. A chance encounter with producer David O. Selznick at a dinner party led to her role as the new Mrs. De Winter in *Rebecca* (1940). Alfred Hitchcock's talent in distilling the raw potential of an actor, combined with Fontaine's fervor to succeed, culminated in a painfully fragile performance that earned Fontaine her first Oscar nomination.

The following year, she reunited with Hitchcock and her *Gunga Din* costar Cary Grant in *Suspicion* (1941), a classic thriller in which Fontaine plays the wife of man she fears is a cold-blooded killer. She was again nominated for an Oscar, finding herself up against her sister — and beating her to the award.

Capitalizing on this success, Fontaine appeared in a series of romantic dramas throughout the 1940s, most notably opposite Orson Welles in *Jane Eyre* (1943) and Charles Boyer in *The Constant Nymph* (1943). However, her strongest performance of the decade was as the reckless, yet willfully determined Lisa Brendle in *Letter from an Unknown Woman* (1948). Sadly, it was followed by a string of mostly forgettable melodramas in the 1950s and the transition to television for the remainder of her career; she retired in the 1990s. Fontaine died in 2013, aged 96. **PG**

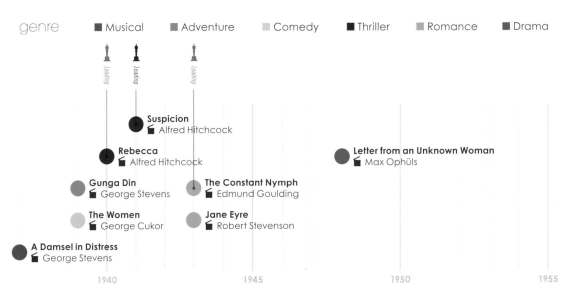

genre   ■ Musical   ■ Adventure   ■ Comedy   ■ Thriller   ■ Romance   ■ Drama

Leading   *Leading*   *Leading*

Suspicion
Alfred Hitchcock

Rebecca
Alfred Hitchcock

Letter from an Unknown Woman
Max Ophüls

Gunga Din
George Stevens

The Constant Nymph
Edmund Goulding

The Women
George Cukor

Jane Eyre
Robert Stevenson

A Damsel in Distress
George Stevens

1940   1945   1950   1955

Action Hero   Character Actor   Rebel

harrison ford 1942

American Graffiti | Star Wars: Episode IV — A New Hope | Raiders of the Lost Ark | Blade Runner | Witness | Patriot Games | The Fugitive | K-19: The Widowmaker

F

As the star of two of the most popular franchises in film history, Harrison Ford is one of the most successful actors of recent times by box-office count alone. An actor of wit and subtle precision, he has maintained his prime box-office position with impressive longevity.

A self-confessed latecomer to acting, Ford began playing small parts in Hollywood in the mid-1960s. He supplemented his acting income as a freelance carpenter and it was through this work that he met George Lucas. The young director cast him in a small part in his 1960s-set teen drama American Graffiti (1973). Ford's role as a hot-headed car racer is brief, but he impressed the director with his roguish charm.

It was from Lucas, four years later, that Ford got his big break. He was cast as Han Solo in Star Wars: Episode IV — A New Hope (1977). With its rousing action scenes and groundbreaking special effects, Star Wars helped usher in the age of the modern blockbuster, but Ford's performance was just as key to the film's popularity: he brought a worldly humor and spiky skepticism to his role as captain of the Millennium Falcon.

Ford's fame was sealed with another collaboration with Lucas. Working with director Steven Spielberg, Lucas cast him as the daring archeologist Indiana Jones in Raiders of the Lost Ark (1981). Ford gave the role an appealing dash of old-style, wisecracking heroism, an astute complement to the film's mood of loving pastiche. In a much darker role for Ridley Scott's Blade Runner (1982), he provided a compelling sci-fi spin on the hard-bitten archetype of film noir, investing the part with a haunting ambiguity. And playing a cop hiding out in a remote Amish community in Peter Weir's 1985 thriller Witness, he gave an Oscar-nominated performance of subtlety and sensitivity. He would reunite with Weir the following year, giving one of his best performances as an eccentric inventor in The Mosquito Coast.

For the next two decades Ford's name was a reliable mark of quality for intelligent Hollywood genre pictures, like Patriot Games (1992) and The Fugitive (1993). A number of his late-career performances are no less compelling — he was on commanding form as the captain of a Soviet submarine in the thriller K19: The Widowmaker (2002). But if his box-office stature today lacks the assurance he previously commanded, Ford still remains a big star, with the reprisal of Han Solo for Star Wars: Episode VII — The Force Awakens, and rumors of a role in a Blade Runner sequel. **EL**

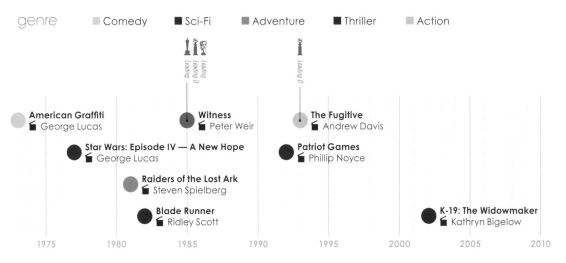

jodie foster 1962

| Napoleon and Samantha | Taxi Driver | Freaky Friday | Bugsy Malone | The Accused | The Silence of the Lambs | Sommersby | Nell |

Jodie Foster is one of the rare performers to have successfully transitioned from child actor to adult star, with a career spanning over four decades. Born in Los Angeles in 1962, Foster first appeared in a television commercial at the age of 3. She was a regular presence on the small screen before expanding her output to family-orientated films like *Napoleon and Samantha* (1972), *Tom Sawyer* (1973) and *One Little Indian* (1973). The precocious Foster was reliably plucky and watchable, but the roles were uncomplicated.

The first sign of her maturing talent was a small role in Martin Scorsese's *Alice Doesn't Live Here Anymore* (1974). The worldly Audrey would be the model for the roles to follow, as Foster specialized in characters who acted older than their years. The best example of this was in her next film with Scorsese, playing 12-year-old prostitute Iris in *Taxi Driver* (1976). Her performance is both confident and insecure, as if the character is aware on some level that she is only outwardly tough. She received her first Oscar nomination for the role.

The disparity between Foster's age and her characters' circumstances could also be observed in the four other films she made in 1976: as a murderous teenager living alone in *The Little Girl Who Lives*

Down the Lane, dying of a heart condition in *Echoes of a Summer*, gleefully playing a gangster's moll in *Bugsy Malone* and swapping bodies with her mother Barbara Harris in the Disney comedy *Freaky Friday*.

After starring in the mischievous *Foxes* (1980) and *Carny* (1980), Foster limited her film appearances in order to concentrate on university. Only *The Hotel New Hampshire* (1984) stands out from this period. On her return to full-time acting she struggled to progress to adult roles, appearing in a run of unsuccessful films that included the moody *Siesta* (1987) and *Stealing Home* (1988). She was reportedly prepared to quit when she won the lead in *The Accused* (1988). Based on the true story of a gang rape victim seeking legal retribution, her raw, angry performance won the actress her first Oscar, with her second arriving just three years later.

Her role as trainee FBI investigator Clarice Starling in Jonathan Demme's hugely successful *The Silence of the Lambs* (1991) assured Foster's star status, and the resourceful, ambitious yet vulnerable character is the one she is most closely associated with. While the serial killer Hannibal Lecter became an instant pop culture icon, the film thrums because of Starling and the unique chemistry between Foster and Anthony Hopkins.

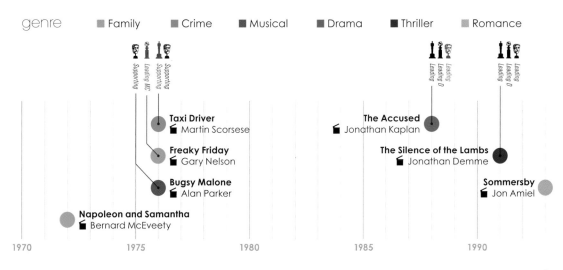

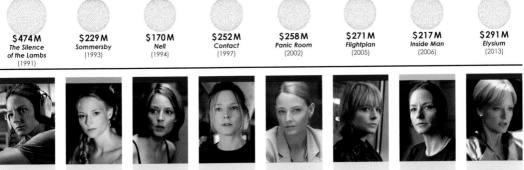

Contact	Anna and the King	Panic Room	Flightplan	Inside Man	The Brave One	Carnage	Elysium

F

Few of the other films Foster made in the 1990s were as popular as *The Silence of the Lambs*, but each was a bold, unconventional choice. In her directorial debut, *Little Man Tate* (1991), she starred as the mother of a child prodigy. She came and went as another prostitute in Woody Allen's *Shadows and Fog* (1991), costarred in the period drama *Sommersby* (1993) and is entertaining as a con-artist in *Maverick* (1994). She received another Oscar nomination for her complex portrayal of a near-feral woman raised in isolation in *Nell* (1994), and is intelligent and passionate in *Contact* (1997), as an astronomer who receives a signal from an extra-terrestrial world. In her last film of the decade, the inert drama *Anna and the King* (1999), she plays the real-life English governess whose experiences inspired *The King And I* (1956).

As Foster entered the third decade of her career, she moved toward roles in more action-orientated films that drew upon her aptitude for playing driven, vulnerable characters. Filling in for Nicole Kidman, she protected a young Kristen Stewart in David Fincher's claustrophobic *Panic Room* (2002), and, after putting her fluent French to use in a small but crucial role in *A Very Long Engagement* (2004), starred as another competent, put-upon woman defending herself against violent outside forces in *Flightplan* (2005).

The success of these movies triggered a more prolific period. She took darker roles as a high-end fixer in the heist thriller *Inside Man* (2006) and as the victim of a brutal assault who becomes a vigilante in *The Brave One* (2007). She also appeared in her first children's film in decades, *Nim's Island* (2008), which was as inconsequential as the earlier films she had starred in.

Returning to the director's chair, Foster also starred in the unsuccessful but strangely admirable *The Beaver* (2011). The film tried to be both a black comedy and a heartwarming family drama, but the two elements canceled each other out, while the scandals unfurling around troubled star Mel Gibson drove audiences away. She was an increasingly distraught mother in *Carnage* (2011), Roman Polanski's adaptation of Yasmine Reza's caustic stage play. And continuing a trend of playing less sympathetic characters, she was the villain in *Elysium* (2013), although her performance, which is hamstrung by a bizarre accent, is markedly different in tone to the rest of the film. In the same year, the 50-year-old star attended the Golden Globes to received a lifetime achievement award. **JWa**

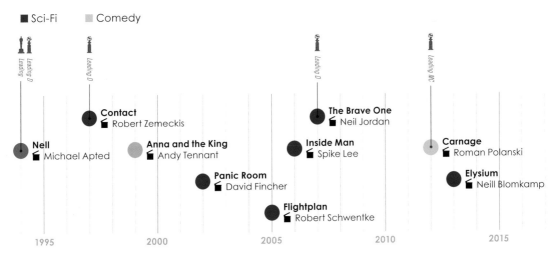

■ Sci-Fi　■ Comedy

Leading D

Leading D

Leading D

Leading MC

Nell
Michael Apted

Contact
Robert Zemeckis

Anna and the King
Andy Tennant

Panic Room
David Fincher

Flightplan
Robert Schwentke

The Brave One
Neil Jordan

Inside Man
Spike Lee

Carnage
Roman Polanski

Elysium
Neill Blomkamp

1995　　　2000　　　2005　　　2010　　　2015

Bugsy Malone
(1976)

Taxi Driver
(1976)

The Accused
(1988)

The Silence of the Lambs
(1991)

Anna and the King
(1999)

Panic Room
(2002)

The Brave One
(2007)

Carnage
(2011)

Bugsy Malone featured Foster as the speakeasy singer Tallulah, girlfriend of crime boss Fat Sam (John Cassisi). Critic Roger Ebert described her as having "as much style as Rita Hayworth brought to *Gilda*."

Foster and Robert De Niro in Martin Scorsese's **Taxi Driver**.

Many other notable actresses were allegedly considered for Foster's role in **Taxi Driver**, including Melanie Griffith, Linda Blair, Bo Derek and Carrie Fisher.

Foster had to fight for the part of Sarah Tobias in **The Accused**, but proved she deserved it by winning an Oscar.

The chemistry between Foster and Anthony Hopkins (as Hannibal Lecter) was central to the success of **The Silence of the Lambs**. The movie became only the third film to win all of the "Big Five" Academy Awards: Best Picture, Best Actor, Best Actress, Best Director and Adapted Screenplay.

Foster reportedly tried to buy the rights for *The Silence of the Lambs* after reading the source novel, but found she had been beaten to it by Gene Hackman.

Set in 19th-century Siam (now Thailand) and based on a true story, *Anna and the King* stars Foster as the English governess Anna Leonowens, who becomes the teacher of King Mongkut's children and wives.

Foster and a young Kristen Stewart as a besieged mother and daughter in David Fincher's thriller *Panic Room.*

The Brave One stars Foster as a radio host-turned-vigilante and Terrence Howard as the cop investigating her crimes.

In Roman Polanski's *Carnage*, Foster starred opposite John C. Reilly, Christoph Waltz and Kate Winslet. Set entirely in one apartment, it is about two bourgeois New York couples meeting to discuss their sons.

jamie foxx 1967

| Any Given Sunday | Collateral | Ray | Jarhead | Dreamgirls | The Kingdom | Django Unchained | The Amazing Spider-Man 2 |

F

Born Eric Marlon Bishop in Terrell, Texas, Jamie Foxx has parlayed his musical and comedic roots into an impressive range as a serious actor. Excelling in sport and music before turning to stand-up comedy in 1989, he joined the Wayans brothers' sketch show *In Living Color* in 1991, and made his film debut in *Toys* (1992).

After supporting roles and occasional leads in several comedies, he made his dramatic debut in *Any Given Sunday* (1999), as a football quarterback with ambitions to branch into music. In *Ali* (2001), he was Muhammad Ali's assistant trainer Drew Bundini Brown.

His breakthrough year was 2004, matching Al Pacino's achievement of a double acting Oscar nomination in the same ceremony and a Best Actor win. This was for *Ray*, a dream role for Foxx as it allowed him to showcase his own considerable musical skills as Ray Charles. His Supporting Actor nomination was for *Collateral*, Michael Mann's neon-lit nocturnal thriller in which Foxx's cab driver is forced to drive Tom Cruise's professional assassin between assignments. As a musician, he scored number one hits on both the U.S. singles and album charts.

He consolidated this success by broadening his acting range. In *Jarhead* (2005), he was a Marine Corps Staff Sergeant. *Miami Vice* (2006) reunited him with Michael Mann for a controversial reimagining of Mann's own seminal 1980s TV series. *Dreamgirls* (2006) returned to the music biz, casting Foxx as a thinly disguised version of Motown's founder Berry Gordy Jr. In *The Kingdom* (2007), he was an FBI agent probing terrorist attacks in Saudi Arabia.

Film acting temporarily took a back seat to his television and music work, although he did appear in *The Soloist* (2009) as a cellist left destitute by schizophrenia, and in *Law Abiding Citizen* (2009) he was a prosecutor forced to confront the vigilante actions of a man who felt betrayed by the justice system.

After supporting roles in comedies *Valentine's Day* and *Due Date* (both 2010), followed by *Horrible Bosses* (2011), Foxx scored another major role in Quentin Tarantino's *Django Unchained* (2012). He plays the freed slave who joins forces with Christoph Waltz's bounty hunter, as garrulous as Django is taciturn. In *White House Down* (2013) his U.S. president's attempt to broker a Middle East peace deal leads to a terrorist assault on the White House, while in *The Amazing Spider-Man 2* (2014) he played the villainous Electro, whose powers resulted from an accident involving electric eels. **MBr**

genre   ■ Drama   ■ Crime   ■ War   ■ Musical   ■ Action   ■ Western

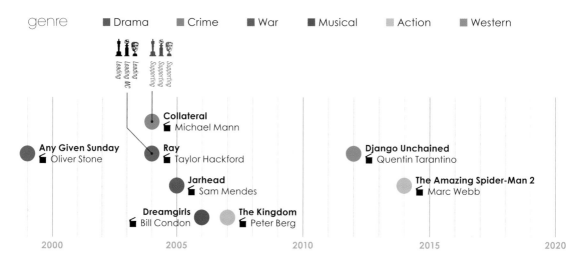

Leading / Leading MC / Leading

Supporting / Supporting

Collateral
Michael Mann

Any Given Sunday
Oliver Stone

Ray
Taylor Hackford

Django Unchained
Quentin Tarantino

Jarhead
Sam Mendes

The Amazing Spider-Man 2
Marc Webb

Dreamgirls
Bill Condon

The Kingdom
Peter Berg

2000   2005   2010   2015   2020

james franco 1978

Spider-Man

Milk

127 Hours

Howl

Rise of the
Planet of
the Apes

This Is
the End

Palo Alto

The
Interview

F

A mainstream celebrity, sex symbol and Oscar nominee who prefers the persona of a bohemian intellectual and prankster, James Franco attracts as much suspicion as admiration. He is not respectful enough of Hollywood to earn a place in its higher echelons — always slipping off its sets to publish some experimental poetry, study for a degree in something or mount an exhibition — while to the art and literature communities he is a starry dilettante, too famous and pretty to be taken seriously as a subversive. Franco continues to mock his own image, playing himself as a narcissistic hipster star in *This Is the End* (2013), as well as authoring artier projects in film, theater, literature, music and art. His 2010 short story collection *Palo Alto* was made into a film by Gia Coppola in 2013; and he became an unlikely poster boy for all-American values with Seth Rogen when their comedy *The Interview* (2014) triggered a security breach at Sony Pictures and diplomatic ructions between the United States and North Korea.

It was alongside Rogen that Franco first found recognition, playing listless stoner teens in Judd Apatow and Paul Feig's television landmark *Freaks and Geeks* (1999–2000). The title role in the television movie *James Dean* (2001) brought him further recognition, and a Golden Globe. Since attaining action figure status via Sam Raimi's *Spider-Man* trilogy (2002–07), he has maintained a balance of big-budget titles such as *Rise of the Planet of the Apes* (2011) and *Oz the Great and Powerful* (2013), goofy comedies like *Pineapple Express* (2008) and *This is the End*, and challenging works by name directors: Gus Van Sant's *Milk* (2008); Danny Boyle's *127 Hours* (2010); Harmony Korine's *Spring Breakers* (2012). He did some of his finest work as poet Allen Ginsberg in the experimental biopic *Howl* (2010). It was *127 Hours*, however, that won him an Oscar nomination. Playing Aron Ralston, a climber who in the wake of an accident faced the real-life horror of cutting his own arm off to save himself, Franco was widely praised. Similar plaudits have tended not to accompany his recurring role as a multimedia artist named Franco in the U.S. soap opera *General Hospital* (2009–12), although the actor himself regards it as performance art. As a director, meanwhile, his projects have included feature film adaptations of Cormac McCarthy's novel *Child of God* (2013) and of William Faulkner's novels *As I Lay Dying* (2013) and *The Sound and the Fury* (2014). **HM**

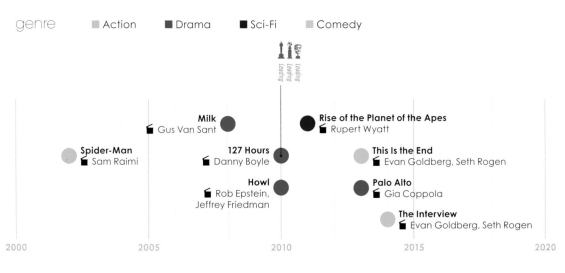

genre ■ Action ■ Drama ■ Sci-Fi ■ Comedy

Leading Leading Leading

Milk
🎬 Gus Van Sant

Rise of the Planet of the Apes
🎬 Rupert Wyatt

Spider-Man
🎬 Sam Raimi

127 Hours
🎬 Danny Boyle

This Is the End
🎬 Evan Goldberg, Seth Rogen

Howl
🎬 Rob Epstein,
Jeffrey Friedman

Palo Alto
🎬 Gia Coppola

The Interview
🎬 Evan Goldberg, Seth Rogen

2000   2005   2010   2015   2020

morgan freeman 1937

| Who Says I Can't Ride a Rainbow | Brubaker | Street Smart | Driving Miss Daisy | Lean on Me | Glory | Robin Hood: Prince of Thieves | Unforgiven |

F

Few actors are able to convince as the president of any country, let alone two. And fewer can get away with playing God. Twice. Such is Morgan Freeman's stature as a star. A prolific actor, he was born in Memphis in 1937 and began his professional acting career in the early 1960s. His first credited screen appearance was a small role in the children's drama *Who Says I Can't Ride a Rainbow* (1971), although he would become better known through his appearances on the soap *Another World* (1982–84) and the children's television show *The Electric Company* (1971–77).

Freeman played a sympathetic inmate in the prison drama *Brubaker* (1980), but his breakthrough role came as a pimp and police suspect in the thriller *Street Smart* (1987). He received an Oscar nomination for his performance. In 1989, he recreated the stage role that won him his third Off-Broadway Theater Award, playing the chauffeur to an elderly Jewish widow in *Driving Miss Daisy*. In the same year, he excelled as a schoolteacher bringing order to an unruly class in *Lean on Me* and a Union soldier fighting the Civil War in the only black regiment, in *Glory*.

Freeman brought gravitas to *Robin Hood: Prince of Thieves* (1991), but it was his performance in Clint Eastwood's *Unforgiven* (1992) that began a string of roles that would see his star rise. As former outlaw Ned Logan, the best friend of Eastwood's Bill Munny, Freeman invests his character with pathos, regretful of the misery his actions have caused, and sees one last journey with his friend, to avenge a brutal attack on a young woman, as a chance to redeem himself.

The Shawshank Redemption (1994) may not have been a huge commercial success on its original release, but it has grown in stature and popularity, and is one of the actor's best-known roles. Freeman is the heart of the film, playing Red, a lifer in a state penitentiary and the closest friend of Tim Robbins' Andy Dufresne. The world-weariness Red exudes is reflected in the somber voice of Detective Somerset in David Fincher's *Se7en* (1995). It is through his eyes that we view the world he polices and reel in horror at the actions of the serial killer John Doe. The performance, quiet but concerned, highlights Freeman's skill at exploring the depths of his characters' feelings.

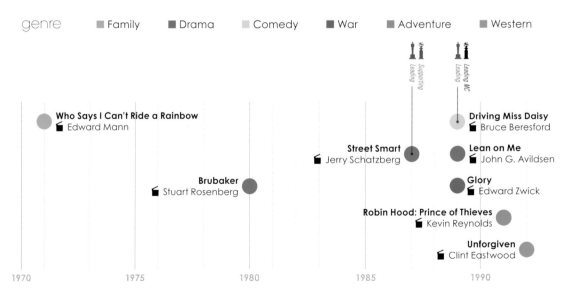

genre ■ Family ■ Drama ■ Comedy ■ War ■ Adventure ■ Western

Supporting
Leading

Leading MC
Leading

Who Says I Can't Ride a Rainbow
Edward Mann

Driving Miss Daisy
Bruce Beresford

Street Smart
Jerry Schatzberg

Lean on Me
John G. Avildsen

Brubaker
Stuart Rosenberg

Glory
Edward Zwick

Robin Hood: Prince of Thieves
Kevin Reynolds

Unforgiven
Clint Eastwood

1970   1975   1980   1985   1990

$275M	$670M	$265M	$502M	$501M	$268M	$448M	$459M
Driving Miss Daisy (1989)	**Robin Hood: Prince of Thieves** (1991)	**Unforgiven** (1992)	**Se7en** (1995)	**Deep Impact** (1998)	**Million Dollar Baby** (2004)	**Batman Begins** (2005)	**Lucy** (2014)

The Shawshank Redemption | **Se7en** | **Deep Impact** | **Million Dollar Baby** | **Batman Begins** | **Gone Baby Gone** | **Invictus** | **Lucy**

Novelist James Patterson's detective Alex Cross should have been perfect for Freeman, but as *Kiss the Girls* (1997) and *Along Came a Spider* (2001) revealed, the stories themselves were not as engaging as their central character. Likewise, *Outbreak* (1995), *Chain Reaction* (1996) and *Hard Rain* (1998) hardly challenged Freeman, although it was good to see him playing a villain in the latter. He was better in *Amistad* (1997), even if the film is weighed down by history.

A decade before Barack Obama was voted into office, Freeman played the U.S. President in the apocalyptic disaster movie *Deep Impact* (1998). His screen persona by this time was that of a respected elder and the role fitted perfectly. In 2003, he played God in *Bruce Almighty* and again, it seemed fitting that if there were a deity he would possess the wisdom that Freeman projected. The actor would play God once more in the inferior sequel *Evan Almighty* (2007).

Freeman won a Best Supporting Actor Oscar for his portrayal of Eddie "Scrap-Iron" Dupris, who convinces his gym owner boss and friend Clint Eastwood to take on a young female boxer in *Million Dollar Baby*

(2004). It is one of his best performances. The following year, he played Lucius Fox in *Batman Begins* (2005). He would go on to appear in the other two entries of Christopher Nolan's *Dark Knight* trilogy and, like Michael Caine's Alfred, is very much the heart of the film. He would also appear alongside Caine in the silly caper movie *Now You See Me* (2013) and in the underwhelming *Transcendence* (2014). He seems to have more fun in Luc Besson's ludicrous *Lucy* (2014).

Freeman occasionally appears in comedies. He starred opposite Jack Nicholson in *The Bucket List* (2007), joined Michael Douglas, Robert De Niro and Kevin Kline on a stag do in *Last Vegas* (2013) and is fun in *RED* (2010). He is dependably solid in the most absurd film projects, from *Wanted* (2008) and *Olympus Has Fallen* (2013) to the somber *Oblivion* (2013). But when he is cast in a role with emotional depth, Freeman is riveting. His police captain in *Gone Baby Gone* (2007) is one of his best roles, conveying the anguish of a man who has to break the law to do the right thing. While his portrayal of Nelson Mandela in *Invictus* (2009) captures the irrepressible spirit and energy of a great man. **IHS**

■ Thriller ■ Action ■ Mystery ■ Sci-Fi

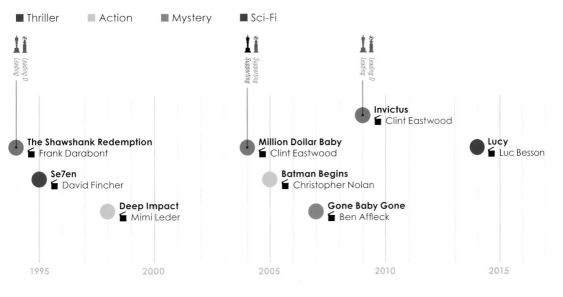

Street Smart
(1987)

Street Smart features Freeman as a pimp called Fast Black, who mistakenly believes that a news story fabricated by Christopher Reeves' journalist is about him.

Driving Miss Daisy
(1989)

Lean on Me
(1989)

The Shawshank Redemption
(1994)

Se7en
(1995)

Million Dollar Baby
(2004)

Batman Begins
(2005)

Invictus
(2009)

Freeman has described his role in **Driving Miss Daisy** as a mistake due to typecasting him as a "wise, old, dignified, black man."

Loosely based on true events, **Lean on Me** starred Freeman as Joe Louis Clark, an inner city high school principal tasked with turning his school's fortunes around.

Freeman and Tim Robbins in **The Shawshank Redemption**. Since 2008 it has topped IMDb's Top 250 film list, as voted by users.

Freeman in one of his best-known roles, as Red in **The Shawshank Redemption**. In Stephen King's original novella, the character is a middle-aged Irishman with greying red hair.

Freeman and Brad Pitt as the detectives hunting a biblically inspired serial killer in **Se7en**.

Hilary Swank and Freeman in *Million Dollar Baby*, for which the actor won an Academy Award after three previous nominations.

Freeman as Lucius Fox in *Batman Begins*, the first instalment in Christopher Nolan's *Batman* trilogy.

Starring Freeman as Nelson Mandela and Matt Damon as François Pienaar, the captain of the South African rugby union team, *Invictus* depicts the events of 1995 Rugby World Cup in the newly post-apartheid South Africa.

In 1995, when Nelson Mandela was asked at a press conference who he would like to play himself in a movie of his life, the statesman replied "Morgan Freeman." The actor finally got the chance with *Invictus*, and was widely praised for his portrayal.

jean gabin 1904–76

| They Were Five | The Lower Depths | Pépé le Moko | La Grande Illusion | Port of Shadows | La Bête Humaine | Le Jour se Lève | Moontide |

Holed up on the top floor of a Paris tenement block, the police closing in, Jean Gabin furiously harangues the rubbernecking crowd below. "Yes, I'm a killer! But the streets are running with killers! Everybody kills!" Even as a murderer, in Marcel Carné's *Le Jour se Lève* (1939), Gabin identifies with the common man. Down-to-earth glamour and anti-romantic romanticism were his stock-in-trade during the 1930s. Gentle beneath a truculent exterior, the doomed proletarian hero at odds with the law, he stoically met his fate without complaining.

Born in Paris in 1904, the son of a café entertainer, Gabin worked briefly as an auto mechanic before branching out into theater, cabaret and vaudeville. He made his screen debut with the coming of sound. Many of his early films, though in French, were shot in Germany for Pathé-Nathan.

It was a run of films directed by Julien Duvivier that brought him to fame; having cast him, rather unexpectedly, as Pontius Pilate in *Behold the Man* (1935), Duvivier gave him the lead role in *La Bandera* (1935), in which he murders a man in Paris and joins the Spanish foreign legion. In *They Were Five* (1936) he is one of a cartel of unemployed workers that buy a winning lottery ticket and open a restaurant together, with uneasy results. Taking the title role in *Pépé le Moko* (1937), he is an expatriate French gangster hiding in the Casbah of Algiers, yearning nostalgically

for Paris and lured to his doom by the love of a visiting Frenchwoman. *Pépé* was the film that consolidated Gabin's stardom and defined his on-screen persona — a tough, streetwise character, outwardly cynical but with an underlying romantic streak that will cause his downfall.

Jean Renoir, with whom Gabin got on exceptionally well, cast him as one of the bunch of dead-end characters in *The Lower Depths* (1936), adapted from Maxim Gorky's play, and in *La Bête Humaine* (1938) as a homicidal train driver, cursed — according to the Émile Zola novel that the film is based on — by a genetic inheritance of tainted blood. Between those two, *La Grande Illusion* (1937) found both director and star at their peak. Set in a German POW camp during World War I, Renoir's impassioned plea for common humanity in the face of class, racial and nationalist conflicts gave Gabin, as a working-class French officer, one of his supreme roles.

Gabin was at his most iconic, though, in two of the richly atmospheric, doom-laden dramas from director Marcel Carné and writer Jacques Prévert that so potently distilled the mood of just-pre-World War II France. *Port of Shadows* (1938), the pair's first masterpiece of poetic realism, offered him a tailor-made role as an army deserter on the run in the titular foggy port, with Michèle Morgan the sad-eyed waif

genre ■ Drama ■ Crime ■ War ▨ Noir ▨ Romance □ Comedy

They Were Five Julien Duvivier	**Port of Shadows** Marcel Carné	
The Lower Depths Jean Renoir	**La Bête Humaine** Jean Renoir	
Pépé le Moko Julien Duvivier	**Le Jour se Lève** Marcel Carné	
La Grande Illusion Jean Renoir		**Moontide** Archie Mayo

1930   1935   1940   1945

| La Marie du port | Le Plaisir | Touchez Pas au Grisbi | French Cancan | Pig Across Paris | Maigret Sets a Trap | Love Is My Profession | The Baron of the Locks |

he takes under his wing. In *Le Jour se Lève* (1939), with Gabin as the trapped, doomed killer, chain-smoking his way through his last night on Earth, the metaphor for France on the brink of catastrophe was umistakable.

There was time for one more good role, as the tough tugboat skipper in Jean Grémillon's *Stormy Waters* (1941), before Gabin lit out for Hollywood. He was miserable there: "In English, I could hear myself speak and I felt that someone else was speaking in my place … Nothing seemed to correspond to what I was saying, neither my gestures, my body or anything I felt physically or thought." He was no happier with the studios' attempts to make him over physically into "the French Spencer Tracy." After two lame vehicles, he fled the United States to join the Free French forces and took part in the Normandy landings.

After the war, with his style of working-class hero out of fashion, Gabin lost his way a little. Attempts to revisit his pre-war triumphs in René Clément's *The Walls of Malapaga* (1949) and Carné's *La Marie du port* (1950) felt flat. Max Ophüls used him well, as the Normandy farmer enchanted by a visiting group of urban prostitutes, in the longest episode of his Guy de Maupassant three-parter *Le Plaisir* (1952). But it was Jacques Becker who put him back on track, as the ageing crime boss looking to pull one final haul in *Touchez Pas au Grisbi* (1954).

The film revived Gabin's screen career, launching him on the series of patriarchal roles that would continue into his old age. Back with his friend Jean Renoir, he was magisterial as the impresario Danglard in *French Cancan* (1954), founding the Moulin Rouge and juggling rich backers, bailiffs and various mistresses to achieve his ambition. The role took in comedy as well as drama, both of which Gabin handled well. Comedy predominated in Claude Autant-Lara's German Occupation-set *Pig Across Paris* (1956), with Gabin as an artist teaming up with Bourvil's cab driver to transport four suitcases of blackmarket pork across the capital.

Now gray-haired, thicker-set and exuding wry experience, Gabin settled into a series of authority-figure roles, sometimes even on the right side of the law; he played Georges Simenon's Inspector Maigret several times, starting with Jean Delannoy's *Maigret Sets a Trap* (1958). Simenon also provided the material for Autant-Lara's *Love Is My Profession* (1958), with Gabin as a wealthy lawyer who falls for a seductive young client played by Brigitte Bardot. In the final decade of his career, increasingly stubborn and averse to taking direction, Gabin took to working only with directors he could dominate, and the quality of his later films declined. But to the last he remained hugely popular with the public. **PK**

■ Mystery

La Marie du port
📷 Marcel Carné

Le Plaisir
📷 Max Ophüls

Touchez Pas au Grisbi
📷 Jacques Becker

French Cancan
📷 Jean Renoir

Pig Across Paris
📷 Claude Autant-Lara

Maigret Sets a Trap
📷 Jean Delannoy

Love Is My Profession
📷 Claude Autant-Lara

The Baron of the Locks
📷 Jean Delannoy

1950   1955   1960   1965

clark gable 1901–60

Hell Divers   **Possessed**   **Red Dust**   **It Happened One Night**   **Mutiny on the Bounty**   **China Seas**   **San Francisco**   **Saratoga**

G

Clark Gable is best remembered for playing Rhett Butler in the Hollywood landmark *Gone with the Wind* (1939). Just as that film was a product — and summation — of Hollywood's golden era, so too was Gable's star persona. Known affectionately as "The King" for his box-office supremacy and commanding screen presence, Gable's best performances are memorable studies of a certain kind of masculinity: rugged, straight-talking, prone to action rather than contemplation. But alongside his image as a guy's guy was a dreamy and romantic adventurousness that saw him partnered with some of Hollywood's most celebrated actresses.

Born 1901, in Ohio, Gable acted as a young man in provincial theater and spent much of his formative experience under the guidance of his first wife, theater manager Josephine Dillon. She helped him develop a more naturalistic style of delivery and beef up his slight figure. An extra in Hollywood silents, Gable began to be noticed in the early 1930s for his supporting roles. It was not all favorable attention, however. "His ears are too big and he looks like an ape," producer Darryl F. Zanuck famously said of him.

Gable provided an early taste of his raw machismo in *Hell Divers* (1931). An aviation action film, the actor brought to it an impressive assurance as a cocky young naval ace on board a U.S. carrier, whose talents threaten his older colleague. Gable gave more tough-guy attitude to his role as a worldly and affluent lawyer who takes on a mistress, played by Joan Crawford, in *Possessed* (1931).

It would be another female costar with whom Gable achieved his early breakthrough. The six pictures that he made with Jean Harlow turned him into a star. In a series of romances set in exotic locales, such as the French colonial rubber plantation of *Red Dust* (1932) or the steamer boat of *China Seas* (1935), Gable tended to be cast as straight-talking guys with a romantic streak, against the brassy, wisecracking characters Harlow played so well. It was an exquisitely well-matched partnership, the couple especially adept at scenes of push-pull banter. Their final collaboration, *Saratoga*, was released after Harlow's untimely death in 1937.

Gable added similar gruff sophistication to his partnership with Claudette Colbert's heiress in Frank Capra's romantic comedy *It Happened One Night*

genre   ■ Adventure   ■ Drama   ■ Romance   ■ Comedy   ■ Western   ■ War

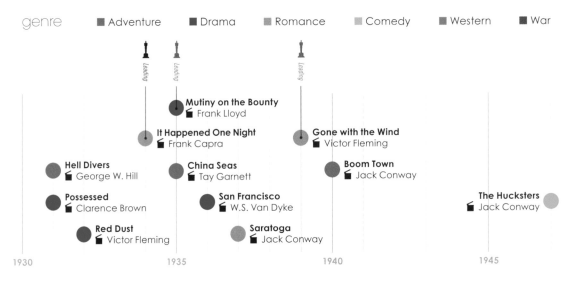

Mutiny on the Bounty
Frank Lloyd

It Happened One Night
Frank Capra

Hell Divers
George W. Hill

China Seas
Tay Garnett

Gone with the Wind
Victor Fleming

Boom Town
Jack Conway

Possessed
Clarence Brown

San Francisco
W.S. Van Dyke

The Hucksters
Jack Conway

Red Dust
Victor Fleming

Saratoga
Jack Conway

Leading   Leading   Leading

1930   1935   1940   1945

$6.8BN
Gone with the Wind
(1939)

| Gone with the Wind | Boom Town | The Hucksters | Mogambo | The Tall Men | Run Silent, Run Deep | It Started in Naples | The Misfits |

G

(1934), winning an Oscar for his performance. He was nominated again the following year for his role as Fletcher Christian in the 1935 version of *Mutiny on the Bounty*, powerfully conveying his character's fiery sense of justice. The actor further established his credentials as a serious actor in three films alongside Spencer Tracy, notably the grandly realized *San Francisco* (1936) and *Boom Town* (1940).

His status as Hollywood's pre-eminent male star was spectacularly confirmed by his role in *Gone with the Wind*. Based on Margaret Mitchell's celebrated novel, it says something for the actor's clout that producer David O. Selznick delayed production for two years to wait for his availability. It was inspired casting. If the film's politics now seem uncomfortably dated, Gable's performance as Rhett, whose air of courtly irony disguises an ardent, even cruel intensity, is mesmerizing.

Gable served in the U.S. Air Force during part of World War II, even flying a few combat missions over Europe. His service put a hiatus on his movie career but it enhanced his persona of uncomplicated masculinity. Playing a serviceman returning back to his old career from the war, he was a New York

advertising executive in the flawed but fun 1947 comedy drama *The Hucksters*. It was a modest success, but Gable struggled to recapture his pre-war glory. The 1950s were a time of turmoil for the studios, and the actor's mixed fortunes were, in some senses, symptomatic of this wider sense of panic in the industry.

There were some fine later performances. In the World War II drama *Run Silent, Run Deep* (1958) he was customarily tough as a driven captain of a U.S. submarine. And he showed a nice light touch in *It Started in Naples* (1960), playing a middle-aged American who falls for Sophia Loren's cabaret singer.

The standout performance from this period would also be his last. In *The Misfits* (1961), Gable plays an ageing cowboy who embarks on a troubled relationship with a young divorcee. Filmed on location in the Nevada desert, it was a notoriously difficult shoot. However, alongside costars Marilyn Monroe and Montgomery Clift, actors with a markedly more naturalistic style, Gable impressed. He was ruggedly convincing, weathered by experience and a little melancholy with advancing years. The film was released following his death in 1960. **EL**

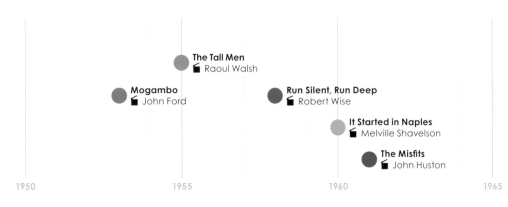

greta garbo 1905–90

Gösta
Berlings
Saga

Flesh and
the Devil

Joyless
Street

The Kiss

Anna
Christie

Romance

Mata Hari

Grand Hotel

Swedish-born Greta Garbo embodied the grace and glamour of Hollywood's Golden Age, yet actively spurned the spotlight. A dazzling screen icon, she cultivated an enigmatic and elusive image through years of self-imposed isolation. She found fame during the late silent era for her progressive acting style, conveying a startlingly deep range of emotions in front of the camera. And yet, for all her celebrity, Garbo's career spanned just 19 years, making the last of 27 screen appearances in 1941, at the age of 36.

Born 1905, in Stockholm, Greta Lovisa Gustafsson was the daughter of a laborer. She left school at the age of 13 to care for her sick father, before eventually being forced into work following his death a year later. It was not until 1921, while working at a department store, that she would first appear in front of the camera. She starred in an advertisement, which led to a series of promotional videos and eventually her feature debut, in the silent comedy *Peter the Tramp* (1922). She studied at Stockholm's Royal Dramatic Theatre Acting School where she was chosen to appear in Mauritz Stiller's *Gösta Berlings Saga* (1924). Louis B. Mayer, then head of MGM, saw the film and offered Stiller a contract. He accepted, but only on the proviso that his lead actress also be signed.

With a new surname — a decision made on her behalf by Stiller — Garbo quickly earned a reputation as the screen's "great sufferer." Playing a series of disillusioned women, scarred by heartbreak and stalked by tragedy, the quality of her performances saw her internationally recognized. G.W. Pabst's *Joyless Street* (1925) made her a huge star in Germany, but her striking presence could be enjoyed by any national audience. Her U.S. debut was an adaptation of a Vicente Blasco-Ibanez story, *Torrent* (1926), which featured Garbo as a Spanish peasant who becomes an opera star. Her performance was so striking that her fee was raised before the film was even released. Blasco-Ibanez was also the source for her follow-up. Appearing opposite John Gilbert, the deeply romantic *Flesh and the Devil* (1926) made Garbo a sensation.

Of the 24 films she made in Hollywood, all were for MGM. However, the relationship with her employer was never easy. She resented Stiller's being fired from *The Temptress* (1926) and was even more infuriated at not being allowed to travel back to Sweden to attend her sister's funeral. Equally, her refusal to attend publicity events and her high wage demands constantly tested the studio's resolve. However, with films such as *Love* (aka *Anna Karenina*, 1927) and *The*

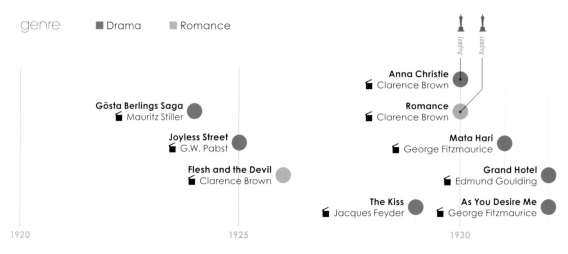

genre   ■ Drama   ■ Romance

Gösta Berlings Saga
📽 Mauritz Stiller

Joyless Street
📽 G.W. Pabst

Flesh and the Devil
📽 Clarence Brown

The Kiss
📽 Jacques Feyder

Anna Christie
📽 Clarence Brown

Romance
📽 Clarence Brown

Mata Hari
📽 George Fitzmaurice

Grand Hotel
📽 Edmund Goulding

As You Desire Me
📽 George Fitzmaurice

Leading   Leading

1920   1925   1930

As You Desire Me | Queen Christina | The Painted Veil | Anna Karenina | Camille | Conquest | Ninotchka | Two-Faced Woman

Kiss (1929) continuing to dominate the box office, the studio could hardly complain. And her reticence to appear in the spotlight only added to audiences' insatiable appetite for her on-screen appearances.

MGM delayed her sound debut, waiting for the appropriate vehicle with which to showcase her talents. The opportunity finally arrived with Clarence Brown's adaptation of Eugene O'Neill's *Anna Christie* (1930) — her husky voice perfect for the titular character, a woman with a secret past. The studio's promotional campaign was simple, but effective: "Garbo Talks!" The film was an international hit, earning the star her first Academy Award nomination. She would receive another nomination the following year, when she reunited with Brown for *Romance* (1930). She also played the eponymous spy *Mata Hari* (1931), which became MGM's biggest hit of the year.

Garbo's popularity reached its peak with the release of *Grand Hotel* (1932). Its unprecedented success gave her more power in negotiations with MGM and allowed her to shy away even more from media and public engagements. She refused interviews, never attended premieres and her sets were closed to all visitors, even, on occasions, to the director of the film. When asked why, Garbo explained: "When people are watching, I'm just a woman making faces for the camera. It destroys the illusion." It was also believed that Garbo felt self-conscious about her English, worried about expressing herself correctly and aware of the media's tendency to twist the meaning of comments. She became known as "the Swedish sphinx," an enigmatic star who fascinated and enthralled in equal measure.

Garbo reprised her role as *Anna Karenina* (1935), following it with similar portrayals of isolated women consumed by an insatiable yearning for love, first in *Camille* (1936) and then in *Conquest* (1937), the latter film one of Garbo's only box-office failures. By the late 1930s, her box-office appeal was waning. MGM's solution was to feature her in a comedy. Ernst Lubitsch's *Ninotchka* (1939), a satire cowritten by Billy Wilder, features Garbo as a gravely serious, egocentric Soviet ambassador, who is gradually won round to the West. It earned her a third and final Oscar nomination. Her last screen appearance paled by comparison. George Cukor's *Two-Faced Woman* (1941) lacks the energy of Lubitsch's sparkling comedy and Garbo's career was halted by the onset of World War II. However, her early retirement saw her bow out on a high, where her star has remained. **PG**

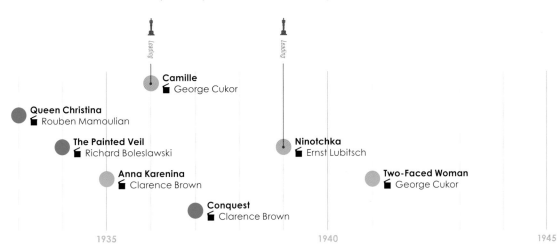

Camille
George Cukor

Queen Christina
Rouben Mamoulian

The Painted Veil
Richard Boleslawski

Anna Karenina
Clarence Brown

Conquest
Clarence Brown

Ninotchka
Ernst Lubitsch

Two-Faced Woman
George Cukor

1935   1940   1945

Gösta Berlings Saga
(1924)

Flesh and the Devil
(1926)

Anna Christie
(1930)

Mata Hari
(1931)

Grand Hotel
(1932)

Anna Karenina
(1935)

Conquest
(1937)

Ninotchka
(1939)

Garbo as Elizabeth Dohna in the romantic drama *Gösta Berlings Saga*, based on the 1891 novel by Selma Lagerlöf.

Anna Christie stars Garbo as a prostitute who reunites with her estranged father and falls in love.

Flesh and the Devil starred Garbo and John Gilbert, who would become lovers offscreen as well as on during shooting of the movie.

John Gilbert, Garbo and Marc McDermott in *Flesh and the Devil*, which tells the story of two childhood friends who fall in love with the same woman.

Garbo and Charles Bickford in *Anna Christie*, Garbo's sound debut. The first words that she said on film were "Gimme a whisky, ginger ale on the side, and don't be stingy, baby!" The introduction of sound posed no problem for Garbo — her stock soared with each new feature.

Mata Hari was loosely based on the life of the eponymous exotic dancer and courtesan, who was convicted of being a spy and executed by firing squad in France under charges of espionage for Germany during World War I.

Unusually, **Grand Hotel** featured five of MGM's top tier stars: Garbo, Joan Crawford, John Barrymore, Lionel Barrymore and Wallace Beery. Garbo insisted on top billing.

Anna Karenina featured Garbo's second performance as the title character after the 1927 silent adaptation *Love*.

The story of the Polish Countess Marie Walewska, who becomes the mistress of Napoleon, **Conquest** made a loss for MGM.

Aping the promotional slogan of her first sound feature ("Garbo Talks!"), the tagline for **Ninotchka** read "Garbo Laughs!"

ava gardner 1922–90

| Whistle Stop | The Killers | The Hucksters | Show Boat | Pandora and the Flying Dutchman | Lone Star | The Snows of Kilimanjaro | Mogambo |

"She can't sing, she can't talk, she can't act, she's terrific!" was the reported content of a telegram sent by Louis B. Mayer, head of MGM, to his head of talent, Al Altman, upon seeing Ava Gardner's 1941 screen test. Gardner's abilities as a performer are no longer subject to such doubt, but it took MGM five years from signing Gardner up to finding her a star-making featured role — in Robert Siodmak's The Killers (1946) — and she would continue to be rather haphazardly cast, primarily in roles that foregrounded her looks.

From the earliest days of her career, which saw her make a swift marriage to MGM's most bankable star Mickey Rooney, her private life was of greater interest to the public than her work. Had there been an Oscar for generating gossip column inches, it might not have taken Gardner until 1954 to be nominated. However, prurient disapproval of her many and brazen liaisons has long since given way to warm public respect and affection for a woman whose sexual confidence and self-effacing smarts now seem to place her well ahead of her time. Accounts proliferate of her friendliness, her lack of inhibitions and her salty sense of humor.

Gardner's discovery was part of a specific drive by MGM to swell its ranks of stars with members of the public in whom talent scouts glimpsed raw potential. Gardner was raw indeed: a poor and unworldly farm girl from North Carolina, she was contracted to MGM even though she had never acted and her accent was considered incomprehensible. Only 19 when she married Rooney, she came into maturity already famous. Though her beauty earned her much attention during her brief marriage, it seemed that even Rooney's influence could not help her to graduate from uncredited bit-parts. No shortage of influential men took an interest once she and Rooney split up: by the time The Killers gave her the spotlight, she had already passed a phase as the object of Howard Hughes' eccentric attentions, and attempted to settle down again, as the fifth wife of big-band leader Artie Shaw — a union that endured only a year.

If life away from the screen had its disappointments, The Killers had revealed that she had something special on it. Siodmak insisted on restraint, presenting his actress in minimal make-up and encouraging

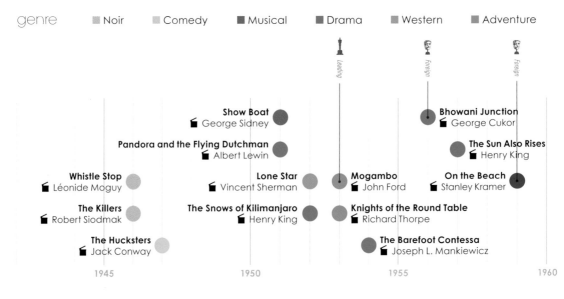

genre ■ Noir ■ Comedy ■ Musical ■ Drama ■ Western ■ Adventure

Leading

foreign

foreign

Show Boat
George Sidney

Bhowani Junction
George Cukor

Pandora and the Flying Dutchman
Albert Lewin

The Sun Also Rises
Henry King

Whistle Stop
Léonide Moguy

Lone Star
Vincent Sherman

Mogambo
John Ford

On the Beach
Stanley Kramer

The Killers
Robert Siodmak

The Snows of Kilimanjaro
Henry King

Knights of the Round Table
Richard Thorpe

The Hucksters
Jack Conway

The Barefoot Contessa
Joseph L. Mankiewicz

1945   1950   1955   1960

Knights of the Round Table	The Barefoot Contessa	Bhowani Junction	The Sun Also Rises	On the Beach	Seven Days in May	The Night of the Iguana	Earthquake

G

her to scale down her gestures and delivery; and her actual screen time was relatively brief. Yet, as her biographer Lee Server puts it, Gardner "haunts the entire film with her compelling presence." The film was a hit and Gardner a star in the making. She could be sure that she had scaled the professional heights when cast opposite her childhood idol Clark Gable in *The Hucksters* (1947). The two would become friends and work together again on *Lone Star* (1952) and *Mogambo* (1953), for which Gardner gained her only Oscar nomination. She would be seen at her most exquisite in Joseph L. Mankiewicz's lavish, soapy Hollywood melodrama *The Barefoot Contessa* (1954) — though she found considerably less common ground with another legendary costar, Humphrey Bogart. Further acclaim followed for her work in *Bhowani Junction* (1956), directed by George Cukor.

This time of professional flourishing also saw Gardner become embroiled in the on-again off-again affair that would dominate her personal life, and enthrall and appall the general public, for a period of years. "I truly felt that no matter what happened, we would always be in love," she said of her early bond with Frank Sinatra. Their affair convinced Sinatra's wife Nancy that despite her Catholicism, it was finally time to stop turning a blind eye to his infidelities and allow a divorce. Gardner and Sinatra wed in 1951, but both were unfaithful and violently jealous — while constant pursuit by paparazzi, whom Sinatra was prone to attack, added further pressure. The marriage finally ended in 1957, though the two would never end their friendship. Ava convalesced in Spain, where she made friends with Ernest Hemingway and had a relationship with famed bullfighter Luis Miguel Dominguín.

Gardner's later career saw her continue to work with fine directors — John Frankenheimer on *Seven Days in May* (1964); John Huston on *The Night of the Iguana* (1964) — although she also entertained lighter content, such as the disaster movies *Earthquake* (1974) and *The Cassandra Crossing* (1976), as well as a stint on the television soap opera *Knots Landing* in 1985. She spent her last two decades living in London, where she died of pneumonia in 1990 at the age of 67. **HM**

■ Sci-Fi ■ Thriller ■ Action

Foreign Leading D

Seven Days in May
🎬 John Frankenheimer

The Night of the Iguana
🎬 John Huston

Earthquake
🎬 Mark Robson

1965   1970   1975

judy garland 1922–69

| Broadway Melody of 1938 | Thorough–breds Don't Cry | Love Finds Andy Hardy | Babes in Arms | The Wizard of Oz | Little Nellie Kelly | Life Begins for Andy Hardy | Presenting Lily Mars |

A brilliant and troubled star, whose own life resembled a Hollywood melodrama, Judy Garland could light up the screen or make you cry. Her best work, a handful of films whose diversity is a testament to the range of her talent, has made her a beloved Hollywood icon.

Born Frances Ethel Gumm in Grand Rapids, Minnesota, 1922, Garland was the youngest child of vaudevillians. She first performed in public at the age of 2, with her sisters on the stage of her parents' cinema, singing the chorus to "Jingle Bells." Moving to California, the siblings were enrolled in a dance school and appeared in a few shorts. They changed their name to the Garland Sisters in 1935, but broke up a year later. Busby Berkeley saw them perform and Judy was signed to MGM, although the studio had no idea what to do with this 13-year-old talent.

After a few odd roles and a performance at Clark Gable's birthday, her major break came when she starred opposite the equally diminutive Mickey Rooney in *Thoroughbreds Don't Cry* (1937). He went on to become a star thanks to the *Andy Hardy* series, which Garland joined on the fourth entry, *Love Finds Andy Hardy* (1938). Their first starring role was in *Babes in Arms* (1939). They would appear in five more films

together, including *Andy Hardy Meets Debutante* (1940) and *Life Begins for Andy Hardy* (1941). Garland appealed to audiences with her girl-next-door persona. However, MGM was ruthless in its treatment of the young stars. To put them through the hectic schedule they were given amphetamines to stay awake and barbiturates to sleep, resulting in the actress' lifelong struggle with drugs.

The Wizard of Oz (1939) made Garland a star at 17. Shot in black and white and color, she plays Dorothy, a young girl who is knocked unconscious when a tornado strikes her Kansas home and is whisked off into a dream world of fairies, munchkins and witches, where she must follow the yellow brick road to find a wizard that can transport her home. Its faultless blend of drama, knockabout comedy, music and spectacle made it universally popular and Garland strikes a perfect balance of small-town naivety and feistiness.

After appearing in Busby Berkeley's *Strike Up the Band* (1940) with Mickey Rooney, Garland was the star of *Little Nellie Kelly* (1940), an adaptation of George M. Cohan's 1920s Broadway hit about familial strife. She was one of three showbiz hopefuls in *Ziegfeld Girl* (1941), appeared alongside Gene Kelly for the first

genre ■ Musical ■ Comedy ■ Romance ■ Drama

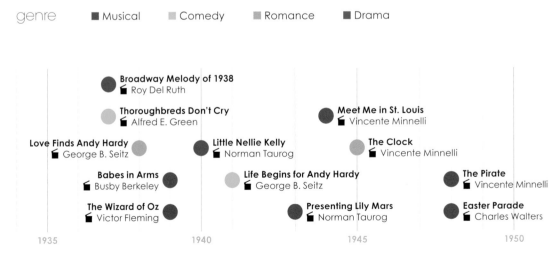

Broadway Melody of 1938 — Roy Del Ruth
Thoroughbreds Don't Cry — Alfred E. Green
Love Finds Andy Hardy — George B. Seitz
Babes in Arms — Busby Berkeley
The Wizard of Oz — Victor Fleming
Little Nellie Kelly — Norman Taurog
Life Begins for Andy Hardy — George B. Seitz
Presenting Lily Mars — Norman Taurog
Meet Me in St. Louis — Vincente Minnelli
The Clock — Vincente Minnelli
The Pirate — Vincente Minnelli
Easter Parade — Charles Walters

1935   1940   1945   1950

$392M
The Wizard of Oz
(1939)

$38M
A Star is Born
(1954)

Meet Me in
St. Louis

The Clock

The Pirate

Easter
Parade

A Star Is Born

Judgment at
Nuremberg

A Child
Is Waiting

I Could Go
on Singing

G

time in *For Me and My Gal* (1942) and was promoted as a more grown-up star by her studio for *Presenting Lily Mars* (1943), in which she appeared opposite Van Helfin as a young woman chasing fame.

Meet Me in St. Louis (1944), directed by Garland's soon-to-be husband Vincente Minnelli, was one of her finest achievements. A sumptuous family melodrama with musical interludes, it details the travails of an upper-middle class family, living in the titular city at the time of the 1904 World's Fair. With the Garland classics "The Trolley Song," "The Boy Next Door" and a heartbreaking rendition of "Have Yourself a Merry Little Christmas," it is a high point of the Hollywood musical and the star excels as one of the opinionated daughters of Leon Ames' businessman. Minnelli also directed Garland in her first dramatic role, *The Clock* (1945), a straightforward romantic drama with the actress solid in the lead, and the excellent musical *The Pirate* (1948), opposite Gene Kelly. The film was a critical success, but audiences were less impressed. Garland and Minnelli divorced in 1951.

Easter Parade (1948) was a huge critical and commercial hit. Garland stars opposite Fred Astaire, who was coaxed out of retirement after Gene Kelly

broke his ankle. Although the film's story is simple, the roll call of songs, written by Irving Berlin, is a joy. It was the biggest hit of the year.

Summer Stock (1950) was Garland's last film with Kelly and MGM. It is now only remembered for an inventive dance sequence and Garland's rendition of "Get Happy." She suffered a number of personal problems during this period and took three years off. Her return, in *A Star Is Born* (1954), found both her and costar James Mason on blistering form. The story of the relationship between a fading star and the aspiring singer he mentors is an emotionally raw, moving drama. As one contemporary critic noted, Garland "gives what is just about the greatest one-woman show in modern movie history." She was nominated for an Oscar. Further acclaim accompanied her dramatic performances in Stanley Kramer's *Judgment at Nuremberg* (1961) and John Cassavetes' *A Child Is Waiting* (1963).

Garland's final role was in *I Could Go on Singing* (1963), playing a superstar who has to choose between love and fame. It is a reflection on the decisions the performer made in her own life and is a perfect epitaph to a remarkable screen presence. **IHS**

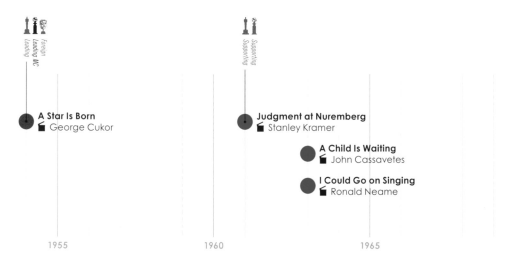

Foreign
Leading MC
Leading

A Star Is Born
George Cukor

Supporting
Supporting

Judgment at Nuremberg
Stanley Kramer

A Child Is Waiting
John Cassavetes

I Could Go on Singing
Ronald Neame

1955

1960

1965

richard gere 1949

| Looking For Mr. Goodbar | Days of Heaven | American Gigolo | An Officer and a Gentleman | Breathless | Pretty Woman | Chicago | I'm Not There |

Born in Philadelphia in 1949, Richard Gere's breakthrough role was in Richard Brooks' *Looking For Mr. Goodbar* (1977), playing a violent street hustler. The following year, he made good on his early promise, offering up a beguiling performance as a murderer on the run in Terrence Malick's poetic *Days of Heaven* (1978).

As he established a reputation for his acting prowess, Gere's game-changing role as a male escort in Paul Schrader's study of masculinity in crisis, *American Gigolo* (1980), saw him launched as a bona fide sex symbol. It would define his career for much of the next decade, bolstered in no small part by his decision to follow it with the steamy romantic drama *An Officer and a Gentleman* (1982).

However, no sooner did Gere hit the big time than his stock took a sudden nosedive. Though he shone in Jim McBride's remake of Jean-Luc Godard's *Breathless* (1983), audiences were nonplussed. Francis Ford Coppola's *The Cotton Club* (1984) was a huge failure, with Gere giving a near-comatose performance. Matters were helped little by his being cast in the dour sword and sandals biblical drama *King David* (1985), the underwhelming action thriller *No Mercy* (1986) and Sidney Lumet's *Power* (1986).

However, salvage came with two films in 1990. He was compelling and wicked in Mike Figgis' police thriller *Internal Affairs*, while his role as a wealthy businessman who falls for Julia Roberts' call girl in *Pretty Woman* reminded audiences just how charming he could be. Both were major box-office successes and propelled Gere back onto the A-list.

His success continued throughout the decade, courtesy of the box-office hits *Sommersby* (1993), *Primal Fear* (1996) and *Runaway Bride* (1999). He struck gold with his all-singing, all-dancing performance in *Chicago* (2002), a glitzy film update of the Broadway musical that saw him win a Best Actor Golden Globe.

Aside from a couple of misses, Gere's recent work is populated with more challenging roles. He was one of the six Bob Dylans in Todd Hanyes' artistic triumph *I'm Not There* (2007) and excellent as real-life forger Clifford Irving in *The Hoax* (2006), then attracted some of the best notices of his career playing a troubled hedge fund magnate in *Arbitrage* (2012). **MB**

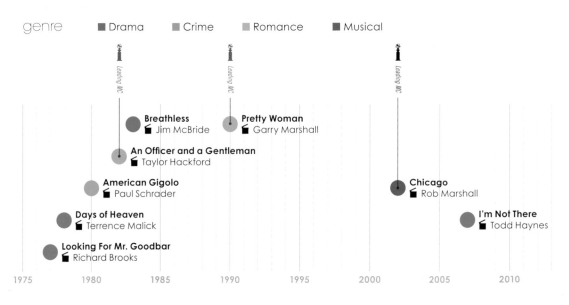

genre   ■ Drama   ■ Crime   ■ Romance   ■ Musical

Breathless
🎬 Jim McBride

Pretty Woman
🎬 Garry Marshall

An Officer and a Gentleman
🎬 Taylor Hackford

American Gigolo
🎬 Paul Schrader

Chicago
🎬 Rob Marshall

Days of Heaven
🎬 Terrence Malick

I'm Not There
🎬 Todd Haynes

Looking For Mr. Goodbar
🎬 Richard Brooks

| 1975 | 1980 | 1985 | 1990 | 1995 | 2000 | 2005 | 2010 |

mel gibson 1956

Mad Max

Gallipoli

Lethal Weapon

The Man Without a Face

Braveheart

Ransom

Payback

The Beaver

It is easy to forget now, but for almost two decades Mel Gibson was one of the most popular movie stars in the world. Despite being commonly thought of as Australian, the actor was born in Peekskill, New York, changing continents at the age of 12. He became known to international audiences for his aggressive portrayal of the eponymous hero of the dystopian sci-fi *Mad Max* (1979) and its 1981 sequel. These parts were followed swiftly by well-received performances in Peter Weir's *Gallipoli* (1981) and *The Year of Living Dangerously* (1982). As his star rose, Gibson relocated to the United States, announcing his arrival in 1984 with lead roles in *Mrs. Soffel*, *The River* and *The Bounty*.

A third installment of the *Mad Max* series in 1985 proved divisive, but Gibson had the biggest hit of his career as suicidal detective Martin Riggs in *Lethal Weapon* (1987). With its fluid action and sharp dialogue, the action comedy was one of the most influential films of the decade and spawned three sequels.

While he continued to be drawn to action films and thrillers such as *Tequila Sunrise* (1988), Gibson expanded his range to dramatic roles, playing the titular Danish prince in Franco Zeffirelli's *Hamlet* (1990), a reanimated 1930s test pilot in *Forever Young* (1992)

and a disfigured recluse who befriends a young boy in his directorial debut *The Man Without a Face* (1993). His second film as director, *Braveheart* (1995), in which he starred as the Scottish rebel William Wallace, won him Oscars for his direction and producing.

Turning his focus fully onto acting again, Gibson starred in the thrillers *Ransom* (1996) and *Conspiracy Theory* (1997), and played against type as a double-crossed criminal in *Payback* (1999). He remained prolific, appearing in *The Million Dollar Hotel*, *What Women Want* and *The Patriot* in 2000 alone, but M. Night Shyamalan's third feature *Signs* (2002) would turn out to be his final lead role for several years.

Gibson withdrew from acting after a series of damaging revelations about his behavior during a 2006 arrest, followed later by criminal allegations of domestic violence. A comeback was tried with the thriller *Edge of Darkness* (2010) and Jodie Foster's comedy-drama *The Beaver* (2011), both of which failed. The actor became almost entirely unemployable. Understanding that he was no longer a believable heroic character, Gibson changed tack, playing a violent antihero in *How I Spent My Summer Vacation* (2012) and villains in both *Machete Kills* (2013) and *The Expendables 3* (2014). **JWa**

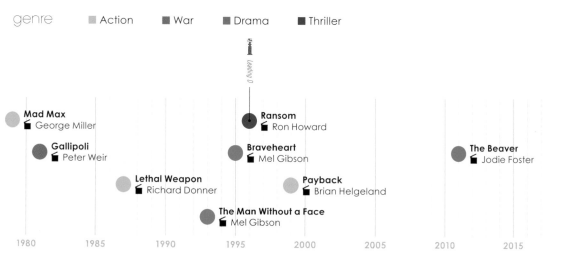

genre   ■ Action   ■ War   ■ Drama   ■ Thriller

Leading 0

Mad Max
🎬 George Miller

Gallipoli
🎬 Peter Weir

Lethal Weapon
🎬 Richard Donner

The Man Without a Face
🎬 Mel Gibson

Ransom
🎬 Ron Howard

Braveheart
🎬 Mel Gibson

Payback
🎬 Brian Helgeland

The Beaver
🎬 Jodie Foster

1980   1985   1990   1995   2000   2005   2010   2015

john gielgud 1904–2000

| Julius Caesar | The Charge of the Light Brigade | Oh! What a Lovely War | Providence | The Elephant Man | Arthur | Plenty | Prospero's Books |

The British actor John Gielgud might be best remembered for his theater performances, but he also made a unique and lasting contribution to the screen. Lacking the matinee idol appeal of Laurence Olivier, a close contemporary, Gielgud emerged as a film actor relatively late in life, but it was a career of remarkable richness and increasing boldness.

Born in 1904 in London into a theatrical dynasty, Gielgud's early acting ambitions were discouraged by his parents. Persisting, he won a place at RADA and received a classical training that was a cornerstone to his subsequent work. By the mid-1920s, he was a star of the London stage and would build a reputation as one of Britain's pre-eminent interpreters of Shakespeare.

Gielgud initially showed little interest in cinema, with only a handful of screen performances pre-World War II, which included a role in Alfred Hitchcock's *Secret Agent* (1936). It was in Hollywood in the early 1950s that Gielgud made his first substantial screen performance, in Joseph L. Mankiewicz's 1953 Shakespeare adaptation *Julius Caesar*. He would return to big-screen Shakespeare adaptations throughout the rest of his career, most memorably in Orson Welles' dazzling *Chimes at Midnight* (1965).

Gielgud was Oscar nominated for his role as the King of France in the historic drama *Becket* (1964). The intelligence and control of his brief appearance set a pattern in which a cameo from the actor could lend disparate productions a touch of class. This was sometimes disastrously ill-judged — he came to regret, for instance, his involvement in the soft-porn Roman epic *Caligula* (1979) — but it also proved rewarding: he won an Oscar for his nimble performance as a disapproving butler in the 1981 comedy *Arthur*.

Gielgud came to be a stalwart fixture of the British screen, with richly detailed performances in key works of postwar UK cinema, including *The Charge of the Light Brigade* (1968), *Oh! What a Lovely War* (1969) and later *The Elephant Man* (1980).

In the 1970s, his film work became bolder, climaxing in a performance of affecting force as an ailing English novelist in Alain Resnais' 1977 drama *Providence*. He delivered a crisply authoritative turn as a disillusioned civil servant in *Plenty* (1985) and in his late eighties he triumphed with one of his greatest film performances, in *Prospero's Books* (1991). Featuring Gielgud in the title role, Peter Greenaway's impressive re-imagining of *The Tempest* was the actor's magisterial swansong. **EL**

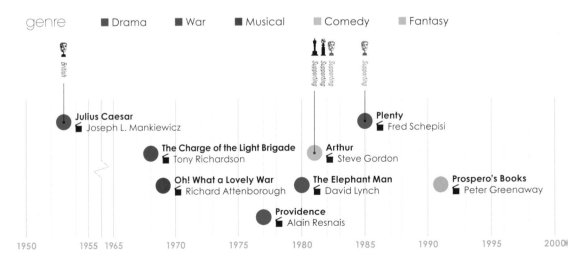

genre ■ Drama ■ War ■ Musical ■ Comedy ■ Fantasy

British

Supporting
Supporting
Supporting

Supporting

Julius Caesar
Joseph L. Mankiewicz

Plenty
Fred Schepisi

The Charge of the Light Brigade
Tony Richardson

Arthur
Steve Gordon

Oh! What a Lovely War
Richard Attenborough

The Elephant Man
David Lynch

Prospero's Books
Peter Greenaway

Providence
Alain Resnais

1950   1955 1965   1970   1975   1980   1985   1990   1995   2000

lillian gish 1893–1993

| The Birth of a Nation | Broken Blossoms | Way Down East | Orphans of the Storm | The Scarlet Letter | The Wind | The Night of the Hunter | The Whales of August |

G

"Stigmatized at the age of 31 as a grasping, silly, sexless antique," wrote former actress Louise Brooks, "the great Lillian Gish left Hollywood forever, but not a head turned to mark her departure." Brooks' indignation was justified. Gish has a good claim to be the finest American screen actress of the silent period and, as her subsequent work showed, was fully capable of making the transition to sound. But for the last half-century of her long career she remained sadly underused.

Acting was something she was virtually born to. She made her stage debut at age 6 and by the time D.W. Griffith discovered her and gave her a start in movies with *An Unseen Enemy* (1912), she had a decade of acting experience behind her. Over the next three years she appeared in nearly 50 films (mostly two- or three-reelers), the great majority of them directed by Griffith.

Griffith's massive, ambitious, woefully racist Civil War epic, *The Birth of a Nation* (1915), consolidated Gish's star status. As the daughter of an idyllically depicted Southern family she projects sweetness and charm without ever becoming cloying, and palpable fear when danger threatens. As the linking figure of The Mother in *Intolerance* (1916) she has little to do but rock a cradle, but does it with gentle affection.

The delicacy and subtlety of her acting never precluded strong emotions. In *Broken Blossoms* (1919) Gish plays the daughter of a brutal East End drunkard,

and her frantic terror when he is about to beat her is painful to watch. *Way Down East* (1920) includes a harrowing scene where she baptizes her dying child, her eyes full of grief and lonely desperation. Her last film for Griffith, *Orphans of the Storm* (1921), has her and her sister Dorothy as siblings divided and imperiled during the French Revolution.

For expat Swedish director Victor Sjöström she was Hester Prynne in his adaptation of *The Scarlet Letter* (1926) and gave perhaps her greatest performance in *The Wind* (1928), as the vulnerable girl from Virginia trapped in the windswept desolation of the Mojave Desert. But then came the sound era, and Gish was written off as hopelessly old-fashioned. Over the next 50 years she appeared in less than 20 features, and even the better ones — *Portrait of Jennie* (1948); *The Cobweb* (1955); *The Unforgiven* (1960); *The Wedding* (1978) — offered her relatively little scope. But *The Night of the Hunter* (1955), Charles Laughton's sole foray into directing, played to her strengths. As the carer of orphans with whom two hunted children find refuge from Robert Mitchum's malevolent preacher, she is at once tender and indomitably tough.

Gish made her last film, *The Whales of August* (1987), at age 91. Teamed with three other veterans — Bette Davis, Ann Sothern and Vincent Price — she showed she had lost nothing of her intelligence, delicacy and screen presence. **PK**

genre   ■ Drama   ■ Thriller

The Birth of a Nation — D.W. Griffith
Broken Blossoms — D.W. Griffith
Way Down East — D.W. Griffith
Orphans of the Storm — D.W. Griffith
The Scarlet Letter — Victor Sjöström
The Wind — Victor Sjöström
The Night of the Hunter — Charles Laughton
The Whales of August — Lindsay Anderson

1915   1920   1925   1930   1950   1955   1960   1985   1990   1990

jeff goldblum 1952

Death Wish

The Big Chill

Into the Night

The Fly

The Tall Guy

Jurassic Park

Independence Day

Le Week-End

With his odd, sometimes awkward features, Jeff Goldblum seemed destined for character actor status, playing oddballs and outsiders, as evinced by his debut, as one of the rapists — Freak #1 — in *Death Wish* (1974). But rather than attempt to hide his uniqueness, he turned it to his advantage and in the process headed up a number of the most successful blockbusters of the last three decades.

Born in Pennsylvania, Goldblum followed his debut with roles in Robert Altman's *California Split* (1974) and as one of the many eccentrics in *Nashville* (1975). He is the man informing someone by phone that he has lost his mantra in *Annie Hall* (1977) and is a victim in the remake of *Invasion of the Body Snatchers* (1978). The size of the roles grew. He was reunited with college friends in *The Big Chill* (1983) and, along with Harry Shearer, is a comical NASA recruiter in *The Right Stuff* (1983). He is a lascivious villain in the western *Silverado* (1985) and takes the lead in John Landis' chase movie *Into the Night* (1985), perfect as the gangly, awkward dupe helping out Michelle Pfeiffer's glamorous jewel smuggler.

Then came *The Fly* (1986) and stardom. He is perfect as Seth Brundle, the scientist who invents a teleportation machine only to have his DNA spliced with that of an insect's the first time he attempts the jump through space. David Cronenberg's body horror profits enormously from the actor's physicality, but it

is in his balancing humor with pathos as Seth's health deteriorates that makes the final act so moving.

He is funny alongside Jim Carrey in *Earth Girls Are Easy* (1988), but the film is neither fast nor furious enough and jokes are in short supply toward the end. *The Tall Guy* (1989) is far better, giving Goldblum one of his best roles as a seemingly unemployable London-based American actor whose burgeoning relationship with Emma Thompson's nurse coincides with his being cast in a new show, "Elephant: The Musical." It also features one of the funniest sex scenes committed to film.

After playing a ruthless drug trafficker in *Deep Cover* (1992), he is devilishly charming and intense as the chaos theorist who finds himself on the menu of an island's dinosaur occupants in *Jurassic Park* (1993). He would return to the role in 1997's *The Lost World*. He is all hips and sex appeal as he walks out of the desert, having just saved the world with Will Smith, in *Independence Day* (1996) and looks set to appear in its belated sequel.

He has made occasional appearances in Wes Anderson's films and is excellent in Paul Schrader's disturbing but flawed Holocaust drama *Adam Resurrected* (2008). His third act appearance in *Le Week-End* (2013) is a delight, the actor exuding charm as a successful writer who has chosen to go with the flow and take whatever life throws him. **IHS**

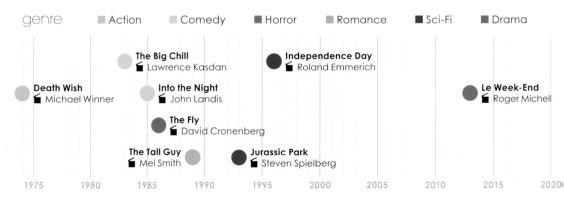

genre ■ Action ■ Comedy ■ Horror ■ Romance ■ Sci-Fi ■ Drama

The Big Chill
Lawrence Kasdan

Independence Day
Roland Emmerich

Death Wish
Michael Winner

Into the Night
John Landis

Le Week-End
Roger Michell

The Fly
David Cronenberg

The Tall Guy
Mel Smith

Jurassic Park
Steven Spielberg

1975   1980   1985   1990   1995   2000   2005   2010   2015   2020

ryan gosling 1980

The Believer — The Notebook — Half Nelson — Lars and the Real Girl — Blue Valentine — Crazy, Stupid, Love — Drive — The Place Beyond the Pines

The early phases of Ryan Gosling's career have arguably followed a reverse trajectory: from the heart of mainstream pop culture toward up-and-coming directors, indie budgets and film festival slots. He began as a member of the Disney Channel's television variety troupe The Mickey Mouse Club, and went on to head up a number of children's television shows before making his break into movies. Yet unlike other erstwhile child stars, Gosling has never seemed seriously dented by early industry exposure, in terms of either character or credibility. This may be because his big-screen breakthrough — in Henry Bean's rigorous and challenging drama *The Believer* (2001) — was as close as a performance comes to being inarguably good and universally acclaimed; or because his subsequent career choices have been marked by an unusual degree of intelligence and restraint.

After *The Notebook* (2004) placed him firmly in the heartthrob ranks, Gosling could presumably have had his pick of superhero franchises and shirtless action roles. Instead, he stuck to fragile, oddball characters, making full use of his off-center handsomeness and fraught, pensive brand of masculinity. It paid off in plaudits, as well as plentiful trips to the Sundance Film Festival. As a crack-addicted schoolteacher in *Half Nelson* (2006), Gosling received an Oscar nomination; as a young man in love with a sex toy in *Lars and the Real Girl* (2007), a Golden Globe nod followed. Within a few years, Gosling was a superstar — without having performed in anything like a blockbuster.

He did his finest work to date in Derek Cianfrance's raw break-up chronicle *Blue Valentine* (2010); went for matinee idol mega-charm in the ensemble comedy *Crazy, Stupid, Love* (2011); was directed by George Clooney in political thriller *The Ides of March* (2011); and offered his offbeat version of an action hero in Nicolas Winding Refn's stylishly murky *Drive* (2011). He stuck with the directors who had helped him establish his arty credentials, working with Winding Refn for a second time on the divisive Cannes competitor *Only God Forgives* (2013), and with Cianfrance again on *The Place Beyond the Pines* (2012).

Less celebrated than his acting was Gosling's directing debut with *Lost River* (2014), widely decried as pretentious and muddled. He has since become a father, with actress Eva Mendes, to daughter Esmeralda; and announced a hiatus from acting, "to assess why I'm doing it and how I'm doing it." **HM**

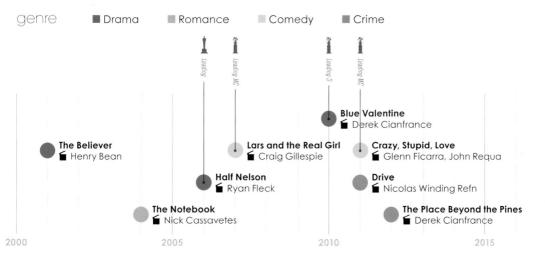

genre ■ Drama ■ Romance ■ Comedy ■ Crime

Blue Valentine — Derek Cianfrance

The Believer — Henry Bean

Lars and the Real Girl — Craig Gillespie

Crazy, Stupid, Love — Glenn Ficarra, John Requa

Half Nelson — Ryan Fleck

Drive — Nicolas Winding Refn

The Notebook — Nick Cassavetes

The Place Beyond the Pines — Derek Cianfrance

2000 — 2005 — 2010 — 2015

the leading man

King Baggot | Richard Barthelmess | Charlie Chaplin | William Powell | James Stewart | Cary Grant | Dustin Hoffman | Robert Redford

"The Man Whose Face Is As Familiar As The Man In The Moon" was one of the taglines used to promote American cinema's first named leading man, King Baggot. Cast together in numerous silent films from 1909, Baggott and his costar Florence Lawrence broke the tradition of film actors working anonymously, and became the first performers whose names were used to promote their films. Though Baggot's face and name are now far from familiar, his prolific career can be traced back to many of the archetypes that continue to define the on-screen personae of male movie stars today. Baggott appeared in historical epics, comedies and crime thrillers alike, playing gallant costume heroes, spies, detectives, dissolute baddies and put-upon husbands. The prototype for the male star was in place, and whether an actor was leading a narrative himself or providing romantic interest for a female bill-topper, his own name and public image was now set to be part of the film's promotional package.

One of the main functions of the cinematic leading man is to embody an idealized form of masculinity — a dream alter ego and/or romantic partner for the audience. Idealized forms, however, can take more than one shape. If brawny, red-blooded leading men have always had their place, from Errol Flynn, Marlon Brando and Burt Lancaster to Russell Crowe and Tom Hardy, the male lead whose appeal owes as much to sensitivity as obvious machismo has a throughline from silent stars Charlie Chaplin, Buster Keaton, Richard Barthelmess and Bobby Harron all the way to contemporary stars like Leonardo DiCaprio, Jake Gyllenhaal and Ryan Gosling. The dashing, grown-up gentleman, meanwhile, who negotiates the world on wit and charm, has just as many embodiments — among them William Powell, twinkly sophisticate of the *Thin Man* series (1934–47); Clark Gable, a shoo-in for the iconic role of Rhett Butler; Cary Grant, Sidney Poitier, George Clooney and Robert Downey Jr. There are those who make it not so much on any brand of sex appeal as on a certain grace and sharpness: Fred Astaire, Jack Lemmon, Kevin Spacey, Mathieu Amalric; decent-seeming everymen like James Stewart and Tom Hanks; and the out-and-out oddities whose magnetism is as hard to define as it is to ignore, among them Spencer Tracy, Gérard Depardieu, Jack Nicholson and Nicolas Cage. Some, of course, can chameleon their way into a dizzying range of roles — like Christian Bale, who has played thugs, superheroes, killers and charmers of virtually every demeanor and body type. And sometimes, an actor finds career renewal simply by playing against his established

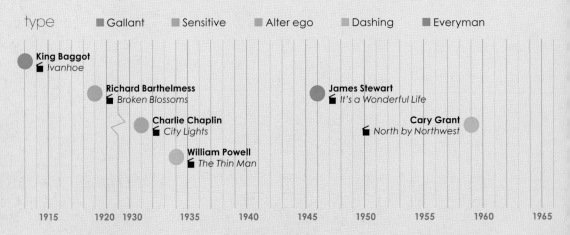

type ■ Gallant   ■ Sensitive   ■ Alter ego   ■ Dashing   ■ Everyman

King Baggot
Ivanhoe

Richard Barthelmess
Broken Blossoms

Charlie Chaplin
City Lights

William Powell
The Thin Man

James Stewart
It's a Wonderful Life

Cary Grant
North by Northwest

1915   1920 1930   1935   1940   1945   1950   1955   1960   1965

| Woody Allen | Jack Nicholson | Robert De Niro | Denzel Washington | George Clooney | Shah Rukh Khan | Colin Firth | Ryan Gosling |

on-screen type — as when Denzel Washington won an Oscar for playing the bad guy in *Training Day* (2001); or ladykiller Colin Firth played a gay professor in *A Single Man* (2009). The phenomenon is not confined to Hollywood: other movie-producing territories have produced their deathless male performers, from 1960s icons Marcello Mastroianni and Jean-Paul Belmondo, to the "Bollywood Tom Cruise," Shah Rukh Khan, and Asia's firmament of action stars, including Jackie Chan, Chow Yun-Fat and Jet Li.

Though most of these individuals are easy on the eye, classical good looks are not an indispensable requirement for iconhood. The pressure to look good affects men as well as women in the movie business, and yet it arguably has its outer limits. Some of the most obviously handsome men in cinema history — Paul Newman, Robert Redford, Warren Beatty, Brad Pitt, Johnny Depp — have claimed frustration at the limitations imposed by playing only beautiful people, and kicked against the trivial, effete associations of being a pin-up. Redford's rejection for the role of Benjamin Braddock in *The Graduate* (1967) provides an interesting case study in casting dynamics. Though the character had been envisaged in the source novel by Charles Webb as a classically good-looking, athletic WASP, and Redford thought himself made

for it, director Mike Nichols knew he was not right for the role when he responded to the question "Have you ever struck out with a girl?" with bafflement. Diminutive, dark and disheveled Dustin Hoffman was cast, and an iconically offbeat leading performance enabled. Hoffman's success in the role paved the way for a host of intense, twitchy, unconventionally attractive 1970s leading men, among them Al Pacino and Robert De Niro. Meanwhile, Robert Redford's successful shift into directing — a trajectory shared by Mel Gibson, Clint Eastwood, George Clooney and Ben Affleck, among others — indicates a determination to display greater gravitas than a mere pampered performer. Other actor-directors, such as Charlie Chaplin and Woody Allen, have created indivisibly complementary on- and offscreen personae: they are their own best leading men, to such an extent that when Woody Allen the director casts another performer as his male lead, an element of imitation of Woody Allen the actor almost inevitably creeps in.

As recognizable as the Man in the Moon? Probably much more so, in many of these cases. Yet what we actually want from our leading men — hero or villain, hard case or sympathetic confidant, joker or naif or know-it-all — has always been as broad a field as the stories in which we want to see them. **HM**

■ Offbeat ■ Handsome ■ Oddity ■ Intense ■ Against type ■ Icon

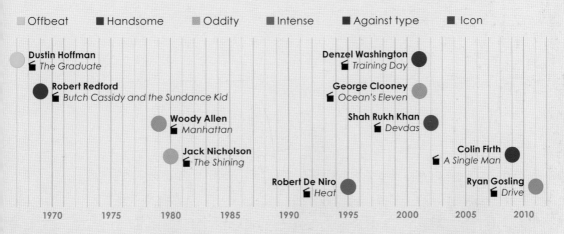

Dustin Hoffman
The Graduate

Robert Redford
Butch Cassidy and the Sundance Kid

Woody Allen
Manhattan

Jack Nicholson
The Shining

Robert De Niro
Heat

Denzel Washington
Training Day

George Clooney
Ocean's Eleven

Shah Rukh Khan
Devdas

Colin Firth
A Single Man

Ryan Gosling
Drive

1970   1975   1980   1985   1990   1995   2000   2005   2010

cary grant 1904–86

She Done
Him Wrong

Sylvia
Scarlett

The Awful
Truth

Bringing
Up Baby

Gunga Din

Only Angels
Have Wings

His Girl
Friday

The
Philadelphia
Story

G

The film critic and historian David Thomson has called Cary Grant "the best and the most important actor in the history of the cinema." And the director Alan J. Pakula observed: "It was genius. He never wasted a motion on the screen." He was a box-office draw for decades, an enduringly handsome leading man, the epitome of debonair sophistication. Yet he communed with the camera so effortlessly that his greatness almost passed unnoticed.

He was born Archibald Alexander Leach in 1904, in Bristol, UK. At 14, he ran off with Bob Pender's troupe of knockabout performers, learning to be an acrobat, stilt walker, juggler and mime. In 1920, he joined the company's tour of the United States, deciding to remain there. A moderately successful Broadway career followed until, in 1931, Archie Leach decided to try his hand in Hollywood. Paramount gave him a contract and told him to find a new name.

Despite matinee idol looks, it took Grant a while to find his feet. He is stiff as Marlene Dietrich's lover in *Blonde Venus* (1932) and only slightly more red-blooded in the Mae West vehicle *She Done Him Wrong* (1933).

He started to find his comic touch as a cockney rogue in George Cukor's *Sylvia Scarlett* (1935), his first pairing with Katharine Hepburn. And in 1937, Leo McCarey's *The Awful Truth* made him a star. Grant and Irene Dunne are perfectly matched as the husband and wife socialites who file for divorce and spend the rest of the film regretting it. Claiming to have based his character's urbane manner on McCarey, the actor now firmly established his persona: impeccably dressed, confident and socially at ease, wryly amused, slightly self-regarding and at times endearingly foolish. Here, too, were the inimitable tools: the clipped, authoritative, mid-Atlantic accent and perfectly timed comic delivery, the knowing gestures and a physicality that was the fruit of his days in vaudeville.

More classic screwballs followed, including *My Favorite Wife* (1940), again with Dunne, and two for Howard Hawks: *Bringing Up Baby* (1938), in which Grant, Hepburn and a leopard run amok in the country, and *His Girl Friday* (1940), with Grant's unscrupulous newspaper editor stopping at nothing to prevent his star reporter — and ex-wife — from leaving

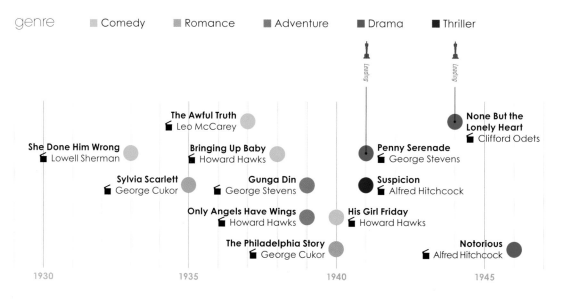

genre   ■ Comedy   ■ Romance   ■ Adventure   ■ Drama   ■ Thriller

Leading

Leading

The Awful Truth
🎬 Leo McCarey

**None But the
Lonely Heart**
🎬 Clifford Odets

She Done Him Wrong
🎬 Lowell Sherman

Bringing Up Baby
🎬 Howard Hawks

Penny Serenade
🎬 George Stevens

Sylvia Scarlett
🎬 George Cukor

Gunga Din
🎬 George Stevens

Suspicion
🎬 Alfred Hitchcock

Only Angels Have Wings
🎬 Howard Hawks

His Girl Friday
🎬 Howard Hawks

The Philadelphia Story
🎬 George Cukor

Notorious
🎬 Alfred Hitchcock

1930   1935   1940   1945

Penny
Serenade

Suspicion

None But
the Lonely
Heart

Notorious

I Was a Male
War Bride

Monkey
Business

North by
Northwest

Charade

him. His and Rosalind Russell's banter is arguably the fastest and funniest ever recorded on screen.

He was twice reunited with Cukor and Hepburn, in *Holiday* (1938) and *The Philadelphia Story* (1940), effervescent romantic comedies spiced with caustic class critique. In 1939, he appeared in two action adventures: *Gunga Din* and *Only Angels Have Wings*.

Grant's only two Oscar nominations were for dramas: *Penny Serenade* (1941), in which he and Dunne struggle to come to terms with the loss of a child, and *None But the Lonely Heart* (1944), the actor convincing as a cockney itinerant attempting to settle down so as to be with his dying mother.

His very best work was for two directors: Hawks and Alfred Hitchcock. With Hawks he continued to be the consummate screwball comedian, performing in drag in *I Was a Male War Bride* (1949) and regressing to childhood while cavorting with Marilyn Monroe in *Monkey Business* (1952). For Hitchcock, the darker side of his persona was brought clearly into view: as Joan Fontaine's playboy husband in *Suspicion* (1941), and the jealous spy tormenting Ingrid Bergman

in *Notorious* (1946). No one played ambiguity and emotional wariness quite so potently as Grant in these films. He made two more for Hitchcock: still agile as a cat burglar opposite Grace Kelly in *To Catch a Thief* (1955) and, in one of his most famous roles, as the ad man pursued by a spy ring in *North by Northwest* (1959).

Sometimes accused of playing safe in his choices, when Grant did make an atypical film the result often misfired, as with the Cole Porter biopic *Night and Day* (1946) and the Napoleonic War film *The Pride and the Passion* (1957). He was bolder behind the scenes, however: in the 1930s, when he chose not to renew his studio contract, he became the first star to go freelance.

He teamed well with Deborah Kerr in the romantic drama *An Affair to Remember* (1957), again with Bergman in the romantic comedy *Indiscreet* (1958) and with Audrey Hepburn in the enjoyable comedy thriller *Charade* (1963). Approaching his sixties, he was conscious that his age was making romantic leads — his stock in trade — untenable. After *Walk Don't Run* (1966), in which the famous romancer was now the matchmaker, he retired. He died in 1986, aged 82. **DM**

■ Mystery

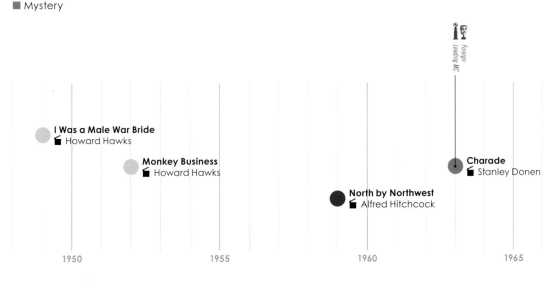

Foreign
Leading MC

I Was a Male War Bride
Howard Hawks

Monkey Business
Howard Hawks

North by Northwest
Alfred Hitchcock

Charade
Stanley Donen

1950   1955   1960   1965

Sylvia Scarlett
(1935)

Bringing Up Baby
(1938)

His Girl Friday
(1940)

Penny Serenade
(1941)

None But the
Lonely Heart
(1944)

I Was a Male War
Bride
(1949)

Monkey Business
(1952)

North by
Northwest
(1959)

Sylvia Scarlett was the first of four films that Grant and Katharine Hepburn made together.

Grant and Hepburn looking for the titular escaped leopard in ***Bringing Up Baby***. A flop upon release, it is now considered one of the definitive screwball comedies.

Grant and Rosalind Russell in ***His Girl Friday***. The movie is renowned for the pair's energetic verbal sparring, which unusually for the time featured overlapping dialogue.

Grant and costar Irene Dunne in ***Penny Serenade***.

None But the Lonely Heart starred Grant as a cockney drifter who returns home to help his ailing mother, played by Ethel Barrymore.

One of Grant's personal favorites, ***None But the Lonely Heart*** gestured toward his own roots as Archie Leach.

I Was a Male War Bride saw Grant dress up in drag in an attempt to beat the bureaucracy of the U.S. Army.

Marilyn Monroe's secretary assists Grant's absent-minded chemist in *Monkey Business*.

French critic Jacques Rivette declared *Monkey Business* "a brilliant film," praising "the artfulness with which Cary Grant twists his gestures into symbols."

Grant runs for his life in an iconic scene from *North by Northwest*. No less iconic is the Kilgour suit that he is wearing (hand-picked by Grant himself), which has even inspired a story that tells the film from its viewpoint.

hugh grant 1960

| Maurice | Four Weddings and a Funeral | Sense and Sensibility | Notting Hill | Bridget Jones's Diary | About a Boy | Love Actually | Music and Lyrics |

Although he was to become famous for romantic comedies, Hugh Grant spent the first part of his career as a dramatic actor. Born in Hammersmith, London, in 1960, he was struggling in a revue comedy troupe when he costarred in the Merchant Ivory production *Maurice* (1987), as James Wilby's illicit lover. After a string of mostly dire European features the next year, he worked primarily in television, with an occasional film role. He is a dashing Chopin in *Impromptu* (1991), excellent opposite Kristin Scott Thomas in Roman Polanski's *Bitter Moon* (1992) and took a small role in Merchant Ivory's *The Remains of the Day* (1993).

At the age of 34, Grant achieved sudden fame as the foul-mouthed lead of *Four Weddings and a Funeral* (1994), directed by Mike Newell and written by Richard Curtis. While the film relied on its ensemble, much of its success was due to his BAFTA-winning performance, portraying a certain type of wry, shambling Englishness. The film became a surprise hit, but Grant had difficulty capitalizing on its success. Following a role in *Sense and Sensibility* (1995) and the middling comedy *Nine Months* (1995), he struggled to escape his typecasting. His excellent performance notwithstanding, the self-produced medical thriller

Extreme Measures (1996) failed at the box office and he has mostly stuck to romcoms ever since.

After a brief hiatus, Grant returned to the familiar with *Mickey Blue Eyes* (1999) and *Notting Hill* (1999), which reunited him with Newell and Curtis. The latter was another hit and reinvigorated his career. He subsequently played a sleazy art dealer in Woody Allen's *Small Time Crooks* (2000) and Renée Zellweger's womanizing love rat in *Bridget Jones's Diary* (2001), signaling his career's next phase, as a self-absorbed, yet alluring cad. He received the best notices of his career as an indolent man reluctantly becoming more responsible in *About a Boy* (2002), which he followed up by playing an immature tycoon in *Two Weeks Notice* (2002), a commercial hit despite its poor reviews.

Grant worked with Curtis for a third time on *Love Actually* (2003), the weakest of their three collaborations. The ensuing decade saw him continue in mainstream romcoms, including the sprightly *Music and Lyrics* (2007). Grant's output slowed after the embarrassing *Did You Hear About the Morgans?* (2009), although he would play a range of villainous characters in the ambitious, yet flawed, *Cloud Atlas* (2012). It was his first straight drama in 16 years. **JWa**

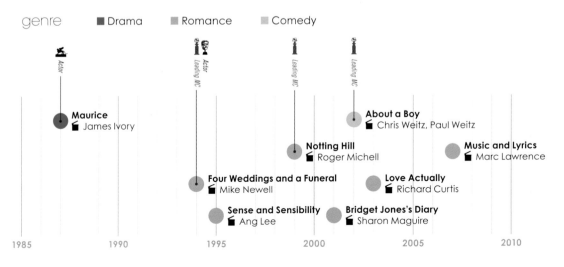

genre ■ Drama ■ Romance ■ Comedy

Actor

Actor Leading MC

Leading MC

Leading MC

Maurice
James Ivory

About a Boy
Chris Weitz, Paul Weitz

Notting Hill
Roger Michell

Music and Lyrics
Marc Lawrence

Four Weddings and a Funeral
Mike Newell

Love Actually
Richard Curtis

Sense and Sensibility
Ang Lee

Bridget Jones's Diary
Sharon Maguire

1985   1990   1995   2000   2005   2010

pam grier 1949

Women in Cages

Black Mama White Mama

Coffy

Foxy Brown

Original Gangstas

Mars Attacks!

Jackie Brown

Larry Crowne

Pam Grier was one of the main faces of Blaxploitation cinema. She played two of the genre's three key action heroines, in turn offering up a stronger, more kick-ass representation of women on the screen.

After an uncredited role in *Beyond the Valley of the Dolls* (1970), the 22-year-old Grier starred in her first women in prison film, *The Big Doll House* (1971), followed by the Roger Corman prison exploitation drama *Women in Cages* (1971). She plays a lesbian in both, but on opposite sides of the law. There was a role in George Armitage's *Hit Man* (1972), but then Grier returned to prison in *The Big Bird Cage* (1972). She appeared in *Cool Breeze* (1972), an all-black remake of *The Asphalt Jungle* (1950), before being incarcerated again, opposite Margaret Markov, in *Black Mama White Mama* (1973).

After playing a voodoo enchantress battling vampirism in *Scream Blacula Scream* (1973), Grier was cast in her breakthrough role as *Coffy* (1973). What it lacks in subtlety, the film makes up in explicit violence as Grier's character dispatches the drug dealers and mob bosses responsible for hooking her younger sister on drugs. She is another angel of vengeance in 1974's *Foxy Brown*, going after the criminals who shot her

government agent boyfriend. Both films employ a mix of bloody violence and sexual provocation as the draw for audiences, who turned out in droves.

The Arena (1974) is one of the silliest Blaxploitation films, featuring Grier and Markov as women in ancient Rome, forced to fight as gladiators. *Sheba, Baby* (1975) attempts to profit from the vengeance narrative of Grier's earlier films but fails. *Friday Foster* (1975) marked her last official entry in the Blaxploitation genre.

For the next 20 years, Grier's career comprised character parts. She plays a prostitute killer in *Fort Apache, The Bronx* (1981) and was a regular on *Miami Vice* between 1985 and 1989. She is a protective mother in *Mars Attacks!* (1996) and makes appearances in *Escape From L.A.* (1996) and *Original Gangstas* (1996).

Grier's finest role came as the eponymous heroine of Quentin Tarantino's *Jackie Brown* (1997). She is a commanding presence, eclipsing Robert De Niro, Samuel L. Jackson and Bridget Fonda. She has been good in roles since, particularly in the television shows *The L Word* (2004–09) and *Smallville* (2010), and as a teacher in *Larry Crowne* (2011). But her Coffy and Foxy Brown notwithstanding, Pam Grier will forever be Jackie Brown. **IHS**

genre ■ Action ■ Crime ■ Sci-Fi ■ Romance

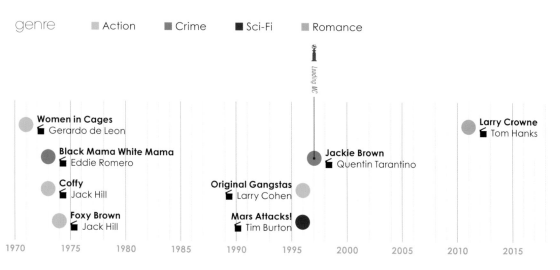

Leading MC

Women in Cages
Gerardo de Leon

Black Mama White Mama
Eddie Romero

Coffy
Jack Hill

Foxy Brown
Jack Hill

Original Gangstas
Larry Cohen

Mars Attacks!
Tim Burton

Jackie Brown
Quentin Tarantino

Larry Crowne
Tom Hanks

1970 | 1975 | 1980 | 1985 | 1990 | 1995 | 2000 | 2005 | 2010 | 2015

alec guinness 1914–2000

| Great Expectations | Oliver Twist | Kind Hearts and Coronets | The Lavender Hill Mob | The Man in the White Suit | Father Brown | The Ladykillers | The Bridge on the River Kwai |

A mercurial talent, Alec Guinness was born in London, in 1914. His first professional theater role came while he was still a drama student and at the age of 22 he acted opposite John Gielgud in *Hamlet*. Although he had an uncredited role in *Evensong* (1934), his first proper film role came after serving in World War II. David Lean's adaptation of Charles Dickens' *Great Expectations* (1946) was to be the start of a career-long collaboration between Guinness and the director.

He played Fagin in Lean's *Oliver Twist* (1948) and although his look was inspired by George Cruikshanks' illustrations that accompanied the first edition of Dickens' novel, it was still a look some viewed as anti-Semitic. They reunited on *The Bridge on the River Kwai* (1957), with Guinness awarded an Oscar for his portrayal of Colonel Nicholson, the senior ranking officer at a Japanese prisoner of war camp whose obsessive behavior divides the lower ranks. Guinness played Prince Faisal in *Lawrence of Arabia* (1962), his skin darkened to resemble the Hashemite leader. He is convincing in the role, although a similar attempt by Lean to cast the actor as an Indian, Professor

Godbole, in his estimable adaptation of E.M. Forster's *A Passage to India* (1984), backfired. Guinness also appeared as Yevgraf Zhivago, the eponymous hero's half-brother in Lean's *Doctor Zhivago* (1965).

Guinness is closely associated with the comedies produced by Ealing studios in the postwar period. He began with one of his finest performances — or eight of them — as the D'Ascoyne family in the mordantly funny *Kind Hearts and Coronets* (1949). Next came his meek bank-clerk-cum-gold-bullion-thief in *The Lavender Hill Mob* (1951). Guinness is a delight as the bookish introvert whose life suddenly becomes more interesting. He plays a variation on the role in *The Man in the White Suit* (1951), as a brilliant chemist who invents an indestructible cloth, much to the chagrin of big business and unions. As the creepy Professor Marcus in *The Ladykillers* (1955), Guiness plays the leader of a gang planning to rob a security van. A study in betrayal, the black comedy features a superb cast with Guinness at his best, trying to prevent the other gang members from killing each other while joyous at how much money he is making with each death.

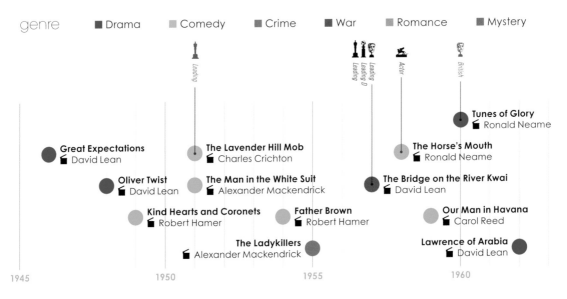

$226 M (U.S.)
The Bridge
on the River Kwai
(1957)

$347 M (U.S.)
Lawrence
of Arabia
(1962)

$829 M (U.S.)
Doctor Zhivago
(1965)

$3 BN
Star Wars
(1977)

$2 M
Little Dorrit
(1988)

| The Horse's Mouth | Our Man in Havana | Tunes of Glory | Lawrence of Arabia | Doctor Zhivago | The Quiller Memorandum | Star Wars: Episode IV — A New Hope | Little Dorrit |

In 1954, the actor took on the titular role in *Father Brown*, based on the character created by G.K. Chesterton. A light entertainment, it was a resounding success with audiences on both sides of the Atlantic, thanks in no small part to Guinness' affability in the role. He was another man of the cloth in the more serious political drama *The Prisoner* (1955), playing a Cardinal in an East European country interrogated by Jack Hawkins' Communist official. Guinness' excellent performance notwithstanding, the film was banned in a number of countries for its controversial content.

He was nominated for an Oscar for his adaptation of Joyce Carey's *The Horse's Mouth* (1958), in which he stars as an artist who has difficulty in finding a sponsor that will allow him to express himself. It is one of his best performances, never allowing his slippery character to earn audiences' sympathy, but remaining devilishly charming nonetheless. He is convincing as Jim Wormwold in Carol Reed's fine adaptation of Graham Greene's *Our Man in Havana* (1959) and playing a lonely teacher and aristocrat in *The Scapegoat* (1959). He received a BAFTA nomination for his performance in the unsettling psychological drama *Tunes of Glory* (1960), playing a bullying commanding officer in a Scottish regiment who cannot accept his peacetime replacement.

Guinness brings intelligence to the role of Marcus Aurelius in Anthony Mann's impressive *The Fall of the Roman Empire* (1964), but the film failed to attract an audience. He also shines as a stiff, officious handler in *The Quiller Memorandum* (1966). He is an entertaining Charles I in the leaden *Cromwell* (1970) and appears to have fun as Jacob Marley's ghost in the musical *Scrooge* (1970). However, his most famous role from this period is Obi-Wan Kenobi in *Star Wars*, beginning with *Episode IV — A New Hope* (1977). He brings gravitas to the role of the veteran Jedi knight and, as one of the few cast members who believed the film would be successful, must have been happy with his percentage of the profits in lieu of a larger salary.

Guinness returned to Dickens at the end of his career, with an Oscar-nominated performance in an epic adaptation of *Little Dorritt* (1988), crowning a remarkable career. **IHS**

■ Sci-Fi

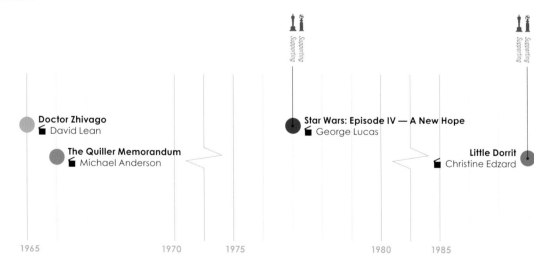

Supporting
Supporting

Supporting
Supporting

Doctor Zhivago
David Lean

The Quiller Memorandum
Michael Anderson

Star Wars: Episode IV — A New Hope
George Lucas

Little Dorrit
Christine Edzard

1965   1970   1975   1980   1985

jake gyllenhaal 1980

Donnie Darko   The Day After Tomorrow   Brokeback Mountain   Jarhead   Zodiac   Source Code   End of Watch   Nightcrawler

Born in 1980, in Los Angeles, Jake Gyllenhaal was raised in a filmmaking family. His parents are producer/screenwriter Naomi Foner and director Stephen Gyllenhaal. He is also the brother of actress Maggie Gyllenhaal, who played his sister in the cult hit *Donnie Darko* (2001), his breakthrough role.

He made his first foray into blockbuster territory with Roland Emmerich's *The Day After Tomorrow* (2004), in which an international storm plunges the world into a new ice age. Gyllenhaal would later beef up for Mike Newell's lackluster action epic, *Prince of Persia: The Sands of Time* (2010).

In 2005, he brought gravitas and depth to the role of a U.S. Marine serving in a pre-Desert Storm Saudi Arabia, in Sam Mendes' *Jarhead*. *Brokeback Mountain* swiftly followed, which allowed the actor to display his range, as a man caught between desire and the norms of the conservative society he lives in. He was awarded a BAFTA for his performance.

Gyllenhaal has continued to act in a wide range of films. In David Fincher's *Zodiac* (2007), he plays a San Francisco cartoonist obsessed with the infamous Zodiac killer. His disturbing turns in *Rendition*

(2007) and *Brothers* (2009) offer further evidence of Gyllenhaal's brooding intensity, while Duncan Jones' clever sci-fi *Source Code* (2011) has the actor play a soldier involved in a mind-bending experimental government program. In the captivating *End of Watch* (2012) he is an LAPD detective faced with a daily diet of brutality and violence, unaware that life for him and his partner is about to get worse.

Taking up producer duties, Gyllenhaal helped bring Dan Gilroy's directorial debut, *Nightcrawler* (2014), to the screen. A sobering look at the rapacious appetite for death and violence in television reportage, Gyllenhaal's Lou Bloom is one of the most terrifying creations in recent screen history. The actor shed pounds for the role and looks disarmingly haunted and harrowed. It is his finest performance to date.

Gyllenhaal has also collaborated with Canadian auteur Denis Villeneuve on two films. *Prisoners* (2013) is an intriguing tale of child abduction, while *Enemy* (2013) sees him play dual roles as a man who seeks out his doppelganger after spotting him in a movie. An unsettling piece, it in many ways encapsulates the daring choices the actor continues to make. **JW**

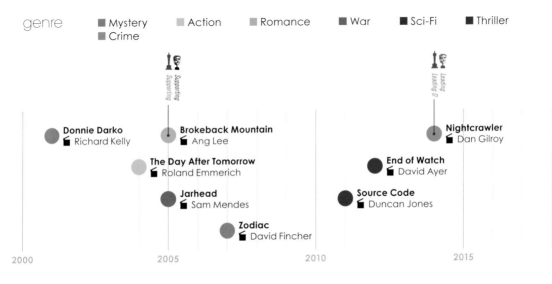

genre   ■ Mystery   ■ Action   ■ Romance   ■ War   ■ Sci-Fi   ■ Thriller
           ■ Crime

Supporting / Supporting

Leading / Leading D

Donnie Darko
🎬 Richard Kelly

Brokeback Mountain
🎬 Ang Lee

Nightcrawler
🎬 Dan Gilroy

The Day After Tomorrow
🎬 Roland Emmerich

End of Watch
🎬 David Ayer

Jarhead
🎬 Sam Mendes

Source Code
🎬 Duncan Jones

Zodiac
🎬 David Fincher

2000   2005   2010   2015

maggie gyllenhaal 1977

| Donnie Darko | Secretary | Casa de los Babys | Sherrybaby | World Trade Center | The Dark Knight | Crazy Heart | Hysteria |

Maggie Gyllenhaal has made a raft of films featuring strong, decisive women. So it may seem strange that she came to fame, in her first lead role, as a secretary who gets bent over a desk and spanked by her boss.

She was born in Manhattan, to filmmaker parents. The actor Jake Gyllenhaal is her younger brother. Growing up in Los Angeles, she started acting from an early age, making her screen debut at age 15 in her father's film *Waterland* (1992). Her next five films were all directed by her father. She was among the title character's band of teenage kidnappers/filmmakers in John Waters' *Cecil B DeMented* (2000) and played her brother Jake's sister in his breakthrough film *Donnie Darko* (2001). Then came *Secretary* (2002), in which her character Lee finds liberation and fulfilment in being disciplined by her boss (James Spader).

Since then, Gyllenhaal has kept her career flexible, taking occasional support roles in big-budget movies to free her for more challenging work in independent productions. In *World Trade Center* (2006) she played the wife of a victim of the 9/11 attacks, without much to do except express anguish; but she brought some depth to the role of Assistant District Attorney Rachel Dawes, ex-girlfriend of Bruce Wayne, in Christopher Nolan's *The Dark Knight* (2008). As the assistant to James Woods' Secret Service boss in Roland Emmerich's slam-bang actioner *White House Down* (2013), she looked flabbergasted to good effect.

On the indie side, she took small roles in Spike Jonze's *Adaptation* and George Clooney's directorial debut *Confessions of a Dangerous Mind* (both 2002), then was one of the women planning to adopt in John Sayles' *Casa de los Babys* (2003). Yet more poignantly, in the lead role of *Sherrybaby* (2006) she was an ex-con desperately trying to get her life back on line and reconnect with her daughter after three years in jail. In *Crazy Heart* (2009) she was touching as the young reporter trying to redeem Jeff Bridges' broken-down country singer.

For the road comedy *Away We Go* (2009), Gyllenhaal turned in a diverting satirical portrayal of a humor-free New Ager living a life of high-minded ideological purity. A more sympathetic variant came in Tanya Wexler's period comedy *Hysteria* (2011), about the invention of the vibrator, where she played a feminist pioneer in Victorian London. And she was powerful, conflicted and ultimately despairing in the BBC television series *The Honourable Woman* (2014). **PK**

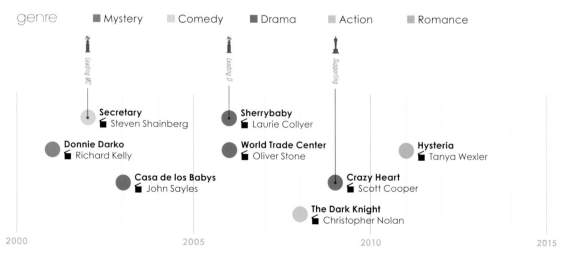

genre   ■ Mystery   ■ Comedy   ■ Drama   ■ Action   ■ Romance

Leading MC

Secretary
Steven Shainberg

Donnie Darko
Richard Kelly

Casa de los Babys
John Sayles

Leading D

Sherrybaby
Laurie Collyer

World Trade Center
Oliver Stone

Supporting

Crazy Heart
Scott Cooper

The Dark Knight
Christopher Nolan

Hysteria
Tanya Wexler

2000   2005   2010   2015

gene hackman 1930

 H

| Lilith | Bonnie and Clyde | Downhill Racer | The French Connection | The Poseidon Adventure | Scarecrow | The Conversation | Night Moves |

Blurring the line between character actor and star, Gene Hackman has been a formidable screen presence for four decades. Born in California in 1930, he joined the Pasadena Playhouse in 1956, where he studied alongside lifelong friend Dustin Hoffman.

In 1964, Hackman starred opposite Warren Beatty in Robert Rossen's *Lilith*. The actors would reunite on *Bonnie and Clyde* (1967), with Hackman playing Clyde Barrow's older brother Buck. It earned him his first Oscar nomination. More importantly, it associated the actor with the new wave of filmmakers that were transforming American cinema. After a number of small screen roles and the melancholy aerial drama *The Gypsy Moths* (1969), Hackman played the U.S. national ski coach in Michael Ritchie's *Downhill Racer* (1969). The film's drama, outside of the race footage, emanates from the turbulent relationship between Hackman's no-nonsense coach and Robert Redford's ruthless young athlete. A similarly fractious dynamic lies at the heart of the father-son drama *I Never Sang for My Father* (1970), with Hackman starring opposite Melvyn Douglas. He was again nominated for an Oscar.

After the brutal *The Hunting Party* (1971), Hackman took on one of his defining roles, as New York narcotics officer Jimmy "Popeye" Doyle in *The French Connection* (1971). He won an Oscar for his portrayal, a blistering performance of pent-up rage. He would return to the character in John Frankenheimer's muscular, Marseilles-set *French Connection II* (1975), which is no less edgy than William Friedkin's original.

After his corrupt, drug-dealing cop in *Cisco Pike* (1972), Hackman starred in Michael Ritchie's sparse *Prime Cut* (1972), as a corrupt Missouri rancher who sells women as sex slaves, grinds his enemies into mincemeat and refuses to settle a debt with the mob. Faced with no alternative, the crime syndicate sends Lee Marvin's enforcer to deal with him, resulting in a bloodbath. Jerry Schatzberg's *Scarecrow* (1973) was a more sedate drama, following Hackman and Al Pacino's misfits on a perambulating road trip. Hackman delivered one of his finest performances in Arthur Penn's detective thriller *Night Moves* (1975), playing an ex-football player-turned-private investigator. However, these films have been eclipsed

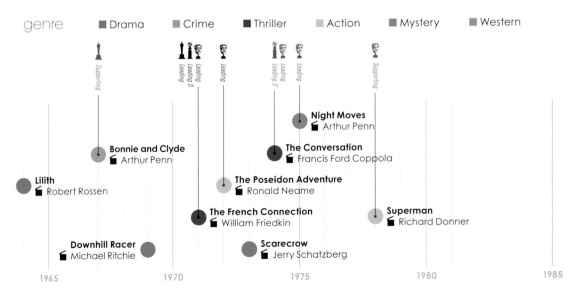

genre ■ Drama ■ Crime ■ Thriller ■ Action ■ Mystery ■ Western

Night Moves
Arthur Penn

Bonnie and Clyde
Arthur Penn

The Conversation
Francis Ford Coppola

Lilith
Robert Rossen

The Poseidon Adventure
Ronald Neame

The French Connection
William Friedkin

Superman
Richard Donner

Downhill Racer
Michael Ritchie

Scarecrow
Jerry Schatzberg

1965   1970   1975   1980   1985

$298M (U.S.)
The French Connection (1971)

$473M (U.S.)
The Poseidon Adventure (1972)

$1.1BN
Superman (1978)

$265M
Unforgiven (1992)

$241M
Crimson Tide (1995)

$177M
Get Shorty (1995)

$359M
Enemy of the State (1998)

$94M
The Royal Tenenbaums (2001)

Superman

Mississippi Burning

Unforgiven

Crimson Tide

Get Shorty

Enemy of the State

The Royal Tenenbaums

Heist

by two of the actor's most celebrated roles from that time. He is excellent as Reverend Scott, who manages to save a small band of passengers in The Poseidon Adventure (1972), elevating the film above most other disaster movies of the 1970s. And his performance as Harry Caul in Francis Ford Coppola's The Conversation (1974), the surveillance expert whose life falls apart as a result of his own paranoia, remains one of his best. It is also a spectral presence over the character he plays in the Will Smith vehicle Enemy of the State (1998).

Hackman is not known for comedy roles but he excelled as the villainous mastermind Lex Luthor in Superman (1978) and was even funnier in the 1980 sequel. He gave one of his best performances as a two-bit movie producer in Get Shorty (1995) and sends himself up brilliantly as a ruthless general in the animated movie Antz (1998). And his irresponsible patriarch in The Royal Tenenbaums (2001) is perfectly in tune with Wes Anderson's vision of familial strife.

The actor's work-rate throughout the 1980s and 1990s was prodigious. He shines as wealthy monomaniac in Eureka (1983) and exudes charisma as a risk-taking journalist in Under Fire (1983). In Power (1986), he convinces as a washed up political media consultant, while as a high school basketball coach in the acclaimed Hoosiers (1986) he brings fiery passion and nobility. His matter-of-fact delivery also suits the roles he played in Mississippi Burning (1988), as an FBI agent returning to the Deep South at the height of the racial tensions in the 1960s, and in Crimson Tide (1995), as a submarine commander caught in a battle of wits with Denzel Washington's second in command. And he is the perfect actor for David Mamet's terse dialogue, playing an expert thief double crossed by those closest to him, in Heist (2001).

No Way Out (1987), like the later thrillers The Firm (1993), Absolute Power (1997) and Runaway Jury (2003), all use Hackman's ability to present an image of decency, behind which is a moral vacuum. It is this combination of misplaced piety and ruthless self-interest that makes his Oscar-winning turn as Little Bill, the bullying Sheriff in Clint Eastwood's Unforgiven (1992) so compelling yet utterly reprehensible. It is one of his best roles in an impressive career. **IHS**

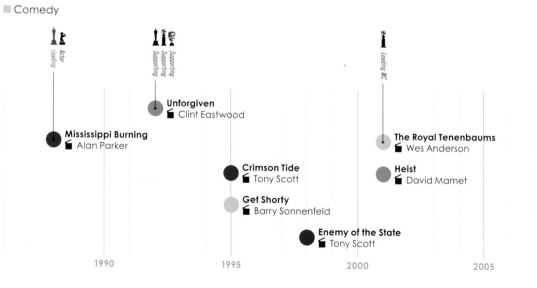

Comedy

Unforgiven
Clint Eastwood

Mississippi Burning
Alan Parker

The Royal Tenenbaums
Wes Anderson

Crimson Tide
Tony Scott

Heist
David Mamet

Get Shorty
Barry Sonnenfeld

Enemy of the State
Tony Scott

1990   1995   2000   2005

tom hanks 1956

Splash

Punchline

Big

A League of Their Own

Philadelphia

Sleepless in Seattle

Forrest Gump

Apollo 13

Over the past 30 years, there have been bigger action heroes, greater heartthrobs, even — albeit few — more award-laden stars. However, no one has consistently combined the critical acclaim, box-office success and all-round everyman popularity of Thomas Jeffrey Hanks.

Born in California in 1956, Hanks made his name in cross-dressing television sitcom *Bosom Buddies* (1980–82). His first hit movie was *Splash* (1984), about a man who falls in love with a mermaid. Hanks' inherent likeability helped sell the fantastical premise, his affable charm and comic timing offsetting any lack of overt sex appeal. Lesser mainstream comedies followed. Then, in 1988, Hanks stepped up with a dazzling one-two combination. *Punchline* cast him as an acerbic small-time stand-up comedian; but it was playing a 12-year-old whose wish to become *Big* puts him inside an adult's body that propelled him toward stardom. Hanks brilliantly captured the physicality of an overgrown child and his guileless performance won him a first Best Actor Oscar nomination.

Despite a few slip-ups, most notably Brian De Palma's wayward *Bonfire of the Vanities* (1990),

the 1990s was Hanks' decade. A delightfully gruff supporting turn as coach to a wartime female baseball team in *A League of Their Own* (1992) confirmed his character actor credentials. He then reaffirmed his leading man status in the hugely popular *Sleepless in Seattle* (1993) opposite Meg Ryan.

Hanks also became the second man to win back-to-back Best Actor Oscars. Jonathan Demme's *Philadelphia* (1993), Hollywood's landmark AIDS drama, reckoned — correctly — that Hanks playing an openly gay man afflicted with the disease would make the stigmatized illness more acceptable. Hanks' emotional acceptance speech only confirmed it. The following year, his turn as *Forrest Gump* (1994), a slow-witted, kind-hearted innocent inadvertently propelled through baby boomer-era U.S. history, endeared Hanks to millions.

Success followed success. As astronaut Jim Lovell, commander of the *Apollo 13* (1995) space mission, Hanks embodied low-key grace under pressure. His voicing of cowboy Woody in Pixar's groundbreaking digital animation *Toy Story* (1995) and its later sequels,

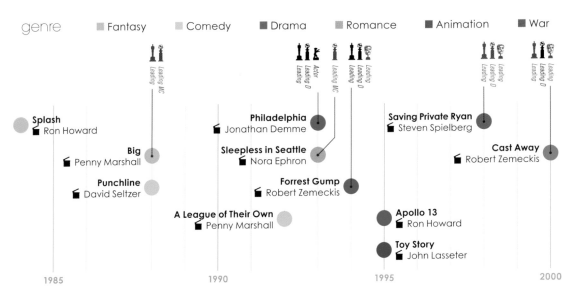

genre ■ Fantasy ■ Comedy ■ Drama ■ Romance ■ Animation ■ War

Leading MC

Actor D / Leading D / Leading

Leading MC

Leading / Leading D

Leading / Leading D

Leading / Leading D

Splash
Ron Howard

Big
Penny Marshall

Punchline
David Seltzer

A League of Their Own
Penny Marshall

Philadelphia
Jonathan Demme

Sleepless in Seattle
Nora Ephron

Forrest Gump
Robert Zemeckis

Saving Private Ryan
Steven Spielberg

Cast Away
Robert Zemeckis

Apollo 13
Ron Howard

Toy Story
John Lasseter

1985   1990   1995   2000

| $334M Philadelphia (1993) | $368M Sleepless in Seattle (1993) | $1.1BN Forrest Gump (1994) | $545M Apollo 13 (1995) | $555M Toy Story (1995) | $691M Saving Private Ryan (1998) | $558M Cast Away (2000) | $879M The Da Vinci Code (2006) |

Toy Story | Saving Private Ryan | Cast Away | Road to Perdition | The Da Vinci Code | Cloud Atlas | Captain Phillips | Saving Mr. Banks

established him as the ultimate proxy family friend. In Steven Spielberg's searing World War II epic *Saving Private Ryan* (1998), the actor's army captain embodied the "Greatest Generation" at their most noble.

All these roles could have become preachy ciphers in lesser hands, but Hanks imparted an honesty and, where appropriate, a wry self-awareness to counteract excessive piety — a claim that could not be made for either his lackluster reteaming with Meg Ryan, *You've Got Mail* (1998), or interminable death-row melodrama *The Green Mile* (1999). Yet both still performed well.

Hanks' most physically transformative role came in *Cast Away* (2000), as a man stranded for years on a deserted island. His poignant survival struggle garnered yet more awards. Another change of pace followed with Depression-era gangster film *Road to Perdition* (2002), Hanks cast atypically as a ruthless mob hit man. Two more Spielberg films came next: *Catch Me If You Can* (2002), as the FBI agent on the trail of Leonardo DiCaprio's con man, and *The Terminal* (2004), as an airport-bound immigrant. His ostentatious thief in the Coen brothers' remake of

The Ladykillers (2004) was a bold choice, but none of these films lived up to their full potential.

Audiences flocked back — though critics did not — to the adaptations of Dan Brown's best selling mysteries *The Da Vinci Code* (2006) and *Angels and Demons* (2009), with the star stiffly cast in a role imagined for Harrison Ford. Mike Nichols' *Charlie Wilson's War* (2007), starring Hanks as a Texas congressman opposite Julia Roberts, was slick fun; but rejoining Roberts for *Larry Crowne* (2011), his second directorial effort, showed how the appeal of two huge stars had waned.

While Hanks has now moved into an "elder statesman" industry role, executive producing passion projects, he is still able to turn out impressive or risky acting work. They range from multiple roles in the ambitious adaptation of David Mitchell's labyrinthine novel *Cloud Atlas* (2012) to carefully maintaining his composure during a ship hijacking in *Captain Phillips* (2013). It was no surprise either, when casting Walt Disney for *Saving Mr. Banks* (2013), that they chose Hanks. The ultimate embodiment of benevolent American entertainment, it is a role he knows well. **LS**

■ Adventure ■ Crime ■ Thriller ■ Sci-Fi

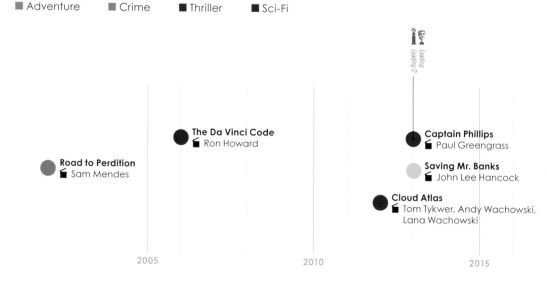

Road to Perdition
🎬 Sam Mendes

The Da Vinci Code
🎬 Ron Howard

Captain Phillips
🎬 Paul Greengrass

Saving Mr. Banks
🎬 John Lee Hancock

Cloud Atlas
🎬 Tom Tykwer, Andy Wachowski, Lana Wachowski

2005   2010   2015

setsuko hara 1920

The Daughter of the Samurai

No Regrets for Our Youth

Late Spring

Early Summer

Repast

Tokyo Story

Sound of the Mountain

The End of Summer

It is simplistic to draw too many direct comparisons between performers, especially those from different cultures, but there are numerous parallels between Greta Garbo and Setsuko Hara: their fondness for tragic roles, their ineffably mysterious faces, and their startlingly early professional retirement when seemingly at the peak of their careers.

Born Masae Aida in Yokohama in 1920, Hara gained early entry into Nikkatsu Studios thanks to her sister marrying a film director. She made her debut at 15, and first came to international attention in *The Daughter of the Samurai* (1937), a coproduction between Nazi Germany and Imperial Japan that saw her character attempting suicide by jumping into an active volcano.

The next few years were dominated by war and the production of overt propaganda vehicles, but she secured a more nuanced role in Akira Kurosawa's *No Regrets for Our Youth* (1946), as a woman who questions her political beliefs after her husband dies in police custody. She made one more film with Kurosawa, the Dostoevsky adaptation *The Idiot* (1951), but it was her six films with Yasujirô Ozu and her four with Mikio Naruse that secured her lasting reputation.

For Ozu, she starred in what was loosely called "the Noriko trilogy," *Late Spring* (1949), *Early Summer* (1951) and *Tokyo Story* (1953), although whether she was actually playing the same character was never made explicit. In the first, she is a daughter who renounces marriage to care for her father; in the second, she shocks her family by revealing her own marriage plans; and in the third, her widow is the only person who truly shows any concern for the well-being of her parents-in-law. In all three cases she gives immensely subtle performances as women largely circumscribed by society's expectations, but who are nonetheless prepared to defy convention if they feel it necessary. She appeared in three more Ozu films, as one of the sisters searching for their mother in *Tokyo Twilight* (1957), and as two more widows in *Late Autumn* (1960) and *The End of Summer* (1961), in both cases having to consider romantic matches arranged by others.

She was equally compelling in her four films for Naruse, in the first three of which she played women facing the prospect of disintegrating marriages. In *Repast* (1951), she is reduced to the role of domestic drudge to an indifferent husband, while in *Sound of the Mountain* (1954) her father-in-law is far more aware of her marital difficulties than is his son. *Sudden Rain* (1956) turns marital failure into rueful black comedy, while in *Daughters, Wives and a Mother* (1960) she is a widow whose substantial inheritance cannot help but disrupt her relationship with relatives and in-laws.

Other roles were less characteristic, including a sun goddess in *The Three Treasures* (1959), a fantasy about the birth of Shintoism. Citing disillusionment with acting, she retired in 1963, shortly after Ozu's death. **MBr**

genre   ■ Drama

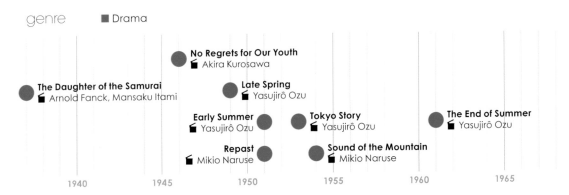

No Regrets for Our Youth
🎬 Akira Kurosawa

The Daughter of the Samurai
🎬 Arnold Fanck, Mansaku Itami

Late Spring
🎬 Yasujirô Ozu

Early Summer
🎬 Yasujirô Ozu

Tokyo Story
🎬 Yasujirô Ozu

The End of Summer
🎬 Yasujirô Ozu

Repast
🎬 Mikio Naruse

Sound of the Mountain
🎬 Mikio Naruse

1940   1945   1950   1955   1960   1965

tom hardy 1977

Layer Cake

Bronson

Inception

Warrior

Lawless

The Dark Knight Rises

Locke

Mad Max: Fury Road

For an actor to carry a whole feature film by himself, with no one else on screen, suggests a player of exceptional power and screen presence. Tom Hardy's one man tour de force in *Locke* (2013) — just him driving a car, with various voices on his cell phone — is an outstanding example of the genre.

He was born in London of Anglo-Irish descent. He studied acting at the Richmond Drama School and later at the London Drama Centre. In his late teens and early twenties, his career was disrupted by alcohol and a crack cocaine addiction, habits that led to the breakdown of his first marriage; but he was able to draw on memories of this dark period for some of his most effective performances, especially in *Bronson* (2008).

Despite his personal problems, Hardy made his screen debut as one of the ill-fated U.S. soldiers in *Black Hawk Down* (2001), and continued to land interesting roles — as the electrical wizard helping a bunch of animal-rights activists in *LD 50 Lethal Dose* (2003), and as a London thug in Matthew Vaughan's gangster thriller *Layer Cake* (2004). He played a cockney lad looking to get lucky in the ensemble piece *Scenes of a Sexual Nature* (2006), and one of those swept away in the disaster movie *Flood* (2007). He was Bill Sikes in a television adaptation of *Oliver Twist* (2007), and another London gangster, this time for Guy Ritchie, in *RocknRolla* (2008).

Then he was *Bronson* — real-life British jailbird Michael Peterson, who adopted the name Charles Bronson to suit his hard man persona — and the critics took notice. His appearance — bull-chested, shaven-headed, macho-mustached — is genuinely scary, all the more so as director Nicolas Winding Refn periodically has him boastfully narrating his life-story in white clown make-up to an appreciative audience. He is scarcely less violent as a boxer in *Warrior* (2011), dangerously nervy as a rogue agent on the run in *Tinker Tailor Soldier Spy* (2011), Tomas Alfredson's adaptation of John le Carré's spy classic, and insidious as one of the dream-stealers in Christopher Nolan's convoluted *Inception* (2010).

Menacing in his stillness, Hardy is the toughest and most taciturn of the three bootlegging brothers in John Hillcoat's Depression-era drama *Lawless* (2012). For Nolan again, he played arch-baddie Bane in the third of the Batman trilogy, *The Dark Knight Rises* (2012) — he is malevolence incarnate, although the mask he wears renders much of his dialogue incomprehensible.

He is mesmerizing as *Locke*, driving and driven, haunted by voices, juggling work, wife and mistress as his life implodes around him. The title role in the revival of the *Mad Max* franchise (2015) seems tailor-made for Hardy and few actors could even be considered suitable for the dual role of the real-life criminal Kray twins in Brian Helgeland's *Legend* (2015). **PK**

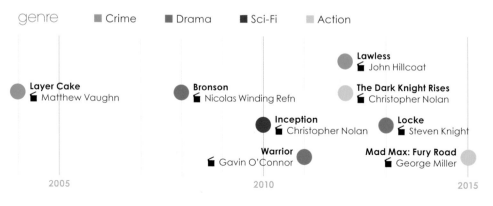

genre   ■ Crime   ■ Drama   ■ Sci-Fi   ■ Action

Lawless
John Hillcoat

Layer Cake
Matthew Vaughn

Bronson
Nicolas Winding Refn

The Dark Knight Rises
Christopher Nolan

Inception
Christopher Nolan

Locke
Steven Knight

Warrior
Gavin O'Connor

Mad Max: Fury Road
George Miller

2005   2010   2015

jean harlow 1911–37

Hell's Angels   The Secret Six   Platinum Blonde   Red-Headed Woman   Bombshell   China Seas   Libeled Lady   Saratoga

The archetypal "Blonde Bombshell," Jean Harlow was one of the biggest stars of the 1930s and one of cinema's earliest sex symbols. Born in Missouri in 1911, she initially struggled to find anything more than extra work and walk-on parts in films such as *The Love Parade* (1929) and the now-lost *This Thing Called Love* (1929). Her most significant early role was a brief appearance as a woman accidentally stripped by Oliver Hardy in the silent short *Double Whoopee* (1929).

Her breakthrough came when Howard Hughes decided to re-shoot his half-completed silent epic *Hell's Angels* (1930) in order to make it a sound film. As the Norwegian lead Greta Nissen was meant to be playing a British aristocrat, Hughes fired the heavily accented star and replaced her with Harlow. Despite some poor reviews, she found the role opened doors for her. She was the female lead in the first of Warner's classic gangster films, *The Public Enemy* (1931), was a boxer's wife in Tod Browning's *Iron Man* (1931) and played opposite Spencer Tracy in the titular role of *Goldie* (1931). *The Secret Six* (1931) initiated the first of six screen appearances opposite costar Clark Gable. And her reputation as a sex symbol and star was cemented by the early Frank Capra-directed romantic comedy *Platinum Blonde* (1931), which was renamed to reference her famous bleached hair.

Soon after, Harlow signed an exclusive contract with MGM and rapidly became one of the studio's most popular stars, in spite of a tumultuous, often scandal-filled personal life. While continuing to act in romantic dramas like *Red Dust* (1932) and *Hold Your Man* (1933), again opposite Gable, she moved into comedy, appearing in *Red-Headed Woman* (1932) and *Bombshell* (1933). Nicknamed both "Baby" and "The Laughing Vamp," she largely played self-assured, ambitious characters in control of their own sexuality and almost exclusively dressed in satin gowns.

Most of Harlow's films were box-office successes, although a rare exception was the World War I drama *Suzy* (1936). Critical acclaim did not always follow in the wake of her profitability, with *The Girl from Missouri* (1934) receiving a particularly disparate commercial and critical response. Her later films, *China Seas* (1935) and the screwball comedy *Libeled Lady* (1936), which was nominated for a Best Picture Oscar, were among her best-received work. Other films from this time include *Reckless* (1935), *Riffraff* (1936), *Wife vs. Secretary* (1936) and *Personal Property* (1937).

After contracting scarlet fever as a teenager, Harlow suffered from a series of illnesses throughout her short life. At the age of just 26, she died of kidney failure, a week after collapsing on the set of *Saratoga* (1937), her last film with Gable. The nearly finished film was completed with look-alikes and a voice double. Released less than two months after her death, the movie was the biggest hit of her career. **JWa**

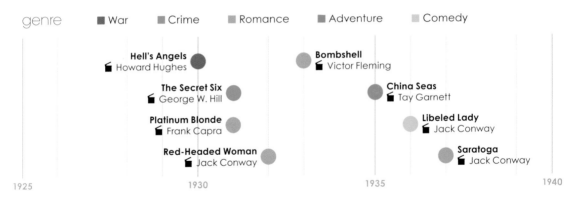

genre   ■ War   ■ Crime   ■ Romance   ■ Adventure   ■ Comedy

Hell's Angels
Howard Hughes

The Secret Six
George W. Hill

Platinum Blonde
Frank Capra

Red-Headed Woman
Jack Conway

Bombshell
Victor Fleming

China Seas
Tay Garnett

Libeled Lady
Jack Conway

Saratoga
Jack Conway

1925   1930   1935   1940

anne hathaway 1982

| The Princess Diaries | Brokeback Mountain | The Devil Wears Prada | Rachel Getting Married | Love & Other Drugs | Alice in Wonderland | Les Misérables | Interstellar |

H

Anne Hathaway's early career was defined by the surprise success of her debut performance in *The Princess Diaries* (2001). Born in Brooklyn in 1982, she had only appeared in a short-lived television program when she starred as Mia Thermopolis, an unpopular teenager who becomes the heir to a tiny European kingdom. The film's commercial success led to a series of features aimed at younger audiences, but by the time the actress starred in *The Princess Diaries 2: Royal Engagement* (2004) she had outgrown family-orientated filmmaking. She subsequently made an effort to transition into adult parts, first with the little seen *Havoc* (2005) and then with a supporting role as Jake Gyllenhaal's rodeo queen wife in the gay cowboy drama *Brokeback Mountain* (2005).

One of the biggest hits of Hathaway's career came when she played Meryl Streep's beleaguered assistant in *The Devil Wears Prada* (2006), although much of the movie's critical praise went to Streep and costar Emily Blunt. Neither Jane Austen biopic *Becoming Jane* (2007) nor the action comedy *Get Smart* (2008) would find an audience, but Hathaway received her first Oscar nomination as a recovering addict in *Rachel Getting Married* (2008). Disappointingly, she would follow up this excellent performance with the anodyne *Bride Wars* (2009) and regrettable ensemble romantic comedy *Valentine's Day* (2010).

Hathaway played royalty again as the White Queen in Tim Burton's *Alice in Wonderland* (2010), which unexpectedly became one of the highest grossing movies of all time. The same year, she acted opposite Gyllenhaal again in the refreshingly frank *Love & Other Drugs* (2010). Another unconventional romantic comedy, *One Day* (2011), followed, but her wandering Yorkshire accent was much pilloried.

In 2012, Hathaway played cat burglar Selina Kyle in *The Dark Knight Rises*, though the final chapter in Christopher Nolan's *Batman* trilogy failed to live up to its predecessors. She also had a key role as the tragic Fantine in Tom Hooper's adaptation of the stage musical *Les Misérables*, winning a Best Supporting Actress Oscar for her raw, sorrowful performance. Hathaway would work again with Nolan, playing a driven astronaut in the space epic *Interstellar* (2014). Her performance, like the film, divided critical opinion. However, it confirmed her status as a leading star. **JWa**

genre   ■ Family   ■ Romance   ■ Comedy   ■ Drama   ■ Fantasy   ■ Musical
■ Sci-Fi

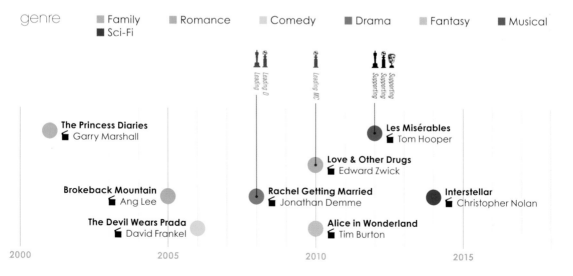

The Princess Diaries
Garry Marshall

Les Misérables
Tom Hooper

Love & Other Drugs
Edward Zwick

Brokeback Mountain
Ang Lee

Rachel Getting Married
Jonathan Demme

Interstellar
Christopher Nolan

The Devil Wears Prada
David Frankel

Alice in Wonderland
Tim Burton

2000   2005   2010   2015

ethan hawke 1970

| Explorers | Dead Poets Society | Before Sunrise | Gattaca | Training Day | Before Sunset | Before the Devil Knows You're Dead | Boyhood |

Born in Austin, Texas, in 1970, Ethan Hawke has become one of the most fascinating actors in contemporary U.S. cinema. Best known for playing likeable characters tinged by failure and weakness, Hawke is also an accomplished screenwriter and novelist.

First coming to attention in Joe Dante's anarchic teen adventure *Explorers* (1985), it was as a timid, impressionable student inspired by Robin Williams' English teacher in *Dead Poets Society* (1989) that Hawke made a formidable early impression.

A role as a philosophical slacker in *Reality Bites* (1994) made Hawke something of a Generation-X heartthrob and was a warm-up for what would become his signature role, in a trilogy of films made with Richard Linklater and Julie Delpy. *Before Sunrise* (1995) follows a young couple who meet on a train in Europe and enjoy a night of passion. In *Before Sunset* (2004) the couple reconnect by chance in Paris. The third encounter with the characters, *Before Midnight* (2013), sees the pair not so happily married and vacationing in Greece. Blessed with an easy naturalism, the films form a compelling trilogy, with Hawke and Delpy perfect as the couple.

Returning to filmmaking after a two-year hiatus, Hawke segued into more mainstream sci-fi territory in Andrew Niccol's riveting *Gattaca* (1997). It was followed by a busy period that saw Hawke move between commercial and independent movies, with roles in *Great Expectations* (1998), *Hamlet* (2000) and three further Linklater collaborations: the commercial failure *The Newton Boys* (1998), a brief cameo in the digitally animated *Waking Life* (2001) and the intense, single-room drama *Tape* (2001). He was also nominated for an Academy Award as a rookie cop schooled by a corrupt partner in *Training Day* (2001).

The final film from Sidney Lumet, *Before The Devil Knows You're Dead* (2007) pitted Hawke and Philip Seymour Hoffman as siblings driven by desperation and greed to rob the store owned by their elderly parents. A dark work that paints a despairing portrait of morality, it is one of the finest crime films in recent memory. A fifth collaboration with Linklater, *Boyhood* (2014), became a sensation and was showered with awards and critical acclaim. Shot over 12 years, the film follows the life of a young boy from the age of 6 to 18. As the boy's feckless but well-intentioned father, Hawke exudes the easy charm and slacker philosophy that, through its many subtle variations, has come to define so many of his performances. **JW**

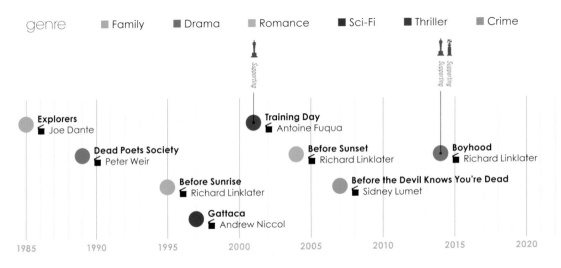

genre ■ Family ■ Drama ■ Romance ■ Sci-Fi ■ Thriller ■ Crime

Explorers
Joe Dante

Dead Poets Society
Peter Weir

Before Sunrise
Richard Linklater

Gattaca
Andrew Niccol

Training Day
Antoine Fuqua
Supporting

Before Sunset
Richard Linklater

Before the Devil Knows You're Dead
Sidney Lumet

Boyhood
Richard Linklater
Supporting Supporting

1985 1990 1995 2000 2005 2010 2015 2020

goldie hawn 1945

Cactus Flower

There's a Girl in My Soup

The Sugarland Express

Shampoo

Private Benjamin

Overboard

The First Wives Club

Everyone Says I Love You

Despite starting out as a dancer, Goldie Hawn came to prominence in the late 1960s as a comic performer on television. With her reputation as a lovable comedienne developing nicely, she made the transition to the big screen, keeping within her comfort zone in *Cactus Flower* (1969), for which she won a Best Supporting Actress Oscar, and *There's a Girl in My Soup* (1970).

As the 1970s progressed, Hawn appeared in Steven Spielberg's *The Sugarland Express* (1974), playing one half of a couple on the run from the law, and excelled as the erratic girlfriend of Warren Beatty's hairdresser in the smart, critically acclaimed political satire *Shampoo* (1975). Both films saw the actress expand her range in an attempt to shake off her "dumb blonde" persona.

She held her own against Chevy Chase and Dudley Moore in the comedy thriller *Foul Play* (1978) and although Mario Monicelli's Rome-set comedy *Lovers and Liars* (1979) bombed, Hawn is a charming presence. However, it was her Oscar-nominated turn in the much-loved comedy *Private Benjamin* (1980), as a grieving newlywed fooled into thinking the army life is for her, that won Hawn favor with audiences.

Over the next few years, she appeared in *Seems Like Old Times* (1980), *Best Friends* (1982) and *Wildcats*

(1986). She also starred, for a third time — after *The One and Only, Genuine, Original Family Band* (1968) and *Swing Shift* (1984) — opposite her partner Kurt Russell in one of her most popular roles, as a spoiled heiress who loses her memory following an accident in the comedy *Overboard* (1987).

After another comic turn in *Bird On a Wire* (1990) and a dramatic role in the thriller *Deceived* (1991), Hawn hit her stride, churning out a series of charming performances in a string of likable hit comedies. *Housesitter* (1992), *Death Becomes Her* (1992) and *The First Wives Club* (1996) each effortlessly showcased Hawn's natural talent for comedy and proved hugely successful with audiences. Meanwhile, her appearance in Woody Allen's *Everyone Says I Love You* (1996) is a joy.

Hawn reunited with her *Housesitter* costar Steve Martin for the disappointing remake *The Out-of-Towners* (1999), while a couple of years later she scored one of her biggest flops in the much-derided *Town & Country* (2001). She followed it with *The Banger Sisters* (2002), starring opposite Susan Sarandon as a pair of ageing groupies recalling their glorious past. However, the film is most notable for being Hawn's final on-screen performance before retirement. **MB**

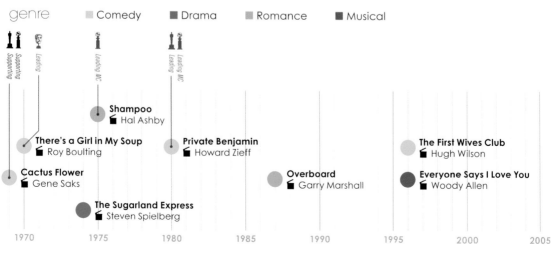

genre ■ Comedy ■ Drama ■ Romance ■ Musical

Supporting
Supporting

Leading

Leading MC

Leading MC
Leading

Shampoo
Hal Ashby

There's a Girl in My Soup
Roy Boulting

Private Benjamin
Howard Zieff

The First Wives Club
Hugh Wilson

Cactus Flower
Gene Saks

Overboard
Garry Marshall

Everyone Says I Love You
Woody Allen

The Sugarland Express
Steven Spielberg

1970   1975   1980   1985   1990   1995   2000   2005

salma hayek 1966

Desperado

The Faculty

Wild Wild West

Frida

Once Upon a Time in Mexico

Grown Ups

Savages

How to Make Love Like an Englishman

H

Born in 1966, in Coatzacoalcos, Mexico, Salma Hayek was raised a Catholic by her Spanish mother and Lebanese/Mexican father, attended a convent school in Louisiana and then lived with her aunt in Texas during her teens. She returned to Mexico to attend university but dropped out to pursue her dream of acting.

Hayek became a national star in 1989 when she was cast in the title role for the television series *Teresa*. However, Hollywood beckoned and after a number of minor television appearances, her major break came in Robert Rodriguez's sophomore feature, *Desperado* (1995). She played the owner of a bookshop that was better known as a local drug drop and the love interest of Antonio Banderas' gun-toting mariachi.

She was an alien in Rodriguez's enjoyable teen sci-fi thriller *The Faculty* (1998) and starred opposite Matthew Perry in *Fools Rush In* (1997). She was wasted — as was everyone else — in the overblown Will Smith vehicle *Wild Wild West* (1999). Better was her performance as Anita Randazzo in Mark Christopher's recreation of New York's disco glory days, *54* (1998).

In 1999, Hayek launched her own production company, Ventanarosa, with *No One Writes to the Colonel*, directed by Arturo Ripstein. The company's

third venture, *Frida* (2002), remains its most prestigious — and also gave Hayek the role of a lifetime. She excels as Mexican artist Frida Kahlo, conveying the ferocity of her lust for life and vulnerability. The film was nominated for six Academy Awards, including a Best Actress nomination for Hayek.

Hayek went on to star in the third part of Rodriguez's mariachi trilogy, *Once Upon a Time in Mexico* (2003), reprising her role of Carolina, unsurprisingly more sultry and more armed than the former offering. Between 2006 and 2010, she executive produced and guest-starred in the award-winning television series *Ugly Betty*. She starred opposite Adam Sandler in the comedy *Grown Ups* (2010) and its 2013 sequel. And she teamed up with Antonio Banderas, albeit offscreen, in the *Shrek* franchise offshoot, *Puss in Boots* (2011). She also voiced the character of Cutlass Liz in Aardman's *The Pirates! Band of Misfits* (2012).

Recent projects have included Oliver Stone's *Savages* (2012), playing the boss of a Mexican cartel who wants to expand her business, and the romantic comedy *How to Make Love like an Englishman* (2014), starring opposite Pierce Brosnan. **MK**

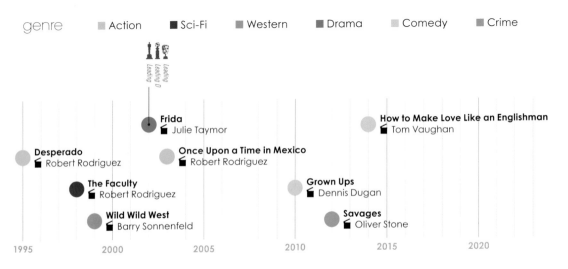

genre ■ Action ■ Sci-Fi ■ Western ■ Drama ▪ Comedy ■ Crime

Leading
Leading
Leading 0

Frida
Julie Taymor

How to Make Love Like an Englishman
Tom Vaughan

Desperado
Robert Rodriguez

Once Upon a Time in Mexico
Robert Rodriguez

The Faculty
Robert Rodriguez

Grown Ups
Dennis Dugan

Wild Wild West
Barry Sonnenfeld

Savages
Oliver Stone

1995   2000   2005   2010   2015   2020

234 **movie star chronicles**

rita hayworth 1918–87

Only Angels Have Wings	The Lady in Question	Strawberry Blonde	You'll Never Get Rich	Cover Girl	Gilda	The Lady from Shanghai	Miss Sadie Thompson

In the 1940s, Rita Hayworth was one of Hollywood's biggest, most beautiful stars. She was a talented dancer, one of the few to partner both Fred Astaire and Gene Kelly. And her innate combination of sensuality and vulnerability made her an ideal femme fatale. Nevertheless, hers was an imperfect career. In her heyday, Hayworth's fame had as much to do with being a forces favorite as it did her acting. For one so renowned, she gave few significant performances.

Margarita Carmen Cansino was born in Brooklyn in 1918, to an Irish-American mother and Spanish father, both dancers. Pushed by her father, Margarita began dance lessons at 4 and by 12 was his stage partner. She was performing in Mexican nightclubs when an executive from Fox spotted her. After some small roles for the studio, she moved to Columbia. By this time, she was married to the Svengali-like Edward Judson, who decided to make her less "Latin" and thus more marketable. Electrolysis altered her hairline, she became a redhead, and took her mother's maiden name.

Her breakthrough was as Cary Grant's old flame in the Howard Hawks adventure *Only Angels Have Wings* (1939), a supporting role whose instant allure pushed female lead Jean Arthur into the shade. Her impact as the object of James Cagney's affections in *Strawberry Blonde* (1941) led to star billing with Astaire in *You'll Never Get Rich* (1941). That musical and its reprise, *You Were Never Lovelier* (1942), were smash hits.

Hayworth then teamed with Kelly in *Cover Girl* (1944), as a dancer whose career takes off after she appears on a magazine cover. The plot mirrored Hayworth's own life — not only the *Life* photo shoot that made her one of the forces' most popular pin-ups during World War II, but the constant presence of controlling men. Among them, Columbia studio head Harry Cohn, who refused his top star the vocal lessons she craved; her singing voice was invariably dubbed.

Her most famous role was as *Gilda* (1946), the frivolous focus of a dangerous love triangle. Her performance is notable for its erotic striptease — of nothing more than her elbow-length, satin gloves. For *The Lady from Shanghai* (1947), director and estranged husband Orson Welles radically transformed her signature look; as a platinum blonde seductress, Hayworth had never been more beautiful, more enigmatic or more thrillingly effective.

But from the late 1940s her career declined, due variously to a turbulent private life (she was married and divorced five times), her deteriorating relationship with Columbia, heavy drinking and finally Alzheimer's disease. She remained a largely superficial actress, though she was moving in the otherwise woeful *Miss Sadie Thompson* (1953) and was a good fit for the somber ensemble of *Separate Tables* (1958). Hayworth's last musical was *Pal Joey* (1957), opposite Frank Sinatra and Columbia's new favorite, Kim Novak. **DM**

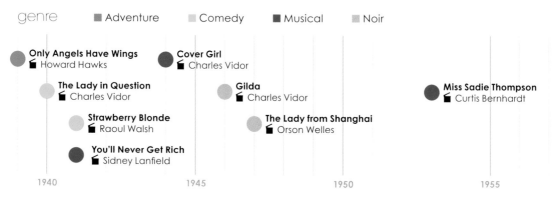

genre   ■ Adventure   ■ Comedy   ■ Musical   ■ Noir

Only Angels Have Wings
🎬 Howard Hawks

The Lady in Question
🎬 Charles Vidor

Strawberry Blonde
🎬 Raoul Walsh

You'll Never Get Rich
🎬 Sidney Lanfield

Cover Girl
🎬 Charles Vidor

Gilda
🎬 Charles Vidor

The Lady from Shanghai
🎬 Orson Welles

Miss Sadie Thompson
🎬 Curtis Bernhardt

1940   1945   1950   1955

audrey hepburn 1929–93

| The Lavender Hill Mob | Roman Holiday | Sabrina | War and Peace | Love in the Afternoon | Funny Face | The Nun's Story | The Unforgiven |

Slim, elegant, nervy, Givenchy-clad — is this not how we all remember Audrey Hepburn? It was not her sole register, of course, but it is the image of her that has remained most vivid. There was a wide-eyed vulnerability about her, a fragile innocence underlying the glamour; it was a combination that gave her an irresistible appeal. She could play women who were misguided, deluded, mischievous, even devious; but her innate gentleness and courtesy make it impossible to imagine her playing anyone truly bad.

Daughter of a Dutch baroness and an Anglo-Irish banker who deserted the family when she was 6, she grew up in wartime privation in the occupied Netherlands. She studied dancing in Arnhem and London, then joined the chorus line in a few stage musicals. In 1951, she made her screen debut with some small roles, including a brief appearance at the start of *The Lavender Hill Mob* (1951). In a more substantial role, she played Valentina Cortese's sister in Thorold Dickinson's political thriller *Secret People* (1952).

After playing the title role in the stage adaptation of *Gigi* (1951) in New York, Hollywood took notice.

William Wyler's *Roman Holiday* (1953) conferred stardom upon her as a princess on a state visit to Rome, briefly escaping the cage of protocol with Gregory Peck's American reporter. For Billy Wilder she took the title role in *Sabrina* (1954) as the chauffeur's daughter wooed by both her father's employers. It was a contrived story, but she gave it heart; it was also the first film where she was costumed by Hubert de Givenchy, who became a personal friend and whose clean simple lines came to define her screen persona.

War and Peace (1956) was hollow and largely miscast, with Hepburn's Natasha the sole exception. There followed her first screen musical — and the first of three films she made with Stanley Donen — *Funny Face* (1957). Partnered with Fred Astaire but in no way overshadowed by him, she plays a bookstore clerk discovered by Astaire's fashion photographer, bringing wit and gamine charm. Back with Wilder for *Love in the Afternoon* (1957), she is the Parisian ingénue romanced by Gary Cooper's playboy; at this stage in her career, being teamed with much older male stars was a frequent occurrence.

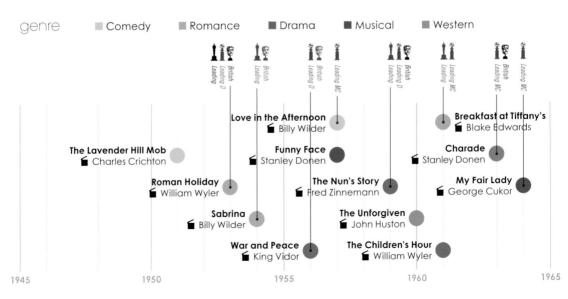

genre   ■ Comedy   ■ Romance   ■ Drama   ■ Musical   ■ Western

Love in the Afternoon — Billy Wilder
The Lavender Hill Mob — Charles Crichton
Roman Holiday — William Wyler
Funny Face — Stanley Donen
Breakfast at Tiffany's — Blake Edwards
Charade — Stanley Donen
Sabrina — Billy Wilder
The Nun's Story — Fred Zinnemann
My Fair Lady — George Cukor
The Unforgiven — John Huston
War and Peace — King Vidor
The Children's Hour — William Wyler

1945   1950   1955   1960   1965

$543M (U.S.)
My Fair Lady
(1964)

$140M (U.S.)
Always
(1989)

**Breakfast
at Tiffany's**

**The
Children's
Hour**

Charade

My Fair Lady

**How to Steal
a Million**

**Two for
the Road**

**Robin and
Marian**

Always

Peter Finch, as the doctor to whom Hepburn's nun is attracted in *The Nun's Story* (1959), was closer to her in age, but it was solemn, slow-moving stuff. In the jungle fantasy *Green Mansions* (1959) she plays the fey "bird" girl Rima, a role undertaken out of loyalty to its director, her then husband Mel Ferrer. For John Huston she played an Indian girl raised by whites in his unconventional western *The Unforgiven* (1960).

And then came *Breakfast at Tiffany's* (1961), the film for which she is still best remembered. As New York good-time girl Holly Golightly, her character was toned down from Truman Capote's trampier original. Even so, sitting on the fire-escape singing "Moon River," she still tugs at the heartstrings. She was borderline lesbian in *The Children's Hour* (1961), and for Donen again she teamed with Cary Grant for the Hitchcockian comedy-thriller *Charade* (1963).

Paris When It Sizzles (1964) was minor-league comedy. Hepburn was a spirited Eliza in *My Fair Lady* (1964) though, to her disappointment, her singing voice was dubbed. *How to Steal a Million* (1966), a caper comedy for Wyler, felt poorly paced; but *Two*

for the Road (1967), her third for Donen, was the film of which she often said she felt proudest. A comedy-drama road movie about a disintegrating relationship, it is told in fragments, spanning 12 years.

She played a blind woman menaced by heavies in *Wait until Dark* (1967), then there was a long gap while she devoted herself to parenthood and, increasingly, worked for UNICEF. In the elegiac *Robin and Marian* (1976), the tentative renewal of romance between her Marian and Sean Connery's Robin Hood was touching. She then made *Bloodline* (1979), a contrived suspense thriller that seemed better than it was.

After this there were only two more films, both offering her support roles: Peter Bogdanovich's would-be romantic comedy *They All Laughed* (1981) — nobody did — and Steven Spielberg's afterworld drama *Always* (1989). It was over-sentimental, but redeemed by Hepburn's serene presence as a guardian angel. However, her lifelong slimness was starting to look ravaged; she was succumbing to cancer. News of her death in 1993 came as a public loss, received with affection and regret. **PK**

H

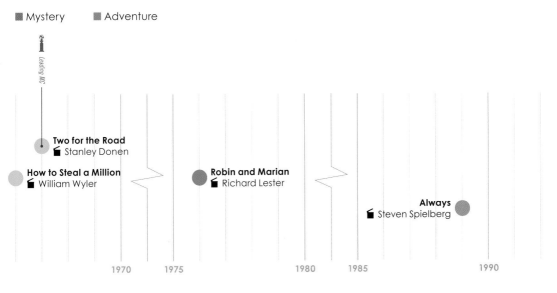

■ Mystery   ■ Adventure

Leading MC

Two for the Road
🎬 Stanley Donen

How to Steal a Million
🎬 William Wyler

Robin and Marian
🎬 Richard Lester

Always
🎬 Steven Spielberg

1970   1975   1980   1985   1990

Roman Holiday
(1953)

Sabrina
(1954)

War and Peace
(1956)

Funny Face
(1957)

**Breakfast at
Tiffany's**
(1961)

Charade
(1963)

My Fair Lady
(1964)

Two for the Road
(1967)

Roman Holiday gave Hepburn her first starring Hollywood role, for which she won a Best Actress Academy Award.

Humphrey Bogart romances Hepburn in *Sabrina*, belying the poor relationship between the costars offscreen.

Hepburn poses in Givenchy for *Sabrina*, marking the start of a lifelong association between the actress and designer. In an interview for *Vanity Fair*, Hubert Givenchy said that Hepburn "gave a life to the clothes—she had a way of installing herself in them that I have seen in no one else since."

Henry Fonda, Hepburn and Mel Ferrer in *War and Peace*. Hepburn received $350,000 for her role, making her the highest paid actress at the time.

Funny Face paired Hepburn with Fred Astaire. "Fred literally swept me off my feet," she later recalled.

Hepburn in her iconic role as Holly Golightly in *Breakfast at Tiffany's*.

Despite not earning back its budget at the box office, *Funny Face* is today regarded as a visually sumptuous classic.

Charade has been described as "the best Hitchcock film that Hitchcock never made."

After finishing shooting on *Charade*, Cary Grant reportedly declared "All I want for Christmas is another picture with Audrey Hepburn."

Despite initial disappointment at Hepburn's casting, Rex Harrison later described his *My Fair Lady* costar as his favorite leading lady.

Two for the Road depicts Hepburn and Albert Finney as a young couple at five different points in their relationship, from romantic first meeting to marital breakdown.

katharine hepburn 1907–2003

A Bill of
Divorcement

Little Women

Sylvia
Scarlett

Mary of
Scotland

Bringing Up
Baby

The
Philadelphia
Story

Woman of
the Year

Adam's Rib

H

"Nature, Mr. Allnut, is what we are put into this world to rise above." The line comes from John Huston's *The African Queen* (1951), scripted by Peter Viertel; but so perfectly does its subtly self-mocking hauteur fit Katharine Hepburn's persona (both on and offscreen) that it is tempting to wonder if she wrote it herself. Her costar, Humphrey Bogart, remarked afterward — evidently still reeling from the experience — "She doesn't give a damn how she looks. I don't think she tries to be a character. I think she is one."

Right from her very first screen role — radiantly holding her own, at 25, against that primest of hams, John Barrymore, in *A Bill of Divorcement* (1932) — Hepburn served notice that she intended to be utterly her own woman. The title of one of her subsequent films, *A Woman Rebels* (1936) is often proposed as summing her up — but rebellion implies a prior subordinate position and Hepburn, raised by wealthy, free-thinking, left-leaning parents, never for a moment thought herself anyone's inferior. If she never quite convinced as Mary Queen of Scots in John Ford's *Mary of Scotland* (1936), it was less through any lack of regal dignity than through the stiff staginess that infected the film as a whole.

Her staunch independence shone through on screen. Studio-era Hollywood liked to make over its stars, especially the women: to change their names, faces, accents and hairstyles; dictate their wardrobes; mold their tastes and personalities to suit the publicity department's demands. But there was nothing synthetic about Hepburn, with her angular but graceful physique and the flattened vowels that invited parody. Pretty she was not, though it seems strange that there were people who could not see she was beautiful. David O. Selznick denied her the role of Scarlett O'Hara, telling her she was not sexy enough.

Inevitably, Hepburn's refusal to compromise aroused hostility. At one point — amazingly, just after her gloriously funny performance as the ditsy socialite disrupting Cary Grant's stuffy paleontologist in *Bringing Up Baby* (1938) — a group of exhibitors labeled her "box-office poison." She responded by asking Philip Barry to rewrite his play *The Philadelphia Story* (1940) for her, secured the movie rights and stormed back in triumph. True, her range was limited. Dorothy Parker's brilliantly catty put-down "She ran the gamut of emotions from A to B," seems unlikely to be forgotten, though it was earned for an early role

genre
■ Drama   ■ Romance   ■ Comedy   ■ Adventure   ■ Mystery

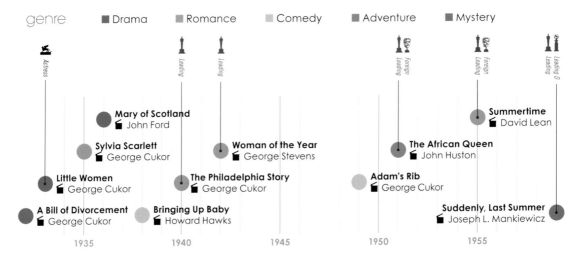

Actress

Leading

Leading

Foreign
Leading

Foreign
Leading

Leading D
Leading

Mary of Scotland
John Ford

Summertime
David Lean

Sylvia Scarlett
George Cukor

Woman of the Year
George Stevens

The African Queen
John Huston

Little Women
George Cukor

The Philadelphia Story
George Cukor

Adam's Rib
George Cukor

A Bill of Divorcement
George Cukor

Bringing Up Baby
Howard Hawks

Suddenly, Last Summer
Joseph L. Mankiewicz

1935   1940   1945   1950   1955

$397M (U.S.)
Guess Who's
Coming to Dinner
(1967)

$307M (U.S.)
On Golden Pond
(1981)

The African
Queen

Summertime

Suddenly,
Last Summer

Long Day's
Journey into
Night

Guess Who's
Coming to
Dinner

The Lion in
Winter

The Trojan
Women

On Golden
Pond

in a reputedly mediocre Broadway play. But playing Chinese for *Dragon Seed* (1944) was ill-advised, and her performance as a wild hillbilly girl in *Spitfire* (1934) makes her namesake Audrey's flower-girl in *My Fair Lady* (1964) look like a tour de force of dirty realism.

On her home ground, though, she was superlative. Sophisticated comedy brought out the best in her; few actresses could match the fun, vitality and sheer relish Hepburn brought to *Bringing Up Baby*, *The Philadelphia Story* and the underrated *Holiday* (1938). Without diminishing the run of nine films she made with Spencer Tracy, to which she brought the added warmth of their off-screen partnership, Cary Grant was perhaps her ideal screen partner; they matched each other for poise, playfulness and a tantalizing sense of sexual ambiguity. For their first film together, *Sylvia Scarlett* (1935), she spent most of the time disguised in drag, and made a deliciously sexy boy.

With Tracy, sexual ambiguity emphatically was not on offer. In films like *Woman of the Year* (1942), *Adam's Rib* (1949) and *Pat and Mike* (1952), much of the joy comes from seeing the irresistible force of Hepburn's patrician hauteur collide with the immovable object of Tracy's down-to-earth redneck stolidity. The pair

of them played out the battle of the sexes with a sense of amused self-awareness (and, in her case, a touching hint of underlying vulnerability) that rescued the situations from conventional cliché. The one-off teaming with Bogart in *The African Queen* reworked the same sexual tension in an earthier, saltier mode.

As was to be expected, Hepburn aged gracefully and with dignity, refusing to play younger than her years. She willingly explored new modes, from the full-tilt grand guignol of *Suddenly, Last Summer* (1959) to the high theatrical tragedy of *Long Day's Journey into Night* (1962). Recognition, at last, was ungrudging; she accumulated four Oscars and 12 nominations, a record yet to be beaten. The awards, admittedly, were not always for the films that should have earned them; her Eleanor of Aquitaine carried *The Lion in Winter* (1968) through sheer force, but *Guess Who's Coming to Dinner* (1967) and *On Golden Pond* (1981) were regrettably swamped with sentiment.

When she died, some accounts described Katharine Hepburn as "the final link with the Golden Age of Hollywood" and "the last of her kind." In actual fact, she was always the only one of her kind, far too individual to be representative of anything. **PK**

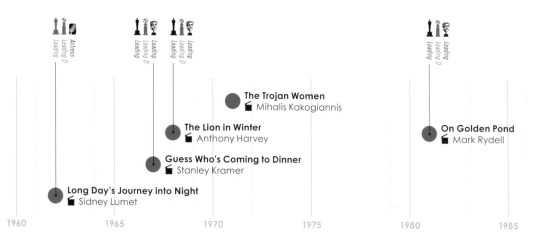

Actress
Leading D
Leading

Leading
Leading D
Leading

Leading
Leading D
Leading

Leading
Leading D
Leading

The Trojan Women
Mihalis Kakogiannis

The Lion in Winter
Anthony Harvey

Guess Who's Coming to Dinner
Stanley Kramer

Long Day's Journey into Night
Sidney Lumet

On Golden Pond
Mark Rydell

1960   1965   1970   1975   1980   1985

charlton heston 1923–2008

| The Greatest Show on Earth | The Ten Command-ments | Touch of Evil | The Big Country | Ben-Hur | Major Dundee | Khartoum | Planet of the Apes |

The star most closely associated with the Golden Age of the Hollywood epic, Charlton Heston stood out like a bronzed Adonis. His square jaw and athletic physique made him the perfect choice to lead a nation toward the promised land or an army into war against marauding force. In real life, he was a divisive figure, particularly in his unwavering defense of the right to bear arms. But with his experience of over 60 years and 100-odd films, he is every inch a star.

After a spell in the army toward the end of World War II, Heston and his wife Lydia moved to New York where they earned money as artists' models before he made a name for himself in theater. His first professional screen role was playing the lead in William Dieterle's film noir *Dark City* (1950), but it was his role as a circus manager in Cecile B. DeMille's *The Greatest Show on Earth* (1952) that not only got him noticed, but put him in the running to play Moses in DeMille's epic *The Ten Commandments* (1956). Before that epic, there was a run of average films that included *Ruby Gentry* (1952), *Pony Express* (1953), *The Naked Jungle* (1954) and *The Far Horizons* (1955).

DeMille chose Heston to play Moses because he believed the actor looked like Michelangelo's statue of Moses and because he had been impressed by his knowledge of Ancient Egyptian history during his audition. It was perfect casting. Heston not only holds his own against another unique star, Yul Brynner, who plays Rameses, but never appears dwarfed by the scale of the enterprise. Even with a vast gray wig, immense beard and make-up that ages him a few generations, Heston convinces.

The actor's ability to carry the weight of such a large production saw him return to the epic a number of times. He was not the first choice to play the lead in *Ben-Hur* (1959) — only winning the role after Marlon Brando, Burt Lancaster and Rock Hudson had turned it down. But he excelled in it even if, as later evidence showed, he was unaware of the homoerotic undercurrent between his character and Stephen Boyd's Messala that cowriter Gore Vidal introduced to the screenplay. Heston would go on to star in Anthony Mann's entertaining *El Cid* (1961) and Nicholas Ray's *55 Days at Peking* (1963); in 1965, he was John the Baptist in *The Greatest Story Ever Told*, Michelangelo in *The Agony and the Ecstasy* and a medieval knight in *The War Lord*. *Khartoum* (1966), in which he played General Gordon to Laurence Olivier's Mahdi, was

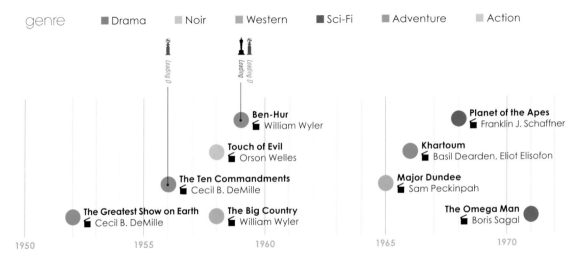

genre ■ Drama ■ Noir ■ Western ■ Sci-Fi ■ Adventure ■ Action

Ben-Hur
William Wyler

Planet of the Apes
Franklin J. Schaffner

Touch of Evil
Orson Welles

Khartoum
Basil Dearden, Eliot Elisofon

The Ten Commandments
Cecil B. DeMille

Major Dundee
Sam Peckinpah

The Greatest Show on Earth
Cecil B. DeMille

The Big Country
William Wyler

The Omega Man
Boris Sagal

1950   1955   1960   1965   1970

$317M (U.S.)	$563M (U.S.)	$18M (U.S.)	$219M	$378M (U.S.)	$78M (U.S.)	$597M	$478M
The Greatest Show on Earth (1952)	*The Ten Commandments* (1956)	*Touch of Evil* (1958)	*Planet of the Apes* (1968)	*Earthquake* (1974)	*Wayne's World 2* (1993)	*True Lies* (1994)	*Planet of the Apes* (2001)

The Omega Man / Soylent Green / The Three Musketeers / Earthquake / Wayne's World 2 / True Lies / Hamlet / Planet of the Apes

the last of the classical epics, which had become unfashionable with audiences.

In 1958, Heston played one of his few supporting roles, as the foreman to a bullying rancher in *The Big Country*. In the same year, he played the seemingly incorruptible drug enforcement officer Miguel Vargas in Orson Welles' *Touch of Evil*. Shot after weeks of rehearsals, during which the cast helped rewrite the dialogue, the film is seen as the last great film noir and Heston's performance ranks among his best. Welles saw how the actor's noble screen persona would offer a stark contrast to the compromised figures living in a limbo world on the U.S.–Mexico border.

Welles' film was recut by the studio and only recently restored to the correct director's version. Sam Peckinpah's cut of what might have been one of his masterpieces, *Major Dundee* (1965), has never been recovered. Heston still excels as the leader of a ragtag band of Unionists and Confederates who cross the border into Mexico in order to hunt down an Apache raiding group, and a recent restoration has gone some way to restoring the film to its original state.

If Heston no longer appeared in biblical blockbusters, two new kinds of epic awaited him. He is the last vestige of a dying or disappeared world in *Planet of the Apes* (1968) and *The Omega Man* (1971), while in *Soylent Green* (1973) he is a cop who discovers the truth behind the food product that supplements the planet's scarce natural resources. The films introduced Heston to a new audience and his larger-than-life stature suited the apocalyptic narratives. Likewise, in *Earthquake* (1974), the actor appeared almost superhuman in his willingness to race against time to save both his wife and lover as Los Angeles crumbles.

Heston excelled as the conniving Cardinal Richelieu in Richard Lester's anarchic *The Three Musketeers* (1973) and its 1974 sequel, but it was one of his last significant roles. He continued to appear in films, but the roles he played were less interesting. His brief appearance in *Wayne's World 2* (1993) highlighted the power of his screen presence, while he offered gentle relief as the head of a spy unit in *True Lies* (1994). His Player King in Kenneth Branagh's *Hamlet* (1996) is a joy, while his role as an ape in Tim Burton's woeful remake of *Planet of the Apes* (2001) offers a sly dig at the actor's gun stance but is also a reminder of what a formidable presence he was in that earlier film. **IHS**

■ Comedy

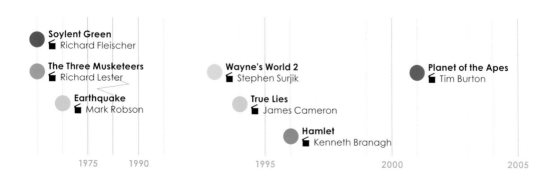

Soylent Green
Richard Fleischer

The Three Musketeers
Richard Lester

Earthquake
Mark Robson

Wayne's World 2
Stephen Surjik

True Lies
James Cameron

Hamlet
Kenneth Branagh

Planet of the Apes
Tim Burton

1975   1990   1995   2000   2005

The Greatest Show on Earth (1952)

The Ten Commandments (1956)

Touch of Evil (1958)

Ben-Hur (1959)

Planet of the Apes (1968)

The Omega Man (1971)

Soylent Green (1973)

Earthquake (1974)

Charlton Heston as the circus manager and an unrecognizable James Stewart as a clown in *The Greatest Show on Earth*.

Heston once commented that playing Moses in *The Ten Commandments* was the high point of his career.

Heston in *Ben-Hur*'s famous chariot race scene, which at the time was the most expensive action sequence ever filmed.

Heston as a young Moses in Cecil B. DeMille's *The Ten Commandments*, which was the highest-grossing film of 1956.

Heston and Janet Leigh in *Touch of Evil*. Originally hired only to act in the movie, Orson Welles was reportedly given directing duties to secure Heston's involvement.

Costing an unprecedented $15 million, *Ben-Hur* boasted 300 sets, 365 speaking parts and 50,000 extras.

In her review of **Planet of the Apes** for The New Yorker, Pauline Kael observed that the story "wouldn't be so forceful or so funny if it weren't for the use of Charlton Heston in the [leading] role. With his perfect, lean-hipped, powerful body, Heston is a god-like hero; built for strength, he is an archetype of what makes Americans win."

Adapted from Richard Matheson's 1954 novel I Am Legend, **The Omega Man** starred Heston as a survivor of a plague that has wiped out most of the human race.

Set in 2022, **Soylent Green** depicted a dystopian future in which the world has become overcrowded, polluted and depleted of resources due to the greenhouse effect.

Earthquake was the first film to be screened in Sensurround, a new sound technique that used special speakers and a soundtrack with very low tones to create the effect of an earthquake happening inside the movie theater.

dustin hoffman 1937

The Graduate	Midnight Cowboy	Straw Dogs	Papillon	Lenny	Marathon Man	All the President's Men	Kramer vs. Kramer

H

Dustin Hoffman's first major screen role was in Mike Nichols' *The Graduate* (1967), and just as that film was a seminal portrait of an emerging generation, Hoffman similarly typified a new kind of leading man. A dedicated Method actor, his portrayal of the conflicted and alienated Benjamin Braddock would herald a wave of antiheroes played by everyman stars who might have been character actors if they had started their careers any earlier, or later.

Hoffman became an instant star with *The Graduate*, which was the highest-grossing film of its year and for which he received the first of seven Oscar nominations. His second nomination would come soon after, for *Midnight Cowboy* (1969), as the limping conman Ratso. He next played the romantic lead, opposite Mia Farrow, in *John and Mary* (1968) and a 121-year-old white man recalling his Native American upbringing in Arthur Penn's revisionist western *Little Big Man* (1970).

As a timid mathematician driven to violent retribution, he was the star of one of the most controversial films of the decade, Sam Peckinpah's home-invasion thriller *Straw Dogs* (1971). While many elements — including a notorious rape scene — are out of touch with contemporary mores, Hoffman's portrayal of the character is among his most compelling roles. Further demonstrating his commitment to variety, he was the dubbed lead of Italian-language comedy *Alfredo, Alfredo* (1972) and Steve McQueen's near-blind prison friend Louis Dega in *Papillon* (1973). He excelled as the comedian Lenny Bruce in Bob Fosse's stylish biopic *Lenny* (1974).

Hoffman has often displayed a gift for choosing films that have captured the zeitgeist. In *All the President's Men* (1976), he played political journalist Carl Bernstein, who along with Bob Woodward was key to revealing the Watergate scandal that led to the resignation of President Nixon. The taut, well-regarded film was released just two years after Woodward and Bernstein's bestselling account of the story was published. Hoffman's other feature that year, *Marathon Man* (1976), saw him play a Ph.D. student and long distance runner who becomes embroiled with a Nazi war criminal. It was a critical and commercial success. *Straight Time* (1978) and *Agatha*

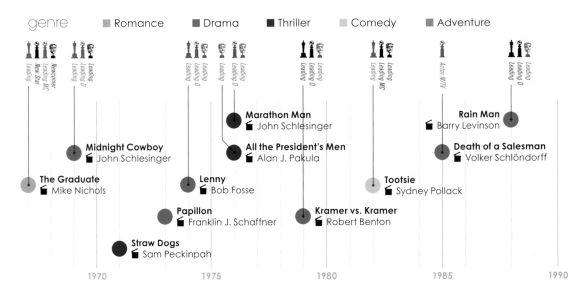

genre ■ Romance ■ Drama ■ Thriller □ Comedy ■ Adventure

Newcomer / Leading MC / New Star / Leading

Leading D / Leading

Leading / Leading D / Leading

Leading / Leading D

Leading / Leading D / Leading

Leading MC / Leading

Actor M/TV

Leading / Leading D / Leading

Marathon Man
John Schlesinger

Rain Man
Barry Levinson

Midnight Cowboy
John Schlesinger

All the President's Men
Alan J. Pakula

Death of a Salesman
Volker Schlöndorff

The Graduate
Mike Nichols

Lenny
Bob Fosse

Tootsie
Sydney Pollack

Papillon
Franklin J. Schaffner

Kramer vs. Kramer
Robert Benton

Straw Dogs
Sam Peckinpah

1970   1975   1980   1985   1990

Tootsie	Death of a Salesman	Rain Man	Hook	Outbreak	Wag the Dog	I Heart Huckabees	Perfume: The Story of a Murderer

(1979) might have lacked the same cultural impact, but the emotive custody drama *Kramer vs. Kramer* (1979) reflected changing attitudes to parenthood and divorce. It won Hoffman his first Oscar.

His next film was as the cross-dressing lead in Sydney Pollack's popular comedy *Tootsie* (1982). After years of dramatic roles it showed Hoffman in a new light. He briefly returned to drama to play Willy Loman in *Death of a Salesman* (1985), the television movie adaptation of Arthur Miller's play, and attempted comedy again with *Ishtar* (1987). Despite being one of the most famous and expensive flops of all time, the film itself is an unexpected pleasure. A year later, Hoffman's portrayal of autistic savant Raymond Babbit in the satisfying, but emotionally manipulative *Rain Man* (1988) would win him another Oscar.

Perhaps reflecting the tonal sea change in popular filmmaking, Hoffman showed a willingness to appear in broader material. A string of disappointing films followed, although his theatrically villainous performance in *Hook* (1991) was the highlight of the otherwise-saccharine movie. He was surprisingly cast as the lead in the disaster film *Outbreak* (1995), one of the bigger box-office successes of his later career.

Hoffman also pursued roles in smaller films including *Sleepers* (1996), and *Mad City* (1997), and had fun as a film producer creating a fake war in Barry Levinson's satirical black comedy *Wag the Dog* (1997). The film was shot quickly while they waited to make their expensive deep-sea science fiction film *Sphere* (1998), and the disparity between the films shows the struggle Hoffman had in finding good material to work with.

Lead roles have become less common in recent years, but Hoffman has never been short of smaller parts. He is excellent in *Confidence* (2003), *Finding Neverland* (2004) and *I Heart Huckabees* (2004). He played Ben Stiller's father in *Meet the Fockers* (2004), reprising the role for the barrel-scraping *Little Fockers* (2010). Two of his better later performances are as Ben Whishaw's olfactory benefactor in *Perfume: The Story of a Murderer* (2006) and as a lonely composer in *Last Chance Harvey* (2008). The horseracing television series *Luck* (2011–12) is one of the few projects in recent years to fully harness the talents of this highly gifted actor. **JWa**

H

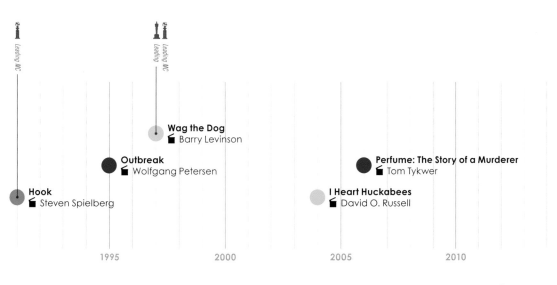

Wag the Dog
Barry Levinson

Outbreak
Wolfgang Petersen

Hook
Steven Spielberg

Perfume: The Story of a Murderer
Tom Tykwer

I Heart Huckabees
David O. Russell

Leading MC

Leading MC

1995   2000   2005   2010

philip seymour hoffman 1967–2014

| Twister | Boogie Nights | The Big Lebowski | Magnolia | The Talented Mr. Ripley | Owning Mahowny | Capote | Mission: Impossible III |

A character actor who became a charismatic leading man, Philip Seymour Hoffman was born in Fairport, New York, in 1967. He started out in theater, which he would constantly return to, before making his first screen appearance in a 1991 episode of *Law & Order*. He auditioned five times for the role of a spoiled student in *Scent of a Woman* (1992), which he credited for setting him on the road to success.

Although he only had a small role in Paul Thomas Anderson's *Hard Eight* (1996), as a craps player, it was the beginning of his most fruitful cinematic partnership. He played a boom operator who lusts after Mark Wahlberg's porn star in Anderson's next film *Boogie Nights* (1997). In *Magnolia* (1999), he plays a nurse caring for Jason Robards' terminal cancer patient, increasingly caught up in a complex web of familial relations. Both these roles are a stark contrast to the two-bit conman who attempts to extort money from Adam Sandler's dupe in *Punch-Drunk Love* (2002) and the controlling head of a religious sect in *The Master* (2012). His scenes alone with Joaquin Phoenix in that film underpin the explosive intensity of his screen presence, quiet one moment then raging against all around him the next.

Hoffman occasionally appeared in bigger Hollywood films. One of his most popular roles is as the slovenly Dustin Davis in *Twister* (1996). He makes for a convincingly sleazy Freddy Lounds in *Red Dragon* (2002) and appears to have fun with his portrayal of Plutarch Heavensbee in *The Hunger Games: Catching Fire* (2013). However, it is his Owen Davian in *Mission: Impossible III* (2006), by far the best and certainly the most malevolent villain in that franchise, which finds the actor chewing the scenery and acting every other performer off the screen. It was shot immediately after his Oscar-winning performance in *Capote* (2005). It was deserved, but the actor has been better when he is not limited to playing a real-life character.

Hoffman's best work lies in his catalogue of obsessives, failures and flawed heroes, although as he showed with his naive yet affable writer in *State and Main* (2000), he was just as capable of commanding the screen with an everyday character. He could do smug to perfection. Aside of his turn in *Scent of a Woman*, he was hilarious as an officious aide in *The Big Lebowski* (1998) and seethed with entitlement and class contempt as Freddy Miles in *The Talented Mr. Ripley* (1999), almost stealing the film from Jude Law

genre ■ Action ■ Drama ■ Comedy ■ Thriller ■ Crime ■ Sci-Fi

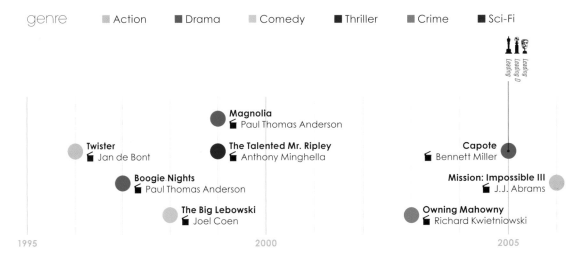

Leading
Leading D
Leading

Magnolia
Paul Thomas Anderson

Twister
Jan de Bont

The Talented Mr. Ripley
Anthony Minghella

Boogie Nights
Paul Thomas Anderson

The Big Lebowski
Joel Coen

Capote
Bennett Miller

Mission: Impossible III
J.J. Abrams

Owning Mahowny
Richard Kwietniowski

1995 2000 2005

| Charlie Wilson's War | Before the Devil Knows You're Dead | Synechdoche, New York | The Ides of March | The Master | A Late Quartet | The Hunger Games: Catching Fire | A Most Wanted Man |

and Matt Damon. His CIA operative in *Charlie Wilson's War* (2007) and campaign manager in *The Ides of March* (2011) both exude malevolence and charm in equal measure, always poised for a fight.

If his lonely onanist in *Happiness* (1998) is too damaged to hide his pain, Hoffman's portrayal of Rusty, the transvestite living next to Robert De Niro's disabled cop in *Flawless* (1999), is all about image as a way of covering a life of victimization. Hoffman steers clear of cliché in his portrayal, which cannot be said of the rest of the film. He is excellent in the title role of *Owning Mahowny* (2003), in which he plays a real-life gambling addict and bank employee who embezzled over $10 million to support his habit. Director Richard Kwietniowski avoids the pitfalls of the gambling film — all flash and little substance — by focusing on Hoffman's performance, creating a claustrophobic atmosphere from which the actor gradually sucks in every last pocket of air.

Following his Oscar win, Hoffman had enough power to green light any project that interested him. He had read a script that director Sidney Lumet had been developing and brought Ethan Hawke on board to star with him in *Before the Devil Knows You're Dead*

(2007). A scathing indictment of the selfish culture that had developed under the administration of George Bush, Lumet's film has no heroes, and Hoffman's Andy Hanson lacks both a spine and a moral compass. A year later, he played the troubled playwright Caden Cotard in Charlie Kaufman's ambitious *Synechdoche, New York* (2008). It is to his credit that Hoffman keeps the mechanics of the film in check and along with Samantha Morton ensures that its formal brilliance never subsumes its emotional core. The more conventional *A Late Quartet* (2012) is far from perfect, but the scenes between Catherine Keener, Mark Ivanir, Christopher Walken and Hoffman, as the four members of a string quartet, possess a quiet energy.

Shortly before his death, Hoffman appeared in *God's Pocket* (2014), an effective low-key drama set in a blue-collar neighborhood of Philadelphia. He followed it with the lead role in Anton Corbijn's adaptation of John le Carré's *A Most Wanted Man* (2014). An espionage thriller in which Hoffman's agent is left wondering who the real enemy is, it ends with his character broken, despairing at the world and its injustice. It is a breathtaking performance and a sad reminder of what a bright talent we have lost. **IHS**

Supporting | Supporting | Supporting

Charlie Wilson's War
Mike Nichols

Before the Devil Knows You're Dead
Sidney Lumet

Synechdoche, New York
Charlie Kaufman

Supporting

Actor | Supporting | Supporting

The Hunger Games: Catching Fire
Francis Lawrence

The Master
Paul Thomas Anderson

A Late Quartet
Yaron Zilberman

The Ides of March
George Clooney

A Most Wanted Man
Anton Corbijn

2010

2015

william holden 1918–81

| Golden Boy | Sunset Boulevard | Stalag 17 | Sabrina | Bridge on the River Kwai | The Wild Bunch | The Towering Inferno | Network |

H

William Holden was one of Hollywood's finest character actors who successfully made the transition to star. His first major role was in Rouben Mamoulian's *Golden Boy* (1939), starring alongside Barbara Stanwyck as Joe Bonaparte, a violinist who dreams of becoming a boxer. His inexperience almost got him fired from the film, but Stanwyck rallied to keep him on board, privately tutoring the actor to forge an impressive partnership. Praise for his performance led to a run of roles as a "boy-next-door" leading man, including a successful turn in *Our Town* (1940) and opposite Robert Mitchum in *Rachel and the Stranger* (1948). However, Holden's major breakthrough was yet to come.

When Montgomery Clift and Fred MacMurray rejected the role of washed-up screenwriter Joe Gillis in Billy Wilder's *Sunset Boulevard* (1950), Holden was hired, turning in a career-best performance as the cynical gigolo to Gloria Swanson's faded movie star.

The 1950s saw Holden's popularity grow and led to his producing his strongest work, including an Oscar-winning performance as a cynical and unpopular POW in Billy Wilder's World War II drama *Stalag 17* (1953).

In the following years he moved seamlessly across genres, starring in westerns like John Ford's *The Horse Soldiers* (1959), romantic comedies like *Sabrina* (1954) and epic war films such as *The Bridge on the River Kwai* (1957). His high fee and percentage of that film's profit allowed Holden to lessen his workload. Openly admitting that he had lost his enthusiasm for acting, he spent most of the 1960s at his nature reserve in Africa.

Not that the quality of his work had diminished. He was on stunning form as the leader of a group of bank robbers in Sam Peckinpah's acclaimed *The Wild Bunch* (1969). There was pain and tenderness in his portrayal of an older man's infatuation with a young woman in Clint Eastwood's *Breezy* (1973). He brought class to the role of a property magnate in *The Towering Inferno* (1974) and in Sidney Lumet's media satire *Network* (1976) he is acerbic and beaten as a television executive aware that his time in the spotlight is over. A few more roles remained, including a starring role in Billy Wilder's little-seen *Fedora* (1978). He died in 1981, leaving behind a body of work shot through with sardonic wit, natural charm and that gravelly, yet commanding voice. **PG**

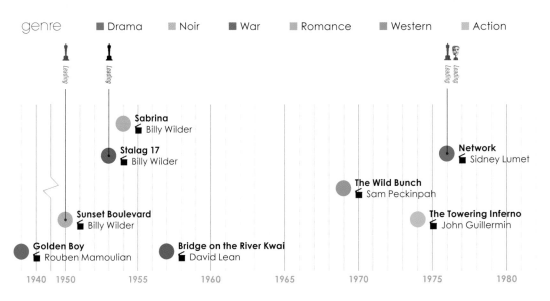

genre ■ Drama ■ Noir ■ War ■ Romance ■ Western ■ Action

Leading *Leading*

Leading *Leading*

Sabrina
🎬 Billy Wilder

Stalag 17
🎬 Billy Wilder

Network
🎬 Sidney Lumet

The Wild Bunch
🎬 Sam Peckinpah

Sunset Boulevard
🎬 Billy Wilder

The Towering Inferno
🎬 John Guillermin

Golden Boy
🎬 Rouben Mamoulian

Bridge on the River Kwai
🎬 David Lean

1940 1950   1955   1960   1965   1970   1975   1980

bob hope 1903–2003

| The Big Broadcast of 1938 | The Cat and the Canary | Road to Singapore | Nothing But the Truth | Road to Morocco | The Paleface | The Great Lover | The Facts of Life |

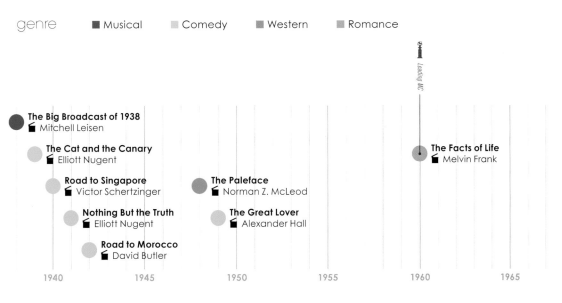

Born in England, Leslie Towne Hope began his career in entertainment at the age of 12. By that time, his family had emigrated to the United States and he was a regular fixture at local talent contests. By the age of 26 he was better known as Bob Hope and had honed his comedic skills through musical theater, soon to transfer them to radio and television. Like many comedy stars of the era, Hope worked in short films, producing eight between 1934 and 1936. These were precursors to *The Big Broadcast of 1938* (1938), where he joined veteran comedian W.C. Fields in what can be seen as a passing of the Hollywood comedy torch.

The archetypal Hope role is all but fully formed in even his earliest films. *The Cat and the Canary* (1939) features him as the hero, but he is neither the most handsome male lead, the most intelligent, nor the bravest. His character, Wally Campbell, is quick with a one-liner but in all other areas of life is hopelessly ill-equipped. By the time of *The Paleface* (1948), the line between Hope and his on-screen persona was impossible to discern. Hiding behind Jane Russell's no-nonsense Calamity Jane, intimidated by her and crazy for her, he is somehow both the hero and the fall guy. It is this nervous man that Hope would perfect over the rest of his career.

His best-known films are the seven *Road to* movies released between 1940 and 1962. Costarring Bing Crosby and Dorothy Lamour, the films are featherlight comedy-musicals, functioning as little more than a platform for the three stars to improvise their way through culture clashes and low-stakes adventures.

While many movie comedians attempt dramatic reinvention, Hope was content to play for laughs. An exception is *The Facts of Life* (1960), with Lucille Ball.

Hope's humor shared certain traits with Jewish or British humor, projecting the self-deprecating male decades before Woody Allen laid bare his anxieties for all to see. He was able to showcase this open, inviting style of humor as the host of the annual Academy Awards ceremony for a record 14 times.

His style of comedy may have evolved little over his career and while it never touched on political or social trends, he was embraced all over the world in a way that very few other actors ever had or have been. **SW**

H

genre ■ Musical ■ Comedy ■ Western ■ Romance

Leading MC

The Big Broadcast of 1938
Mitchell Leisen

The Cat and the Canary
Elliott Nugent

Road to Singapore
Victor Schertzinger

Nothing But the Truth
Elliott Nugent

Road to Morocco
David Butler

The Paleface
Norman Z. McLeod

The Great Lover
Alexander Hall

The Facts of Life
Melvin Frank

1940   1945   1950   1955   1960   1965

anthony hopkins 1937

| Young Winston | A Bridge Too Far | Magic | The Elephant Man | The Bounty | 84 Charing Cross Road | The Silence of the Lambs | Howards End |

Anthony Hopkins is among Britain's most admired screen actors. Although he made regular film appearances as a young man, it was in middle age that he delivered his career-defining performance as Hannibal Lecter in *The Silence of the Lambs* (1991). As an actor, he is renowned for his impeccable technique, exquisitely judged restraint and piercing emotional power.

He was born in 1937, to working-class parents in Port Talbot, Wales, which was also the home town of Richard Burton. As a teenager, Hopkins briefly met him. But despite sharing a classically trained background, the two performers were quite different: more a character actor than a star, Hopkins immerses himself in his roles, and has been more discriminating about his choice of material than the notoriously uneven Burton. If any actor stands as his mentor, it is Laurence Olivier, who employed the young actor at the National Theatre in the mid-1960s.

At the start of his career, Hopkins was known primarily as a stage actor, but he admitted to disliking the repetitive nature of theater. Among his early film roles was his countryman Lloyd George in Richard Attenborough's glossy account of Churchill's early years *Young Winston* (1972), a part Hopkins would

reprise a year later for BBC television. The film marked a long association with Attenborough, a director celebrated for his sensitive approach to actors.

Hopkins brought unaffected authority to his role as a besieged British officer in Attenborough's World War II epic *A Bridge Too Far* (1977), his appearance alongside more high-profile cast members like Sean Connery a recognition of his potential. The next year he took the lead in Attenborough's psychological horror *Magic* (1978). Playing a ventriloquist who seems possessed by his dummy, Hopkins gave a performance of quiet virtuosity and lasting unease.

Throughout the 1980s, Hopkins gave distinguished performances, mostly in prestige productions. He was a subtle and intelligent Captain Bligh in the famous tale of mutiny at sea *The Bounty* (1984), and poignant as the bookseller who has a transatlantic epistolary friendship with a New Yorker in *84 Charing Cross Road* (1987). But of his films from this period, his standout role is in David Lynch's *The Elephant Man* (1980), as the humane doctor who takes charge of John Hurt's profoundly disfigured Joseph Merrick.

In the late 1980s, after a long spell in Los Angeles, Hopkins returned to London with a sense, he later

genre   ■ Drama   ■ War   ■ Horror   ■ Adventure   ■ Thriller   ■ Romance

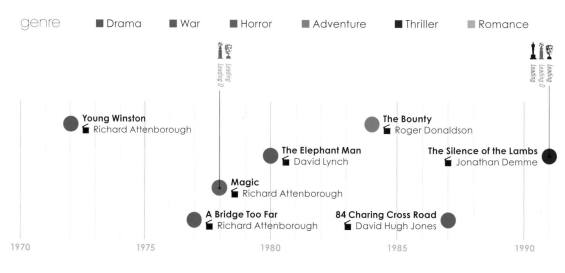

Young Winston
Richard Attenborough

The Bounty
Roger Donaldson

The Elephant Man
David Lynch

The Silence of the Lambs
Jonathan Demme

Magic
Richard Attenborough

A Bridge Too Far
Richard Attenborough

84 Charing Cross Road
David Hugh Jones

1970   1975   1980   1985   1990

$196M (U.S.)
A Bridge Too Far
(1977)

$74M (U.S.)
The Elephant Man
(1980)

$474M
*The Silence
of the Lambs*
(1991)

$43M (U.S.)
Howards End
(1992)

$38M (U.S.)
*The Remains
of the Day*
(1993)

$42M (U.S.)
Shadowlands
(1993)

$464M
Hannibal
(2001)

$86M
Bad Company
(2002)

The Remains
of the Day

Shadowlands

Nixon

Hannibal

Bad
Company

The Human
Stain

You Will
Meet a
Tall Dark
Stranger

Hitchcock

admitted, that his career in Hollywood was over. Things changed spectacularly when he took the role of Lecter for Jonathan Demme's landmark thriller. He was a grotesque villain, but Hopkins played him with a precise, almost minimalist touch: with his character confined for most of the picture to a high-security cell, the actor made small gestures count. He was rewarded with an Oscar for his performance. (Reprising the role for *Hannibal* [2001] and *Red Dragon* [2002] Hopkins was less accomplished, introducing an unwelcome note of camp to the performance.)

Discussing acting, Hopkins adopts a matter-of-fact, pointedly demystifying tone; but his attitude is belied by the exacting level of preparation he brings to every role. Committing an entire script to memory, he prefers only a few takes to capture the moment, while it is still fresh. This approach has made him one of the finest purveyors of screen naturalism.

During the 1990s, Hopkins played a number of substantial roles that revealed his expressive range. He was outstanding in Merchant-Ivory's 1992 adaptation of E.M. Forster's *Howards End* (as a stiff but ruthless Edwardian businessman) and in their 1993 adaptation of Kazuo Ishiguro's novel *The Remains of the Day* (as a

buttoned-down butler). Reuniting with Attenborough, he was devastatingly moving as the novelist C.S. Lewis, who falls in love with an American poet in *Shadowlands* (1993). All three roles were studies in a very British form of emotional restraint, a sensibility that Hopkins' finely calibrated style captures brilliantly.

But Hopkins has also impressed playing wildly expressive, emotionally unrestrained characters. For Oliver Stone's *Nixon* (1995), his portrayal of the president was marked by a dark intensity and fervid paranoia: a note-perfect impersonation of a public figure that Hopkins made his own, it is among his finest performances. If Hopkins' more recent roles have not challenged him so much — his portrayal of *Hitchcock* in the eponymous 2012 drama being a rare exception — he tends to remain solid, no matter the quality of the film. He is assured as a CIA agent in the lackluster thriller *Bad Company* (2002), is a game murderer in *Fracture* (2007) and offers fierce authority as the Norse god Odin in *Thor* (2011). However, given the right part — the challenging role of an academic with a secret in *The Human Stain* (2003) or his delicate study of a late-mid-life crisis in *You Will Meet a Tall Dark Stranger* (2010) — he can still dazzle. **EL**

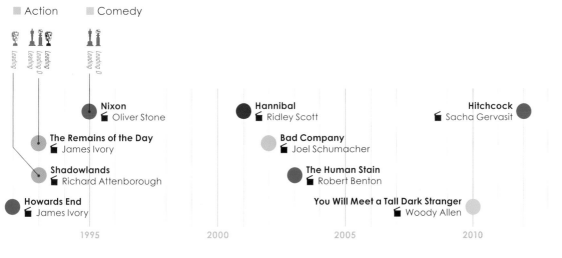

dennis hopper 1936–2010

| Rebel Without a Cause | The Sons of Katie Elder | Cool Hand Luke | Easy Rider | True Grit | The Last Movie | Mad Dog Morgan | The American Friend |

Dennis Hopper was a studio star who embraced the 1960s counterculture; a celebrated photographer, artist and hell-raiser; and an unpredictable presence in indie films who was just as comfortable playing a villain in a Hollywood blockbuster. His life was one of the more outrageous stories in Peter Biskind's account of New Hollywood, *Easy Riders, Raging Bulls* (1998). He seemed incapable of playing by the rules, yet he managed to find a place for himself both in and outside the Hollywood system.

He was born in Dodge City, Kansas, in 1936. After a few television roles, his first major film appearance was in Nicholas Ray's *Rebel Without a Cause* (1955), with James Dean. The two actors became friends and appeared together again in George Stevens' *Giant* (1956). He clashed with director Henry Hathaway on the set of *From Hell to Texas* (1958) and was informed he would never work again. A decade of minor film and television roles followed. He took up photography, covering the Civil Rights movement, as well as documenting life in Hollywood.

Hopper credits John Wayne with salvaging his career. He secured him a role on *The Sons of Katie Elder* (1965), as the son of the film's villain. He would star opposite Wayne again in *True Grit* (1969), but by that time he was well on the way to becoming an important member of the New Hollywood.

Hopper starred alongside Peter Fonda in *The Trip* (1967), then played prison inmates in *Cool Hand Luke* (1967) and *Hang 'Em High* (1968), before teaming up with Fonda to make a key film of the era, *Easy Rider* (1969). Written by and starring both, and directed by Hopper, it tells the story of two bikers who set out from Los Angeles, heading for New Orleans, in search of the notion of "America." What they find is a world of bigotry, prejudice and violence, which closes in on them in the film's bleak final moments. It is hard to tell whether the leads are acting or just stoned, but the film's tone of optimism quashed remains powerful.

Hopper's next film as director is one of the great stories of cinematic indulgence. *The Last Movie* (1971) is an account of a film director losing control on location, but is a sterling example of life reflecting art. It took over a year to edit and when it was finally released, the film was met with derision. However, it has improved with time, as has Hopper's central performance.

The actor ventured to Australia to appear in *Mad Dog Morgan* (1976), a typically bizarre Ozploitation

genre ■ Drama ■ Western ■ Crime ■ Thriller ■ War ■ Horror

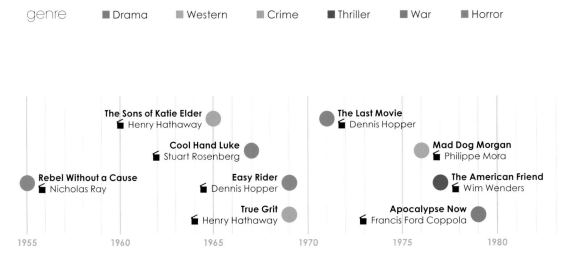

The Sons of Katie Elder
Henry Hathaway

The Last Movie
Dennis Hopper

Cool Hand Luke
Stuart Rosenberg

Mad Dog Morgan
Philippe Mora

Rebel Without a Cause
Nicholas Ray

Easy Rider
Dennis Hopper

The American Friend
Wim Wenders

True Grit
Henry Hathaway

Apocalypse Now
Francis Ford Coppola

1955   1960   1965   1970   1975   1980

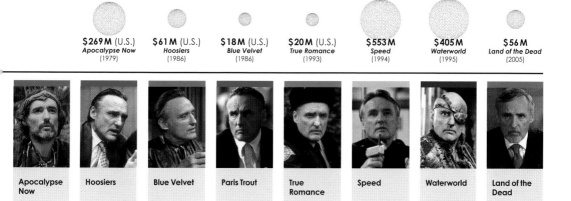

$269 M (U.S.)	$61 M (U.S.)	$18 M (U.S.)	$20 M (U.S.)	$553 M	$405 M	$56 M
Apocalypse Now (1979)	Hoosiers (1986)	Blue Velvet (1986)	True Romance (1993)	Speed (1994)	Waterworld (1995)	Land of the Dead (2005)

Apocalypse Now | Hoosiers | Blue Velvet | Paris Trout | True Romance | Speed | Waterworld | Land of the Dead

movie about an infamous antipodean outlaw. He returned to America for Henry Jaglom's *Tracks* (1977), playing a U.S. soldier returning from Vietnam with his friend's body, before traveling to Germany to appear in *The American Friend* (1977), Wim Wenders' adaptation of Patricia Highsmith's 1974 novel *Ripley's Game*. Hopper is excellent as the eponymous killer. From there, he traveled to the Philippines to play a drug-addled photojournalist in Francis Ford Coppola's *Apocalypse Now* (1979). He is convincing in the role, but his behavior on set led to fellow star Marlon Brando demanding that Hopper steer well clear of him.

He stepped in for another director on *Out of the Blue* (1980) and also played the ex-con father of a dysfunctional family. It is a strong performance, which hinted at the power Hopper would display in roles over the next decade. There were minor appearances in *Rumble Fish* (1983) and *The Osterman Weekend* (1983), as well as the lead in Tobe Hooper's hilarious 1986 horror comedy *The Texas Chainsaw Massacre 2*. In the same year, Hopper's profile increased significantly. He received an Academy Award nomination for his performance as a town drunk in the sports movie *Hoosiers* and is chilling as a loner driven insane by

guilt in *River's Edge*. However, it is his performance as Frank, an unhinged gang leader and drug dealer, in David Lynch's *Blue Velvet*, that set a new standard for Hopper. It is an incendiary performance, one of the best of the decade. He was no less compelling — and repulsive — as the eponymous racist and wife beater in Stephen Gyllenhaal's *Paris Trout* (1991).

If *Blue Velvet* gave Hopper cultural kudos, his role as Christian Slater's cop father, who delivers a withering speech to Christopher Walken's consigliore in *True Romance* (1993) strengthened his appeal, while his villain in *Speed* (1994) made him a star. He added more fun to *Waterworld* (1995) than it actually deserved, playing a maniacal, chain-smoking baddie searching the waterlogged planet for land. He was enjoyable in the low-rent sci-fi adventure *Space Truckers* (1996) and reveled in playing a criminal mastermind in the television series *24* (2002).

Hopper continued to work prodigiously up to his death in 2010. He is gleefully corrupt as the unofficial mayor of a city besieged by zombies in George A. Romero's post-Katrina satire *Land of the Dead* (2005) and is uncharacteristically restrained as the poet friend of Ben Kingsley's professor in *Elegy* (2008). **IHS**

■ Action　　■ Sci-Fi

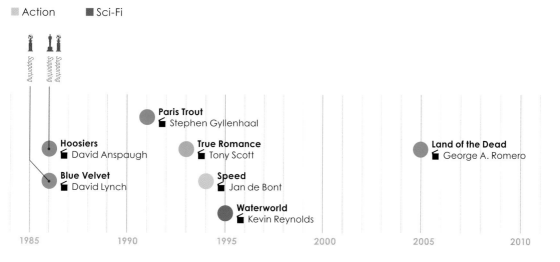

dennis hopper 255

Rebel Without a Cause
(1955)

Easy Rider
(1969)

The Last Movie
(1971)

Apocalypse Now
(1979)

Blue Velvet
(1986)

Hoosiers
(1986)

True Romance
(1993)

Speed
(1994)

Hopper in his big screen debut as Goon, one of the teen delinquents in *Rebel Without a Cause*.

Hopper's subdued turn as Billy in *Easy Rider* belied his behavior offscreen as director, which was notoriously chaotic with drunken, drug-crazed screaming fits.

Playing a photojournalist in *Apocalypse Now* was an apt role for Hopper, who was an accomplished and respected photographer in real life.

Hopper and Peter Fonda in *Easy Rider*. The pair later became embroiled in a longstanding feud over the credit and profits.

Filmed on location in Peru, *The Last Movie* has been dismissed by many critics as a drug-fueled disaster.

Hopper later said of the *Apocalypse Now* shoot, "Ask anybody who was out there, we all felt like we fought the war."

Upon seeing the script for **Blue Velvet** (which had already begun filming), Hopper phoned director David Lynch to say "I have to play Frank Booth, because I *am* Frank Booth."

osely based on a true story, **Hoosiers** starred Hopper and Gene Hackman as high school basketball aches who lead their team to the state championships.

Although Hopper's role in **True Romance** is fairly small, this scene (with Christopher Walken) is widely viewed as the movie's best.

Speed saw Hopper go up against Keanu Reeves' cop as a vengeful former bomb squad technician who holds a bus full of people ransom. The actor said of the film, "This is what an action movie really should have been — and was."

trevor howard 1913–88

Brief
Encounter

The Third
Man

Outcast of
the Islands

The Key

Sons and
Lovers

Mutiny on
the Bounty

Battle of
Britain

Ryan's
Daughter

Trevor Howard's feature debut was in an uncredited role as a ship's officer in *The Way Ahead* (1944) — a fitting beginning for a man who would be seen as the very definition of the stiff upper-lipped, rarely ruffled British military officer. Born in Margate, Kent, he learned his craft at the Royal Academy for Dramatic Arts before honing his skills on stage throughout the 1930s. He was called up to the Royal Signals in 1940 and although the veracity of his military record remains contentious, it proved a fruitful vein to mine for many years to come.

It was with his third film role that Howard's stardom was assured, lending his clipped tones to the character of Dr. Alec Harvey, opposite Celia Johnson, in David Lean's restrained train station romance *Brief Encounter* (1945). The military still played a significant role on the screen postwar, and Howard soon found himself playing Lt. David Baynes in *I See a Dark Stranger* (1946) and an ex-RAF man in *I Became a Criminal* (1947), a gritty British noir. Howard would return to a variation of the genre two years later in Carol Reed's exquisite *The Third Man* (1949), playing military policeman Major Calloway.

Howard reunited with Reed for the Joseph Conrad adaptation *Outcast of the Islands* (1951), which features an impressive performance by the actor as reprobate Peter Willems. Left in a village in Borneo, his plans to double-cross his friend are engulfed by a madness that Howard masterfully renders. Work flowed throughout the 1950s, including BAFTA nominations for *The Heart of the Matter* (1953) and *Manuela* (1957). He finally won the award for his role as a World War II tugboat captain in Reed's *The Key* (1958).

Howard's sole Oscar nomination followed two years later, for his leading role in Jack Cardiff's *Sons and Lovers* (1960). That film launched a decade that saw Howard back on the open sea as Captain Bligh to Marlon Brando's Fletcher Christian in *Mutiny on the Bounty* (1962), opposite Frank Sinatra in *Von Ryan's Express* (1965), playing a memorable Lord Cardigan in *The Charge of the Light Brigade* (1968) — for which he was also BAFTA nominated — and Air Vice Marshal Keith Park in Guy Hamilton's *Battle of Britain* (1969). His arguably career best turn came as Father Collins in David Lean's much-maligned *Ryan's Daughter* (1970).

Before his death at the age of 74 in 1988, he ventured to the planet Krypton for *Superman* (1978), played a mad Russian in *Light Years Away* (1981), and an aged Native American in *Windwalker* (1980), was hilarious as the eccentric Lord Henry Ames in *The Missionary* (1982) and took a small role as a judge in Richard Attenborough's *Gandhi* (1982). **BN**

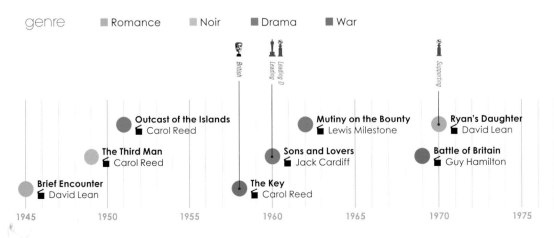

genre   ■ Romance   ■ Noir   ■ Drama   ■ War

Outcast of the Islands
Carol Reed

The Third Man
Carol Reed

Brief Encounter
David Lean

Mutiny on the Bounty
Lewis Milestone

Sons and Lovers
Jack Cardiff

The Key
Carol Reed

Ryan's Daughter
David Lean

Battle of Britain
Guy Hamilton

1945   1950   1955   1960   1965   1970   1975

rock hudson 1925–85

| Magnificent Obsession | All That Heaven Allows | Giant | Written on the Wind | Pillow Talk | Man's Favorite Sport? | Seconds | Ice Station Zebra |

With his good looks and instinctive screen presence, aspiring actor Roy Harold Scherer Jr. seemed to have it all. Apart from the name, that is. So in the late 1940s, under the advice of a Hollywood talent scout, the rising star became Rock Hudson and a legend was born.

The actor's first few years in the business proved busy if not terribly fruitful. However, everything changed when melodrama maestro Douglas Sirk cast the actor in his lavish weepy *Magnificent Obsession* (1954). It was Hudson's breakthrough performance, balancing his physical beauty with a sensitivity lacking in many leading men. Over the next few years, Sirk continued to cast Hudson, in such films as *All That Heaven Allows* (1955) and the operatic *Written on the Wind* (1956), which propelled him to superstardom. He also flexed his dramatic muscles in George Stevens' acclaimed epic *Giant* (1956), playing opposite Elizabeth Taylor and James Dean in a role that saw him nominated for an Academy Award.

Toward the end of the 1950s, he reunited with Sirk for *The Tarnished Angels* (1957), before starring in the adaptation of Ernest Hemingway's *A Farewell To Arms* (1957). While the latter proved something of a misstep, his pairing with Doris Day in the romantic comedy *Pillow Talk* (1959) proved a hit and paved the way for the direction his career would take in the early 1960s.

Hudson cashed in on his newfound success in gentle romantic fare with appearances in the fluffy but hugely enjoyable comedies *Lover Come Back* (1961), *Come September* (1961), *Send Me No Flowers* (1964) and *Man's Favorite Sport?* (1964). If the star seemed to be merely treading water with his screen choices, his performance in John Frankenheimer's mind-bending masterpiece *Seconds* (1966) would make critics sit up and take notice once more, giving Hudson his most satisfying role outside of a Douglas Sirk film.

Roles in *Ice Station Zebra* (1968), *Showdown* (1973) and *Avalanche* (1978) would see Hudson sporadically hit the big screen, but from the late 1960s onward his star had begun to wane. In the early 1980s, Hudson was once again thrust into the public eye. In 1984, the actor was diagnosed with HIV and the following year he publicly announced his condition, also coming out as homosexual. In addition to his legacy as one of Hollywood's great leading men, Hudson's decision to be so open about his illness proved a significant turning point in the public awareness of AIDS and HIV. He died from AIDS-related complications in 1985, aged 59. **MB**

genre ■ Romance ■ Drama ■ Comedy ■ Sci-Fi ■ Thriller

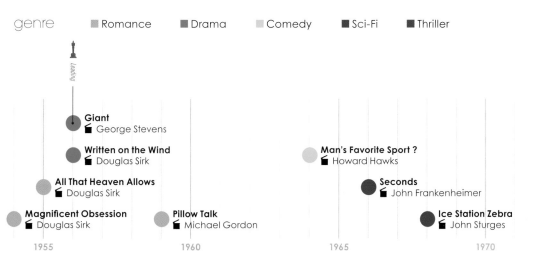

Leading

Giant
George Stevens

Written on the Wind
Douglas Sirk

Man's Favorite Sport ?
Howard Hawks

All That Heaven Allows
Douglas Sirk

Seconds
John Frankenheimer

Magnificent Obsession
Douglas Sirk

Pillow Talk
Michael Gordon

Ice Station Zebra
John Sturges

1955   1960   1965   1970

isabelle huppert 1953

| Les Valseuses | The Lacemaker | Violette Noziere | Heaven's Gate | Loulou | Passion | Madame Bovary | Amateur |

Isabelle Huppert is undoubtedly one of the most accomplished, fearless and prolific actresses in contemporary French cinema. An incredibly versatile performer unafraid to tackle provocative roles, Huppert has formed a close association with auteur directors including Claude Chabrol and Michael Haneke.

A graduate of the Paris Conservatoire d'Art Dramatique, she first came to attention in Bertrand Blier's sexually explicit Les Valseuses (1974), a film that made a star of Gérard Depardieu as one of two thugs who lie, cheat, steal and screw their way across France. In 1978, she won a BAFTA for Best Newcomer for her role in The Lacemaker (1977), a Normandy-set tale of sexual awakening. Violette Noziere (1978), which marked Huppert's first collaboration with Chabrol, is a powerful thriller about a woman who eschews her bourgeois upbringing in favor of a life of crime.

Her first experience of Hollywood proved chastening. Michael Cimino's Heaven's Gate (1980), a dramatization of the 1890 Johnson County War in Wyoming, was a fraught production and a financial disaster. However, the film, whose analysis of class is at the heart of much of the actress' work, is now rightly viewed as an ambitious masterpiece. She returned to France for Bertrand Tavernier's Coup de Torchon (1981) and Maurice Pialat's Loulou (1980). Reuniting Huppert and Depardieu, Pialat's drama is an erotic account of an affair between two young Parisian's from disparate backgrounds. Huppert is utterly convincing as a bored, middle-class executive who decides to experience the seedier side of Paris.

After playing a factory worker who tries to unionize her fellow employees in Jean-Luc Godard's Passion (1982), Huppert attracted international acclaim as the eponymous heroine in Chabrol's Gustave Flaubert adaptation, Madame Bovary (1991). Huppert's Emma Bovary is a revelation — radiating frustration, desire and desperation. Putting the experience of Heaven's Gate behind her, Huppert reached out to U.S indie auteur Hal Hartley, who responded by writing the part of a pornography-writing nymphomaniac nun — who does not actually have sex — especially for her. The resulting Amateur (1994) proved to be the director's most successful work to date. Huppert would only periodically work again in the United States, most notably in David O. Russell's I Heart Huckabees (2004).

A powerful portrait of a failing marriage, La Séparation (1995) sees the actress reach Kristin Scott-

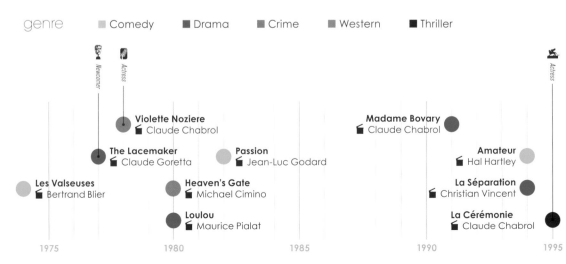

genre   ■ Comedy   ■ Drama   ■ Crime   ■ Western   ■ Thriller

Violette Noziere
Claude Chabrol

The Lacemaker
Claude Goretta

Passion
Jean-Luc Godard

Madame Bovary
Claude Chabrol

Amateur
Hal Hartley

Les Valseuses
Bertrand Blier

Heaven's Gate
Michael Cimino

La Séparation
Christian Vincent

Loulou
Maurice Pialat

La Cérémonie
Claude Chabrol

1975   1980   1985   1990   1995

| La Séparation | La Cérémonie | The Piano Teacher | Time of the Wolf | Gabrielle | The Sea Wall | White Material | Amour |

Thomas levels of chilliness. Chabrol's Hitchcockian *La Cérémonie* (1995) ranks among Huppert's finest achievements. Radiating malice, she is excellent as the exploitative Jeanne, a provincial misfit who takes a newly hired maid under her wing, thus precipitating a wave of deception, murder and class hatred.

The Piano Teacher (2001), the first of three films with Haneke, also ranks as one of Huppert's best. Giving a performance of astounding emotional intensity, she plays Erika Kohut, a repressed woman who teaches piano at the Vienna Conservatory and lives with her tyrannical mother, with whom she has a volatile love-hate relationship. But when one of Erika's students attempts to seduce her, the barriers that she has carefully erected around her claustrophobic world are shattered, unleashing an uncontrollable desire. The Best Actress prize at Cannes was just reward.

After a little light relief in François Ozon's *8 Women* (2002), Huppert was back with Haneke again for the disturbing and divisive *Time of the Wolf* (2003). Set in an unnamed European country at an undisclosed time, this bleak apocalyptic drama tells the story of a family who flee the city, hoping to find refuge and security in their country home, only to discover a group of unwelcoming strangers occupying it. In the ensuing confrontation their lives are changed forever.

Patrice Chéreau's somber Joseph Conrad adaptation, *Gabrielle* (2005), offered only marginal relief. Pascal Gregory and Huppert are impeccable as a well-heeled Parisian couple whose chaste marriage is a synthetic veneer of respectability.

The Rithy Panh-directed *The Sea Wall* (2008) is another notable addition to her filmography. Based on the novel by Marguerite Duras and set in the rich landscape of French colonial Indochina, the film helped earn Huppert the European Film Academy's 2009 Achievement in World Cinema award. Her portrayal of a mother fighting to protect her family and her crops in a hostile foreign environment was a theme revisited in Clare Denis' superlative *White Material* (2009), a highly charged examination of the legacy of colonialism.

A third collaboration with Haneke on *Amour* (2012) brought the director his second Palme d'Or. Huppert takes a smaller part as the daughter of a devoted elderly couple who are thrown into crisis by the onset of age and illness. It is an unflinching story of sacrifice, devotion and the limits that love can drive us to. **JW**

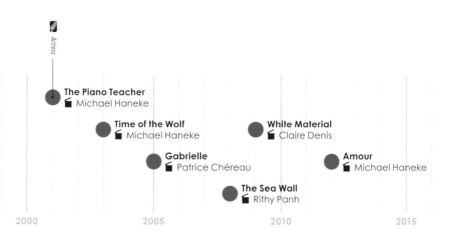

Actress

The Piano Teacher
Michael Haneke

Time of the Wolf
Michael Haneke

White Material
Claire Denis

Gabrielle
Patrice Chéreau

Amour
Michael Haneke

The Sea Wall
Rithy Panh

2000   2005   2010   2015

william hurt 1950

Altered States

Body Heat

Gorky Park

Kiss of the Spider Woman

Children of a Lesser God

Broadcast News

A History of Violence

Into the Wild

Blessed with patrician good looks that established him as a leading man from his very first on-screen appearance, William Hurt all but started at the top. And with an Oscar six years after his debut, he may have felt that he had little left to prove — hence his later reinvention as a character actor.

Born in Washington, D.C. in 1950, Hurt graduated in drama from Juilliard and made a name for himself in the theater before making his screen debut as the lead Ken Russell's *Altered States* (1980). He was perfectly cast as the scientist obsessed with investigating heightened perception through sensory deprivation. The following year, he had a knockout turn opposite Kathleen Turner in the steamy noir update *Body Heat* (1981), whose writer–director Lawrence Kasdan then cast him as a troubled Vietnam veteran in *The Big Chill* (1983). *Gorky Park* (1983) saw him adopting an incongruous English accent for the role of Russian detective Arkady Renko.

Kiss of the Spider Woman (1985) was both a career peak, winning him multiple awards (including an Oscar), and a transitional film, bringing a new boldness to his choice of roles. He played a gay drag queen who shares a South American jail cell with Raul

Julia's political activist. He was also Oscar-nominated for *Children of a Lesser God* (1986), as a teacher who falls in love with a deaf student, and for *Broadcast News* (1987), as an inexperienced anchorman who falls for Holly Hunter's ultra-professional producer. His excessively cautious travel writer in Kasdan's *The Accidental Tourist* (1988) was also much acclaimed.

Hurt has kept busy ever since, acting for Woody Allen in *Alice* (1990) and Wim Wenders in *Until the End of the World* (1991), and headlining more mainstream movies such as *The Doctor* (1991), *Second Best* (1994), *Jane Eyre* (1996) and *Lost in Space* (1998). More recently, he has become increasingly drawn to supporting parts, and indeed once described himself as "a character actor in a leading man's body." He was a Communist policeman in *Sunshine* (1999) and the scientist who oversaw the creation of the robot boy at the heart of *A.I. Artificial Intelligence* (2001), and gave a brief but riveting performance as the crime boss in *A History of Violence* (2005), securing a Best Supporting Actor Oscar nomination. He was also praised for his portrayal of a man concerned about his son's proposal to live off the Alaskan wilderness in *Into the Wild* (2007). **MBr**

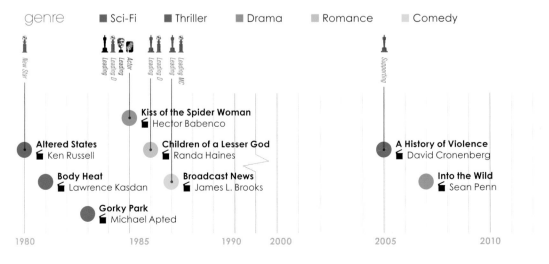

genre ■ Sci-Fi ■ Thriller ■ Drama ■ Romance □ Comedy

New Star

Actor / Leading / Leading D / Leading

Leading / Leading D / Leading MC

Supporting

Kiss of the Spider Woman
Hector Babenco

Altered States
Ken Russell

Children of a Lesser God
Randa Haines

A History of Violence
David Cronenberg

Body Heat
Lawrence Kasdan

Broadcast News
James L. Brooks

Into the Wild
Sean Penn

Gorky Park
Michael Apted

1980   1985   1990   2000   2005   2010

hugh jackman 1968

X-Men

Van Helsing

Happy Feet

The Prestige

The Fountain

Australia

Les Misérables

Prisoners

Hugh Jackman was born in Sydney in 1968. His film roles had been limited to the Australian movies *Erskineville Kings* (1999) and *Paperback Hero* (1999) when he was cast in *X-Men* (2000) as the emotionally damaged mutant Wolverine.

The success of Bryan Singer's film sparked a trend for superhero movies, and within a decade they were the dominant form of blockbuster filmmaking. *X-Men*, made on a relatively slim budget, is notable now for how thoughtful and small-scale it is in comparison to the increasingly labyrinthine efforts that followed.

After *X-Men*, Jackman starred in the romantic comedies *Animal Attraction* (2001) and *Kate & Leopold* (2001), as well as the misfiring *Swordfish* (2001). He played Wolverine again in the series' strongest entry *X2* (2003), and attempted to start another franchise as a monster hunter in *Van Helsing* (2004). While the film was a reasonable commercial success it was poorly received and no sequels were produced.

Including voiceover roles in *Flushed Away* and *Happy Feet*, Jackman appeared in half a dozen films in 2006. The boldest of these was Darren Aronofsky's *The Fountain*. Audiences were confounded by the equally ridiculous and profound film, but it has since amassed a cult following. The other significant film Jackman made that year was *The Prestige*, directed by Christopher Nolan. He gave an intense performance alongside Christian Bale as competing magicians driven to extremes measures.

Baz Luhrmann's World War II epic *Australia* (2008) struggled to feel more than an impression of other, better pictures. After years of serious work and the needless spin-off *X-Men Origins: Wolverine* (2009) it was an unexpected pleasure to see Jackman as a robot boxing trainer in the fun *Real Steel* (2011) and a used car salesman in the butter-carving comedy *Butter* (2011). These were followed by his emotive performance as Jean Valjean in *Les Misérables* (2012), for which he received an Oscar nomination.

Jackman persuaded Darren Aronofsky to make a one-off Wolverine film, but the director dropped out in pre-production. While James Mangold's eventual *The Wolverine* (2013) was an improvement on its predecessor, it still lacked bite. Jackman would play the character again in *X-Men: First Class* (2011) and its sequel *X-Men: Days of Future Past* (2014), but a better use of his time was Denis Villeneuve's compelling thriller *Prisoners* (2013). **JWa**

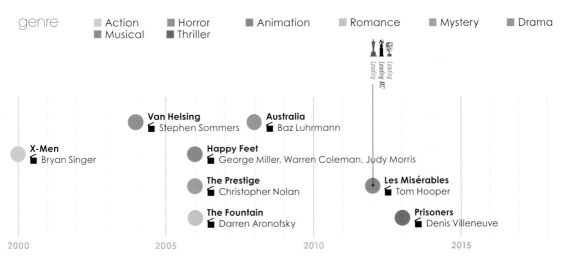

genre ■ Action ■ Horror ■ Animation ■ Romance ■ Mystery ■ Drama
       ■ Musical ■ Thriller

X-Men
🎬 Bryan Singer

Van Helsing
🎬 Stephen Sommers

Happy Feet
🎬 George Miller, Warren Coleman, Judy Morris

The Prestige
🎬 Christopher Nolan

The Fountain
🎬 Darren Aronofsky

Australia
🎬 Baz Luhrmann

Les Misérables
🎬 Tom Hooper

Prisoners
🎬 Denis Villeneuve

2000   2005   2010   2015

singers on the screen

Bing Crosby · Frank Sinatra · Elvis Presley · Mick Jagger · Jimmy Cliff · Bob Dylan · Adam Faith · David Bowie

Singers and film have been frequent bedfellows. From the early "race movies" starring Louis Jordan and Bessie Smith, the star crossover always seemed perfectly natural. Bing Crosby, Frank Sinatra, Cliff Richard, Adam Faith and Elvis Presley kicked open the doors for David Bowie, Mick Jagger and Björk. A stampede followed that continues today with figures including Madonna (great in *Desperately Seeking Susan*, 1985, dire in everything else) Ice Cube, Whitney Houston, Prince, Justin Timberlake and, most recently, Andre 3000 in Hendrix biopic *Jimi: All Is by My Side* (2013).

Quietly rebellious crooner Bing Crosby sustained a long and successful acting career, most notably alongside a perennially wisecracking Bob Hope in a series of globe-trotting comedic road movies. *Road to Singapore* (1940), with Hope and Crosby as two playboys turning their back on love started the cycle. Frank Sinatra had a surprisingly eclectic range but was excellent in Otto Preminger's *The Man with the Golden Arm* (1955) as Frankie Machine, an ex-addict trying to make it as a jazz musician. Elvis Presley was ruthlessly exploited and made a quickfire series of mediocre movies. *Jailhouse Rock* (1957) and *King Creole* (1958) probably come closest to replicating his huge appeal but *Charro!* (1969), a western of the

spaghetti variety is the movie in which Presley shows some actual acting ability, as an unjustly accused man seeking to right his reputation.

The music industry is given short shrift in Perry Henzell's *The Harder They Come* (1972). Jimmy Cliff, who also provides the theme song, is a wannabe reggae artist who must navigate unscrupulous producers and the drug-infected Kingston ghettos. The film was one of the first to emerge from Jamaica.

Nicolas Roeg has an uncanny gift when it comes to pop star casting and the act of persona transference. Co-directed with Donald Cammell, *Performance* (1970) features Jagger as a reclusive pop star hiding out in his Notting Hill mansion. When James Fox's gangster on the run comes calling, both men seek refuge in the other. Influenced by Borges, the film is a kaleidoscopic look at 1960s counterculture and is undoubtedly a masterpiece. Roeg repeated the trick in *The Man Who Fell To Earth* (1976), casting an otherworldly Bowie as an alien who lands on Earth to amass the financial fortune that may save his home planet. An examination of consumer culture and the perils of alcoholism, it makes perfect use of Bowie's sense of otherness. Likewise, Art Garfunkel is eerily effective as an American psychologist with unhealthy sexual appetites in Roeg's Vienna-set *Bad Timing*

type ■ Crooner ■ Rock 'n' roll ■ Rock ■ Reggae ■ Folk/Rock ■ Pop

Bing Crosby
🎬 *Road to Singapore*

Frank Sinatra
🎬 *The Man with the Golden Arm*

Elvis Presley
🎬 *Charro!*

Mick Jagger
🎬 *Performance*

Jimmy Cliff
🎬 *The Harder They Come*

Bob Dylan
🎬 *Pat Garrett and Billy the Kid*

Adam Faith
🎬 *Stardust*

1940   1945   1950   1955   1960   1965   1970   1975

Art Garfunkel | John Lydon | Madonna | Nick Cave | Tupac Shakur | P.J. Harvey | Björk | Will Oldham

(1980). The director's favorite of his own works, it is characteristically full of metaphor and allusion.

Peckinpah's *Pat Garrett and Billy the Kid* (1973) is undoubtedly the best performance from Bob Dylan. The film instead belongs to Kris Kristofferson, exuding swagger, charm and menace as the outlaw who becomes the quarry of former partner turned lawman, Pat Garrett (James Coburn). Kristofferson would go on to excel in *Heaven's Gate* (1980), *Trouble in Mind* (1985) and John Sayles' *Lone Star* (1996). With a filmography that includes *Down By Law* (1986) and *Short Cuts* (1993), picking a signature film for Tom Waits is a tall order, but Robert Frank and Rudy Wurlitzer's *Candy Mountain* (1987) wins out. An iconic road movie featuring the dead ends and wrong turns common in life, Waits plays it just to the right of eccentric as a golf loving self-made man.

Like Tom Waits, Nick Cave has acquired elder statesman status and as well as his songwriting has found equal success as a screenwriter for John Hillcoat with *The Proposition* (2005) and *The Assassination of Jesse James by the Coward Robert Ford* (2007, in which Cave also cameos). He stepped in front of the camera as Maynard, a psychotic inmate at a maximum security Australian jail in Hillcoat's bleak and uncompromising *Ghosts of the Civil Dead* (1988).

The global explosion of hip-hop in the 1990s saw a number of top rap stars courted by directors and producers with Ice Cube, Ice-T and Tupac Shakur all taking on acting duties. Shakur was the most successful and the most natural dramatic actor. Ernest R. Dickerson's 1992 drama *Juice* is a particular highpoint, with Shakur outstanding as a youth corrupted by a thirst for power and respect among his peers. *Gridlock'd* (1997) is another standout film in a career cruelly curtailed. P.J. Harvey and Björk only made one film apiece and more's the pity. Harvey played Mary Magdalene in Hal Hartley's millennial drama *The Book of Life* (1998). Björk won a Best Actress award at Cannes as a factory worker with dwindling eyesight in Lars von Trier's manipulative *Dancer in the Dark* (2000).

If there is a favorite among the vast array of singers' appearances on the screen — with little space here to list them all — it has to be Will Oldham (aka Bonnie Prince Billy) in Kelly Reichardt's *Old Joy* (2006). Oldham began his career as an actor, with a role in John Sayles' *Matewan* (1987), and in Reichardt's meditative look at two old friends who on a road trip to a restorative hot spring, realizing they now have little in common, Oldham exudes an impressive naturalism and melancholy. **JW**

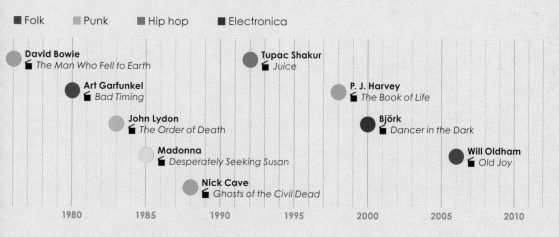

■ Folk ■ Punk ■ Hip hop ■ Electronica

David Bowie
The Man Who Fell to Earth

Art Garfunkel
Bad Timing

John Lydon
The Order of Death

Madonna
Desperately Seeking Susan

Nick Cave
Ghosts of the Civil Dead

Tupac Shakur
Juice

P. J. Harvey
The Book of Life

Björk
Dancer in the Dark

Will Oldham
Old Joy

1980   1985   1990   1995   2000   2005   2010

samuel l. jackson 1948

Coming to America

Do the Right Thing

Jungle Fever

Jurassic Park

Fresh

Pulp Fiction

Die Hard: With a Vengeance

A Time to Kill

J

Samuel L. Jackson's first film role was in the 1972 mixed-race relationship drama *Together for Days*. It took some time for his career to take off, but with appearances in over 100 movies, he is now one the most prolific and popular stars in Hollywood.

Born in Washington, D.C., in 1948, Jackson was a prominent Civil Rights activist and closely associated with the Black Panther movement in his youth. One of his earliest notable roles is as a robber holding up a fast food restaurant, who is overpowered by Eddie Murphy's African prince, in *Coming to America* (1988). A minor cameo, it introduced audiences to the edginess in his performances — a sense that he could explode with rage at any moment — that has since come to be his stock in trade. He followed it with his radio DJ, commenting on the day's unrest, in Spike Lee's incendiary *Do the Right Thing* (1989). Further small roles followed, but he was also grappling with drug addiction at the time. He credits his role as a junkie in Lee's *Jungle Fever* (1991) with turning his life around. The performance, raw and splenetic, was awarded a special prize by the jury at the Cannes Film Festival.

Jackson made an impression in the opening scenes of *Menace II Society* (1993), is a commanding presence in *Jurassic Park* (1993) and his chess expert, advising a young boy in *Fresh* (1994), gave him one of his best roles prior to his memorable breakthrough in *Pulp Fiction* (1994). The role of Jules Winnfield transformed Jackson's career. Delivering Quentin Tarantino's rich dialogue with aplomb, his Jules is a fascinating, funny and often terrifying creation. He is even better as the vicious Ordell Robbie in the director's *Jackie Brown* (1997) and Stephen, the conniving manservant, in *Django Unchained* (2012).

Jackson brought vitality to *Die Hard: With a Vengeance* (1995) and makes for an amiable pairing with Bruce Willis. He is also an excellent foil to Geena Davis' action heroine in *The Long Kiss Goodnight* (1996), employing an easygoing charm, interspersed with expletives, that has come to define one element of his screen persona.

In *A Time to Kill* (1996), Jackson plays the father of a young girl who is raped by a two men and is subsequently charged with murder when he kills them. An adaptation of John Grisham's novel and a huge box-office success, it widened Jackson's appeal, although the film is mediocre. By contrast, *One Eight Seven* (1997) offered a violent riposte to the glut of

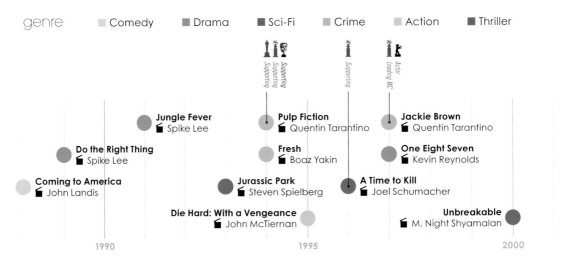

genre   ■ Comedy   ■ Drama   ■ Sci-Fi   ■ Crime   ■ Action   ■ Thriller

Supporting Supporting Supporting

Supporting

Actor Leading MC

Jungle Fever
🏺 Spike Lee

Pulp Fiction
🏺 Quentin Tarantino

Jackie Brown
🏺 Quentin Tarantino

Do the Right Thing
🏺 Spike Lee

Fresh
🏺 Boaz Yakin

One Eight Seven
🏺 Kevin Reynolds

Coming to America
🏺 John Landis

Jurassic Park
🏺 Steven Spielberg

A Time to Kill
🏺 Joel Schumacher

Die Hard: With a Vengeance
🏺 John McTiernan

Unbreakable
🏺 M. Night Shyamalan

1990   1995   2000

$570M	$1.7BN	$337M	$561M	$337M	$1BN	$433M	$715M
Coming to America (1988)	Jurassic Park (1993)	Pulp Fiction (1994)	Die Hard: With a Vengeance (1995)	Unbreakable (2000)	Star Wars: Episode III — Revenge of the Sith (2005)	Django Unchained (2012)	Captain America: The Winter Soldier (2014)

| Jackie Brown | One Eight Seven | Unbreakable | Changing Lanes | Star Wars: Episode III — Revenge of the Sith | Lakeview Terrace | Django Unchained | Captain America: The Winter Soldier |

inspirational high school teacher movies produced in the 1990s. The first film to feature Jackson as star, he is compelling as a teacher who decides to take action against the escalating gang culture problem, but the film's bleak tone failed to engage with audiences.

Jackson has appeared in countless, effects-driven blockbusters, from *Sphere* (1998) and the entertaining *Deep Blue Sea* (1999), to *xXx* (2002), *Jumper* (2008) and *Kingsman: The Secret Service* (2014), playing a lisping villain. He is one of the few highlights of the second *Star Wars* trilogy, particularly *Episode III — Revenge of the Sith* (2005). However, his biggest impact has come from his appearance as Nick Fury, the irascible head of S.H.I.E.L.D., in the ever-expanding Marvel *Avengers* enterprise. First appearing in *Iron Man* (2008), Fury has become a mainstay of the franchise, his role growing with each entry. *Captain America: The Winter Soldier* (2014) is his largest role to date, revealing some of his backstory, but plans are afoot for Fury to have his own feature.

Unsurprisingly for so prolific an actor, Jackson has appeared in more than a few bad movies. Most famously, there is *Snakes on a Plane* (2006), whose title says it all. *Freedomland* (2006) failed to capture

the complexity of Richard Price's source novel and Jackson looks uncomfortable in it, while *Black Snake Moan* (2006) is a bizarre Deep South drama with the actor playing a bluesman attempting to cure Christina Ricci's young woman of nymphomania.

Outside of his work with Spike Lee, he has confronted the issue of race in a number of films. He had fun with John Singleton in recreating *Shaft* (2000), which features the detective hunting down Christian Bale's racist killer. *Changing Lanes* (2002) offered up a more penetrating study of class and racial difference in contemporary America, albeit through the prism of an effective thriller that pits Jackson's divorcee against Ben Affleck's slick businessman. And in Neil LaBute's *Lakeview Terrace* (2008), the actor plays an LAPD cop who is disturbed by the arrival next door of a mixed-race couple and starts to terrorize them.

Jackson's presence, even in a cameo role, often lifts a film. At his best, he leaves audiences feeling both exhilarated and unsettled. In *Unbreakable* (2000), his screen persona initially has audiences perplexed as to the kind of character he is, although these days it is clear that if anyone could convincingly play a criminal mastermind, Jackson could. **IHS**

■ Western

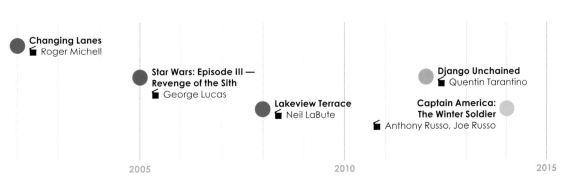

Changing Lanes
Roger Michell

Star Wars: Episode III — Revenge of the Sith
George Lucas

Lakeview Terrace
Neil LaBute

Django Unchained
Quentin Tarantino

Captain America: The Winter Soldier
Anthony Russo, Joe Russo

2005   2010   2015

Jungle Fever
(1991)

Pulp Fiction
(1994)

Die Hard: With a Vengeance
(1995)

A Time to Kill
(1996)

Jackie Brown
(1997)

Star Wars: Episode III — Revenge of the Sith
(2005)

Lakeview Terrace
(2008)

Django Unchained
(2012)

Jackson as the crack addict Gator in Spike Lee's *Jungle Fever*.

Pulp Fiction was the movie that launched Jackson to stardom. The scenes featuring his Jules Winnfield and John Travolta's Vincent Vega are some of the film's most memorable.

Die Hard: With a Vengeance saw Jackson play a Harlem shopkeeper called Zeus Carver, who helps Bruce Willis' John McClane save New York from terrorists.

Robert De Niro and Jackson as Louis Gara and Ordell Robbie in *Jackie Brown*.

Jackson as Carl Lee Hailey, the father on trial for killing his daughter's rapists in the John Grisham adaptation *A Time to Kill*.

Jackie Brown was Jackson's second picture with director Quentin Tarantino.

Jackson as the Jedi master Mace Windu in *Star Wars: Episode III — Revenge of the Sith*. A huge fan of the original trilogy, Jackson was offered the role after mentioning on a talk show that he would like to work with director George Lucas.

Receiving mixed reviews upon release, *Lakeview Terrace* nonetheless won praise for Jackson's performance from critic Roger Ebert, who observed that "for such a nice man [he] can certainly play vicious."

Almost unrecognizable as the tyrannical butler Stephen in *Django Unchained*, Jackson was widely lauded for his performance. The *Rolling Stone* review of the movie praised the actor for being "outstanding at locating the complexities in this Uncle Tom with an agenda."

emil jannings 1884–1950

| Madame DuBarry | The Last Laugh | Tartuffe | Faust | The Last Command | The Blue Angel | Der Herrscher | Uncle Kruger |

There was a time, in the heyday of German silent cinema, when Emil Jannings was considered one of the greatest screen actors in the world — perhaps even *the* greatest. To latter-day eyes those acclaimed performances can now appear a little hammy, but, seen in the context of the period, he had few equals in terms of sheer screen presence.

Before World War I, Jannings was a member of one of the finest theatrical troupes of the period, Max Reinhart's Berliner Ensemble. His fellow actor Ernst Lubitsch, as director, gave him some of his best early roles, most notably as Louis XV in *Madame DuBarry* (1919) and Henry VIII in *Anna Boleyn* (1920).

Jannings suited these and similar heavyweight roles, often in historical dramas. He took the title roles in *Danton* (1921) and *Peter the Great* (1922), and played the Pharaoh Amenes in *Loves of Pharaoh* (1922), the Caliph Haroun al-Raschid in *Waxworks* (1924) and Nero in *Quo Vadis* (1924). Rulers and authority figures came naturally to him. But his best roles were those where his vainglorious self-confidence was undermined by insecurity and doubt. E.A. Dupont captured this side of Jannings in *Variety* (1925), where he plays a trapeze artist who leaves his wife and child for a younger woman only to realize that she is cheating on him.

This aspect of Jannings' screen persona was even more tellingly explored in the film that brought him to international fame, F.W. Murnau's *The Last Laugh* (1924), where his majestic hotel head porter is humiliatingly reduced to the status of lavatory attendant. This was the first of his three films for Murnau; the next was *Tartuffe* (1925), adapted from Molière's classic satire on religious hypocrisy. Jannings here seems like a monster parasite avidly sucking the lifeblood out of his host household. Third came *Faust* (1926), where Jannings' mocking, lecherous Mephisto acted the rest of the cast straight off the screen.

He was lured to Hollywood, where Paramount fashioned several majesty-brought-low vehicles for him, the best of which was Josef von Sternberg's *The Last Command* (1928). With the coming of sound he returned to Germany, where Sternberg gave him his last great role in *The Blue Angel* (1930), as the pompous schoolmaster ruined by lust for Marlene Dietrich's cabaret singer.

An enthusiastic pro-Nazi, Jannings was made head of UFA under the Third Reich and appeared in various propaganda films, playing such characters as President Krüger. Blacklisted at the end of the war, he lived out his final years in bitter retirement. **PK**

genre   ■ Drama

Leading

Actor

Madame DuBarry
🎬 Ernst Lubitsch

The Last Command
🎬 Josef von Sternberg

The Last Laugh
🎬 F.W. Murnau

The Blue Angel
🎬 Josef von Sternberg

Tartuffe
🎬 F.W. Murnau

Der Herrscher
🎬 Veit Harlan

Faust
🎬 F.W. Murnau

Uncle Kruger
🎬 Hans Steinhoff

1920   1925   1930   1935   1940   1945

Femme Fatale   Girl Next Door   Lover   Superhero

scarlett johansson 1984

| Ghost World | Girl with a Pearl Earring | Lost in Translation | Vicky Cristina Barcelona | The Avengers | Her | Under the Skin | Lucy |

Born in 1984, Scarlett Johansson made her film debut aged 9 and at 13 was cast opposite Robert Redford in *The Horse Whisperer* (1998), as a young girl traumatized after a riding accident. Already working steadily, it was her appearance in indie comedy *Ghost World* (2001) that suggested her true potential.

In 2003, still only 18-years-old, Johansson announced herself as an adult screen presence to be reckoned with. In *Girl With a Pearl Earring*, she played the serving girl who inspires 17th century Dutch painter Johannes Vermeer to create his enigmatic portrait. The expressive silences and chaste sexual tension between Johansson and Colin Firth proved irresistible. Johansson entranced another older male costar in Sofia Coppola's *Lost in Translation*. Bill Murray's world-weary actor and Johansson's lonely young bride bond in a shimmering, dreamlike Tokyo, another unconsummated union that only enhanced her mystique.

These roles emphasized Johansson's seductiveness as much as her acting ability, so it was little surprise that Woody Allen hired her as an ill-fated femme fatale in his London-set thriller *Match Point* (2005). It began a run of European-based roles as Allen's muse, most successfully in the beguiling *Vicky Cristina Barcelona* (2008), which allowed her to display a comic timing and sweetness to go with the sex appeal.

Though in constant demand — Christopher Nolan's *The Prestige*, Brian De Palma's *The Black Dahlia* (both 2006) — Johansson's commercial appeal temporarily waned. But she bounced back with the key recurring role of Natasha Romanoff, aka "Black Widow," appearing in Marvel franchise builders *Iron Man 2* (2010), *Captain America: The Winter Soldier* (2014) and the billion-dollar-grossing *The Avengers* (2012).

Johansson's action credentials were solidified in Luc Besson's cheerfully ludicrous *Lucy* (2014), as a naive drug mule turned superhuman. Besson tapped into her otherworldly poise and allure — but so too, to far greater effect, did Spike Jonze's futuristic romance *Her* (2013). Using only her voice, she creates a remarkably fully-rounded "character" as sentient computer operating system Samantha, the object of owner Joaquin Phoenix's affections. Jonathan Glazer's semi-improvised, lo-fi sci-fi masterpiece *Under the Skin* (2013) featured her as a predatory alien in Scotland who starts to question her own identity. Daring and original, these films bode well for Johansson, marking her out as an actress unafraid to experiment. **LS**

genre   ■ Comedy   ■ Drama   ■ Action   ■ Sci-Fi

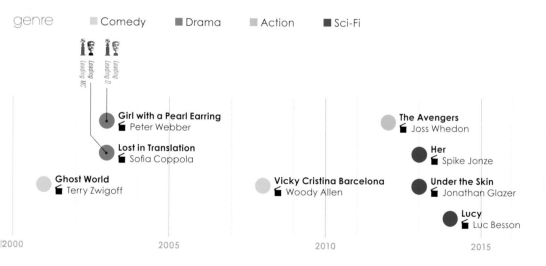

Leading W   Leading D

Girl with a Pearl Earring
🎬 Peter Webber

The Avengers
🎬 Joss Whedon

Lost in Translation
🎬 Sofia Coppola

Her
🎬 Spike Jonze

Ghost World
🎬 Terry Zwigoff

Vicky Cristina Barcelona
🎬 Woody Allen

Under the Skin
🎬 Jonathan Glazer

Lucy
🎬 Luc Besson

2000   2005   2010   2015

angelina jolie 1975

Hackers

Girl, Interrupted

Lara Croft: Tomb Raider

Alexander

Mr. & Mrs. Smith

A Mighty Heart

Changeling

Maleficent

The daughter of actor Jon Voight, Angelina Jolie made her fleeting screen debut at the age of 7, playing opposite her father in *Lookin' To Get Out* (1982). Parts in a few music videos and small budget features followed, but it was her role in *Hackers* (1995) that first got Jolie noticed by critics and the industry.

The next few years saw Jolie's stock rise. She won Golden Globes for her performances in the television movies *George Wallace* (1997) and *Gia* (1998). She starred opposite Denzel Washington in *The Bone Collector* (1999) and held her own against Cate Blanchett, John Cusack and soon-to-be second husband Billy Bob Thornton in *Pushing Tin* (1999). However, it was her performance in *Girl, Interrupted* (1999) that elevated her stock, and won her an Academy Award for Best Supporting Actress.

After the emotional demands of playing a young sociopath, Jolie's next role was in the flimsy *Gone in 60 Seconds* (2000), which nevertheless showcased how well-suited she is for action roles, something she further explored when playing the titular video game heroine in *Lara Croft: Tomb Raider* (2001).

After the box-office failure of Oliver Stone's *Alexander* (2004), Jolie once again hit the headlines when rumors surfaced of an on-set relationship with the married Brad Pitt, while the pair worked on *Mr. & Mrs. Smith* (2005). They publicly acknowledged their relationship the following year and were married in 2014. The film, meanwhile, proved to be a huge hit.

Jolie appeared in a string of high-profile films over the next few years, including Robert De Niro's *The Good Shepherd* (2006), Michael Winterbottom's *A Mighty Heart* (2007), the animated *Beowulf* (2007), action thriller *Wanted* (2008) and, most notably, the Clint Eastwood directed drama *Changeling* (2008). It saw her garner rave reviews and numerous award nominations. Roles in *Salt* (2010) and the critically mauled *The Tourist* (2010) followed, but then she took a hiatus from acting, during which she made her directorial debut with *In the Land of Blood and Honey* (2011) and embarked on a number of trips as a Goodwill Ambassador for the UN. Despite her return to the screen in the Disney smash hit *Maleficent* (2014), Jolie's humanitarian work has taken precedence over her acting and she has expressed a wish to remain behind the camera. She directed her second feature *Unbroken* (2014) and for her third, *By the Sea* (2015), appears alongside Pitt. **MB**

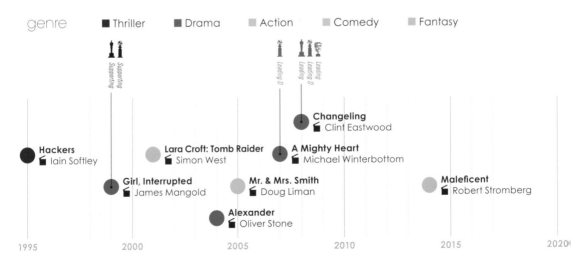

genre ■ Thriller ■ Drama ■ Action ■ Comedy ■ Fantasy

Supporting / Supporting

Leading D

Leading D

Leading D

Changeling
Clint Eastwood

Hackers
Iain Softley

Lara Croft: Tomb Raider
Simon West

A Mighty Heart
Michael Winterbottom

Girl, Interrupted
James Mangold

Mr. & Mrs. Smith
Doug Liman

Maleficent
Robert Stromberg

Alexander
Oliver Stone

1995   2000   2005   2010   2015   2020

tommy lee jones 1946

Eyes of
Laura Mars

The Fugitive

Cobb

Men in
Black

The Three
Burials of
Melqiades
Estrada

No Country
for Old Men

Lincoln

The
Homesman

Grizzled Texan Tommy Lee Jones was born in San Seba in 1946. After attending Harvard, he moved to New York City to become an actor, playing a variety of Broadway roles. His first film was the wildly successful *Love Story* (1970), playing a Harvard student.

After a brief return to Broadway, Jones worked extensively on television. During this time, he turned in fine performances in *Rolling Thunder* (1977), *The Betsy* (1978) and *Eyes of Laura Mars* (1978). A stunning turn in *Coal Miner's Daughter* (1980), as Loretta Lynn's husband, won him his first Golden Globe nomination. He also excelled as a gangster in *Stormy Monday* (1988).

Jones hit his stride in the 1990s. His role in Oliver Stone's *JFK* (1991) led to his first nomination for a Best Supporting Actor Oscar. He would win one two years later as the lawman pursuing Harrison Ford's wrongfully convicted prison escapee in *The Fugitive* (1993).

Jones balanced commercial fare like the enjoyable actioner *Under Siege* (1992), disaster movie *Volcano* (1997) and *Small Soldiers* (1998), with more serious roles such as a 1950s military officer dealing with his wife's mental illness in *Blue Sky* (1994) and an exceptional turn as the repellent baseball player in *Cobb* (1994). He also brought gravitas to the otherwise lightweight

Men in Black (1997) and its sequels. Opinion is divided on his outrageous portrayal of the prison governor in Oliver Stone's controversial *Natural Born Killers* (1994).

A new decade saw Jones step behind the camera. *The Three Burials of Melquiades Estrada* (2005) is a fascinating portrait of life on the border between the United States and Mexico, with Jones playing a ranch hand who exacts revenge on the man who killed his Mexican friend, while in *The Homesman* (2014) he is a vagabond saved by Hilary Swank's frontierswoman, who accompanies her on a perilous journey back east.

He is exceptional as a father searching for his disappeared son in Paul Haggis' post-9/11 themed *In the Valley of Elah* (2007) and delivered an outstanding performance as a beleaguered sheriff in the Coen brother's lyrical *No Country for Old Men* (2007).

Reliable in the dramas *The Company Men* (2010) and *Emperor* (2012), as well as comedies like *Hope Springs* (2012) and *The Family* (2013), Jones' most impressive performance in recent years — and one of the best of his career — is as Thaddeus Stevens in Steven Spielberg's *Lincoln* (2012). Holding his own against Daniel Day-Lewis, Jones brings gravitas and depth to his portrayal of the elder statesman. **CGD**

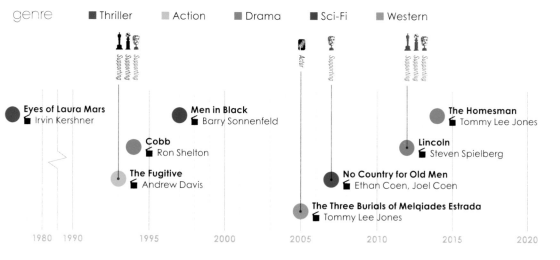

genre   ■ Thriller   ■ Action   ■ Drama   ■ Sci-Fi   ■ Western

Supporting
Supporting
Supporting

Actor   Supporting

Supporting
Supporting
Supporting

Eyes of Laura Mars
🎬 Irvin Kershner

Men in Black
🎬 Barry Sonnenfeld

Cobb
🎬 Ron Shelton

The Fugitive
🎬 Andrew Davis

The Homesman
🎬 Tommy Lee Jones

Lincoln
🎬 Steven Spielberg

No Country for Old Men
🎬 Ethan Coen, Joel Coen

The Three Burials of Melqiades Estrada
🎬 Tommy Lee Jones

1980   1990   1995   2000   2005   2010   2015   2020

shashi kapoor 1938

Shakespeare
Wallah

Jab Jab
Phool Khile

Haseena
Maan
Jayegi

Siddhartha

Aa Gale
Lag Jaa

Junoon

New Delhi
Times

In Custody

While enjoying a very successful career at home in the Hindi film industry, Shashi Kapoor is perhaps the first Indian star to have had a global presence, thanks to his collaborations with the Merchant-Ivory team. He was born into the first family of Hindi popular cinema, his father being the actor Prithivaj Kapoor and his brothers Raj, the renowned actor/director/producer, and Shammi, the "rebel star" of Hindi cinema.

Kapoor debuted as a child actor with *Aag* (1948), followed by *Awaara* (1951). In both he played the younger screen version of his brother Raj. His debut as a leading man was in Yash Chopra's *Dharmputra* (1961), where he played a Hindu fundamentalist who discovers that he is adopted and is actually Muslim. In 1963, Kapoor began a long collaboration with producer Ismail Merchant, director James Ivory and writer Ruth Prawer Jhabvala, with the English-language drama *The Householder*, in which he plays a college lecturer struggling to save his marriage.

With *Waqt* (1965), Yash Chopra created the template for the modern Bollywood blockbuster, with multiple stars, including Kapoor, and a story unfolding across generations, in exotic foreign locations. In *Jab Jab Phool Khile* (1965), another blockbuster, Kapoor played the romantic lead. That year started a mode of working that became common practice for him; he would star in a mainstream Hindi language hit and then act in or produce an arthouse film.

In the mid-1950s, he met and fell in love with British actress Jennifer Kendal. Their paths had crossed while Kapoor was working with his father's theater group and Kendal was with her father's Shakespearean theater company. They married in 1958. *Shakespeare Wallah* (1965), a Merchant-Ivory production about the journeys of a Shakespearean troupe through India, starred Kapoor as a dashing playboy.

Hits galore like *Pyar Kiye Jaa* (1966), *Haseena Maan Jayegi* (1968) and *Aa Gale Lag Jaa* (1973) continued. At the same time, Kapoor starred in Merchant-Ivory's *Bombay Talkie* (1970), alongside his wife, and Conrad Rooks' adaptation of Herman Hesse's *Siddhartha* (1972). Though he had acted opposite Amitabh Bachchan in *Roti Kapda Aur Makaan* (1974), *Deewar* (1975) began a phase of Kapoor's career where he played an able foil to his costar. The partnership continued over many years and included *Kabhi Kabhi* (1976), *Trishul* (1978), *Kaala Patthar* (1979) and *Silsila* (1981).

Arthouse features produced by Kapoor included *Junoon* (1979), *Kalyug* (1981), *Vijeta* (1982) and *Utsav* (1984). He directed the mainstream fantasy *Ajooba* (1991), starring Bachchan, whose career was on the wane. The film was a critical and commercial disaster. Notable later roles include a fearless newspaper editor in *New Delhi Times* (1986), for which he won an Indian National Award for Best Actor, and *In Custody* (1994), where he played a debauched Urdu poet. **NR**

genre ■ Drama ■ Romance

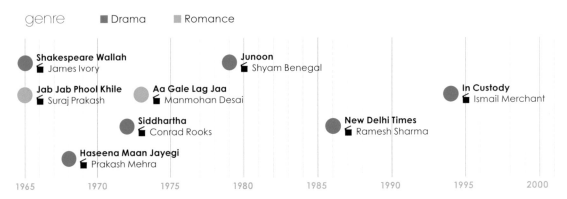

Shakespeare Wallah
🎬 James Ivory

Junoon
🎬 Shyam Benegal

Jab Jab Phool Khile
🎬 Suraj Prakash

Aa Gale Lag Jaa
🎬 Manmohan Desai

In Custody
🎬 Ismail Merchant

Siddhartha
🎬 Conrad Rooks

New Delhi Times
🎬 Ramesh Sharma

Haseena Maan Jayegi
🎬 Prakash Mehra

1965 1970 1975 1980 1985 1990 1995 2000

anna karina 1940

Une Femme est Une Femme | **Vivre Sa Vie** | **Bande à Part** | **Pierrot le Fou** | **The Nun** | **The Stranger** | **Vivre Ensemble** | **Chinese Roulette**

Born in Denmark, Anna Karina hitchhiked to Paris aged 17 and became a model. Spied in an advertisement by director Jean-Luc Godard, he asked Karina to appear naked in a small role in *Breathless* (1960). She refused, though he subsequently hired her for *Le Petit Soldat*, which remained unreleased until 1963. That meant the first glimpse movie audiences had of Karina was in *Une Femme est Une Femme* (1961), a vibrant, semi-musical love triangle comedy. Her striking looks marked her out as much as her unaffected ease and contemporary attitude on camera. She and Godard married and Karina won Best Actress at the Berlin Film Festival.

Vivre Sa Vie (1962) is another, more twisted love letter to Karina, this time portraying a woman who falls into prostitution. Again Godard seems to be deliberately contextualizing her in movie history, her dark bob reminiscent of Louise Brooks in *Pandora's Box* (1929). Indeed, despite their turbulent relationship, Karina appears as the perfect conduit for Godard's cinematic inventiveness, the wellspring for much of his most celebrated work during this period: *Bande à Part*'s (1964) impromptu dance with Sami Frey and Claude Brasseur and sprint through the Louvre; and

the audience-referencing road trip with Jean-Paul Belmondo in *Pierrot le Fou* (1965). The pair seem to erase the boundaries between life and art, so much so that the crumbling relationship between Belmondo's Pierrot and Karina's Marianne is a distillation of her and Godard's own traumatic split.

Thanks to these films and the other Karina/Godard collaborations, *Alphaville* (1965) and *Made in U.S.A.* (1966), she began to garner good roles for other filmmakers. In Jacques Rivette's controversial *The Nun* (1966), she played a novice railing against Church-sanctioned abuse. She was winning opposite Marcello Mastroianni in Luchino Visconti's *The Stranger* (1967). In 1973 she wrote, directed and starred in *Vivre Ensemble*, playing a free-spirit who "corrupts" a stiff professor, but reviews were mixed. Better was Rainer Werner Fassbinder's *Chinese Roulette* (1976), with Karina as the mistress caught up in a bourgeois couple's exposed hypocrisies and prejudices.

Though Karina has continued to work, cameos in Rivette's *Up, Down, Fragile* (1995) or Jonathan Demme's *The Truth About Charlie* (2002) are largely nods to her New Wave legacy; a heritage of which Karina herself still seems justifiably proud. **LS**

K

genre ■ Comedy ■ Drama ■ Crime

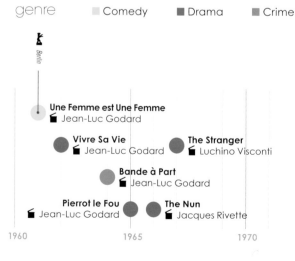

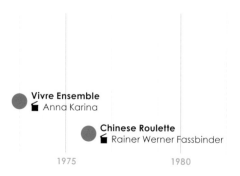

Berlin

Une Femme est Une Femme
Jean-Luc Godard

Vivre Sa Vie
Jean-Luc Godard

The Stranger
Luchino Visconti

Bande à Part
Jean-Luc Godard

Vivre Ensemble
Anna Karina

Pierrot le Fou
Jean-Luc Godard

The Nun
Jacques Rivette

Chinese Roulette
Rainer Werner Fassbinder

1960   1965   1970   1975   1980

boris karloff 1887–1969

Frankenstein

The Mummy

The Ghoul

The Lost Patrol

The Raven

Targets

Dozens of actors have portrayed the wretched creature from Mary Shelley's 1818 novel for the stage and screen, but the definitive image of Frankenstein's monster in popular culture remains that of Boris Karloff. His most famous role was the source of his enduring popularity, leading to a prolific career.

Born in London in 1887, Karloff moved to Canada in 1909 to pursue stage acting, traveling to Hollywood a decade later. After working as an extra in silent films, he progressed to small supporting parts, often as foreign villains. In 1931, he emerged from relative obscurity with roles in *The Criminal Code* and *Five Star Final*, but it was another of the 15 films he made that year that brought worldwide stardom. Enduring grueling hours of make-up, Karloff played Henry Frankenstein's abominable creation in *Frankenstein*.

While the creature is remembered as a lumbering monster, *Frankenstein*'s power comes from the sympathy Karloff generated for his character. The inevitable sequel *The Bride of Frankenstein* (1935) is arguably superior, but the commercially successful *Son of Frankenstein* (1939) marked a decline in quality, after which he stepped away from the character.

The success of *Frankenstein* gave Karloff the opportunity to explore other genres in *The Mask of Fu Manchu* (1932), *Scarface* (1932) and *The Lost Patrol*

(1934), as well as a series of five crime films playing the Chinese-American detective Mr. Wong. He would be most closely associated with horror, however, and was one of the genre's biggest early stars. The year after his breakthrough, he starred as another iconic monster in *The Mummy* (1932), before exploring Egyptian mysticism again in *The Ghoul* (1933). During this period he starred in a number of popular horror films, several of which were alongside Bela Lugosi, like *The Black Cat* (1934) and *The Body Snatcher* (1945).

Horror's appeal was waning by the time Karloff starred in the B-movie *Bedlam* (1946) and he focused increasingly on theater and television. In the 1960s he starred in several low-budget horror films, including Mario Bava's *Black Sabbath* (1963) and two directed by Roger Corman, *The Raven* (1963) and *The Terror* (1963). Corman had 20 minutes of footage left over from the latter and was owed two days' work from the actor, so persuaded Peter Bogdanovich to make another film: *Targets* (1968). Bogdanovich cast Karloff as Byron Orlok, an ageing, outmoded horror actor who confronts a man on a shooting rampage. With its motiveless real-world killer, *Targets* signaled a shift in horror away from the fantastical films that he had built his career upon, and yet his presence also constituted a fitting tribute to them. **JWa**

genre   ■ Horror   ■ War   ■ Thriller

Frankenstein
James Whale

The Mummy
Karl Freund

The Ghoul
T. Hayes Hunter

The Lost Patrol
John Ford

The Raven
Roger Corman

Targets
Peter Bogdanovich

1930   1935   1940   1945   1950   1955   1960   1965

shintarô katsu 1931–97

The Loyal 47 Ronin

Samurai Vendetta

Buddha

The Tale of
Zatoichi

Hanzo the Razor:
Sword of Justice

Zatoichi

Shintarô Katsu is primarily associated with one role: Zatoichi, the blind masseur with uncanny skill as a swordsman, who he played in 26 features and multiple television series. He was born Toshio Okumura near Tokyo, the son of a shamisen player who performed in the kabuki theater. Katsu originally intended to follow in his father's footsteps, and by his teens had become a professional musician. In 1953, he was talent-spotted by a film actor, introduced to the head of Daiei Studios and offered a contract. He made his film debut in 1954, and his filmography was well into double figures before he played his first leading role in 1960.

Examples of his early output include supporting roles in the anti-capitalist satire *An Osaka Story* (1957), originally to have been directed by Kenji Mizoguchi, but completed after his death; Kunio Wanatabe's *The Loyal 47 Ronin* (1958), in which Katsu played a boozy servant; and as a virtuoso swordsman in Kazuo Mori's *Samurai Vendetta* (1959). In 1961, he played the major role of the villainous Devadatta in *Buddha* (1961). He also appeared as an escaped convict in Kon Ichikawa's *An Actor's Revenge* (1963).

But it was *The Tale of Zatoichi* (1962) that established Katsu's lasting fame. Picking up where Akira Kurosawa and Toshiro Mifune's 1961 film *Yojimbo* left off, the character caught the popular imagination from the start: an irrepressibly cheeky gambler and conman who was more than capable of rising to the occasion when it came to seeking righteous vengeance on behalf of himself or others, his disability doing little to impede his prowess as both a swordsman and a dice player.

In 1967, Katsu formed his own production company, overseeing a further ten *Zatoichi* films until 1973, before the character transferred to television (1974–79). In 1972 Katsu headlined *Hanzo the Razor: Sword of Justice*, inaugurating a cycle of three films in which his law enforcement official is as likely to make use of his oversized penis as any more conventional weapon, especially when interrogating female suspects. At the same time he began producing the more successful *Lone Wolf and Cub* series (1972–74) as a six-film vehicle for his brother Tomisaburo Wakayama.

Increasingly involved with television by the late 1970s, he also became equally if not more notorious for his off-screen activities. He was arrested three times for drug possession and clashed with veteran director Akira Kurosawa to the point of his being fired from the lead role of *Kagemusha* (1980), while an attempt at reviving *Zatoichi* in 1989 (with Katsu as director as well as star) proved a one-off. He retired from film acting the following year, and died in 1997. **MBr**

K

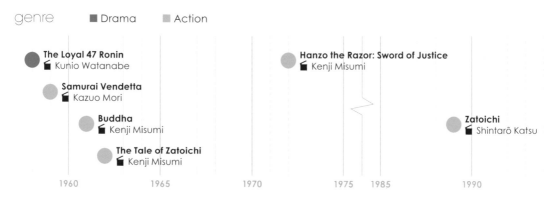

genre ■ Drama ■ Action

The Loyal 47 Ronin
Kunio Watanabe

Samurai Vendetta
Kazuo Mori

Buddha
Kenji Misumi

The Tale of Zatoichi
Kenji Misumi

Hanzo the Razor: Sword of Justice
Kenji Misumi

Zatoichi
Shintarô Katsu

1960   1965   1970   1975 1985   1990

buster keaton 1895–1966

The Butcher Boy

The Saphead

One Week

The Frozen North

Three Ages

Our Hospitality

Sherlock Jr.

The Navigator

Buster Keaton was the supreme poet of silent film comedy. His straight-faced stoicism in the face of huge recalcitrant objects (a train, an ocean liner, a landslide, a collapsing house) or overwhelming odds has led critics to reach for words like "fatalistic" and "existential." But the Keaton persona was also endlessly resourceful, rarely accepting defeat. Straight-faced he might be (though never expressionless), but there was a determination in the dark-eyed stare and the set of his jaw. And unlike almost all his silent-comedy coevals, he had an instinctive and inventive feeling for the use of cinematic space.

A member of his parents' vaudeville act from infancy, Buster soon learned that a solemn reaction to comic mishaps got him extra laughs. His first screen appearance, at the invitation of his friend Roscoe "Fatty" Arbuckle, in *The Butcher Boy* (1917), shows him instilling a deliberate calm into the frenetic activity around him. Over the next three years he made some 15 two-reelers with Arbuckle, first in New York and then in California, before his producer, Joe Schenck, set him up with his own company in Charlie Chaplin's former studios. Here he made a forgettable first feature, *The Saphead* (1920) and 19 shorts.

These shorts show him perfecting and enriching his craft, exploring the recurrent themes and situations

he would further develop in his features. In *One Week* (1920) a build-it-yourself house is first assembled then gradually disintegrates before Buster's somber gaze. The house as entrapment machine would show up again in *The Scarecrow* (1920), *The Haunted House* (1921) and *The Electric House* (1922). Happy endings were not obligatory: *The Boat* (1921), a superbly structured chain of catastrophes, ends with Keaton's entire family shipwrecked and benighted. The final shot of *Cops* (1922) shows the trademark Keaton porkpie hat adorning a tombstone.

On principle, Keaton would never fake a stunt, shooting in unbroken long-shot takes to prove nothing was being falsified, but he was happy to exploit all the special effects that the camera could offer. In *The Playhouse* (1921), making virtuoso use of multiple exposure, he plays every part in a theater: the actors, the whole orchestra, all nine blackface minstrels and every member of the audience, male and female, young and old — all with impeccable coordination.

Three Ages (1923) felt like a hedged bet: three two-reelers skillfully intertwined into a feature, showing the vicissitudes of love through the ages; but *Our Hospitality* (1923) was his first feature-length triumph. Set in the Deep South of 1831, with all Keaton's concern for period and location, it deploys scrupulous

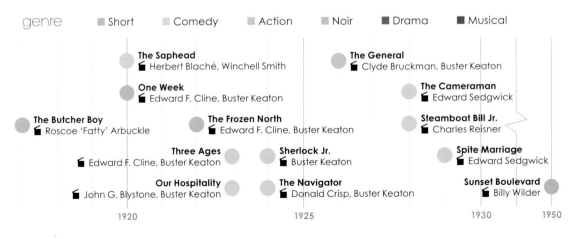

genre   ■ Short   ■ Comedy   ■ Action   ■ Noir   ■ Drama   ■ Musical

The Saphead
🎬 Herbert Blaché, Winchell Smith

The General
🎬 Clyde Bruckman, Buster Keaton

One Week
🎬 Edward F. Cline, Buster Keaton

The Cameraman
🎬 Edward Sedgwick

The Butcher Boy
🎬 Roscoe 'Fatty' Arbuckle

The Frozen North
🎬 Edward F. Cline, Buster Keaton

Steamboat Bill Jr.
🎬 Charles Reisner

Three Ages
🎬 Edward F. Cline, Buster Keaton

Sherlock Jr.
🎬 Buster Keaton

Spite Marriage
🎬 Edward Sedgwick

Our Hospitality
🎬 John G. Blystone, Buster Keaton

The Navigator
🎬 Donald Crisp, Buster Keaton

Sunset Boulevard
🎬 Billy Wilder

1920   1925   1930   1950

| The General | The Cameraman | Steamboat Bill Jr. | Spite Marriage | Sunset Boulevard | Limelight | It's a Mad, Mad, Mad, Mad World | A Funny Thing Happened on the Way to the Forum |

dramatic logic along with witty gags and some of his most breathtaking athletic feats. *Sherlock Jr.* (1924) boasted a montage sequence set in a dream context, where Buster slips through a dozen settings without any apparent cuts in his own movements, and a virtuoso stunt sequence with him careering headlong on the handlebars of a riderless motor-bike. As usual, Keaton did all his own stunts.

Gifted with a natural mechanical bent, Keaton loved devising ingenious contraptions. In *The Navigator* (1924) his rich-ninny character and girlfriend find themselves alone at sea in a huge liner — but within weeks have rigged up intricate devices to run the boat. *Seven Chances* (1925) was let down by its material; *Go West* (1925) introduced an unwonted hint of Chaplinesque pathos; and *Battling Butler* (1926), adapted from another stage play, suffered from uncertainty of tone.

Then came his masterpiece. *The General* (1926) is set during the Civil War, with Buster driving a train for the Confederacy. Again, the period sense is impeccably authentic, the gags flow from the action, and the photography is spare and beautiful. Astonishingly, it was poorly received. *College* (1927) found Keaton straying into formulaic Harold Lloyd territory, but *Steamboat Bill Jr.* (1928) was a return

to form, with a cyclone sequence that elevates stuntwork into an elegant, dreamlike ballet.

Ill-advisedly, Keaton signed a contract with MGM. The studio, baffled by his improvisatory genius, tried to tie him down with closely budgeted scripts and armies of studio gagwriters. For *The Cameraman* (1928) he managed to retain some freedom, but *Spite Marriage* (1929), his last silent movie and the last real Keaton film, betrayed the influence of the studio. With the advent of sound his career fell apart. Drinking heavily, his marriage breaking up, he appeared in eight sound movies for MGM, ranging from the mediocre to the abysmal. In 1933 the studio fired him. He appeared in a poor film in France, a terrible one in England and a series of Poverty Row two-reelers. For 10 years he vanished, a hopeless has-been.

Gradually he resurfaced, with cameos in Billy Wilder's *Sunset Boulevard* (1950), his old rival Chaplin's *Limelight* (1952) and *Around the World in 80 Days* (1956). His films were rediscovered, restored and shown at retrospectives. Samuel Beckett wrote a 22-minute short for him, simply called *Film* (1965), which was shown at the Venice Film Festival where he received a standing ovation. He was touched and delighted; but as he told film historian Lotte Eisner afterward, "Sure, it's great — but it's all 30 years too late." **PK**

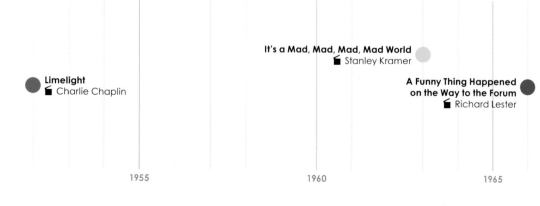

It's a Mad, Mad, Mad, Mad World
Stanley Kramer

Limelight
Charlie Chaplin

A Funny Thing Happened on the Way to the Forum
Richard Lester

1955 1960 1965

movie clowns

| Harold Lloyd | Raymond Griffith | Buster Keaton | Laurel & Hardy | The Marx brothers | Peter Sellers | Jacques Tati | Mel Brooks |

What defines a movie clown? One decisive factor is that they are more dependent on physical comedy than verbal sparring: Harpo Marx is a movie clown, Cary Grant is not. Charlie Chaplin has too much pathos, while W.C. Fields is too dependent on verbal humor. As with the earliest practitioners of commedia dell'arte, clowning around, broadly speaking, adopts a more physical style, setting up a scenario in which the actor can make their body perform ridiculous feats that usually result in harm to their person — or very nearly. It is not the humor of realism or observational comedy. Sight gags and absurd behavior are the key weapons in the clown's armory.

Time is not kind to the clown princes of comedy. Aside from horror, comedy is the only genre that relies on an impulsive response from the viewer. Horror is intended to make you scream; comedy is meant to make you scream with laughter. And while the effect of jump scares can dull over repeated viewings, they can still affect the first-time viewer. Comedy, however, is much more at the mercy of trends and styles, and changing tastes. What was outrageous or surprising in the earliest comedy films is often passé or twee by modern standards.

The earliest comedy stars of the Mack Sennett and Hal Roach silent short films depended on simple

scenes that evolved into complex slapstick or farce. Serials like *Keystone Cops* (1912–17) were hugely successful and Buster Keaton created ambitious, dangerous routines for the sake of a laugh. With the arrival of sound, some actors, such as Laurel and Hardy, were able to make the transition and stay current, whereas other popular draws were left behind: Harold Lloyd, Mabel Normand and Harry Langdon. Their humor no longer translated to viewers and could not compete with the comedians using dialogue as part of their act.

The Marx brothers, comprised of Groucho, Chico, Harpo and sometimes Zeppo, utilized deft wordplay ("Will you marry me? Do you have any money? Answer the second question first.") with perfectly calibrated routines born from their stage work. The mirror scene or the teasing-toying of the peanut seller in *Duck Soup* (1933) exemplify this perfectly. Their spirit was anarchic and surreal. Less sophisticated but still anarchic was The Three Stooges: Larry, Curly and Moe. More in line with cartoons, their brutal, raucous, blunt style was hugely popular from the late 1920s all the way to the 1970s.

Films built around the particular well-practiced routines of comedians became less prolific as vaudeville died out. Stand-ups began to make the

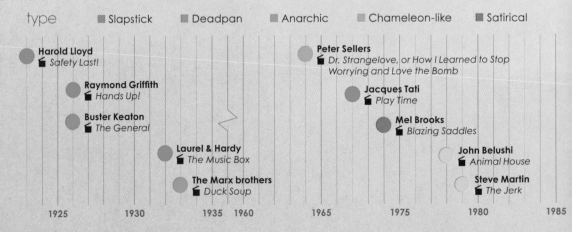

type ■ Slapstick ■ Deadpan ■ Anarchic ■ Chameleon-like ■ Satirical

Harold Lloyd
Safety Last!

Raymond Griffith
Hands Up!

Buster Keaton
The General

Laurel & Hardy
The Music Box

The Marx brothers
Duck Soup

Peter Sellers
Dr. Strangelove, or How I Learned to Stop Worrying and Love the Bomb

Jacques Tati
Play Time

Mel Brooks
Blazing Saddles

John Belushi
Animal House

Steve Martin
The Jerk

1925   1930   1935   1960   1965   1975   1980   1985

John Belushi | Steve Martin | Robin Williams | Jim Carrey | Mike Myers | Ben Stiller | Will Ferrel | Kristen Wiig

transition into thinly veiled versions of themselves in film and a new breed of chameleon-like comic actors arrived, such as Alec Guinness. Peter Sellers, one of the most gifted comic actors of all time, was able to tell jokes in an expression, or an inflection, or in more overt displays such as the deranged scientist in *Dr. Strangelove, or How I Learned to Stop Worrying and Love the Bomb* (1964). In his best work, Sellers ensured that the jokes always fit with the character. This was nowhere more so than in his early appearance as Inspector Clouseau in *A Shot in the Dark* (1964), where the detective's confidence in his ability seems delusional alongside his utter incompetence.

While Woody Allen's neuroses physically manifested themselves — in his early films, at least — in the anxieties of the 1960s, Britain's *Carry On* series offered an unashamedly bawdy time at the cinema. In France, the classiest act of clowning around came from Jacques Tati. As an actor, writer and director, Tati used the silent Monsieur Hulot to find his way through scenarios brimming with comic possibilities.

Female actors have had fewer opportunities to establish themselves as movie clowns, often being relegated instead to supporting roles for a leading man. However, notable actresses who displayed both verbal sparring skills and impeccable

physicality include Madeline Kahn and Gilda Radner. Arguably, they were able to show greater range and disappear into their characters more than their male counterparts, who had to be recognizable for the movie-going public.

In the 1980s, Steve Martin took physical comedy to a new level, representing a new breed of clown. Like the Marx brothers or Laurel and Hardy, Martin worked the live circuit before becoming a film star. Along with Chevy Chase, John Belushi, John Candy and Robin Williams, he helped pave the way for modern clowns such as Jim Carrey. Theirs was an era of riotous, high-concept films that made major stars of their leading men. But by the end of the 1990s, their style of comedy was overtaken by the emergence of the "man child." Lovable (in theory), badly adjusted males, they created jokes from their stupidity and the chaos they left in their wake. These comedies of no manners turned comedians such as Adam Sandler and Will Ferrell into major box-office draws.

"Gross out" comedies and R-rated humor quickly became the trend du jour, with films such as *Knocked Up* (2007). *The Hangover* (2009) produced a movie clown in Zach Galifianakis and *Bridesmaids* (2011) gave the world new female comedy stars in Kristen Wiig and Melissa McCarthy. **SW**

■ Riotous ■ Spoof ■ Man child ■ Female

Robin Williams *Aladdin*

Jim Carrey *The Mask*

Mike Myers *Austin Powers: International Man of Mystery*

Ben Stiller *Zoolander*

Will Ferrel *Anchorman: The Legend of Ron Burgundy*

Kristen Wiig *Bridesmaids*

1990 1995 2000 2005 2010 2015 2020

diane keaton 1946

The Godfather

Sleeper

Love and Death

Annie Hall

Looking for Mr. Goodbar

Interiors

Manhattan

Reds

Equally adept at comedy and drama, Diane Keaton is noted for bringing eccentricity, emotional directness and a refreshing lightness of touch to both.

Born in 1946, in Los Angeles, Keaton started her career as a stage actress before receiving her on-screen breakthrough as Kay Adams in *The Godfather* (1972). While the protagonist of the film was Michael Corleone (Al Pacino), the urbane, non-Italian outsider Kay was the audience surrogate — it was through her eyes that the viewer was introduced to the Corleones and the Mafia world. That identification would be key throughout. Keaton returned to the character in the equally impressive *The Godfather: Part II* (1974), and her increasing disillusionment was once again crucial to the film's emotional arc. Unfortunately, the magic would be gone by the much-derided third installment, although its high point remains the sad, regretful reunion between Kay and Michael.

The first of several film appearances with Woody Allen took place in the other film Keaton made in 1972, as she reprised her Tony-nominated stage role in *Play It Again, Sam*. The pair's natural chemistry made them a terrific comedy double act — she was game and happy where he was neurotic and dismayed. She costarred with him in two of his best early comedies, *Sleeper* (1973) and *Love and Death* (1975).

Keaton's next collaboration with Allen, *Annie Hall* (1977), would win her an Oscar and provide the defining role of her career. Annie Hall is a complicated, enormously appealing character — intelligent and loopy, insecure and courageous. It is unsurprising that it is the role Keaton is most closely associated with: not only is the character one of the most indelible women in modern cinema, but she also is largely based on Keaton's own personality, history — her real surname is Hall and her nickname was Annie — and stylishly androgynous dress sense.

Taking a step away from comedies, Keaton starred in the erotic drama *Looking for Mr. Goodbar* (1977), and took a lead role in Allen's first straight dramatic work, the poorly received *Interiors* (1978). The two would have more luck the following year with the comedy-drama *Manhattan* (1979), which is among Allen's strongest efforts. Except for a brief cameo in *Radio Days* (1987), the only other time Keaton worked with Allen was on the charming *Manhattan Murder Mystery* (1993), in a part originally written for Mia Farrow, before their acrimonious separation.

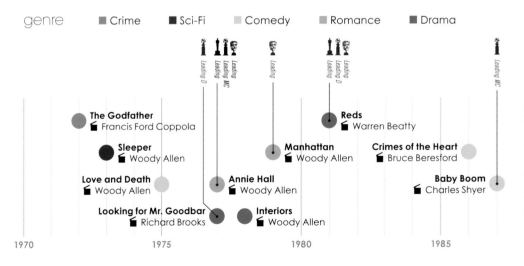

genre ■ Crime ■ Sci-Fi ■ Comedy ■ Romance ■ Drama

The Godfather
Francis Ford Coppola

Sleeper
Woody Allen

Love and Death
Woody Allen

Looking for Mr. Goodbar
Richard Brooks

Annie Hall
Woody Allen

Interiors
Woody Allen

Reds
Warren Beatty

Manhattan
Woody Allen

Crimes of the Heart
Bruce Beresford

Baby Boom
Charles Shyer

1970   1975   1980   1985

Crimes of
the Heart

Baby Boom

Father of
the Bride

Manhattan
Murder
Mystery

Marvin's
Room

The First
Wives Club

Something's
Gotta Give

The Family
Stone

As the resilient journalist Louise Bryant, Keaton gave one of her best performances in *Reds* (1981). Warren Beatty's 194-minute epic about the socialist John Reed and the political upheavals of the early 20th century took an entire year to shoot, but at its heart was the complex, moving love story between Bryant and Reed. Another troubled relationship between a married couple was the basis of *Shoot the Moon* (1982), while in *Mrs. Soffel* (1984) she played a prison warden's wife who goes on the run with inmate Mel Gibson.

In a rare departure into darker material, Keaton starred as an actress and double agent in *The Little Drummer Girl* (1984), based on John le Carré's spy novel. She seemed ill-at-ease in the role and the film was a commercial failure, which led to an uneven period of work — while the Southern melodrama comedy *Crimes of the Heart* (1986) and *Baby Boom* (1987) were generally well-received, *The Good Mother* (1988) was another flop and the release of *The Lemon Sisters* (1989) was delayed for over a year.

The beguiling uncertainty that had defined Keaton's early performances started to evolve into a more confident, yet still defiantly eccentric, screen persona. She was the straight wife to a panicked Steve Martin in *Father of the Bride* (1991) and its 1995 sequel, and sought revenge on her estranged husband in the unexpected hit *The First Wives Club* (1996). She also costarred with Meryl Streep and Leonardo DiCaprio in an adaptation of the stage drama *Marvin's Room* (1996). Increasingly interested in pursuits outside acting, her only other films that decade were middling: *The Only Thrill* (1997), *The Other Sister* (1999) and *Hanging Up* (2000), which she also directed.

After recovering from the flop *Town & Country* (2001), Keaton received her third Oscar nomination for *Something's Gotta Give* (2003). Starring opposite her *Reds* costar Jack Nicholson, she was delightful as a playwright who falls for an ageing lotario, both actors drawing amusingly on their public personas. Despite the film's contrivances, it was refreshing to see mature love depicted in a mainstream Hollywood picture. In the later part of her career, Keaton has been typecast as a matriarch in the comedy dramas *The Family Stone* (2005), *Because I Said So* (2007) and *The Big Wedding* (2013), as well as the out-and-out comedies *Mama's Boy* (2007) and *Smother* (2007). A welcome exception was as the host of a low-rated television show in *Morning Glory* (2010). **JWa**

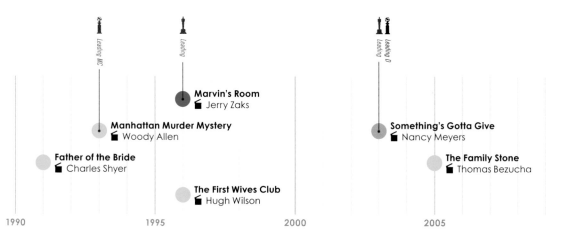

Leading MC

Leading

Leading

Leading O

Marvin's Room
Jerry Zaks

Manhattan Murder Mystery
Woody Allen

Something's Gotta Give
Nancy Meyers

Father of the Bride
Charles Shyer

The Family Stone
Thomas Bezucha

The First Wives Club
Hugh Wilson

1990   1995   2000   2005

michael keaton 1951

| Night Shift | Beetlejuice | Clean and Sober | Batman | Pacific Heights | Jackie Brown | White Noise | Birdman |

Michael Keaton started out as a stand-up comedian. It did not work out, but the nervous energy required to perform in front of a live audience remained. He is a brilliant comic actor, as evinced by his Oscar-nominated turn in 2014's *Birdman: Or (The Unexpected Virtue of Ignorance)*, but he has employed that same energy to startling effect as a villain.

Born in 1951, Keaton's attempts at live comedy introduced him to James Belushi and the pair worked on the short-lived television series *Working Stiffs* (1979). That brought him to the attention of Ron Howard, who cast him alongside Henry Winkler in *Night Shift* (1982), set in a city morgue. Keaton steals every scene with his manic energy. He played a stay-at-home dad in *Mr. Mom* (1983), an unlikely hoodlum in the gangster parody *Johnny Dangerously* (1984) and the foreman of a car plant who attempts to convince a Japanese company to take over operations in *Gung Ho* (1986). However, it was his boisterous turn as the exorcist of the living, the titular villain in Tim Burton's *Beetlejuice* (1988), that audiences were able to see Keaton in full flow, his physical comedy as frenetic as his speech.

Burton cast Keaton as the eponymous hero of *Batman* (1989), much to the chagrin of the comic book hero's fans. However, the move worked. His caped crusader fulfilled the requirements, but he was a far more interesting Bruce Wayne. Keaton and Burton reunited for the darker *Batman Returns* (1992), then wisely dropped out of the series. It was the actor's only brush with the superhero genre until *Birdman*, in which director Alejandro González Iñárritu draws on audience's awareness of Keaton's previous role to add depth to the character of Riggan, an actor haunted by a fictional superhero.

A year before *Batman*, Keaton played a cocaine addict in *Clean and Sober* (1988). It remains one of his best performances. He is excellent as a psychopath in *Pacific Heights* (1990), but nothing he did in *My Life* (1993), playing a family man dying of cancer, could save the film from drowning in a pool of sentimentality.

Aside of *Birdman*, recent roles have been less interesting. His Ray Nicolette in *Jackie Brown* (1997) and *Out of Sight* (1998) is fun but slight and *White Noise* (2005), in which he plays a man who believes he can hear the dead through electronic transmissions, is unsettling but ultimately silly. His recent performance, showcasing how good an actor he is, will hopefully attract more roles deserving of his talent. **IHS**

genre　■ Comedy　■ Fantasy　■ Drama　■ Action　■ Thriller　■ Crime

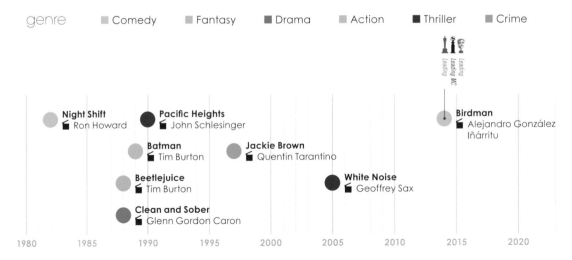

Night Shift
Ron Howard

Pacific Heights
John Schlesinger

Batman
Tim Burton

Jackie Brown
Quentin Tarantino

Beetlejuice
Tim Burton

White Noise
Geoffrey Sax

Clean and Sober
Glenn Gordon Caron

Birdman
Alejandro González Iñárritu

| 1980 | 1985 | 1990 | 1995 | 2000 | 2005 | 2010 | 2015 | 2020 |

harvey keitel 1939

Who's That Knocking at My Door

Mean Streets

Taxi Driver

Fingers

Bugsy

Reservoir Dogs

Pulp Fiction

Smoke

The unacknowledged patron saint of first-time directors, Harvey Keitel has given his blessing to a remarkable array of emerging talent. Starting with Martin Scorsese in 1965, Keitel's extraordinary run of luck extends across four decades. Whether Keitel considers himself lucky is another matter. His career has been defined by its openness to risk and experience. If it is hard to imagine other actors in Keitel's signature roles, then that is surely down to the nature of Keitel's performances and the sense that he has spared nothing of himself.

In 1965, Keitel was working as a court stenographer when he saw an advertisement in a trade paper. A New York University student was looking for an actor for what was then intended as a graduation project. The student was Martin Scorsese, and the film would go on to become the director's first feature, *Who's That Knocking at My Door* (1967). Although the film did well on the festival circuit, its real significance lay in its fraternal pairing of actor and director. Raised in different boroughs, under different faiths, the two New Yorkers had enough of a shared background to realize Scorsese's Lower East Side story. A bond was forged.

Mean Streets (1973) saw Keitel reprise his role as Scorsese's alter ego, making up for his sins not "in the church but on the street." He appeared in Scorsese's next two films, *Alice Doesn't Live Here Anymore* (1974) and *Taxi Driver* (1976). Keitel began to show his range and appeal to first-time directors: he was undaunted by difficult material. The films he made with Ridley Scott (*The Duellists*, 1977), Paul Schrader (*Blue Collar*, 1978) and James Toback (*Fingers*, 1978) represent a high-watermark in his career. By comparison, the 1980s were something of a fallow period, though he emerged from the wilderness with the role of Judas in Scorsese's *The Last Temptation of Christ* (1988).

He began the next decade alongside Jack Nicholson in *The Two Jakes* (1990), though the much anticipated sequel to *Chinatown* (1974) performed poorly at the box office. But then Keitel embarked on a terrific run of films: *Thelma & Louise* (1991), *Bugsy* (1991), *Bad Lieutenant* (1992), *Reservoir Dogs* (1992), *The Piano* (1993), *Pulp Fiction* (1994) and *Smoke* (1995). And with recent roles in *Moonrise Kingdom* (2012) and *The Grand Budapest Hotel* (2014), he seems to have found a place in Scorsese devotee Wes Anderson's repertory company — a home from home. **MM**

genre   ■ Drama   ■ Crime   ■ Comedy

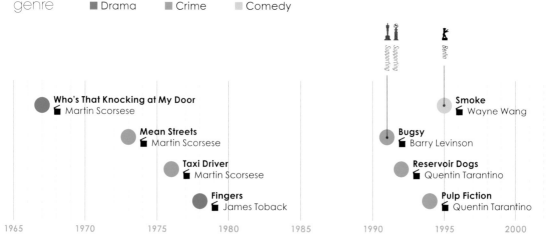

Supporting / Supporting

Berlin

Who's That Knocking at My Door
🎬 Martin Scorsese

Mean Streets
🎬 Martin Scorsese

Taxi Driver
🎬 Martin Scorsese

Fingers
🎬 James Toback

Bugsy
🎬 Barry Levinson

Reservoir Dogs
🎬 Quentin Tarantino

Pulp Fiction
🎬 Quentin Tarantino

Smoke
🎬 Wayne Wang

1965   1970   1975   1980   1985   1990   1995   2000

gene kelly 1912–96

| For Me and My Gal | Anchors Aweigh | The Pirate | Take Me Out to the Ball Game | On the Town | Black Hand | Summer Stock | An American in Paris |

More than just a star of musicals, Gene Kelly was a driving force behind the genre for over two decades, responsible for some of the most lyrical moments in the history of cinema.

Born in 1912, Kelly enrolled at university to study economics but was soon sidetracked by musical theater. He became a dance teacher before moving to New York. His stage breakthrough was in 1939's *The Time of Your Life*; further success followed on Broadway in 1940, with the leading role in *Pal Joey*.

Producer David O. Selznick signed him, but on arrival in Hollywood Kelly discovered half his contract had been sold to MGM and he was to star in *For Me and My Gal* (1942), opposite Judy Garland. The film was a success and the studio bought the other half of his contract. Next came the pedestrian drama *Pilot 5* (1943) and a role opposite Lucille Ball in the Cole Porter penned *Du Barry Was a Lady* (1943). He choreographed his own moves in *Thousands Cheer* (1943), but his real breakthrough on film came opposite Rita Hayworth in *Cover Girl* (1944) and a sequence where he danced with his own reflection.

He entered World War II as a photographer and on his return starred opposite Frank Sinatra in the first of several films together, *Anchors Aweigh* (1945). Although Kelly was Oscar nominated for his acting, it was the dance routines, which he devised and choreographed himself, that drew audiences, making it the biggest hit of the year. In *Ziegfeld Follies* (1946), two legends of Hollywood dance met when Kelly faced off against Fred Astaire.

After being forced to pull out of *Easter Parade* (1948) due to a broken ankle, he appeared with Judy Garland in the critically acclaimed *The Pirate* (1948). Vincente Minnelli's luscious, knowing take on the swashbuckler film found both stars on top form, but it failed commercially. He had better success with the fun *The Three Musketeers* (1948) and his second film with Sinatra, *Take Me Out to the Ball Game* (1949).

Then came the innovative *On the Town* (1949). The success of *Ball Game* gave Kelly some bargaining power with Arthur Freed at MGM, who green lit the film that starred Kelly, Sinatra and Jules Munshin as three sailors let loose in New York. With music by

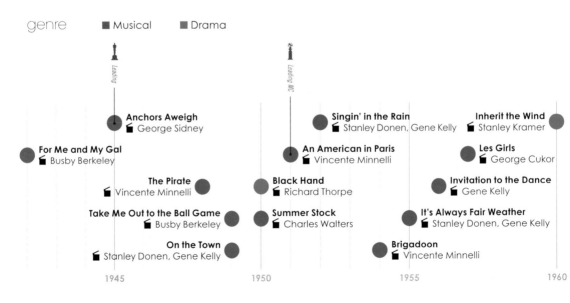

genre   ■ Musical   ■ Drama

Leading

Leading MC

Anchors Aweigh
George Sidney

Singin' in the Rain
Stanley Donen, Gene Kelly

Inherit the Wind
Stanley Kramer

For Me and My Gal
Busby Berkeley

An American in Paris
Vincente Minnelli

Les Girls
George Cukor

The Pirate
Vincente Minnelli

Black Hand
Richard Thorpe

Invitation to the Dance
Gene Kelly

Take Me Out to the Ball Game
Busby Berkeley

Summer Stock
Charles Walters

It's Always Fair Weather
Stanley Donen, Gene Kelly

On the Town
Stanley Donen, Gene Kelly

Brigadoon
Vincente Minnelli

1945   1950   1955   1960

$15M (U.S.)
Singin' in the Rain
(1952)

$65M
Xanadu
(1980)

Singin' in
the Rain

Brigadoon

It's Always
Fair Weather

Invitation to
the Dance

Les Girls

Inherit the
Wind

The Young
Girls of
Rochefort

Xanadu

Leonard Bernstein and Roger Edens, and codirected by Kelly and acclaimed Broadway choreographer Stanley Donen, the film is a marvel of Technicolor and invention in its use of actual locations.

Rather than make another musical, the actor gave one of his few straight dramatic performances in *Black Hand* (1950). Set in the early 20th century, he plays an Italian who returns to New York to avenge his father's death, at the hands of a crime syndicate. A low-key film noir, Kelly is impressive as a man seeking justice. He brought the same passion to his other notable dramatic role, in *Inherit the Wind* (1960), as a newspaperman who supports the notion of Darwinism.

Kelly's last pairing with Garland was *Summer Stock* (1950), an indifferent musical that pales in comparison to his remarkable collaboration with Minnelli, *An American in Paris* (1951). Inspired by George Gershwin's 1928 composition, Kelly and his director create a magical world. The song and dance routines are perfectly executed, but it is the film's climax that attracted acclaim. Brokenhearted, Kelly dances to Gershwin's score in a 15-minute sequence that blends the modern and classical, against a backdrop inspired by French painters.

He went further with *Singin' in the Rain* (1952). One of the greatest films ever made and a brilliant parody of the period when Hollywood introduced sound, Kelly reunited with Donen to direct and also star. He was rarely better. The whole thing rockets along with audiences barely allowed to catch their breath between jokes, songs and inspired dance routines.

The Hollywood musical began to wane by the mid-1950s. *Brigadoon* (1954) was dull compared to Kelly's previous films. *It's Always Fair Weather* (1955) was fun, but audiences stayed away. George Cukor's *Les Girls* (1957) was stylish and attracted a sizeable box office, but lost money because of the scale of its production.

Kelly's best musical in later years was made in France. *The Young Girls of Rochefort* (1967) was Jaques Demy's homage to the kinds of film Kelly made at the height of his fame. He directed the hugely successful *Hello Dolly!* (1969) and a decade later appeared in *Xanadu* (1980). Not the finest musical to go out on, but then Kelly had nothing to prove. **IHS**

K

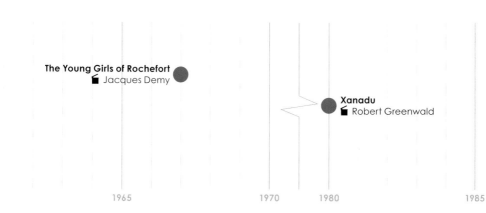

The Young Girls of Rochefort
Jacques Demy

Xanadu
Robert Greenwald

1965   1970   1980   1985

gene kelly 287

grace kelly 1929–82

Fourteen Hours

High Noon

Mogambo

The Country Girl

Dial M for Murder

Rear Window

When Grace Kelly died in a car accident, aged 52, it was a tragic end to what most people saw as a fairy-tale life. Blonde, blue-eyed, classically beautiful, Kelly became a major Hollywood star at 23. Her image was one of cool serenity, desirable but chaste — "the pious man's Marilyn Monroe." But after a screen career lasting just five years and 11 films, she married a reigning European monarch and retired from acting.

Wherever Hollywood is involved, the gap between image and reality is considerable, but this is perhaps never greater than in the case of Grace Kelly. Even by Tinseltown standards, the list of Kelly's lovers is impressive. Most of her leading men, several of her directors, Marlon Brando, Frank Sinatra, David Niven, Prince Aly Khan, the Shah of Iran and many more. That, despite all this, she still managed to preserve that public image of white-gloved purity, says a lot for the power of the Hollywood studios in the 1950s.

And also for Kelly herself. A few wronged wives apart, everybody genuinely liked her. She was sweet, friendly and gentle. On-set she was the complete professional. And, intentionally or not, she exuded an air of vulnerability — people wanted to protect her.

Her first screen role, in Henry Hathaway's taut thriller *Fourteen Hours* (1951), was small and attracted little attention. But stardom beckoned with Fred Zinnemann's classic western *High Noon* (1952), where she played Gary Cooper's newlywed Quaker wife, torn between her rejection of violence and loyalty to her husband. *Mogambo* (1953) was minor-league John Ford, but by now Alfred Hitchcock, always on the lookout for another cool blonde had taken notice.

Dial M for Murder (1954), hampered by its stage origins and the studio's insistence on 3D, did not give Kelly much scope as the woman whose husband (Ray Milland) plans to have her killed. But then came *Rear Window* (1954), her finest film, with Hitch on top form. Kelly's scenes with her fiancé James Stewart's photographer, immobilized with his leg in plaster, allowed her to explore a wealth of sexual teasing.

genre ■ Drama ■ Western ■ Adventure ■ Thriller ■ War ■ Romance

Fourteen Hours — Henry Hathaway
High Noon — Fred Zinnemann
Mogambo — John Ford
Supporting

1950 · 1951 · 1952 · 1953

$110M (U.S.)
Dial M for Murder
(1954)

$321M (U.S.)
Rear Window
(1954)

The Bridges at
Toko-Ri

Green Fire

To Catch a Thief

The Swan

High Society

Hard-working as ever, Kelly made five films in 1954 alone. Neither *The Bridges at Toko-Ri*, a routine war movie, nor *Green Fire*, a routine action-adventure, had much to offer her apart from standard romantic interest parts. But *The Country Girl*, rarely seen these days, won Kelly her sole Oscar. As the cynical wife of a washed-up actor, she dressed down, playing older than her years. It suggested that, given a longer career and more flexibility from the studios, she could have encompassed a much wider range of roles.

But in the spring of 1955, Kelly was introduced to Prince Rainier III of Monaco, who urgently needed an heir. The press leapt avidly on the romance, and the future pattern of her life began to be laid down for her. There was one final film for Hitchcock, though: *To Catch a Thief* (1955), set on the Riviera. This was Hitch in light-comedy mode, with Cary Grant as a retired cat burglar and Kelly as a pretty American tourist turned on by the idea of sex with a crook. She plays it with a light touch, relishing the innuendoes.

The Swan (1956) was creaky, old-fashioned stuff. *High Society* (1956) had more life to it; a musical remake of *The Philadelphia Story* (1940), with Kelly in the Katharine Hepburn role of a divorcee about to remarry who realizes she still has feelings for her ex. It was diverting enough, if you could forget the original.

Then came the wedding. On Kelly's side of the bargain she came through. Three children and the succession was secured. Drawn by the fairy-tale glamour, tourists started to flock to Monaco, turning around the mini-state's economy. Meanwhile, Rainier, diverted himself with a string of girlfriends.

Kelly now found herself trapped in the decorous image she had fostered. Bored by state protocol and desperately homesick, she tried to revive her acting career — for Hitchcock in *The Birds* (1963), then for Herbert Ross with *The Turning Point* (1977) — but both times the idea was vetoed. Lonely and alienated, Kelly took to drinking. To many of her friends, her death, horrible as it was, seemed something of a release. **PK**

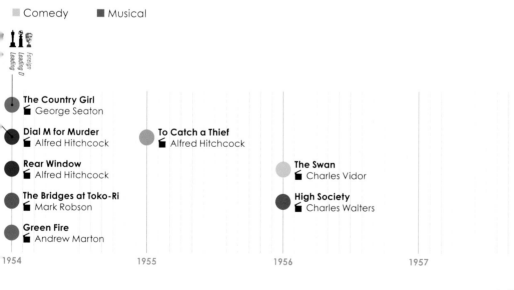

Comedy ■ Musical

Foreign
Leading D
Leading

The Country Girl
George Seaton

Dial M for Murder
Alfred Hitchcock

Rear Window
Alfred Hitchcock

The Bridges at Toko-Ri
Mark Robson

Green Fire
Andrew Marton

To Catch a Thief
Alfred Hitchcock

The Swan
Charles Vidor

High Society
Charles Walters

1954   1955   1956   1957

deborah kerr 1921–2007

The Life and Death of Colonel Blimp

I See a Dark Stranger

Black Narcissus

From Here to Eternity

The King and I

Heaven Knows, Mr. Allison

Separate Tables

The Sundowners

Born in Glasgow in 1921, Deborah Kerr trained as a ballerina but soon crossed over to drama. Talent-spotted by producer Gabriel Pascal, she was cast in a minor role in *Major Barbara* (1941) but promoted to leads in *Love on the Dole* (1941), *Penn of Pennsylvania*, *Hatter's Castle* and *The Day Will Dawn* (all 1942).

Her big artistic — if not commercial — break came with *The Life and Death of Colonel Blimp* (1943) in which Michael Powell and Emeric Pressburger cast her as the three women who loomed largest in the title character's life. She would later headline their extraordinary *Black Narcissus* (1947) as the most senior of the nuns in a Himalayan convent. Before that she worked for Alexander Korda on the acclaimed *Perfect Strangers* (1945) and starred with Trevor Howard in *I See a Dark Stranger* (1946).

Pascal then sold her contract to MGM, propelling her across the Atlantic where she starred opposite Clark Gable (*The Hucksters*, 1947), Spencer Tracy (*Edward, My Son*, 1949) and fellow expat Stewart Granger (*King Solomon's Mines*, 1950). The Oscar nomination for *Edward, My Son* notwithstanding, her roles in this period were not especially challenging. That changed with *From Here to Eternity* (1953), which

cast her against type. Her character's adulterous clinch in the surf with Burt Lancaster caused a sensation — and led to a second Oscar nomination.

The End of the Affair (1955) saw her as another adulteress, while *The Proud and the Profane* (1956) was a transparent attempt at copying her earlier hit. But she then changed gear again, appearing in *The King and I* (1956) at costar Yul Brynner's insistence, her singing voice dubbed by Marni Nixon. *Heaven Knows, Mr. Allison* (1957) cast her as another nun, this time opposite Robert Mitchum's U.S. marine, with whom she is stranded on an island during World War II. These secured two more Oscar nominations, with yet more for *Separate Tables* (1958) and *The Sundowners* (1960).

She then played one of her greatest roles, as the repressed governess in *The Innocents* (1961) whose various ghostly encounters may or may not be happening in her feverish imagination. But her films thereafter were mainly undistinguished, and after performing her first nude scene in *The Gypsy Moths* (1969) she abandoned the big screen in favor of stage and television work. She made a brief return to the cinema in *The Assam Garden* (1985), before ill health dictated a permanent retirement. She died in 2007. **MBr**

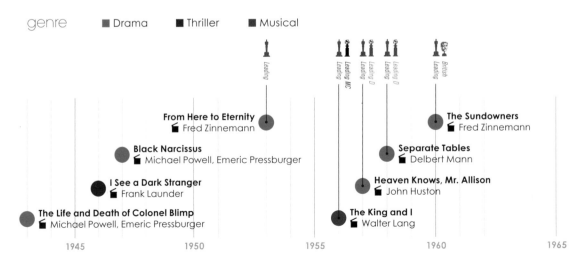

genre ■ Drama ■ Thriller ■ Musical

From Here to Eternity
🎬 Fred Zinnemann

The Sundowners
🎬 Fred Zinnemann

Black Narcissus
🎬 Michael Powell, Emeric Pressburger

Separate Tables
🎬 Delbert Mann

I See a Dark Stranger
🎬 Frank Launder

Heaven Knows, Mr. Allison
🎬 John Huston

The Life and Death of Colonel Blimp
🎬 Michael Powell, Emeric Pressburger

The King and I
🎬 Walter Lang

1945   1950   1955   1960   1965

shah rukh khan 1965

Darr

Karan Arjun

Dilwale
Dulhania Le
Jayenge

Devdas

Main
Hoon Na

Swades

Chakde!
India

My Name
Is Khan

The year 1965 was an important one for Indian cinema. It witnessed the birth of the (unrelated) Khan triumvirate Shah Rukh, Salman and Aamir, who would go on to dominate Bollywood from the early 1990s to the present day. Salman has cornered the action market, while Aamir acts in mostly intelligent projects. However, it is Shah Rukh Khan who is considered India's biggest movie star globally, with appearances from him bringing Berlin, Paris, London and Los Angeles to a standstill due to the sheer numbers of fans desperate to catch a glimpse. The *Los Angeles Times* described him as "the biggest movie star you've never heard of."

Shah Rukh Khan does not generally act in genre movies, unless you count Bollywood as a genre. His films have a bit of everything, although primarily romance, where he is India's biggest lover after 1970s icon Rajesh Khanna. There is also goofy humor, melodrama and some action thrown into the mix.

He debuted with *Deewana* (1992), but it was his turns as an obsessive lover in *Baazigar* and *Darr* (both 1993) that catapulted him into the big time. *Dilwale Dulhania Le Jayenge* (1995), the longest running Indian film of all time — it is still playing in Mumbai's Maratha Mandir cinema — cemented his position as the ultimate romantic icon. His long roster of romantic hits includes *Pardes* (1997), *Dil To Pagal Hai* (1997), *Kuch Kuch Hota Hai* (1998), *Mohabbatein* (2000), *Kabhi Khushi Kabhi Gham* (2001), *Devdas* (2002),

Kal Ho Naa Ho (2003) and *Veer Zaara* (2004), among many others.

As a producer, Khan has had the freedom to dabble in various genres, with the historical *Asoka* (2001), the fantasy *Paheli* (2005) and sci-fi *Ra.One* (2011), but his Bollywood ventures with director Farah Khan, *Main Hoon Naa* (2004), *Om Shanti Om* (2007) and *Happy New Year* (2014), have proven the most successful. And despite his image as a being primarily a romantic entertainer, Khan has also displayed his acting prowess, most notably in *Swades* (2004), where he plays a NASA scientist who returns to India to help bring electricity to his village; *Chakde! India* (2007), as a hockey coach in quest of redemption; and *My Name Is Khan* (2010), as a man with Asperger's syndrome who journeys across post 9/11 America to highlight the plight of Muslims. He won the Filmfare Award for Best Actor for all three performances.

A shrewd businessman, Khan has a range of interests, including the film and television production company Red Chillies and the cricket team Kolkata Knight Riders. He also tours the world with a Bollywood troupe, his concerts selling out any arenas they are booked into. His net worth is estimated to be more than $600 million, a proportion of which he donates to charities of his choice, as anonymously as it is possible in a country where he lives like goldfish in a bowl and with paparazzi lenses trained on his every move. **NR**

K

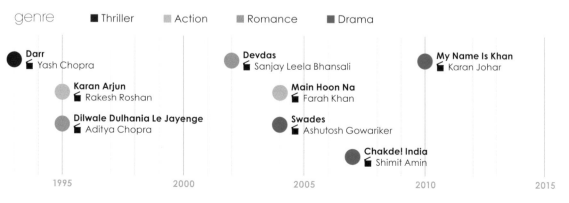

genre   ■ Thriller   ■ Action   ■ Romance   ■ Drama

Darr
🎬 Yash Chopra

Karan Arjun
🎬 Rakesh Roshan

Dilwale Dulhania Le Jayenge
🎬 Aditya Chopra

Devdas
🎬 Sanjay Leela Bhansali

Main Hoon Na
🎬 Farah Khan

Swades
🎬 Ashutosh Gowariker

Chakde! India
🎬 Shimit Amin

My Name Is Khan
🎬 Karan Johar

1995   2000   2005   2010   2015

nicole kidman 1967

| Flirting | Far and Away | To Die For | The Portrait of a Lady | Eyes Wide Shut | Moulin Rouge! | The Others | The Hours |

Nicole Kidman is, in some senses, a throwback to the stars of the studio heyday — an emblem of old-fashioned elegance and high glamour. But for all her cover-star poise, she has earned her high profile through her skill as an actress and at her best she is a performer with an adventurous range and directness.

Born in Hawaii to Australian parents, Kidman featured as a teenager in a number of low-budget Australian films. Her breakthrough came with a compelling performance in the sailing thriller *Dead Calm* (1989). With her blaze of tightly curled red hair, Kidman was also a strikingly beautiful lead, and unsurprisingly, Hollywood came calling.

Her U.S. debut was not the most auspicious of beginnings: the car-racing drama *Days of Thunder* (1990). It was one of the biggest hits of the year and Kidman, starring alongside soon-to-be husband Tom Cruise, did well to get noticed among the bombast of Tony Scott's fireworks. Following a lively turn in the coming-of-age comedy *Flirting* (1991), she reunited with Cruise for *Far and Away* (1992), Ron Howard's visually sweeping tale about two Irish immigrants

in 1890s America. Her performance as the lively daughter of an affluent landlord received better reviews than the overblown film. Kidman made more of an impact in smaller, less commercial fare. She was outstanding in Gus Van Sant's *To Die For* (1995) — witty and commandingly seductive as a ruthlessly ambitious television weatherwoman. She also gave a performance of intelligence and poignancy as the tragic heroine of the 1996 adaptation of Henry James' *The Portrait of a Lady*. While the film was flawed, Kidman's commitment to the role revealed her depth and subtlety as an actress.

Kidman's next big role was her most challenging yet. In Stanley Kubrick's *Eyes Wide Shut* (1999), she played a young married woman whose confession of sexual desire for another man profoundly unsettles her husband, played by Cruise. Her enormously nuanced performance suggests, with moving subtlety, her character's interior torments, of a piece with the film's larger sense of ambiguity and teasing mystery.

Over the course of the next decade, she continued to pursue ambitious roles that tested her range. Her

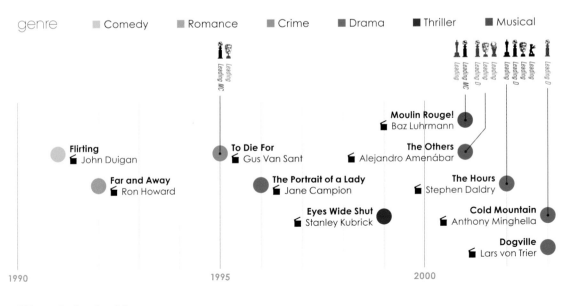

genre   ■ Comedy   ■ Romance   ■ Crime   ■ Drama   ■ Thriller   ■ Musical

Flirting
John Duigan

Far and Away
Ron Howard

To Die For
Gus Van Sant

The Portrait of a Lady
Jane Campion

Eyes Wide Shut
Stanley Kubrick

Moulin Rouge!
Baz Luhrmann

The Others
Alejandro Amenábar

The Hours
Stephen Daldry

Cold Mountain
Anthony Minghella

Dogville
Lars von Trier

1990   1995   2000

$231 M	$33 M (U.S.)	$228 M	$238 M	$278 M	$142 M	$221 M	$230 M
Far and Away (1992)	To Die For (1995)	Eyes Wide Shut (1999)	Moulin Rouge! (2001)	The Others (2001)	The Hours (2002)	Cold Mountain (2003)	Australia (2008)

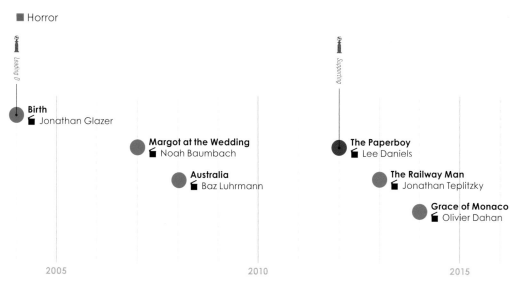

| Cold Mountain | Dogville | Birth | Margot at the Wedding | Australia | The Paperboy | The Railway Man | Grace of Monaco |

decision to collaborate with the provocative Danish director Lars von Trier for his bleak, radically minimalist small-town drama *Dogville* (2003), surprised many. However, her brave performance, which lent a fleshy and poignant humanity to von Trier's occasionally didactic script, was widely admired.

For Alejandro Amenábar she gave another assured turn in the clever ghost story *The Others* (2001), her outward poise gradually disintegrating to reveal her character's profound distress. A year later, she was Virginia Woolf in Stephen Daldry's *The Hours* (2002); her melancholy turn as the novelist on the day of her suicide wining her an Oscar.

It was for Jonathan Glazer, that Kidman gave one of her richest performances. *Birth* (2004) saw her play an affluent Manhattan widow who becomes convinced that her deceased husband has been reincarnated as a 10-year-old boy. She is deeply affecting in a film now recognized as one of the best of that decade.

Kidman has also excelled in lighter roles. Her gutsy performance in the 2001 musical *Moulin Rouge!* matched the film's camp exuberance, and she was wickedly good fun as the scheming title character in the caustic *Margot at the Wedding* (2007). Her attempts at more mainstream comedy have fared less well. Both *The Stepford Wives* (2004) and *Bewitched* (2005) were commercial and critical failures.

Kidman has also made some dubious choices with heavyweight dramas. Her Southern belle, separated from her lover by the Civil War in Anthony Minghella's *Cold Mountain* (2003), was alternately muted and mannered. While her performance in Baz Luhrmann's kitsch epic *Australia* (2008) veers erratically between the unfunny and melodramatic. And she was stiffly unconvincing as the lead of the critical flop *Grace of Monaco* (2014).

But she can still impress. She was unsettling in *Fur: An Imaginary Portrait of Diane Arbus* (2006) and several recent performance have revealed a new range. She is magnificently uninhibited in Lee Daniels' lurid 2012 melodrama *The Paperboy*, while she brings restraint and quiet dignity to *The Railway Man* (2013). And who can begrudge a little archness in her portrayal of the villainous taxidermist in *Paddington* (2014). **EL**

■ Horror

Leading D / Supporting

Birth
Jonathan Glazer

Margot at the Wedding
Noah Baumbach

Australia
Baz Luhrmann

The Paperboy
Lee Daniels

The Railway Man
Jonathan Teplitzky

Grace of Monaco
Olivier Dahan

2005　　　　2010　　　　2015

Far and Away
(1992)

Moulin Rouge!
(2001)

The Others
(2001)

The Hours
(2002)

Cold Mountain
(2003)

Birth
(2004)

Australia
(2008)

The Paperboy
(2012)

Far and Away starred Kidman and her then-husband Tom Cruise as Irish immigrants seeking their fortune in 1890s America. It was the second film to feature the pair, after 1990's *Days of Thunder*.

Kidman and Ewan McGregor in Baz Luhrmann's lavish jukebox musical ***Moulin Rouge!*** Despite being terrified of singing in front of an audience, the actress received widespread acclaim and an Academy Award nomination for her performance.

Set in the immediate aftermath of World War II, **The Others** starred Kidman as the mother of two children who cannot be exposed to sunlight due to a rare disease.

Kidman scooped numerous awards for her turn as Virginia Woolf in **The Hours**, including a Best Actress Oscar.

ased on the bestselling novel by Charles Frazier, **Cold Mountain** starred Kidman and Jude Law as lovers
parated by the American Civil War.

Booed when it premiered at the Venice Film Festival, several
critics have now called for a reappraisal of the chilling **Birth**.

euniting Kidman with director Baz Luhrmann, **Australia** told the story of English aristocrat Sarah Ashley and her fight to save the outback cattle station she unexpectedly inherits.
med on location in Western Australia, the movie was used by Tourism Australia as part of a campaign to increase visitor numbers to the country.

dman and **Australia** costar Hugh Jackman. Director Baz Luhrmann envisaged the movie as the Australian
one with the Wind (1939).

The Guardian review of **The Paperboy** described Kidman's
performance as "funny, sexy, poignantly vulnerable."

klaus kinski 1926–91

| For a Few Dollars More | Doctor Zhivago | A Bullet for the General | The Great Silence | Count Dracula | Aguirre, Wrath of God | Jack the Ripper | Woyzeck |

There will never be another actor like Klaus Kinski. Director Werner Herzog stresses this in his entertaining documentary about his relationship with the German actor, *My Best Fiend* (1999). They made five films together but the link between them stretched far beyond cinema. The film opens with the actor standing before a packed auditorium, playing his own interpretation of Jesus, haranguing an audience as they hurl abuse at him. It is a startling sight. But little about the actor was conventional.

He was born Klaus Gunther Nakszynski in 1926, to German parents in the Free City of Danzig. He fought very briefly in the German Wehrmacht during World War II, but was injured by British troops and served out the remainder of the conflict in the UK. On his release, he returned to Germany, entered the theater and made his screen debut as a Dutch concentration camp prisoner in *Morituri* (1948). He followed it with uncredited appearances in Anatole Litvak's *Decision Before Dawn* (1951) and Roberto Rossellini's *Fear* (1954), before taking on a number of roles in German productions and ending the decade as a cast member in Douglas Sirk's war drama, *A Time to Love and a Time to Die* (1958).

Kinski appeared in more than 50 films in the 1960s alone. They ranged from exploitation and horror to European westerns and more prestige studio productions. With his odd features and intense presence, he was the perfect character actor. Highlights include *Doctor Zhivago* (1965), in which he played an anarchist being transported to a gulag, a bizarre performance as the controversial French libertine and author in *Marquis de Sade: Justine* (1969), an embattled German officer fighting off American G.I.s in the "macaroni combat" war film *Five for Hell* (1969), and a tortured Renfield in *Count Dracula* (1970).

His most famous appearance from this period was as the hunchback gunslinger, a member of Gian Maria Volenté's gang, in *For a Few Dollars More* (1965). It was the first of a number of spaghetti westerns the actor appeared in, which also included *A Bullet for the General* (1966), *Pride and Vengeance* (1967), *The Ruthless Four* (1968) and *The Great Silence* (1968).

Kinski kept up the frenetic rate of film roles in the early 1970s, starring in an average of five films a year. The genres remained the same, although by mid-way through the decade the demand for European westerns was wearing thin. The key role from this period was as the eponymous explorer in Werner Herzog's *Aguirre, Wrath of God* (1972). It presents an account of a mission undertaken by Spanish conquistadors deep into the Amazonian jungle in search of the mythical city of El Dorado. As the journey progresses the men lose heart, leaving Lope

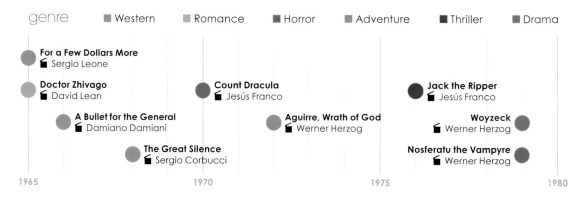

genre ■ Western ■ Romance ■ Horror ■ Adventure ■ Thriller ■ Drama

For a Few Dollars More
Sergio Leone

Doctor Zhivago
David Lean

A Bullet for the General
Damiano Damiani

The Great Silence
Sergio Corbucci

Count Dracula
Jesús Franco

Aguirre, Wrath of God
Werner Herzog

Jack the Ripper
Jesús Franco

Woyzeck
Werner Herzog

Nosferatu the Vampyre
Werner Herzog

1965 1970 1975 1980

Nosferatu
the Vampyre

Buddy
Buddy

Fitzcarraldo

Android

The Little
Drummer
Girl

Cobra
Verde

Paganini

My Best
Fiend

de Aguirre alone in his determination to continue. From its breathtaking opening shot, of soldiers traveling along the path that leads to Machu Picchu, to the film's final moments, with Aguirre floating aimlessly on a raft populated by monkeys, the drama profits enormously from Kinski's wild performance. He is convincing in his portrayal of a man gradually unhinged by the immensity of his mission and the sense of abjection at his failure, not only to complete his task, but at the realization that he will die in this world.

He played the title character in Herzog's *Nosferatu the Vampyre* (1979), the director's homage to F.W. Murnau's 1922 film. Unlike contemporary versions of the Dracula myth, Kinski's vampire is a sad, pathetic creature whom, one senses, feels genuine emotion for Isabelle Adjani's Lucy Harker, but cannot help his baser instincts. Aided by the film's ethereal lighting and stunning production design, Kinski's monster is a remarkable creation. Sadly, one of the actor's last films, *Vampire in Venice* (1988), is a pale imitation.

In the same year, Kinski and Herzog worked on an adaptation of Georg Büchner's play *Woyzeck* (1979). Originally written as a commentary on class and the privations of poverty, Herzog's film also tackles the psychological impact of institutionalized behavior. Kinski's simple soldier is put through a battery of unnecessary tests on the orders of his captain and his severe mental breakdown results in his violent outburst. Once again, the actor is startling in his portrayal, conveying the pain and despair of the character, even as he loses any last grasp on the real world.

The actor was apparently offered a role in Steven Spielberg's 1981 blockbuster *Raiders of the Lost Ark*, turning it down because the script was "moronically shitty." Instead, that year he played a sexual therapist who has eloped with Jack Lemmon's wife in Billy Wilder's *Buddy Buddy*. The following year he appeared as an industrialist who decides to build an opera house deep in the Peruvian jungle in *Fitzcarraldo*. Herzog's most ambitious film, it also features one of Kinski's finest performances, although his behavior on set, as can be seen in Les Blank's making of film, *Burden of Dreams* (1982), had become erratic at best. However, like his Aguirre, on film Kinski is a magnetic presence.

The actor and director's final feature together, *Cobra Verde* (1987), based on Bruce Chatwin's 1980 novel *The Viceroy of Ouidah* about the life of a fictional Brazilian slave trader, lacks the power of their earlier films. Kinski's career slowed down at the end of the 1980s and he died in 1991, leaving behind a controversial legacy, both on film and in his personal life. **IHS**

K

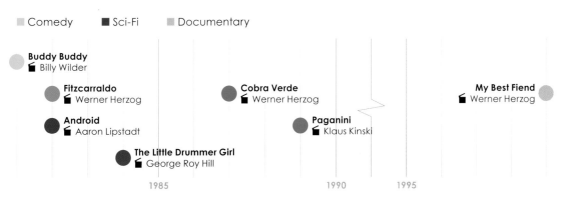

■ Comedy   ■ Sci-Fi   ■ Documentary

Buddy Buddy
 Billy Wilder

Fitzcarraldo
 Werner Herzog

Android
 Aaron Lipstadt

The Little Drummer Girl
 George Roy Hill

Cobra Verde
 Werner Herzog

Paganini
 Klaus Kinski

My Best Fiend
 Werner Herzog

1985   1990   1995

takeshi kitano 1947

Merry Christmas Mr. Lawrence | Violent Cop | Sonatine | Hana-Bi | Gohatto | Battle Royale | Zatoichi | Outrage

With a screen persona that is as much inspired by Buster Keaton's deadpan loner as it is a Melville antihero, "Beat" Takeshi Kitano is an internationally acclaimed actor and filmmaker, while in his native Japan he is also regarded as something of a renaissance man: comedian, writer, poet, columnist, television presenter, producer and visiting professor at Tokyo University. On screen, he has played sadistic gangsters and violent cops, but his best roles are those informed by his early career as a stand-up comic, allowing him to undermine masculine stereotypes.

Born in Tokyo in 1947, Kitano began his career as a comedian in a double act called"The Two Beats." A film career began after he abandoned the act, his breakthrough role being the personable sergeant in Nagisa Ôshima's Merry Christmas Mr. Lawrence (1983), charged with guarding British and Commonwealth troops in a prisoner of war camp.

Violent Cop (1989) marked Kitano's directorial debut. He plays a police officer whose response to his colleague's suicide and sister's kidnapping by local yakuza thugs drives him to commit unspeakable acts of violence. In Boiling Point (1990) he is a psychotic yakuza thug whose actions threaten the lives of all around him, while in Sonatine (1993) he is a veteran gangster tired of his life and desperate to find a way out. The three films found Kitano quickly developing his on-screen persona, from a cruel, taciturn figure to something warmer, albeit no less violent. Sonatine is the best of the three, both as director and actor. The persona that has come to inform his characters since is fully formed by the film's nihilistic end.

Hana-Bi (1997) features his best performance to date. A touching, funny and occasionally violent drama, it tells the story of a disgraced cop who takes his dying wife on a second honeymoon. His subsequent film, Kikujiro (1999), felt slight by comparison. He then directed himself in his only period feature, playing the legendary blind swordsman Zatoichi (2003). It is one of his most enjoyable, playful performances. He has continued to star in his own films, the best of which is his recent crime diptych Outrage (2010) and Beyond Outrage (2012), although like his earlier, brutal Brother (2000), his character's acts of violence are sometimes hard to stomach.

Elsewhere, Kitano was wasted in Johnny Mnemonic (1995), but is superb as the sadistic games organizer in the blackly comic Battle Royale (2000). However, the actor's best performance outside his own films is in his second feature with Ôshima. Gohatto (1999) is a exploration of homosexuality within a samurai elite and Kitano excels as a powerful commander, offering up a subdued performance that stands in stark contrast to his more violent gangsters. **IHS**

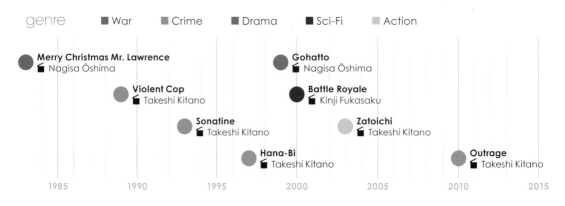

genre ■ War ■ Crime ■ Drama ■ Sci-Fi ■ Action

alan ladd 1913–64

| This Gun For Hire | The Glass Key | The Blue Dahlia | Two Years Before the Mast | O.S.S. | The Great Gatsby | Shane | The Carpet-baggers |

Alan Ladd specialized in playing stoic-but-soft-spoken tough guys. Born in Arkansas, he was primarily a stage and radio actor in the first part of his career. Aside from small supporting roles in films like *Rulers of the Sea* (1939) and *Joan of Paris* (1942), he was a prolific and often uncredited presence among other bit players in a range of films that included *Citizen Kane* (1941).

His breakthrough finally came playing the doubled-crossed hit man Raven in *This Gun For Hire* (1942). His unsmiling performance would shepherd in a new portrayal of gangsters on screen, which he continued with his first starring role, as the title-character in *Lucky Jordan* (1942). *This Gun For Hire* was also Ladd's first role alongside Veronica Lake, with whom he would be paired with on three further occasions: the noir classics *The Glass Key* (1942) and *The Blue Dahlia* (1946) and *Saigon* (1948).

Firmly established as a star and under contract with Paramount, Ladd appeared in a series of popular films for the studio throughout the 1940s. They included *China* (1943), *And Now Tomorrow* (1944), *Two Years Before the Mast* (1946), *O.S.S.* (1946), *Beyond Glory* (1948) and *The Great Gatsby* (1949).

Ladd continued to star in film noirs like *Chicago Deadline* (1949) and *Appointment with Danger* (1951), but increasingly worked in westerns, appearing in *Whispering Smith* (1948), *Branded* (1950) and *Red Mountain* (1951). His best known role was as the titular drifter in George Stevens' classic western *Shane* (1953); the film's ambiguous final scene became Ladd's most indelible cinematic moment.

After a successful partnership with Paramount a dissatisfied Ladd chose to move on. Although he continued to star in films, including *The Red Beret* (1953), *Hell Below Zero* (1954) and *The Black Knight* (1954), his career lost its momentum. He mistakenly turned down the role of Jet Rink in Stevens' *Giant* (1956), which went on to become one of the biggest hits of the 1950s. He formed his own production company, frequently producing as well as starring in films such as *Hell on Frisco Bay* (1955), *The Big Land* (1957) and the Michael Curtiz-directed noir *The Man in the Net* (1959). He was also the star of *Boy on a Dolphin* (1957), which is notable now for being Sophia Loren's English-language debut. However, he struggled to recapture his earlier popularity and was barely working at all by the time he starred in the crime drama *13 West Street* (1962). Ladd appeared likely to have a late career resurgence after playing an ageing cowboy turned actor in *The Carpetbaggers* (1964), but passed away of an accidental overdose before the film's release and substantial commercial success. **JWa**

genre   ■ Crime   ■ Adventure   ■ War   ■ Drama   ■ Western

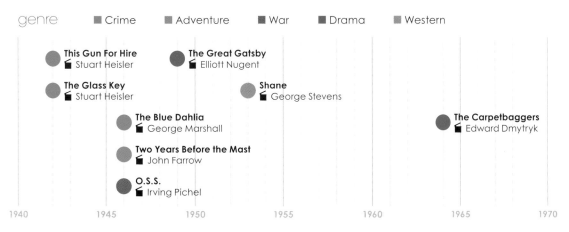

burt lancaster 1913–94

The Killers

Brute Force

The Crimson Pirate

From Here to Eternity

Vera Cruz

Apache

Gunfight at the O.K. Corral

Sweet Smell of Success

Through all Burt Lancaster's best roles — and through his own personality — there runs an element of ambiguity. Director Lindsay Anderson spotted it very early on in the actor's career, noting "this odd mixture of violence and decency, this goodwill that has not quite found a satisfactory channel of expression." Put certain descriptions side by side, and it is hard to believe they are referring to the same person. Writer Andrew Collins described the dominant features of Lancaster's face as "the jutting jaw and the pleading, kind eyes." Novelist Norman Mailer wrote of "the coldest eyes I've ever looked into."

Lancaster came to screen acting late. He was born in east Harlem and started out as an acrobat, quitting New York University to join the circus. The daredevil trapeze act that he developed with Nick Cravat — who partnered him in several of his films — supplied him with an athlete's dexterity of movement. Right into old age he moved with a catlike grace.

By the time Lancaster made his screen debut in The Killers (1946) he was 33. As an ex-prizefighter passively awaiting death at the hands of hit men, he was already showing the flipside of his dominant physical presence. The very first time we see him on screen,

he is lying on his back in the dark — not hiding, simply succumbing to the oblivion that he knows he cannot escape. In real life, though, Lancaster was anything but passive. Together with New York agent Harold Hecht and producer-writer James Hill, he formed Hecht-Hill-Lancaster. Not since the formation of United Artists in 1920 had an independent combine exerted such muscle against the power of the studios.

The arrangement enabled Lancaster to secure much better terms from the studios and, more importantly, allowed him to choose his roles. Following The Killers, he often found himself typecast as neurotic tough guys, his eyes shaded by snap-brim hats. With his growing power as an independent he could break away and explore a multiplicity of roles, including those no big studio would ever allow a contract star of Lancaster's stamp. Not that all his early films conformed to formula. He was powerful as a convict driven beyond endurance in Dassin's Brute Force (1947), while The Flame and the Arrow (1950) and The Crimson Pirate (1952) were sheer exuberant self-indulgence, with Lancaster showing off by doing his own stunts.

Those swashbucklers gave free rein to the barnstorming hamminess in Lancaster's acting, the

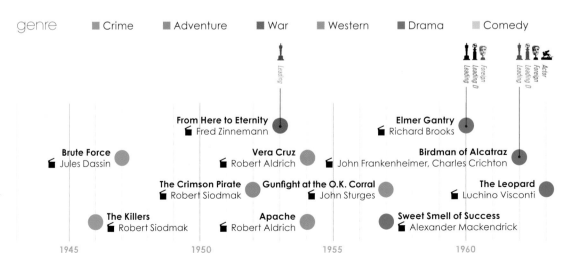

genre ■ Crime ■ Adventure ■ War ■ Western ■ Drama ■ Comedy

Brute Force — Jules Dassin

From Here to Eternity — Fred Zinnemann

The Crimson Pirate — Robert Siodmak

The Killers — Robert Siodmak

Vera Cruz — Robert Aldrich

Gunfight at the O.K. Corral — John Sturges

Apache — Robert Aldrich

Elmer Gantry — Richard Brooks

Birdman of Alcatraz — John Frankenheimer, Charles Crichton

Sweet Smell of Success — Alexander Mackendrick

The Leopard — Luchino Visconti

1945   1950   1955   1960

| Elmer Gantry | Birdman of Alcatraz | The Leopard | The Train | Ulzana's Raid | Conversation Piece | Buffalo Bill and the Indians | Local Hero |

larger-than-life gestures and the wide toothy grin that earned him the nickname "Crockery Joe." He could turn this side of his persona to good use, as a megalomaniac general in *Seven Days in May* (1964), or in his Oscar-winning portrayal of *Elmer Gantry* (1960), where it perfectly fitted the con-artist preacher, hyped up on his own verbal charlatanry. But in the same film he can tone right down to the tenderness of his scenes with Jean Simmons.

The more quietly the power and danger in the actor's persona are deployed, the greater their effect. In *Sweet Smell of Success* (1957) his vindictive columnist J.J. Hunsecker always speaks in calm, measured tones. His movements are reined in and closed off, his arms rigid with the tension of a powerful man channeling his force into devious psychological outlets.

The subtlety of Lancaster's performance in *Sweet Smell* — as well as the gentleness of his lifer in *Birdman of Alcatraz* (1962), and the pathos of his alcoholic husband in *Come Back, Little Sheba* (1952) — makes it the more surprising that Luchino Visconti was initially opposed to casting him as the Prince in *The Leopard* (1963). Even dubbed, Lancaster brings to the role an instinctive nobility colored by regret at the

changes and deterioration he sees but cannot stem. It is something of the same quality that he found in his veteran scout McIntosh in *Ulzana's Raid* (1972), too clear-eyed to deny that things are going steadily from bad to worse and too wearily fatalistic to try to prevent them.

Lancaster could also play vulnerable characters — as in *The Swimmer* (1968), embodying the disintegration of the suburban American Dream, or in *Atlantic City* (1981), where he is a former small-time mobster washed up in the New Jersey seaside resort, living on odd jobs, numbers-running and fantasies of his one-time intimacy with Al Capone and Lucky Luciano.

The teaming for which Lancaster is best remembered — with Kirk Douglas in *Gunfight at the O.K. Corral* (1957), *Seven Days in May*, *Tough Guys* (1986) and several more — though entertaining and generally good box office, produced some of his least interesting work. By contrast with the yin-yang clash with Tony Curtis that fuels the conflict in *Trapeze* (1956) and *Sweet Smell*, Lancaster and Douglas are too similar as actors to strike more than superficial sparks. Even so, Lancaster rarely took the easy route, and there is a mix of audacity, conscience and sheer enjoyment in his filmography. **PK**

L

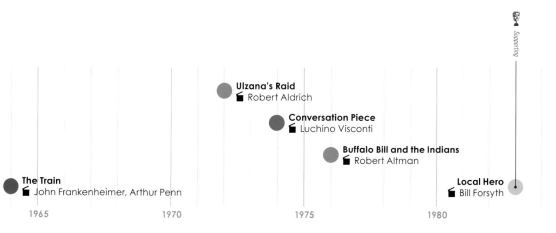

Supporting

Ulzana's Raid
Robert Aldrich

Conversation Piece
Luchino Visconti

Buffalo Bill and the Indians
Robert Altman

The Train
John Frankenheimer, Arthur Penn

Local Hero
Bill Forsyth

1965   1970   1975   1980

jessica lange 1949

| King Kong | The Postman Always Rings Twice | Tootsie | Frances | Country | Sweet Dreams | Music Box | Cape Fear |

It was while working as a model in New York in the 1970s that Jessica Lange was spotted by movie mogul Dino De Laurentis, who quickly cast the young beauty in his big-budget remake of the classic monster movie *King Kong* (1976). Although the film proved a hit with audiences, it was savaged by critics. Lange's performance in particular attracted almost universal criticism. It would be another three years before she appeared on screen, this time as an angel of death in Bob Fosse's Palm d'Or-winning *All That Jazz* (1979).

With the memories of *King Kong* fading, Lange appeared in another remake, this time the steamy noir *The Postman Always Rings Twice* (1981). Although the film did not fare well at the box office, it has since undergone a critical re-evaluation, with special praise given to Lange's performance. If the role showed her promise, she more than delivered the following year with two of her most acclaimed roles. She is sparkling as Dustin Hoffman's soap opera costar in *Tootsie* (1982), a performance that won her the Oscar for Best Supporting Actress. In *Frances* (1982), she played the troubled actress and television host Frances Farmer.

Lange continued to give a host of acclaimed performances, most notably in *Country* (1984), opposite her partner Sam Shepard, playing country music legend Patsy Cline in *Sweet Dreams* (1985) and in *Music Box* (1989), as a lawyer who defends her father of war crimes. She held her own against Diane Keaton and Sissy Spacek in Bruce Beresford's *Crimes of the Heart* (1986) and excels as the wife of a football star undergoing a crisis after his career ends in Taylor Hackford's *Everybody's All-American* (1988).

In the early 1990s, Lange appeared in yet another high-profile remake, Martin Scorsese's potent update of the classic thriller *Cape Fear* (1991). She gives a wonderfully brittle performance as the wife of a compromised lawyer. It was followed by an Oscar-winning turn, this time for Best Actress, as a manic depressive in Tony Richardson's *Blue Sky* (1994).

Roles in *Rob Roy* (1995), *Hush* (1998), *Titus* (1999), *Prozac Nation* (2001) and *Big Fish* (2003) kept the actress in the spotlight, but it was her unexpected casting in the hit television show *American Horror Story* in 2011 that has introduced her to a new generation of admirers. Appearances in *The Gambler* (2014) and *Wild Oats* (2015) notwithstanding, it is her thrilling role on the small screen that reveals what an exciting and enticing presence Lange can be. **MB**

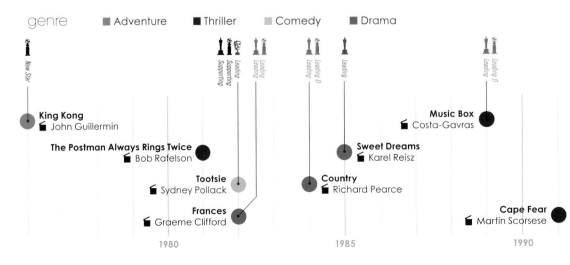

genre   ■ Adventure   ■ Thriller   ■ Comedy   ■ Drama

New Star

Leading
Supporting
Leading

Leading D
Leading

Leading

Leading D
Leading

King Kong
John Guillermin

The Postman Always Rings Twice
Bob Rafelson

Tootsie
Sydney Pollack

Frances
Graeme Clifford

Sweet Dreams
Karel Reisz

Country
Richard Pearce

Music Box
Costa-Gavras

Cape Fear
Martin Scorsese

1980   1985   1990

charles laughton 1899–1962

Island of Lost Souls

The Private Life of Henry VIII

Mutiny on the Bounty

Rembrandt

The Hunchback of Notre Dame

Hobson's Choice

Spartacus

Advise and Consent

"You can't direct a Laughton picture," remarked Alfred Hitchcock resignedly after making *Jamaica Inn* (1939). "The best you can hope for is to referee." Charles Laughton was a notoriously difficult actor and if given his head he could ham outrageously. At other times he would agonize over how to "get into" a role, often with recourse to grossly physical expedients. To play the stuttering future emperor in Josef von Sternberg's aborted *I Claudius* (1937), he required someone to physically and brutally kick him onto the set. Yet at his best he created a handful of the greatest performances ever committed to the screen.

Self-loathing hampered Laughton for much of his life. Conflicted about his homosexuality, he thought himself ugly. Yet in many ways his looks were his greatest asset; his features were highly expressive, as he showed in 1932 in his first significant role as one of the benighted visitors in James Whale's *The Old Dark House*. That same year, his Nero was the best thing in Cecil B. DeMille's *The Sign of the Cross*, and he delivered a wordless, five-minute tour de force in Ernst Lubitsch's episode of *If I Had a Million*.

His larger-than life performance in *The Private Life of Henry VIII* (1933) earned him major fame, but his

reading of Doctor Moreau in *Island of Lost Souls* (1932) strikes deeper. Implacable Inspector Javert in *Les Misérables* (1935) and inflexible Captain Bligh in *Mutiny on the Bounty* (1935) added to his rich gallery of villains, but perhaps his most deeply felt performance came in the title role of Alexander Korda's *Rembrandt* (1936). Sensitive, intimate, deeply moving, it is one of the most convincing portraits of an artist in all cinema.

He was the best on-screen Quasimodo in *The Hunchback of Notre Dame* (1939), and affecting as a timid village schoolteacher in Jean Renoir's *This Land Is Mine* (1943). All too often, though, character acting shaded into caricature, as in his re-run of Bligh in *Captain Kidd* (1945). Increasingly, Laughton came to see film as a means of subsidizing his true love, the theater, and his performances suffered accordingly. The response to his foray into directing, *The Night of the Hunter* (1955), did not help. On the evidence of this gothic thriller he could have made a great director, but it met with critical incomprehension and Laughton, discouraged, never directed again. He gave one last fine screen performance, as a wily, corrupt senator in *Advise and Consent* (1962), completing it with some difficulty just before his death. **PK**

L

genre
■ Adventure   ■ Comedy   ■ Drama   ■ Romance   ■ Thriller

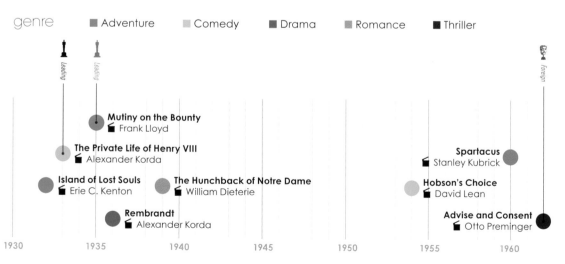

Leading

Leading

Foreign

Mutiny on the Bounty
🎬 Frank Lloyd

The Private Life of Henry VIII
🎬 Alexander Korda

Spartacus
🎬 Stanley Kubrick

Island of Lost Souls
🎬 Erie C. Kenton

The Hunchback of Notre Dame
🎬 William Dieterie

Hobson's Choice
🎬 David Lean

Rembrandt
🎬 Alexander Korda

Advise and Consent
🎬 Otto Preminger

1930   1935   1940   1945   1950   1955   1960

Clown Hero

laurel and hardy

Putting Pants on Philip

Big Business

Unaccust-omed as We Are

Wrong Again

Pardon Us

The Music Box

Sons of the Desert

Babes in Toyland

We have producer Hal Roach to thank for the greatest comic pairing in movie history: skinny Lancashire-born Stan Laurel (Arthur Stanley Jefferson, 1890–1965) and tubby Southern gent Oliver Hardy (Norvell Hardy Jr., 1892–1957). Not only the greatest, but the most lovable. The scrupulous respectability (much courtly raising of those bowler hats), the ill-fated eagerness to please, the helplessness with women (check out Ollie's Freudian tie-twiddling), and above all, their respective reactions to inevitable snowballing disaster, Stan dissolving in tears, Ollie glaring incredulously into camera — all were executed with impeccable timing, seamless mutual chemistry and an innocent resilience in the face of catastrophe. Quality suffered after their 1940 split with Roach, but the classic shorts and the best of the 1930s features are still peerless.

Laurel (he took his stage-name at the outset of his film career) was born in Ulverston, Lancashire, into a theatrical family. He started out in British music hall and came to the United States in 1910 with the Fred Karno Company, on the same boat as the then equally unknown Charlie Chaplin. He made his screen debut in 1917 and over the next nine years appeared in over 70 shorts, usually writing his own material and occasionally directing. His range was wider than one might guess from his later incarnation with Hardy: he was quite capable of wicked impersonations of Rudolph Valentino — as "Rhubarb Vaselino" in *Mud and Sand* (1922) — or John Barrymore (in *Dr. Pyckle and Mr. Pryde*, 1925).

Hardy was born into a middle-class family in Georgia and became a popular stage singer in his teens. For a while he ran a cinema, before making his screen debut in 1914. Generally billed as "Babe" Hardy, he appeared in several hundred films over the next decade — mostly shorts, though he took a small role in Buster Keaton's *Three Ages* (1923). One or two of his films were directed by Laurel; the pair had both featured in *The Lucky Dog* (1921), and then again in 10 two-reelers for the Hal Roach Company after joining it in 1926. But not until *Putting Pants on Philip* (1927) did Roach decide to pair them as a double act.

Over the next four years, they made over 40 two- or three-reelers, the majority of them directed by Leo McCarey. Unlike the social loners played by Keaton and Chaplin, Laurel and Hardy generally aspired to bourgeois respectability, only to be undone by their own incompetence. Hardy, rotund and double-chinned, with a tiny toothbrush mustache, fancied himself the more intelligent of the pair, often rebuking the gormlessly grinning, slighter-built Laurel for his ineptitude ("Here's another nice mess you've gotten me into!"), although when push came to shove Laurel usually proved the more resourceful. Sometimes they

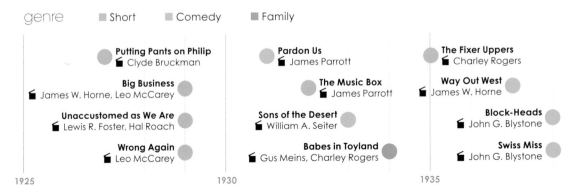

genre ■ Short ■ Comedy ■ Family

Putting Pants on Philip
Clyde Bruckman

Big Business
James W. Horne, Leo McCarey

Unaccustomed as We Are
Lewis R. Foster, Hal Roach

Wrong Again
Leo McCarey

Pardon Us
James Parrott

The Music Box
James Parrott

Sons of the Desert
William A. Seiter

Babes in Toyland
Gus Meins, Charley Rogers

The Fixer Uppers
Charley Rogers

Way Out West
James W. Horne

Block-Heads
John G. Blystone

Swiss Miss
John G. Blystone

1925   1930   1935

| The Fixer Uppers | Way Out West | Block-Heads | Swiss Miss | The Flying Deuces | A Chump at Oxford | Saps at Sea | Robinson Crusoeland |

were married, and generally henpecked by their wives, often played by Mae Busch, Anita Garvin or Daphne Pollard — though in *Twice Two* (1933) they played each other's wives. (And in *Brats*, 1930, they played both themselves and their own children.)

Their humor was unashamedly slapstick, often involving paint, buckets of water or custard pies (*The Battle of the Century*, 1927, possibly features more people throwing more pies than any other movie ever made), bangs on the head, kicks up the backside and the like. Frequently, they came up against infuriated cops or indignant members of the public, often played by such classic stooges as Edgar Kennedy or — in some 33 of their films — the small, bald and irascible Scotsman, James Finlayson, master of the slow burn. In *Big Business* (1929), trying to sell Christmas trees off the back of a truck, the pair wind up demolishing Finlayson's house, while he wrecks their truck and their trees.

Reversing their screen personas, it was Laurel who was the brains of the combo; he devised the subjects, wrote the scripts, created the gags and often acted as de facto director, though was never credited as such. Hardy, a more easy-going character, was happy to go and play golf, showing up when it was time to shoot — and never resenting that Laurel got paid twice as much as he did. In 1930, the pair transitioned, quite painlessly, to sound, and the

next year made their first feature, *Pardon Us* (1931), in which they played convicts. Their features, while containing classic sequences, never sustained quite the same level of comic excellence as the shorts; the best of them were *Sons of the Desert* (1933), where they sneak away from their wives to attend a licentious fraternity supper, and the western *Way Out West* (1937), in which they duet, rather charmingly, on the song "Trail of the Lonesome Pine." Their masterpiece, though, was the short *The Music Box* (1932), playing countless variations on the single gag of Stan and Ollie doggedly trying to maneuver an upright piano up a precipitous flight of steps. These steps, in the Silver Lake district of Los Angeles, are now named "Music Box Steps," near what is now Laurel and Hardy Park.

In 1940, the pair split with Roach and moved over to MGM, where they made eight features from 1941 to 1945. These were mediocre, studio-dictated fare; as Laurel observed, "We had no say on those films, and it sure looked it." The act broke up, though they remained good friends, and Hardy took one or two straight roles. The duo reunited for one last feature, made in France, *Robinson Crusoeland* (aka *Atoll K*, 1951); they were both visibly ageing, and the slapstick looked painful. After this they embarked on a few international tours, and were received everywhere with overwhelming affection. **PK**

jennifer lawrence 1990

| The Burning Plain | Winter's Bone | X-Men: First Class | Silver Linings Playbook | The Hunger Games | American Hustle | X-Men: Days of Future Past | Serena |

In an early breakout role, Jennifer Lawrence played a young Charlize Theron. Just six years later, aged only 24, she had eclipsed Theron and every other award-winning actress around, as the most commercial and popular female American star since Julia Roberts' heyday.

Born in Kentucky in 1990, Lawrence started acting on television in 2007, before coming to wider attention in *The Burning Plain* (2008), as the daughter of an unfaithful woman whose actions inadvertently lead to tragedy. Her alluring combination of maturity and vulnerability attained even greater potency as Ree Dolly in *Winter's Bone* (2010), a gritty thriller about a teenager struggling to support her impoverished family and forced to find her missing small-time crook father. Lawrence's justly acclaimed performance brought her an Oscar nomination, aged just 20.

Solid work followed as the "other woman" in indie romance *Like Crazy* (2011) and terrorized teen in thriller *House at the End of the Street* (2012). Her profile rising, Lawrence snagged a key role in the superhero prequel/reboot *X-Men: First Class* (2011) as the shape-shifting mutant Mystique. Given a more nuanced background than the character had previously been allowed, Lawrence made for an engaging antihero.

She quickly found herself headlining the next big young adult franchise adaptation, cast as Katniss Everdeen, reluctant heroine of *The Hunger Games* (2012). Pitched into a merciless, dystopian gladiatorial arena, it is a role requiring a tricky balance of both everygirl and superwoman — a combination that Lawrence seems to embody naturally.

David O. Russell's offbeat romantic comedy *Silver Linings Playbook* (2012) was another triumph. Lawrence's young widow Tiffany is refreshingly complex and again she exhibited a startling assurance opposite older costar Bradley Cooper. Once more audiences, critics and peers were smitten, resulting in a Best Actress Academy Award.

Russell's follow-up, the full-throttle con artist caper *American Hustle* (2013) offered Lawrence a flashy supporting role as a high-maintenance housewife. Such critically acclaimed roles were the ideal balance to her ongoing *X-Men* and *Hunger Games* series. Lawrence's meteoric career rise and off-screen accessibility and goofy persona have made her a firm audience favorite. It is so far a bulletproof combination that not even a misfire-like period melodrama *Serena* (2014) can derail. **LS**

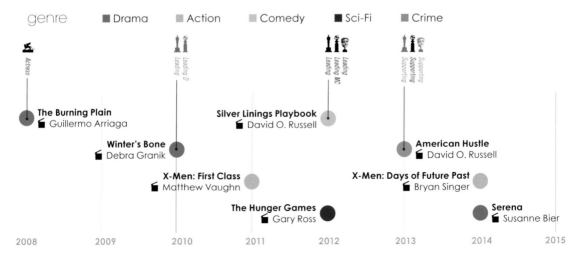

genre   ■ Drama   ■ Action   ■ Comedy   ■ Sci-Fi   ■ Crime

The Burning Plain
🎬 Guillermo Arriaga

Winter's Bone
🎬 Debra Granik

X-Men: First Class
🎬 Matthew Vaughn

Silver Linings Playbook
🎬 David O. Russell

The Hunger Games
🎬 Gary Ross

American Hustle
🎬 David O. Russell

X-Men: Days of Future Past
🎬 Bryan Singer

Serena
🎬 Susanne Bier

2008   2009   2010   2011   2012   2013   2014   2015

jean-pierre léaud 1944

| The 400 Blows | Masculin, Féminin | La Chinoise | Love on the Run | Détective | I Hired a Contract Killer | Irma Vep | The Pornographer |

Born in Paris in 1944, Jean-Pierre Léaud was cast at the age of 14 as Antoine Doinel in François Truffaut's first feature-length film, *The 400 Blows* (1959). The director and star would unite on a further four features tracing Doinel's progress to adulthood, through marriage, fatherhood and ultimately divorce. The films, *Love at Twenty* (1962); *Stolen Kisses* (1968); *Bed & Board* (1970) and *Love on the Run* (1979) are ranked as landmarks of cinema history and recognized as among the finest screen works about the transition from childhood to adulthood. Characterized by a fresh-faced innocence and a gift for improvization, Léaud and Truffaut would work together frequently, on films such as *Anne and Muriel* (1971) and *Day for Night* (1973).

Léaud, whose best performances exude a wry humor, would work with Jean-Luc Godard on many of the director's most influential films, including *Made In U.S.A* (1966), *Masculin, Féminin* (1966), *La Chinoise* (1967) and *Weekend* (1967). The pair last worked together on *Détective* (1985), a typically opaque crime thriller that is mesmerizingly shot and structured. In demand with leading European auteurs, Léaud worked with Bernardo Bertolucci, who cast him in a small role in *Last Tango in Paris* (1972), but was far more prominent in Aki Kaurismäki's *I Hired a Contract Killer* (1990), playing a menial worker whose redundancy causes him to hire a killer to murder him at some unspecified point in the future. *Le Havre* (2011) marked a second collaboration with the Finnish filmmaker, with the actor playing a xenophobic neighbor of the film's gentle lead.

Oliver Assayas' *Irma Vep* (1996) and Bertand Bonello's *The Pornographer* (2001) both cast the actor as an ageing filmmaker, albeit of very different temperaments. In Assayas' tribute to early cinema, Léaud is a filmmaker close to the edge of a breakdown, with the film reflecting his losing grip on reality. By contrast, Bonello's film — a study of a former porn filmmaker who embarks on a new film — is a more provocative affair, attracting controversy at the time for featuring male ejaculation. The films gave Léaud two of his best roles in years.

Finding favor with a new generation of enfants terribles, Léaud has also appeared in *I Saw Ben Barka Get Killed* (2005) and Noémie Lvovsky's *Camille Rewinds* (2012). In 2009, Léaud teamed up with fellow veterans Jeanne Moreau and Fanny Ardant in Ming-Liang Tsai's exploration of the Salome myth, *Face*. **JW**

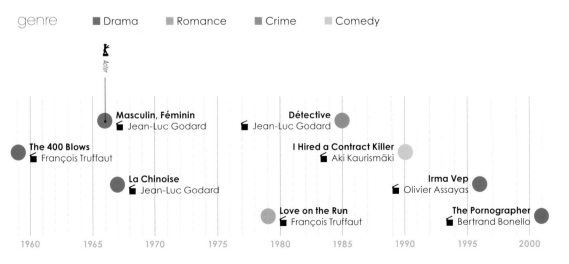

genre   ■ Drama   ■ Romance   ■ Crime   ■ Comedy

Actor

Masculin, Féminin
Jean-Luc Godard

Détective
Jean-Luc Godard

The 400 Blows
François Truffaut

I Hired a Contract Killer
Aki Kaurismäki

La Chinoise
Jean-Luc Godard

Irma Vep
Olivier Assayas

Love on the Run
François Truffaut

The Pornographer
Bertrand Bonello

1960   1965   1970   1975   1980   1985   1990   1995   2000

heath ledger 1979–2008

| 10 Things I Hate About You | A Knight's Tale | Ned Kelly | The Brothers Grimm | Brokeback Mountain | I'm Not There | The Dark Knight | The Imaginarium of Doctor Parnassus |

From his early roles on daytime Australian television, through his breakthrough years as a young heartthrob in Hollywood, and on to his later period as a respected acting talent, Heath Ledger made a lasting impression during his all too brief time in the spotlight.

Following a few youthful screen appearances in his native Australia, Ledger's big break came when he was cast in the teen comedy *10 Things I Hate About You* (1999). The film, a modern take on Shakespeare's *The Taming of The Shrew*, received widespread acclaim, with Ledger attracting positive notices.

The success of the film led to supporting roles in Roland Emmerich's bloated American Revolution drama *The Patriot* (2000) and playing Billy Bob Thornton's morose son in Marc Forster's Oscar-winning *Monster's Ball* (2001). He landed his first starring role in the lightweight medieval romp *A Knight's Tale* (2001). With its contemporary soundtrack and playful engagement with history, it was an entertaining showcase for the actor's winning charm. He returned to Australia to film *Ned Kelly* (2003), in which he played the titular outlaw. He would play another mythic historical character two years later, as the eponymous lothario in Lasse Hallström's underwhelming *Casanova* (2005).

Ledger worked with Terry Gilliam for the first time on *The Brothers Grimm* (2005), a shoot reported to have been plagued with difficulties. That year he also starred in Catherine Hardwicke's *Lords of Dogtown* (2005), a biographical drama about a group of skateboarders. However, it was his role in Ang Lee's *Brokeback Mountain* (2005) that demonstrated the breadth of the young actor's talent. His performance as a cowboy who falls in love with his friend received universal praise and garnered much award recognition, including a Best Actor Oscar nomination.

He continued to impress, first in the Australian romance *Candy* (2006) and then in Todd Haynes' esoteric tribute to Bob Dylan *I'm Not There* (2007). Then came *The Dark Knight* (2008) and the performance of a lifetime. Ledger's Joker was edgier, more violent and brutal than previous incarnations, but the actor also brought a cruel wit and offbeat charm. Unfortunately, he would never see the finished film. He died six months before its release, following an accidental drug overdose. He was halfway through filming *The Imaginarium of Doctor Parnassus* (2009).

Ledger's performance in *The Dark Knight* was awarded with a posthumous Oscar. **MB**

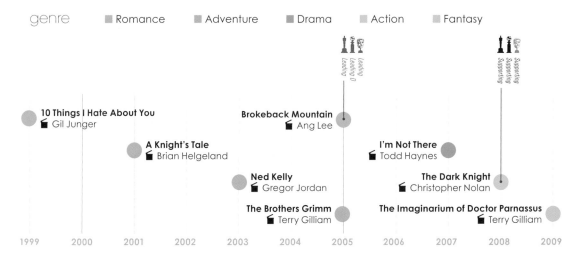

genre ■ Romance ■ Adventure ■ Drama ■ Action ■ Fantasy

10 Things I Hate About You
Gil Junger

A Knight's Tale
Brian Helgeland

Ned Kelly
Gregor Jordan

The Brothers Grimm
Terry Gilliam

Brokeback Mountain
Ang Lee

I'm Not There
Todd Haynes

The Dark Knight
Christopher Nolan

The Imaginarium of Doctor Parnassus
Terry Gilliam

1999 2000 2001 2002 2003 2004 2005 2006 2007 2008 2009

bruce lee 1940–73

| The Kid | The Orphan | Marlowe | The Big Boss | Fist of Fury | Way of the Dragon | Enter the Dragon | Game of Death |

An actor more famous than the roles he played, Bruce Lee was, in a career cut short by his early death, able to define himself as arguably the most famous Eastern film star of all time. Born in the United States, but raised in Hong Kong, Lee was a child actor with 21 films to his name by the age of 20. Until the mid-1960s, Lee worked exclusively in Hong Kong, where he studied the martial art of Wing Chun. In 1966, his career received a huge boost when he took a part in the U.S. television series *The Green Hornet* (1966–67), playing Kato, the chauffer and sidekick of the hero. As with many of his roles, the part functioned primarily as a showcase for his incredible physical talents.

His first major Hollywood film was a supporting role in *Marlowe* (1969), playing a bouncer in a brief fight sequence that ends with a vertiginous exit for the nascent star. However, his big break came with the 1971 Hong Kong actioner, *The Big Boss*. His first film for Golden Harvest studio and producer Raymond Chow, *The Big Boss* was at the vanguard of films that prompted the huge popularity of martial arts movies across the world. For many Western audiences, it was their first exposure to both the martial arts action film and a leading Asian actor as the protagonist. It was Hong Kong's biggest commercial success until Lee's next film, *Fist of Fury* (1972).

The majority of Lee's hit films were revenge-infused crime dramas, employing exploitation-style narratives and characters as a springboard for the breathtaking fights. However, *Fist of Fury* stands apart for its political themes, an element that was important to Lee. It shows a China under siege by foreign powers and the hero battling them with honor and nobility.

Now an international superstar, Lee wrote, produced, directed and starred in his next project, *Way of the Dragon* (1972). More comedic than his previous work, but still delivering thrilling action sequences, it successfully made inroads into Hollywood, as Lee battled an American nemesis, played by Chuck Norris, in a European city. The film led to what many see as his masterpiece, *Enter the Dragon* (1973). Once again playing the hero, he is aided by John Saxon and sports legend and Blaxploitation star Jim Kelly. With a plot that involves a legendary martial arts competition run by a drugs kingpin and vengeance for a murdered sister, Lee was at the height of his powers. The one-inch punch sequence and the nunchuks display are legendary in action cinema, but also evident is the star's self-awareness and sense of humor.

Upon his sudden death of a cerebral edema at the age of 32, Lee left one unfinished film in his wake. Assembled by his *Enter the Dragon* director Robert Clouse, *Game of Death* (1978) may feel incomplete, but Lee is as powerful as ever and his striking, black-striped yellow jumpsuit was instantly iconic — as proved by its reappearance in *Kill Bill: Vol. 1* (2003). **SW**

genre   ■ Drama   ■ Mystery   ■ Action

The Kid
Fung Fung

Marlowe
Paul Bogart

Fist of Fury
Wei Lo

The Big Boss
Wei Lo and Chia-Hsiang

Way of the Dragon
Bruce Lee

The Orphan
Sun-Fung Lee

Enter the Dragon
Robert Clouse

Game of Death
Robert Clouse and Sammo Kam-Bo Hung

1950   1955   1960   1965   1970   1975

christopher lee 1922–2015

| The Curse of Frankenstein | Dracula | The Mummy | The Gorgon | The Face of Fu Manchu | The Devil Rides Out | Dracula Prince of Darkness | The Wicker Man |

Christopher Lee is best known for playing some of cinema's most iconic villains, his long association with Hammer Films and a late career revival that saw him feature in a number of major blockbusters. Appearing in over 200 films across six decades, he claimed to have had more swordfights on screen than any other actor in the history of the medium. Recognizable for his operatic bass voice, imposing stature and menacing, sunken features, the secret of his appeal was his ability to charm audiences as he scared them, making darkness and the occult seem oddly compelling and seductive.

Born in London in 1922, Lee served in the RAF during World War II before being recruited to J. Arthur Rank's legendary "Charm School." His feature debut was a single line delivered in *Corridor of Mirrors* (1948), sitting at a table to mask his height. He spent the following decade in supporting roles and uncredited bit-parts before his breakthrough — his first appearance for Hammer, in *The Curse of Frankenstein* (1957), playing the monster to Peter Cushing's Baron Frankenstein.

The film revived gothic cinema and established "Hammer Horror" as a popular worldwide brand, with Lee as one of their biggest stars. He and Cushing starred in 22 films together, one of which made him a star: *Dracula* (1958). With growing reticence, Lee reprised the sinister-yet-alluring Count for six sequels, the strongest of which was *Dracula: Prince of Darkness*

(1966), shot back-to-back on the same sets as his previous feature, *Rasputin: The Mad Monk* (1966).

The actor's association with Hammer continued for two decades and included the popular titles *The Mummy* (1959), playing the revived high priest Kharis, and *The Gorgon* (1964). For the most part he was cast as the villain. An exception was the impressive *The Devil Rides Out* (1968), possibly the studio's creative high point. An adaptation of Dennis Wheatley's novel, Lee plays an investigator who comes face to face with a devil-worshipping cult.

Outside of horror, Lee played the criminal mastermind Dr. Fu Manchu in five films, starting with *The Face of Fu Manchu* (1965), as well as Mycroft Holmes in Billy Wilder's *The Private Life of Sherlock Holmes* (1970), after having portrayed the detective himself in *Sherlock Holmes and the Deadly Necklace* (1962) and Sir Henry Baskerville in Hammer's *The Hound of the Baskervilles* (1959). He would play Sherlock again in a pair of films in the early 1990s.

Perhaps owing to his upbringing as the son of a countess and lieutenant colonel, Lee was always at his most effective playing characters from an aristocratic or privileged background, whose corruption and malign intent are obscured by their status. Count Dracula is a key example, but the most compelling is Lord Summerisle, the hiding-in-plain-sight antagonist of *The Wicker Man* (1973). Deceptively jovial in a

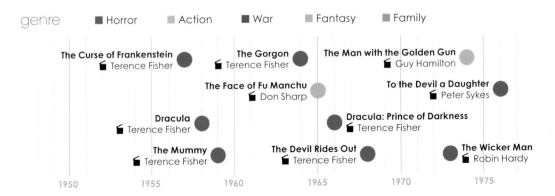

genre ■ Horror ■ Action ■ War ■ Fantasy ■ Family

The Curse of Frankenstein
 Terence Fisher

The Gorgon
 Terence Fisher

The Man with the Golden Gun
 Guy Hamilton

The Face of Fu Manchu
 Don Sharp

To the Devil a Daughter
 Peter Sykes

Dracula
 Terence Fisher

Dracula: Prince of Darkness
 Terence Fisher

The Mummy
 Terence Fisher

The Devil Rides Out
 Terence Fisher

The Wicker Man
 Robin Hardy

1950   1955   1960   1965   1970   1975

$99M (U.S.)	$289M	$1.2B	$844M	$568M	$1B
The Man with the Golden Gun (1974))	Sleepy Hollow (1999)	The Lord of the Rings: The Fellowship of the Ring (2001)	Star Wars: Episode II — Attack of the Clones (2002)	Charlie and the Chocolate Factory (2005)	The Hobbit: An Unexpected Journey (2012)

The Man with the Golden Gun | To the Devil a Daughter | Jinnah | Sleepy Hollow | The Lord of the Rings: The Fellowship of the Ring | Star Wars: Episode II — Attack of the Clones | Charlie and the Chocolate Factory | The Hobbit: An Unexpected Journey

yellow turtleneck and tweeds, Lee managed to make "Come, it is time to keep your appointment with the Wicker Man" one of the most ominous lines in cinema history. The film slipped into obscurity for several years before finding later popularity.

The Wicker Man marked a shift away from the gothic horror that had made him a star. He followed the film with roles as the Comte de Rochefort in Richard Lester's knockabout The Three Musketeers (1973) and its 1974 sequel, and as the three-nippled Francisco Scaramanga in The Man with the Golden Gun (1974). Despite a poor response to the film itself, Scaramanga became one of the most popular Bond villains. His last film for Hammer was To the Devil a Daughter (1976). After that, he mostly avoided horror.

He moved to the United States in 1977, starring in films such as Airport '77 (1977) and Steven Spielberg's overblown comedy 1941 (1979). He continued to work solidly throughout the 1980s and 1990s, but few of his films found a wide audience: an earnest performance as the founder of Pakistan, Mohammed Ali Jinnah, in the epic biopic Jinnah (1998) bypassed cinemas altogether, although Lee said it was his favorite. The following year, Tim Burton cast him in a small role in the Hammer-tribute Sleepy Hollow (1999). He provided voices or near-cameos in four other films for the director, including a role in Charlie and the Chocolate Factory (2005) as Johnny Depp's disapproving dentist father.

The resurgence of his career began when he played the evil wizard Saruman in the Lord of the Rings series, making his most significant appearance in the first installment, The Fellowship of the Ring (2001). The trilogy was a massive commercial and critical success, although he was dismayed when his part was cut from the theatrical version of the concluding episode, The Return of the King (2003).

A noticeably frail Lee returned as Saruman in the adaptation of The Hobbit, a book in which the character does not even appear. Like much of the bloated second trilogy, his appearances in An Unexpected Journey (2012) and The Battle of the Five Armies (2014) were largely unnecessary.

He played a villain, Count Dooku, in another hugely profitable trilogy — George Lucas' Star Wars prequels. His most substantial contribution is in Episode II — Attack of the Clones (2002), a film now remembered for a laughably odd duel between Lee and Yoda. Other recent appearances include The Golden Compass (2007), Glorious 39 (2009) and Martin Scorsese's delightful homage to early cinema Hugo (2011), in which Lee towers over the film's heroes as an imposing but benevolent bookshop owner.

Lee's concentration on genre films resulted in his absence from most awards ceremonies. However, in 2011 he received a BAFTA Fellowship, in recognition of his vital contribution to British cinema. **JWa**

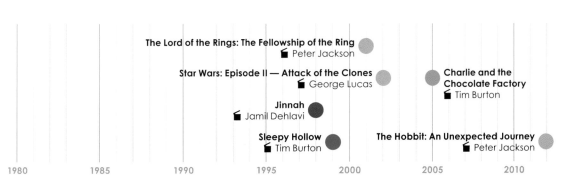

The Lord of the Rings: The Fellowship of the Ring
Peter Jackson

Star Wars: Episode II — Attack of the Clones
George Lucas

Charlie and the Chocolate Factory
Tim Burton

Jinnah
Jamil Dehlavi

Sleepy Hollow
Tim Burton

The Hobbit: An Unexpected Journey
Peter Jackson

1980 | 1985 | 1990 | 1995 | 2000 | 2005 | 2010

The Curse of Frankenstein (1957)

Dracula (1958)

The Mummy (1959)

The Wicker Man (1973)

The Man with the Golden Gun (1974)

The Lord of the Rings: The Fellowship of the Ring (2001)

Star Wars Episode II: Attack of the Clones (2002)

The Hobbit: An Unexpected Journey (2012)

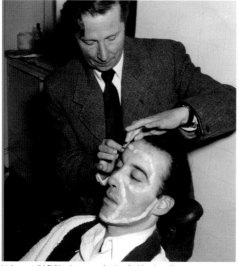

Make-up artist Phil Leakey preparing Lee for his role as the eponymous monster in *The Curse of Frankenstein* ...

... the result was suitably gruesome, deliberately avoiding any resemblance to Jack Pierce's design for the Universal films.

Lee in the iconic role of *Dracula*. The actor only spoke 13 lines in the entire movie.

The Mummy starred Lee as Kharis, a mummified Egyptian priest who is unintentionally brought back to life by 19th-century archeologists.

John Banning (Peter Cushing) fends off Kharis (Lee) in *The Mummy*. Ostensibly, a remake of Universal's 1932 film, most of the plot actually comes from *The Mummy's Hand* (1940) and *The Mummy's Tomb* (1942).

In a 2013 article in the *Guardian*, *The Wicker Man* director Robin Hardy said that Lee "was the obvious choice or Lord Summerisle. He had a patrician air, and this wonderful voice for incantations to the gods."

Lee as Francisco Scaramanga in ***The Man with the Golden Gun***. The actor is in fact a cousin of Bond creator Ian Fleming.

Lee as Saruman, the White Wizard, in ***The Lord of the Rings: The Fellowship of the Ring***. He once said that the only reason he took a part in the television series *The New Adventures of Robin Hood* (1997–98) "was to show anyone who was watching that I could play a wizard and that I would be ideal casting for *The Lord of the Rings*."

Star Wars: Episode II — Attack of the Clones featured Lee as he fallen Jedi Master Count Dooku.

Lee reprised his role as Saruman in ***The Hobbit: An Unexpected Journey*** and its sequels, *The Desolation of Smaug* (2013) and *The Battle of the Five Armies* (2014).

stars of horror

Max Schreck | Bela Lugosi | Boris Karloff | Fay Wray | Peter Cushing | Christopher Lee | Anthony Perkins | Deborah Kerr

Peter Cushing once said that he found a creaking door and half open coffin more terrifying than the visceral shocks for which many horror films are renowned. That may seem odd considering that the early Hammer films that made his name in the late 1950s were notorious at the time for their goriness. Not that this infamy, which has dogged the genre throughout its history, has ever been a bad thing.

German director F.W. Murnau's silent classic *Nosferatu* (1922), though not the first horror film, was one of the first to ignite the public's imagination, turning audiences onto the genre while making an icon of Max Schreck, who played the vampire Count Orloc. It took until the advent of sound for horror to come into its own in Hollywood. Two studios in particular, Universal and RKO, set themselves up as the natural home for the genre. Plundering the archives of Victorian gothic literature, films like *Dracula* (1931) and *Frankenstein* (1931), both made at Universal, made stars of Bela Lugosi and Boris Karloff. Lugosi's talent was limited and he ended up in Ed Wood's rickety productions, while Karloff possessed more range. But even though his career was both longer and greater, neither he nor Lugosi was ever able to shake off the roles that made their names. Over at RKO, directors Merian C. Cooper and Ernest B. Schoedsack did

the same for Fay Wray, placing her at the mercy of a mighty gorilla in *King Kong* (1933), a film whose popularity made it one of cinema's first blockbusters, as well as immortalizing its hapless heroine.

Over the next two decades, horror continued to prosper, although it would be some time before the genre achieved the crossover success that saw A-list actors attached to projects. And on the rare occasions when they did, such as Warner Brothers' largely forgotten Humphrey Bogart vehicle *The Return of Doctor X* (1939), the film would be marketed as something else — in this case a mystery — in order to attract a wider audience.

It was not until the success of *The Curse of Frankenstein* (1957), which established independent British studio Hammer Films as a worldwide force, that horror gained a degree of acceptance, if not respectability, within the film industry and among the wider cinema-going public. Hammer's next film, *Dracula* (1958), not only bolstered the reputation of Christopher Lee, but also introduced a startling level of sexuality to the story of the legendary vampire, furthering Hammer's reputation as a risk-taking studio.

Horror became more of a mainstay, but still some industry figures balked at associating their film so overtly with the genre. Although Alfred

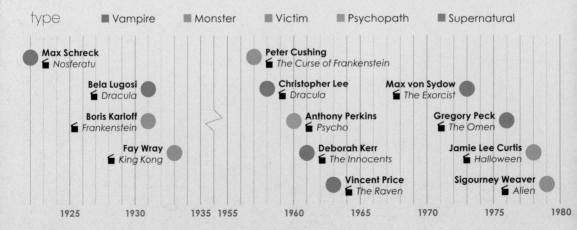

type   ■ Vampire   ■ Monster   ■ Victim   ■ Psychopath   ■ Supernatural

Max Schreck
🎬 *Nosferatu*

Bela Lugosi
🎬 *Dracula*

Boris Karloff
🎬 *Frankenstein*

Fay Wray
🎬 *King Kong*

Peter Cushing
🎬 *The Curse of Frankenstein*

Christopher Lee
🎬 *Dracula*

Anthony Perkins
🎬 *Psycho*

Deborah Kerr
🎬 *The Innocents*

Vincent Price
🎬 *The Raven*

Max von Sydow
🎬 *The Exorcist*

Gregory Peck
🎬 *The Omen*

Jamie Lee Curtis
🎬 *Halloween*

Sigourney Weaver
🎬 *Alien*

1925   1930   1935 1955   1960   1965   1970   1975   1980

| Vincent Price | Max von Sydow | Gregory Peck | Jamie Lee Curtis | Sigourney Weaver | Anthony Hopkins | Tom Cruise | Brad Pitt |

Hitchcock's *Psycho* (1960) is now considered a classic psychological horror, it was marketed as a thriller upon its release. The next year, Deborah Kerr starred in the gothic chiller *The Innocents* (1961), with any doubts over her involvement in so "tawdry" a genre assuaged by the fact that the film, no matter how scary, was an adaptation of Henry James' novella *The Turn of the Screw* (1898) and therefore a "respectable" chiller.

Roger Corman was not quite so reticent in taking classic literature and soaking it in blood. Adapting a series of Edgar Allan Poe stories, often with science fiction author Richard Matheson writing the screenplays, he created a series of highly stylized shockers, replete with a lurid use of color. He also rejuvenated the careers of many a veteran Hollywood actor. In *The Raven* (1963), Corman's regular star Vincent Price appeared opposite Boris Karloff and Peter Lorre, as well as a young Jack Nicholson.

The horror film, at least the version of it we recognize today, came into being in the late 1960s and early 1970s, as the rule of the Hollywood studios came to an end and the strictures of the Hays Code dissipated, allowing directors to offer up more brutal representations of violence. Even the Oscars paid attention, unable to ignore huge successes like *The Exorcist* (1973), which starred Swedish actor and Bergman regular Max von Sydow. Then came *The Omen* (1976), with Gregory Peck in the lead, and the horror as blockbuster entertainment was born.

Halloween (1978) followed suit, with Jamie Lee Curtis as a young woman stalked by a mask-wearing killer, while *Alien* (1979) offered up a feminist icon in the form of Sigourney Weaver's Ripley. In *The Silence of the Lambs* (1991), Jodie Foster's Clarice Starling gave audiences another strong female in a genre not always known for such positive representations of women, although she was always going to be secondary to Anthony Hopkins' memorable villain, Hannibal Lecter. The film is also significant for being the first horror to win major awards and one of the few films to win the five most coveted Oscars.

By the time Tom Cruise appeared in *Interview with the Vampire* (1994), horror had become commonplace at the local multiplex. Torture porn such as the *Saw* or *Hostel* series featured on the mainstream program and even the zombie movie, once a sub-genre that only the hardened horror fan could stomach, had come a long way since George A. Romero's *Night of the Living Dead* (1968). *The Walking Dead* television series has been a huge success, while Brad Pitt produced and starred in the blockbuster zombie movie *World War Z* (2013). **CP**

☐ Zombie

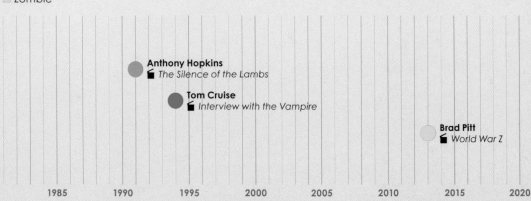

Anthony Hopkins
The Silence of the Lambs

Tom Cruise
Interview with the Vampire

Brad Pitt
World War Z

1985   1990   1995   2000   2005   2010   2015   2020

Girl Next Door | Femme Fatale | Saint | Sinner

janet leigh 1927–2004

The Romance of Rosy Ridge

Little Women

Angels in the Outfield

Scaramouche

Houdini

The Naked Spur

The Black Shield of Falworth

Prince Valiant

Janet Leigh has been so defined by a single role that it comes as a shock to realize that her doomed secretary Marion Crane in Alfred Hitchcock's *Psycho* (1960) not only comes relatively late in her filmography, but is also an atypical outlier in a career more characterized by light comedies and historical romps, including several opposite her then-husband Tony Curtis.

Born Jeanette Helen Morrison in Merced, California, in 1927, she had no particular ambition to act until former star Norma Shearer visited the ski resort where her parents were working, saw a picture of their daughter, and recommended her for a screen test. Offered an MGM contract before she turned 20, it took the newly renamed Janet Leigh just three weeks to be cast as the female lead in the post-Civil War drama *The Romance of Rosy Ridge* (1947).

It was a big hit and a huge career boost: over the next decade she would typically make three to five films a year. Her third, the Lassie vehicle *Hills of Home* (1948), gave her above-the-title billing and her popularity was cemented by being dubbed "Hollywood's No.1 Glamour Girl" later that year. She

was part of the ensemble cast of the popular *Little Women* (1949) and hopped easily across genres: from period dramas (*That Forsyte Woman*, 1949), comedies (*Angels in the Outfield*, 1951) and westerns (*The Naked Spur*, 1953), to thrillers (*Rogue Cop*, 1954), musicals (*My Sister Eileen*, 1955) and Jazz Age gangster melodramas (*Pete Kelly's Blues*, 1955). She also supported Dean Martin and Jerry Lewis in *Living It Up* (1954). Other on-screen partners included Robert Mitchum (*Holiday Affair*, 1949), John Wayne (*Jet Pilot*, 1957), Stewart Granger (*Scaramouche*, 1952), Robert Wagner (*Prince Valiant*, 1954) and Victor Mature (*Safari*, 1956).

But her most enduring on-screen partnership was with Tony Curtis, whom she married in 1951. In *Houdini* (1953), he was the famous escapologist, she his long-suffering wife. In medieval drama *The Black Shield of Falworth* (1954), he was the up-and-coming knight, she the love interest. In *The Vikings* (1958), her Princess Morgana attracts the attention of Vikings Erik (Curtis) and Einar (Kirk Douglas), while in *The Perfect Furlough* (1958), she is an army psychiatrist supervising Curtis' fish-out-of-water corporal in Paris. Finally, in

genre ■ Romance ■ Family ■ Adventure ■ Drama ■ Western

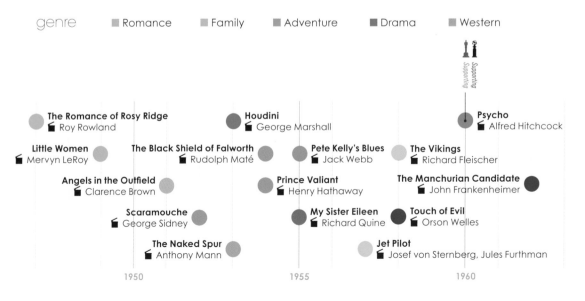

Supporting

The Romance of Rosy Ridge
Roy Rowland

Little Women
Mervyn LeRoy

Angels in the Outfield
Clarence Brown

Scaramouche
George Sidney

The Naked Spur
Anthony Mann

Houdini
George Marshall

The Black Shield of Falworth
Rudolph Maté

Prince Valiant
Henry Hathaway

Pete Kelly's Blues
Jack Webb

My Sister Eileen
Richard Quine

Jet Pilot
Josef von Sternberg, Jules Furthman

Psycho
Alfred Hitchcock

The Vikings
Richard Fleischer

The Manchurian Candidate
John Frankenheimer

Touch of Evil
Orson Welles

1950   1955   1960

$18M (U.S.)
Touch of Evil
(1958)

$253M (U.S.)
Psycho
(1960)

$21M (U.S.)
*The Manchurian
Candidate*
(1962)

$61M (U.S.)
The Fog
(1980)

Pete Kelly's
Blues

My Sister
Eileen

Jet Pilot

The Vikings

Touch of
Evil

Psycho

The
Manchurian
Candidate

The Fog

Who Was That Lady? (1960), she played a gullible wife convinced by her straying husband that he is actually an undercover agent.

But among all this lighthearted fare came the two masterpieces that have contributed the most to keeping her reputation alive. The first was Orson Welles' belated return to Hollywood, *Touch of Evil* (1958), in which she played the wife of Charlton Heston's Mexican drug official. Their first post-nuptial kiss comes at the very end of the film's legendary extended opening shot, accompanied by the explosion that kickstarts the plot.

Alfred Hitchcock's stunning journey into suspense, *Psycho*, was Leigh's most daringly adventurous role on multiple levels. Aside from the fact that Marion is killed off well before the halfway mark — which came as an unprecedented shock to the film's original audience — her opening scenes with her lunch-break lover John Gavin were daringly frank for the time. Leigh is rarely off the screen prior to the famous shower scene, conveying a characterization more complex and nuanced than many actors achieve across an entire

feature, and she was rewarded with a Golden Globe Award and an Oscar nomination.

Despite *Psycho*'s box-office and cultural impact, Leigh found big-screen pickings surprisingly slim thereafter. John Frankenheimer's *The Manchurian Candidate* (1962), in which she played the sympathetic lover of Frank Sinatra's understandably paranoid U.S. Army major, was a worthy successor to her work with Welles and Hitchcock, and the musical comedy *Bye Bye Birdie* (1963) was a popular hit, although Leigh was overshadowed by Ann-Margret's star-making supporting turn. She was the wife of Paul Newman's eponymous *Harper* (1966), but had little screen time, while all her leading roles from this period were in forgettable fluff. A reunion with Jerry Lewis for *Three on a Couch* (1966) proved ill advised.

From the late 1960s, Leigh forged a second career on television. Her last cinema roles were generally undistinguished, although she made an effective pairing with her real-life daughter Jamie Lee Curtis in John Carpenter's spooky ghost story *The Fog* (1980). She died of a heart attack in 2004. **MBr**

■ Crime   ■ Musical   ■ Action   ■ Thriller   ■ Horror

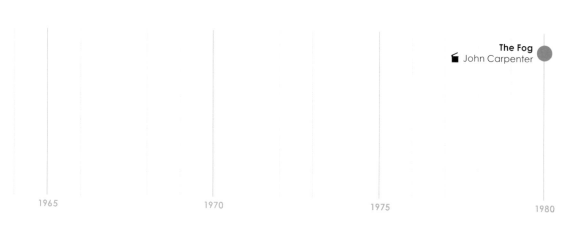

The Fog
John Carpenter

1965   1970   1975   1980

vivien leigh 1913–67

| Fire Over England | Dark Journey | Storm in a Teacup | A Yank at Oxford | Sidewalks of London | Gone with the Wind | Waterloo Bridge | 21 Days |

On the strength of just two movies and a checkered private life, stands Vivien Leigh's reputation as one of the great movie stars. Other actresses may have more impressive résumés, but when your signature role is perhaps the most famous casting coup in film history and your major relationship with the most acclaimed British actor of his generation is constantly under the spotlight, they tend to print the legend. Fortunately, Leigh also had the talent, beauty and spirit to back it up.

Born Vivian Mary Hartley in India, 1913, she declared at a young age her desire to be a celebrated actress. She enrolled at the prestigious Royal Academy of Dramatic Arts in 1931, only to drop out when she married a barrister 13 years her senior and had a child.

Undeterred, she ventured back into acting, changing her name to Vivien Leigh and becoming an overnight sensation in her very first professional play. Film mogul Alexander Korda promptly signed her up for movies. Her first significant role was in the Elizabeth I drama *Fire Over England* (1937), playing a frisky lady-in-waiting who falls in love with a court nobleman. Her on-screen lover was played by rising British stage star Laurence Olivier and, despite their respective marriages, the two soon began a real love affair.

Though Leigh's part in *Fire Over England* was minor, she featured heavily in the publicity, shown as a very glamorous and atypical English actress. Her next roles confirmed this: cast as double-agent lover to Conrad Veidt in spy romance *Dark Journey* (1937); trying to emulate U.S. screwball comedies with Rex Harrison in *Storm in a Teacup* (1937); and a vamp in MGM's first UK-based production, *A Yank at Oxford* (1938). *Sidewalks of London* (1938) saw her play a seductive pickpocket and sidekick to Charles Laughton. While most reviewers noted her physical charms, Leigh herself continued to diligently improve her craft on the stage.

Leigh had a reputation for chasing down her dreams (she had seen Olivier perform before they met and declared she would one day marry him). Margaret Mitchell's 1936 American Civil War novel *Gone with the Wind* was a best-seller and Leigh, although still relatively unknown, believed she should play its Southern belle heroine, Scarlett O'Hara. Following Olivier to Hollywood, she somehow inveigled her way onto the set through his agent Myron Selznick, brother of the film's producer David. The rest is history. Leigh won the role against far higher-profile, home-advantaged competition, then

genre   ■ Adventure   ■ Thriller   ■ Comedy   ■ Romance   ■ War   ■ Drama

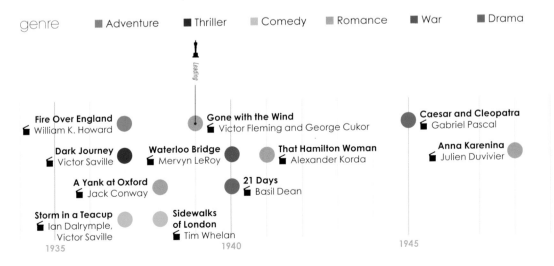

Leading

Fire Over England
William K. Howard

Gone with the Wind
Victor Fleming and George Cukor

Caesar and Cleopatra
Gabriel Pascal

Dark Journey
Victor Saville

Waterloo Bridge
Mervyn LeRoy

That Hamilton Woman
Alexander Korda

Anna Karenina
Julien Duvivier

A Yank at Oxford
Jack Conway

21 Days
Basil Dean

Storm in a Teacup
Ian Dalrymple, Victor Saville

Sidewalks of London
Tim Whelan

1935   1940   1945

| That Hamilton Woman | Caesar and Cleopatra | Anna Karenina | A Streetcar Named Desire | The Deep Blue Sea | The Roman Spring of Mrs. Stone | Ship of Fools |

worked incessantly on a chaotic, extended shoot. Her Scarlett is indelible: flighty and spoiled, driven and resilient, exasperating but utterly enchanting. The film's success and her Best Actress Academy Award meant she was, once again, an overnight sensation.

Now married, Leigh and Olivier were cinema's golden couple, but World War II's ominous shadow affected their work choices. Her MGM follow-up, *Waterloo Bridge* (1940), was another doomed romance, Leigh playing a dancer forced into prostitution. Capitalizing on her success, Leigh's crime drama with Olivier, *21 Days* (1940), was released. The pair then reteamed for *That Hamilton Woman* (1941), a lavish period drama about the scandalous affair between Admiral Nelson and noblewoman Emma Hamilton. Very much a wartime propaganda piece, it soars on the real-life couple's tangible chemistry.

She and Olivier then returned to Britain. Theater and work for the troops occupied her for the rest of the war, as well as bouts of ill health. Would-be British epic *Caesar and Cleopatra* (1945) failed to rival Hollywood counterparts and an on-set fall resulted in a miscarriage and her first noted bout of depression. Another 1940s melodrama, an adaptation of Tolstoy's

Anna Karenina (1948), also misfired. She seemed unable to channel the necessary passion of previous successes.

Leigh's long-running West End stage portrayal of a very different Southern belle, *A Streetcar Named Desire*'s ageing, fragile Blanche DuBois, won her the 1951 movie role opposite the U.S. cast, featuring naturalistic "Method" sensation Marlon Brando. Their contrasting acting styles synergized the film, Leigh's tragic fantasist winning her a second Oscar.

Streetcar was Leigh's final great movie role. Struggles with her severe bipolar disorder went on to dominate her life and eventually contributed to the end of her marriage. A somewhat starchy performance as a married woman desperately seeking emancipation in *The Deep Blue Sea* (1955) was followed by another wretchedly abused older woman in *The Roman Spring of Mrs. Stone* (1961). Her final screen role, as a bitter, melancholy divorcée aboard heavy-handed floating metaphor *Ship of Fools* (1965), was inauspicious. And although her stage career continued with some success, her tragically premature death came in 1967, aged just 53. For cinephiles, however, Leigh's enduring Scarlett provides eternal promise that tomorrow is another day. **LS**

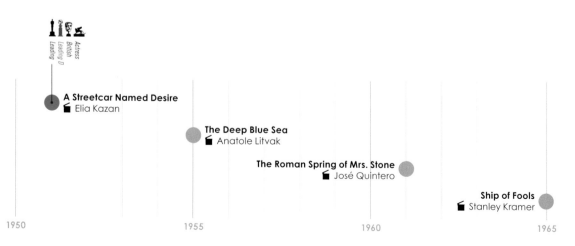

Actress
British
Leading D
Leading

A Streetcar Named Desire
Elia Kazan

The Deep Blue Sea
Anatole Litvak

The Roman Spring of Mrs. Stone
José Quintero

Ship of Fools
Stanley Kramer

1950　　　　1955　　　　1960　　　　1965

jack lemmon 1925–2001

It Should Happen to You

Mister Roberts

Cowboy

Some Like It Hot

The Apartment

Days of Wine and Roses

The Fortune Cookie

The Odd Couple

Billy Wilder once said, "Happiness is working with Jack Lemmon." The actor's collaboration with the filmmaker, on seven films over 25 years, is the pivotal partnership of his career. Lemmon was good elsewhere, sometimes brilliant, but there was a spark with Wilder that only a few actors encounter with a director.

Lemmon made his screen debut, at 24, in *The Lady Takes a Sailor* (1949). He followed that with an Oscar-winning performance as a lackadaisical ensign aboard a naval vessel in the World War II comedy drama *Mister Roberts* (1955). The role highlights Lemmon's physical and verbal dexterity. The musical *My Sister Eileen* (1955) and a number of comedies followed, before *Some Like It Hot* (1959) with Wilder.

Wilder saw in Lemmon's nervous energy huge comic potential and a capacity for pathos. Although Marilyn Monroe is the star attraction and Tony Curtis the romantic lead, it is Lemmon who walks away with the movie's best scenes, from his hilarious post-date dance with maracas, having just been proposed to by a wealthy millionaire, to the film's brilliant final scene, as the two oddball couples escape from a police raid.

He gave one of his finest comic performances in *The Apartment* (1960), as a lowly corporate employee who is pressured to lend out his apartment so that his superiors can conduct their extra-marital affairs, but who falls for one of the women, played by Shirley MacLaine. The actor's presence takes the edge off Wilder's customary cynicism and the film's bittersweet ending is genuinely affecting.

Irma La Douce (1963) was another success for Wilder and Lemmon, but its story of a former Parisian police officer who invents a character to be the only client of a prostitute (Shirley MacLaine) he has fallen in love with in order for her not to sleep with other men has not dated so well. However, the film is sumptuously made and Lemmon offers up another breathless performance. It is a stark contrast to his appearance opposite Lee Remick in Blake Edwards' *Days of Wine and Roses* (1962). They play a young couple who succumb to alcoholism and find their lives spiraling out of control. Lemmon's performance was nominated for an Academy Award. He went on to star in Edwards' *The Great Race* (1965), opposite Tony Curtis again. An attempt to cash in on the trend for huge ensemble caper movies, such as *It's a Mad, Mad, Mad, Mad World* (1963) and *Those Magnificent Men in their Flying Machines* (1965), it failed at the box office.

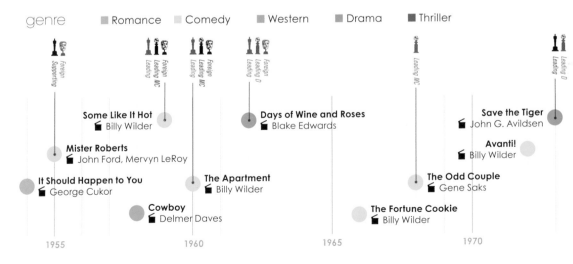

genre   ■ Romance   ■ Comedy   ■ Western   ■ Drama   ■ Thriller

Foreign Supporting

Foreign Leading MC / Leading

Foreign Leading MC / Leading

Foreign Leading D / Leading

Leading MC

Leading D / Leading

Some Like It Hot
Billy Wilder

Mister Roberts
John Ford, Mervyn LeRoy

It Should Happen to You
George Cukor

Cowboy
Delmer Daves

The Apartment
Billy Wilder

Days of Wine and Roses
Blake Edwards

The Fortune Cookie
Billy Wilder

The Odd Couple
Gene Saks

Save the Tiger
John G. Avildsen

Avanti!
Billy Wilder

1955   1960   1965   1970

$299M (U.S.)
The Odd Couple
(1968)

$166M (U.S.)
The China Syndrome
(1979)

$26M (U.S.)
Tribute
(1980)

$19M (U.S.)
Buddy Buddy
(1981)

$34M (U.S.)
Missing
(1982)

$18M (U.S.)
Glengarry Glen Ross
(1992)

$10M (U.S.)
Short Cuts
(1993)

Avanti!

Save
the Tiger

The China
Syndrome

Tribute

Buddy
Buddy

Missing

Glengarry
Glen Ross

Short Cuts

Wilder's cynical view of the world is more present in *The Fortune Cookie* (1966), whose account of a sports cameraman's attempts to dupe his insurance company out of a huge indemnity has lost none of its satirical bite. Lemmon is hilarious as the injured man, while Walter Matthau is his straight-faced attorney, "Whiplash Willie" Gingrich. It was the first pairing of the two actors. Their most famous role together is as the bickering roommates in Neil Simon's *The Odd Couple* (1968). Lemmon would direct Matthau in the comedy drama *Kotch* (1971) and the pair would remain a fixture on the screen into the 1990s with the amiable *Grumpy Old Men* (1993) and its 1995 sequel. For Wilder, they starred opposite each other in *The Front Page* (1974), a fast-paced adaptation of Ben Hecht and Charles MacArthur's 1928 play. If it lacks the brilliance of *His Girl Friday* (1940), Lemmon and Matthau remain galvanizing as two journalists racing against time to help prevent an innocent man being executed. The pair also starred in Wilder's last film, *Buddy Buddy* (1981). It is hardly the director's best work, but Lemmon is paranoia personified as a man contemplating suicide after his wife has left him, only to become an accomplice to Matthau's assassin.

Lemmon also starred in Wilder's *Avanti!* (1972), as a businessman who travels to Italy to collect his deceased father's body. There, he discovers his father had been having an affair for years and embarks on a relationship with the dead lover's daughter. One of Wilder's gentlest films, Lemmon is a much calmer presence. It is a marked contrast to his Oscar-winning turn in *Save the Tiger* (1973), as an executive who finds himself heading toward a breakdown. A powerful performance, it presaged the more serious roles that would dominate his later years.

He is brilliant in *The China Syndrome* (1979), as an engineer at a nuclear power plant who locks himself in the control room to raise awareness of the dangers of this relatively new fuel. He won the Best Actor prize at Cannes for his performance in *Missing* (1982), playing a father searching for his son following the Chilean coup in 1973. He exudes desperation as a salesman in *Glengarry Glen Ross* (1992) and in his brief, single-scene appearance in *Short Cuts* (1993), he plays a man who tries and fails to make peace with his estranged son. The nervous energy remains, but it is imbued with incalculable sadness at the mistakes we make in life and our inability to undo them. **IHS**

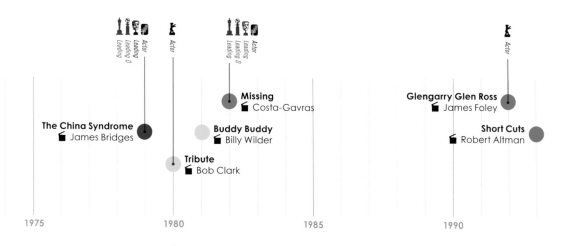

The China Syndrome
James Bridges

Actor
Leading
Leading D
Leading

Actor

Tribute
Bob Clark

Buddy Buddy
Billy Wilder

Actor
Leading
Leading D
Leading

Missing
Costa-Gavras

Actor

Glengarry Glen Ross
James Foley

Short Cuts
Robert Altman

1975   1980   1985   1990

tony leung 1962

A City of Sadness

Hard Boiled

Chungking Express

Happy Together

In the Mood for Love

Infernal Affairs

Hero

The Grandmaster

Best known as Wong Kar-wai's long-time collaborator, Tony Leung successfully made the transition from 1980s television idol to one of Hong Kong's greatest movie stars. He traverses both popular and arthouse cinema, national and transnational, setting him apart from the majority of Hong Kong movie stars, who have become globally famous via kung fu or action comedy.

Leung was born in Hong Kong in 1962. His father left when he was 8, and Leung quit school at 15 and worked in retail to help support his family. It was during this time that he befriended actor Stephen Chow, and it was on his advice that Leung enrolled in Hong Kong's television channel TVB's training program in 1982.

Leung's natural talent immediately won him roles in various television shows and he became a household name. His international breakthrough came with a stunning performance in Taiwanese director Hsiao-Hsien Hou's *A City of Sadness* (1989), which won the Golden Lion at the Venice Film Festival. His next major role was alongside Chow Yun-fat in John Woo's popular action film *Hard Boiled* (1992), in which he played a cool killer, before starring in Wong Kar-wai's wuxia-themed *Ashes of Time* (1994) and *Chungking Express* (1994). Their next collaboration was

the Palme d'or nominated *Happy Together* (1997), in which Leung and fellow Wong regular Leslie Cheung navigate a complex romantic relationship.

His performance in Wong's atmospheric masterpiece *In the Mood for Love* (2000) remains his most memorable role to date. Set in 1960s Hong Kong, Lee and costar Maggie Cheung, with whom the actor regularly appeared throughout the previous decade, play two people who find out their respective partners are having an affair. Moodily lit, with stunning costumes, the film is gorgeous to look at and their pairing is one of the most seductive in modern cinema.

In 2002, Leung starred in Andrew Lau's *Infernal Affairs*, playing an undercover cop and criminal. A smart thriller, it would be remade by Martin Scorsese as *The Departed* (2006). In the same year, he starred in Zhang Yimou's resplendent wuxia blockbuster *Hero*, which reunited him with Cheung. No less beautiful, but a great deal steamier, was Ang Lee's World War II erotic drama *Lust, Caution* (2007), with Leung taking on the role of a spy.

More recently, Leung reunited with Wong to star as the legendary Yip Man in the auteur's martial arts epic, *The Grandmaster* (2013). **CMB**

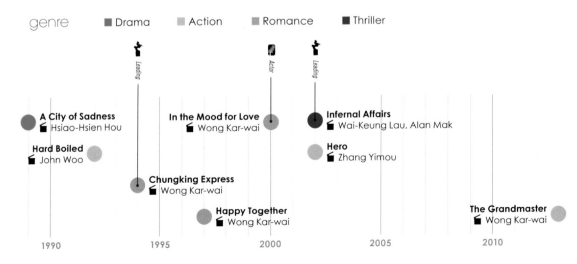

genre ■ Drama ■ Action ■ Romance ■ Thriller

A City of Sadness
Hsiao-Hsien Hou

Hard Boiled
John Woo

In the Mood for Love
Wong Kar-wai

Chungking Express
Wong Kar-wai

Happy Together
Wong Kar-wai

Infernal Affairs
Wai-Keung Lau, Alan Mak

Hero
Zhang Yimou

The Grandmaster
Wong Kar-wai

1990   1995   2000   2005   2010

jerry lewis 1926

| Artists and Models | Cinderfella | The Bellboy | The Nutty Professor | The Patsy | The Disorderly Orderly | The King of Comedy | Funny Bones |

For years, the achievement of Jerry Lewis was eclipsed by his status as a standing joke of U.S. cinema. By the late 1960s, he had become identified with an already passé stridency in American humor, while his public persona came to be tainted by the arduous sentiment of his charity telethons. It took a persona-redefining role in Martin Scorsese's The King of Comedy (1983) to show that Lewis was a much more complex performer than had generally been realized.

Lewis' breakthrough as a live performer came when he teamed up with crooner Dean Martin in 1945. From 1949 on, the duo made 17 films, most notably Artists and Models (1955) with director Frank Tashlin, who later made solo Lewis vehicles including Cinderfella (1960) and The Disorderly Orderly (1964).

When the duo split rancorously in 1956, Lewis reinvented himself as a successful solo star, then quickly went on to direct himself. Early ventures such as The Bellboy (1960) and The Patsy (1964) mix physical farce with benign but high-octane satire. The hyper-stylized mise-en-scène of The Ladies' Man (1961) impressed no less an admirer than Jean-Luc Godard. Arguably the star's defining performance, The Nutty Professor (1963) is one of several films that play on perceptions of the "Jerry Lewis" character; this Jekyll-and-Hyde parable pits the familiar goof against a lounge lizard alter ego, seemingly a merciless lampoon of Dean Martin.

Lewis' career flagged when he opted for a "mature" persona in the late 1960s. An unreleased movie about the Holocaust, The Day the Clown Cried (1972), remains legendary among celebrity missteps. Subsequent comedies such as Hardly Working (1980) were appreciated mainly in France, where he starred in two films made for the French market.

Perceptions of Lewis were transformed by his role as a hardened chat show host in The King of Comedy. In a taut, chilly performance, Lewis seems to offer a pitiless self-portrait as a man who has toiled too long in the showbiz mill and emerged without illusions. A decade later, Lewis impressed in a supporting role in another contemplation of the rewards and sacrifices of comedy, the eccentric Funny Bones (1995).

The sheer frenzy of Lewis' youthful style can feel jarring today, and much of his output has not aged well. But as American embarrassment about the kitsch aspects of his career is gradually forgotten, the originality, ingenuity and ferocious energy of Lewis' best performances continue to impress. **JR**

genre   ■ Musical   ■ Family   ■ Comedy

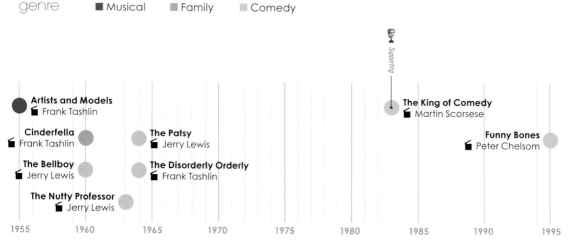

Supporting

Artists and Models
Frank Tashlin

Cinderfella
Frank Tashlin

The Bellboy
Jerry Lewis

The Nutty Professor
Jerry Lewis

The Patsy
Jerry Lewis

The Disorderly Orderly
Frank Tashlin

The King of Comedy
Martin Scorsese

Funny Bones
Peter Chelsom

1955   1960   1965   1970   1975   1980   1985   1990   1995

gong li 1965

| Red Sorghum | Ju Dou | Raise the Red Lantern | The Story of Qiu Ju | Farewell My Concubine | To Live |

Emerging as the face of a new China in the 1980s, Gong Li has played a key role in the nation's international cinematic reawakening. Gong found immediate success with her debut role as the subjugated yet headstrong My Grandma in Zhang Yimou's *Red Sorghum* (1987). Her subsequent partnership with Zhang would create an image of steadfast determinism, playing women overcoming oppressive structures throughout China's often-brutal history.

She was born in Shenyang, China, in 1965, during the Cultural Revolution. Failing the entrance exam into a prestigious music school, she took a place in the Central Academy of Drama in Beijing. Before she graduated she was cast in *Red Sorghum*, which received international acclaim and would be the beginning of a fruitful partnership between actor and director. She later starred in Zhang's controversial *Ju Dou* (1990), which was initially banned in China, allegedly due to its sexual content. It was also the first Chinese film to be nominated for an Academy Award.

More international successes followed with *Raise the Red Lantern* (1991), *Farewell My Concubine* (1993), *To Live* (1994) and *The Story of Qiu Ju* (1992), for which she won the Best Actress prize at the Venice Film Festival. She plays the eponymous heroine, a heavily pregnant rural peasant navigating China's justice system amid bureaucratic corruption. Directed yet again by Zhang the film was a stylistic and thematic departure for both director and actor, with its modern social realist setting and themes. Her collaboration with Zhang on *Shanghai Triad* (1995) would be their last for many years and would also mark the end of her highly publicized affair with the married director.

In 1997, Gong starred alongside Jeremy Irons and Maggie Cheung in the independent U.S. production, *Chinese Box* (1997), her first English-speaking role. She eventually made her major Hollywood debut as Hatsuomo in *Memoirs of a Geisha* (2005), followed closely by a key role in Michael Mann's *Miami Vice* (2006) and as Lady Murasaki in *Hannibal Rising* (2007). Cast in roles playing both Chinese and Japanese characters, Gong fell in line with a distinctly Hollywood idea of Asian female identity.

At the age of 41, Gong starred as Empress Phoenix opposite Chow Yun-fat in Zhang's wuxia blockbuster *Curse of the Golden Flower* (2006). She also starred in *Coming Home* (2014), which received its international premiere at the Cannes Film Festival. **CMB**

genre ■ War ■ Drama

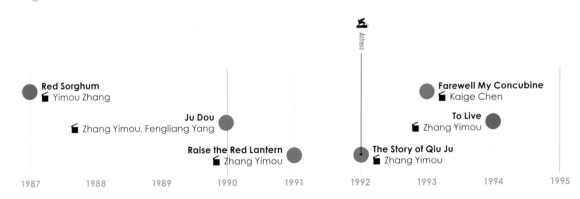

| Red Sorghum — Yimou Zhang | Ju Dou — Zhang Yimou, Fengliang Yang | Raise the Red Lantern — Zhang Yimou | The Story of Qiu Ju — Zhang Yimou | To Live — Zhang Yimou | Farewell My Concubine — Kaige Chen |

1987 1988 1989 1990 1991 1992 1993 1994 1995

ruan lingyu 1910–35

A Married Couple
in Name Only

Spring Dream in
the Old Capital

Love
and Duty

The Goddess

New Women

National
Customs

Often referred to as China's Greta Garbo, Ruan Lingyu is a legend of the Golden Age of Chinese cinema. A popular movie star of the silent era, Ruan came to represent the modern, urban, working "new woman" of Republican Shanghai. However, her fame and lifestyle led to constant scrutiny by the Chinese press and Ruan committed suicide in 1935 at the age of 24. It is reported that over 100,000 people attended her funeral.

Born Ruan Fenggen in Shanghai in 1910, her mother was a housemaid and her father a manual worker who died when she was 6 years old. In 1926, aged 16, Ruan responded to an advertisement in a newspaper calling for actors. She was immediately signed with the Shanghai-based Mingxing Film Company and starred in Bu Wangcan's A Married Couple in Name Only (1927), under the stage name Lingyu. However, it was her performance as a prostitute named Yan Yan, in Lianhua Studio's hugely successful Spring Dream in the Old Capital (1930), that made Ruan a star.

With the powerhouse Lianhua behind her, Ruan's popularity grew. She worked with the best filmmakers of the era, and was cast in lead roles as predominantly downtrodden yet heroic women, the best example of which is Love and Duty (1931). In 1933, she was cast in Bu Wangcan's Three Modern Women. This stronger, more fashionable role aligned her star image with that of the new urban women of Shanghai, increasing her popularity.

Ruan found herself increasingly cast as strong and complex women, making the most of her roles in films such as Fei Mu's debut Night in the City (1933) and The Goddess (1934), in which she plays a prostitute and single mother who kills her pimp. Also during this period, she married and divorced Zhang Damin, a bankrupt gambler, and began an affair with the tea tycoon Tang Jishan. Zhang sued Ruan following their divorce, and as a result she suffered intense tabloid scrutiny.

Her penultimate film, New Women (1935), was based on the tragic life of actress Ai Xia, who committed suicide in 1934, following a painful life under the glare of the press. Ruan plays Wei Ming, an independent and talented writer, who kills herself after being subjected to a tabloid scandal. The film was highly critical of the press, showing them to be heartless in their pursuit of a story. Unsurprisingly, it prompted a media backlash upon its release, and intensified scrutiny of Ruan. Imitating the desperate act of the film's tragic heroine, Ruan swallowed poison and died a month after the film's release. Her suicide note is reported to have contained the line, "Gossip is a fearful thing," singling out the press, who hounded her to her death. Later research indicates it was her relationship with the abusive Tang Jishan that was the more likely cause, suggesting he in fact forged the note. Ming-Yau Lo's National Customs would be Ruan's final film, released posthumously in 1935. **CMB**

genre   ■ Drama

● **A Married Couple in Name Only**
  🎬 Bu Wangcang

● **The Goddess**
  🎬 Yonggang Wu

● **Spring Dream in the Old Capital**
  🎬 Sun Yu

● **New Women**
  🎬 Chusheng Cai

● **Love and Duty**
  🎬 Bu Wangcang

● **National Customs**
  🎬 Ming-Yau Lo, Shilin Zhu

1927   1928   1929   1930   1931   1932   1933   1934   1935   1936

harold lloyd 1893–1971

Grandma's Boy

Safety Last!

Girl Shy

The Freshman

The Kid Brother

Feet First

Movie Crazy

The Sin of Harold Diddlebock

During the heyday of American silent comedy in the 1920s, Harold Lloyd was probably the most popular screen comedian of all, at least if box-office returns are any guide. Today he is generally ranked a poor third to Charlie Chaplin and Buster Keaton. His films lack the pathos of Chaplin's and the inventiveness of Keaton's, often relying on routine gags. And his classic screen persona — the all-American, go-getting young man — has not worn as well as Keaton's dogged loner or Chaplin's rebellious tramp. But there is a likeability about Lloyd, and his best films are highly watchable.

In his early shorts for Hal Roach, from 1915 to 1917, Lloyd appeared as a character called Lonesome Luke, obviously copied from Chaplin's tramp, and working strictly to formula; as Lloyd himself recalled, they "always ended with two hundred feet of chase." He never much liked the character and, in 1917, persuaded Roach to let him try out a new persona, whom Lloyd referred to as "Glasses": straw-hatted, bespectacled, invincibly keen, flashing a manic grin whenever he spots a pretty girl.

Lloyd played this character, usually billed as "The Boy," in around 100 shorts for Roach, before moving on to feature-length films in 1921. His short films have never enjoyed the same enduring popularity as those

of Keaton, Chaplin or Laurel and Hardy, and it is not hard to see why: they feel carelessly slung together, and often end just because they have run out of gags.

High and Dizzy (1920), one of Lloyd's last shorts, includes a brief ledge-walking scene that anticipates his skyscraper-climbing antics in *Safety Last!* (1923), the most successful of all his films and one of the year's top money-makers. *Girl Shy* (1924) did almost as well, with Lloyd embarking on a hair-raising ride on top of a runaway streetcar. Almost always he started off shy only to triumph in the last reel; in *The Freshman* (1925) he scores the winning goal in a football match, and in the western *The Kid Brother* (1927), he recovers the stolen gold that had been entrusted to his father, the sheriff.

Lloyd made the transition to sound relatively easily: his first film, *Feet First* (1930), with more high-building acrobatics, fell flat, but the Hollywood in-jokes of *Movie Crazy* (1932) fared better. But gradually over the decade he reached "the conclusion nobody had any particular use for me as a comedian any more." A shrewd businessman, he had invested wisely during his glory years, so it was only out of nostalgia that he made one last film, *The Sin of Harold Diddlebock* (1947). It was directed by Preston Sturges, but found neither him nor his star on form. **PK**

genre　■ Comedy　■ Action　■ Family

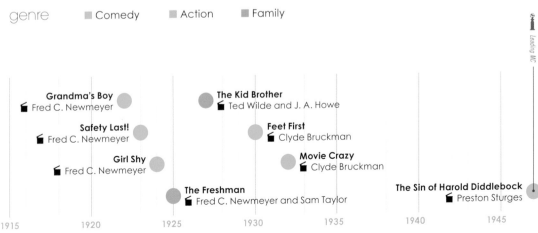

Grandma's Boy
Fred C. Newmeyer

Safety Last!
Fred C. Newmeyer

Girl Shy
Fred C. Newmeyer

The Freshman
Fred C. Newmeyer and Sam Taylor

The Kid Brother
Ted Wilde and J. A. Howe

Feet First
Clyde Bruckman

Movie Crazy
Clyde Bruckman

The Sin of Harold Diddlebock
Preston Sturges

1915　　1920　　1925　　1930　　1935　　1940　　1945

Leading MC

carole lombard 1908–42

| Man of the World | No Man of Her Own | Twentieth Century | My Man Godfrey | Nothing Sacred | Made for Each Other | Mr. & Mrs. Smith | To Be or Not To Be |

Carole Lombard was one of early Hollywood's most effervescent, brilliant comediennes. Born Jane Alice Peters to a wealthy family in Indiana, 1908, she was considered a tomboy and excelled at sports as a youngster, qualities which won her a small-screen role aged just 12. Encouraged by the experience, she changed her name, found work on a series of comedy shorts and, as the "talkies" caught on, began to find her métier. In 1931, she appeared opposite dashing star William Powell in *Man of the World*, playing a young American girl romanced in Paris by a novelist who is also blackmailing her wealthy uncle. Despite a 16-year age-gap, she and Powell married.

No Man of Her Own (1932) cast her against the actor who would become her second husband, Clark Gable. Although the drama is uninspired, the chemistry in their only screen pairing is palpable. Lombard's true strengths on screen were not harnessed until *Twentieth Century* (1934). Howard Hawks' fizzing, early screwball comedy costarred Lombard as a vainglorious diva dueling with John Barrymore's egotistical theater impresario. Her unfettered physicality, zinging dialogue and game matching of Barrymore's deliberate hamminess, made her a star.

Though divorced from Powell, she costarred with him to fine effect in *My Man Godfrey* (1936), a savvy, class-based comedy, in which Lombard's ditzy heiress hires a homeless man as the family butler. She and Powell shimmer off each other perfectly; as Lombard does with Fredric March, in *Nothing Sacred* (1937).

Despite her comedic success, Lombard evidently wanted to be taken more seriously. Though she acquits herself well in *In Name Only* (1939) with Cary Grant, or alongside James Stewart in *Made for Each Other* (1939), one misses Lombard's wilder side. Alfred Hitchcock's rare comedy *Mr. & Mrs. Smith* (1941) is labored material that is far from the star or director's best.

Her best was her last. In *To Be or Not To Be* (1942), Ernst Lubitsch's savagely funny farce about a hapless Polish acting troupe who thwart a Nazi spy plot, Lombard's wonderfully vapid ingénue gets immersed in, yet is somehow blissfully removed from, the real horrors; a stunning balancing act that heightens the daring humor. Sadly, before the movie even opened, Lombard was killed in a plane crash. She was just 33 and broke the heart of Clark Gable and movie lovers everywhere — her huge untapped potential destined to remain tragically unfulfilled. **LS**

genre ◼ Romance ◻ Comedy ◼ Drama

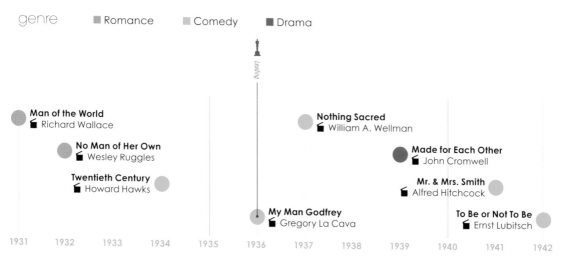

Man of the World
Richard Wallace

No Man of Her Own
Wesley Ruggles

Twentieth Century
Howard Hawks

My Man Godfrey
Gregory La Cava

Nothing Sacred
William A. Wellman

Made for Each Other
John Cromwell

Mr. & Mrs. Smith
Alfred Hitchcock

To Be or Not To Be
Ernst Lubitsch

Leading

1931   1932   1933   1934   1935   1936   1937   1938   1939   1940   1941   1942

sophia loren 1934

Aida

Scandal in Sorrento

The Pride and the Passion

The Black Orchid

Houseboat

That Kind of Woman

It Started in Naples

Two Women

Sophia Loren's career features almost 100 credits over seven decades, including a Best Actress Oscar. She is also regarded as one of the most beautiful women in the history of cinema. However, the captivating star power that apparently once saw Cary Grant begging for her hand in marriage came from humble beginnings. Born Sofia Villani Scicolone in Rome, 1934, she spent an impoverished childhood in her mother's hometown of Pozzuoli during World War II. By the age of 15, she had blossomed into a striking young woman and was shortly to begin her journey to stardom.

It was in Pozzuoli that she caught the eye of producer Carlo Ponti, who would later become her husband. Adopting the stage surname "Loren," she appeared in a series of films as an extra before her first starring role, as the titular *Aida* (1953), in a film adaptation of Verdi's opera. Her performance garnered much critical acclaim and from there her stock began to rise. She was cast in Vittorio De Sica's multi-narrative drama *The Gold of Naples* (1954), in which she played the wife of a pizzeria owner searching for her lost wedding ring. That same year saw the completion of *Too Bad She's Bad*

(1954), the first of 11 films with Marcello Mastroianni. They were soon reunited in *The Miller's Wife* (1955) and roles in *Scandal in Sorrento* (1955) and *What a Woman!* (1956) followed, before Hollywood came knocking.

Her American debut, *Boy on a Dolphin* (1957), saw Loren playing little more than an exotic beauty. The next few years were littered with roles that would propel her to international stardom: opposite Cary Grant and Frank Sinatra in *The Pride and the Passion* (1957); John Wayne in *Legend of the Lost* (1957); Anthony Perkins in *Desire Under the Elms* (1958); Grant again in *Houseboat* (1958); and as mistress to an industrialist in Sidney Lumet's oft-maligned *That Kind of Woman* (1959). These roles did little to suggest Loren's ability to act, but ensured that her looks attracted audiences in their droves. However, in the same year that she starred opposite Clark Gable in *It Started in Naples* (1960), Vittorio De Sica gave Loren the role that would finally change perceptions of her.

In returning her to native soil for *Two Women* (1960), De Sica stripped Loren of the frivolous glamour for which she was known internationally. His gritty

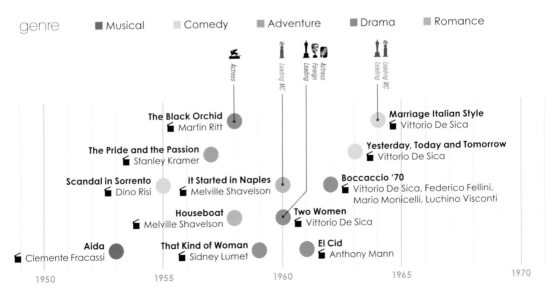

genre   ■ Musical   ■ Comedy   ■ Adventure   ■ Drama   ■ Romance

Actress

Leading MC

Leading

Actress Foreign

Leading

Actress MC

The Black Orchid
🎬 Martin Ritt

Marriage Italian Style
🎬 Vittorio De Sica

The Pride and the Passion
🎬 Stanley Kramer

Yesterday, Today and Tomorrow
🎬 Vittorio De Sica

Scandal in Sorrento
🎬 Dino Risi

It Started in Naples
🎬 Melville Shavelson

Boccaccio '70
🎬 Vittorio De Sica, Federico Fellini, Mario Monicelli, Luchino Visconti

Houseboat
🎬 Melville Shavelson

Two Women
🎬 Vittorio De Sica

Aida
🎬 Clemente Fracassi

That Kind of Woman
🎬 Sidney Lumet

El Cid
🎬 Anthony Mann

1950   1955   1960   1965   1970

| El Cid | Boccaccio '70 | Yesterday, Today and Tomorrow | Marriage Italian Style | The Verdict | The Voyage | A Special Day | Ready to Wear |

drama required an emotionally raw and physically demanding performance. Recalling the talent evident in her early work, Loren impressed her critics and audiences, becoming the first person to win an Oscar for a performance in a language other than English. Her profile sky-rocketed, allowing her to move with ease between Hollywood and Europe.

Loren romanced with Peter Sellers in *The Millionairess* (1960) and Charlton Heston in *El Cid* (1961). Further collaborations with De Sica included his segment of *Boccaccio '70* (1962), *Yesterday, Today and Tomorrow* (1963) and *Marriage Italian Style* (1964), for which she received rave reviews and a second Academy Award nomination. Meanwhile, she collected a record $1 million pay cheque for Anthony Mann's commercially catastrophic *The Fall of the Roman Empire* (1964). It had little measurable effect on its leading lady, however, and she continued to appear alongside the brightest male stars Hollywood could offer: Paul Newman in *Lady L* (1965), Gregory Peck in *Arabesque* (1966) and Marlon Brando in *A Countess from Hong Kong* (1967). Her first child was born in 1968 and acting

took a backseat to motherhood. What work she did do in the 1970s was largely away from the United States. De Sica's trailblazing *Sunflower* (1970) was the first western movie to shoot in the USSR and followed Loren's Giovanna as she traveled in search of her husband, still missing after World War II. And in De Sica's final film, *The Voyage* (1974), Loren was cast opposite Richard Burton in a misguided family drama. The rest of the decade also involved appearances in *The Verdict* (1974), the over-baked disaster movie *The Cassandra Crossing* (1976) and Ettore Scola's lauded drama *A Special Day* (1977).

In 1991, Loren was recognized by both the Oscars and the Césars with honorary awards, prior to another celebrated turn, in Robert Altman's *Ready to Wear* (1994). She appeared in a number of television movies before taking on the role of Daniel Day-Lewis' glamorous mother in Rob Marshall's *Nine* (2009), a glitzy musical interpretation of Federico Fellini's *8½* (1963). She recently published her memoirs, *Yesterday, Today, Tomorrow: My Life* (2014), which look back over a life of stardom, celebrity and glamour. **BN**

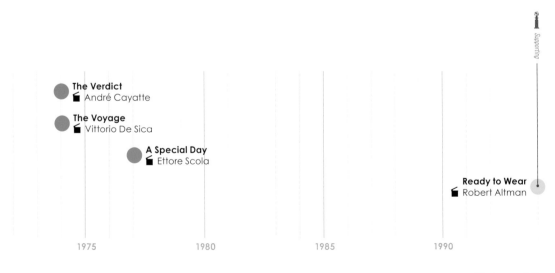

Supporting

The Verdict
André Cayatte

The Voyage
Vittorio De Sica

A Special Day
Ettore Scola

Ready to Wear
Robert Altman

1975   1980   1985   1990

Aida
(1953)

**The Pride
and the Passion**
(1957)

Houseboat
(1958)

**That Kind
of Woman**
(1959)

El Cid
(1961)

Boccaccio '70
(1962)

**Marriage Italian
Style**
(1964)

The Voyage
(1974)

Loren in her fist starring role as the eponymous **Aida**, an Ethiopian slave who falls in love with an Egyptian military commander.

Loren and Frank Sinatra in **The Pride and the Passion**, which was shot on location in Spain.

Houseboat was the second of two movies that Loren starred in with Cary Grant. Grant — 30 years her senior and married — became infatuated with Loren on their first film together, *The Pride and the Passion* (1957), begging her to leave her partner Carlo Ponti for him.

Sidney Lumet's **That Kind of Woman** starred Loren as the mistress of a millionaire industrialist who falls in love with a paratrooper played by Tab Hunter.

Loren and director Anthony Mann on the set of **El Cid**, about the legendary 11th-century Castillian knight.

oren received her second Oscar nomination for her role in *arriage Italian Style*, opposite Marcello Mastroianni.

The anthology film *Boccaccio '70* contains four episodes, by different directors, on the subject of morality and love. Loren starred in the episode "La riffa," directed by Vittorio De Sica.

arriage Italian Style stars Loren as a prostitute who embarks on an affair with a successful businessman, and ventually tricks him into marrying her.

Loren as the reluctant wife of Ian Bannen in Vittorio De Sica's final film, *The Voyage*.

peter lorre 1904–64

M

The Man Who Knew Too Much

Think Fast, Mr. Moto

The Maltese Falcon

Casablanca

Arsenic and Old Lace

Der Verlorene

The Raven

"I want to escape … to escape from myself! … But it's impossible! I can't. I can't escape … Who knows what it's like to be me? How I'm forced to act …" Cringing, pathetic, grotesque, the cornered child-killer makes his agonized plea to a grim-faced kangaroo court of criminals. Peter Lorre's leading role debut was also one of his finest performances, making him internationally famous. Yet at the same time it trapped him, sentencing him to 30 years of playing sad-eyed psychopaths. Throughout his career, the lines from Fritz Lang's M (1931) echo in ironic commentary.

But Lorre was also trapped by his own distinctive physique. Squat, stocky, round-faced, at once pitiable and terrifying: the eyes, liquid and soulful, that could abruptly bulge with murderous rage or ungovernable terror; the voice, a gentle mittel-European whisper, pitching without warning into a shrill fury of frustration and hate; the caged, prowling walk, driven by some intolerable restlessness of spirit. Small wonder if he found himself typecast as madmen and murderers.

Lorre himself, longing to extend his range, always claimed that his true bent lay in comedy, and often his best roles were a fine balance of comic and sinister. Hitchcock appreciated this quirky ambiguity, casting him in The Man Who Knew Too Much (1934) as the soft-spoken nihilist gang-leader, switching in an instant from coy affability to chilling menace; and in Secret Agent (1936) as a hit man known as the "Hairless Mexican," flamboyantly overdressed, giggling over the death of a wrongly identified innocent. And in The Maltese Falcon (1941) his high-camp villain, Joel Cairo, perfumed and querulous, fastidiously steals several scenes. This led to a teaming with the stately, orotund Sydney Greenstreet for eight more movies, Lorre's scuttering nervousness playing off the British actor's plump urbanity like a noir-tinged Laurel and Hardy.

There is a similarly fruitful play of opposites in the matching of Lorre, as squeamish plastic surgeon Dr. Einstein, with Raymond Massey's hulking, malevolent Jonathan Brewster in Arsenic and Old Lace (1944). Occasionally he was cast on the side of virtue, as in the eight Mr. Moto movies (1937–39) in which he improbably played a Japanese secret agent.

A bid for high seriousness in an adaptation of Crime and Punishment (1935) foundered on Josef von Sternberg's flaccid direction. But for the most part Lorre's 80-odd films offered him little more than what he sardonically referred to as "latrine duty." In 1951, he made his sole attempt at direction with Der Verlorene, playing a doctor in postwar Germany burdened with wartime guilt. A powerful, expressionist piece, it undeservedly flopped. After that he wandered with resigned sadness through some woefully bad films. Only the full-blooded gothickry of Roger Corman's Edgar Allan Poe adaptations (1962–63) offered a temporary respite, and his death at age 59 seemed a release. **PK**

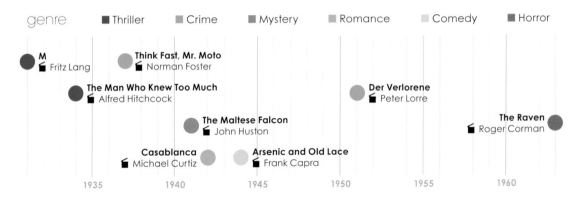

genre   ■ Thriller   ■ Crime   ■ Mystery   ■ Romance   ■ Comedy   ■ Horror

M
🎬 Fritz Lang

Think Fast, Mr. Moto
🎬 Norman Foster

The Man Who Knew Too Much
🎬 Alfred Hitchcock

Der Verlorene
🎬 Peter Lorre

The Maltese Falcon
🎬 John Huston

The Raven
🎬 Roger Corman

Casablanca
🎬 Michael Curtiz

Arsenic and Old Lace
🎬 Frank Capra

1935   1940   1945   1950   1955   1960

shirley maclaine 1934

The Trouble with Harry

The Apartment

Irma La Douce

Sweet Charity

Two Mules for Sister Sara

Being There

Terms of Endearment

In Her Shoes

Shirley MacLaine plays human beings. Many of her roles, and all her best ones, have portrayed women very far from movie-star perfection: fallible, misguided, vulnerable, affectionate, lovable, exasperating.

She was born in Richmond, Virginia, the older sister of Warren Beatty. In 1950, while still in high school, she joined the chorus line in a New York revival of *Oklahoma*. Talent-spotted while playing second lead in *The Pajama Game* (1954), her screen debut was auspicious; she landed the lead in Alfred Hitchcock's *The Trouble with Harry* (1955), as Harry's young widow.

She played a model in the Jerry Lewis and Dean Martin comedy *Artists and Models* (1955), but did not find it much fun, as the partnership was heading for its acrimonious rupture. Then she was the Indian princess hijacked by David Niven in *Around the World in 80 Days* (1956); utterly un-Indian, but delightful. She was a tomboy who attracts Glenn Ford's sheep-farmer in *The Sheepman* (1958), then the small-town floozie who scoops Frank Sinatra's ex-serviceman in *Some Came Running* (1958). Her rapport with Sinatra earned her honorary membership of the Rat Pack.

Ask Any Girl (1959) reunited her with Niven as a country girl in the big city, then she hit the jackpot with Billy Wilder's *The Apartment* (1960). Perfectly teamed with Jack Lemmon, her gamine charm as funny, sweet, wounded lift-girl Fran Kubelik marked a high point in her career. But after this she seemed to lose her way. She was a closeted lesbian in *The Children's Hour* (1961) with a crush on Audrey Hepburn, and a Parisian prostitute in *Irma La Douce* (1963), which reunited her with Wilder and Lemmon, but to disappointing effect.

She was off the screen for a while, then played another prostitute in *Sweet Charity* (1969), the musical version of Federico Fellini's *Nights of Cabiria* (1957). Then a prostitute again, this time disguised as a nun, in *Two Mules for Sister Sara* (1970).

Another hiatus, developing her live act, then superbly matched with Anne Bancroft as two old friends/rivals in *The Turning Point* (1977). She was the politico's wife trying to arouse passion in Peter Sellers in *Being There* (1979), a neurotic mother in *Terms of Endearment* (1983), and a domineering piano teacher in *Madame Sousatzka* (1988). Since the 1990s, MacLaine has increasingly portrayed grandmothers, always with spirit and never trying to play younger than her age. Since she never aimed for conventional screen glamour, old age suits her fine. **PK**

M

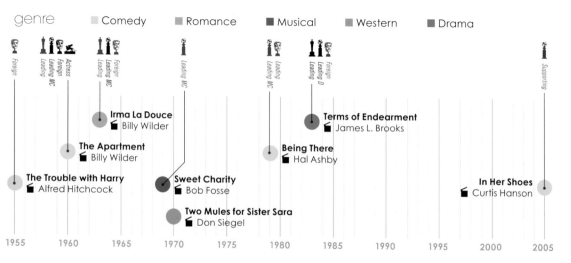

genre   ■ Comedy   ■ Romance   ■ Musical   ■ Western   ■ Drama

Irma La Douce
Billy Wilder

The Apartment
Billy Wilder

The Trouble with Harry
Alfred Hitchcock

Sweet Charity
Bob Fosse

Two Mules for Sister Sara
Don Siegel

Being There
Hal Ashby

Terms of Endearment
James L. Brooks

In Her Shoes
Curtis Hanson

1955   1960   1965   1970   1975   1980   1985   1990   1995   2000   2005

fred macmurray 1908–91

Grand
Old Girl

Alice
Adams

Hands
Across the
Table

Double
Indemnity

The Egg
and I

The Caine
Mutiny

The Shaggy
Dog

The
Apartment

Fred MacMurray was the "everyman" of postwar Hollywood cinema. Even if his name is less familiar now, his warm, fatherly smile and chiselled jaw is likely to evoke fond memories of the wholesome family movies he starred in throughout the 1950s and 1960s.

Born in Illinois in 1908, MacMurray was raised in Wisconsin. A proficient saxophonist and singer, he toured America before finding himself cast alongside Bob Hope in Jerome Kern's musical *Roberta* (1933). Success on the stage led to a contract with Paramount and MacMurray made his official on-screen debut in the romantic drama *Grand Old Girl* (1935). He then starred opposite Katharine Hepburn in *Alice Adams* (1935), as well as Henry Fonda and Sylvia Sidney in *The Trail of the Lonesome Pine* (1936). He also found himself cast as the romantic interest of Carole Lombard and Claudette Colbert in films such as *Hands Across the Table* (1935), *The Princess Comes Across* (1936), *Swing High, Swing Low* (1937) and *Maid of Salem* (1937). A string of popular comedies such as *Remember the Night* (1940) and *One Night in Lisbon* (1941) gave MacMurray a reputable image as one of Hollywood's busiest and most loved actors — a reputation that director Billy Wilder hoped to exploit in his hardboiled film noir *Double Indemnity* (1944).

A number of Hollywood A-Listers had turned down the role of gullible insurance agent Walter Neff before MacMurray was approached. He also voiced concerns, worried that his fans would disapprove of such a dark film and that he would struggle with the demands of the role. Nonetheless, his performance opposite Barbara Stanwyck was a roaring success and signaled a turning point in his career. His repertoire expanded, allowing him to appear in a wide range of roles. In the years that followed he starred as a naval officer opposite Humphrey Bogart in *The Caine Mutiny* (1954), a cop turned murderer in *Pushover* (1954) and as a husband who buys a rural chicken farm in the quaint romantic comedy *The Egg and I* (1947).

MacMurray appeared in an increasing number of wholesome Disney-produced family films in the later stages of his career. However, Billy Wilder had another trick up his sleeve, wanting the actor to play a morally compromised senior manager who coerces Jack Lemmon's youthful employee to rent out his home in *The Apartment* (1960). Released around the same time as Disney's *The Shaggy Dog* (1959), it was inspired casting and MacMurray once again delivered.

Moving into television, MacMurray appeared in the immensely popular *My Three Sons* (1960–72). He continued to make movies, mostly for Disney, such as *The Absent-Minded Professor* (1961) and *Son of Flubber* (1963), but a series of flops led him to focus more on his television work. After a long battle with cancer, MacMurray died in 1991. He will be remembered as one of Hollywood's most likeable figures. **PG**

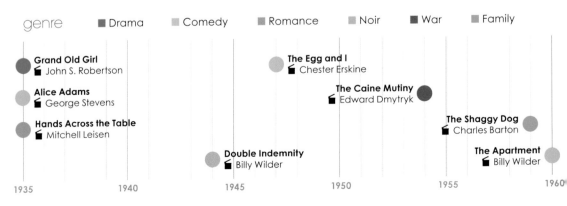

genre ■ Drama ■ Comedy ■ Romance ■ Noir ■ War ■ Family

Grand Old Girl
🎬 John S. Robertson

Alice Adams
🎬 George Stevens

Hands Across the Table
🎬 Mitchell Leisen

Double Indemnity
🎬 Billy Wilder

The Egg and I
🎬 Chester Erskine

The Caine Mutiny
🎬 Edward Dmytryk

The Shaggy Dog
🎬 Charles Barton

The Apartment
🎬 Billy Wilder

1935   1940   1945   1950   1955   1960

anna magnani 1908–73

| | | | | | | | | |

Rome, Open City   L'Amore   Bellissima   The Golden Coach   The Rose Tattoo   The Fugitive Kind   Mamma Roma   The Secret of Santa Vittoria

One of the great presences of postwar Italian cinema, Anna Magnani rarely did things by halves. From a desperately impoverished background herself, she breathed vivid life into a lengthy parade of working-class characters, defying cliché and stereotype.

She was born in 1908 and grew up in Rome. Funding acting studies by performing as a nightclub singer, she began her busy screen career with *The Blind Woman of Sorrento* (1934). Her breakthrough role was in Roberto Rossellini's *Rome, Open City* (1945), in which she played a World War II resistance activist, a performance singled out by international reviews.

Despite this new fame, she remained loyal to Italian cinema. Career highlights of this period include *L'Amore* (1948), in which she reteamed with her off-screen lover Rossellini for a diptych in which she played a woman trying to rescue a relationship over the telephone and a pregnant peasant convinced that she is the Virgin Mary. In Luchino Visconti's *Bellissima* (1951), she is the ultimate stage mother.

In 1951, Tennessee Williams premiered his play *The Rose Tattoo*, creating the character of Louisiana-based Italian-American widow Serafina with Magnani in mind, although she turned down the part on linguistic grounds. But she then starred in Jean Renoir's *The Golden Coach* (1952), in English, and felt confident enough to play Serafina in the 1955 film version of Williams' play, opposite Burt Lancaster. Her performance made her the first Italian actor to receive an Oscar. Williams wrote another play for her, *Orpheus Descending* (1957), although again she eschewed the stage part in favor of the film version, retitled *The Fugitive Kind* (1959).

She won awards for George Cukor's *Wild is the Wind* (1957, Berlin Silver Bear), as a Nevada-based Italian immigrant; Mario Camerini's *The Awakening* (1956, Silver Ribbon), as a nun who befriends a young boy; and Renato Castellani's *Behind Closed Shutters* (David di Donatello award) as a convict who takes new inmate Giulietta Masina under her wing. In 1962, she played the title role in *Mamma Roma*, as a reformed prostitute whose past threatens to catch up with her.

After professing disenchantment with earthy working-class roles, she largely abandoned the big screen, the major exception being *The Secret of Santa Vittoria* (1969). Her final film was Federico Fellini's *Roma* (1972), a brief cameo as herself, which was released the year before her death from pancreatic cancer. **MBr**

M

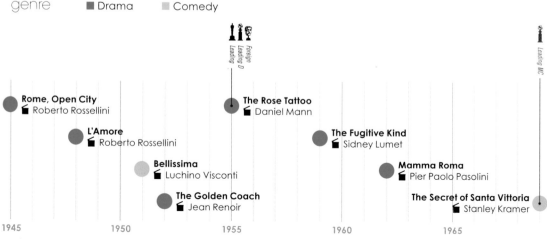

genre   ■ Drama   ■ Comedy

Foreign Leading D
Leading

Leading MC

Rome, Open City
Roberto Rossellini

The Rose Tattoo
Daniel Mann

L'Amore
Roberto Rossellini

The Fugitive Kind
Sidney Lumet

Bellissima
Luchino Visconti

Mamma Roma
Pier Paolo Pasolini

The Golden Coach
Jean Renoir

The Secret of Santa Vittoria
Stanley Kramer

1945   1950   1955   1960   1965

tobey maguire 1975

The Ice Storm | Pleasantville | The Cider House Rules | Ride with the Devil | Wonder Boys | Spider-Man | Seabiscuit | Brothers

Tobey Maguire's breakthrough came with the role of Paul Hood, an awkward college student in Ang Lee's 1970s-set drama *The Ice Storm* (1997). He accurately captures both the earnestness and embarrassment of youth as he attempts — and fails — to seduce Katie Holmes' wealthy Manhattanite. He next played the sex-obsessed fictional character of a writer in Woody Allen's *Deconstructing Harry* (1997).

After a small role as a hitchhiker in *Fear and Loathing in Las Vegas* (1998), Maguire turned in one of his best performances, playing alongside Reese Witherspoon as siblings who find themselves trapped in a 1950s television show in *Pleasantville* (1998). He is particularly convincing as a modern teen passing himself off as a member of Eisenhower's America. Ang Lee then cast him again in the underrated western *Ride with the Devil* (1999), which detailed the travails of immigrants along the border between north and south during the American Civil War. He plays the central character in the John Irving adaptation *The Cider House Rules* (1999), but the film fails to embrace the novelist's savage wit. He is excellent as the aspiring young writer who is bedded by Robert Downey Jr.'s literary agent in the hilarious *Wonder Boys* (2000).

Then came *Spider-Man* (2002) and stardom. Maguire was 28 when he was cast as Peter Parker but easily passes for 10 years younger and perfectly captures the awkwardness of late adolescence. His burgeoning romance with Kirsten Dunst's Mary Jane Watson is sweet without being sentimental. *Spider-Man 2* (2004) was even better, but 2007's third entry in the franchise was a mess, narratively and tonally.

The actor conveys the spirit of goodness in the solid *Seabiscuit* (2003) and proved to be surprisingly nasty in Steven Soderbergh's *The Good German* (2006). He further developed the dark side of his screen persona with *Brothers* (2009), as a soldier who returns a broken man from his captivity in Afghanistan and begins to suspect his wife of having an affair with his brother.

Maguire is hilarious in one of the spoof trailers at the start of *Tropic Thunder* (2008); this willingness to send himself up is also visible in the television comedy *The Spoils of Babylon* (2014). More serious roles have been less impressive. His Nick Carraway in Baz Luhrmann's adaptation of *The Great Gatsby* (2013) is too timid, while his cameo in *Labor Day* (2013) adds nothing to an insipid film. His portrayal of Bobby Fischer in *Pawn Sacrifice* (2014) is a more appealing prospect. **IHS**

genre ■ Drama ■ Fantasy ■ War ▢ Comedy ■ Action ■ Thriller

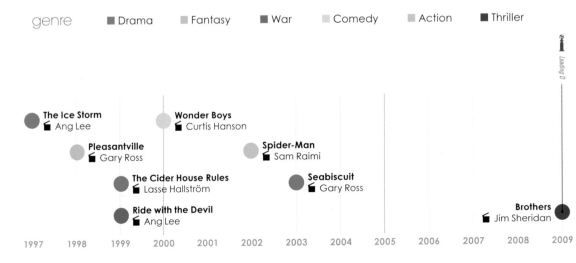

The Ice Storm
🎬 Ang Lee

Wonder Boys
🎬 Curtis Hanson

Pleasantville
🎬 Gary Ross

Spider-Man
🎬 Sam Raimi

The Cider House Rules
🎬 Lasse Hallström

Seabiscuit
🎬 Gary Ross

Ride with the Devil
🎬 Ang Lee

Brothers
🎬 Jim Sheridan

Leading D

1997   1998   1999   2000   2001   2002   2003   2004   2005   2006   2007   2008   2009

john malkovich 1953

The Killing
Fields

Dangerous
Liaisons

In the Line
of Fire

The Portrait
of a Lady

Con Air

Being John
Malkovich

Burn After
Reading

Changeling

A charter member of the Steppenwolf Theater Company, John Malkovich was an acclaimed stage actor before he began a career in film. His first success came with an Oscar nomination for his performance in *Places in the Heart* (1984), which was soon followed by an Emmy award for his portrayal of Biff in the CBS television adaptation of *Death of a Salesman* (1985).

He built a reputation for playing anti-authoritarian rogues thanks to solid performances in *The Killing Fields* (1984) and *Empire of the Sun* (1987). However, it was his stunning portrayal of the amoral Valmont in Stephen Frear's *Dangerous Liaisons* (1988) that saw him become a star. He followed it with an equally compelling performance in Bernardo Bertolucci's *The Sheltering Sky* (1990).

He starred with Steppenwolf colleague Gary Sinise in a fine adaptation of *Of Mice and Men* (1992) and excelled as the psychotic assassin in Clint Eastwood's *In the Line of Fire* (1993). *Mary Reilly* (1996) was a misfire, but he seethed contempt in Jane Campion's *The Portrait of a Lady* (1996). Then came a shock. He was surprising, but perfect, casting as Cyrus "The Virus" Grissom in the action blockbuster *Con Air* (1997). It is the first of numerous appearances in

big-budget mainstream titles that range from the good to the risible and include *The Man in the Iron Mask* (1998), *Joan of Arc* (1999), *Johnny English* (2003), *The Hitchhiker's Guide to the Galaxy* (2005), *Eragon* (2006), *RED* (2010) and its 2013 sequel, *Transformers: Dark of the Moon* (2011) and *Warm Bodies* (2013).

Between his Hollywood films, Malkovich has worked for some of the world's greatest directors. He appears in Wim Wenders and Michelangelo Antonioni's visually ravishing *Beyond the Clouds* (1995), had a key role in Raul Ruiz's ambitious *Time Regained* (1999) and is a fine Ripley in Liliana Cavani's *Ripley's Game* (2002). He returned to Ruiz to portray the great Austrian symbolist painter in *Klimt* (2006) and brought a similar artistry to his one feature — so far — as director, the sublime *The Dancer Upstairs* (2000).

His impressive appearances in the Coens' *Burn After Reading* (2008) and Clint Eastwood's *Changeling* (2008) notwithstanding, Malkovich's most celebrated role after *Dangerous Liaisons* is playing both himself and countless other John Malkovichs in Spike Jonze's madcap *Being John Malkovich* (1999). It goes to show that being a serious actor does not always mean having to be serious. **CGD**

M

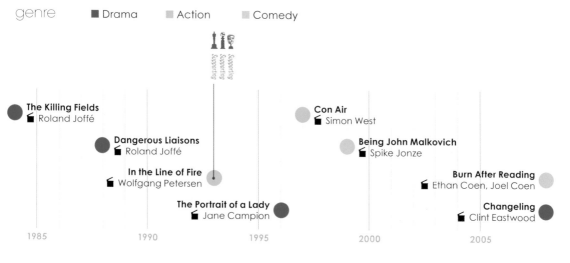

genre ■ Drama ■ Action ■ Comedy

Supporting
Supporting
Supporting

The Killing Fields
Roland Joffé

Con Air
Simon West

Dangerous Liaisons
Roland Joffé

Being John Malkovich
Spike Jonze

In the Line of Fire
Wolfgang Petersen

Burn After Reading
Ethan Coen, Joel Coen

The Portrait of a Lady
Jane Campion

Changeling
Clint Eastwood

1985   1990   1995   2000   2005

jayne mansfield 1933–67

Illegal

The Girl Can't Help It

The Burglar

The Wayward Bus

Will Success Spoil Rock Hunter?

Kiss Them For Me

The Sheriff of Fractured Jaw

Promises! Promises!

Jayne Mansfield's film career lasted a little over a decade, but encompassed one of the medium's most dramatic rise-and-falls. She was also one of the most famous sex symbols of her era, her blonde bombshell image eclipsing her work as an actress.

Born in Bryn Mawr, Pennsylvania, in 1933, Mansfield was a beauty queen and glamour model for *Playboy* when she first started working in film. After making her debut as a nymphomaniac in the B-movie noir *Female Jungle* (1955), her earliest appearances were uncredited bit-parts in *Pete Kelly's Blues* (1955), *Underwater!* (1955) and *Hell on Frisco Bay* (1955), followed by a small dramatic role in *Illegal* (1955).

Almost entirely ignored by the major studios, Mansfield's breakthrough came on stage, starring as the Marilyn Monroe-like film star Rita Marlowe in the play *Will Success Spoil Rock Hunter?* (1955). The role would fix the two actresses together in the public's imagination, with Mansfield often viewed as a gaudy facsimile of Monroe. The popular comedy ran on Broadway for over a year, during which time Mansfield had become a tabloid fixture and an attractive prospect as a new movie star. Twentieth Century Fox signed her to a lengthy contract and bought the film rights to the play in order to shut it down.

Her first major screen role was in the musical *The Girl Can't Help It* (1956), a sizeable commercial hit. While she became recognized for her comedic work,

the following year, in 1957, she gave two dramatic performances in *The Burglar* and the John Steinbeck-adaptation *The Wayward Bus*, the latter of which won her a Golden Globe as that year's "New Star." She also appeared in the film version of *Will Success Spoil Rock Hunter?*. These movies comprised the peak of her career, after which her decline was precipitous. In her final picture of the year, she starred with Cary Grant in the flop *Kiss Them For Me*. The overwhelmingly negative response caused Fox to lose interest, choosing to lend her to low-budget international productions until her contract ran out.

Aside from the British western *The Sheriff of Fractured Jaw* (1958) and sex comedy *Promises! Promises!* (1963) — promoted solely on the basis of it featuring Mansfield naked — the rest of her career was devoid of commercial success. Unable to find work in the United States, she mostly appeared in cheaply made foreign films like *Homesick for St. Pauli* (1963) and *Panic Button* (1964), with her last major role being in *The Las Vegas Hillbillys* (1966). Her voluptuous appearance and overtly sexual persona had become unfashionable, and while she remained famous she had become better known as a celebrity than a movie star. After a turbulent few years marked by alcoholism and an abusive relationship, she died in a car accident — the news of which received more attention than any of her final performances. **JWa**

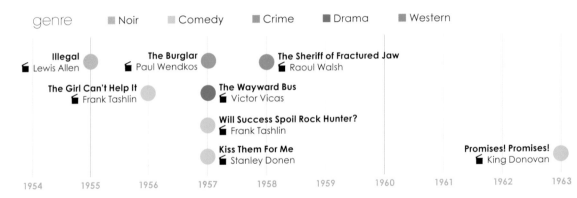

genre   ■ Noir   ■ Comedy   ■ Crime   ■ Drama   ■ Western

Illegal
Lewis Allen

The Burglar
Paul Wendkos

The Sheriff of Fractured Jaw
Raoul Walsh

The Girl Can't Help It
Frank Tashlin

The Wayward Bus
Victor Vicas

Will Success Spoil Rock Hunter?
Frank Tashlin

Kiss Them For Me
Stanley Donen

Promises! Promises!
King Donovan

1954   1955   1956   1957   1958   1959   1960   1961   1962   1963

sophie marceau 1966

The Party

Mad Love

Fanfan

Braveheart

A Midsummer Night's Dream

Nelly

Trivial

Female Agents

Sophie Marceau is an actress who thrives on interesting and challenging roles. She first caught the attention of audiences and critics when she was 14, in *The Party* (1980), a charming domestic comedy about a teenager navigating her way through high school and her parents' relationship dilemmas. Marceau would reprise the role, winning a César award for Most Promising Actress, in the 1982 sequel.

Following a key role in Alain Corneau's Foreign Legion drama *Fort Saganne* (1984), Marceau starred in her first collaboration with Andrzej Zulawski, *Mad Love* (1985). They would also work together on *My Nights Are More Beautiful Than Your Days* (1989), *La note bleu* (1991) and *Fidelity* (2000). Working with Maurice Pialat, Marceau gave a riveting turn as the object of fascination and desire for Gérard Depardieu's cop in *Police* (1985).

Fanfan (1993), an adaptation by Alexandre Jardin of his best-selling novel, saw Marceau take on a lighter role. However, the film failed to ignite the box office. The following year she convinced as the daughter of a famous musketeer, in Bertrand Tavernier's enjoyably silly period romp *Revenge of the Musketeers* (1994).

Already a much in-demand actress in Europe, by the mid-1990s Hollywood had taken notice. She was cast as Isabella of France in Mel Gibson's historically questionable Oscar-winner *Braveheart* (1995). While other supporting actors chew on the scenery,

Marceau plays Isabella with a subtlety missing from the rest of the film. In the same year, she was an ethereal presence in Michelangelo Antonioni's portmanteau movie *Beyond the Clouds* (1995).

Marceau's strong performance notwithstanding, Bernard Rose's *Anna Karenina* (1997) failed to capture the spirit of Leo Tolstoy's sweeping novel. Continuing her appearance in big-budget, English-speaking films, Marceau played Elektra King, one of the more interesting female Bond villains, in *The World Is Not Enough* (1999).

Entering a new decade, Marceau returned to Europe and embarked on a series of character-driven films. They included a moving performance as the wife of a recently deceased doctor in *Nelly* (2004), directing and starring in the period crime drama *Trivial* (2007) and, recalling her own youthful cinematic debut, playing the mother of a young 14 year old with love on her mind, in *LOL* (2008).

One of the biggest French hits of 2008, *Female Agents* saw Marceau cast among a host of leading French actresses as resistance members fighting the Nazis during World War II. Handsomely made, the film demands little of its cast, who nevertheless turn in uniformly excellent performances.

In 2013, Marceau appeared in the Hitchcockian-style thriller *Stop Me*, about a woman who admits to the murder of her abusive husband. She also reunited with *LOL* director Lisa Azuelos on *Quantum Love* (2014). **SW**

M

genre ■ Comedy ■ Drama ■ Romance

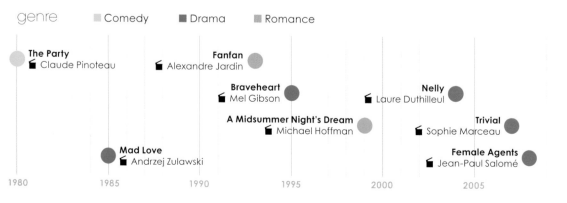

The Party
🎬 Claude Pinoteau

Fanfan
🎬 Alexandre Jardin

Braveheart
🎬 Mel Gibson

Nelly
🎬 Laure Duthilleul

A Midsummer Night's Dream
🎬 Michael Hoffman

Trivial
🎬 Sophie Marceau

Mad Love
🎬 Andrzej Zulawski

Female Agents
🎬 Jean-Paul Salomé

1980   1985   1990   1995   2000   2005

dean martin 1917–95

My Friend Irma

Artists and Models

The Young Lions

Some Came Running

Rio Bravo

Ocean's 11

Kiss Me, Stupid

The Silencers

There is an argument that Dean Martin only really ever played "Dean Martin" on screen. There is a counter-argument that, as one of America's most charismatic, easygoing, beloved all-round entertainers, it is all that audiences — and he himself — required.

Born Dino Paul Crocetti in Ohio, 1917, he left school early. His attempted career as a nightclub singer was unspectacular — until he met comedian Jerry Lewis. The duo developed an improvisatory musical-comedy act, Lewis as wild-card, man child and Martin as unruffled straight man, the stage sensation quickly graduating to television, radio and, inevitably, the movies. The pair debuted with supporting roles in *My Friend Irma* (1949), with Martin as smooth suitor to one of the leading ladies, and Lewis as his nutty sidekick.

Martin and Lewis popularized their star double-act across another 15 films, plugging Dean's crooning and Jerry's slapstick into various near-interchangeable templates. Perhaps their best is the vibrant *Artists and Models* (1955), buoyed by ex-Looney Tunes director Frank Tashlin and Shirley MacLaine. But in 1956 the pair split acrimoniously, never to re-team on film again.

Keen to move on, Martin was a left-field choice to star opposite Marlon Brando and Montgomery Clift in the war movie *The Young Lions* (1958); but, playing a cowardly showbiz entertainer forced to fight, Martin's natural charm helps him hold his own. *Some Came Running* (1958) was his first on-screen appearance

with Frank Sinatra; their real-life friendship is evident throughout, with Sinatra as the author/soldier returning to his hometown and Martin perfect as the resident smooth-talking, Stetson-wearing gambler.

Martin's most acclaimed performance came in Howard Hawks' classic western *Rio Bravo* (1959). His town drunk, who redeems himself as a member of John Wayne's outnumbered posse, showed a vulnerability he seldom exposed and confirmed his genuine skill as an actor. But then Martin drifted into Sinatra's "Rat Pack," the epitome of early-1960s, liquor-fueled, tuxedo-clad cool. It is a seductive but shallow mirage, and breezy, Vegas-set heist caper *Ocean's 11* (1960) is basically an excuse to pay homage at the Pack's court.

Further attempts at serious work — *Ada* (1961), *Toys in the Attic* (1963) — were not well received, which left either more Rat Pack hijinks or gamely sending up his own womanizing image as "Dino" in Billy Wilder's ribald *Kiss Me, Stupid* (1964). His Matt Helm spy spoof series, beginning with *The Silencers* (1966), was casual fun, but Martin was evidently more invested in his music and eponymous hit television show. Further movie roles — *Airport* (1970), *The Cannonball Run* (1981) — are less than perfunctory and he died, never voicing career regrets, a somewhat reclusive enigma in 1995. But then effortlessness is the essence of Dean Martin's appeal; for his many fans, the nonchalant, velvet-voiced charmer image is compensation enough. **LS**

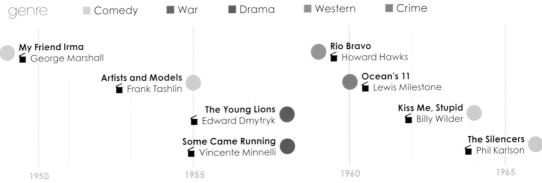

genre   ■ Comedy   ■ War   ■ Drama   ■ Western   ■ Crime

My Friend Irma
George Marshall

Artists and Models
Frank Tashlin

The Young Lions
Edward Dmytryk

Some Came Running
Vincente Minnelli

Rio Bravo
Howard Hawks

Ocean's 11
Lewis Milestone

Kiss Me, Stupid
Billy Wilder

The Silencers
Phil Karlson

1950   1955   1960   1965

lee marvin 1924–87

The Big Heat

The Man Who Shot Liberty Valance

The Killers

Cat Ballou

The Dirty Dozen

Point Blank

The Iceman Cometh

The Big Red One

One of Hollywood's great tough guys, Lee Marvin's best roles succeeded in revealing characters whose bravado hid doubts and insecurities. A native of New York, Marvin served in the Pacific during World War II. His experiences left him psychologically scarred. He became an actor by chance, when he was fixing the plumbing of a theater and was asked to stand in for a performer who was ill. He moved to Hollywood in 1950 and had various roles on television before he gave a memorable performance as a sadistic gangster in *The Big Heat* (1953). In the same year, he was a rival biker to Marlon Brando in *The Wild One* (1953). He went on to play a crewmember in *The Caine Mutiny* (1954) and one of the racists in *Bad Day at Black Rock* (1955).

He starred opposite John Wayne for the first time in *The Comancheros* (1961) and is the ill-fated gunfighter whose death lies at the heart of John Ford's *The Man Who Shot Liberty Valance* (1962). Ford, Wayne and Marvin collaborated again on the knockabout *Donovan's Reef* (1963) and the actor is outstandingly menacing in Don Siegel's remake of *The Killers* (1964).

Marvin's Oscar-winning turn in *Cat Ballou* (1965) highlighted his skill at comedy. An offbeat western, he is superb as the drunken bum Jane Fonda's

landowner hires to avenge her father's death at the hands of a gunslinger, also played by Marvin. He would return to the role of lovable rogue in *Paint Your Wagon* (1969) and *Shout at the Devil* (1976).

As the commanding officer taking 12 convicts on a deadly mission in *The Dirty Dozen* (1967), Marvin balances humor with gravitas. However, director John Boorman gave him two meatier roles. He is brilliant as Walker, a man hell-bent on revenge in *Point Blank* (1967). The film blended noir with the 1960s psychedelic scene to produce an edgy thriller and in Marvin an existential hero for the times. *Hell in the Pacific* (1968) might be more traditional, but Marvin and Toshiro Mifune are compelling as two soldiers playing a cat and mouse game on an island in World War II.

Prime Cut (1972) features another great face-off, this time between Marvin and Gene Hackman as two vicious gangsters, while his Hickey in *The Iceman Cometh* (1973) is a sad, pathetic figure of a man. As his career came to an end, Marvin turned in one of his best performances as a sergeant experiencing the worst of World War II in Sam Fuller's *The Big Red One* (1980). The character may be tough, but Marvin invests him with humor and humility. **IHS**

M

genre ■ Noir ■ Western ■ Crime □ Comedy ■ War ■ Drama

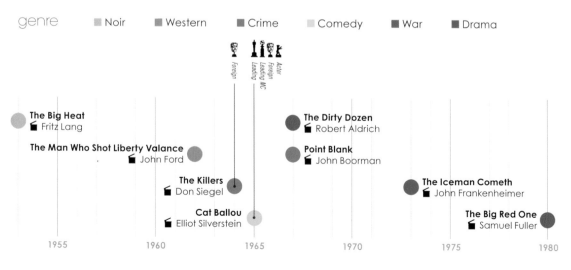

Foreign

Actor Foreign Leading MC Leading

The Big Heat
Fritz Lang

The Man Who Shot Liberty Valance
John Ford

The Killers
Don Siegel

Cat Ballou
Elliot Silverstein

The Dirty Dozen
Robert Aldrich

Point Blank
John Boorman

The Iceman Cometh
John Frankenheimer

The Big Red One
Samuel Fuller

1955   1960   1965   1970   1975   1980

the marx brothers

The Cocoanuts · **Animal Crackers** · **Monkey Business** · **Horse Feathers** · **Duck Soup** · **A Night at the Opera** · **A Day at the Races** · **Go West**

Groucho, Chico and Harpo — and perennial afterthought Zeppo — were genuine brothers, and the sibling rivalry ran high. That mutually relished aggression fuels the rampant anarchy of their best films, where nothing and nobody is safe from assault. Groucho (Julius, 1890–1977) had the caustic wisecracks, the cigar, the glasses, the loping walk and the greasepaint mustache; Chico (Leonard, 1887–1961) had the pixie hat, the cod-Italian accent and the flashy piano solos; curly-wigged Harpo (Adolph/Arthur, 1888–1964) was willfully dumb, larcenous and lecherous; Zeppo (Herbert, 1901–79) was the straight man, but quit the act after *Duck Soup* (1933).

Starting out before World War I in vaudeville, the brothers rose to become Broadway headliners in the 1920s. They scored a major stage success in 1925 with *The Cocoanuts*, which, in 1929, furnished the material for their debut film. It was the first of five innovative, subversive and borderline-deranged comedies they made for Paramount, the others being *Animal Crackers* (1930), *Monkey Business* (1931), *Horse Feathers* (1932) and *Duck Soup*. From their days onstage, the brothers brought their anarchic slapstick stylings to the screen and combined them with dialogue too intricate to be used in their vaudeville work. Sacred cows — always excepting their greatest stooge, the majestically impervious Margaret Dumont — tumbled at their approach. Self-lacerating humor

has never been sharper. Riotous physical comedy, such as the climactic football game/chariot run in *Horse Feathers*, could sit alongside one-liners like Groucho's "I was going to get a flat bottom — but the girl at the boathouse didn't have one."

Their Paramount run climaxed with the barbed satire of *Duck Soup*, with Groucho the leader of an armed European nation eager to start a war because, "I've paid a month's rent on the battlefield." It now looks like their greatest film, but at the time it flopped and the brothers (minus Zeppo) moved over to MGM, where studio head Irving Thalberg packaged them into a more commercially acceptable form. In the MGM films, from *A Night at the Opera* (1935) to *The Big Store* (1941), anarchy is toned down, pre-code naughtiness is dropped and tedious love-interest plots are added. There were still inspired moments, but increasingly the brothers looked like sub-plots in their own films.

The screen act broke up after *The Big Store*, but reunited for *A Night in Casablanca* (1946) and *Love Happy* (1949), reputedly to help Chico pay off his gambling debts. After that all three appeared, but in separate scenes, in Irwin Allen's rambling *The Story of Mankind* (1957), with Harpo playing Sir Isaac Newton. Groucho, in between stints on television as a gameshow host, featured in a few more films. His final appearance was in Otto Preminger's *Skidoo* (1968) where, suitably enough, he was cast as God. **PK**

genre ■ Musical ■ Comedy

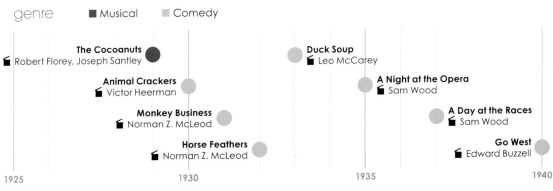

The Cocoanuts · Robert Florey, Joseph Santley
Animal Crackers · Victor Heerman
Monkey Business · Norman Z. McLeod
Horse Feathers · Norman Z. McLeod
Duck Soup · Leo McCarey
A Night at the Opera · Sam Wood
A Day at the Races · Sam Wood
Go West · Edward Buzzell

1925 · 1930 · 1935 · 1940

giulietta masina 1921–94

Variety
Lights

The White
Sheik

Europa '51

La Strada

Il Bidone

The Nights
of Cabiria

Juliet of
the Spirits

Ginger
and Fred

The female half of one of Italian cinema's greatest creative partnerships, Giulietta Masina made her deepest impression in her husband Federico Fellini's films, most notably *La Strada* (1954) and *The Nights of Cabiria* (1957), where her blend of comedy and pathos drew deserved comparisons with Charlie Chaplin.

She was born near Bologna in 1921 and grew up in Rome. She began acting at university and met Fellini when she was cast in one of his radio plays. They married in 1943. After a small, uncredited role in Roberto Rossellini's *Paisan* (1946), she made her formal film debut in *Without Pity* (1948). The film was directed by Alberto Lattuada and cowritten by her husband, who then jointly directed *Variety Lights* (1950), casting Masina as the jealous mistress of the owner of a shabby touring theatrical company. Fellini's solo debut, *The White Sheik* (1952), cast her as another prostitute. She then worked for Rossellini again on *Europa '51* (1952), as an impoverished mother-of-six taken under Ingrid Bergman's solicitous wing.

Masina then played her first lead role as Gelsomina, the naive young woman who becomes the reluctant assistant to Anthony Quinn's washed-up strongman in the masterly *La Strada*. It won the Silver Lion at Venice, the inaugural Oscar for Best Foreign Language Film and is still regarded as one of Italian cinema's supreme achievements.

She continued working with Fellini as the wife of Richard Basehart's frustrated painter-turned-crook in *Il Bidone* (1955). She then reprised the role of the prostitute Cabiria from *The White Sheik* in *The Nights of Cabiria*, eternally optimistic in the face of implacably grim social realities. *Juliet of the Spirits* (1965) was a lavish fantasy in which Masina's middle-aged housewife explores her own psyche to escape life with her unsympathetic husband. Two decades later, *Ginger and Fred* (1986) cast her opposite Marcello Mastroianni as a raffish pair of vaudeville performers who specialize in Rogers-Astaire impersonations.

She made a handful of other films and some television roles, none of which had the same profile. *Fortunella* (1958) was a winsome drudge, *Caged* (1959) was a woman-in-prison film costarring Anna Magnani, while the failure of *The High Life* (1960) triggered a career hiatus. Her final film was *A Day to Remember* (1991), in which her elderly matriarch falls victim to scheming descendants. She died in 1994, only a few months after her husband. **MBr**

M

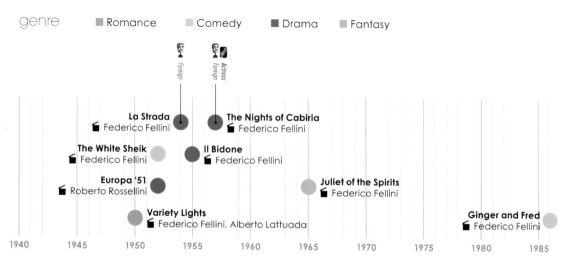

genre   ■ Romance   ■ Comedy   ■ Drama   ■ Fantasy

Foreign   Actress Foreign

La Strada
🎬 Federico Fellini

The Nights of Cabiria
🎬 Federico Fellini

The White Sheik
🎬 Federico Fellini

Il Bidone
🎬 Federico Fellini

Europa '51
🎬 Roberto Rossellini

Juliet of the Spirits
🎬 Federico Fellini

Variety Lights
🎬 Federico Fellini, Alberto Lattuada

Ginger and Fred
🎬 Federico Fellini

1940   1945   1950   1955   1960   1965   1970   1975   1980   1985

james mason 1909–84

| The Man in Grey | The Wicked Lady | Odd Man Out | Caught | Pandora and the Flying Dutchman | The Desert Rats | Julius Caesar | A Star Is Born |

James Mason, born in Huddersfield, England, in 1909, graduated from Cambridge University with a degree in architecture, but was drawn to acting. After a short time on stage he began to appear in "quota quickies," followed by roles in *Fire Over England* (1937) and *Thunder Rock* (1942), before making a name for himself in a series of Gainsborough melodramas.

The Man in Grey (1943) made him a star in the UK. He excelled as the bullying rake Lord Rohan. In *Fanny by Gaslight* (1944) he continued his run of dastardly villains, playing another selfish aristocrat. His attraction to audiences grew and in 1945 he made his international breakthrough with appearances in three films. *They Were Sisters* was the biggest success of the year in Britain and stands apart from other popular Gainsborough productions for its near-contemporary setting. Although he is still a villain in *The Wicked Lady*, he is a charming, dashing one, playing a highwayman who falls under Margaret Lockwood's spell. And in *The Seventh Veil*, Mason once again revels in his role, this time as a bullying pianist and music teacher whose malevolence toward his cousin hides his love for her.

In Carol Reed's *Odd Man Out* (1947) he had his most challenging film to date, playing an injured IRA robber on the run from the police, who gradually close in on him. Unlike his previous, more flamboyant roles, Mason expertly captures the fear of a man who faces certain death. He is no less impressive in his first American production, *Caught* (1949), Max Ophüls' film noir about a doctor entangled in a dangerous love affair with a married woman. He also starred in the director's *The Reckless Moment* (1949), as a blackmailer who falls in love with his quarry. Ophüls identified the actor's skill at conveying complex emotions with a glance.

Mason starred opposite Ava Gardner in the opulent fantasy drama *Pandora and the Flying Dutchman* (1951), one of the strangest, most visually resplendent films of the era, with the stars playing would-be lovers and the latest incarnation of mythical figures. Mason is less mercurial and more grounded playing Field Marshall Rommel in *The Desert Fox* (1951). He returned to the character again in *The Desert Rats* (1953), a less biographical but more dramatic account of the battle for North Africa during World War II. He would continue to play Germans in *The Blue Max* (1966) and Sam Peckinpah's *Cross of Iron* (1977), as well as a Nazi hiding out in South America in *The Boys from Brazil* (1978).

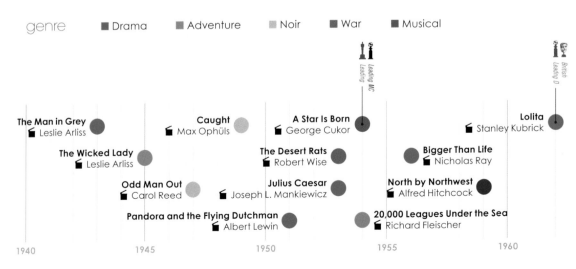

genre ■ Drama ■ Adventure ■ Noir ■ War ■ Musical

The Man in Grey — Leslie Arliss
Caught — Max Ophüls
A Star Is Born — George Cukor
Lolita — Stanley Kubrick
The Wicked Lady — Leslie Arliss
The Desert Rats — Robert Wise
Bigger Than Life — Nicholas Ray
Odd Man Out — Carol Reed
Julius Caesar — Joseph L. Mankiewicz
North by Northwest — Alfred Hitchcock
Pandora and the Flying Dutchman — Albert Lewin
20,000 Leagues Under the Sea — Richard Fleischer

1940   1945   1950   1955   1960

$38M
A Star Is Born
(1954)

$131M
The Verdict
(1982)

20,000
Leagues
Under the
Sea

Bigger
Than Life

North by
Northwest

Lolita

Age of
Consent

The Cross
of Iron

The Verdict

The
Shooting
Party

He is a captivating Brutus in Joseph L. Mankiewicz's starry production of *Julius Caesar* (1953) and gives an outstanding performance as Judy Garland's husband, a former matinee idol whose career is in decline, in *A Star Is Born* (1954). As Norman Maine descends into alcoholism, lashing out at his loved ones, Mason reminds us of the man's sense of helplessness — his actions a by-product of his desperation. The actor's study of mental illness is even more acute in Nicholas Ray's *Bigger Than Life* (1956), in which he plays a small-town schoolteacher whose bouts of pain are remedied by a new drug, only for it to have an adverse effect on his personality. The film failed to attract audiences, but it now ranks as one of Mason's best. He also starred as Captain Nemo in Disney's *20,000 Leagues Under the Sea* (1954).

Mason still relished a villain and is outstanding as Philip Vandamm, the smooth-talking killer in Alfred Hitchcock's *North by Northwest* (1959). He is the perfect counterpart to Cary Grant's confused, but no less slippery advertising executive. Stanley Kubrick also saw something fascinating in Mason's ability to present respectability while hiding something darker, casting him as Humbert Humbert in *Lolita* (1962). The

film features one of Mason's best scenes. After his wife has died in a road accident, Humbert runs a bath and pours himself a whisky. A neighbor arrives to find him in the bath, the whisky glass balanced between his chest and lip, and thinks he might be suicidal when he is, in fact, celebrating. It is a deliciously cruel scene and Mason plays it perfectly.

Back in England, he appeared in *Georgy Girl* (1966), as an older man lusting after Lynn Redgrave's happy-go-lucky Londoner, and a cuckolded spy in Sidney Lumet's bleak *The Deadly Affair* (1966). He plays a fictional version of Australian artist Norman Lindsay opposite Helen Mirren's youthful muse in Michael Powell's *Age of Consent* (1969) and convinces as a strict tutor at a Catholic boarding school in Lumet's *Child's Play* (1972). The director would exploit Mason's powerful screen presence again, this time as a feared attorney, battling Paul Newman's ambulance chaser, in *The Verdict* (1982). It was one of his final great roles, along with another patriarch, Sir Randolph Nettleby, in the pre-World War I drama *The Shooting Party* (1985). Mason invests Nettleby with dignity, a wiser man than those around him, who knows the world is changing and that he no longer has a role to play in it. **IHS**

M

■ Adventure   ■ Thriller   ■ Comedy

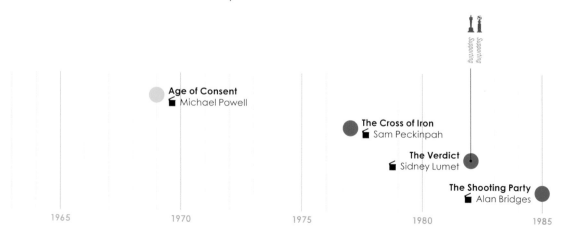

Supporting
Supporting

Age of Consent
◄ Michael Powell

The Cross of Iron
◄ Sam Peckinpah

The Verdict
◄ Sidney Lumet

The Shooting Party
◄ Alan Bridges

1965   1970   1975   1980   1985

marcello mastroianni 1924–96

Big Deal on Madonna Street

La Dolce Vita

Il Bell'Antonio

Divorce Italian Style

La Notte

Yesterday, Today and Tomorrow

8½

The Tenth Victim

If any one actor could be said to have embodied almost every aspect of being a modern Italian male, it was surely Marcello Mastroianni. Born in 1924, he grew up in Turin and Rome. He became a film extra in his mid-teens, graduating to small parts by his early twenties, and playing his first significant dramatic role in *The Charge is Murder* (1950). He kept busy throughout the 1950s, appearing in several films per year, winning the first of a record seven Silver Ribbon awards, presented by Italian film journalists, for *Days of Love* (1954). His second was for Luchino Visconti's *White Nights* (1957), in which he convincingly filtered a Dostoyevsky protagonist through a recognizably Italian psyche. By then an established presence in Italian cinema, he became a major international star with this and Mario Monicelli's crime caper *Big Deal on Madonna Street* (1958), in which the actor's washed-up photographer tries to juggle childcare duties with the planning of a jewel heist.

Federico Fellini's *La Dolce Vita* (1960) definitively established the Mastroianni persona: a would-be intellectual who is more professionally comfortable writing gossip-column drivel, a job that allowed both him and Fellini to take the cultural temperature of Rome at the turn of the 1960s, reveling in the glamour even as they expressed disapproval. Mastroianni would not work as frequently with Fellini as his reputation later suggested, but other key roles included a stunning performance as the creatively blocked director in *8½* (1963), the bewildered man trying to understand the inhabitants of the *City of Women* (1980), the washed-up Fred Astaire impersonator in the satire *Ginger and Fred* (1986), and as himself in the autobiographical *Intervista* (1987).

Other major Italian directors that Mastroianni worked with include Michelangelo Antonioni, Marco Bellocchio, Vittorio De Sica, Marco Ferreri, Elio Petri, Ettore Scola, Paolo and Vittorio Taviani, Giuseppe Tornatore and Lina Wertmüller. He also headlined a vast number of popular hits, notably *Il Bell'Antonio* (1960) and *Divorce Italian Style* (1961). He appeared in two of the more neglected films by John Boorman (*Leo the Last*, 1970) and Roman Polanski (*What?*, 1972), as well as forging a screen partnership with Sophia Loren that spanned a dozen films between 1954 and 1994, including the delightful *Yesterday, Today and Tomorrow* (1963), in which they played three separate couples in Naples, Milan and Rome.

genre ■ Comedy ■ Drama ■ Sci-Fi ■ Romance

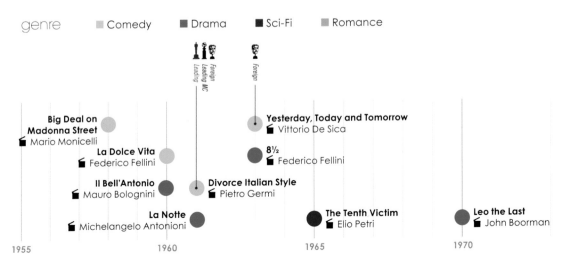

Big Deal on Madonna Street
Mario Monicelli

La Dolce Vita
Federico Fellini

Il Bell'Antonio
Mauro Bolognini

La Notte
Michelangelo Antonioni

Divorce Italian Style
Pietro Germi

Yesterday, Today and Tomorrow
Vittorio De Sica

8½
Federico Fellini

The Tenth Victim
Elio Petri

Leo the Last
John Boorman

1955 1960 1965 1970

| Leo the Last | Allonsanfan | A Special Day | City of Women | The Beekeeper | Dark Eyes | Everybody's Fine | Ready to Wear |

Mastroianni's filmography is vast. Standout performances include his ostensibly virile Romeo, privately struggling with personal problems, in *Il bell'Antonio*; his partnership with Jeanne Moreau as a couple watching their marriage fracture in Antonioni's *La Notte* (1961); the bleached-blond assassin playing a deadly sci-fi game in Petri's *The Tenth Victim* (1965); the would-be rake who can only become aroused in perilous situations in Monicelli's *Casanova '70* (1965); the man obsessed with balloons in Ferreri's *The Man with the Balloons* (1965); the exiled royal turned political radical in *Leo the Last*; one of a quartet of libertine gourmands gorging themselves to death in Ferreri's *La Grande Bouffe* (1973); the hesitant revolutionary in *Allonsanfan* (1974); the gay broadcaster in fascist Italy in Scola's *A Special Day* (1977); the title role in Marco Bellocchio's adaptation of Pirandello's *Henry IV* (1984); the misguidedly optimistic patriarch who decides to pay his neglectful offspring surprise visits in Tornatore's ironically titled *Everybody's Fine* (1990); and the laid-back Neapolitan foil to Jack Lemmon's overstressed American businessman in Scola's *Macaroni* (1985).

Mastroianni also shared with Lemmon the rare distinction of two Cannes Best Actor awards — his were for *Jealousy, Italian Style* (1970) and *Dark Eyes* (1987). He also achieved Best Actor Oscar nominations for *A Special Day* and *Dark Eyes*. He won a Golden Globe for *Divorce Italian Style* and a further nomination for *Used People* (1992), as well as a BAFTA for *Yesterday, Today and Tomorrow*. And there are countless Italian awards, culminating in a Venice Film Festival Golden Lion for his entire body of work.

As the Italian film industry ran into financial difficulties in the early 1980s, Mastroianni mainly worked abroad in his final years. He made *The Beekeeper* (1986) and *The Suspended Step of the Stork* (1991) for Theo Angelopolous, *Dark Eyes* for Nikita Mikhalkov, *Miss Arizona* (1988) for Pál Sándor, *The Children Thief* (1991) for Christian de Chalonge, *Used People* for Beeban Kidron, *1, 2, 3, Sun* (1993) for Bertrand Blier, *I Don't Want To Talk About It* (1993) for María Luisa Bemberg, *Ready to Wear* (1994) for Robert Altman, *One Hundred and One Nights* (1995) for Agnès Varda, *Three Lives and Only One Death* (1996) for Raoúl Ruiz, and his final film, Manoel de Oliveira's *Voyage to the Beginning of the World* (1997). When he died in 1996, Rome's Trevi Fountain, through which he so memorably waded in *La Dolce Vita*, was symbolically draped in black. **MBr**

M

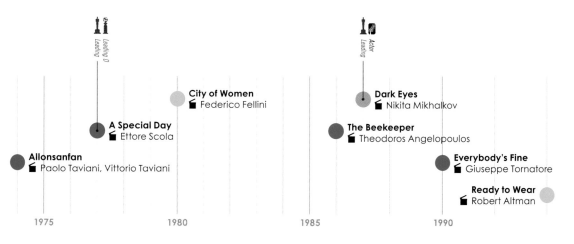

Leading D
Leading

City of Women
Federico Fellini

A Special Day
Ettore Scola

Allonsanfan
Paolo Taviani, Vittorio Taviani

Actor
Leading

Dark Eyes
Nikita Mikhalkov

The Beekeeper
Theodoros Angelopoulos

Everybody's Fine
Giuseppe Tornatore

Ready to Wear
Robert Altman

1975   1980   1985   1990

Big Deal on Madonna Street (1958)

La Dolce Vita (1960)

La Notte (1961)

Divorce Italian Style (1961)

8½ (1963)

Leo the Last (1970)

A Special Day (1977)

Ready to Wear (1994)

Mastroianni as the hapless, small-time criminal Tiberio in **Big Deal on Madonna Street**.

Federico Fellini's **La Dolce Vita** depicts a week in the life of Mastroianni's tabloid journalist, as he navigates the decadent high society of 1960 Rome.

Set during a single day, **La Notte** starred Mastroianni as a disillusioned novelist husband in a failing marriage.

Mastroianni as Guido Anselmi, the on-screen alter ego of Federico Fellini in the director's hugely influential **8½**.

Mastroianni as the unfaithful husband plotting to kill wife Daniela Rocca in **Divorce Italian Style**, Pietro Germi's satire of Sicilian male-chauvinist culture.

Leo the Last starred Mastroianni as an exiled prince living in London with his fiancée (Billie Whitelaw), who finds himself drawn to the life of West Indian immigrants living in the shadow of his mansion.

Mastroianni in ***A Special Day***, a role for which he received a Best Actor Academy Award nomination.

Ready to Wear was the final on-screen pairing of Mastroianni and Sophia Loren. The two first worked together in 1954, on *Too Bad She's Bad*.

carmen maura 1945

Tigres de papel	Pepi, Luci, Bom	What Have I Done to Deserve This?	Law of Desire	Women on the Verge of a Nervous Breakdown	¡Ay, Carmela!	Common Wealth	Volver

Carmen Maura's early life never hinted that she would become one of the most celebrated actresses in Spanish cinema. She was born in Madrid, 1945, into an illustrious family that featured a number of statesmen. She married at a young age and had two children. But in the late 1960s, a rebellious streak took hold and she chose to become an actress. The choice cost Maura her marriage, as acting was not seen as a respectable profession at the time.

Her first notable film role was in Fernando Colomo's *Tigres de papel* (1977). She was 32 years old and had just met the young filmmaker Pedro Almodóvar. She appeared in his first feature, *Folle... Folle... Fólleme, Tim!* (1978). The filmmaker found in Maura the perfect partner to embody characters experiencing a rollercoaster of extreme emotions, and capable of handling his signature mix of comedy and melodrama.

In *Pepi, Luci, Bom* (1980) she plays Pepi, who plots her revenge on the policeman who raped her by convincing his wife to leave him. In Miguel Picazo's *Extramuros* (1985), she is a lesbian nun in the 16th century. He regular appearances on television broadened her fan base, but she continued working with Almodóvar, starring in *Dark Habits* (1983), *What Have I Done to Deserve This?* (1984), *Matador* (1986) and *Law of Desire* (1987), in which she played a man who changed sex out of love for his father. The hugely popular *Women on the Verge of a Nervous Breakdown* (1988), earned Maura her first Goya, as well as the Best Actress award at the Venice Film Festival. But Maura's working relationship with the filmmaker was notoriously fractious and they parted company. She received two more Goya awards for Carlos Saura's *¡Ay, Carmela!* (1990) and Alex de la Iglesia's *Common Wealth* (2000).

In 2006, Maura reunited with Almodóvar on *Volver*, playing a dead woman who re-enters her daughters' life. The comeback was a celebration for all. The film was a huge success, both with critics and audiences; there is no doubt that Almodóvar's partnership with Maura is one of the most fruitful in his career. *Volver* earned its female cast a collective prize for Best Actress in Cannes, and Maura her fourth Goya.

A resident of Paris for more than 20 years, Maura was recognized by her French colleagues in 2010 with a César for Best Actress in a Supporting Role for *The Women on the 6th Floor*, and continues working with both French and Spanish filmmakers. **AG**

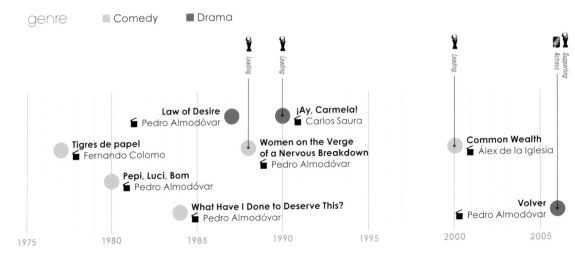

genre ■ Comedy ■ Drama

Leading   *Leading*   *Leading*   *Supporting Actress*

Law of Desire
▪ Pedro Almodóvar

¡Ay, Carmela!
▪ Carlos Saura

Tigres de papel
▪ Fernando Colomo

Women on the Verge of a Nervous Breakdown
▪ Pedro Almodóvar

Common Wealth
▪ Álex de la Iglesia

Pepi, Luci, Bom
▪ Pedro Almodóvar

What Have I Done to Deserve This?
▪ Pedro Almodóvar

Volver
▪ Pedro Almodóvar

1975   1980   1985   1990   1995   2000   2005

matthew mcconaughey 1969

Dazed and Confused	A Time to Kill	Contact	The Wedding Planner	Killer Joe	Mud	Dallas Buyers Club	Interstellar

Born in Texas, 1969, Matthew McConaughey's screen debut was as Wooderson, the 20-something slacker who hangs out with high schoolers in Richard Linklater's 1970s-set, coming-of-age classic *Dazed and Confused* (1993). Wooderson's boastful seduction of vulnerable teenage girls should be creepy, but McConaughey's laidback drawl and shameless charm created an iconic, much-loved character.

Great as *Dazed* was, it remained a cult hit. What set the mainstream media buzzing was his starring role as a straight-arrow lawyer defending a poor black father in racist Mississippi, in the John Grisham adaptation *A Time to Kill* (1996). The rippling physique, square jaw and blue eyes drew Paul Newman comparisons and McConaughey exuded star quality. Leading roles for major filmmakers — Robert Zemeckis' probing sci-fi *Contact* and Steven Spielberg's slavery drama *Amistad* (both 1997) — duly followed. However, despite decent work, the actor seemed to somehow disappear amid the effects, award-bait histrionics and higher-profile costars.

Hollywood kept trying — and failing — to make him a star, with the likes of media satire *EdTV* (1999) and submarine thriller *U-571* (2000). Then *The Wedding Planner* (2001) began an almost 10-year run of sunny, unfunny romantic comedies. Banking far too heavily on his good ol' boy allure, it seemed a creative dead-end.

Thankfully a new decade brought renewed career focus, and a succession of eye-catching, diverse performances in challenging projects: in William Friedkin's grim neo-noir *Killer Joe* (2011), he mined the chilling flipside of his Texan propriety, excelling as a sinister, black-clad cop who moonlights as a contract killer; in *Mud* (2012), he was a grizzled Mississippi fugitive who befriends two children; and in *Magic Mike* (2012), he reveled in his role as the cocky owner/performer of a male strip club. This much-vaunted "McConnaissance" was sealed with *Dallas Buyers Club* (2013), loosely based on the true 1980s tale of an HIV-positive homophobic rodeo worker who provided cheap AIDS medicine to the gay community. Gaunt, desperate but driven, McConaughey rode this underdog/antihero role all the way to Oscar glory.

His upward trajectory then ascended all the way to the stars in Christopher Nolan's sci-fi epic *Interstellar* (2014), playing an astronaut hero charged with finding mankind a new home. It is a role that would have been inconceivable for him even five years prior. **LS**

M

genre   ■ Comedy   ■ Thriller   ■ Sci-Fi   ■ Romance   ■ Crime   ■ Drama

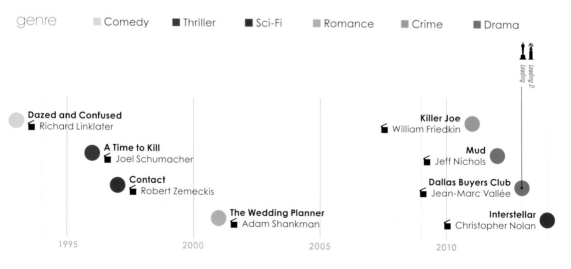

Leading D
Leading

Dazed and Confused
Richard Linklater

A Time to Kill
Joel Schumacher

Contact
Robert Zemeckis

The Wedding Planner
Adam Shankman

Killer Joe
William Friedkin

Mud
Jeff Nichols

Dallas Buyers Club
Jean-Marc Vallée

Interstellar
Christopher Nolan

1995   2000   2005   2010

hattie mcdaniel 1895–1952

| Judge Priest | Alice Adams | China Seas | Show Boat | Saratoga | Gone with the Wind | In This Our Life | Thank Your Lucky Stars |

Hattie McDaniel probably holds the record for the longest walk to the stage to collect an Oscar. She won Best Supporting Actress for her performance as Mammy, Scarlett O'Hara's house servant in *Gone with the Wind* (1939). Whereas most nominees are located close to the stage, McDaniel was seated at the back of the room. The first African-American to win an Oscar, her location in the room says much about the role of non-white actors in Hollywood at this time.

Born to former slaves in Wichita, Kansas, McDaniel started out as a musical performer before making her screen debut as a maid in *The Golden West* (1932). She was more prominent in the Mae West vehicle *I'm No Angel* (1933). A year later she was on contract with Fox and the roles became slightly bigger, but still limited to the kind of occupations that most African-American actors found themselves playing in films. Her most prominent role was in John Ford's *Judge Priest* (1934), which led to the comical Malena, who destroys a meal in *Alice Adams* (1935) and Jean Harlow's maid-cum-traveling companion in *China Seas* (1935). She played opposite Harlow again in the star's last film, *Saratoga* (1937). The year before, she starred opposite Irene Dunn and Paul Robeson in *Show Boat* (1936).

If she was criticized for cozying up a little too closely to Hollywood and playing roles that were seen as reductive in their representation of African-Americans, her most famous role showed that she was able to transcend the limitations of a character and offer up a more rounded screen persona than had been conceived on the page. Over 70 years on, *Gone with the Wind*'s romantic representation of the old South is hackneyed. But McDaniel's performance retains a spikiness that is is missing from so many of the other performances. Whether it's a smart put down or one of her withering looks, McDaniel is a dominant presence. Because of the Jim Crow laws, McDaniel could not attend the premiere in Atlanta, but she was at the opening in Hollywood and Selznick insisted that her face feature prominently in the marketing. Nonethless, she still had to sit separately from her fellow cast members at the Oscars.

In 1942, McDaniel played a maid confronting racism in John Huston's *In This Our Life*. The following year she was the best thing about *Thank Your Lucky Stars*, opposite Humphrey Bogart and Bette Davis. Her last role was in *Family Honeymoon* (1949). She had appeared in over 80 films in 17 years. **IHS**

genre   ■ Comedy   ■ Adventure   ■ Musical   ■ Romance   ■ Drama

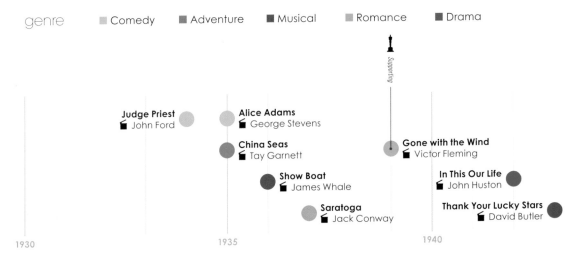

Supporting

Judge Priest
John Ford

Alice Adams
George Stevens

China Seas
Tay Garnett

Gone with the Wind
Victor Fleming

Show Boat
James Whale

In This Our Life
John Huston

Saratoga
Jack Conway

Thank Your Lucky Stars
David Butler

1930   1935   1940

ewan mcgregor 1971

Shallow Grave

Trainspotting

Velvet Goldmine

Star Wars: Episode I — The Phantom Menace

Moulin Rouge!

Young Adam

Beginners

The Impossible

Ewan Gordon McGregor was born in 1971, in Fife, Scotland. His first movie role was as one of a trio of Edinburgh housemates who uncover a dead body, a pile of money and their worst impulses, in Danny Boyle's hit thriller *Shallow Grave* (1994). McGregor's boyish good looks hinted at a danger beneath the charm, a quality even better utilized in his next film with Boyle, *Trainspotting* (1996). Based on the Irvine Welsh novel, the unapologetic tale of a group of young heroin addicts became the coolest British film of the time.

McGregor continued to do daring work in edgy films for unorthodox filmmakers, like *The Pillow Book* (1996) for Peter Greenaway or as a gay, 1970s glam rock star in the trippy *Velvet Goldmine* (1998) for Todd Haynes. It was not just that the actor took risks and let it all hang out, but evidently delighted in doing so. It was perhaps surprising, then, to see him accept the role of a young Obi-Wan Kenobi in the hugely anticipated *Star Wars* prequel *The Phantom Menace* (1999).

McGregor unerringly mimicked Alec Guinness' vocal inflections and was a natural for derring-do and lightsaber duels; whatever the defects of that film and its two sequels, he is not one of them. It also raised his profile and popularity enormously. As did Baz Luhrmann's *Moulin Rouge!* (2001), a delirious musical in which the actor played a writer in turn-of-the-20th century Paris, who is drawn into a tragic romance with Nicole Kidman's consumptive courtesan. McGregor's exuberance and supple tenor voice helped the film's devotees to swoon at its unashamed romanticism.

Amid a number of big U.S. movies — Ridley Scott's *Black Hawk Down* (2001) and Tim Burton's *Big Fish* (2003) among them — David Mackenzie's grim 1950s-set tale of adultery and murder, *Young Adam* (2003), was a welcome return to Scotland for the actor. Substantially more risqué, McGregor was effortlessly convincing as an amoral drifter.

Nonetheless, he remains in high demand with A-list directors like Woody Allen, Roman Polanski and Steven Soderbergh, who respectively cast him in *Cassandra's Dream* (2007), *The Ghost* (2010) and *Haywire* (2011).

If he has yet to find another role of the caliber of *Trainspotting*, some roles have still found him on excellent form. Recent highlights include *Beginners* (2010), playing an introverted man whose father comes out as gay, and a moving performance in *The Impossible* (2012), as a man separated from his wife and children in Thailand, following the tsunami in 2004. **LS**

M

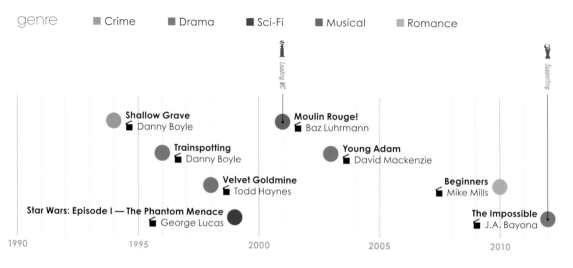

genre ■ Crime ■ Drama ■ Sci-Fi ■ Musical ■ Romance

Leading MC

Supporting

Shallow Grave
Danny Boyle

Moulin Rouge!
Baz Luhrmann

Trainspotting
Danny Boyle

Young Adam
David Mackenzie

Velvet Goldmine
Todd Haynes

Beginners
Mike Mills

Star Wars: Episode I — The Phantom Menace
George Lucas

The Impossible
J.A. Bayona

1990　　　1995　　　2000　　　2005　　　2010

steve mcqueen 1930–80

The
Magnificent
Seven

The Great
Escape

The
Cincinnati
Kid

The Sand
Pebbles

Nevada
Smith

The Thomas
Crown Affair

Bullitt

The Reivers

Steve McQueen was a fine actor and an even greater star. In his late-1960s prime, he brought to his roles a presence and attitude that made him one of the leading box-office draws of his day. But he was — and is — a style icon as well as an actor. An undeniably handsome leading man, with keen, watchful blue eyes and wiry blond hair, he perfected an acting style that was minimalist and inscrutable, and stood as a transitional figure between the laconic, no-nonsense approach of earlier actors like Gary Cooper and the laidback attitude of the Beat generation: even now, he can still be considered the King of Cool.

Born in Indiana in 1930, McQueen's background was troubled: he had a difficult relationship with his reportedly violent stepfather, and spent his mid-teens remanded to a boys' school. As a young man he joined the Marines; at first demoted for insubordination, he was eventually commended for his service and honorably discharged. His formative years, then, were marked at once by an attitude of anti-authoritarianism and by a sense of professional discipline, features that would go on to distinguish some of his finest roles.

After a brief spell on Broadway, he moved to California, scoring a handful of movie roles, notably supporting his future *The Towering Inferno* (1974) costar Paul Newman in *Somebody Up There Likes Me* (1956) and as the lead of the schlocky B-movie *The Blob* (1958). In the same year, an appearance in the television western *Wanted: Dead or Alive* (1958–61) gave McQueen his first big break.

He had a rugged charisma that suited the genre, and throughout his career he would return to the western. His first major screen role was in a western: John Sturges' *The Magnificent Seven* (1960). His was a supporting role, but he commanded the screen when he appeared, bringing a compelling combination of almost feline stillness and bursts of purposeful, often violent action that would become his trademark.

Sturges cast McQueen in his next film, this time in the lead. In World War II drama *The Great Escape* (1963) he played an anti-authoritarian U.S. captain held in a prisoner of war camp, who eventually helps with a tunnel break-out. The film was rousing entertainment and it made McQueen a star. He proved a natural rebel and carried off the rare trick of turning insolence into a form of charm.

Following solid performances in the 1965 depression-era drama *The Cincinnati Kid* and the

genre ■ Western ■ Adventure ■ Drama ■ Crime ■ Thriller

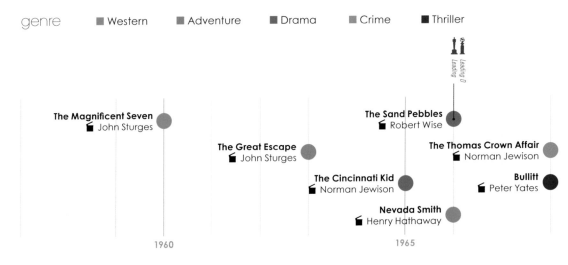

The Magnificent Seven
John Sturges

The Great Escape
John Sturges

The Cincinnati Kid
Norman Jewison

Nevada Smith
Henry Hathaway

The Sand Pebbles
Robert Wise

The Thomas Crown Affair
Norman Jewison

Bullitt
Peter Yates

1960

1965

Le Mans

Junior
Bonner

The
Getaway

Papillon

The
Towering
Inferno

An Enemy
of the
People

Tom Horn

The Hunter

1966 western *Nevada Smith*, McQueen took two contemporary roles that were to boost his profile. In *The Thomas Crown Affair* (1968) he played a rich bank executive who believes he has perpetrated the perfect heist; if the film now seems a little mannered, McQueen handled the role with suave assurance. Even better was his turn as the detective hero of San Fransisco-set police thriller *Bullitt* (1968): gifting the role a sense of serious, even somber professionalism that perfectly suited the film's hardboiled tone.

McQueen's personal obsession with cars figured throughout his career: he followed *Bullitt* with *The Reivers* (1969), an idiosyncratic comedy set in 1905, whose plot partly revolves around a stolen car, as well as a performance of ramshackle charm by McQueen. And in 1971 he played a racing driver in the auto-sports drama *Le Mans* — although he could do little to enliven the film's dramatic flatness.

In pointed contrast was the slick and fast-moving thriller *The Getaway* (1972), in which McQueen was a model of brutal efficiency as an ex-con on the run with his wife (Ali McGraw, whom he was to marry in real life). Director Sam Peckinpah had previously elicited one of McQueen's warmest and gentlest performances, as a veteran rodeo rider in the modern-day western *Junior Bonner* (1972).

By the early 1970s, McQueen was one of the biggest stars in Hollywood, his box-office supremacy confirmed by the top billing he received over a high-profile cast in the lavish disaster movie *The Towering Inferno*. But he was also acquiring a reputation for difficulty on set, and in the mid 1970s he took a break from filming, returning only for a strange, critically drubbed stab at a more serious role in the stagey 1978 adaptation of Ibsen's *An Enemy of the People*. (His earlier attempt at a prestige role in 1973's *Papillon* also received mixed reviews.)

In 1980, he attempted a comeback. The thriller *The Hunter* was a poor vehicle for his talents, but he had better luck with *Tom Horn*, a decent western that featured a strong performance from him as an ageing cowboy out of step with changing times. It proved especially poignant because McQueen was, at the time of shooting, suffering from cancer that would soon claim his life at the age of 50. He showed every sign of delivering great roles as he aged, but if his loss robbed us of those mature performances, the actor, in a screen career that lasted two decades, still wields enormous cultural influence. **EL**

M

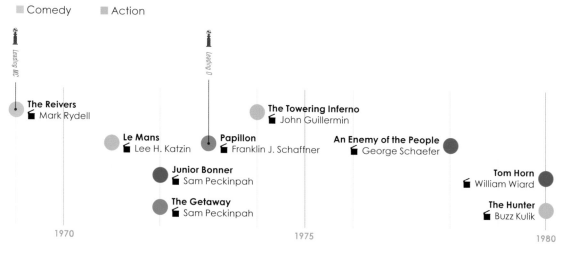

■ Comedy   ■ Action

Leading MC

Leading D

The Reivers
🎬 Mark Rydell

The Towering Inferno
🎬 John Guillermin

Le Mans
🎬 Lee H. Katzin

Papillon
🎬 Franklin J. Schaffner

An Enemy of the People
🎬 George Schaefer

Junior Bonner
🎬 Sam Peckinpah

Tom Horn
🎬 William Wiard

The Getaway
🎬 Sam Peckinpah

The Hunter
🎬 Buzz Kulik

1970

1975

1980

bette midler 1945

The Rose

Divine Madness!

Down and Out in Beverley Hills

Ruthless People

Beaches

For the Boys

Gypsy

The First Wives Club

Loud and sassy, Bette Midler did not so much arrive on the screen as explode onto it with her screen debut in *The Rose* (1979). By then, she was already an established stage act; as The Divine Miss M she was a gay icon and her acerbic, frequently foul-mouthed act offended as many as it entertained. Her move into film seemed a natural step.

She was 34 when she starred in *The Rose*. The character of Mary Rose Foster allowed Midler the opportunity to channel the energy of her live performance with a showcase for her acting talent. The result is edgy and driven, with Midler investing enough of her own persona into the role for it to feel more than a fictional account of Janis Joplin's last days. She followed it with *Divine Madness!* (1980), Michael Ritchie's documentary film, capturing her hilarious live performance at the Pasadena Civic Auditorium in 1979.

Paul Muzursky skillfully deploys Midler's comic skills in *Down and Out in Beverly Hills* (1986), his remake of Jean Renoir's 1932 film *Boudou Saved from Drowning*. She stars alongside Richard Dreyfuss as a wealthy couple who allow Nick Nolte's drifter into their home, with disastrous results. She would also star in Mazursky's *Scenes From a Mall* (1991), opposite Woody Allen.

Ruthless People (1986) followed. Less scabrous than Mazursky's satire, Midler is good as the kidnapped wife of a company boss who discovers her husband is not particularly interested in her being returned. However, the role hinted at a softening of her persona, which was confirmed by her roles in *Outrageous Fortune* (1987) and *Big Business* (1988). *Beaches* (1988) covers the 30-year friendship between Midler and Barbara Hershey's close friends. Featuring her rendition of "The Wind Beneath My Wings," Garry Marshall's film is unashamedly sentimental and was a hit with audiences. It also cemented Midler's position as a major mainstream star.

If *Stella* (1990) was a resounding failure, Midler was strong in *For the Boys* (1991), a fictional account of the life of Dixie Leonard. And she was outstanding as Mama Rose in the television adaptation of *Gypsy* (1993). She is entertaining as one of the witches in *Hocus Pocus* (1993) and relishes the role of a divorcée looking to avenge her philandering husband in *The First Wives Club* (1996). Since then, film roles suited to her talent have been thin on the ground. *Parental Guidance* (2012) was mildly successful but a pale shadow of her best work. **IHS**

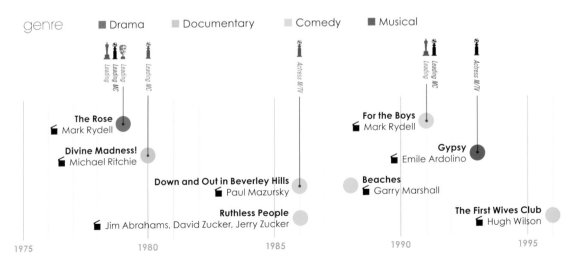

genre   ■ Drama   ■ Documentary   ■ Comedy   ■ Musical

The Rose
Mark Rydell

Divine Madness!
Michael Ritchie

Down and Out in Beverley Hills
Paul Mazursky

Ruthless People
Jim Abrahams, David Zucker, Jerry Zucker

For the Boys
Mark Rydell

Gypsy
Emile Ardolino

Beaches
Garry Marshall

The First Wives Club
Hugh Wilson

1975   1980   1985   1990   1995

toshiro mifune 1920–97

Stray Dog

Rashomon

Seven Samurai

Throne of Blood

The Hidden Fortress

Yojimbo

Samurai Rebellion

Hell in the Pacific

Toshiro Mifune first burst upon an astounded Western audience at the 1951 Venice Film Festival, in Akira Kurosawa's *Rashomon* (1950). The force and vitality of his performance brought him overnight global fame.

Mifune was born in Tsingtao, China, to Japanese parents. In 1945, following military service as an aerial photographer, he applied to Toho Studios for work in the photography department. According to legend, he was misdirected to the acting auditions, where he responded with a startling performance of such raw fury that Kurosawa immediately snapped him up.

Although he worked with almost every Japanese director of note, it is for his films with Kurosawa that Mifune will always be best remembered. The vigor of his acting perfectly matched the director's dynamic style of filmmaking. At his best, he was capable of performances of such gleefully savage energy as to make every other action star of the movies seem flatfooted. Kurosawa often liked to team him with Takashi Shimura, with the older and more staid Shimura playing the voice of experience to Mifune's impulsive hothead, as in the police drama *Stray Dog* (1949).

Beginning with *Drunken Angel* (1948), with Mifune electrifying as a young gangster, the actor and

director made 15 films together over the next 17 years. Mifune's commanding screen presence fitted him perfectly for period dramas — as the peasant would-be samurai in *Seven Samurai* (1954), the scruffy, scratching itinerant warrior of *Yojimbo* (1961) and its sequel *Sanjuro* (1962), or the Macbeth figure, dying a spectacular death in *Throne of Blood* (1957). Yet he was no less powerful in modern-dress roles, such as the beleaguered industrialist of *High and Low* (1963), or the Hamlet figure in Kurosawa's modern-dress Shakespeare, *The Bad Sleep Well* (1960).

Due to an estrangement of obscure origin, Mifune never again worked with Kurosawa after *Red Beard* (1965). He formed his own production company and remained constantly in demand; perhaps his finest role outside his work for Kurosawa was in Masaki Kobayashi's *Samurai Rebellion* (1967), as a samurai pitting himself against an unjust overlord. He also took on non-Japanese assignments, but few did him justice. It was only John Boorman's World War II drama, *Hell in the Pacific* (1968), where he played a Japanese naval officer stuck on a tiny island with a U.S. pilot (played by Lee Marvin), that captured something of his range, humor and power. **PK**

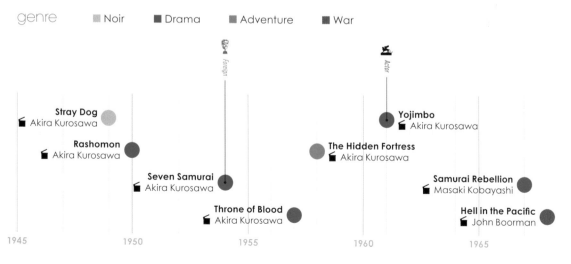

genre ■ Noir ■ Drama ■ Adventure ■ War

Stray Dog Akira Kurosawa

Rashomon Akira Kurosawa

Seven Samurai Akira Kurosawa

Throne of Blood Akira Kurosawa

The Hidden Fortress Akira Kurosawa

Yojimbo Akira Kurosawa

Samurai Rebellion Masaki Kobayashi

Hell in the Pacific John Boorman

1945   1950   1955   1960   1965

mads mikkelsen 1965

| Pusher | After the Wedding | Casino Royale | Coco Chanel & Igor Stravinsky | Valhalla Rising | A Royal Affair | The Hunt | The Salvation |

Born in 1965 in the Østerbro area of Copenhagen, Mads Mikkelsen is one of Europe's most recognizable, versatile and in-demand actors. Segueing effortlessly between arthouse and Hollywood productions, he made a startling debut in Nicolas Winding Refn's *Pusher* (1996), a violent portrayal of Copenhagen's criminal underbelly. He would reprise his role as Tonny in *Pusher II* (2004), this time taking center stage. The actor secured star status in his homeland with Susanne Bier's *After The Wedding* (2006), in which he discovers a life-changing secret upon returning to Denmark after running an orphanage in India.

Mikkelsen's brooding intensity catapulted him into another stratosphere when he was cast as the suave but twisted villain Le Chiffre in *Casino Royale* (2006). The scenes between Le Chiffre and Daniel Craig's Bond simmered with homoeroticism, especially during a critical scene in which Le Chiffre beats a naked 007. The actor did not allow the role to pigeon-hole him, however, by next appearing as Igor Stravinsky in Jan Kounen's classy romantic biopic *Coco Chanel & Igor Stravinsky* (2009). A third collaboration with Refn saw Mikkelsen deliver arguably his greatest performance to date as a one-eyed warrior in *Valhalla Rising* (2009).

Nikolaj Arcel's *A Royal Affair* (2012) witnessed a return to a more lush and opulent period drama, with Mikkelsen exceptional as a king's physician who attracts the lustful attentions of the monarch's young wife (Alicia Viklander). A sizeable European hit, the film followed another brief foray into more mainstream territory as Rochefort in Paul W.S. Anderson's unremarkable *The Three Musketeers* (2011). Heightened critical acclaim greeted Thomas Vinterberg's *The Hunt* (2012), a role for which Mikkelsen won the Best Actor prize at Cannes.

Returning to his small-screen roots in 2013 (from 2000 to 2004 he starred in the long-running Danish television drama *Unit One*), Mikkelsen offered a viable alternative to Anthony Hopkins as a debonair, sharp-suited Hannibal Lecter in the acclaimed *Hannibal*.

The actor's recent role in Kristian Levring's *The Salvation* (2014) makes Lars von Trier the one Danish director of note with whom he is yet to collaborate. Set in the American West in the 1870s, the film tells the story of a settler who kills his family's murderer, unleashing the fury of a notorious gang leader. When the cowardly townspeople betray him, he is forced to adopt *High Noon* tactics and go it alone. **JW**

genre   ■ Crime   ■ Drama   ■ Action   ■ Adventure   ■ Western

Actor

Pusher
📽 Nicolas Winding Refn

Coco Chanel & Igor Stravinsky
📽 Jan Kounen

After the Wedding
📽 Susanne Bier

The Hunt
📽 Thomas Vinterberg

Casino Royale
📽 Martin Campbell

A Royal Affair
📽 Nikolaj Arcel

Valhalla Rising
📽 Nicolas Winding Refn

The Salvation
📽 Kristian Levring

1996   2000   2005   2010

john mills 1908–2005

In Which We Serve

Great Expectations

Scott of the Antarctic

Hobson's Choice

Ice Cold in Alex

Tunes of Glory

Swiss Family Robinson

Ryan's Daughter

British actor John Mills' screen debut was in the comedy *The Midshipmaid* (1932), followed by the musical *Britannia of Billingsgate* (1933) and thriller *The Ghost Camera* (1933). The roles grew, but his major breakthrough came as Ordinary Seaman Shorty Blake, one of the survivors of a German U-boat raid in Noel Coward and David Lean's *In Which We Serve* (1942). Moving between the past, as a crew prepares to engage in battle, and the present, with a few survivors awaiting rescue, Mills represents the common man. He carried the role into *We Dive at Dawn* (1943).

Mills took one of the leads in *This Happy Breed* (1944), which tells the story of a British family in the years between the two world wars. He is excellent as a soldier who goes AWOL to prevent his wife succumbing to the advances of a draft-dodging cad in *Waterloo Road* (1945) and moved up to officer status for Anthony Asquith's *The Way to the Stars* (1945).

Though almost 40, Mills' youthful looks allowed him to carry off the role of the grown-up Pip in David Lean's first Charles Dickens adaptation, *Great Expectations* (1946). Only two years later, he looks understandably weathered as the tragic, eponymous explorer in Charles Frend's visually breathtaking *Scott of the Antarctic* (1948). He then returned to a more youthful look as the titular hero of H.G. Wells' *The History of Mr. Polly* (1949). He is equally impressive, holding his own against Charles Laughton's bullying patriarch, in Lean's comical *Hobson's Choice* (1954).

Mills continued to appear in war roles. He played legendary escapee Pat Reid in *The Colditz Story* (1955) and is one of a group on a mission in *Above Us the Waves* (1955). In 1958 alone, he played the head of an embattled unit in the African campaign drama *Ice Cold in Alex*, led a group of men out of *Dunkirk* and adopted a more suave persona as a spy trainer in *I Was Monty's Double*. There were also roles in *King Rat* (1965) and the anti-war satire *Oh! What a Lovely War* (1969).

Outside military uniform, Mills was excellent as a police officer investigating two murders in *Town on Trial* (1957) and the best dad any shipwrecked family could ask for in *Swiss Family Robinson* (1960). He confronted racism as the father of a woman who embarks on a relationship with a West Indian man in *Flame in the Streets* (1961) and won an Oscar for his portrayal of a mentally impaired man in Lean's uneven drama *Ryan's Daughter* (1970). More films followed, of varying quality, but Mills brought nobility to each role. **IHS**

M

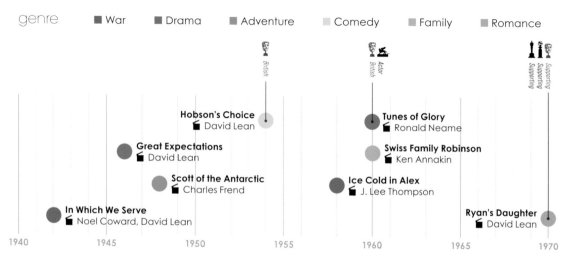

genre   ■ War   ■ Drama   ■ Adventure   ☐ Comedy   ■ Family   ■ Romance

British

Actor British

Supporting Supporting Supporting

Hobson's Choice
David Lean

Tunes of Glory
Ronald Neame

Great Expectations
David Lean

Swiss Family Robinson
Ken Annakin

Scott of the Antarctic
Charles Frend

Ice Cold in Alex
J. Lee Thompson

In Which We Serve
Noel Coward, David Lean

Ryan's Daughter
David Lean

1940   1945   1950   1955   1960   1965   1970

liza minnelli 1946

In the Good Old Summertime

Charlie Bubbles

The Sterile Cuckoo

Tell Me That You Love Me, Junie Moon

Cabaret

Lucky Lady

One of show business' most striking personalities, Liza May Minnelli was born in 1946 in Los Angeles, into Hollywood royalty. Her father, Vincente Minnelli, was making a name for himself as the director of classy musicals and melodramas, while her mother, Judy Garland, had been a superstar since the release of *The Wizard of Oz* in 1939.

She made her first movie appearance aged 3, in a vehicle for her mother, *In the Good Old Summertime* (1949). She was only a child when her parents divorced and remarried, and she witnessed her mother's professional highs and subsequent lows because of depression and substance abuse. As a result of her mother's emotional state, Minnelli matured early, taking care of domestic issues.

Influenced by her parents' tastes and gifted with her mother's vocal abilities, there was little doubt where she would end up. At the age of 13 she appeared on television, singing and dancing with Gene Kelly. She quit school at 16, moved to New York, and tried her luck with Broadway. Her deep and sonorous voice immediately attracted admirers, and the success of the 1963 show *Best Foot Forward* won her a recording contract. She was

the toast of the town once again in 1965, when her performance in *Flora the Red Menace* made her the youngest performer ever to be awarded a Tony. Her extravagant personality charmed audiences and she played to sold-out theaters.

Her first significant film role was in *Charlie Bubbles* (1967). However, critics first took notice when she appeared in Alan J. Pakula's directorial debut, *The Sterile Cuckoo* (1969), playing the funny, needy teenager, Poolie Adams. She was 23 and was nominated for an Oscar, Golden Globe and BAFTA for the role. She played a similar character in Otto Preminger's *Tell Me That You Love Me, Junie Moon* (1970). However, the glitter of her nascent fame was dulled by her mother's premature death in 1969. She dealt with grief by throwing herself into her work, taking one of her acclaimed musicals on tour.

The watershed in her career was Bob Fosse's decision to cast her in *Cabaret* (1972), a musical drama about life in Weimar Germany and the rise of the Nazis, set mostly in a nightclub and based on the writings of Christopher Isherwood. Minnelli was a perfect fit for Sally Bowles. If her mother had come to represent classical Hollywood, Minnelli represented

genre   ■ Musical   ■ Drama   ■ Romance   ■ Musical   ▢ Comedy

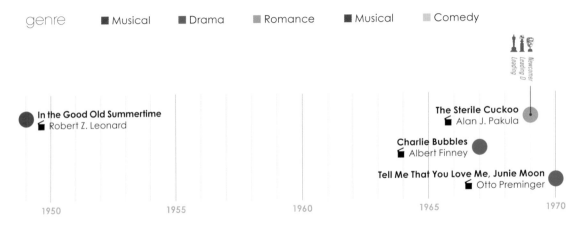

Newcomer
Leading D
Leading

In the Good Old Summertime
Robert Z. Leonard

The Sterile Cuckoo
Alan J. Pakula

Charlie Bubbles
Albert Finney

Tell Me That You Love Me, Junie Moon
Otto Preminger

1950   1955   1960   1965   1970

$239 M (U.S.)
Cabaret
(1972)

$106 M (U.S.)
Lucky Lady
(1975)

$148 M (U.S.)
Silent Movie
(1976)

$63 M (U.S.)
New York, New York
(1977)

$245 M
Arthur
(1981)

$29 M
Arthur 2:
On the Rocks
(1988)

A Matter of Time

Silent Movie

New York,
New York

Arthur

Arthur 2:
On the Rocks

Stepping Out

both the break with that time and, unsurprisingly, an echo of it. She was vivid and life-loving, but also flawed. Yet she still had the aura of an old star. Her Sally Bowles is a magnificent creation and she carries the film. A colossal success, it won her an Oscar, Golden Globe, BAFTA and countless other awards. She would work with Fosse again on the made-for-television musical extravaganza *Liza with a Z* (1972), which broke new ground for the medium and earned Minnelli an Emmy, making her one of the few performers to win major awards in theater, film and television.

Sadly, few roles offered the range of Sally Bowles and Minnelli's career began to fade following the failure of *Lucky Lady* (1975). She appeared in her father's film, *A Matter of Time* (1976), opposite Ingrid Bergman, but all three had done better work. Then Martin Scorsese approached her about the lead female role in a period musical he was developing. *New York, New York* (1977) is a coruscating account of the relationship between Minnelli's nightclub singer and Robert De Niro's jazz musician. Minnelli gives her all in a performance that ranks alongside Sally Bowles. Her rendition of the title song became a smash hit and was subsequently hijacked by Frank

Sinatra. But the film not only failed at the box office, it also confounded critics. Time has been kind to it and the film is now quite rightly hailed as one of Scorsese's best by many critics. However, another failure was too much for the star and Minnelli took a break from the movies and returned to the stage.

Her 1979 show at Carnegie Hall was another sell-out, bolstering her career. She was persuaded to return to film with a script about a rich drunk, his sarcastic butler and a working-class woman he falls in love with. Steve Gordon's *Arthur* (1981) was a breakout hit, thanks in no small part to Minnelli's sparkling performance. She went on a world tour, her popularity greater than ever.

Minnelli's life since has been a rollercoaster. There have been a number of relationships made public by constant paparazzi attention and her health has suffered. But then there was the 1987 residency at Carnegie Hall, another huge success. She toured with Frank Sinatra and Sammy Davis Jr. The films have been mixed. *Arthur 2: On the Rocks* (1988) was a mistake, but she was charming in *Stepping Out* (1991). Best of all are her appearances on the television series *Arrested Development* (2003–13). She sends herself up hilariously and, once again, proves herself a star. **AG**

■ Fantasy

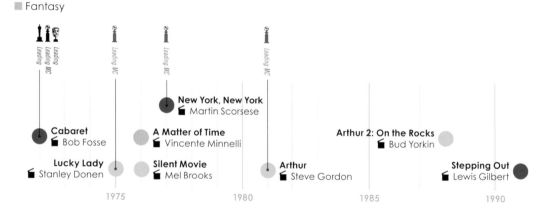

Cabaret
Bob Fosse

Lucky Lady
Stanley Donen

A Matter of Time
Vincente Minnelli

Silent Movie
Mel Brooks

New York, New York
Martin Scorsese

Arthur
Steve Gordon

Arthur 2: On the Rocks
Bud Yorkin

Stepping Out
Lewis Gilbert

1975   1980   1985   1990

helen mirren 1945

Age of Consent

O Lucky Man!

Caligula

The Long Good Friday

Excalibur

Cal

The Mosquito Coast

The Cook, the Thief, His Wife and Her Lover

Helen Mirren's own life has had flashes of the kind of moments that inspire films. Her grandfather was a Russian diplomat who became a taxi driver when he was stranded in London after the 1917 Russian Revolution. Mirren's name is an anglicized approximation of her birth name Ilyena Mironoff. To go from the granddaughter of a refugee to a Dame of the British Empire — via an Oscar, three Golden Globes and four BAFTAs — is an impressive journey.

Mirren was convinced from the age of 6 that she was destined to be an actress. She joined the National Youth Theatre aged 18, which led to a position with the Royal Shakespeare Company. Her first major screen role came in Michael Powell's *Age of Consent* (1969), playing the young muse to James Mason's ageing and jaded artist. As the somewhat wild and impetuous Cora, she offers glimpses of the sensuality that would define her as an actress. Art also provided the backdrop for her role in *Savage Messiah* (1972), Ken Russell's biopic of sculptor Henri Gaudier-Brzeska. Mirren again played a sensual artist's muse, but suffragette Gosh Boyle Smith is the antithesis of Cora — her sexuality appearing more deliberate and practical.

Two vastly different films with Malcolm McDowell followed. *O Lucky Man!* (1973) was Lindsay Anderson's brilliant and surreal follow-up to *If...* (1968). *Caligula* (1979) was widely reviled, with both screenwriter Gore Vidal and director Tinto Brass removing their names from the story of decadence and corruption in Ancient Rome, following the producer's decision to insert hardcore sex scenes. However, Mirren has always stood by the vilified film.

The most iconic of Mirren's early roles followed in *The Long Good Friday* (1980), generally considered one of the best British crime films. Mirren plays the wife of Bob Hoskins' gang boss. She plays her character with regal poise, hinting at the roles she would play later in her career. In fact, royalty — albeit of the legendary kind — was present in *Excalibur* (1981). While the film itself may have only been a moderate success, Mirren was commended for her chilling portrayal of vengeful sorceress Morgana.

She was also impressive in Pat O'Connor's *Cal* (1984), a romantic drama set against the backdrop of 1980s Northern Ireland. She revealed a softer, more tender side in her performance, adding immeasurably to the heartbreaking tale of two lovers caught up in

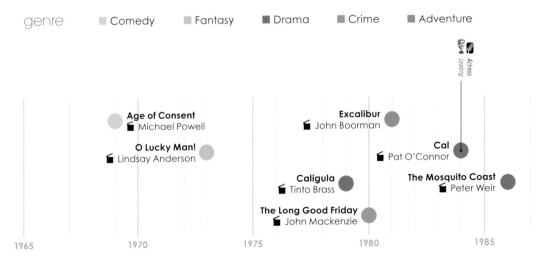

genre ■ Comedy ■ Fantasy ■ Drama ■ Crime ■ Adventure

Actress Leading

Age of Consent ▸ Michael Powell

O Lucky Man! ▸ Lindsay Anderson

Excalibur ▸ John Boorman

Caligula ▸ Tinto Brass

Cal ▸ Pat O'Connor

The Mosquito Coast ▸ Peter Weir

The Long Good Friday ▸ John Mackenzie

1965 1970 1975 1980 1985

$90M (U.S.)	$30M (U.S.)	$24M (U.S.)	$116M	$123M	$143M	$213M	$24M
Excalibur (1981)	*The Mosquito Coast* (1986)	*The Madness of King George* (1994)	*Gosford Park* (2001)	*Calendar Girls* (2003)	*The Queen* (2006)	*RED* (2010)	*Hitchcock* (2012)

The Madness of King George | Some Mother's Son | Gosford Park | Calendar Girls | The Queen | The Tempest | RED | Hitchcock

a violent and harsh outside world. Two years later, she was attempting to escape the world in a different way, in Peter Weir's survival adventure, *The Mosquito Coast* (1986). She is the loyal wife of Harrison Ford's eccentric inventor, forced into a difficult position by his insistence on moving their family to the jungle.

In the shocking and brilliant *The Cook, the Thief, His Wife and Her Lover* (1989), Mirren was anything but loyal as the alluring spouse of Michael Gambon's sadistic crook and restaurant owner. Her performance is remarkable for the way she transforms from the all-but-silent wife to the lover who finds freedom in another man's arms and, finally, a voice to counter the rasp of her bullying spouse. It is one of her finest performances. In 1991, she appeared on television in the role that would define her career, playing no-nonsense DCI Jane Tennyson in the BBC's critically acclaimed series *Prime Suspect*. The series dominated her career throughout the 1990s, and only her Oscar-nominated performance as Queen Charlotte in *The Madness of King George* (1994) stood out among her film roles of the decade.

The 2000s saw Mirren finally rewarded at the Oscars. Many felt she was unlucky to lose out on Best Supporting Actress for *The Madness of King George*, or when she was nominated for her excellent turn as the housekeeper in Robert Altman's British period drama *Gosford Park* (2001). It was for her heartfelt portrayal of Queen Elizabeth II in Stephen Frears' *The Queen* (2006) that she received the Best Actress prize, three years after she was made a Dame by the Queen herself. She was nominated for Best Supporting Actress a third time for *The Last Station* (2009), giving a fine performance as the wife of Leo Tolstoy.

Subsequent years have seen Mirren taking on a wide range of roles. She appeared alongside Bruce Willis and John Malkovich in the action movie *RED* (2010) and its 2013 sequel. She lent her voice to animated adventure *Legend of the Guardians: The Owls of Ga'hoole* (2010), and returned to the world of British gangsters in *Brighton Rock* (2010). She received BAFTA and Golden Globe nominations for her performance as Alma Hitchcock in *Hitchcock* (2012) and voiced the imposing Dean Hardscrabble in the Pixar sequel *Monsters University* (2013). She was nominated for her sixth feature film Golden Globe for her role as a snobbish restaurant owner in *The Hundred Foot Journey* (2014). **MG**

■ Mystery   ■ Action

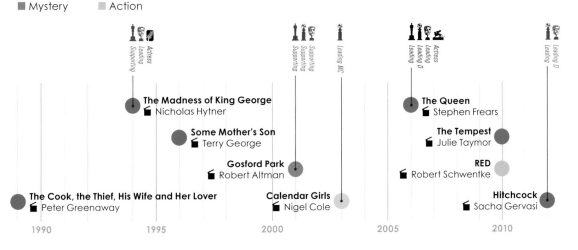

Age of Consent
(1969)

O Lucky Man!
(1973)

Caligula
(1979)

The Mosquito Coast
(1986)

Some Mother's Son
(1996)

Calendar Girls
(2003)

The Queen
(2006)

Hitchcock
(2012)

Age of Consent gave Mirren her first major film role, as a youthful muse to James Mason's ageing artist.

Causing controversy upon its release, *Caligula* is now a cult classic.

Mirren and Malcolm McDowell in the magical-realist *O Lucky Man!*.

Mirren and River Phoenix as mother and son in *The Mosquito Coast*. Her costar Harrison Ford later described her as "a wonderful blend of natural talent, understanding and technique and, dare we say it, balls."

Based on a true story, **Some Mother's Son** starred Mirren and Fionnula Flanagan as the mothers of two imprisoned IRA members participating in a hunger strike, facing the dilemma of watching their sons die or saving their lives.

critic Roger Ebert described Mirren's Oscar-winning turn as Queen Elizabeth II in **The Queen** as "a masterful performance, built on suggestion, implication and understatement." The actress went on to reprise the role on stage in 2013, for *The Audience*, to further acclaim.

Mirren as Chris Harper, one of the Women's Institute members who bares all in **Calendar Girls**.

Set during the filming of *Psycho* (1960), **Hitchcock** stars Mirren as the eponymous director's wife, Alma. The actress briefly met the real-life Hitchcock during an audition for *Frenzy* (1972), but the pair did not like each other.

robert mitchum 1917–97

The Story of G.I. Joe

Out of the Past

Crossfire

The Night of the Hunter

Heaven Knows, Mr. Allison

The Sundowners

Robert Mitchum may not have been revered like his costars and peers, such as Henry Fonda, Gregory Peck or Kirk Douglas. He may not be remembered as the diverse actor he was. His broad physique, dark features, heavily lidded eyes and laconic manner may have made him ideal for antiheroes or villains, and he especially excelled at the latter, but there was far more to the man than that. And if it seems like he was underappreciated, watching the body of work he left behind makes it almost impossible to deduce why.

Mitchum turned to acting after a nervous breakdown left him unfit for manual labor. He starred in a series of low-budget westerns, before breaking through in World War II drama The Story of G.I. Joe (1945). He played Bill Walker, the world-weary and ultimately heroic commanding officer of a company of infantrymen, being observed through campaigns in Africa and Europe by journalist Ernie Pyle. The film was commended for being one of the most realistic war films of its era and Mitchum was nominated for a Best Supporting Actor Oscar. It is no accident that Mitchum would forge his name through war films, westerns and film noir. His unquestionable physicality and masculinity made him utterly convincing as

soldiers, cowboys and detectives. He would earn a BAFTA nomination for his portrayal of a marine corporal shipwrecked alongside a nun in Heaven Knows, Mr. Allison (1957), directed by John Huston and costarring Deborah Kerr. He reunited with Kerr for The Sundowners (1960) and proved a useful talisman for her. Twice Kerr was nominated for Best Actress when starring opposite Mitchum, and this time she won. Mitchum would return to the military as Brigadier General Norman Cota in the epic depiction of the D-Day landing, The Longest Day (1962), alongside an all-star cast. Mitchum bid farewell to war films with Midway (1976), another all-star spectacular about an iconic World War II battle, but it was not received anywhere near as well as The Longest Day.

Mitchum found the perfect home in film noir, the genre that would come to define his career. He starred in several crime thrillers over the space of two years, the most enduring being Crossfire (1947) and Out of the Past (aka Build My Gallows High, 1947). The latter sees him as a true hardboiled antihero, consuming more cigarettes than would seem humanly possible as he tries to outwit Jane Greer's devious femme fatale. He delivers each fatalistic one-

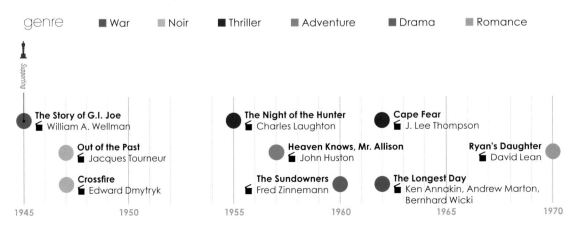

genre ■ War ■ Noir ■ Thriller ■ Adventure ■ Drama ■ Romance

Supporting

The Story of G.I. Joe
🎬 William A. Wellman

Out of the Past
🎬 Jacques Tourneur

Crossfire
🎬 Edward Dmytryk

The Night of the Hunter
🎬 Charles Laughton

Heaven Knows, Mr. Allison
🎬 John Huston

The Sundowners
🎬 Fred Zinnemann

Cape Fear
🎬 J. Lee Thompson

The Longest Day
🎬 Ken Annakin, Andrew Marton, Bernhard Wicki

Ryan's Daughter
🎬 David Lean

1945   1950   1955   1960   1965   1970

Cape Fear | The Longest Day | Ryan's Daughter | The Friends of Eddie Coyle | Farewell, My Lovely | Dead Man

liner with such aplomb that it is no wonder he would go on to play the Hamlet of film noir, private eye Phillip Marlowe, twice in the 1970s. Of these, *Farewell, My Lovely* (1975) is superior to the poor remake of *The Big Sleep* (1978), but his traditional take on Marlowe suffered in comparison to the updated version of the sleuth that Elliott Gould played in Robert Altman's *The Long Goodbye* (1973). He also produced, starred in and supposedly directed much of *Thunder Road* (1958), along with singing the theme song.

Mitchum was at his best when channeling a seam of malevolence. His turn as Reverend Harry Powell, the preacher with love and hate on his knuckles and murder in his heart, in Charles Laughton's nightmarish fairy tale *The Night of the Hunter* (1955) is unforgettably sinister and remains one of the greatest screen villains. Powell's nonchalance toward violence, often singing and whistling as he goes about his evil work, makes him unsettling company. Seven years later, Mitchum played the vengeful rapist Max Cady in *Cape Fear* (1962). His menacing performance is the highlight of the film. (Robert De Niro's psychopath in Martin Scorsese's 1991 version of *Cape Fear* draws heavily on Powell and the earlier version of Cady as influences.)

Mitchum also appeared in that film, albeit taking the side of the law.)

It would be disingenuous to imply that Mitchum was limited to villains or roughly hewn physical heroes. For instance, in 1970 he played a gentle schoolteacher in David Lean's *Ryan's Daughter*, set against the backdrop of the Irish fight for independence. The film was derided on its release — although it has fared better retrospectively — except for Mitchum, whose performance was praised by critics. Another riveting performance followed in *The Friends of Eddie Coyle* (1973), adapted from a novel by George Higgins. Peter Yates' downbeat crime drama concerns a low-level criminal whose days are numbered when his associates discover he has turned police informant. Mitchum is flawless as the downtrodden eponymous hero.

Of his work toward the end of his life, Mitchum's unmistakable tones lend added gravitas as the narrator of *Tombstone* (1993), and he was on fearsome form in his very brief but brilliant cameo in Jim Jarmusch's existential western *Dead Man* (1995). It is a wonderful sight to see Mitchum still so terrifying in his later years. He died in 1997. **MG**

■ Crime ■ Mystery ■ Western

The Friends of Eddie Coyle
Peter Yates

Farewell, My Lovely
Dick Richards

Dead Man
Jim Jarmusch

1975   1980   1985   1990   1995

marilyn monroe 1926-62

Ladies of
the Chorus

All About
Eve

The Asphalt
Jungle

Don't Bother
to Knock

Monkey
Business

Niagara

Gentlemen
Prefer
Blondes

How to
Marry a
Millionaire

Has there ever been a more iconic star than Marilyn Monroe? A symbol of all the glamour and beauty Hollywood can muster and possessing an incomparable screen presence, the girl once christened Norma Jeane Baker might just be the most perfect star the silver screen has ever known.

Born in Los Angeles, in 1926, Monroe had a difficult childhood spent mostly in foster homes, where she was more than once the victim of sexual assault. Intent on making an escape from such misery, aged just 16 Monroe married childhood sweetheart Jimmy Dougherty and went to work in a factory in California. Her beauty and photogenic looks soon led to work as a model. By 1946, her marriage had ended and she was on contract to Twentieth Century Fox. While there, Monroe made fleeting film appearances, but failed to land any speaking roles.

The next year, Monroe signed a six-month contract with Columbia, landing her first significant part in the musical Ladies of the Chorus (1948). The film failed to ignite the box office and her time with the studio proved short lived. Over the next few years, she would have small roles in a number of significant films, including John Huston's crime drama The Asphalt Jungle (1950), the iconic All About Eve (1950) and Fritz Lang's riveting Clash by Night (1952). Following these minor successes, she signed once again with Fox.

Monroe's first starring role came in 1952, in the form of Don't Bother to Knock. In the same year she played a ditzy secretary in Howard Hawks' screwball comedy Monkey Business. She is a beguiling presence in Niagara (1953), in which she plays a woman scheming to murder her husband. Although the film received much attention, many critics focused more on her looks than the quality of her performance.

The deliriously entertaining Gentlemen Prefer Blondes (1953) confirmed Monroe's superstar status. The story of two young women looking for love in Paris, the film was a runaway hit and featured some of the star's most memorable on-screen moments, including her dizzying rendition of "Diamonds Are a Girl's Best Friend." She followed it up with another smash hit, the comedy How To Marry a Millionaire (1953), playing opposite Betty Grable and Lauren Bacall.

Otto Preminger's western River of No Return (1954) may not be very well known, but it showcases a different side to Monroe and remains one of her most underrated performances. Unfortunately, the

genre   ■ Musical   ■ Crime   ■ Drama   ■ Thriller   ☐ Comedy   ■ Western

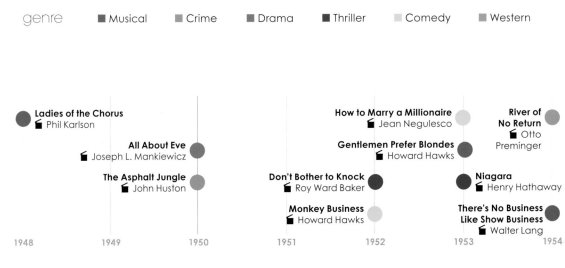

Ladies of the Chorus
Phil Karlson

All About Eve
Joseph L. Mankiewicz

The Asphalt Jungle
John Huston

Don't Bother to Knock
Roy Ward Baker

Monkey Business
Howard Hawks

How to Marry a Millionaire
Jean Negulesco

Gentlemen Prefer Blondes
Howard Hawks

Niagara
Henry Hathaway

There's No Business
Like Show Business
Walter Lang

River of
No Return
Otto
Preminger

1948   1949   1950   1951   1952   1953   1954

River of No Return

There's No Business Like Show Business

The Seven Year Itch

Bus Stop

The Prince and the Showgirl

Some Like It Hot

Let's Make Love

The Misfits

lackluster vaudevillian musical *There's No Business Like Show Business* (1954) displays almost no such qualities, and was a critical and commercial failure. Monroe also made headlines that year when she married the baseball legend Joe DiMaggio in a short-lived union.

Critical opinion of Monroe took a happy upswing with her acclaimed performance in *The Seven Year Itch* (1955). Its success earned her significant creative control on subsequent projects. At the same time, she became increasingly concerned with her on-screen persona. She took to studying with Lee Strasberg at the Actors Studio, determined to refine her craft.

Bus Stop (1956) marked a notable change from the light comedies and musicals for which she was known. Her performance, balancing lost-girl innocence with a raw sexuality, was met with positive reviews. She continued to surprise when she married the playwright and screenwriter Arthur Miller. Following the wedding, she traveled to England to star opposite Laurence Olivier in his film adaptation of the Terence Rattigan stage play *The Prince and the Showgirl* (1957). The shoot was problematic from the start, with the star reported to be incredibly difficult to work with. The film was a critical and commercial failure.

Following an absence from the screen in 1958, Monroe returned with the smash hit comedy *Some Like It Hot* (1959), playing Sugar Kane Kowalczyk — one of her best-loved roles. But despite the apparent harmony on screen, filming was once again plagued by reports of the actress' disruptive behavior.

The new decade saw her appear opposite Yves Montand in George Cukor's frothy *Let's Make Love* (1960), although there is little of merit to the film beyond the star's rendition of "My Heart Belongs to Daddy." The following year, she made her final complete performance in the magnificent but melancholic drama *The Misfits* (1961), which costarred Clark Gable and Montgomery Clift, and was written by Miller, whose relationship with Monroe had irreparably deteriorated.

Monroe had become almost entirely dependent on medication by this time. When she started work on her next film, *Something's Got To Give* (1962), opposite Dean Martin, she was suffering from severe anxiety and depression and was soon removed from the film, which was eventually abandoned. The scenes that Monroe shot would prove to be her last. That August, she was found in her home, having died from an overdose. She was just 36 years old. **MB**

M

■ Romance

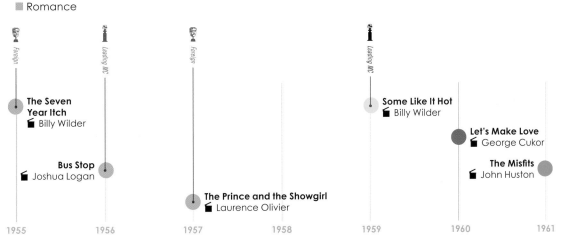

The Seven Year Itch
🎬 Billy Wilder — Foreign

Bus Stop
🎬 Joshua Logan

The Prince and the Showgirl
🎬 Laurence Olivier — Foreign

Some Like It Hot
🎬 Billy Wilder — Leading MC

Let's Make Love
🎬 George Cukor

The Misfits
🎬 John Huston

1955 1956 1957 1958 1959 1960 1961

Ladies of the Chorus
(1948)

Niagara
(1953)

Gentlemen Prefer Blondes
(1953)

How to Marry a Millionaire
(1953)

There's No Business Like Show Business
(1954)

The Seven Year Itch
(1955)

Some Like It Hot
(1959)

The Misfits
(1961)

Monroe sparkles as burlesque chorus girl Peggy Martin in **Ladies of the Chorus**, her first significant screen role.

Joseph Cotten and Monroe as a murderous husband and wife in the thriller-film noir **Niagara**.

Gentlemen Prefer Blondes cast Monroe in the star-making role of gold-digger Lorelei Lee.

Monroe as one of three resourceful women seeking rich husbands in **How to Marry a Millionaire**. Although Hollywood gossips predicted a battle of the blondes on set, the relationship between Monroe and costars Betty Grable and Lauren Bacall was very supportive.

A box office flop, *There's No Business Like Show Business* featured Monroe as a sexy nightclub singer.

Between 2,000 and 5,000 spectators watched Monroe film this iconic scene from *The Seven Year Itch* in New York, despite the shoot taking place at 1 a.m.

Despite vowing never to work with her again, *Some Like It Hot* director Billy Wilder always admitted that few performers had Monroe's brilliance for comic timing.

Clark Gable and Monroe in *The Misfits*, which tragically would be the final film released by both stars.

screen sirens

Pola Negri | Clara Bow | Louise Brooks | Jean Harlow | Hedy Lamarr | Jane Russell | Rita Hayworth | Dorothy Dandridge

Read any story about Hollywood's Golden Age and chances are you will soon hit upon the phrase "screen siren"; a variation on the concept of Greek mythology's treacherous sea creatures, manifested as gorgeous women, whose captivating voices lured sailors to their doom. From its infancy, cinema deliberately cast a number of its female stars as mystical entities, potent enough to emotionally capsize willing (male) audiences.

Silent films exalted in the visual power of these exotic women's ability to enthrall. Pola Negri, a Polish beauty who emerged through early German film, was the eroticized "other": her *Madame DuBarry* (1919), re-released as U.S. sensation *Passion*, showed a highly sexualized woman who could teasingly manipulate men, and, by extension, spectators. Louise Brooks, an American who ventured into German cinema, had a similarly intoxicating effect. In the classic *Pandora's Box* (1929), her Lulu is so threateningly seductive that the film's only way to nullify its power is for Jack the Ripper to murder her.

The notion of a screen siren, then, inherently objectifies, and several early female stars were openly branded. Clara Bow was "The It Girl," ostensibly due to the provocative *It* (1927). However, given her scandalized private life, there was no mistaking what

that "It" denoted. Jean Harlow was "The Platinum Blonde," similarly in reference to the title of her hit 1931 movie, which fetishized her overt sexuality. Austrian actress Hedy Lamarr's infamous nude frolicking in Czech film *Ecstasy* (1933) labeled her "The Ecstasy Lady" and directly hastened her move to Hollywood.

All three benefited from Hollywood's pre-Code days when films were far more risqué. The Hays Code did not entirely muffle its sirens, but it certainly muted them. The coming of sound, too, affected stars like Negri and Bow, whose heavy accents somehow spoiled the fantasy they embodied. Nevertheless, sexual exploitation continued. Howard Hughes endorsed new star Jane Russell for his film *The Outlaw* (1943) with a racy poster of her leaning back, displaying her ample cleavage, and the epithet, "There are two good reasons why men go to see her." Unsurprisingly, when the film was eventually released, it was a huge hit.

Sirens are also strongly linked with femme fatales, deadly agents of film noir, the dark crime dramas featuring scheming temptresses that Hollywood gravitated toward in the 1940s. Such films helped Lauren Bacall, Barbara Stanwyck and Jane Greer find stardom, but the epitome of the genre is Rita Hayworth as *Gilda* (1946). Tossing her stunning red hair (it matters not that the film is black-and-white) and

type   ■ Exotic   ■ Racy   ■ Blonde bombshell   ■ Femme fatale

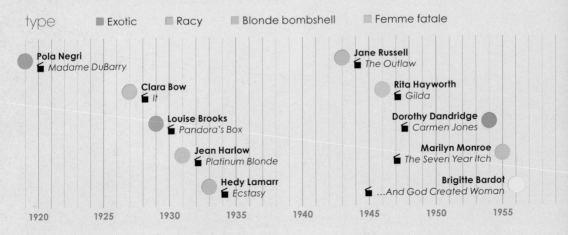

Pola Negri
🎬 *Madame DuBarry*

Clara Bow
🎬 *It*

Louise Brooks
🎬 *Pandora's Box*

Jean Harlow
🎬 *Platinum Blonde*

Hedy Lamarr
🎬 *Ecstasy*

Jane Russell
🎬 *The Outlaw*

Rita Hayworth
🎬 *Gilda*

Dorothy Dandridge
🎬 *Carmen Jones*

Marilyn Monroe
🎬 *The Seven Year Itch*

Brigitte Bardot
🎬 *...And God Created Woman*

1920   1925   1930   1935   1940   1945   1950   1955

Marilyn Monroe | Brigitte Bardot | Anita Ekberg | Ursula Andress | Farrah Fawcett | Kathleen Turner | Angelina Jolie | Scarlett Johansson

strutting her infamous striptease dance, Hayworth became an instant cultural icon of desire.

Into the 1950s only one type — moreover one woman — dominated. The Blonde was back and Marilyn Monroe remains perhaps the single most iconic female movie star ever: bubbly, buxom and fun; somehow attainable yet still a goddess. The image of her skirt blown up over her head by a subway street grille is known by people who have never seen that scene in *The Seven Year Itch* (1955). With Monroe, Jayne Mansfield, Betty Grable and Kim Novak dominating the screen, you would be forgiven for thinking they represented all womankind. The likes of the stunning Dorothy Dandridge, the first African-American woman to get Hollywood starring roles like *Carmen Jones* (1954), remain a minority in every way.

Which came first, a growing interest in international cinema, or in France's Brigitte Bardot, whose languid, pouting charms caused a stampede toward the appropriately titled *...And God Created Woman* (1956)? Popular too were full-bodied Italian stars like Sophia Loren and Gina Lollobrigida, or Sweden's Anita Ekberg, whose gravity-defying curves induce hypnotic lust in Marcello Mastroianni during *La Dolce Vita* (1960). Switzerland's Ursula Andress began the trend of the "Bond girl" with her bikini-clad ocean

entrance in *Dr. No* (1962). But while the 1940s and 1950s sirens often subverted the objectifying male gaze, these parts tended to offer a far less playful role.

Once feminism became a more prominent force in the 1970s, there was far less mention of "sirens," its sexist connotations no longer justified. Naturally there were — and always will be — men and women feted for their physical beauty, but generally movies seemed to seek more balance. Attempts to promote television star and the era's most popular pin-up, Farrah Fawcett, on the big screen, in 1978's *Somebody Killed Her Husband*, failed miserably. In fact, to find the next female figure designed to drop jaws, Hollywood had to draw her. *Who Framed Roger Rabbit*'s (1988) Jessica Rabbit, was modeled on 1940s femme fatales and voiced with smoky sensuality by Kathleen Turner. It was both ironic acknowledgment and affectionate send-up of old-fashioned sirens.

Today, actresses cited for their sexuality often use this trope's knowingness as part of their armory and agency. Action stars Angelina Jolie in *Lara Croft: Tomb Raider* (2001) or Scarlett Johansson in *Lucy* (2014) are good examples of this more recent image. Arguably more perplexing is Johansson's otherworldly predator in *Under the Skin* (2013). She is a disturbing, complex object of desire, and all the more fascinating for it. **LS**

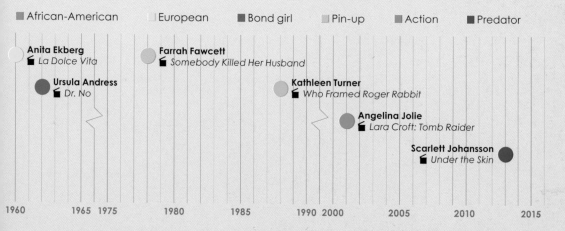

■ African-American □ European ■ Bond girl ▨ Pin-up ▨ Action ■ Predator

Anita Ekberg
🎬 *La Dolce Vita*

Ursula Andress
🎬 *Dr. No*

Farrah Fawcett
🎬 *Somebody Killed Her Husband*

Kathleen Turner
🎬 *Who Framed Roger Rabbit*

Angelina Jolie
🎬 *Lara Croft: Tomb Raider*

Scarlett Johansson
🎬 *Under the Skin*

1960   1965 1975   1980   1985   1990 2000   2005   2010   2015

yves montand 1921–91

| Gates of the Night | The Wages of Fear | Let's Make Love | The War Is Over | Grand Prix | Z | Le Cercle Rouge | Jean de Florette |

Famous as both an actor and a singer, Yves Montand was the cinematic embodiment of debonair Gallic charm. Born in Italy, his family relocated to France when he was two. After being discovered by Édith Piaf, he initially found success as a singer, but soon progressed to acting, with a notable early role as a member of the French resistance in *Gates of the Night* (1946).

In Montand's early career he made only occasional screen appearances, before starring in one of his best-known films, the claustrophobic thriller *The Wages of Fear* (1953). Its success led him to become a more prolific actor. Subsequent performances included a small part in the historical biopic *Napoléon* (1955) and starring roles in *Marguerite of the Night* (1955), *Men and Wolves* (1957) and *The Crucible* (1957), adapted by Jean-Paul Sartre from Arthur Miller's stage play.

International recognition came when Montand appeared opposite Marilyn Monroe in *Let's Make Love* (1960), although much of that was due to their well-publicized affair rather the film itself. He remained in the United States to appear in *Sanctuary* (1961), *Goodbye Again* (1961) and *My Geisha* (1962), but none were especially successful. Afterward, he mostly kept to French films, with rare exceptions being John

Frankenheimer's *Grand Prix* (1966) and Vincente Minnelli's *On a Clear Day You Can See Forever* (1970).

On returning to France, Montand had more success, working solidly throughout the 1960s with films that included *The War Is Over* (1966), *Is Paris Burning?* (1966) and *Live for Life* (1967). Of the films he made during this time, *Z* (1969) had the greatest impact, although his role in it was brief. He would work with director Costa-Gavras on four other films: *The Sleeping Car Murders* (1965), *The Confession* (1970), the stunning *State of Siege* (1972) and *Womanlight* (1979).

Remaining an international star into the 1970s, he appeared in a variety of genres, from comedies such as *Delusions of Grandeur* (1971) and *The Big Operator* (1976) to thrillers like *Police Python 357* (1976). While his looks and natural charm made him well suited to playing romantic leads in films such as *César and Rosalie* (1972), he was at his most compelling in Jean-Pierre Melville's terrific noir *Le Cercle Rouge* (1970). His work-rate slowed during his later career, although he received some of his best reviews for his formidable performance as the ageing patriarch César Soubeyran in Claude Berri's beautiful adaptations of *Jean de Florette* (1986) and *Manon des Sources* (1986). **JWa**

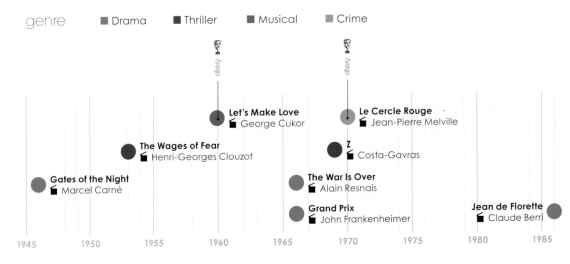

genre ■ Drama ■ Thriller ■ Musical ■ Crime

Foreign

Foreign

Let's Make Love
George Cukor

Le Cercle Rouge
Jean-Pierre Melville

The Wages of Fear
Henri-Georges Clouzot

Z
Costa-Gavras

Gates of the Night
Marcel Carné

The War Is Over
Alain Resnais

Grand Prix
John Frankenheimer

Jean de Florette
Claude Berri

| 1945 | 1950 | 1955 | 1960 | 1965 | 1970 | 1975 | 1980 | 1985 |

M

julianne moore 1960

| Short Cuts | Vanya on 42nd Street | Boogie Nights | Magnolia | Far From Heaven | The Hours | The Kids Are All Right | Still Alice |

Julianne Moore had already won an Emmy for her work in television by the time Hollywood caught up with her. A supporting role in *The Hand That Rocks the Cradle* (1992) received stand-out reviews, but her real breakthrough came in *The Fugitive* (1993), where she played a doctor suspicious of Harrison Ford's strange behavior. On screen for less than five minutes, Moore's resolute presence still registered. She stood out again in a fine ensemble cast in Robert Altman's *Short Cuts* (1993). In one scene, Moore appeared naked from the waist down, drawing accusations of prurience on the part of Altman. But Moore was undaunted by the intimacy of the scene, emboldened by the challenging material. The underwriter of her own risks, Moore established a pattern of working that continues to this day: roles in Hollywood movies offset by candid portraits of troubled women in films by auteur directors.

Vanya on 42nd Street (1994) began as a theater project in 1989, but was transformed by Louis Malle into an unusual hybrid: a rehearsal of Anton Chekhov's play *Uncle Vanya* (1897) that turns into a full-on performance. Moore won Best Actress at the Boston Society of Film Critics' Awards, as well as the attention of a new wave of U.S. filmmakers.

In Todd Haynes' existential horror *Safe* (1995), Moore seemed to collapse in on herself; while in Paul Thomas Anderson's *Boogie Nights* (1997), she was maternal and bereft as a 1970s porn star. The Coen brothers were next, with *The Big Lebowski* (1998).

Of all *Magnolia*'s (1999) desperate characters, Moore's anxious young wife seemed the most attuned to the film's rising hysteria. She was glamourous, God-fearing and guilt-ridden in *The End of the Affair* (1999), and perfectly at home in the Nova Scotia setting of *The Shipping News* (2001). But her finest performances of the new decade came in *The Hours* (2002) and *Far from Heaven* (2002), where she captured the despair of two 1950s housewives, earning Oscar nominations in both the leading and supporting categories.

Moore is by now such an established figure that her presence immediately enriches a project, whether mainstream (*The Hunger Games* series) or independent (2010's *The Kids Are All Right* and David Cronenberg's 2014 Hollywood satire, *Maps to the Stars*). Soulful, incandescent and fearless, she was rewarded with a Best Actress Oscar for her performance as a university professor with Alzheimer's in *Still Alice* (2014). **MM**

M

genre ■ Drama

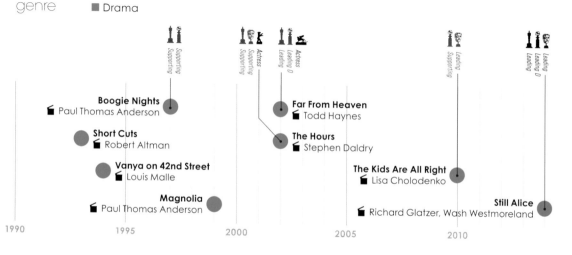

Supporting / Supporting

Actress / Leading D / Supporting

Actress / Leading D / Leading

Leading / Supporting

Leading / Leading D / Leading

Boogie Nights
Paul Thomas Anderson

Short Cuts
Robert Altman

Vanya on 42nd Street
Louis Malle

Magnolia
Paul Thomas Anderson

Far From Heaven
Todd Haynes

The Hours
Stephen Daldry

The Kids Are All Right
Lisa Cholodenko

Still Alice
Richard Glatzer, Wash Westmoreland

1990   1995   2000   2005   2010

jeanne moreau 1928

Lift to the Scaffold

Seven Days... Seven Nights

La Notte

Jules et Jim

Viva Maria!

The Bride Wore Black

Querelle

Time to Leave

Jeanne Moreau might be termed "the auteur's actor." Few cinema performers have racked up work for such a comprehensive and international roll call of revered directors; but then, few stars bring such intelligence and questing aesthetic ambition to their work.

At 20, Moreau became the youngest-ever member of the legendary Comedie Française, and was soon regarded as the best French stage actress of her generation. Her cinema career was initially low-key, with appearances in B-movies through the 1950s; but a role in Louis Malle's stylish thriller *Lift to the Scaffold* (1958) propelled her firmly in the direction of stardom. Their next collaboration, *The Lovers* (1958), affirmed her status as a sex symbol, but even as the 1960s fell in love with French beauties, her appeal was too complex for her to be mistaken for a mere screen beauty.

Moreau's looks are characterized by an electrifying changeability — sullen and heavy one moment, delicately pretty or childishly insouciant the next — and her performances have a similar mutability, making her a particular find for directors with an interest in the ambiguities of human behavior. International fame followed her iconic turn as the object of two men's desires in François Truffaut's *Jules et Jim* (1962). The director would also provide her with the title role of a vengeful widow in *The Bride Wore Black* (1968). She was at the center of surreal sexual shenanigans in Luis Bunuel's *The Diary of a Chambermaid* (1964), and romped opposite Brigitte Bardot in Lpuis Malle's comic western *Viva Maria!* (1965). Moreau also worked extensively with significant British directors, among them Peter Brook, Anthony Asquith and Tony Richardson, who left his wife, Vanessa Redgrave, for a short-lived relationship with her.

Hollywood saw less of her, although she was directed by John Frankenheimer in *The Train* (1964), with Burt Lancaster, and by Elia Kazan in the F. Scott Fitzgerald adaptation *The Last Tycoon* (1976), with Robert De Niro. In her later career, she might have been accused of favoring esoteric obscurity for its own sake — "Moreau is commonly the only excuse for the films she's in," a critic observed in the 1970s. However, she still hit on intriguing and challenging projects — including *Querelle* (1982), the dark, dreamy final film by Rainer Werner Fassbinder, and *Time to Leave* (2005), by François Ozon. She has also directed two feature films, *Lumiere* (1976) and *The Adolescent* (1979), and a documentary, *Lillian Gish* (1983). **HM**

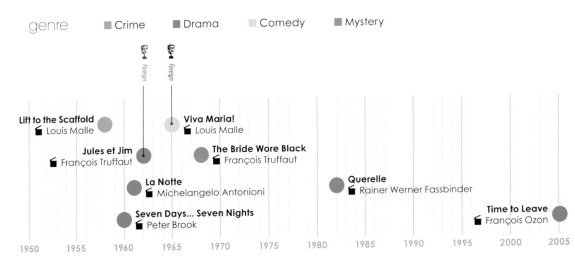

genre ■ Crime ■ Drama ■ Comedy ■ Mystery

Foreign   Foreign

Lift to the Scaffold
Louis Malle

Viva Maria!
Louis Malle

Jules et Jim
François Truffaut

The Bride Wore Black
François Truffaut

La Notte
Michelangelo Antonioni

Querelle
Rainer Werner Fassbinder

Seven Days... Seven Nights
Peter Brook

Time to Leave
François Ozon

1950   1955   1960   1965   1970   1975   1980   1985   1990   1995   2000   2005

viggo mortensen 1958

Witness

The Reflecting Skin

Crimson Tide

Lord of the Rings: The Fellowship of the Ring

A History of Violence

Eastern Promises

The Road

The Two Faces of January

Born in Manhattan, 1958, Viggo Mortensen is a fascinating and unpredictable actor, frequently using his post *The Lord of the Rings* (2001–03) fame to act in more esoteric fare. Running his own poetry imprint, he is also an established painter and photographer.

Mortensen debuted as an Amish farmer in Peter Weir's *Witness* (1985), standing out in a small but pivotal role. In British auteur Philip Ridley's singular *The Reflecting Skin* (1990), he is mesmerizing as an older brother seeking to protect his young sibling from the harsh realities of the world. He was equally impressive in Sean Penn's *The Indian Runner* (1991) and Brian De Palma's exuberant *Carlito's Way* (1993).

Stardom might have beckoned following Tony Scott's naval drama *Crimson Tide* (1995), but the actor instead reunited with Ridley for *The Passion of Darkly Noon* (1995), worked with Jane Campion on *The Portrait of a Lady* (1996) and bossed Demi Moore around in Ridley Scott's *G.I. Jane* (1997). Then, Peter Jackson's *The Lord of the Rings* trilogy changed everything. Cast as the dashing and heroic Aragorn, he became an unlikely sex symbol.

Visibly uncomfortable with the newfound attention, the quietly spoken actor threw himself into a diverse range of projects. First was *Hidalgo* (2004), an enigmatic western. And then came his critically acclaimed turn in David Cronenberg's *A History of Violence* (2005). Playing a mild-mannered small-town man with a dark, hidden past, Mortensen is electric. Further collaborations with Cronenberg followed. For his role as Nikolai, a Russian mafiosi in *Eastern Promises* (2007) the actor was rewarded with an Oscar nomination. As Sigmund Freud in *A Dangerous Method* (2011), he was unlucky to miss out on a Golden Globe.

John Hillcoat's unforgiving adaptation of Cormac McCarthy's *The Road* (2009) superbly illustrates Mortensen's commitment to his craft. The actor spent the entire shoot in dank rags as the father of a young boy trying to negotiate a post-apocalyptic landscape. From another acclaimed literary source (Patricia Highsmith), Mortensen excelled as a dapper conman on the run in *The Two Faces of January* (2014).

Two of Mortensen's most recent projects see him expanding his horizons still further. Lisandro Alonso's *Jauja* (2014) is a Herzog-influenced trek across unforgiving foreign terrain, while David Oelhoffen's *Far From Men* (2014) is a North African existential western, set during the Algerian War. **JW**

M

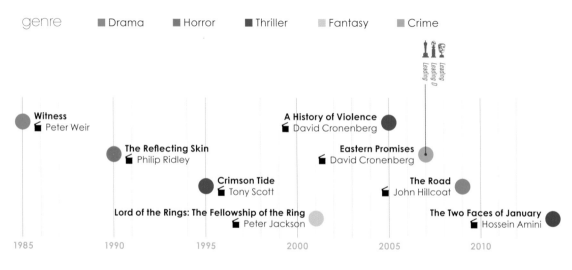

genre ■ Drama ■ Horror ■ Thriller ■ Fantasy ■ Crime

Leading O
Leading

Witness
Peter Weir

The Reflecting Skin
Philip Ridley

Crimson Tide
Tony Scott

Lord of the Rings: The Fellowship of the Ring
Peter Jackson

A History of Violence
David Cronenberg

Eastern Promises
David Cronenberg

The Road
John Hillcoat

The Two Faces of January
Hossein Amini

1985   1990   1995   2000   2005   2010

eddie murphy 1961

| 48 Hrs | Trading Places | Beverly Hills Cop | Coming to America | Harlem Nights | The Nutty Professor | Shrek | Dreamgirls |

A dynamic, electrifying, exhaustively inventive comic performer, Eddie Murphy was one of many cast members from the television show *Saturday Night Live* (*SNL*) to graduate to the big screen. Heading up a string of box-office hits in the 1980s, he was also one of the first African-American actors whose name alone could "open" a movie.

Like his hero Richard Pryor, Brooklyn-born Murphy cut his teeth on the New York stand-up scene. Joining *SNL* in 1980, Murphy is credited with boosting the show's reputation, which had suffered following the departure of several cast members. A supremely confident, bracingly charismatic performer, Murphy made his screen debut in *48 Hrs* (1982), an action comedy in which he played a convict on a two-day release pass partnered with Nick Nolte's tough-guy cop.

His dazzling performance helped make the film a box-office hit. He would enjoy greater success alongside fellow *SNL* alumnus Dan Aykroyd in the comedy *Trading Places* (1983). But it was as the title character of the 1984 comedy thriller *Beverly Hills Cop* that Murphy scored his biggest hit. In a film originally written for Sylvester Stallone, about a Detroit cop relocated to one of Los Angeles' more exclusive neighborhoods, Murphy was wholly convincing as the gun-toting action hero, but with his fast-talking, street-smart humor he lent the film's high-concept script some flesh-and-blood personality. The movie was one of the signature films of the 1980s and made Murphy a star.

Murphy remained a big draw for the rest of the decade, but never quite recaptured the incendiary appeal of those early films. Nonetheless, he was still capable of revealing his versatility. In *Coming to America* (1988), which he cowrote, he was appealing in the lead role as a guileless African prince, but it was in playing some of the eccentric New Yorker supporting characters that Murphy really shone.

Murphy would go on to play multiple characters in several other films, notably the garrulous Klump family in *The Nutty Professor* (1996). That film marked a turn in Murphy's career toward roles in more family-friendly fare. It continued with his most popular recent role as the voice to Donkey in the *Shrek* series (2001–10). He received his first Oscar nomination for his acclaimed performance in the 2006 musical *Dreamgirls*. The movie was a spectacular showcase for Murphy's vocal gifts, and offered hope that he will continue in a more adventurous vein with future roles. **EL**

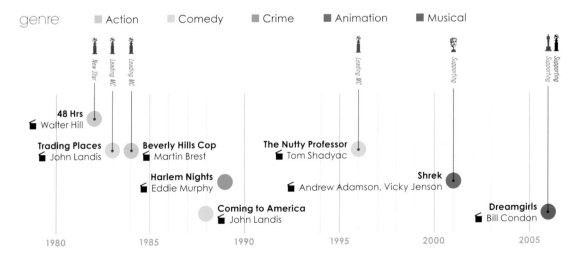

genre ■ Action ■ Comedy ■ Crime ■ Animation ■ Musical

New Star Leading MC Leading MC Leading MC Supporting Supporting / Supporting

48 Hrs
Walter Hill

Trading Places
John Landis

Beverly Hills Cop
Martin Brest

Harlem Nights
Eddie Murphy

Coming to America
John Landis

The Nutty Professor
Tom Shadyac

Shrek
Andrew Adamson, Vicky Jenson

Dreamgirls
Bill Condon

| 1980 | 1985 | 1990 | 1995 | 2000 | 2005 |

bill murray 1950

| Meatballs | Ghostbusters | Scrooged | Groundhog Day | Rushmore | Lost in Translation | Broken Flowers | St. Vincent |

Bill Murray was introduced to audiences when he joined *Saturday Night Live* in 1977. Shortly before leaving the program, he made his film debut in *Meatballs* (1979), as summer camp counselor Tripper Harrison. Sardonic and quick-witted, but with depths of previously unexplored compassion, Tripper would became a template for Murray's screen persona.

After playing Hunter S. Thompson in *Where the Buffalo Roam* (1980), he starred in a succession of the biggest comedies of the 1980s: as a gopher-hunting greenskeeper in *Caddyshack* (1980), irreverent army recruit in *Stripes* (1981), Dustin Hoffman's roommate in *Tootsie* (1982), and the infinitely-quotable Dr. Peter Venkman in *Ghostbusters* (1984) and its 1989 sequel.

Murray agreed to star in *Ghostbusters* in order to cowrite and star in his dramatic debut, a fascinating but ultimately flawed adaptation of M. Somerset Maugham's *The Razor's Edge* (1984). After the film's disastrous reception he took a hiatus from performing, returning with the perennial Christmas favorite *Scrooged* (1988). He continued to stretch himself in *Quick Change* (1990), *What About Bob?* (1991) and *Mad Dog and Glory* (1993), before starring in one of his finest films, the sublime *Groundhog Day* (1993).

After a small role in *Ed Wood* (1994), Murray returned to broad comedy in movies such as *Kingpin* (1996) and *The Man Who Knew Too Little* (1997), but he appeared to have outgrown goofier work. A major turning point came playing sad sack Herman Blume in Wes Anderson's *Rushmore* (1998). Blume was a maturation of his cinematic persona: still the cynical iconoclast, but lonely, regretful and beaten by life. He would go on to appear in all of the director's subsequent films, most notably *The Life Aquatic with Steve Zissou* (2004).

Murray's resurgence continued with a soulful, emotionally open performance as the compromised movie star Bob Harris in *Lost in Translation* (2003). The Oscar-nominated role would be the signature one of his middle age. He was equally impressive in the existential *Broken Flowers* (2005).

Outside of his sterling work with Anderson, Murray has starred in *City of Ember* (2008), *Get Low* (2009), *Hyde Park on Hudson* (2012) and *The Monuments Men* (2014), none of which has fully exploited his talent. He remains adept at elevating weaker material, as seen in *St. Vincent* (2014): while its tale of Murray befriending a teenager invites disappointing comparisons to *Rushmore* and *Meatballs*, he is still wonderful. **JW**

M

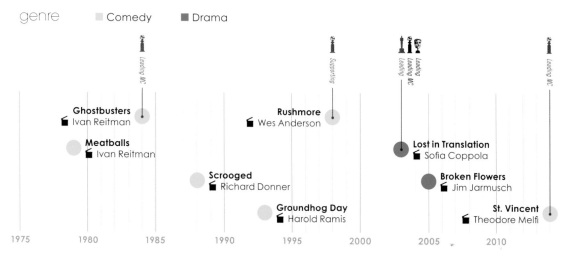

genre ■ Comedy ■ Drama

Leading MC

Supporting

Leading
Leading MC
Leading

Leading MC

Ghostbusters
Ivan Reitman

Rushmore
Wes Anderson

Lost in Translation
Sofia Coppola

Meatballs
Ivan Reitman

Scrooged
Richard Donner

Broken Flowers
Jim Jarmusch

Groundhog Day
Harold Ramis

St. Vincent
Theodore Melfi

1975   1980   1985   1990   1995   2000   2005   2010

nargis 1929–81

Barsaat

Andaz

Awaara

Deedar

Anhonee

Chori Chori

Mother India

Raat Aur Din

Nargis Dutt will forever be associated with the 1957 movie *Mother India*, playing the long-suffering and endlessly courageous heroine. It was the first and, so far, one of only three Indian films to secure a nomination in the Best Foreign Language Film category at the Oscars.

Nargis was born Fatima Rashid to a Hindu father and Muslim mother. One of her earliest successes under her new name was *Mela* (1948), in which she appeared opposite Dilip Kumar. The same year, she starred in *Aag* (1948), the directorial debut of actor and producer Raj Kapoor. The alleged romance between Kapoor and Nargis, fueled by their appearance together in several blockbuster films, kept the Indian gossip press in copy for years. One of those hits was *Barsaat* (1949), with the two playing star-crossed lovers. She starred opposite both Kapoor and Kumar in Mehboob Khan's love triangle, *Andaz* (1949).

Deedar (1951) is considered one of the finest tragedies in the history of Hindi-language cinema, with the actress giving a stunning performance. Kapoor and Nargis also appeared in *Awaara* (1951), which examined the intertwining lives of a poor man and rich girl. Beyond its astonishing success in South Asia, the film was popular throughout East Asia, Africa and the Soviet Union. In the complex psychodrama *Anhonee* (1952), she played dual roles of twin sisters, while in *Chori Chori* (1956), a remake of Frank Capra's

It Happened One Night (1934), she displayed her flair for comedy, taking on Claudette Colbert's role.

In *Mother India* (1957), Nargis is heartbreaking as a single mother living in a small village, who brings up her sons in extreme poverty and is ultimately faced with a terrible decision. Sunil Dutt, who played her son in the film, saved Nargis from a fire on set and they eventually married. Nargis reduced her acting assignments significantly after this. One of her last memorable roles was in *Raat Aur Din* (1967), playing a woman with dissociative identity disorder. A brave and uncompromising performance, she was rewarded with India's then newly introduced National Award for Best Actress.

In 1980, Nargis was nominated to India's upper house of parliament, the Rajya Sabha. During her tenure there she famously accused India's greatest filmmaker, Satyajit Ray, of peddling Indian poverty abroad in order to win awards, with films like *Pather Panchali* (1955). She succumbed to pancreatic cancer in 1981, days before the premiere of *Rocky*, the debut feature of her son Sanjay Dutt, who would go on to have a successful career as a Bollywood leading man before serving time in prison for his involvement in the 1993 Mumbai blasts. Today, Nargis' name is invoked annually as India's National Award for Best Feature Film on National Integration is named after her. For the rest of the world, she will always be Mother India. **NR**

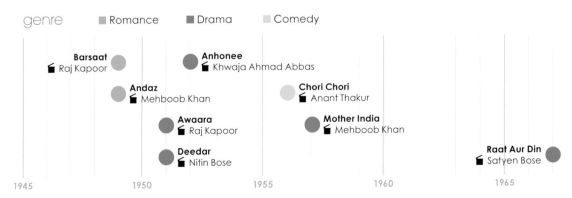

genre   ■ Romance   ■ Drama   ■ Comedy

Barsaat
Raj Kapoor

Andaz
Mehboob Khan

Awaara
Raj Kapoor

Deedar
Nitin Bose

Anhonee
Khwaja Ahmad Abbas

Chori Chori
Anant Thakur

Mother India
Mehboob Khan

Raat Aur Din
Satyen Bose

1945   1950   1955   1960   1965

liam neeson 1952

Excalibur   The Mission   Schindler's List   Rob Roy   Michael Collins   Kinsey   Batman Begins   Taken

Liam Neeson was a stage actor in Ireland when he was spotted by John Boorman and cast as Sir Gawain in *Excalibur* (1981). For the next decade he worked solidly, with supporting parts in films including *Krull* (1983), *The Bounty* (1984) and *The Mission* (1986).

By the time he costarred with Diane Keaton in *The Good Mother* (1988), Neeson had progressed to leading roles, starring in 1990 as a Scottish-miner-turned-bareknuckle-boxer in *The Big Man* and then as a disfigured superhero in Sam Raimi's *Darkman*. After roles in Woody Allen's *Husbands and Wives* (1992) and as the title character in *Ethan Frome* (1993), he received his major breakthrough playing the titular character in *Schindler's List* (1993). His Oscar-nominated portrayal of German businessman Oskar Schindler made him an international star. He next appeared as a compassionate doctor in *Nell* (1994), followed by rousing turns as the titular historical heroes of *Rob Roy* (1995) and *Michael Collins* (1996).

His career floundered in the late 1990s, but his fortunes seemed to rally when he was cast as Qui-Gon Jinn in the *Star Wars* prequel *The Phantom Menace* (1999). However, despite its box-office success, the film was widely viewed as a disappointment. He continued to play parental figures, first as Leonardo DiCaprio's father in Martin Scorsese's *Gangs of New York* (2002), and then as a bereaved father in *Love Actually* (2003).

He was at his most compelling as the pioneering sex researcher Alfred Kinsey in *Kinsey* (2004), but it failed at the box office. He had a slim role in *Kingdom of Heaven* (2005), managing to convince when he spoke the line, "I once fought two days with an arrow through my testicle." The characters that suit him best encompass both steadfast determination and hard edges — qualities displayed as Bruce Wayne's mentor Henri Ducard in *Batman Begins* (2005).

Neeson has often played physical characters, but this became the key focus of his work after starring in *Taken* (2008) as a former CIA operative tracking his kidnapped daughter. An unexpected global hit, it established him as a genuine action star at the age of 56. Neeson went on to star in a wave of genre efforts, including two *Taken* sequels (2012 and 2014), along with *Unknown* (2011), *Non-Stop* (2014) and the flops *The A-Team* (2010) and *Battleship* (2012). Best is *The Grey* (2011), in which he fights wolves. While a far cry from *Schindler's List*, these films succeed thanks to the warmth and solemn tenacity conveyed by Neeson. **JWa**

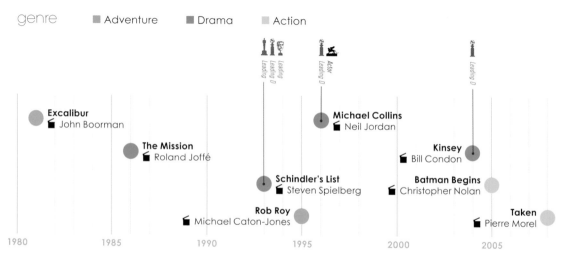

genre   ■ Adventure   ■ Drama   ■ Action

Excalibur
John Boorman

The Mission
Roland Joffé

Schindler's List
Steven Spielberg

Rob Roy
Michael Caton-Jones

Michael Collins
Neil Jordan

Kinsey
Bill Condon

Batman Begins
Christopher Nolan

Taken
Pierre Morel

1980   1985   1990   1995   2000   2005

paul newman 1925–2008

| Somebody Up There Likes Me | Cat on a Hot Tin Roof | The Left-Handed Gun | The Hustler | Hud | Cool Hand Luke | Butch Cassidy and the Sundance Kid | The Sting |

Actor, filmmaker, philanthropist, culinary entrepreneur and perennial heartthrob, Paul Newman is one of Hollywood's most beloved stars and role models. Born in Ohio, in 1925, he served in World War II as a radioman-gunner, narrowly escaping death because an ear infection grounded his pilot; the other members of their unit were killed in the Battle of Okinawa.

After graduating from college, Newman worked in touring theater and studied under Lee Strasberg at the Actors Studio. He almost starred opposite James Dean in *East of Eden* (1955) and worked alongside Eva Marie Saint and Frank Sinatra in a television production of *Our Town* (1955). His first Hollywood film was *The Silver Chalice* (1954), but he attracted attention with his boxer in *Somebody Up There Likes Me* (1956). *The Left-Handed Gun* and *Cat on a Hot Tin Roof* (both 1958) made him a box-office attraction.

Newman was building a reputation as a heavyweight actor as well as a star with matinee idol looks. *The Young Philadelphians* (1959) and *Exodus* (1960) tapped into his dramatic skills, but it was *The Hustler* (1961) that proved a perfect platform for his persona. As "Fast" Eddie Nelson, Newman delivers a whip-smart cocktail of youthful rebellion and raw

ambition in a drama that explores the price of success. He is equally compelling in *Hud* (1963), playing a selfish upstart in a small Texas town who finds himself constantly at odds with his rancher father. In between, he played a jazz musician in *Paris Blues* (1961) and scored less successfully with his second Tennessee Williams adaptation, *Sweet Bird of Youth* (1962).

He starred in two international espionage thrillers. In *The Prize* (1963), he plays a novelist visiting Stockholm to accept the Nobel Prize for Literature, only to discover that a leading physicist and fellow prizewinner has been kidnapped. Its knockabout humor is a stark contrast to Alfred Hitchcock's darker *Torn Curtain* (1966), with Newman's scientist posing as a potential defector to the Communist East in order to steal a secret formula. Hitchcock and the actor did not get along and the film lacks momentum, but it does feature an impressively brutal fight between Newman and Wolfgang Kieling's security officer.

Cool Hand Luke (1967) gave Newman another cool, rebellious role — a drunk sentenced to hard labor for a misdemeanor, who earns the respect of fellow convicts by standing up to authority. *Butch Cassidy and the Sundance Kid* (1969) offered

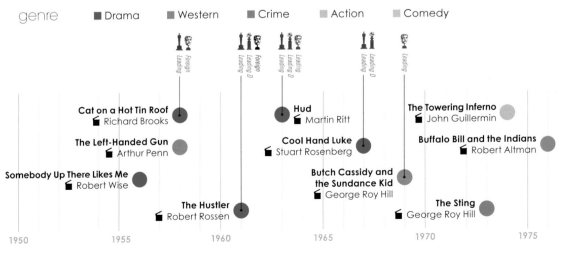

genre ■ Drama ■ Western ■ Crime ■ Action ■ Comedy

Cat on a Hot Tin Roof — Richard Brooks	Hud — Martin Ritt	The Towering Inferno — John Guillermin
The Left-Handed Gun — Arthur Penn	Cool Hand Luke — Stuart Rosenberg	Buffalo Bill and the Indians — Robert Altman
Somebody Up There Likes Me — Robert Wise	Butch Cassidy and the Sundance Kid — George Roy Hill	
The Hustler — Robert Rossen		The Sting — George Roy Hill

1950   1955   1960   1965   1970   1975

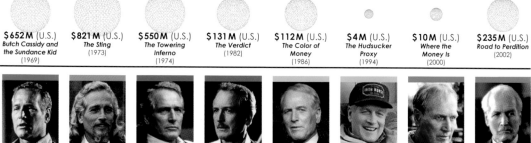

| $652M (U.S.) Butch Cassidy and the Sundance Kid (1969) | $821M (U.S.) The Sting (1973) | $550M (U.S.) The Towering Inferno (1974) | $131M (U.S.) The Verdict (1982) | $112M (U.S.) The Color of Money (1986) | $4M (U.S.) The Hudsucker Proxy (1994) | $10M (U.S.) Where the Money Is (2000) | $235M (U.S.) Road to Perdition (2002) |

The Towering Inferno

Buffalo Bill and the Indians

The Verdict

The Color of Money

Nobody's Fool

The Hudsucker Proxy

Where the Money Is

Road to Perdition

another anti-establishment role and a fine pairing with Robert Redford. Newman's eyes were rarely as bright as they are in the film's first hour, his laconic attitude and playful nature setting the pace, before director George Roy Hill sends the antiheroes off on an overlong travelogue and the charm of the earlier scenes is lost. The two actors teamed up with Hill again for *The Sting* (1973), an enjoyable caper movie.

Newman continued with a number of offbeat westerns. John Huston directed him as the eponymous law enforcer in *The Life and Times of Judge Roy Bean* (1972), while Robert Altman cast him as the legendary hero in *Buffalo Bill and the Indians, or Sitting Bull's History Lesson* (1976). His second film with Altman, *Quintet* (1979) may be set in the future, but its iconography and Newman's silent stranger align it with the western. Likewise, Sam Mendes' 1930s-set crime drama *Road to Perdition* (2002) has all the hallmarks of a western, with Newman as the grizzled patriarch of a crime family.

Newman and Steve McQueen bring dignity to *The Towering Inferno* (1974), an overblown soap opera with flames, while his second outing as Lew Harper in *The Drowning Pool* (1975) takes the cool Californian

detective down to Louisiana in a film that lacks the spark of 1966's *The Moving Target*. He is better as a businessman falsely linked to a murder by a journalist in *Absence of Malice* (1981) and an ambulance-chasing lawyer who fights the church and a respected law firm in *The Verdict* (1982).

The Color of Money (1986) found Newman returning to the role of Eddie Nelson, who sees his younger self in Tom Cruise's hustler. The actor received an Oscar for his performance. However, it lacks the drama of *The Hustler*, save a thrilling scene with Forest Whitaker and the final moments, with Eddie announcing, "I'm back!"

The Hudsucker Proxy (1994) gave Newman a rare comedy role, playing a ruthless corporate shark who plans to take over a vast corporation only to be stymied by Tim Robbins' inept new employee. However, his best work prior to his death in 2008 was in Robert Benton's *Nobody's Fool* (1994). He plays a small-time hustler who ekes out a living in a town in upstate New York, only to have it disturbed by the arrival of his estranged son and grandson. It is a lovely performance by the actor — charming without being unsentimental and up there with his best work. **IHS**

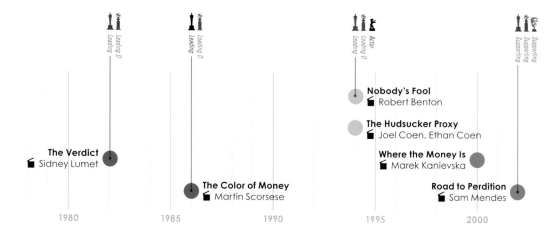

Nobody's Fool
Robert Benton

The Hudsucker Proxy
Joel Coen, Ethan Coen

Where the Money Is
Marek Kanievska

The Verdict
Sidney Lumet

The Color of Money
Martin Scorsese

Road to Perdition
Sam Mendes

1980   1985   1990   1995   2000

jack nicholson 1937

| Easy Rider | Five Easy Pieces | The Last Detail | Chinatown | One Flew Over the Cuckoo's Nest | The Passenger | The Shining | Terms of Endearment |

There has always been a little bit of the devil in Jack Nicholson. After coming to prominence during the New Hollywood of the 1970s and starring in several of its defining films, he maintained the period's emphasis on antiheroes over subsequent decades, while remaining one of America's most successful and compelling leading men. Ever the rebel or the villain, he excels at playing unconventional, off-balance characters of shifting morality and wolfish charm.

Born in Neptune City, New Jersey, in 1937, Nicholson emerged from a convoluted family background to become a fixture in the work of B-movie auteur Roger Corman, whom he had met in an acting class. He made his screen debut in *The Cry Baby Killer* (1958) as a teen who incorrectly believes he is a murderer, and subsequently appeared in a number of cheaply made horror films for Corman, including *The Little Shop of Horrors* (1960) and *The Raven* (1963). While eminently watchable, even at this early stage, he gave some of his career's weakest performances in compelling-yet-terrible material like *The Terror* (1963).

After a decade of struggling, Nicholson's breakthrough role was as a disillusioned, alcoholic lawyer in *Easy Rider* (1969). It received the first of his record 12 Oscar nominations. Another nomination arrived with his turn as playing a piano-prodigy-turned-oil-field-worker in *Five Easy Pieces* (1970), directed by Bob Rafelson. It remains one of his best performances. The pair would reunite on the intense *The King of Marvin Gardens* (1972), steamy noir remake *The Postman Always Rings Twice* (1981) and the crime drama *Blood and Wine* (1996).

The establishment of Nicholson as a star coincided directly with the birth of New Hollywood, and over the next few years he would be one of the era's biggest names. Following roles in Mike Nichols' contemplation of sexual mores in *Carnal Knowledge* (1971) and the foul-mouthed *The Last Detail* (1973), he delivered a stunning performance in one of the decade's finest films, Roman Polanski's *Chinatown* (1974). He would return to the role of dogged PI Jake Gittes in 1990's *The Two Jakes*, which he also directed.

A year later, Nicholson worked with Michelangelo Antonioni, on *The Passenger* (1975). It was unsuccessful at the box office but is greatly admired, with Nicholson giving a subtley nuanced performance. It is a contrast to his remarkable turn in *One Flew Over the Cuckoo's Nest* (1975). Randle McMurphy, an unwilling inmate

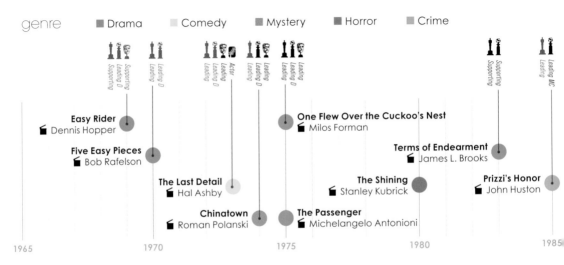

genre ■ Drama ■ Comedy ■ Mystery ■ Horror ■ Crime

Easy Rider — Dennis Hopper (Supporting / Leading D Supporting)

Five Easy Pieces — Bob Rafelson (Leading D Leading)

The Last Detail — Hal Ashby (Leading D Leading)

Chinatown — Roman Polanski (Actor / Leading / Leading D Leading)

One Flew Over the Cuckoo's Nest — Milos Forman (Leading D Leading D Leading)

The Passenger — Michelangelo Antonioni (Leading / Leading D Leading)

The Shining — Stanley Kubrick

Terms of Endearment — James L. Brooks (Supporting / Supporting)

Prizzi's Honor — John Huston (Leading MC / Leading)

1965   1970   1975   1980   1985

| $140M (U.S.)
Chinatown
(1974) | $473M (U.S.)
One Flew Over
the Cuckoo's Nest
(1975) | $254M (U.S.)
Terms of
Endearment
(1983) | $775M
Batman
(1989) | $405M
A Few Good Men
(1992) | $457M
As Good as
It Gets
(1997) | $137M
About Schmidt
(2002) | $336M
The Departed
(2006) |

Prizzi's Honor | The Witches of Eastwick | Batman | A Few Good Men | As Good as It Gets | The Pledge | About Schmidt | The Departed

at a psychiatric hospital, is perhaps his definitive role: the electric outsider, stood in fruitless defiance of unyielding authority. Though he is impressive in all, he had less success with *The Missouri Breaks* (1976), *The Last Tycoon* (1976) and his second feature as director, *Goin' South* (1978).

Audiences and critics were initially left cold by *The Shining* (1980), Stanley Kubrick's masterful adaptation of Stephen King's bestseller, although it would eventually become one of the actor's most popular films. Its singularly unnerving quality was due in part to Kubrick's fastidious approach: at one point he demanded 127 retakes of a single shot.

Nicholson gave one of most engaging performances as playwright Eugene O'Neill in *Reds* (1981). Warren Beatty's epic was one of the final films of New Hollywood, but Nicholson continued to attract audiences, starring in *Terms of Endearment* (1983), for which he won his second Oscar, *Prizzi's Honor* (1985) and *The Witches of Eastwick* (1987), while also impressing in smaller efforts like *Ironweed* (1987). He had his biggest commercial success with a cartoonish performance as The Joker in *Batman* (1989). Billed above Michael Keaton, Nicholson's canny deal-making entitled him to a significant share of the film's box-office and merchandising revenue.

By the 1990s Nicholson increasingly veered toward hammy self-parody, often with enjoyable results in films like *A Few Good Men* (1992), *Mars Attacks!* (1996) and *As Good as It Gets* (1997). He won his third Oscar for playing the misanthropic Melvin Udall in the latter film, which remains one of his most likable characters. He did not appear on screen again until *The Pledge* (2001) and *About Schmidt* (2002), playing a pair of compelling, against-type roles as a somber detective and a retired actuary respectively. *About Schmidt* was particularly revelatory: stripped of his natural charm, he gave one of his finest later performances.

Nicholson was on more familiar territory in *Anger Management* (2003), *Something's Gotta Give* (2003) and as the powerful mob boss Frank Costello in *The Departed* (2006). Even if he was on autopilot in Martin Scorsese's crime drama, it remained a pleasure to watch him play a seductively amoral character one more time. He has been mostly inactive since, only starring in the unexpected sleeper hit *The Bucket List* (2007) and his fourth film with James L. Brooks, the underperforming *How Do You Know* (2010). **JWa**

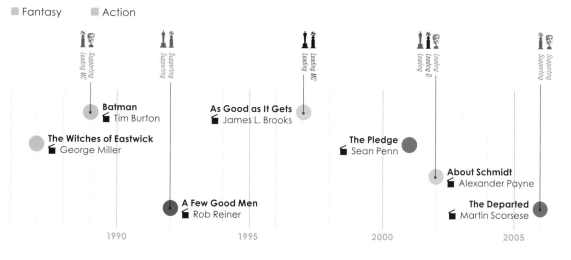

■ Fantasy　■ Action

Batman
🎬 Tim Burton

The Witches of Eastwick
🎬 George Miller

A Few Good Men
🎬 Rob Reiner

As Good as It Gets
🎬 James L. Brooks

The Pledge
🎬 Sean Penn

About Schmidt
🎬 Alexander Payne

The Departed
🎬 Martin Scorsese

1990　　1995　　2000　　2005

Easy Rider
(1969)

The Last Detail
(1973)

Chinatown
(1974)

**One Flew Over
the Cuckoo's Nest**
(1975)

The Shining
(1980)

Batman
(1989)

A Few Good Men
(1992)

The Departed
(2006)

Written by Peter Fonda and Dennis Hopper (who also directed), *Easy Rider* gave Nicholson his first Oscar nomination. Made on a budget of $300,000, it earned $40 million at the box office and was key in heralding the coming of the New Hollywood age.

The Last Detail starred Nicholson as a U.S. Navy petty officer escorting a sailor to a naval prison.

Nicholson as PI Jake Gittes in *Chinatown*. Nominated for 11 Oscars, the film is considered one of the best ever made.

The role of Randle McMurphy in *One Flew Over the Cuckoo's Nest* is widely viewed to be one of the actor's greatest performances.

This famous scene from *The Shining* reportedly took three days to film and required the use of 60 doors.

f his role in **Batman**, Nicholson told critic Roger Ebert that "I did The Joker not for a ommercial success but because I wanted to work in a mask."

Vincent Canby's review of **A Few Good Men** for The New York Times paid particular praise to Nicholson's "vicious, funny, superbly reptilian turn."

The Departed saw Nicholson finally work with Martin Scorsese after a 30-year acquaintace. The director commented: "I wanted something iconic from Nicholson. It may have taken a long time, but it was worth the wait."

david niven 1910–83

| The Charge of the Light Brigade | The Dawn Patrol | Wuthering Heights | A Matter of Life and Death | The Moon Is Blue | Around the World in 80 Days | Separate Tables | The Pink Panther |

When David Niven published his autobiography *The Moon's a Balloon* (1972), he reinforced the image of a man who effortlessly swanned through life on the back of a naturally debonair charm. It is an impression that is hard to shake off, even if a fact-check of his account reveals that he tended to print the legend.

Born James David Graham Niven in London in 1910, he graduated from Sandhurst military college in 1930, but resigned his commission in 1933 and crossed the Atlantic. Ending up in California, he worked his way up the Hollywood hierarchy from the position of an extra. Spotted and signed by producer Sam Goldwyn, in just two years he moved from an uncredited part in *Mutiny on the Bounty* (1935) to significant supporting roles in *Dodsworth* (1936), *The Charge of the Light Brigade* (1936) and *The Prisoner of Zenda* (1937).

His first leading role was as Bertie Wooster in *Thank You, Jeeves!* (1936), but meatier parts came via *The Dawn Patrol* (1938), as a World War I aviator, and *Wuthering Heights* (1939), bringing pathos to the thankless role of Cathy's would-be paramour Edgar. He took up his Army commission again in 1939, and spent much of the war in active service, occasionally appearing in films like *The Way Ahead* (1944).

Soon after the war ended, he played one of his most fondly remembered roles, that of the pilot who finds himself suspended between Earth and Heaven in Powell and Pressburger's lavish fantasy *A Matter of Life and Death* (1946). Back in Hollywood, he made the equally fantastical *The Bishop's Wife* (1947), in which his bishop's prayers are answered by Cary Grant's angel. But he was not happy with his blond wig as *Bonnie Prince Charlie* (1948), and a dispute over *The Elusive Pimpernel* (1950) led to him severing ties with Goldwyn under the mistaken impression that he would be inundated with offers. However, he still occasionally achieved a high profile, as with Otto Preminger's controversial *The Moon Is Blue* (1953) and as Phileas Fogg in *Around the World in 80 Days* (1956).

His Oscar as the disgraced Major Pollock in *Separate Tables* (1958) re-established Niven as a star and he maintained a prolific output until his death in 1983. Highlights include his intrepid corporal in *The Guns of Navarone* (1961), the suave criminal Sir Charles Litton in *The Pink Panther* (1963), the oldest of multiple James Bonds in *Casino Royale* (1967), Count Dracula in *Vampira* (1974) and a sort of Doctor Watson to Peter Ustinov's Hercule Poirot in *Death on the Nile* (1978). **MBr**

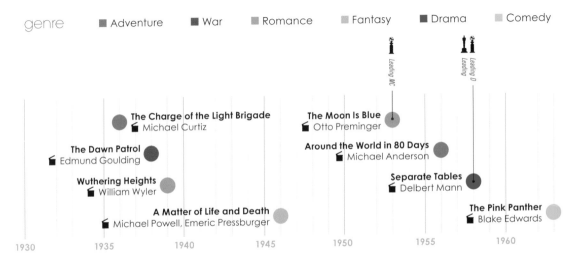

genre   ■ Adventure   ■ War   ■ Romance   ■ Fantasy   ■ Drama   ■ Comedy

Leading MC

Leading D
Leading

The Charge of the Light Brigade
Michael Curtiz

The Dawn Patrol
Edmund Goulding

Wuthering Heights
William Wyler

A Matter of Life and Death
Michael Powell, Emeric Pressburger

The Moon Is Blue
Otto Preminger

Around the World in 80 Days
Michael Anderson

Separate Tables
Delbert Mann

The Pink Panther
Blake Edwards

1930   1935   1940   1945   1950   1955   1960

philippe noiret 1930–2006

Zazie dans le métro | Thérèse Desqueyroux | The Watchmaker of St. Paul | Let Joy Reign Supreme | The Judge and the Assassin | Coup de Torchon | Cinema Paradiso | Il Postino

Heavy-set and jowly, Philippe Noiret scarcely exuded movie-star glamour. Yet in a career encompassing some 140 features, it would be hard to pick out a bad performance he gave in any of them. When, in Michael Radford's *Il Postino* (1984), he portrayed Pablo Neruda, he was utterly convincing despite looking and sounding nothing like the real-life Chilean poet.

Born in Lille, Noiret studied theater in Paris and made his screen debut in Jacqueline Audry's *Gigi* (1949). His first significance role came in Agnès Varda's *La Pointe Courte* (1955), generally reckoned the first film of the New Wave. His knack for comedy was revealed in Louis Malle's *Zazie dans le métro* (1960), playing the titular child's transvestite uncle. He was an unscrupulous property developer in René Clair's comedy *Tout l'or du monde* (1961), and in *Thérèse Desqueyroux* (1962) his smug dullness as the heroine's husband made her desire to poison him totally credible.

Noiret took the occasional supporting role in English-language movies (*The Night of the Generals*, 1967; *Justine*, 1969; Hitchcock's flawed *Topaz*, 1969), but was always more at ease in French. In the title role of *Very Happy Alexander* (1968) he was a happy hedonist, unfazed by the death of his wife, while his degenerate judge in *La Grande Bouffe* (1973) took hedonism to excess, literally eating himself to death.

Then began his partnership with Bertrand Tavernier. In *The Watchmaker of St. Paul* (1974), Noiret's slow-burning anger seared the screen. He was the 18th-century regent Philippe d'Orléans in *Let Joy Reign Supreme* (1975), and gave a telling portrayal of high-minded hypocrisy in *The Judge and the Assassin* (1976). *Coup de Torchon* (1981) featured Noiret as a despised local police chief who one day decides to turn against his abusers. In a more melancholy register, he was the World War I major tasked with identifying the war dead in *Life and Nothing But* (1989), and a shabby ex-musketeer in *La Fille de d'Artagnan* (1994).

Noiret's versatility was remarkable. He played a despicable petty crook in *Monsieur Albert* (1976), a pompous professor of Greek in *Dear Detective* (1978), a sad elderly homosexual in *I Don't Kiss* (1991) and a self-satisfied stage actor in *The King of Paris* (1995). His biggest international hit was as the gentle Italian village projectionist in *Cinema Paradiso* (1988). Interviewed in 1989 he asked, "I mean, what is acting for the movies? I've never really understood." His impressive screen career suggests otherwise. **PK**

genre   ■ Comedy   ■ Drama   ■ Romance

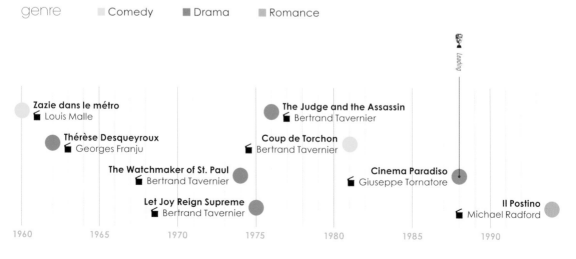

Zazie dans le métro — Louis Malle
Thérèse Desqueyroux — Georges Franju
The Watchmaker of St. Paul — Bertrand Tavernier
Let Joy Reign Supreme — Bertrand Tavernier
The Judge and the Assassin — Bertrand Tavernier
Coup de Torchon — Bertrand Tavernier
Cinema Paradiso — Giuseppe Tornatore
Il Postino — Michael Radford

1960   1965   1970   1975   1980   1985   1990

kim novak 1933

Picnic

The Man
with the
Golden Arm

Pal Joey

Vertigo

Bell, Book
and Candle

Middle of
the Night

Kiss Me,
Stupid

Liebestraum

Kim Novak's start in the film industry reads like a corny, rags to riches story. While waiting to be an extra in the Jane Russell musical *The French Line* (1954), the 21-year-old was spotted by an agent, who signed her to a contract with Columbia Pictures soon after. Within a year, she was a fully-fledged movie star, envisioned by Columbia as their answer to Marilyn Monroe.

Her first key role was in the noir *Pushover* (1954), displaying poise and confidence as a gangster's moll who seduces Fred MacMurray's cop into a life of crime. She was next in *Phffft* (1954), then played a nightclub singer in *5 Against the House* (1955). Two of her biggest early successes were as the true object of heroin addict Frank Sinatra's affection in the then shocking *The Man with the Golden Arm* and opposite William Holden in the overheated drama *Picnic* (both 1955).

Firmly established as a major star, Novak appeared in three commercially successful films by George Sidney: playing a love-struck socialite in *The Eddy Duchin Story* (1956), the eponymous troubled stage actress in biopic *Jeanne Eagels* (1957) and opposite Frank Sinatra again in the musical *Pal Joey* (1957).

Now rightly viewed as one of the greatest films of all time, Alfred Hitchcock's dark psychological thriller *Vertigo* (1958) was regarded as a misstep upon its release, with Novak's haunting, complex portrayal of two overlapping characters coming under particular scrutiny. She and costar James Stewart were paired together again in the popular romantic comedy *Bell, Book and Candle* (1958), with Novak playing a witch who meddles in the life of her neighbor.

Even though their working relationship had been fraught, the death of tyrannical Columbia head Harry Cohn in 1958 was a turning point in Novak's career. "The choice of good scripts seemed to die with him," she later recollected. After another terrific performance in *Middle of the Night* (1959), the actress was suddenly adrift, starring in simplistic sex-symbol roles in films like *The Notorious Landlady* (1962) and *The Amorous Adventures of Moll Flanders* (1965), with only Billy Wilder's *Kiss Me, Stupid* (1964) standing out.

Disappointed by the lack of good material and dealing with mental health issues, Novak left the film industry in 1965. She would return sporadically to act in films only to disappear again afterward. In 1991 she played a dying writer in *Liebestraum*, but had a combative relationship with director Mike Figgis and after the experience decided to retire for good. **JWa**

genre   ■ Drama   ■ Musical   ■ Thriller   ■ Romance   □ Comedy   ■ Mystery

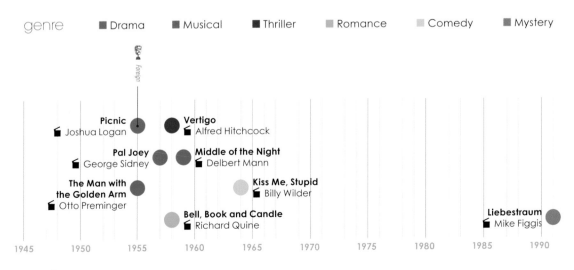

Foreign

Picnic
Joshua Logan

Vertigo
Alfred Hitchcock

Pal Joey
George Sidney

Middle of the Night
Delbert Mann

**The Man with
the Golden Arm**
Otto Preminger

Kiss Me, Stupid
Billy Wilder

Bell, Book and Candle
Richard Quine

Liebestraum
Mike Figgis

1945   1950   1955   1960   1965   1970   1975   1980   1985   1990

maureen o'hara 1920

| The Hunchback of Notre Dame | Jamaica Inn | How Green Was My Valley | Miracle on 34th Street | Rio Grande | The Quiet Man | The Parent Trap | McLintock! |

In telling an interviewer, "I'm very lucky, I really had some wonderful movies," red-haired Maureen O'Hara may have credited her cinematic achievements to the proverbial fortune of her homeland. In truth, her stardom was due in equal measure to her tenacity and a dedication to her craft.

Born Maureen FitzSimons in 1920, in the Dublin suburb of Ranelagh, the Irish actress — dubbed the Queen of Technicolor at the height of her fame during the 1940s and 1950s — knew from a young age the direction in which her future lay. However, despite her mother being a former operatic contralto, O'Hara's father was less happy about his daughter's theatrical aspirations, insisting she had some practical training to fall back on. He need not have worried.

From the age of 6, O'Hara trained in acting, singing and dancing. Her theater work led to a screen test in London and despite a less than auspicious performance, it was seen by actor Charles Laughton who sensed a certain sparkle to her. With business partner Erich Pommer, he signed O'Hara to a seven-year contract with their new production company Mayflower Pictures. Her first major role was in Alfred Hitchcock's *Jamaica Inn* (1939), an adaptation of Daphne du Maurier's novel. So pleased was Laughton with her performance that he cast her as Esmeralda opposite his Quasimodo in *The Hunchback of Notre Dame* (1939), filmed at the RKO Studios in Hollywood.

The outbreak of World War II saw O'Hara move permanently to Hollywood and following the sale of her contract with Mayflower Pictures to RKO, her career blossomed. It is during this period that she appeared in many of her best remembered films: the box-office hits *How Green Was My Valley* (1941), the first of many collaborations with director John Ford, the swashbuckler *The Black Swan* (1942) and the perennial Christmas favorite *Miracle on 34th Street* (1947). During the 1950s, O'Hara featured often alongside John Wayne, and their work together, which included the westerns *Rio Grande* (1950) and *McLintock!* (1963), are among both stars' most popular screen appearances. Ford's Irish-based comedy romance *The Quiet Man* (1952) not only returned O'Hara to her roots, but also showcased her fiery temperament, which perfectly mirrored Wayne's laconic style.

Despite a memorable turn in Disney's hit *The Parent Trap* (1961), O'Hara appeared on screen less frequently from the 1960s on. Her final outing was the appropriately named television movie *The Last Dance* (2000). She received a British Film Institute Fellowship in 1993 and an honorary Oscar in 2015 in recognition of a career spanning over 60 years. In 2010, she offered up typically forthright advice for those wishing to follow in her footsteps: "If you really want it," she said, "go after it — but learn how to speak properly, for God's sake!" **CP**

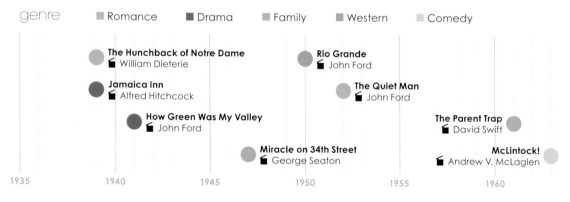

genre   ■ Romance   ■ Drama   ■ Family   ■ Western   ■ Comedy

The Hunchback of Notre Dame
🎬 William Dieterie

Jamaica Inn
🎬 Alfred Hitchcock

How Green Was My Valley
🎬 John Ford

Miracle on 34th Street
🎬 George Seaton

Rio Grande
🎬 John Ford

The Quiet Man
🎬 John Ford

The Parent Trap
🎬 David Swift

McLintock!
🎬 Andrew V. McLaglen

1935   1940   1945   1950   1955   1960

gary oldman 1958

| Meantime | Sid and Nancy | Bram Stoker's Dracula | Leon | Air Force One | Batman Begins | Tinker Tailor Soldier Spy | Dawn of the Planet of the Apes |

Gary Oldman led the way for a generation of British actors, among them Daniel Day-Lewis, Alfred Molina and Tim Roth. Schooled in the theater, Oldman and his cohorts claimed as their rightful inheritance the screen legacy of the "Method." The remarkable films that came out of the New Hollywood were key to this development, particularly the work of Robert De Niro.

Like De Niro, Oldman was capable of extreme physical transformations. Already an award-winning stage actor, Oldman enhanced his reputation with a run of films that showed a talent for deep immersion. He made his screen debut in *Remembrance* (1982), followed by a supporting role in *Meantime* (1983). The latter hinted at his capacity for danger and volatility, albeit with an innate sense of comic timing — qualities that would go on to serve him well. But it was his performances as Sid Vicious in *Sid and Nancy* (1986) and as Joe Orton in *Prick Up Your Ears* (1987) that revealed the depth of Oldman's talent. Putting flesh on the bones of biography, he went beyond impersonation. With his ear for accents and a great vocal facility, Oldman now laid claim to roles that previously would have gone to an American. His migration to Hollywood was inevitable and desired,

though the films he made on his arrival, *Criminal Law* (1988) and *Chattahoochee* (1989), were unremarkable.

Not that Oldman had finished with England. In Alan Clarke's *The Firm* (1989), he was exuberant, menacing and funny as an estate agent-cum-football hooligan. He brought the same unpredictability to his Irish-American gangster in *State of Grace* (1990), which saw him go head to head with Sean Penn. Both actors had drawn from the same wellspring of artistic influence, though it was Oldman who landed eye-catching roles in films by Oliver Stone and Francis Ford Coppola. In *JFK* (1991), Oldman vanished into the void that was Lee Harvey Oswald; while as the lead in *Bram Stoker's Dracula* (1992), he lowered his voice an octave and made the "undead" soulful in perpetuity.

For the rest of the 1990s, Oldman lit up big-budget movies with extravagant star turns, and in the process typecast himself. But he delved deep for his directorial debut, the autobiographical *Nil By Mouth* (1997). Benevolent but pivotal roles in two franchises, *Harry Potter* (2004–11) and *The Dark Knight* (2005–12), established his cumulative box-office eminence. And as George Smiley in *Tinker Tailor Soldier Spy* (2011), both actor and spy came in from the cold. **MM**

genre ◼ Drama ◼ Horror ◼ Thriller ◼ Action

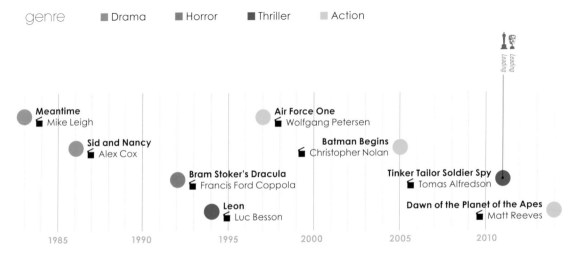

Meantime
Mike Leigh

Air Force One
Wolfgang Petersen

Sid and Nancy
Alex Cox

Batman Begins
Christopher Nolan

Bram Stoker's Dracula
Francis Ford Coppola

Tinker Tailor Soldier Spy
Tomas Alfredson

Leon
Luc Besson

Dawn of the Planet of the Apes
Matt Reeves

Leading

1985   1990   1995   2000   2005   2010

laurence olivier 1907–89

Fire Over England

Rebecca

Hamlet

The Prince and the Showgirl

The Entertainer

Sleuth

Marathon Man

War Requiem

As actor, director and a founder of the National Theatre, Laurence Olivier is a major figure of the British postwar stage. He is also one of Britain's greatest screen actors of the sound era. One of few genuine British stars in the Hollywood studio system, he combined matinee-idol charisma with a precise, demonstrative style that drew on his theater experience.

Born in Surrey in 1907, Olivier trained at the Central School of Speech in Drama in London. By the 1930s he was a major theatrical star. He was dismissive of cinema, but his classical good looks and penetrating presence made him suited to film, and he was cast in leading roles in popular British movies. In the patriotic Elizabethan drama *Fire Over England* (1937) he exuded sprightly charm as a young English spy.

Olivier was soon noticed by Hollywood, and was brought over to feature alongside Merle Oberon in *Wuthering Heights* (1939). He chafed against the dictates of the studio system, but his performance was less mannered than his English roles. He was even more assured playing another brooding romantic in *Rebecca* (1940), this time for Alfred Hitchcock.

His U.S. celebrity cemented by his marriage in 1940 to Vivien Leigh, Olivier was set for a Hollywood career, but with the outbreak of World War II he returned to the UK and to the stage. Revisiting an acclaimed stage role, he directed and starred in *Henry V* (1944), a morale-booster built around the actor's rousing performance.

After the war, Olivier directed himself in two further notable Shakespeare adaptations. An actor whose approach to his role was an intensely physical process, Olivier nonetheless conveyed with immense power the internal agonies of Hamlet in his 1948 screen version. And he gave what many regard as one of his greatest performances, as Richard III, in his 1955 adaptation.

He gave a blistering performance of a down-on-his-luck song and dance man in *The Entertainer* (1960). It was a bold, confrontational turn that connected Olivier to a new generation of filmmakers (following stiff performances in mainstream films like *The Prince and the Showgirl*, 1957). It was one of Olivier's last leading roles, though there were fine performances to follow, including a manipulative crime writer in *Sleuth* (1972) and a terrifying Nazi war criminal in *Marathon Man* (1976). His best late screen work was in television, although he was sublime in 1989's *War Requiem*, his final appearance before his death that year. **EL**

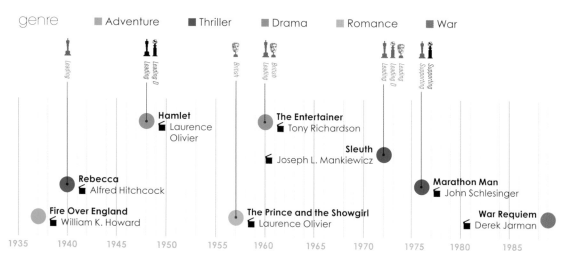

genre ■ Adventure ■ Thriller ■ Drama ■ Romance ■ War

Hamlet
Laurence Olivier

The Entertainer
Tony Richardson

Sleuth
Joseph L. Mankiewicz

Rebecca
Alfred Hitchcock

Marathon Man
John Schlesinger

Fire Over England
William K. Howard

The Prince and the Showgirl
Laurence Olivier

War Requiem
Derek Jarman

1935 1940 1945 1950 1955 1960 1965 1970 1975 1980 1985

peter o'toole 1932–2013

The Day
They Robbed
the Bank
of England

The Savage
Innocents

Lawrence
of Arabia

Becket

Lord Jim

What's New
Pussycat?

The Night
of the
Generals

The Lion
in Winter

The off-screen reputation of Peter O'Toole as a hard-living hell-raiser stands in sharp contrast to his screen work, in which the talented actor was acclaimed for committed performances in serious dramas. He suffered through several slumps in a long career that often played out like a cautionary tale and yet also featured notable highs, including one of the most outstanding performances in cinema history.

O'Toole was born in 1932 in Connemara, Ireland. After completing his national service and becoming a rebellious presence at the Royal Academy of Dramatic Arts, he started working on the stage. His cinematic career began in 1960, with small roles in a trio of films: Kidnapped, The Savage Innocents and The Day They Robbed the Bank of England.

It was O'Toole's role in the latter film that caught the attention of David Lean. He subsequently cast the actor as T.E. Lawrence, the near-mythic British army officer who contributed to the Arab Revolt, in Lawrence of Arabia (1962). The film is rightfully acclaimed as one of the finest epics ever made — a rewarding, stirring work about a deeply complex

figure. Aged just 28 when the 16-month shoot began, O'Toole is extraordinary as Lawrence. He received his first of eight Best Actor Oscar nominations for the performance — famously, he became the most nominated actor to never win.

Lawrence of Arabia made O'Toole a worldwide star and is his most significant role by some margin. He followed it up with another Oscar-nominated performance in Becket (1964), playing Henry II opposite Richard Burton's Thomas Becket, and was then miscast in the lavish, commercially disastrous Joseph Conrad adaptation Lord Jim (1965). Seeking to break free from epics, he pursued a range of different films, including the Woody Allen-penned comedy What's New Pussycat? (1965), John Huston's ambitious The Bible: In the Beginning... (1966) and the World War II drama The Night of the Generals (1967).

He played a much older Henry II in The Lion in Winter (1968). As the 50-year-old monarch, he was captivating as a sparring partner for Katharine Hepburn's feisty Eleanor of Aquitaine. The following year he took one of his most popular roles as the Latin

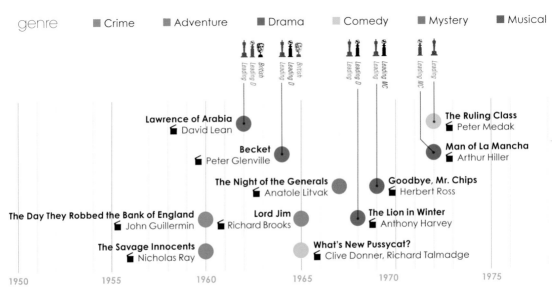

genre ■ Crime ■ Adventure ■ Drama ■ Comedy ■ Mystery ■ Musical

Lawrence of Arabia
David Lean
British / Leading D / Leading

Becket
Peter Glenville
Leading D / Leading

The Night of the Generals
Anatole Litvak

The Day They Robbed the Bank of England
John Guillermin

Lord Jim
Richard Brooks

The Savage Innocents
Nicholas Ray

What's New Pussycat?
Clive Donner, Richard Talmadge

The Lion in Winter
Anthony Harvey
Leading D / Leading MC

Goodbye, Mr. Chips
Herbert Ross
Leading MC

The Ruling Class
Peter Medak
Leading

Man of La Mancha
Arthur Hiller

1950   1955   1960   1965   1970   1975

| Goodbye, Mr. Chips | The Ruling Class | Man of La Mancha | The Stunt Man | My Favorite Year | The Last Emperor | Troy | Venus |

teacher Arthur Chipping in *Goodbye, Mr. Chips* (1969), a musical remake of the superior 1939 original.

O'Toole's predilection for flamboyant performances found an appropriate platform in *The Ruling Class* (1972), a dark satire in which he played the 14th Earl of Gurney, a paranoid schizophrenic believing himself to be either the second coming of Christ or Jack the Ripper. A passion project for the actor, the film was a commercial disappointment upon release but subsequently became a cult favorite.

As the 1970s progressed, O'Toole's heavy drinking and excessive lifestyle took its toll on both his body and career, and he starred in an increasing number of poorly received films and lost most of his stomach to a major illness. He continued to make daring choices like *Man of La Mancha* (1972) and the bizarre, erotic biopic *Caligula* (1979), but these received a largely negative response and he mostly kept to the stage. One of the few occasions when O'Toole's idiosyncratic approach paid off was his role as the tyrannical director Eli Cross in *The Stunt Man* (1980), a refreshing and clever film ahead of its time.

In sweeter, more conventional fare he was also effective as a drunkard swashbuckling actor in *My Favorite Year* (1982), receiving his seventh Oscar nomination. Aside of his portrayal of a kindly tutor in *The Last Emperor* (1987), a hilarious turn as the owner of a haunted castle in *High Spirits* (1988) and the television movie of arguably his most famous stage role, *Jeffrey Bernard is Unwell* (1999), the 1980s and 1990s were mostly populated by minor roles or cameos.

After much hesitation on his part O'Toole accepted an honorary Oscar in 2003, despite his stated desire to win one outright. The following year he took a role as King Priam in *Troy*, but with typical candor was publicly critical of the final result. On the opposing end of cinematic scale, he starred as an elderly actor attracted to a young woman in the tender *Venus* (2006).

Along with providing the voice of an exacting food critic in the Pixar film *Ratatouille* (2007), *Venus* would be one of his last major acting roles. In 2012 the 79-year-old O'Toole announced his retirement from acting, saying "The heart of it has gone out for me: it won't come back." He died a little over a year later. **JWa**

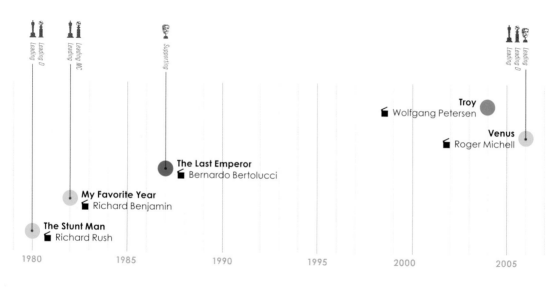

when good stars turn bad

James Cagney

Burt Lancaster

James Stewart

Tony Curtis

Henry Fonda

Glenn Close

Bill Murray

Harrison Ford

If the essence of acting is to experience a wide variety of different characters, it is astounding how limited the roles of many early movie thespians were. Silent cinema stars were often defined by a single persona: Charlie Chaplin's "Little Tramp," Rudolph Valentino's lovers, Greta Garbo's stone-faced sufferers. The tradition continued well into Hollywood's Golden Age, particularly with leading men: were Errol Flynn, Gary Cooper or John Wayne ever anything less than heroic? In Alfred Hitchcock's *Suspicion* (1941), preview audiences simply would not accept debonair Cary Grant murdering his wife, so the ending was reshot.

However, there were rare exceptions. James Cagney started out as a vaudeville dancer and in gangster film *The Public Enemy* (1931), he was originally cast as the good guy. Mid-shoot, he and costar Edward Woods switched roles. Now it was Cagney who, in one of cinema's iconic moments, shoved a half-grapefruit into Mae Clarke's face. A villain was born; and though Cagney continued to play nice and nasty, that initial shocking role remained a career keystone.

Blame — or commend — the vogue for "Method" acting and a more naturalistic commitment to character, but whatever the reason, from the 1950s onward, stars seemed more at ease moving to the dark side. Hitchcock delighted in casting decent, wholesome James Stewart as a voyeur in *Rear Window* (1954) and even a virtual necrophiliac, desperately trying to recreate the woman he loved and lost, in *Vertigo* (1958). Burt Lancaster, athletic hero of *The Crimson Pirate* (1952) and *Gunfight at the O.K. Corral* (1957) used his considerable physical presence to intimidating effect as vindictive gossip columnist J.J. Hunsecker in *Sweet Smell of Success* (1957). Hunsecker is the corrupt king of a phony court, and Lancaster's pathological contempt for everyone made for a terrifying villain.

Lancaster's *Sweet Smell* costar, Tony Curtis, turned his back on pretty-boy good guys in *The Boston Strangler* (1968), a compelling look at real-life serial killer Albert DeSalvo. That same year came perhaps the defining example of a screen good-guy-gone-bad. For decades, Henry Fonda was Hollywood's epitome of honest decency, so it probably took an outsider like Italian Sergio Leone to subvert those blue eyes as sadistic killer Frank in his epic *Once Upon a Time in the West* (1968). The film is a masterpiece but a huge part of its thrill is the shock of seeing *Young Mr. Lincoln* (1939) gun down a child. A later, comparable example, is Ben Kingsley's benign aura after *Gandhi* (1982). Nothing he had done on screen previously

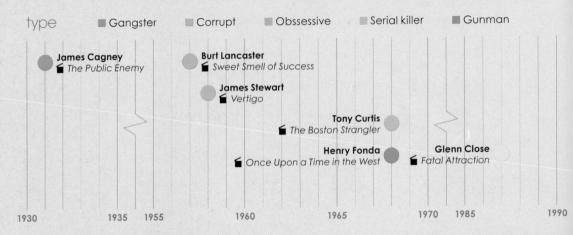

type ■ Gangster ■ Corrupt ■ Obssessive ■ Serial killer ■ Gunman

James Cagney
🏴 *The Public Enemy*

Burt Lancaster
🏴 *Sweet Smell of Success*

James Stewart
🏴 *Vertigo*

Tony Curtis
🏴 *The Boston Strangler*

Henry Fonda
🏴 *Once Upon a Time in the West*

Glenn Close
🏴 *Fatal Attraction*

1930   1935   1955   1960   1965   1970   1985   1990

Ben Kingsley | Denzel Washington | Robin Williams | Tom Cruise | Elijah Wood | Albert Brooks | Cameron Diaz | Steve Carell

prepared for the shock of a vicious, foul-mouthed loose cannon gangster in *Sexy Beast* (2000).

In American cinema's late 1960s and 1970s resurgence, a generation of actors came of age — Jack Nicholson, Robert De Niro, Al Pacino, Dustin Hoffman — who were much more comfortable playing flawed antiheroes in the likes of *The Godfather* (1972) or *Taxi Driver* (1976). Their inherent unpredictability is enmeshed with their allure. As a result, any shift into outright villainy, such as Nicholson in *Batman* (1989) or Hoffman in *Hook* (1991), no matter how enjoyable, did not seem so radical.

It is necessary to jump forward to more recent times for another Fonda-like revelation. Denzel Washington's corrupt cop in *Training Day* (2001) took so many people aback that they gave him the Oscar that his noble and equally deserving Steve Biko and Rubin "Hurricane" Carter were denied. Perennial hero Tom Cruise utilized his laser-like drive and focus for more nefarious ends as a relentless hit man in Michael Mann's *Collateral* (2004). Making Harrison Ford the surprisingly cowardly bad guy of *What Lies Beneath* (2000) was a highly unexpected late twist. And baby-faced Elijah Wood, innocent hobbit in *The Lord of the Rings* trilogy (2001–03) was surely the last person you would expect as *Sin City*'s (2005) cannibalistic serial killer. Wood obviously enjoyed the experience, though, playing another gruesome psychopath in *Maniac* (2012).

The welcome tendency among movie comedians to seek out more serious roles also sometimes delves into outright villainy. Probably the most celebrated is Robin Williams, supremely creepy as both obsessive voyeur in *One Hour Photo* (2002) and *Insomnia*'s (2002) sneering serial killer. Casting Bill Murray as a fearsome mobster opposite Robert De Niro in *Mad Dog and Glory* (1993) was a great switch, while those used to seeing Albert Brooks as a soft-centered neurotic were thrilled to see his stony-faced killer in *Drive* (2011). And Steve Carell, the amiable *Anchorman* (2004) and *The 40-Year-Old Virgin* (2005) star, was chilling as real-life sociopath John DuPont in *Foxcatcher* (2014).

Women, as is often the case in Hollywood, have fewer options. Most actresses who go dark do so with a pantomime-like fantasy element involved — Susan Sarandon in *Enchanted* (2007) or *Stardust*'s (2007) Michelle Pfeiffer. Yet those rare serious opportunities — Glenn Close switching from sensible or long-suffering good women roles to deranged harpy in *Fatal Attraction* (1987); or Cameron Diaz's fun-loving screen persona subverted into a calculating predator in *The Counselor* (2013) — prove them every bit as capable and versatile as their male counterparts. **LS**

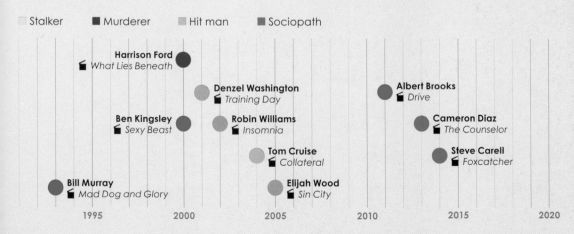

Stalker ■ Murderer ■ Hit man ■ Sociopath

Harrison Ford
What Lies Beneath

Denzel Washington
Training Day

Albert Brooks
Drive

Ben Kingsley
Sexy Beast

Robin Williams
Insomnia

Cameron Diaz
The Counselor

Tom Cruise
Collateral

Steve Carell
Foxcatcher

Bill Murray
Mad Dog and Glory

Elijah Wood
Sin City

1995 | 2000 | 2005 | 2010 | 2015 | 2020

al pacino 1940

The Panic in Needle Park	The Godfather	Serpico	Scarecrow	The Godfather: Part II	Dog Day Afternoon	Scarface	Sea of Love

Few, if any, actors have ever achieved the incendiary power of Alfredo James Pacino. His signature roles, often as either cop or criminal, are among the most acclaimed and iconic in American cinema.

Born in Manhattan, 1940, the young Pacino had an unruly adolescence. Eventually accepted into the Actors Studio, he studied under "Method" guru Lee Strasberg, going on to award-winning stage work. His film breakthrough came as a livewire heroin addict in gritty love story *The Panic in Needle Park* (1971). This film brought him to the attention of Francis Ford Coppola, then casting *The Godfather* (1972). Despite studio misgivings, Coppola insisted on Pacino as Michael Corleone, the youngest son of a mafia don, who first reluctantly, then ruthlessly assumes control of the family business. Though Marlon Brando played the title role, Pacino's Michael is the central protagonist; his gradual descent from ambivalent outsider to cold-blooded murderer is both tragic and utterly chilling.

Pacino's emergence amid the 1970s New Hollywood moviemaking boom ushered in an incredible run of work. In under-appreciated road movie *Scarecrow* (1973), his sweet-natured clown is a wonderful foil to Gene Hackman's tough-nut ex-con.

As *Serpico* (1973), based on the real-life whistle-blowing New York police officer, Pacino's wounded eyes reflect his building rage at the endemic corruption around him and the fear of potential retribution. And his return to Michael Corleone in *The Godfather: Part II* (1974) showed a man become a monster. Taken as one whole arc, it is one of the most remarkable performances in film history.

Incredibly, Pacino's next role was its equal. In *Dog Day Afternoon* (1975), his character Sonny's attempt to rob a bank — to pay for his male lover's sex change operation, no less — goes badly wrong. Portraying Sonny's desperate attempts to juggle the cops, his hapless colleague Sal, the hostages and a growing media circus, Pacino's jittery defiance and vulnerability is electrifying.

It is tempting to speculate that such soul-baring efforts forced Pacino to ease up, taking on lighter roles in far less demanding work. Although he committed to William Friedkin's controversial *Cruising* (1980), as a cop hunting a killer in New York's gay underground scene, there is a sense of miscasting. Brian De Palma's *Scarface* (1983), on the other hand, could not be played by anyone else. Tony Montana,

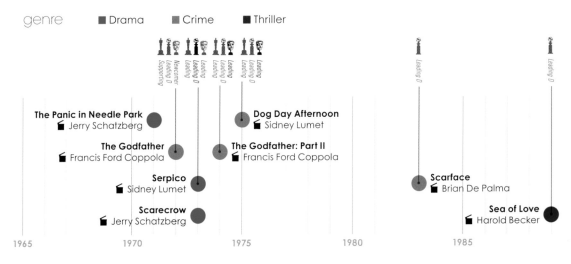

genre ■ Drama ■ Crime ■ Thriller

The Panic in Needle Park
Jerry Schatzberg

The Godfather
Francis Ford Coppola

Serpico
Sidney Lumet

Scarecrow
Jerry Schatzberg

Dog Day Afternoon
Sidney Lumet

The Godfather: Part II
Francis Ford Coppola

Scarface
Brian De Palma

Sea of Love
Harold Becker

1965   1970   1975   1980   1985

$1.4BN	$225M (U.S.)	$217M (U.S.)	$209M	$245M	$223M	$287M	$182M
The Godfather (1972)	The Godfather: Part II (1974)	Dog Day Afternoon (1975)	The Sea of Love (1989)	The Godfather: Part III (1990)	Scent of a Woman (1992)	Heat (1995)	Donnie Brasco (1997)

The Godfather: Part III

Scent of a Woman

Carlito's Way

Heat

Donnie Brasco

The Insider

Insomnia

Manglehorn

a vicious Cuban immigrant ready to seize his slice of the American Dream, is Pacino in excelsis, strutting, hustling, relishing every exaggerated syllable of his outrageous accent and one-liners. Though widely reviled on release, *Scarface* has gone on to become perhaps his most notorious role.

The disastrous reception to American Civil War epic *Revolution* (1985) saw Pacino take a four-year hiatus. His comeback, sexy thriller *Sea of Love* (1989), showed he had lost none of his charisma as a cop whose new lover may be a serial killer. Now seen as a veteran, the industry clearly felt uncomfortable that, unlike his peers, Pacino had never won an Oscar. Denied by a redundant *The Godfather: Part III* (1990), compensation came with a win for *Scent of a Woman* (1992), playing a blind, alcoholic ex-Army colonel who serves as mentor to a clean-cut preppie. It is an award-bait role, which, while effective, is far removed from Pacino's 1970s heyday. Another spin as a De Palma gangster, in the more elegiac *Carlito's Way* (1993), saw him tone things down again.

Michael Mann's crime epic *Heat* (1995) was heralded as the long awaited on-screen meeting between Pacino and his contemporary Robert De

Niro. The pair only share two scenes, but as cop and criminal, obsessive professionals who are flip sides of the same coin, they live up to their heavyweight billing. *Donnie Brasco* (1997) returned Pacino to the wrong side of the law, deftly playing an ageing, fading wise guy betrayed by Johnny Depp's undercover agent. In between these crime sagas came his highly personal directorial debut *Looking for Richard* (1996), a documentary analyzing Shakespeare's *Richard III*.

Gripping real-life drama *The Insider* (1999) found Pacino excelling as canny television producer trying to convince Russell Crowe's chemist to expose the toxic tobacco industry. His guilt-ridden, sleep-deprived detective in *Insomnia* (2002) was solid, but too many generic thrillers and cop flicks — *The Recruit* (2003), *88 Minutes* (2007), woeful De Niro reunion *Righteous Kill* (2008) — and over-the-top escapades began to clog up his resumé. Despite some fine made-for-television work, it is telling that no movie since *Donnie Brasco* has been deemed award-worthy. The double bill of *The Humbling* and *Manglehorn*, which both premiered at the 2014 Venice Film Festival, hinted at the greatness of Pacino when he worked with the right material. **LS**

P

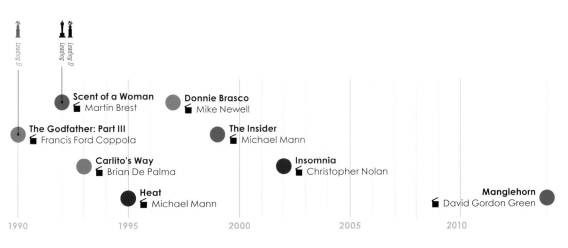

Leading D

Leading D
Leading

Scent of a Woman
Martin Brest

Donnie Brasco
Mike Newell

The Godfather: Part III
Francis Ford Coppola

The Insider
Michael Mann

Carlito's Way
Brian De Palma

Insomnia
Christopher Nolan

Heat
Michael Mann

Manglehorn
David Gordon Green

1990   1995   2000   2005   2010

The Panic in Needle Park
(1971)

Serpico
(1973)

The Godfather:
Part II
(1974)

Dog Day
Afternoon
(1975)

Scarface
(1983)

Scent of
a Woman
(1992)

Donnie Brasco
(1997)

Pacino with Kitty Winn in his breakthrough movie *The Panic in Needle Park*, which was controversial for its depiction of drug use.

Based on the true story of New York cop Frank Serpico, *Serpico* was filmed in reverse order, with Pacino's hair starting long and then being trimmed for each scene.

Pacino almost quit his role as Sonny in *Dog Day Afternoon*, but changed his mind when it was offered to Dustin Hoffman.

Insomnia
(2002)

The Godfather: Part II saw Pacino's character, Michael Corleone, descend even further into the dark heart of the criminal underworld, becoming a vampiric, remorseless killer of his own brother, isolated by his paranoia and misanthropy.

...ay hello to my little friend!" — Pacino as the Cuban drug kingpin Tony Montana ...*Scarface*.

The *Rolling Stone* review of **Donnie Brasco** described Pacino and Depp as "a match made in acting heaven, riffing off each other with astonishing subtlety and wit."

...cino and Chris O'Donnell in **Scent of a Woman**, the movie that finally won Pacino a ...st Actor Academy Award.

A remake of a Norwegian thriller, **Insomnia** starred Pacino as a homicide detective and Robin Williams as the prime suspect in a murder case he is investigating.

robert pattinson 1986

Vanity Fair

Harry Potter and the Goblet of Fire

Twilight

Little Ashes

Bel Ami

Cosmopolis

The Rover

Map to the Stars

London-born Robert Pattinson started out in amateur theater, where he caught the attention of an agent. This led to his first screen role, an uncredited appearance in Mira Nair's *Vanity Fair* (2004). He was cut from the film's theatrical release, but later reinstated for the DVD version. Following a small role in the television film *Curse of the Ring* (2004), the actor first attracted attention playing Cedric Diggory in *Harry Potter and the Goblet of Fire* (2005). He was named "British Star of Tomorrow" by *The Times* newspaper, and following roles in a couple of television movies was cast as the lead in *How to Be* (2008) and *Little Ashes* (2008), the latter of which saw him give a sensitive portrait of a young Salvador Dalí.

However, Pattinson's major break came with his role as Edward Cullen, the heartthrob vampire in the adaptation of Stephanie Meyer's blockbuster young adult fiction series, *Twilight* (2008–12). It made him one of the most recognizable faces in Hollywood and his off-screen romance with costar Kristen Stewart made for countless headlines around the world. Although the critical reception to the films has been mixed, their popularity with audiences has made the series one of the most successful Hollywood film franchises.

Keenly aware of his own screen persona and the risk of being typecast, Pattinson has opted for more challenging work since completing the final *Twilight* film, steering clear of easy roles in favor of complex, often troubled individuals. *Bel Ami* (2012) might have seemed a safe option, playing a young man whose good looks find him the object of attraction for a number of women, but the adaptation of Guy de Maupassant's story paints Pattinson's character, Georges Duroy, as a ruthless social climber.

The actor then took the lead in David Cronenberg's study of capitalism out of control in *Cosmopolis* (2012). An adaptation of Don DeLillo's novel, it competed for the Palme d'Or at the Cannes Film Festival and gave Pattinson one of his most challenging roles yet.

The actor took on another demanding role in the post-apocalyptic *The Rover* (2014), playing a simpleton con who helps Guy Pearce's embattled traveler retrieve a stolen car. The film premiered at Cannes, as did Pattinson's second collaboration with Cronenberg. A coruscating satire of Hollywood, *Map to the Stars* (2014) featured Pattinson as a limo driver who finds himself attracted to Mia Wasikowska's misfit.

Pattinson plays T.E. Lawrence opposite Nicole Kidman in *Queen of the Desert* (2015), Werner Herzog's biopic of Gertrude Bell. He also takes on another real-life character, Dennis Stock — the celebrated U.S. photojournalist who befriended James Dean — in Anton Corbijn's *Life* (2015). Such roles show Pattinson's continued desire to distance himself from his teen heartthrob persona in favor of a career as an actor unafraid to take on challenging material. **OC**

genre   ■ Drama   ■ Fantasy   ■ Thriller

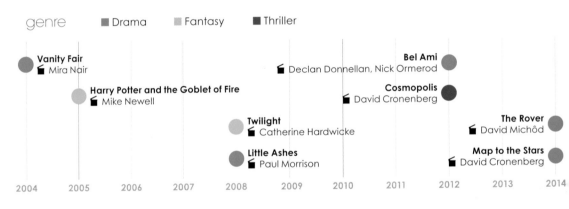

Vanity Fair
Mira Nair

Harry Potter and the Goblet of Fire
Mike Newell

Twilight
Catherine Hardwicke

Little Ashes
Paul Morrison

Bel Ami
Declan Donnellan, Nick Ormerod

Cosmopolis
David Cronenberg

The Rover
David Michôd

Map to the Stars
David Cronenberg

2004   2005   2006   2007   2008   2009   2010   2011   2012   2013   2014

gregory peck 1916–2003

Spellbound

The Gunfighter

Roman Holiday

The Big Country

To Kill a Mockingbird

Cape Fear

Arabesque

The Boys from Brazil

With his square jaw, upright bearing and intense, dark-eyed gaze, Gregory Peck appeared an icon of integrity — and was often cast as just that. At times this could lead him to appear stiff, even wooden; but if the role allowed for humor to temper the righteousness the humanity showed through.

Lead roles were his from the start. He was a Soviet patriot combatting German invaders in his screen debut, *Days of Glory* (1944), and a Scots missionary in China in *The Keys of the Kingdom* (1944). On the strength of these he was picked up by Hitchcock for two flawed films: the thriller *Spellbound* (1945) and the courtroom drama *The Paradine Case* (1947). In between these he was cast against type as a lecherous baddie in the western *Duel in the Sun* (1946) and, in line with his liberal principles, as a journalist rooting out prejudice in *Gentleman's Agreement* (1947).

As black-clad Johnny Ringo, broodingly waiting for the next gunslinger to challenge his reputation, Peck dominated *The Gunfighter* (1950). In contrast, he brought lightness and warmth to *Roman Holiday* (1953), as the journalist helping Audrey Hepburn's princess enjoy her brief taste of freedom. His performance as Captain Ahab in John Huston's misconceived *Moby Dick* (1956), however, felt inhibited and uncomfortable. Far more attuned to his persona was his mild-mannered easterner in *The Big Country* (1958), come west to join his fiancée and finding himself the unheeded voice of reason in a local feud.

Clear-cut action roles, as with the leader of the guerrilla band in *The Guns of Navarone* (1961), fitted him well, though he brought an intriguing hint of moral fallibility to the lawyer menaced by Robert Mitchum in *Cape Fear* (1962). Then came the role he was born to play: Atticus Finch, the single parent, liberal-minded lawyer fighting racism in a 1930s Alabama small town in *To Kill a Mockingbird* (1962). Goodness is notoriously tough to portray without edging into priggishness, but Peck here brings it off with apparent ease.

Mirage (1965) and *Arabesque* (1966) were enjoyable thrillers, with Peck handling the twisty intrigues competently. From here on it was mostly staunch, upright authority figures, but *The Boys from Brazil* (1978) offered something unexpected: Peck, for the first and only time in his career, playing sheer unregenerate evil as Dr. Joseph Mengele. His face-off with Laurence Olivier's Nazi-hunter prompted suggestions that he should have played evil more often. **PK**

P

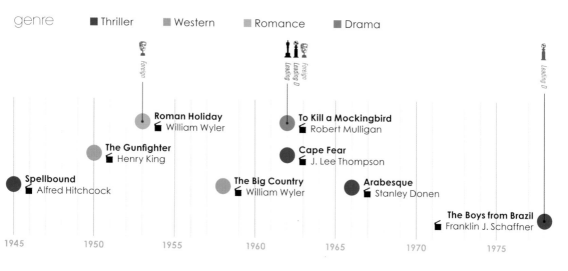

genre ■ Thriller ■ Western ■ Romance ■ Drama

Foreign

Foreign
Leading D
Leading

Leading D

Roman Holiday
🎬 William Wyler

To Kill a Mockingbird
🎬 Robert Mulligan

The Gunfighter
🎬 Henry King

Cape Fear
🎬 J. Lee Thompson

Spellbound
🎬 Alfred Hitchcock

The Big Country
🎬 William Wyler

Arabesque
🎬 Stanley Donen

The Boys from Brazil
🎬 Franklin J. Schaffner

1945 1950 1955 1960 1965 1970 1975

cheng pei-pei 1946

The Lotus Lamp

Lovers Rock

Come Drink With Me

Hong Kong Nocturne

The Lady Hermit

Flirting Scholar

Crouching Tiger, Hidden Dragon

Lilting

Known as the Queen of Swordplay, Cheng Pei-pei shot to fame in Hong Kong in the 1960s, when the Shaw brothers were redefining and popularizing the martial arts genre. She worked with the Hong Kong studio giants for over a decade, honing her legendary swordplay skills in kung fu classics such as King Hu's *Come Drink with Me* (1966) and *The Lady Hermit* (1971). Despite taking a 20-year hiatus, Cheng has starred in over 60 films, 21 of which were with the Shaw brothers. She continues to act, recently starring opposite Ben Whishaw in Hong Khaou's low-budget British drama *Lilting* (2014).

Born in Shanghai in 1946, Cheng trained as a classical dancer. Moving to Hong Kong in 1962, she spent a year training with the Shaw brothers, one of the second group of actors sent by the producers to Japan in order to hone their skills. Prior to her career-defining wuxia debut, she starred mostly in musicals and romantic dramas, such as *The Lotus Lamp* (1963) playing a male character, and *Lovers' Rock* (1964). She also landed the lead role in Inoue Imetsugu's *Hong Kong Nocturne* (1967), one of the best musicals of the period.

However, it was Cheng's appearance in the highly influential *Come Drink with Me* that provided her big break. King Hu cast her because of her background as a dancer, which he believed made her more graceful and skilled as a martial artist. Cheng claims that Run Run Shaw had initially wanted to destroy the movie, because it did not conform to the conventions of the wuxia genre. In particular, it featured a female protagonist. But the film was a huge commercial success and transformed Cheng into a bona fide star of this brand of martial arts film, which she continued to star in.

During the 1970s, with the popularity of Bruce Lee, Hong Kong martial arts cinema focused more on men. Cheng's last great film with the Shaws was 1971's stunning *The Lady Hermit*. Playing the eponymous heroine, Cheng's performance is regarded as her best from this era. Shortly after the film's release, she married and moved to Los Angeles, where she spent 20 years working in television and raising a family.

In 1993, following her divorce, she returned to Hong Kong and starred alongside Stephen Chow and Gong Li as Madam Wah in Chow's comedy *Flirting Scholar* (1993), which became a huge success in mainland China. Cheng subsequently remained in Hong Kong, taking smaller film roles and working in television, until she was cast as Jade Fox in Ang Lee's multiple Oscar-winning wuxia drama *Crouching Tiger, Hidden Dragon* (2000). A wonderful villain and easily the film's most colorful character, it earned her the accolade of Best Supporting Actress at the Hong Kong Film Awards. Her subtle, moving performance in *Lilting* aside, she continues to work in Hong Kong and China. **CMB**

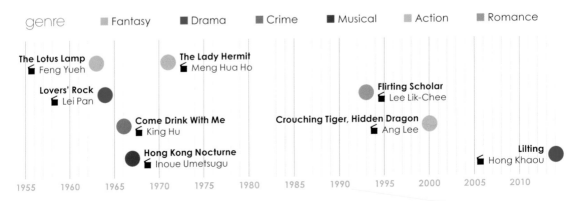

genre   ■ Fantasy   ■ Drama   ■ Crime   ■ Musical   ■ Action   ■ Romance

The Lotus Lamp
🎬 Feng Yueh

The Lady Hermit
🎬 Meng Hua Ho

Lovers' Rock
🎬 Lei Pan

Flirting Scholar
🎬 Lee Lik-Chee

Come Drink With Me
🎬 King Hu

Crouching Tiger, Hidden Dragon
🎬 Ang Lee

Hong Kong Nocturne
🎬 Inoue Umetsugu

Lilting
🎬 Hong Khaou

1955   1960   1965   1970   1975   1980   1985   1990   1995   2000   2005   2010

| Character Actor | Fighter | Sinner | Saint | Villain |

sean penn 1960

| Taps | At Close Range | Carlito's Way | Dead Man Walking | Mystic River | 21 Grams | Milk | This Must Be the Place |

Confident and charismatic from the start, Sean Penn drew early comparisons with Robert De Niro. Unfortunately for Penn, he came of age when high-concept movies had become dominant, with the "personal" auteur-driven films of the previous decade finding fewer champions in a Hollywood underwritten by multinational corporations. Still, Penn flourished, his willfulness apparent from his big-screen debut in *Taps* (1981). Here, Penn stood out in a cast that included George C. Scott, Timothy Hutton and Tom Cruise, in what was only his second movie. If Cruise went on to enjoy huge box-office success, Penn was quickly regarded as the best actor of his generation. Critic Pauline Kael singled him out as early as *Bad Boys* (1983): "Each time, Penn comes as a complete surprise."

He had already demonstrated his range with an influential comedic turn in *Fast Times at Ridgemont High* (1982), a rare feat in itself for a heavyweight talent conscious of his place within a tradition of sullen but poetic American actors. But what Penn needed — great material, a Scorsese to his De Niro — was simply not there. Instead he gravitated toward mavericks and mentors, befriending John Cassavetes, Marlon Brando and Dennis Hopper, while conspiring to act opposite the previous generation's best actors. One by one they lined up: Christopher Walken in *At Close Range* (1986), Robert Duvall in *Colors* (1988), De Niro in *We're No Angels* (1989) and Al Pacino in *Carlito's Way* (1993). On each occasion Penn acquitted himself, but then he threatened to quit acting in favor of directing.

His absence only seemed to incite a clamor for his return. He began to work with directors deserving of his talent: Brian De Palma, David Fincher, Terrence Malick and Woody Allen. He was nominated for an Academy Award for his work in *Dead Man Walking* (1995). He received another nomination for his egotistical, though oddly endearing jazz guitarist in Allen's *Sweet and Lowdown* (1999). He won his first Oscar for his performance in Clint Eastwood's *Mystic River* (2003), where he is turbulent and vengeful, as well as tender. And then in *Milk* (2008), as the eponymous gay rights activist and politician, Penn reminded audiences that he could be light on his feet and no less sorrowful. He received a second Oscar. In recent years acting has taken a back seat to his activism and humanitarian aid work, but he has has still found time for projects such as *This Must Be the Place* (2011) and *Gangster Squad* (2013). **MM**

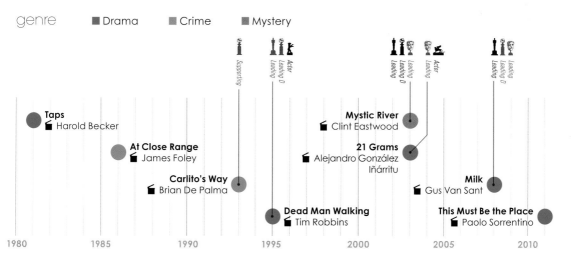

genre ■ Drama ■ Crime ■ Mystery

Taps — Harold Becker

At Close Range — James Foley

Carlito's Way — Brian De Palma

Dead Man Walking — Tim Robbins

Mystic River — Clint Eastwood

21 Grams — Alejandro González Iñárritu

Milk — Gus Van Sant

This Must Be the Place — Paolo Sorrentino

1980   1985   1990   1995   2000   2005   2010

anthony perkins 1932–92

The Actress

Friendly Persuasion

Psycho

Goodbye Again

The Trial

Catch-22

Winter Kills

Psycho II

If ever an actor were associated with a single defining character, Anthony Perkins and the towering role of Norman Bates in the influential *Psycho* (1960) is arguably the best example. However, his career extended far further than Alfred Hitchcock's thriller.

Born in New York in 1932, Perkins began appearing on stage from an early age, making his feature debut in *The Actress* (1953), alongside Spencer Tracy and Jean Simmons. William Wyler's *Friendly Persuasion* (1956) saw him cast as a young Quaker caught between his spiritual, pacifist upbringing and military obligation during the Civil War. It earned him a Best Supporting Actor Oscar nomination and a Golden Globe for Most Promising Newcomer, a title he shared that year with Paul Newman and John Kerr. A couple of westerns, *The Tin Star* and *The Lonely Man* (both 1957) were followed by more romantic fare such as *The Matchmaker* (1958), opposite Shirley MacLaine, and *Green Mansions* (1959), with Audrey Hepburn.

Cast by Alfred Hitchcock as the seemingly innocent innkeeper, Perkins excelled in the brilliantly executed, still shocking and explicit *Psycho*. The synthesis of sensitivity and sociopathic tendencies in many ways became the shadow from which Perkins

as an actor could never escape. He would reprise the role in a number of inferior sequels, although *Psycho II* (1983) still managed to muster up some thrills.

He appeared in Anatole Litvak's *Goodbye Again* (1961), an adaptation of the novel by Françoise Sagan, in which he is commendable as a young lawyer embarking on an affair with an older woman. *The Trial* (1962) may well be the finest film of Perkins' career. Shot and funded in Europe, Orson Welles' expressionistic take on Franz Kafka's novel makes phenomenal use of space and architecture and effectively translates its source material. As Josef K., a man persecuted for unknown crimes, Perkins communicates the paranoia of an innocent man trapped in a labyrinthine bureaucratic system.

Though a less successful translation of an acclaimed novel, Mike Nichols' tilt at Joseph Heller's anti-war novel *Catch-22* (1970) is not without interest and Perkins equips himself well among a starry cast. He then drifted in and out of European and American productions, making a couple of strong films — William Richert's psychological thriller *Winter Kills* (1979) and Ken Russell's risqué *Crimes of Passion* (1984) — before his untimely death in 1992. **JW**

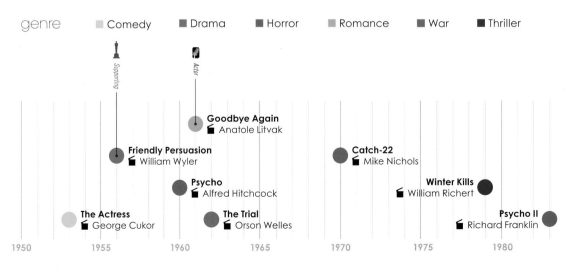

genre ■ Comedy ■ Drama ■ Horror ■ Romance ■ War ■ Thriller

Supporting

Actor

Goodbye Again
Anatole Litvak

Friendly Persuasion
William Wyler

Catch-22
Mike Nichols

Psycho
Alfred Hitchcock

Winter Kills
William Richert

The Actress
George Cukor

The Trial
Orson Welles

Psycho II
Richard Franklin

1950   1955   1960   1965   1970   1975   1980

michelle pfeiffer 1958

| Grease 2 | Scarface | The Witches of Eastwick | Dangerous Liaisons | The Fabulous Baker Boys | Love Field | Batman Returns | The Age of Innocence |

Michelle Pfeiffer's film career did not get off to a promising start. Her breakthrough role in the much derided musical sequel *Grease 2* (1982) could have ended it all before it began, with rumors that following her portrayal of heroine Stephanie Zinone, nobody wanted to be associated with her. Luckily for Pfeiffer, Brian De Palma gave her the benefit of the doubt and she landed a role in his infamous *Scarface* (1983).

She subsequently worked with Richard Donner on the fantasy epic *Ladyhawke* (1985) and with John Landis on *Into the Night* (1985), but it was opposite heavyweights Jack Nicholson, Susan Sarandon and Cher in *The Witches of Eastwick* (1987) that Pfeiffer hit box-office gold again. She followed it with a couple of moderate successes, as a gangster's widow who embarks on a relationship with an undercover FBI agent in *Married to the Mob* (1988) and caught between Kurt Russell and Mel Gibson in *Tequila Sunrise* (1988), until she scored one of her most critically acclaimed roles, as Madame Marie de Tourvel in Stephen Frears' *Dangerous Liaisons* (1988). She received an Oscar nomination for her performance and followed it with another, playing feisty singer Susie Diamond in *The Fabulous Baker Boys* (1989).

One of Pfeiffer's most iconic roles came courtesy of Tim Burton's *Batman Returns* (1992), in which she gave a particularly seductive performance as Catwoman. She was moving as a woman devastated by the assassination of John F. Kennedy in *Love Field* (1992). She returned to period drama the following year, beautifully capturing the pain of a spurned woman in Martin Scorsese's *The Age of Innocence* (1993), before having fun opposite Jack Nicholson again in *Wolf* (1994).

Pfeiffer had some modest hits over the next few years, with the urban school drama *Dangerous Minds* (1995) and comedy *One Fine Day* (1996), but it was not until the new millennium that she would have another smash on her hands, with the supernatural thriller *What Lies Beneath* (2000). After roles in *I Am Sam* (2001) and *White Oleander* (2002), Pfeiffer took a hiatus from her film career to spend time with her family. She returned as a bullying mother in *Hairspray* (2007), a witch in the fantasy adventure *Stardust* (2007), reunited with Frears on the less successful *Cheri* (2009) and appeared in the low-key drama *Personal Effects* (2009). She has continued to work regularly, most notably reuniting with Burton for his big screen adaptation of cult television show *Dark Shadows* (2012). **MB**

genre   ■ Musical   ■ Crime   ■ Fantasy   ■ Drama   ■ Romance   ■ Action

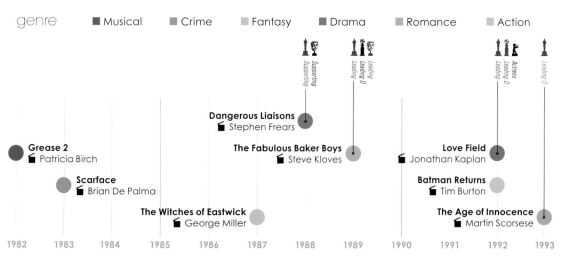

joaquin phoenix 1974

| Parenthood | To Die For | Inventing the Abbotts | 8MM | Gladiator | The Yards | Buffalo Soldiers | The Village |

Brooding, intense and prodigiously gifted, Joaquin Phoenix has been described as one of his generation's best actors. He is a risk taker, whose abilities have produced astonishing performances, sometimes from the unlikeliest of roles.

Born Joaquín Rafael Bottom in 1974, the actor was initially known to audiences as Leaf Phoenix. He appeared in a number of television shows and the films *SpaceCamp* (1986) and *Russkies* (1987) before making an impression as Dianne Weist's troubled son in *Parenthood* (1989). He then left the screen for a few years. When he returned, as Joaquin Phoenix in 1995's *To Die For*, playing one of the youths Nicole Kidman's weather forecaster dupes into killing her husband, he showed himself to be a compelling screen presence.

He is sweet opposite Liv Tyler in *Inventing the Abbotts* (1997) and one of the more interesting elements of Oliver Stone's oddly unsatisfying modern noir *U Turn* (1997). He plays sleaze to the hilt in Joel Schumacher's repugnant *8MM* (1999) but shows real depth in *The Yards* (2000), which began a rewarding collaboration with director James Gray. Their second film, *We Own the Night* (2007), continues the murky, noirish mood of the earlier film, with Phoenix playing

the manager of a nightclub to the disdain of his family, most of whom are cops. He then played a man caught between two women from very different backgrounds in *Two Lovers* (2008) and, in 2013's *The Immigrant*, he is a resident of New York who falls in love with Marion Cotillard's new arrival at Ellis Island. Phoenix's style of performance is perfectly attuned to Gray's low-key character studies.

Then came *Gladiator* (2000). Phoenix's portrayal of Commodus is a marked contrast to his earlier performances. A raging storm of insecurity, incestuous desire and lust for power, Phoenix's emperor may bear little resemblance to the actual leader of Rome, but it makes for compelling viewing. He toned his performance back down again to play Abbé du Coulmier, a young priest charged with watching over the incarcerated Marquis de Sade in *Quills* (2000).

Phoenix is perfect as an anti-authoritarian soldier on a U.S. base some time around the fall of the Berlin Wall in Gregor Jordan's smart satire *Buffalo Soldiers* (2001), but looks lost — like everyone else — in Thomas Vinterberg's bizarre, apocalyptic sci-fi drama *It's All About Love* (2003). If he is peripheral to Mel Gibson's grieving patriarch in M. Night Shyamalan's *Signs*

genre ■ Comedy ■ Crime ■ Romance ■ Drama ■ Mystery ■ Sci-Fi

Parenthood
Ron Howard

To Die For
Gus Van Sant

Inventing the Abbotts
Pat O'Connor

8MM
Joel Schumacher

Gladiator
Ridley Scott

The Yards
James Gray

Buffalo Soldiers
Gregor Jordan

1990   1995   2000

Walk the Line · We Own the Night · Two Lovers · I'm Still Here · The Master · The Immigrant · Her · Inherent Vice

(2002), he is one of the few highlights in the director's *The Village* (2004), an engaging if ultimately silly drama.

After a small role in *Hotel Rwanda* (2004), Phoenix played Jack Morrison, a Baltimore fireman, in Jay Russell's *Ladder 49* (2004). Trapped in a warehouse as fire rages around him, the film cuts to flashbacks of the character's early life and entry into the service. The actor imbues Jack with quiet nobility as he realizes there is little chance of escaping the furnace.

Walk the Line (2005), in which he plays country singer Johnny Cash, was another huge hit for the star. Although his musical performances impress, it is the domestic scenes, opposite Reese Witherspoon's June Carter, that make the film so engrossing. Phoenix excels at characters tormented by guilt, as he proved again with *Reservation Road* (2007), playing a lawyer who hits a boy with his car and flees the scene, only to end up representing the dead boy's father.

Phoenix's recent output has been dominated by his collaborations with Paul Thomas Anderson and Spike Jonze, and the pseudo-documentary he made with his friend and brother-in-law Casey Affleck. *I'm Still Here* (2010) was the result of Phoenix disappearing for two years, with the exception of bizarre appearances on David Letterman's talk show. Premiering at the Venice International Film Festival, the film divided critics. A smart, often funny, dissection of our obsession with celebrity, the lengths that Phoenix goes to have us believe he has lost the plot are impressive.

The actor returned to narrative film with *The Master* (2012) in which he played Freddie, a sex-obsessed alcoholic who finds himself drawn into the inner circle of a modern-day shaman, played by Philip Seymour Hoffman. Both actors have rarely been better, with Phoenix startling in his exploration of Freddie's baser, more feral behavior. The actor's portrayal of Doc Sportello in Anderson's faithful adaptation of Thomas Pynchon's *Inherent Vice* (2014) is a calmer beast. Phoenix excels at conveying Doc's sense of growing disquiet at the bizarre world he finds himself trapped in.

The world of *Her* (2013) is no less strange. Set in a future metropolis, Phoenix plays Theodore Twombly, a lonely divorcé who embarks on a relationship with Samantha, an intelligent computer operating system. Scarlett Johansson's sultry voice notwithstanding, Phoenix brings immense warmth and humanity to his performance, one of his best and further evidence of his status as a commanding screen presence. **IHS**

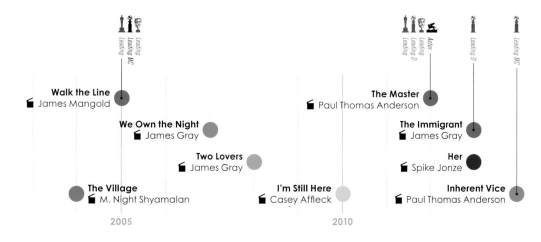

Walk the Line — James Mangold

We Own the Night — James Gray

Two Lovers — James Gray

The Village — M. Night Shyamalan

I'm Still Here — Casey Affleck

The Master — Paul Thomas Anderson

The Immigrant — James Gray

Her — Spike Jonze

Inherent Vice — Paul Thomas Anderson

2005   2010

mary pickford 1892–1979

| The Female of the Species | Friends | Hearts Adrift | Stella Maris | Daddy Long-Legs | Pollyanna | My Best Girl | Coquette |

The woman about whom the soubriquet "America's Sweetheart" was first used can also lay claim to being the movie industry's first marquee name, half of its first power couple and one of its earliest moguls. Within three years of appearing in her first feature, Mary Pickford was producing her own films. Her place in America's affections had been secured via appearances in myriad silent shorts, initially for D.W. Griffith's Biograph company. So popular did she instantly become that Biograph drew audiences with the promise of "The Girl with the Golden Curls" long before it ever credited actors by name.

Born Gladys Smith in Toronto in 1892, Pickford took to the stage in childhood. Cinema was her natural medium, however, as Griffith identified when she screen-tested for him as a teenager in 1909. Her combination of limpid prettiness with an air of street-smart self-reliance made her a draw for audiences of many social types — at the height of her fame she was described by one critic as "the best-known woman who has ever lived … loved by more people than any other woman that has been in all history."

Pickford recognized the power that this level of fame conferred, and used it. She was still in her 20s when she joined with Griffith, Charlie Chaplin and Douglas Fairbanks to found United Artists, which sought to challenge the stranglehold of the Hollywood studios and permit opportunities for independent productions. Fairbanks became Pickford's second husband in 1920. The two made their own films at their Pickford-Fairbanks studios, and became well known for entertaining high-profile guests at their Hollywood mansion, Pickfair. They were also founding members of the Academy of Arts and Motion Picture Sciences.

Pickford's career began to slide in the 1930s. Having fallen in love with her as an ingénue, the public was less keen on seeing her in adult roles such as she played in *Coquette* (1929). It won her an Academy Award, but scandalized her fans, not least because it saw her crop her famous curls into a fashionable bob. Moreover, Pickford was one of many silent film stars for whom the advent of sound failed to provide new opportunities; she largely retired from acting as the medium became dominant. She also divorced Fairbanks, although she continued to live at Pickfair. Indeed, in later life she rarely left it; when the Academy presented her with an honorary Oscar in 1976, she recorded her acceptance speech at her home. **HM**

genre ■ Short ■ Romance ■ Drama ■ Comedy ■ Family

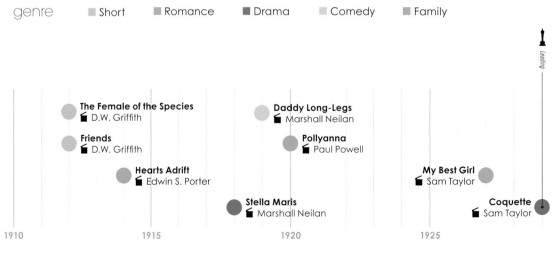

The Female of the Species
D.W. Griffith

Daddy Long-Legs
Marshall Neilan

Friends
D.W. Griffith

Pollyanna
Paul Powell

Hearts Adrift
Edwin S. Porter

My Best Girl
Sam Taylor

Stella Maris
Marshall Neilan

Coquette
Sam Taylor

1910   1915   1920   1925

brad pitt 1963

Thelma & Louise

A River Runs Through It

Twelve Monkeys

Se7en

Fight Club

The Assassination of Jesse James …

Inglourious Basterds

The Tree of Life

Born in 1963, William Bradley Pitt grew up in Missouri, studying journalism at university before quitting to try his luck in Hollywood. After a run of forgettable television work, he burst into the public consciousness in *Thelma & Louise* (1991) as J.D., the charming thief who sexually liberates Geena Davis. His chiseled golden boy looks were seized upon and compared to Robert Redford, who chose Pitt to star as the free-spirited rebel lead in *A River Runs Through It* (1992).

Starring roles in major movies followed, such as *Interview with the Vampire* and *Legends of the Fall* (both 1994), but his ill-fated detective in David Fincher's hugely influential *Se7en* (1995) provided Pitt's next major hit. That same year, he brought livewire intensity to Terry Gilliam's dystopian sci-fi *Twelve Monkeys* (1995), earning a Golden Globe and his first Oscar nomination.

Uneven lead roles continued, but reteaming with Fincher for cult classic *Fight Club* (1999) was the adrenaline shot his career needed. As Tyler Durden, Pitt was an antihero for pre-millennial male angst. The role also showcased the actor's sly humor, usually only displayed in scene-stealing comic parts like *Snatch*'s (2000) unintelligible Irish gypsy or the vacuous would-be-blackmailer in *Burn After Reading* (2008).

Despite twice being voted "Sexiest Man Alive," Pitt's best or most popular work is rarely in a romantic role. The exception is spy actioner *Mr. & Mrs. Smith* (2005), where he met his future wife, Angelina Jolie, spawning the "Brangelina" tabloid phenomenon.

On screen, however, Pitt seems more comfortable as one of the guys: slick heist caper *Ocean's Eleven* (2001) and its sequels; *The Assassination of Jesse James by the Coward Robert Ford* (2007), a brooding, lyrical western featuring Pitt as James; or hamming it up as good ol' boy Aldo "The Apache," leader of Quentin Tarantino's *Inglourious Basterds* (2009).

Such later roles demonstrate Pitt's shift toward collaborations with edgier filmmakers like Alejandro González Iñárritu for *Babel* (2006); or Bennett Miller's *Moneyball* (2011), a film that, along with David Fincher's reverse-time love story *The Curious Case of Benjamin Button* (2008) won Pitt Best Actor nominations. Even more acclaimed were his stern 1950s Texas patriarch in Terrence Malick's *The Tree of Life* (2011) and a supporting role in *12 Years a Slave* (2013). Should Pitt continue to combine artistic highs with commercial hits like zombie apocalypse thriller *World War Z* (2013), his ongoing respected star status looks assured. **LS**

P

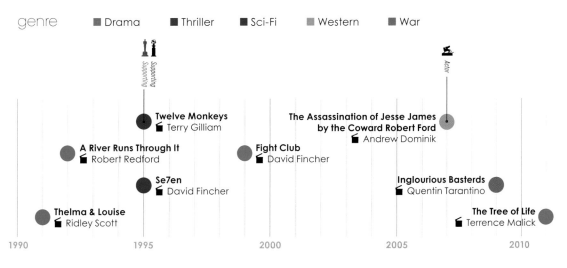

genre ■ Drama ■ Thriller ■ Sci-Fi ■ Western ■ War

Supporting
Supporting

Actor

Twelve Monkeys Terry Gilliam

The Assassination of Jesse James by the Coward Robert Ford Andrew Dominik

A River Runs Through It Robert Redford

Fight Club David Fincher

Se7en David Fincher

Inglourious Basterds Quentin Tarantino

Thelma & Louise Ridley Scott

The Tree of Life Terrence Malick

1990   1995   2000   2005   2010

sidney poitier 1927

| No Way Out | Blackboard Jungle | Edge of the City | The Defiant Ones | Porgy and Bess | A Raisin in the Sun | Lilies of the Field | A Patch of Blue |

In 2002 Sidney Poitier was awarded an honorary Oscar. Introducing him, Denzel Washington explained the unique significance of the actor: "He was the reason a movie got made. The first solo, above-the-title African-American movie star." It is a succinct description of Poitier's historical importance — an actor who challenged the racial discrimination of Hollywood, and paved the way for successive generations of African-Americans. But with roles that combined precision and fierce emotional power, Poitier was also a magnetic screen presence.

Although born in Miami, in 1927, Poitier grew up in the Bahamas. It was a hardscrabble upbringing, one relatively isolated from the ugly racial politics of segregation that prevailed in the United States at the time. As a young man, Poitier moved to New York and joined the American Negro Theater. His performances got him noticed by Hollywood and in 1950 he enjoyed an early breakthrough role in *No Way Out*. He was a young doctor who endures racist taunts from one of his patients, an injured bank robber. Breaking from Hollywood's tendency to cast black actors in subservient roles, Poitier played the part of the doctor with poise, intelligence and understated dignity.

Poitier's next notable role was a little more abrasive. Controversial at the time, *Blackboard Jungle* (1955) saw him play a student in a class of delinquent youths, and the cool, commanding charisma he brought to the part stood out among his fellow actors. (The scenario reversed in 1967 when Poitier played a teacher in the London-set drama *To Sir, With Love*.) In the 1957 New York-set drama *Edge of the City*, he was steely and street-smart as a longshoreman and friend to his fiery young colleague, played with typical passion by John Cassavetes. An exploration of labor relations, the film enhanced Poitier's association with films engaged with politically loaded topics.

The most well known of Poitier's social conscience movies were the two he made with Stanley Kramer, one of Hollywood's most outspoken liberals. As an escaped convict chained to Tony Curtis' white prisoner, *The Defiant Ones* (1958) tackled the racism of the still-segregated American South. Nominated for an Oscar, Poitier played his escapee with a tough intensity and fierce intelligence, providing the role with a complexity that transcended the script's sometimes heavyhanded aspects. And in 1967, he was the doctor fiancé of a young white woman,

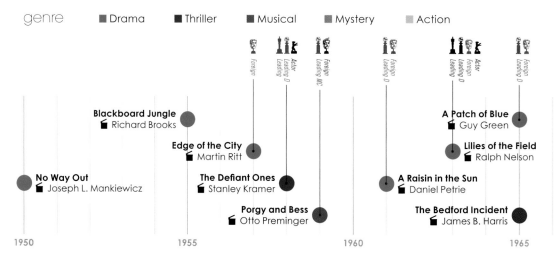

genre ■ Drama ■ Thriller ■ Musical ■ Mystery ■ Action

Blackboard Jungle
Richard Brooks

Edge of the City
Martin Ritt

No Way Out
Joseph L. Mankiewicz

The Defiant Ones
Stanley Kramer

Porgy and Bess
Otto Preminger

A Patch of Blue
Guy Green

Lilies of the Field
Ralph Nelson

A Raisin in the Sun
Daniel Petrie

The Bedford Incident
James B. Harris

1950   1955   1960   1965

The Bedford Incident	In the Heat of the Night	Guess Who's Coming to Dinner	To Sir, with Love	They Call Me Mister Tibbs!	Shoot to Kill	Mandela and de Klerk	The Jackal

attempting to persuade her parents to agree to their marriage in *Guess Who's Coming to Dinner*. Made on the eve of a Supreme Court ruling striking down laws that banned racially mixed marriages, it was a timely production, and Poitier gave a polished performance alongside Spencer Tracy and Katharine Hepburn.

But for all Poitier's grace and charisma, the role of the black suitor was improbably upstanding. Poitier may have been the first African-American to head up mainstream Hollywood movies, but the roles were often unbelievably wholesome (as in his Oscar-winning turn as an illiterate handyman who helps a group of nuns build a church in 1963's *Lilies of the Field*) or curiously sexless. *A Patch of Blue* (1965) did see his character fall in love with a white woman, but she was blind, and their on-screen kiss was excised from prints in the American South.

But Poitier was always watchable, and with more challenging material his performances were richly compelling. He was superb in *A Raisin in the Sun* (1961) as the young husband in a large African-American family recently located to the suburbs. A study of the tensions across the family's generations, the film depicted black American experience with a vividness

rare for the times. And he lent a watchful skepticism to his part as a journalist onboard a U.S. submarine in the tense Cold War drama *The Bedford Incident* (1965).

In the same year that Poitier made *Guess Who's Coming to Dinner*, he starred in the far tougher *In the Heat of the Night* (1967). As northern detective Virgil Tibbs who reluctantly joins a murder case in Mississippi, Poitier played the part with grit and assurance, confronting the vile racial prejudices of the South. It was a memorable performance that Poitier revived in the 1970 thriller *They Call Me Mister Tibbs!*.

In the Heat of the Night caught the mood of the ongoing Civil Rights movement. Its release marked the end of a defining decade for Poitier, but in the years that followed he withdrew from the screen to focus on a directing career. The non-threatening figure that he represented on screen was perhaps out of sync with the more assertive and radically orientated black Civil Rights movement of the 1970s. His late-career cameos have been infrequent, although he lent class to the excellent action film *Shoot to Kill* (aka *Deadly Pursuit*, 1988) and the entertainingly silly *The Jackal* (1997); and he was widely admired for playing Nelson Mandela in the 1997 television drama *Mandela and de Klerk*. **EL**

Foreign
Leading 0

They Call Me Mister Tibbs!
Gordon Douglas

In the Heat of the Night
Norman Jewison

Guess Who's Coming to Dinner
Stanley Kramer

To Sir, with Love
James Clavell

Shoot to Kill
Roger Spottiswoode

Mandela and de Klerk
Joseph Sargent

The Jackal
Michael Caton-Jones

1970   1985   1990   1995

natalie portman 1981

Léon

Heat

Star Wars:
Episode I —
The Phantom
Menace

Garden
State

Closer

V for
Vendetta

Black Swan

Thor

Natalie Portman was just 12 years old when she gave her stunning debut performance as the fiery, resourceful orphan Mathilda in Luc Besson's hit man thriller Léon (1994). This star-making turn was followed by a succession of small roles in high-profile efforts, including Heat (1995), Everyone Says I Love You (1996) and Mars Attacks! (1996). As a self-proclaimed "old soul" in Beautiful Girls (1996), she was the standout in a fine ensemble cast.

Inescapable worldwide fame arrived when Portman was cast as Queen Amidala in Star Wars: Episode I — The Phantom Menace (1999), the long-awaited prequel to George Lucas' space opera trilogy. But despite her efforts, she never seemed entirely comfortable in the role.

After starring in the low-key dramas Anywhere but Here (1999) and Where the Heart Is (2000), Portman partially withdrew from film to focus on her studies at Harvard University; Star Wars: Episode II — Attack of the Clones (2002) was shot during her summer break, followed a year later by an extended cameo as a young widow in Cold Mountain (2003).

She made a successful return to acting in 2004, first as writer–director Zach Braff's whimsical love interest in Garden State and then with an Oscar-nominated turn in Closer. This was followed by Star Wars: Episode III — Revenge of the Sith (2005), the trilogy's best entry by far. Other films during the period, including Mr. Magorium's Wonder Emporium (2007) and The Other Boleyn Girl (2008), were passable. She excelled in the otherwise-underwhelming V for Vendetta (2005) and made an appearance in Wong Kar-wai's English-language debut My Blueberry Nights (2007).

Darren Aronofsky's Black Swan (2010), would provide the defining role of her adult career so far. Portman trained for half a year to be convincing as Nina, a ballerina driven to hallucinatory madness by a desire for creative perfection. Her committed performance sold the excesses of Aronofsky's frenzied visual style and saw her win an Oscar for Best Actress.

After the heights of Black Swan, Portman's output slowed again as she focused on parenthood, with her only significant roles being a pair of uneven bawdy comedies, No Strings Attached (2011) and Your Highness (2011). She was game in Thor (2011), a canny career move but not one to have yielded great dramatic results, as demonstrated by its middling sequel Thor: The Dark World (2013). **JWa**

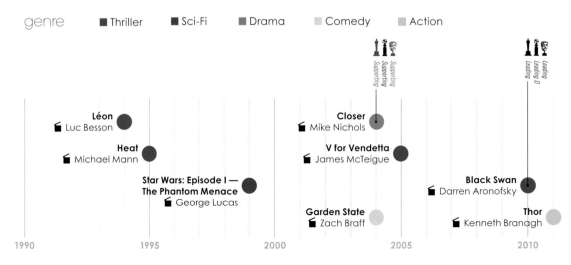

genre   ■ Thriller   ■ Sci-Fi   ■ Drama   ■ Comedy   ■ Action

Léon
Luc Besson

Heat
Michael Mann

Star Wars: Episode I —
The Phantom Menace
George Lucas

Closer
Mike Nichols

V for Vendetta
James McTeigue

Garden State
Zach Braff

Black Swan
Darren Aronofsky

Thor
Kenneth Branagh

Supporting
Supporting
Supporting

Leading
Leading D
Leading

1990   1995   2000   2005   2010

dick powell 1904–63

42nd Street | Gold Diggers of 1935 | It Happened Tomorrow | Murder, My Sweet | Cornered | Pitfall | The Tall Target | The Bad and the Beautiful

Hollywood heartthrob Dick Powell may have been many things, but he would have been the first to admit that a brilliant actor was not one of them. He was an accomplished all-rounder, an attribute that often meant more than rugged matinee idol appeal or Shakespearian ability. In a career spanning 33 years, he played many roles in Hollywood, from a hot hoofer-cum-songster for Warner Bros. in many of their Busby Berkeley musicals during the 1930s, to reinventing himself as a private eye in several gritty thrillers for RKO during the 1940s, before finishing as a successful television executive in the 1950s, a transition cut short only by his untimely death from cancer at the age of 58 in 1963.

Richard Ewing Powell was born in Mountain View, Arkansas, in 1904. His wholesome, cheeky looks and melodious voice — honed through years of singing in a church choir as a child — perfectly suited a career touring with a band as an instrumentalist and singer. It was during this period that a scout from Warner Bros. discovered Powell, signing him to a long-term contract with the studio. After a number of bit-parts in largely forgettable films, he found fame with roles in big-budget musical extravaganzas such as *42nd Street* (1933) and *Gold Diggers of 1935* (1935), starring alongside leading ladies Ruby Keeler and Gloria Stuart.

By the end of the decade, Powell had tired not only of the all-singing, all-dancing roles he was

being cast in, but of Warner Bros. itself. Following his departure from the studio, he expanded his range, appearing in a range of comedies that included *Model Wife* (1941), *True to Life* (1943) and René Clair's delightful fantasy *It Happened Tomorrow* (1944). But it was his move to RKO and appearances in a series of thrillers that would see Powell's popularity rise again. After losing out to Fred MacMurray for the role of Walter Neff in Billy Wilder's 1944 classic *Double Indemnity*, the same year saw him play the first major screen appearance of Raymond Chandler's private detective Philip Marlowe in *Murder, My Sweet*. His success would continue with *Cornered* (1945) and the critically lauded *Pitfall* (1948).

During the 1950s, despite roles in acclaimed productions like the period adventure *The Tall Target* (1951) and romantic drama *The Bad and the Beautiful* (1952), Powell's big-screen appearances became less frequent. As the decade progressed, he moved into television, producing his own eponymous series *The Dick Powell Show* (1961–63), as well as directing a series of television movies that included *Woman on the Run* (1959). Married three times, Powell was the epitome of the old-school Hollywood movie star. Charming, handsome and debonair, many of his best films still sparkle thanks to his presence and the range of his work is a reminder of how important diversity can be in order to survive the fickleness of Hollywood. **CP**

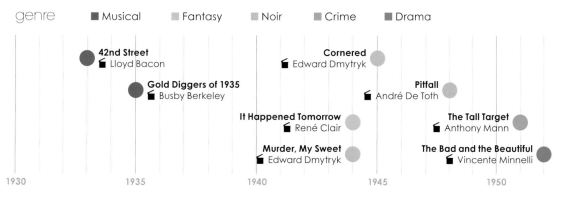

genre ■ Musical ■ Fantasy ■ Noir ■ Crime ■ Drama

42nd Street
Lloyd Bacon

Cornered
Edward Dmytryk

Gold Diggers of 1935
Busby Berkeley

Pitfall
André De Toth

It Happened Tomorrow
René Clair

The Tall Target
Anthony Mann

Murder, My Sweet
Edward Dmytryk

The Bad and the Beautiful
Vincente Minnelli

1930 — 1935 — 1940 — 1945 — 1950

elvis presley 1935–77

Love Me
Tender

Jailhouse
Rock

King Creole

Flaming
Star

G.I. Blues

Blue Hawaii

Wild in the
Country

Kid
Galahad

Born in 1935, in Tupelo, Mississippi, Elvis Presley is primarily remembered as one of the most popular musical acts of the 20th century and a seminal figure in the ascension of pop music and teen culture. But he was also a prolific screen actor. Over a period of 13 years, the performer starred in 31 feature films, all of which were designed as vehicles for him and his music. Churned out regularly to a loyal audience, these quickly shot, cheaply produced films — mostly formulaic melodramas set in exotic locations, sprinkled with Presley songs — were uneven at best and their overall quality waned deciduously. However, several of his pictures are genuinely successful and he remains a charismatic presence throughout, in spite of his evident loss of interest. While he is now best known for the music, he spent much of his career focused on cinema, and many of his songs come from the soundtracks to those films.

By 1956, Presley had become the most famous singer in the world and was keen to move into the film industry. Several projects had already fallen through when he came to star in the American Civil War-era western Love Me Tender (1956), which had its name changed to capitalize on the potential popularity of a forthcoming song. Even though the part of Clint Reno was intended as a purely dramatic role, Presley's controlling manager Colonel Tom Parker insisted on his singing in the film, and four musical numbers

were added arbitrarily. Presley would later point to this decision as shaping the course of his cinematic career for the worse: the film was a financial success, and thus became the template for almost all of his subsequent efforts.

Following the popularity of Love Me Tender, Presley starred in three more films in the short period before he joined the U.S. Army: Loving You (1957), Jailhouse Rock (1957) and King Creole (1958), directed by Michael Curtiz. He was perhaps never more virile, energetic and compelling on screen than during his hip-swinging performance of the title number in Jailhouse Rock, but King Creole is his best film. Playing an aspiring singer who tangles with crime boss Walter Matthau, Presley's committed performance now hints at potential unfulfilled.

Presley returned from his spell in the army hoping to further explore dramatic roles, but his first film was the clean-cut, hackneyed G.I. Blues (1960), directed by Norman Taurog. He had more of an opportunity to stretch himself in the Don Siegel-directed Flaming Star (1960) and as a troubled aspiring writer in Wild in the Country (1961), the latter of which was scripted by the playwright Clifford Odets. Neither film was anywhere near as commercially successful as G.I. Blues, however, with Wild in the Country an outright flop. Discouraged from taking such risks again, he returned to the profitable formula with Blue Hawaii

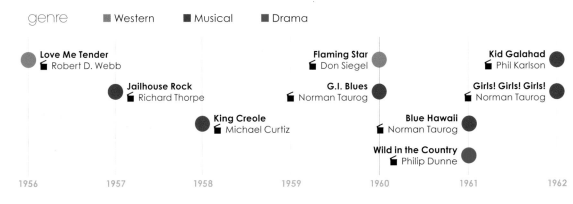

genre ■ Western ■ Musical ■ Drama

Love Me Tender Robert D. Webb		**Flaming Star** Don Siegel	**Kid Galahad** Phil Karlson
Jailhouse Rock Richard Thorpe		**G.I. Blues** Norman Taurog	**Girls! Girls! Girls!** Norman Taurog
	King Creole Michael Curtiz	**Blue Hawaii** Norman Taurog	
		Wild in the Country Philip Dunne	

| 1956 | 1957 | 1958 | 1959 | 1960 | 1961 | 1962 |

| Girls! Girls! Girls! | Viva Las Vegas | Roustabout | Girl Happy | Spinout | Live a Little, Love a Little | Charro! | Change of Habit |

(1961), which was also directed by Taurog. The journeyman filmmaker would direct a total of nine of Presley's films, all of which are cut from the same cloth.

While *Blue Hawaii* was responsible for the dispiriting wave of almost interchangeable features to come, the film itself is among his most enjoyable. A lightweight travelogue, it depicts Presley as a returning solider trying to avoid joining his father's pineapple company by working as a tour guide. The film is as simplistic and uneven as his other efforts, but if the "Elvis movie" is a genre in itself then it is the quintessential example.

After *Blue Hawaii* proved to be another profitable venture, Presley tried to repeat the trick again — and again and again. He reliably turned out a film every four months for the remainder of the decade, with *Follow That Dream* (1962), *Kid Galahad* (1962), *Girls! Girls! Girls!* (1962), *It Happened at the World's Fair* (1963), *Fun in Acapulco* (1963), *Kissin' Cousins* (1964), *Viva Las Vegas* (1964), *Roustabout* (1964), *Girl Happy* (1965), *Tickle Me* (1965), *Harum Scarum* (1965), *Frankie and Johnny* (1966), *Paradise, Hawaiian Style* (1966), *Spinout* (1966), *Easy Come, Easy Go* (1967), *Double Trouble* (1967), *Clambake* (1967), *Stay Away, Joe* (1968), *Speedway* (1968) and *Live a Little, Love a Little* (1968). These movies were increasingly tired exercises that did not seem to understand his appeal or best qualities, and which existed in a world isolated from the fast-changing 1960s they were released into. While there were occasional, semi-decent efforts in that exhausting series of films, particularly *Kid Galahad*, *Viva Las Vegas* and *Spinout*, most are dull.

For Presley's long-term producer Hal Wallis, the films existed solely to make profit — the money from *Blue Hawaii* financed the Richard Burton and Peter O'Toole period drama *Becket* (1964) — while for Colonel Tom Parker they were essentially promotional material for the soundtrack albums. For Presley himself, the films were a job, and he would sign contracts for several movies at once. The numbing relentlessness of his output inevitably caused saturation, however, and by the end of the decade they had become dated and were close to unprofitable.

Worse, perhaps, for Presley, he had lost his mystique. He grew a beard for his sole non-musical film, *Charro!* (1969), made two more musicals, *The Trouble with Girls* (1969) and *Change of Habit* (1969), and then he was done. To reinvigorate his flagging career he decided that he needed to turn from cinema and back to the medium that made him famous in the first place: television. His wildly successful 1968 comeback special would lead to the next, final stage in his career before his death at the age of 42 in 1977. **JWa**

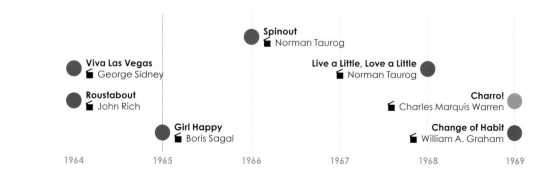

	Spinout 🎬 Norman Taurog	
Viva Las Vegas 🎬 George Sidney		**Live a Little, Love a Little** 🎬 Norman Taurog
Roustabout 🎬 John Rich		**Charro!** 🎬 Charles Marquis Warren
	Girl Happy 🎬 Boris Sagal	**Change of Habit** 🎬 William A. Graham

1963   1964   1965   1966   1967   1968   1969

vincent price 1911–93

| Laura | His Kind of Woman | House of Wax | The Masque of the Red Death | Witchfinder General | Theatre of Blood | The Whales of August | Edward Scissorhands |

Vincent Price, the Dark Prince of Hollywood horror, was not a man who believed in curtailing his behavior, either on screen or in life. Although he was primarily known for his appearances in films of the macabre, his work in this niche genre actually made up a relatively small part of a prodigious career spanning over 50 years and almost 200 screen appearances.

An avid art collector and accomplished chef who published several popular cookery books, Price was born in 1911, into a respected middle-class family in St. Louis, Missouri. He planned to go to London to study for a Masters in Fine Art, but his academic aspirations were soon overshadowed by an interest in theater and he made his stage debut in 1935, performing with Orson Welles' Mercury Theater. Within a year, he was starring alongside Helen Hayes in the Broadway production of the controversial play *Victoria Regina*.

It was inevitable that Hollywood would discover Price, though he did not find success overnight. After making his debut in 1938's *Service de Luxe*, it was six years before he made any impression on audiences, playing raffish playboy Shelby Carpenter in the noir classic *Laura* (1944). Over the next decade, he starred in a slew of potboilers — mostly in support of bigger name stars, such as Robert Mitchum and Jane Russell in the comedy noir *His Kind of Woman* (1951) — before taking the lead as the mad sculptor in André De Toth's groundbreaking 3D horror *House of Wax* (1953).

Though Price had previously featured in films that could loosely be described as horror, *House of Wax* was the film that established him in the genre he would be associated with for the remainder of his career. In the early 1960s, he appeared in a number of Roger Corman films, including the director's masterpiece, *The Masque of the Red Death* (1964). Other features the two made together, inspired by the writings of Edgar Allan Poe, included *Pit and the Pendulum* (1961), *Tales of Terror* (1962), *The Comedy of Terrors* (1963) and *The Raven* (1963).

Price traveled to the UK in the late 1960s to appear in Michael Reeves' *Witchfinder General* (1968), now hailed as a milestone of horror cinema. In the early 1970s he appeared in the black comedy *Theatre of Blood* (1973), which he considered among his finest achievements, and played the lead in *The Abominable Dr. Phibes* (1971) and its 1972 sequel.

Price's screen appearances, though still frequent, lacked the vitality of his early work. His voice was introduced to a new generation with his rap on Michael Jackson's "Thriller" (1982) and a final blaze of glory came with his appearance alongside Bette Davis and Lillian Gish in the bittersweet drama *The Whales of August* (1987), and a brief cameo as the eccentric inventor in Tim Burton's fairy tale *Edward Scissorhands* (1990). Price died three years later, one of the last great stars of Hollywood horror. **CP**

genre ■ Noir ■ Horror ■ Drama ■ Fantasy

Laura
Otto Preminger

His Kind of Woman
John Farrow

House of Wax
André De Toth

The Masque of the Red Death
Roger Corman

Witchfinder General
Michael Reeves

Theatre of Blood
Douglas Hickox

The Whales of August
Lindsay Anderson

Edward Scissorhands
Tim Burton

1940   1945   1950   1955   1960   1965   1970   1975   1980   1985   1990

claude rains 1889–1967

| The Invisible Man | The Adventures of Robin Hood | Mr. Smith Goes to Washington | The Wolf Man | Casablanca | Mr. Skeffington | Notorious | Lawrence of Arabia |

Born in London in 1889, Claude Rains' father was a theater actor. The young Claude soon followed suit, gradually building an impressive reputation as a performer and teacher. After serving in World War I, he made his way to New York and Broadway, before his rich and sonorous voice made him the perfect actor to play Dr. Jack Griffin in *The Invisible Man* (1933), one of Universal Studios' classic horror films.

Despite his inexperience on screen, Rains performed terrifically. He traded on this initial reputation as a star of horror with several supernatural dramas, including *The Clairvoyant* (1934) and *Mystery of Edwin Drood* (1935), before landing the role of Napoleon in the musical *Hearts Divided* (1936). It was a busy period for the actor, not least with appearances in two of the most enduring pictures from the latter part of the decade. First he played the dastardly Prince John to Errol Flynn's dashing archer in *The Adventures of Robin Hood* (1938), and then the conniving senator opposed by James Stewart's eponymous hero in *Mr. Smith Goes to Washington* (1939). The latter saw Rains receive the first of his four Oscar nominations for Best Supporting Actor.

Rains returned to his roots at Universal, bringing gravitas to the role of Sir John Talbot in *The Wolf Man*

(1941). However, it is his wry performance in *Casablanca* (1942) for which he will be best remembered, playing the gleefully corrupt Captain Louis Renault. It is an Oscar-nominated performance that stole the thunder from many bigger stars and confirmed Rains' position as a classy supporting player. In the same year, he would convince as the psychiatrist coming to the aid of Bette Davis in *Now, Voyager* (1942) before returning to Universal and the lead role in *Phantom of the Opera* (1943). Rains' third Oscar nomination acknowledged his excellent turn as the suffering *Mr. Skeffington* (1944).

Rains' final Academy nomination was for his mesmerizing performance in Alfred Hitchcock's *Notorious* (1946), in which he plays a Nazi sympathizer intent on continuing the work of the dismantled Third Reich. He was also on impressive form as a husband desperate to please his unhappy wife in *The Passionate Friends* (1949), David Lean's follow-up to *Brief Encounter* (1945). Before his death in 1967, Rains would work again with Lean on *Lawrence of Arabia* (1962) and appear in the biblical epic *The Greatest Story Ever Told* (1965). In both, he employs his trademark resonance to winning effect, capping off a hugely successful career that was sorely missing the awards recognition it deserved. **BN**

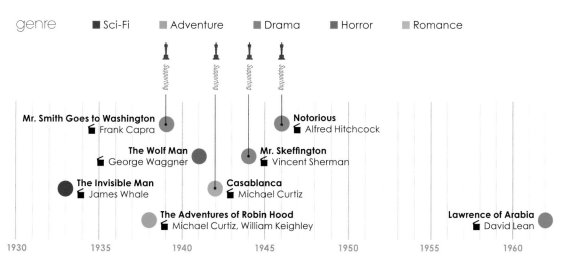

genre ■ Sci-Fi ■ Adventure ■ Drama ■ Horror ■ Romance

Supporting · Supporting · Supporting · Supporting

Mr. Smith Goes to Washington
🎬 Frank Capra

Notorious
🎬 Alfred Hitchcock

The Wolf Man
🎬 George Waggner

Mr. Skeffington
🎬 Vincent Sherman

The Invisible Man
🎬 James Whale

Casablanca
🎬 Michael Curtiz

The Adventures of Robin Hood
🎬 Michael Curtiz, William Keighley

Lawrence of Arabia
🎬 David Lean

1930　　1935　　1940　　1945　　1950　　1955　　1960

basil rathbone 1892–1967

The Masked Bride | David Copperfield | Captain Blood | Romeo and Juliet | The Adventures of Robin Hood | The Hound of the Baskervilles | Sherlock Holmes and the Voice of Terror | The Last Hurrah

Born in Johannesburg, Philip St. John Basil Rathbone moved with his parents to the UK aged 2. He made his first stage appearance in a production of *The Taming of the Shrew*, in 1911. He was an intelligence officer in World War I and at its end returned to the theater, continuing his series of Shakespearean roles. His first screen appearance was in the British film *Innocent* (1921), playing a villain. A few other roles in British films followed before he made his American debut in *Trouping with Ellen* (1924).

In *The Bishop Murder Case* (1930), Rathbone took over the role of detective Nick Grinde from William Powell, who had played the character in three films. It suited him, but Powell returned to the character again in 1933, before handing the role on to other actors.

With his angular features, Rathbone suited villainous characters. And his experience on stage gave him an advantage with more classical material. He is a cruel Mr. Mudstone in *David Copperfield* (1935) and an imposing Pontius Pilate in *The Last Days of Pompey* (1935). However, his most acclaimed role from this period is his Tybalt in George Cukor's acclaimed production of *Romeo and Juliet* (1936) for which he received an Oscar nomination. He was

also nominated for his performance as King Louis XI of France in *If I Were a King* (1938).

After playing the treacherous Captain Levasseur opposite Errol Flynn's hero in *Captain Blood* (1935), Rathbone appeared as the Sheriff of Nottingham to Flynn's eponymous hero in *The Adventures of Robin Hood* (1938). One of the high points of 1930s Hollywood, Michael Curtiz's film features a wonderful villainous double act from Rathbone and Claude Rains as King John.

In 1939, Rathbone played Sherlock Holmes for the first time, in *The Hound of the Baskervilles*. His performance, combining erudition and wit with a hint of mockery, is wonderfully contrasted with the buffoonery of Nigel Bruce's Watson. The film was a success and 13 sequels followed, ending with *Dressed to Kill* (1946). The first two entries are the best, although the attempt to bring the character into modern times is fascinating in light of the recent television incarnations of the character.

Rathbone continued to act up until his death in 1967, but it is his period as Holmes and as one of Hollywood's most charismatic villains that he will be remembered. **IHS**

genre   ■ Romance   ■ Drama   ■ Adventure   ■ Mystery

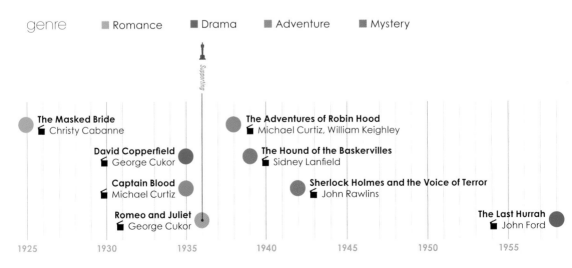

Supporting

The Masked Bride
🎬 Christy Cabanne

David Copperfield
🎬 George Cukor

Captain Blood
🎬 Michael Curtiz

Romeo and Juliet
🎬 George Cukor

The Adventures of Robin Hood
🎬 Michael Curtiz, William Keighley

The Hound of the Baskervilles
🎬 Sidney Lanfield

Sherlock Holmes and the Voice of Terror
🎬 John Rawlins

The Last Hurrah
🎬 John Ford

1925   1930   1935   1940   1945   1950   1955

ronald reagan 1911–2004

Love Is on
the Air

Secret
Service of
the Air

Knute
Rockne,
All American

Kings Row

Desperate
Journey

Bedtime for
Bonzo

Hellcats of
the Navy

The Killers

It is occasionally remarked that the most famous role Ronald Reagan ever played was that of the U.S. President, which he did from 1981 to 1989. Born in 1911 in Tampico, Illinois, his long film career is understandably less significant than the political one that followed, but is an interesting illustration of the life of an unremarkable mid-20th century journeyman actor.

When Reagan signed his first contract with Warner Bros. he had never acted professionally before. Four months later, the studio released his first film, *Love Is on the Air* (1937). The role led to a position within the studio's B-movie unit, starring in quickies like *Girls on Probation* (1938) and *Hell's Kitchen* (1939), intended to pad out double features. An engaging but stiff lead, Reagan appeared in seven such pictures in 1938 alone. When *Secret Service of the Air* (1939) became a small hit, Warners produced three more installments featuring Reagan's Agent "Brass" Bancroft character in 15 months. In addition to the endless stream of B-movies, he also took occasional supporting roles in larger films, opposite Bette Davis in *Dark Victory* (1939) and Errol Flynn in *Santa Fe Trail* (1940).

Reagan suited authoritative figures: military men, lawyers, government agents. His best-known role is in *Knute Rockne, All American* (1940), although he only appears in it briefly. He played George Gipp, a star halfback whose premature death inspires his team

to victory. His deathbed speech, imploring his coach to tell his teammates to "win just one for the Gipper" serves as an insight into his later political appeal, as well being responsible for his alternately derisive or affectionate nickname.

The United States joined World War II just as Reagan's career was taking off with a supporting role as a double amputee in *Kings Row* (1942), which was nominated for a Best Picture Oscar. After playing an RAF pilot in *Desperate Journey* (1942), he joined the First Motion Picture unit to produce training and propaganda films. His career never quite recovered its momentum and within a few years of returning he was making films like *Bedtime for Bonzo* (1951), opposite a chimpanzee. But by then he was more interested in his role as president of the Screen Actors Guild.

As his career wound down, the soldiers and airmen he had once played gave way to cowboys and marshals in westerns like *Law and Order* (1953) and *Tennessee's Partner* (1955), although he did play a naval commander in *Hellcats of the Navy* (1957). Reagan would only appear in one more film after that, as a crime boss in Don Siegel's *The Killers* (1964), the sole occasion he played a villain and quite possibly his best role. The same year he started making stump speeches in support of Republican presidential candidate Barry Goldwater; his second career was about to begin. **JWa**

R

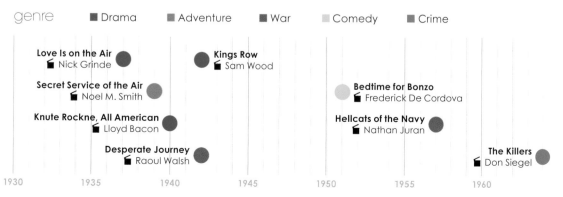

genre   ■ Drama   ▲ Adventure   ■ War   □ Comedy   ■ Crime

Love Is on the Air
🎬 Nick Grinde

Kings Row
🎬 Sam Wood

Secret Service of the Air
🎬 Noel M. Smith

Bedtime for Bonzo
🎬 Frederick De Cordova

Knute Rockne, All American
🎬 Lloyd Bacon

Hellcats of the Navy
🎬 Nathan Juran

Desperate Journey
🎬 Raoul Walsh

The Killers
🎬 Don Siegel

1930   1935   1940   1945   1950   1955   1960

robert redford 1936

| The Chase | Butch Cassidy and the Sundance Kid | Downhill Racer | The Candidate | Jeremiah Johnson | The Sting | The Way We Were | Three Days of the Condor |

Charles Robert Redford Jr. was born in Santa Monica, California, in 1936, but his acting career began in New York, where he appeared on stage and in various television shows. His good looks made him an easy attraction and within a few years he made his transition to film, appearing in *The Tall Story* (1960). He also made an impression in Sidney Lumet's television production of Eugene O'Neil's *The Iceman Cometh* (1960).

Redford earned positive notices playing a closet homosexual in *Inside Daisy Clover* (1965) and starred in *This Property Is Condemned* (1966), the first of many films with director Sydney Pollack. However, it was with his role in *The Chase* (1966), which costarred Marlon Brando and Jane Fonda, that Redford's career took off. He plays an escaped convict desperate to return to his wife, with the small town she lives in divided over how to deal with him when he arrives. Redford and Fonda starred opposite each other again in Neil Simon's romantic drama, *Barefoot in the Park* (1967), an adaptation of his play.

The actor's breakthrough year was 1969, with the release of three key films. *Butch Cassidy and the Sundance Kid* was hugely popular. The pairing of Redford with Paul Newman was so successful that

director George Roy Hill would reunite them for the comedy caper *The Sting* (1973); Redford would also return to Hill for 1975's *The Great Waldo Pepper*, playing a stunt pilot in 1920s America. Abraham Polonsky's *Tell Them Willie Boy Is Here* is based on a true story of a Native American who ran away with his girlfriend after killing her father in self-defense. Redford plays the sheriff pursuing them. And in the third film, *Downhill Racer*, Redford stars as an ambitious young skier who finds himself battling with the ski team's coach. The films made Redford a major star, but they also suggested that his screen persona required more than a handsome character to be compelling. His best work has always explored the conflict between his outward appearance and the more problematic personality that lies beneath. He was never meant to play the nice guy and, like Cary Grant and George Clooney, he is better when his roles feature an element of moral ambivalence.

The Candidate (1972) is a case in point. As the idealistic son of a former Governor, Redford's Bill McKay seems perfect. But he only becomes interesting as the film progresses, when we see that even the most virtuous can be corrupted. Redford

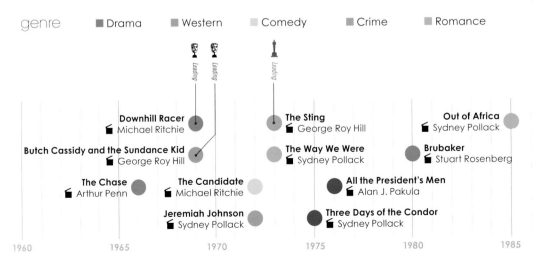

genre ■ Drama ■ Western ■ Comedy ■ Crime ■ Romance

Leading Leading Leading

Downhill Racer
Michael Ritchie

Butch Cassidy and the Sundance Kid
George Roy Hill

The Chase
Arthur Penn

The Candidate
Michael Ritchie

Jeremiah Johnson
Sydney Pollack

The Sting
George Roy Hill

The Way We Were
Sydney Pollack

All the President's Men
Alan J. Pakula

Three Days of the Condor
Sydney Pollack

Out of Africa
Sydney Pollack

Brubaker
Stuart Rosenberg

1960   1965   1970   1975   1980   1985

All the President's Men	Brubaker	Out of Africa	Indecent Proposal	The Horse Whisperer	The Company You Keep	All Is Lost	Captain America: The Winter Soldier

also impressed as the gruff loner seeking solace in the wilderness in his second film with Sydney Pollack, *Jeremiah Johnson* (1972). His films with Pollack range in quality. Although Barbra Streisand and Meryl Streep shine in, respectively, *The Way We Were* (1973) and *Out of Africa* (1985), Redford's roles are too passive. He is excellent as a researcher on the run from assassins in *Three Days of the Condor* (1975); and convinces as an embittered rodeo star in *The Electric Horseman* (1979). Redford and Pollack's final collaboration, *Havana* (1990), set prior to the Cuban Revolution, failed to repeat the success of their best work.

Like Alan Ladd before him and Leonardo DiCaprio since, Redford is unable to capture the spirit of Fitzgerald's antihero in Jack Clayton's handsome adaptation of *The Great Gatsby* (1974). He is far better in *All the President's Men* (1976) as Bob Woodward who, with Carl Bernstein (Dustin Hoffman), broke the story of the Watergate affair that led to President Nixon's downfall. Like his prison warden, who fights corruption and better facilities for prisoners in *Brubaker* (1980), Redford excels at portraying self-righteous individuals who risk everything for a cause. It is what makes his baseball star, Roy Hobbs, so

compelling in *The Natural* (1984) — the exploration of a character who is single-minded in their ambition to achieve a goal, and who is often unaware of their weaknesses or where their real enemy lurks.

Redford directed his first film, the Oscar-winning *Ordinary People*, in 1980 and thereafter would juggle his own projects with appearances on screen. As a result, he has starred in fewer films over the last three decades. If *Indecent Proposal* (1993) marks a creative nadir — notwithstanding its box-office success — and *The Horse Whisperer* (1998) wallowed a little too much in its own mythology, Redford makes for a fine villain in *Captain America: The Winter Soldier* (2014) and is quietly compelling as the former Weather Underground militant whose identity has been discovered in *The Company You Keep* (2012). However, his finest performance in recent years — and one of the best of his career — is in *All Is Lost* (2013). His nameless yachtsman, who battles for his life after his craft collides with a drifting shipping container, is not dissimilar to Jeremiah Johnson. He is a loner who is resilient and seems more at ease in his own company, but also possesses a ruthless streak. It is the perfect role for Redford and he excels in it. **IHS**

■ Thriller　　■ Adventure　　■ Action

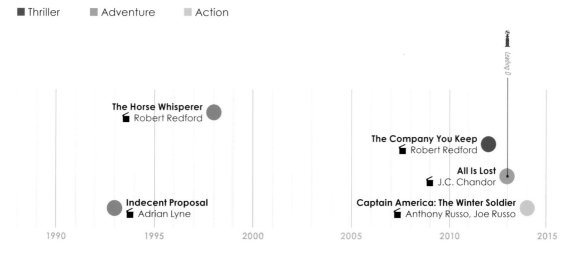

Leading ⌀

The Horse Whisperer
Robert Redford

The Company You Keep
Robert Redford

All Is Lost
J.C. Chandor

Indecent Proposal
Adrian Lyne

Captain America: The Winter Soldier
Anthony Russo, Joe Russo

| 1990 | 1995 | 2000 | 2005 | 2010 | 2015 |

Butch Cassidy and the Sundance Kid (1969)

The Candidate (1972)

Jeremiah Johnson (1972)

The Way We Were (1973)

The Sting (1973)

Out of Africa (1985)

Indecent Proposal (1993)

Captain America: The Winter Soldier (2014)

Paul Newman, Katharine Ross and Redford in *Butch Cassidy and the Sundance Kid*, which was the highest grossing film of 1969.

Redford and Will Geer in *Jeremiah Johnson*, a western based in part on the life of the legendary mountain man Liver-Eating Johnson.

A satirical comedy-drama, *The Candidate* reunited Redford with *Downhill Racer* (1969) director Michael Ritchie.

Redford and Barbra Streisand as doomed lovers in the romantic drama *The Way We Were*.

Reteaming Redford with Paul Newman, *The Sting* starred the pair as two professional grifters plotting to con a mob boss.

Released in 1973, Redford did not watch *The Sting* until 2004, upon the suggestion of his grandson. "I thought it was a really good movie," was his verdict.

Based on the autobiography of Karen Blixen, *Out of Africa* starred Redford as a big-game hunter who develops a romantic relationship with the author, played by Meryl Streep.

Redford as the handsome billionaire who offers $1 million dollars to spend the night with the married Demi Moore in *Indecent Proposal*.

Redford took the role of the head of S.H.I.E.L.D. in *Captain America: The Winter Soldier* because he "thought it would be interesting" to experience high-tech filmmaking.

vanessa redgrave 1937

Morgan! A Suitable Case for Treatment — **A Man for All Seasons** — **Blow-Up** — **Isadora** — **The Devils** — **Julia** — **The Bostonians** — **Prick Up Your Ears**

There was perhaps an inevitability about Vanessa Redgrave's calling as an actress. A member of a British theatrical dynasty, she is the daughter of the celebrated stage and screen actor Michael and sister to actors Corin and Lynn; she was married to film director Tony Richardson, and is the mother of actresses Joely and Natasha. But while her remarkable screen career has contributed to the vaunted reputation of the Redgrave name, her gifts are entirely her own.

She was born in London in 1937. Trained at the Central School of Speech and Drama, by the early 1960s she was a stage actress of enormous promise, winning acclaim for her role as Rosalind in a 1961 production of As You Like It. Redgrave has combined roles for the theater with screen appearances throughout her career, and like many British classically trained performers of her generation, there is an impressive rigor and precision to her approach.

Her breakthrough screen performance came in 1966 with Morgan! A Suitable Case for Treatment, a comedy about a working-class artist determined to stop his middle-class ex-wife (played by Redgrave) from marrying an affluent gallery owner. The film was directed by Karel Reisz, one a number of filmmakers

injecting some stylistic brio into British cinema of the day. A key film in the so-called British New Wave, Morgan! now seems a little mannered, but Redgrave's performance is delicate and lively, striking an attitude that mixes pity with residual love for her former lover.

A handsome woman with strong, elegant features, Redgrave was soon cast in major roles in some of the standout British films of the 1960s. In the same year Morgan! was released she appeared (alongside her brother Corin) in the Oscar-laden Tudor drama A Man for All Seasons; and she was also acclaimed for her role in Blow-Up, Michelangelo Antonioni's defining snapshot of London in the swinging sixties. Playing a young woman whose tryst with her lover is captured by a hip photographer, she gave a performance of affecting anxiety, leaving an impression that deepened the film's discomfiting, enigmatic mood.

Her first major starring role was as Isadora Duncan in Isadora (1968), Karel Reisz's epic portrait of the groundbreaking 1920s dancer. Bringing to her dance scenes an imposing physicality and forceful agility, she was at once exuberant and subtle, and was duly Oscar-nominated for Best Actress that year. Even more impressive was her turn in Ken Russell's The Devils

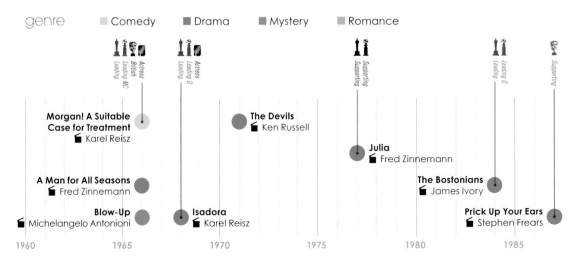

| $80M (U.S.)
Julia
(1977) | $3M (U.S.)
Prick Up Your Ears
(1987) | $43M (U.S.)
Howards End
(1992) | $5M (U.S.)
Mrs. Dalloway
(1997) | $39M
The Pledge
(2001) | $146M
Atonement
(2007) | $177M
The Butler
(2013) | $12M
Foxcatcher
(2014) |

Howards End | Wilde | Mrs. Dalloway | The Pledge | Atonement | Coriolanus | The Butler | Foxcatcher

(1971). A lastingly controversial portrait of political and religious fervor in 17th-century France, the film features one of Redgrave's wildest performances, notably uninhibited in the scenes of sexual fantasy.

In the more conventional, 1930s-set drama *Julia* (1977), Redgrave was mysterious and magnetic as the title character, a fearless anti-fascist, and friend from childhood of Lillian Hellman (Jane Fonda). Redgrave won an Oscar for the role, but her divisive acceptance speech — in which she attacked a strand of Zionism — suggested hers was too independent-minded a talent to adapt to a sustained Hollywood career.

Redgrave did continue to take roles in American cinema, quite often delivering brilliant performances in small roles in less commercial fare. She provided a piercing cameo as an elderly woman grieving for her granddaughter in Sean Penn's haunting *The Pledge* (2001), and more recently in Lee Daniels' *The Butler* (2013) she made a vivid albeit brief appearance as the caretaker of a cotton plantation in 1920s Georgia.

It is for British cinema that Redgrave has given her finest late-career performances. She was witty and sly as Joe Orton's literary agent in *Prick Up Your Ears* (1987), the acclaimed drama about of

the playwright's doomed relationship with Kenneth Halliwell. It was a role that returned Redgrave to the convulsive cultural scene of London in the 1960s — an era she helped define in her youth.

But her more memorable roles of recent years generally belong to an earlier period. Always a subtle, intelligent performer, Redgrave has become adept at conveying the nuances and import of unspoken conventions of late Victorian and Edwardian society. She was luminous as the wife of a rich businessman in James Merchant's adaptation of *Howards End* (1992), continuing a relationship with the director from her exquisite performance in his 1984 Henry James adaptation *The Bostonians*. In 1997 she contributed fine work as one of the ensemble cast of the Oscar Wilde biopic *Wilde*, and as the heroine of the adaptation of Virginia Woolf's *Mrs. Dalloway*, poignantly hinting at her character's unarticulated, complex sorrows.

Her more recent appearances might be brief, but Redgrave can still command the screen, as she did playing a novelist with failing memory in *Atonement* (2007), Volumnia in Ralph Fiennes' *Coriolanus* (2011) and as the fiercely disapproving mother of an unstable millionaire in *Foxcatcher* (2014). **EL**

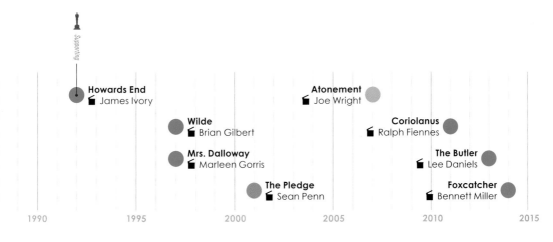

Supporting

Howards End
James Ivory

Wilde
Brian Gilbert

Mrs. Dalloway
Marleen Gorris

The Pledge
Sean Penn

Atonement
Joe Wright

Coriolanus
Ralph Fiennes

The Butler
Lee Daniels

Foxcatcher
Bennett Miller

1990 1995 2000 2005 2010 2015

keanu reeves 1964

River's Edge

Dangerous Liaisons

Bill & Ted's Excellent Adventure

Point Break

My Own Private Idaho

Speed

The Matrix

A Scanner Darkly

You might be hard pressed to argue for Keanu Reeves being a heavyweight acting talent, but his instinctive screen presence and laid-back sense of charm far outweighs his limited range.

With a handful of commercial and television credits under his belt, Reeves made his cinematic breakthrough in the melancholic teen drama *River's Edge* (1986). The relative success of that film led to his being cast in another dark tale of adolescent ennui, *Permanent Record* (1988). He was adequate in Stephen Frears' *Dangerous Liaisons* (1988) but excelled as a wayward teen who befriends his girlfriend's younger brother in *Parenthood* (1989), and created a legend as slacker hero Ted "Theodore" Logan in the smash hit comedy *Bill & Ted's Excellent Adventure* (1989). He would revisit the character in 1991 for the even sillier *Bill & Ted's Bogus Journey*.

Now a bankable star, Reeves found himself working with heavyweight directors. He was FBI agent Johnny Utah in Kathryn Bigelow's *Point Break* (1991). Utah is described by his new boss as "young, dumb and full of cum," an apt phrase for a number of roles Reeves played during this period. He starred opposite River Phoenix in Gus Van Sant's *My Own Private Idaho* (1991) and was Jonathan Harker in Francis Ford Coppola's *Bram Stoker's Dracula* (1992), although his performance was widely mocked, mostly because of his unconvincing British accent. However,

it was an exercise in subtlety and nuance compared with his dismal turn in Kenneth Branagh's otherwise effervescent *Much Ado About Nothing* (1993).

Reeves' leading role in the kinetic smash hit *Speed* (1994) repositioned him as an action hero, although subsequent action movies *Johnny Mnemonic* (1995) and *Chain Reaction* (1996) failed to repeat its success. Fortunately for Reeves, his career-defining role as Neo in *The Matrix* (1999) played to his strengths. With its state-of-the-art effects and end of days scenario, Reeves' performance as a blank canvas with an as yet-to-be-realized future is a perfect fit.

While his blockbuster career was going strong, Reeves' dramatic endeavors fared less well. *The Watcher* (2000) and *Sweet November* (2001) were both dismissed by critics. Still, *The Matrix Reloaded* (2003) and *The Matrix Revolutions* (2003) were successful, if increasingly confounding. Reeves also had fun as a cynical exorcist in *Constantine* (2005), another box-office hit.

Reeves worked with Richard Linklater on his Rotoscope adaptation of Philip K. Dick's brilliant head-scratcher *A Scanner Darkly* (2006) and appeared in the sci-fi remake *The Day the Earth Stood Still* (2008). He produced and played the lead in fantasy action film *47 Ronin* (2013) and made the transition to director with *Man of Tai Chi* (2013), a martial arts actioner that met with some critical success. **MB**

genre ■ Drama ■ Comedy ■ Crime ■ Action ■ Sci-Fi ■ Animation

River's Edge
Tim Hunter

Point Break
Kathryn Bigelow

Dangerous Liaisons
Stephen Frears

Speed
Jan de Bont

Bill & Ted's Excellent Adventure
Stephen Herek

The Matrix
Andy Wachowski, Lana Wachowski

My Own Private Idaho
Gus Van Sant

A Scanner Darkly
Richard Linklater

1985   1990   1995   2000   2005

rekha 1954

Ghar

Muqaddar
Ka Sikandar

Khubsoorat

Umrao
Jaan

Utsav

Khoon Bhari
Maang

Khiladiyon
Ka Khiladi

Aastha

Every film industry in the world has a diva and Rekha certainly answers to that description in Indian cinema. Born Bhanurekha to Tamil industry megastar Gemini Ganesan and Telugu industry heroine Pushpavalli, she debuted as a child artiste in the Telugu language *Rangula Ratnam* (1966). Later, known by then simply by the contracted screen name of Rekha, at 15 she played a femme fatale in the Kannada language spy thriller *Operation Jackpot Nalli CID 999* (1969), opposite Rajkumar, a legend of the industry.

It was in the Hindi language industry that Rekha would go on to make her mark, debuting in *Sawan Bhadon* (1970). Though the film was a success, the vicious Bombay gossip press, obsessed with North Indian fair skin, derided this plump dusky beauty from the south. Ironically, one of the films she appeared in during this period, *Gora Aur Kala* (1972), had Rajendra Kumar playing twins, one fair and one dark-skinned, both of whom are in love with the fair-skinned princess Hema Malini, while the dusky Rekha played yet another village girl on the sidelines. Years later, in an interview with India's *The Telegraph*, Rekha would say: "I was called the 'Ugly Duckling' of Hindi films because of my dark complexion and South Indian features. I used to feel deeply hurt when people compared me with the leading heroines of the time and said I was no match for them. I was determined to make it big on sheer merit."

And make it she did, after a process where she transformed herself from the so-called "Ugly Duckling" to a swan. She won acclaim for *Do Anjaane* (1976) and *Ghar* (1978) playing, respectively, an actress and gang rape victim. However, it was in *Muqaddar Ka Sikandar* (1978), as a courtesan opposite Amitabh Bachchan, that she captured the national imagination. Rekha's alleged affair with Bachchan also fired the nation's heart. Next, she appeared in Yash Chopra's *Silsila* (1981), playing the other woman to Bachchan and his real-life actress wife Jaya Bhaduri's married couple.

Rekha displayed her range by starring in the comedy *Khubsoorat* (1980), period drama *Umrao Jaan* (1981) and the erotic *Utsav* (1984). She was also considered a fashion icon, which was capitalized on in *Khoon Bhari Maang* (1988), in which she transforms from a plain Jane into a glamorous diva who takes revenge upon her philandering and murderous husband.

Khiladiyon Ka Khiladi (1996) saw Rekha playing a mafia boss in Canada; together with *Aastha* (1997), it was one of her last successes as lead. In later years she tried to maintain her image, but her comeback attempt as a glamorous granny in *Super Nani* (2014) found little favor with audiences. In her personal life, apart from an alleged affair with Bachchan, Rekha was married briefly to businessman Mukesh Agarwal, until he committed suicide. **NR**

R

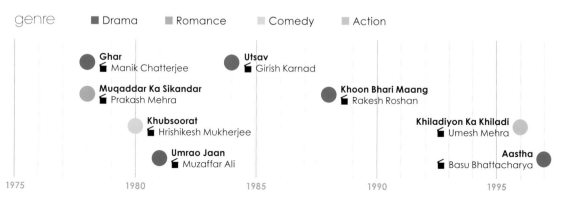

genre   ■ Drama   ■ Romance   ■ Comedy   ■ Action

Ghar
☙ Manik Chatterjee

Utsav
☙ Girish Karnad

Muqaddar Ka Sikandar
☙ Prakash Mehra

Khoon Bhari Maang
☙ Rakesh Roshan

Khubsoorat
☙ Hrishikesh Mukherjee

Khiladiyon Ka Khiladi
☙ Umesh Mehra

Umrao Jaan
☙ Muzaffar Ali

Aastha
☙ Basu Bhattacharya

1975   1980   1985   1990   1995

jean reno 1948

| The Big Blue | Nikita | The Visitors | Léon | Ronin | Godzilla | The Crimson Rivers | The Da Vinci Code |

While considered one of France's most recognizable actors, Jean Reno was actually born to Spanish parents in Casablanca, Morocco, in 1948. He moved to the French mainland as a 17-year-old. After struggling in bit-parts, he agreed to star in a short by first-time filmmaker Luc Besson. It would turn out to be the beginning of a long-term professional relationship. He starred in Besson's feature debut *The Last Battle* (1983) and appeared in the director's breakthrough, *Subway* (1985). However, it was not until he played champion diver Enzo Molinari in the director's 1988 drama *The Big Blue* that he became a star. It was the most financially successful French film of the decade.

The pair worked together again on *Nikita* (1990), in which Reno played an assassin called The Cleaner, who helps a teenage girl join the profession. They would return to a similar premise four years later, but in the meantime,Reno made a name for himself in other directors' work. Of these, the medieval time-travel comedy *The Visitors* (1993) would be the most enduring.

Reno is best known for his soulful yet tough portrayal of the eponymous hit man taking care of a 12-year-old Natalie Portman in *Léon* (1994), which was both his and Besson's first American film. The conflicting sides of the character were perfectly embodied by Reno, who was believable in both the film's action sequences as well as more tender ones.

The role brought Reno international recognition and in its wake he mostly focused on U.S. productions. Like many foreign actors who make the transition to Hollywood, he would have difficulty finding substantial roles, taking supporting parts in films like *French Kiss* (1995) and *Mission: Impossible* (1996). One of his better roles around this time was opposite Robert De Niro in John Frankenheimer's tense *Ronin* (1998), but he was wasted in *Godzilla* (1998).

Reno had to return to France to find lead roles, starring in a mix of thrillers and comedies, including *The Crimson Rivers* (2000), *Wasabi* (2001), *Jet Lag* (2002) and *The Corsican File* (2004). Despite their respective qualities, few of these films received a significant international release. He played a police officer in two Paris-set films — *The Da Vinci Code* (2006) and the reboot of *The Pink Panther* (2006) — both of which were huge financial successes of dubious merit. He continued to split his time between countries, usually playing small roles in American films like *Couples Retreat* (2009) and *Alex Cross* (2012), while starring in *22 Bullets* (2010) and *The Chef* (2012) back home. Often typecast as criminals or law enforcement officers, a satisfying exception was his role as an anti-Semitic boyfriend in Kenneth Lonergan's extraordinary *Margaret* (2011), although the film's release was delayed for four years due to Lornegan struggling to create a final cut. **JWa**

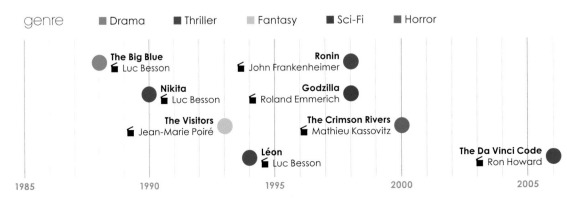

genre ■ Drama ■ Thriller ■ Fantasy ■ Sci-Fi ■ Horror

The Big Blue
Luc Besson

Ronin
John Frankenheimer

Nikita
Luc Besson

Godzilla
Roland Emmerich

The Visitors
Jean-Marie Poiré

The Crimson Rivers
Mathieu Kassovitz

Léon
Luc Besson

The Da Vinci Code
Ron Howard

1985   1990   1995   2000   2005

burt reynolds 1936

Deliverance

Nickelodeon

Smokey and the Bandit

Hooper

The Best Little Whorehouse in Texas

Breaking In

Striptease

Boogie Nights

During the 1970s and into the 1980s, Burt Reynolds was one of the biggest names in Hollywood. A handsome, physically imposing actor, he shared some of the rugged charisma of earlier stars like Clark Gable, with an air of self-deprecation that suggested he did not take himself too seriously. But his seemingly effortless image belied a versatile, often underrated talent.

Reynolds was a talented college football player, but when injury ended his sporting ambitions he started acting classes. His first screen roles were in television drama. Following Clint Eastwood, Reynolds took an early big-screen role in Europe as the title hero of the violent 1966 Spaghetti Western *Navajo Joe*.

It was under John Boorman that Reynolds scored his breakout hit. The British filmmaker's gritty backwoods adventure drama *Deliverance* (1972) saw Reynolds impress in the physically demanding role of a city tourist terrorized by a gang of hillbillies on a river-rafting trip in remote Georgia. He performed his own stunts, the outtakes from which were re-used for his 1978 comedy-drama *Hooper*, in which he gave one of his most affable performances, as a veteran stuntman.

He could be just as skilled in lighter roles. An accomplished country singer (who would sing alongside Dolly Parton in 1982's overblown *The Best Little Whorehouse in Texas*), Reynolds starred in 1975 musical *At Long Last Love*. A flop at the time, Peter Bogdanovich's Cole Porter-scored 1930s pastiche drew a performance of great throwaway charm by the actor. Reynolds also gave the liveliest performance of Bogdanovich's 1976 period comedy *Nickelodeon*, as a silent movie actor.

In 1977, Reynolds provided a winning combination of action and humor as a renegade high-speed driver in *Smokey and the Bandit*. It marked the high point in his popularity and he would spend too much time and energy on sequels and cast-offs, like *The Cannonball Run* (1981), trying to replicate its success. With a few exceptions, such as his droll turn as an ageing con in the comedy-drama *Breaking In* (1989), he rarely gave the impression of stretching himself as an actor.

He launched a comeback of sorts, having fun as a sleazy congressman in the 1996 comedy *Striptease*, but the film was poorly received. Much more successful was his turn as a veteran porn director in *Boogie Nights* (1997), exuding a kingly charm that saw him Oscar nominated, providing a reminder — perhaps the last — of Reynolds' ample gifts as an actor. **EL**

R

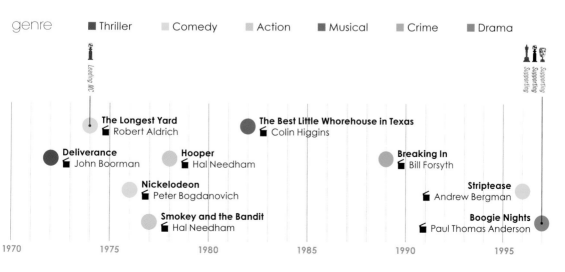

genre   ■ Thriller   ■ Comedy   ■ Action   ■ Musical   ■ Crime   ■ Drama

Leading MC

Supporting
Supporting
Supporting

The Longest Yard
Robert Aldrich

The Best Little Whorehouse in Texas
Colin Higgins

Deliverance
John Boorman

Hooper
Hal Needham

Breaking In
Bill Forsyth

Nickelodeon
Peter Bogdanovich

Striptease
Andrew Bergman

Smokey and the Bandit
Hal Needham

Boogie Nights
Paul Thomas Anderson

1970   1975   1980   1985   1990   1995

debbie reynolds 1932

| Three Little Words | Singin' in the Rain | The Catered Affair | How the West Was Won | The Unsinkable Molly Brown | What's the Matter with Helen? | Mother | Behind the Candelabra |

Born in El Paso, Texas, in 1932, Debbie Reynolds was still at school when she was signed by Warner Bros., making her film debut as an uncredited extra in *June Bride* (1948) and receiving her first speaking part in *The Daughter of Rosie O'Grady* (1950). After a role as the singer and Betty Boop-inspiration Helen Kane in *Three Little Words* (1950), she appeared in the musicals *Two Weeks with Love* (1950) and *Mr. Imperium* (1951).

Reynolds' breakthrough came a year later, playing the enthusiastic ingénue Kathy Selden alongside Gene Kelly and Donald O'Connor in the great Hollywood musical *Singin' in the Rain* (1952). An unseasoned dancer at the time, she later claimed that making the film was the hardest experience of her life. She progressed to leading roles in a series of musicals of variable quality, including *I Love Melvin* (1953), *The Affairs of Dobie Gillis* (1953) and *Athena* (1954).

As the popularity of musicals diminished, Reynolds started to appear in straight comedies and romantic films, such as *The Tender Trap* (1955) and *Tammy and the Bachelor* (1957). Despite showing an aptitude for drama in *The Catered Affair* (1956), her work was mostly restricted to light comedies, with occasional exceptions like *How the West Was Won* (1962). She

returned to musicals as the title character in *The Unsinkable Molly Brown* (1964), receiving her only Oscar nomination for playing the colorful *Titanic*-survivor.

Like her contemporary Doris Day, as the 1960s progressed Reynolds' perkily innocent persona fell out of fashion. As a result, she focused instead on the stage and Las Vegas revues. After starring with Shelley Winters in the campy thriller *What's the Matter with Helen?* (1971), she barely worked for the next two decades, making infrequent appearances in films such as the MGM compendium *That's Entertainment!* (1974), a cameo as herself in *The Bodyguard* (1992) and Oliver Stone's Vietnam War drama *Heaven & Earth* (1993).

Reynolds made a partial comeback with a well-received performance as the eponymous matriarch in *Mother* (1996). The following year, she took a supporting role in *In & Out* (1997), then later starred as an ageing actress alongside Shirley MacLaine, Joan Collins and Elizabeth Taylor in *These Old Broads* (2001), which was written by her daughter Carrie Fisher. After another quiet decade, she donned a prosthetic nose to portray the controlling mother of Michael Douglas' Liberace in Steven Soderbergh's portrait of the pianist, *Behind the Candelabra* (2013). **JWa**

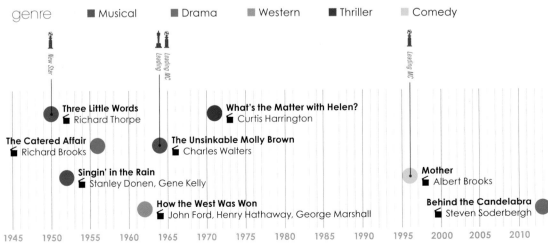

genre ■ Musical ■ Drama ▨ Western ■ Thriller ▧ Comedy

New Star

Leading MC

Leading MC

Three Little Words
🎬 Richard Thorpe

What's the Matter with Helen?
🎬 Curtis Harrington

The Catered Affair
🎬 Richard Brooks

The Unsinkable Molly Brown
🎬 Charles Walters

Singin' in the Rain
🎬 Stanley Donen, Gene Kelly

Mother
🎬 Albert Brooks

How the West Was Won
🎬 John Ford, Henry Hathaway, George Marshall

Behind the Candelabra
🎬 Steven Soderbergh

1945   1950   1955   1960   1965   1970   1975   1980   1985   1990   1995   2000   2005   2010

tim robbins 1958

Bull Durham

Jacob's Ladder

Bob Roberts

The Player

The Shawshank Redemption

Arlington Road

Mystic River

War of the Worlds

Born in 1958 in West Covina, California, Tim Robbins pursued stage acting from his early teens, later forming an experimental theater group and taking small roles in television and film, most notably in *Top Gun* (1986). After surviving the failure that was *Howard the Duck* (1986), his breakthrough came playing the egocentric baseball pitcher Ebby Calvin LaLoosh in *Bull Durham* (1988). Lead roles followed in *Miss Firecracker* (1989) and *Erik the Viking* (1989). There was more substance to his performance as a Vietnam veteran in the hallucinatory *Jacob's Ladder* (1990).

Robbins took to writing and directing in 1992, starring as a folk singer and right-wing senatorial candidate in *Bob Roberts*. He would stay behind the camera in all his subsequent films as director. Also that year, Robbins starred in Robert Altman's outstanding Hollywood satire *The Player*, a role that perfectly utilized his gift for chilliness and won him the Best Actor prize at Cannes. He would work with Altman again on *Short Cuts* (1993) and *Ready to Wear* (1994).

The year 1994 was decidedly mixed for the actor. As well as the tepid Albert Einstein romance *I.Q.*, he starred in the Coen brothers' *The Hudsucker Proxy*, an expensive flop that proved damaging for everyone

involved. Robbins' other commercially disappointing film that year was *The Shawshank Redemption*. However, the film developed an extraordinary second life and is now a popular favorite.

For the remainder of the decade, Robbins focused more on directing. Aside from the comedy *Nothing to Lose* (1997) and a well-received turn in conspiracy thriller *Arlington Road* (1999), his only other work was a cameo in *Austin Powers: The Spy Who Shagged Me* (1999).

His work-rate increased at the start of the next decade. He played against type, as John Cusack's New Age antagonist in *High Fidelity* (2000). Neither Brian De Palma's *Mission to Mars* (2000) nor Michel Gondry's *Human Nature* (2001) were especially successful, but he gave an Oscar-winning turn as a man traumatized by childhood molestation in *Mystic River* (2003).

Since starring in the underrated *Code 46* (2003), Robbins' work has mainly been in supporting roles. The most significant was a deranged man in Steven Spielberg's *War of the Worlds* (2005), a divisive role that weakened the film. Robbins has since contributed solid work to middling films like *City of Ember* (2008), *Thanks for Sharing* (2012) and *Life of Crime* (2014), none of which managed to find an audience. **JWa**

R

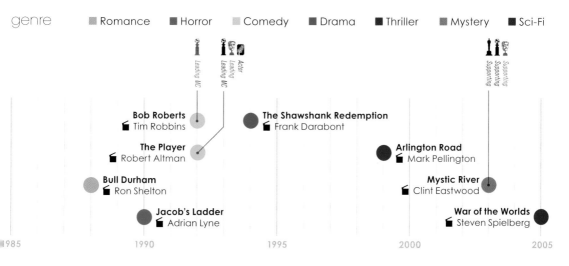

genre   ■ Romance   ■ Horror   ■ Comedy   ■ Drama   ■ Thriller   ■ Mystery   ■ Sci-Fi

Leading MC

Actor
Leading
Leading MC

Supporting
Supporting
Supporting

Bob Roberts
🏴 Tim Robbins

The Shawshank Redemption
🏴 Frank Darabont

The Player
🏴 Robert Altman

Arlington Road
🏴 Mark Pellington

Bull Durham
🏴 Ron Shelton

Mystic River
🏴 Clint Eastwood

Jacob's Ladder
🏴 Adrian Lyne

War of the Worlds
🏴 Steven Spielberg

1985   1990   1995   2000   2005

julia roberts 1967

| Mystic Pizza | Steel Magnolias | Pretty Woman | Flatliners | Sleeping With the Enemy | Hook | The Pelican Brief | Conspiracy Theory |

One of Hollywood's most successful actresses, Julia Roberts has been generating box-office gold since she hit it big in the early 1990s. Success came fairly quickly for the actress, who achieved positive recognition for her first significant film role in the indie hit *Mystic Pizza* (1988). The following year she took a further step toward the A-list, landing an Oscar nomination for the melodrama *Steel Magnolias* (1989), opposite Shirley MacLaine and Sally Field.

If Roberts was on the brink of stardom, her next role launched her into the stratosphere. She excelled in the role of a Beverly Hills prostitute with a heart of gold in Garry Marshall's smash hit romantic comedy *Pretty Woman* (1990). Roberts received another Oscar nomination and her second Golden Globe.

Keen not to be typecast, Roberts tried her hand at a number of thrillers. *Flatliners* (1990) felt like a post Brat Pack film, with a group of medical students experimenting with the afterlife. In *Sleeping with the Enemy* (1991) she played the wife of an abusive husband who escapes his clutches and settles down to a new life and identity, only for him to catch up with her. She also took the lead in the saccharine sob-fest *Dying Young* (1991), but neither critics nor

audiences were convinced. Steven Spielberg cast her as Tinkerbell in his Peter Pan adaptation *Hook* (1991), while Robert Altman had her play herself, playing a character in a fictional film, in his brilliant Hollywood satire, *The Player* (1992).

Roberts took the starring role, opposite Denzel Washington, in the John Grisham thriller *The Pelican Brief* (1993), then returned to Altman for his much-maligned — but actually rather enjoyable — *Ready to Wear* (1994). She played the lead in *Mary Reilly* (1996), for which she was universally mocked because of her unconvincing Irish accent. It had improved by the time of Neil Jordan's *Michael Collins* (1996). Then came the popular mainstream hits *My Best Friend's Wedding* (1997), for which she received another Golden Globe nomination, and the enjoyably far-fetched *Conspiracy Theory* (1997), which paired her with Mel Gibson.

She was an executive producer on the lightweight, but enjoyable drama *Stepmom* (1998), also starring opposite Susan Sarandon. For the rest of the decade she seemed to tread water. There was *Notting Hill* (1999), opposite Hugh Grant, which demanded little of its stars, while *Runaway Bride* (1999), which reunited

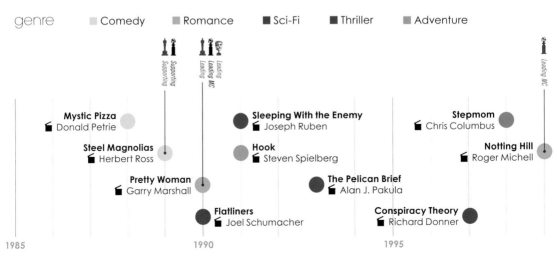

genre   ■ Comedy   ■ Romance   ■ Sci-Fi   ■ Thriller   ■ Adventure

Supporting
Supporting

Leading
Leading MC
Leading

Leading MC

Mystic Pizza
Donald Petrie

Steel Magnolias
Herbert Ross

Pretty Woman
Garry Marshall

Flatliners
Joel Schumacher

Sleeping With the Enemy
Joseph Ruben

Hook
Steven Spielberg

The Pelican Brief
Alan J. Pakula

Conspiracy Theory
Richard Donner

Stepmom
Chris Columbus

Notting Hill
Roger Michell

1985   1990   1995

$832M	$302M	$516M	$317M	$230M	$513M	$349M	$598M
Pretty Woman (1990)	Sleeping with the Enemy (1991)	Hook (1991)	The Pelican Brief (1993)	Stepmom (1998)	Notting Hill (1999)	Erin Brockovich (2000)	Ocean's Eleven (2001)

Stepmom | Notting Hill | Erin Brockovich | Ocean's Eleven | Mona Lisa Smile | Closer | Eat Pray Love | August: Osage County

Roberts with *Pretty Woman* director Garry Marshall and costar Richard Gere, was underwhelming at best. Both films were huge hits, but there was a danger that Roberts would remain saddled with such roles.

The new century saw the beginning of one of the most vital collaborations of Roberts' career, with Steven Soderbergh. She took everyone by surprise with her Oscar-winning turn in *Erin Brockovich* (2000). She plays a blue-collar mother who joins a legal firm as a secretary but whose passion for the victims of industrial pollution finds her spearheading their class action. Balancing brassiness with intelligence, Roberts is sensational. She reunited with Soderbergh as George Clooney's ex and Andy Garcia's current girlfriend in *Ocean's Eleven* (2001), easily holding her own against an impressive cast. Then in 2002 she was one of the cast in Soderbergh's meta-exercise *Full Frontal*. Panned though the film was, it showed Roberts' willingness to experiment.

She starred in *The Mexican* (2001) and *America's Sweethearts* (2001), before joining her *Ocean's* costar George Clooney in his directorial debut, *Confessions of A Dangerous Mind* (2002). It was a smart role, like her supporting turn in Mike Nichols' satire *Charlie Wilson's War* (2007), for which she was praised and received yet another Golden Globe nomination.

Roberts was on safer ground with the gentle *Mona Lisa Smile* (2003), which earned her a record-breaking $25 million — the highest fee ever negotiated for an actress. Her first collaboration with Mike Nichols was on his film version of Patrick Marber's coruscating stage play *Closer* (2004). She was cast opposite Jude Law, Natalie Portman and Clive Owen, the latter of whom would play her partner in crime in Tony Gilroy's convoluted, semi-successful corporate espionage comedy thriller *Duplicity* (2009).

Garry Marshall's *Valentine's Day* (2010) found Roberts working with an ensemble cast, filling the box-office tills, if not the heart. Genuine sentiment was also hard to find in Ryan Murphy's *Eat Pray Love* (2010) and the Tom Hanks-directed romantic drama *Larry Crowne* (2011). It was interesting, if no more than diverting to see Roberts cast against type as the villainous Evil Queen Clementianna in the slight fairy tale-fantasy *Mirror Mirror* (2012). She won Academy Award recognition for her portrayal of Barbara Weston in *August: Osage County* (2013). It was one of her most satisfying roles for some time. **MB**

R

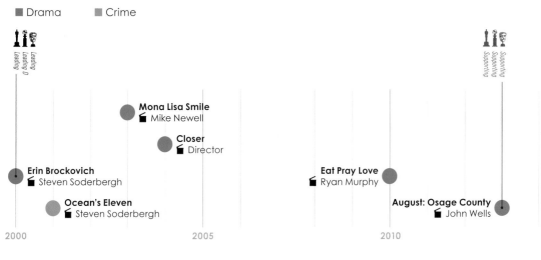

■ Drama   ■ Crime

Leading / Leading D / Leading

Supporting / Supporting / Supporting

Mona Lisa Smile Mike Newell

Closer Director

Erin Brockovich Steven Soderbergh

Ocean's Eleven Steven Soderbergh

Eat Pray Love Ryan Murphy

August: Osage County John Wells

2000 | 2005 | 2010

Steel Magnolias
(1989)

Pretty Woman
(1990)

**Sleeping
With The Enemy**
(1991)

The Pelican Brief
(1993)

Erin Brockovich
(2000)

Ocean's Eleven
(2001)

Eat Pray Love
(2010)

**August: Osage
County**
(2013)

Roberts' *Steel Magnolias* costar Shirley MacLaine once said of the actress that "the moment she walked into the rehearsal room it was obvious she was a born movie star."

Roberts in her star-making role as Vivian Ward, the prostitute who melts the heart of Richard Gere's wealthy businessman in *Pretty Woman*.

Poorly received by critics, *Sleeping with the Enemy* nonetheless became a box-office hit.

Adapted from John Grisham's 1992 novel, *The Pelican Brief* starred Roberts as law student Darby Shaw.

oberts in her Oscar-winning role as **Erin Brockovich**. David Ansen's review of the movie for *Newsweek* declared her performance to be "flat-out terrific."

Filmed on location in New York, Rome, India and Bali, **Eat Pray Love** saw Roberts play a woman seeking answers to life's big questions.

he real-life Erin Brockovich has declared the events depicted in the movie to be probably 98 percent accurate."

s the only female cast member in **Ocean's Eleven**, Roberts said that she "felt like the mboy sister with all these motley brothers."

August: Osage County allowed Roberts to show a darker side, as a member of the dysfunctional Weston family.

paul robeson 1898–1976

Body
and Soul

Borderline

The Emperor
Jones

Sanders
of the River

Show Boat

Song of
Freedom

King
Solomon's
Mines

The Proud
Valley

"A voice so pure, a vision so clear / I've got to learn to live like you / learn to sing like you," declares the Manic Street Preachers' 2001 single "Let Robeson Sing." What was so special about this "giant man with a heavenly voice"? Known to some as a stage and theater actor, to others as the bearer of one of the most soul-shaking bass voices in the history of popular music, and to still others as an impassioned political activist, Paul Robeson was one of few African-American performers to attain movie stardom in pre-civil rights Hollywood.

Born in 1898 in New Jersey, the son of a runaway slave turned minister, Robeson was only the third African-American student ever to attend Rutgers University, where he excelled in athletics, theater and debating, and was valedictorian of his class. A law degree at Columbia, which Robeson funded by playing professional football, followed; but the racism he encountered drove him away from law practice, and toward a full-time life in the arts. Finding racial discrimination to be less entrenched in Europe than in America, he spent time living in London, where he graced the stages of the West End. Movie success came with his appearances in films such as *The Emperor Jones* (1933), *Sanders of the River* (1935) and *Show Boat* (1936), in which he performed what would become one of his signature songs, "Ol' Man River."

Robeson became more politically active as his professional stature increased, lending his support to the Republican forces fighting in the Spanish Civil War as well as to labor and civil rights interests at home in the United States. His political sympathy for Josef Stalin and advocacy for a thawing of relations between America and the USSR, as well as his outspoken criticism of institutional racism in the United States and vocal support for the rights of colonial African peoples, made him a target for government suspicion: he was investigated by the House Un-American Activities Committee, and — damagingly for his career — his passport was withdrawn from 1950 to 1958. During this period, his films and recordings became difficult to source in the United States — a situation that contributes to his continuing relative lack of prominence among pioneering black artists and celebrated civil rights activists.

He continued to rally support for the causes he supported, however, including the striking miners in Wales who had been the subject of his 1940 film *The Proud Valley*. The miners were amid the many signatories to petitions to have Robeson's passport reinstated; when it was, he immediately embarked upon a world tour, visiting Moscow and adding to his catalogue of concerns the condition of aboriginal citizens of Australia and New Zealand. Stress over his continued surveillance by MI5 and the CIA contributed to the breakdown of his health in the 1960s, and he withdrew from public life, dying from a stroke in 1976. **HM**

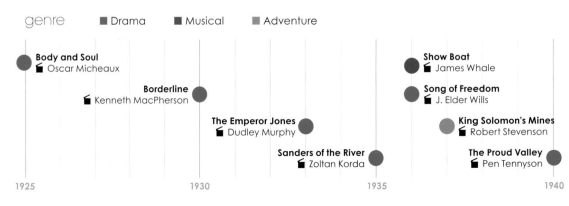

genre　■ Drama　■ Musical　■ Adventure

Body and Soul
Oscar Micheaux

Borderline
Kenneth MacPherson

The Emperor Jones
Dudley Murphy

Sanders of the River
Zoltan Korda

Show Boat
James Whale

Song of Freedom
J. Elder Wills

King Solomon's Mines
Robert Stevenson

The Proud Valley
Pen Tennyson

1925　　　　　　1930　　　　　　1935　　　　　　1940

edward g. robinson 1893–1973

| Little Caesar | The Woman in the Window | Double Indemnity | The Stranger | Key Largo | House of Strangers | The Ten Command- ments | The Cincinnati Kid |

A stocky, intense actor known for portraying authoritative and vicious gangsters, Edward G. Robinson's 50-year acting career spanned the Golden Age of Hollywood. His first roles were in the silent films *Arms and the Woman* (1916) and *The Bright Shawl* (1923), followed several years later by *The Hole in the Wall* (1929), most notable for being his first screen role as a gangster.

Robinson would be cast as a criminal throughout his career, developing underworld figures in *Outside the Law* (1930) and *The Widow from Chicago* (1930) before his breakthrough performance as the nascent gangster Rico in *Little Caesar* (1931). His famous and much-imitated vocal delivery became emblematic of the character type.

The success of *Little Caesar* made Robinson a star and, along with *The Public Enemy* (1931), created a trend for gangster films. Even when not playing habitual criminals, in films such as *The Last Gangster* (1937), he was almost invariably cast as the tough guy, no matter if it was a barber running a gambling den in *Smart Money* (1931), a tabloid editor in *Five Star Final* (1931) or a restaurant owner in *Barbary Coast* (1935).

As gangster films were superseded by film noir in the 1940s, Robinson continued to thrive, starring in Fritz Lang's acclaimed *The Woman in the Window* (1944) and Orson Welles' middling *The Stranger* (1946). His most famous role from the period was as the claims adjuster Barton Keyes in Billy Wilder's *Double Indemnity* (1944). Robinson's other notable role was as the exiled gangster Johnny Rocco in *Key Largo* (1948), his fifth and final screen appearance alongside Humphrey Bogart.

While never officially blacklisted, Robinson was repeatedly called before the House Un-American Activities Committee and his star began to wane. There was some reprieve with a key role in Cecil B. DeMille's grand *The Ten Commandments* (1956). After that, he mostly took supporting roles in films such as *My Geisha* (1962), *The Prize* (1963) and *The Cincinnati Kid* (1965), alongside appearances in such European films as *Grand Slam* (1967) and *It's Your Move* (1968).

After shooting a screen test opposite Charlton Heston for *Planet of the Apes* (1968), he decided not to take the part of ape Dr. Zaius, wishing to avoid lengthy sessions in make-up. His final role was opposite Heston in *Soylent Green* (1973). Having never been nominated for any of his 101 films, in 1972 Robinson was awarded an honorary Oscar for his achievements, but passed away before the ceremony took place. **JWa**

genre ■ Crime ■ Noir ■ Drama

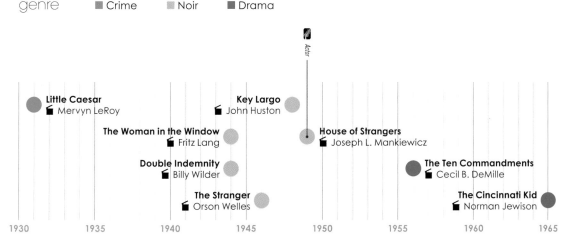

Little Caesar — Mervyn LeRoy
The Woman in the Window — Fritz Lang
Double Indemnity — Billy Wilder
The Stranger — Orson Welles
Key Largo — John Huston
House of Strangers — Joseph L. Mankiewicz
The Ten Commandments — Cecil B. DeMille
The Cincinnati Kid — Norman Jewison

1930 1935 1940 1945 1950 1955 1960 1965

jean rochefort 1930

| Hearth Fires | The Tall Blond Man with One Black Shoe | Let Joy Reign Supreme | An Elephant Can Be Extremely Deceptive | Drummer-Crab | The Hairdresser's Husband | Wild Target | Man on the Train |

A familiar and beloved figure in French cinema, Jean Rochefort's long and productive career began on stage, in 1953. He was 23 years old and he would continue working with the same theater company for several years, which he later described as happy and fulfilling. He also appeared in films as early as the mid-1950s, eventually quitting the theater for cinema following the success of mainstream comedies *Cartouche* (1962) and *Up to His Ears* (1965). He was a recurring character in the popular period series *Angélique* (1964–66), starring Michèle Mercier as a feisty woman in search of her disappeared lover.

Rochefort's friendly personality had him frequently cast in comedies, such as box-office hits *The Tall Blond Man with One Black Shoe* (1972) and *An Elephant Can Be Extremely Deceptive* (1976), and their respective sequels. But director Bertrand Tavernier allowed the actor to demonstrate the range of his skills in the dramas *The Watchmaker of St. Paul* (1974) and *Let Joy Reign Supreme* (1975). Rochefort's performance as a debauched abbot in the latter film earned him a César for Best Supporting Actor. Two years later, his commanding performance in Pierre Schoendoerffer's *Drummer-Crab* (1977) was acknowledged with the César for Best Actor.

Rochefort's grandfather owned horse stables and as a young man the actor took up horse riding, moving into horse breeding later in life and becoming recognized for his expertise on the subject through his commentaries for French television on the various equine disciplines at the Olympic Games. This lifelong passion led Rochefort to accept a number of films that allowed him to ride horses despite the quality of some projects, a concession he has admitted with good humor. Horse riding is the subject of two of his three documentaries as a director, and he spoke out against Terry Gilliam because of the mistreatment of the animal playing Don Quixote's horse during the production of the aborted *The Man Who killed Don Quixote*. The production underwent a series of disasters, including a severe back injury sustained by Rochefort, and the project's failure was the subject of the documentary, *Lost in La Mancha* (2002).

He remained active late into his life, turning in fine performances in Leconte's *Man on the Train* (2002) and Guillaume Canet's *Tell No One* (2006). In later years, Rochefort's pleasant voice became much deeper and made him a natural choice for voiceover narration and animation films. In his last film, Fernando Trueba's *The Artist and his Model* (2012), he played an ageing sculptor whose inspiration is revived when he encounters a young Spanish woman. After its release Rochefort announced his retirement. However, in 2014 Philippe le Guay announced that his new film, *Florida* (2015), would feature the iconic actor whose mustache must be the most famous in cinema. **AG**

genre ■ Drama ■ Comedy ■ Romance ■ Crime

Hearth Fires
🎬 Serge Korber

Drummer-Crab
🎬 Pierre Schoendoerffer

The Tall Blond Man with One Black Shoe
🎬 Yves Robert

The Hairdresser's Husband
🎬 Patrice Leconte

Let Joy Reign Supreme
🎬 Bertrand Tavernier

Wild Target
🎬 Pierre Salvadori

An Elephant Can Be Extremely Deceptive
🎬 Yves Robert

Man on the Train
🎬 Patrice Leconte

1965   1970   1975   1980   1985   1990   1995   2000

sam rockwell 1968

Confessions of a Dangerous Mind

Matchstick Men

Choke

Moon

Iron Man 2

Conviction

Seven Psychopaths

The Way Way Back

Sam Rockwell seemed to have a decent career marked out as a darkly humorous, energetically odd sideshow to the main attraction. On the back of his excellent turn opposite Nicolas Cage in Ridley Scott's twisty thriller *Matchstick Men* (2003), *Entertainment Weekly* even resigned him to his sidekick fate, citing his "excessive interestingness." But a career as charmingly villainous secondary characters, in films like *Matchstick Men* and *Charlie's Angels* (2000), was foiled by George Clooney. For his directorial debut, the pitch-black *Confessions of a Dangerous Mind* (2002), Clooney chose to put his *Welcome To Collinwood* (2002) costar front and center as U.S. game show pioneer and self-professed CIA assassin Chuck Barris. As Barris, Rockwell displayed a kinetic, magnetic, self-destructive charisma that seemed wholly apart from other leading men. He won the Best Actor prize at the Berlin International Film Festival for his performance.

It would be six years before another significant central role came along, but when it did, in the form of *Choke* (2008), based on the novel by Chuck Palahniuk, Rockwell seized the opportunity. Again, he showed his talent for playing charming misanthropes,

as a man who preys on sex addicts and pretends to choke in restaurants as an elaborate ploy to extract money from his saviors. While *Confessions of A Dangerous Mind* and *Choke* had both offered offbeat glimpses of what Rockwell could do when given center stage, it was Duncan Jones' existential sci-fi *Moon* (2009) that proved beyond all doubt that Rockwell could carry a film on his own. And for the vast majority of it, he is very much on his own, manning a lunar outpost, waiting to return to his life on Earth. Both the film and Rockwell earned rave reviews.

The following two years would see Rockwell team up twice with Jon Favreau for *Iron Man 2* (2010) and *Cowboys and Aliens* (2011), nine years after he had a small role in Favreau's *Made* (2001). He also earned critical acclaim for his performances in the downbeat true story *Conviction* (2010), as a man wrongly imprisoned for murder, and as a hilariously unhinged dognapper in *Seven Psychopaths* (2012). In more recent years, Rockwell has shown a softer side, as an unlikely mentor in the charming coming-of-age comedy drama *The Way Way Back* (2013), and demonstrated he can do vulnerable and romantic, opposite Keira Knightley, in *Say When* (2014). **MG**

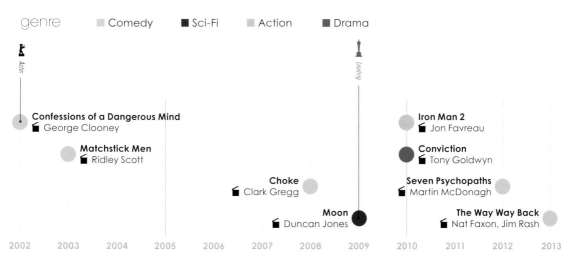

genre ■ Comedy ■ Sci-Fi ■ Action ■ Drama

Actor

Leading

Confessions of a Dangerous Mind
George Clooney

Matchstick Men
Ridley Scott

Choke
Clark Gregg

Moon
Duncan Jones

Iron Man 2
Jon Favreau

Conviction
Tony Goldwyn

Seven Psychopaths
Martin McDonagh

The Way Way Back
Nat Faxon, Jim Rash

2002   2003   2004   2005   2006   2007   2008   2009   2010   2011   2012   2013

ginger rogers 1911–95

Flying Down to Rio

Top Hat

Swing Time

Stage Door

Vivacious Lady

Kitty Foyle

The Major and the Minor

Monkey Business

Ginger Rogers was half of one of the most famous on-screen couples in movie history. In 10 musicals, she and Fred Astaire personified Hollywood at its most rarified and uplifting. Even away from Astaire, Rogers enjoyed a career in comedy and drama, working with high caliber directors and costars.

She was born Virginia Katherine McMath, in Missouri, in 1911. "Ginger" made her Broadway debut in 1929, the same year as her first film. In 1933 she made a strong impression in three screen musicals: *42nd Street*, *Gold Diggers of 1933* and her first with Astaire, *Flying Down to Rio*. Astaire was 12 years her senior, and a renowned Broadway dancer, but had come later to films; *Flying Down to Rio* was his second, Rogers' 20th. Though they both featured down the credits, the romantic leads were quickly overshadowed by the chemistry of the two supporting players.

Astaire and Rogers' musicals included *The Gay Divorcee* (1934), *Top Hat* (1935) and *Swing Time* (1936). He was the supreme dancer, she the better actor; he was all precision, she suggested spontaneity; he was an odd-looking, sexless sprite, she earthy and gorgeous. As Katharine Hepburn once remarked: "He gives her class. She gives him sex."

Their last RKO film together was *The Story of Vernon and Irene Castle* (1939). By this time Rogers had started to go it alone with the drama *Stage Door* (1937), impressive as a wisecracking yet sensitive dancer in a theatrical boarding house. She won an Oscar for *Kitty Foyle* (1940), as a shopgirl reflecting on her failed affair with an upper-class heir. Most of her characters were working-class, independent women, falling in love with men socially above her.

She was a likeable comedienne: in *Vivacious Lady* (1938) opposite James Stewart, and in *Bachelor Mother* (1939) with David Niven; in Billy Wilder's *The Major and the Minor* (1942) she gamely attempted a character pretending to be a child; *Once Upon a Honeymoon* (1942) was a misfiring wartime comedy, though Rogers and Cary Grant generated a sexual frisson that was still apparent as a middle-aged couple in Howard Hawks' *Monkey Business* (1952).

Rogers and Astaire reteamed for the final time for *The Barkleys of Broadway* (1949), an unplanned reunion that was the result of Judy Garland being dropped. By this time Rogers was struggling to find strong mature roles on screen, but in the 1960s she made a successful return to stage musicals. **DM**

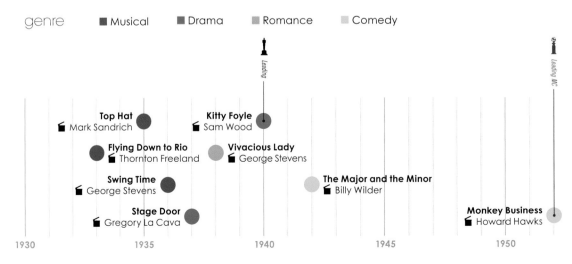

genre   ■ Musical   ■ Drama   ■ Romance   ■ Comedy

Leading

Leading MC

Top Hat
Mark Sandrich

Kitty Foyle
Sam Wood

Flying Down to Rio
Thornton Freeland

Vivacious Lady
George Stevens

Swing Time
George Stevens

The Major and the Minor
Billy Wilder

Stage Door
Gregory La Cava

Monkey Business
Howard Hawks

1930   1935   1940   1945   1950

mickey rooney 1920–2014

A Family Affair

Thorough-breds Don't Cry

Boys Town

National Velvet

Breakfast at Tiffany's

Pulp

The Black Stallion

Night at the Museum

Inducted into his parents' vaudeville act before he had reached his second birthday, Mickey Rooney spent his entire life performing. Born in 1920, his acting career is one of the longest in cinema history, spanning 88 years, from silent films to the modern era.

Rooney's film debut was in the silent short *Not to be Trusted* (1926), but his breakthrough came playing the eponymous protagonist of the comedy short series *Mickey McGuire*. Starting with *Mickey's Circus* (1927), over nine years he starred in 78 films, legally changing his name to Mickey McGuire before settling on Mickey Rooney. A second significant film series began when he was cast as Andy Hardy, who began life as a supporting character in *A Family Affair* (1937). The role established Rooney as a star, and by the time the series ended, 14 films later with *Love Laughs at Andy Hardy* (1946), his name appeared in every title.

Of the seven films he shot in 1937, *Thoroughbreds Don't Cry* featured Rooney's first pairing with Judy Garland. Closely associated throughout their early careers, the young stars' jaunty appearances together include three *Andy Hardy* features and the Busby Berkley musicals *Babes in Arms* (1939), *Strike Up the Band* (1940) and *Babes on Broadway* (1941).

Now established as a comic and musical performer, Rooney expanded into drama with *Boys Town* (1938), playing a delinquent youth.

By 1941, Rooney had spent three years as Hollywood's biggest box-office attraction. After completing *The Human Comedy* (1943) and *National Velvet* (1944) with Elizabeth Taylor, he was drafted into the U.S. Army. His career failed to recover upon his return to the screen, having outgrown the teen roles that made him a star. He increasingly worked in television, including hosting his own show. When he did appear on screen, the results were mixed. He received an Oscar nomination for *The Bold and the Brave* (1956), but an attempt to revive his signature series with *Andy Hardy Comes Home* (1958) proved unsuccessful.

Of all the characters Rooney played following his teen stardom, the most famous is his dubious portrayal of Audrey Hepburn's Japanese neighbor, Mr. Yunioshi, in *Breakfast at Tiffany's* (1961). There were roles in *The Extraordinary Seaman* (1969), *Pulp* (1972) and an Oscar-nominated performance in *The Black Stallion* (1979). He was awarded an honorary Oscar in 1983. His final years featured amiable cameos in *Night at the Museum* (2006) and *The Muppets* (2011). **JW**

R

genre   ■ Comedy   ■ Drama   ■ Family   ■ Romance

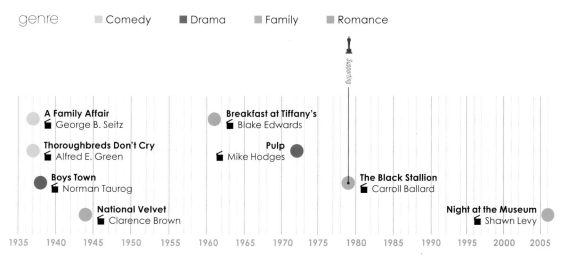

Supporting

A Family Affair
George B. Seitz

Breakfast at Tiffany's
Blake Edwards

Thoroughbreds Don't Cry
Alfred E. Green

Pulp
Mike Hodges

Boys Town
Norman Taurog

The Black Stallion
Carroll Ballard

National Velvet
Clarence Brown

Night at the Museum
Shawn Levy

1935 1940 1945 1950 1955 1960 1965 1970 1975 1980 1985 1990 1995 2000 2005

gena rowlands 1930

A Child Is Waiting

Faces

Minnie and Moskowitz

A Woman Under the Influence

Opening Night

Gloria

Another Woman

The Neon Bible

Gena Rowlands is best known for the remarkable films she made with her husband John Cassavetes. Although she appeared in his directorial debut, *Shadows* (1959), and had a supporting role in *A Child Is Waiting* (1963), it was not until *Faces* (1968) that their collaboration began in earnest. Hers is the first face we see after that film's post-title sequence: closer than close-up, looking straight into the camera, every inch a movie star.

Rowlands started out in live television, but it was on Broadway, in Paddy Chayefsky's *Middle of the Night* (1956), where she made her name. Rave reviews invited attention from Hollywood and a contract with MGM led to work in the movies: *The High Cost of Loving* (1958); *Lonely Are the Brave* (1962); *The Spiral Road* (1962); *Tony Rome* (1967) and *Machine Gun McCain* (1969), with Cassavetes in the lead role. But then from 1968 to 1984, she acted almost exclusively in her husband's films: *Minnie and Moskowitz* (1971), *A Woman Under the Influence* (1974), *Opening Night* (1977), *Gloria* (1980) and *Love Streams* (1984). With the exception of *Gloria*, all of them could be described as "home movies" — even *Minnie and Moskowitz*, which puts its own heady spin on the screwball comedy, feels personal, if not downright autobiographical.

The sense that this singular body of work was very much a family affair is intensified by the way the films were made. Cassavetes and Rowlands mortgaged their home to fund each project; friends and family were cast in significant roles; in-laws' houses were used as locations; and at the heart of this enterprise was Gena Rowlands' galvanic presence. To see her in her prime is to realize how much her influence has been absorbed by other filmmakers. Pedro Almodóvar had her in mind when he made *All About My Mother* (1999) and *Blue Jasmine* (2013) had traces of Rowlands' Mabel Longhetti — but then Woody Allen had worked with Rowlands on *Another Woman* (1988).

After Cassavetes' death in 1989, Rowlands began to work more regularly: Jim Jarmusch's *Night On Earth* (1991), Terence Davies' *The Neon Bible* (1995), and then for her son Nick Cassavetes, in *Unhook the Stars* (1996), *She's So Lovely* (1997) and *The Notebook* (2004). She lent her voice to *Persopolis* (2007), and further family support — this time for her daughter, Zoe Cassavetes — to *Broken English* (2007). But it is the films that John Cassavetes wrote with Rowlands in mind that will be remembered, and that cry out for an Almodóvar-inspired rubric: All About Gena. **MM**

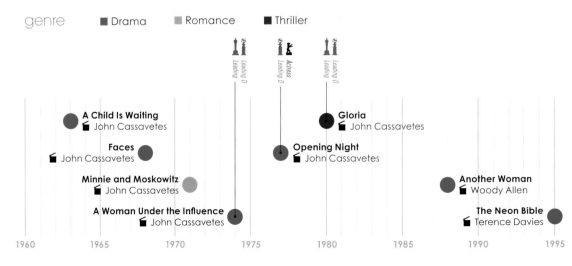

genre   ■ Drama   ■ Romance   ■ Thriller

Leading D / Leading D

Actress / Leading D

Leading D / Leading D

A Child Is Waiting
John Cassavetes

Faces
John Cassavetes

Minnie and Moskowitz
John Cassavetes

A Woman Under the Influence
John Cassavetes

Gloria
John Cassavetes

Opening Night
John Cassavetes

Another Woman
Woody Allen

The Neon Bible
Terence Davies

1960   1965   1970   1975   1980   1985   1990   1995

jane russell 1921–2011

| The Outlaw | The Paleface | His Kind of Woman | The Las Vegas Story | Road to Bali | Gentlemen Prefer Blondes | The French Line | Johnny Reno |

Jane Russell reclines seductively on a pile of straw, a six-shooter pressed to her hip, her body clothed yet scandalously uncovered. The most famous image of the actress comes not from one of her features, but from a series of publicity stills for her debut *The Outlaw* (1943). The film would make her one of the era's major sex symbols, synonymous with a kind of charged eroticism that was unfamiliar to many cinemagoers of the time.

Born in Bemidji, Minnesota, in 1921, Russell's breakthrough came when she won a much-publicized nationwide search by filmmaker Howard Hughes. Signed to a lengthy contract, her first role was in *The Outlaw* as Rio McDonald, a fiery woman caught in a love triangle with Billy the Kid and Doc Holliday. Despite being shot in 1941 and premiering in 1943, *The Outlaw* was not released widely until 1946, a consequence of the battle between Hughes and censors over the film's emphasis on Russell's bust. The publicity over the delay made her a star years before its release, with most audiences first seeing her in *Young Widow* (1946).

Hughes ruthlessly managed Russell's early career and as a result she worked infrequently. She did not star in another film until the Bob Hope comedy western *The Paleface* (1948). She would return for its 1952 sequel, *Son of Paleface*. By the time she starred in her fourth film, *His Kind of Woman* (1951), with Robert

Mitchum, she had already been in the industry for a decade. The 1950s was busier. She worked in a variety of genres, starring in *The Las Vegas Story* (1952), *Montana Belle* (1952), *Road to Bali* (1952) and *Macao* (1952), opposite Mitchum again.

Her biggest hit was the musical comedy *Gentlemen Prefer Blondes* (1953), Howard Hawks' smart battle of the sexes, which makes much from the chemistry between Russell and costar Marilyn Monroe. With her popularity at its peak, Russell starred in another musical, *The French Line* (1954), produced by Hughes and shot in 3-D. Much like *The Outlaw*, the film was structured almost entirely around her physique, with some posters claiming "It'll knock both your eyes out!"

Gentlemen Marry Brunettes (1955), alongside Jeanne Crain, floundered without the combination of Russell and Monroe. After impressing in *The Tall Men* (1955) and *The Revolt of Mamie Stover* (1956), Russell's career tailed off as she struggled to find worthy material, with nine years between *The Fuzzy Pink Nightgown* (1957) and the western *Johnny Reno* (1966). After a small part in *Darker Than Amber* (1970), she left film acting behind for good, citing the disheartening lack of roles for women of her age. In total, she appeared in just 24 features over her 27-year film career, mostly during a white-hot, too-brief period of less than a decade. **JWa**

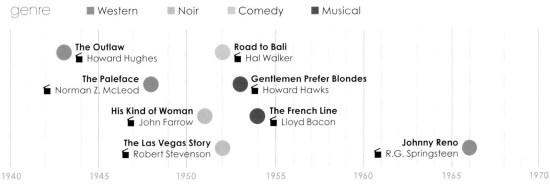

genre   ■ Western   ■ Noir   ■ Comedy   ■ Musical

The Outlaw
Howard Hughes

Road to Bali
Hal Walker

The Paleface
Norman Z. McLeod

Gentlemen Prefer Blondes
Howard Hawks

His Kind of Woman
John Farrow

The French Line
Lloyd Bacon

The Las Vegas Story
Robert Stevenson

Johnny Reno
R.G. Springsteen

1940   1945   1950   1955   1960   1965   1970

meg ryan 1961

| When Harry Met Sally | The Doors | Sleepless in Seattle | Courage Under Fire | You've Got Mail | Kate & Leopold | In the Cut | The Women |

Has there ever been a name more synonymous with the romantic comedy genre than Meg Ryan? For well over a decade the actress moved from one gentle love story to the next. But such close association can be a hard thing to shake. More recent bold choices notwithstanding, she has struggled to free herself from the light entertainment chains of her defining years.

After the false start that was the schlocky *Amityville 3-D* (1983), and a few smaller roles in films including *Top Gun* (1986), Meg Ryan's first significant role was in Joe Dante's family sci-fi adventure *Innerspace* (1987). She followed it with the remake of the 1950 noir *D.O.A.* (1988) and *The Presidio* (1988), but it was her role in the hit rom-com *When Harry Met Sally* (1989) that would turn Ryan into a household name. Her performance as Sally charmed both critics and audiences, and saw her nominated for a Golden Globe.

Ryan's choices immediately following the Rob Reiner smash included the oddball comedy *Joe Versus the Volcano* (1990) with Tom Hanks, and Oliver Stone's vaguely ridiculous music biopic *The Doors* (1991), although the role was an early indication of her desire to carve a more diverse career. While neither of these films set the box office alight, Ryan struck gold

again when she starred opposite Hanks in *Sleepless in Seattle* (1993), Nora Ephron's modern-day riff on *An Affair To Remember* (1957). It cemented Ryan's reputation as the go-to girl for sweeping love stories.

Over the next decade, Ryan impressed in *When A Man Loves A Woman* (1994), stretching herself more than any other film that decade to play an alcoholic, *Restoration* (1995) and *Courage Under Fire* (1996). She also starred in the lighter *I.Q.* (1994), *French Kiss* (1995) and the hit *You've Got Mail* (1998), which paired her again with Tom Hanks, in a remake of Ernst Lubitsch's vastly superior *The Shop Around the Corner* (1940).

Roles in fluffy fare such as *Hanging Up* (2000) and *Kate & Leopold* (2001) provided little scope for Ryan to test her abilities, but her performance in Jane Campion's *In the Cut* (2003) was a radical departure, casting her in an erotic thriller that stands as possibly her most complex and interesting performance.

Alas, Ryan's willingness to experiment proved short lived, and she has done little to push herself in other films. One of her most notable recent roles came in the form of the unconvincing remake *The Women* (2008), which saw Ryan retreat to her comfort zone, albeit lacking the charm she once effortlessly exuded. **MB**

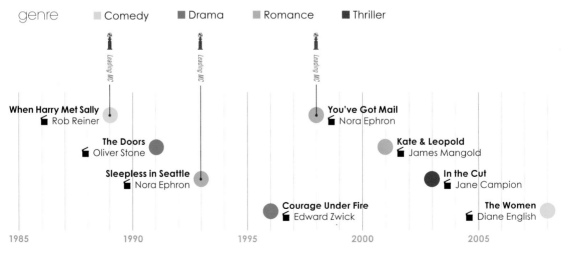

genre ■ Comedy ■ Drama ■ Romance ■ Thriller

Leading MC
Leading MC
Leading MC

When Harry Met Sally
📷 Rob Reiner

You've Got Mail
📷 Nora Ephron

The Doors
📷 Oliver Stone

Kate & Leopold
📷 James Mangold

Sleepless in Seattle
📷 Nora Ephron

In the Cut
📷 Jane Campion

Courage Under Fire
📷 Edward Zwick

The Women
📷 Diane English

1985   1990   1995   2000   2005

robert ryan 1909–73

Crossfire

On Dangerous Ground

The Naked Spur

Bad Day at Black Rock

Men in War

Billy Budd

The Wild Bunch

The Outfit

Robert Ryan looked dangerous when he scowled. He could look even more dangerous when he smiled. He made a highly effective villain, but he could also express warmth and tenderness — and, when given the chance, both aspects in the same film.

Ryan graduated from Dartmouth College in 1931, then spent the next few years in a variety of hardscrabble jobs before enrolling in acting school in 1939. Excluding a couple of bit-parts in his teens, he was over 30 before he made his screen debut.

Edward Dmytryk's *Tender Comrade* (1943) gave him his first major role, cast opposite Ginger Rogers, though the film later hit trouble when it was accused of being Communist propaganda. Dmytryk cast him as a vicious racist in *Crossfire* (1947), earning the actor an Oscar nomination; then Joseph Losey gave him a benevolent role in his anti-racist parable *The Boy with Green Hair* (1948). In Max Ophüls' *Caught* (1949) he was a control-freak millionaire reminiscent of Howard Hughes. His first two films for Nicholas Ray, *Born to Be Bad* (1950) and *Flying Leathernecks* (1951), were negligible, but in *On Dangerous Ground* (1951) Ray gave him his most ambiguous role to date: a tough cop redeemed by his relationship with a blind girl.

He was nasty again in a couple of good westerns: a dangerously articulate outlaw in *The Naked Spur* (1953) and the chief heavy menacing Spencer Tracy in *Bad Day at Black Rock* (1955). Westerns suited what he himself called his "long, seamy face." In *Men in War* (1957), he was the lieutenant striving to keep his men alive when his platoon is cut off in hostile territory. Hard-bitten thriller *Odds Against Tomorrow* (1959) had him as a gang leader trying to bring off a doomed bank heist.

Ryan was an unexpected choice as John the Baptist in biblical epic *King of Kings* (1961), but made almost mandatory casting for Claggart, malevolence personified, in *Billy Budd* (1962). Known for his unfailing reliability, he was increasingly offered cameos and support roles. Sam Peckinpah's seminal western *The Wild Bunch* (1969), though, called for something more. As a former gang member coerced into helping hunt down his associates, Ryan's whole body seems weighed down with a consciousness of betrayal.

In his final years he was visibly ill, battling cancer, but still managed to add two highly distinctive performances to his rich gallery of gang bosses: in René Clément's bizarre fantasy-thriller *And Hope to Die* (1972), and John Flynn's taut, tough *The Outfit* (1973). **PK**

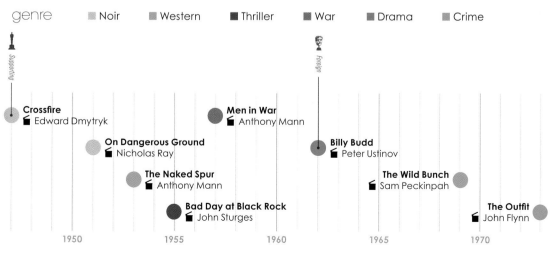

genre   ■ Noir   ■ Western   ■ Thriller   ■ War   ■ Drama   ■ Crime

Supporting

Foreign

Crossfire
Edward Dmytryk

Men in War
Anthony Mann

On Dangerous Ground
Nicholas Ray

Billy Budd
Peter Ustinov

The Naked Spur
Anthony Mann

The Wild Bunch
Sam Peckinpah

Bad Day at Black Rock
John Sturges

The Outfit
John Flynn

1950   1955   1960   1965   1970

george sanders 1906–72

| Foreign Correspond-ent | Man Hunt | The Moon and Sixpence | The Picture of Dorian Gray | The Private Affairs of Bel Ami | All About Eve | The Jungle Book | The Kremlin Letter |

George Sanders was the smoothest of villains; a cool cad who could outsneer Basil Rathbone and outpurr Vincent Price. He deployed irresistible charm with an edge of menace, qualified by a disconcerting sense of languid disengagement. Given the quality of many of his films, this feeling of ennui was often justified.

Despite his proclaimed laziness and contempt for the whole business of acting, Sanders made an impressive number of movies. Now and then he was on the side of virtue, as in Alfred Hitchcock's *Foreign Correspondent* (1940), where he helps out Joel McCrea's bemused hero, as the sympathetic detective in *The Lodger* (1944), or the series of programers where he played freelance investigator The Saint (1939–41) or his American equivalent The Falcon (1941–42). Occasionally he was even cast as a romantic lead, teamed with the young Ingrid Bergman in *Rage in Heaven* (1941).

During World War II Sanders was inevitably cast as suave but nasty Nazis, most notably in *Man Hunt* (1941), and as a quisling in Jean Renoir's *This Land Is Mine* (1943). But it was the morally ambiguous roles, the charmingly cynical bounders that suited him best. He was ideal, then, for Charles II in *Forever Amber* (1947).

Highly literate and multilingual, Sanders responded thankfully to intelligent scripts. Albert Lewin, master of overblown cultural decadence, served him well in three films: *The Moon and Sixpence* (1942), adapted from Somerset Maugham's novel inspired by the life of Gauguin, where he played the stockbroker-turned-artist; epigram-spouting Lord Henry Wooton in *The Picture of Dorian Gray* (1945); and over-age but effective as Maupassant's womanizing social climber in *The Private Affairs of Bel Ami* (1947). But Sanders' finest role came from Joseph Mankiewicz, in *All About Eve* (1950). As the adder-tongued drama critic Addison de Witt, he deservedly netted an Oscar.

His most highly regarded film, though one he hated making, was Roberto Rossellini's *Journey to Italy* (1954), which reunited him with Bergman. He costarred with Ethel Merman for the Irving Berlin musical *Call Me Madam* (1953), but after that the quality of his material started to slip. He made a couple of late comebacks, suave as ever as the voice of Shere Khan in Disney's *The Jungle Book* (1967), and as a drag queen in *The Kremlin Letter* (1970), but the weariness was winning out. His suicide note was wholly in character. "Dear World, I am leaving because I am bored." **PK**

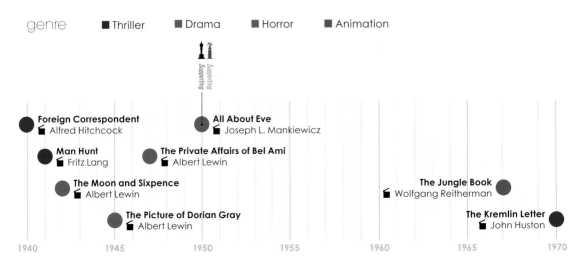

genre   ■ Thriller   ■ Drama   ■ Horror   ■ Animation

Supporting

Foreign Correspondent
Alfred Hitchcock

All About Eve
Joseph L. Mankiewicz

Man Hunt
Fritz Lang

The Private Affairs of Bel Ami
Albert Lewin

The Moon and Sixpence
Albert Lewin

The Jungle Book
Wolfgang Reitherman

The Picture of Dorian Gray
Albert Lewin

The Kremlin Letter
John Huston

1940   1945   1950   1955   1960   1965   1970

Clown   Sinner

adam sandler 1966

Happy Gilmore

The Wedding Singer

Big Daddy

Punch-Drunk Love

Spanglish

50 First Dates

Funny People

Grown Ups

It is difficult to think of another contemporary comedian who is simultaneously as commercially successful and critically maligned as Adam Sandler. Born in 1966, he performed stand-up comedy as a teenager before progressing to television. He made his film debut at 23, starring in the best-forgotten *Going Overboard* (1989), after which he joined the long-running sketch show *Saturday Night Live (SNL)* as a writer, rising to become one of the show's biggest stars.

Sandler's first post-*SNL* effort was *Billy Madison* (1995), concerning a spoiled hotel heir forced to return to school. The first of many hits for the comedian, its apoplectic man-child protagonist, broad physical humor and anti-authoritarian narrative set the template for subsequent films. Of this specific sub-genre, *Happy Gilmore* (1996) remains probably the strongest, although *The Waterboy* (1998) and *Big Daddy* (1999) had their own particular charms.

Stepping aside from his usual fare, in 1998 Sandler costarred with Drew Barrymore in the warm romantic-comedy *The Wedding Singer*. Like his other characters, Sandler's heartbroken 1980s crooner was defined by comedic anger, but the film's appeal was broader thanks to its softer tone. Sandler later re-teamed with Barrymore for the underrated *50 First Dates* (2004) and *Blended* (2014), but neither would achieve the same enduring popularity.

While continuing to dutifully turn out films like *Little Nicky* (2000) Sandler starred in Paul Thomas Anderson's strange, beautiful *Punch-Drunk Love* (2002). Anderson was able to employ Sandler's boyish behavior to create scenes of suffocating tension and oddly touching romance. The role portended a new direction for the actor, but aside from the comedy-dramas *Spanglish* (2004) and *Reign Over Me* (2007), he largely stuck to his tested formula, albeit with diminishing quality and audience sizes — although *You Don't Mess with the Zohan* (2008) was a return to form.

In Judd Apatow's *Funny People* (2009), Sandler played a successful comedian stuck making formulaic films, blighted by creative inertia and a sense of ennui. Apatow — Sandler's old roommate — wrote the part especially for him, and it demonstrated what impressive work the actor was capable of. That he followed it up with *Grown Ups* (2010) and the widely-reviled *Jack and Jill* (2011) suggested that, once again, *Funny People* was more a tantalizing anomaly than a sea change in an increasingly bland career. **JWa**

S

genre   ■ Comedy   ■ Romance

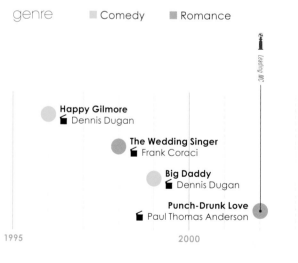

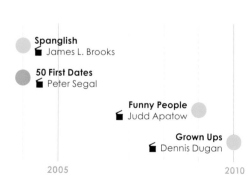

Leading Me

Happy Gilmore
🎬 Dennis Dugan

The Wedding Singer
🎬 Frank Coraci

Big Daddy
🎬 Dennis Dugan

Punch-Drunk Love
🎬 Paul Thomas Anderson

Spanglish
🎬 James L. Brooks

50 First Dates
🎬 Peter Segal

Funny People
🎬 Judd Apatow

Grown Ups
🎬 Dennis Dugan

1995   2000   2005   2010

susan sarandon 1946

| The Rocky Horror Picture Show | Pretty Baby | Atlantic City | The Hunger | The Witches of Eastwick | Bull Durham | Thelma & Louise | Lorenzo's Oil |

"Jimmy, what colour are my eyes?" Susan Sarandon's Louise challenges her lover in *Thelma & Louise* (1991). Feckless as Michael Madsen's Jimmy may be, this is hardly much of a test: could anyone who'd looked more than once at Sarandon mistake the color of the roundest, brownest orbs in the business?

The Sarandon eyes are elements of a complex beauty, at once frank and subtle, that has aided its owner in playing roles that range from the unworldly to the world-weary, from the self-sacrificing to the self-serving, and from the saintly to the super-sexed. Despite her distinctive looks, Sarandon really has no type on screen. Perhaps the one characteristic it is hard to imagine Sarandon embodying convincingly is stupidity. Despite frequently playing parts that emphasize her sex appeal, Sarandon's conspicuous cleverness has ensured that she is never confined to being decorative; and though in later life she has played many matriarchs (including one of American literature's most iconic, Marmee March in 1994's *Little Women*), these have tended toward the complex and unsentimental. The trajectory of her career, meanwhile — with her greatest success and prominence coming in her forties — flies in the face of

the truism that Hollywood cannot help but sideline its best actresses at that time of life.

Born Susan Tomalin in New York City in 1946, Sarandon adopted the surname with which she would become famous on her marriage to actor Chris Sarandon. The union ended in 1979, but she chose to keep the name. Her screen debut came opposite Peter Boyle in John G. Avildsen's *Joe* (1970) — largely forgotten now and by her recent estimation, "so bad," but impactful at the time for its portrayal of an America angrily divided over the Vietnam War. Sarandon showed her game sense of humor and her counterculture cool as the readily corruptible Janet in the indelible cult megahit *The Rocky Horror Picture Show* (1975); risked controversy as a prostitute who auctions off her daughter's virginity in Louis Malle's *Pretty Baby* (1978) and gained her first Oscar nomination for the same director's *Atlantic City* (1980).

Throughout the 1980s, she accrued fame, solid roles and heavy-hitting costars, with titles including *The Hunger* (1983), *The Witches of Eastwick* (1987) and *Bull Durham* (1988) confirming her ability to simultaneously project maternal authority, potent sensuality and a certain intelligent mystique. It was on

S

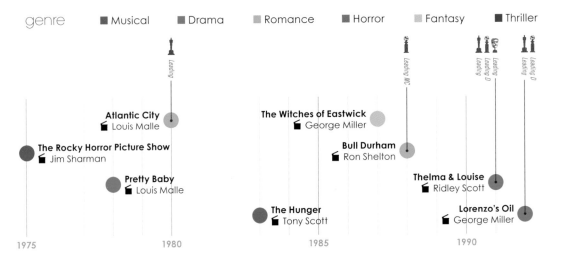

genre ■ Musical ■ Drama ■ Romance ■ Horror ■ Fantasy ■ Thriller

Atlantic City
Louis Malle

The Witches of Eastwick
George Miller

The Rocky Horror Picture Show
Jim Sharman

Bull Durham
Ron Shelton

Pretty Baby
Louis Malle

Thelma & Louise
Ridley Scott

The Hunger
Tony Scott

Lorenzo's Oil
George Miller

1975　　　　　1980　　　　　1985　　　　　1990

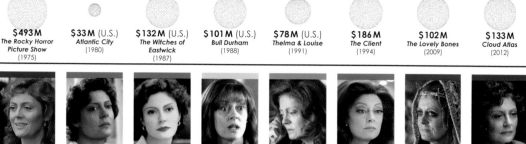

$493M	$33M (U.S.)	$132M (U.S.)	$101M (U.S.)	$78M (U.S.)	$186M	$102M	$133M
The Rocky Horror Picture Show (1975)	Atlantic City (1980)	The Witches of Eastwick (1987)	Bull Durham (1988)	Thelma & Louise (1991)	The Client (1994)	The Lovely Bones (2009)	Cloud Atlas (2012)

The Client | Dead Man Walking | Cradle Will Rock | The Banger Sisters | In the Valley of Elah | The Lovely Bones | Cloud Atlas | The Company You Keep

the set of *Bull Durham* that Sarandon met the up-and-coming actor Tim Robbins, who would be her partner for the ensuing 23 years, and father her two sons.

But it was in the 1990s that Sarandon did her finest and most celebrated work. She was Oscar-nominated not only for her performance in *Thelma & Louise*, but also for her work in family weepie *Lorenzo's Oil* (1992), slick legal thriller *The Client* (1994) and death row drama *Dead Man Walking* (1995), for which she finally won the Best Actress Academy Award.

Since then, leading roles playing to Sarandon's full capacities have not been especially thick on the ground, although she has the undoubted ability to make the most of second-string roles as steely moms, wives or women with mysterious pasts. Some parts — *The Banger Sisters* (2002), in which she costarred with Goldie Hawn as a former rock'n'roll groupie; Robert Redford's *The Company You Keep* (2012), in which she played a former member of the radical action group The Weather Underground — have played explicitly on another aspect of her persona: that of an unreconstructed relic of the 1960s, still wedded to free love and left-wing idealism. Indeed, Sarandon's off-screen political activism makes her, for some,

a radical of a distinctly unpleasant if not dangerous stripe. She frequently provides voiceover work for documentaries covering matters of equality and social justice, and has also sought far broader attention for certain issues. In 1993, she and Robbins briefly hijacked the Oscars ceremony to draw attention to the plight of Haitian refugees interned at Guantanamo Bay. Hate mail followed, as well as a two-year ban from the event; the refugees, meanwhile, were released. Both actors were also vocal in their opposition to the Iraq war. The nihilistic satire *Team America: World Police* (2004) caricatured them — along with Sarandon's *Dead Man Walking* costar Sean Penn, and a clutch of other Hollywood liberals — as humorless, vapid do-gooders with an anti-American agenda. Whether or not you align with her specific causes, the charge of lacking wit is one easily disproved. Sarandon's lively gift for comedy has been showcased not only on the big screen, but in a number of fun television guest spots. As to lacking patriotism? "I love America," she countered in a 2006 interview with *The Independent*. "I can't think of anywhere else that I'd want to be. My feeling is I'm going to stick around until they throw me out." **HM**

S

■ Comedy ■ Mystery ■ Sci-Fi

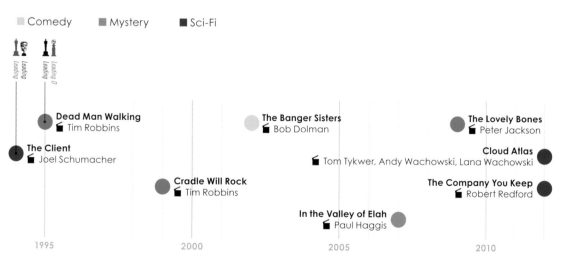

Dead Man Walking — Tim Robbins
The Client — Joel Schumacher
Cradle Will Rock — Tim Robbins
The Banger Sisters — Bob Dolman
In the Valley of Elah — Paul Haggis
The Lovely Bones — Peter Jackson
Cloud Atlas — Tom Tykwer, Andy Wachowski, Lana Wachowski
The Company You Keep — Robert Redford

1995   2000   2005   2010

roy scheider 1932–2008

| The French Connection | Jaws | Marathon Man | All That Jazz | Last Embrace | 2010 | Naked Lunch | The Myth of Fingerprints |

Roy Scheider was born in New Jersey in 1932. At college, he traded boxing gloves for the stage and made his way into film shortly after, taking a role in the low-rent horror movie *The Curse of the Living Corpse* (1964).

Scheider might have remained a character actor had Hollywood not undergone a radical transformation in the late 1960s. He is a straight guy in *Puzzle of a Downfall Child* (1970) and an upmarket pimp in *Klute* (1971). His breakthrough came playing Russo, Gene Hackman's more sensible partner in *The French Connection* (1971). He is perfect as the solid, by the book cop, although that persona is given more of an edge in *The Seven-Ups* (1973), Scheider's first leading role.

Fame arrived with *Jaws* (1975). The actor excels as the water-averse police chief of a coastal resort who is forced to battle a great white shark. Scheider balances the role of bemused cop, concerned parent and action hero with ease, but the film comes into its own when he is teamed with Richard Dreyfuss' earnest oceanographer and Robert Shaw's salty sea dog. A sequel followed and Scheider is the best thing in it, but Spielberg's magic was noticeably absent.

He is effective as Dustin Hoffman's cynical older brother in *Marathon Man* (1976), playing a spy who falls foul of Laurence Olivier's Nazi, but is better as an increasingly paranoid government agent in Jonathan Demme's Hitchcock-esque *Last Embrace* (1979). He would return to similar territory with 1982's *Still of the Night*, playing a psychiatrist who suspects that Meryl Streep's character might be a psychopathic killer.

Scheider took on his finest role, as Bob Fosse's on-screen alter ego Joe Gideon, in *All That Jazz* (1979). In a stunning performance, he plays Gideon as a selfish narcissist whose passion is the stage, no matter how many women he professes to love. Scheider is in every scene and invests himself fully in the role.

The 1980s began to see him feature in less interesting roles. *Blue Thunder* (1983) is a fun action film and *2010* (1984) an enjoyable but pedestrian sequel to Stanley Kubrick's masterpiece *2001: A Space Odyssey* (1968). *52 Pick-Up* (1986) was a better-than-average Elmore Leonard adaptation and he is excellent as the maniacal Dr. Benway in David Cronenberg's adaptation of William Burroughs' *Naked Lunch* (1991). His remaining films were mostly unworthy of his talent. Only *The Myth of Fingerprints* (1997) stands out, with Scheider on blistering form as the caustic head of a family that has gathered for Thanksgiving. **IHS**

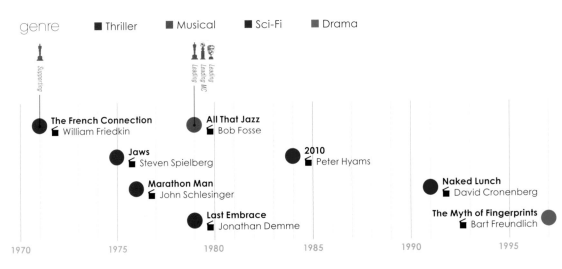

genre ■ Thriller ■ Musical ■ Sci-Fi ■ Drama

Supporting

Leading
Leading MC
Leading

The French Connection
William Friedkin

All That Jazz
Bob Fosse

Jaws
Steven Spielberg

2010
Peter Hyams

Marathon Man
John Schlesinger

Naked Lunch
David Cronenberg

Last Embrace
Jonathan Demme

The Myth of Fingerprints
Bart Freundlich

1970　　　　1975　　　　1980　　　　1985　　　　1990　　　　1995

romy schneider 1938–82

Sissi

Purple Noon

What's New Pussycat

La Piscine

The Things of Life

Ludwig

That Most Important Thing: Love

Death Watch

The memory of Romy Schneider, one of the most famous actresses from the German-speaking world, carries with it an air of melancholy. Certainly, her personal life was full of tragedy and then there was her untimely death. But to watch her films — the ones she will be remembered for — is to witness high drama.

She was born Rosemarie Albach in Vienna, in 1938. Although both of her parents were actors, her mother Magda Schneider was the more famous, counting Adolf Hitler as a fan. Romy came to fame in the 1950s, with the hugely popular *Sissi* trilogy (1955–57), in which she played the title role of a 19th-century Bavarian princess who went on to become Empress of Austria. For a while, she found it difficult to be taken seriously as an actress due to the flowery nature of the character. Nonetheless, she would return to the role in 1972, for Luchino Visconti's *Ludwig*, which charted the life and death of King Ludwig II of Bavaria.

She met Alain Delon on the set of the romantic period drama *Christine* (1958). She moved to Paris to live with him and they worked together on stage and in a number of films, most memorably in René Clément's Patricia Highsmith adaptation, *Purple Noon* (1960). They appeared in one final film following the end of their relationship — Jacques Deray's *La Piscine* (1969), which profited greatly from her presence. During this period she also made her Hollywood debut, *Good Neighbor Sam* (1964), opposite Jack

Lemmon, and appeared with Peter Sellers and Woody Allen in *What's New Pussycat* (1965).

The 1970s saw Schneider come into her own. In addition to *Ludwig*, she appeared opposite Michel Piccoli in Claude Sautet's romantic drama *The Things of Life* (1970). She and the director would reunite for another four features, including the noirish thriller *Max and the Junkmen* (1971) and *César and Rosalie* (1972).

Two outstanding performances would win Schneider Best Actress Césars: Andrzej Zulawski's *That Most Important Thing: Love* (1975), a disturbing film that featured her as a porn actress attempting to go legit by staging a production of Shakespeare's *Richard III*; and her final collaboration with Sautet, *A Simple Story* (1978). She excelled in Claude Chabrol's *Innocents with Dirty Hands* (1975) and was moving as the dying woman in Bertrand Tavernier's *Death Watch* (1980).

Her life spiraled out of control in the 1980s. Shortly after a messy divorce, her son David was killed in an accident. She turned to drink. In her last film, Jacques Rouffio's *The Passerby* (1982), she portrayed a mother whose son dies. The film, dedicated to David, had just been released when she died of a heart attack at her Paris home. Rumors of a suicide were quashed by her family and friends, who explained that her heart had been weakened by a recent kidney operation. In 2008, she was posthumously honored with a César, presented by her former partner Alain Delon. **AG**

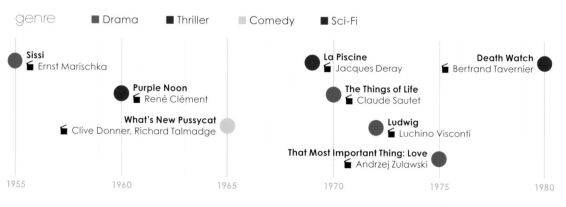

genre   ■ Drama   ■ Thriller   ■ Comedy   ■ Sci-Fi

Sissi
Ernst Marischka

Purple Noon
René Clément

What's New Pussycat
Clive Donner, Richard Talmadge

La Piscine
Jacques Deray

The Things of Life
Claude Sautet

Ludwig
Luchino Visconti

That Most Important Thing: Love
Andrzej Zulawski

Death Watch
Bertrand Tavernier

1955   1960   1965   1970   1975   1980

sci-fi and the stars

Brigitte Helm   Claude Rains   Spencer Tracy   Michael Rennie   Leslie Nielsen   Eddie Constantine   Jane Fonda   Charlton Heston

Back in cinema's early days, the only stars on view in science-fiction films were those twinkling in the heavens. Even though sci-fi dates back to the very first movies — images from George Méliès' *A Trip to the Moon* (1902) are still recognized today — Hollywood stars did not sully themselves with so lowbrow a genre. The very idea of, say, Greta Garbo or Clark Gable onboard a spaceship or fighting aliens was simply inconceivable. To find an actor whose breakthrough came in sci-fi, one must look to Germany and Fritz Lang's groundbreaking *Metropolis* (1927). Brigitte Helm, who played both its heroine and the film's robot antagonist, founded a — short-lived, admittedly — screen career from her iconic work here.

While another disreputable genre, horror, created its own stars (Bela Lugosi, Boris Karloff, Lon Chaney, Jr.) sci-fi still languished. Olympic gold medalist Buster Crabbe did well on serials *Flash Gordon* and *Buck Rogers*; but in features, other than Britain's Claude Rains, who went on to a stellar career after starring in H.G. Wells' *The Invisible Man* (1933), possibly the only major actor who featured in the genre was Spencer Tracy, playing the title roles in *Dr. Jekyll and Mr. Hyde* (1941). This too, like the Wells adaptation, had the literary prestige of its author Robert Louis Stevenson to bolster its credentials.

The next explosion of sci-fi movies came in the 1950s, the post-atomic age, with interest in nascent technology and space travel at a new peak. Several sci-fi classics from this era endure — *The Day the Earth Stood Still* (1951), *The War of the Worlds* (1953), *Forbidden Planet* (1956) — although, the decade's A-list stars are conspicuously absent from these so-called B-movies. *Forbidden Planet* allowed actors like Leslie Nielsen a certain cult status, although television was the more likely career option, especially when shows like *Star Trek* (1966–69) helped push sci-fi further into the mainstream in the 1960s.

Outside of Hollywood, *Alphaville* (1965) is a film noir-inspired dystopia, in which Jean-Luc Godard used the popular Eddie Constantine alongside his regular muse Anna Karina. Slowly, bigger names moved into the genre. After her Oscar-winning *Cat Ballou* (1965) Jane Fonda took on camp classic *Barbarella* (1968). In fact, 1968 was a key milestone in sci-fi cinema. Stanley Kubrick's cerebral *2001: A Space Odyssey* is still the genre's masterpiece, although Kubrick no doubt deliberately chose "faceless" actors Gary Lockwood and Keir Dullea to highlight mankind's necessary evolution; but in box-office terms, the real breakthrough was *Planet of the Apes* (1968), with its heavyweight star Charlton Heston. Sci-fi

type ◼ Robot ◼ Scientist ◼ Alien ◼ Astronaut ◼ Dystopia

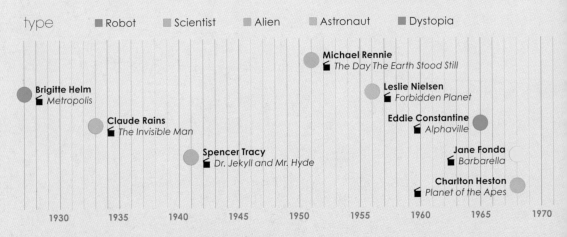

Michael Rennie
The Day The Earth Stood Still

Brigitte Helm
Metropolis

Leslie Nielsen
Forbidden Planet

Claude Rains
The Invisible Man

Eddie Constantine
Alphaville

Spencer Tracy
Dr. Jekyll and Mr. Hyde

Jane Fonda
Barbarella

Charlton Heston
Planet of the Apes

1930   1935   1940   1945   1950   1955   1960   1965   1970

Yul Brynner | Sean Connery | Richard Dreyfuss | Harrison Ford | Arnold Schwarze-negger | Sigourney Weaver | Tom Cruise | Jennifer Lawrence

cinema started to flourish, with films like *Silent Running* (1972) and *Westworld* (1973) — in which Yul Brynner deconstructed his heroic *Magnificent Seven* image as a killer cowboy robot — tackling serious themes with bigger-name actors. Heston did more than most to aid this renaissance, with two more sci-fi hits, *The Omega Man* (1971), based on Richard Matheson's classic novel *I Am Legend*, and *Soylent Green* (1973).

However, not every big star carried off the transition. John Boorman's *Zardoz* (1974), featuring its star Sean Connery kitted out in what resembles a mankini/nappy combination, hardly helped him move on from 007. In fact, many of the great 1970s actors — Pacino, De Niro, Burstyn, Dunaway — had far too much of a naturalistic, contemporary edge to seem at home in any world other than this one.

Then, in 1977, another watershed: George Lucas' *Star Wars* phenomenon, an old-fashioned cliffhanger in shiny new trappings, consolidated by Steven Spielberg's *Close Encounters of the Third Kind*. The cast of *Star Wars* was largely unknown; *Close Encounters*' Richard Dreyfuss was a rising star (winning the Oscar for the same year's *The Goodbye Girl*). But regardless, the enormous financial success meant that no studio — or actor — could afford to dismiss the genre any longer.

Harrison Ford, *Star Wars*' breakout star, bolstered his success with *Blade Runner* (1982), a much bleaker sci-fi that initially flopped but is now seen as a masterpiece. Austrian bodybuilder Arnold Schwarzenegger seemed a ludicrous Hollywood proposition. Being cast as an indestructible cyborg in *The Terminator* (1984) launched his ascent to superstardom. Great roles for women were — and still are — scandalously scarce. It's science fiction, in *Terminator*'s Sarah Connor (Linda Hamilton) and, especially, the *Alien* series' Ellen Ripley (Sigourney Weaver), that provided the female screen icons so desperately needed. The outstanding *Aliens* (1986) is effectively about two mothers battling to the death to preserve their offspring.

Today's biggest names routinely attempt sci-fi: Brad Pitt and Bruce Willis in *Twelve Monkeys* (1995), George Clooney in *Solaris* (2002), Leonardo DiCaprio in *Inception* (2010), although none as successfully as Tom Cruise, who seemed completely at home in the futuristic Spielberg collaborations *Minority Report* (2002) and *War of the Worlds* (2005). For contemporary stars, the choice is clear: find an action, superhero or sci-fi franchise. Jennifer Lawrence was lucky enough to combine all three with her blockbuster series *The Hunger Games* (2012). For a star-driven sci-fi cinema, the future is now. **LS**

Space traveler　■ Alien encounter　■ Future world

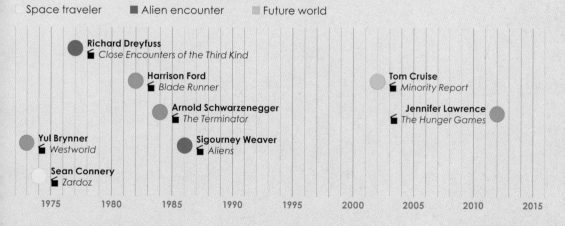

Richard Dreyfuss
Close Encounters of the Third Kind

Harrison Ford
Blade Runner

Tom Cruise
Minority Report

Arnold Schwarzenegger
The Terminator

Jennifer Lawrence
The Hunger Games

Yul Brynner
Westworld

Sigourney Weaver
Aliens

Sean Connery
Zardoz

1975　1980　1985　1990　1995　2000　2005　2010　2015

arnold schwarzenegger 1947

Stay Hungry

Conan the Barbarian

The Terminator

Predator

Total Recall

Terminator 2: Judgment Day

True Lies

Escape Plan

A pumped-up, oversized action star of almost super-human proportions, Arnold Schwarzenegger was always destined to play a mythical hero like Conan the Barbarian. What is perhaps most surprising about his career is its longevity. A smart businessman, the actor and occasional politician has always confounded expectations.

Born in Austria, 1947, Schwarzenegger used his success on the bodybuilding circuit to move to the United States and break into movies. His first role was in the abysmal *Hercules in New York* (1969). He played a henchman in Robert Altman's *The Long Goodbye* (1973), before the documentary *Pumping Iron* (1977) made the athlete a celebrity. However, the year before he impressed with a role in *Stay Hungry* (1976), performing bluegrass songs with a violin. It won him a Best Newcomer Golden Globe.

John Milius' *Conan the Barbarian* (1982) gave Schwarzenegger his breakthrough role but James Cameron understood the actor's strengths and weaknesses better and made him a star as *The Terminator* (1984). He is perfect as the seemingly indestructible humanoid. So much so that he returned for a sequel, this time as the good guy, in 1991's

Terminator 2: Judgment Day. He was back again for further sequels in 2003 and 2015.

The winning formula of brawn and one-liners became his staple in action films such as *Commando* (1985), *Predator* (1987), *The Running Man* (1987) and the superior *Total Recall* (1990). He attempted a postmodern take on the genre with the ambitious but flawed *Last Action Hero* (1993) and was reunited with James Cameron for a third time on *True Lies* (1994).

He also tried his hand at comedy. *Twins* (1988) and *Junior* (1994) are throwaway fun, the latter seeing him nominated for a Golden Globe. *Kindergarten Cop* (1990) is too violent, *Jingle All the Way* (1996) is too silly and his Mr. Freeze, like everything else in Joel Schumacher's *Batman & Robin* (1997), is embarrassing.

Then came politics. He won the vote for Governor of California and took a hiatus from film. When his term in office ended, he returned as one of the ageing action stars in *The Expendables* (2010) and its two sequels. *The Last Stand* (2013) and *Escape Plan* (2013) are entertaining throwbacks to his 1980s movies, while *Maggie* (2015) finds the star in one of his most dramatic roles as a father racing against time to find a cure for his daughter before she turns into a zombie. **IHS**

genre   ■ Drama   ■ Fantasy   ■ Sci-Fi   ■ Action   ■ Thriller

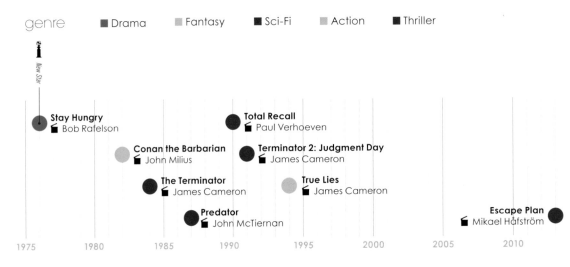

New Star

Stay Hungry
Bob Rafelson

Total Recall
Paul Verhoeven

Conan the Barbarian
John Milius

Terminator 2: Judgment Day
James Cameron

The Terminator
James Cameron

True Lies
James Cameron

Predator
John McTiernan

Escape Plan
Mikael Håfström

1975   1980   1985   1990   1995   2000   2005   2010

kristin scott thomas 1960

| Bitter Moon | Four Weddings and a Funeral | The English Patient | The Horse Whisperer | I've Loved You So Long | Nowhere Boy | Leaving | Only God Forgives |

With award nominations for performances in English and French, aloof beauty Kristin Scott Thomas has pursued a fascinating double career, in the process defying the adage that leading actresses struggle to maintain their careers as they enter middle age.

Born in Cornwall, she trained at drama school in London before dropping out to work as an au pair in Paris. She completed her studies in the French capital, and was cast as a spoiled heiress in rock star Prince's vanity project *Under the Cherry Moon* (1986). An inauspicious start, things rapidly improved.

The Evelyn Waugh adaptation *A Handful of Dust* (1988) won her plaudits and a double pairing with Hugh Grant, in sexual psychodrama *Bitter Moon* (1992) and the comedy smash hit *Four Weddings and a Funeral* (1994), showcased her ability to add depth to characters who might have come across as buttoned-up caricatures on the page. The Fascist Britain update of *Richard III* (1995) cast her as the target of Ian McKellen's predatory dictator, and she was dramatically killed off at the start of *Mission: Impossible* (1996). In *The English Patient* (1996), she is moving as a woman who betrays her husband for Ralph Fiennes' Hungarian adventurer, with fatal consequences.

That film was her ticket to Hollywood: she was the distraught mother who hires Robert Redford's *The Horse Whisperer* (1998), the U.S. politician who finds herself drawn to Harrison Ford's police officer after the deaths of their adulterous spouses in *Random Hearts* (1999) and the hostess of the gathering in *Gosford Park* (2001). On a smaller British scale, she was the frustrated wife of Rowan Atkinson's vicar in *Keeping Mum* (2005) and a snobbish mother-in-law in *Easy Virtue* (2008). In *Nowhere Boy* (2009) she was John Lennon's aunt, while her foul-mouthed gangster in *Only God Forgives* (2013) offered an exhilarating if controversial image overhaul.

From the late 1980s, she also pursued a prolific parallel career in France. *Autobus* (1991), in which the schoolbus she is in charge of is hijacked, was the first to gain international exposure. In *I've Loved You So Long* (2008), she returns to her family after a 15-year prison sentence, for reasons only gradually drip-fed to the audience. It won her the European Film Award for Best Actress. In *Leaving* (2009), she sacrifices her comfortable middle-class lifestyle for an affair with a Spanish builder, while in the Paris-set thriller *The Woman in the Fifth* (2011), her mysterious Hungarian émigrée is the only character who never speaks French. **MBr**

S

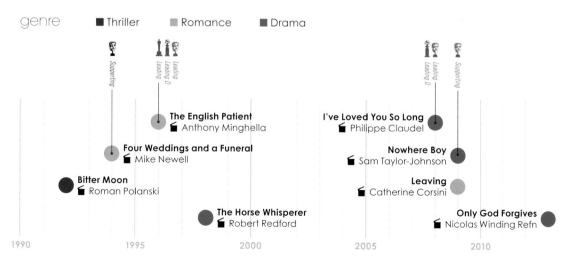

genre ■ Thriller ▨ Romance ■ Drama

Supporting

Leading *D Leading* *Leading*

D Leading *Leading* *Supporting*

The English Patient
🎬 Anthony Minghella

Four Weddings and a Funeral
🎬 Mike Newell

Bitter Moon
🎬 Roman Polanski

The Horse Whisperer
🎬 Robert Redford

I've Loved You So Long
🎬 Philippe Claudel

Nowhere Boy
🎬 Sam Taylor-Johnson

Leaving
🎬 Catherine Corsini

Only God Forgives
🎬 Nicolas Winding Refn

1990   1995   2000   2005   2010

jean seberg 1938–79

| Saint Joan | Bonjour Tristesse | The Mouse That Roared | Breathless | Lilith | Line of Demarcation | Paint Your Wagon | Airport |

Best known for her iconic role in one of French cinema's most influential films, American actress Jean Seberg gave a number of strong performances over the course of a regrettably brief career. Born in Marshalltown, Iowa, in 1938, she won a worldwide talent search run by Otto Preminger to star as Joan of Arc in *Saint Joan* (1957). The inexperienced Seberg was just 17 at the time. She received overwhelmingly negative reviews for her performance, but Preminger cast her again in his adaptation of Françoise Sagan's *Bonjour Tristesse* (1958). Again, she attracted heavy criticism, but the film has dated well and Seberg gives a compelling performance. The following year she was one of the few characters not played by Peter Sellers in *The Mouse That Roared* (1959).

After making *Bonjour Tristesse*, Seberg moved to France, where she appeared opposite Jean-Paul Belmondo in Jean-Luc Godard's sensational *Breathless* (1960). One of the earliest films of the French New Wave, it is regarded as a landmark for its challenge to the conventions of cinematic language. As an American exchange student and aspiring journalist, Seberg is capricious, teasing, uninhibited, glamorous, and almost impossibly youthful.

Over the next few years Seberg worked primarily in France, appearing in *Love Play* (1961), *Infidelity* (1961) and *Backfire* (1964), once again starring opposite Belmondo. She returned to America for *Lilith* (1964), playing a schizophrenic patient in a psychiatric institute and the object of obsession for Warren Beatty's trainee therapist. The role ranks among her best, but the film was a commercial failure. For the rest of the decade she split her energies between France and America: her French movies included Claude Chabrol's *Line of Demarcation* (1966) and *Who's Got the Black Box* (1967), while her American efforts included Mervyn LeRoy's *Moment to Moment* (1965), *A Fine Madness* (1966) and two of her biggest hits, the western musical *Paint Your Wagon* (1969) and ensemble disaster movie *Airport* (1970).

In reaction to her support of the Black Panthers, the FBI was successful in ensuring Hollywood blacklisted Seberg. She continued to act in European films of variable quality, including *Dead of Summer* (1970), *Plot* (1972), *The Big Delirium* (1975) and *The Wild Duck* (1976). However, after a decade of harassment from the U.S. government and a turbulent personal life, Seberg committed suicide in 1979, aged 40. **JWa**

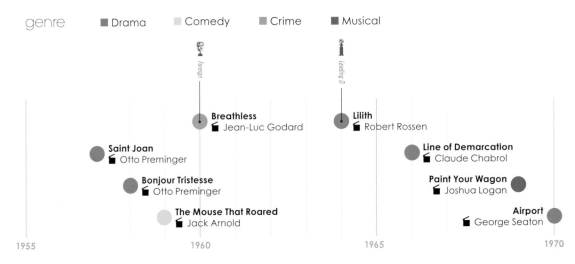

genre ■ Drama ■ Comedy ■ Crime ■ Musical

peter sellers 1925–80

The
Ladykillers

I'm All
Right Jack

Lolita

The Pink
Panther

Dr.
Strangelove

After the Fox

The Party

Being There

Peter Sellers' first major film role was as one of the criminals in the Ealing comedy classic *The Ladykillers* (1955). By that time he was a veteran of radio and television, and had appeared in five films, including the Goons vehicle *Down Among the Z Men* (1952).

He was born Richard Henry Sellers in 1925 and from an early age displayed a gift for comedy. His film work ranges from broad slapstick to subtle character studies. His next key film after *The Ladykillers*, *The Mouse That Roared* (1959), saw him play three roles. It was not the first time he took on a number of roles in one film; in *Let's Go Crazy* (1951), Sellers and Spike Milligan both played several characters. Also in 1959, Sellers turned in an excellent performance as a trade union shop steward in *I'm All Right Jack*, which is one of the first displays of his ability as an actor. He is equally impressive as a meek accountant in *The Battle of the Sexes* (1960), a convincing con in the British caper movie *Two Way Stretch* (1960) and gives one of his most understated performances as a philandering Welsh librarian in *Only Two Can Play* (1962).

Sellers' Claire Quilty is the perfect foil to James Mason's Humbert Humbert in Stanley Kubrick's *Lolita* (1962). The director identified a malevolence in the

actor's screen persona and mines it brilliantly. Sellers would work with Kubrick again on *Dr. Strangelove or: How I Learned to Stop Worrying and Love the Bomb* (1964). He played three roles: an increasingly desperate President of the United States, the deeply disturbed Dr. Strangelove and, perhaps his best performance in the film, a terribly polite British officer attempting to disarm a U.S. General who has gone mad.

With *The Pink Panther* (1963), the hilarious *A Shot in the Dark* (1964) and three sequels that followed over the next 14 years, Sellers' bumbling French police inspector Jacques Clouseau became his most memorable character. However, it also became an albatross. The roles that made Sellers such an exciting presence early in his career became less frequent. He is funny as the conman turned director in *After the Fox* (1966) and there are inspired moments in *The Party* (1968). But the anarchy of *The Wrong Arm of the Law* (1963) or charm of *Heavens Above!* (1963) is absent from most of his films from the late 1960s and 1970s. He did return to form toward the end of his life, giving one of his most affecting performances as a man mistaken for a genius in *Being There* (1979). It highlighted what a unique screen presence Sellers could be. **IHS**

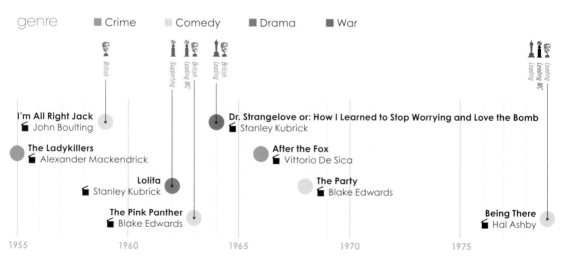

genre   ■ Crime   ■ Comedy   ■ Drama   ■ War

I'm All Right Jack
John Boulting — *British*

The Ladykillers
Alexander Mackendrick

Lolita
Stanley Kubrick — *Supporting*

The Pink Panther
Blake Edwards

Dr. Strangelove or: How I Learned to Stop Worrying and Love the Bomb
Stanley Kubrick — *British Leading MC / British Leading*

After the Fox
Vittorio De Sica

The Party
Blake Edwards

Being There
Hal Ashby — *Leading / Leading MC / Leading*

1955   1960   1965   1970   1975

Character Actor	Charmer	Sinner

toni servillo 1959

One Man Up	The Conse-quences of Love	The Girl by the Lake	Gomorrah	Il Divo	A Quiet Life	Gorbaciof	The Great Beauty

Born in 1959 in Afragola, Italy, Toni Servillo spent over a decade performing and directing for the stage prior to founding the Teatri Uniti in 1987. Across the course of an impressive theater career, he has become one of Italy's most respected actors. And in expanding his repertoire to cinema he has gained considerable international recognition. Often likened to a middle-aged Marcello Mastroianni, Servillo's film career has benefited greatly from his formidable partnership with director Paolo Sorrentino, winning David de Donatello Awards for his turns in each of their four films together.

It was almost a decade after his first big-screen outing in *Death of a Neapolitan Mathematician* (1992) before Sorrentino's feature debut provided Servillo with his first notable role. In *One Man Up* (2001), Servillo plays washed-up nightclub singer Tony Pisapia. It is a commendable performance in an otherwise uneven drama. However, their sophomore collaboration, *The Consequences of Love* (2004), gave the actor an impressive platform from which to reveal his skills. As a former stockbroker cow-towed into serving the Mafia, Titta di Girolamo finds himself incarcerated in a Swiss hotel with little to do each month but carry out his money laundering assignations, observe the hotel's other residents and alleviate his boredom with heroin. Servillo transforms the impassive Giralomo into an enigmatic character, inflecting the hollowness of this sharply elegant man with subtle nuances.

Servillo brought a similar degree of depth to the character of Commissario Sanzio in Andrea Molaioli's otherwise unremarkable *The Girl by the Lake* (2007). However, leading roles in two far more successful and widely exported ventures followed. Matteo Garrone's realist gangster drama *Gomorrah* (2008) was a major critical success and featured Servillo in one of its many narrative strands as a noxious businessman dealing with the illegal dumping of poisonous waste. In the same year, Servillo played former Italian Prime Minister Giulio Andreotti in Sorrentino's *Il Divo* (2008). While Andreotti himself dismissed the representation, the general consensus was adulatory and Servillo's international profile rose significantly.

Despite the weaknesses of Stefano Incerti's drama, Servillo's performance at the heart of *Gorbaciof* (2010) was strong enough to gain the film plaudits, once again showing the actor's innate skill in enabling audiences to engage with emotionally isolated men. Another riveting turn dominated Claudio Cupellini's *A Quiet Life* (2010), with Servillo playing a mobster living in exile. Back in Rome was Jep Gambardella, the enigmatic character at the center of Sorrentino's Oscar-winning masterpiece *The Great Beauty* (2013). The filmmaker's Fellini-esque critique of modern Italy, it is an ideal fit for the weathered face of Servillo, who perfectly embodies the ennui of the Italian capital's cultural elite. **BN**

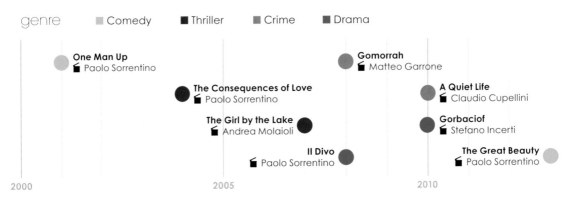

genre ■ Comedy ■ Thriller ■ Crime ■ Drama

One Man Up
🏳 Paolo Sorrentino

The Consequences of Love
🏳 Paolo Sorrentino

The Girl by the Lake
🏳 Andrea Molaioli

Il Divo
🏳 Paolo Sorrentino

Gomorrah
🏳 Matteo Garrone

A Quiet Life
🏳 Claudio Cupellini

Gorbaciof
🏳 Stefano Incerti

The Great Beauty
🏳 Paolo Sorrentino

2000   2005   2010

omar sharif 1932

| Sira` Fi al-Wadi | Lawrence of Arabia | Doctor Zhivago | Genghis Khan | The Night of the Generals | Funny Girl | Che! | Hidalgo |

Born Michel Demitri Shalhoub in Egypt in 1932, the actor who would rise to fame as Omar Sharif began his acting career with a role in the Egyptian romantic drama *Sira` Fi al-Wadi* (1954), appearing opposite Faten Hamama, whom he later married. Over the remainder of the decade Sharif rose to prominence in Egypt, appearing in *No Tomorrow* (1957), *Lady of the Castle* (1959) and *The River of Love* (1961). However it was his first English-language role that saw Sharif attract international recognition, not to mention a Golden Globe and an Academy Award nomination. He played Sherif Ali in David Lean's grandiose *Lawrence of Arabia* (1962). With his dark, handsome looks, expressive eyes and calm demeanor, it is no surprise he became an overnight sensation.

Sharif then appeared in *Behold a Pale Horse* (1964) and *The Fall of the Roman Empire* (1964), before reuniting with Lean for another sweeping drama, this time in titular role of *Doctor Zhivago* (1965). It added immeasurably to his appeal. He continued appearing in historical epics such as *Genghis Khan* (1965) and *The Night of the Generals* (1967), before taking on the lighter role of gambler Nick Arnstein in the romantic musical *Funny Girl* (1968) opposite Barbra Streisand.

True to form, Sharif concluded his most successful decade by taking on another historical legend, appearing as Marxist revolutionary Che Guevara in Richard Fleischer's *Che!* (1969). He was fine in *The Horsemen* (1971) and seduced Julie Andrews in *The Tamarind Seed* (1974), before reuniting with Streisand on *Funny Lady* (1975), the sequel to their hit musical.

As an actor with highly distinctive looks, good roles were not always so easy to find. *Bloodline* (1979), *Top Secret!* (1984) and *The Possessed* (1988) wasted his talent. He fared better in television, with notable appearances in *Peter the Great* (1986) and a star-studded adaptation of *Gulliver's Travels* (1996).

More recently, Sharif returned to bigger scale films. *The 13th Warrior* (1999) and *Hidalgo* (2004) were solid entertainments but failed to attract audiences. His biggest success in recent years, *Monsieur Ibrahim* (2003), also saw him receive a great deal of acclaim for his performance as a Turkish shop owner in 1960s Paris who befriends a Jewish boy in his teens. He received a Best Actor Award at the Venice Film Festival and the Césars. Outside of film, he has racked up countless accolades as one of the world's finest Bridge players. He retired from the game in 2006. **MB**

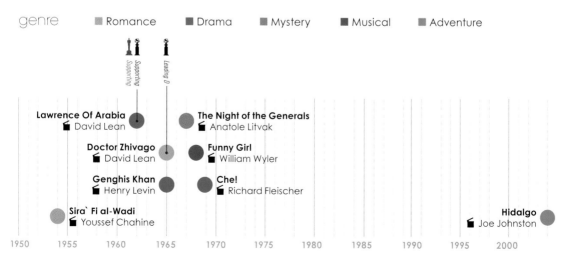

genre   ■ Romance   ■ Drama   ■ Mystery   ■ Musical   ■ Adventure

Supporting / Supporting

Leading D

Lawrence Of Arabia — David Lean

The Night of the Generals — Anatole Litvak

Doctor Zhivago — David Lean

Funny Girl — William Wyler

Genghis Khan — Henry Levin

Che! — Richard Fleischer

Sira` Fi al-Wadi — Youssef Chahine

Hidalgo — Joe Johnston

1950   1955   1960   1965   1970   1975   1980   1985   1990   1995   2000

Crook	Character Actor	Killer	Villain	Sinner

robert shaw 1927–78

From Russia with Love

Battle of the Bulge

A Man for All Seasons

The Birthday Party

The Sting

The Taking of Pelham One Two Three

Jaws

Black Sunday

An actor known for his intensity on stage and screen, as well as an acclaimed novelist, Robert Shaw was born in Lancashire, England, in 1927. After a stint in the Royal Air Force during World War II, he first made a name for himself on stage before his role as Guy Gisbon's co-pilot in *The Dam Busters* (1955).

Shaw was one of six investors to produce a radical adaptation of Harold Pinter's *The Caretaker* (1963), which won a prize at the Berlin Film Festival. He then followed it with his ultra-fit SMERSH operative Donald Grant in *From Russia with Love* (1963). Almost a match for James Bond, Shaw is one of the franchise's best villains. However, the actor never seemed interested in a conventional movie star career and was always drawn back to more low-key, character-driven work, such as Irvin Kershner's *The Luck of Ginger Coffey* (1964).

After his excellent German adversary to a U.S. Army unit attempting to destabilize the Nazi's ranks in *Battle of the Bulge* (1965), Shaw scored one of his biggest successes playing Henvy VIII in *A Man for All Seasons* (1966). Detailing the souring relationship between the monarch and Sir Thomas More, Shaw's Henry is by turns playful and bullying. It earned the actor his only Oscar nomination.

In 1968, Shaw returned to Harold Pinter, taking the lead in William Friedkin's *The Birthday Party*. It is one of the best performances of his career, channeling his intensity into a troubled character. He is no less impressive as Francisco Pizarro in *The Royal Hunt of the Sun* (1969) and Lord Randolph Churchill in *Young Winston* (1972), although both films lack focus. He is an excellent foil to Sarah Miles in *The Hireling* (1973) and a slick mob boss in *The Sting* (1973). However, his best films in the last few years of his life were in *The Taking of Pelham One Two Three* (1974) and *Jaws* (1975). In the former he plays Mr. Blue, the mastermind behind the hijacking of a New York Subway train. The film may smack of B-movie clichés, but the cast elevates the material, making it one of the most enjoyable thrillers of the decade. As for his salty sea dog in Steven Spielberg's blockbuster, it is the one role above all others for which Shaw will be remembered. His Quint is a wonderful creation, both amusing and irascible.

Shaw went on to play a ruthless Sheriff of Nottingham in *Robin and Marian* (1976) and brought gravitas to the lead investigator in *Black Sunday* (1977). He died of a heart attack shortly after completing *Avalanche Express* (1979). **IHS**

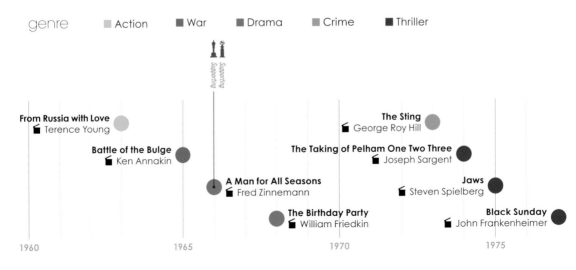

genre ■ Action ■ War ■ Drama ■ Crime ■ Thriller

Supporting / Supporting

From Russia with Love — Terence Young

Battle of the Bulge — Ken Annakin

A Man for All Seasons — Fred Zinnemann

The Birthday Party — William Friedkin

The Sting — George Roy Hill

The Taking of Pelham One Two Three — Joseph Sargent

Jaws — Steven Spielberg

Black Sunday — John Frankenheimer

1960   1965   1970   1975

martin sheen 1940

The Subject Was Roses · Badlands · Apocalypse Now · The Dead Zone · Wall Street · The Departed · Bobby · The Way

Born Ramon Estevez in 1940, to an Irish mother and Hispanic father, Sheen moved to New York in his early twenties to become an actor, changing his name to avoid prejudicial casting. His movie breakthrough came in the adaptation of an early stage success, The Subject Was Roses (1968).

Mostly television work followed, until his boyish looks saw him cast opposite Sissy Spacek as the murderous young lovers-on-the-run in Badlands (1973). Inspired by a real-life killing spree, Terrence Malick's debut feature is a lyrical, savage masterpiece, with Sheen hypnotic as the pseudo-philosophizing, dead-eyed lost boy. The performance is echoed in his portrayal of a stranger who attempts to ingratiate himself with Jodie Foster's young girl living alone in the unsettling The Little Girl Who Lives Down the Lane (1976).

His next major role only came about when Francis Ford Coppola summoned him to replace Harvey Keitel on the Vietnam epic Apocalypse Now (1979). A notoriously out-of-control production, Sheen famously broke down for real when filming the opening scene and later suffered a heart attack. Incredibly he was back filming within a month, providing powerful witness to Coppola's phantasmagoric heart of darkness.

Sheen's own famously outspoken liberal profile perhaps influenced his later work, with noble turns in prestige blockbusters like Gandhi (1982) and contemporary dramas such as Wall Street (1987). Sometimes movies tapped into his darker side — the Stephen King adaptation The Dead Zone (1983) slyly used his political fervor to cast him as a maniacal U.S. President — but such subversion was rare.

Shamefully underrated and underused by major filmmakers, Sheen was consigned to lackluster fare like the horror flick The Believers (1987) and comic-book movie Spawn (1997). Better work came as an advisor to Michael Douglas in The American President (1995), before his award-winning role as President Bartlett on hit television show The West Wing (1999–2006).

Sheen projected paternal authority as the police captain shepherding Leonardo DiCaprio's undercover agent in The Departed (2006). He worked under his son Emilio's direction in Bobby (2006), about Robert Kennedy's assassination, and The Way (2010), about a man undertaking a grueling Spanish pilgrimage to honor his dead son. His aura of kind, moral authority was utilized again as Peter Parker's wise Uncle Ben in superhero reboot The Amazing Spider-Man (2012). LS

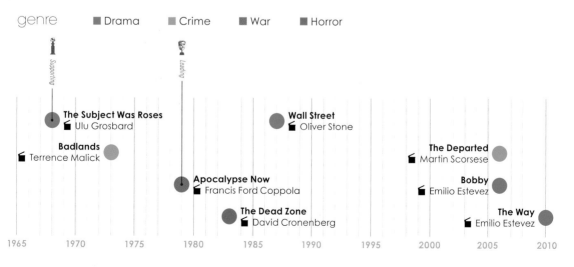

simone signoret 1921–85

La Ronde

Les Diaboliques

Room at the Top

Is Paris Burning?

The Army of Shadows

The Confession

Le Chat

L'Étoile du Nord

Born in 1921, in Wiesbaden, Germany, Simone Signoret was for many years one of the most recognizable faces in French cinema. She had a long film apprenticeship during World War II, mostly as an extra as she was working without an official permit during the Nazi occupation of France, because her father, who had fled to England, was Jewish.

Signoret's first role of major significance came in Max Ophüls' hugely influential *La Ronde* (1950), playing one of the characters involved in a series of amorous encounters in the Vienna of 1900. Henri-Georges Clouzot's *Les Diaboliques* (1955) was another key film in her ascent. One of the greatest postwar French films, it is a potent psychological thriller in which the wife and mistress of a cruel headmaster conspire to kill him, before being driven to the brink of madness when his corpse mysteriously disappears.

Jack Clayton's *Room at the Top* (1959), a faithful adaptation of John Braine's novel, is a cornerstone of the kitchen sink cycle of films that emanated from Britain in the mid- to late-1950s. Laurence Harvey's ambitious young accountant schemes to wed a wealthy factory owner's daughter, played by Heather Sears, despite falling in love with a married older woman. Signoret is outstanding as the object of his affection and earned the Oscar for Best Actress.

Signoret's next two features must have had great personal significance given that they deal with Nazi occupied France. *Is Paris Burning?* (1966) looks at the true story of the occupying forces' departure from Paris in 1944, while *The Army of the Shadows* (1969) is a taut account of underground resistance fighters. If her role in the former was relegated to that of a bar owner, in the latter she is a tragic member of the Resistance, whose capture seals her fate.

Signoret's work remained within the political spectrum for *The Confession* (1970), Costa-Gavras' account of Czechoslovakian Communist Artur London, played by her husband Yves Montand. In *Le Chat* (1971), Signoret plays the wife of Jean Gabin, who develops an intense hatred of the family cat when it replaces her in her husband's affections. The role would win her a Silver Bear at the Berlin Film Festival.

Signoret's final film was *L'Ètoile du Nord* (1982). Based on a novel by Georges Simenon, it is most notable for the interplay between Philippe Noiret and Signoret, who plays an elderly landlady. She won a second César for her performance. **JW**

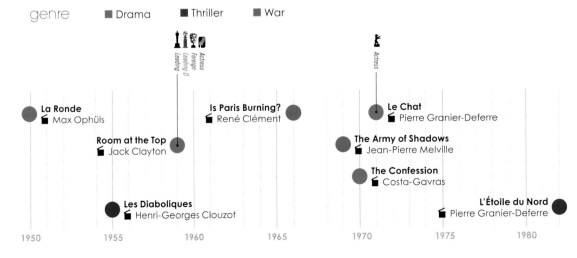

genre   ■ Drama   ■ Thriller   ■ War

La Ronde
Max Ophüls

Room at the Top
Jack Clayton

Les Diaboliques
Henri-Georges Clouzot

Is Paris Burning?
René Clément

Le Chat
Pierre Granier-Deferre

The Army of Shadows
Jean-Pierre Melville

The Confession
Costa-Gavras

L'Étoile du Nord
Pierre Granier-Deferre

1950   1955   1960   1965   1970   1975   1980

simone simon 1910–2005

La Bête
Humaine

The Devil
and Daniel
Webster

Cat People

Madem-
oiselle Fifi

La Ronde

Le Plaisir

The Extra
Day

The Woman
in Blue

Hailing from French city of Béthune, Simone Simon led something of a nomadic life during her formative years, following her parents around Africa and Europe, from Madagascar and Budapest to Marseille via Turin and Berlin. The family eventually settled in Paris, where the artistic Simon originally harbored aspirations to be a fashion designer. However, work as a model and occasional appearances in stage musicals brought her to the attention of Swiss director Marc Allégret, whose patronage resulted in her entry into films during the early 1930s. Years of small — frequently uncredited — roles followed before she was spotted by legendary studio mogul Darryl F. Zanuck, who whisked her to Hollywood in 1935 with the promise of fame and fortune.

Tinseltown had a love affair with Europeans during the 1930s and 1940s, and a cavalcade of actors and actresses from across the pond descended on America's West Coast, imbuing lavish studio productions with an added air of sophistication. Simon should have been a sure-fire success. However, her beguiling looks and exotic accent proved an enigma to many in Hollywood: a limited grasp of the English language and reputation for onset volatility resulted in her dismissal from several productions. Disillusioned, Simon returned to France where she appeared in a number of successful films, the most notable being Jean Renoir's La Bête Humaine (1938).

But Simon had not completely written off a career in Hollywood. With the outbreak of World War II, she returned to America where, after a leading role in the cult fantasy The Devil and Daniel Webster (1941), she featured in the film for which she will be forever remembered: Cat People (1942). The role of mysterious and troubled Serbian immigrant Irena in producer Jacques Tourneur's cult chiller — and its 1944 sequel — was tailor-made for Simon and assured her place in the annals of cinema history. But the success in America was short-lived and, following a final performance in the wartime drama Mademoiselle Fifi (1944), she returned permanently to France.

During her later years Simon's screen appearances decreased. There were roles in several French dramas, including Max Ophüls' La Ronde (1950) and Le Plaisir (1952), as well as the English comedy The Extra Day (1956). However, she never again achieved the success she found in Tourneur's masterpiece. Her final screen appearance was in the French comedy drama The Woman in Blue (1973). With a romantic reputation as exotic as her looks, which included stories of her trysts with World War II Serbian double agent Duško Popov, Simon's private life proved as capricious as her career. She never married, instead living in quiet retirement until her death in Paris in 2005. But she will be remembered for the enigmatic presence she brought to one of the classic Hollywood horror films. **CP**

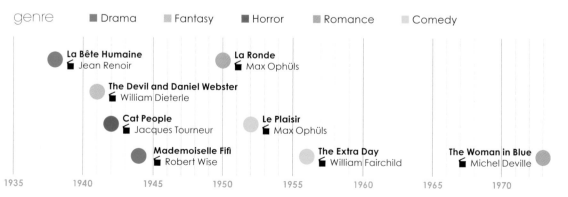

genre ■ Drama ■ Fantasy ■ Horror ■ Romance ■ Comedy

La Bête Humaine
Jean Renoir

La Ronde
Max Ophüls

The Devil and Daniel Webster
William Dieterle

Cat People
Jacques Tourneur

Le Plaisir
Max Ophüls

Mademoiselle Fifi
Robert Wise

The Extra Day
William Fairchild

The Woman in Blue
Michel Deville

1935 1940 1945 1950 1955 1960 1965 1970

frank sinatra 1915–98

| Anchors Aweigh | On the Town | From Here to Eternity | Suddenly | Guys and Dolls | The Man with the Golden Arm | High Society | Pal Joey |

Frank Sinatra was a star before he ever took a lead role in a film. By the early 1940s, he was one of the most popular singers in America. He managed to escape from his contract with bandleader Tommy Dorsey, but not before he appeared, uncredited, with the band in *Las Vegas Nights* (1941) and *Ship Ahoy* (1942).

Sinatra, who was born in Hoboken, New Jersey, in 1915, made his first significant screen appearance opposite Gene Kelly in *Anchors Aweigh* (1945). They play Navy sailors on leave in Hollywood. A knockabout comedy with musical numbers, it began a brief string of films for the pair, which included *Take Me Out to the Ball Game* (1949) and their best collaboration, *On the Town* (1949), which repeated *Anchors'* formula but in Manhattan.

Sinatra's career then stalled. His popularity as a singer was waning and the publicity surrounding his affair with Ava Gardner was destroying his clean image. The record company he was signed to dropped him and it looked like his career was over. Then came his performance as the doomed Maggio in *From Here to Eternity* (1953). It revealed a depth hitherto missing from previous roles and he was rewarded with an Oscar for Best Supporting Actor. At the same time, he signed to Capitol Records and would begin his finest run of recordings.

Suddenly (1954) is a taut thriller about a psychotic killer's plan to assassinate the president. Sinatra is effective in his first role as a villain, wild eyed and continually on the brink of exploding. Otto Preminger made the most of this nervous energy when he cast Sinatra as jazz drummer and heroin addict Frankie Machine in *The Man with the Golden Arm* (1955). It is another surprisingly raw performance from a singer who was better known for his slick stage presence. In the same year, he played Nathan Detroit opposite Marlon Brando's Sky Masterson in *Guys and Dolls* (1955). The two famously disliked each other, with Sinatra resentful that Brando took the role he wanted. Their acting styles were also markedly different, with Sinatra calling Brando "mumbles." Their approach to film was not just in how they played a role. Singing and recording albums was work to Sinatra. He had little time for the mechanics of film and tired after the first take.

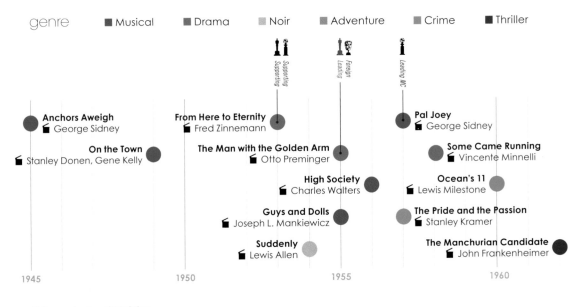

genre ■ Musical ■ Drama ■ Noir ■ Adventure ■ Crime ■ Thriller

Supporting / Supporting

Foreign / Leading

Leading MC

Anchors Aweigh
George Sidney

From Here to Eternity
Fred Zinnemann

Pal Joey
George Sidney

On the Town
Stanley Donen, Gene Kelly

The Man with the Golden Arm
Otto Preminger

Some Came Running
Vincente Minnelli

High Society
Charles Walters

Ocean's 11
Lewis Milestone

Guys and Dolls
Joseph L. Mankiewicz

The Pride and the Passion
Stanley Kramer

Suddenly
Lewis Allen

The Manchurian Candidate
John Frankenheimer

1945   1950   1955   1960

The Pride and the Passion

Some Came Running

Ocean's 11

The Manchurian Candidate

Von Ryan's Express

The Naked Runner

Tony Rome

The First Deadly Sin

High Society (1956) cast Sinatra alongside one of his heroes, Bing Crosby, and the two perform well together, although the film is a pale shadow of *The Philadelphia Story* (1940), which was also adapted from the same Philip Barry play. He is excellent in *Pal Joey* (1957), which features one of his best on-screen performances, singing "The Lady is a Tramp." And he is outstanding as the writer Dave Hirsh, returning to his small hometown and a heap of trouble, in Vincente Minnelli's *Some Came Running* (1958). Between the two was *The Pride and the Passion* (1957), with Sinatra and Cary Grant both looking awkward as a Spanish guerilla and British officer fighting Napoleon's forces.

There was Delmer Davies' *Kings Go Forth* (1958), with Sinatra and Tony Curtis falling in love with the same girl during World War II, and Frank Capra's domestic comedy *A Hole in the Head* (1959). Neither was impressive, with the latter film only memorable for featuring the first performance of "High Hopes."

Ocean's 11 (1960) marked the first of the "Rat Pack" films and was followed by *Sergeants 3* (1962), *4 for Texas* (1963) and *Robin and the 7 Hoods* (1964). None

of the films are especially good, but the concerts that Sinatra, Dean Martin and Sammy Davis Jr. performed while they were in Las Vegas shooting *Ocean's* have become the stuff of legend.

All but one of Sinatra's movies after the Rat Pack films is inconsequential. *Von Ryan's Express* (1965) is an overlong but entertaining World War II yarn, while *Tony Rome* (1967) offers up a leisurely paced detective thriller. Sinatra mustered up some energy for *The First Deadly Sin* (1980), playing a cop desperate to catch a serial killer while coping with his terminally ill wife.

If Sinatra had shown as much commitment to all his roles as he did to Major Bennett Marco, the lead in *The Manchurian Candidate* (1962), his films might be regarded with the same level of esteem as his recordings. He is excellent as the army officer who believes something happened when North Korean forces captured him and his men and that Laurence Harvey's Raymond Shaw has something to do with it. It is a tense conspiracy thriller with Sinatra convincing as a man almost driven insane by his nightmares. This performance alone made the singer a movie star. **IHS**

■ War   ■ Mystery

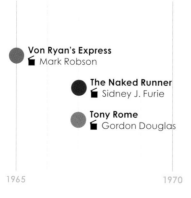

Von Ryan's Express
🎬 Mark Robson

The Naked Runner
🎬 Sidney J. Furie

Tony Rome
🎬 Gordon Douglas

The First Deadly Sin
🎬 Brian G. Hutton

1965   1970   1975   1980

stellan skarsgård 1951

The Simple-Minded Murderer   Breaking the Waves   Good Will Hunting   Timecode   Mamma Mia!   The Girl with the Dragon Tattoo   Thor   Nymphomaniac

One of Sweden's most internationally recognized movie stars, Stellan Skarsgård is a prolific character actor who has appeared in a wide range of films. Closely associated with Lars von Trier, he has featured in six projects created by the provocative director.

Born in Gothenburg, Sweden, in 1951, Skarsgård worked in television as a teenager before making his big screen debut in *Strandhugg I Somras* (1972). Over the next 16 years he mixed stage work with films such as *Taboo* (1977), *The Simple-Minded Murderer* (1982) and *False as Water* (1985). He was first introduced to international audiences with parts in *The Unbearable Lightness of Being* (1988) and *The Hunt for Red October* (1990). His performance in Sven Nykvist's *The Ox* (1991) also received significant recognition.

Skarsgård's breakthrough performance came in von Trier's *Breaking the Waves* (1996), impressing as Emily Watson's paralyzed husband. He subsequently appeared in *Dancer in the Dark* (2000), *Dogville* (2003) and *Melancholia* (2011) for the director. Following the success of *Breaking the Waves*, he worked increasingly in America, although the Norwegian thriller *Insomnia* (1997) provided one of his best roles. He appeared in Steven Spielberg's *Amistad* (1997),

was truculent as a lecturer in *Good Will Hunting* (1997), and was part of *Ronin* (1998) and *Timecode*'s (2000) impressive ensemble casts.

Most of the characters Skarsgård has played since his transition to America have been supporting ones, playing Bootstrap Bill in two *Pirates of the Caribbean* films, *Dead Man's Chest* (2006) and *At World's End* (2007), and a Swiss commander in *Angels & Demons* (2009). The most notable role of his big-budget work is astrophysicist Dr. Erik Selvig, a recurring character in the Marvel universe, from *Thor* (2011) and its 2013 sequel to the hugely popular *The Avengers* (2012).

While all these films have been commercial hits, the roles have demanded little from Skarsgård. Welcome respite from blockbusters have included an amusing turn in the ABBA musical *Mamma Mia!* (2008), the riveting portrayal of brutal warden at a youth prison in *King of Devil's Island* (2010), and a key role as the ruling member of a fractious family in *The Girl with the Dragon Tattoo* (2011). His finest performance in recent years found him mostly confined to one room, in von Trier's punishing two-volume *Nymphomaniac* (2013), playing an overeducated yet naive man with a fondness for pedantry. **JWa**

genre   ■ Drama   ■ Romance   ■ Musical   ■ Mystery   ■ Action

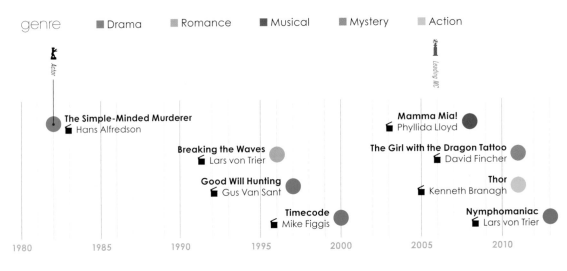

Actor

Leading MC

The Simple-Minded Murderer
Hans Alfredson

Breaking the Waves
Lars von Trier

Good Will Hunting
Gus Van Sant

Timecode
Mike Figgis

Mamma Mia!
Phyllida Lloyd

The Girl with the Dragon Tattoo
David Fincher

Thor
Kenneth Branagh

Nymphomaniac
Lars von Trier

1980   1985   1990   1995   2000   2005   2010

maggie smith 1934

| Nowhere to Go | The Pumpkin Eater | Othello | The Prime of Miss Jean Brodie | Travels with My Aunt | A Room with a View | The Lonely Passion of Judith Hearne | Gosford Park |

Now in her eighties, Maggie Smith shows no sign of slowing down. With a stage career dating back over 60 years and 50-odd films behind her, she triumphed on television as the Dowager Countess of Grantham in *Downton Abbey* (2010–15). Awards have been showered on her, including Oscars, Emmys, BAFTAs, Golden Globes, a CBE and a Damehood.

Smith's film career was relatively slow to take off. She was striking as the society girl caught up in crime in *Nowhere to Go* (1958), but the film, made in the dying days of Ealing, attracted little notice. Smith was nominated for an Oscar for her Desdemona in Laurence Olivier's *Othello* (1965), but that was little more than a filmed record of the stage production.

True screen-acting recognition came with the title role in *The Prime of Miss Jean Brodie* (1969), in which Smith played the fascist-loving, pre-war Edinburgh schoolmistress and won a Best Actress Oscar. Her exchanges with Celia Johnson's disapproving headmistress were a model of acid-tinged comedy. Comedy with an edge has always suited her: she was Anne Bancroft's treacherous friend in *The Pumpkin Eater* (1964), the music-hall singer luring gullible youngsters to enlist in *Oh! What a Lovely War* (1969)

and the social-climbing wife of Michael Palin's chiropodist in *A Private Function* (1984).

By way of contrast, Smith was heartbreaking in the title role of *The Lonely Passion of Judith Hearne* (1987): a middle-aged spinster, grasping at one last doomed chance of happiness. She has never scrupled to play her age; at 38 she had already played nearly twice her age in the disappointing Graham Greene adaptation, *Travels with my Aunt* (1972), as the hero's imperious Aunt Augusta. She was by far the best thing in the film.

Authority figures soon beckoned, and she played them with stern grace. She made a severe Duchess of York in *Richard III* (1995); a reluctantly amused Mother Superior in *Sister Act* (1992) and its 1993 sequel; and in the *Harry Potter* franchise (2001–11) played Professor Minerva McGonagall, a stalwart presence throughout the cycle. Anticipating her *Downton Abbey* role, she portrayed another period aristo in Robert Altman's country-house drama, *Gosford Park* (2001).

In a recent release, *My Old Lady* (2014), her character, a 92-year-old Frenchwoman, utters a line that evokes the sharpness and savor of Maggie Smith's acting at its best: "Precision is the key to a long life. Precision — and wine." **PK**

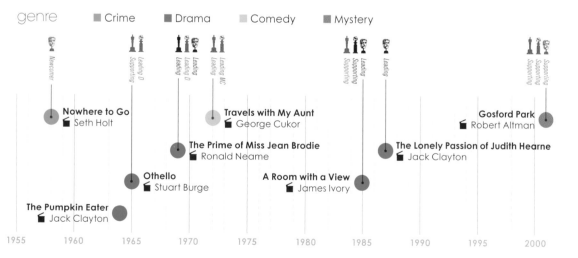

genre ■ Crime ■ Drama ■ Comedy ■ Mystery

Newcomer — Nowhere to Go / Seth Holt

Leading D / Supporting — Othello / Stuart Burge

The Pumpkin Eater / Jack Clayton

Leading MC: Leading D Leading — The Prime of Miss Jean Brodie / Ronald Neame

Leading — Travels with My Aunt / George Cukor

A Room with a View / James Ivory

Leading Supporting Supporting — The Lonely Passion of Judith Hearne / Jack Clayton

Leading

Supporting Supporting Supporting — Gosford Park / Robert Altman

| 1955 | 1960 | 1965 | 1970 | 1975 | 1980 | 1985 | 1990 | 1995 | 2000 |

will smith 1968

| Six Degrees of Separation | Bad Boys | Indepen-dence Day | Men in Black | Ali | The Pursuit of Happyness | I Am Legend | After Earth |

A confident, immensely affable performer with a flair for comedy, Will Smith was already a successful rapper and television personality before launching his screen career. But this early celebrity was soon eclipsed by his phenomenal popularity as a movie star.

Born in 1968, Smith found fame as a teenager as the MC of hip-hop outfit DJ Jazzy Jeff and the Fresh Prince, and he adopted his French Prince persona — wise-cracking, cheeky, street smart — as the fish-out-of-water lead character of the NBC sitcom *The Fresh Prince of Bel Air* (1990–96). The show was a big hit, and led, inevitably, to offers from Hollywood. His first major role was as a young con artist who deceives a wealthy New York couple in *Six Degrees of Separation* (1993), where he impressed alongside established actors like Donald Sutherland and Stockard Channing.

Smith's high-energy, motor-mouth performance as a cop matched the big-impact, over-the-top style of action comedy *Bad Boys* (1995), but it was with his role as an Air Force pilot who helps defeat an invasion of aliens in *Independence Day* (1996) that Smith scored his major breakthrough. He injected humor and a boyish sense of mischief into his character, delivering a true star performance in a film that was otherwise dominated by special effects. It set the tone for his winning performances in the *Men in Black* franchise (1997–2012), where his trademark ebullience was amusingly contrasted with the deadpan delivery of his costar Tommy Lee Jones.

Throughout the 2000s, Smith was a major box-office draw. He might have dampened down his youthful brio, but he was still in commanding form in action-hero roles, notably in *I Am Legend* (2007), which for long stretches features the actor alone. He was less impressive in the recent *After Earth* (2013) — but it would be impossible to write off Smith's box-office clout given his continued run of success.

Besides, he has also proven himself in smaller, more intimate dramas. In *The Pursuit of Happyness* (2006) he was surprisingly subdued — as well as movingly convincing — as a homeless father, a performance that saw him Oscar nominated. He was also nominated for what was arguably his most challenging role: as Muhammad Ali in boxing biopic, *Ali* (2001). It was a magnificent turn, and suggests that Smith could develop into an actor of even more richness once he passes his box-office prime and accepts more diverse projects. **EL**

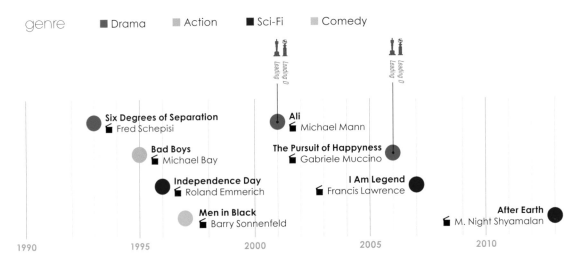

genre ■ Drama ■ Action ■ Sci-Fi ■ Comedy

Leading D Leading

Leading D Leading

Six Degrees of Separation
🎬 Fred Schepisi

Bad Boys
🎬 Michael Bay

Independence Day
🎬 Roland Emmerich

Men in Black
🎬 Barry Sonnenfeld

Ali
🎬 Michael Mann

The Pursuit of Happyness
🎬 Gabriele Muccino

I Am Legend
🎬 Francis Lawrence

After Earth
🎬 M. Night Shyamalan

1990   1995   2000   2005   2010

alberto sordi 1920-2003

I Vitelloni

The Bachelor

Everybody Go Home

A Difficult Life

To Bed or Not to Bed

The Scientific Cardplayer

An Average Little Man

Traffic Jam

A titan of Italian cinema, with an unequaled talent for parodying the worst of the Italian man, Alberto Sordi's career encompassed more than 150 films. Together with actors Marcello Mastroianni and Vittorio Gassman, he was the exemplar of "Italian-style" comedy.

Sordi was born in Rome in 1920. He displayed a precocious inclination to entertain at a young age. After his heavy Roman accent and patois got him fired from a Milanese drama school, he returned to the capital, where he polished his talent in music hall shows and became a dubbing actor.

His popularity began to grow after the war with radio programs, on which he created a number of popular characters. However, he was less lucky in the movies, only being cast in small, insignificant roles. Things changed for him in the early 1950s, when he was offered significant parts in Federico Fellini's *The White Sheik* (1952) and *I Vitelloni* (1953), as well as four films by Steno. In these latter films he embodied lazy and cowardly men, a particular brand of mockery that Mario Monicelli transposed with great success onto the military world in the comedy *The Great War* (1959), for which Sordi won his first Donatello Award. Monicelli later employed the actor's uncanny ability

to embody characters of such pathetic smallness in his masterpiece *An Average Little Man* (1977), a caustic satire of society's acceptance of mediocrity.

Over the years, the actor continued to bring to the screen the changing face of the average Italian, mostly in comedies such as *Everybody Go Home* (1960), Luigi Comencini's depiction of the panic among Italian troops at the end of World War II, or *Be Sick… It's Free!* (1968). Sordi also impressed in more sophisticated comedy dramas, giving his all in *The Scientific Cardplayer* (1972), a blackly humorous take on class warfare. Admired by his peers, both at home and internationally, he was awarded a Golden Globe for *To Bed or Not to Bed* (1963), and a Silver Bear for Best Actor in Berlin for the drama *In Prison Awaiting Trial* (1971).

He also directed 18 films, mostly comedies, in which he also appeared. They include *Smoke Over London* (1966) and *Everybody in Jail* (1984). His final film, which he also directed, was 1998's *Incontri Proibiti*.

The following year, the Donatello Awards presented Sordi with a Career David, marking his retirement from the film industry. When he died in 2003, aged 82, more than a million people gathered on the streets of Rome for his funeral. **AG**

genre   ■ Comedy   ■ Drama

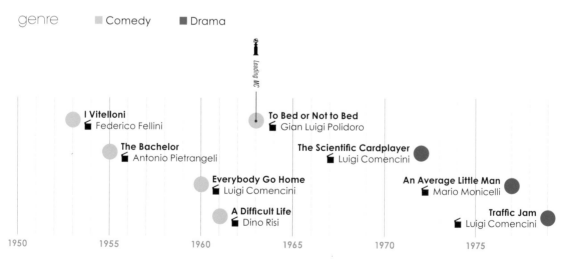

Leading MC

I Vitelloni
Federico Fellini

The Bachelor
Antonio Pietrangeli

Everybody Go Home
Luigi Comencini

A Difficult Life
Dino Risi

To Bed or Not to Bed
Gian Luigi Polidoro

The Scientific Cardplayer
Luigi Comencini

An Average Little Man
Mario Monicelli

Traffic Jam
Luigi Comencini

1950   1955   1960   1965   1970   1975

the movie villain

Gilbert "Broncho Billy" Anderson

Werner Krauss

Colin Clive

James Mason

Gert Frobe

Lee Van Cleef

Ian McDiarmid

Max von Sydow

As long as there have been movies there have been movie villains. In the earliest silents, filmmakers had to create a memorable way to make the villain of the piece easily identifiable without dialogue. *The Great Train Robbery* (1903) introduced a costume motif that became a ready symbol for villains: the black hat. From then on in westerns, the hero wore a white hat and the villain black, and the audience knew where their allegiances lay. In *Once Upon a Time in the West* (1968), pillar of heroism Henry Fonda is transformed into a villain by his dark wardrobe.

A villain is associated with totems or symbols of danger: anyone bearing skull and crossbones is surely the bad guy. The theatricality of early motion pictures carried over clear, morally unambiguous portrayals of antagonists to signpost their actions to the viewer. This resulted in the mustache-twirling, arch camp versions of Long John Silver in various *Treasure Island* adaptations, as well as mad scientists from as early as *The Cabinet of Dr. Caligari* (1920) and *Metropolis* (1927). The most famous is Dr. Frankenstein, portrayed memorably by Colin Clive in the 1931 film and by Peter Cushing over several films, before parody set in.

Villains are a projection of fears, informed by genuine danger, as well as paranoia, in culture. When presented on screen, they return the audience's anxiety, reinforcing stereotypes. In the 1950s, at the height of the Cold War, fears of the spread of Communism resulted in a wealth of powerful on-screen masterminds hell-bent on destroying Western culture. Instead of actual physical fighting, the villain would be highly intelligent and an arch manipulator. The result was such sinister and suave antagonists as Phillip Vandamm in *North by Northwest* (1959) and Mrs. Iselin in *The Manchurian Candidate* (1962).

The glamour of the 1960s gave rise to high-concept villainy and a series featuring cinema's greatest rogues' gallery: the James Bond franchise. Over his 50-year career Bond has faced colorful and maniacal characters who are clearly the villain, not only because of their mad schemes, but by simple logic: if our hero is a perfect physical and heroic ideal, whatever is the opposite to that is bad. Hence Dr. No and his replacement hands, the grotesque Rosa Klebb and Auric Goldfinger, Francisco Scaramanga and his third nipple, and — the more unattractive the villain the more evil they are — the very ugly Ernst Stavro Blofeld.

It seems to be typical that what is unusual or alien is not to be trusted and this translates to villains,

type   ■ Bandit   ■ Mad scientist   ■ Arch manipulator   ■ Bond villain   ■ Mercenary
■ Nazi

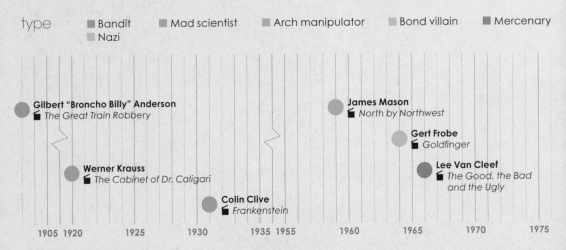

Gilbert "Broncho Billy" Anderson
The Great Train Robbery

James Mason
North by Northwest

Gert Frobe
Goldfinger

Werner Krauss
The Cabinet of Dr. Caligari

Lee Van Cleef
The Good, the Bad and the Ugly

Colin Clive
Frankenstein

1905 1920   1925   1930   1935 1955   1960   1965   1970   1975

| Arnold Schwarze-negger | Dennis Hopper | Alan Rickman | Anthony Hopkins | Daniel Day Lewis | Vincent Cassel | Heath Ledger | Christoph Waltz |

with the depressing result that Hollywood has been happy to simply make the enemy non-American. After the fall of the Iron Curtain, action movies began to identify Middle Eastern terrorists as the catchall opposing force. Such characters, as evinced by James Cameron's *True Lies* (1994), were never developed further than vague personas ready for the hero to obliterate.

More interesting were the British and European character actors who breathed life into roles that called for "otherness," albeit mixed with sophistication and sensuality. Peter Cushing and Ian McDiarmid played Grand Moff Tarkin and Emperor Palpatine in the *Star Wars* franchise; *Flash Gordon*'s Ming the Merciless was portrayed by Max von Sydow (1980); Alan Rickman was arguably at his most appealing as Hans Gruber in *Die Hard* (1988) and a wonderfully hammy Sheriff of Nottingham in *Robin Hood: Prince of Thieves* (1991); Daniel Day-Lewis chewed the scenery in Martin Scorsese's *Gangs of New York* (2002); and Anthony Hopkins won an Oscar for his impeccably mannered maniac Hannibal Lecter in *The Silence of the Lambs* (1991). Such villains did away with preconceived notions of black hearts and hid their evil behind a façade of respectability.

Countless villains projected a more psychological threat, breaking down the hero and disturbing the audience with their ideology. Placing Frank Booth in middle-class suburbia in *Blue Velvet* (1986) rips open the comfortable, entitled façade of American life and represents a hideous, unfathomable id that strikes at the heart of all viewers. He is not a pantomime villain or an impossible megalomaniac — he is something darker and stranger than even pure evil.

From a plot perspective, the antagonist is the catalyst for the story, disrupting the hero's status quo, but from a psychological angle the villain can act as a distorted mirror image of the protagonist. As with the Joker and Bruce Wayne in *Batman* (1989) and *The Dark Knight* (2008), both characters are a response to the other and could not exist without their opposites. Batman wants to exert order and live in a rational world without mindless killing while the Joker is a wild, uncontrollable genie out of the bottle. They validate one another. If either ceased to be, so would the other. Things are more complex in *Fight Club* (1999), *Memento* (2000) and *Inception* (2010), where the protagonist is also the antagonist. These characters are deep into the inner world of their heroes and raise the question, "what is a villain?" **SW**

■ Dark lord　■ Supervillain　■ Cyborg　■ Gangster　■ Pantomime villain　■ Maniac

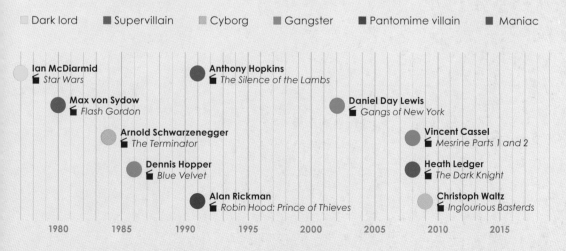

Ian McDiarmid
🎬 *Star Wars*

Anthony Hopkins
🎬 *The Silence of the Lambs*

Max von Sydow
🎬 *Flash Gordon*

Daniel Day Lewis
🎬 *Gangs of New York*

Arnold Schwarzenegger
🎬 *The Terminator*

Vincent Cassel
🎬 *Mesrine Parts 1 and 2*

Dennis Hopper
🎬 *Blue Velvet*

Heath Ledger
🎬 *The Dark Knight*

Alan Rickman
🎬 *Robin Hood: Prince of Thieves*

Christoph Waltz
🎬 *Inglourious Basterds*

| 1980 | 1985 | 1990 | 1995 | 2000 | 2005 | 2010 | 2015 |

kevin spacey 1959

| Working Girl | Henry & June | Glengarry Glen Ross | Consenting Adults | The Ref | Swimming with Sharks | The Usual Suspects | Se7en |

There is something of the old school performer in Kevin Spacey, as was evinced in a scene from the third series of *House of Cards* (2015), when his President Underwood performs a number, with piano accompaniment, in the presence of Russia's visiting premier. It is the showman in him; why he played Bobby Darin in *Beyond the Sea* (2004) and why his villains are so charismatic.

Spacey was born in New Jersey in 1959 and attended Juilliard before appearing on stage in the early 1980s. He earned notices for his performance in Jonathan Miller's 1986 production of *Long Day's Journey Into Night*, which was televised the following year. He made his feature debut as a subway thief in *Heartburn* (1986), but was more prominent as a sleazy stockbroker in *Working Girl* (1988). He took on a larger role in *Henry & June* (1990) and offered up his first villain with the creepy *Consenting Adults* (1992).

He joined an impressive cast for James Foley's adaptation of David Mamet's *Glengarry Glen Ross* (1992), playing John Williamson, the office manager. Unlike the other salesmen, whose selfish behavior is derived as much from desperation to make a sale and keep their jobs as it is bravado, Williamson is a ruthless bastard who relishes the failure of those too weak to keep up. It is a chilling performance by Spacey. He would play out a variation of the role in other films, such as *Swimming with Sharks* (1994), as a studio executive breaking in a new assistant, and the comedy *Horrible Bosses* (2011), but neither displays the cold malice of Williamson.

Spacey's major breakthrough came in 1995. Alongside *Swimming with Sharks*, he played a scientist in *Outbreak*. However, it was his role as the quiet member of a gang who plan an elaborate heist, only to get caught up in a much bigger game involving a legendary criminal mastermind, that made him a star. *The Usual Suspects* was a critical and commercial success. Spacey was rewarded with an Oscar for his portrayal of the devious Verbal Kint, whose testimony about an explosion aboard a ship at the Port of Los Angeles and the events leading up to it provide the labyrinthine film with its spine. He confirmed his star status by appearing uncredited — at his behest so as not to spoil the surprise — as the serial killer John Doe in David Fincher's *Se7en*. He plays himself and the Duke of Buckingham in Al Pacino's inventive documentary about Shakespeare's *Richard III*,

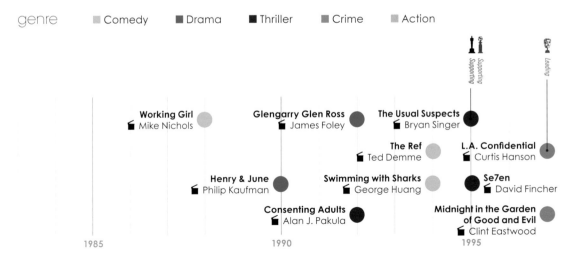

genre ■ Comedy ■ Drama ■ Thriller ■ Crime ■ Action

Working Girl — Mike Nichols

Glengarry Glen Ross — James Foley

The Usual Suspects — Bryan Singer

The Ref — Ted Demme

L.A. Confidential — Curtis Hanson

Henry & June — Philip Kaufman

Swimming with Sharks — George Huang

Se7en — David Fincher

Consenting Adults — Alan J. Pakula

Midnight in the Garden of Good and Evil — Clint Eastwood

1985   1990   1995

L.A.
Confidential

Midnight in
the Garden
of Good
and Evil

The
Negotiator

American
Beauty

Beyond
the Sea

Superman
Returns

Margin
Call

Horrible
Bosses

Looking for Richard (1996), while in *A Time to Kill* (1996), he is solid as the prosecuting attorney in a murder trial.

He gives one of his best performances in Clint Eastwood's *Midnight in the Garden of Good and Evil* (1997). Based on a real-life murder case in Savannah, Georgia, the film traces the events surrounding the murder of a local celebrity. However, the drama focuses more on the society in which the murder takes place and the fascinating character of the victim, Jim Williams. Spacey plays him as a charming raconteur — a *bon vivant* whose warm generosity belies a more complex, troubled personality. He played another charmer in Curtis Hanson's sumptuous adaptation of James Ellroy's *L.A. Confidential* (1997). Detective Sergeant Jack Vincennes initially seems more interested in celebrity than fighting crime, but Spacey portrays him as a sad individual who uses fame as a cloak and who craves a way to redeem himself.

In *The Negotiator* (1998), Spacey and costar Samuel L. Jackson play police hostage negotiators who find themselves on opposite sides of the law. The setup was perfect for two actors known for their rich delivery, but the script fails to engage and the film, though still entertaining, is a disappointment.

Spacey had already featured in one portrait of familial strife before his Oscar-winning turn in Sam Mendes' *American Beauty* (1999). He was perfectly cast opposite Judy Davis in *The Ref* (1994). They play a bickering couple who are taken hostage and refuse to stop arguing, even at gunpoint. However, his Lester Burnham is a more complex individual. He is fed up with life and is desperate to find a way to feel once again. He fixates on his daughter's school friend, even though he knows that his malaise lies deeper than mere sexual gratification. Spacey's portrayal refuses audiences the satisfaction of sympathizing with him too much, but perfectly conveys the fears of middle age and despondency with life.

With his involvement in London's Old Vic theater, Spacey's film output since *American Beauty* has been sporadic. There have been a number of disappointments, including an underwhelming *The Shipping News* (2002). However, he excelled as Ron Klain in *Recount* (2008) and the middle manager of a bank on the cusp of the 2008 financial crisis in *Margin Call* (2011). In television's *House of Cards*, Spacey is at his best, playing the President with the perfect balance of charm and malice. **IHS**

S

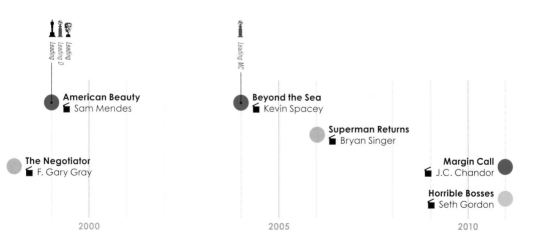

Leading
Leading D
Leading

American Beauty
Sam Mendes

Leading MC

Beyond the Sea
Kevin Spacey

Superman Returns
Bryan Singer

The Negotiator
F. Gary Gray

Margin Call
J.C. Chandor

Horrible Bosses
Seth Gordon

2000   2005   2010

sylvester stallone 1946

Rocky

Paradise
Alley

Victory

First Blood

Cliffhanger

Cop Land

Rocky
Balboa

The
Expendables

Sylvester Gardenzio Stallone is an action star and filmmaker whose own career echoes the tenacity, longevity and proclivity for comebacks of his two signature screen personas, Rocky Balboa and John Rambo. Stallone's big break is part of Hollywood lore: he wrote a script about an underdog boxer given a shot to challenge the world heavyweight champion and, despite financial offers to cast a known star, held out to play the lead himself. Stallone's brawny physique and mumbling charm helped *Rocky* (1976) become a cultural phenomenon, and won him the Best Picture Academy Award.

Stallone's next projects — union drama *F.I.S.T.* and his directorial debut *Paradise Alley* (both 1978) — underperformed. It set a trend for the actor to focus on lavish *Rocky* sequels and crowd-pleasing action roles. Perhaps the most enjoyably outrageous of these was World War II POW football movie *Victory* (1981).

In *First Blood* (1982), Stallone played a traumatized Vietnam vet, John Rambo, waging war on the U.S. law enforcement that push him over the edge; it is a far more thoughtful, serious film than its cartoonish sequels. As the 1980s swaggered on, Stallone became the big-screen epitome of Reagan-era America, his

tales of revisionist macho jingoism resonating strongly with audiences of the time.

An early 1990s foray into comedy was soon halted by a return to blockbuster action, most emphatically in *Cliffhanger* (1993). But amid a run of faltering heroics — *Judge Dredd* (1995) and *Get Carter* (2000) — came the unexpectedly effective *Cop Land* (1997): a slow-burn drama that cast Stallone as a small-town sheriff fighting police corruption, and leading a cast including Harvey Keitel and Robert De Niro. It was his best performance in years and his reluctance to pursue similar work still seems like a missed opportunity.

Into the 2000s, Stallone, then pushing 60 but still in great physical shape, resurrected both his iconic roles. *Rocky Balboa* (2006) was surprisingly powerful; *Rambo* (2008) was less artistically successful but it proved popular. Then Stallone corralled his former 1980s screen rivals — Schwarzenegger, Bruce Willis and co. — into action hit *The Expendables* (2010). Reunions with Schwarzenegger for *Escape Plan* (2013) and De Niro for *Grudge Match* (2013) largely traded on their former screen glories. Still, if one thing remains clear from Stallone's four-decade stretch as a star, one should never fully count him out. **LS**

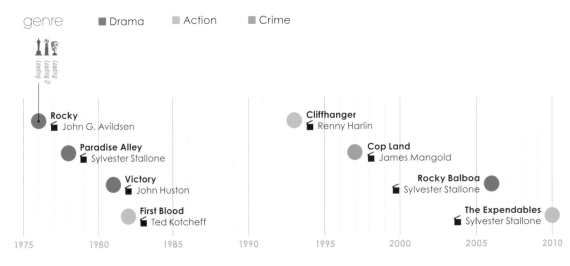

genre ■ Drama ■ Action ■ Crime

Rocky
John G. Avildsen

Paradise Alley
Sylvester Stallone

Victory
John Huston

First Blood
Ted Kotcheff

Cliffhanger
Renny Harlin

Cop Land
James Mangold

Rocky Balboa
Sylvester Stallone

The Expendables
Sylvester Stallone

1975   1980   1985   1990   1995   2000   2005   2010

Character Actor	Femme Fatale	Lover	Sinner

barbara stanwyck 1907–90

The Miracle Woman	The Bitter Tea of General Yen	Stella Dallas	The Lady Eve	Double Indemnity	The File on Thelma Jordon	Forty Guns	Walk on the Wild Side

In Billy Wilder's *Double Indemnity* (1944) Barbara Stanwyck plays seductive and calculating Phyllis Dietrichson, who suckers Walter Neff (Fred MacMurray) into killing her husband. We do not see the murder, but we hear it. Neff's hidden in the back of their car; Phyllis is driving, her husband sitting beside her. Wilder's camera moves into a close-up on Stanwyck's face, and as she listens to the dying man's strangulated gasps her eyes widen just a fraction and her lips part — enough to tell us she is aroused by hearing her lover kill her husband. It is acting of the utmost subtlety.

Stanwyck was always one of the most versatile actresses in Hollywood. She started out dancing in nightclubs, made her stage debut at 16 and her screen debut four years later. Frank Capra provided some of her best early roles. In *The Miracle Woman* (1931) she is convincing as a phoney evangelist, while *The Bitter Tea of General Yen* (1933) extended her range into new terrain as a missionary in war-torn China, at once attracted to and repelled by the urbane warlord who has captured her.

Typically hard-bitten but soft-hearted, she served as love-interest for the young William Holden in *Golden Boy* (1939), then hit her comic peak tying naive brewery heir Henry Fonda in helpless knots in *The Lady Eve* (1941). Stanwyck shimmers between mercenary manipulator and starry-eyed romantic, at one point shrewdly impersonating a high-toned English aristocrat. In Howard Hawks' screwball *Ball of Fire* (1941) she plays a feisty gangster's moll, Sugarpuss O'Shea, persuading a shy lexicographer (Gary Cooper) to experience life outside the library.

Poignancy was well within her range, as seen in the melodrama *There's Always Tomorrow* (1956), which reunited her with Fred MacMurray. He is a married man whose family take him for granted. Back into his life comes Stanwyck, an ex-colleague from his younger days; she movingly portrays a woman who has channeled erotic disappointment into career success.

Her gallery of tough, cynical dames reached delirious heights in Sam Fuller's western *Forty Guns* (1957). Flagrant Freudian imagery rampages across the screen as Stanwyck's whip-wielding ranch-owner sweeps into town at the head of her forty-strong harem of gunmen. The hint of sexual ambiguity that had always shadowed her screen persona came into focus in *Walk on the Wild Side* (1962), where she presides over a brothel as its lesbian madam. **PK**

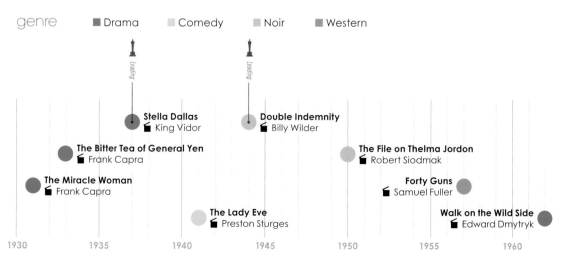

genre ■ Drama ■ Comedy ■ Noir ■ Western

Leading

Stella Dallas
King Vidor

The Bitter Tea of General Yen
Frank Capra

The Miracle Woman
Frank Capra

The Lady Eve
Preston Sturges

Leading

Double Indemnity
Billy Wilder

The File on Thelma Jordon
Robert Siodmak

Forty Guns
Samuel Fuller

Walk on the Wild Side
Edward Dmytryk

1930   1935   1940   1945   1950   1955   1960

femmes fatales

Mary Astor • Barbara Stanwyck • Rita Hayworth • Lana Turner • Jane Greer • Nina van Pallandt • Faye Dunaway • Isabella Rossellini

The shadowy world of film noir has offered many lasting cinematic tropes, but none more enduring or alluring than the femme fatale. She is the yang to the yin of the cynical, hard-drinking and chain-smoking antihero. She is beautiful, clever, irresistible, deadly and never to be trusted. The things that are bad for us have a magnetic pull and, in most cases, she will prove worse for those tangled in her web than all the cigarettes and scotch in the world.

Although the legacy of the femme fatale stretches back to biblical man-eaters such as Delilah, Salome and Jezebel, the term more readily evokes the brightest lights of Hollywood's Golden Age. None epitomizes her better than Rita Hayworth in *Gilda* (1946), a siren who uses her sexuality to drive her new husband and her old flame insane with love, lust and hatred, all at the same time. Our introduction to Gilda reveals a lot. Her new husband knocks on the door, asking, "Gilda, are you decent?" With a flick of her hair, an iridescent Hayworth beams, "Me? Sure, I'm decent." In a single moment, she is both angelic and sultry, completely apart from other women of the era in her brazenly flirtatious nature.

There are rival schools of thought on the femme fatale. One argues that she is a feminist symbol, a break from traditional female roles and a sign of

woman's dominance of man. Gilda certainly fits into this argument, as her games have exactly the desired effect. As does the unseen but omnipresent Rebecca in *Rebecca* (1940), whose power over her husband extends beyond the grave, or Lynn Bracken, the Veronica Lake lookalike played by Kim Basinger in *L.A. Confidential* (1997), whose happy ending may be seen as a moral reward for the fact that she is driven mainly by love rather than greed or revenge.

The second theory is that the femme fatale is a symbol of misogyny, evidenced by how she is usually punished or destroyed for stepping outside of the traditional female roles of mother or wife. In *Build My Gallows High* (1947), Kathie (Jane Greer) pays the ultimate price for her scheming. She is so irresistible, even her mobster boyfriend (Kirk Douglas), who she robbed and shot, wants her back. Jeff (Robert Mitchum) is sent to track her down and falls for her, getting drawn into the middle of her treachery, and spurning his virtuous girlfriend (Virginia Huston).

The classic image that the term "femme fatale" conjures up is one of the beautiful mysterious woman who slinks into a private detective's office, enlisting his help and luring him into a sordid and complicated plot. This device has never been used better than in *The Maltese Falcon* (1941), where Sam Spade

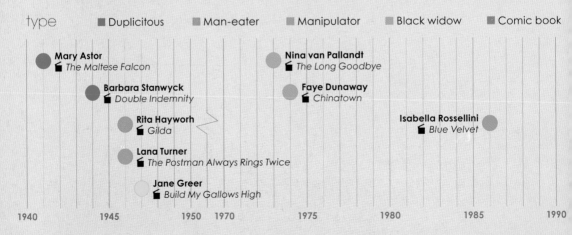

type   ■ Duplicitous   ■ Man-eater   ■ Manipulator   ■ Black widow   ■ Comic book

Mary Astor
The Maltese Falcon

Barbara Stanwyck
Double Indemnity

Rita Hayworh
Gilda

Lana Turner
The Postman Always Rings Twice

Jane Greer
Build My Gallows High

Nina van Pallandt
The Long Goodbye

Faye Dunaway
Chinatown

Isabella Rossellini
Blue Velvet

1940   1945   1950   1970   1975   1980   1985   1990

Michelle Pfieffer

Nicole Kidman

Kim Basinger

Nora Zehetner

Anne Hathaway

Eva Green

Katherine Waterstone

(Humphrey Bogart) is hired by the duplicitous Brigid O'Shaughnessy/Ruth Wonderly (Mary Astor) and is almost immediately up to his ears in murder.

If private detectives should learn anything from film noir, it is to avoid working for beautiful women with missing or recently deceased husbands. Philip Marlowe (Elliott Gould) falls foul of the former in *The Long Goodbye* (1973), although he is smart enough not to sleep with the alluring Eileen Wade (Nina van Pallandt). In Roman Polanski's *Chinatown* (1974), Jake Gittes (Jack Nicholson) lacks that vital self-control and lands himself in seriously hot water when he succumbs to the charms of Evelyn Mulwray (Faye Dunaway).

At times, the men ensnared by these temptresses get what they deserve. Take Frank (John Garfield) in *The Postman Always Rings Twice* (1946). Not ten minutes after being hired by Nick, the kind older proprietor of a diner and gas station, Frank is under the spell of Nick's young wife Cora (Lana Turner) and trying to convince her to run off with him. Nick and Cora deserve each other. "Stealing a man's wife, that's nothing, but stealing a man's car, that's larceny," Frank says. Cora plays him like a fiddle, running off with him, then changing her mind a couple of miles down the road, bit by bit encouraging the morally challenged Frank to kill her husband.

The flipside to men like Frank are those too naive to ever know they are being played. In *To Die For* (1995), a modern spin on a truly noirish tale, Nicole Kidman vamps it up brilliantly as a weather girl with big aspirations and a thoroughly thick stooge (Joaquin Phoenix) to help her realize them. The same could be said for Kyle MacLachlan's Jeffrey in David Lynch's *Blue Velvet* (1986), drawn to Dorothy (Isabella Rossellini), an emotionally damaged lounge singer whose son and husband are being held captive by the psychotic Frank. Dorothy is more ambiguous than the average femme fatale in that she appears to be a victim and it is never made clear whether or not she intentionally manipulates Jeffrey to kill Frank.

The femme fatale remains a part of modern cinema. Michelle Pfeiffer and Anne Hathaway delivered indelible performances as Catwoman in *Batman Returns* (1992) and *The Dark Knight Rises* (2012). *Sin City* (2005) and its sequel are both teeming with dangerous women (particularly Eva Green's titular dame in the latter), Nora Zehetner shows how young it can start in Rian Johnson's high school noir *Brick* (2005), and it seems as if all the women in Paul Thomas Anderson's psychedelic noir *Inherent Vice* (2015) are hell-bent on leading Doc Sportello on a merry dance. **MG**

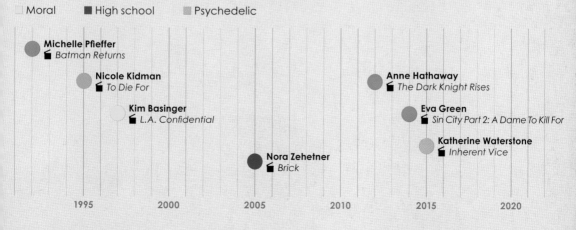

■ Moral ■ High school ■ Psychedelic

Michelle Pfieffer
Batman Returns

Nicole Kidman
To Die For

Kim Basinger
L.A. Confidential

Nora Zehetner
Brick

Anne Hathaway
The Dark Knight Rises

Eva Green
Sin City Part 2: A Dame To Kill For

Katherine Waterstone
Inherent Vice

1995   2000   2005   2010   2015   2020

barbara steele 1937

| Black Sunday | The Pit and the Pendulum | The Horrible Dr. Hichcock | 8½ | Curse of the Crimson Altar | Caged Heat | Shivers | Piranha |

Barbara Steele's idiosyncratic career began when she abandoned a lead role in an Elvis Presley vehicle, finding a different path instead as the star of a number of Italian gothic horror films during the 1960s. In a genre in which women had been typically cast as damsels-in-distress, she became known for playing assertive characters that wreaked havoc, driven by forbidden emotions. While these women would inevitably be punished violently for their transgressions, Steele's persona as a "predatory bitch goddess," as she later described it, was a breakthrough in horror.

Steele was painting scenery for a repertory company when the lead actress was taken ill and she was asked to fill in. Spotted by a talent scout and recruited into J. Arthur Rank's "Charm School," she made her debut with small roles in a trio of comedies that included Bachelor of Hearts (1958). After 20th Century Fox bought her contract, she was miscast as the American love interest in Flaming Star (1960), quitting without warning days into filming.

Having burned her bridges in Hollywood, Steele decamped to Italy to star in Mario Bava's influential debut Black Sunday (1960), playing dual parts as Asa Vajda, a witch put to her death by her brother, and her descendant Katia. The stark contrast between Asa and the simpering princess Katia — a character without agency and wholly dependent upon male instruction — portends the roles she would play throughout her career. The following year, she made a brief return to America to play Vincent Price's wife in Roger Corman's The Pit and the Pendulum, although her voice was once again dubbed.

Black Sunday inspired a vibrant wave of Italian horror films, many of which featured Steele. Typecast as scheming, usually adulterous vixens, her Italian films from this period include The Ghost (1963), The Long Hair of Death (1964), Nightmare Castle (1965), The She Beast (1966) and An Angel for Satan (1966), as well as a rare appearance as a victim in The Horrible Dr. Hichcock (1962). During this time she attempted to work in other genres, most notably in Federico Fellini's 8½ (1963) and the German drama Young Törless (1966), but was unable to escape her association with horror.

After starring with Christopher Lee and Boris Karloff in Curse of the Crimson Altar (1968), she stepped away from acting for several years, making her return, against type, as a sexually repressed wheelchair-bound prison warden in Jonathan Demme's debut Caged Heat (1974). She later moved into producing. Infrequent screen appearances were mostly limited to films made by admiring directors: for David Cronenberg in Shivers (1975) and for Joe Dante in his B-movie Piranha (1978). Frustrated by her restrictive career at the time, she has since embraced, albeit warily, her place within the history of the genre. **JWa**

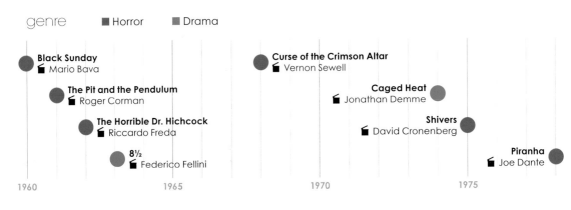

genre ■ Horror ■ Drama

Black Sunday — Mario Bava
The Pit and the Pendulum — Roger Corman
The Horrible Dr. Hichcock — Riccardo Freda
8½ — Federico Fellini
Curse of the Crimson Altar — Vernon Sewell
Caged Heat — Jonathan Demme
Shivers — David Cronenberg
Piranha — Joe Dante

1960　　1965　　1970　　1975

rod steiger 1925–2002

On the
Waterfront

The
Pawnbroker

In the Heat
of the Night

The
Illustrated
Man

Waterloo

A Fistful of
Dynamite

Lucky
Luciano

Mars
Attacks!

None of the major roles in the last two decades of Rod Steiger's career hint at the power of the roles he played in his first twenty years. Born in 1925, he started out in television. In 1953, he played the role of Marty in Paddy Chayefsky's eponymous teleplay. He could have taken the role in the film version, which saw Ernest Borgnine win an Oscar, but he balked at being tied to a long-term contract with a studio. It was his blistering performance as Marlon Brando's mob enforcer brother in *On the Waterfront* (1954) that got him noticed. In the film's most famous scene, Steiger holds his own against Brando's towering performance, railing against his older brother for destroying his life.

A run of fine performances followed. He is a suitably grim-faced Jud Fry in *Oklahoma!* (1955), a bully personified as studio head Stanley Shriner Hoff in *The Big Knife* (1955), a ruthless prosecutor in Otto Preminger's *The Court-Martial of Billy Mitchell* (1955) and convincingly plays a corrupt boxing promoter opposite Humphrey Bogart in *The Harder They Fall* (1956).

With his heavy features and baritone voice, Steiger made screen villainy look easy. In *Jubal* (1956), he is a rancher hell-bent on destroying Glenn Ford's cowboy. The actor turned down the role of Al Capone in the

1959 biopic of the gangster several times before playing the character as a brute. His Napoleon in the 1970 epic *Waterloo* is a full-blooded performance, as is his Italian dictator in *Last Days of Mussolini* (1975).

The actor's best performances lay in more ambiguous roles. He is moving as a Holocaust survivor who cannot escape the past in *The Pawnbroker* (1964), which saw him nominated for an Academy Award. Steiger plays Sol Nazerman as a man removed from the world, barely able to communicate on an emotional level. He is no less impressive as Victor Komarovsky in *Doctor Zhivago* (1966).

Steiger's Oscar-winning performance as racist Southern police chief Bill Gillespie in Norman Jewison's *In the Heat of the Night* (1967) has come to define his career. Again, the actor takes a difficult character and presents him in a way that may not have had audiences liking him, but at least allows us to understand the way he thinks and behaves.

He is solid in Sergio Leone's hit-and-miss *A Fistful of Dynamite* (1971) but the roles became less interesting. His priest in *The Amityville Horror* (1979) is the best thing in the film and his General in *Mars Attacks!* (1996) is fun, but pales compared to his earlier work. **IHS**

S

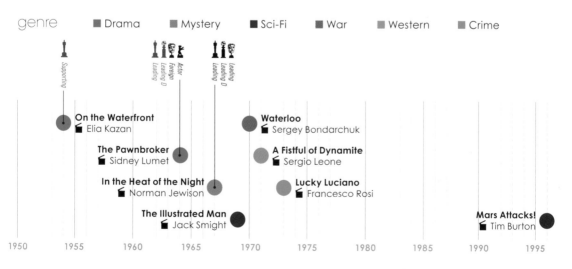

genre ■ Drama ■ Mystery ■ Sci-Fi ■ War ■ Western ■ Crime

Supporting

On the Waterfront
Elia Kazan

Actor
Foreign
Leading D

The Pawnbroker
Sidney Lumet

Leading D

Leading D
Leading

In the Heat of the Night
Norman Jewison

Waterloo
Sergey Bondarchuk

A Fistful of Dynamite
Sergio Leone

Lucky Luciano
Francesco Rosi

The Illustrated Man
Jack Smight

Mars Attacks!
Tim Burton

1950 1955 1960 1965 1970 1975 1980 1985 1990 1995

james stewart 1908–97

You Can't Take It with You

Mr. Smith Goes to Washington

Destry Rides Again

The Philadelphia Story

It's a Wonderful Life

Rope

Harvey

Winchester '73

James Stewart began his film career as the boy next door; he was a fresh-faced youth whose ideals espoused the best of American middle-class life. Even if he was a little naive at times, he understood people. He also knew a good director when he worked with one and over the course of his career he encouraged them to transform his screen persona into a darker, more complex figure. His film career spanned almost 60 years and his resulting filmography is one of the richest of any star to come out of Hollywod.

His first few films floundered, with studio bosses unsure what to do with this gangly actor whose speech pattern felt so different. Cary Grant recognized brilliance in it: "He had the ability to talk naturally. He knew that in conversations people do often interrupt one another and it's not always so easy to get a thought out. It took a little time for the sound men to get used to him, but he had an enormous impact. And then, some years later, Marlon [Brando] came out and did the same thing all over again — but what people forget is that Jimmy did it first."

It was in his 16th film and first for Frank Capra that Stewart found a vehicle that suited his nervous energy. You Can't Take It With You (1938) is a screwball comedy in which Stewart plays the son of Edward Arnold's industrialist, who falls for Jean Arthur's stenographer and is part of an eccentric family whose house his father wants to tear down. Stewart is the befuddled calm amidst the family's madcap storm. The following year he appeared in Capra's Mr. Smith Goes to Washington, in which his innocent head of the boy rangers becomes a junior senator and battles the corrupt forces in government.

Stewart's balance of innocence and understanding of human nature makes him the perfect foil to Marlene Dietrich and Brian Donlevy in Destry Rides Again (1939), while in Ernst Lubitsch's The Shop Around the Corner (1940), he balances sweet charm with mischievousness. He won an Oscar for his role in The Philadelphia Story (1940), his persona standing in stark contrast to Cary Grant and Katharine Hepburn's sophisticates, adding to the comic mix.

Frank Borzage's The Mortal Storm (1940) was one of the few films to condemn the Nazis prior to America's entry into World War II. It was the last significant film Stewart made before signing up for active service. On his return, Stewart appeared in his third and final film with Frank Capra, It's a Wonderful Life (1946). Although

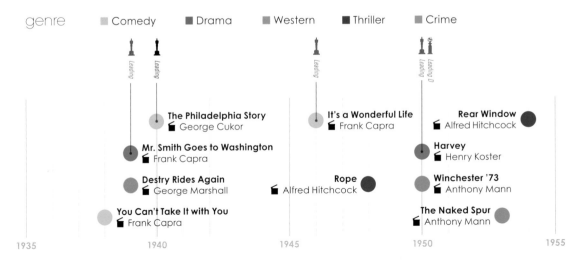

genre ■ Comedy ■ Drama ■ Western ■ Thriller ■ Crime

The Philadelphia Story
George Cukor

Mr. Smith Goes to Washington
Frank Capra

Destry Rides Again
George Marshall

You Can't Take It with You
Frank Capra

It's a Wonderful Life
Frank Capra

Rope
Alfred Hitchcock

Rear Window
Alfred Hitchcock

Harvey
Henry Koster

Winchester '73
Anthony Mann

The Naked Spur
Anthony Mann

1935   1940   1945   1950   1955

| The Naked Spur | Rear Window | The Spirit of St. Louis | Vertigo | Anatomy of a Murder | The Man Who Shot Liberty Valance | The Flight of the Phoenix | The Shootist |

regarded as one of the great Hollywood movies now, the critical and commercial response to the film was muted. The documentary-style noir *Call Northside '77* (1948) followed. Stewart then began one of his most fruitful collaborations, with Alfred Hitchcock.

A cinematic experiment, *Rope* (1948) appears to play out in one single take. Stewart is a college professor who uncovers a crime committed by two students, a situation based on the Leopold and Loeb case. More noteworthy was how differently the director employed his actor. Over the course of the next three films, Hitchcock played a major role not only in maturing Stewart, but imbuing him with emotional depth and a complexity that hinted at a darker, less wholesome character. He is mostly stationary in *Rear Window* (1954), a voyeur on the world outside his window, where he thinks he has witnessed a murder. In *The Man Who Knew Too Much* (1956), Hitchcock has the loyalty of Stewart's character tested, to see how far he is willing to go to protect his family. And in *Vertigo* (1958), the actor's early screen persona disappears completely, replaced by a man obsessed by feelings of responsibility for a woman's suicide.

Hitchcock was not the only director fascinated by Stewart's persona. Anthony Mann directed the actor in the westerns *Winchester '73* (1950), *Bend of the River* (1952), *The Naked Spur* (1953), *The Far Country* (1954) and *The Man From Laramie* (1955). Hugely popular, they were darker films in which Stewart's characters often edged toward moral ambivalence. Mann also directed Stewart in the drama *Thunder Bay* (1953) and the popular biopic *The Glenn Miller Story* (1954).

Stewart still retained an innocence in some roles, most notably *Harvey* (1950) and is two-dimensionally heroic in Billy Wilder's underwhelming *The Spirit of St. Louis* (1957). He is far better as the lawyer in Otto Preminger's searing courtroom drama, *Anatomy of a Murder* (1959) and the senator who choses legend over fact in John Ford's *The Man Who Shot Liberty Valance* (1962). He also starred in the director's last western *Cheyenne Autumn* (1964), as Wyatt Earp, but gave a more committed performance in *The Flight of the Phoenix* (1965) as the pilot of a plane that crashes in a desert, who works with his crew to find a way to fly out of there. Stewart's last great role was opposite his friend John Wayne in Don Siegel's elegiac *The Shootist* (1976), although he continued acting into his 80s. **IHS**

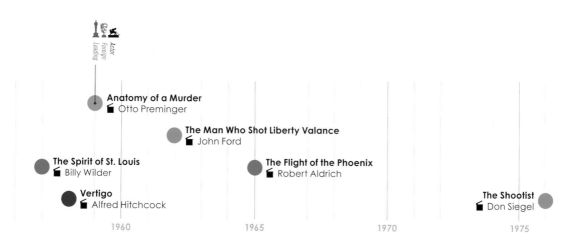

Leading
Actor
Foreign

Anatomy of a Murder
Otto Preminger

The Man Who Shot Liberty Valance
John Ford

The Spirit of St. Louis
Billy Wilder

The Flight of the Phoenix
Robert Aldrich

Vertigo
Alfred Hitchcock

The Shootist
Don Siegel

1960   1965   1970   1975

Mr. Smith Goes
to Washington
(1939)

The Philadelphia
Story
(1940)

It's a
Wonderful Life
(1946)

Harvey
(1950)

Rear Window
(1954)

Vertigo
(1958)

Anatomy
of a Murder
(1959)

The Shootist
(1976)

In one of the actor's defining roles, Frank Capra's comedy-drama **Mr. Smith Goes to Washington**, Stewart plays an idealistic senator fighting political corruption.

Katharine Hepburn handpicked costar James Stewart to act alongside her in **The Philadelphia Story**, having bought the film rights after appearing in the stage version.

Stewart plays struggling small-town savings and loan manager George Bailey in **It's a Wonderful Life**.

Now a much-loved Christmas classic, **It's a Wonderful Life** was Stewart's personal favorite of his feature films.

The eccentric Elwood P. Dowd (Stewart) converses with his best friend — a six-foot tall, invisible rabbit in **Harvey**.

Stewart's wheelchair-bound photographer turns voyeur in Hitchcock's tense thriller **Rear Window**.

Anatomy of a Murder saw Stewart in the role of small-town lawyer Paul Biegler. It was to be his last Oscar-nominated performance.

Hitchcock's masterpiece **Vertigo** was the first film to use a dolly zoom. The unsettling in-camera effect helped convey the acrophobia suffered by Stewart's character.

Stewart as Dr. Hostetler, who dying gunfighter John Bernard Books (John Wayne) consults for a second opinion in Don Siegel's **The Shootist**.

ben stiller 1965

Reality Bites

Flirting with Disaster

Your Friends & Neighbours

There's Something About Mary

Meet the Parents

The Royal Tenenbaums

Tropic Thunder

Greenberg

The son of comedians Jerry Stiller and Anne Meara, Ben Stiller spent his childhood on television shows with his parents before making a name for himself as one of America's most popular comedy actors. Stiller focused equally on comedy writing and performing before producing, co-writing and starring in his self-titled television sketch show in 1992. He split his time between creative disciplines, culminating in a costarring role in his directorial debut, *Reality Bites* (1994), now seen as a key Generation X film.

Stiller made further appearances in other directors' films. He played the lead in David O. Russell's screwball comedy *Flirting with Disaster* (1996) and was a philandering husband in Neil LaBute's scathing ensemble piece *Your Friends & Neighbors* (1998). The Farrelly brothers' surprisingly warm-hearted *There's Something About Mary* (1998) made Stiller one of the biggest comic names of the decade, although a reunion with the siblings years later for a remake of *The Heartbreak Kid* (2007) found them unable to replicate the winning formula.

Two years after his breakout performance, Stiller had another huge hit as Robert De Niro's hapless future son-in-law in *Meet the Parents* (2000). The duo would play the leads in two sequels, albeit with diminishing returns. *Meet the Parents* also marked the first of many on-screen appearances alongside Owen Wilson, with the pair becoming key figures in

the group of comedians often referred to as the "Frat Pack." The next year, Stiller joined Wilson again in Wes Anderson's idiosyncratic comedy-drama *The Royal Tenenbaums* and *Zoolander*, which he also directed. That film was a commercial disappointment but has since gained a cult following. The pair's attempt to start a franchise with a big-screen remake of *Starsky & Hutch* (2004) went nowhere beyond the first entry.

It is a common fate for modern American comedians to be subsumed by toothless-yet-lucrative family films as they age, which Stiller has mostly limited to the *Night at the Museum* (2006) franchise and voice-work for the *Madagascar* series. He had one of his biggest successes as a director with *Tropic Thunder* (2008), in which he took a back seat to Robert Downey Jr.'s barnstorming performance. Beyond *Tropic Thunder*, the sheer number of remakes and sequels in his later career disheartens, considering his early commitment to independent comedies, but original efforts like *Tower Heist* (2011) were also below par.

When faced with strong material, Stiller can deliver, as was proven by his superb performances in Noah Baumbach's *Greenberg* (2010) and *While We're Young* (2014). Stiller directed himself once again in the long-gestating *The Secret Life of Walter Mitty* (2013), but the film's technical excellence was let down by a saccharine tone and shedding of the premise that made James Thurber's short story so moving. **JWa**

genre ■ Comedy

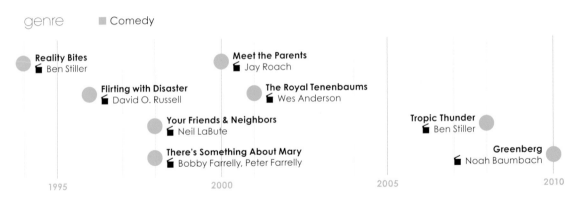

● Reality Bites
🎬 Ben Stiller

● Meet the Parents
🎬 Jay Roach

● Flirting with Disaster
🎬 David O. Russell

● The Royal Tenenbaums
🎬 Wes Anderson

● Your Friends & Neighbors
🎬 Neil LaBute

● Tropic Thunder
🎬 Ben Stiller

● There's Something About Mary
🎬 Bobby Farrelly, Peter Farrelly

● Greenberg
🎬 Noah Baumbach

1995   2000   2005   2010

sharon stone 1958

Total Recall

Basic Instinct

Sliver

The Specialist

Casino

The Quick and The Dead

The Mighty

Broken Flowers

Although her infamous breakthrough came in 1992 with *Basic Instinct*, former model Sharon Stone had been attempting to hit the big time in Hollywood for over a decade before Paul Verhoeven made her a star. Her first substantial role was in Wes Craven's Amish shocker *Deadly Blessing* (1981) and roles in low-end fare like *King Solomon's Mines* (1985) kept the actress working, but did not give her the lift she truly needed.

In the early 1990s things changed, firstly with a supporting role alongside Arnold Schwarzenegger in the enjoyable sci-fi actioner *Total Recall* (1990). That introduced her to director Verhoeven, arguably the single most defining collaborator in Stone's career. Two years later, he cast her as bisexual murder suspect Catherine Trammell in *Basic Instinct* (1992), which propelled the actress to international recognition. It is a stunning performance, that keeps the audience guessing as to her character's guilt.

While the role, and in particular the infamous leg crossing scene, would make her a superstar, it was one she struggled to escape from as her career progressed. There was also the uneasy relationship between the director and star, with Stone claiming to the press that she had been exploited by Verhoeven

and was unclear how sexually explicit the film would be. Verhoeven hit back, saying, "As much as I love her, I hate her, too, especially after the lies she told the press."

Her next film, the voyeuristic erotic thriller *Sliver* (1993) seemed little more than a cynical attempt to cash in on Stone's image of a sexually predatory femme fatale, while her performances in *Intersection* and *The Specialist* (both 1994) landed her a double "win" at the Razzies. However, Stone's credibility took a sudden upturn when she was cast in Martin Scorsese's *Casino* (1995). It attracted favorable reviews and an Oscar nomination. She continued to receive good notices for her performances in *The Mighty* (1998) and *The Muse* (1999), even if her celebrity status was dwindling. A "comeback" in *Catwoman* (2004) failed to materialize when the film was unveiled to savage reviews. She was a charming ex of Bill Murray's character in Jim Jarmusch's *Broken Flowers* (2005), winning her back some credibility. Although that soon disappeared with *Basic Instinct 2* (2006). Once again, the film follows the exploits of Catherine Trammell, albeit with the action relocated to London and David Morrissey filling Michael Douglas' shoes. No one emerged from the film with their dignity intact. **MB**

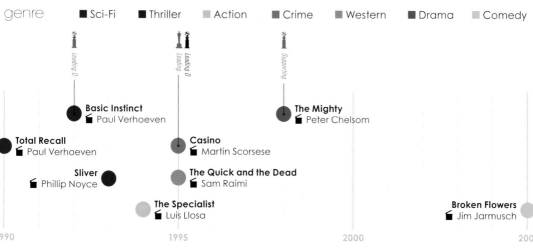

genre   ■ Sci-Fi   ■ Thriller   ■ Action   ■ Crime   ■ Western   ■ Drama   ■ Comedy

Basic Instinct
Paul Verhoeven

The Mighty
Peter Chelsom

Total Recall
Paul Verhoeven

Casino
Martin Scorsese

Sliver
Phillip Noyce

The Quick and the Dead
Sam Raimi

The Specialist
Luis Llosa

Broken Flowers
Jim Jarmusch

1990   1995   2000   2005

meryl streep 1949

| The Deer Hunter | Kramer vs. Kramer | Sophie's Choice | Silkwood | Out of Africa | A Cry in the Dark | Death Becomes Her | The River Wild |

Judging the greatest U.S. male actor from Hollywood's post-1969 "Movie Brat" resurgence usually produces a split decision between Pacino, Nicholson, De Niro or Hoffman. On the female side, it is simply a consensual coronation: Meryl Streep's supreme technical ability and versatility (from tragic melodrama to screwball comedy); a late-career box-office boom to go with her record 19 Oscar nominations and 3 wins; plus untold accolades and admiration from her peers and audiences alike make her the undisputed U.S. screen actress of her generation.

Mary Louise Streep studied drama at Yale and showed early promise on stage, leading to a notable film debut opposite Jane Fonda in period drama *Julia* (1977). Her next role, in Vietnam War-era epic *The Deer Hunter* (1978), as the small-town woman left behind by two men who both love her, resulted in her first Oscar nomination. The following year, she won the Best Supporting Actress award for *Kramer vs. Kramer*, playing a troubled woman who abandons her husband and young son, before trying to win back custody. It was a role that could easily have been a caricatured villain, but Streep's disquieting restraint imbued it with more complexity.

Dual roles across two time periods in *The French Lieutenant's Woman* (1981) first demonstrated Streep's remarkable facility for accents (here, English); *Sophie's Choice* (1982) confirmed it. For her role as a holocaust survivor, recounting the terrible decision she was forced to make in the concentration camp, Streep's flawless Polish (and German) and utterly unaffected, heartrending work won her the Best Actress Oscar.

The 1980s continued this trend of accented roles in hvv eavyweight awards contenders: as Danish writer Karen Blixen in *Out of Africa* (1985); as a Depression-era hobo in *Ironweed* (1987) and as real-life Australian mother Lindy Chamberlain, accused of murdering her infant daughter in *A Cry in the Dark* (1988). The latter is possibly her most impressive showing in a serious decade's work, along with her quietly stunning portrayal of ill-fated plutonium processing plant whistleblower Karen Silkwood in 1983.

A conscious if floundering attempt at comedy in *She-Devil* (1989) was followed up with a more successful, special-effects-driven farce, *Death Becomes Her* (1992), which directly spoofed the specter of ageing actresses' limited choices. She next tackled her first action movie, *The River Wild*

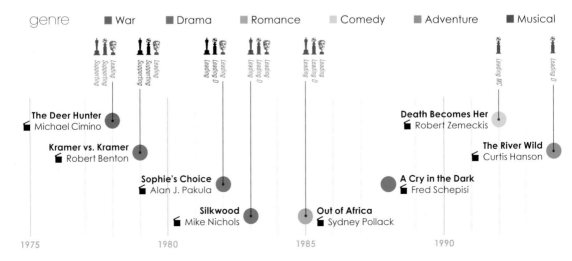

genre ■ War ■ Drama ■ Romance ■ Comedy ■ Adventure ■ Musical

The Deer Hunter — Michael Cimino (Leading / Supporting / Supporting)

Kramer vs. Kramer — Robert Benton (Leading / Supporting / Supporting)

Sophie's Choice — Alan J. Pakula (Leading / Leading)

Silkwood — Mike Nichols (Leading / Leading D)

Out of Africa — Sydney Pollack (Leading / Leading D)

A Cry in the Dark — Fred Schepisi (Leading / Leading D)

Death Becomes Her — Robert Zemeckis (Leading MC)

The River Wild — Curtis Hanson (Leading D)

1975　　　　1980　　　　1985　　　　1990

$176M (U.S.)
The Deer Hunter
(1978)

$343M (U.S.)
Kramer vs. Kramer
(1979)

$280M
Out of Africa
(1985)

$149M
The River Wild
(1994)

$280M
The Bridges of
Madison County
(1995)

$380M
The Devil
Wears Prada
(2006)

$665M
Mamma Mia!
(2008)

$202M
Into the Woods
(2014)

The Bridges of Madison County

Adaptation

The Devil Wears Prada

A Prairie Home Companion

Mamma Mia!

Julie & Julia

The Iron Lady

Into the Woods

(1994), surprisingly adept in her rugged surroundings and physically holding her own opposite villain Kevin Bacon. Then, back again to serious matters, playing an Italian-American farmer's wife who briefly falls for Clint Eastwood's worldly photographer in *The Bridges of Madison County* (1995). Streep's intimate, mature passion underplayed, yet enhanced the melodrama.

Despite near-universal acclaim, a backlash still exists that brands Streep as some kind of "acting machine" (misappropriating a quote from her friend and *Silkwood* costar Cher), churning out overtly technique-based roles in middlebrow, unchallenging fare. Streep's career does include portrayals that could be deemed excessively mannered — *Doubt*'s (2008) vindictive nun or *August: Osage County*'s (2013) grandstanding matriarch. However, what this criticism overlooks is the variety of modest, naturalistic performances Streep has given: sweet and funny in *Defending Your Life* (1991); an easygoing but wistful country singer in *A Prairie Home Companion* (2006); and wonderful as Susan Orlean, a writer whose investigation into orchids sends her spiraling into emotional crisis in Spike Jonze's *Adaptation* (2002). Regardless, at this stage Streep was still seen as a critical, rather than popular, favorite. *The Devil Wears Prada* (2006) changed that. Her turn as fashionista boss-from-hell Miranda Priestly, reputedly based on *Vogue*'s Anna "Nuclear" Wintour, was both gloriously glacial, and when necessary, painfully vulnerable. It was also a huge hit, easily the biggest of her career — that is, until *Mamma Mia!* (2008). Based on the hit stage musical, whatever this box-office phenomenon's merits (or lack of), no one could deny Streep's unashamed, full-throated gusto, which made her, aged almost sixty, a mainstream global star.

With *Julie & Julia* (2009) and *The Iron Lady* (2011) Streep tackled two markedly different real-life icons: U.S. chef Julia Childs and British Prime Minister Margaret Thatcher. Nailing Thatcher from her ruthless pomp to frail dotage won Streep her third Oscar.

Although Streep has appeared in classics, one might argue she has never headlined her own *Godfather*, *Chinatown*, *Raging Bull* or *Tootsie*, although perhaps that is more a valid critique of the dearth of quality female-driven films. Given her illustrious career, balanced with a stable marriage and family, perhaps Streep's greatest, lifelong performance is inspirational role model. **LS**

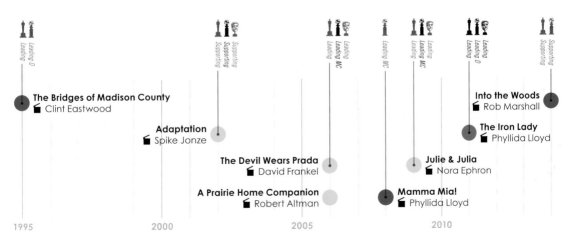

Leading D

Supporting
Supporting

Leading MC
Leading
Leading

Leading MC

Leading MC
Leading
Leading

Leading D
Leading
Leading

Supporting
Supporting

The Bridges of Madison County
Clint Eastwood

Adaptation
Spike Jonze

The Devil Wears Prada
David Frankel

A Prairie Home Companion
Robert Altman

Mamma Mia!
Phyllida Lloyd

Julie & Julia
Nora Ephron

The Iron Lady
Phyllida Lloyd

Into the Woods
Rob Marshall

1995   2000   2005   2010

Kramer vs.Kramer
(1979)

Sophie's Choice
(1982)

Out of Africa
(1985)

Adaptation
(2002)

**The Devil
Wears Prada**
(2006)

Mamma Mia!
(2008)

The Iron Lady
(2011)

Into the Woods
(2014)

The tale of a young couple's divorce and the impact on their young son, *Kramer vs. Kramer* won five Academy Awards, including Best Supporting Actress for Meryl Streep.

Sophie's Choice centers on a love triangle between a Polish immigrant (Streep), her husband and writer Stingo (Peter McNichol) who they befriend.

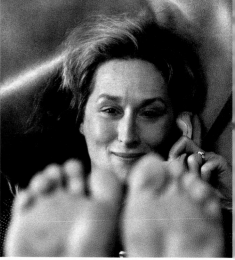

In Charlie Kaufman's metafilm *Adaptation*, Streep keeps the narrative fireworks grounded in Susan Orlean's heartache.

Streep worked on her accent for *Out of Africa* by listening to recordings of Danish writer Isak Dinesen (Karen Blixen) reading her works.

Anne Hathaway plays the smart assistant to Streep's demanding fashion magazine editor-in-chief in *The Devil Wears Prada*.

Although **Mamma Mia!** cast actors not noted for their singing abilities, Streep was generally judged to have performed well. "There's a freedom of expression that women of my age are not normally asked to portray, so it was wonderful to have that musical, physical and emotional opportunity to release everything in one character," said the actress.

Streep spent months watching broadcasts of Margaret Thatcher to develop her mannerisms and speech for **The Iron Lady.** Despite not sharing Thatcher's political views, Streep admired the politician's personal strength and her achievements in pushing the boundaries for women leaders.

Streep's performance as Margaret Thatcher in **The Iron Lady** was widely acclaimed, earning her the Academy Award for Best Actress, 29 years after she first won it.

Into the Woods, adapted from Stephen Sondheim's fairy-tale musical, saw Streep once again steal the show — and songs — as the conflicted witch.

barbra streisand 1942

Funny Girl

Hello, Dolly!

On a Clear Day You Can See Forever

The Owl and The Pussycat

Up the Sandbox

What's Up, Doc?

The Way We Were

Funny Lady

By the time she appeared in *Funny Girl* (1968), Barbra Streisand had released 10 albums and was a regular on TV variety shows. It was only natural that she would move to the big screen and the musical biopic of comedienne Fanny Brice's life, which the singer had already performed on Broadway, was a perfect start. Producer Ray Stark had no doubts about Streisand's ability to play the role on film: "I just felt she was too much a part of Fanny, and Fanny was too much a part of Barbra to have it go to someone else." Director William Wyler saw her as a challenge — an actress who had never appeared in a film carrying the entire production — but also saw in her the enthusiasm of Bette Davis, who he had worked with on a number of films. The gamble worked. Streisand's freshness, both in appearance and the energy she employs on screen offers up a sassy, captivating character that saw her awarded with an Oscar for Best Actress. She returned to Fanny Brice's life in 1975 with *Funny Lady*, but neither the film nor Streisand capture the freewheeling spirit of *Funny Girl*.

She stayed with the musical for her next two films. Directed by Gene Kelly, *Hello, Dolly!* (1969) is also based on a stage show, telling the story of Dolly Levi, a strong-willed widow and matchmaker who goes in search of the perfect partner for the ornery but well-off Horace Vandergelder, even though she desires marriage with him herself. Although Streisand plays a feisty Dolly, the film is weighed down by its running time and excessive exposition. She then appeared in *On a Clear Day You Can See Forever* (1970), which was directed by Vincente Minnelli and features a number of visually ravishing moments. However, it lacks pace in its tale of a young chain-smoker who, at the behest of her priggish fiancé, sees a psychiatrist who, in the process of hypnotizing her, falls in love with a woman she inhabited in a previous life.

Streisand's film work to date not only highlighted her stunning voice, it revealed an aptitude for comedy. Her first non-musical films were aimed at channeling this talent. Based on Bill Manhoff's Broadway play, *The Owl and the Pussycat* (1970) was adapted by Buck Henry to suit Streisand and costar George Segal. She plays an uneducated actress, model and occasional prostitute, he an educated aspiring writer. The clash of cultures allowed for witty interplay and Streisand shines with her delivery. The film was a critical and commercial success.

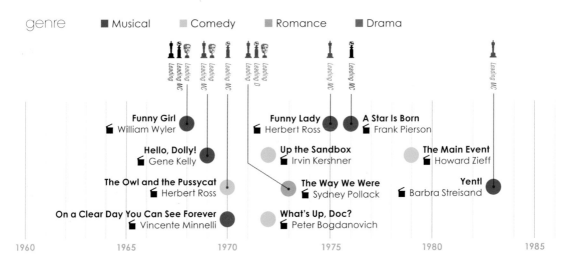

genre ■ Musical ☐ Comedy ■ Romance ■ Drama

Funny Girl
William Wyler

Hello, Dolly!
Gene Kelly

The Owl and the Pussycat
Herbert Ross

On a Clear Day You Can See Forever
Vincente Minnelli

Funny Lady
Herbert Ross

Up the Sandbox
Irvin Kershner

The Way We Were
Sydney Pollack

What's Up, Doc?
Peter Bogdanovich

A Star Is Born
Frank Pierson

The Main Event
Howard Zieff

Yentl
Barbra Streisand

1960   1965   1970   1975   1980   1985

$370M (U.S.)
What's Up, Doc?
(1972)

$238M (U.S.)
The WayWe Were
(1973)

$170M (U.S.)
Funny Lady
(1975)

$330M (U.S.)
A Star Is Born
(1976)

$138M (U.S.)
The Main Event
(1979)

$95M (U.S.)
Yentl
(1983)

$129M (U.S.)
The Prince of Tides
(1991)

$642M
Meet the Fockers
(2004)

A Star
Is Born

The Main
Event

Yentl

Nuts

The Prince
of Tides

The Mirror
Has Two
Faces

Meet the
Fockers

The Guilt
Trip

Director Peter Bogdanovich had just shot *The Last Picture Show* (1971) and teamed up with Buck Henry, David Newman and Robert Benton to come up with a screenplay that emulated the Golden Age of the screwball comedy. The result, *What's Up, Doc?* (1972), is a fast-talking, furiously paced and hilariously funny farce, set in and around a hotel, and concerns four identical plaid bags. Ryan O'Neal, playing an academic, unfortunately attracts the attention of Streisand's troublemaker when their two bags are mixed up. It is a perfect role for the actress and she is as charming as she is kooky. O'Neal and Streisand teamed up for a sequel of sorts, *The Main Event* (1979), but the film lacked the fizz of Bogdanovich's near-masterpiece.

Streisand starred in Sydney Pollack's *The Way We Were* (1973), faring better than her costar Robert Redford, who is passive to her hyperactive. The title song gave her one of her biggest hits from a film, but aside of her performance the drama is lackluster. Likewise, many critics thought it was a mistake to have remade *A Star Is Born* (1976), but audiences disagreed. Time has not been good to the film or the performances in it.

The actress began to appear in fewer films from the 1980s, as she moved into writing, directing and producing. *Yentl* (1983) was her first production. A musical version of a play by Leah Napolin and Isaac Bashevis Singer, with Streisand as an Ashkenazi Jewish girl in Poland who dresses as a boy in order to receive an education, the film tends to divide audiences. It is usually liked only by ardent admirers of Streisand.

Martin Ritt's *Nuts* (1987) was the first fully dramatic outing for Streisand, playing a prostitute facing a murder charge, whose parents want her declared mentally incompetent. Like its unfortunate title, the film lacks subtlety. She is on better form in her own *The Prince of Tides* (1991), a faithful adaptation of Pat Conroy's novel, although Nick Nolte steals his costar's thunder with a stunning portrayal of a man going through a midlife crisis.

Streisand's most recent films have seen her return to comedy. *The Guilt Trip* (2012) and *Little Fockers* (2010) are desperately in need of a better script, while *The Mirror Has Two Faces* (1996) features a strong first half, with Streisand and Jeff Bridges complementing each other. However, *Meet the Fockers* (2004) finds the actress channeling the anarchic spirit of her early films. **IHS**

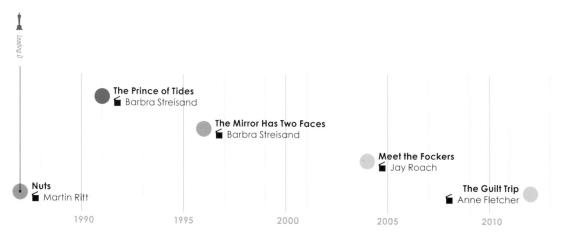

Leading Ø

The Prince of Tides
Barbra Streisand

The Mirror Has Two Faces
Barbra Streisand

Meet the Fockers
Jay Roach

Nuts
Martin Ritt

The Guilt Trip
Anne Fletcher

1990   1995   2000   2005   2010

donald sutherland 1935

M*A*S*H

Klute

Don't Look Now

Fellini's Casanova

Ordinary People

JFK

Pride & Prejudice

The Hunger Games

Donald Sutherland was a star in 1970s Hollywood who was associated with a wave of films that broke from the strictures of the studio system to produce more adult, politically engaged work. Consummate craftsmanship underlined his status as a countercultural icon. He is as renowned for his villainous turns as he is his leading-men roles, and in recent years he has distinguished himself as a character actor.

Physically imposing, the unconventionally handsome actor was often cast as a villain, and there was an avowedly antiheroic aspect to his first big-screen role, as one of a group of convicts on a mission into Nazi Germany in *The Dirty Dozen* (1967). His breakthrough followed as army surgeon Hawkeye Pierce in war-torn Korea in Robert Altman's *M*A*S*H* (1970). Sutherland is outstanding as the jokey, anti-authoritarian medic, an inspired comic turn that underlines the film's mood of freewheeling irreverence. *M*A*S*H* brought Sutherland a degree of fame and led to his being cast in high-profile Hollywood movies, albeit playing characters of some color and eccentricity. In another World War II caper, *Kelly's Heroes* (1970), he was the tellingly named Oddball, a part he played with laid-back humor.

Yet it was with less obviously mainstream projects that Sutherland made his greatest impact. In *Klute* (1971), one of the key early films of the so-called New Hollywood, his performance as a private detective was quiet, intelligent and astutely attuned to the unsettling psychological complexities of the thriller. He was even better in Nic Roeg's *Don't Look Now* (1973) as a husband struggling to come to terms with the loss of his child in a wintry Venice — a performance of mournful interiority and quiet eloquence.

Sutherland has been bold in his career choices, too, often working with maverick European directors. He took the title role of the serial seducer in *Fellini's Casanova* (1976). Wearing heavy make-up for the performance, Sutherland exuded a sly sensuality; that same year he was terrifyingly intense as a fascist thug in Bernardo Bertolucci's epic drama *1900*.

From the 1980s onward, Sutherland has been a prolific character actor. He was electrifying as an informant in Oliver Stone's *JFK* (1991) and was a wry, sardonic Mr. Bennet in the 2005 adaptation of *Pride & Prejudice*. Playing President Snow in *The Hunger Games* franchise, Sutherland has captivated a younger audience unaware of his storied past. **EL**

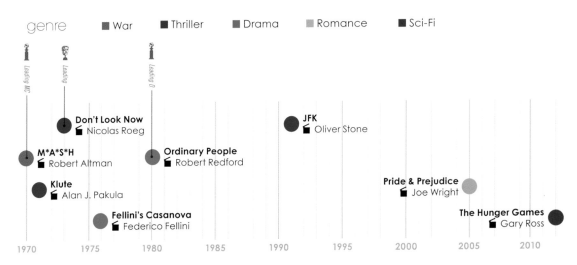

genre ■ War ■ Thriller ■ Drama ■ Romance ■ Sci-Fi

Leading MC | Leading | Leading D

Don't Look Now Nicolas Roeg
JFK Oliver Stone
M*A*S*H Robert Altman
Ordinary People Robert Redford
Klute Alan J. Pakula
Pride & Prejudice Joe Wright
Fellini's Casanova Federico Fellini
The Hunger Games Gary Ross

1970 | 1975 | 1980 | 1985 | 1990 | 1995 | 2000 | 2005 | 2010

gloria swanson 1899–1983

| The Pullman Bride | Male and Female | Beyond the Rocks | Sadie Thompson | The Trespasser | Queen Kelly | Indiscreet | Sunset Boulevard |

Most people will immediately think of Gloria Swanson as Norma Desmond, the has-been silent movie star lurking in her crumbling mansion in *Sunset Boulevard* (1950), Billy Wilder's scathing satire on Hollywood. In real life Swanson was a lot livelier and funnier than Norma, and got a little tired of being identified with her last great role. She remarked, "I never was Norma Desmond, and I don't know anyone who lived like that!" She could be imperious, though. "I will be every inch and every moment the star!" she declared at the height of her fame in the mid-1920s.

Her career started with uncredited bit-parts in slapstick comedies. Several of them starred Wallace Beery; they married in 1916 and headed for Hollywood, where she signed with Mack Sennett and made about ten two-reelers for him. She disliked slapstick, so it was with relief that she broke with Sennett and moved to Triangle, where she secured dramatic roles in a series of marital dramas, starting with *Society for Sale* (1918), that lifted her to stardom.

When Triangle went bust Swanson was snapped up by Cecil B. DeMille at Paramount and made six films with him: more marital dramas with titles like *Male and Female* and *Don't Change Your Husband* (both 1919),

offering the standard DeMillian mix of salaciousness and moralizing. Swanson was never the most flexible of actresses, tending to stiffness, but she suited DeMille's stolid directorial style. She was working with other directors, too, and by 1926 was Paramount's highest-paid star.

Comedy gave her more scope. Allan Dwan used her well in *Manhandled* (1924), as a shopgirl taken up by society, and she went to France to star in *Madame Sans-Gêne* (1925), playing Napoleon's laundress. She quit Paramount in 1926 to form Gloria Swanson Productions under the auspices of United Artists. For *Queen Kelly* (1929) she was a convent schoolgirl who attracts royal attention when she accidentally drops her knickers; she was charmingly unaffected in the role, but director, Erich von Stroheim, went badly over-budget, and she fired him with the film left unfinished.

Swanson made the transition to sound without problems, but in the early 1930s her career unraveled with startling speed and by 1934 she was on the shelf. One attempt at a comeback, *Father Takes a Wife* (1941) vanished without trace; and then eight years later came the call from Wilder. Three trashy films post-*Sunset Boulevard* are best forgotten. **PK**

genre ■ Short ■ Adventure ■ Drama ■ Comedy ■ Noir

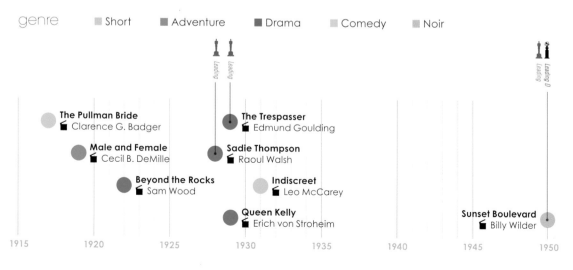

The Pullman Bride — Clarence G. Badger
Male and Female — Cecil B. DeMille
Beyond the Rocks — Sam Wood
Queen Kelly — Erich von Stroheim
The Trespasser — Edmund Goulding
Sadie Thompson — Raoul Walsh
Indiscreet — Leo McCarey
Sunset Boulevard — Billy Wilder

1915   1920   1925   1930   1935   1940   1945   1950

max von sydow 1929

| The Seventh Seal | Winter Light | The Greatest Story Ever Told | Hour of the Wolf | The Emigrants | The Exorcist | Three Days of the Condor | Flash Gordon |

Max von Sydow has long displayed a talent for playing a bewilderingly wide range of roles. Equally comfortable as a man of God (Jesus Christ, Father Merrin) or his polar opposite (Ming the Merciless, Ernst Stavro Blofeld), he can be dapper and charming in one film, then gaunt and sinister in the next. His career has spanned six decades and multiple languages, and his imposing height has contributed greatly to an abiding air of stern authority.

Born in Sweden in 1929, von Sydow acted at school before training professionally at Stockholm's Royal Dramatic Theatre. By his graduation in 1951, he had already appeared in films, although his career breakthrough came four years later, when he joined Ingmar Bergman's repertory company and alternated between stage and screen roles. The most famous of these was as Antonius Block, the knight who plays chess with Death (Bengt Ekerot) in *The Seventh Seal* (1957), in which von Sydow's craggy good looks were counterbalanced by Ekerot's smoothly sinister make-up. Von Sydow appeared in most of Bergman's films over the next six years; lead roles included the murderously vengeful father in *The Virgin Spring* (1959) and the priest in *Winter Light* (1963). He made

four more Bergman films at the turn of the 1970s, as the painter beset by demonic visions in *Hour of the Wolf* (1968), as one half of a couple trying to survive a devastating war in *Shame* (1968), as the emotionally fragile lover of the title character in *The Passion of Anna* (1969) and the husband cuckolded by Elliott Gould's visitor in *The Touch* (1971).

Between those blocks of Bergman, von Sydow established himself as a major international star, via the lead role of Jesus Christ in the all-star mega-production *The Greatest Story Ever Told* (1965). His attraction to producer-director George Stevens was that he combined amply proven screen presence while being unknown to mainstream U.S. audiences. This did not last long — indeed, von Sydow relocated to Los Angeles for a time because he was receiving so many Hollywood offers, including *The Quiller Memorandum* and *Hawaii* (both 1966), the parts of Anne Frank's father Otto in the 1967 TV adaptation of *The Diary of Anne Frank*, the Soviet counter-intelligence officer in *The Kremlin Letter* (1970) and a cameo in *Cabaret* (1972).

His comparatively late appearance as Father Merrin in the title role of *The Exorcist* (1973) injected

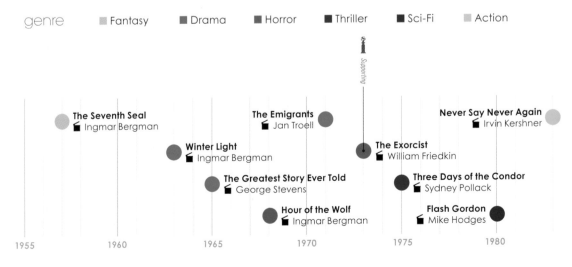

genre ■ Fantasy   ■ Drama   ■ Horror   ■ Thriller   ■ Sci-Fi   ■ Action

Supporting

The Seventh Seal
🎬 Ingmar Bergman

Winter Light
🎬 Ingmar Bergman

The Greatest Story Ever Told
🎬 George Stevens

Hour of the Wolf
🎬 Ingmar Bergman

The Emigrants
🎬 Jan Troell

The Exorcist
🎬 William Friedkin

Three Days of the Condor
🎬 Sydney Pollack

Flash Gordon
🎬 Mike Hodges

Never Say Never Again
🎬 Irvin Kershner

1955   1960   1965   1970   1975   1980

| Never Say Never Again | Hannah and Her Sisters | Pelle the Conqueror | Awakenings | The Best Intentions | Minority Report | The Diving Bell and the Butterfly | Extremely Loud & Incredibly Close |

the demonic proceedings with some much-needed solemnity. *Steppenwolf* (1974) cast him in the lead role of Harry Haller, torn between human and primal, but the film was little seen. His ice-cool professional assassin in *Three Days of the Condor* (1975) made a far bigger impact, as did his captain of the ship undertaking the *Voyage of the Damned* (1976); although, perhaps his most fondly remembered role was that of Emperor Ming the Merciless in Mike Hodges' riotously camp remake of *Flash Gordon* (1980). Another iconic villain, James Bond's nemesis Blofeld, followed soon after in *Never Say Never Again* (1983), while his fussily perfectionist, emotionally controlling painter Frederick in Woody Allen's *Hannah and Her Sisters* (1986) was almost an homage to his Bergman characters.

Throughout this entire period, he remained in close touch with his Scandinavian roots. In addition to his work with Bergman, he appeared in several films by Jan Troell, notably in the two-part epic *The Emigrants* (1971) and *The New Land* (1973), as the head of an impoverished Swedish family emigrating to the United States. The following decade, he appeared in the first of two Palme d'Or winners directed by Bille August,

Pelle the Conqueror (1987), as the title character's eternally optimistic father (which earned him a rare Best Actor Oscar nomination for a foreign-language role), and *The Best Intentions* (1992), as a semi-fictionalized version of screenwriter Ingmar Bergman's maternal grandfather, before playing Knut Hamsun in Troell's *Hamsun* (1996). His only collaboration with Lars von Trier is offscreen, but his sepulchral voice as the narrator of *Europa* (1991) is unmistakable.

His prodigious work rate has shown no sign of slackening either side of the millennium, as he moved smoothly between Hollywood tear-jerkers (*Awakenings*, 1990), European art movies (*Until the End of the World*, 1991), noir-tinged thrillers (*A Kiss Before Dying*, 1991), supernatural horror (*Needful Things*, 1993) and sci-fi (*Judge Dredd*, 1995; *Star Wars Episode VII — The Force Awakens*, 2015). A cameo in *The Diving Bell and the Butterfly* (2007) proved that he could be heartbreaking in French, while his dialogue-free supporting performance in *Extremely Loud & Incredibly Close* (2011) saw him communicating purely with hands tattooed with "yes" and "no" and his infinitely expressive face. It earned him a second Oscar nomination. **MB**

■ Comedy

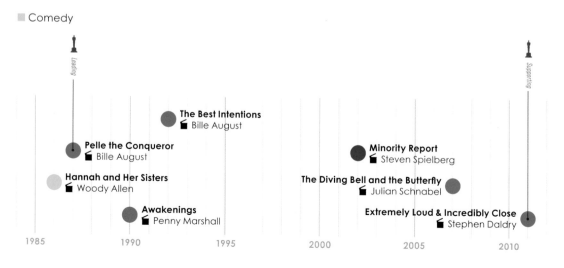

Leading

Supporting

The Best Intentions
Bille August

Pelle the Conqueror
Bille August

Hannah and Her Sisters
Woody Allen

Awakenings
Penny Marshall

Minority Report
Steven Spielberg

The Diving Bell and the Butterfly
Julian Schnabel

Extremely Loud & Incredibly Close
Stephen Daldry

1985　　1990　　1995　　2000　　2005　　2010

kinuyo tanaka 1910-77

Dragnet Girl

Shunkinsho: Okoto to Sasuke

Utamaro and His Five Women

The Life of Oharu

Ugetsu Monogatari

Sansho the Bailiff

Ballad of Narayama

Sandakan 8

Kinuyo Tanaka is widely considered the finest actress in Japanese cinema. She was astonishingly versatile, capable of playing good or evil characters, strong or victimized, honest or crooked, aristocratic or peasant. She worked with all the great Japanese directors of her era: Kenji Mizoguchi, Yasujiro Ozu, Akira Kurosawa, Keisuke Kinoshita, Heinosuke Gosho, Kon Ichikawa, Mikio Naruse, Yoshitaro Nomura, Masaki Kobayashi and many more. Her career lasted over 50 years, and she appeared in nearly 250 films. In defiance of convention (female directors being virtually unheard of in Japan), she also directed several excellent films.

Tanaka's career began in the silent era (which lasted longer in Japan than in other movie-making countries), making her screen debut at 15. Relatively few of her silent films have survived; among the earliest are Ozu's student comedies (*I Graduated, But...*, 1929; *I Flunked, But...*, 1930) and the last of his short-lived cycle of gangster movies, *Dragnet Girl* (1933). By the late 1930s she had become Japan's most popular female star, with Nomura's *Yearning Laurel* (1938) her biggest hit of the decade.

She made her first film for Mizoguchi, *Osaka Elegy*, in 1936, but did not start working with him regularly until 1944. They made twelve films together in ten years, including several of her most famous roles. In *Utamaro and His Five Women* (1946) she was one of the great painter's acolytes, and a prostitute in *Women of the Night* (1948). A trio of Mizoguchi films in the early 1950s include some of her finest work. In *The Life of Oharu* (1952) she played a 17th-century woman of the Japanese Imperial court who declines from concubine to streetwalker. She was a potter's wife in *Ugetsu Monogatari* (1953), abandoned by her husband and murdered by bandits, returning as a gentle ghost to welcome her faithless man home. *Sansho the Bailiff* (1954), set in the feudal 11th century, traces the fate of an aristocratic woman and her two children after her husband is exiled. Tanaka's work for other directors was scarcely less distinguished. For Ozu she made, among others, the bleak and violent *A Hen in the Wind* (1948). She played 20 years older than her age in Kinoshita's *Ballad of Narayama* (1958), as a self-sacrificing peasant.

The feminist sympathies of Mizoguchi's films did not always extend into real life. When Tanaka, his finest actress — and his lover — wanted to turn director he opposed her, causing the end of their personal and professional relationship. With the support of Ozu, she directed six films between 1953 and 1962, paving the way for future female Japanese directors. **PK**

genre ■ Drama ■ Mystery

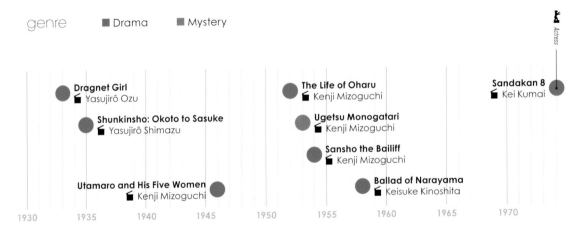

Actress

Dragnet Girl
Yasujirô Ozu

Shunkinsho: Okoto to Sasuke
Yasujirô Shimazu

Utamaro and His Five Women
Kenji Mizoguchi

The Life of Oharu
Kenji Mizoguchi

Ugetsu Monogatari
Kenji Mizoguchi

Sansho the Bailiff
Kenji Mizoguchi

Ballad of Narayama
Keisuke Kinoshita

Sandakan 8
Kei Kumai

1930   1935   1940   1945   1950   1955   1960   1965   1970

audrey tautou 1976

| Venus Beauty | Amélie | Dirty Pretty Things | The Da Vinci Code | Priceless | Coco Before Chanel | Thérèse | Mood Indigo |

Audrey Tautou had appeared in a number of television films by the time she left drama school. Within two years, the French actress was cast in her feature debut, *Venus Beauty* (1999), for which she won a César for most promising actress. Tautou's breakthrough came as the eponymous heroine of Jean-Pierre Jeunet's worldwide hit *Amélie* (2001). The whimsical, winsome and warm Amélie Poulain made Tautou an internationally recognized figure. Jeunet and Tautou worked together again on *A Very Long Engagement* (2004), about a woman trying to discover whether her fiancé died during the Battle of the Somme. The film was seen as a disappointment after *Amélie*, but it possesses its own minor charms.

Other roles from this time include *God Is Great and I'm Not* (2001), *He Loves Me... He Loves Me Not* (2002) and Cédric Klapisch's *The Spanish Apartment* (2002), the first of a trilogy of films with the director and actor Romain Duris, which was followed by *Russian Dolls* (2005) and *Chinese Puzzle* (2013). Tautou and Duris also appeared together in *Mood Indigo* (2013), with Tautou playing Duris' effervescent love interest.

Alongside the whimsy of Jeunet and Gondry, Tautou has appeared in grittier fare, such as Stephen Frears' London-set drama *Dirty Pretty Things* (2002), playing an illegal immigrant who falls foul of Sergei Lopez's insidious concierge. She also starred alongside Tom Hanks in *The Da Vinci Code* (2006), her first Hollywood production. After the experience she decided to not star in films that would bring her to a wider audience — "I don't want to become more popular," she explained in a 2012 interview. Instead, the charming but small-scale *Priceless* (2006) in which she portrays a deliciously amoral gold digger, set a benchmark for the types of roles to come.

Tautou's choice to avoid "the superstar road," as she has described it, was combined with a purposeful slowing in work rate. Since 2006 she has typically appeared in a film a year at most, including *Hunting and Gathering* (2007) and *Delicacy* (2011). The most successful effort from this period was *Coco Before Chanel* (2009).

One of Tautou's most challenging roles to date was in *Thérèse* (2012). In a largely internal performance — quite unlike anything she had attempted before — she conveys the troubled inner life of an intelligent woman unhappily ahead of her time and driven to extreme measures. **JWa**

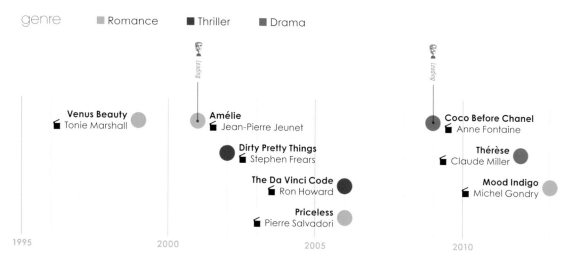

genre ■ Romance ■ Thriller ■ Drama

Venus Beauty
Tonie Marshall

Amélie
Jean-Pierre Jeunet

Dirty Pretty Things
Stephen Frears

The Da Vinci Code
Ron Howard

Priceless
Pierre Salvadori

Coco Before Chanel
Anne Fontaine

Thérèse
Claude Miller

Mood Indigo
Michel Gondry

1995   2000   2005   2010

shirley temple 1928–2014

Little Miss Marker

Bright Eyes

Curly Top

The Littlest Rebel

Wee Willie Winkie

Heidi

The Little Princess

Fort Apache

In the aphotic depths of the Great Depression, U.S. President Franklin D. Roosevelt commented, "As long as our country has Shirley Temple, we will be all right." He was not alone in that belief. Battered by unprecedented economic hardship, the United States turned to the cherubic all-singing-all-dancing Temple for cheer, and for three years in the 1930s she was the nation's box-office star.

Born in Santa Monica, California in 1928, Temple's natural gift for performing was capitalized upon by her ambitious mother, who arranged for her to take dance lessons and put her hair in Mary Pickford-like ringlets. Her first on-screen appearances were in 1932 in a series of one-reel parodies called *Baby Burlesks*. Her breakthrough came performing "Baby Take a Bow" with James Dunn in *Stand Up and Cheer!* (1934). She also had her first starring role that year, in *Little Miss Marker*, playing a girl cared for by gangsters after her father loses her in a bet and commits suicide. Her ascent was immediate; by the end of 1934, she had starred in her first star vehicle, *Bright Eyes*, in which she performed her signature song "On the Good Ship Lollipop." A few months later, she was awarded the first Juvenile Oscar, recognition of her status in the industry.

Temple was as much a cultural phenomenon as she was a movie star, responsible for a wide range of merchandise, including over $45 million worth of Shirley Temple dolls. A story development team of 19 writers was set up at Twentieth Century Fox to create projects for her, and hit after hit followed, including *The Little Colonel* (1935), *Curly Top* (1935), *The Littlest Rebel* (1935), *Dimples* (1936) and *Stowaway* (1936). She played ten orphans in five years, specializing in the portrayal of indefatigably optimistic characters taken in by gruff older men in need of uplift.

As Temple aged and her films became more ambitious. She appeared in more adaptations of children's literature, such as the John Ford-directed *Wee Willie Winkie* (1937) — now more famous for novelist Graham Greene's review than the film itself — *Heidi* (1937) and *The Little Princess* (1939). Her career survived her transition to teenagehood, but after *The Blue Bird* and *Young People* both flopped in 1940 she was no longer quite the box-office attraction she had been. Aside of the features *Since You Went Away* (1944), *The Bachelor and the Bobby-Soxer* (1947) and her second film with John Ford, *Fort Apache* (1948), Temple's work was mostly indifferent and was received by audiences and critics accordingly. She also tired of her career and, after 19 years in the profession, Shirley Temple retired from the film industry forever. She was 22 years old. Later, she would pursue a diplomatic career, becoming the U.S. ambassador to Ghana and then to Czechoslovakia during the Velvet Revolution. **JWa**

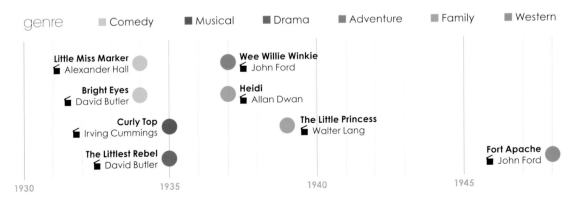

genre   ■ Comedy   ■ Musical   ■ Drama   ■ Adventure   ■ Family   ■ Western

Little Miss Marker
Alexander Hall

Bright Eyes
David Butler

Curly Top
Irving Cummings

The Littlest Rebel
David Butler

Wee Willie Winkie
John Ford

Heidi
Allan Dwan

The Little Princess
Walter Lang

Fort Apache
John Ford

1930   1935   1940   1945

Character Actor | Charmer | Saint | Sinner

emma thompson 1959

| Howards End | Much Ado About Nothing | The Remains of the Day | In the Name of the Father | Sense and Sensibility | Love Actually | An Education | Saving Mr. Banks |

It is a well-known and depressing fact that few successful actresses are guaranteed as high-profile a career once they pass a certain age. The number of films featuring roles for older women is pathetically small. It is a testament then to Emma Thompson's enduring appeal that she has continued to build such a formidable body of work over the last 20 years.

Thompson's skills as both a comic and serious actor led to appearances in the television comedy shows *The Comic Strip Presents...* (1984) and *The Young Ones* (1984) before taking on more significant roles in *Tutti Frutti* (1987) and *Fortunes of War* (1987) — where she met husband Kenneth Branagh. Her film debut was in the Richard Curtis-penned comedy *The Tall Guy* (1989). In the same year, she starred in Branagh's directorial debut, *Henry V*. The pair collaborated on *Dead Again* (1991), *Peter's Friends* (1992) and the joyful *Much Ado About Nothing* (1993), although by that time they were divorced.

In her first collaboration with the directing-producing team of Merchant Ivory, Thompson gave an Oscar-winning performance as Margaret Schlegel, the moral spine of E.M. Forster's *Howards End* (1992), a story of class division in turn-of-the-20th-century England. She and costar Anthony Hopkins reunited for *The Remains of the Day* in 1993. Her performance is a masterclass in balancing passion and restraint.

Thompson's greatest accomplishment is arguably her joint role of lead actress in and screenwriter of Ang Lee's *Sense and Sensibility* (1995). Her adaptation of Jane Austen's sprawling novel is a cinematic feast, losing none of the novel's themes, which deals with women who are not just searching for love, but looking for a life and the means by which to live it.

Thompson has seldom ventured into blockbuster territory, such as the *Harry Potter* franchise. She has played strong individuals, including the wife of a philandering president in *Primary Colors* (1998) and P.L. Travers in *Saving Mr. Banks* (2013). In *Love Actually* (2003), her role sidesteps the sentimentality affecting every other narrative thread of the film, instead offering a credible portrait of emotional distress. *Stranger than Fiction* (2006) was a fascinating role in terms of gender balance. She plays an author suffering from writer's block, who discovers that her manuscript is narrating the life of an ordinary man. It is a fine example of how Thompson has become one of the most versatile talents in contemporary cinema. **SW**

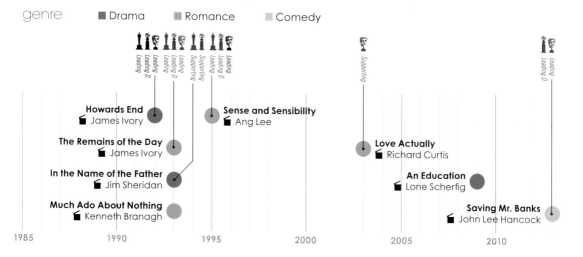

genre ■ Drama ■ Romance ■ Comedy

Leading / Leading D / Leading / Leading D / Leading / Supporting / Supporting / Leading / Leading D / Leading

Supporting

Leading / Leading D

Howards End
James Ivory

Sense and Sensibility
Ang Lee

The Remains of the Day
James Ivory

Love Actually
Richard Curtis

In the Name of the Father
Jim Sheridan

An Education
Lone Scherfig

Much Ado About Nothing
Kenneth Branagh

Saving Mr. Banks
John Lee Hancock

1985 | 1990 | 1995 | 2000 | 2005 | 2010

the three stooges

| Soup to Nuts | Woman Haters | Men in Black | Grips, Grunts and Groans | Rockin' in the Rockies | Brideless Groom | Have Rocket, Will Travel | The Three Stooges in Orbit |

The Three Stooges were the last surviving screen presence of the U.S. vaudeville tradition, continuing to appear in wild slapstick farces long after the form had lost its foothold in popular culture. While the most famous permutation of the ensemble consisted of Larry Fine (Louis Feinberg, 1902–75) and brothers Curly (Jerome Lester Horwitz, 1903–52) and Moe Howard (Moses Horwitz, 1897–1975), the long-running comedy act featured several different lineups throughout their 220 films, with Larry and Moe as the only constants.

Initially the Stooges were created as the support to lead comedian Ted Healy. After several years as a live act the group starred in their first film, *Soup to Nuts* (1930), but its lack of success led to a difficult period in which the Stooges and a marginalized, alcoholic Healy argued frequently. At this point the third Stooge was Shemp Howard, who would be replaced by his younger brother Curly when Shemp left to pursue a successful solo career. The troupe starred in a series of shorts, including *Nertsery Rhymes* (1933), and also provided comic relief in films like *Meet the Baron* (1933).

In 1934, the trio separated acrimoniously from Healy and renamed themselves the Three Stooges, their screen personalities by now fully developed: Moe, the bullying leader, Curly, the man-child innocent and Larry, the acquiescent intermediary. Signing a contract with Columbia, they starred in many short films, the best of which were *Woman Haters* (1934), *Hoi Polloi* (1935) and *Grips, Grunts and Groans* (1937). Filled with broad physical comedy, the films remained popular despite shorts falling out of fashion. They even received an Oscar nomination for 1934's *Men in Black*.

Even though they are best known for the 190 short films they made for Columbia between 1934 and 1959, the Three Stooges made appearances in other films, including *Start Cheering* (1938) and *Time Out for Rhythm* (1941). Their own feature vehicles, such as *Rockin' in the Rockies* (1945) and *Swing Parade of 1946* (1946), were less common. Unlike Laurel and Hardy or the Marx brothers, they appeared to show little ambition in pushing the format of their act.

The most prominent lineup of Larry, Curly and Moe ended in 1946 when Curly retired due to a period of prolonged illness. He was reluctantly succeeded by a returning Shemp Howard, who starred in *Brideless Groom* (1947), *The Hot Scots* (1948) and *Who Done It?* (1949). He remained until his death in 1955. By this point, the quality of the Stooges' work had diminished considerably. They continued with Joe Besser, whose entries are the least well-regarded, until Columbia canceled their contract. After "Curly Joe" DeRita joined in 1958 the group mounted a late comeback, appearing on television and starring in several popular features including *Have Rocket, Will Travel* (1959) and *The Three Stooges in Orbit* (1962). **JWa**

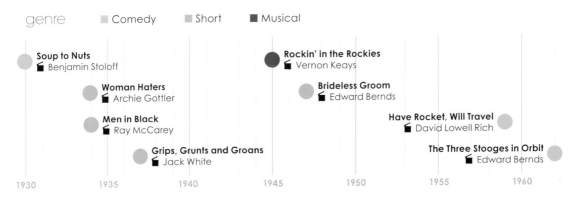

genre ■ Comedy ■ Short ■ Musical

Soup to Nuts
Benjamin Stoloff

Woman Haters
Archie Gottler

Men in Black
Ray McCarey

Grips, Grunts and Groans
Jack White

Rockin' in the Rockies
Vernon Keays

Brideless Groom
Edward Bernds

Have Rocket, Will Travel
David Lowell Rich

The Three Stooges in Orbit
Edward Bernds

1930 1935 1940 1945 1950 1955 1960

uma thurman 1970

Dangerous Liaisons | Henry & June | Even Cowgirls Get the Blues | Pulp Fiction | Beautiful Girls | Gattaca | Kill Bill: Vol. 1 | Nympho-maniac

Having begun her career as a fashion model at the age of 15, Uma Thurman made the transition to the big screen in 1987 with *Kiss Daddy Goodnight*. The following year, her breakthrough came with a cameo in Terry Gilliam's enchanting *The Adventures of Baron Munchausen* and, more crucially, her role as Cecile de Volanges in Stephen Frears' acclaimed *Dangerous Liaisons*. The promise she showed in that film was followed by her portrayal of June Miller in the sexually explicit *Henry & June* (1990), playing a blind woman in thriller *Jennifer 8* (1992) and holding her own against Robert De Niro and Bill Murray in *Mad Dog and Glory* (1993). Around this time, she married actor Gary Oldman, but their relationship only lasted two years.

Thurman's performance in the notorious flop *Even Cowgirls Get The Blues* (1994) was met with universal derision. Fortunately, her next appearance was as a feisty gangster's moll in Quentin Tarantino's *Pulp Fiction* (1994). With her Louise Brooks' bob, sparky dialogue and a memorable dance scene opposite John Travolta, she is one of the most iconic images of 1990s cinema. She reunited with Tarantino in 2003 for *Kill Bill: Vol. 1* and its sequel (2004). A cinematic love letter from director to star, with a role that they created together, Thurman is compelling as the kick-ass heroine. She followed up *Pulp Fiction* with indie charmer *Beautiful Girls* (1996) and romcom *The Truth About Cats and Dogs* (1996). Thurman was Ethan Hawke's love interest in the visionary sci-fi drama *Gattaca* (1997). The pair married shortly after. Unfortunately, she followed a string of successes with arguably her worst film choices; firstly, in the woeful *Batman and Robin* (1997) and then the disastrous big-screen version of TV series *The Avengers* (1998).

Over the next few years, Thurman focused on raising her family. Her most notable roles in this period were a smart cameo in Woody Allen's *Sweet and Lowdown* (1999), one of the leads in Merchant Ivory's lustrous *The Golden Bowl* (2000) and opposite Hawke in the tense drama *Tape* (2001). She also won a Golden Globe for her performance in the HBO TV movie *Hysterical Blindness* (2002). Roles in moderate hits like the underwhelming *Get Shorty* (1995) sequel *Be Cool* (2005) and a turn as Medusa in *Percy Jackson & the Lightning Thief* (2010) kept her in the public eye. But, it was a role in Lars von Trier's *Nymphomaniac* (2013) that provided Thurman with her most exciting and unexpected appearance for some years. **MB**

genre   ■ Drama   ■ Crime   ■ Comedy   ■ Romance   ■ Sci-Fi   ■ Action

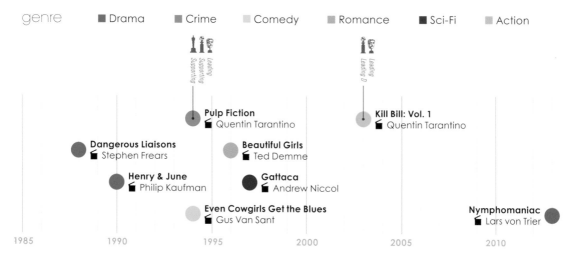

Leading / Supporting / Supporting

Pulp Fiction
Quentin Tarantino

Leading / Leading O

Kill Bill: Vol. 1
Quentin Tarantino

Dangerous Liaisons
Stephen Frears

Beautiful Girls
Ted Demme

Henry & June
Philip Kaufman

Gattaca
Andrew Niccol

Even Cowgirls Get the Blues
Gus Van Sant

Nymphomaniac
Lars von Trier

1985   1990   1995   2000   2005   2010

spencer tracy 1900–67

| 20,000 Years in Sing Sing | Man's Castle | Fury | Captains Courageous | Edison, the Man | Dr. Jekyll and Mr. Hyde | Woman of the Year | State of the Union |

Spencer Tracy was Hollywood's all-American everyman. The characters he played were typically no-nonsense, gruff-spoken proletarians, often truculent or pugnacious, sometimes brooding or stubborn to the point of pig-headedness, but rarely vicious. In his early career he was occasionally cast as bad guys, but after that there were few villains in his filmography. And, especially by his peers, he was one of the most respected actors in U.S. cinema.

He was born into an Irish-American working-class family, and after military academy and Ripon College entered the American Academy of Dramatic Art in New York. Success on Broadway brought him to the attention of John Ford, who cast him in the lead of *Up the River* (1930), a comedy about an ex-con. It was minor Ford, but noticed enough for Fox to put Tracy under contract. His first few roles for them, often typecast as a gangster, were no great shakes, so he was happy to be loaned out to Warner's for *20,000 Years in Sing Sing* (1932) — a criminal again, but a role with more complexity.

Impressed, Fox gave him *The Power and the Glory* (1933), the rise and fall of a railroad tycoon (scripted by Preston Sturges), and one of the first films to use voice-over narration. He was the best thing in *Man's Castle* (1933), a Depression-set romance, and a cynical carnie-owner in *Dante's Inferno* (1935). That same year he served a brief jail term for drunkenness. Fox dropped him, but MGM snapped him up and gave him some of his best roles; not least Fritz Lang's first U.S. film, *Fury* (1936), as the lynch-mob victim plotting his revenge. He was a priest, not for the last time, sparring with Clark Gable in the earthquake drama *San Francisco* (1936), and an earthy Portuguese fisherman (with a dubious accent) in *Captains Courageous* (1937). Back with Borzage, he played a cab-driver defying the crime bosses in *Big City* (1937); and he was a priest again, barely surmounting the sentimentality, in the urban morality-play of *Boys Town* (1938).

By now he was a shoo-in for prestige biopics, and he got two of them: *Stanley and Livingstone* (1939 — he was Stanley), and *Edison, the Man* (1940). He was suitably heroic in King Vidor's period adventure *Northwest Passage* (1940). More sparring with Gable in *Boom Town* (1940), then for once he played evil in *Dr. Jekyll and Mr. Hyde* (1941). It was generally felt that Fredric March had done a better job.

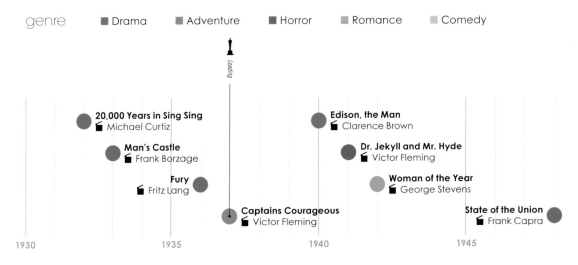

genre ■ Drama ■ Adventure ■ Horror ■ Romance ■ Comedy

Leading

20,000 Years in Sing Sing
🎬 Michael Curtiz

Man's Castle
🎬 Frank Borzage

Fury
🎬 Fritz Lang

Captains Courageous
🎬 Victor Fleming

Edison, the Man
🎬 Clarence Brown

Dr. Jekyll and Mr. Hyde
🎬 Victor Fleming

Woman of the Year
🎬 George Stevens

State of the Union
🎬 Frank Capra

1930   1935   1940   1945

| Adam's Rib | Father of the Bride | The Actress | Bad Day at Black Rock | The Old Man and the Sea | Inherit the Wind | Judgment at Nuremberg | Guess Who's Coming to Dinner |

Then came the first of his nine films — and his off-screen partnership — with Katharine Hepburn. *Woman of the Year* (1942) set the battle-of-the-sexes pattern: she is a patrician political columnist, he is a down-to-earth sports journalist, and their mutual attraction snags on their disagreement over a woman's role. The ending is appallingly sexist, but the crackling chemistry between them makes for great comedy. Although Tracy's marriage was dead, as a Catholic he could not divorce; but his relationship with Hepburn became an open secret.

Of their films together, *Adam's Rib* (1949), *Pat and Mike* (1952) and, to lesser effect, *Without Love* (1945) and *The Desk Set* (1957), replayed the teaming for comedy; *Keeper of the Flame* (1942) and *State of the Union* (1948) took a slightly more serious stance; and there was a so-so western, *The Sea of Grass* (1947). Meanwhile Tracy took on war movies, of which *The Seventh Cross* (1944), where he played an anti-Nazi German on the run, was the best. Several routine movies filled out the decade before he took the title role in *Father of the Bride* (1950).

He made one good western in the 1950s, *Broken Lance* (1954), as a domineering cattle baron, and one great one: *Bad Day at Black Rock* (1955), a one-armed World War II veteran up against larceny and ingrained racism in a desert township. Back with John Ford for only the second time in his career, he played a lovably corrupt politico in *The Last Hurrah* (1958), but as a Mexican fisherman in the Hemingway adaptation *The Old Man and the Sea* (1958) he appeared stiff. He was becoming cantankerous and difficult to work with, although Stanley Kramer made good use of him in *Inherit the Wind* (1960), as the liberal lawyer defending a 1925 Tennessee schoolteacher's right to expound Darwinian theory.

He played his final priest in *The Devil at Four O'Clock* (1961) and a judge in the self-consciously solemn *Judgment at Nuremberg* (1961). That was for Kramer again, as was the comedy *It's a Mad, Mad, Mad, Mad World* (1963). He was suffering from emphysema and diabetes, and made no films for four years. Kramer and Hepburn talked him into doing *Guess Who's Coming to Dinner* (1967), as the liberal father dismayed to find his daughter's engaged to a black man. A sententious, self-satisfied film, it is redeemed by the final teaming of Hepburn with a visibly ill Tracy. He died barely a week after shooting wrapped. **PK**

■ Thriller

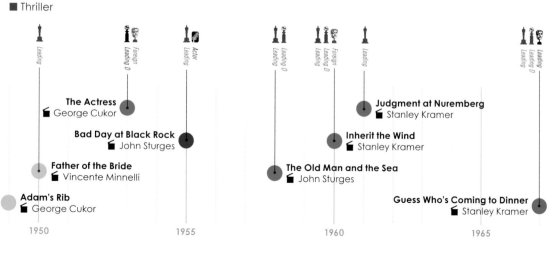

The Actress
📽 George Cukor

Bad Day at Black Rock
📽 John Sturges

Father of the Bride
📽 Vincente Minnelli

Adam's Rib
📽 George Cukor

Judgment at Nuremberg
📽 Stanley Kramer

Inherit the Wind
📽 Stanley Kramer

The Old Man and the Sea
📽 John Sturges

Guess Who's Coming to Dinner
📽 Stanley Kramer

1950　　　　1955　　　　1960　　　　1965

john travolta 1954

Saturday Night Fever

Grease

Blow Out

Look Who's Talking

Pulp Fiction

Get Shorty

Face/Off

Hairspray

Having gained notoriety for his role in the hit television sitcom *Welcome Back Kotter* (1975–79), John Travolta's cinematic breakthrough came with Brian De Palma's masterful horror opus *Carrie* (1976). However, it was the following year that his career went stratospheric thanks to his stunning portrayal of disco dancing lothario Tony Manero in *Saturday Night Fever* (1977). A brilliant, riveting performance, it earned the young actor his first Academy Award nomination.

Travolta's stardom continued to rocket the following year with his role as Danny Zucko in the film adaptation of hit musical *Grease* (1978). It remains one of his most enduring, beloved and iconic roles. Unfortunately, no sooner did Travolta become one of Hollywood's biggest stars, his fame took a nosedive with a string of films that underperformed at the box office. *Urban Cowboy* (1980) and *Blow Out* (1981), both showcased Travolta's impressive dramatic range (the latter proving arguably Travolta's most accomplished performance), but failed to rival the successes of his previous hits, while the misstep that was *Staying Alive* (1983) saw him revisit the role of Tony Manero to disastrous effect. The rest of the 1980s saw the decline continue, with films like *Two of a Kind* (1983) failing to

excite either critics or audiences. *Look Who's Talking* (1989) looked briefly promising, but Travolta followed this up with a series of duds.

Pulp Fiction (1994) put Travolta back on the map. Ever the cinephile, Quentin Tarantino cast the actor based on his performance in *Blow Out* and the role of hit man Vincent Vega saw Travolta earn his second Academy Award nomination. In one of Hollywood's greatest comebacks, the years that followed saw the actor rise to prominence with acclaimed performances in the smart *Get Shorty* (1995), action thriller *Broken Arrow* (1996) and the delirious bullet ballet *Face/Off* (1997), serious dramas *Mad City* (1997) and *A Civil Action* (1998) and the political satire *Primary Colors* (1998). Yet, true to form, Travolta made some bad decisions, the worst of which being the film adaptation of Church of Scientology founder L. Ron Hubbard's *Battlefield Earth* (2000). The following years saw a string of disappointments. He may have hit box-office gold with his role as Edna Turnblad in *Hairspray* (2007), but there are few other roles in which the actor could display his talent. He starred in Oliver Stone's *Savages* (2012), but like most of his recent films, neither audiences or critics were impressed. **MB**

genre ■ Drama ■ Musical ■ Thriller ■ Comedy ■ Action

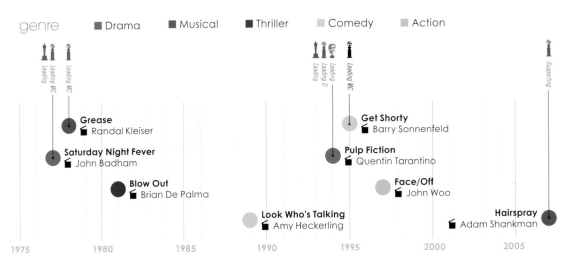

Grease
Randal Kleiser

Saturday Night Fever
John Badham

Blow Out
Brian De Palma

Look Who's Talking
Amy Heckerling

Get Shorty
Barry Sonnenfeld

Pulp Fiction
Quentin Tarantino

Face/Off
John Woo

Hairspray
Adam Shankman

1975   1980   1985   1990   1995   2000   2005

kathleen turner 1954

Body Heat

Romancing the Stone

Crimes of Passion

Prizzi's Honor

Peggy Sue Got Married

The War of the Roses

Serial Mom

The Virgin Suicides

With a commanding screen presence and trademark gravelly voice, the latter often drawing comparisons to deep-toned icon Lauren Bacall, Kathleen Turner burst onto the screen playing the seductive femme fatale in Lawrence Kasdan's neo-noir *Body Heat* (1981). It propelled her to instant stardom. Rather than cash in on her vampy persona, Turner followed it with a role in the Steve Martin vehicle *The Man With Two Brains* (1983), in which she starred as a villainous gold digger. Turner continued to display her comic prowess as Joan Wilder in Robert Zemeckis' *Romancing the Stone* (1984). Playing a romantic novelist who discovers life is far more thrilling than fiction, she won a Golden Globe for her performance, which was the first of three opposite Michael Douglas and Danny DeVito. They followed it with the disappointing sequel *The Jewel of the Nile* (1985), but then offered audiences something much darker. A caustic, hilarious account of a marriage gone sour, *The War of the Roses* (1989), which DeVito directed.

She excelled as the prostitute being stalked in Ken Russell's controversial *Crimes of Passion* (1984) and earned another Golden Globe for her portrayal of an assassin who falls in love with Jack Nicholson's mobster in John Huston's *Prizzi's Honor* (1985). However, it was as a despondent housewife in Francis Ford Coppola's whimsical *Peggy Sue Got Married* (1986) that Turner showed her range, moving from the present day back in time, to chart where the rot set into her marriage and to possibly offer her another chance. She was deservedly nominated for an Oscar.

Turner put her distinctive vocals to good use, playing Jessica Rabbit in *Who Framed Roger Rabbit* (1988), while that same year she worked with Kasdan again on the understated *The Accidental Tourist*. The good reviews for her performance in that film were a stark contrast to the universal drubbing she received for *V.I. Warshawski* (1991).

Due to personal illness, Turner appeared in few films during the 1990s. Her standout performance from this period was as the murderous matriarch in John Waters' black comedy *Serial Mom* (1994). She gave one of her best performances, as a conservative, domineering mother in Sofia Coppola's directorial debut *The Virgin Suicides* (1999). More recently, Turner played Chandler Bing's father in a few episodes of sitcom *Friends* and she dabbled in extremely broad comedy in the sequel *Dumb and Dumber To* (2014). **MB**

genre ■ Thriller ■ Adventure ■ Crime ■ Comedy ■ Drama

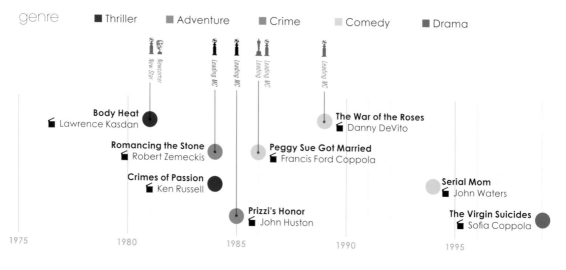

Newcomer / New Star

Leading MC

Leading MC

Leading MC

Leading MC

Body Heat
Lawrence Kasdan

Romancing the Stone
Robert Zemeckis

Crimes of Passion
Ken Russell

Prizzi's Honor
John Huston

Peggy Sue Got Married
Francis Ford Coppola

The War of the Roses
Danny DeVito

Serial Mom
John Waters

The Virgin Suicides
Sofia Coppola

1975 1980 1985 1990 1995

lana turner 1921–95

Ziegfeld Girl

Slightly
Dangerous

The Postman
Always
Rings Twice

Green
Dolphin
Street

The Bad
and the
Beautiful

Peyton
Place

Imitation
of Life

Madame X

To Lana Turner belongs the quintessential Hollywood discovery story. Born poor in rural Idaho, she moved to Los Angeles with her mother soon after her father was murdered in a robbery. Things changed for Lana (then Julia) Turner when, as a 16-year-old schoolgirl, she skipped a typing class and went for a soda on Sunset Boulevard. She was spotted by the publisher of *The Hollywood Reporter* and, via his industry contacts, fast-tracked into a contract with MGM. Turner's first film, *They Won't Forget* (1937), saw her costumed in a manner that led to the nickname "The Sweater Girl" — and commenced a pattern of Turner being cast in roles that required little more of her than prettiness.

It was Tay Garnett's superior noir *The Postman Always Rings Twice* (1946), based on the novel by James M. Cain, that expanded what was offered to her. Although glamour was still crucial to the role — her white-hot wardrobe offering an electrifying challenge to the notion that femmes fatales can be relied upon to dress in black — she also captured with painful acuity the frustration and repressed rage of a woman trapped in poverty and underappreciated in a passionless marriage. The late 1940s saw her ensconced as MGM's most popular star, headlining

titles such as *Cass Timberlane* (1947) with Spencer Tracy, *Homecoming* (1948) with Clark Gable and *The Three Musketeers* (1948) with Gene Kelly. However, the following decade provided her with more enduring projects: Vincente Minnelli's sweeping melodrama *The Bad and the Beautiful* (1952); the huge hit *Peyton Place* (1957), for which she was Oscar-nominated, and Douglas Sirk's lush tearjerker *Imitation of Life* (1959).

The year 1958 also saw Turner struck by one of the most intriguing scandals ever to afflict a major Hollywood star, when her mobster lover Johnny Stompanato was stabbed to death in her home during a fight. In a sensational trial, at which Turner was required to testify for over an hour, her 14-year-old daughter Cheryl Crane was found to have committed justifiable homicide while defending her mother from Stompanato's violence. Turner feared the case would damage her career; in fact, the publicity — as well as the fact that the film coincidentally focused upon the stormy relationship between a mother and teenage daughter — helped *Imitation of Life* to succeed. Still, Turner worked sporadically over the 1960s, and by the 1970s had largely retired, although she had a guest role on the soap opera *Falcon Crest* in 1982. **HM**

genre   ■ Musical   ■ Romance   ■ Noir   ■ Drama

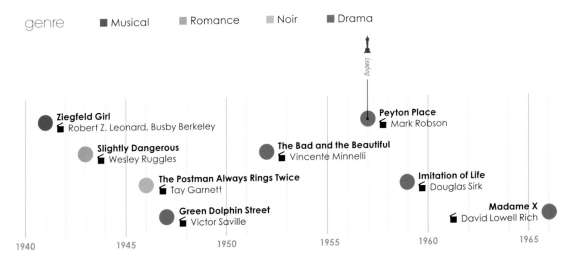

Leading

Ziegfeld Girl
Robert Z. Leonard, Busby Berkeley

Peyton Place
Mark Robson

Slightly Dangerous
Wesley Ruggles

The Bad and the Beautiful
Vincente Minnelli

The Postman Always Rings Twice
Tay Garnett

Imitation of Life
Douglas Sirk

Green Dolphin Street
Victor Saville

Madame X
David Lowell Rich

1940   1945   1950   1955   1960   1965

liv ullmann 1938

Persona

Hour of
the Wolf

The
Emigrants

Cries and
Whispers

A Bridge
Too Far

Autumn
Sonata

Speriamo
che sia
femmina

Saraband

The most internationally successful female member of Ingmar Bergman's repertory company, Liv Ullmann's career has alternated psychologically intense leading roles in the Swedish master's films with a wide range of other dramatic and even comedic roles.

Born in Tokyo to Norwegian parents, she grew up in Toronto and New York before commencing a stage career in her ancestral homeland. Ullmann secured her first leading role in *Young Sinners* (1959). When she made her first Swedish film, *Kort är sommaren* (1962), she and costar Bibi Andersson unexpectedly bumped into Bergman in a Stockholm street and he had the idea for *Persona* (1966) after he was struck by their physical resemblance. *Persona* cast Ullmann as an inexplicably mute actress cared for by Andersson's garrulous nurse, their faces ultimately merging in an iconic European arthouse cinema image. Ullmann became Bergman's lover and muse. She was war-stricken in *Shame* (1968), beset by demons in *Hour of the Wolf* (1968), bereaved in *The Passion of Anna* (1969), sexually vivacious in *Cries and Whispers* (1972), half of a disintegrating marriage in the searing *Scenes from a Marriage* (1973) and one of two married psychiatrists in *Face to Face* (1976). After playing

David Carradine's sibling in *The Serpent's Egg* (1977), she forged another beautifully calibrated female partnership as Ingrid Bergman's daughter in *Autumn Sonata* (1978). She also starred in Jan Troell's two-part epic *The Emigrants* (1971) and *The New Land* (1972).

Her English-language roles were less memorable. She was Charles Bronson's kidnapped wife in *Cold Sweat* (1970), the medieval *Pope Joan* (1972), the older half of a May-September romance in the comedy *40 Carats* (1973) and a Himalayas-stranded teacher in the musical *Lost Horizon* (1973). She also played Queen Christina of Sweden in *The Abdication* (1975) and the real-life "Angel of Arnhem," Kate ter Horst, in Richard Attenborough's epic but unfocused *A Bridge Too Far* (1977).

Increasingly drawn to the stage, Ullmann was absent from cinema screens for almost a decade before starring in Ingmar Bergman's swansong *Saraband* (2003), which saw her share the screen with her costar of many Bergman films — Erlund Josephson. More recently, *Two Lives* (2012) cast her as a woman whose decision to testify against the Norwegian state over a shameful World War II secret has a life-changing impact on her daughter. **MBr**

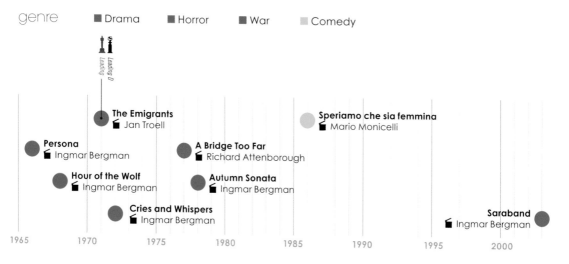

genre   ■ Drama   ■ Horror   ■ War   ■ Comedy

Leading D

The Emigrants
Jan Troell

Speriamo che sia femmina
Mario Monicelli

Persona
Ingmar Bergman

A Bridge Too Far
Richard Attenborough

Hour of the Wolf
Ingmar Bergman

Autumn Sonata
Ingmar Bergman

Cries and Whispers
Ingmar Bergman

Saraband
Ingmar Bergman

1965   1970   1975   1980   1985   1990   1995   2000

rudolph valentino 1895–1926

The Four Horsemen of the Apocalypse

Camille

The Conquering Power

The Sheik

Blood and Sand

The Eagle

The Son of the Sheik

A Sainted Devil

It is said that women fainted on hearing the news that Rudolph Valentino had died on August 23, 1926, as a result of complications following surgery for appendicitis. Over 100,000 people attended his funeral in New York City. People apparently committed suicide that day. There was even a small riot that had to be quelled by police officers on horseback. Such was the star's immense popularity. In the years since, it has only bolstered his legend. Unfortunately, most of his films have not lived up to his reputation.

He was born Rodolfo Alfonso Raffaello Pierre Filibert Guglielmi di Valentina d'Antonguolla in Apulia, a region of Italy, in 1895. At 18, he passed through Ellis Island's immigration center to become a citizen of the United States. His first years in the country were tough and he subsequently found himself homeless. He eventually made his way to the West Coast with Al Jolson's traveling theater company and was cast in bit-parts before he appeared as Julio Desnoyers in Rex Ingram's World War I drama *The Four Horsemen of the Apocalypse* (1921). It was a huge commercial and critical success but the studio and Ingram had insufficient faith in either his ability or screen presence. He was cast in the now-missing *Uncharted Seas* (1921) and *The Conquering Power* (1921), which was another commercial success. He developed *Camille* (1921) outside the studio,

but the resulting film was dismissed by critics as too experimental for audience's tastes.

Valentino then moved to Famous Players-Lasky Corporation and his reputation as the screen's great lover was sealed with *The Sheik* (1921). The story of an Arab Sheik Ahmed Ben Hassan — whom we actually discover is not Arab at all but a mix of British and Spanish — who falls in love with a British aristocrat. The film played for almost a year in some countries. The actor returned to the role with the superior *The Son of the Sheik* (1926), which features one of his best performances. It was released shortly after his death.

He worked on four Famous Players-Lasky films over the course of the next year and a half. *Moran of the Lady Letty* (1921) was dismissed by critics but lapped up by audiences eager to see Valentino steal hearts. *Beyond the Rocks, Blood and Sand* and *The Young Rajah*, all produced in 1922, were no better. There was a hiatus as the actor went on strike, unhappy once again at the way he was being financially treated by a studio. When he returned, in 1924, he starred in the critical and commercial failures *Monsieur Beaucaire* and *A Sainted Devil*.

He moved to United Artists and starred in *The Eagle* (1925). His best film, it plays up his romantic image while also offering a slyly amusing commentary on it. Although not as successful as his final movie, it is his most enduring. **IHS**

genre   ■ War   ■ Romance   ■ Drama   ■ Action   ■ Adventure

The Four Horsemen of the Apocalypse
Rex Ingram

Camille
Ray C. Smallwood

The Conquering Power
Rex Ingram

The Sheik
George Melford

Blood and Sand
Fred Niblo

The Eagle
Clarence Brown

The Son of the Sheik
George Fitzmaurice

1921   1922   1923   1924   1925   1926

Cop	Crook	Killer	Hero

lino ventura 1919–87

| Touchez Pas au Grisbi | Elevator to the Gallows | Classe Tous Risques | Le Deuxième Souffle | The Sicilian Clan | Army of the Shadows | Illustrious Corpses | Garde à vue |

Many of his films were hard-boiled thrillers and his physically imposing presence made him a natural heavy, but Lino Ventura was also a subtle character player with a particular gift for portraying people weighed down either by their conscience or by circumstances that they cannot control.

Despite being largely associated with French cinema, he was born in Parma, Italy, in 1919. His family moved to France when he was 7 and he initially made his name as a champion Greco-Roman wrestler before breaking into films, by chance, when director Jacques Becker, struck by his distinctive appearance, cast him as an Italian gangster in the classic thriller *Touchez Pas au Grisbi* (1954). He acted opposite French cinema idol Jean Gabin, who was sufficiently impressed to encourage the younger man to keep up acting. They made five more films together.

Ventura initially played criminals, but by the mid-1950s he was also being cast as cops. In *Elevator to the Gallows* (1958), he is the detective who ultimately solves the crime. In *Classe Tous Risques* (1960) he gave one of his definitive performances as career criminal Abel Davos, desperately trying to maintain his code of honor as things go wrong and the police close in. He made a rare appearance speaking his native Italian in Vittorio De Sica's *The Last Judgment* (1961), but generally stuck with French cinema — unsurprisingly, as by then he was a major star in his own right, thanks to popular hits like *Monsieur Gangster* (1963) and *The Great Spy Chase* (1964)

In 1966, he appeared in the first of a number of films directed by Jean-Pierre Melville. The two men did not get on, which is unfortunate as Ventura was in many ways the perfect protagonist for Melville's stylized, fatalistic thrillers. *Le Deuxième Souffle* (1966) was one of his best, a complex web of intrigue and double-crossing in which Ventura's crook proves more upright than Paul Frankeur's corrupt cop. *Army of the Shadows* (1969) was even better, with Ventura as the head of a French Resistance cell, his weary performance conveying the full moral weight of the frequently terrible decisions that he has to make, including abandoning comrades to their certain death for the sake of the movement as a whole.

Ventura kept up a prolific output until his relatively early death in 1987. He reunited with Jean Gabin for *The Sicilian Clan* (1969) as the police commissioner hell-bent on catching Alain Delon's thief turned cop killer. He was the jailed head of an Italian crime family in *The Valachi Papers* (1972), convinced that fellow prisoner Charles Bronson is an informant. He played the increasingly stymied police inspector in *Illustrious Corpses* (1976), attempting to solve a complex, highly politicized series of murders. While his inspector in *Garde à vue* (1980) painstakingly and self-revealingly interrogates Michel Serrault's murder suspect. **MBr**

genre ■ Crime ■ War ■ Thriller

Touchez Pas au Grisbi
Jacques Becker

Elevator to the Gallows
Louis Malle

Classe Tous Risques
Claude Sautet

Le Deuxième Souffle
Jean-Pierre Melville

The Sicilian Clan
Henri Verneuil

Army of the Shadows
Jean-Pierre Melville

Illustrious Corpses
Francesco Rosi

Garde à vue
Claude Miller

1950   1955   1960   1965   1970   1975   1980

monica vitti 1931

L'Avventura

La Notte

L'Eclisse

Red Desert

Modesty Blaise

The Pacifist

Flirt

Secret Scandal

To international audiences, Monica Vitti was Michelangelo Antonioni's muse, the aloof blonde beauty who starred in many of his greatest films, but to her fellow Italians, she was a popular and prolific comedy actress, although few of these films traveled abroad. Born Maria Luisa Ceciarelli, she worked as a stage actress before breaking into films in 1954.

Her first significant screen role was in *Le Dritte* (1958). By then, she had started working with Antonioni in the theater. They became lovers and their four successive films established her as a major star. In *L'Avventura* (1960), she is the best friend of a woman who vanishes during a Mediterranean cruise, the search becoming increasingly irrelevant as she and her friend's boyfriend are drawn to each other. In *La Notte* (1961), she flirts with Marcello Mastroianni at a party, but refuses to help him destroy his marriage. In *L'Eclisse* (1962) she breaks up her own relationship to be with Alain Delon's stockbroker, only to be alienated by his materialism. And in *Red Desert* (1964), her traumatized reaction to the modern world is matched by a deliberately artificial color scheme.

She continued to make comedies throughout this period and English-speaking audiences saw this side of her when she played the title role of *Modesty Blaise* (1966), an ex-criminal recruited as a British government agent. Kitschy fun, Joseph Losey's film was denounced by fans of Peter O'Donnell's comic-strip source, but retains a cult following to this day. Of her Italian comedies, Mario Monicelli's *The Girl with a Pistol* (1968) had some international exposure thanks to an Oscar nomination for Best Foreign Language Film.

By then, her relationship with Antonioni was over, but she worked with two more great European auteurs, starring in Miklós Jancsó's *The Pacifist* (1970) and in the large ensemble cast of Luis Buñuel's *The Phantom of Liberty* (1974). *Flirt* (1983), directed by future husband Roberto Russo and co-written by the couple, won a Berlin Silver Bear for her performance as a woman whose husband has an imaginary lover. Her last film, *Secret Scandal* (1989), was also her directorial debut. Its failure led to her retirement from the cinema, although she continued to work in television and the theater into the 1990s. **MBr**

genre ■ Mystery ■ Drama ■ Comedy

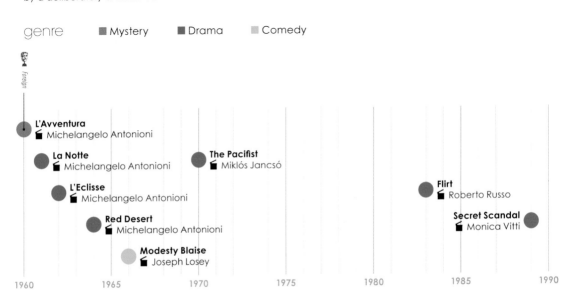

L'Avventura
Michelangelo Antonioni

La Notte
Michelangelo Antonioni

The Pacifist
Miklós Jancsó

L'Eclisse
Michelangelo Antonioni

Flirt
Roberto Russo

Red Desert
Michelangelo Antonioni

Secret Scandal
Monica Vitti

Modesty Blaise
Joseph Losey

1960   1965   1970   1975   1980   1985   1990

gian maria volonté 1933–94

| A Fistful of Dollars | Wind from the East | Investigation of a Citizen Above Suspicion | Le Cercle Rouge | The Mattei Affair | Christ Stopped at Eboli | The Moro Affair | Chronicle of a Death Foretold |

One part matinee idol, two parts killer. Gian Maria Volonté, who was born in Milan in 1933, was devilishly handsome in his youth, but his eyes gave away something darker, wild even. It made him the perfect choice for Sergio Leone's spaghetti westerns.

He started out in theater and made his film debut with a small role in Duilio Coletti's World War II naval drama *Under Ten Flags* (1960). There were roles in a number of low-rent sword and sandal films, including Edward G. Ulmer's silly, little-seen *Journey Beneath the Desert* (1961) and the Reg Park vehicle *Hercules and the Captive Women* (1961). Valerio Zurlini's *Girl with a Suitcase* (1961) was better. He had a starring role in the Taviani brothers' collaboration with Valentino Orsini, *Un uomo da bruciare* (1962), playing a Sicilian who attempts to rally people against Mafia oppression.

Volonté's international breakthrough came with his compelling performance as Ramón Rojo in Leone's *A Fistful of Dollars* (1964). The narrative required his character to be the worst of a bad bunch and the actor delivers a rich, malevolent performance, always on the edge of erupting with violence and a perfect adversary to Clint Eastwood's marginally nicer antihero. He was even better in *For a Few Dollars More* (1965), with Leone zooming in on his expressive eyes, which range from the manic, relishing the moment before a killing, to near-comatose, drifting into a drug-

induced sleep where he dreams of a young woman who killed herself rather than be with him. Audiences may have loved the films and his villain, but Volonté dismissed them. He returned to the genre for Damiano Damiani's *A Bullet for the General* (1966).

Volonté began to work with some of the best filmmakers of the era. He starred in Elio Petri's *We Still Kill the Old Way* (1967), then returned to the director for the excellent satirical thriller *Investigation of a Citizen Above Suspicion* (1970), playing a police inspector who decides to commit a crime to see how corrupt the system he operates in really is. He is part of the ensemble in the Dziga Vertov Group's radical political tract *Wind from the East* (1970) and a member of a gang in Jean-Pierre Melville's masterly *Le Cercle Rouge* (1970). Volonté also worked with Marco Bellicchio on the newspaper-set drama *Slap the Monster on Page One* (1972) and Gillo Pontecorvo on the political drama *Ogro* (1979). However, his most important collaboration was with Francesco Rosi. He is compelling as the titular character in *The Mattei Affair* (1972) and *Lucky Luciano* (1973), and gives a riveting performance as in *Christ Stopped at Eboli* (1979).

Volonté died in 1994, while filming Theo Angelopoulos' *Ulysses' Gaze* (1995). All that remains from that shoot are a few enigmatic images taken by the photographer Joseph Koudelka. **IHS**

V

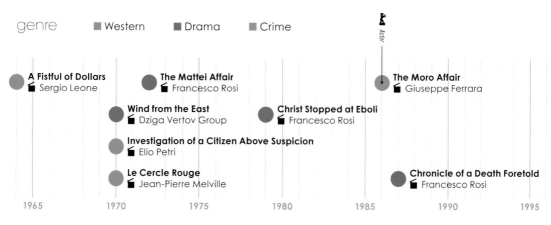

genre ■ Western ■ Drama ■ Crime

Actor

A Fistful of Dollars
Sergio Leone

The Mattei Affair
Francesco Rosi

The Moro Affair
Giuseppe Ferrara

Wind from the East
Dziga Vertov Group

Christ Stopped at Eboli
Francesco Rosi

Investigation of a Citizen Above Suspicion
Elio Petri

Le Cercle Rouge
Jean-Pierre Melville

Chronicle of a Death Foretold
Francesco Rosi

1965   1970   1975   1980   1985   1990   1995

christopher walken 1943

| The Anderson Tapes | Annie Hall | The Deer Hunter | Heaven's Gate | King of New York | Pulp Fiction | The Addiction | A Late Quartet |

Ronald Walken was a child actor who trained as a dancer. By the time of his feature debut, in the Sidney Lumet thriller *The Anderson Tapes* (1971), he was Christopher. Right away, there was something different about him — good-looking but pallid; charismatic but strange. As such, he was perfectly cast as Diane Keaton's bizarre brother Duane in Woody Allen's *Annie Hall* (1977). Allen's line on extricating himself from Duane's disturbing car crash fantasies about "being due back on Planet Earth" summed up Walken's otherworldly appeal.

Michael Cimino's Vietnam epic *The Deer Hunter* (1978) exploited this, with Walken as one of three small-town Pennsylvania friends shattered by their combat experience. The actor is devastating in some of the most intense scenes in U.S. cinema, with Nick little more than a haunted shell of a man as he plays Russian roulette. Walken largely survived the critical mauling given Cimino's notorious follow-up, *Heaven's Gate* (1980) and was able to show off his virtuoso dance skills in the adaptation of Dennis Potter's *Pennies from Heaven* (1981). Yet leading roles in mainstream films seemed an odd fit for him. The only

effective one, the Stephen King adaptation *The Dead Zone* (1983), took advantage of his left-field fragility. Instead, Walken seemed better suited to scene-stealing villainy, be it as a Bond villain (*A View to a Kill*, 1985) or a deranged father in *At Close Range* (1986). That chilling performance established a long roll-call of bad guys. Arguably his best are in Abel Ferrara's searing *King of New York* (1990) and in Tony Scott's *True Romance* (1993). By now, Walken's trademark offbeat line delivery made him ideal to juice up a film: cameo monologues in *Pulp Fiction* (1994) and *The Addiction* (1995) are a highlight of both films. The former confirmed his comedic skills too, another strand in his prolific career much capitalized upon.

Lest Walken's career be reduced to gimmicks, when called upon to offer more, he delivers. His role as father to Leonardo DiCaprio's con artist in *Catch Me If You Can* (2002) is touching and *A Late Quartet* (2012) saw him play a cellist suffering from Parkinson's disease, which he rendered with understated sensitivity. Still, if reassuring weirdness is what you want, villainous or humorous, Walken remains Hollywood's go-to elder statesman of eccentricity. **LS**

W

genre ■ Crime ■ Comedy ■ War ■ Western ■ Thriller ■ Horror ■ Drama

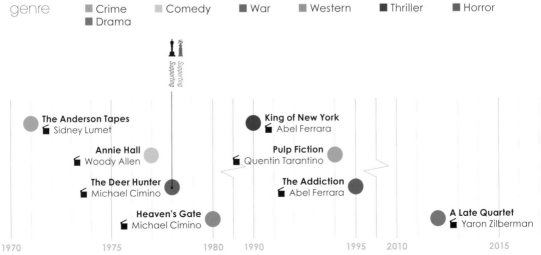

Supporting
Supporting

The Anderson Tapes
Sidney Lumet

Annie Hall
Woody Allen

The Deer Hunter
Michael Cimino

Heaven's Gate
Michael Cimino

King of New York
Abel Ferrara

Pulp Fiction
Quentin Tarantino

The Addiction
Abel Ferrara

A Late Quartet
Yaron Zilberman

1970   1975   1980 1990   1995 2010   2015

christoph waltz 1956

| Inglourious Basterds | The Green Hornet | Carnage | Water for Elephants | The Three Musketeers | Django Unchained | The Zero Theorem | Big Eyes |

Not so much a late bloomer as an untapped well, Christoph Waltz had already enjoyed a lengthy career before the collaboration with Quentin Tarantino that catapulted him into the limelight. His show-stealing turn in *Inglourious Basterds* (2009) not only made him instantly recognizable, but also clinched him Oscar glory from his first nomination. Such an outcome had not always seemed likely for the Austrian-born actor who spent decades on the stage and the small screen, primarily in Germany.

Waltz's well-regarded cinematic debut was in *Kopfstand* (1981), playing a young man incarcerated in an asylum. Much of the 1980s were spent in movies and guest roles on television with a leading part in British miniseries *The Gravy Train* (1990). Throughout the next decade his status grew domestically. He gave an acclaimed turn in *Du bist nicht allein — Die Roy Black Story* (1996), which also began a fruitful collaborative relationship with Peter Keglevic. Over the proceeding years Waltz made intermittent appearances outside Germany — *Ordinary Decent Criminal* (2000) for instance — but remained largely on television, with a growing penchant for memorable villains. He had always resisted playing a Nazi, but when Tarantino came knocking Waltz found his big chance.

A wonderfully enjoyable performance, Waltz's Colonel Hans Landa — the ostentatious antagonist to Brad Pitt's band of vengeful Allies — is at his most captivating in the film's nail-biting opening scene, set in a French farmhouse. After awards recognition came further nefarious roles in studio action movies. They may have done Waltz no harm, but they failed to wow audiences or critics.

More appreciated was his turn in Roman Polanski's *Carnage* (2011), a savage comedy based on Yasmina Reza's stage play. Brimming with sharp dialogue and expansive discourse, it proved another suitable showcase for Waltz's loquacious style. However, it was his second appearance for Tarantino that turned heads once again, in *Django Unchained* (2012). A second Academy Award for supporting actor beckoned.

Terry Gilliam cast Waltz as the lead in his futuristic dystopian satire *The Zero Theorem* (2013) and Tim Burton drew on the actor's propensity for malevolence in *Big Eyes* (2014). And few could quibble with Waltz being cast as the villain in Bond film, *Spectre* (2015). **BN**

W

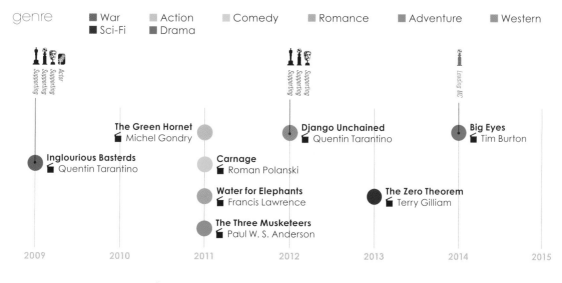

genre
- ■ War
- ■ Sci-Fi
- ■ Action
- ■ Drama
- ■ Comedy
- ■ Romance
- ■ Adventure
- ■ Western

Actor
Supporting
Supporting

Supporting
Supporting

Leading MC

The Green Hornet
Michel Gondry

Inglourious Basterds
Quentin Tarantino

Carnage
Roman Polanski

Water for Elephants
Francis Lawrence

The Three Musketeers
Paul W. S. Anderson

Django Unchained
Quentin Tarantino

The Zero Theorem
Terry Gilliam

Big Eyes
Tim Burton

2009   2010   2011   2012   2013   2014   2015

denzel washington 1954

Carbon Copy

Cry Freedom

Glory

Mo' Better Blues

Malcolm X

The Pelican Brief

Philadelphia

Crimson Tide

Denzel Washington's first major screen role was in the comedy *Carbon Copy* (1981), playing George Segal's son from a short-lived relationship. However, he was better known for his role in the popular U.S. hospital drama *St. Elsewhere*, which ran from 1982 to 1988.

He had a small part in *A Soldier's Story* (1984) and gave an indication of the kind of role he would play in the future with his portrayal of a confident political consultant in *Power* (1986). However, it was as Steve Biko in *Cry Freedom* (1987) that Washington was able to show how charismatic a screen actor he could be. Two low-key films followed: the British thriller *For Queen and Country* (1988) and the Jamaican-set *The Mighty Quinn* (1989). Washington plays an outspoken soldier in the only African-American army unit to fight in the Civil War in *Glory* (1989). He received an Oscar for his performance. It was not the most significant role in the film, but his performance highlighted what a powerful presence he could be.

However, the key development during this period was his work with Spike Lee. He plays a jazz trumpeter in *Mo' Better Blues* (1990), a drama that focuses on the right and wrong decisions we make in life. Washington is impressive, but the film is marred by its

dubious representation of two Jewish characters. Their next film, *Malcolm X* (1992) is a hugely accomplished biopic of the controversial activist, from his early criminal life and subsequent incarceration and conversion to Islam, to his rise in the Nation of Islam, ultimate break away from it and assassination in 1965. It is a powerhouse performance from Washington as he transforms from a cocky chancer into a man of great intelligence, wit and wisdom.

He Got Game (1998), Washington's third collaboration with Lee, should be better known than it is. The film features one of the actor's best performances as a prison inmate who has to convince his estranged son, a promising basketball player, to choose the right university in order to get a reduction in his sentence. In their most recent collaboration, *Inside Man* (2006), Washington is a police inspector investigating a bank robbery in which nothing seems to have been stolen. He brings a laconic air to the character that chimes with the film's pace.

After an impressive appearance as Don Pedro of Aragon in Kenneth Branagh's *Much Ado About Nothing* (1993), playing a reporter investigating a conspiracy in *The Pelican Brief* (1993) and a lawyer

W

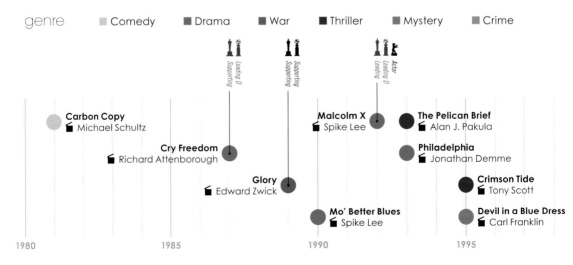

genre ■ Comedy ■ Drama ■ War ■ Thriller ■ Mystery ■ Crime

Carbon Copy
Michael Schultz

Cry Freedom
Richard Attenborough

Glory
Edward Zwick

Mo' Better Blues
Spike Lee

Malcolm X
Spike Lee

The Pelican Brief
Alan J. Pakula

Philadelphia
Jonathan Demme

Crimson Tide
Tony Scott

Devil in a Blue Dress
Carl Franklin

1980   1985   1990   1995

$336 M	$317M	$242M	$139M	$215M	$302M	$181M	$165M
Philadelphia (1993)	The Pelican Brief (1993)	Crimson Tide (1995)	Training Day (2001)	Inside Man (2006)	American Gangster (2007)	Unstoppable (2010)	Flight (2012)

| Devil in a Blue Dress | The Hurricane | Training Day | Inside Man | American Gangster | The Great Debaters | Unstoppable | Flight |

representing a man with AIDS in *Philadelphia* (1993), Washington excelled as the executive officer on a submarine who faces off against his commanding officer when they disagree over the possibility of a nuclear threat, in *Crimson Tide* (1995). It was the first — and most impressive — of five collaborations with Tony Scott, whose visual style has been adopted by countless directors.

Washington's performance as detective Easy Rawlins in *Devil in a Blue Dress* (1995) is one of his most likeable, although Don Cheadle's psychotic Mouse steals every scene. He reunited with *Glory* director Ed Zwick for *Courage Under Fire* (1996), an intelligent examination of friendly fire and the cost of war, with Washington emotionally engaging as an officer whose mistake cost lives. The pair also worked on *The Siege* (1998), which dramatizes a possible terrorist attack on New York. It is an uneven film but elements of it are uncanny as they presage a post-9/11 world.

Washington is at his best playing flawed or haunted characters. He is mesmerizing as the boxing champion wrongly sentenced for triple homicide in Norman Jewison's *The Hurricane* (1999). As with his Malcolm X, Washington's transformation, spanning

years of Rubin Carter's life, is compelling, particularly in the sequence that unfolds during his spell in isolation. He crossed to the other side of the law for *Training Day* (2001) and turns in one of his most compelling performances, as corrupt cop Alonzo Harris, who deals as much dope as he and his men capture on the streets of Los Angeles. The actor deservedly won an Oscar for his portrayal.

In his only film for Ridley Scott, Washington played real-life drug baron Frank Lucas in *American Gangster* (2007). The film traces his ascent during the late 1960s through to his arrest and conviction, a decade later. Washington's best scenes in the film are during his first recces in Asia and as he moves through his local neighborhood, the actor capturing the spirit of a man who feels he is the king of all he sees.

In *Flight* (2012), he plays an alcoholic, drug-taking pilot who saves passengers from certain death but must face up to the consequences of his addiction. It is an audacious performance by Washington, resisting the sympathy of audiences, instead playing the man as a callous, self-interested loner who can only rebuild his life when he comes to terms with how far he has gone off the rails. **IHS**

W

■ Action

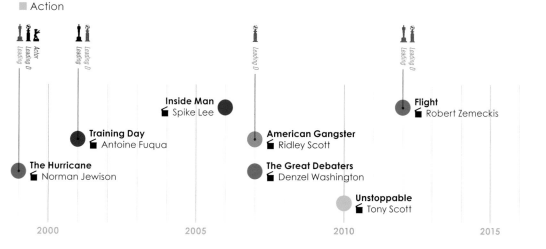

Leading | Actor / Leading D

Leading D

Leading D

Leading D / Leading

Inside Man
Spike Lee

Flight
Robert Zemeckis

Training Day
Antoine Fuqua

American Gangster
Ridley Scott

The Hurricane
Norman Jewison

The Great Debaters
Denzel Washington

Unstoppable
Tony Scott

2000   2005   2010   2015

john wayne 1907–79

Brown of Harvard

Stagecoach

The Long Voyage Home

Seven Sinners

The Spoilers

They Were Expendable

Fort Apache

Red River

An enduring symbol of American masculinity, John Wayne starred in over 200 films during his 50-year career. His roles often perpetuated the frontier myth of the Wild West, as well as romanticizing U.S. ideals of honor, loyalty and virtue. Wayne saddled up to play some of the western genre's most recognizable characters, cutting a rugged and imposing image. During World War II and the subsequent Cold War, audiences could seek refuge from this state of fear by living vicariously through cinema and Wayne's embodiment of the American dream.

Born Marion Robert Morrison, Wayne was a solid student at school but he excelled on the football field. He won a sports scholarship to the University of Southern California (USC), but an ankle injury cut short his football career. While in college, he found work as a scenery mover at Fox before becoming an extra in silent films like *Drop Kick* (1927) and *Brown of Harvard* (1926). In 1928 Wayne met director John Ford and the pair forged a friendship that would last a lifetime.

Wayne's early work with Ford on films like *Men Without Women* (1930) gave him experience and the chance to hone his craft. Between 1930 and 1933,

Wayne made a total of 36 films, including *Ride Him, Cowboy* (1932), but it was Ford who gave the actor his star-making break, casting him as Ringo the Kid in the Academy Award-winning *Stagecoach* (1939). The film was an overnight sensation, transforming the genre from a pulpy, throwaway attraction into a more respectable genre, commanding critical attention.

Wayne's next major roles steered clear of the western genre. While his unyielding facial expressions conveyed little emotion, there was no denying that his presence and calm demeanor made him a striking on-screen presence. His handsome, yet rugged looks made him a suitable action hero and a satisfactory romantic lead. He starred opposite Marlene Dietrich in three films — *Seven Sinners* (1940), *Pittsburgh* (1943) and *The Spoilers* (1942) — and reunited with Ford to play a Swedish sailor in *The Long Voyage Home* (1940). Later that decade he appeared in a string of films that became known as Ford's "cavalry trilogy" — *Fort Apache* (1948), *She Wore a Yellow Ribbon* (1949) and *Rio Grande* (1950). He also took the lead, opposite Montgomery Clift, in Howard Hawks' classic, *Red River* (1948), playing a ruthless cattle baron.

W

genre ■ Drama   ■ Western   ■ Romance   ■ War

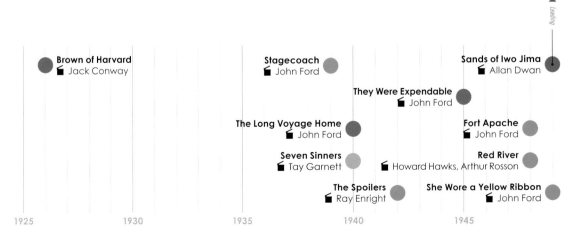

Leading

Brown of Harvard
🎬 Jack Conway

Stagecoach
🎬 John Ford

Sands of Iwo Jima
🎬 Allan Dwan

They Were Expendable
🎬 John Ford

The Long Voyage Home
🎬 John Ford

Fort Apache
🎬 John Ford

Seven Sinners
🎬 Tay Garnett

Red River
🎬 Howard Hawks, Arthur Rosson

The Spoilers
🎬 Ray Enright

She Wore a Yellow Ribbon
🎬 John Ford

1925   1930   1935   1940   1945

| Sands of Iwo Jima | She Wore a Yellow Ribbon | Rio Grande | The Searchers | The Man Who Shot Liberty Valance | How the West Was Won | In Harm's Way | True Grit |

Despite his star having shone for over a decade, Wayne's best performances were still to come. One of these was playing the antihero in Ford's *The Searchers* (1956). Wayne is Ethan Edwards, an embittered Civil War veteran hunting the Indians who kidnapped his niece. The moral ambiguity of Wayne's character allowed his cold, unaffected stare to become the backbone of his character's terrifying and pitiless persona, and added a palpable sense of dread to proceedings. It was a brave and complex role for the actor.

Wayne enrolled in a cinematic tour-of-duty in which he protected U.S. "freedom" against all its enemies. In his role as Captain Rockwell Torrey in Otto Preminger's *In Harm's Way* (1965), Wayne is quoted as saying, "All battles are fought by scared men who'd rather be someplace else," yet ironically, despite starring in war epics like *Sands of Iwo Jima* (1949), Wayne never actually served in the U.S. Army, his exemption due to his age and family status. This absence from the battlefield might explain his continued attempts to star as U.S. protector, including his controversial role in *The Green Berets* (1965).

As his star rose during the 1940s, Wayne took an interest behind the scenes. *Angel and the Badman* (1947) was the first film he produced and over the years he was involved with several production companies. In 1960, he invested $1.2 million in his passion project *The Alamo* (1960). Sadly, the film failed, but Wayne continued to star in popular westerns like *The Man Who Shot Liberty Valance* (1962) and *How the West Was Won* (1963). He played with his western persona in *True Grit* (1969), which earned him a Best Actor Oscar for his portrayal of the dishonorable one-eye drunkard Rooster Cogburn.

In the final decades of his career, Wayne became a divisive figure due to his outspoken, anti-communist views. However, for many Wayne existed on the big screen as a larger than life embodiment of the strained dichotomy between good and evil, that was as present in his final film, the elegiac *The Shootist* (1976), as it was in his earlier work. While the archaic image of hard-drinking, gunslinging, wisecracking alpha males remains the western prototype of virility, John Wayne will be forever remembered as the exemplar of a certain kind of masculinity. **PG**

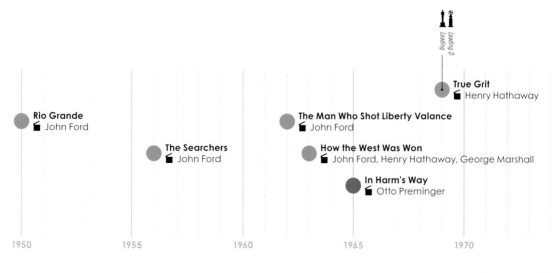

Rio Grande
John Ford

The Searchers
John Ford

The Man Who Shot Liberty Valance
John Ford

How the West Was Won
John Ford, Henry Hathaway, George Marshall

In Harm's Way
Otto Preminger

True Grit
Henry Hathaway

1950   1955   1960   1965   1970

the western hero

Henry Fonda Alan Ladd John Wayne Burt Lancaster Paul Newman Robert Redford William Holden Kevin Kline

Throughout the 20th century, the cowboy was one of the most iconic figures in cinema, a symbol of true manliness in a lawless world. From John Wayne to Clint Eastwood, so many legendary stars are as integral to the classic western as palominos, six-shooters and the red rock formations of Utah. Typically, the western hero was a serious, silent man of action who bravely forged an uncompromising path through the new frontiers of America at the tail end of the 19th century, battling evildoers, Native Americans and nature itself.

The defining image of the cowboy as the lone hero is arguably Alan Ladd in *Shane* (1953). Shane is a drifter and a relic of the old Wild West, a gunfighter who takes up a cause solely because his conscience will not let him walk away from injustice. Taken in by a kind family of sharecroppers, he adopts the fight of their community, who live under the tyranny of an evil cattle baron. Shane may be a killer, but it is when he is seen through the eyes of the family he rescues, particularly their young son Joey, that he becomes a hero.

John Wayne was probably the purest incarnation of the classic western hero. His first starring role came in *The Big Trail* (1930), but it was his turn in John Ford's *Stagecoach* (1939) that made him a true star. Of his 142 films, *The Searchers* (1956) and *True Grit* (1969)

stand out most. Wayne's characters were often heroic well past the point of credulity: clean-cut, brave, possessing a clear moral compass and strong enough to knock a man out with one punch. Yet Ethan Edwards and Rooster Cogburn deviate from this significantly. Edwards, a serial campaigner through the Civil and Mexican wars, leads a search party to track down the Comanche who have kidnapped his young niece. The character is humorless, vengeful and driven by an unconditional hatred of the Comanche, to the point that he would rather kill his niece than leave her with them.

Wayne won his only Oscar for the role of the amusingly irascible Marshal Rooster Cogburn in *True Grit*, a role that also earned an Oscar nomination for Jeff Bridges in the Coen brothers' remake in 2010. Cogburn may be a drunk and something of a mercenary but that masks a bravery and loyalty that shine through, as hard as he tries to disguise them.

Not that Cogburn is the only roguish hero to grace a western. The most famous were on the opposite side of the law and on the run, in George Roy Hill's *Butch Cassidy and the Sundance Kid* (1969). Played with no small charm and palpable chemistry by Paul Newman and Robert Redford, Butch and Sundance, for all their quips and escapades, represent the idea

type   ■ Classic hero   ■ Lone hero   ■ Antihero   ■ Rogue   ■ Fading hero

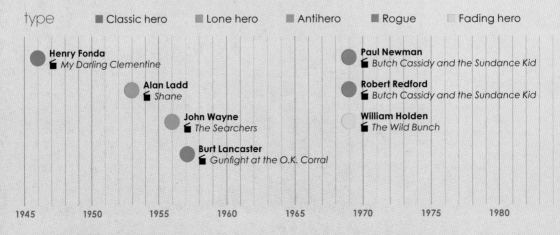

Henry Fonda
🎬 *My Darling Clementine*

Alan Ladd
🎬 *Shane*

John Wayne
🎬 *The Searchers*

Burt Lancaster
🎬 *Gunfight at the O.K. Corral*

Paul Newman
🎬 *Butch Cassidy and the Sundance Kid*

Robert Redford
🎬 *Butch Cassidy and the Sundance Kid*

William Holden
🎬 *The Wild Bunch*

1945   1950   1955   1960   1965   1970   1975   1980

Emilio Estevez | Clint Eastwood | Kurt Russell | Kevin Costner | Guy Pearce | Tommy Lee Jones | Jeff Bridges | Arnold Schwarzenegger

of the western hero as a fading ideal, a concept that was prevalent in the late 1960s, as also evidenced in Sam Peckinpah's furiously violent *The Wild Bunch* (1969). In both films, the protagonists are fleeing from the death of the world they embody as much as they are from their own inevitable ends.

The 1980s also proved fertile ground for further heroic outlaws in westerns, even if few of the films were notable for their quality. Kevin Costner's turn as the trigger-happy, excitable misfit Jake in the entertaining *Silverado* (1985) is one such exception, as is Emilio Estevez's "heroic outlaw" take on Billy the Kid in the Brat Pack westerns *Young Guns* (1988) and *Young Guns II* (1990).

The western had faded in popularity by the time Estevez and Kiefer Sutherland mounted up, but the 1990s saw something of a resurgence in the genre. Rival Wyatt Earp biopics duked it out on the big screen, with Kurt Russell's all-guns blazing "Hell's comin' with me" *Tombstone* (1993) taking on Kevin Costner's more thoughtful *Wyatt Earp* (1994). Earp and the shootout at the O.K. Corral has proved fertile ground for filmmakers, the famous lawman traditionally portrayed as the epitome of righteousness, bravery and moral decency. His story has been told repeatedly since *Frontier Marshal*

(1934), but most notably in John Ford's *My Darling Clementine* (1946), starring Henry Fonda as Earp, and *Gunfight at the O.K. Corral* (1957) with Burt Lancaster.

Of the 1990s renaissance in the genre, the most important film is unquestionably Clint Eastwood's *Unforgiven* (1992). Eastwood is Bill Munny, a classic, roughly hewn western hero, a retired gunslinger who returns to action to earn the reward for an attack on a prostitute. Munny's last stand mirrors that of Eastwood, who used the picture as his farewell to the genre.

Eastwood stands alongside Wayne as the most iconic actor in the genre, especially for his work with Sergio Leone on the trilogy: *A Fistful of Dollars* (1964), *For a Few Dollars More* (1965) and *The Good, the Bad and the Ugly* (1966). As "The Man With No Name" Eastwood embodied the ideal of the reactionary western hero: mysterious, silent, gruff and lethal with a six-shooter, but not always morally upstanding.

In recent years, the traditional western has proved a rarity, but its influence is still felt. Contemporary set films such as *No Country For Old Men* (2007) and *The Last Stand* (2013) feature small-town sheriffs fighting seemingly unstoppable evil, while John Hillcoat's *The Proposition* (2005) transposed the genre to Australia, creating a memorable antihero in Guy Pearce's Charlie Burns. **MG**

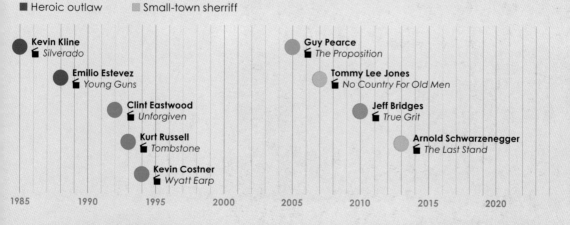

■ Heroic outlaw   ■ Small-town sherriff

Kevin Kline — *Silverado*

Emilio Estevez — *Young Guns*

Clint Eastwood — *Unforgiven*

Kurt Russell — *Tombstone*

Kevin Costner — *Wyatt Earp*

Guy Pearce — *The Proposition*

Tommy Lee Jones — *No Country For Old Men*

Jeff Bridges — *True Grit*

Arnold Schwarzenegger — *The Last Stand*

1985   1990   1995   2000   2005   2010   2015   2020

sigourney weaver 1949

| Alien | The Year of Living Dangerously | Ghostbusters | Aliens | Working Girl | Gorillas in the Mist | The Ice Storm | Avatar |

With no more than a few small roles to her name, the most significant being in *Annie Hall* (1977), Sigourney Weaver was cast as the lead in Ridley Scott's sci-fi shocker *Alien* (1979). It is the role for which the actress will forever be synonymous. She infused Ripley with a strength and determination that would see her widely regarded as a feminist icon. She reprised the character in James Cameron's sequel *Aliens* (1986), which not only proved a more challenging experience physically, but also offered Weaver the chance to further develop the emotional complexities of her character. The film was a huge success and she received her first in a string of Academy Award nominations. A second sequel, David Fincher's *Alien 3* (1992), required Weaver to shave her head. It was a darker, dirtier film than the previous entries and, like Jean-Pierre Jeunet's fourth installment, *Alien Resurrection* (1997), it proved less popular, although in both films Weaver gives committed performances.

Her next role after *Alien* was opposite Mel Gibson in Peter Weir's acclaimed *The Year of Living Dangerously* (1982). Then, in 1984 she starred in another blockbuster role, as Bill Murray's love interest-turned possessed demon, in the supernatural comedy *Ghostbusters* (1984). It remains another iconic role in her career.

Weaver's second Oscar nod came courtesy of her portrayal of naturalist Dian Fossey in *Gorillas in the Mist* (1988), while in the same year she was also nominated for a supporting role in Mike Nichols' *Working Girl* (1988), in which she shone as a Machiavellian business woman. The underwhelming *1492: Conquest of Paradise* (1992) was followed by several acclaimed performances, including roles in Roman Polanski's searing *Death and the Maiden* (1994), serial killer thriller *Copycat* (1995) and Ang Lee's *The Ice Storm* (1997). Her portrayal of a bored housewife in a sleepy 1970s Connecticut town remains one of her most striking performances.

Weaver has rarely had the chance to show off her deft comic skills, so her performance in the space opera parody *Galaxy Quest* (1999) came as a surprise to many. It was when Weaver worked again with Cameron that she scored her biggest box-office hit, with the technically groundbreaking *Avatar* (2009). **MB**

W

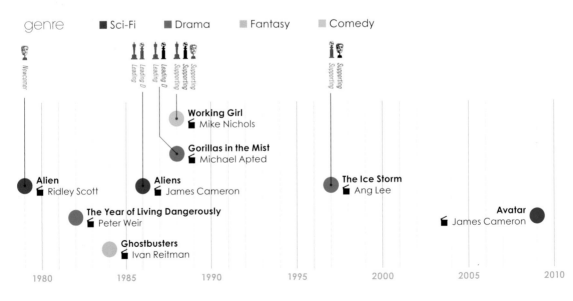

genre   ■ Sci-Fi   ■ Drama   ■ Fantasy   ■ Comedy

Newcomer
Leading D
Leading D
Leading D
Supporting
Supporting
Supporting
Supporting

Working Girl
Mike Nichols

Gorillas in the Mist
Michael Apted

Alien
Ridley Scott

Aliens
James Cameron

The Ice Storm
Ang Lee

The Year of Living Dangerously
Peter Weir

Avatar
James Cameron

Ghostbusters
Ivan Reitman

1980   1985   1990   1995   2000   2005   2010

johnny weissmuller 1904–84

Glorifying the American Girl

Tarzan the Ape Man

Tarzan and His Mate

Tarzan Escapes

Swamp Fire

Jungle Jim

Valley of the Head Hunters

Devil Goddess

Johnny Weissmuller was born in 1904 in the former Austro-Hungarian Empire, near the present-day city of Timisoara, Romania. His family emigrated to the United States when he was still a baby. Or was he born in Pennsylvania, as he later declared? Was he christened Peter Johann or Johann Peter? And did he take his brother's name, because John Weissmüller was an American citizen by birth? These little mysteries only add to the myth of the man best known for his performance as Tarzan, but who first rose to glory as a record-breaking member of the U.S. Olympic team.

He had taken up swimming at age 9 on the advice of a doctor, after contracting polio, and grew to be a tall, impressive athlete. While working as a lifeguard at a Lake Michigan beach, he was spotted by swim coach Bill Bachrach, who trained him to be a champion. Weissmuller broke his first world record at the age of 17 and went on to win five Olympic gold medals, 67 world and 52 national titles, and regularly broke the freestyle swimming records for distances ranging from 100 yards to the half-mile. He remained undefeated at retirement, when he went to Hollywood.

The 25-year-old phenomenon made his first film appearance as an Adonis clad only in a fig leaf in Milliard Webb's *Glorifying the American Girl* (1929). Cyril Hume, working on the adaptation of Edgar Rice Burroughs' *Tarzan the Ape Man* for MGM, noticed Weissmuller swimming in the pool of his hotel and suggested him for the part of Tarzan. The studio released him from an exclusive contract with a swimwear company, and promoted him as "the only man in Hollywood who's natural in the flesh and can act without clothes." Maureen O'Sullivan was cast as Jane Parker, the British woman who leaves her fiancé to go and live with Tarzan in the jungle. The film was an immediate box-office hit. Critics were also positive, at least for the first three films in the series: *Tarzan the Ape Man* (1932), *Tarzan and His Mate* (1934) and *Tarzan Escapes* (1936). But Weissmuller maintained the screen role for 16 years and completed 12 Tarzan films, despite audiences' growing fatigue with the repetitive plot. Half of them were produced by RKO, after MGM dropped the series. Weissmuller was then hired by Columbia as the lead in *Jungle Jim* (1948), playing the adventurer in a safari suit for no less than 16 films, plus a television series.

The good-natured Weissmuller once joked that he got lucky with Tarzan because it was a part tailor-made for him: it satisfied his taste for athletic prowess, involved some swimming, little dialogue ("Me Tarzan, you Jane") and earned him millions. He retired to a house in Acapulco, close to the shooting location of his last Tarzan film, where he died in 1979 after a series of strokes. Upon his request, the famous Tarzan howl, which he invented and is still used in film and television productions, was played three times at his funeral. **AG**

W

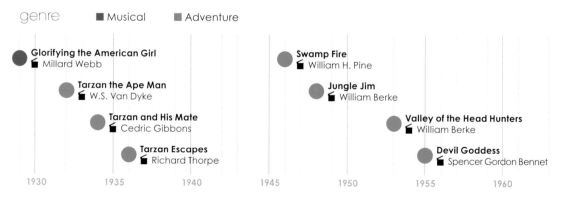

genre ■ Musical   ■ Adventure

Glorifying the American Girl
Millard Webb

Tarzan the Ape Man
W.S. Van Dyke

Tarzan and His Mate
Cedric Gibbons

Tarzan Escapes
Richard Thorpe

Swamp Fire
William H. Pine

Jungle Jim
William Berke

Valley of the Head Hunters
William Berke

Devil Goddess
Spencer Gordon Bennet

1930   1935   1940   1945   1950   1955   1960

orson welles 1915–85

Citizen Kane

Jane Eyre

The Stranger

The Lady from Shanghai

Macbeth

The Third Man

Othello

Confidential Report

Orson Welles is a star of the movies, without ever really being a movie star. As writer–director, he is one of world cinema's giants; solely as an actor, his stature is considerably diminished; yet as the lead in many of his own films, his performances are integral to their success. That he rarely, if ever, achieved the same potency appearing in other people's films, provides a fascinating glimpse into his abilities.

The young prodigy's meteoric rise is the stuff of legend, treading the boards in Dublin and on Broadway in his teens, and producing such notorious shows as an all-black voodoo *Macbeth* and scaremongering *War of the Worlds* radio broadcast. Given carte blanche aged 24 for his film debut, *Citizen Kane* (1941), he played the hubristic newspaper magnate from callow youth to dying old man. Dazzling filmmaking aside, Welles' dynamic charisma plus several autobiographical congruences, are so entwined with the character that, even today, Welles is as much Kane as the character's intended target, William Randolph Hearst. It would be churlish not to attribute that, at least partly, to his acting skills.

Welles' directorial travails are well-documented elsewhere; as an actor, his brooding Rochester in *Jane Eyre* (1943) looks the part but seems too self-involved to make the love story convincing. Back in his own work, his covert ex-Nazi in *The Stranger* (1946) is compellingly sinister, even if the film feels a touch impersonal, and his reckless sailor entranced by his then-wife Rita Hayworth in film noir *The Lady from Shanghai* (1947) is a credible stooge, despite a wandering Irish brogue. In his rapidly filmed, inventive *Macbeth* (1948) his driven intensity and haunting visuals largely cancel out performance anxieties.

Whereas *Macbeth* was shot in three weeks, *Othello* (1952) took three years, shot piecemeal, on the fly. Although modern audiences might feel discomfort at his "blackface" appearance, Welles' rich, mellifluous voice produces persuasive evidence for his expertise in putting the Bard on screen. All these roles highlight the fact that, with his imposing stature and darkly cherubic looks, Welles conveyed nothing of straightforward heroism. He is habitually larger-than-life, and too seldom comes across as a generous actor. It is why he suits Shakespeare: soliloquies let him engage with his favorite scene partner — himself. When not directing, he is often a distraction, looming just removed from the drama.

W

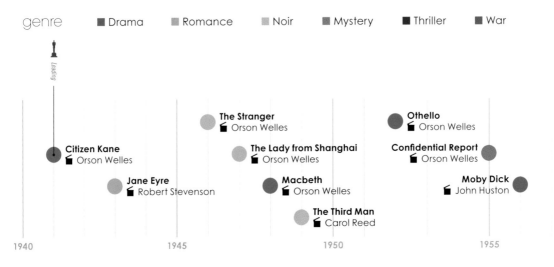
genre   ■ Drama   ■ Romance   ■ Noir   ■ Mystery   ■ Thriller   ■ War

Leading

The Stranger
🎬 Orson Welles

Othello
🎬 Orson Welles

Citizen Kane
🎬 Orson Welles

The Lady from Shanghai
🎬 Orson Welles

Confidential Report
🎬 Orson Welles

Jane Eyre
🎬 Robert Stevenson

Macbeth
🎬 Orson Welles

Moby Dick
🎬 John Huston

The Third Man
🎬 Carol Reed

1940   1945   1950   1955

$25 M (U.S.)
Citizen Kane
(1941)

$6 M (U.S.)
The Third Man
(1949)

$18 M (U.S.)
Touch of Evil
(1958)

Moby Dick

The Long
Hot Summer

Touch of Evil

The Trial

Chimes at
Midnight

A Man for
All Seasons

Catch-22

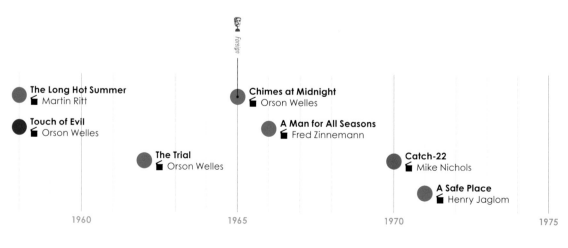

A Safe
Place

This quality is perfect for easily his greatest role outside his own work. In the classic thriller *The Third Man* (1949), Welles' Harry Lime is an amoral, murderous black-market racketeer in postwar Vienna. He is also the story's most devilishly charming, insouciant character, given one of cinema's great delayed entrances and (partly self-penned) speeches.

Ensconced in European "exile," *Confidential Report* (1955) is a strange, near-parody of Kane, wherein an ominous tycoon Arkadin hires a man to investigate his own life. Now weightier than ever, Welles, shot from low angles, scowls down the lens from behind a thick beard but neither he nor the film ever feels sincere — if that were even the point. Then came an unexpected olive branch from Hollywood. Welles was hired to write, direct and appear in *Touch of Evil* (1958), playing the border town cop Hank Quinlan, seemingly bloated with corruption, the largest freak in a carnival of grotesques. The film is Welles at his brilliant best, his force-of-nature performance an unsettling mix of grandstanding and self-loathing, but utterly effective.

He continued to grace films with either flamboyant supporting or cameo roles, to mixed success. His overblown Southern patriarch in *The Long Hot Summer*

(1958) is a dud. On the other hand, his performance as *Compulsion*'s (1959) Clarence Darrow surrogate, defending two young Leopold-and-Loeb-inspired murderers from the death penalty, is far more nuanced. It is as if the studios could only stomach Welles in small, potent doses. But whatever the size of the part, or the man, he makes a vivid impression: puce of face and robe as Cardinal Wolsey in *A Man for All Seasons* (1966) or suitably officious and dominant as trigger-happy General Dreedle in *Catch-22* (1970). And he evidently enjoyed Henry Jaglom's experimental, oft-overlooked *A Safe Place* (1971).

The rest of his dwindling career for hire is a study in ignominy. In his own final films, however, Welles still took star billing. Falstaff in *Chimes at Midnight* (1965) is a well-rounded, touching portrait, jovial and bawdy in his pomp, yet self-aware enough to understand being mercilessly ostracized. In the innovative *F For Fake* (1973), a film-essay about and including trickery and fraud, Welles has a blast playing himself as a self-confessed "charlatan." What he really means, though, is "showman" — a role that goes some way to defining his genius as a filmmaker, as well as his strengths and weaknesses as an actor. **LS**

W

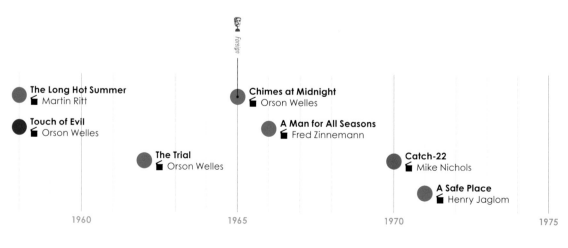

Foreign

The Long Hot Summer
Martin Ritt

Touch of Evil
Orson Welles

The Trial
Orson Welles

Chimes at Midnight
Orson Welles

A Man for All Seasons
Fred Zinnemann

Catch-22
Mike Nichols

A Safe Place
Henry Jaglom

1960   1965   1970   1975

mae west 1893–1980

| Night After Night | I'm No Angel | She Done Him Wrong | Belle of the Nineties | Go West Young Man | Klondike Annie | My Little Chickadee | Sextette |

Mary Jane West was born in Brooklyn in 1893. As a child she showed early signs of her artistic talents in shows aimed at family members and neighbors. A born entertainer, whose natural self-confidence was further enhanced by her mother, she started performing professionally as a teenager, under the stage name Baby Mae.

A smart woman with a flair for business, West quickly garnered attention on Broadway, where she wrote and produced her own shows, shrewdly tickling the censors with risqué topics and content. She explored sexuality in a rare confrontational manner and was an early supporter of gay rights. This strategy once led to her arrest for "corrupting the morals of youth," but it worked like a charm, with every show's cancellation multiplying the attention directed at this provocative performer.

West was almost 40 years old when her notoriety reached the studios of Paramount Pictures, under whose aegis she became a star. For her first film, *Night After Night* (1932), she was allowed to edit her lines, and she continued to do so, taking on the role of co-writer or sole screenwriter on all of her films. As a result, her characters had the wit and sex appeal befitting her persona. West cast a 28-year-old Cary Grant as her male lead in *She Done Him Wrong* and *I'm No Angel* (1933), box-office hits that contributed to making the actor famous. It was her most productive

period. After *Belle of the Nineties* (1934) and *Goin' to Town* (1935), West worked with Raoul Walsh on *Klondike Annie* (1936), an interesting take on religion, and with Henry Hathaway on *Go West Young Man* (1936). *Every Day's a Holiday* (1937) was a failure and an ungrateful Paramount studio, having been rescued by her smash hits only four years earlier, turned its back on the actress. Universal Pictures produced *My Little Chickadee* (1940), which West wrote with costar W.C. Fields, while Columbia backed *The Heat's On* (1943). The latter's commercial and critical failure led the actress to distance herself from Hollywood.

Mae West is one of the most iconic figures in 20th-century popular culture. Her name was given to the title of a 1935 painting by Salvador Dalí. Her face emblazons the flag planted by a half-mad alpinist at the peak of a vertiginous icy mountain in Werner Herzog's *Scream of Stone* (1991). Dalí also modeled his famous wood and satin *Mae West Lips Sofa* upon the actress' sensuous, inimitable smile. And it seems that West herself never doubted her glamour and uniqueness — she even made a screen comeback at the age of 85 as a seductress in the chaotic musical homage to her glory years, *Sextette* (1978), an adaptation of her own 1926 stage play *Sex*. The film bombed upon its release, although the star was sheltered from the debacle by her adoring fans. She died two years later, at her home in Los Angeles. **AG**

genre ■ Drama   ■ Comedy

Night After Night
🎬 Archie Mayo

I'm No Angel
🎬 Wesley Ruggles

She Done Him Wrong
🎬 Lowell Sherman

Belle of the Nineties
🎬 Leo McCarey

Go West Young Man
🎬 Henry Hathaway

Klondike Annie
🎬 Raoul Walsh

My Little Chickadee
🎬 Edward F. Cline

Sextette
🎬 Ken Hughes

1935   1940   1975   1980

| Character Actor | Hero | Villain |

forest whitaker 1961

The Color of Money

Good Morning, Vietnam

Bird

The Crying Game

Ghost Dog: The Way of the Samurai

Panic Room

The Last King of Scotland

The Butler

Forest Whitaker has specialized in playing unexpected roles, from a cricket-obsessed English soldier to a tranquil assassin. A soulful dramatic actor, his hulking dimensions are complemented by his distinctive countenance and gentle demeanor. Whitaker was still at college when he shot his first on-screen role, as a quarterback in *Fast Times at Ridgemont High* (1982). He then struggled to find good work until his memorable cameo as a pool shark in *The Color of Money* (1986), Martin Scorsese's sequel-of-sorts to *The Hustler* (1961). Recruited after it emerged that the previously cast actor could not play pool, Whitaker spent two weeks training in order to play well enough — an early sign of his dedication to the craft.

His career picked up pace with supporting roles in two Vietnam War films: *Platoon* (1986) and *Good Morning, Vietnam* (1987). His breakthrough came playing jazz saxophonist Charlie Parker in Clint Eastwood's *Bird* (1988), for which he won best actor at Cannes. He worked solidly through the 1990s, starring in *Downtown* (1990) and *Diary of a Hitman* (1991) before becoming primarily a character actor in films like *Blown Away* (1994) and *Phenomenon* (1996). Although he appeared in few truly great pictures during this time, he was powerful as a British soldier captured by the IRA in *The Crying Game* (1992).

One of his few starring roles from this time is also among his best, playing the samurai code-following hit man in Jim Jarmusch's offbeat *Ghost Dog: The Way of the Samurai* (1999). It is one of his most emblematic roles. Unfortunately he followed it up by donning dreadlocks and what looked like a swimmer's nose plug to costar in the terrible *Battlefield Earth* (2000). He soon recovered and was excellent in high-concept thrillers, *Panic Room* (2002) and *Phone Booth* (2002).

The most acclaimed role of Whitaker's career to date came with his portrayal of Idi Amin in Kevin Macdonald's *The Last King of Scotland* (2006). As the brutal Ugandan dictator he is compelling, charming, unpredictable and terrifying. He won most major awards that year for his performance, including a Best Actor Oscar. After its success, he had difficulty finding a part as rewarding. He gained positive reviews for *The Butler* (2013), loosely based on the 34-year tenure of White House valet Cecil Gaines. While the film is hampered by uneven presidential caricatures, Whitaker remains understated as a man living with dignity during a turbulent period of U.S. history. **JWa**

W

genre   ■ Drama   ■ War   ■ Action   ■ Thriller

Bird
Clint Eastwood

Good Morning, Vietnam
Barry Levinson

The Color of Money
Martin Scorsese

The Crying Game
Neil Jordan

The Last King of Scotland
Kevin Macdonald

Panic Room
David Fincher

Ghost Dog: The Way of the Samurai
Jim Jarmusch

The Butler
Lee Daniels

1985   1990   1995   2000   2005   2010   2015

richard widmark 1914–2008

| Kiss of Death | Night and the City | Panic in the Streets | Pickup on South Street | The Alamo | Judgment at Nuremberg | The Bedford Incident | Coma |

Richard Widmark came to prominence in his very first screen role, as the psychopathic hoodlum Tommy Udo in Henry Hathaway's film noir, *Kiss of Death* (1947). He was nominated for an Academy Award and won a Golden Globe for Most Promising Newcomer. However, it found him typecast for a number of years.

An adaptation of the novel by Gerald Kersh, *Night and the City* (1950) cemented Widmark's stardom. Arguably the actor's signature role, Widmark is exceptional as Harry Fabian, a small-time grifter and nightclub tout who gets in way over his head when he tries to step up a league and go partly legit as a wrestling promoter. Director Jules Dassin makes tremendous use of London locations and Widmark's face is etched with fear and desperation as he sees his dreams and ambitions crumble.

Widmark's run of fine features continued with Elia Kazan's *Panic in the Streets* (1950): the tale of a New Orleans doctor and policeman joining forces over a 48-hour period to locate a killer infected with a pneumonic plague. In Sam Fuller's *Pickup on South Street* (1953), he plays Skip McCoy, a cocksure New York pickpocket who inadvertently steals a message with classified information and becomes a target for a Communist spy ring. A synthesis of Cold War spy thriller and film noir, Widmark again artfully articulates a criminal with the capacity to be in the wrong place, doing the wrong thing at the wrong time.

A detour from crime thrillers into westerns was precipitated by Delmer Daves' *The Last Wagon* (1956) and continued with sterling work in Edward Dmytryk's *Warlock* (1959). It was followed by a starring role as Col. Jim Bowie in John Wayne's loosely historical *The Alamo* (1960).

Displaying his trademark versatility, Widmark segued into courtroom drama with Stanley Kramer's intense *Judgment at Nuremberg* (1961). An account of the trail of Nazi war criminals by a U.S.-led court, the film also featured Spencer Tracy (one of Widmark's screen idols), Burt Lancaster and Marlene Dietrich. *The Bedford Incident* (1965) teamed Widmark with Sidney Poitier in a naval standoff between a U.S. destroyer and a Soviet submarine caught violating territorial waters. He was excellent in Don Siegel's *Madigan* (1968), playing an ageing New York police detective.

Widmark's last great performance was in medical conspiracy thriller *Coma* (1978), which reminded audiences of his sense of craft and composure. **JW**

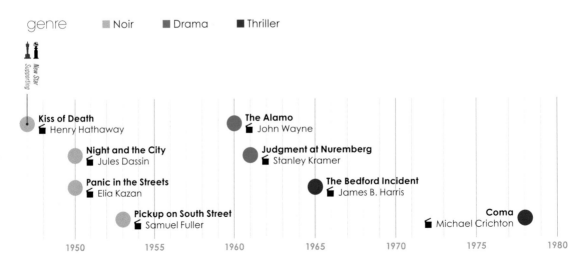

genre   ■ Noir   ■ Drama   ■ Thriller

New Star
Supporting

Kiss of Death
Henry Hathaway

Night and the City
Jules Dassin

Panic in the Streets
Elia Kazan

Pickup on South Street
Samuel Fuller

The Alamo
John Wayne

Judgment at Nuremberg
Stanley Kramer

The Bedford Incident
James B. Harris

Coma
Michael Crichton

1950   1955   1960   1965   1970   1975   1980

robin williams 1951–2014

Popeye

Good Morning, Vietnam

Dead Poets Society

The Fisher King

Aladdin

Mrs. Doubtfire

Good Will Hunting

One Hour Photo

Robin Williams was one of his generation's greatest comedians, unusual among comics in that his free-associating dynamism ran alongside his classical training at the Juilliard performing arts school. As an adult he rapidly established himself on California's stand-up circuit. His break came when a guest appearance as alien Mork on television hit *Happy Days* led to the hugely successful spin-off, *Mork & Mindy* (1978–82). His first lead movie role showed his uncanny impersonation of a cartoon favorite, *Popeye* (1980).

Early film work was patchy, the best probably in *The World According to Garp* (1982). Then in 1987 came the perfect star vehicle. As real-life maverick DJ Adrian Cronauer, stationed with U.S. troops in *Good Morning, Vietnam*, Williams could combine wild on-air improvisations with genuine pathos.

He showed dramatic versatility and largely contained the comic riffing for his inspirational English teacher in *Dead Poets Society* (1989), and tapped into the deranged grief of a homeless widower seeking a redemptive Holy Grail in Terry Gilliam's *The Fisher King* (1991). If Vietnam offered one encapsulation for his singular talents, Williams found another as the voice of the Genie in Disney's animation *Aladdin* (1992).

Given free rein, the animators literally designed their characters and scenarios around his freewheeling gags and Williams' work changed the face (or voice) of animation, ushering in a new star-driven approach.

Meanwhile, Williams was still toplining major movies, from serious dramas like *Awakenings* (1990) to a reimagined Peter Pan in Steven Spielberg's *Hook* (1991). His biggest solo hit, *Mrs. Doubtfire* (1993), cast him as a desperate divorced dad who disguises himself as a female housekeeper to stay with his family. *Good Will Hunting* (1997) offered a better blend of tough sentiment, Williams excelling as the psychiatrist who takes Matt Damon's headstrong prodigy under his wing. Later attempts at villainy, the creepy, repressed stalker of *One Hour Photo* (2002) and the chilling serial killer of *Insomnia* (2003) were strikingly successful.

If Williams never again matched his 1990s heyday, he remained a popular presence on and offscreen. However, like many clowns, his more troubled roles and previous drink and drug addictions hinted at personal demons that he struggled to contain and Williams tragically committed suicide in 2014. The outpouring of public grief only confirmed his place in popular culture as a truly beloved one-off. **LS**

W

genre   Comedy   War   Drama   Animation   Family   Thriller

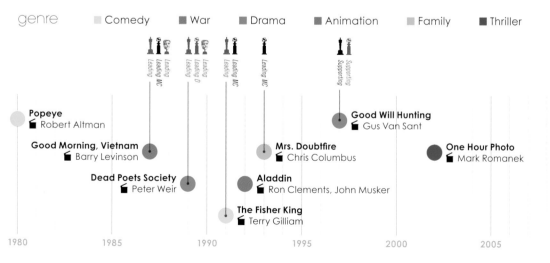

Popeye
Robert Altman

Good Morning, Vietnam
Barry Levinson

Dead Poets Society
Peter Weir

The Fisher King
Terry Gilliam

Aladdin
Ron Clements, John Musker

Mrs. Doubtfire
Chris Columbus

Good Will Hunting
Gus Van Sant

One Hour Photo
Mark Romanek

Leading MC
Leading
Leading
Leading D
Leading MC
Leading MC
Supporting
Supporting

1980   1985   1990   1995   2000   2005

the action hero

Douglas Fairbanks Toshiro Mifune Cary Grant Sean Connery Tura Satana Harrison Ford Eddie Murphy Sylvester Stallone

Encompassing a variety of genres, the action film has had various incarnations. Its first major star was Douglas Fairbanks. He rejuvenated the moribund period adventure film with *The Mask of Zorro* in 1920 and produced its masterpiece with *The Thief of Bagdad* (1924). Thrilling, romantic and featuring a non-stop succession of chases, fights and acrobatics, it is regarded as one of the finest films in pre-sound cinema.

Fairbanks' spectaculars set the template for the action film over the next few decades. However, in early 1950s Japan, a new director was offering up a more visceral kind of action movie. With *Seven Samurai* (1954), Akira Kurosawa made action more brutal and bloody. Toshiro Mifune plays the temperamental upstart who desperately wants to join Takashi Shimura's small gang of *ronin* and the battle scenes, in mud and rain, are breathtaking.

Alfred Hitchcock's mastery over suspense included set-pieces that often involved chases, such as the climax on the top of the British Museum in *Blackmail* (1929). Yet in *North by Northwest* (1959), he created the ultimate chase film, comprised of one set-piece after another. At the heart of it is Cary Grant's suave Roger O. Thornhill, very much a precursor to a new kind of hero, the jet-setting spy.

James Bond first appeared in *Dr. No* (1962), but it was *From Russia with Love* (1963) that created the template of action and sex for the entries that followed. Sean Connery possessed elements of Grant's smooth operator, but there was also malevolence in his Bond — he could be nasty if required. As other Bonds took over, this became less of a trait, until Daniel Craig returned the role to its roots.

Women, particularly in Bond films, were mostly relegated to being a love interest, with the odd character — such as Pussy Galore in *Goldfinger* (1964) — offering up a few moves. But other films gave women a more central role. Russ Meyer's exploitation feature *Faster Pussycat! Kill! Kill!* (1965) introduced Tura Satana to the world. She plays Varla, a violence-loving, go-go dancer who goes on the rampage with some friends, wreaking havoc and in the process offering up a very different female screen persona to what had come before.

Martial arts cinema dominated the action movie scene of the 1970s, with Bruce Lee, Jackie Chan and the films of the Shaw brothers providing violent entertainment. If these stars were sinewy, the 1980s action hero took on bulkier proportions. Sylvester Stallone had made a name for himself as Rocky Balboa. But Ted Kotcheff's taut *First Blood* (1982) hinted at what

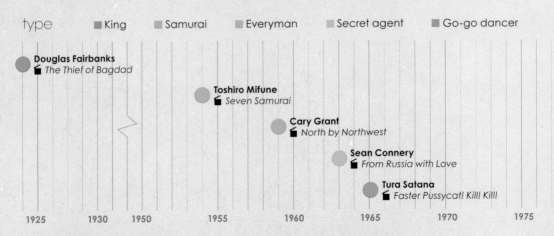

type   ■ King   ■ Samurai   ■ Everyman   ■ Secret agent   ■ Go-go dancer

Douglas Fairbanks
The Thief of Bagdad

Toshiro Mifune
Seven Samurai

Cary Grant
North by Northwest

Sean Connery
From Russia with Love

Tura Satana
Faster Pussycat! Kill! Kill!

1925   1930   1950   1955   1960   1965   1970   1975

Arnold Schwarze-negger | **Mel Gibson & Danny Glover** | **Bruce Willis** | **Patrick Swayze** | **Akshay Kumar** | **Tom Cruise** | **Geena Davis** | **Jason Statham**

was to come. John Rambo is a Vietnam veteran who falls foul of a sheriff in a small rural town and unleashes hell on it. There were three sequels and in each the actor's muscles seemed to grow. Yet he paled next to Arnold Schwarzenegger. The two stars dominated much of the 1980s action box office. *Total Recall* (1990) was one of the Austrian-born actor's highpoints, with a script as ingenious as the film's set-pieces.

Sci-fi in the 1980s action blockbuster was dominated by two franchises, both led by women. Sigourney Weaver was Ripley in *Alien* (1979) and Linda Hamilton played Sarah Connor in The Terminator (1984). Yet it was the sequels, *Aliens* (1986) and *Terminator 2: Judgment Day* (1991) that saw the two cast as bona fide action stars. It was not until Geena Davis' spirited turn as the assassin in *The Long Kiss Goodnight* (1996) and then Angelina Jolie's athletic performances in *Lara Croft: Tomb Raider* (2001), *Mr. & Mrs. Smith* (2005), *Wanted* (2008) and *Salt* (2010) that an actress dominated the action film so thoroughly.

Toward the end of the 1980s, a more ordinary hero took center stage, in the form of Mel Gibson and Danny Glover's cops in *Lethal Weapon* (1987) and Bruce Willis' John McClane in Die Hard (1988). Aside of Kathryn Bigelow's smart undermining of the action genre in *Point Break* (1991), with Keanu Reeves

and Patrick Swayze not so much playing characters as cyphers of the action genre, the everyday hero dominates the action hero in cinema. Even in Hong Kong and India. John Woo took over from the martial arts films produced in Hong Kong until the mid-1980s. He created the bullet ballet, with guns replacing fists and Chow Yun-fat, his favorite actor, a master with any firearm. *Hard Boiled* (1992) is the best example of their collaboration, made before Woo moved to the United States and bested himself with *Face/Off* (1991). In India, Akshay Kumar has been the country's biggest action star since his breakthrough performance in *Khiladi* (1992). Again, he is an ordinary hero who finds himself in extraordinary circumstances and uses his physical prowess to win through.

The action film over the last few years has turned its attention to Europe. The Tom Cruise vehicle *Mission: Impossible* (1996) offered a template, along with Luc Besson's slick style of filmmaking. And the success of Jason Statham's *The Transporter* (2002) unleashed a Euro-thriller industry. As well as offering roles to contemporary stars like Scarlett Johansson (*Lucy*, 2014), the Euro-thriller has given us a new kind of film — the veteran action movie — with stars Liam Neeson (*Taken*, 2008), Kevin Costner (*3 Days to Kill*, 2014) and Sean Penn (*The Gunman*, 2015) leading the way. **IHS**

■ Treasure hunter ■ Cop ■ Special forces ■ Surfer ■ Prankster ■ Hit man

Harrison Ford
🔖 *Raiders of the Lost Ark*

Patrick Swayze
🔖 *Point Break*

Eddie Murphy
🔖 *Beverly Hills Cop*

Akshay Kumar
🔖 *Khiladi*

Sylvester Stallone
🔖 *Cobra*

Tom Cruise
🔖 *Mission: Impossible*

Arnold Schwarzenegger
🔖 *Predator*

Geena Davis
🔖 *The Long Kiss Goodnight*

Mel Gibson & Danny Glover
🔖 *Lethal Weapon*

Bruce Willis
🔖 *Die Hard*

Jason Statham
🔖 *Crank*

1980   1985   1990   1995   2000   2005   2010

bruce willis 1955

| Blind Date | Die Hard | Mortal Thoughts | Pulp Fiction | Twelve Monkeys | The Sixth Sense | Unbreakable | Looper |

Bruce Willis returned the action hero to the blue-collar working stiff. After the muscular antics of the Stallones and Schwarzeneggers, Willis' John McClane, the hero of *Die Hard* (1988), was an everyman cop who happened to find himself in the wrong place at the wrong time, but uses his anonymity to gain an advantage over a collection of heavily armed crooks. The film played up the cheeky persona that was already known to millions of viewers of television show *Moonlighting* (1985–89).

The son of a U.S father and German mother, Willis was born on a U.S. military base in Kassel, Germany, in 1955. He had a few roles on *Miami Vice* and *The Twilight Zone* before being chosen from several thousand candidates to play David Addison Jr. opposite Cybill Shepherd in *Moonlighting* in 1985. He stayed with the show for three years, during which time it became one of the most popular series on television.

His first cinematic outing in Blake Edwards' comedy *Blind Date* (1987) did little more than offer up a variation of his small-screen persona. *Sunset* (1988) was an uneven comedy about the early days of the western in Hollywood. Then came *Die Hard* (1988). With its blend of high-octane thrills, smart dialogue and satirical swipes at law enforcement and the media, the film was an enormous success. A 1990 sequel followed, keeping the same formula but swapping a building for an airport. *Die Hard: With a Vengeance* (1995) was an improvement, thanks to Willis' pairing with Samuel L. Jackson. *Live Free or Die Hard* (2007) was unnecessary and *A Good Day to Die Hard* (2013) terrible.

Willis' subsequent career has adopted a pattern of commercial and critical success followed by a slump, only to find the actor resurrected by another success. So *Die Hard* was followed by an admirable turn as a Vietnam veteran in the overly dour *In Country* (1989) and the woeful *The Bonfire of the Vanities* (1990), terrible *Hudson Hawk* (1991) and dodgy *Color of Night* (1994). He returned to form with his boxer in *Pulp Fiction* (1994). Likewise, aside of *Twelve Monkeys* (1995), there was little of worth after his collaboration with Tarantino until his quiet, moving turn as a child psychologist in the excellent *The Sixth Sense* (1999). He was even better in M. Night Shyamalan's *Unbreakable* (2000), as a blue-collar worker who gradually realizes he is a superhero.

There has been a clutch of good roles since. He is taciturn as the good cop in the violent *Sin City* (2005), fun in the admittedly throwaway cop drama *16 Blocks* (2006), an unassuming officer in Wes Anderson's *Moonrise Kingdom* (2012) and on form in the smart sci-fi thriller *Looper* (2012). Recent films have been less impressive so another resurrection should be upon us any time soon. **IHS**

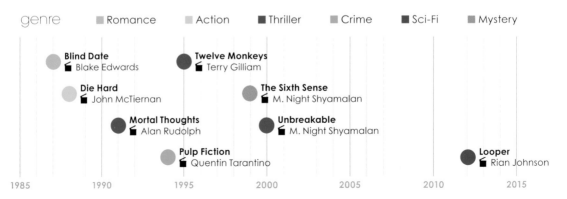

genre ■ Romance ■ Action ■ Thriller ■ Crime ■ Sci-Fi ■ Mystery

Blind Date
Blake Edwards

Die Hard
John McTiernan

Mortal Thoughts
Alan Rudolph

Pulp Fiction
Quentin Tarantino

Twelve Monkeys
Terry Gilliam

The Sixth Sense
M. Night Shyamalan

Unbreakable
M. Night Shyamalan

Looper
Rian Johnson

| 1985 | 1990 | 1995 | 2000 | 2005 | 2010 | 2015 |

oprah winfrey 1954

The Color Purple | Native Son | The Women of Brewster Place | There Are No Children Here | Before Women Had Wings | Beloved | The Butler | Selma

Oprah Winfrey was hosting daytime talk show *AM Chicago* when she caught the attention of music and film producer Quincy Jones. Admiring her self-assurance, Jones persuaded Steven Spielberg to cast her in his adaptation of Alice Walker's Pulitzer Prize-winning novel *The Color Purple* (1985). Winfrey received an Oscar nomination for the performance as the headstrong Sofia, the brightest role of an overwrought film that sentimentalized Walker's powerful prose. Winfrey parlayed her association with the irrepressible character into a hugely successful talk show, becoming one of America's most wealthy, powerful media personalities over the next decade.

Occupied by her television program and a burgeoning media empire, Winfrey's acting appearances have been limited since her promising debut, with a focus on socially conscious output that she has produced herself. She played a struggling mother in *Native Son* (1986) and took the lead in the acclaimed miniseries *The Women of Brewster Place* (1989). The television movie *There Are No Children Here* (1993) saw her portray another mother enduring poverty and trying circumstances, although her performance was noticeably mannered.

Winfrey did not act again until the television movie, *Before Women Had Wings* (1997). The following year she starred with *Color Purple* costar Danny Glover in another adaptation of a Pulitzer Prize-winning novel by a significant African-American female author, Toni Morrison's *Beloved*. Despite a brave, anguished performance from Winfrey as a former slave literally haunted by the past, the film failed to have the same impact as her earlier collaboration with Glover.

Winfrey put her acting on hold for nearly 15 years, with only a few voiceover roles in animated films. She made a well-received return to the screen in *The Butler* (2013) as the troubled wife of Forest Whitaker's eponymous valet. The film itself — one of the few Winfrey has starred in that she has not also produced — was both heavy-handed and powerful, lumpen and rousing, and had a mixed critical reception.

In 2014, Winfrey appeared in the excellent Martin Luther King Jr. biopic *Selma*. Producing once again, she took a small role as a civil rights activist, who, in one of the film's most moving scenes, tries to register to vote and is rejected. The quiet dignity of the portrayal underlines how regrettable it is that she is not a more prolific actress. **JWa**

W

genre ■ Drama

Supporting
Supporting

The Color Purple
🎬 Steven Spielberg

Before Women Had Wings
🎬 Lloyd Kramer

Native Son
🎬 Jerrold Freedman

Beloved
🎬 Jonathan Demme

Selma
🎬 Ava DuVernay

The Women of Brewster Place
🎬 Donna Deitch

The Butler
🎬 Lee Daniels

There Are No Children Here
🎬 Anita W. Addison

1985   1990   1995   2000   2005   2010   2015   2020

kate winslet 1975

| Heavenly Creatures | Sense and Sensibility | Jude | Hamlet | Titanic | Enigma | Iris | Eternal Sunshine of the Spotless Mind |

According to legend, Kate Winslet was 17 and in the middle of making a sandwich when she received the call confirming her part in Peter Jackson's *Heavenly Creatures* (1994). Juliet sets in motion both joy and horror as she and her friend Pauline collude to create a fantasy world for two, which ends in a brutal murder. Winslet captured the impetuousness and selfishness of the young girl — a perfect start for one of the finest screen actors of the last two decades.

No less feisty was her Marianne Dashwood, opposite Emma Thompson in Ang Lee's gorgeous *Sense and Sensibility* (1995). Michael Winterbottom hardened her for Sue in his adaptation of Thomas Hardy, *Jude* (1996), whereas Kenneth Branagh transformed her into a pained Ophelia in his epic, monochrome vision of *Hamlet* (1996).

Winslet was gradually making a name for herself when *Titanic* (1997) happened. James Cameron's recreation of the famous disaster, told through the fictional cross-class romance of Jack and Rose, became the first film to gross over $1 billion at the box office. It won eleven Oscars and became a cultural phenomenon. Neither Winslet nor costar Leonardo DiCaprio won that night, but the film propelled both onto the Hollywood A-List. It would be another 20 years before the pair appeared together on screen again. When they did, it was in a darker, even more tragic vein. Sam Mendes' soulful adaptation of Richard Yates' *Revolutionary Road* (2008) profits from the two leads' outstanding performances.

After *Titanic*, Winslet opted for a series of low-key films. She played a peripatetic mother in *Hideous Kinky* (1998), then worked with Jane Campion on the bizarre *Holy Smoke* (1999). After a foray into Napoleonic France, starring in Philip Kaufman's beguiling *Quills* (2000), she made an appearance in the Bletchley Park-set thriller *Enigma* (2001) and excelled as a young Iris Murdoch in *Iris* (2001).

Michel Gondry's inspired decision to cast Winslet in *Eternal Sunshine of the Spotless Mind* (2004) gave the actress one of her most fascinating roles and the resulting performance remains one of her most engaging. Charlie Kaufman's story of love, loss and memory erasure features Winslet as Clementine, the love interest of Jim Carrey's troubled soul. The character she plays became known as a "manic pixie dreamgirl," a trope writer Nathan Rabin defined as, "That bubbly, shallow cinematic creature that exists

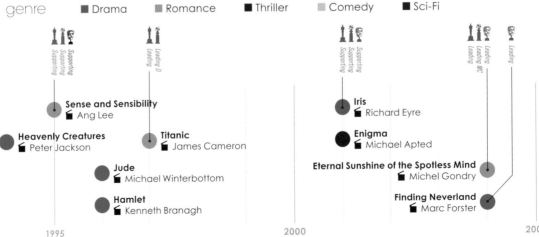

genre ■ Drama ■ Romance ■ Thriller ■ Comedy ■ Sci-Fi

Sense and Sensibility
Ang Lee

Heavenly Creatures
Peter Jackson

Titanic
James Cameron

Jude
Michael Winterbottom

Hamlet
Kenneth Branagh

Iris
Richard Eyre

Enigma
Michael Apted

Eternal Sunshine of the Spotless Mind
Michel Gondry

Finding Neverland
Marc Forster

1995 2000 2005

| Finding Neverland | Little Children | The Reader | Revolutionary Road | Carnage | Contagion | Labor Day | Divergent |

solely in the fevered imaginations of sensitive writer–directors to teach broodingly soulful young men to embrace life and its infinite mysteries and adventures." For Winslet it was a chance to exhibit a wider range of emotions and to eschew the image some audiences had of her as being a "period" actress.

However, she did return to period drama for the engaging *Finding Neverland* (2004), as a dying mother opposite Johnny Depp's J.M. Barrie. After a brief, hilarious cameo playing a variation of herself in an episode of Ricky Gervais and Stephen Merchant's television comedy *Extras* (2005), she turned in a stunning performance, replete with a song and dance number, as a white trash mistress in John Tuturro's enjoyable *Romance & Cigarettes* (2005). She was on desperate form as the unhappy housewife in *Little Children* (2006) and adopted a convincing Deep South accent for Stephen Zallian's *All the King's Men* (2006).

Winslet's *annus mirabilis* was 2008. In *The Reader*, David Hare's adaptation of Bernard Schlink's novel, she plays Hanna, a tram inspector who embarks on a sexual relationship with a young boy only for him to discover years later that she had been a guard in a concentration camp. Even by Winslet's standards, her performance is raw and intense, and she won an Oscar for it. She was on feisty form in Roman Polanski's *Carnage* (2011), an adaptation of Yasmina Reza's stage play, and she brought integrity to the role of a CDC operative investigating a plague in Steven Soderberg's *Contagion* (2011). A brief appearance in the woeful comedy sketch film *Movie 43* (2013) was a misstep and while Jason Reitman's *Labor Day* (2013) might have appeared great on the page, something was lost in its transfer to the screen.

Winslet's best performance in recent years was on Todd Hayne's gorgeous miniseries *Mildred Pierce* (2011). It is a sublime character study of a woman striving to make the best of her life, only to be undermined by her family. It won Winslet her second Golden Globe and ranks as a key entry in her filmography.

Returning to the big screen, Winslet is a fine villain in *Divergent* (2014) and *Insurgent* (2015), and is set to appear in subsequent episodes of the young adult drama. She is due to appear in John Hillcoat's crime drama *Triple Nine* (2015) and the long in gestation Steve Jobs biopic, opposite Michael Fassbender and directed by Danny Boyle. **SMK**

W

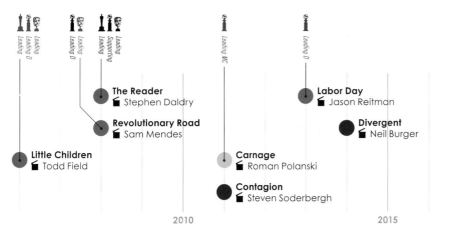

The Reader
Stephen Daldry

Revolutionary Road
Sam Mendes

Little Children
Todd Field

Carnage
Roman Polanski

Contagion
Steven Soderbergh

Labor Day
Jason Reitman

Divergent
Neil Burger

2010

2015

Heavenly Creatures
(1994)

Sense and Sensibility
(1995)

Titanic
(1997)

Eternal Sunshine of the Spotless Mind (2004)

Finding Neverland
(2004)

The Reader
(2008)

Carnage
(2011)

Labor Day
(2013)

Winslet was one of 175 girls who auditioned for the part of Juliet Hume in Peter Jackson's murder drama *Heavenly Creatures*.

Winslet briefly dated *Sense and Sensibility* costar Greg Wise, who went on to marry actress and screenwriter Emma Thompson.

Jack (Leonardo DiCaprio) and Rose (Kate Winslet) in one of the most memorable (and much imitated/parodied) scenes of shipwreck-love story *Titanic*. The most expensive film ever made at the time, many critics predicted that it would be a failure at the box office.

Winslet's performance as Clementine Kruczynski opposite Jim Carrey in in Michel Gondry's *Eternal Sunshine of the Spotless Mind* is the actress' personal favorite.

Finding Neverland centers on the friendship between Sylvia Llewelyn Davies (Winslet) and Peter Pan author J.M. Barrie.

Winslet's portrayal of a tram conductor who later resurfaces in a war crimes trial in *The Reader* earned her several awards, including the Academy Award for Best Actress.

Black comedy-drama *Carnage* was shot in real time, without breaks, to add to the sense of escalating tension between the parents.

In *Labor Day* Winslet gives a solid performance as a depressed mother who has an affair with Josh Brolin's escaped convict.

natalie wood 1938–81

| Miracle on 34th Street | Rebel Without a Cause | Splendor in the Grass | West Side Story | Love with the Proper Stranger | Inside Daisy Clover | This Property Is Condemned | Bob & Carol & Ted & Alice |

"Curtain up! Light the lights! You've got nothing to hit but the heights!" enthuses the big number from *Gypsy* (1962), addressed to Natalie Wood as the stripper Gypsy Rose Lee. Wood was a star for over 30 years of her sadly curtailed life. From one of the most likable and least mawkish child stars of her era she matured into a beautiful, appealing young woman with a touching air of vulnerability. Yet somehow she never did quite hit the heights; all too often, her performances betrayed a lack of emotional range.

Making her screen debut at age 5, she was an unaffected child star, wide-eyed with wonder at meeting the real Santa Claus in *Miracle on 34th Street* (1947). Unlike many child actors she made the transition to teenage roles and then to adult parts fluently and with no loss of technique. In *Rebel Without a Cause* (1955) she, along with James Dean and Sal Mineo, captures the unfocused discontentment of a whole generation. As the girl abducted by Comanche her role in *The Searchers* (1956) is brief, but the moment when John Wayne's Ethan Edwards, who has sworn to kill her for becoming a squaw, cradles her in his arms and says, "Let's go home, Debbie" is unforgettable.

Wood made a charming Maria in *West Side Story* (1961), although her singing voice was dubbed, and she topped that performance in Elia Kazan's *Splendor in the Grass* (1961). She was teamed with Warren Beatty (his screen debut) as a pair of teenagers tormented by the sexual prudery of small-town 1920s America; Wood is moving in her brief erotic joy and final desolation. Equally impressive was her performance in *Love with the Proper Stranger* (1963), as a young woman who gets pregnant, decides against an abortion and marries the father (Steve McQueen), only to regret her decision.

In *Gypsy*, Wood's tentative presence in the title role is steamrollered straight off the screen by Rosalind Russell's powerhouse performance as her mother. *Inside Daisy Clover* (1965) saw Wood as the seafront urchin snapped up by a reptilian studio head (Christopher Plummer) to be molded for stardom. Wood does feisty and street-smart well, and at age 27 acts 15 quite convincingly. She could play comedy, but was often let down by her material, as in *Sex and the Single Girl* (1964). Best of her comedies was *Bob & Carol & Ted & Alice* (1969), Paul Mazursky's satire on sexual mores in 1960s America. **PK**

W

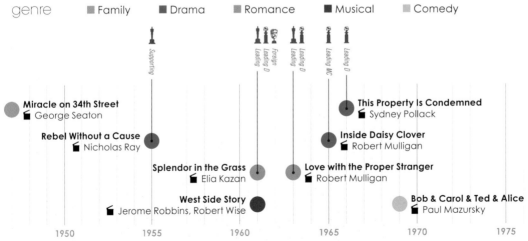

genre   ■ Family   ■ Drama   ■ Romance   ■ Musical   ■ Comedy

Miracle on 34th Street
George Seaton

Rebel Without a Cause
Nicholas Ray

Splendor in the Grass
Elia Kazan

West Side Story
Jerome Robbins, Robert Wise

This Property Is Condemned
Sydney Pollack

Inside Daisy Clover
Robert Mulligan

Love with the Proper Stranger
Robert Mulligan

Bob & Carol & Ted & Alice
Paul Mazursky

Supporting   Foreign   Leading D   Leading   Leading D   Leading MC   Leading D

1950   1955   1960   1965   1970   1975

fay wray 1907–2004

| The Wedding March | The Four Feathers | Dirigible | The Most Dangerous Game | Mystery of the Wax Museum | King Kong | Viva Villa! | The Clairvoyant |

Cinema's first "scream queen," Fay Wray was a silent movie actress who successfully transitioned into talkies, but struggled to break free from her later association with the horror genre. Despite her long and varied career, she is primarily remembered as the object of King Kong's obsession in the eponymous monster movie: the beauty that killed the beast.

Wray's first feature-length film was *The Coast Patrol* (1925), but many of her earliest appearances were in two-reeler comedy shorts like *Thundering Landlords* (1925) and *Moonlight and Noses* (1925). As with all film performers of that time, Wray's output depended upon which studio she was signed to: after moving from Hal Roach Studios to Universal she worked in westerns such as *The Wild Horse Stampede* (1926), before joining Paramount.

It was with Paramount that she had her first major role, as an innkeeper's daughter in Eric von Stroheim's lustrous romantic drama *The Wedding March* (1928). However, the film's lengthy and difficult post-production process meant that other appearances, in *The First Kiss* (1928) and *The Legion of the Condemned* (1928) — both costarring Gary Cooper — came out first.

In 1929, Wray starred in one of the final major silent films, *The Four Feathers*. With the arrival of sound she appeared in *The Texan* (1930) and Frank Capra's thrilling *Dirigible* (1931). Her capacity for screaming and portraying terror found her increasingly starring in horror movies such as *Doctor X* (1933) and *Mystery of the Wax Museum* (1933), both directed by Michael Curtiz and produced before the Hays Code limited what these films could depict.

Her consummate performances in other films notwithstanding, Wray will always be remembered for *King Kong* (1933), in which she played Ann Darrow, the struggling Depression-era actress whose waifish charm literally drives the "Eighth Wonder of the World" to his downfall. Beyond its groundbreaking technical achievements and influence on filmmaking, *King Kong* remains a moving, gripping and wonderfully creepy film, while the climactic moment of the giant ape astride the Empire State Building, clutching Darrow as biplanes attack him, is one of the most iconic images in cinema history. As was typical of Hollywood then, Wray and the creative team also worked on *The Most Dangerous Game* (1932), shooting the film on the same sets, but at night.

Following *King Kong*'s success Wray acted in a spate of films, including *Shanghai Madness* (1933) with Spencer Tracy, *One Sunday Afternoon* (1933), *The Clairvoyant* (1934) and *Viva Villa!* (1934). Her work rate slowed later in the decade, finally calling it a day after the release of *Not a Ladies' Man* (1942). In the decades that followed, she took occasional small roles and worked in television, but appeared to harbor no further desire to be a star. **JWa**

W

genre ■ Drama ■ War ■ Adventure ■ Horror ■ Mystery ■ Western

The Wedding March
🎬 Erich von Stroheim

The Four Feathers
🎬 Merian C. Cooper, Lothar Mendes, Ernest B. Schoedsack

The Most Dangerous Game
🎬 Irving Pichel, Ernest B. Schoedsack

Dirigible
🎬 Frank Capra

King Kong
🎬 Merian C. Cooper, Ernest B. Schoedsack

Mystery of the Wax Museum
🎬 Michael Curtiz

Viva Villa!
🎬 Jack Conway

The Clairvoyant
🎬 Maurice Elvey

1925   1930   1935

michelle yeoh 1962

| Yes, Madam | Police Story 3: Super Cop | The Soong Sisters | Tomorrow Never Dies | Crouching Tiger, Hidden Dragon | Memoirs of a Geisha | Reign of Assassins | The Lady |

One of the most popular female action stars in the world, Michelle Yeoh first became known for starring in Hong Kong martial arts films, but in recent years has received acclaim for her dramatic performances.

Born in Malaysia, she was studying to be a ballet dancer in London when a back injury halted her career. Her decision to focus on choreography instead was also curtailed when she became Miss Malaysia, which led to small roles in two Sammo Hung vehicles, *Owl vs. Dumbo* (1985) and *Twinkle, Twinkle Lucky Stars* (1985). Hung also produced *Yes, Madam* (1985), which provided Yeoh with her breakthrough.

Yeoh's graceful physicality made her uniquely suited to the kinetic, highly choreographed action films made in Hong Kong during this period, and she prided herself on doing her own stunts. Like much of Hong Kong action cinema, these films were often retitled and bowdlerized by the time they reached western audiences.

In 1988 Yeoh officially retired from acting but returned four years later to costar with Jackie Chan in *Police Story 3: Super Cop* (1992). The film is one of the strongest efforts in both actors' careers, with their acrobatic, go-for-broke fighting styles complementing each other. Following its success she was the prolific star of *The Heroic Trio* (1993) and its

sequel *Executioners* (1993), *Butterfly and Sword* (1993), *Holy Weapon* (1993), *Police Story* spin-off *Once a Cop* (1993), *Wonder Seven* (1994) and *Wing Chun* (1994), along with dramatic roles in *The Stunt Woman* (1996) and *The Soong Sisters* (1997). Her first appearance outside of Hong Kong was as the Chinese spy Wai Lin in *Tomorrow Never Dies* (1997).

Two years later she starred in the Ang Lee-directed *Crouching Tiger, Hidden Dragon*. Beyond its action sequences, what impressed most were the emotive, curiously melancholy performances of Yeoh and her costars Chow Yun-fat, Zhang Ziyi and Chang Chen. She later recruited *Crouching Tiger* cinematographer Peter Pau to direct *The Touch* (2002), which she also produced. She also starred opposite Zhang Ziyi in the Hollywood drama *Memoirs of a Geisha* (2005).

Yeoh continued to act in action films, both in Hong Kong and abroad, appearing as a masked vigilante in *Silver Hawk* (2004), a Mongolian nun in *Babylon A.D.* (2008), a sorceress in *The Mummy: Tomb of the Dragon Emperor* (2008) and a former hired killer in *Reign of Assassins* (2010). These were balanced with a series of dramatic roles that included Danny Boyle's sci-fi thriller *Sunshine* (2007), *The Children of Huang Shi* (2008) and her passion project, *The Lady* (2011), playing Burmese politician Aung San Suu Kyi. **JWa**

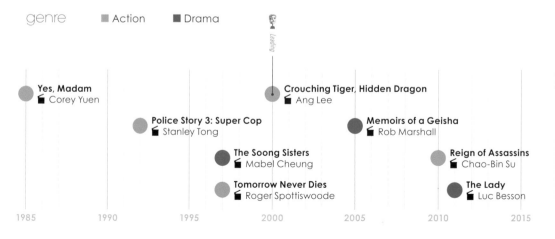

genre   ■ Action   ■ Drama

Yes, Madam
Corey Yuen

Crouching Tiger, Hidden Dragon
Ang Lee

Police Story 3: Super Cop
Stanley Tong

Memoirs of a Geisha
Rob Marshall

The Soong Sisters
Mabel Cheung

Reign of Assassins
Chao-Bin Su

Tomorrow Never Dies
Roger Spottiswoode

The Lady
Luc Besson

1985   1990   1995   2000   2005   2010   2015

chow yun-fat 1955

An Autumn's Tale

The Killer

God of Gamblers

Hard Boiled

The Replacement Killers

Anna and the King

Crouching Tiger, Hidden Dragon

Pirates of the Caribbean: At World's End

Known for his everyman appearance, cool tough demeanor and quiet nobility, Chow Yun-fat became the most prominent star of Hong Kong action cinema, the worldwide emergence of which turned him into an internationally recognized figure.

Born on Lamma Island in 1955, Chow started his career as a popular television star in his native Hong Kong before moving into feature films. Initially struggling to find worthy material, his breakthrough came in John Woo's Triad thriller *A Better Tomorrow* (1986). Hugely influential, the film established the Heroic Bloodshed genre: stylized operatic action films about criminals and cops bound by codes of honor and seeking redemption through gun violence.

Becoming popular far beyond Hong Kong, Woo and Chow became synonymous with the genre, producing a series of increasingly outrageous thrillers such as *A Better Tomorrow II* (1987), *The Killer* (1989), *Once a Thief* (1991) and *Hard Boiled* (1992). Starring Chow as the clarinet-playing Inspector "Tequila" Yuen, *Hard Boiled* is arguably the high point of these films, celebrated for its stunning opening — a shoot-em up in a teahouse — and the climax, where he defends a maternity ward full of babies from gun-toting gangsters. The genre's other notable filmmaker was Ringo Lam, who would direct the actor in *City on Fire* (1987), *Prison on Fire* (1987), *A Better Tomorrow III* (1990), *Prison on Fire II* (1991) and *Full Contact* (1992).

Chow also took roles in romances such as *An Autumn's Tale* (1987) and comedy-dramas like Wong Jing's *God of Gamblers* (1989) and its numerous spin-offs.

The popularity of Hong Kong action cinema in America ultimately led to its demise, as talent like Woo and Chow were tempted to work abroad, albeit with mostly vapid results. The transition never quite worked for Chow: his first American films, *The Replacement Killers* (1998) and *The Corruptor* (1999), were weak imitations of his early efforts, while later films like the period drama *Anna and the King* (1999) and *Bulletproof Monk* (2003) failed to resonate with audiences. The biggest hit of his career, however, was a blend of East and West, costarring with Michelle Yeoh in Ang Lee's ravishing wuxia drama *Crouching Tiger, Hidden Dragon* (2000).

After *Crouching Tiger, Hidden Dragon* Chow mostly worked in Hong Kong and China, starring in *The Postmodern Life of My Aunt* (2006), Zhang Yimou's visually intoxicating *Curse of the Golden Flower* (2006), *Let the Bullets Fly* (2010), as the eponymous philosopher in the biopic *Confucius* (2010), *The Assassins* (2012), *The Last Tycoon* (2012) and *The Monkey King* (2014). His most notable American film during this time was as pirate lord Sao Feng, one of the few redeeming elements in the overlong and needlessly complicated *Pirates of the Caribbean: At World's End* (2007). **JWa**

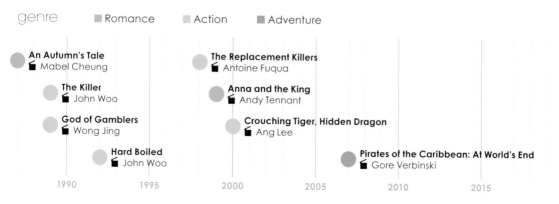

genre   ■ Romance   ■ Action   ■ Adventure

An Autumn's Tale
Mabel Cheung

The Killer
John Woo

God of Gamblers
Wong Jing

Hard Boiled
John Woo

The Replacement Killers
Antoine Fuqua

Anna and the King
Andy Tennant

Crouching Tiger, Hidden Dragon
Ang Lee

Pirates of the Caribbean: At World's End
Gore Verbinski

1990   1995   2000   2005   2010   2015

catherine zeta-jones 1969

The Mask
of Zorro

Entrapment

Traffic

Chicago

Intolerable
Cruelty

Ocean's
Twelve

No
Reservations

Side Effects

By the age of 11, Welsh-born Catherine Zeta-Jones was already a British tap dancing champion. Having spent her early years on stage, she traveled to France to play the lead role in her first feature, Philippe de Broca's *Les 1001 Nuits* (1990). Soon after, she played Mariette in the much-loved television series *The Darling Buds of May* (1991–93).

Over the next few years, Zeta-Jones appeared in a number of television dramas and modest features. However, it was her feisty performance in *The Mask of Zorro* (1998) that hinted at her potential for big-screen stardom. Holding her own against Anthony Hopkins and Antonio Banderas, particularly in the film's action scenes, she proved to be a charismatic presence.

Her lead role in *Entrapment* (1999), playing an investigator attempting to catch Sean Connery's thief in the act, made much of Zeta-Jones' action movie persona. Her skills as a serious actor were evinced the following year, playing the wife of an imprisoned drug dealer in Steven Soderbergh's *Traffic* (2000). What could have been a perfunctory role becomes an intriguing portrait of a woman initially shocked by her husband's profession, who transforms herself into a formidable force in it. It earned her a Golden Globe

nomination for Best Supporting Actress and began the first of three projects with the filmmaker. If *Ocean's Twelve* (2004) was a disappointment, *Side Effects* (2013) proved to be an effective Hitchcockian thriller.

Oscar and BAFTA success came with Zeta-Jones' performance in *Chicago* (2002), playing Velma Kelly. Employing her considerable skills as a dancer, Zeta-Jones' musical sequences are matched by the archness of her dialogue scenes, recalling femmes fatales from Hollywood's Golden Age. She returned to the musical with *Rock of Ages* (2012), although the film failed to win over critics and audiences.

The Coen brothers' *Intolerable Cruelty* (2003) gave Zeta-Jones her best comedy role, playing opposite George Clooney as a woman for whom romance is not so much an ideal as the first step in a divorce settlement. Her charm, alongside Clooney's, softens the edges of the Coen's sour, cynical tale.

Recent years have seen Zeta-Jones take roles in films that have failed to perform at the box office or are dramatically underwhelming. However, she excelled in Gillian Armstrong's *Death Defying Acts* (2007) and was impressive as the wife of Russell Crowe's mayor in the flawed *Broken City* (2013). **OC**

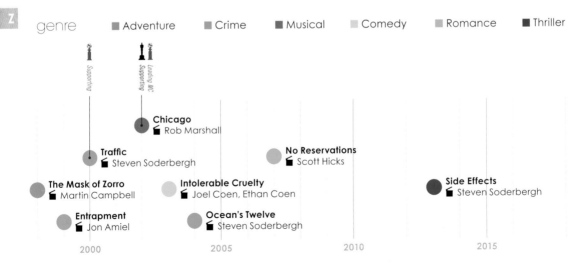

genre ■ Adventure ■ Crime ■ Musical ■ Comedy ■ Romance ■ Thriller

Supporting

Leading MC
Supporting

Chicago
Rob Marshall

Traffic
Steven Soderbergh

No Reservations
Scott Hicks

The Mask of Zorro
Martin Campbell

Intolerable Cruelty
Joel Coen, Ethan Coen

Side Effects
Steven Soderbergh

Entrapment
Jon Amiel

Ocean's Twelve
Steven Soderbergh

2000   2005   2010   2015

zhang ziyi 1979

The Road Home   **Crouching Tiger, Hidden Dragon**   **Rush Hour 2**   **House of Flying Daggers**   **2046**   **Princess Raccoon**   **Sophie's Revenge**   **The Grandmaster**

In 2000 Zhang Ziyi was named one of China's "Four Dan Actresses." An accolade that pays homage to the Beijing Opera stars of the 1920s, at the turn of the millennium it established the arrival of a new era of superstardom in Chinese cinema. She is also one of a handful of contemporary East Asian actors to establish a career in Hollywood, having starred in transnational blockbusters such as *Crouching Tiger, Hidden Dragon* (2000), *Hero* (2002) and *Memoirs of a Geisha* (2005). Since her breakthrough role in *Crouching Tiger* at the age of 22, she has been known for playing predominantly wuxia roles, yet she claims, "I can do better than just kicking ass."

Zhang attended the Beijing Dance Academy before enrolling at the Central Academy of Drama. She was cast in a lead role in Zhang Yimou's *The Road Home* (1999), which was a huge success in China. Soon after, she played one of the leads in *Crouching Tiger*. Working alongside a legendary cast including Cheng Pei Pei and Chow Yun-fat, Zhang claims to have been nervous during filming, feeling that she had to work hard to earn Lee's trust.

After *Crouching Tiger*, Zhang received many offers to star in U.S. movies, choosing *Rush Hour 2* (2001), in which she starred alongside Jackie Chan and Chris Tucker as the villainous Hu Li. She was subsequently cast in various kung fu and action parts, including Zhang Yimou's *Hero* (2002). Over the next four years, she starred in several wuxia films, such as *House of Flying Daggers* (2004), while also taking on auteur projects, including yakuza genre film legend Seijun Suzuki's *Princess Raccoon* (2005), Lou Ye's *Purple Butterfly* (2003) and Wong Kar-wai's *2046* (2004).

In 2005, Zhang was cast as the lead in the Hollywood adaptation of *Memoirs of a Geisha*. The film was banned in China a week before its release and Zhang was criticized by officials who called her "an embarrassment to China." She spoke out against this accusation, claiming that the ban probably had more to do with "intense historical problems between China and Japan" than anything else.

As the film industry boomed in the late 2000s, Zhang starred in successful domestic films including the romantic comedy *Sophie's Revenge* (2009) and *Love for Life* (2011), the first mainstream film to deal with the AIDS epidemic that swept China in the 1990s. In 2013, she worked again with Wong Kar-wai on *The Grandmaster*, in another kung fu role. **CMB**

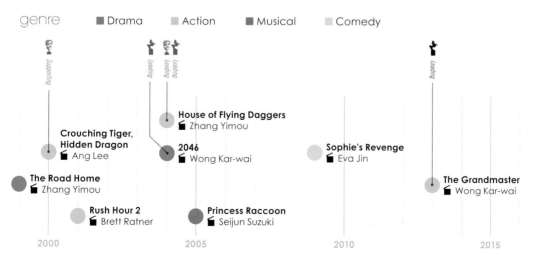

genre   ■ Drama   ■ Action   ■ Musical   ■ Comedy

Supporting   *Leading*   *Leading*   *Leading*   *Leading*

House of Flying Daggers
Zhang Yimou

Crouching Tiger, Hidden Dragon
Ang Lee

2046
Wong Kar-wai

Sophie's Revenge
Eva Jin

The Road Home
Zhang Yimou

The Grandmaster
Wong Kar-wai

Rush Hour 2
Brett Ratner

Princess Raccoon
Seijun Suzuki

2000   2005   2010   2015

awards directory

BEST ACTOR | BEST ACTRESS

Film (Actor)	Best Actor	Year	Best Actress	Film (Actress)
The Last Command / The Way of All Flesh	Emil Jannings	1929	Janet Gaynor	7th Heaven / Street Angel / Sunrise
In Old Arizona	Warner Baxter	1930	Mary Pickford	Coquette
Disraeli	George Arliss	1931	Norma Shearer	The Divorcee
A Free Soul	Lionel Barrymore	1932	Marie Dressler	Min and Bill
The Champ	Wallace Beery (tie)	1933	Helen Hayes	The Sin of Madelon Claudet
Dr. Jekyll and Mr. Hyde	Fredric March (tie)			
The Private Life of Henry VIII	Charles Laughton	1934	Katharine Hepburn	Morning Glory
It Happened One Night	Clark Gable	1935	Claudette Colbert	It Happened One Night
The Informer	Victor McLaglen	1936	Bette Davis	Dangerous
The Story of Louis Pasteur	Paul Muni	1937	Luise Rainer	The Great Ziegfeld
Captains Courageous	Spencer Tracy	1938	Luise Rainer	The Good Earth
Boys Town	Spencer Tracy	1939	Bette Davis	Jezebel
Goodbye, Mr. Chips	Robert Donat	1940	Vivien Leigh	Gone with the Wind
The Philadelphia Story	James Stewart	1941	Ginger Rogers	Kitty Foyle
Sergeant York	Gary Cooper	1942	Joan Fontaine	Suspicion
Yankee Doodle Dandy	James Cagney	1943	Greer Garson	Mrs. Miniver
Watch on the Rhine	Paul Lukas	1944	Jennifer Jones	The Song of Bernadette
Going My Way	Bing Crosby	1945	Ingrid Bergman	Gaslight
The Lost Weekend	Ray Milland	1946	Joan Crawford	Mildred Pierce
The Best Years of Our Lives	Fredric March	1947	Olivia de Havilland	To Each His Own
A Double Life	Ronald Colman	1948	Loretta Young	The Farmer's Daughter
Hamlet	Laurence Olivier	1949	Jane Wyman	Johnny Belinda
All the King's Men	Broderick Crawford	1950	Olivia de Havilland	The Heiress
Cyrano de Bergerac	José Ferrer	1951	Judy Holliday	Born Yesterday
The African Queen	Humphrey Bogart	1952	Vivien Leigh	A Streetcar Named Desire
High Noon	Gary Cooper	1953	Shirley Booth	Come Back, Little Sheba
Stalag 17	William Holden	1954	Audrey Hepburn	Roman Holiday
On the Waterfront	Marlon Brando	1955	Grace Kelly	The Country Girl
Marty	Ernest Borgnine	1956	Anna Magnani	The Rose Tattoo
The King and I	Yul Brynner	1957	Ingrid Bergman	Anastasia
The Bridge on the River Kwai	Alec Guinness	1958	Joanne Woodward	The Three Faces of Eve
Separate Tables	David Niven	1959	Susan Hayward	I Want to Live!
Ben-Hur	Charlton Heston	1960	Simone Signoret	Room at the Top
Elmer Gantry	Burt Lancaster	1961	Elizabeth Taylor	BUtterfield 8
Judgment at Nuremberg	Maximilian Schell	1962	Sophia Loren	Two Women
To Kill a Mockingbird	Gregory Peck	1963	Anne Bancroft	The Miracle Worker
Lilies of the Field	Sidney Poitier	1964	Patricia Neal	Hud
My Fair Lady	Rex Harrison	1965	Julie Andrews	Mary Poppins
Cat Ballou	Lee Marvin	1966	Julie Christie	Darling
A Man for All Seasons	Paul Scofield	1967	Elizabeth Taylor	Who's Afraid of Virginia Woolf?
In the Heat of the Night	Rod Steiger	1968	Katharine Hepburn	Guess Who's Coming to Dinner
Charly	Cliff Robertson	1969	Katharine Hepburn (tie)	The Lion in Winter
			Barbra Streisand (tie)	Funny Girl
True Grit	John Wayne	1970	Maggie Smith	The Prime of Miss Jean Brodie
Patton	George C. Scott	1971	Glenda Jackson	Women in Love
The French Connection	Gene Hackman	1972	Jane Fonda	Klute
Save the Tiger	Jack Lemmon	1973	Liza Minnelli	Cabaret
The Godfather	Marlon Brando	1974	Glenda Jackson	A Touch of Class
Harry and Tonto	Art Carney	1975	Ellen Burstyn	Alice Doesn't Live Here Anymore
One Flew Over the Cuckoo's Nest	Jack Nicholson	1976	Louise Fletcher	One Flew Over the Cuckoo's Nest
Network	Peter Finch	1977	Faye Dunaway	Network
The Goodbye Girl	Richard Dreyfuss	1978	Diane Keaton	Annie Hall
Coming Home	Jon Voight	1979	Jane Fonda	Coming Home
Kramer vs. Kramer	Dustin Hoffman	1980	Sally Field	Norma Rae
Raging Bull	Robert De Niro	1981	Sissy Spacek	Coal Miner's Daughter
On Golden Pond	Henry Fonda	1982	Katharine Hepburn	On Golden Pond
Gandhi	Ben Kingsley	1983	Meryl Streep	Sophie's Choice
Tender Mercies	Robert Duvall	1984	Shirley MacLaine	Terms of Endearment
Amadeus	F. Murray Abraham	1985	Sally Field	Places in the Heart
Kiss of the Spider Woman	William Hurt	1986	Geraldine Page	The Trip to Bountiful
The Color of Money	Paul Newman	1987	Marlee Matlin	Children of a Lesser God
Wall Street	Michael Douglas	1988	Cher	Moonstruck
Rain Man	Dustin Hoffman	1989	Jodie Foster	The Accused
My Left Foot	Daniel Day-Lewis	1990	Jessica Tandy	Driving Miss Daisy
Reversal of Fortune	Jeremy Irons	1991	Kathy Bates	Misery
The Silence of the Lambs	Anthony Hopkins	1992	Jodie Foster	The Silence of the Lambs
Scent of a Woman	Al Pacino	1993	Emma Thompson	Howards End
Philadelphia	Tom Hanks	1994	Holly Hunter	The Piano
Forrest Gump	Tom Hanks	1995	Jessica Lange	Blue Sky
Leaving Las Vegas	Nicolas Cage	1996	Susan Sarandon	Dead Man Walking
Shine	Geoffrey Rush	1997	Frances McDormand	Fargo
As Good as It Gets	Jack Nicholson	1998	Helen Hunt	As Good as It Gets
Life Is Beautiful	Roberto Benigni	1999	Gwyneth Paltrow	Shakespeare in Love
American Beauty	Kevin Spacey	2000	Hilary Swank	Boys Don't Cry
Gladiator	Russell Crowe	2001	Julia Roberts	Erin Brockovich
Training Day	Denzel Washington	2002	Halle Berry	Monster's Ball
The Pianist	Adrien Brody	2003	Nicole Kidman	The Hours
Mystic River	Sean Penn	2004	Charlize Theron	Monster
Ray	Jamie Foxx	2005	Hilary Swank	Million Dollar Baby
Capote	Philip Seymour Hoffman	2006	Reese Witherspoon	Walk the Line
The Last King of Scotland	Forest Whitaker	2007	Helen Mirren	The Queen
There Will Be Blood	Daniel Day-Lewis	2008	Marion Cotillard	La Vie en Rose
Milk	Sean Penn	2009	Kate Winslet	The Reader
Crazy Heart	Jeff Bridges	2010	Sandra Bullock	The Blind Side
The King's Speech	Colin Firth	2011	Natalie Portman	Black Swan
The Artist	Jean Dujardin	2012	Meryl Streep	The Iron Lady
Lincoln	Daniel Day-Lewis	2013	Jennifer Lawrence	Silver Linings Playbook
Dallas Buyers Club	Matthew McConaughey	2014	Cate Blanchett	Blue Jasmine
The Theory of Everything	Eddie Redmayne	2015	Julianne Moore	Still Alice

BEST SUPPORTING ACTOR

Film	Actor	Year
Come and Get It	Walter Brennan	1937
The Life of Emile Zola	Joseph Schildkraut	1938
Kentucky	Walter Brennan	1939
Stagecoach	Thomas Mitchell	1940
The Westerner	Walter Brennan	1941
How Green Was My Valley	Donald Crisp	1942
Johnny Eager	Van Heflin	1943
The More the Merrier	Charles Coburn	1944
Going My Way	Barry Fitzgerald	1945
A Tree Grows in Brooklyn	James Dunn	1946
The Best Years of Our Lives	Harold Russell	1947
Miracle on 34th Street	Edmund Gwenn	1948
The Treasure of the Sierra Madre	Walter Huston	1949
Twelve O'Clock High	Dean Jagger	1950
All About Eve	**George Sanders**	1951
A Streetcar Named Desire	Karl Malden	1952
Viva Zapata!	Anthony Quinn	1953
From Here to Eternity	**Frank Sinatra**	1954
The Barefoot Contessa	Edmond O'Brien	1955
Mister Roberts	**Jack Lemmon**	1956
Lust for Life	Anthony Quinn	1957
Sayonara	Red Buttons	1958
The Big Country	Burl Ives	1959
Ben-Hur	Hugh Griffith	1960
Spartacus	Peter Ustinov	1961
West Side Story	George Chakiris	1962
Sweet Bird of Youth	Ed Begley	1963
Hud	Melvyn Douglas	1964
Topkapi	Peter Ustinov	1965
A Thousand Clowns	Martin Balsam	1966
The Fortune Cookie	Walter Matthau	1967
Cool Hand Luke	George Kennedy	1968
The Subject Was Roses	Jack Albertson	1969
They Shoot Horses, Don't They?	Gig Young	1970
Ryan's Daughter	**John Mills**	1971
The Last Picture Show	Ben Johnson	1972
Cabaret	Joel Grey	1973
The Paper Chase	John Houseman	1974
The Godfather Part II	**Robert De Niro**	1975
The Sunshine Boys	George Burns	1976
All the President's Men	Jason Robards	1977
Julia	Jason Robards	1978
The Deer Hunter	**Christopher Walken**	1979
Being There	Melvyn Douglas	1980
Ordinary People	Timothy Hutton	1981
Arthur	**John Gielgud**	1982
An Officer and a Gentleman	Louis Gossett, Jr.	1983
Terms of Endearment	**Jack Nicholson**	1984
The Killing Fields	Haing S. Ngor	1985
Cocoon	Don Ameche	1986
Hannah and Her Sisters	**Michael Caine**	1987
The Untouchables	**Sean Connery**	1988
A Fish Called Wanda	Kevin Kline	1989
Glory	**Denzel Washington**	1990
Goodfellas	Joe Pesci	1991
City Slickers	Jack Palance	1992
Unforgiven	**Gene Hackman**	1993
The Fugitive	**Tommy Lee Jones**	1994
Ed Wood	Martin Landau	1995
The Usual Suspects	**Kevin Spacey**	1996
Jerry Maguire	Cuba Gooding Jr.	1997
Good Will Hunting	**Robin Williams**	1998
Affliction	James Coburn	1999
The Cider House Rules	**Michael Caine**	2000
Traffic	**Benicio del Toro**	2001
Iris	Jim Broadbent	2002
Adaptation	Chris Cooper	2003
Mystic River	**Tim Robbins**	2004
Million Dollar Baby	**Morgan Freeman**	2005
Syriana	**George Clooney**	2006
Little Miss Sunshine	Alan Arkin	2007
No Country for Old Men	**Javier Bardem**	2008
The Dark Knight	**Heath Ledger**	2009
Inglourious Basterds	**Christoph Waltz**	2010
The Fighter	**Christian Bale**	2011
Beginners	Christopher Plummer	2012
Django Unchained	**Christoph Waltz**	2013
Dallas Buyers Club	Jared Leto	2014
Whiplash	J. K. Simmons	2015

BEST SUPPORTING ACTRESS

Gale Sondergaard	1937	Anthony Adverse
Alice Brady	1938	In Old Chicago
Fay Bainter	1939	Jezebel
Hattie McDaniel	1940	Gone with the Wind
Jane Darwell	1941	The Grapes of Wrath
Mary Astor	1942	The Great Lie
Teresa Wright	1943	Mrs. Miniver
Katina Paxinou	1944	For Whom the Bell Tolls
Ethel Barrymore	1945	None but the Lonely Heart
Anne Revere	1946	National Velvet
Anne Baxter	1947	The Razor's Edge
Celeste Holm	1948	Gentleman's Agreement
Claire Trevor	1949	Key Largo
Mercedes McCambridge	1950	All the King's Men
Josephine Hull	1951	Harvey
Kim Hunter	1952	A Streetcar Named Desire
Gloria Grahame	1953	The Bad and the Beautiful
Donna Reed	1954	From Here to Eternity
Eva Marie Saint	1955	On the Waterfront
Jo Van Fleet	1956	East of Eden
Dorothy Malone	1957	Written on the Wind
Miyoshi Umeki	1958	Sayonara
Wendy Hiller	1959	Separate Tables
Shelley Winters	1960	The Diary of Anne Frank
Shirley Jones	1961	Elmer Gantry
Rita Moreno	1962	West Side Story
Patty Duke	1963	The Miracle Worker
Margaret Rutherford	1964	The V.I.P.s
Lila Kedrova	1965	Zorba the Greek
Shelley Winters	1966	A Patch of Blue
Sandy Dennis	1967	Who's Afraid of Virginia Woolf?
Estelle Parsons	1968	Bonnie and Clyde
Ruth Gordon	1969	Rosemary's Baby
Goldie Hawn	1970	Cactus Flower
Helen Hayes	1971	Airport
Cloris Leachman	1972	The Last Picture Show
Eileen Heckart	1973	Butterflies Are Free
Tatum O'Neal	1974	Paper Moon
Ingrid Bergman	1975	Murder on the Orient Express
Lee Grant	1976	Shampoo
Beatrice Straight	1977	Network
Vanessa Redgrave	1978	Julia
Maggie Smith	1979	California Suite
Meryl Streep	1980	Kramer vs. Kramer
Mary Steenburgen	1981	Melvin and Howard
Maureen Stapleton	1982	Reds
Jessica Lange	1983	Tootsie
Linda Hunt	1984	The Year of Living Dangerously
Peggy Ashcroft	1985	A Passage to India
Anjelica Huston	1986	Prizzi's Honor
Dianne Wiest	1987	Hannah and Her Sisters
Olympia Dukakis	1988	Moonstruck
Geena Davis	1989	The Accidental Tourist
Brenda Fricker	1990	My Left Foot
Whoopi Goldberg	1991	Ghost
Mercedes Ruehl	1992	The Fisher King
Marisa Tomei	1993	My Cousin Vinny
Anna Paquin	1994	The Piano
Dianne Wiest	1995	Bullets over Broadway
Mira Sorvino	1996	Mighty Aphrodite
Juliette Binoche	1997	The English Patient
Kim Basinger	1998	L.A. Confidential
Judi Dench	1999	Shakespeare in Love
Angelina Jolie	2000	Girl, Interrupted
Marcia Gay Harden	2001	Pollock
Jennifer Connelly	2002	A Beautiful Mind
Catherine Zeta-Jones	2003	Chicago
Renée Zellweger	2004	Cold Mountain
Cate Blanchett	2005	The Aviator
Rachel Weisz	2006	The Constant Gardener
Jennifer Hudson	2007	Dreamgirls
Tilda Swinton	2008	Michael Clayton
Penélope Cruz	2009	Vicky Cristina Barcelona
Mo'Nique	2010	Precious
Melissa Leo	2011	The Fighter
Octavia Spencer	2012	The Help
Anne Hathaway	2013	Les Misérables
Lupita Nyong'o	2014	12 Years a Slave
Patricia Arquette	2015	Boyhood

BEST ACTOR — DRAMA

Watch on the Rhine	Paul Lukas	1944
Wilson	Alexander Knox	1945
The Lost Weekend	Ray Milland	1946
The Yearling	**Gregory Peck**	1947

BEST ACTRESS — DRAMA

Jennifer Jones	The Song of Bernadette
Ingrid Bergman	Gaslight
Ingrid Bergman	The Bells of St. Mary's
Rosalind Russell	Sister Kenny

Film (Actor)	Best Actor	Year	Best Actress	Film (Actress)
A Double Life	Ronald Colman	1948	Rosalind Russell	Mourning Becomes Electra
Hamlet	Laurence Olivier	1949	Jane Wyman	Johnny Belinda
All the King's Men	Broderick Crawford	1950	Olivia de Havilland	The Heiress
Cyrano de Bergerac	José Ferrer	1951	Gloria Swanson	Sunset Boulevard
Death of a Salesman	Fredric March	1952	Jane Wyman	The Blue Veil
High Noon	Gary Cooper	1953	Shirley Booth	Come Back, Little Sheba
The Actress	Spencer Tracy	1954	Audrey Hepburn	Roman Holiday
On the Waterfront	Marlon Brando	1955	Grace Kelly	The Country Girl
Marty	Ernest Borgnine	1956	Anna Magnani	The Rose Tattoo
Lust for Life	Kirk Douglas	1957	Ingrid Bergman	Anastasia
The Bridge on the River Kwai	Alec Guinness	1958	Joanne Woodward	The Three Faces of Eve
Separate Tables	David Niven	1959	Susan Hayward	I Want to Live!
Career	Anthony Franciosa	1960	Elizabeth Taylor	Suddenly, Last Summer
Elmer Gantry	Burt Lancaster	1961	Greer Garson	Sunrise at Campobello
Judgment at Nuremberg	Maximilian Schell	1962	Geraldine Page	Summer and Smoke
To Kill a Mockingbird	Gregory Peck	1963	Geraldine Page	Sweet Bird of Youth
Lilies of the Field	Sidney Poitier	1964	Leslie Caron	The L-Shaped Room
Becket	Peter O'Toole	1965	Anne Bancroft	The Pumpkin Eater
Doctor Zhivago	Omar Sharif	1966	Samantha Eggar	The Collector
A Man for All Seasons	Paul Scofield	1967	Anouk Aimée	A Man and a Woman
In the Heat of the Night	Rod Steiger	1968	Edith Evans	The Whisperers
The Lion in Winter	Peter O'Toole	1969	Joanne Woodward	Rachel, Rachel
True Grit	John Wayne	1970	Geneviève Bujold	Anne of the Thousand Days
Patton	George C. Scott	1971	Ali MacGraw	Love Story
The French Connection	Gene Hackman	1972	Jane Fonda	Klute
The Godfather	Marlon Brando	1973	Liv Ullmann	The Emigrants
Serpico	Al Pacino	1974	Marsha Mason	Cinderella Liberty
Chinatown	Jack Nicholson	1975	Gena Rowlands	A Woman Under the Influence
One Flew Over the Cuckoo's Nest	Jack Nicholson	1976	Louise Fletcher	One Flew Over the Cuckoo's Nest
Network	Peter Finch	1977	Faye Dunaway	Network
Equus	Richard Burton	1978	Jane Fonda	Julia
Coming Home	Jon Voight	1979	Jane Fonda	Coming Home
Kramer vs. Kramer	Dustin Hoffman		Sally Field	Norma Rae
Raging Bull	Robert De Niro	1981	Mary Tyler Moore	Ordinary People
On Golden Pond	Henry Fonda	1982	Meryl Streep	The French Lieutenant's Woman
Gandhi	Ben Kingsley	1983	Meryl Streep	Sophie's Choice
The Dresser	Tom Courtenay (tie)	1984	Shirley MacLaine	Terms of Endearment
Tender Mercies	Robert Duvall (tie)			
Amadeus	F. Murray Abraham	1985	Sally Field	Places in the Heart
Runaway Train	Jon Voight	1986	Whoopi Goldberg	The Color Purple
Mona Lisa	Bob Hoskins	1987	Marlee Matlin	Children of a Lesser God
Wall Street	Michael Douglas	1988	Sally Kirkland	Anna
Rain Man	Dustin Hoffman	1989	Jodie Foster (tie)	The Accused
			Shirley MacLaine (tie)	Madame Sousatzka
			Sigourney Weaver (tie)	Gorillas in the Mist
Born on the Fourth of July	Tom Cruise	1990	Michelle Pfeiffer	The Fabulous Baker Boys
Reversal of Fortune	Jeremy Irons	1991	Kathy Bates	Misery
The Prince of Tides	Nick Nolte	1992	Jodie Foster	The Silence of the Lambs
Scent of a Woman	Al Pacino	1993	Emma Thompson	Howards End
Philadelphia	Tom Hanks	1994	Holly Hunter	The Piano
Forrest Gump	Tom Hanks	1995	Jessica Lange	Blue Sky
Leaving Las Vegas	Nicolas Cage	1996	Sharon Stone	Casino
Shine	Geoffrey Rush	1997	Brenda Blethyn	Secrets & Lies
Ulee's Gold	Peter Fonda	1998	Judi Dench	Mrs. Brown
The Truman Show	Jim Carrey	1999	Cate Blanchett	Elizabeth
The Hurricane	Denzel Washington	2000	Hilary Swank	Boys Don't Cry
Cast Away	Tom Hanks	2001	Julia Roberts	Erin Brockovich
A Beautiful Mind	Russell Crowe	2002	Sissy Spacek	In the Bedroom
About Schmidt	Jack Nicholson	2003	Nicole Kidman	The Hours
Mystic River	Sean Penn	2004	Charlize Theron	Monster
The Aviator	Leonardo DiCaprio	2005	Hilary Swank	Million Dollar Baby
Capote	Philip Seymour Hoffman	2006	Felicity Huffman	Transamerica
The Last King of Scotland	Forest Whitaker	2007	Helen Mirren	The Queen
There Will Be Blood	Daniel Day-Lewis	2008	Julie Christie	Away from Her
The Wrestler	Mickey Rourke	2009	Kate Winslet	Revolutionary Road
Crazy Heart	Jeff Bridges	2010	Sandra Bullock	The Blind Side
The King's Speech	Colin Firth	2011	Natalie Portman	Black Swan
The Descendants	George Clooney	2012	Meryl Streep	The Iron Lady
Lincoln	Daniel Day-Lewis	2013	Jessica Chastain	Zero Dark Thirty
Dallas Buyers Club	Matthew McConaughey	2014	Cate Blanchett	Blue Jasmine
The Theory of Everything	Eddie Redmayne	2015	Julianne Moore	Still Alice

BEST ACTOR — MUSICAL/COMEDY · BEST ACTRESS — MUSICAL/COMEDY

Film (Actor)	Best Actor	Year	Best Actress	Film (Actress)
Three Little Words	Fred Astaire	1951	Judy Holliday	Born Yesterday
On the Riviera	Danny Kaye	1952	June Allyson	Too Young to Kiss
Singin' in the Rain	Donald O'Connor	1953	Susan Hayward	With a Song in My Heart
The Moon Is Blue	David Niven	1954	Ethel Merman	Call Me Madam
A Star Is Born	James Mason	1955	Judy Garland	A Star Is Born
The Seven Year Itch	Tom Ewell	1956	Jean Simmons	Guys and Dolls
Around the World in Eighty Days	Cantinflas	1957	Deborah Kerr	The King and I
Pal Joey	Frank Sinatra	1958	Taina Elg (tie)	Les Girls
			Kay Kendall (tie)	Les Girls
Me and the Colonel	Danny Kaye	1959	Rosalind Russell	Auntie Mame
Some Like It Hot	Jack Lemmon	1960	Marilyn Monroe	Some Like It Hot
The Apartment	Jack Lemmon	1961	Shirley MacLaine	The Apartment
Pocketful of Miracles	Glenn Ford	1962	Rosalind Russell	A Majority of One
Divorce, Italian Style	Marcello Mastroianni	1963	Rosalind Russell	Gypsy
The Devil	Alberto Sordi	1964	Shirley MacLaine	Irma la Douce

My Fair Lady	Rex Harrison	1965	**Julie Andrews**	Mary Poppins
Cat Ballou	**Lee Marvin**	1966	**Julie Andrews**	The Sound of Music
The Russians Are Coming	Alan Arkin	1967	Lynn Redgrave	Georgy Girl
Camelot	Richard Harris	1968	Anne Bancroft	The Graduate
Oliver!	Ron Moody	1969	**Barbra Streisand**	Funny Girl
Goodbye, Mr. Chips	**Peter O'Toole**	1970	Patty Duke	Me, Natalie
Scrooge	Albert Finney	1971	Carrie Snodgress	Diary of a Mad Housewife
Fiddler on the Roof	Topol	1972	Twiggy	The Boy Friend
Avanti!	**Jack Lemmon**	1973	**Liza Minnelli**	Cabaret
A Touch of Class	George Segal	1974	Glenda Jackson	A Touch of Class
Harry and Tonto	Art Carney	1975	Raquel Welch	The Three Musketeers
The Sunshine Boys	George Burns (tie)	1976	Ann-Margret	Tommy
The Sunshine Boys	Walter Matthau (tie)			
A Star Is Born	Kris Kristofferson	1977	**Barbra Streisand**	A Star Is Born
The Goodbye Girl	**Richard Dreyfuss**	1978	**Diane Keaton (tie)**	Annie Hall
			Marsha Mason (tie)	The Goodbye Girl
Heaven Can Wait	**Warren Beatty**	1979	Ellen Burstyn (tie)	Same Time, Next Year
			Maggie Smith (tie)	California Suite
Being There	**Peter Sellers**	1980	**Bette Midler**	The Rose
The Idolmaker	Ray Sharkey	1981	Sissy Spacek	Coal Miner's Daughter
Arthur	Dudley Moore	1982	Bernadette Peters	Pennies from Heaven
Tootsie	**Dustin Hoffman**	1983	**Julie Andrews**	Victor Victoria
Educating Rita	**Michael Caine**	1984	Julie Walters	Educating Rita
Micki + Maude	Dudley Moore	1985	**Kathleen Turner**	Romancing the Stone
Prizzi's Honor	**Jack Nicholson**	1986	**Kathleen Turner**	Prizzi's Honor
"Crocodile" Dundee	Paul Hogan	1987	Sissy Spacek	Crimes of the Heart
Good Morning, Vietnam	**Robin Williams**	1988	Cher	Moonstruck
Big	**Tom Hanks**	1989	Melanie Griffith	Working Girl
Driving Miss Daisy	**Morgan Freeman**	1990	Jessica Tandy	Driving Miss Daisy
Green Card	**Gérard Depardieu**	1991	**Julia Roberts**	Pretty Woman
The Fisher King	**Robin Williams**	1992	**Bette Midler**	For the Boys
The Player	**Tim Robbins**	1993	Miranda Richardson	Enchanted April
Mrs. Doubtfire	**Robin Williams**	1994	Angela Bassett	What's Love Got to Do with It
Four Weddings and a Funeral	**Hugh Grant**	1995	Jamie Lee Curtis	True Lies
Get Shorty	John Travolta	1996	**Nicole Kidman**	To Die For
Jerry Maguire	Tom Cruise	1997	Madonna	Evita
As Good as It Gets	**Jack Nicholson**	1998	Helen Hunt	As Good as It Gets
Little Voice	**Michael Caine**	1999	Gwyneth Paltrow	Shakespeare in Love
Man on the Moon	**Jim Carrey**	2000	Janet McTeer	Tumbleweeds
O Brother, Where Art Thou?	**George Clooney**	2001	Renée Zellweger	Nurse Betty
The Royal Tenenbaums	**Gene Hackman**	2002	**Nicole Kidman**	Moulin Rouge!
Chicago	**Richard Gere**	2003	Renée Zellweger	Chicago
Lost in Translation	**Bill Murray**	2004	**Diane Keaton**	Something's Gotta Give
Ray	**Jamie Foxx**	2005	Annette Bening	Being Julia
Walk the Line	**Joaquin Phoenix**	2006	Reese Witherspoon	Walk the Line
Borat	**Sacha Baron Cohen**	2007	**Meryl Streep**	The Devil Wears Prada
Sweeney Todd	**Johnny Depp**	2008	**Marion Cotillard**	La Vie en Rose
In Bruges	Colin Farrell	2009	Sally Hawkins	Happy-Go-Lucky
Sherlock Holmes	**Robert Downey, Jr.**	2010	**Meryl Streep**	Julie & Julia
Barney's Version	Paul Giamatti	2011	Annette Bening	The Kids Are All Right
The Artist	Jean Dujardin	2012	Michelle Williams	My Week with Marilyn
Les Misérables	**Hugh Jackman**	2013	**Jennifer Lawrence**	Silver Linings Playbook
The Wolf of Wall Street	Leonardo DiCaprio	2014	Amy Adams	American Hustle
Birdman	**Michael Keaton**	2015	**Amy Adams**	Big Eyes

BEST SUPPORTING ACTOR   BEST SUPPORTING ACTRESS

For Whom the Bell Tolls	Akim Tamiroff	1944	Katina Paxinou	For Whom the Bell Tolls
Going My Way	Barry Fitzgerald	1945	Agnes Moorehead	Mrs. Parkington
A Medal for Benny	J. Carrol Naish	1946	Angela Lansbury	The Picture of Dorian Gray
The Razor's Edge	Clifton Webb	1947	Anne Baxter	The Razor's Edge
Miracle on 34th Street	Edmund Gwenn	1948	Celeste Holm	Gentleman's Agreement
The Treasure of the Sierra Madre	Walter Huston	1949	Ellen Corby	I Remember Mama
Battleground	James Whitmore	1950	Mercedes McCambridge	All the King's Men
Mister 880	Edmund Gwenn	1951	Josephine Hull	Harvey
Quo Vadis	Peter Ustinov	1952	Kim Hunter	A Streetcar Named Desire
My Six Convicts	Millard Mitchell	1953	Katy Jurado	High Noon
From Here to Eternity	**Frank Sinatra**	1954	**Grace Kelly**	Mogambo
The Barefoot Contessa	Edmond O'Brien	1955	Jan Sterling	The High and the Mighty
Trial	Arthur Kennedy	1956	Marisa Pavan	The Rose Tattoo
The Rainmaker	Earl Holliman	1957	Eileen Heckart	The Bad Seed
Sayonara	Red Buttons	1958	Elsa Lanchester	Witness for the Prosecution
The Big Country	Burl Ives	1959	Hermione Gingold	Gigi
Ben-Hur	Stephen Boyd	1960	Susan Kohner	Imitation of Life
Exodus	Sal Mineo	1961	**Janet Leigh**	Psycho
West Side Story	George Chakiris	1962	Rita Moreno	West Side Story
Lawrence of Arabia	**Omar Sharif**	1963	Angela Lansbury	The Manchurian Candidate
The Cardinal	John Huston	1964	Margaret Rutherford	The V.I.P.s ·
Seven Days in May	Edmond O'Brien	1965	Agnes Moorehead	Hush… Hush, Sweet Charlotte
The Spy Who Came in from the Cold	Oskar Werner	1966	Ruth Gordon	Inside Daisy Clover
The Sand Pebbles	Richard Attenborough	1967	Jocelyne LaGarde	Hawaii
Doctor Dolittle	Richard Attenborough	1968	Carol Channing	Thoroughly Modern Millie
Star!	Daniel Massey	1969	Ruth Gordon	Rosemary's Baby
They Shoot Horses, Don't They?	Gig Young	1970	**Goldie Hawn**	Cactus Flower
Ryan's Daughter	**John Mills**	1971	Karen Black (tie)	Five Easy Pieces
The Last Picture Show	Ben Johnson	1972	Maureen Stapleton (tie)	Airport
Cabaret	Joel Grey	1973	Ann-Margret	Carnal Knowledge
The Paper Chase	John Houseman	1974	Shelley Winters	The Poseidon Adventure
The Towering Inferno	**Fred Astaire**	1975	Linda Blair	The Exorcist

	Best Actor		Best Actress	
The Sunshine Boys	Richard Benjamin	1976	Karen Black	*The Great Gatsby*
Marathon Man	**Laurence Olivier**	1977	Brenda Vaccaro	*Jacqueline Susann's Once Is Not Enough*
Equus	Peter Firth	1978	Katharine Ross	*Voyage of the Damned*
Midnight Express	John Hurt	1979	**Vanessa Redgrave**	*Julia*
Being There	Melvyn Douglas (tie)	1980	Dyan Cannon	*Heaven Can Wait*
Apocalypse Now	Robert Duvall (tie)		**Meryl Streep**	*Kramer vs. Kramer*
Ordinary People	Timothy Hutton	1981	Mary Steenburgen	*Melvin and Howard*
Arthur	**John Gielgud**	1982	Joan Hackett	*Only When I Laugh*
An Officer and a Gentleman	Louis Gossett, Jr.	1983	**Jessica Lange**	*Tootsie*
Terms of Endearment	**Jack Nicholson**	1984	Cher	*Silkwood*
The Killing Fields	Haing S. Ngor	1985	Peggy Ashcroft	*A Passage to India*
Out of Africa	Klaus Maria Brandauer	1986	Meg Tilly	*Agnes of God*
Platoon	Tom Berenger	1987	**Maggie Smith**	*A Room with a View*
The Untouchables	**Sean Connery**	1988	Olympia Dukakis	*Moonstruck*
Tucker: The Man and His Dream	Martin Landau	1989	**Sigourney Weaver**	*Working Girl*
Glory	**Denzel Washington**	1990	**Julia Roberts**	*Steel Magnolias*
Longtime Companion	Bruce Davison	1991	Whoopi Goldberg	*Ghost*
City Slickers	Jack Palance	1992	Mercedes Ruehl	*The Fisher King*
Unforgiven	**Gene Hackman**	1993	Joan Plowright	*Enchanted April*
The Fugitive	**Tommy Lee Jones**	1994	Winona Ryder	*The Age of Innocence*
Ed Wood	Martin Landau	1995	Dianne Wiest	*Bullets Over Broadway*
12 Monkeys	**Brad Pitt**	1996	Mira Sorvino	*Mighty Aphrodite*
Primal Fear	Edward Norton	1997	**Lauren Bacall**	*The Mirror Has Two Faces*
Boogie Nights	**Burt Reynolds**	1998	Kim Basinger	*L.A. Confidential*
The Truman Show	Ed Harris	1999	Lynn Redgrave	*Gods and Monsters*
Magnolia	**Tom Cruise**	2000	**Angelina Jolie**	*Girl, Interrupted*
Traffic	**Benicio del Toro**	2001	Kate Hudson	*Almost Famous*
Iris	Jim Broadbent	2002	Jennifer Connelly	*A Beautiful Mind*
Adaptation	Chris Cooper	2003	**Meryl Streep**	*Adaptation.*
Mystic River	**Tim Robbins**	2004	Renée Zellweger	*Cold Mountain*
Closer	Clive Owen	2005	**Natalie Portman**	*Closer*
Syriana	**George Clooney**	2006	Rachel Weisz	*The Constant Gardener*
Dreamgirls	**Eddie Murphy**	2007	Jennifer Hudson	*Dreamgirls*
No Country for Old Men	**Javier Bardem**	2008	**Cate Blanchett**	*I'm Not There*
The Dark Knight	**Heath Ledger**	2009	**Kate Winslet**	*The Reader*
Inglourious Basterds	**Christoph Waltz**	2010	Mo'Nique	*Precious*
The Fighter	**Christian Bale**	2011	Melissa Leo	*The Fighter*
Beginners	Christopher Plummer	2012	Octavia Spencer	*The Help*
Django Unchained	**Christoph Waltz**	2013	**Anne Hathaway**	*Les Misérables*
Dallas Buyers Club	Jared Leto	2014	**Jennifer Lawrence**	*American Hustle*
Whiplash	J. K. Simmons	2015	Patricia Arquette	*Boyhood*

BEST ACTOR / BEST ACTRESS

	Best Actor		Best Actress	
The Sound Barrier (British)	Ralph Richardson	1953	**Vivien Leigh**	*A Streetcar Named Desire (British)*
Viva Zapata! (Foreign)	**Marlon Brando**		Simone Signoret	*Golden Helmet (Foreign)*
Julius Caesar (British)	John Gielgud	1954	**Audrey Hepburn**	*Roman Holiday (British)*
Julius Caesar (Foreign)	**Marlon Brando**		Leslie Caron	*Lili (Foreign)*
Doctor in the House (British)	Kenneth More	1955	Yvonne Mitchell	*The Divided Heart (British)*
On the Waterfront (Foreign)	**Marlon Brando**		Cornell Borchers	*The Divided Heart (Foreign)*
Richard III (British)	**Laurence Olivier**	1956	Katie Johnson	*The Ladykillers (British)*
Marty (Foreign)	Ernest Borgnine		Betsy Blair	*Marty (Foreign)*
A Town Like Alice (British)	Peter Finch	1957	Virginia McKenna	*A Town Like Alice (British)*
Gervaise (Foreign)	François Périer		**Anna Magnani**	*The Rose Tattoo (Foreign)*
The Bridge on the River Kwai (British)	**Alec Guinness**	1958	Heather Sears	*The Story of Esther Costello (British)*
12 Angry Men (Foreign)	Henry Fonda		**Simone Signoret**	*The Crucible (Foreign)*
The Key (British)	Trevor Howard	1959	Irene Worth	*Orders to Kill (British)*
The Defiant Ones (Foreign)	Sidney Poitier		**Simone Signoret**	*Room at the Top (Foreign)*
I'm All Right Jack (British)	**Peter Sellers**	1960	**Audrey Hepburn**	*The Nun's Story (British)*
Some Like It Hot (Foreign)	Jack Lemmon		Shirley Maclaine	*Ask Any Girl (Foreign)*
The Trials of Oscar Wilde (British)	Peter Finch	1961	Rachel Roberts	*Saturday Night and Sunday Morning (British)*
The Apartment (Foreign)	Jack Lemmon		**Shirley Maclaine**	*The Apartment (Foreign)*
No Love for Johnnie (British)	Peter Finch	1962	Dora Bryan	*A Taste of Honey (British)*
The Hustler (Foreign)	**Paul Newman**		**Sophia Loren**	*Two Women (Foreign)*
Lawrence of Arabia (British)	**Peter O'Toole**	1963	Leslie Caron	*The L-Shaped Room (British)*
Birdman of Alcatraz (Foreign)	**Burt Lancaster**		Anne Bancroft	*The Miracle Worker (Foreign)*
The Servant (British)	**Dirk Bogarde**	1964	Rachel Roberts	*This Sporting Life (British)*
Divorzio all'italiana (Foreign)	**Marcello Mastroianni**		Patricia Neal	*Hud (Foreign)*
Guns at Batasi / Seance on a Wet Afternoon (British)	Richard Attenborough	1965	**Audrey Hepburn**	*Charade (British)*
Ieri, oggi, domani (Foreign)	**Marcello Mastroianni**		Anne Bancroft	*The Pumpkin Eater (Foreign)*
Darling (British)	Dirk Bogarde	1966	**Julie Christie**	*Darling (British)*
Cat Ballou / The Killers (Foreign)	Lee Marvin		Patricia Neal	*In Harm's Way (Foreign)*
The Spy Who Came in from the Cold / Who's Afraid of Virginia Woolf? (British)	**Richard Burton**	1967	Elizabeth Taylor	*Who's Afraid of Virginia Woolf? (British)*
The Pawnbroker (Foreign)	**Rod Steiger**		Jeanne Moreau	*Viva Maria! (Foreign)*
A Man for All Seasons (British)	Paul Scofield	1968	Edith Evans	*The Whisperers (British)*
In the Heat of the Night (Foreign)	**Rod Steiger**		Anouk Aimée	*A Man and a Woman (Foreign)*
Guess Who's Coming to Dinner	**Spencer Tracy**	1969	**Katharine Hepburn**	*The Lion in Winter & Guess Who's Coming to Dinner*
John and Mary / Midnight Cowboy	**Dustin Hoffman**	1970	**Maggie Smith**	*The Prime of Miss Jean Brodie*
Butch Cassidy and the Sundance Kid / Downhill –Racer / Tell Them Willie Boy Is Here	**Robert Redford**	1971	Katharine Ross	*Butch Cassidy and the Sundance Kid / Tell Them Willie Boy Is Here*
Sunday Bloody Sunday	Peter Finch	1972	Glenda Jackson	*Sunday Bloody Sunday*
The French Connection / The Poseidon Adventure	**Gene Hackman**	1973	**Liza Minnelli**	*Cabaret*
Charley Varrick / Pete 'n' Tillie	Walter Matthau	1974	Stéphane Audran	*Just Before Nightfall & The Discreet Charm of the Bourgeoisie*
Chinatown / The Last Detail	**Jack Nicholson**	1975	Joanne Woodward	*Summer Wishes, Winter Dreams*
The Godfather Part II / Dog Day Afternoon	Al Pacino	1976	Ellen Burstyn	*Alice Doesn't Live Here Anymore*
One Flew Over the Cuckoo's Nest	**Jack Nicholson**	1977	Louise Fletcher	*One Flew Over the Cuckoo's Nest*
Network	Peter Finch	1978	**Diane Keaton**	*Annie Hall*

Film	Best Actor	Year	Best Actress	Film
The Goodbye Girl	**Richard Dreyfuss**	1979	Jane Fonda	Julia
The China Syndrome	**Jack Lemmon**	1980	Jane Fonda	The China Syndrome
The Elephant Man	John Hurt	1981	Judy Davis	My Brilliant Career
Atlantic City	**Burt Lancaster**	1982	**Meryl Streep**	The French Lieutenant's Woman
Gandhi	Ben Kingsley	1983	Katharine Hepburn	On Golden Pond
Educating Rita	**Michael Caine (tie)**	1984	Julie Walters	Educating Rita
Tootsie	**Dustin Hoffman (tie)**			
The Killing Fields	Haing S. Ngor	1985	**Maggie Smith**	A Private Function
Kiss of the Spider Woman	**William Hurt**	1986	Peggy Ashcroft	A Passage to India
Mona Lisa	Bob Hoskins	1987	**Maggie Smith**	A Room with a View
The Name of the Rose	**Sean Connery**	1988	Anne Bancroft	84 Charing Cross Road
A Fish Called Wanda	John Cleese	1989	**Maggie Smith**	The Lonely Passion of Judith Hearne
My Left Foot	**Daniel Day-Lewis**	1990	Pauline Collins	Shirley Valentine
Cinema Paradiso	**Philippe Noiret**	1991	Jessica Tandy	Driving Miss Daisy
The Silence of the Lambs	**Anthony Hopkins**	1992	**Jodie Foster**	The Silence of the Lambs
Chaplin	**Robert Downey, Jr.**	1993	**Emma Thompson**	Howards End
Shadowlands	**Anthony Hopkins**	1994	Holly Hunter	The Piano
Four Weddings and a Funeral	**Hugh Grant**	1995	**Susan Sarandon**	The Client
The Madness of King George	Nigel Hawthorne	1996	**Emma Thompson**	Sense and Sensibility
Shine	Geoffrey Rush	1997	Brenda Blethyn	Secrets & Lies
The Full Monty	Robert Carlyle	1998	**Judi Dench**	Mrs. Brown
Life Is Beautiful (La vita è bella)	Roberto Benigni	1999	**Cate Blanchett**	Elizabeth
American Beauty	**Kevin Spacey**	2000	Annette Bening	American Beauty
Billy Elliot	Jamie Bell	2001	**Julia Roberts**	Erin Brockovich
A Beautiful Mind	**Russell Crowe**	2002	**Judi Dench**	Iris
Gangs of New York	**Daniel Day-Lewis**	2003	**Nicole Kidman**	The Hours
Lost in Translation	**Bill Murray**	2004	Scarlett Johansson	Lost in Translation
Ray	**Jamie Foxx**	2005	Imelda Staunton	Vera Drake
Capote	**Philip Seymour Hoffman**	2006	Reese Witherspoon	Walk the Line
The Last King of Scotland	**Forest Whitaker**	2007	**Helen Mirren**	The Queen
There Will Be Blood	**Daniel Day-Lewis**	2008	**Marion Cotillard**	La Vie en Rose
The Wrestler	Mickey Rourke	2009	**Kate Winslet**	The Reader
A Single Man	**Colin Firth**	2010	Carey Mulligan	An Education
The King's Speech	**Colin Firth**	2011	Natalie Portman	Black Swan
The Artist	Jean Dujardin	2012	**Meryl Streep**	The Iron Lady
Lincoln	**Daniel Day-Lewis**	2013	Emmanuelle Riva	Amour
12 Years a Slave	Chiwetel Ejiofor	2014	**Cate Blanchett**	Blue Jasmine
The Theory of Everything	Eddie Redmayne	2015	**Julianne Moore**	Still Alice

BEST SUPPORTING ACTOR · BEST SUPPORTING ACTRESS

Film	Best Supporting Actor	Year	Best Supporting Actress	Film
The Bofors Gun	Ian Holm	1969	Billie Whitelaw	Charlie Bubbles & Twisted Nerve
Oh! What a Lovely War	**Laurence Olivier**	1970	Celia Johnson	The Prime of Miss Jean Brodie
Kes	Colin Welland	1971	Susannah York	They Shoot Horses, Don't They?
The Go-Between	Edward Fox	1972	Margaret Leighton	The Go-Between
The Last Picture Show	Ben Johnson	1973	Cloris Leachman	The Last Picture Show
O Lucky Man!	Arthur Lowe	1974	Valentina Cortese	Day for Night
Murder on the Orient Express	**John Gielgud**	1975	**Ingrid Bergman**	Murder on the Orient Express
The Towering Inferno	**Fred Astaire**	1976	Diane Ladd	Alice Doesn't Live Here Anymore
One Flew Over the Cuckoo's Nest	Brad Dourif	1977	**Jodie Foster**	Taxi Driver & Bugsy Malone
A Bridge Too Far	Edward Fox	1978	Jenny Agutter	Equus
Midnight Express	John Hurt	1979	Geraldine Page	Interiors
Apocalypse Now	Robert Duvall	1980	Rachel Roberts	Yanks
	No award this year	1981	No award this year	
Chariots of Fire	Ian Holm	1982	No award this year	
Reds	**Jack Nicholson**	1983	Maureen Stapleton (tie)	Reds
			Rohini Hattangadi (tie)	Gandhi
Trading Places	Denholm Elliott	1984	Jamie Lee Curtis	Trading Places
A Private Function	Denholm Elliott	1985	Liz Smith	A Private Function
Defence of the Realm	Denholm Elliott	1986	Rosanna Arquette	Desperately Seeking Susan
The Mission	Ray McAnally	1987	**Judi Dench**	A Room with a View
Jean de Florette	**Daniel Auteuil**	1988	Susan Wooldridge	Hope and Glory
A Fish Called Wanda	Michael Palin	1989	**Judi Dench**	A Handful of Dust
My Left Foot	Ray McAnally	1990	**Michelle Pfeiffer**	Dangerous Liaisons
Cinema Paradiso (Nuovo cinema Paradiso)	Salvatore Cascio	1991	Whoopi Goldberg	Ghost
Robin Hood: Prince of Thieves	Alan Rickman	1992	Kate Nelligan	Frankie and Johnny
Unforgiven	**Gene Hackman**	1993	Miranda Richardson	Damage
Schindler's List	**Ralph Fiennes**	1994	Miriam Margolyes	The Age of Innocence
Pulp Fiction	**Samuel L. Jackson**	1995	**Kristin Scott Thomas**	Four Weddings and a Funeral
Rob Roy	Tim Roth	1996	**Kate Winslet**	Sense and Sensibility
The Crucible	Paul Scofield	1997	Juliette Binoche	The English Patient
The Full Monty	Tom Wilkinson	1998	Sigourney Weaver	The Ice Storm
Elizabeth	Geoffrey Rush	1999	**Judi Dench**	Shakespeare in Love
The Talented Mr. Ripley	Jude Law	2000	**Maggie Smith**	Tea with Mussolini
Traffic	**Benicio del Toro**	2001	Julie Walters	Billy Elliot
Moulin Rouge!	Jim Broadbent	2002	Jennifer Connelly	A Beautiful Mind
Catch Me If You Can	Christopher Walken	2003	**Catherine Zeta-Jones**	Chicago
Love Actually	Bill Nighy	2004	Renée Zellweger	Cold Mountain
Closer	Clive Owen	2005	**Cate Blanchett**	The Aviator
Brokeback Mountain	**Jake Gyllenhaal**	2006	Thandie Newton	Crash
Little Miss Sunshine	Alan Arkin	2007	Jennifer Hudson	Dreamgirls
No Country for Old Men	**Javier Bardem**	2008	Tilda Swinton	Michael Clayton
The Dark Knight	**Heath Ledger**	2009	**Penélope Cruz**	Vicky Cristina Barcelona
Inglourious Basterds	**Christoph Waltz**	2010	Mo'Nique	Precious
The King's Speech	Geoffrey Rush	2011	Helena Bonham Carter	The King's Speech
Beginners	Christopher Plummer	2012	Octavia Spencer	The Help
Django Unchained	**Christoph Waltz**	2013	**Anne Hathaway**	Les Misérables
Captain Phillips	Barkhad Abdi	2014	**Jennifer Lawrence**	American Hustle
Whiplash	J. K. Simmons	2015	Patricia Arquette	Boyhood

BEST ACTOR · BEST ACTRESS

Best Actor (film)	Best Actor	Year	Best Actress	Best Actress (film)
The Lost Weekend	Ray Milland	1946	Michèle Morgan	La Symphonie Pastorale
	No award this year	1947	No award this year	
	Festival not held	1948	Festival not held	
House of Strangers	**Edward G. Robinson**	1949	Isa Miranda	The Walls of Malapaga
	Festival not held	1950	Festival not held	
The Browning Version	Michael Redgrave	1951	**Bette Davis**	All About Eve
Viva Zapata!	**Marlon Brando**	1952	Lee Grant	Detective Story
	No award this year	1953	No award this year	
	No award this year	1954	No award this year	
Bolshaya Semya	Whole cast	1955	Whole cast	Bolshaya Semya
Bad Day at Black Rock	**Spencer Tracy**			
	No award this year	1956	Susan Hayward	I'll Cry Tomorrow
Valley of Peace	John Kitzmiller	1957	**Giulietta Masina**	Nights of Cabiria
The Long, Hot Summer	**Paul Newman**	1958	Bibi Andersson / Eva Dahlbeck /	Brink of Life
			Barbro Hiort af Ornäs / Ingrid Thulin	
Compulsion	Bradford Dillman	1959	**Simone Signoret**	Room at the Top
	No award this year	1960	Melina Mercouri	Never on Sunday
			Jeanne Moreau	Moderato Cantabile
Goodbye Again	**Anthony Perkins**	1961	**Sophia Loren**	Two Women
Long Day's Journey into Night	Dean Stockwell / Jason	1962	**Katharine Hepburn**	Long Day's Journey into Night
	Robards / Ralph Richardson /		Rita Tushingham	A Taste of Honey
	Murray Melvin			
A Taste of Honey	Richard Harris	1963	Marina Vlady	The Conjugal Bed (L'Ape Regina)
This Sporting Life	Antal Páger	1964	Anne Bancroft	The Pumpkin Eater
Pacsirta	Saro Urzi		Barbara Barrie	One Potato, Two Potato
Seduced and Abandoned	Terence Stamp	1965	Samantha Eggar	The Collector
The Collector	Per Oscarsson	1966	**Vanessa Redgrave**	Morgan!
Three Days and a Child	Oded Kotler	1967	Pia Degermark	Elvira Madigan
	Festival not held	1968	Festival not held	
Z	Jean-Louis Trintignant	1969	**Vanessa Redgrave**	Isadora
The Pizza Triangle	**Marcello Mastroianni**	1970	Ottavia Piccolo	Metello
Sacco e Vanzetti	Riccardo Cucciolla	1971	Kitty Winn	The Panic in Needle Park
Nous ne vieillirons pas ensemble	Jean Yanne	1972	Susannah York	Images
Love and Anarchy	Giancarlo Giannini	1973	Joanne Woodward	The Effect of Gamma Rays…
The Last Detail	**Jack Nicholson**	1974	Marie-José Nat	Les violons du bal
Profumo di donna	Vittorio Gassman	1975	Valérie Perrine	Lenny
Pascual Duarte	José Luis Gómez	1976	Dominique Sanda	L'eredità Ferramonti
			Mari Törocsik	Déryné hol van?
Elisa, vida mía	Fernando Rey	1977	Shelley Duvall	3 Women
			Monique Mercure	J.A. Martin Photographe
Coming Home	Jon Voight	1978	Jill Clayburgh	An Unmarried Woman
			Isabelle Huppert	Violette Nozière
The China Syndrome	**Jack Lemmon**	1979	Sally Field	Norma Rae
A Leap in the Dark	Michel Piccoli	1980	Anouk Aimée	A Leap in the Dark
La tragedia di un uomo ridicolo	Ugo Tognazzi	1981	**Isabelle Adjani**	Quartet / Possession
Missing	**Jack Lemmon**	1982	Jadwiga Jankowska-Cieslak	Another Way
La Mort de Mario Ricci	**Gian Maria Volonté**	1983	Hanna Schygulla	Storia di Piera
Los santos inocentes	Alfredo Landa	1984	**Helen Mirren**	Cal
	Francisco Rabal			
Kiss of the Spider Woman	**William Hurt**	1985	Norma Aleandro / Cher	The Official Story / Mask
Ménage	Michel Blanc	1986	Barbara Sukowa	Rosa Luxemburg
Mona Lisa	Bob Hoskins		Fernanda Torres	Eu Sei Que Vou Te Amar
Dark Eyes	**Marcello Mastroianni**	1987	Barbara Hershey	Shy People
Bird	**Forest Whitaker**	1988	Barbara Hershey / Jodhi	A World Apart
			May / Linda Mvusi	
Sex, Lies, and Videotape	James Spader	1989	**Meryl Streep**	A Cry in the Dark
Cyrano de Bergerac	**Gérard Depardieu**	1990	Krystyna Janda	Przesluchanie
Barton Fink	John Turturro	1991	Irène Jacob	The Double Life of Véronique
The Player	**Tim Robbins**	1992	Pernilla August	The Best Intentions
Naked	David Thewlis	1993	Holly Hunter	The Piano
To Live	Ge You	1994	Virna Lisi	La Reine Margot
Carrington	Jonathan Pryce	1995	**Helen Mirren**	The Madness of King George
Le huitième jour	Pascal Duquenne	1996	Brenda Blethyn	Secrets & Lies
	Daniel Auteuil			
She's So Lovely	**Sean Penn**	1997	Kathy Burke	Nil by Mouth
My Name Is Joe	Peter Mullan	1998	Élodie Bouchez	The Dreamlife of Angels
			Natacha Régnier	
Humanité	Emmanuel Schotté	1999	Séverine Caneele	Humanité
			Émilie Dequenne	Rosetta
In the Mood for Love	**Tony Leung**	2000	Björk	Dancer in the Dark
The Piano Teacher (La pianiste)	Benoît Magimel	2001	**Isabelle Huppert**	The Piano Teacher
The Son (Le fils)	Olivier Gourmet	2002	Kati Outinen	The Man Without a Past
Uzak	Muzaffer Ozdemir	2003	Marie-Josée Croze	The Barbarian Invasions
	Mehmet Emin Toprak			
Nobody Knows	Yūya Yagira	2004	**Maggie Cheung**	Clean
The Three Burials of Melquiades Estrada	**Tommy Lee Jones**	2005	Hanna Laslo	Free Zone
Days of Glory (Indigènes)	Jamel Debbouze / Samy	2006	**Penélope Cruz / Carmen Maura /**	Volver
	Naceri / Roschdy Zem / Sami		Lola Dueñas / Chus Lampreave /	
	Bouajila / Bernard Blancan		Blanca Portillo / Yohana Cobo	
The Banishment (Izgnanie)	Konstantin Lavronenko	2007	Jeon Do-yeon	Secret Sunshine
Che	**Benicio del Toro**	2008	Sandra Corveloni	Linha de Passe
Inglourious Basterds	**Christoph Waltz**	2009	Charlotte Gainsbourg	Antichrist
Biutiful / La nostra vita	**Javier Bardem** / Elio Germano	2010	**Juliette Binoche**	Certified Copy
The Artist	Jean Dujardin	2011	Kirsten Dunst	Melancholia
The Hunt	**Mads Mikkelsen**	2012	Cristina Flutur / Cosmina Stratan	Beyond the Hills
Nebraska	Bruce Dern	2013	Bérénice Bejo	The Past
Mr. Turner	Timothy Spall	2014	**Julianne Moore**	Maps to the Stars
The Measure of a Man	Vincent Lindon	2015	Rooney Mara	Carol
			Emmanuelle Bercot	Mon roi

BEST ACTOR · BEST ACTRESS

Film (Actor)	Best Actor	Year	Best Actress	Film (Actress)
Trapeze	Burt Lancaster	1956	Elsa Martinelli	Donatella
Tizoc	Pedro Infante	1957	Yvonne Mitchell	Woman in a Dressing Gown
The Defiant Ones	Sidney Poitier	1958	Anna Magnani	Wild Is the Wind
Archimède le clochard	Jean Gabin	1959	Shirley MacLaine	Ask Any Girl
Inherit The Wind	Fredric March	1960	Juliette Mayniel	Kirmes
No Love for Johnnie	Peter Finch	1961	Anna Karina	Une femme est une femme
Mr. Hobbs Takes a Vacation	James Stewart	1962	Rita Gam / Viveca Lindfors	No Exit
Lilies of the Field	Sidney Poitier	1963	Bibi Andersson	Älskarinnan
The Pawnbroker	Rod Steiger	1964	Sachiko Hidari	Nippon Konchuki and Kanojo to kare
Cat Ballou	Lee Marvin	1965	Madhur Jaffrey	Shakespeare Wallah
Masculin, féminin	Jean-Pierre Léaud	1966	Lola Albright	Lord Love a Duck
Le vieil homme et l'enfant	Michel Simon	1967	Edith Evans	The Whisperers
L'Homme qui ment	Jean-Louis Trintignant	1968	Stéphane Audran	Les Biches
Le Chat	Jean Gabin	1971	Simone Signoret	Le Chat
			Shirley MacLaine	Desperate Characters
Detenuto in attesa di giudizio	Alberto Sordi	1972	Elizabeth Taylor	Hammersmith Is Out
Jakob der Lügner	Vlastimil Brodský	1975	Kinuyo Tanaka	Sandakan hachibanshokan, bohkyo
Verlorenes Leben	Gerhard Olschewski	1976	Jadwiga Baranska	Noce i dnie
El anacoreta	Fernando Fernán Gómez	1977	Lily Tomlin	The Late Show
Outrageous!	Craig Russell	1978	Gena Rowlands	Opening Night
Ernesto	Michele Placido	1979	Hanna Schygulla	Die Ehe der Maria Braun
Dyrygent	Andrzej Seweryn	1980	Renate Krößner	Solo Sunny
Dvadtsat shest dney iz zhizni Dostoevskogo	Anatoly Solonitsyn	1981	Barbara Grabowska	Goraczka
Tribute	Jack Lemmon			
Den Enfaldige Mördaren	Stellan Skarsgård	1982	Katrin Saß	Bürgschaft für ein Jahr
Une étrange affaire	Michel Piccoli			
That Championship Season	Bruce Dern	1983	Yevgeniya Glushenko	Vlyublyon po sobstvennomu zhelaniyu
The Dresser	Albert Finney	1984	Inna Churikova	Voenno-polevoy roman
			Monica Vitti	Flirt
Stico	Fernando Fernán Gómez	1985	Jo Kennedy	Wrong World
Hiuch HaGdi	Tuncel Kurtiz	1986	Charlotte Valandrey	Rouge Baiser
			Marcélia Cartaxo	Hour of the Star
Il Caso Moro	Gian Maria Volonté	1987	Ana Beatriz Nogueira	Vera
Einer trage des anderen Last	Jörg Pose	1988	Holly Hunter	Broadcast News
	Manfred Möck			
Mississippi Burning	Gene Hackman	1989	Isabelle Adjani	Camille Claudel
Silent Scream	Iain Glen	1990	No award this year	
Mister Johnson	Maynard Eziashi	1991	Victoria Abril	Amantes
Utz	Armin Mueller-Stahl	1992	Maggie Cheung	Ruan Ling Yu
Malcolm X	Denzel Washington	1993	Michelle Pfeiffer	Love Field
Philadelphia	Tom Hanks	1994	Crissy Rock	Ladybird, Ladybird
Nobody's Fool	Paul Newman	1995	Josephine Siao	Nu ren si shi
Dead Man Walking	Sean Penn	1996	Anouk Grinberg	Mon homme
Romeo + Juliet	Leonardo DiCaprio	1997	Juliette Binoche	The English Patient
Jackie Brown	Samuel L. Jackson	1998	Fernanda Montenegro	Central do Brasil
Night Shapes (Nachtgestalten)	Michael Gwisdek	1999	Juliane Köhler	Aimée & Jaguar
			Maria Schrader	
The Hurricane	Denzel Washington	2000	Bibiana Beglau	Die Stille nach dem Schuß
			Nadja Uhl	
Traffic	Benicio del Toro	2001	Kerry Fox	Intimacy
Laissez-passer	Jacques Gamblin	2002	Halle Berry	Monster's Ball
Confessions of a Dangerous Mind	Sam Rockwell	2003	Nicole Kidman / Julianne Moore / Meryl Streep	The Hours
Lost Embrace (El abrazo partido)	Daniel Hendler	2004	Charlize Theron	Monster
			Catalina Sandino Moreno	Maria Full of Grace
Thumbsucker	Lou Taylor Pucci	2005	Julia Jentsch	Sophie Scholl - Die letzten Tage
Elementarteilchen	Moritz Bleibtreu	2006	Sandra Hüller	Requiem
The Other (El otro)	Julio Chávez	2007	Nina Hoss	Yella
The Song of Sparrows (Avaze gonjeshk-ha)	Reza Naji	2008	Sally Hawkins	Happy-Go-Lucky
London River	Sotigui Kouyaté	2009	Birgit Minichmayr	Alle Anderen
How I Ended This Summer (Kak Ya Provel Etim Letom)	Grigoriy Dobrygin	2010	Shinobu Terajima	Caterpillar
	Sergei Puskepalis			
A Separation	Peyman Moaadi / Shahab Hosseini / Ali-Asghar Shahbazi / Babak Karimi	2011	Sareh Bayat / Sarina Farhadi / Leila Hatami / Kimia Hosseini	A Separation
A Royal Affair	Mikkel Følsgaard	2012	Rachel Mwanza	War Witch
An Episode in the Life of an Iron Picker	Nazif Mujic	2013	Paulina García	Gloria
Black Coal, Thin Ice	Liao Fan	2014	Haru Kuroki	The Little House
45 Years	Tom Courtenay	2015	Charlotte Rampling	45 Years

BEST ACTOR · BEST ACTRESS

Film (Actor)	Best Actor	Year	Best Actress	Film (Actress)
Viva Villa!	Wallace Beery	1934	Katharine Hepburn	Little Women
Crime et Châtiment	Pierre Blanchar	1935	Paula Wessely	Episode
The Story of Louis Pasteur	Paul Muni	1936	Annabella	Wings of the Morning
Der Herrscher	Emil Jannings	1937	Bette Davis	Kid Galahad
Pygmalion	Leslie Howard	1938	Norma Shearer	Marked Woman & Marie Antoinette
	No award this year	1939	No award this year	
	No award this year	1940	No award this year	
Don Buonaparte	Ermete Zacconi	1941	Luise Ullrich	Annelie
Bengasi	Fosco Giachetti	1942	Kristina Söderbaum	Die goldene Stadt
Monsieur Vincent	Pierre Fresnay	1947	Anna Magnani	Angelina
The Trial	Ernst Deutsch	1948	Jean Simmons	Hamlet
Portrait of Jennie	Joseph Cotten	1949	Olivia de Havilland	The Snake Pit
The Asphalt Jungle	Sam Jaffe	1950	Eleanor Parker	Caged
La Nuit est Mon Royaume	Jean Gabin	1951	Vivien Leigh	A Streetcar Named Desire

Death of a Salesman	Fredric March	1952	**Ingrid Bergman**	Europe '51[7][8]
Le Bon Dieu Sans Confession	Henri Vilbert	1953	Lilli Palmer	The Four Poster
Air of Paris / Grisbi	**Jean Gabin**	1954	No award this year	No award this year
Les Héros Sont Fatigués / Des Teufels General	Curd Jürgens	1955	No award this year	No award this year
The Deep Blue Sea	Kenneth More			
La Traversée de Paris	Bourvil	1956	Maria Schell	Gervaise
A Hatful of Rain	Anthony Franciosa	1957	Dzidra Ritenberga	Malva
The Horse's Mouth	**Alec Guinness**	1958	**Sophia Loren**	The Black Orchid
Anatomy of a Murder	**James Stewart**	1959	Madeleine Robinson	À Double Tour
Tunes of Glory	**John Mills**	1960	**Shirley MacLaine**	The Apartment
Yojimbo	**Toshiro Mifune**	1961	Suzanne Flon	Tu ne tueras point
Birdman of Alcatraz	**Burt Lancaster**	1962	Emmanuelle Riva	Thérèse Desqueyroux
Tom Jones	Albert Finney	1963	Delphine Seyrig	Muriel
King and Country	Tom Courtenay	1964	Harriet Andersson	Loving Couples
Red Beard	**Toshiro Mifune**	1965	Annie Girardot	Three Rooms in Manhattan
Almost A Man / The Search	Jacques Perrin	1966	Natalya Arinbasarova	The First Teacher
Jutro	Ljubisa Samardzic	1967	Shirley Knight	Dutchman
Faces	John Marley	1968	Laura Betti	Teorema
	BREAK IN AWARDS		BREAK IN AWARDS	
Streamers	Guy Boyd / George Dzundza / David Alan Grier / Mitchell Lichtenstein / Matthew Modine / Michael Wright	1983	Darling Legitimus	Sugar Cane Alley
Paar	Naseeruddin Shah	1984	Pascale Ogier	Full Moon in Paris
Police	**Gérard Depardieu**	1985	No award this year	
Regalo di Natale	Carlo Delle Piane	1986	Valeria Golino	A Tale of Love
Maurice	**Hugh Grant** / James Wilby	1987	Kang Soo-yeon	The Surrogate Mother
Things Change	Don Ameche / Joe Mantegna	1988	**Isabelle Huppert**	Story of Women
			Shirley MacLaine	Madame Sousatzka
What Time Is It?	**Marcello Mastroianni** / Massimo Troisi	1989	Peggy Ashcroft / Geraldine James	She's Been Away
The Only Witness	Oleg Borisov	1990	Gloria Münchmeyer	The Moon in the Mirror
My Own Private Idaho	River Phoenix	1991	Tilda Swinton	Edward II
Glengarry Glen Ross	**Jack Lemmon**	1992	Gong Li	The Story of Qiu Ju
Un'anima divisa in due	Fabrizio Bentivoglio	1993	**Juliette Binoche**	Three Colors: Blue
In the Heat of the Sun	Xia Yu	1994	Maria de Medeiros	Três Irmãos
Der Totmacher	Götz George	1995	Sandrine Bonnaire / **Isabelle Huppert**	La Cérémonie
Michael Collins	**Liam Neeson**	1996	Victoire Thivisol	Ponette
One Night Stand	Wesley Snipes	1997	Robin Tunney	Niagara, Niagara
Hurlyburly	**Sean Penn**	1998	**Catherine Deneuve**	Place Vendôme
Topsy-Turvy	Jim Broadbent	1999	Nathalie Baye	An Affair of Love
Before Night Falls	**Javier Bardem**	2000	Rose Byrne	The Goddess of 1967
Light of My Eyes	Luigi Lo Cascio	2001	Sandra Ceccarelli	Light of My Eyes
A Journey Called Love	Stefano Accorsi	2002	**Julianne Moore**	Far from Heaven
21 Grams	**Sean Penn**	2003	Katja Riemann	Rosenstrasse
The Sea Inside	**Javier Bardem**	2004	Imelda Staunton	Vera Drake
Good Night, and Good Luck	David Strathairn	2005	Giovanna Mezzogiorno	Don't Tell
Hollywoodland	**Ben Affleck**	2006	**Helen Mirren**	The Queen
The Assassination of Jesse James	**Brad Pitt**	2007	**Cate Blanchett**	I'm Not There
Giovanna's Father	Silvio Orlando	2008	Dominique Blanc	L'Autre
A Single Man	**Colin Firth**	2009	Kseniya Rappoport	The Double Hour
Essential Killing	Vincent Gallo	2010	Ariane Labed	Attenberg
Shame	**Michael Fassbender**	2011	Deanie Ip	A Simple Life
The Master	**Philip Seymour Hoffman** / **Joaquin Phoenix**	2012	Hadas Yaron	Fill the Void
Miss Violence	Themis Panou	2013	Elena Cotta	A Street in Palermo
Hungry Hearts	Adam Driver	2014	Alba Rohrwacher	Hungry Hearts

BEST ACTOR			BEST ACTRESS	
Mambrú Went to War	Fernando Fernán Gómez	1987	Amparo Rivelles	Hay que deshacer la casa
The Living Forest	Alfredo Landa	1988	Verónica Forqué	The Happy Life
Winter Diary	Fernando Rey	1989	**Carmen Maura**	Women on the Verge of a Nervous Breakdown
If They Tell You I Fell	Jorge Sanz	1990	Rafaela Aparicio	The Sea and the Weather
¡Ay, Carmela!	Andrés Pajares	1991	**Carmen Maura**	¡Ay, Carmela!
Don Juan in Hell	Fernando Guillén	1992	Silvia Munt	Butterfly Wings
La marrana	Alfredo Landa	1993	Ariadna Gil	The Age of Beauty
Madregilda	Juan Echanove	1994	Verónica Forqué	Kika
Días contados	Carmelo Gómez	1995	Cristina Marcos	All Men Are the Same
Mouth to Mouth	**Javier Bardem**	1996	Victoria Abril	Nobody Will Speak of Us When We're Dead
Como un relámpago	Santiago Ramos	1997	Emma Suárez	The Dog in the Manger
La buena estrella	Antonio Resines	1998	Cecilia Roth	Martín (Hache)
The Grandfather	Fernando Fernán Gómez	1999	**Penélope Cruz**	The Girl of Your Dreams
Goya in Bordeaux	Francisco Rabal	2000	Cecilia Roth	All About My Mother
Goodbye from the Heart	Juan Luis Galiardo	2001	**Carmen Maura**	Common Wealth
Fausto 5.0	Eduard Fernández	2002	Pilar López de Ayala	Mad Love
Mondays in the Sun	**Javier Bardem**	2003	Mercedes Sampietro	Common Places
Take My Eyes	Luis Tosar	2004	Laia Marull	Take My Eyes
The Sea Inside	**Javier Bardem**	2005	Lola Dueñas	The Sea Inside
Camarón: When Flamenco Became Legend	Óscar Jaenada	2006	Candela Peña	Princesses
Go Away from Me	Juan Diego	2007	**Penélope Cruz**	Volver
Under the Stars	Alberto San Juan	2008	Maribel Verdú	Seven Billiard Tables
Che I: The Argentine	**Benicio del Toro**	2009	Carme Elías	Camino
Cell 211	Luis Tosar	2010	Lola Dueñas	Me Too
Biutiful	**Javier Bardem**	2011	Nora Navas	Black Bread
No Rest for the Wicked	José Coronado	2012	Elena Anaya	The Skin I Live In
The Dead Man and Being Happy	José Sacristán	2013	Maribel Verdú	Blancanieves
Living Is Easy with Eyes Closed	Javier Cámara	2014	Marian Álvarez	Wounded
Marshland	Javier Gutiérrez	2015	Bárbara Lennie	Magical Girl

Film	Best Supporting Actor	Year	Best Supporting Actress	Film
Tata mía	Miguel Rellán	1987	Verónica Forqué	The Year of the Awakening
Divine Words	Juan Echanove	1988	Verónica Forqué	Moors and Christians
Espérame en el cielo	José Sazatornil	1989	María Barranco	Women on the Verge of a Nervous Breakdown
Esquilache	Adolfo Marsillach	1990	María Asquerino	The Sea and the Weather
¡Ay Carmela!	Gabino Diego	1991	María Barranco	The Ages of Lulu
The Dumbfounded King	Juan Diego	1992	Kiti Manver	Anything for Bread
Belle Époque	Fernando Fernán Gómez	1993	Chus Lampreave	The Age of Beauty
Sombras en una batalla	Fernando Valverde	1994	Rosa María Sardà	Why Do They Call It Love When They Mean Sex?
Running Out of Time	Javier Bardem	1995	María Luisa Ponte	Cradle Song
Así en el cielo como en la tierra	Luis Ciges	1996	Pilar Bardem	Nobody Will Speak of Us When We're Dead
La buena vida	Luis Cuenca	1997	Mary Carrillo	Beyond the Garden
Live Flesh	José Sancho	1998	Charo López	Secrets of the Heart
Torrente, el brazo tonto de la ley	Tony Leblanc	1999	Adriana Ozores	A Time for Defiance
París Tombuctú	Juan Diego	2000	María Galiana	Alone
Common Wealth	Emilio Gutiérrez Caba	2001	Julia Gutiérrez Caba	You're the One
Ten Days Without Love	Emilio Gutiérrez Caba	2002	Rosa María Sardà	No Shame
Mondays In The Sun	Luis Tosar	2003	Mercedes Sampietro	Common Places
In the City	Eduard Fernández	2004	Candela Peña	Take My Eyes
The Sea Inside	Celso Bugallo	2005	Mabel Rivera	The Sea Inside
The Method	Carmelo Gómez	2006	Elvira Mínguez	Tapas
DarkBlueAlmostBlack	Antonio de la Torre	2007	Carmen Maura	To Return
13 Roses	José Manuel Cervino	2008	Amparo Baró	Seven Billiard Tables
Camino	Jordi Dauder	2009	Penélope Cruz	Vicky Cristina Barcelona
Gordos	Raúl Arévalo	2010	Marta Etura	Cell 211
Even the Rain	Karra Elejalde	2011	Laia Marull	Black Bread
Eva	Lluís Homar	2012	Ana Wagener	La voz dormida
Unit 7	Julián Villagrán	2013	Candela Peña	A Gun in Each Hand
Family United	Roberto Álamo	2014	Terele Pávez	Witching and Bitching
Spanish Affair	Karra Elejalde	2015	Carmen Machi	Spanish Affair

Film	Best Actor	Year	Best Actress	Film
The Pistol	Wang Yin	1962	You Min	Sun, Moon and Star
From Dusk Till Dawn	Tang Ching	1963	Betty Loh Ti	The Love Eterne
	Awards not held	1964	Awards not held	
Beautiful Duckling	Ke Hsiang-Ting	1965	Li Lihua	Between Tears and Laughter
Hsi Shih: Beauty of Beauties	Zhao Lei	1966	Kuei Ya-Lei	Misty Rain
The Country Calamity	Ou Wei	1967	Chiang Ching	Many Enchanting Nights
The Road	Tsui Fu-Sheng	1968	Ivy Lin Po	Too Late for Love
Storm Over the Yangtse River	Peter Yang Kwan	1969	Li Lihua	Storm Over the Yangtse River
The Evergreen Mountains	Ke Hsiang-Ting	1970	Gua Ah-Leh	Home Sweet Home
The Story of Tin-Ying	Wang Yin	1971	Lisa Lu	The Arch
Execution in Autumn	Ou Wei	1972	Judy Ongg	Love Can Forgive and Forget
The Escape	Peter Yang Kwan	1973	Polly Kuan	Back Alley Princess
	Awards not held	1974	Awards not held	
Long Way From Home	Charlie Shin	1975	Lisa Lu	The Empress Dowager
Fragrant Flower Versus Noxious Grass	Chang Feng	1976	Hsu Feng	Assassin
Far Away From Home	Charlie Chin	1977	Chelsia Chan	Chelsia My Love
He Never Gives Up	Qi Han	1978	Tien Niu	The Diary of Di-Di
A Teacher of Great Soldiers	Ko Chun Hsiung	1979	Lin Feng-Jiao	The Story of a Small Town
White Jasmine	Wang Kuan-Hsiung	1980	Hsu Feng	The Pioneers
If I Were for Real	Alan Tam	1981	Sylvia Chang	My Grandfather
Man on the Brink	Eddie Chen	1982	Wang Ping	Tiger Killer
Papa, Can You Hear Me Sing?	Sun Yueh	1983	Monica Lu	A Flower in the Raining Night
Law with Two Phases	Danny Lee	1984	Loretta Hui-Shan Yang	The Young Runaway
Hong Kong 1941	Chow Yun Fat	1985	Loretta Hui-Shan Yang	Kuei-Mei, a Woman
Braveheart	Ti Lung	1986	Sylvia Chang	Passion
An Autumn's Tale	Chow Yun Fat	1987	Anita Mui	Rouge
Gangland Odyssey	Man Tsz Leung	1988	Dodo Cheng	Moon, Star & Sun
A City of Sadness	Sung Young Chen	1989	Maggie Cheung	Full Moon in New York
Farewell, China	Tonyy Leung Ka Fai	1990	Lin Chin Hsia	Till the End of the World
Pushing Hands	Lang Hsiung	1991	Maggie Cheung	Ruan Ling Yu
Police Story III Supercop	Jackie Chan	1992	Lindzay Chan	To Liv(e)
Crime Story	Jackie Chan	1993	Ng Kar Lai	Remains of a Woman
Chung King Express	Lin Yang	1994	Joan Chen	Red Rose, White Rose
Super Citizen Ko	Lin Yang	1995	Josephine Siao	Summer Snow
In The Heat Of the Sun	Xia Yu	1996	Josephine Siao	Stage Door
The Mad Phoenix	Tse Kwan Ho	1997	Maggie Cheung	Comrades-Almost A Love Story
Xiu Xiu-The Sent Down Girl	Lopsang	1998	Lu Lu	Xiu Xiu-The Sent Down Girl
Generation Pendragon	Ko Chun Hsiung	1999	Rachel Lee	Ordinary Heroes
The Mission	Francis Ng	2000	Maggie Cheung	In the Mood for Love
Lanyu	Liu Ye	2001	Qin Hailu	Durian Durian
Three-Going Home	Leon Lai	2002	Lee Sinje	The Eye
Infernal Affairs	Tony Leung Chiu Wai	2003	Sandra Ng	Golden Chicken
Infernal Affairs III	Andy Lau	2004	Yang Kuei-Mei	The Moon Also Rises
Divergence	Aaron Kwok	2005	Shu Qi	Three Times
After This Our Exile	Aaron Kwok	2006	Zhou Xun	Perhaps Love
Lust, Caution	Tony Leung Chiu Wai	2007	Joan Chen	The Home Song Stories
Assembly	Zhang Hanyu	2008	Prudence Liew	True Women For Sale
Cow	Bo Huang (tie)	2009	Li Bingbing	The Message
The Beast Stalker	Cheung Ka Fai (tie)			
MONGA	Ethan Juan	2010	Lv Li Ping	City Monkey
A Simple Life	Andy Lau	2011	Deanie Ip	A Simple Life
Life without Principle	Lau Ching Wan	2012	Gwei Lun-Mei	Gf * Bf
Stray Dogs	Lee Kang Sheng	2013	Zhang Ziyi	The Grandmaster
A Fool	Chen Jian-Bin	2014	Chen Shiang Chyi	Exit

contributors

Carol Mei Barker (CMB) is a film academic and writer, specializing in contemporary Chinese cinema.

Michael Blyth (MB) is a film programmer for both the BFI London Film Festival and BFI Flare: London LGBT Film Festival. He also contributes to various print and online publications, specializing in queer cinema and the horror genre.

Michael Brooke (MBr) is a regular contributor to *Sight & Sound*, one of the creators of multimedia British film and TV encyclopaedia BFI Screenonline, and a Blu-ray and DVD producer equally comfortable with arthouse and exploitation cinema, sometimes in the same package.

Ollie Charles (OC) works in film distribution, specializing in independent arthouse cinema. He is the contributing editor for *Front Row Reviews* and is currently completing his first web series and short film.

Charles Graham-Dixon (CGD) is a London-based journalist and writer. He has written for *Vice*, *Grolsch Film Works*, *The Guardian*, *Somesuch*, *Little White Lies* and *Film4*.

Patrick Gamble (PG) is a freelance film writer and deputy editor of the film website CineVue. He has contributed to *Indiewire*, *The Skinny* and BBC 5Live's *The HitList*.

Aurélie Godet (AG) was born in Paris and is a programmer for the Locarno International Film Festival. She has an extensive knowledge of the film industry through her work in script development, shooting and distribution. Aurélie also programs for the IFF Colombo in Sri Lanka and writes for *Cahiers du Cinéma*.

Mark Grassick: (MG) is a film and music journalist and deputy editor of *Vue Magazine*. He is guaranteed to love almost any independent film about small-town America, crime and troubled antiheroes.

Ian Haydn Smith (IHS) is a London-based writer and the editor of *Curzon Magazine*. He is the update editor for *1001 Movies You Must See Before You Die*.

Mariayah Kaderbhai (MK) began her career at the British Film Institute before joining BAFTA, where she has been for the last 11 years and where she is the Film Programme Manager. She has also worked on Al Jazeera's former flagship film show, *The Fabulous Picture Show*, as a producer and journalist.

Sophie Monks Kaufman (SMK) is a staff writer at *Little White Lies*.

Philip Kemp (PK) is a critic and film historian, a regular contributor to *Sight & Sound*, *Total Film*, *Times Higher Educational* and *Curzon Magazine*. He teaches Film Journalism at the University of Leicester.

Edward Lawrenson (EL) is a London-based freelance writer.

Mick McAloon (MM) is a freelance writer and film programmer.

Hannah McGill (HM) is a critic and writer based in Edinburgh. She writes a monthly cinema column for *Sight & Sound* magazine and reviews books for *The Scotsman* and *The Independent*. From 2006 to 2010 she was Artistic Director of the Edinburgh International Film Festival.

Demetrios Matheou (DM) is a London-based journalist, author and programmer. He has been the film critic of *The Sunday Herald* since 2004, is the film editor of The Arts Desk website and a regular contributor to *Sight & Sound* magazine. He is the author of *The Faber Book of New South American Cinema*.

Ben Nicholson (BN) is a freelance film journalist living and working in London. The editor of award-winning film blog CineVue, he

also contributes to film magazines including *Vérité* and *The Skinny*.

Cleaver Patterson (CP) is a regular contributor to the *Film International*, *Flickfeast* and *The People's Movies* websites. He has also written for *Curzon Magazine*, *Rue Morgue*, *Starburst* and *Video Watchdog*.

Naman Ramachandran (NR) writes for *Sight & Sound*, *Variety* and *Cineuropa*. He is the author of *Rajinikanth: The Definitive Biography* and *Lights Camera Masala: Making Movies in Mumbai*.

Jonathan Romney (JR) is a weekly online reviewer for *Film Comment*, and also contributes regularly to *The Observer*, *Sight & Sound*, *Screen Daily* and others. He is Associate Lecturer at the London College of Communication.

Leigh Singer (LS) is a freelance film journalist whose work has appeared in many major UK newspapers, magazines and websites. He is also a video essayist, filmmaker and program advisor for the London Film Festival

Jason Ward (JWa) is the Associate Editor of *Oh Comely* magazine and a freelance film journalist.

Simon Ward (SW) is a writer and editor, currently working at Titan Books. He has written extensively on cinema and graphic novels for a range of publications. His official companion book to Nicolas Winding Refn's film *The Neon Demon* is due to be published in 2016.

Jason Wood (JW) is the Artistic Director for Film at HOME and Visiting Professor at Manchester School of Art. His books include *The Faber Book of Mexican Cinema*, and three collections of interviews with filmmakers, including the forthcoming *New British Cinema from 'Submarine' to '12 Years a Slave': The Resurgence of British Film-making*.

index

index continued

index continued

picture credits

Every effort has been made to credit the copyright holders of the images used in this book. We apologize for any unintentional omissions or errors and would be pleased to insert the appropriate acknowledgement to any companies or individuals in any subsequent editions of the work.
Quintessence would like to give special thanks to Phil Moad and Darren Thomas at The Kobal Collection for their help supplying images.

KEY

Thumbnail images: numbered, left to right or top to bottom (1), (2), (3), (4), (5), (6), (7), (8)
Image-only pages: top = t / bottom = b / left = l / right = r / center = c / top left = tl / top right = tr / center top = ct / center bottom = cb / center left = cl / center right = cr / center left top = clt / center left bottom = clb / center right top = crt / center right bottom = crb / bottom left = bl / bottom right = br

2 Christopher Polk/Getty Images **6** John Kobal Foundation/Getty Images **16** LOIC VENANCE/AFP/Getty Images **18 (1)** DreamWorks SKG/Kemp Company/Splendid Pictures/Parkes+MacDonald Image Nation/Muse Entertainment Enterprises **(2)** Junebug Movie/Epoch Films **(3)** Walt Disney Pictures/Josephson Entertainment/Andalasia Productions/Right Coast Productions **(4)** Goodspeed Productions/Scott Rudin Productions **(5)** Closest to the Hole Productions/Fighter/Mandeville Films/Relativity Media/The Weinstein Company **(6)** The Weinstein Company/Ghoulardi Film Company/Annapurna Pictures **(7)** Columbia Pictures/Annapurna Pictures/Atlas Entertainment **(8)** The Weinstein Company/Silverwood Films/Tim Burton Productions/Electric City Entertainment **19 (1)** Les Artistes Associés/Les Films du Carrosse/Les Productions Artistes Associés **(2)** EMI Films/20th Century Fox Film Corporation **(3)** Werner Herzog Filmproduktion/Gaumont **(4)** Gaumont/Oliane Productions/Marianne Productions/Soma Film Produktion **(5)** Société Nouvelle de Cinématographie/C.A.P.A.C./TF1 Films Production **(6)** Les Films Christian Fechner/Lilith Films I.A./Gaumont/Antenne-2/Films A2/DD Productions **(7)** Renn Productions/France 2 Cinéma/D.A. Films/N.E.F. Filmproduktion und Vertriebs/Degeto Film/ARD/WMG Film/RCS Films & TV **(8)** Mascaret Films/Arte France **20 (1)** Too Askew Prod. Inc./View Askew Productions **(2)** Be Gentlemen Limited Partnership/Lawrence Bender Productions/Miramax **(3)** Touchstone Pictures/Jerry Bruckheimer Films/Valhalla Motion Pictures **(4)** Paramount Pictures/Scott Rudin Productions **(5)** Marvel Enterprises/New Regency Pictures/Horseshoe Bay Productions/Epsilon Motion Pictures/Regency Enterprises/20th Century Fox Film Corporation **(6)** Back Lot Pictures/Focus Features/Miramax/TJ Film Productions **(7)** Warner Bros/GK Films/Smokehouse Pictures **(8)** 20th Century Fox Film Corporation/Regency Enterprises/TSG Entertainment **21 (1)** Jack Rollins & Charles H. Joffe Productions **(2)** Jack Rollins & Charles H. Joffe Productions **(3)** Jack Rollins & Charles H. Joffe Productions **(4)** Jack Rollins & Charles H. Joffe Productions **(5)** Jack Rollins & Charles H. Joffe Productions **(6)** Orion Pictures/Jack Rollins & Charles H. Joffe Productions **(7)** TriStar Pictures **(8)** Sweetland Films/Magnolia Pictures **22 (1)** Walt Disney Productions **(2)** MGM/Filmways Pictures **(3)** Robert Wise Productions/Argyle Enterprises **(4)** Universal Pictures **(5)** Geoffrey Productions/Orion Pictures **(6)** MGM/Peerford Ltd./Artista Management/Blake Edwards Entertainment/Ladbroke **(7)** Golan-Globus Productions **(8)** Walt Disney Pictures/BrownHouse Productions/Bottom of the Ninth Productions **23 (1) (2)** TV Man Union **(3)** Oshima Productions/Shôchiku Eiga/Kadokawa Shoten Publishing Co./Imagica Corp./BS Asahi/Eisei Gekijo/Bac Films/Canal+/Recorded Picture Company **(4)** Omega Project/Omega Micott Inc./Emperor Multimedia Group/Star Max/Alpha Group/Spike Co. Ltd./Excellent Film **(5)** Bohemian Films/Cinemasia **(6)** Asahi National Broadcasting Company/Bandai Visual Company/DENTSU Music And Entertainment/Office Kitano/Saitô Entertainment/TV Asahi/Tokyo FM Broadcasting Co. **(7)** CTB Film Company/Andreevsky Flag Film Company/X-Filme Creative Pool/Eurasia Film Production/Kinofabrika **(8)** Paramount Pictures/Marvel Entertainment/Marvel Studios **24 (1)** Warner Bros. **(2)** Paramount Pictures **(3)** Warner Bros. **(4)** RKO Radio Pictures **(5)** Warner Bros. **(6)** MGM **(7)** MGM/Loew's **(8)** MGM **25 (1)** Walt Disney Productions **(2)** Columbia Pictures Corporation/Rastar Productions **(3)** Universal Pictures **(4)** Allied Artists Pictures/ ABC Pictures/A Feuer and Martin Production/Bavaria Film **(5)** Paramount Pictures/Robert Stigwood Organization/Allan Carr Production **(6)** 20th Century Fox Film Corporation/Bazmark Films **(7)** Imagine Entertainment/Mikona Productions GmbH & Co. KG **(8)** Walt Disney Animation Studios/Walt Disney Pictures **26 (1)** MGM **(2)** RKO Radio Pictures **(3)** RKO Radio Pictures **(4)** RKO Radio Pictures **(5)** RKO Radio Pictures **(6)** RKO Radio Pictures **(7)** Paramount Pictures **(8)** MGM/Loew's **27 (1)** MGM **(2)** MGM **(3)** Paramount Pictures **(4)** Stanley Kramer Productions **(5)** Warner Brothers/Seven Arts **(6)** Warner Bros./20th Century Fox Film Corporation **(7)** Golden **(8)** Universal Pictures **28 (1)** DD Productions/Films A2/RAI Radiotelevisione Italiana/Renn Productions **(2)** Cinéa/Cofimage/Eniloc Films/France 3/France 3 Cinéma/Soficas/Sofinergie Films **(3)** Film Par Film/Cinéa/Orly Films/Sédif Productions/Paravision International S.A./D.A. Films/France 3 Cinéma/Sofinergie 1/Investimage 3/Sofica Créations **(4)** Renn Productions/France 2 Cinéma/D.A. Films/N.E.F. Filmproduktion und Vertriebs/Degeto Film/ARD/WMG Film/RCS Films & TV **(5)** Canal+/Center for Film and Audiovisual Arts of the French Community of Belgium/Centre National de la Cinématographie/D.A. Films/Eurimages/Homemade Films/Pan Européenne Production/Polygram Filmed Entertainment/RTL-TVi/TF1 Films Production/Working Title Films **(6)** Axiom Films/Canal+/Centre Européen Cinématographique Rhône-Alpes/Centre National de la Cinématographie/France 2 Cinéma/France Télévision Images 2/Procirep/Rhône-Alpes Cinéma/Rézo Films/Rézo Productions/Sofica Sofinergie 5 **(7)** Les Films du Losange/Wega Film/Bavaria Film/BIM Distribuzione **(8)** Les Films Alain Sarde/Zack Films/Pathé **29 (1)** Warner Bros. **(2)** Warner Bros. **(3)** 20th Century Fox Film Corporation **(4)** Universal International Pictures **(5)** EMI Film Distributors/G.W. Films Limited **(6)** Paramount Pictures **(7)** TriStar Pictures/Phoenix Pictures/Barwood Films **(8)** 20th Century Fox Film Corporation/Scott Free Productions/ApolloProMedia GmbH & Co. 1. Filmproduktion KG/Stillking Films/QI Quality International GmbH & Co. KG/Epsilon Motion Pictures/Franchise Pictures/World 2000 Entertainment **30 (1)** Prakash Mehra Productions **(2)** R.S.J. Productions **(3)** United Producers/Sippy Films/Sholay Media & Entertainment **(4)** Trimurti Films Pvt. Ltd. **(5)** Yash Raj Films **(6)** Hirawat Jain and Company/M.K.D. Films Combine/Manmohan Films **(7)** Nariman Films **(8)** Yash Raj Films **31 (1)** Yash Raj Films **(2)** Shemaroo **(3)** Aasia Films Pvt. Ltd./M.K.D. Films Combine **(4)** Dharma Productions **(5)** Yash Raj Films **(6)** B.R. Films **(7)** K Sera Sera/RGV Film Company **(8)** MAD Entertainment Ltd. **32 (1)** Paramount Pictures/Georgetown Productions Inc./Sean S. Cunningham Films **(2)** MGM/SLM Production Group **(3)** Paramount Pictures/IndieProd Company Productions **(4)** Hemdale Film/Northwood Productions **(5)** Universal Pictures/No Frills Film Production **(6)** Columbia Pictures Corporation/Stonebridge Entertainment **(7)** Columbia Pictures Corporation/Castle Rock Entertainment **(8)** Universal Pictures/Turman-Foster Company/David Foster Productions **33 (1)** Warner Bros./Canal+/The Wolper Organization **(2)** Universal Pictures/Imagine Entertainment **(3)** Mandalay Entertainment **(4)** Artisan Entertainment **(5)** Warner Bros./Village Roadshow Pictures/NPV Entertainment/Malpaso Productions **(6)** Dash Films/Lee Daniels Entertainment/The Woodsman LLC **(7)** Universal Pictures/Imagine Entertainment/Working Title Films/StudioCanal/Relativity Media **(8)** 20th Century Fox Film Corporation/Marvel Entertainment/Dune Entertainment/Bad Hat Harry Productions/Donners' Company **34 (1)** Amblin Entertainment/Warner Bros. **(2)** Channel Four Films/Goldwyn Films/Killer Films/Miramax/Newmarket Capital Group/Single Cell Pictures/Zenith Entertainment **(3)** Am Psycho Productions/Edward R. Pressman Film/Lions Gate Films/Muse Productions/P.P.S. Films/Quadra Entertainment/Universal Pictures **(4)** Filmax Group/Castelao Producciones/Canal+ España **(5)** Andrea Sperling Productions/Crave Films/Harsh Times **(6)** Warner Bros./Syncopy/DC Comics/ Legendary Pictures/Patalex III Productions Limited **(7)** Closest to the Hole Productions/Fighter/Mandeville Films/The Park Entertainment/Relativity Media/The Weinstein Company **(8)** Columbia Pictures/Annapurna Pictures/Atlas Entertainment **35 (1)** Columbia Pictures Corporation **(2)** RKO Radio Pictures **(3)** RKO Radio Pictures **(4)** RKO Radio Pictures **(5)** MGM **(6)** 20th Century Fox Film Corporation **(7)** Hunt Stromberg Productions **(8)** MGM **36 (1)** El Deseo/Laurenfilm **(2)** El Deseo **(3)** TriStar Pictures/Clinica Estetico **(4)** Columbia Pictures Corporation/Los Hooligans Productions **(5)** Hollywood Pictures/Cinergi Pictures Entertainment/Dirty Hands Productions/Summit Entertainment **(6)** TriStar Pictures/Amblin Entertainment/David Foster Productions/Global Entertainment Productions GmbH & Company Medien KG/Zorro Productions **(7)** DreamWorks Animation **(8)** Blue Haze Entertainment/Canal+ España/El Deseo/FilmNation Entertainment/Instituto de Crédito Oficial/Instituto de la Cinematografía y de las Artes Audiovisuales/Televisión Española **37 (1)** Lolafilms/Ovídeo TV S.A./Sogepaq **(2)** CiBy 2000/El Deseo/France 3 Cinéma **(3)** El Mar Pictures/Grandview Pictures **(4)** Sogepaq/Sogecine/Himenóptero/Union Générale Cinématographique/Eyescreen S.r.l. **(5)** Paramount Vantage/Miramax/Scott Rudin Productions/Mike Zoss Productions **(6)** The Weinstein Company/Mediapr/Gravier Productions/Antena 3 Films/Antena 3 Televisión/Televisió de Catalunya **(7)** Menageatro/Mod Producciones/Focus Features/Televisión Española/Televisió de Catalunya/Ikiru Films **(8)** Eon Productions/Danjaq/B23 **38 (1)** Group Film Productions Limited **(2)** Filmsonor/Rizzoli Film/S.E.C.A./Cinétel **(3)** Cocinor/Iéna Productions/Union Cinématographique Lyonnaise **(4)** Les Films Ariane/Filmsonor/Cinétel/Rizzoli Film **(5)** Iéna Productions/Union Cinématographique Lyonnaise/Compagnia Edizioni Internazionali Artistiche Distribuzione **(6)** Dear Film Produzione/Gray-Film/Progéfi/Société Nouvelle Pathé Cinéma **(7)** Cinédis/Les Editions Cinégraphiques **(8)** Han Productions/C.E.I.A.P. **39 (1)** Compagnia Cinematografica Montoro/Compagnie Internationale de Productions Cinématographiques/Progéfi **(2)** Francos Films/Incei Film **(3)** Les Films Concordia/Rome Paris Films/Compagnia Cinematografica Champion **(4)** Nouvelles Éditions de Films/Les Productions Artistes Associés/Vides Cinematografica **(5)** Les Films du Quadrangle/Francos Films/Kenwood Productions/Les Films Pomereu/Paramount Pictures **(6)** Les Films Marceau/Produzioni Europee Associati/Cocinor **(7)** Palomar Pictures International/Kingston Film Productions Ltd./Central Cinema Company Film **(8)** FGL Productions/Copercines, Cooperativa Cinematográfica/Films EGE/Francos Films/Hemdale Group/Société Nouvelle de Cinématographie/Vides Cinematografica **40 (1)** FilmFour/Kalima Productions GmbH & Co. KG/StudioCanal/TalkBack Productions/WT2 Productions/Working Title Films **(2)** Four by Two/Everyman Pictures/Dune Entertainment/Major Studio Partners/One America/Four by Two Films **(3)** Columbia Pictures/Relativity Media/Apatow Productions/Mosaic Media Group/GH One **(4)** Warner Bros./DreamWorks Pictures/Parkes+MacDonald Image Nation/The Zanuck Company/Tim Burton Productions **(5)** Universal Pictures/Media Rights Capital/Four by Two/Everyman Pictures/Four by Two Films **(6)** Paramount Pictures/GK Films/Infinitum Nihil **(7)** Paramount Pictures/Four by Two Films **(8)** Universal Pictures/Relativity Media/Working Title Films/Cameron Mackintosh Ltd. **41 (1)** Universal Pictures/Amblin Entertainment **(2)** Dino De Laurentiis Company/Universal Pictures **(3)** Zeta Entertainment **(4)** Dimension Films/Woods Entertainment **(5)** Juno Pix/New Line Cinema/Robert Simonds Productions **(6)** Columbia Pictures Corporation/Flower Films/Tall Trees Productions/Global Entertainment Productions GmbH & Company Medien KG **(7)** Pandora Cinema/Flower Films/Adam Fields Productions/Gaylord Films **(8)** Mandate Pictures/Vincent Pictures/Flower Films/Rye Road Productions/Babe Ruthless Productions/Barry Mendel Productions/Dune Entertainment **42 (1)** DD Productions/Films A2/RAI Radiotelevisione Italiana/Renn Productions **(2)** Pierre Grise Productions/George Reinhart Productions/FR3 Films Production/Centre National de la Cinématographie/Canal+/Investimage 2 et 3/Région Languedoc-Roussillon **(3)** Film Par Film/Cinéa/Orly Films/Sédif Productions/Paravision International S.A./D.A. Films/France 3 Cinéma/Sofinergie 1/Investimage 3/Sofica Créations/Canal+/Centre National de la Cinématographie **(4)** Cecchi Gori Group Tiger Cinematografica/Les Films Alain Sarde/Prokino Filmproduktion/ TF1 Films Production/Tiger Cinematografica **(5)** Asap Films/Sintra S.r.l./Man's Films/Bitters End/France 2 Cinéma/DD Productions/RTL-TVi/Canal+/CinéCinéma/Centre National de la Cinématographie/Région Ile-de-France/RAI Radiotelevisione Italiana/Eurimages **(6)** Paramount Pictures/Cruise/Wagner Productions **(7)** Gemini Films/France 2 Cinéma/Les Films du Lendemain/Blu Cinematografica/Madragoa Filmes/Eurimages/Canal+/Centre National de la Cinématographie **(8)** HAL Films **43 (1)** Arcade/Arena Films/CAB Productions/Canal+/Centre National de la Cinématographie/Cofimage 11/Office Fédéral de la Culture/Procirep/TF1 Films Production/Télévision Suisse-Romande **(2)** BIM/Canal+/Centre National de la Cinématographie/Fidélité Productions/France 2 Cinéma/Gimages 5/Local Films/Mars Distribution **(3)** Les Films Pelléas/Giorno Films/Cinémaginaire Inc./StudioCanal/Pyramide Productions/Glem Production/Gimages 4 **(4)** FIT Productions/Spice Factory/France 2 Cinéma/Canal+/Gimages 6/Centre National de la Cinématographie/Conseil Régional Midi-Pyrénées **(5)** France 2 Cinéma/DD Productions/Vértigo Films/Canal+/Studio Images 9/Les Films Alain Sarde **(6)** Pierre Grise Productions/Cinemaundici/Arte France Cinéma/V.M. Productions/FM2B Productions **(7)** Asap Films/Sintra S.r.l./Man's Films/Bitters End **(8)** UGC Distribution/SBS Films/France 2 Cinéma/Soficinéma 2 & 3/Media Programme of the European Community/Sofica UGC 1/Canal+/TPS Star/Région Ile-de-France **44 (1)** DD Productions/Films A2/RAI Radiotelevisione Italiana/Renn Productions **(2)** Pierre Grise Productions/George Reinhart Productions/FR3 Films Production/Centre National de la Cinématographie/Canal+/Investimage 2 et 3/Région Languedoc-Roussillon **(3)** Film Par Film/Cinéa/Orly Films/Sédif Productions/Paravision International S.A./D.A. Films/France 3 Cinéma/Sofinergie 1/Investimage 3/Sofica Créations/Canal+/Centre National de la Cinématographie **(4)** Paramount Pictures/Cruise/Wagner Productions **(5)** Arcade/Arena Films/CAB Productions/Canal+/Centre National de la Cinématographie/Cofimage 11/Office Fédéral de la Culture/Procirep/TF1 Films Production/Télévision Suisse-Romande **(6)** BIM/Canal+/Centre National de la Cinématographie/Fidélité Productions/France 2 Cinéma/Gimages 5/Local Films/Mars Distribution **(7)** France 2 Cinéma/DD Productions/Vértigo Films/Canal+/Studio Images 9/Les Films Alain Sarde **(8)** Pierre Grise Productions/Cinemaundici/Arte France Cinéma/V.M. Productions/FM2B Productions **tl** RENN/A2/RAI-2/THE KOBAL COLLECTION **tr** GRISE/FR3/CANAL +/THE KOBAL COLLECTION **c** GRISE/FR3/CANAL +/THE KOBAL COLLECTION **bl** PAR/ORLY/SEDIF/PARAVISION/FR3/THE KOBAL COLLECTION **br** PARAMOUNT/THE KOBAL COLLECTION/CLOSE, MURRAY **45 tr** CANAL +/FIDELITE PRODUCTIONS/THE KOBAL COLLECTION/MOIREAU, JEAN-CLAUDE **cl** Arcade/Arena Films/CAB/Canal+/Cnc/The Kobal Collection **cr** Canal+/The Kobal Collection **br** PIERRE GRISE PRODS/THE KOBAL COLLECTION **46 (1)** Warner Bros./Newton Productions/NBI Productions **(2)** Columbia Pictures Corporation **(3)** Florin/Tatira **(4)** Warner Brothers/Seven Arts/Tatira-Hiller Productions **(5)** David Foster Productions/Warner Bros. **(6)** Doubleday Productions/Gus/Harbor Productions **(7)** Persky-Bright/Vista/Columbia Pictures Corporation/Rubeeker Films **(8)** Columbia Pictures Corporation/Vista **47 (1)** Paramount Pictures **(2)** Barclays Mercantile Industrial Finance/JRS Productions **(3)** Columbia Pictures Corporation/Delphi V Productions **(4)** Touchstone Pictures/Silver Screen Partners IV/Mulholland Productions **(5)** TriStar Pictures/Mulholland Productions/Baltimore Pictures **(6)** Mulholland Productions **(7)** 20th Century Fox Film Corporation **(8)** New Line Cinema/Sidney Kimmel Entertainment/FR Production/Longfellow Pictures/Simon Fields Productions **48 (1)** Les Films Impéria/Les Productions Georges de Beauregard/Société Nouvelle de Cinématographie **(2)** Concordia Compagnia Cinematografica/Rome Paris Films **(3)** Dear Film Produzione/Les Films Ariane/Les Productions Artistes Associés **(4)** Films Georges de Beauregard/Rome Paris Films/Société Nouvelle de Cinématographie/Dino de Laurentiis Cinematografica **(5)** Les Films du Carrosse/Les Productions Artistes Associés/Produzioni Associate Delphos **(6)** Cerito Films/Les Films Ariane/Simar Films/Euro International Film **(7)** Canal+/Les Films 13/TF1 **(8)** F Comme Film/France 2 Cinéma/Fidela SAP/Canal+/CinéCinéma/ARD Degeto Film **49 (1)** Selznick International Pictures **(2)** Warner Bros. **(3)** MGM **(4)** Vanguard Films/RKO Radio Pictures **(5)** Italia Film/Junior Film/Sveva Film/Les Films Ariane/Francinex/Société Générale de Cinématographie **(6)** 20th Century Fox Film Corporation **(7)** United Artists/The Kobal Collection **(8)** Personafilm/Filmédis/Incorporated Television Company/Suede Film **50 (1)** Altavista Films/Zeta Film **(2)** Anhelo Producciones/Besame Mucho Pictures/Producciones Anhelo **(3)** FilmFour/Wildwood Enterprises/Tu Vas Voir Productions/BD Cine/Inca Films S.A./Sahara Films/Senator Film Produktion/Sound for Film **(4)** Canal+ España/El Deseo/Televisión Española **(5)** Partizan Films/Gaumont/France 3 Cinéma/Canal+/TPS Star/Mikado Film **(6)** AXN/Alebrije Cine y Video/Canal+ España/Canal+ **(7)** Fabula/Participant Media/Funny Balloons/Canana Films **(8)** Busboy Productions/International Traders/OddLot Entertainment **51 (1)** Universal Pictures/40 Acres & A Mule Filmworks **(2)** Paramount Pictures/Imagine Films Entertainment/Eddie Murphy Productions **(3)** 20th Century Fox Film Corporation **(4)** 20th Century Fox Film Corporation/Marvel Enterprises/Donners' Company/Bad Hat Harry Productions **(5)** Lee Daniels Entertainment/Lions Gate Films **(6)** Eon Productions/Danjaq/MGM/United Artists **(7)** DreamWorks Pictures/Neal Street Productions/DreamWorks SKG **(8)** Cloud Atlas Productions/X-Filme Creative Pool/Anarchos Pictures/A Company Filmproduktionsgesellschaft/ARD Degeto Film/Ascension Pictures/Dreams of Dragon Picture/Five Drops/Media Asia Group **52 (1)** Films A2/T. Films **(2)** Les Films Plain Chant/Soprofilms/FR3 Films Production/Unité Trois **(3)** The Saul Zaentz Company **(4)** Films A2/Gaumont International/Les Films Christian Fechner **(5)** Nouvelles Éditions de Films/Skreba Films/StudioCanal **(6)** MK2 Productions/CED Productions/France 3 Cinéma/CAB Productions/Zespol Filmowy "Tor"/Canal+ **(7)** Hachette Première/Canal+/Centre Européen Cinématographique Rhône-Alpes/Compagnie Européenne Cinématographique/Entree Europees Cineatografique/France 2 Cinéma **(8)** Tiger Moth/Miramax/The Kobal Collection **53 (1)** Miramax/Fat Free Ltd/David Brown Productions **(2)** Cinémaginaire Inc./Epithète Films/France 2 Cinéma/France 3 Cinéma **(3)** Les Films du Losange/Wega Film/Bavaria Film/BIM Distribuzione **(4)** 3H Productions/Margo Films/Les Films du Lendemain/Arte France Cinéma **(5)** MK2 Productions/BiBi Film/Abbas Kiarostami Productions/France 3 Cinéma/Canal+ France **(6)** 3B Productions/Arte France Cinema/C.R.R.A.V. Nord Pas De Calais/Canal+/Region Paca/The Kobal Collection **(7)** Warner Bros./Legendary Pictures/Disruption Entertainment/Dune Entertainment/Toho Company **(8)** CG Cinéma/Pallas Film/CAB Productions/Vortex Sutra/Arte France Cinéma/ZDF/Arte/Orange Studi/Radio Télévision Suisse/SRG SSR idée suisse/Ezekiel Film Production **54 (1)** Saul Zaentz Company/The Kobal Collection **(2)** Films A2/Gaumont International/Les Films Christian Fechner **(3)** MK2/CED/CAB/The Kobal Collection **(4)** Fat Free Ltd/Miramax/The Kobal Collection **(5)** Tiger Moth/Miramax/The Kobal Collection **(6)** MK2 Productions/BiBi Film/Abbas Kiarostami Productions/France 3 Cinéma/Canal+ France **(7)** 3B Productions/Arte France Cinema/C.R.R.A.V. Nord Pas De Calais/Canal+/Region Paca/The Kobal Collection **(8)** CG Cinéma/Pallas Film/CAB Productions/Vortex Sutra/Arte France Cinéma/ZDF/Arte/Orange Studi/Radio Télévision Suisse/SRG SSR idée suisse/Ezekiel Film Production **tl** Saul Zaentz Company/The Kobal Collection **tr** Saul Zaentz Company/The Kobal Collection **cl** Films Christian Fechner/The Kobal Collection **cr** MK2/CED/CAB/The Kobal Collection **b** Fat Free Ltd/Miramax/The Kobal Collection **55 tr** Tiger Moth/Miramax/The Kobal Collection **cl** Canal+/The Kobal Collection **cr** Canal+/The Kobal Collection **bl** 3B Productions/Arte France Cinema/C.R.R.A.V. Nord Pas De Calais/Canal+/Region Paca/The Kobal Collection **br** CG Cinema/Pallas Film/CAB Productionsvortex Sutra/Arte France Cinema/Zdf/Rts/The Kobal Collection **56 (1)** Australian Film Finance Corporation/Dalton Films/Fox Searchlight Pictures/Meridian Films/New South Wales Film & Television Office **(2)** PolyGram Filmed Entertainment/Working Title Films/Channel Four Films **(3)** New Line Cinema/WingNut Films/The Saul Zaentz Company **(4)** Forward Pass/Appian Way/IMF Internationale Medien und Film GmbH & Co. 3. Produktions KG/Initial Entertainment Group/Warner Bros./Miramax **(5)** Fox Searchlight Pictures/DNA Films/UK Film Council/BBC Films/Scott Rudin Productions/Ingenious Film Partners **(6)** Killer Films/John Wells Productions/John Goldwyn Productions/Endgame Entertainment/Dreamachine/Film & Entertainment VIP Medienfonds 4 GmbH & Co. KG/Grey Water Park Productions/Rising Star/Wells Productions **(7)** Warner Bros./Paramount Pictures/The Kennedy/Marshall Company **(8)** Gravier Productions/Perdido Productions **57 (1)** Ealing Studios **(2)** J. Arthur Rank Organisation **(3)** The Rank Organisation **(4)** The Rank Organisation **(5)** Elstree Distributors/Springbok Productions **(6)** Royal Avenue Chelsea **(7)** Ital-Noleggio Cinematografico/Praesidens/Pegaso Cinematografica/Eichberg-Film **(8)** Alfa Cinematografica **58 (1)** Warner Bros. **(2)** Warner Bros. **(3)** Warner Bros. **(4)** Warner Bros. **(5)** Warner Bros. **(6)** Warner Bros. **(7)** Warner Bros. **(8)** Warner Bros. **59 (1)** Warner Bros. **(2)** Warner Bros. **(3)** Columbia Pictures Corporation/Santana Pictures Corporation **(4)** Romulus Films/Horizon Pictures **(5)** Columbia Pictures Corporation **(6)** Paramount Pictures **(7)** Paramount Pictures **(8)** Columbia Pictures Corporation **60 (1)** Stanley Kramer Productions **(2)** Charles K. Feldman Group/Warner Bros. **(3)** Stanley Kramer Productions **(4)** Columbia Pictures Corporation/Horizon Pictures **(5)** The Samuel Goldwyn Company **(6)** Pennebaker Productions **(7)** Pennebaker Productions **(8)** Warner Brothers/Seven Arts **61 (1)** Paramount Pictures/Alfran Productions **(2)** United Artists/Les Productions Artistes Associés/Produzioni Europee Associati **(3)** Devon/Persky-Bright **(4)** Dovemead Films/Film Export A.G./International Film Production **(5)** Zoetrope Studios **(6)** Davros Films/Star Partners II Ltd./Sundance Productions **(7)** TriStar Pictures **(8)** Paramount Pictures/Mandalay Pictures/Horseshoe Bay Productions/Lee Rich Productions/Cineartists AG/MP Film Management/Vierte Beteiligung KC Medien AG & Co. KG **62 (1)** Stanley Kramer Productions **(2)** Charles K. Feldman Group/Warner Bros. **(3)** Columbia Pictures Corporation/Horizon Pictures **(4)** The Samuel Goldwyn Company **(5)** Paramount Pictures/Alfran Productions **(6)** United Artists/Les Productions Artistes Associés/Produzioni Europee Associati **(7)** Zoetrope Studios **(8)** Davros Films/Star Partners II Ltd./Sundance Productions **tl** United Artists/The Kobal Collection **tr** Warner Bros/The Kobal Collection **cl** Columbia/The Kobal

Collection **cr** Warner Bros/The Kobal Collection **bl** Paramount/The Kobal Collection **br** Paramount/The Kobal Collection **63 tl** MGM/Samuel Goldwyn/The Kobal Collection **tr** Pea/The Kobal Collection **cr** Zoetrope/United Artists/The Kobal Collection **bc** Zoetrope/United Artists/The Kobal Collection **br** MGM/The Kobal Collection **64 (1)** Nero/The Kobal Collection **(2)** Warner Bros/The Kobal Collection **(3)** RKO/THE KOBAL COLLECTION/KAHLE, ALEX **(4)** Columbia/The Kobal Collection **(5)** Warner Bros/The Kobal Collection **(6)** Warner Bros/The Kobal Collection **(7)** Columbia/The Kobal Collection **(8)** Warner Bros/The Kobal Collection **65 (1)** Columbia/The Kobal Collection **(2)** Paramount/The Kobal Collection **(3)** Bandai Media/Shochiku-Fuji/The Kobal Collection **(4)** MGM/Pathe/The Kobal Collection **(5)** Lazennec/Canal +/La Sept/The Kobal Collection **(6)** Dreamworks/The Kobal Collection **(7)** Wild Bunch/Morena Films/The Kobal Collection **(8)** Highlook Communications Group/Razor Film/Ndr/Br/Rotana Studios/The Kobal Collection **66 (1)** Columbia Pictures Corporation/BBS Productions **(2)** Columbia Pictures Corporation/Rastar Pictures **(3)** Jaffilms/Paramount Pictures **(4)** The Malpaso Company **(5)** Partisan Productions **(6)** Gurian Entertainment **(7)** Walt Disney Productions/Lisberger/Kushner **(8)** Columbia Pictures Corporation/Delphi IV Productions **67 (1)** Lucasfilm **(2)** Gladden Entertainment/Mirage/Tobis **(3)** Columbia Pictures Corporation **(4)** Spring Creek Productions/Warner Bros. **(5)** Polygram Filmed Entertainment/Working Title Films **(6)** Paramount Pictures/Marvel Enterprises/Marvel Studios/Fairview Entertainment/Dark Blades Films **(7)** Fox Searchlight Pictures/Informant Media/Butcher's Run Films **(8)** Paramount Pictures/Skydance Productions/Scott Rudin Productions/Mike Zoss Productions **68 (1)** Columbia/The Kobal Collection **(2)** Columbia/The Kobal Collection **(3)** United Artists/The Kobal Collection **(4)** Walt Disney Pictures/The Kobal Collection **(5)** Columbia Pictures Corporation **(6)** Polygram/Working Title/The Kobal Collection **(7)** Fox Searchlight/The Kobal Collection **(8)** Skydance Productions/The Kobal Collection **tl** Columbia/The Kobal Collection **tr** Columbia/The Kobal Collection **cl** United Artists/The Kobal Collection **cr** United Artists/The Kobal Collection **bl** Walt Disney Pictures/The Kobal Collection **69 tl** Polygram/Working Title/The Kobal Collection **tr** Fox Searchlight/The Kobal Collection **cr** Fox Searchlight/The Kobal Collection **bl** Tri-Star/Hill-Obst/The Kobal Collection **br** Skydance Productions/The Kobal Collection **70 (1)** The Mirisch Company/Alpha Productions **(2)** The Mirisch Company **(3)** MGM/MKH/Seven Arts Pictures **(4)** Rafran Cinematografica/Finanzia San Marco/Paramount Pictures **(5)** Chartoff-Winkler Productions/Carlino Productions **(6)** The Mirisch Company **(7)** Dino De Laurentiis Company/Paramount Pictures **(8)** Columbia Pictures Corporation/Claridge Productions **71 (1)** Famous Players-Lasky Corporation **(2)** Famous Players-Lasky Corporation **(3)** Fox Film Corporation **(4)** Paramount Famous Lasky Corporation **(5)** Paramount Pictures **(6)** Nero-Film AG **(7)** Pabst-Film/Hom-AG für Filmfabrikation **(8)** Sofar-Film **72 (1)** Cameo Film- und Fernsehproduktion/Kunsthochschule für Medien Köln (KHM) **(2)** X-Filme Creative Pool/Westdeutscher Rundfunk/ARTE **(3)** Y3 Film/Coop 99/Südwestrundfunk/ARTE **(4)** Future Films/Mediapro **(5)** Serenity Film/Celluloid Dreams/EMC Filmproduktion/Fanes Film/Mirabelle Pictures/Social Capital/The Steel Company/Tempête Sous un Crâne/X-Filme Creative Pool **(6)** Universal Pictures/The Weinstein Company/A Band Apart/Studio Babelsberg/Visiona Romantica **(7)** DreamWorks SKG/Reliance Entertainment/Participant Media/Anonymous Content/FBO/Reliance Entertainment **(8)** Exclusive Media Group/Cross Creek Pictures/Imagine Entertainment/Revolution Films/Working Title Films/Double Negative **73 (1)** Aubrey Schenck Productions/Samba Films **(2)** 20th Century Fox Film Corporation **(3)** Paramount Pictures/Motion Picture Associates **(4)** Avon Productions (II)/MGM **(5)** Cinédis/Les Editions Cinégraphiques **(6)** The Mirisch Company/Alpha Productions **(7)** Jet Films/Lubicz Productions/The Bryna Company/Triumfilm **(8)** MGM **74 (1)** 20th Century Fox Film Corporation **(2)** Columbia Pictures Corporation/Winkler Films **(3)** Hollywood Pictures/Caravan Pictures **(4)** Castle Rock Entertainment/Village Roadshow Pictures/NPV Entertainment/Fortis Films **(5)** Bob Yari Productions/DEJ Productions/Blackfriars Bridge Films/Harris Company/ApolloProScreen Filmproduktion/Bull's Eye Entertainment **(6)** Touchstone Pictures/Mandeville Films/Kurtzman/Orci **(7)** Alcon Entertainment/Left Tackle Pictures/Zucker/Netter Productions **(8)** Warner Bros./Esperanto Filmoj/Heyday Films **75 (1)** 20th Century Fox Film Corporation **(2)** Orion/Woodfall Film Productions **(3)** 20th Century Fox Film Corporation/MCL Films S.A./Walwa Films S.A. **(4)** Salem Films Limited **(5)** Warner Bros./Chenault Productions **(6)** MGM/Jerry Gershwin Productions/Elliott Kastner Productions/Winkast Film Productions **(7)** Persky-Bright Productions/Winkast Film Productions **(8)** Umbrella-Rosenblum Films Production/Virgin Benelux/Virgin Schallplatten/Virgin **76 (1)** Paramount Pictures/Alfran Productions **(2)** Paramount Pictures **(3)** Columbia Pictures Corporation/Rastar Pictures/Vista **(4)** Joseph E. Levine Productions **(5)** Mann/Caan Productions **(6)** ML Delphi Premier Productions/TriStar Pictures/Zoetrope Studios **(7)** Castle Rock Entertainment/Nelson Entertainment **(8)** Castle Rock Entertainment/New Line Cinema **77 (1)** TriStar Pictures/Rastar Pictures/Zoetrope Studios/Delphi V Productions **(2)** Circle Films **(3)** PolyGram Filmed Entertainment/Propaganda Films **(4)** Lumiere Pictures/A Lila Cazès Production/Initial Productions **(5)** Hollywood Pictures/Don Simpson/Jerry Bruckheimer Films **(6)** Permut Presentations/Touchstone Pictures/Paramount Pictures/Douglas/Reuther Productions/WCG Entertainment Productions/Krane Entertainment **(7)** Beverly Detroit/Clinica Estetico/Good Machine/Intermedia/Magnet Productions/Propaganda Films **(8)** Millennium Films/Edward R. Pressman Film/Saturn Films/Polsky Films/Osiris Productions/Lieutenant Productions/Nu Image Films **78 (1)** Warner Bros. **(2)** Warner Bros. **(3)** Warner Bros./The Vitaphone Corporation **(4)** Fox Searchlight Pictures/Regency Enterprises/Taurus Film/ Panoramica **(5)** First National Pictures **(6)** Warner Bros. **(7)** Warner Bros. **(8)** Warner Bros. **79 (1)** Warner Bros. **(2)** MGM **(3)** Warner Bros./Orange **(4)** MGM **(5)** Universal International Pictures (UI) **(6)** Barna-Alper Productions/Halifax Film Company/Head Gear Films/Seville Productions **(7)** Bavaria Film/The Mirisch Corporation/Pyramid Productions **(8)** Dino De Laurentiis Company/Sunley Productions Ltd. **80 (1)** Diamond Films **(2)** The Rank Organisation/Lowndes Productions Limited/Steven S.A. **(3)** Lewis Gilbert/Sheldrake Films **(4)** MGM British Studios **(5)** Columbia Pictures Corporation/Devon/Persky-Bright/Allied Artists Pictures **(6)** Acorn Pictures **(7)** Orion Pictures/Jack Rollins & Charles H. Joffe Productions **(8)** HandMade Films/Palace Production **81 (1)** Orion Pictures **(2)** Recorded Picture Company (RPC)/Fox Searchlight Pictures/Marmont Productions/Blood & Wine Productions/Majestic Films International **(3)** FilmColony/Miramax/Nina Saxon Film Design **(4)** Giai Phong Film Studio/IMF Internationale Medien und Film GmbH & Co. 2. Produktions KG/Intermedia Films/Mirage Enterprises/Pacifica Film/Saga **(5)** Warner Bros./Syncopy/DC Comics/Legendary Pictures/Patalex III Productions Limited **(6)** Universal Pictures/Strike Entertainment/Hit & Run Productions **(7)** Marv Films/UK Film Council/HanWay Films/Prescience Film Fund/Framestore/Prescience **(8)** Paramount Pictures/Warner Bros./Legendary Pictures/Lynda Obst Productions/Syncopy **82 (1)** Cinecittà/Lux Film/Lux Film **(2)** Titanus/Les Films Marceau **(3)** Cineriz/Francinex **(4)** Titanus/Société Nouvelle Pathé Cinéma/Société Générale de Cinématographie (S.G.C.) **(5)** Mirisch G-E Productions **(6)** Pax Enterprises/Columbia Pictures Corporation **(7)** Rafran Cinematografica/Finanzia San Marco/Paramount Pictures **(8)** Werner Herzog Filmproduktion/Pro-ject Filmproduktion/Filmverlag der Autoren/Zweites Deutsches Fernsehen (ZDF)/Wildlife Films Peru **83 (1)** Morgan Creek Productions **(2)** New Line Cinema/Dark Horse Entertainment **(3)** New Line Cinema/Motion Picture Corporation of America (MPCA) **(4)** Paramount Pictures/Scott Rudin Productions **(5)** Universal Pictures/Mutual Film Company /Jersey Films/Cinehaus/Shapiro/West Productions/Tele München Fernseh Produktionsgesellschaft (TMG)/British Broadcasting Corporation (BBC)/Marubeni/Toho-Towa **(6)** Focus Features/Anonymous Content/This Is That Productions **(7)** Paramount Pictures/DreamWorks Pictures/Nickelodeon Movies/Kumar Mobiliengesellschaft mbH & Co. Projekt Nr. 2 KG/Parkes+MacDonald Image Nation/Scott Rudin Productions **84 (1)** David Susskind Productions, Jonathan Productions, MGM **(2)** Revue Studios **(3)** MGM/MKH/Seven Arts Pictures **(4)** American International Pictures (AIP)/Globo Vídeo/ MGM Home Entertainment (Europe)/MGM/UA Home Entertainment/Nickes Sound City **(5)** William Castle Productions **(6)** Euro International Film (EIA)/Euroatlantica **(7)** Faces Music **(8)** Santa Fe Productions (I) **85 (1)** Filmways Pictures/Universal Pictures **(2)** Faces Distribution **(3)** Frank Yablans Presentations/20th Century Fox Film Corporation **(4)** UNITED ARTISTS/THE KOBAL COLLECTION **(5)** MGM/SLM Production Group **(6)** John M. Eckert Productions Ltd./Kings Road Productions Ltd./Mark Films Ltd. **(7)** Major Productions/Marvin Film Partners **(8)** Cannon Films **86 (1)** Canal+/Cofinergie 6/Egg Pictures/Kasso Inc. Productions/La Sept Cinéma/Les Productions Lazennec/Polygram Filmed Entertainment/Studio Image **(2)** Cecchi Gori Group Tiger Cinematografica/IMA Productions/La Sept Cinéma/M6 Films/Mate Producciones S.A./Union Générale Cinématographique (UGC) **(3)** 120 Films/Canal+/Eskwad/Les Cinémas de la Zone/Nord-Ouest Productions/StudioCanal/Wild Bunch **(4)** Warner Bros. /Village Roadshow Pictures/Jerry Weintraub Productions/Section Eight/WV Films III **(5)** Focus Features/BBC Films/Astral Media/Corus Entertainment/Téléfilm Canada/Kudos Film and Television/Serendipity Point Films/Scion Films/Shine Pictures **(6)** La Petite Reine/Remstar Productions/Novo RPI/M6 Films **(7)** Fox Searchlight Pictures/Cross Creek Pictures /Protozoa Pictures/Phoenix Pictures/Dune Entertainment **(8)** Pathé/Cloud Eight Films/Decibel Films **87 (1)** Seasonal Film Corporation **(2)** Seasonal Film Corporation **(3)** Authority Films/Golden Harvest Company/Paragon Films Ltd. **(4)** Golden Way Films Ltd./Paragon Films Ltd./Toho-Towa **(5)** Golden Harvest Company/Golden Way Films Ltd./Jadran Film/Paragon Films Ltd. **(6)** Golden Harvest Company/Maple Ridge Films/Toho-Towa **(7)** New Line Cinema/Roger Birnbaum Productions **(8)** Touchstone Pictures/Spyglass Entertainment/Roger Birnbaum Productions/Jackie Chan Films Limited **88 (1)** Dai Lei Film Company/Wing Yiu Film Company/Yau Kiu Film Company **(2)** Kurosawa Production Co./Toho Company **(3)** Daiei Motion Picture Company **(4)** Shaw Brothers **(5)** Warner Bros./Concord Productions Inc./Golden Harvest Company/Sequoia Productions **(6)** Toei Company **(7)** Shaw Brothers **(8)** Shaw Brothers **89 (1)** Seasonal Film Corporation **(2)** Golden Harvest Company/Film Workshop **(3)** Largo Entertainment/JVC Entertainment Networks/Signature Pictures/Renaissance Pictures/Dark Horse Entertainment **(4)** Asia Union Film & Entertainment Ltd./China Film Co-Production Corporation/Columbia Pictures Film Production Asia Edko Films/Good Machin/Sony Pictures Classics/United China Vision/Zoom Hunt International Productions **(5)** Baa-Ram-Ewe/Sahamongkolfilm Co. **(6)** Columbia Pictures Film Production Asia/Huayi Brothers Media/Taihe Film Investment Co. Ltd./Beijing Film Studio/China Film Group/Fourth Production Company Film Group, The/Star Overseas/China Film Co-Production Corporation **(7)** Pt. Merantau Films/Celluloid Dreams/XYZ Films **(8)** Block 2 Pictures/Jet Tone Films/Sil-Metropole Organisation/Bona International Film Group **90 (1)** Keystone Film Company **(2)** Keystone Film Company **(3)** The Essanay Film Manufacturing Company **(4)** The Essanay Film Manufacturing Company **(5)** Lone Star Corporation **(6)** Lone Star Corporation **(7)** First National Pictures **(8)** Charles Chaplin Productions **91 (1)** Charles Chaplin Productions **(2)** Charles Chaplin Productions **(3)** Charles Chaplin Productions **(4)** Charles Chaplin Productions **(5)** Charles Chaplin Productions **(6)** Celebrated Productions **(7)** Attica Film Company **(8)** Chaplin Film Productions Ltd./Universal Pictures **92 (1)** In-Gear Film Production **(2)** In-Gear Film Production **(3)** Cos Group **(4)** Golden Way Films Ltd. **(5)** Dacia Films/Canal+ **(6)** Block 2 Pictures/Jet Tone Production/Paradis Films **(7)** Beijing New Picture Film Co./China Film Co-Production Corporation/Elite Group Enterprises/Sil-Metropole Organisation/Zhang Yimou Studio **(8)** Journeyman Films Ltd./Rectangle Productions/Haystack Productions/Rhombus Media/Arte France Cinéma **93 (1)** Vic Films Productions/Waterfall Prouctions **(2)** Joseph Janni Production/Vic Films Productions/Appia Films Ltd. **(3)** MGM/Vic Films Productions **(4)** David Foster Productions/Warner Bros. **(5)** Casey Productions/Eldorado Films/D.L.N. Ventures Partnership **(6)** Elysian Dreams/Moonstone Entertainment/Sandcastle 5 Productions **(7)** Miramax/FilmColony **(8)** Foundry Films/Capri Releasing/HanWay Films/Echo Lake Entertainment **94 (1)** Charles K. Feldman Group/Monterey Productions **(2)** Paramount Pictures **(3)** Paramount Pictures **(4)** Columbia Pictures Corporation **(5)** Warner Bros. **(6)** Columbia Pictures Corporation/Horizon Pictures (II)/Academy Pictures Corporation/Camp Films **(7)** Roxlom Films Inc. **(8)** Seven Arts Pictures **95 (1)** Dimension Films/A Band Apart/Los Hooligans Productions/Miramax **(2)** Universal Pictures/Jersey Films **(3)** Touchstone Pictures/Universal Pictures/StudioCanal/Working Title Films/Mike Zoss Productions **(4)** Warner Bros./Baltimore Spring Creek Productions/Radiant Productions **(5)** Warner Bros./Village Roadshow Pictures/NPV Entertainment/Jerry Weintraub Productions/Section Eight/WV Films II **(6)** Warner Bros./Participant Media/4M/Section Eight/FilmWorks/MID Foundation **(7)** Samuels Media/Castle Rock Entertainment/Mirage Enterprises/Section Eight/Clayton Productions **(8)** Warner Bros./Esperanto Filmoj/Heyday Films **96 (1)** Jolly Film/Constantin Film Produktion/Ocean Films **(2)** Universal Pictures **(3)** Black Rhino Productions/Columbia Pictures Corporation/Delphi Films **(4)** Paramount Pictures/Eddie Murphy Productions **(5)** The Zanuck Company/Majestic Films International **(6)** TriStar Pictures/Clinica Estetico **(7)** Regency Enterprises/The Wolper Organization/Warner Bros. **(8)** Warner Bros./Village Roadshow Pictures/NPV Entertainment/Outlaw Productions (I)/WV Films II **97 (1)** Columbia Pictures Corporation/Forward Pass/Initial Entertainment Group (IEG)/Moonlighting Films/Overbrook Entertainment/Peters Entertainment/Picture Entertainment Corporation **(2)** DreamWorks SKG/Universal Pictures/Scott Free Productions/Mill Film/C & L/Dawliz/Red Wagon Entertainment **(3)** Miramax/Producers Circle/Storyline Entertainment/Kalis Productions GmbH & Co. KG **(4)** Universal Pictures/Bristol Bay Productions/Anvil Films/Baldwin Entertainment Group **(5)** Warner Bros./Participant Media/4M/Section Eight/FilmWorks/MID Foundation **(6)** The Weinstein Company **(7)** Paramount Pictures/Marvel Entertainment/Marvel Studios **(8)** Paramount Pictures/Marvel Enterprises/Marvel Studios/Fairview Entertainment/Dark Blades Films **98 (1)** Columbia Pictures Corporation **(2)** Paramount Pictures **(3)** 20th Century Fox Film Corporation **(4)** Paramount Pictures **(5)** Paramount Pictures **(6)** Paramount Pictures **(7)** Universal International Pictures **(8)** Lorimar Telepictures **99 (1)** Eon Productions **(2)** Alfred J. Hitchcock Productions **(3)** MGM/Seven Arts Pictures **(4)** Columbia Pictures Corporation/Devon/Persky-Bright/Allied Artists Pictures **(5)** Neue Constantin Film/Cristaldifilm/Les Films Ariane/Zweites Deutsches Fernsehen (ZDF) **(6)** Paramount Pictures **(7)** Paramount Pictures/Lucasfilm **(8)** Paramount Pictures/Mace Neufeld Productions/Nina Saxon Film Design **100 (1)** Paramount Pictures **(2)** Paramount Pictures **(3)** Paramount Pictures **(4)** Paramount Pictures **(5)** Columbia Pictures Corporation **(6)** Paramount Pictures **(7)** Paramount Pictures **(8)** Paramount Pictures **101 (1)** The Samuel Goldwyn Company **(2)** Warner Bros. **(3)** Frank Capra Productions **(4)** International Pictures/Cinema Artists **(5)** Warner Bros. **(6)** Stanley Kramer Productions **(7)** Billy Wilder Productions **(8)** Ashton Productions/Walter Mirisch Productions **102 (1)** Columbia Pictures Corporation/Delphi IV Productions **(2)** Orion Pictures **(3)** Paramount Pictures **(4)** Gordon Company **(5)** Tig Productions/Majestic Films International **(6)** Universal Pictures/Gordon Company/Davis Entertainment/Licht/Mueller Film Corporation **(7)** Touchstone Pictures/Cobalt Media Group/Beacon Pictures/Tig Productions **(8)** Warner Bros./Legendary Pictures/Syncopy **103 (1)** ARP Sélection/TF1 Films Production/Canal+ **(2)** C.A.P.A.C./Hugo Films/M6 Films **(3)** 2003 Productions/Warner Bros./Tapioca Films/TF1 Films Production **(4)** Légende Films/TF1 International/TF1 Films Production/Okko Productions/Songbird Pictures **(5)** The Weinstein Company/Relativity Media/Marc Platt Productions/Lucamar Productions **(6)** Warner Bros./Legendary Pictures/Syncopy **(7)** Why Not Productions/Page 114/France 2 Cinéma/Les Films du Fleuve/Radio Télévision Belge Francophone (RTBF)/Lumière/Lunanime **(8)** Les Films du Fleuve/Archipel 35/BIM Distribuzione/Eyeworks/France 2 Cinéma/Radio Télévision Belge Francophone (RTBF)/Belgacom **104 (1)** RKO Radio Pictures/Mercury Productions **(2)** Mercury Productions **(3)** Skirball Productions/Universal Pictures **(4)** The Selznick Studio/Vanguard Films **(5)** Vanguard Films/Selznick International Pictures **(6)** Carol Reed's Production/London Film Productions **(7)** Transatlantic Pictures **(8)** Universal International Pictures (UI) **105 (1)** British Broadcasting Corporation (BBC) **(2)** DreamWorks SKG/20th Century Fox Film Corporation/The Zanuck Company **(3)** BBC Films/British Film Council/Capitol Films/Focus Features/Ruby Films **(4)** Pathé Pictures International/UK Film Council/FilmFour/Inside Track Films **(5)** Sony Pictures Classics/Marv Films **(6)** Columbia Pictures/Eon Productions/Casino Royale Productions/Stillking Films/Casino Royale/Danjaq/United Artists **(7)** Universal Pictures/DreamWorks SKG/Reliance Entertainment **(8)** Columbia Pictures/MGM/Scott Rudin Productions/Yellow Bird **106 (1)** MGM **(2)** MGM **(3)** MGM **(4)** MGM **(5)** Warner Bros. **(6)** Warner Bros. **(7)** Warner Bros. **(8)** 20th Century Fox Film Corporation **107 (1)** Michael Curtiz Productions/Warner Bros. **(2)** Warner Bros. **(3)** Joseph Kaufmann Productions **(4)** MGM **(5)** Republic Pictures (I) **(6)** The Associates & Aldrich Company/Seven Arts Pictures/Warner Bros. **(7)** William Castle Productions **(8)** Herman Cohen Productions **108 (1)** Paramount Pictures **(2)** Paramount Pictures **(3)** Rainbow Productions **(4)** Bing Crosby Productions/Hope Enterprises/Paramount Pictures **(5)** Paramount Pictures **(6)** Paramount Pictures **(7)** MGM/Sol C. Siegel Productions/Bing Crosby Productions **(8)** P-C Productions/Essex Productions/Meadway-Claude Productions Company (I) (II) **109 (1)** The Australian Film Commission/Film Victoria/Romper Stomper Pty. Ltd./Seon Film Productions **(2)** Regency Enterprises/The Wolper Organization/Warner Bros. **(3)** Blue Lion Entertainment/Forward Pass/Kaitz Productions/Mann/Roth Productions/Spyglass Entertainment/Touchstone Pictures **(4)** DreamWorks SKG/Universal Pictures/Scott Free Productions/Mill Film/C & L/Dawliz/Red Wagon Entertainment **(5)** Universal Pictures/DreamWorks SKG/Imagine Entertainment **(6)** 20th Century Fox Film Corporation/Miramax/Universal Pictures/Samuel Goldwyn Films **(7)** Universal Pictures/Imagine Entertainment/Relativity Media/Scott Free Productions/Film Rites/WR Universal Group **(8)** Paramount Pictures/Regency Enterprises/Protozoa Pictures/Disruption Entertainment **110 (1)** 20th Century Fox Film Corporation **(2)** The Geffen Company **(3)** Legend Production Company/Embassy International Pictures **(4)** Paramount Pictures **(5)** Touchstone Pictures/Silver Screen Partners II **(6)** United Artists/The Guber-Peters Company/Star Partners II Ltd./Mirage Enterprises **(7)** Ixtlan **(8)** Davis Entertainment/Mirage Enterprises/Paramount Pictures/Scott Rudin Productions **111 (1)** Geffen Pictures **(2)** Paramount Pictures/Cruise/Wagner Productions **(3)** Ghoulardi Film Company/New Line Cinema/The Magnolia Project **(4)** Warner Bros./Stanley Kubrick Productions/Hobby Films/Pole Star **(5)** 20th Century Fox Film Corporation/DreamWorks SKG/Cruise/Wagner Productions/Blue Tulip Productions/Ronald Shusett/Gary Goldman/Amblin Entertainment **(6)** Paramount Pictures/DreamWorks SKG/Parkes+MacDonald Image Nation/Edge City **(7)** DreamWorks SKG/Red Hour Films/Goldcrest Pictures/Internationale Filmproduktion Stella-del-Sud Second **(8)** Warner Bros./Village Roadshow Pictures/RatPac-Dune Entertainment **112 (1)** Lolafilms/Ovídeo TV S.A./Sogepaq **(2)** Canal+ España/Las Producciones del Escorpión/Les Films Alain Sarde/Lucky Red/Sociedad General de Televisión (Sogetel) **(3)** El Deseo/Renn Productions/France 2 Cinéma/Vía Digital **(4)** Columbia Pictures Corporation/Miramax **(5)** Canal+ España/El Deseo/Ministerio de Cultura/Televisión Española (TVE) **(6)** The Weinstein Company/Mediapro/Gravier Productions **(7)** Universal Pictures International (UPI)/Canal+ España/El Deseo **(8)** Walt Disney Pictures/Jerry Bruckheimer Films/Moving Picture Company (MPC) **113 (1)** BBC Films/HBO Films/Neal Street Productions **(2)** DreamWorks SKG/Reliance Entertainment/Amblin Entertainment/The Kennedy/Marshall Company **(3)** StudioCanal/Karla Films/Paradis Films/Kinowelt Filmproduktion/Working Title Films **(4)** Paramount Pictures/Skydance Productions/Bad Robot/Auckland Audio **(5)** Regency Enterprises/River Road Entertainment/Plan B Entertainment/New Regency Pictures/Film4 **(6)** The Weinstein Company/Mediapr/Gravier Productions/Antena 3 Films/Antena 3 Televisión/Televisió de Catalunya **(7)** MGM/New Line Cinema/WingNut Films **(8)** Black Bear Pictures/Bristol Automotive **114 (1)** Paramount Pictures **(2)** Norma Productions/Curtleigh Productions/Hill-Hecht-Lancaster Productions **(3)** Curtleigh Productions/Stanley Kramer Productions **(4)** Ashton Productions/The Mirisch Corporation **(5)** Universal International Pictures (UI)/Granart Company **(6)** Bryna Productions **(7)** 20th Century Fox Film Corporation **(8)** Recorded Picture Company (RPC)/Zenith Entertainment **115 (1)** Hal Roach Studios **(2)** Two Cities Films **(3)** British Broadcasting Corporation (BBC) **(4)** Warner Bros./Hammer Film Productions **(5)** Hammer Film Productions **(6)** Hammer Film Productions **(7)** Lucasfilm/20th Century Fox Film Corporation **(8)** London-Cannon Films **116 (1)** Fox 2000 Pictures **(2)** Be Gentlemen Limited Partnership/Lawrence Bender Productions/Miramax **(3)** Constellation Entertainment/Douglas/Reuther Productions/American Zoetrope **(4)** DreamWorks SKG/Paramount Pictures/Amblin Entertainment/Mutual Film Company/Mark Gordon Productions **(5)** Miramax/Paramount Pictures/Mirage Enterprises/Timnick Films **(6)** Warner Bros./Village Roadshow Pictures/NPV Entertainment/Jerry Weintraub Productions/Section Eight/WV Films II **(7)** Epsilon Motion Pictures/My Cactus/Tango Films **(8)** Universal Pictures/The Kennedy/Marshall Company/Hypnotic/Kalima Productions GmbH & Co. KG/Stillking Films **117 (1)** Warner Bros./Plan B Entertainment/Initial Entertainment Group (IEG)/Vertigo Entertainment/Media Asia Films **(2)** Universal Pictures/Morgan Creek Productions/Tribeca Productions/American Zoetrope **(3)** Be Gentlemen Limited Partnership/Lawrence Bender Productions/Miramax **(4)** Warner Bros./Participant Media/Groundswell Productions/Section Eight/Jaffe/Braunstein Enterprise **(5)** Paramount Pictures/Skydance Productions/Scott Rudin Productions/Mike Zoss Productions **(6)** Fox Searchlight Pictures/Gilbert Films/Mirage Enterprises/Scott Rudin Productions **(7)** Jerry Weintraub Productions/HBO Films **(8)** Paramount Pictures/Warner Bros./Legendary Pictures/Lynda Obst Productions/Syncopy **118 (1)** RKO Radio Pictures **(2)** Warner Bros. **(3)** Warner Bros. **(4)** Warner Bros. **(5)** Warner Bros. **(6)** Warner Bros. **(7)** Warner Bros. **(8)** The Samuel Goldwyn Company **119 (1)** Warner Bros. **(2)** Warner Bros. **(3)** Warner Bros. **(4)** 20th Century Fox Film Corporation **(5)** The Associates & Aldrich Company/Seven Arts Pictures/Warner Bros. **(6)** Columbia Broadcasting System (CBS)/Highschool Sweethearts/Sternin & Fraser Ink/TriStar Television **(7)** Hammer Film Productions/Seven Arts Pictures **(8)** Nelson Entertainment **120 (1)** Otto Preminger Films **(2)** MGM/Seven Arts Pictures **(3)** Bristol Films/Norlan Productions **(4)** Slaves Company/Theatre Guild **(5)** 40 Acres & A Mule Filmworks **(6)** Columbia Pictures/15 Black Men/40 Acres & A Mule Filmworks **(7)** Silver Sphere Corporation **(8)** THEntertainment **121 (1)** The Samuel Goldwyn Company **(2)** Dorchester/Warner Bros. **(3)** Essex Productions/Meadway-Claude Productions Company (I) (II) **(4)** P-C Productions/Essex Productions/Meadway-Claude Productions Company (I) (II) **(5)** Trace-Mark Productions **(6)** Universal Pictures **(7)** Golden Harvest Company/Eurasia Investments **(8)** Beco Films/TriStar Pictures **122 (1)** Warner Bros./Michael Curtiz Productions **(2)** Michael Curtiz Productions/Warner Bros. **(3)** Warner Bros. **(4)** Warner Bros. **(5)** Warner Bros. **(6)** Arwin Productions **(7)** MGM **(8)** Paramount Pictures/Filwite Productions **123 (1)** Warner Bros. **(2)** Perlsea Company **(3)** Arwin Productions/Universal International Pictures (UI) **(4)** Universal International Pictures (UI)/7 Pictures/Nob Hill Productions Inc./Arwin Productions **(5)** Universal/The Kobal Collection/The Kobal Collection **(6)** Martin Melcher Productions/Universal Pictures **(7)** Universal Pictures **(8)** Arwin Productions/Cinema Center Films **124 (1)** International Film Investors/National Film Development Corporation of India (NFDC)/Goldcrest Films International/Indo-British/Carolina Bank **(2)** Dino De Laurentiis Company/Bounty Productions Ltd. **(3)** Working Title Films/SAF Productions/Channel Four Films **(4)** Goldcrest Films International/National Film Finance Corporation (NFFC)/Curzon Film Distributors/Film Four International/Merchant Ivory Productions **(5)** Columbia Pictures Corporation/Stars and Bars Limited **(6)** The Saul Zaentz Company **(7)** Ferndale Films/Granada Television/Radio Telefís Éireann (RTÉ) **(8)** Morgan Creek Productions **125 (1)** Hell's Kitchen Films/Universal Pictures **(2)** Columbia Pictures Corporation/Cappa Production **(3)** 20th Century Fox Film Corporation **(4)** Universal Pictures/Hell's Kitchen Films **(5)** Miramax/Initial Entertainment Group (IEG)/Alberto Grimaldi Productions **(6)** IFC Productions/IFC Productions/Elevation Filmworks/Jack and Rose Productions **(7)** Paramount Vantage/Miramax/Ghoulardi Film Company **(8)** DreamWorks SKG/20th Century Fox Film Corporation/Reliance Entertainment **126 (1)** West End Films **(2)** Warner Bros./Taplin - Perry - Scorsese Productions **(3)** Paramount Pictures/The Coppola Company **(4)** Columbia Pictures Corporation/Bill/Phillips/Italo/Judeo Productions **(5)** Chartoff-Winkler Productions **(6)** EMI Films/Universal Pictures **(7)** United Artists/The Kobal Collection **(8)** Embassy International Pictures/20th Century Fox Film Corporation **127 (1)** Paramount Pictures **(2)** Universal Pictures/City Light Films **(3)** Warner Bros. **(4)** Amblin Entertainment/Cappa Films/Tribeca Productions **(5)** Warner Bros./Regency Enterprises/Forward Pass/Art Linson Productions/Monarchy Enterprises B.V. **(6)** Miramax/A Band Apart/Lawrence Bender Productions/Mighty Mighty Afrodite Productions **(7)** Universal Pictures/DreamWorks SKG/Nancy Tenenbaum Films/Tribeca Productions **(8)** The Weinstein Company **128 (1)** Chartoff-Winkler Productions **(2)** EMI Films/Universal Pictures **(3)** United Artists/The Kobal Collection **(4)** Warner Bros./Taplin - Perry - Scorsese Productions **(5)** Columbia Pictures Corporation/Bill/Phillips/Italo/Judeo Productions **(6)** Universal Pictures/City Light Films **(7)** Warner Bros. **(8)** Universal Pictures/DreamWorks SKG/Nancy Tenenbaum Films/Tribeca Productions **tl** UNITED ARTISTS/THE KOBAL COLLECTION **ct** The Deer Hunter, FILM Copyright © 1978 STUDIOCANAL FILMS LTD. ALL RIGHTS RESERVED/THE KOBAL COLLECTION **cb** Taplin-Perry-Scorsese/The Kobal Collection **bl** United Artists/The Kobal Collection **129 tl** Emi/Columbia/Warners/The Kobal Collection **ct** Universal/The Kobal Collection **cb** WARNER BROS/THE KOBAL COLLECTION **bl** Columbia/The Kobal Collection **br** UNIVERSAL/DREAMWORKS/THE KOBAL COLLECTION/CARUSO, PHILLIP **130 (1)** Universal Pictures **(2)** MGM **(3)** Nero-Film AG **(4)** RKO Radio Pictures **(5)** Selznick International Pictures/MGM **(6)** Hecht-Lancaster Productions **(7)** 20th Century-Fox Productions **(8)** Michael Laughlin Enterprises/Universal Pictures **131 (1)** Fantasy Films **(2)** McElroy & McElroy/MGM **(3)** Castle Rock Entertainment/Nelson Entertainment **(4)** PolyGram Filmed Entertainment/Working Title Films **(5)** Polygram Filmed Entertainment/Working Title Films **(6)** SenArt Films/Next Wednesday Productions/Station Agent, The **(7)** Sidney Kimmel Entertainment/Likely Story/Projective Testing Service/Russia **(8)** Lionsgate/Lee

Daniels Entertainment/Smokewood Entertainment Group 132 (1) Warner Bros. (2) Warner Bros. (3) Giant Productions/Warner Bros. 133 (1) PolyGram Filmed Entertainment/Spelling Films International/Blue Parrot (2) Fear and Loathing LLC/Rhino Films/Shark Productions/Summit Entertainment/Universal Pictures (3) The Bedford Falls Company/Compulsion Inc./Initial Entertainment Group (IEG)/Splendid Medien AG/USA Films (4) This Is That Productions/Y Productions/Mediana Productions Filmgesellschaft (5) Lakeshore Entertainment/Alphaville Films (6) Dimension Films/Troublemaker Studios (7) Wild Bunch/Telecinco/Laura Bickford Productions/Morena Films (8) Universal Pictures/Relativity Media/Stuber Productions 134 (1) Euro International Film (EIA)/Transcontinental Films S.A. (2) Robert et Raymond Hakim/Paris Film/Paritalia/Titanus (3) Titanus/Les Films Marceau (4) Cineriz/Interopa Film/Paris Film (5) Titanus/Société Nouvelle Pathé Cinéma/Société Générale de Cinématographie (S.G.C.) (6) Compagnie Industrielle et Commerciale Cinématographique (CICC)/Fida Cinematografica/Filmel/TC Productions (7) Les Films Marceau/Produzioni Europee Associati (PEA)/Cocinor (8) Société Nouvelle de Cinématographie (SNC)/Tritone Cinematografica 135 (1) Adel Productions/Marianne Productions/Mars Film (2) Euro International Film (EIA)/Les Films Corona/Selenia Cinematografica (3) Euro International Film (EIA)/Oceania Produzioni Internazionali Cinematografiche (4) Adel Productions/Lira Films/Mondial Televisione Film (5) Lira Films/Adel Productions/Nova Films/Mondial Televisione Film (6) Adel Productions (7) Adel Productions/Films A2/Sara Films (8) Vega Film/Sara Films/Canal+/Peripheria/Films A2/Centre National de la Cinématographie (CNC)/Soficas Investimages/Télévision Suisse-Romande (TSR) 136 (1) Les Films Plain Chant/Soprofilms/FR3 Films Production/Unité Trois (2) Central Cinema Company Film (CCC)/Les Films du Losange/Telmar Film International Ltd./Zespol Filmowy "Perspektywa" (3) Davis-Films/Live Entertainment/PFG Entertainment (4) MK2 Productions/France 3 Cinéma/CAB Productions (5) Castle Rock Entertainment/Detour Filmproduction/Filmhaus Wien Universa Filmproduktions (6) Warner Independent Pictures (WIP)/Castle Rock Entertainment/Detour Filmproduction (7) Polaris Film Production & Finance/Tempête Sous un Crâne/3L Filmproduktion (8) Faliro House Productions/Venture Forth/Castle Rock Entertainment/Detour Filmproduction 137 (1) Eon Productions/United Artists (2) BBC Scotland/Ecosse Films/Irish Screen/WGBH (3) Universal Pictures/Miramax/The Bedford Falls Company (4) Miramax/David Brown Productions/Fat Free (5) British Broadcasting Corporation (BBC)/Fox Iris Productions/Intermedia Films/Mirage Enterprises/Miramax (6) Fox Searchlight Pictures/DNA Films/UK Film Council/BBC Films (7) Blueprint Pictures (8) The Weinstein Company/Yucaipa Films/Pathé/BBC Films 138 (1) Parc Film/Madeleine Films/Beta Film (2) Compton Films/Tekli British Productions (3) Robert et Raymond Hakim/Paris Film Productions/Five Film (4) Madeleine Films/Parc Film (5) Les Films du Carrosse/Les Productions Artistes Associés/Produzioni Associate Delphos (6) Época Films/Talia Films/Selenia Cinematografica/Les Films Corona (7) Les Films du Carrosse/Sédif Productions/TF1 Films Production/Société Française de Production (SFP) (8) MGM/Peerford Ltd. 139 (1) T. Films/Films A2 (2) Paradis Films/La Générale d'Images/Bac Films/Orly Films/Ciné Cinq (3) Les Films Alain Sarde/TF1 Films Production/Les Films de l'Etang/Alhena Films/Angel's Company (4) Gemini Films/Gemini Films/Les Films du Lendemain/Blu Cinematografica (5) Zentropa Entertainments/Trust Film Svenska/Film i Väst/Liberator Productions (6) BIM/Canal+/Centre National de la Cinématographie (CNC)/Fidélité Productions (7) Why Not Productions/France 2 Cinéma/Wild Bunch/Bac Films (8) Mandarin Films/FOZ/France 2 Cinéma/Mars Films/Wild Bunch/Scope Pictures 140 (1) Parc Film/Madeleine Films/Beta Film (2) Compton-Tekli/Royal/The Kobal Collection (3) Paris Film/Five Film/The Kobal Collection (4) Les Films du Carrosse/Les Productions Artistes Associés/Produzioni Associate Delphos (5) Les Films du Carrosse/Sédif Productions/TF1 Films Production/Société Française de Production (SFP) (6) Paradis Films/La Générale d'Images/Bac Films/Orly Films/Ciné Cinq (7) Gemini Films/Gemini Films/Les Films du Lendemain/Blu Cinematografica (8) Mandarin Films/FOZ/France 2 Cinéma/Mars Films/Wild Bunch/Scope Pictures tl Parc Films/Madeleine Films/The Kobal Collection tr Compton-Tekli/Royal/The Kobal Collection cl Paris Film/Five Film/The Kobal Collection cr Paris Film/Five Film/The Kobal Collection bl Moviestore Collection/REX br Moviestore Collection/REX 141 tr Moviestore Collection/REX cr Paradis/General D'Images/The Kobal Collection bl Moviestore Collection/REX br Music Box Films/The Kobal Collection 142 (1) C.A.P.A.C./S.N. Prodis/Universal Pictures France (UPF) (2) Produzioni Europee Associati (PEA)/Les Productions Artistes Associés/Artemis Film (3) Les Films du Carrosse/Sédif Productions/TF1 Films Production/Société Française de Production (SFP) (4) Gaumont/TF1 Films Production (5) DD Productions/Films A2/RAI Radiotelevisione Italiana/Renn Productions/Télévision Suisse-Romande (TSR) (6) Erato Films/Films A2/Flach Film/Action Films (7) Caméra One/Centre National de la Cinématographie (CNC)/DD Productions/Films A2/Hachette Première/Investors Club/Sofinergie 1/Union Générale Cinématographique (UGC) (8) Touchstone Pictures/Australian Film Finance Corporation (AFFC)/ 143 (1) Gaumont/Légende Entreprises/France 3 Cinéma/Due West (2) Canal+/DD Productions/Film Par Film/Orly Films/Paravision International S.A./Sidonie/Sédif roductions/TF1 Films Production (3) United Artists Corporation (4) AMLF/Bavaria Entertainment/Canal+/Cecchi Gori Group Tiger Cinematografica/Centre National de la Cinématographie (CNC) (5) La Petite Reine/Remstar Productions/Novo RPI/M6 Films (6) Mandarin Films/FOZ/France 2 Cinéma/Mars Films/Wild Bunch/Scope Pictures (7) Fox 2000 Pictures/Dune Entertainment/Ingenious Media/Haishang Films (8) Belladonna Productions 144 (1) 20th Century Fox Film Corporation (2) Universal Pictures/Imagine Entertainment (3) Paramount Pictures (4) Touchstone Pictures (5) Pandora Filmproduktion/JVC Entertainment Networks/Newmarket Capital Group/12 Gauge Productions (6) Fear and Loathing LLC/Rhino Films/Shark Productions/Summit Entertainment/Universal Pictures (7) Walt Disney Pictures/Jerry Bruckheimer Films (8) Miramax/FilmColony 145 (1) Paramount Pictures (2) Bazmark Films/20th Century Fox Film Corporation (3) 20th Century Fox Film Corporation/Paramount Pictures/Lightstorm Entertainment (4) Figment Films (5) Forward Pass/Appian Way/IMF Internationale Medien und Film GmbH & Co. 3. Produktions KG (6) DreamWorks SKG/BBC Films/Evamere Entertainment/Neal Street Productions/Goldcrest Pictures (7) Warner Bros./Legendary Pictures/Syncopy (8) Paramount Pictures/Red Granite Pictures/Appian Way/Sikelia Productions/EMJAG Productions 146 (1) Universum Film (UFA) (2) Paramount Pictures (3) Dishonored (4) Paramount Pictures (5) Paramount Pictures (6) Paramount Pictures (7) Paramount Pictures (8) London Film Productions 147 (1) Universal Pictures (2) Universal Pictures (3) Paramount Pictures (4) Warner Bros. (5) Fidelity Pictures Corporation (6) Edward Small Productions (7) Universal International Pictures (UI) (8) Roxlom Films Inc. 148 (1) UFA/The Kobal Collection (2) Paramount Pictures (3) Paramount Pictures (4) Paramount Pictures (5) London Film Productions (6) Universal Pictures (7) Fidelity Pictures Corporation (8) Edward Small Productions t UFA/The Kobal Collection cl Paramount/The Kobal Collection cr Paramount/The Kobal Collection bl Paramount/The Kobal Collection br Paramount/The Kobal Collection 149 tl ITV/REX tr RKO/The Kobal Collection cl Universal/The Kobal Collection b United Artists/The Kobal Collection 150 (1) MGM (2) Universal Pictures (3) Warner Bros. (4) Vanguard Films/RKO Radio Pictures (5) Paramount Pictures (6) George Stevens Productions (7) The Mirisch Corporation (8) Scimitar Productions 151 (1) Carolco Pictures/Carolco International N.V. (2) Touchstone Pictures/Australian Film Finance Corporation (AFFC)/ (3) Gaumont/Les Films du Dauphin (4) Columbia Pictures Corporation/Los Hooligans Productions (5) Miramax/Tiger Moth Productions (6) Paramount Vantage/Miramax/Scott Rudin Productions/Mike Zoss Productions (7) Universal Pictures/Relativity Media/Forward Pass/Misher Films (8) The Weinstein Company/Columbia Pictures 152 (1) Dreamland (2) Dreamland (3) Dreamland (4) ITV/REX (5) Westdeutscher Rundfunk (WDR) (6) New Line Cinema (7) Fox Run Productions Inc. (8) New Line Cinema/Ingenious Film Partners 153 (1) Hal Wallis Productions (2) Screen Plays/Stanley Kramer Productions (3) Paramount Pictures (4) MGM (5) MGM (6) Bryna Productions (7) Bryna Productions (8) Joel Productions 154 (1) MGM (2) Columbia Pictures/IPC Films (3) Frank Yablans Presentations/20th Century Fox Film Corporation (4) 20th Century Fox Film Corporation/El Corazon Producciones S.A./Nina Saxon Film Design/SLM Production Group (5) Paramount Pictures (6) 20th Century Fox Film Corporation/American Entertainment Partners L.P. /Amercent Films (7) 20th Century Fox Film Corporation (8) Carolco Pictures/Canal+ 155 (1) Alcor Films/Canal+/Regency Enterprises/Warner Bros. (2) Warner Bros./Baltimore Pictures/Constant c Productions (3) Universal Pictures/Castle Rock Entertainment/Wildwood Enterprises/Columbia Pictures Corporation (4) Polygram Filmed Entertainment/Propaganda Films/A&B Producoes, Lda. (5) British Broadcasting Corporation (BBC)/Curtis Hanson Productions/MFF Feature Film Productions/Marubeni/Mutual Film Company/Paramount Pictures (6) The Bedford Falls Company/Compulsion Inc./Initial Entertainment Group (IEG)/Splendid Medien AG/USA Films (7) 20th Century Fox Film Corporation/Edward R. Pressman Film/Dune Entertainment/Dune Entertainment III (8) Jerry Weintraub Productions/HBO Films 156 (1) Lippert Pictures (2) Dovemead Films/Film Export A.G./International Film Production (3) Swampfilms (4) Warner Bros./The Guber-Peters Company/PolyGram Filmed Entertainment (5) Walt Disney Pictures/Touchstone Pictures/Silver Screen Partners IV/Gordon Company/Dark Horse Entertainment (6) Crowvision Inc./Edward R. Pressman Film/Entertainment Media Investment Corporation/Jeff Most Productions/Miramax (7) 20th Century Fox Film Corporation/Marvel Enterprises/Donners' Company/Bad Hat Harry Productions (8) Columbia Pictures Corporation/Marvel Enterprises/Laura Ziskin Productions 157 (1) Warner Bros./Syncopy/DC Comics/Patalex III Productions Limited (2) Paramount Pictures/Marvel Enterprises/Marvel Studios/Fairview Entertainment/Dark Blades Films (3) Marv Films/Plan B Entertainment (4) Paramount Pictures/Marvel Entertainment/Marvel Studios (5) Paramount Pictures/Marvel Entertainment/Marvel Studios (6) Columbia Pictures/Marvel Entertainment/Laura Ziskin Productions (7) Warner Bros./Legendary Pictures/Syncopy (8) Marvel Studios/Marvel Enterprises/Moving Picture Company (MPC) 158 (1) 20th Century Fox Film Corporation/Amercent Films/American Entertainment Partners L.P. (2) Carolco Pictures/Japan Satellite Broadcasting (JBS)/Canal+/RCS Video (3) Fine Line Features/Spelling Films International/Avenue Pictures Productions (4) Warner Bros./Regency Enterprises/Alcor Films/Ixtlan/New Regency Pictures/J D Productions (5) TriStar Pictures/Fried/Woods Films/Yorktown Productions (6) Mayfair Entertainment International/British Screen/Bayly/Paré Productions/United Artists Pictures/First Look International (7) New Line Cinema/Red Mullet Productions (8) British Broadcasting Corporation (BBC)/Curtis Hanson Productions/MFF Feature Film Productions/Marubeni/Mutual Film Company/Paramount Pictures/Scott Rudin Productions/Tele München Fernseh Produktionsgesellschaft (TMG)/Toho-Towa 159 (1) Warner Bros./Silver Pictures (2) Warner Independent Pictures (WIP)/2929 Productions/Participant Media (3) Warner Independent Pictures (WIP)/Thousand Words/Section Eight/Detour Filmproduction/3 Arts Entertainment (4) Paramount Pictures/Warner Bros./Phoenix Pictures (5) DreamWorks SKG/Red Hour Films (6) Paramount Pictures/Marvel Enterprises/Marvel Studios (7) Warner Bros./Village Roadshow Pictures/Silver Pictures/Wigram Productions/Internationale Filmproduktion Blackbird Dritte (8) Marvel Studios/Paramount Pictures 160 (1) Universal Pictures/Lucasfilm/The Coppola Company (2) American International Pictures (AIP) (3) Astral Bellevue Pathé/Canadian Film Development Corporation (CFDC)/Duddy Kravitz Syndicate/Famous Players/International Cinemedia Center/United Welco (4) Zanuck/Brown Productions/Universal Pictures (5) Warner Bros /The Kobal Collection (6) Warner Bros./MGM/Rastar Pictures (7) Columbia Pictures Corporation/EMI Films/Julia Phillips and Michael Phillips Productions (8) MGM/SLM Production Group 161 (1) Touchstone Pictures/Silver Screen Partners II (2) Bandai Films/Silver Screen Partners III/Touchstone Pictures (3) Touchstone Pictures/Silver Screen Partners II/Cinderella (4) Universal Pictures/United Artists/Amblin Entertainment/U-Drive Productions (5) Touchstone Pictures/Touchwood Pacific Partners 1 (6) Hollywood Pictures/Interscope Communications/Polygram Filmed Entertainment/The Charlie Mopic Company (7) Universal Pictures/Castle Rock Entertainment/Wildwood Enterprises/Columbia Pictures Corporation (8) Summit Entertainment/Di Bonaventura Pictures/DC Entertainment 162 (1) Otto Preminger Films (2) Warner Brothers/Seven Arts/Tatira-Hiller Productions (3) United Artists/Irish DreamTime/MGM (4) Universal Pictures (5) Cinema Center Films/Stockbridge-Hiller Productions (6) Film Trust S.A./Este Films (7) Paramount Pictures/Penthouse/Long Road Productions (8) Warner Bros./20th Century Fox Film Corporation/Irwin Allen Productions/United Films 163 (1) Wildwood Enterprises/Dino De Laurentiis Company (2) MGM/United Artists (3) Columbia Pictures Corporation (4) Paramount Pictures (5) Golan-Globus Productions/Zoetrope Studios (6) Bioskop Film/Cinecom Entertainment Group/Cinétudes Films/Daniel Wilson Productions Inc./Master Partners/Odyssey (7) HBO Pictures/Marvin Worth Productions/Citadel Entertainment/Kahn Power Pictures/Gia Productions (8) Miramax/Industry Entertainment 164 (1) First National Pictures (2) 20th Century Fox Film Corporation (3) Columbia Pictures Corporation (4) Universal International Pictures (UI) (5) The Mirisch Corporation (6) Warner Bros./The Malpaso Company (7) Artists Entertainment Complex/Produzioni De Laurentiis International Manufacturing Company (8) Paramount Pictures/Eddie Murphy Productions 165 (1) Lightning Precision Films/Precision Films/Mack-Taylor Productions/Vestron Pictures (2) Bad Lt. Productions (3) Cecchi Gori Pictures/Juno Pix/New Line Cinema (4) PolyGram Filmed Entertainment/Working Title Films (5) Warner Bros./Village Roadshow Pictures/NPV Entertainment/Outlaw Productions (I)/WV Films II (6) Paramount Pictures/Lions Gate Films/Cruise/Wagner Productions (7) Paramount Vantage/Miramax/Scott Rudin Productions/Mike Zoss Productions (8) Screen Gems/Overbrook Entertainment 166 (1) Jolly Film/Constantin Film Produktion/Ocean Films (2) Produzioni Europee Associati (PEA)/Arturo González Producciones Cinematográficas, S.A/Constantin Film Produktion/United Artists (3) Universal Pictures/The Malpaso Company (4) Universal Pictures/The Malpaso Company (5) Warner Bros./The Malpaso Company (6) Universal Pictures/The Malpaso Company (7) Warner Bros./The Malpaso Company (8) Paramount Pictures/The Malpaso Company 167 (1) The Malpaso Company/Warner Bros. (2) Malpaso Productions/Rastar Pictures/Warner Bros. (3) Warner Bros./Malpaso Productions (4) Columbia Pictures Corporation/Castle Rock Entertainment (5) Warner Bros./Amblin Entertainment/Malpaso Productions (6) Castle Rock Entertainment/Malpaso Productions (7) Million Dollar Baby/Lakeshore Entertainment/Malpaso Productions/Albert S. Ruddy Productions/Epsilon Motion Pictures (8) Matten Productions/Double Nickel Entertainment/Gerber Pictures/Malpaso Productions/Village Roadshow Pictures/WV Films IV/Warner Bros. 168 (1) Jolly Film/Constantin Film Produktion/Ocean Films (2) Produzioni Europee Associati (PEA)/Arturo González Producciones Cinematográficas, S.A/Constantin Film Produktion/United Artists (3) Universal Pictures/The Malpaso Company (4) Warner Bros./The Malpaso Company (5) Paramount Pictures/The Malpaso Company (6) Warner Bros./Malpaso Productions (7) Million Dollar Baby/Lakeshore Entertainment/Malpaso Productions/Albert S. Ruddy Productions/Epsilon Motion Pictures (8) Matten Productions/Double Nickel Entertainment/Gerber Pictures/Malpaso Productions/Village Roadshow Pictures/WV Films IV/Warner Bros. tl Jolly/Constantin/Ocean/The Kobal Collection tr P.E.A/The Kobal Collection c P.E.A/The Kobal Collection bl Universal/The Kobal Collection br Warner Bros/The Kobal Collection 169 tl Paramount/Malpaso/The Kobal Collection tr Warner Bros/The Kobal Collection cl Warner Bros./The Kobal Collection br Warner Bros/The Kobal Collection 170 (1) William Castle Productions (2) Paramount Pictures/Newdon Productions (3) EMI Films/Mersham Productions Ltd. (4) Orion Pictures (5) Orion Pictures (6) Orion Pictures/Jack Rollins & Charles H. Joffe Productions (7) TriStar Pictures (8) 20th Century Fox Film Corporation/20th Century-Fox Productions/Mace Neufeld Productions 171 (1) Film4/Channel Four Film (2) BBC Films/UK Film Council (3) Universal Pictures/The Weinstein Company/A Band Apart (4) See-Saw Films/Film4/UK Film Council (5) Recorded Picture Company (RPC)/Lago Film/Prospero Pictures (6) 20th Century Fox/Dune Entertainment/Scott Free Productions/Brandywine Productions (7) Regency Enterprises/River Road Entertainment/Plan B Entertainment/New Regency Pictures/Film4 (8) Runaway Fridge Productions/Element Pictures/Film4/Indieproduction 172 (1) Allarts/Union Générale Cinématographique (UGC)/La Sept (2) Universal Pictures/Amblin Entertainment (3) Baltimore Pictures/Hollywood Pictures/Wildwood Enterprises (4) Lightstorm Entertainment (5) Miramax/Tiger Moth Productions (6) Columbia Pictures Corporation (7) DNA Films/Ingenious Film Partners/Moving Picture Company (MPC)/UK Film Council (8) Odeon Films/Capitol Films/Artists Independent Network 173 (1) Focus Features/UK Film Council/Potboiler Productions (2) Paramount Vantage/Pathé/BBC Films (3) The Weinstein Company/Mirage Enterprises/Studio Babelsberg (4) Blueprint Pictures/Focus Features/Scion Films (5) Warner Bros./Heyday Films/Moving Picture Company (MPC) (6) Hermetof Pictures/Magna Films/Icon Entertainment International (7) BBC Films/Headline Pictures/Magnolia Mae Films/Taeoo Entertainment (8) Fox Searchlight Pictures/Indian Paintbrush/Studio Babelsberg 174 (1) Goldcrest Films International/National Film Finance Corporation (NFFC) (2) Channel Four Films/Euston Films/PfH Ltd. (3) British Broadcasting Corporation (BBC)/British Screen Finance Ltd./CiBy 2000/European Co-production Fund (4) Universal Pictures/Miramax/The Bedford Falls Company (5) Miramax/Universal Pictures/StudioCanal/Working Title Films/Little Bird (6) Archer Street Productions/Delux Productions/Pathé Pictures International/Film Fund Luxembourg/UK Film Council/Wild Bear Films (7) Fade to Black Productions/Depth of Field/Artina Films (8) The Weinstein Company/UK Film Council 175 (1) Warner Bros. (2) Warner Bros. (3) Warner Bros. (4) Warner Bros. (5) Warner Bros. (6) Warner Bros. (7) Warner Bros. (8) Warner Bros. 176 (1) MGM (2) Gainsborough Pictures (3) 20th Century Fox Film Corporation (4) Warner Bros. (5) Screen Plays/Stanley Kramer Productions (6) The Mirisch Corporation (7) British Lion Film Corporation/Quintra (8) Warner Brothers/Seven Arts/Tatira-Hiller Productions 177 (1) Columbia Pictures Corporation/Pando Company Inc./Raybert Productions (2) Warner Bros./Gus Productions (3) De Laurentiis Entertainment Group (DEG) (4) 20th Century Fox Film Corporation/American Entertainment Partners L.P./Amercent Films (5) Carolco Pictures (6) Spelling-Goldberg Productions (7) Slough Pond/TwoPoundBag Productions/double A Films (8) Focus Features/River Road Entertainment/Alberta Film Entertainment/Good Machine 178 (1) Fox Film Corporation (2) Walter Wanger Productions (3) Warner Bros. (4) 20th Century Fox Film Corporation (5) The Grapes of Wrath (6) 20th Century Fox Film Corporation (7) 20th Century Fox Film Corporation (8) 20th Century Fox Film Corporation 179 (1) Warner Bros./Orange (2) Orion-Nova Productions (3) Otto Preminger Films/Alpha Alpina (4) Columbia Pictures Corporation (5) Rafran Cinematografica/Finanzia San Marco/Paramount Pictures (6) Rafran Cinematografica/Les Films Jacques Leitienne/Imp.Ex.Ci./Alcinter/Rialto Film Preben-Philipsen (7) Warner Bros. (8) IPC Films/Incorporated Television Company (ITC) 180 (1) MGM/Seven Arts Pictures (2) Columbia Pictures Corporation/Harold Hecht Productions (3) Paramount Pictures/Hal Wallis Productions/Nancy Enterprises Inc. (I) (4) American Broadcasting Company (ABC)/Palomar Pictures (I) (5) Dino de Laurentiis Cinematografica/Marianne Productions (6) Warner Bros./Gus Productions (7) Anouchka Films/Vieco Films/Empire Films (8) 20th Century Fox Film Corporation 181 (1) Columbia Pictures Corporation (2) Jerome Hellman Productions/Jayne Productions Inc. (3) Columbia Pictures/IPC Films (4) IPC Films/20th Century Fox Film Corporation (5) IPC Films/Incorporated Television Company (ITC) (6) American Filmworks/Lorimar Productions (7) MGM/Lantana/Star Partners II Ltd. (8) New Line Cinema/BenderSpink/Spring Creek Productions/Kumar Mobiliengesellschaft mbH & Co. Projekt Nr. 1 KG 182 (1) RKO Radio Pictures (2) RKO Radio Pictures (3) MGM (4) Selznick International Pictures (5) RKO Radio Pictures (6) Warner Bros. (7) 20th Century Fox Film Corporation (8) Rampart Productions (I) 183 (1) Universal Pictures/Lucasfilm/The Coppola Company (2) Lucasfilm/20th Century Fox Film Corporation (3) Paramount Pictures/Lucasfilm (4) The Ladd Company/Shaw Brothers/Warner Bros./Blade Runner Partnership (5) Paramount Pictures/Edward S. Feldman Production (6) Mace Neufeld Productions/Paramount Pictures (7) Warner Bros. (8) First Light Production/IMF Internationale Medien und Film GmbH & Co. 2. Produktions KG/Intermedia Films/K-19 Film Production/National Geographic Society/New Regency Pictures/Palomar Pictures (II) 184 (1) Walt Disney Productions (2) Columbia Pictures Corporation/Bill/Phillips/Italo/Judeo Productions (3) Walt Disney Productions (4) The Rank Organisation/Goodtimes Enterprises/Bugsy Malone Productions (5) Paramount Pictures (6) Strong Heart/Demme Production/Orion Pictures (7) Canal+/Regency Enterprises/Alcor Films (8) Egg Pictures/PolyGram Filmed Entertainment/20th Century Fox Film Corporation 185 (1) Warner Bros./South Side Amusement Company (2) Fox 2000 Pictures/Lawrence Bender Productions (3) Columbia Pictures Corporation/Hofflund/Polone/Indelible Pictures (4) Touchstone Pictures/Imagine Entertainment (5) Universal Pictures/Imagine Entertainment/40 Acres & A Mule Filmworks/GH Two (6) Warner Bros./Village Roadshow Pictures/Silver Pictures (7) SBS Productions/Constantin Film Produktion/SPI Film Studio/Versátil Cinema/Zanagar Films/France 2 Cinéma (8) TriStar Pictures/Media Rights Capital/QED International/Genre Films/Sony Pictures Entertainment (SPE) 186 (1) The Rank Organisation/Goodtimes Enterprises/Bugsy Malone Productions (2) Columbia Pictures Corporation/Bill/Phillips/Italo/Judeo Productions (3) Paramount Pictures (4) Strong Heart/Demme Production/Orion Pictures (5) Fox 2000 Pictures/Lawrence Bender Productions (6) Columbia Pictures Corporation/Hofflund/Polone/Indelible Pictures (7) Warner Bros./Village Roadshow Pictures/Silver Pictures (8) SBS Productions/Constantin Film Produktion/SPI Film Studio/Versátil Cinema/Zanagar Films/France 2 Cinéma tl ITV/REX tr Columbia/The Kobal Collection cl Columbia/The Kobal Collection cl Columbia/The Kobal Collection cr Paramount/The Kobal Collection b Orion/The Kobal Collection 187 tr Orion/The Kobal Collection cl 20th Century Fox/The Kobal Collection cr Columbia/The Kobal Collection bl ITV/REX br SBS Productions/The Kobal Collection 188 (1) Warner Bros./Ixtlan/Donners' Company (2) Paramount Pictures/DreamWorks SKG/Parkes+MacDonald Image Nation/Edge City (3) Universal Pictures/Bristol Bay Productions/Anvil Films/Baldwin Entertainment Group (4) Universal Pictures/Red Wagon Entertainment/Neal Street Productions/Motion Picture KAPPA Produktionsgesellschaft (5) DreamWorks SKG/Paramount Pictures/Laurence Mark Productions (6) Universal Pictures/Relativity Media/Forward Pass/FilmWorks/MDBF Zweite Filmgesellschaft/thinkfilm (7) The Weinstein Company/Columbia Pictures (8) Marvel Enterprises/Avi Arad Productions/Columbia Pictures/Matt Tolmach Productions 189 (1) Columbia Pictures Corporation/Marvel Enterprises/Laura Ziskin Productions (2) Focus Features/Axon Films/Groundswell Productions/Jinks/Cohen Company/Cinema Vehicle Services (3) Fox Searchlight Pictures/Pathé/Everest Entertainment/Cloud Eight Films/Decibel Films/Darlow Smithson Productions/Dune Entertainment/Big Screen Productions/Warner Bros. (4) Werc Werk Works/Telling Pictures/RabbitBandini Productions/Radiant Cool (5) 20th Century Fox Film Corporation/Dune Entertainment/Chernin Entertainment/Ingenious Media/Big Screen Productions/Ingenious Film Partners (6) Columbia Pictures/Point Grey Pictures/Mandate Pictures (7) RabbitBandini Productions (8) Columbia Pictures/LStar Capital/Point Grey Pictures 190 (1) Equine Productions (2) 20th Century Fox Film Corporation (3) Golan-Globus Productions (4) Zanuck Company/Majestic Films International (5) Norman Twain Productions/Warner Bros. (6) TriStar Pictures/Freddie Fields Productions (7) Warner Bros./Morgan Creek Productions (8) Warner Bros./Malpaso Productions 191 (1) Castle Rock Entertainment (2) Cecchi Gori Pictures/Juno Pix/New Line Cinema (3) Paramount Pictures/DreamWorks SKG/Zanuck/Brown Productions/Manhattan Project (4) Warner Bros./Lakeshore Entertainment/Malpaso Productions/Albert S. Ruddy Productions (5) Warner Bros./Syncopy/DC Comics/Legendary Pictures/Patalex III Productions Limited (6) LivePlanet/Miramax/Ladd Company, The (7) Warner Bros./Spyglass Entertainment/Revelations Entertainment/Malpaso Productions/Liberty Pictures (8) Canal+/Ciné+/EuropaCorp/TF1 Films Production 192 (1) Golan-Globus Productions (2) Zanuck Company/Majestic Films International (3) Norman Twain Productions/Warner Bros. (4) Castle Rock Entertainment (5) Cecchi Gori Pictures/Juno Pix/New Line Cinema (6) Warner Bros./Lakeshore Entertainment/Malpaso Productions/Albert S. Ruddy Productions (7) Warner Bros./Syncopy/DC Comics/Legendary Pictures/Patalex III Productions Limited (8) Warner Bros./Spyglass Entertainment/Revelations Entertainment/Malpaso Productions/Liberty Pictures tl Cannon/The Kobal Collection tr Warner Bros/The Kobal Collection cl Warner Bros/The Kobal Collection cr Castle Rock Entertainment/The Kobal Collection bl Castle Rock Entertainment/The Kobal Collection br New Line/The Kobal Collection 193 tc Warner Bros./The Kobal Collection tr Warner Bros/DC Comics/The Kobal Collection cr Warner Bros /The Kobal Collection br Warner Bros /The Kobal Collection 194 (1) Ciné-Arys (2) Films Albatros (3) Paris Film (4) Réalisation d'art cinématographique (5) Ciné-Alliance (6) Paris Film (7) Productions Sigma (8) 20th Century Fox Film Corporation 195 (1) Films Sacha Gordine (2) Compagnie Commerciale Française Cinématographique/Stera Films (3) Del Duca Films/Antares Produzione Cinematografica (4) Franco London Films/Jolly Film (5) Continental Produzione/Franco London Films (6) Intermondia Films/Jolly Film (7) Union Cinématographique Lyonnaise/Iéna Productions/CEI Incom (8) Filmsonor/Intermondia Films/Cinétel/Vides Cinematografica 196 (1) MGM (2) MGM (3) MGM (4) Columbia Pictures Corporation (5) MGM (6) MGM (7) MGM (8) MGM 197 (1) Selznick International Pictures/MGM (2) MGM (3) MGM (4) MGM (5) 20th Century Fox Film Corporation (6) Hill-Hecht-Lancaster Productions/Jeffrey Pictures Corp. (7) Capri Productions/Paramount Pictures (8) Seven Arts Pictures 198 (1) Svensk Filmindustri (2) MGM (3) Sofar-Film (4) MGM (6) MGM (5) MGM (7) MGM (8) MGM 199 (1) MGM (2) MGM (3) MGM (4) MGM (5) MGM (6) MGM (7) MGM (8) MGM 200 (1) MGM (2) MGM (3) MGM (4) MGM (5) MGM (6) MGM (7) MGM (8) MGM tl Svensk Filmindustri/The Kobal Collection tr MGM/The Kobal Collection cl MGM/The Kobal Collection cr MGM/The Kobal Collection b MGM/The Kobal Collection 201 t MGM/The Kobal Collection cl MGM/The Kobal Collection cr MGM/The Kobal Collection bl MGM/The Kobal Collection br MGM/The

Kobal Collection **202 (1)** Nero Films **(2)** Mark Hellinger Productions/Universal Pictures **(3)** MGM **(4)** MGM **(5)** Dorkay Productions/Romulus Films **(6)** MGM **(7)** 20th Century Fox Film Corporation **(8)** MGM **203 (1)** MGM **(2)** Figaro/Transoceanic Film **(3)** MGM **(4)** 20th Century Fox Film Corporation **(5)** Stanley Kramer Productions **(6)** Seven Arts Pictures/Joel Productions **(7)** MGM/Seven Arts Pictures **(8)** Universal Pictures/The Filmakers Group **204 (1)** MGM **(2)** MGM **(3)** MGM **(4)** MGM **(5)** MGM **(6)** MGM **(7)** MGM **(8)** MGM **205 (1)** MGM **(2)** MGM **(3)** MGM **(4)** MGM **(5)** Transcona Enterprises/Warner Bros. **(6)** Roxlom Films Inc. **(7)** Stanley Kramer Productions **(8)** Barbican Films **206 (1)** Paramount Pictures **(2)** Paramount Pictures **(3)** Paramount Pictures **(4)** Lorimar Film Entertainment/Paramount Pictures **(5)** Breathless Associates/Miko Productions **(6)** Touchstone Pictures/Silver Screen Partners IV **(7)** Miramax/Producers Circle/Storyline Entertainment/Kalis Productions GmbH & Co. KG **(8)** Killer Films/John Wells Productions/John Goldwyn Productions/Endgame Entertainment/Dreamachine/Film & Entertainment VIP Medienfonds 4 GmbH & Co. KG/Grey Water Park Productions/Rising Star/Wells Productions **207 (1)** Kennedy Miller Productions/Crossroads/Mad Max Films **(2)** Australian Film Commission, The/R & R Films **(3)** Warner Bros./Silver Pictures **(4)** Icon Entertainment International **(5)** Icon Entertainment International/Ladd Company, The/B.H. Finance C.V. **(6)** Touchstone Pictures/Imagine Entertainment/Ransom Productions **(7)** Icon Entertainment International **(8)** Summit Entertainment/Participant Media/Imagenation Abu Dhabi FZ/Anonymous Content **208 (1)** Commonwealth United Entertainment **(2)** Woodfall Film Productions **(3)** Accord Productions **(4)** Action Films/Société Française de Production/France 3/Citel Films **(5)** Brooksfilms **(6)** Orion Pictures **(7)** Pressman Productions/RKO Pictures **(8)** Allarts/Cinéa/Caméra One/Penta Film/Elsevier-Vendex Film Beheer/Channel 4 International/Vrijzinnig Protestantse Radio Omroep/Canal+/NHK **209 (1)** David W. Griffith Corp./Epoch Producing Corporation **(2)** D.W. Griffith Productions **(3)** D.W. Griffith Productions **(4)** D.W. Griffith Productions **(5)** MGM **(6)** MGM **(7)** Paul Gregory Productions **(8)** Nelson Entertainment **210 (1)** Dino De Laurentiis Company/Paramount Pictures **(2)** Columbia Pictures Corporation/Carson Productions **(3)** Universal Pictures **(4)** SLM Production Group/Brooksfilms **(5)** London Weekend Television/Virgin Vision/Working Title Films **(6)** Universal Pictures/Amblin Entertainment **(7)** 20th Century Fox Film Corporation/Centropolis Entertainment **(8)** Film4/Free Range Films/Le Bureau **211 (1)** Fuller Films/Seven Arts Pictures **(2)** New Line Cinema/Gran Via **(3)** Hunting Lane Films/Journeyman Pictures/Silverwood Films/Original Media/Traction Media/Verisimilitude **(4)** MGM/Sidney Kimmel Entertainment/Lars Productions **(5)** Incentive Filmed Entertainment/Silverwood Films/Hunting Lane Films/Chrysler Corporation/Shade Pictures/Motel Movies/Cottage Industries **(6)** Carousel Productions **(7)** FilmDistrict/Bold Films/OddLot Entertainment/Marc Platt Productions/Motel Movies/Newbridge Film Capital **(8)** Sidney Kimmel Entertainment/Electric City Entertainment/Verisimilitude **212 (1)** MGM **(2)** D.W. Griffith Productions **(3)** Charles Chaplin Productions **(4)** MGM **(5)** Liberty Films **(6)** MGM **(7)** Lawrence Turman **(8)** 20th Century Fox Film Corporation/Campanile Productions/Newman-Foreman Company **213 (1)** Jack Rollins & Charles H. Joffe Productions **(2)** Warner Bros./Hawk Films/Peregrine/Producers Circle **(3)** Warner Bros./Regency Enterprises/Forward Pass/Art Linson Productions/Monarchy Enterprises B.V. **(4)** Warner Bros./Village Roadshow Pictures/NPV Entertainment/Outlaw Productions/WV Films II **(5)** Warner Bros./Village Roadshow Pictures/NPV Entertainment/Jerry Weintraub Productions/Section Eight/WV Films II **(6)** Mega Bollywood **(7)** Fade to Black Productions/Depth of Field/Artina Films **(8)** FilmDistrict/Bold Films/OddLot Entertainment/Marc Platt Productions/Motel Movies/Newbridge Film Capital **214 (1)** Paramount Pictures **(2)** RKO Radio Pictures **(3)** Columbia Pictures Corporation **(4)** RKO Radio Pictures **(5)** RKO Radio Pictures **(6)** Columbia Pictures Corporation **(7)** Columbia Pictures Corporation **(8)** MGM/Loew's **215 (1)** Columbia Pictures Corporation **(2)** RKO Radio Pictures **(3)** RKO Radio Pictures **(4)** Vanguard Films/RKO Radio Pictures **(5)** 20th Century Fox Film Corporation **(6)** 20th Century Fox Film Corporation **(7)** MGM **(8)** Stanley Donen Films **216 tl** RKO/The Kobal Collection **tr** RKO/The Kobal Collection **cl** Columbia/The Kobal Collection **cr** Columbia/The Kobal Collection **bl** RKO/The Kobal Collection **br** RKO/The Kobal Collection **217 tl** 20th Century Fox/The Kobal Collection **tr** 20th Century Fox/The Kobal Collection **cl** 20th Century Fox/The Kobal Collection **br** MGM/The Kobal Collection **218 (1)** Merchant Ivory Productions/Cinecom Pictures/Film Four International **(2)** PolyGram Filmed Entertainment/Channel Four Films/Working Title Films **(3)** Columbia Pictures Corporation/Mirage Enterprises **(4)** Polygram Filmed Entertainment/Working Title Films/Bookshop Productions/Notting Hill Pictures **(5)** Miramax/Universal Pictures/StudioCanal/Working Title Films/Little Bird **(6)** Universal Pictures/StudioCanal/Tribeca Productions/Working Title Films/Cinema Vehicle Services **(7)** Universal Pictures/StudioCanal/Working Title Films/DNA Films **(8)** Castle Rock Entertainment/Village Roadshow Pictures/Reserve Room/Flower Films (II) **219 (1)** Balatbat Productions/New World Pictures **(2)** American International Pictures/Four Associates Ltd. **(3)** American International Pictures **(4)** American International Pictures **(5)** Po' Boy Productions **(6)** Tim Burton Productions/Warner Bros. **(7)** Miramax/A Band Apart/Lawrence Bender Productions/Mighty Mighty Afrodite Productions **(8)** Universal Pictures/Vendome Pictures/Playtone Productions **220 (1)** Cineguild **(2)** Cineguild **(3)** Ealing Studios **(4)** Ealing Studios **(5)** J. Arthur Rank Organisation/Ealing Studios **(6)** Facet Productions **(7)** The Rank Organisation/Ealing Studios **(8)** Columbia Pictures Corporation/Horizon Pictures (II) **221 (1)** Knightsbridge Films **(2)** Kingsmead Productions/Columbia Pictures Corporation **(3)** Knightsbridge Films **(4)** Horizon Pictures (II) **(5)** MGM/Carlo Ponti Production/Sostar S.A **(6)** The Rank Organisation/Ivan Foxwell Productions **(7)** Lucasfilm/20th Century Fox Film Corporation **(8)** Sands/Sands Films **222 (1)** Pandora Cinema/Flower Films (II)/Adam Fields Productions/Gaylord Films **(2)** 20th Century Fox Film Corporation/Centropolis Entertainment/Lions Gate Films/Mark Gordon Productions/Mel's Cite du Cinema **(3)** Focus Features/River Road Entertainment/Alberta Film Entertainment/Good Machine **(4)** Universal Pictures/Red Wagon Entertainment/Neal Street Productions/Motion Picture KAPPA Produktionsgesellschaft **(5)** Paramount Pictures/Warner Bros./Phoenix Pictures **(6)** Vendome Pictures/The Mark Gordon Company/Mel's Cite du Cinema **(7)** Exclusive Media Group/Emmett/Furla Films/Hedge Fund Film Partners/Le Grisbi Productions/Crave Films/5150 Action/Knightsbridge Entertainment **(8)** Bold Films/Sierra/Affinity/Nightcrawler **223 (1)** Pandora Cinema/Flower Films (II)/Adam Fields Productions/Gaylord Films **(2)** Slough Pond/TwoPoundBag Productions/double A Films **(3)** IFC Films/Springall Pictures/Blue Magic Pictures **(4)** Big Beach Films/Elevation Filmworks/Red Envelope Entertainment **(5)** Paramount Pictures/Double Feature Films/Intermedia Films/Ixtlan/Kernos Filmproduktionsgesellschaft & Company/Saturn Films **(6)** Warner Bros./Legendary Pictures/Syncopy/DC Comics **(7)** Fox Searchlight Pictures/Informant Media/Butcher's Run Films **(8)** Informant Media/Forthcoming Productions/Beachfront Films/Chimera Films LLC/by alternative pictures/Delux Productions/Arte France Cinéma/Tatfilm/Silver Reel/Lankn Media/The UK Film & TV Production Company PLC/Film Fund Luxembourg/WDR/Arte/Canal+/CinéCinéma **224 (1)** Columbia Pictures Corporation **(2)** Warner Brothers/Seven Arts/Tatira-Hiller Productions **(3)** Wildwood/Wildwood Enterprises **(4)** D'Antoni Productions/Schine-Moore Productions **(5)** 20th Century Fox Film Corporation/Kent Productions **(6)** Warner Bros. **(7)** The Directors Company/The Coppola Company/American Zoetrope/Paramount Pictures **(8)** Warner Bros. **225 (1)** Dovemead Films/Film Export A.G./International Film Production **(2)** Orion Pictures **(3)** Warner Bros./Malpaso Productions **(4)** Hollywood Pictures/Don Simpson/Jerry Bruckheimer Films **(5)** MGM/Jersey Films **(6)** Touchstone Pictures/Jerry Bruckheimer Films/Don Simpson/Jerry Bruckheimer Films/Scott Free Productions/No Such Productions **(7)** Touchstone Pictures/American Empirical Pictures **(8)** Morgan Creek Productions/Franchise Pictures/Indelible Pictures **226 (1)** Touchstone Pictures **(2)** Columbia Pictures Corporation/Fogwood/IndieProd Company Productions **(3)** American Entertainment Partners II L.P./Gracie Films/20th Century Fox Film Corporation **(4)** Columbia Pictures Corporation/Parkway Productions **(5)** TriStar Pictures/Clinica Estetico **(6)** TriStar Pictures **(7)** Paramount Pictures **(8)** Universal Pictures/Imagine Entertainment **227 (1)** Pixar Animation Studios/Walt Disney Pictures **(2)** DreamWorks SKG/Paramount Pictures/Amblin Entertainment/Mutual Film Company/Mark Gordon Productions **(3)** 20th Century Fox Film Corporation/DreamWorks SKG/ImageMovers/Playtone **(4)** DreamWorks SKG/20th Century Fox Film Corporation/The Zanuck Company **(5)** Columbia Pictures/Imagine Entertainment/Skylark Productions/Government of Malta **(6)** Cloud Atlas Productions/X-Filme Creative Pool/Anarchos Pictures/A Company Filmproduktionsgesellschaft/ARD Degeto Film/Ascension Pictures/Dreams of Dragon Picture/Five Drops/Media Asia Group **(7)** Scott Rudin Productions/Michael De Luca Productions/Trigger Street Productions **(8)** Walt Disney Pictures/Ruby Films/Essential Media & Entertainment **228 (1)** Dr. Arnold Fanck-Film/Berlin, J.O. Studios/Nikkatsu/Towa Shoji-Film **(2)** Toho Company **(3)** Shôchiku Eiga **(4)** Shôchiku Eiga **(5)** Toho Company **(6)** Shôchiku Eiga **(7)** Toho Company **(8)** Toho Company/Takarazaka Productions **229 (1)** Sony Pictures Classics/Marv Films **(2)** Vertigo Films/Aramid Entertainment Fund/ Str8jacket Creations/EM Media/4DH Films/Perfume Films **(3)** Warner Bros./Legendary Pictures/Syncopy **(4)** Lionsgate/Mimran Schur Pictures/Solaris/Filmtribe **(5)** The Weinstein Company/Yucaipa Films/Revolt Films/Benaroya Pictures/Annapurna Pictures/Red Wagon Entertainment/Blum Hanson Allen Films /v **(6)** Warner Bros./Legendary Pictures/DC Entertainment/Syncopy **(7)** IM Global/Shoebox Films **(8)** Kennedy Miller Productions/Village Roadshow Pictures/Village Roadshow Pictures **230 (1)** The Caddo Company **(2)** MGM **(3)** Columbia Pictures Corporation **(4)** MGM **(5)** MGM **(6)** MGM **(7)** MGM **(8)** MGM **231 (1)** Walt Disney Pictures/BrownHouse Productions/Bottom of the Ninth Productions **(2)** Focus Features/River Road Entertainment/Alberta Film Entertainment/Good Machine **(3)** Fox 2000 Pictures/Dune Entertainment/Major Studio Partners/Peninsula Films/20th Century Fox Film Corporation **(4)** Armian Pictures/Clinica Estetico/Marc Platt Productions **(5)** Fox 2000 Pictures/Regency Enterprises/New Regency Pictures/Stuber Productions/The Bedford Falls Company/Dune Entertainment **(6)** Walt Disney Pictures/Roth Films/Team Todd/The Zanuck Company/Tim Burton Productions **(7)** Universal Pictures/Relativity Media/Working Title Films/Cameron Mackintosh Ltd. **(8)** Paramount Pictures/Warner Bros./Legendary Pictures/Lynda Obst Productions/Syncopy **232 (1)** Paramount Pictures **(2)** Touchstone Pictures/Silver Screen Partners IV **(3)** Castle Rock Entertainment/Detour Filmproduction/Filmhaus Wien Universa Filmproduktions/Sunrise Production/Columbia Pictures Corporation **(4)** Columbia Pictures Corporation/Jersey Films **(5)** Warner Bros./Village Roadshow Pictures/NPV Entertainment/Outlaw Productions (I)/WV Films II **(6)** Warner Independent Pictures/Castle Rock Entertainment/Detour Filmproduction **(7)** Capitol Films/Funky Buddha Productions/Unity Productions/Linsefilm/Michael Cerenzie Productions **(8)** IFC Productions/Detour Filmproduction **233 (1)** Columbia Pictures Corporation/Frankovich Productions **(2)** Charter Film Productions/Ascot Productions/Frankovich Productions **(3)** Universal Pictures/Zanuck/Brown Productions **(4)** Persky-Bright/Vista/Columbia Pictures Corporation/Rubeeker Films **(5)** Warner Bros. **(6)** Hawn/Sylbert Movie Company/MGM/Star Partners **(7)** Paramount Pictures **(8)** Miramax/Buena Vista Pictures/Magnolia Productions/Sweetland Films **234 (1)** Columbia Pictures Corporation/Los Hooligans Productions **(2)** Dimension Films/Los Hooligans Productions **(3)** Peters Entertainment/Sonnenfeld Josephson Worldwide Entertainment/Todman, Simon, LeMasters Productions/Warner Bros. **(4)** Handprint Entertainment/Lions Gate Films/Miramax/Ventanarosa Productions **(5)** Columbia Pictures Corporation/Dimension Films/Troublemaker Studios **(6)** Columbia Pictures/Relativity Media/Happy Madison Productions **(7)** Ixtlan/Onda Entertainment/Relativity Media **(8)** PalmStar Media/Southpaw Entertainment (I)/Irish DreamTime/Das Films/Envision Entertainment/Knightsbridge Entertainment/Landafar Entertainment/Landafar **235 (1)** Columbia Pictures Corporation **(2)** Columbia Pictures Corporation **(3)** Warner Bros. **(4)** Columbia Pictures Corporation **(5)** Columbia Pictures Corporation **(6)** Columbia Pictures Corporation **(7)** Columbia Pictures Corporation/Mercury Productions **(8)** Columbia Pictures Corporation/The Beckworth Corporation **236 (1)** Ealing Studios **(2)** Paramount Pictures **(3)** Paramount Pictures **(4)** Ponti-De Laurentiis Cinematografica/Paramount Pictures **(5)** Billy Wilder Productions **(6)** Paramount Pictures **(7)** Warner Bros. **(8)** Hill-Hecht-Lancaster Productions **237 (1)** Paramount/The Kobal Collection **(2)** The Mirisch Corporation **(3)** Universal/The Kobal Collection **(4)** Warner Bros. **(5)** Paramount Pictures **(6)** Stanley Donen Films **(7)** Columbia Pictures Corporation/Rastar Pictures **(8)** Universal Pictures/United Artists/Amblin Entertainment/U-Drive Productions **238 tl** Paramount/The Kobal Collection **tr** Paramount/The Kobal Collection **c** Paramount/The Kobal Collection **bl** Paramount/The Kobal Collection **br** Paramount/The Kobal Collection **239 tl** Paramount/The Kobal Collection **tr** Paramount/The Kobal Collection **cl** Paramount/The Kobal Collection **cr** Universal/The Kobal Collection **bl** Warner Bros/The Kobal Collection **br** 20th Century Fox/The Kobal Collection **240 (1)** RKO Radio Pictures **(2)** RKO Radio Pictures **(3)** RKO Radio Pictures **(4)** RKO Radio Pictures **(5)** RKO Radio Pictures **(6)** MGM/Loew's **(7)** MGM **(8)** MGM **241 (1)** Romulus Films/Horizon Pictures **(2)** London Film Productions **(3)** Columbia Pictures Corporation/Horizon Pictures (II)/Academy Pictures Corporation/Camp Films **(4)** Landau Productions **(5)** Columbia Pictures Corporation **(6)** AVCO Embassy/Haworth Productions **(7)** Josef Shaftel Productions Inc. **(8)** IPC Films/Incorporated Television Company (ITC) **242 (1)** Paramount Pictures **(2)** Paramount Pictures/Motion Picture Associates **(3)** Universal International Pictures (UI) **(4)** United Artists/Anthony Productions/Worldwide Productions **(5)** MGM/The Kobal Collection **(6)** Columbia Pictures Corporation/Jerry Bresler Productions **(7)** Julian Blaustein Productions Ltd. **(8)** APJAC Productions/20th Century Fox Film Corporation **243 (1)** Walter Seltzer Productions **(2)** MGM **(3)** Constantin Film Produktion/Impact Pictures/Nouvelles Éditions de Films/Studio Babelsberg **(4)** Universal Pictures/The Filmakers Group **(5)** Paramount Pictures **(6)** 20th Century Fox Film Corporation/Lightstorm Entertainment **(7)** Castle Rock Entertainment/Turner Pictures (I)/Fishmonger Films **(8)** APJAC Productions/20th Century Fox Film Corporation **244 tl** Paramount/The Kobal Collection **tr** Paramount/The Kobal Collection **cl** Paramount/The Kobal Collection **cr** Universal/The Kobal Collection **bl** MGM/The Kobal Collection **br** MGM/The Kobal Collection **245 t** 20th Century Fox/The Kobal Collection **cl** Warner Bros/The Kobal Collection **cr** MGM/The Kobal Collection **br** Universal/The Kobal Collection **246 (1)** Lawrence Turman **(2)** Jerome Hellman Productions/Florin Productions **(3)** ABC Pictures/Talent Associates/Amerbroco **(4)** Allied Artists Pictures/Corona-General/Solar Productions **(5)** Marvin Worth Productions **(6)** Paramount Pictures **(7)** Warner Bros./Wildwood/Wildwood Enterprises **(8)** Columbia Pictures **247 (1)** Columbia Pictures Corporation/Mirage Enterprises/Punch Productions/Delphi Films **(2)** Roxbury Productions/Punch Productions **(3)** United Artists/The Guber-Peters Company/Star Partners II Ltd./Mirage Enterprises **(4)** Amblin Entertainment/TriStar Pictures **(5)** Warner Bros./Arnold Kopelson Productions/Punch Productions/Kopelson Entertainment **(6)** Baltimore Pictures/New Line Cinema/Punch Productions/Tribeca Productions **(7)** Fox Searchlight Pictures/Qwerty Films/Kanzeon/Scott Rudin Productions/N1 European Film Produktions GmbH & Co. KG/Huckabee's **(8)** Constantin Film Produktion/VIP 4 Medienfonds/Nouvelles Éditions de Films/Castelao Producciones/Davis-Films/Ikiru Films/Rising Star **248 (1)** Warner Bros./Universal Pictures/Amblin Entertainment/Constant c Productions **(2)** New Line Cinema/Lawrence Gordon Productions/Ghoulardi Film Company **(3)** Polygram Filmed Entertainment/Working Title Films **(4)** Ghoulardi Film Company/New Line Cinema/The Magnolia Project **(5)** Miramax/Paramount Pictures/Mirage Enterprises/Timnick Films **(6)** Alliance Atlantis Communications/Astral Media/Canadian Film or Video Production Tax Credit/Natural Nylon Entertainment/Ontario Film and Television Tax Credit/Téléfilm Canada **(7)** Sony Pictures Classics/A-Line Pictures/Cooper's Town Productions/Infinity Media/Eagle Vision/Manitoba Film & Sound/Manitoba Film and Video Production Tax Credit/British Columbia Production Services Tax Credit/Capote Productions/Columbia Pictures/United Artists **(8)** Paramount Pictures/Cruise/Wagner Productions/MI 3 Film/China Film Co-Production Corporation/The Fourth Production Company Film Group/China Film Group Corporation/Studio Babelsberg **249 (1)** Universal Pictures/Relativity Media/Participant Media/Playtone/MP Munich Pape Filmproductions/Good Time Charlie Productions **(2)** Capitol Films/Funky Buddha Productions/Unity Productions/Linsefilm/Michael Cerenzie Productions **(3)** Sidney Kimmel Entertainment/Likely Story/Projective Testing Service/Russia **(4)** Cross Creek Pictures/Exclusive Media Group/Smokehouse Pictures/Crystal City Entertainment **(5)** The Weinstein Company/Ghoulardi Film Company/Annapurna Pictures **(6)** Opening Night Productions/Concept Entertainment/Unison Films/Spring Pictures/RKO Pictures **(7)** Color Force/Lionsgate **(8)** Lionsgate/Film4/Demarest Films/FilmNation Entertainment/Senator Film Produktion/Potboiler Productions/The Ink Factory/Amusement Park Films **250 (1)** Columbia Pictures Corporation **(2)** Paramount Pictures **(3)** Paramount Pictures **(4)** Paramount Pictures **(5)** Columbia Pictures Corporation/Horizon Pictures (II) **(6)** Warner Brothers/Seven Arts **(7)** Warner Bros./20th Century Fox Film Corporation/Irwin Allen Productions/United Films **(8)** MGM/United Artists **251 (1)** Paramount Pictures **(2)** Paramount Pictures **(3)** Paramount Pictures **(4)** Paramount Pictures **(5)** Paramount Pictures **(6)** Paramount Pictures **(7)** Hope Enterprises/Paramount Pictures **(8)** HLP **252 (1)** Open Road Films (II)/Columbia Pictures Corporation **(2)** Joseph E. Levine Productions **(3)** 20th Century Fox Film Corporation/Joseph E. Levine Productions **(4)** Brooksfilms **(5)** Dino De Laurentiis Company/Bounty Productions Ltd. **(6)** Brooksfilms/Columbia Pictures Corporation **(7)** Strong Heart/Demme Production/Orion Pictures **(8)** Merchant Ivory Productions/Sumitomo Corporation/Imagica/Cinema Ten/Japan Satellite Broadcasting/Idle Productions/Film Four International **253 (1)** Merchant Ivory Productions/Columbia Pictures Corporation **(2)** Price Entertainment/Spelling Films International/Shadowlands Productions **(3)** Cinergi Pictures Entertainment/Hollywood Pictures/Illusion Entertainment **(4)** MGM/Universal Pictures/Dino De Laurentiis Company/Scott Free Productions **(5)** Touchstone Pictures/Jerry Bruckheimer Films/Stillking Films **(6)** Miramax/Lakeshore Entertainment/Stone Village Pictures/Cinerenta Medienbeteiligungs KG/Cinepsilon **(7)** Mediapro/Versátil Cinema/Gravier Productions/Antena 3 Films/Antena 3 Televisión/Dippermouth **(8)** Fox Searchlight Pictures/Cold Spring Pictures/The Montecito Picture Company/Dune Entertainment/Ingenious Media/Big Screen Productions/Prana Studios **254 (1)** Warner Bros. **(2)** Paramount/The Kobal Collection **(3)** Jalem Productions **(4)** Columbia Pictures Corporation/Pando Company Inc./Raybert Productions **(5)** Paramount Pictures/Skydance Productions/Scott Rudin Productions/Mike Zoss Productions **(6)** Alta-Light **(7)** Mad Dog/Motion Picture Productions **(8)** Bavaria Film/Filmverlag der Autoren/Les Films du Losange/Road Movies Filmproduktion/Westdeutscher Rundfunk/Wim Wenders Productions/Wim Wenders Stiftung **255 (1)** Zoetrope Studios **(2)** De Haven Productions/Hemdale Film **(3)** De Laurentiis Entertainment Group **(4)** Palace Pictures/Viacom **(5)** Morgan Creek Productions/Davis-Films/August Entertainment/Sterling MacFadden **(6)** 20th Century Fox Film Corporation **(7)** Universal Pictures/Gordon Company/Davis Entertainment **(8)** Universal Pictures/Atmosphere Entertainment MM/Exception Wild Bunch/Romero-Grunwald Productions **256 tl** Warner Bros/The Kobal Collection **tr** Columbia/The Kobal Collection **cl** Columbia/The Kobal Collection **cr** Universal/The Kobal Collection **bl** Zoetrope/United Artists/The Kobal Collection **br** Zoetrope/United Artists/The Kobal Collection **257 tr** De Laurentiis/The Kobal Collection **cl** Orion/The Kobal Collection **cr** Morgan Creek/Davis Films/The Kobal Collection **br** 20th Century Fox/The Kobal Collection **258 (1)** Cineguild **(2)** Carol Reed's Production/London Film Productions **(3)** London Film Productions **(4)** Highroad/Open Road Films (II) **(5)** 20th Century-Fox Productions/The Company of Artists **(6)** MGM/Arcola Pictures **(7)** Spitfire Productions **(8)** Faraway Productions **259 (1)** Universal International Pictures **(2)** Universal International Pictures **(3)** Giant Productions/Warner Bros. **(4)** Universal International Pictures **(5)** Arwin Productions/Universal International Pictures **(6)** Gibraltar Productions/Laurel Productions/Universal Pictures **(7)** Joel Productions/John Frankenheimer Productions Inc./Gibraltar Productions **(8)** Filmways Pictures **260 (1)** C.A.P.A.C./S.N. Prodis/Universal Pictures France **(2)** Action Films/Citel Films/Filmproduktion Janus/France 3 **(3)** Filmel/France Régions 3/Cinévidéo **(4)** Partisan Productions **(5)** Action Films,/Gaumont **(6)** Sara Films/Sonimage/Films A2/Film et Video Productions/Société Suisse de Radiodiffusion et Télévision **(7)** MK2 Productions/CED Productions/FR3 Films Production/Canal+/Le Club des Investisseurs/Credit Lyonnais/Conseil Général de l'Eure/Conseil Régional de Haute Normandie **(8)** American Playhouse/Channel Four Films/La Sept Cinéma/True Fiction Pictures/Union Générale Cinématographique/Zenith Entertainment **261 (1)** CMV Produzione Cinematografica/Canal+/D.A. Films/France 2 Cinéma/Renn Productions **(2)** France 3 Cinéma/MK2 Productions/Olga Film GmbH/Prokino Filmproduktion/Zweites Deutsches Fernsehen **(3)** Arte France Cinéma/Arte/Bavaria Film International/Bayerischer Rundfunk/Canal+/Centre National de la Cinématographie/Eurimages/Filmfonds Wien/Les Films Alain Sarde/MK2 Productions/Wega Film/Österreichischer Rundfunk/Österreichisches Filminstitut **(4)** Arte France Cinéma/Bavaria Film/Canal+/Centre National de la Cinématographie/Eurimages/France 3 Cinéma/Les Films du Losange/Wega Film **(5)** Azor Films/Arte France Cinéma/StudioCanal/Love Streams Productions/Albachiara/Network Movie Film-und Fernsehproduktion/Zweites Deutsches Fernsehen/Canal+/arte France Développement/Eurimages/Région Ile-de-FranceMedia Programme of the European Community **(6)** Catherine Dussart Productions/Studio 37/France 2 Cinéma/Scope Pictures/Canal+/CinéCinéma/France 2/Bophana Production/Centre National de la Cinématographie/La Banque postale Image/Films Distribution/Sofica Soficinéma 4/Le Tax Shelter du Gouvernement Fédéral de Belgique/Media Programme of the European Community/SCOPE Invest/Scope Pictures **(7)** Why Not Productions/Wild Bunch/France 3 Cinéma/Canal+/France Télévision/TPS Star/Centre National de la Cinématographie/Les Films Terre Africaine/Cinémage 2/Sofica UGC 1/Procirep **(8)** Les Films du Losange/X-Filme Creative Pool/Wega Film/France 3 Cinéma/ARD Degeto Film/Bayerischer Rundfunk/Westdeutscher Rundfunk **262 (1)** Warner Bros. **(2)** The Ladd Company **(3)** Eagle Associates **(4)** HB Filmes/FilmDallas Pictures **(5)** Paramount Pictures **(6)** Amercent Films/American Entertainment Partners L.P./Gracie Films **(7)** New Line Cinema/BenderSpink/Media !! Filmproduktion München & Company/New Line Productions **(8)** Paramount Vantage/Art Linson Productions/Into the Wild/River Road Entertainment **263 (1)** 20th Century Fox Film Corporation/Marvel Enterprises/Donners' Company/Bad Hat Harry Productions/Springwood Productions/Genetics Productions **(2)** Universal Pictures/The Sommers Company/Stillking Films/Carpathian Pictures **(3)** Warner Bros./Village Roadshow Pictures/Kennedy Miller Productions/Animal Logic/Kingdom Feature Productions **(4)** Touchstone Pictures/Warner Bros./Newmarket Productions/Syncopy **(5)** Warner Bros./Regency Enterprises/Protozoa Pictures/New Regency Pictures/Muse Entertainment Enterprises/Mel's Cite du Cinema **(6)** 20th Century Fox Film Corporation/Bazmark Films/ScreenWest/Dune Entertainment III/Ingenious Film Partners **(7)** Universal Pictures/Relativity Media/Working Title Films/Cameron Mackintosh Ltd. **(8)** Alcon Entertainment/8:38 Productions/Madhouse Entertainment **264 (1)** Paramount Pictures **(2)** Otto Preminger Films/Carlyle Productions **(3)** National General Pictures **(4)** Goodtimes Enterprises **(5)** International Films/Xenon Pictures **(6)** MGM **(7)** Paramount Pictures/Marv Films/Vaughn Productions/Di Bonaventura Pictures/Ingenious Film Partners/Truenorth Productions **(8)** British Lion Film Corporation/Cinema 5 **265 (1)** Recorded Picture Company/ The Rank Organisation **(2)** Cooperativa Jean Vigo/RAI Radiotelevisione Italiana/Aura Film **(3)** Orion Pictures **(4)** Correctional Services/Outlaw Values **(5)** Island World **(6)** Haut et Court/La Sept-Arte/True Fiction Pictures **(7)** Zentropa Entertainments/Trust Film Svenska/Film i Väst/Liberator Productions/Pain Unlimited GmbH Filmproduktion/Cinematograph A/S/What Else? B.V./Icelandic Film/Blind Spot Pictures Oy/France 3 Cinéma/Danmarks Radio/Arte France Cinéma/SVT Drama/Arte/Angel Films/Canal+/FilmFour/Fine Line Features/Filmek A/S/Constantin Film Produktion/Lantia Cinema & Audiovisivi/TV 1000/Vrijzinnig Protestantse Radio Omroep/Westdeutscher Rundfunk/Yleisradio/Memfis Film **(8)** Film Science/Van Hoy/Knudsen Productions/Washington Square Films **266 (1)** Eddie Murphy Productions/Paramount Pictures **(2)** 40 Acres & A Mule Filmworks **(3)** Universal Pictures/40 Acres & A Mule Filmworks **(4)** Universal Pictures/Amblin Entertainment **(5)** Lumière Pictures/Miramax **(6)** Miramax/A Band Apart/Jersey Films **(7)** Cinergi Pictures Entertainment/20th Century Fox Film Corporation **(8)** Regency Enterprises/Warner Bros. **267 (1)** Miramax/A Band Apart/Lawrence Bender Productions/Mighty Mighty Afrodite Productions **(2)** Icon Entertainment International/R U Dun Productions **(3)** Touchstone Pictures/Blinding Edge Pictures/Barry Mendel Productions/ **(4)** Paramount/The Kobal Collection **(5)** Lucasfilm **(6)** Screen Gems/Overbrook Entertainment **(7)** The Weinstein Company/Columbia Pictures **(8)** Marvel Entertainment/Marvel Studios/Sony Pictures Imageworks **268 tl** Universal/The Kobal Collection **tr** Miramax/Buena Vista/The Kobal Collection **cl** Cinergi Pictures/The Kobal Collection **cr** Miramax/The Kobal Collection **bl** Warner Bros/The Kobal Collection **br** Miramax/The Kobal Collection **269 t** Lucasfilm/20th Century Fox/The Kobal Collection **cr** Overbrook Entertaiment/The Kobal Collection **b** Columbia Pictures/The Kobal Collection **270 (1)** Projektions-AG Union **(2)** Universum Film **(3)** Universum Film **(4)** Universum Film **(5)** Paramount Pictures **(6)** Universum Film **(7)** Tobis-Magna-Filmproduktion **(8)** Tobis Filmkunst **271 (1)** United Artists/Granada Film Productions/Jersey Shore/Mr. Mudd/Advanced Medien/Capitol Films **(2)** Archer Street Productions/Delux Productions/Pathé Pictures International/Film Fund Luxembourg/UK Film Council/Wild Bear Films **(3)** Focus Features/Tohokushinsha Film Corporation/American Zoetrope/Elemental Films **(4)** The Weinstein Company/Mediapro/Gravier Productions/Antena 3 Films/Antena 3 Televisión/Televisió de Catalunya **(5)** Marvel Studios/Paramount Pictures **(6)** Annapurna Pictures **(7)** Film4/British Film Institute/Silver Reel/Creative Scotland/FilmNation Entertainment/Nick Wechsler Productions/JW Films/Scottish Screen/UK Film Council **(8)** Canal+/Ciné+/EuropaCorp/TF1 Films Production **272 (1)** United Artists/Suftley **(2)** 3 Arts Entertainment/Columbia Pictures Corporation/Global Entertainment Productions GmbH & Company Medien KG/Red Wagon Entertainment **(3)** Paramount Pictures/Mutual Film Company/British Broadcasting

Corporation/Lawrence Gordon Productions/Marubeni/Eidos Interactive/KFP Produktions GmbH & Co. KG/Tele München Fernseh Produktionsgesellschaft/Toho-Towa (4) Warner Bros./Intermedia Films/Pacifica Film/Egmond Film & Television/France 3 Cinéma/IMF Internationale Medien und Film GmbH & Co. 3. Produktions KG/Pathé Renn Productions/WR Universal Group (5) Regency Enterprises/New Regency Pictures/Summit Entertainment/Weed Road Pictures/Epsilon Motion Pictures (6) Paramount Vantage/Plan B Entertainment/Revolution Films/Kailash Picture Company (7) Imagine Entertainment/Malpaso Productions/Relativity Media (8) Roth Films/Walt Disney Pictures **273** (1) Columbia Pictures Corporation (2) Warner Bros. (3) Alcor Films/Aleor Films/Regency Enterprises/Warner Bros. (4) Columbia Pictures Corporation (5) EuropaCorp/The Javelina Film Company (6) Paramount Vantage/Miramax/Scott Rudin Productions/Mike Zoss Productions (7) DreamWorks SKG/20th Century Fox Film Corporation/Reliance Entertainment/Participant Media/Dune Entertainment/Amblin Entertainment/The Kennedy/Marshall Company/Walt Disney Studios Motion Pictures (8) EuropaCorp/Ithaca/The Javelina Film Company **274** (1) Merchant Ivory Productions (2) Lime Light (3) Mangatram Films (4) Lotus Films (5) A.K. Movies (6) Film-Valas (7) P.K. Communications (8) Merchant Ivory Productions/Channel Four Films **275** (1) Euro International Film (EIA)/Rome Paris Films (2) Les Films de la Pléiade/Pathé Consortium Cinéma (3) Columbia Film/Anouchka Films/Orsay Films (4) Films Georges de Beauregard/Rome Paris Films/Société Nouvelle de Cinématographie (SNC)/Dino de Laurentiis Cinematografica (5) Rome Paris Films/Société Nouvelle de Cinématographie (SNC) (6) Dino de Laurentiis Cinematografica/Raster Film/Marianne Productions/Casbah Film (7) Raska Productions/Société Nouvelle de Cinématographie (SNC) (8) Albatros Filmproduktion/Les Films du Losange **276** (1) Universal Pictures (2) Universal Pictures (3) Gaumont British Picture Corporation (4) RKO Radio Pictures (5) Universal Pictures (6) Saticoy Productions **277** (1) Daiei Studios (2) Daiei Studios (3) Daiei Motion Picture Company (4) Daiei Motion Picture Company (5) Katsu Production Co. Ltd./Toho Company (6) Katsu Production Co. Ltd. **278** (1) Comique Film Company (2) Metro Pictures Corporation (3) Joseph M. Schenck Productions (4) First National Pictures (5) Buster Keaton Productions (6) Joseph M. Schenck Productions (7) Buster Keaton Productions (8) Buster Keaton Productions **279** (1) Buster Keaton Productions/Joseph M. Schenck Productions (2) Buster Keaton Productions/Joseph M. Schenck Productions (3) MGM (4) MGM/Joseph M. Schenck Productions (5) Paramount Pictures (6) Celebrated Productions (7) Casey Productions (8) United Artists/Melvin Frank Production **280** (1) Hal Roach Studios (2) Famous Players-Lasky Corporation (3) Buster Keaton Productions/Joseph M. Schenck Productions (4) Hal Roach Studios (5) Paramount Pictures (6) Columbia Pictures Corporation/Hawk Films (7) Jolly Film/Specta Films (8) Crossbow Productions **281** (1) Universal Pictures/Oregon Film Factory/Stage III Productions (2) Aspen Film Society (3) Walt Disney Pictures (4) New Line Cinema/Dark Horse Entertainment (5) Capella International/Eric's Boy/KC Medien/Moving Pictures/New Line Cinema (6) Paramount Pictures/Village Roadshow Pictures/VH1 Television/NPV Entertainment/Scott Rudin Productions/Red Hour Films/MFP Munich Film Partners GmbH & Company I. Produktions KG/Red Hour Productions/Tenth Planet Productions (7) DreamWorks SKG/Apatow Productions/Herzog-Cowen Entertainment (8) Universal Pictures/Relativity Media/Apatow Productions **282** (1) Paramount Pictures/Alfran Productions (2) Rollins-Joffe Productions (3) Rollins-Joffe Productions (4) Rollins-Joffe Productions (5) Paramount Pictures (6) Rollins-Joffe Productions (7) Rollins-Joffe Productions (8) Barclays Mercantile Industrial Finance/JRS Productions **283** (1) De Laurentiis Entertainment Group (DEG) (2) United Artists/Meyers/Shyer (3) Sandollar Productions/Touchstone Pictures/Touchwood Pacific Partners 1 (4) TriStar Pictures (5) Scott Rudin Productions/Tribeca Productions/Marvin Productions (6) Paramount Pictures (7) Columbia Pictures Corporation/Warner Bros./Waverly Films (8) The Family Stone/Fox 2000 Pictures/Michael London Productions/Pan Productions **284** (1) Ladd Company, The (2) Geffen Company, The (3) Imagine Films Entertainment/Warner Bros. (4) Warner Bros./Guber-Peters Company, The/PolyGram Filmed Entertainment (5) Morgan Creek Productions (6) Miramax/A Band Apart/Lawrence Bender Productions/Mighty Mighty Afrodite Productions (7) Universal Pictures (presents)/Gold Circle Films/White Noise UK Ltd/Brightlight Pictures/Endgame Entertainment/Corus/Movie Network, The/Province of British Columbia Film Incentive BC/Canadian Film or Video Production Tax Credit (8) New Regency Pictures/M Prods/Grisbi Productions, Le/TSG Entertainment/Worldview Entertainment **285** (1) Trimod Films (2) Warner Bros./Taplin - Perry - Scorsese Productions (3) Columbia Pictures Corporation/Bill/Phillips/Italo/Judeo Productions (4) Brut Productions/Fingers Productions Inc. (5) TriStar Pictures/Mulholland Productions/Baltimore Pictures (6) Live Entertainment/Dog Eat Dog Productions Inc. (7) Miramax/A Band Apart/Jersey Films (8) Miramax/Neue Deutsche Filmgesellschaft (NDF)/Euro Space/Internal/Smoke Productions **286** (1) MGM (2) MGM (3) MGM (4) MGM (5) MGM (6) MGM (7) MGM (8) MGM **287** (1) MGM (2) MGM (3) MGM (4) MGM (5) Sol C. Siegel Productions/MGM (6) Stanley Kramer Productions (7) Madeleine Films/Parc Film (8) Universal Pictures **288** (1) 20th Century Fox Film Corporation (2) Stanley Kramer Productions (3) MGM (4) Paramount Pictures (5) Warner Bros. (6) Paramount Pictures/Patron Inc. **289** (1) Paramount Pictures/Perlberg-Seaton Productions (2) MGM (3) Paramount Pictures (4) MGM (5) MGM/Sol C. Siegel Productions/Bing Crosby Productions **290** (1) Rank Organisation, The/Archers, The/Independent Producers (2) Individual Pictures (3) Archers, The/Independent Producers (4) Columbia Pictures Corporation (5) 20th Century Fox Film Corporation (6) 20th Century Fox Film Corporation (7) The Kobal Collection (8) Warner Bros. Productions **291** (1) Yash Raj Films (2) Film Kraft (3) Yash Raj Films (4) Mega Bollywood (5) Red Chillies Entertainment/Venus Films (6) Ashutosh Gowariker Productions Pvt. Ltd./Dillywood/UTV Motion Pictures (7) Yash Raj Films International Ltd. (8) Dharma Productions/Fox Searchlight Pictures/Fox Star Studios/Imagenation Abu Dhabi FZ/Red Chillies Entertainment **292** (1) Kennedy Miller Productions (2) Imagine Films Entertainment/Universal Pictures (3) Columbia Pictures Corporation/Rank Organisation, The (4) Polygram Filmed Entertainment/Propaganda Films (5) Warner Bros./Stanley Kubrick Productions/Hobby Films/Pole Star (6) 20th Century Fox Film Corporation/Bazmark Films (7) Cruise/Wagner Productions/Sogecine/Las Producciones del Escorpión/Dimension Films/Canal+/Lucky Red/Miramax (8) The Kobal Collection/Paramount/Miramax/Coote, Clive **293** (1) Miramax/Mirage Enterprises/Bona Fide Productions/Castel Film Romania/Cattleya (2) Zentropa Entertainments (3) New Line Cinema/Fine Line Features/Lou Yi Inc./Academy Films/March Entertainment (4) Scott Rudin Productions (5) 20th Century Fox Film Corporation/Bazmark Films/ScreenWest/Dune Entertainment III/Ingenious Film Partners (6) Millennium Films/The Kobal Collection (7) Archer Street Productions/Latitude Media/Lionsgat/Pictures in Paradise/Silver Reel/Thai Occidental Productions (8) Stone Angels/YRF Entertainment **294** (1) 20th Century Fox Film Corporation/Scott Free Productions/ApolloProMedia GmbH & Co. 1. Filmproduktion KG/Stillking Films/QI Quality International GmbH & Co. KG/Epsilon Motion Pictures/Franchise Pictures/World 2000 Entertainment (2) 20th Century Fox Film Corporation/Bazmark Films (3) Cruise/Wagner Productions/Sogecine/Las Producciones del Escorpión/Dimension Films/Canal+/Lucky Red/Miramax (4) Paramount Pictures/Miramax/Scott Rudin Productions (5) Miramax/Mirage Enterprises/Bona Fide Productions/Castel Film Romania/Cattleya (6) New Line Cinema/Fine Line Features/Lou Yi Inc./Academy Films/March Entertainment (7) 20th Century Fox Film Corporation/Bazmark Films/ScreenWest/Dune Entertainment III/Ingenious Film Partners (8) Millennium Films/Nu Image Films/Lee Daniels Entertainment/Benaroya Pictures **t** UNIVERSAL/THE KOBAL COLLECTION **c** 20th Century Fox/The Kobal Collection **bl** Miramax/Canal+/Sogecine/The Kobal Collection/Isasi, Teresa **br** The Kobal Collection/Paramount/Miramax/Coote, Clive **295** **tl** MIRAMAX/THE KOBAL COLLECTION **tr** NEW LINE/THE KOBAL COLLECTION/BRIDGES, JAMES **c** THE KOBAL COLLECTION/20TH CENTURY FOX/BAZMARK FILMS **bl** THE KOBAL COLLECTION/20TH CENTURY FOX/BAZMARK FILMS **br** Millennium Films/The Kobal Collection **296** (1) Produzioni Europee Associati (PEA)/Arturo González Producciones Cinematográficas/Constantin Film Produktion (2) MGM (MGM/Carlo Ponti Production/Sostar S.A. (3) M. C. M. (4) Adelphia Compagnia Cinematografica/Les Films Corona (5) Filmar Compagnia Cinematografica/Fénix Cooperativa Cinematográfica/Corona Filmproduktion/Towers of London (6) Werner Herzog Filmproduktion/Hessischer Rundfunk (HR) (7) Elite Film/Ascot Film/Cinemec (8) Werner Herzog Filmproduktion/Zweites Deutsches Fernsehen (ZDF) **297** (1) Werner Herzog Filmproduktion/Gaumont/Zweites Deutsches Fernsehen (ZDF) (2) MGM (3) Werner Herzog Filmproduktion/Pro-ject Filmproduktion/Filmverlag der Autoren/Zweites Deutsches Fernsehen (ZDF)/Wildlife Films Peru (4) New World Pictures (5) Bavaria Film/Pan Arts/Warner Bros. (6) Werner Herzog Filmproduktion/Zweites Deutsches Fernsehen (ZDF/Ghana Film Industry Corporation/De Laurentiis Entertainment Group (DEG) (7) Scena Film/Reteitalia/Président Films (8) Werner Herzog Filmproduktion/Cafe Productions Ltd/Zephir Film/British Broadcasting Corporation/Independent Film Channel (IFC)/Filmstiftung Nordrhein-Westfalen /Outpost Studios **298** (1) Recorded Picture Company (RPC)/National Film Trustees/Oshima Productions/Antares-Nova/Asahi National Broadcasting Company/Broadbank Investments (2) Bandai Media Department/Shochiku-Fuji Company (3) Bandai Visual Company/Shouchiku Co./Shôchiku Eiga/Yamada Right Vision Corporation (4) Bandai Visual Company/Office Kitano/TV Tokyo/Tokyo FM Broadcasting Co. (5) Oshima Productions/Shôchiku Eiga/Kadokawa Shoten Publishing Co./Imagica Corp./BS Asahi/Eisei Gekijo (6) AM Associates/Fukasaku-gumi/GAGA/Kobi Co./MF Pictures/Nippon Shuppan Hanbai (Nippan) K.K./Toei Company/WOWOW (7) Asahi National Broadcasting Company/Bandai Visual Company/DENTSU Music And Entertainment/Office Kitano/Saitô Entertainment/TV Asahi/Tokyo FM Broadcasting Co. (8) Bandai Visual Company/Office Kitano/Omnibus Japan/TV Tokyo/Tokyo FM Broadcasting Co. **299** (1) Paramount Pictures (2) Paramount Pictures (3) Paramount Pictures (4) Paramount Pictures (5) Paramount Pictures (6) Paramount Pictures (7) Paramount Pictures (8) Embassy Pictures/Paramount Pictures **300** (1) Mark Hellinger Productions/Universal Pictures (2) Mark Hellinger Productions/Universal International Pictures (UI) (3) Hecht-Lancaster Productions (4) Columbia Pictures Corporation (5) Hecht-Lancaster Productions (6) Hecht-Lancaster Productions (7) Paramount Pictures/Wallis-Hazen (8) Norma Productions/Curtleigh Productions/Hill-Hecht-Lancaster Productions **301** (1) Elmer Gantry Productions (2) Norma Productions (3) Titanus/Société Nouvelle Pathé Cinéma/Société Générale de Cinématographie (S.G.C.) (4) Les Films Ariane/Les Productions Artistes Associés/Dear Film Produzione (5) Universal Pictures/Associates & Aldrich Company, The/De Haven Productions (6) Rusconi Film/Gaumont International (7) Dino De Laurentiis Company/Lion's Gate Films/Talent Associates-Norton Simon (8) Enigma Production/Goldcrest Films International **302** (1) Dino De Laurentiis Company (2) CIP Filmproduktion GmbH/Lorimar Film Entertainment/MGM (MGM/New Gold Entertainment/Northstar International (3) Columbia Pictures Corporation/Mirage Enterprises/Punch Productions/Delphi Films (4) Brooksfilms/EMI Films (5) Far West/Panagea/Touchstone Pictures (6) Home Box Office (HBO)/Silver Screen Partners (7) Carolco Pictures (8) Amblin Entertainment/Cappa Films/Tribeca Productions **303** (1) Paramount Pictures (2) London Film Productions (3) MGM (4) London Film Productions (5) RKO Radio Pictures (6) London Film Productions/British Lion Film Corporation (7) Bryna Productions (8) Otto Preminger Films/Alpha Alpina **304** (1) Hal Roach Studios (2) Hal Roach Studios (3) Hal Roach Studios (4) Hal Roach Studios (5) Hal Roach Studios (6) Hal Roach Studios (7) Hal Roach Studios (8) Hal Roach Studios **305** (1) Hal Roach Studios (2) Hal Roach Studios (3) Hal Roach Studios (4) Hal Roach Studios (5) Boris Morros Productions (6) Hal Roach Studios (7) Hal Roach Studios (8) Films EGE/Fortezza Film/Franco London Films/La Société des Films Sirius **306** (1) 2929 Productions/Costa Films/Parkes+MacDonald Image Nation (2) Anonymous Content/Winter's Bone Productions (3) 20th Century Fox Film Corporation/Marvel Entertainment/Dune Entertainment/Bad Hat Harry Productions/Donners' Company/Ingenious Media/Big Screen Productions/Ingenious Film Partners/Dune Entertainment III (4) Weinstein Company, The (5) Lionsgate/Color Force (6) Columbia Pictures/Annapurna Pictures/Atlas Entertainment (7) 20th Century Fox Film Corporation/Marvel Entertainment/TSG Entertainment/Bad Hat Harry Productions/Donners' Company/Ingenious Media/Down Productions (8) 2929 Productions/Chockstone Pictures/Nick Wechsler Productions/StudioCanal **307** (1) Les Films du Carrosse/Sédif Productions (2) Anouchka Films/Argos Films/Sandrews/Svensk Filmindustri (SF) (3) Anouchka Films/Les Productions de la Guéville/Athos Films/Parc Film/Simar Films (4) Les Films du Carrosse (5) JLG Films/Sara Film (6) Esselte Video/Finnkino/Megamania/Pandora Filmproduktion/Pyramide Films/Svenska Filminstitutet (SFI)/Villealfa Filmproduction Oy (7) Dacia Films/Canal+ (8) Haut et Court/In Extremis Images **308** (1) Touchstone Pictures/Mad Chance/Jaret Entertainment (2) Columbia Pictures Corporation/Escape Artists/Finestkind/Black and Blu Entertainment (3) Australian Film Commission, The/Australian Film Finance Corporation (AFFC)/Endymion Films/StudioCanal/WTA/Working Title Films/Woss/Group Film Productions (4) Dimension Films/MGM/Mosaic Media Group/Reforma Films/Atlas Entertainment (5) Focus Features/River Road Entertainment/Alberta Film Entertainment/Good Machine (6) Killer Films/John Wells Productions/John Goldwyn Productions/Endgame Entertainment (7) Warner Bros./Legendary Pictures/DC Comics (8) Infinity Features Entertainment/ Poo Poo Pictures/Parnassus Productions **309** (1) Chester Films Inc./Junction/Walt Disney Pictures (2) Cherokee Productions/Katzka-Berne Productions (3) Golden Harvest Company (4) Golden Harvest Company (5) Concord Productions Inc./Golden Harvest Company (6) Warner Bros./Concord Productions Inc./Golden Harvest Company/Sequoia Productions (7) Concord Productions Inc./Columbia Pictures/Golden Harvest Company **310** (1) Warner Bros./Hammer Film Productions (2) Hammer Film Productions (3) Hammer Film Productions (4) Hammer Film Productions (5) Hallam Productions/Constantin Film Produktion (6) Associated British-Pathé/Hammer Film Productions/Seven Arts Pictures (7) Seven Arts Pictures/Hammer Film Productions (8) British Lion Film Corporation **311** (1) Eon Productions/Danjaq (2) Hammer Film Productions/Terra-Filmkunst (3) Dehlavi Films/Petra Film/The Quaid Project (4) Paramount Pictures/Mandalay Pictures/American Zoetrope/Dieter Geissler Filmproduktion/Karol Film Productions/Tim Burton Productions (5) New Line Cinema/WingNut Films/The Saul Zaentz Company (6) Lucasfilm (7) Warner Bros./Village Roadshow Pictures/Zanuck Company, The/Plan B Entertainment/Theobald Film Productions/Tim Burton Productions (8) New Line Cinema/MGM/WingNut Films **312** (1) Warner Bros./Hammer Film Productions (2) Hammer Film Productions (3) Hammer Film Productions (4) British Lion Film Corporation (5) Eon Productions/Danjaq (6) New Line Cinema/WingNut Films/The Saul Zaentz Company (7) Lucasfilm (8) New Line Cinema/MGM/WingNut Films **tl** The Kobal Collection/Hammer **tr** The Kobal Collection/Hammer **cl** The Kobal Collection/Hammer **cr** The Kobal Collection/Hammer **bl** The Kobal Collection/Hammer **313** **tl** © 1973 STUDIOCANAL FILMS LTD. ALL RIGHTS RESERVED/THE KOBAL COLLECTION **tr** THE KOBAL COLLECTION/DANJAQ/EON/UA **c** NEW LINE/SAUL ZAENTZ/WING NUT/THE KOBAL COLLECTION/VINET, PIERRE **bl** The Kobal Collection/Lucasfilm/20th Century Fox **br** New Line Cinema/The Kobal Collection **314** (1) Jofa-Atelier Berlin-Johannisthal/Prana-Film GmbH (2) Universal Pictures (3) Universal Pictures (4) RKO Radio Pictures (5) Warner Bros./Hammer Film Productions (6) Hammer Film Productions (7) Shamley Productions (8) Achilles/20th Century Fox Film Corporation **315** (1) Alta Vista Productions (2) Warner Bros./Hoya Productions (3) 20th Century Fox Film Corporation/Mace Neufeld Productions (4) Compass International Pictures/Falcon International Productions (5) Brandywine Productions/20th Century-Fox Productions (6) Strong Heart/Demme Production/Orion Pictures (7) Geffen Pictures (8) Paramount Pictures/Skydance Productions/Hemisphere Media Capital/GK Films/Plan B Entertainment/2DUX²/Apparatus Productions/Latina Pictures **316** (1) MGM (2) MGM/Loew's (3) Loew's/MGM (4) MGM (5) Paramount Pictures (6) MGM (7) Universal International Pictures (UI) (8) 20th Century Fox Film Corporation **317** (1) Mark VII Ltd. (2) Columbia Pictures Corporation (3) RKO Radio Pictures (4) Bavaria Film/Brynaprod S.A./Curtleigh Productions (5) Universal International Pictures (UI) (6) Shamley Productions (7) M.C. Productions (8) AVCO Embassy Pictures/EDI/Debra Hill Productions **318** (1) London Film Productions (2) London Film Productions (3) Victor Saville Productions/London Film Productions (4) MGM British Studios (5) Mayflower Pictures Corporation (6) Selznick International Pictures/MGM (7) MGM (8) London Film Productions **319** (1) Alexander Korda Films/London Film Productions (2) Gabriel Pascal Productions/Independent Producers (3) London Film Productions (4) Silver Screen Collection/Getty Images (5) London Film Productions (6) Seven Arts Pictures (7) Stanley Kramer Productions **320** (1) Columbia Pictures Corporation (2) Warner Bros./Orange (3) Columbia Pictures Corporation (4) Ashton Productions/Mirisch Corporation, The (5) Mirisch Corporation, The (6) Jalem Productions (7) Mirisch Corporation, The/Phalanx-Jalem (8) Paramount Pictures **321** (1) Jalem Productions/Mirisch Corporation, The/Phalanx Productions/Produzioni Europee Associati (PEA) (2) Filmways Pictures/Cirandinha Productions/Jalem Productions (3) Columbia Pictures/IPC Films (4) Tiberius Film Productions (5) MGM (6) PolyGram Filmed Entertainment/Universal Pictures (7) GGR/New Line Cinema/Zupnik Cinema Group II (8) Fine Line Features/Spelling Films International/Avenue Pictures Productions **322** (1) 3-H Films/ERA International (2) Golden Princess Film Production Limited/Milestone Pictures/Pioneer LDC (3) Jet Tone Production (4) Block 2 Pictures/Jet Tone Production/Prénom H Co. Ltd./Seowoo Film Company (5) Block 2 Pictures/Jet Tone Production/Paradis Films (6) Media Asia Films/Basic Pictures (7) Beijing New Picture Film Co./China Film Co-Production Corporation/Elite Group Enterprises/Sil-Metropole Organisation/Zhang Yimou Studio (8) Block 2 Pictures/Jet Tone Films/Sil-Metropole Organisation/Bona International Film Group **323** (1) Paramount Pictures/Wallis-Hazen (2) Jerry Lewis Productions (3) Jerry Lewis Pictures/Paramount Pictures (4) Paramount Pictures/Jerry Lewis Enterprises (5) Paramount Pictures/Patti Enterprises (6) Jerry Lewis Productions/York Pictures Corporation (7) Embassy International Pictures/20th Century Fox Film Corporation (8) Hollywood Pictures **324** (1) Xi'an Film Studio (2) China Film Co-Production Corporation/China Film Release Import and Export Company/Cineplex Odeon Films/Tokuma Shoten/Xi'an Film Studio (3) ERA International/China Film Co-Production Corporation/Century Communications/Salon Films (4) Sil-Metropole Organisation/Youth Film Studio of Beijing Film Academy (5) Beijing Film Studio/China Film Co-Production Corporation/Maverick Picture Company/Tomson Films (6) ERA International/Shanghai Film Studios **325** (1) Mingxing Film Company (2) Lianhua Film Company (3) Lianhua Film Company (4) Lianhua Film Company (5) Lianhua Film Company (6) Lianhua Film Company **326** (1) Hal Roach Studios (2) Hal Roach Studios (3) The Harold Lloyd Corporation (4) The Harold Lloyd Corporation (5) The Harold Lloyd Corporation (6) The Harold Lloyd Corporation (7) The Harold Lloyd Corporation (8) California Pictures **327** (1) Paramount Pictures (2) Paramount Pictures (3) Columbia Pictures Corporation (4) Universal Pictures (5) Selznick International Pictures (6) Selznick International Pictures (7) RKO Radio Pictures (8) Romaine Film Corporation **328** (1) Oscar Film (2) Titanus/Société Générale de Cinématographie (S.G.C.) (3) Stanley Kramer Productions (4) Paramount Pictures (5) Paramount Pictures (6) Paramount Pictures (7) Capri Productions/Paramount Pictures (8) Compagnia Cinematografica Champion/Cocinor/Les Films Marceau/Société Générale de Cinématographie (S.G.C.) **329** (1) Samuel Bronston Productions/Dear Film Produzione (2) Cineriz/Concordia Compagnia Cinematografica/Francinex/Gray-Film (3) Compagnia Cinematografica Champion/Les Films Concordia (4) Compagnia Cinematografica Champion/Les Films Concordia (5) Compagnia Cinematografica Champion/Les Films Concordia/PECF (6) C.A.P.A.C./Compagnia Cinematografica Champion (7) Compagnia Cinematografica Champion/Canafox Films/New Gold Entertainment (8) Etalon Film/Miramax **330** (1) Oscar Film (2) Stanley Kramer Productions (3) Paramount Pictures (4) Paramount Pictures (5) Samuel Bronston Productions/Dear Film Produzione (6) Cineriz/Concordia Compagnia Cinematografica/Francinex/Gray-Film (7) Compagnia Cinematografica Champion/Les Films Concordia (8) C.A.P.A.C./Compagnia Cinematografica Champion **tl** OSCAR FILM/THE KOBAL COLLECTION **tr** UNITED ARTISTS/THE KOBAL COLLECTION **c** PARAMOUNT/THE KOBAL COLLECTION **bl** PARAMOUNT/THE KOBAL COLLECTION **br** THE KOBAL COLLECTION/ALLIED ARTISTS **331** **tr** The Kobal Collection/CCC/Cineriz/Francinex/Tcf **cl** CHAMPION/CONCORDIA/THE KOBAL COLLECTION **bl** Champion/Concordia/The Kobal Collection **br** CCC FILMKUNST/THE KOBAL COLLECTION **332** (1) Nero-Film AG (2) Gaumont British Picture Corporation (3) 20th Century Fox Film Corporation (4) Warner Bros. (5) Warner Bros. (6) Warner Bros. (7) Arnold Pressburger Filmproduktion (8) Alta Vista Productions **333** (1) Alfred J. Hitchcock Productions (2) Mirisch Corporation, The (3) Mirisch Corporation, The/Phalanx Productions (4) Universal Pictures (5) Universal Pictures/Malpaso Company, The/Sanen Productions (6) BSB/CIP/Lorimar Film Entertainment/NatWest Ventures/New Gold Entertainment/Northstar Media (7) Paramount Pictures (8) Fox 2000 Pictures/Scott Free Productions/Deuce Three Productions **334** (1) RKO Radio Pictures (2) RKO Radio Pictures (3) Paramount Pictures (4) Paramount Pictures (5) Universal International Pictures (UI) (6) Columbia Pictures Corporation (7) Walt Disney Productions (8) Mirisch Corporation, The **335** (1) Excelsa Film (2) Finecine/Tevere Film (3) CEI Incom (4) Delphinus/Hoche Productions/Panaria Film (5) Paramount Pictures (6) Pennebaker Productions (7) Arco Film (8) Stanley Kramer Productions **336** (1) Fox Searchlight Pictures/Good Machine/Canal+ Droits Audiovisuels (2) New Line Cinema/Larger Than Life Productions (3) FilmColony/Miramax/Nina Saxon Film Design (4) Universal Pictures/Good Machine (5) British Broadcasting Corporation (BBC)/Curtis Hanson Productions/MFF Feature Film Productions/Marubeni/Mutual Film Company/Paramount Pictures/Scott Rudin Productions/Tele München Fernseh Produktionsgesellschaft (TMG)/Toho-Towa (6) Columbia Pictures Corporation/Marvel Enterprises/Laura Ziskin Productions (7) Universal Pictures/DreamWorks SKG/Spyglass Entertainment/Larger Than Life Productions/Kennedy/Marshall Company, The (8) Lionsgate/Relativity Media/Sighvatsson Films/Michael De Luca Productions **337** (1) Goldcrest Films International/International Film Investors/Enigma Productions (2) Lorimar Film Entertainment/NFH Productions/Warner Bros. (3) Columbia Pictures Corporation/Castle Rock Entertainment (4) Polygram Filmed Entertainment/Propaganda Films (5) Touchstone Pictures/Jerry Bruckheimer Films/Kouf/Bigelow Productions/Runway Pictures/Hiett Designs of Las Vegas (6) Astralwerks/Gramercy Pictures (I)/Propaganda Films/Single Cell Pictures (7) Focus Features/StudioCanal/Relativity Media/Working Title Films/Mike Zoss Productions (8) Imagine Entertainment/Malpaso Productions/Relativity Media **338** (1) Warner Bros. (2) © 20th Century-Fox (3) Columbia Pictures Corporation/Samson Productions (4) 20th Century Fox Film Corporation (5) © Screen Captures (6) 20th Century Fox Film Corporation/Jerry Wald Productions (7) Angel Productions/20th Century Fox Film Corporation (8) Noonan-Taylor Production **339** (1) Gaumont/Gaumont International/Production Marcel Dassault (2) Sara Films (3) Alter Films/Gaumont/France 3 Cinéma/Canal+ (4) Icon Entertainment International/Ladd Company, The/B.H. Finance C.V. (5) Fox Searchlight Pictures/Regency Enterprises/Taurus Film/Panoramica (6) Marie-Amélie Productions/StudioCanal/Canal+/CinéCinéma/Centre National de la Cinématographie (CNC) (7) Iliade and Films/France 3 Cinéma/SND/Canal+ (8) Les Chauves-Souris **340** (1) Paramount Pictures (2) Paramount Pictures/Wallis-Hazen (3) 20TH CENTURY FOX/THE KOBAL COLLECTION (4) MGM (5) Warner Bros./Armada Productions (6) Dorchester/Warner Bros. (7) Mirisch Corporation, The/Phalanx Productions/Claude Productions (8) Columbia Pictures Corporation/Meadway-Claude Productions Company (I) (II) **341** (1) Columbia Pictures Corporation (2) Paramount Pictures/John Ford Productions (3) Mark Hellinger Productions/Universal Pictures (4) Columbia Pictures Corporation/Harold Hecht Productions (5) MGM/MKH/Seven Arts Pictures (6) MGM (7) Cinévision Ltée/The American Film Theatre (8) Lorimar Productions/Lorac Productions **342** (1) Paramount Pictures (2) Paramount Pictures (3) Paramount Pictures (4) Paramount Pictures (5) Paramount Pictures (6) MGM (7) MGM (8) MGM **343** (1) Capitolium (2) OFI/P.D.C. (3) Ponti-De Laurentiis Cinematografica (4) Ponti-De Laurentiis Cinematografica (5) Ponti-De Laurentiis Cinematografica (6) Dino de Laurentiis Cinematografica/Les Films Marceau (7) Rizzoli Film/Francoriz Production (8) Produzioni Europee Associati (PEA)/Les Films Ariane/France 3 Cinéma/Revcom Films/Stella Film **344** (1) Gainsborough Pictures/Rank Organisation, The (2) Gainsborough Pictures (3) Two Cities Films (4) MGM/Enterprise Productions (5) Dorkay Productions/Romulus Films (6) 20th Century Fox Film Corporation (7) MGM (8) Transcona Enterprises/Warner Bros. **345** (1) Walt Disney Productions (2) 20th Century Fox Film Corporation (3) MGM (4) MGM /Seven Arts Pictures/A.A. Productions Ltd./Anya/Harris-Kubrick Productions/Transworld Pictures (5) Nautilus Productions (6) Anglo-EMI Productions Ltd/Rapid Film/Terra-Filmkunst/Incorporated Television Company (ITC)/Radiant Film GmbH (7) 20th Century Fox Film Corporation (8) Edenflow/Geoff Reeve Films & Television Ltd./Castle Hill Productions/Gavin/Geoffrey Reeve and Associates/Premier **346** (1) © Cinecitt‡ (2) Riama Film/Gray-Film/Pathé Consortium Cinéma (3) Arco Film/Cino del Duca/Societé Cinématographique Lyre (4) Lux Film/Vides Cinematografica/Galatea Film (5) Nepi Film/Silver Films/Sofitedip (6) Compagnia Cinematografica Champion/Les Films Concordia (7) Cineriz/Francinex (8) Compagnia Cinematografica Champion/Les Films Concordia **347** (1) Caribury Films Ltd./Chartoff/Winkler/Boorman (2) Una Cooperativa Cinematografica/Ministero del Turismo e dello Spettacolo (3) Compagnia Cinematografica Champion/Canafox Films/New Gold Entertainment (4) Gaumont/Opera Film Produzione (5) Greek Television ET-1/Theo Angelopoulos Films/International Cinema Company (ICC) (6) Excelsior Film-TV/RAI Radiotelevisione Italiana/Adriana International Corporation/Sovinfilm (7) Erre Produzioni/Les Films Ariane/TF1 Films Production (8) Etalon Film/Miramax **348** (1) Cinecittà (Stabilimenti Cinematografici)/Lux Film/Vides Cinematografica (2) Riama Film/Gray-Film/Pathé Consortium Cinéma (3) Nepi Film/Silver Films/Sofitedip (4) Lux Film/Vides Cinematografica/Galatea Film (5) Cineriz/Francinex (6) Caribury

Films Ltd./Chartoff/Winkler/Boorman **(7)** Compagnia Cinematografica Champion/Canafox Films/New Gold Entertainment **(8)** Etalon Film/Miramax **tl** Lux Film/The Kobal Collection **tr** Riama-Pathe/The Kobal Collection **cl** NEPI/SOTILEDIP/SILVER FILMS/THE KOBAL COLLECTION **bl** The Kobal Collection/Cineriz **br** Lux/Vides/Galatea/The Kobal Collection **349 tr** UNITED ARTISTS/THE KOBAL COLLECTION **bl** CCC/CANAFOX/THE KOBAL COLLECTION **br** Miramax/The Kobal Collection/Georges, E **350 (1)** La Salamandra **(2)** Fígaro Films **(3)** Kaktus Producciones Cinematográficas/Tesauro S.A. **(4)** EL DESEO/THE KOBAL COLLECTION **(5)** El Deseo/Laurenfilm **(6)** Iberoamericana Films Internacional/Televisión Española (TVE)/Ellepi Films **(7)** Antena 3 Televisión/Lolafilms/Vía Digital **(8)** Canal+ España/El Deseo/Ministerio de Cultura/Televisión Española (TVE) **351 (1)** ©GramercyPictures/Courtesy Everett Collection **(2)** Regency Enterprises/Warner Bros. **(3)** Warner Bros/South Side Amusement Company **(4)** Columbia Pictures Corporation/Dee Gee Entertainment/IMF Internationale Medien und Film GmbH & Co. Produktions KG/Intermedia Films/Prufrock Pictures/Tapestry Films **(5)** Voltage Pictures/Picture Perfect (I)/Worldview Entertainment/ANA Media **(6)** Lionsgate/Everest Entertainment/Brace Cove Productions/FilmNation Entertainment **(7)** Truth Entertainment (II)/Voltage Pictures/r2 films/Evolution Independent/CE **(8)** Paramount Pictures/Warner Bros./Legendary Pictures/Lynda Obst Productions/Syncopy **352 (1)** Fox Film Corporation **(2)** RKO Radio Pictures **(3)** MGM **(4)** Universal Pictures **(5)** MGM **(6)** MGM Studios/Getty Images **(7)** Warner Bros. **(8)** Warner Bros. **353 (1)** Channel Four Films/The Glasgow Film Fund/Figment Films **(2)** Channel Four Films/Figment Films/The Noel Gay Motion Picture Company **(3)** Channel Four Films/Goldwyn Films/Killer Films/Miramax/Newmarket Capital Group/Single Cell Pictures/Zenith Entertainment **(4)** Lucasfilm **(5)** 20th Century Fox Film Corporation/Bazmark Films **(6)** Recorded Picture Company (RPC)/Scottish Screen/Film Council/Future Films/HanWay Films/Sigma Films/StudioCanal/Sveno Media/Young Adam Productions **(7)** Olympus Pictures/Parts and Labor/Northwood Productions (II) **(8)** Mediaset España/Summit Entertainment/Apaches Entertainment/Telecinco Cinema/Canal+ España/La Trini/Instituto de la Cinematografía y de las Artes Audiovisuales (ICAA)/Generalitat Valenciana/Institut Valenciã de Cinematografia (IVAC) **354 (1)** Mirisch Company, The/Alpha Productions **(2)** MIRISCH/UNITED ARTISTS/THE KOBAL COLLECTION **(3)** MGM /Filmways Pictures /Solar Productions **(4)** Robert Wise Productions/Solar Productions/20th Century Fox Film Corporation **(5)** Embassy Pictures/Paramount Pictures/Solar Productions **(6)** Mirisch Corporation, The/Simkoe/Solar Productions **(7)** Warner Brothers/Seven Arts/Solar Productions **(8)** Cinema Center Films/Duo Films/Solar Productions **355 (1)** Cinema Center Films/Solar Productions **(2)** American Broadcasting Company (ABC)/Joe Wizan-Booth Gardner Productions/Solar Productions **(3)** First Artists/Solar Productions/Foster-Brower Productions **(4)** Allied Artists Pictures/Corona-General/Solar Productions **(5)** Warner Bros./20th Century Fox Film Corporation/Irwin Allen Productions/United Films **(6)** First Artists/Solar Productions **(7)** First Artists/Solar Productions/Warner Bros. **(8)** Rastar Pictures **356 (1)** 20th Century Fox Film Corporation **(2)** Ladd Company, The **(3)** Touchstone Pictures/Silver Screen Partners II **(4)** Touchstone Pictures/Silver Screen Partners II **(5)** All Girl Productions/Silver Screen Partners IV/Touchstone Pictures **(6)** Moviestore Collection/REX **(7)** RHI Entertainment **(8)** Paramount Pictures **357 (1)** Film Art Association/Shintoho Film Distribution Committee/Toho Company **(2)** Daiei Motion Picture Company **(3)** Toho Company **(4)** Toho Company/Kurosawa Production Co. **(5)** Toho Company **(6)** Kurosawa Production Co./Toho Company **(7)** Mifune Productions Co. Ltd./Toho Company **(8)** Selmur Productions/Henry G. Saperstein Enterprises Inc. **358 (1)** Balboa Entertainment **(2)** Zentropa Entertainments/After the Wedding/Sigma Films/Sveriges Television (SVT/Det Danske Filminstitut/Nordisk Film/Invicta Capital **(3)** Columbia Pictures/Eon Productions/Casino Royale Productions/Stillking Films/Casino Royale/Studio Babelsberg **(4)** Eurowide Film Production/Hexagon Pictures **(5)** BBC Films/Belle Allee Productions, La/NWR Film Productions/Nimbus Film Productions/One Eye Production/Savalas Audio Post-Production **(6)** Zentropa Entertainments/Danmarks Radio (DR)/Trollhättan Film AB/Film i Väst/Sveriges Television (SVT)/Sirena Film **(7)** Danmarks Radio (DR)/Det Danske Filminstitut/Eurimages/Film i Väst/Media Programme of the European Community/Nordisk Film- & TV-Fond /Svenska Filminstitutet (SFI) /Sveriges Television (SVT) /Zentropa Entertainments/Zentropa International Sweden **(8)** Zentropa Entertainments/Forward Films/Spier Films **359 (1)** Two Cities Films **(2)** Cineguild **(3)** Ealing Studios **(4)** London Film Productions/British Lion Film Corporation **(5)** Associated British Picture Corporation **(6)** Knightsbridge Films **(7)** Walt Disney Productions **(8)** Faraway Productions **360 (1)** MGM **(2)** Memorial Enterprises/Universal Pictures **(3)** Boardwalk Productions **(4)** Otto Preminger Films **(5)** Allied Artists Pictures/ABC Pictures/Feuer and Martin Production, A/Bavaria Film **(6)** Gruskoff/Venture Films **361 (1)** American International Pictures/Coralta Cinematografica/Deux Femmes Service Company/General International Film Company **(2)** Crossbow Productions **(3)** Chartoff-Winkler Productions **(4)** Orion Pictures **(5)** Warner Bros./Havlin-Robert Shapiro Production **(6)** Paramount Pictures **362 (1)** Nautilus Productions **(2)** Memorial Enterprises/Sam **(3)** Penthouse Films International/Felix Cinematografica **(4)** British Lion Film Corporation/Calendar Productions/HandMade Films **(5)** Orion Pictures **(6)** Enigma Productions/Goldcrest Films International/Warner Bros. **(7)** The Saul Zaentz Company/Jerome Hellman Productions **(8)** Allarts/Elsevier-Vendex Film Beheer/Allarts Cook/Erato Films/Films Inc. **363 (1)** Samuel Goldwyn Company, The/Channel Four Films/Close Call Films **(2)** Castle Rock Entertainment/Hell's Kitchen Films **(3)** USA Films/Capitol Films/Film Council/Sandcastle 5 Productions/Chicagofilms/Medusa Film **(4)** Touchstone Pictures/Harbour Pictures/Buena Vista International **(5)** Pathé Pictures International/Granada Film Productions/Pathé Renn Productions/BIM Distribuzione/France 3 Cinéma/Canal+/Future Films/Scott Rudin Productions **(6)** Miramax/TalkStory Productions/Artemis Films/Mumbai Mantra Media/Prologue Films/Chartoff Hendee Productions/Chartoff Productions/Touchstone Pictures **(7)** Summit Entertainment/Di Bonaventura Pictures/DC Entertainment **(8)** Fox Searchlight Pictures/Cold Spring Pictures/Montecito Picture Company, The/Dune Entertainment/Ingenious Media/Big Screen Productions **364 (1)** Nautilus Productions **(2)** Memorial Enterprises/Sam **(3)** Penthouse Films International/Felix Cinematografica **(4)** The Saul Zaentz Company/Jerome Hellman Productions **(5)** Castle Rock Entertainment/Hell's Kitchen Films **(6)** Touchstone Pictures/Harbour Pictures/Buena Vista International **(7)** Pathé Pictures International/Granada Film Productions/Pathé Renn Productions/BIM Distribuzione/France 3 Cinéma/Canal+/Future Films/Scott Rudin Productions **(8)** Fox Searchlight Pictures/Cold Spring Pictures/Montecito Picture Company, The/Dune Entertainment/Ingenious Media/Big Screen Productions **tl** Columbia/Nautilus/The Kobal Collection **tr** GTO/Felix/Penthouse/The Kobal Collection **cr** Warner Bros/The Kobal Collection **b** Saul Zaentz Company/The Kobal Collection **365 tr** Castle Rock/Hell'S Kitchen Prod/The Kobal Collection **c** Pathe/The Kobal Collection **bl** Buena Vista/Touchstone Pictures/The Kobal Collection **br** Montecito Picture Company, The/The Kobal Collection **366 (1)** Lester Cowan Productions **(2)** RKO Radio Pictures **(3)** RKO Radio Pictures **(4)** Paul Gregory Productions **(5)** 20th Century Fox Film Corporation **(6)** Warner Bros. Productions **367 (1)** Melville Productions/Talbot Productions **(2)** Darryl F. Zanuck Productions/20th Century Fox Film Corporation **(3)** Faraway Productions **(4)** Paramount Pictures **(5)** EK/ITC Entertainment **(6)** Pandora Filmproduktion/JVC Entertainment Networks/Newmarket Capital Group/12 Gauge Productions **368 (1)** Columbia Pictures Corporation **(2)** 20th Century Fox Film Corporation **(3)** MGM **(4)** 20th Century Fox Film Corporation **(5)** 20th Century Fox Film Corporation **(6)** 20th Century Fox Film Corporation **(7)** 20th Century Fox Film Corporation **(8)** 20th Century Fox Film Corporation **369 (1)** 20th Century Fox Film Corporation **(2)** 20th Century Fox Film Corporation **(3)** Charles K. Feldman Group/20th Century Fox Film Corporation **(4)** 20th Century Fox Film Corporation **(5)** Warner Bros./Marilyn Monroe Productions **(6)** Ashton Productions/Mirisch Corporation, The **(7)** 20th Century Fox/Company of Artists, The **(8)** Seven Arts Pictures **370 (1)** Columbia Pictures Corporation **(2)** 20th Century Fox Film Corporation **(3)** 20th Century Fox Film Corporation **(4)** 20th Century Fox Film Corporation **(5)** 20th Century Fox Film Corporation **(6)** Charles K. Feldman Group/20th Century Fox Film Corporation **(7)** Ashton Productions/Mirisch Corporation, The **(8)** Seven Arts Pictures **tl** Columbia/The Kobal Collection **tr** 20th Century Fox/The Kobal Collection **cr** 20th Century Fox/The Kobal Collection **b** 20th Century Fox/The Kobal Collection **371 tl** 20th Century Fox/The Kobal Collection **tr** 20th Century Fox/The Kobal Collection **bl** United Artists/The Kobal Collection **br** United Artists/Seven Arts/The Kobal Collection **372 (1)** Projektions-AG Union **(2)** Famous Players-Lasky Corporation/Paramount Pictures **(3)** Nero-Film AG **(4)** Columbia Pictures Corporation **(5)** Elektafilm **(6)** Howard Hughes Productions **(7)** Columbia Pictures Corporation **(8)** Carlyle Productions **373 (1)** 20th Century Fox Film Corporation **(2)** Cocinor/Iéna Productions/Union Cinématographique Lyonnaise **(3)** Riama Film/Gray-Film/Pathé Consortium Cinéma **(4)** Eon Productions **(5)** Fawcett-Majors Productions/Melvin Simon Productions **(6)** Touchstone Pictures/Amblin Entertainment/Silver Screen Partners III **(7)** Paramount Pictures/Mutual Film Company/BBC/Lawrence Gordon Productions/Marubeni/Eidos Interactive/KFP Produktions GmbH & Co. KG/Tele München Fernseh Produktionsgesellschaft/Toho-Towa **(8)** Film4/BFI/Silver Reel/Creative Scotland/FilmNation Entertainment/Nick Wechsler Productions/JW Films/Scottish Screen/UK Film Council **374 (1)** Société Nouvelle Pathé Cinéma **(2)** Compagnie Industrielle et Commerciale Cinématographique/Filmsonor/Vera Films/Fono Roma **(3)** 20th Century Fox/Company of Artists, The **(4)** Europa Film/Sofracima **(5)** Cherokee Productions/Douglas & Lewis Productions/Joel Productions/John Frankenheimer Productions Inc./MGM **(6)** Office National pour le Commerce et l'Industrie Cinématographique/Reggane Films/Valoria Films **(7)** Euro International Film/Les Films Corona/Selenia Cinematografica **(8)** DD Productions/Films A2/RAI Radiotelevisione Italiana/Renn Productions/Télévision Suisse-Romande **375 (1)** Fine Line Features/Spelling Films International/Avenue Pictures Productions **(2)** Channel Four Films/Mayfair Entertainment/The Vanya Company **(3)** New Line Cinema/Lawrence Gordon Productions/Ghoulardi Film Company **(4)** Ghoulardi Film Company/New Line Cinema/The Magnolia Project **(5)** Focus Features/Vulcan Productions/Killer Films/John Wells Productions/Section Eight **(6)** Paramount Pictures/Miramax/Scott Rudin Productions **(7)** Artist International/Focus Features/Gilbert Films/Saint Aire Production/10th Hole Productions/Antidote Films/Mandalay Vision **(8)** Lutzus-Brown/Killer Films/BSM Studio/Big Indie Pictures/Shriver Films **376 (1)** Nouvelles Éditions de Films **(2)** Documento Film/Iéna Productions **(3)** Nepi Film/Silver Films/Sofitedip **(4)** Les Films du Carrosse/Sédif Productions **(5)** Nouvelles Éditions de Films/Les Productions Artistes Associés/Vides Cinematografica **(6)** Les Films du Carrosse/Les Productions Artistes Associés/Dino de Laurentiis Cinematografica **(7)** Planet Film/Albatros Filmproduktion/Gaumont **(8)** Fidélité Productions/France 2 Cinéma/StudioCanal/Canal+/TPS Star/Banque Populaire Images 5 **377 (1)** Paramount Pictures/Edward S. Feldman Production **(2)** British Screen Productions/BBC Films/Zenith Entertainment/Fugitive Features/Bialystock & Bloom Limited **(3)** Hollywood Pictures/Don Simpson/Jerry Bruckheimer Films **(4)** New Line Cinema/WingNut Films/The Saul Zaentz Company **(5)** New Line Cinema/BenderSpink/Media !! Filmproduktion München & Company/New Line Productions **(6)** Focus Features/BBC Films/Astral Media/Corus Entertainment/Téléfilm Canada/Kudos Film and Television/Serendipity Point Films/Scion Films/Shine Pictures **(7)** Dimension Films/ 2929 Productions/Nick Wechsler Productions/Chockstone Pictures **(8)** Timnick Films/StudioCanal/Working Title Films **378 (1)** Paramount Pictures/Lawrence Gordon Productions **(2)** Cinema Group Ventures/Paramount Pictures **(3)** Paramount Pictures/Eddie Murphy Productions **(4)** Eddie Murphy Productions/Paramount Pictures **(5)** Eddie Murphy Productions/Paramount Pictures **(6)** Imagine Entertainment **(7)** DreamWorks Animation/DreamWorks SKG/Pacific Data Images **(8)** DreamWorks SKG/Paramount Pictures/Laurence Mark Productions **379 (1)** Canadian Film Development Corporation/Famous Players/Haliburton Films/Paramount Pictures **(2)** Black Rhino Productions/Columbia Pictures Corporation/Delphi Films **(3)** Paramount Pictures/Mirage Productions **(4)** Columbia Pictures Corporation **(5)** American Empirical Pictures/Touchstone Pictures **(6)** Focus Features/Tohokushinsha Film Corporation/American Zoetrope/Elemental Films **(7)** Focus Features/Five Roses/Bac Films **(8)** Chernin Entertainment/Crescendo Productions/Goldenlight Films/Weinstein Company, The **380 (1)** All India Film Corporation/R.K. Films Ltd. **(2)** Mehboob Productions **(3)** All India Film Corporation/R.K. Films Ltd. **(4)** Filmkar Productions **(5)** Naya Sansar **(6)** A.V.M. Productions **(7)** Mehboob Productions **(8)** A.A.N. Productions **381 (1)** Orion Pictures **(2)** Warner Bros./Goldcrest Films International/Kingsmere Productions Ltd./Enigma Productions/AMLF **(3)** Universal Pictures/Amblin Entertainment **(4)** United Artists/Talisman Productions **(5)** Warner Bros./Geffen Pictures **(6)** Fox Searchlight Pictures/Qwerty Films/N1 European Film Produktions GmbH & Co. KG/Pretty Pictures **(7)** Warner Bros./Syncopy/DC Comics/Legendary Pictures/Patalex III Productions Limited **(8)** EuropaCorp/M6 Films/Grive Productions/Canal+/TPS Star/M6/All Pictures Media/Wintergreen Productions **382 (1)** MGM **(2)** MGM/Avon Productions **(3)** Haroll Productions/Warner Bros. **(4)** Rossen Films/20th Century Fox Film Corporation **(5)** Paramount Pictures/Salem-Dover Productions **(6)** Jalem Productions **(7)** 20th Century Fox Film Corporation/Campanile Productions/Newman-Foreman Company **(8)** Zanuck/Brown Productions/Universal Pictures **383 (1)** Warner Bros./20th Century Fox Film Corporation **(2)** Dino De Laurentiis Company/Lion's Gate Films/Talent Associates-Norton Simon **(3)** 20th Century Fox Film Corporation **(4)** Touchstone Pictures/Silver Screen Partners II **(5)** PolyGram Filmed Entertainment, PolyGram Filmproduktion, Silver Pictures, Warner Bros., Working Title Films **(6)** Capella International, Cinehaus, Paramount Pictures **(7)** Gramercy Pictures/IMF Internationale Medien und Film GmbH & Co. Produktions KG/Intermedia Films/Pacifica Film/Polygram Filmed Entertainment/Scott Free Productions **(8)** DreamWorks SKG/20th Century Fox Film Corporation/Zanuck Company, The **384 (1)** Columbia Pictures Corporation/Pando Company Inc./Raybert Productions **(2)** BBS Productions/Columbia Pictures Corporation/Raybert Productions **(3)** Columbia Pictures Corporation/Bright-Persky Associates/Acrobat Productions **(4)** Paramount Pictures/Penthouse/Long Road Productions **(5)** Compagnia Cinematografica Champion/CIPI Cinematografica S.A./Les Films Concordia **(6)** Fantasy Films **(7)** Warner Bros./Hawk Films/Peregrine/Producers Circle **(8)** Paramount Pictures **385 (1)** ABC Motion Pictures **(2)** Warner Bros./Guber-Peters Company, The/Kennedy Miller Productions **(3)** Warner Bros./Guber-Peters Company, The/PolyGram Filmed Entertainment **(4)** Columbia Pictures Corporation/Castle Rock Entertainment **(5)** TriStar Pictures/Gracie Films **(6)** Morgan Creek Productions/Franchise Pictures/Clyde Is Hungry Films/Pledge Productions/Epsilon Motion Pictures **(7)** New Line Cinema/Avery Pix **(8)** Warner Bros./Plan B Entertainment/Initial Entertainment Group/Vertigo Entertainment/Media Asia Films **386 (1)** Columbia Pictures Corporation/Pando Company Inc./Raybert Productions **(2)** Columbia Pictures Corporation/Bright-Persky Associates/Acrobat Productions **(3)** Paramount Pictures/Penthouse/Long Road Productions **(4)** Fantasy Films **(5)** Warner Bros./Hawk Films/Peregrine/Producers Circle **(6)** Warner Bros./Guber-Peters Company, The/PolyGram Filmed Entertainment **(7)** Columbia Pictures Corporation/Castle Rock Entertainment **(8)** Warner Bros./Plan B Entertainment/Initial Entertainment Group/Vertigo Entertainment/Media Asia Films **t** COLUMBIA/THE KOBAL COLLECTION **cl** COLUMBIA/THE KOBAL COLLECTION **cr** PARAMOUNT/THE KOBAL COLLECTION **bl** UNITED ARTISTS/FANTASY FILMS/THE KOBAL COLLECTION **br** WARNER BROS/HAWK FILMS/THE KOBAL COLLECTION **387 tl** WARNER BROS/DC COMICS/THE KOBAL COLLECTION **tr** COLUMBIA/THE KOBAL COLLECTION/BALDWIN, SIDNEY **br** WARNER BROS./THE KOBAL COLLECTION/COOPER, ANDREW **388 (1)** Warner Bros. **(2)** Warner Bros. **(3)** Samuel Goldwyn Company, The **(4)** Archers, The **(5)** Otto Preminger Films **(6)** Michael Todd Company **(7)** Hill-Hecht-Lancaster Productions/Clifton Productions **(8)** Mirisch G-E Productions **389 (1)** Nouvelles Éditions de Films **(2)** Filmel **(3)** Lira Films **(4)** Fildebroc/Les Productions de la Guéville/Universal Pictures France **(5)** Lira Films/Société Française de Production et de Création Audiovisuelles/France Régions 3 **(6)** Les Films de la Tour/Films A2/Little Bear **(7)** Cristaldifilm/Les Films Ariane/RAI 3/TF1 Films Production/Forum Picture **(8)** Cecchi Gori Group Tiger Cinematografica/Penta Film/Esterno Mediterraneo Film/Blue Dahlia Productions/K2 Two/Canal+ **390 (1)** Columbia Pictures Corporation **(2)** Otto Preminger Films/Carlyle Productions **(3)** Essex Productions/George Sidney Productions **(4)** Alfred J. Hitchcock Productions **(5)** Columbia Pictures Corporation/Julian Blaustein Productions Ltd. **(6)** Sudan Productions **(7)** Mirisch Corporation, The/Phalanx Productions/Claude Productions/Mirisch Corporation, The **(8)** Initial Entertainment Group/Pathé Entertainment **391 (1)** RKO Radio Pictures **(2)** Mayflower Pictures Corporation **(3)** 20th Century Fox Film Corporation **(4)** 20th Century Fox Film Corporation **(5)** Republic Pictures/Argosy Pictures **(6)** Argosy Pictures **(7)** Walt Disney Productions **(8)** Batjac Productions **392 (1)** Central Production/Mostpoint/Channel 4 Television Corporation **(2)** Initial Pictures/U.K. Productions Entity/Zenith Entertainment **(3)** American Zoetrope/Columbia Pictures Corporation/Osiris Films **(4)** Gaumont/Les Films du Dauphin **(5)** Columbia Pictures Corporation/Beacon Communications/Radiant Productions **(6)** Warner Bros./Syncopy/DC Comics/Legendary Pictures/Patalex III Productions Limited **(7)** StudioCanal/Karla Films/Paradis Films/Kinowelt Filmproduktion/Working Title Films/Canal+/CinéCinéma **(8)** Chernin Entertainment/Ingenious Media/TSG Entertainment **393 (1)** London Film Productions **(2)** Selznick International Pictures **(3)** Two Cities Films **(4)** Warner Bros./Marilyn Monroe Productions **(5)** Woodfall Film Productions **(6)** Palomar Pictures **(7)** Paramount Pictures **(8)** Anglo International Films/BBC/Liberty Film Sales **394 (1)** MGM/Summit Film Productions **(2)** Gray Films/Joseph Janni/Appia Films/Magic Film/Play Art/Société Nouvelle Pathé Cinéma **(3)** Horizon Pictures **(4)** Paramount Pictures/Keep Films **(5)** Columbia Pictures Corporation/Keep Films **(6)** Famous Artists Productions **(7)** Columbia Pictures/Horizon Pictures/Filmsonor **(8)** AVCO Embassy/Haworth Productions **395 (1)** APJAC Productions/MGM **(2)** Keep Films **(3)** Produzioni Europee Associati/United Artists **(4)** Simon Productions/20th Century Fox Film Corporation **(5)** MGM/Brooksfilms **(6)** Recorded Picture Company/Hemdale Film/Yanco Films Limited/TAO Film/Screenframe/AAA Soprofilms **(7)** Warner Bros./Helena Productions/Latina Pictures/Radiant Productions/Plan B Entertainment/Nimar Studios **(8)** Miramax/FilmFour/UK Film Council/Free Range Films **396 (1)** Warner Bros. **(2)** Norma Productions/Curtleigh Productions/Hill-Hecht-Lancaster Productions **(3)** Alfred J. Hitchcock Productions **(4)** 20th Century Fox Film Corporation **(5)** Rafran Cinematografica/Finanzia San Marco/Paramount Pictures **(6)** Paramount Pictures **(7)** Universal Pictures/Mad Dog Productions **(8)** DreamWorks SKG/20th Century Fox Film Corporation/ImageMovers **397 (1)** Recorded Picture Company/FilmFour/Chronopolis Films/Kanzaman/Sexy RPC **(2)** Warner Bros./Village Roadshow Pictures/NPV Entertainment/Outlaw Productions/WV Films II **(3)** Alcon Entertainment/Witt/Thomas Productions/Section Eight/Insomnia Productions/Summit Entertainment **(4)** Paramount Pictures/DreamWorks SKG/Parkes+MacDonald Image Nation/Edge City **(5)** Dimension Films/Troublemaker Studios **(6)** FilmDistrict/Bold Films/OddLot Entertainment/Marc Platt Productions/Motel Movies/Newbridge Film Capital **(7)** Fox 2000 Pictures/Scott Free Productions/Nick Wechsler Productions/Chockstone Pictures/TSG Entertainment/Ingenious Media/Big Screen Productions **(8)** Annapurna Pictures/Likely Story/Media Rights Capital **398 (1)** Gadd Productions Corp./Didion-Dunne **(2)** Paramount Pictures/Alfran Productions **(3)** Artists Entertainment Complex/Produzioni De Laurentiis International Manufacturing Company **(4)** Warner Bros. **(5)** Paramount Pictures/The Coppola Company **(6)** Warner Bros./Artists Entertainment Complex **(7)** Universal Pictures **(8)** Universal Pictures **399 (1)** Paramount Pictures/Zoetrope Studios **(2)** Universal Pictures/City Light Films **(3)** Universal Pictures/Epic Productions/Bregman/Baer Productions **(4)** Warner Bros./Regency Enterprises/Forward Pass/Art Linson Productions/Monarchy Enterprises B.V. **(5)** Mandalay Entertainment/Baltimore Pictures/Mark Johnson Productions **(6)** Blue Lion Entertainment/Forward Pass/Kaitz Productions/Spyglass Entertainment/Touchstone Pictures **(7)** Alcon Entertainment/ Witt/Thomas Productions/Section Eight/Insomnia Productions/Summit Entertainment **(8)** Worldview Entertainment/Dreambridge Films/Muskat Filmed Properties/Rough House Pictures **400 tl** Gadd Productions/The Kobal Collection **tr** Universal/The Kobal Collection **cl** Paramount/The Kobal Collection **cr** Warner Bros/The Kobal Collection **b** Paramount/The Kobal Collection **401 tr** Mandalay Entertainment/Baltimore Pictures/The Kobal Collection **bl** Universal/The Kobal Collection **br** Alcon Entertainment/Section Eight Ltd/The Kobal Collection **402 (1)** Focus Features/Tempesta Films/Granada Film Productions/Inside Track Films/Mirabai Films/Cine Mosaic **(2)** Warner Bros./Heyday Films/Patalex IV Productions Limited **(3)** Summit Entertainment/Temple Hill Entertainment/Maverick Films/Imprint Entertainment/Goldcrest Pictures/Twilight Productions **(4)** APT Films/Aria Films/Factotum Barcelona S.L./Met Film Production/Met Film **(5)** Redwaves Film/19 Entertainment/Protagonist Pictures/Rai Cinema **(6)** Alfama Fictures/Prospero Pictures/Kinology/France 2 Cinéma/Talandracas/Téléfilm Canada/Leopardo Filmes/Canal +/Rai Cinema/Radiotelevisão Portuguesa (RTP)/Jouror Productions **(7)** Porchlight Films/Lava Bear Films/Blue-Tongue Films/Screen Australia **(8)** Prospero Pictures/Sentient Entertainment/SBS Productions/Integral Film **403 (1)** Selznick International Pictures/Vanguard Films **(2)** 20th Century Fox Film Corporation **(3)** Paramount Pictures **(4)** United Artists/Anthony Productions/Worldwide Productions **(5)** Universal International Pictures (UI)/Pakula-Mulligan/Brentwood Productions **(6)** Melville Productions/Talbot Productions **(7)** Stanley Donen Films **(8)** Lew Grade/Producers Circle/Incorporated Telivision Company **404 (1)** Shaw Brothers **(2)** Shaw Brothers **(3)** Shaw Brothers **(4)** Shaw Brothers **(5)** Shaw Brothers **(6)** Win's Movie Productions **(7)** Asia Union Film & Entertainment Ltd./China Film Co-Production Corporation/Columbia Pictures Film Production Asia/Edko Films/Good Machine/Sony Pictures Classics/United China Vision/Zoom Hunt International Productions **(8)** London Film Productions/Lilting Production/Microwave/BBC Films/Stink Films/SUMS* Film and Media/Dominic Buchanan Productions **405 (1)** 20th Century Fox Film Corporation **(2)** Hemdale Film **(3)** Universal Pictures/Epic Productions/Bregman/Baer Productions **(4)** Havoc/Polygram Filmed Entertainment/Working Title Films **(5)** Warner Bros./Village Roadshow Pictures/NPV Entertainment/Malpaso Productions **(6)** This Is That Productions/Y Productions/Mediana Productions Filmgesellschaft **(7)** Focus Features/Axon Films/Groundswell Productions/Jinks/Cohen Company/Cinema Vehicle Services **(8)** Indigo Film/Lucky Red/Medusa Film/ARP Sélection/France 2 Cinéma/Element Pictures/Bord Scannan na hEireann/Irish Film Board/Media Programme of the European Community/Eurimages Council of Europe/Section 481/Sky/Canal +/CinéCinéma/France Télévision/Intesa San Paolo/Pathé **406 (1)** MGM/The Kobal Collection **(2)** Allied Artists Pictures/B-M Productions **(3)** Shamley Productions **(4)** Argus Film/Mercury Productions (I) **(5)** Paris-Europa Productions/Hisa-Film/Finanziaria Cinematografica Italiana (FICIT) **(6)** Paramount Pictures/Filmways Productions **(7)** Winter Gold Productions **(8)** Universal Pictures/Oak **407 (1)** Paramount Pictures **(2)** Universal Pictures **(3)** Warner Bros./The Guber-Peters Company/Kennedy Miller Productions **(4)** Lorimar Film Entertainment/NFH Productions/Warner Bros. **(5)** Gladden Entertainment/Mirage/Tobis **(6)** Sanford/Pillsbury Productions/Via Rosa Productions **(7)** Warner Bros./Syncopy/DC Comics/Legendary Pictures/Patalex III Productions Limited **(8)** Columbia Pictures Corporation/Cappa Production **408 (1)** Imagine Entertainment/Universal Pictures **(2)** Columbia Pictures Corporation/The Rank Organisation **(3)** Fox 2000 Pictures/Imagine Entertainment/20th Century Fox Film Corporation **(4)** Columbia Pictures Corporation/Hofflund/Polone/Global Entertainment Productions GmbH & Company Medien KG **(5)** DreamWorks SKG/Universal Pictures/Scott Free Productions/Mill Film/C & L/Dawliz/Red Wagon Entertainment **(6)** Miramax/Industry Entertainment **(7)** FilmFour/Good Machine/Gorilla Entertainment/Grosvenor Park Productions/Miramax/Odeon Film/Strange Fiction **(8)** Touchstone Pictures/Blinding Edge Pictures/Scott Rudin Productions **409 (1)** Fox 2000 Pictures/Tree Line Film/Konrad Pictures/Catfish Productions/Mars Media Beteiligungs **(2)** Columbia Pictures/2929 Productions/Industry Entertainment **(3)** 2929 Productions/Wild Bunch/Tempesta Films **(4)** They Are Going to Kill Us Productions **(5)** The Weinstein Company/Ghoulardi Film Company/Annapurna Pictures **(6)** Keep Your Head/Kingsgate Films/Worldview Entertainment **(7)** Annapurna Pictures **(8)** Ghoulardi Film Company/IAC Films/Warner Bros. **410 (1)** Biograph Company **(2)** Biograph Company **(3)** Famous Players Film Company **(4)** Pickford Film **(5)** Mary Pickford Company **(6)** Mary Pickford Company **(7)** Mary Pickford Company **(8)** Pickford Corporation **411 (1)** Pathé Entertainment/Percy Main/Star Partners III Ltd./MGM **(2)** Allied Filmmakers/Wildwood Enterprises **(3)** Universal Pictures/Atlas Entertainment/Classico **(4)** Cecchi Gori Pictures/Juno Pix/New Line Cinema **(5)** Fox 2000 Pictures/Regency Enterprises/Linson Films/Atman Entertainment/Knickerbocker Films/Taurus Film **(6)** Warner Bros./Jesse Films Inc./Scott Free Productions/Plan B Entertainment/Alberta Film Entertainment/Virtual Studios **(7)** Universal Pictures/The Weinstein Company/A Band Apart/Studio Babelsberg/Visiona Romantica **(8)** Cottonwood Pictures/River Road Entertainment/Brace Cove Productions/Plan B Entertainment **412 (1)** 20th Century Fox Film Corporation **(2)** MGM **(3)** David Susskind Productions/Jonathan Productions/MGMs **(4)** Curtleigh Productions/Stanley Kramer Productions **(5)** The Samuel Goldwyn Company **(6)** Columbia Pictures/Columbia Broadcasting System/Columbia TriStar/Monterey Video **(7)** Rainbow Productions **(8)** MGM **413 (1)** Columbia Pictures/Bedford Productions Ltd. **(2)** The Mirisch Corporation **(3)** Columbia Pictures Corporation **(4)** Columbia Pictures Corporation/Columbia British Productions **(5)** The Mirisch Corporation **(6)** Touchstone Pictures/Silver Screen Partners III/Century Park Pictures **(7)** Film Afrika Worldwide/Hallmark Entertainment/Showtime Networks **(8)** Universal Pictures/Mutual Film Company/Alphaville Films/Tele München Fernseh Produktionsgesellschaft/UGC PH/British Broadcasting Corporation/Marubeni/Toho-Tawa/Mel's Cite du Cinema **414 (1)** Gaumont/Les Films du Dauphin **(2)** Warner Bros./Regency Enterprises/Forward Pass/Art Linson Productions/Monarchy Enterprises B.V. **(3)** Lucasfilm **(4)** Camelot Pictures/Jersey Films/Double Feature Films/Large's Ark Productions **(5)** Columbia Pictures/Inside Track 2/Aquarium Productions **(6)** Warner Bros./Virtual Studios/Silver Pictures/Anarchos Productions/Studio Babelsberg/Medienboard

Berlin-Brandenburg/DC Comics **(7)** Fox Searchlight Pictures/Cross Creek Pictures/Protozoa Pictures/Phoenix Pictures/Dune Entertainment **(8)** Paramount Pictures/Marvel Entertainment/Marvel Studios **415 (1)** Warner Bros. **(2)** Warner Bros. **(3)** Arnold Pressburger Films **(4)** RKO Radio Pictures **(5)** RKO Radio Pictures **(6)** Regal Films **(7)** MGM **(8)** MGM **416 (1)** 20th Century Fox Film Corporation **(2)** MGM/Avon Productions (II) **(3)** Paramount Pictures/Hal Wallis Productions **(4)** 20th Century Fox Film Corporation **(5)** Paramount Pictures/Hal Wallis Productions **(6)** Paramount Pictures/Hal Wallis Productions **(7)** The Company of Artists/20th Century Fox Film Corporation **(8)** The Mirisch Corporation **417 (1)** Hal Wallis Productions **(2)** MGM/Jack Cummings Productions/Winters Hollywood Entertainment Holdings Corporation **(3)** Hal Wallis Productions **(4)** Euterpe/MGM **(5)** MGM/Euterpe **(6)** MGM **(7)** National General Pictures **(8)** National Broadcasting Company/Universal Pictures **418 (1)** 20th Century Fox Film Corporation **(2)** RKO Radio Pictures **(3)** Bryan Foy Productions/Warner Bros. **(4)** Alta Vista Productions **(5)** Tigon British Film Productions/American International Productions **(6)** Harbour Productions Limited/Cineman Films **(7)** Nelson Entertainment **(8)** 20th Century Fox Film Corporation **419 (1)** Universal Pictures **(2)** Warner Bros. **(3)** Columbia Pictures Corporation **(4)** Universal Pictures **(5)** Warner Bros. **(6)** Warner Bros. **(7)** Vanguard Films/RKO Radio Pictures **(8)** Horizon Pictures (II) **420 (1)** MGM **(2)** MGM **(3)** Warner Bros. **(4)** MGM **(5)** Warner Bros. **(6)** 20th Century Fox Film Corporation **(7)** Universal Pictures **(8)** Columbia Pictures Corporation **421 (1)** Warner Bros. **(2)** Warner Bros. **(3)** Warner Bros. **(4)** Warner Bros. **(5)** Warner Bros. **(6)** Universal International Pictures **(7)** Morningside Productions **(8)** Revue Studios **422 (1)** Horizon Pictures/Columbia Pictures Corporation **(2)** 20th Century Fox Film Corporation **(3)** Wildwood/Wildwood Enterprises **(4)** Redford-Ritchie Productions/Wildwood Enterprises **(5)** Sanford Productions (III)/Warner Bros. **(6)** Zanuck/Brown Productions/Universal Pictures **(7)** Columbia Pictures Corporation/Rastar Productions/Tom Ward Enterprises **(8)** Wildwood Enterprises/Dino De Laurentiis Company **423 (1)** Warner Bros./Wildwood/Wildwood Enterprises **(2)** 20th Century Fox Film Corporation **(3)** Mirage Enterprises/Universal Pictures **(4)** Paramount Pictures **(5)** Touchstone Pictures/Wildwood Enterprises **(6)** Voltage Pictures/Wildwood Enterprises/Brightlight Pictures/Kingsgate Films/TCYK North Productions **(7)** Before The Door Pictures/FilmNation Entertainment/Sudden Storm Productions/Black Bear Pictures/Treehouse Pictures/Washington Square Films **(8)** Marvel Entertainment/Marvel Studios/Sony Pictures Imageworks **424 tl** 20th Century Fox/The Kobal Collection **tr** Warner Bros/The Kobal Collection **cr** Columbia/The Kobal Collection **bl** Warner Bros/The Kobal Collection **br** Universal/The Kobal Collection **425 tl** Universal/The Kobal Collection **tr** Universal/The Kobal Collection **cl** Paramount/The Kobal Collection **br** Marvel Entertainment/Perception/Spi/The Kobal Collection **426 (1)** British Lion Film Corporation/Quintra **(2)** Highland Films **(3)** Bridge Films/Carlo Ponti Production/MGM **(4)** Hakim/Paris Film/Universal Pictures **(5)** Russo Productions **(6)** 20th Century Fox Film Corporation **(7)** Merchant Ivory Productions/WGBH/Rediffusion/Almi Entertainment Finance Corporation **(8)** Civilhand/Zenith Entertainment **427 (1)** Merchant Ivory Productions/Sumitomo Corporation/Imagica/Cinema Ten/Japan Satellite Broadcasting/Idle Productions/Film Four International **(2)** British Broadcasting Corportation/Capitol Films/Dove International/NDF International/Pandora Filmproduktion/Pony Canyon/Samuelson Entertainment/Samuelson Productions/The Greenlight Fund/Wall to Wall Television **(3)** First Look International/Bayly/Paré Productions/Bergen Film & TV/Newmarket Capital Group/BBC Films/European Co-production Fund/Nederlandse Programma Stichting/Dutch Co-Production Fund/Nederlands Fonds voor de Film **(4)** Morgan Creek Productions/Franchise Pictures/Clyde is Hungry Films/Pledge Productions/Epsilon Motion Pictures **(5)** Universal Pictures/StudioCanal/Relativity Media/Working Title Films **(6)** Hermetof Pictures/Magna Films/Icon Entertainment International/Lipsync Productions/BBC Films/Kalkronkie/Atlantic Swiss Productions/Artemis Films/Magnolia Mae Films/Synchronistic Pictures/Lonely Dragon **(7)** Follow Through Productions/Salamander Pictures/Al-Film/Laura Ziskin Productions/Lee Daniels Entertainment/Pam Williams Productions/Windy Hill Pictures **(8)** Annapurna Pictures/Likely Story/Media Rights Capital **428 (1)** Hemdale Film/Island **(2)** Lorimar Film Entertainment/NFH Productions/Warner Bros. **(3)** De Laurentiis Entertainment Group/De Laurentiis Film Partners/Interscope Communications/Nelson Entertainment/Soisson/Murphey Productions **(4)** Largo Entertainment/JVC Entertainment Networks **(5)** New Line Cinema **(6)** 20th Century Fox Film Corporation **(7)** Warner Bros./Village Roadshow Pictures/Groucho II Film Partnership/Silver Pictures **(8)** Warner Independent Pictures/Thousand Words/Section Eight/Detour Filmproduction/3 Arts Entertainment **429 (1)** N.N. Sippy Productions **(2)** Prakash Mehra Productions **(3)** Rupam Pictures **(4)** Integrated Films **(5)** Film-Valas **(6)** Film Kraft **(7)** D.M.S. Films/Time Magnetics **(8)** Aarohi Film Makers **430 (1)** Gaumont/Les Films du Loup **(2)** Gaumont/Les Films du Loup/Cecchi Gori Group Tiger Cinematografica **(3)** Alpilles Productions/Amigo Productions/Canal+/France 3 Cinéma/Gaumont International **(4)** Gaumont/Les Films du Dauphin **(5)** FGM Entertainment/United Artists Corporation/United Artists **(6)** Centropolis Film Production/Fried Films/Independent Pictures (II)/Toho Company/TriStar Pictures **(7)** Gaumont/Légende Entreprises/TF1 Films Production/Canal + **(8)** Columbia Pictures/Imagine Entertainment/Skylark Productions/Government of Malta **431 (1)** Warner Bros./Elmer Enterprises **(2)** British Lion Film Corporation/Columbia Pictures Corporation/EMI Films **(3)** Universal Pictures/Rastar Pictures/Pat Hustis Camera Cars **(4)** Warner Bros. **(5)** Universal Pictures/RKO Pictures/Miller-Milkis-Boyett Productions **(6)** The Samuel Goldwyn Company/Act III Communications/Breaking In Productions **(7)** Castle Rock Entertainment/Lobell/Bergman Productions **(8)** New Line Cinema/Lawrence Gordon Productions/Ghoulardi Film Company **432 (1)** MGM **(2)** MGM **(3)** MGM **(4)** MGM/Cinerama Productions Corp **(5)** MGM **(6)** Filmways Pictures/Raymax Productions **(7)** Paramount Pictures/Scott Rudin Productions **(8)** Jerry Weintraub Productions/HBO Films **433 (1)** The Mount Company **(2)** Carolco Pictures **(3)** Miramax/Live Entertainment/PolyGram Filmed Entertainment/Rank Organisation, The/Working Title Films **(4)** Avenue Pictures Productions/Spelling Entertainment/Addis Wechsler Pictures/Guild **(5)** Castle Rock Entertainment **(6)** Screen Gems/Lakeshore Entertainment/Arlington Road Productions Corporation/Gorai/Samuelson Productions/Samuelson Productions **(7)** Warner Bros./Village Roadshow Pictures/NPV Entertainment/Malpaso Productions **(8)** Paramount Pictures/DreamWorks SKG/Amblin Entertainment/Cruise/Wagner Productions **434 (1)** Night Life Inc./The Samuel Goldwyn Company/Virgin Vision **(2)** TriStar Pictures/Rastar Films **(3)** Touchstone Pictures/Silver Screen Partners IV **(4)** Columbia Pictures Corporation/StoneBridge Entertainment **(5)** 20th Century Fox Film Corporation **(6)** Amblin Entertainment/Tristar Pictures **(7)** Warner Bros. **(8)** Warner Bros./Silver Pictures/Donner/Shuler-Donner Productions **435 (1)** TriStar Pictures/1492 Pictures **(2)** Polygram Filmed Entertainment/Working Title Films/Bookshop Productions/Notting Hill Pictures **(3)** Universal Pictures/Columbia Pictures/Jersey Films **(4)** Warner Bros./Village Roadshow Pictures/NPV Entertainment/Jerry Weintraub Productions/Section Eight/WV Films II **(5)** Revolution Studios/Red Om Films **(6)** Columbia Pictures/Inside Track 2/Aquarium Productions **(7)** Columbia Pictures/Plan B Entertainment/Red Om Films **(8)** The Weinstein Company/Jean Doumanian Productions/Smokehouse Pictures/Battle Mountain Films/Yucaipa Films **436 tl** Tri-Star/The Kobal Collection **tr** 20th Century Fox/The Kobal Collection **cr** Warner Bros./The Kobal Collection **bl** Touchstone/The Kobal Collection **br** Warner Bros/The Kobal Collection **437 tl** Universal/The Kobal Collection **tr** EAT010AM **cl** Universal/The Kobal Collection **br** Jean Doumanian Productions/The Kobal Collection **438 (1)** Micheaux Film **(2)** Pool Films **(3)** John Krimsky and Gifford Cochran Inc. **(4)** London Film Productions **(5)** Universal Pictures **(6)** British Lion Films/Hammer Film Productions **(7)** Gaumont British Picture Corporation **(8)** CAPAD/Ealing Studios **439 (1)** First National Pictures **(2)** Christie Corporation/International Pictures (I) **(3)** Paramount Pictures **(4)** International Pictures (I)/The Haig Corporation **(5)** Warner Bros. **(6)** 20th Century Fox Film Corporation **(7)** Paramount Pictures/Motion Picture Associates **(8)** MGM/Filmways Pictures/Solar Productions **440 (1)** Mega Film/Société Nouvelle de Cinématographie **(2)** Gaumont/Les Productions de la Guéville/Madeleine Films **(3)** Fildebroc/ Les Productions de la Guéville/Universal Pictures France **(4)** Gaumont International/Les Productions de la Guéville **(5)** AMLF/Bela Productions/Lira Films/Renn Productions/TF1 **(6)** Lambart Productions/TF1 Films Production/Centre National de la Cinématographie/Investimage 2/**Investimage 3** **(7)** Les Films Pelléas/Locofilms/M6 Films/France 2 Cinéma/Sofica Investimage 4/Canal+/Procirep **(8)** Ciné B/Zoulou Films/Rhône-Alpes Cinéma/FCC/Tubedale Films/Pandora Filmproduktion/Cinema Parisien/Media Suits/Film Council/Centre National de la Cinématographie/Canal +/Eurimages/Sofica Sofinergie 5/Natexis Banques Populaires Images 2 **441 (1)** Miramax/Mad Chance/Section Eight/Mel's Cite du Cinema/JVS & Co. **(2)** Warner Bros./ImageMovers/Scott Free Productions/Rickshaw Productions/LivePlanet/HorsePower Entertainment/Saturn Films **(3)** Fox Searchlight Pictures/ATO Pictures/Contrafilm/Aramid Entertainment Fund/Dune Entertainment III/Choke Film **(4)** Liberty Films UK/Xingu Films/Limelight Fund/Lunar Industries **(5)** Paramount Pictures/Marvel Entertainment/Marvel Studios/Fairview Entertainment **(6)** Omega Entertainment/Longfellow Pictures/Oceana Media Finance/Prescience/Innocence Productions/Pantheon Entertainment Corporation **(7)** CBS Films/Film4/British Film Institute/Blueprint Pictures **(8)** Sycamore Pictures/The Walsh Company/OddLot Entertainment/What Just Happened Productions **442 (1)** RKO Radio Pictures **(2)** RKO Radio Pictures **(3)** RKO Radio Pictures **(4)** RKO Radio Pictures **(5)** RKO Radio Pictures **(6)** RKO Radio Pictures **(7)** Paramount Pictures **(8)** 20th Century Fox Film Corporation **443 (1)** MGM **(2)** MGM **(3)** MGM **(4)** MGM **(5)** Jurow-Shepherd **(6)** Three Michaels Film Productions **(7)** Omni Zoetrope **(8)** 20th Century Fox Film Corporation/Ingenious Film Partners/1492 Pictures/21 Laps Entertainment/Dune Entertainment/Sun Canada Productions **444 (1)** Stanley Kramer Productions **(2)** Walter Reade Organization **(3)** Universal Pictures **(4)** Faces **(5)** Faces Distribution **(6)** Columbia Pictures Corporation **(7)** Jack Rollins & Charles H. Joffe Productions **(8)** Academy/Channel Four Films/Iberoamerica Films/Mayfair Films/Scala Productions/Screen Partners Ltd./Three Rivers Production **445 (1)** Howard Hughes Productions **(2)** Paramount Pictures **(3)** RKO Radio Pictures **(4)** RKO Radio Pictures **(5)** Bing Crosby Productions/Hope Enterprises/Paramount Pictures **(6)** 20th Century Fox Film Corporation **(7)** RKO Radio Pictures **(8)** Cinema Center Films/Major Pictures Production **446 (1)** Castle Rock Entertainment/Nelson Entertainment **(2)** Bill Graham Films/Carolco International N.V./Carolco Pictures/Imagine Entertainment/Ixtlan **(3)** TriStar Pictures **(4)** Fox 2000 Pictures **(5)** Warner Bros. **(6)** Konrad Pictures/Miramax **(7)** Pathe Productions/Pathé Pictures International/Red Turtle **(8)** Picturehouse/Pathé Pictures International/Inferno Distribution/Jagged Films/New Line Cinema/Shukovsky English Entertainment **447 (1)** RKO Radio Pictures **(2)** RKO Radio Pictures **(3)** MGM **(4)** MGM **(5)** Security Pictures **(6)** Allied Artists Pictures/Anglo Allied **(7)** Warner Brothers/Seven Arts **(8)** MGM **448 (1)** Walter Wanger Productions **(2)** 20th Century Fox Film Corporation **(3)** David L. Loew-Albert Lewin **(4)** MGM **(5)** David L. Loew-Albert Lewin **(6)** 20th Century Fox Film Corporation **(7)** Walt Disney Productions **(8)** 20th Century Fox Film Corporation **449 (1)** Universal Pictures/Brillstein-Grey Entertainment/Robert Simonds Productions **(2)** Juno Pix/New Line Cinema/Robert Simonds Productions **(3)** Jack Giarraputo Productions/Out of the Blue... Entertainment **(4)** New Line Cinema/Revolution Studios/Ghoulardi Film Company **(5)** Columbia Pictures Corporation/Gracie Films **(6)** Columbia Pictures Corporation/Happy Madison Productions/Anonymous Content/Flower Films (II) **(7)** Universal Pictures/Columbia Pictures/Relativity Media/Apatow Productions/Madison 23 **(8)** Columbia Pictures/Relativity Media/Happy Madison Productions **450 (1)** 20th Century Fox Film Corporation/Michael White Productions **(2)** Paramount Pictures **(3)** International Cinema Corporation/Selta Films/Canadian Film Development Corporation/Cine-Neighbor/Famous Players Limited **(4)** MGM/Peerford Ltd. **(5)** Warner Bros./The Guber-Peters Company/Kennedy Miller Productions **(6)** The Mount Company **(7)** Pathé Entertainment/Percy Main/Star Partners III Ltd./MGM **(8)** Universal Pictures/Kennedy Miller Productions **451 (1)** Warner Bros./Regency Enterprises/Alcor Films **(2)** Havoc/Polygram Filmed Entertainment/Working Title Films **(3)** Cradle Productions Inc./Havoc/Touchstone Pictures **(4)** Fox Searchlight Pictures/Gran Via/Elizabeth Cantillon Productions **(5)** Warner Independent Pictures/NALA Films/Summit Entertainment/Samuels Media/Blackfriars Bridge Films **(6)** DreamWorks SKG/Film4/WingNut Films/New Zealand Large Budget Screen Production Grant/Goldcrest Pictures/Key Creatives **(7)** Cloud Atlas Productions/X-Filme Creative Pool/Anarchos Pictures/A Company Filmproduktionsgesellschaft/ARD Degeto Film/Ascension Pictures/Dreams of Dragon Picture/Five Drops/Media Asia Group **(8)** Voltage Pictures/Wildwood Enterprises/Brightlight Pictures/Kingsgate Films/TCYK North Productions **452 (1)** D'Antoni Productions/Schine-Moore Productions **(2)** Zanuck/Brown Productions/Universal Pictures **(3)** Paramount Pictures **(4)** Columbia Pictures Corporation/20th Century Fox Film Corporation **(5)** Taylor-Wigutow Productions **(6)** MGM **(7)** Film Trustees Ltd./Naked Lunch Productions/Nippon Film Development and Finance/The Ontario Film Development Corporation/Recorded Picture Company/Téléfilm Canada **(8)** Eureka Pictures/Good Machine **453 (1)** Erma-Film **(2)** Robert et Raymond Hakim/Paris Film/Paritalia/Titanus **(3)** Société Nouvelle de Cinématographie/Tritone Cinematografica **(4)** Fida Cinematografica/Lira Films/Sonocam **(5)** Mega Film/Cinétel/Dieter Geissler Filmproduktion/Divina-Film **(6)** Albina Productions S.a.r.l./Rizzoli Film/TIT Filmproduktion GmbH **(7)** Les Productions Artistes Associés/Mercure Productions/TIT Filmproduktion GmbH **(8)** Films A2/Gaumont International/Little Bear/Sara Films/Selta Films/Société Française de Production/TV13 Filmproduktion **454 (1)** Universum Film **(2)** Universal Pictures **(3)** MGM **(4)** 20th Century Fox Film Corporation **(5)** MGM **(6)** Athos Films/Chaumiane/Filmstudio **(7)** Dino de Laurentiis Cinematografica/Marianne Productions **(8)** APJAC Productions/20th Century Fox Film Corporation **455 (1)** MGM **(2)** John Boorman Productions **(3)** Columbia Pictures Corporation/EMI Films/Julia Phillips and Michael Phillips Productions **(4)** The Ladd Company/Shaw Brothers/Warner Bros./Blade Runner Partnership **(5)** Hemdale Film/Pacific Western/Euro Film Funding/Cinema 84 **(6)** 20th Century Fox Film Corporation/Brandywine Productions/SLM Production Group **(7)** 20th Century Fox Film Corporation/DreamWorks SKG/Cruise/Wagner Productions/Blue Tulip Productions/Ronald Shusett/Gary Goldman/Amblin Entertainment **(8)** Lionsgate/Color Force **456 (1)** Outov Productions **(2)** Universal Pictures/Dino De Laurentiis Company **(3)** Hemdale Film/Pacific Western/Euro Film Funding/Cinema 84 **(4)** Amercent Films/American Entertainment Partners L.P./Davis Entertainment/Lawrence Gordon Productions/Silver Pictures/20th Century Fox Film Corporation **(5)** Carolco Pictures/Carolco International N.V. **(6)** Carolco Pictures/Pacific Western/Lightstorm Entertainment/Canal+/T2 Productions **(7)** 20th Century Fox Film Corporation/Lightstorm Entertainment **(8)** Summit Entertainment/Emmett/Furla Films/Mark Canton Productions/Envision Entertainment/Boies/Schiller Film Group/Atmosphere Entertainment MM/Knightsbridge Entertainment **457 (1)** Canal+/Columbia Pictures Corporation/Les Films Alain Sarde/R.P. Productions/Timothy Burrill Productions **(2)** PolyGram Filmed Entertainment/Channel Four Films/Working Title Films **(3)** Miramax/Tiger Moth Productions **(4)** Touchstone Pictures/Wildwood Enterprises **(5)** UGC YM/Integral Film/France 3 Cinéma/UGC Images/Sofica UGC 1/Sofica Soficinéma 4/Fonds Eurimages du Conseil de l'Europe/Région Lorraine/Ville de Nancy/Communaute Urbaine du Grand Nancy/Canal+/TPS Star **(6)** Ecosse Films/Film4/UK Film Council/Aver Media/North West Vision/Lipsync Productions **(7)** Pyramide Productions/Caméra One/VMP/Solaire Production/Canal+/CinéCinéma/Cofinova 5/Région Languedoc-Roussillon/Centre National de la Cinématographie/Cofinova 3/Procirep/Angoa-Agicoa **(8)** Space Rocket Nation/A Grand Elephant/Bold Films/Film i Väst/Gaumont/Wild Bunch **458 (1)** Wheel Productions **(2)** Wheel Productions **(3)** Columbia Pictures Corporation/Highroad Productions **(4)** Les Films Impéria/Les Productions Georges de Beauregard/Société Nouvelle de Cinématographie **(5)** Columbia Pictures Corporation **(6)** Les Productions Georges de Beauregard/Rome Paris Films/Société Nouvelle de Cinématographie **(7)** Alan Jay Lerner Productions/The Malpaso Company **(8)** Universal Pictures/Ross Hunter Productions **459 (1)** The Rank Organisation/Ealing Studios **(2)** Charter Film Productions/Boulting Brothers **(3)** MGM/Seven Arts Pictures/A.A. Productions Ltd./Anya/Harris-Kubrick Productions/Transworld Pictures **(4)** Mirisch G-E Productions **(5)** Columbia Pictures Corporation/Hawk Films **(6)** Cinecitta Italiana Stabilimenti Cinematografici/Compagnia Cinematografica Montoro/Nancy Enterprises (I) **(7)** The Mirisch Corporation **(8)** BSB/CIP/Lorimar Film Entertainment/NatWest Ventures/New Gold Entertainment /Northstar Media **460 (1)** Indigo Film **(2)** Fandango/Indigo Film/Medusa Film **(3)** Indigo Film/Medusa Film/Sky/Friuli Venezia Giulia Film Commission/Ministero per i Beni e le Attività Culturali/Media Programme of the European Community **(4)** Fandango/Rai Cinema/Sky/Ministero per i Beni e le Attività Culturali/Media Programme of the European Community **(5)** Indigo Film/Lucky Red/Parco Film/Babe Film/StudioCanal/Arte France Cinéma/Sky Cinema/Ministero per i Beni e le Attività Culturali/Fonds Eurimages du Conseil de l'Europe/Film Commission Torino-Piemonte/Regione Campania/Campania Film Commission/Centre National de la Cinématographie **(6)** Acaba Produzioni/Babe Film/EOS Entertainment/Rai Cinema/Canal+/CinéCinéma/Ministero per i Beni e le Attività Culturali/Media Programme of the European Community/Deutsche Filmförderfonds **(7)** Devon Cinematografica/Surf Film/The Bottom Line/Immagine e Cinema/Teatri Uniti/Rai Cinema/Ministero per i Beni e le Attività Culturali **(8)** Indigo Film/Medusa Film/Babe Film/Pathé/France 2 Cinéma/Mediaset/Canal+/Ciné+/France Télévisions/Regione Lazio/Ministero per i Beni e le Attività Culturali/Banca Popolare di Vicenza/Lazio Film Commission/Fonds Eurimages du Conseil de l'Europe/Media Programme of the European Community/Biscottificio Verona **461 (1)** Nile Cinema Company **(2)** Horizon Pictures (II) **(3)** MGM/Carlo Ponti Production/Sostar S.A. **(4)** Columbia Pictures Corporation/Irving Allen Productions/Central Cinema Company Film/Avala Film **(5)** Columbia Pictures/Horizon Pictures (II)/Filmsonor **(6)** Columbia Pictures Corporation/Rastar Productions **(7)** Richard Fleischer/Sy Bartlett/20th Century Fox Film Corporation **(8)** Touchstone Pictures/Casey Silver Productions/Dune Films **462 (1)** Eon Productions/Danjaq **(2)** Warner Bros./Cinerama Productions Corp./United States Pictures **(3)** Highland Films **(4)** American Broadcasting Company/Palomar Pictures International **(5)** Zanuck/Brown Productions/Universal Pictures **(6)** Palomar Pictures (I)/Palladium Productions **(7)** Zanuck/Brown Productions/Universal Pictures **(8)** Paramount Pictures **463 (1)** MGM/Edgar Lansbury Productions Inc./T.D.J. Productions Inc./Delos Productions Inc. **(2)** Warner Bros./Pressman-Williams/Jill Jakes Production/Badlands Company **(3)** Zoetrope Studios **(4)** Dino De Laurentiis Company/Lorimar Film Entertainment **(5)** 20th Century Fox Film Corporation/American Entertainment Partners L.P./Amercent Films **(6)** Warner Bros./Plan B Entertainment/Initial Entertainment Group/Vertigo Entertainment/Media Asia Films **(7)** The Weinstein Company/Bold Films/Bobby/Holly Wiersma Productions **(8)** Filmax Entertainment/Icon Entertainment International/Elixir Films **464 (1)** Films Sacha Gordine **(2)** Filmsonor/Vera Films **(3)** Romulus Films/Remus **(4)** Marianne Productions/Transcontinental Films **(5)** Les Films Corona/Fono Roma **(6)** Les Films Corona/Les Films Pomereu/Produzione Intercontinentale Cinematografica/Fono Roma/Selenia Cinematografica **(7)** Lira Films/Cinétel/Gafer/Comacico **(8)** Sara Films/Films A2 **465 (1)** Paris Film **(2)** William Dieterle Productions **(3)** RKO Radio Pictures **(4)** RKO Radio Pictures **(5)** Films Sacha Gordine **(6)** Compagnie Commerciale Française Cinématographique/Stera Films **(7)** British Lion Film Corporation **(8)** Eléfilm/Italian International Film/Les Films de la Boétie **466 (1)** MGM **(2)** MGM **(3)** Columbia Pictures Corporation **(4)** Libra Productions Inc. **(5)** The Samuel Goldwyn Company **(6)** Otto Preminger Films/Carlyle Productions **(7)** MGM/Sol C. Siegel Productions/Bing Crosby Productions **(8)** Essex Productions/George Sidney Productions **467 (1)** Stanley Kramer Productions **(2)** MGM **(3)** Warner Bros./Village Roadshow Pictures/NPV Entertainment/Jerry Weintraub Productions/Section Eight/WV Films II **(4)** M.C. Productions **(5)** 20th Century Fox Film Corporation/P-R Productions Picture **(6)** Artanis Productions/Sinatra Enterprises **(7)** Arcola Pictures **(8)** Artanis Productions Inc./Cinema VII **468 (1)** Svensk Filmindustri/Svenska Filminstitutet/Svenska Ord **(2)** Argus Film Produktie/Arte/Canal+/CoBo Fonds/Det Danske Filminstitut/Eurimages/European Script Fund/Finnish Film Foundation/Icelandic Film/La Sept Cinéma/Liberator Productions/Lucky Red/Media Investment Club/Memfis Film/Nederlands Fonds voor de Film/Nordisk Film- & TV-Fond/Northern Lights/Norwegian Film Institute/October Films/Philippe Bober/SVT Drama/Svenska Filminstitutet/TV1000 AB/Trust Film Svenska/Villealfa Filmproduction Oy/Vrijzinnig Protestantse Radio Omroep/Yleisradio/Zentropa Entertainments/Zweites Deutsches Fernsehen **(3)** Be Gentlemen Limited Partnership/Lawrence Bender Productions/Miramax **(4)** Screen Gems/Red Mullet Productions **(5)** Universal Pictures/Relativity Media/Littlestar/Playtone/Internationale Filmproduktion Richter **(6)** Columbia Pictures/MGM/Scott Rudin Productions/Yellow Bird/Film Rites/Ground Control **(7)** Paramount Pictures/Marvel Entertainment/Marvel Studios **(8)** Zentropa Entertainments/Zentropa International Köln /Heimatfilm/Film i Väst /Slot Machine /Caviar Films/Concorde Filmverleih/Artificial Eye/Les Films du Losange/European Film Bonds/Caviar **469 (1)** MGM/Ealing Films **(2)** Romulus Films **(3)** BHE Films/National Theatre of Great Britain Production **(4)** 20th Century-Fox Productions **(5)** MGM **(6)** Goldcrest Films International/National Film Finance Corporation/Curzon Film Distributors/Film Four International/Merchant Ivory Productions **(7)** HandMade Films/United British Artists **(8)** USA Films/Capitol Films/Film Council/Sandcastle 5 Productions/Chicagofilms/Medusa Film **470 (1)** MGM/Maiden Movies/New Regency Pictures **(2)** Don Simpson/Jerry Bruckheimer Films **(3)** 20th Century Fox Film Corporation/Centropolis Entertainment **(4)** Columbia Pictures Corporation/Amblin Entertainment/Parkes+MacDonald Image Nation **(5)** Columbia Pictures Corporation/Forward Pass/Initial Entertainment Group/Moonlighting Films/Overbrook Entertainment/Peters Entertainment/Picture Entertainment Corporation **(6)** Columbia Pictures Corporation/Relativity Media/Overbrook Entertainment/Escape Artists **(7)** Warner Bros./Village Roadshow Pictures/Weed Road Pictures/Overbrook Entertainment/3 Arts Entertainment/Heyday Films/Original Film **(8)** Columbia Pictures/Overbrook Entertainment/Blinding Edge Pictures **471 (1)** Cité Films/Peg-Films **(2)** Film Costellazione Produzione/Águila Films **(3)** Dino de Laurentiis Cinematografica/Orsay Films **(4)** Dino de Laurentiis Cinematografica **(5)** Dino de Laurentiis Cinematografica **(6)** C.I.C./Dino de Laurentiis Cinematografica/Produzione Cinematografiche Inter.Ma.Co. **(7)** Auro Cinematografica **(8)** Clesi Cinematografica/Greenwich Film Productions/José Frade Producciones Cinematográficas S.A./Albatros Filmproduktion/Filmédis/Gaumont International **472 (1)** Edison Manufacturing Company **(2)** Decla-Bioscop AG **(3)** Universal Pictures **(4)** MGM **(5)** Eon Productions **(6)** Produzioni Europee Associati/Arturo González Producciones Cinematográficas, S.A/Constantin Film Produktion/United Artists **(7)** Lucasfilm **(8)** Starling Films/Dino De Laurentiis Company **473 (1)** Hemdale Film/Pacific Western/Euro Film Funding/Cinema 84 **(2)** De Laurentiis Entertainment Group **(3)** Warner Bros./Morgan Creek Productions **(4)** Strong Heart/Demme Production/Orion Pictures **(5)** 20th Century Fox Film Corporation **(6)** La Petite Reine/Remstar Productions/Novo RPI/M6 Films/Canal+/TPS Star/120 Films/Région Haute-Normandie/Procirep/Angoa-Agicoa/Centre National de la Cinématographie/Téléfilm Canada/Société de Développement des Entreprises Culturelles/Uni Etoile 4/Uni Etoile 5/Banque Populaire Images 8/Cinémage 2 **(7)** Warner Bros./Legendary Pictures/Syncopy/DC Comics **(8)** Universal Pictures/The Weinstein Company/A Band Apart/Studio Babelsberg/Visiona Romantica **474 (1)** 20th Century Fox Film Corporation **(2)** Walrus & Associates **(3)** GGR/New Line Cinema/Zupnik Cinema Group II **(4)** Hollywood Pictures/Touchwood Pacific Partners 1/Permut Presentations **(5)** Touchstone Pictures/Don Simpson/Jerry Bruckheimer Films **(6)** Cineville/Keystone Studios/Mama'Z Boy Entertainment/NeoFight Film **(7)** PolyGram Filmed Entertainment/Spelling Films International/Blue Parrot/Bad Hat Harry Productions/Rosco Film GmbH **(8)** Cecchi Gori Pictures/Juno Pix/New Line Cinema **475 (1)** Regency Enterprises/The Wolper Organization/Warner Bros. **(2)** Malpaso Productions/Silver Pictures/Warner Bros. **(3)** Regency Enterprises/Mandeville Films/New Regency Pictures/Monarchy Enterprises B.V./Taurus Film **(4)** DreamWorks SKG/Jinks/Cohen Company **(5)** Lions Gate Films/Archer Street Productions/QI Quality International GmbH & Co. KG/Trigger Street Productions/Visionview Production/Studio Babelsberg/Endgame Entertainment/Element X/Media 8 Entertainment/Medienboard Berlin-Brandenburg **(6)** Warner Bros./Legendary Pictures/Peters Entertainment/Bad Hat Harry Productions/DC Comics/Red Sun Productions Pty. Ltd. **(7)** Before The Door Pictures/Benaroya Pictures/Washington Square Films/Untitled Entertainment **(8)** New Line Cinema/Rat Entertainment **476 (1)** Chartoff-Winkler Productions/United Artists **(2)** Force Ten Productions Inc. **(3)** Lorimar Film Entertainment/Victory Company/New Gold Entertainment **(4)** Anabasis N.V./Elcajo Productions **(5)** Carolco Pictures/Canal+/Pioneer/RCS Video/Cliffhanger Productions **(6)** Miramax/Woods Entertainment/Across the River Productions **(7)** MGM/Columbia Pictures/Revolution Studios/Rogue Marble **(8)** Millennium Films/Nu Image Films/Nimar Studios/Rogue Marble **477 (1)** Columbia Pictures Corporation **(2)** Columbia Pictures Corporation **(3)** The Samuel Goldwyn Company **(4)** Paramount Pictures **(5)** Paramount Pictures **(6)** Hal Wallis Productions **(7)** 20th Century Fox Film Corporation/Globe Enterprises **(8)** Famous Artists Productions/Famartists Productions S.A./Columbia Pictures Corporation **478 (1)** Warner Bros. **(2)** Paramount Pictures **(3)** Columbia Pictures Corporation **(4)** MGM **(5)** RKO Radio Pictures **(6)** E-K-Corporation/Lion's Gate Films **(7)** Paramount Pictures/Penthouse/Long Road Productions **(8)** De Laurentiis Entertainment Group **479 (1)** Warner Bros./PolyGram Filmed Entertainment **(2)** Columbia Pictures Corporation/The Rank Organisation **(3)** Regency Enterprises/The Wolper Organization/Warner Bros. **(4)** Bergman Lustig Productions **(5)** Warner Bros./Legendary Pictures/Syncopy/DC Comics **(6)** Aldamisa Entertainment/Demarest Films/Miramax/Solipsist Film/Troublemaker Studios **(7)** Ghoulardi Film Company/IAC Films/Warner Bros. **480 (1)** Galatea Film/Jolly Film/Alta Vista Productions **(2)** Alta Vista Productions **(3)** Panda Film **(4)** Cineriz/Francinex **(5)** Tigon British Film Productions **(6)** Artists Entertainment Complex/New World Video/Renegade Women Co **(7)** Canadian

RECEIVED OCT 2 9 2015

Film Development Corporation (CFDC)/Cinépix/DAL Productions (8) New World Pictures 481 (1) Columbia Pictures Corporation/Horizon Pictures (2) Landau Company/The Pawnbroker Company (3) The Mirisch Corporation (4) SKM (5) Dino de Laurentiis Cinematografica/Mosfilm (6) Rafran Cinematografica/Euro International Film/San Miura (7) Harbor Productions/Les Films de la Boétie/Vides Cinematografica (8) Tim Burton Productions/Warner Bros. 482 (1) Columbia Pictures Corporation (2) Columbia Pictures Corporation (3) Universal Pictures (4) MGM/Loew's (5) Liberty Films (II) (6) Warner Bros./Transatlantic Pictures (7) Universal International Pictures (8) Universal International Pictures 483 (1) MGM (2) Paramount Pictures/Paton Inc. (3) Leland Hayward Productions/Warner Bros./Billy Wilder Productions (4) Alfred J. Hitchcock Productions (5) Carlyle Productions (6) Paramount Pictures/ John Ford Productions (7) The Associates & Aldrich Company (8) Columbia/The Kobal Collection tl RKO/The Kobal Collection tr RKO/The Kobal Collection bl MGM/The Kobal Collection br RKO/The Kobal Collection 485 tr Universal/The Kobal Collection ctr Paramount/The Kobal Collection cbr Columbia/The Kobal Collection bl Paramount/The Kobal Collection br Paramount/The Kobal Collection 486 (1) Jersey Films/Universal Pictures (2) Miramax (3) Polygram Filmed Entertainment/Propaganda Films/Fleece (4) 20th Century Fox Film Corporation (5) Universal Pictures/DreamWorks SKG/Nancy Tenenbaum Films/Tribeca Productions (6) Touchstone Pictures/ American Empirical Pictures (7) DreamWorks SKG/Red Hour Films/Goldcrest Productions (8) Scott Rudin Productions/Twins Financing 487 (1) Carolco Pictures/Carolco International N.V. (2) Carolco Pictures/Canal+ (3) Paramount Pictures (4) Warner Bros./Jerry Weintraub Productions/Iguana Productions (5) Universal Pictures/Syalis DA/Légende Entreprises/De Fina-Cappa (6) TriStar Pictures/Japan Satellite Broadcasting (JBS)/IndieProd Company Productions (7) Chaos Productions/Jane Startz Productions/Miramax/Scholastic Productions (8) Focus Features/Five Roses/Bac Films 488 (1) IFM Films/Universal Pictures (2) Columbia Pictures (3) Incorporated Television Company/ Keith Barish Productions (4) ABC Motion Pictures (5) Mirage Enterprises/Universal Pictures (6) Casen Productions/Golan-Globus Productions/Cinema Verity/Evil Angels Films/Warner Bros. (7) Universal Pictures (8) Universal Pictures/Turman-Foster Company/David Foster Productions 489 (1) Warner Bros./Amblin Entertainment/Malpaso Productions (2) Beverly Detroit/Clinica Estetico/Good Machine/Intermedia/Magnet Productions/Propaganda Films (3) Fox 2000 Pictures/Dune Entertainment/Major Studio Partners/Peninsula Films (4) Picturehouse/GreeneStreet Films/River Road Entertainment/Sandcastle 5 Productions/Prairie Home Productions (5) Universal Pictures/Relativity Media/Littlestar/Playtone/Internationale Filmproduktion Richter (6) Lucamar Productions/Marc Platt Productions/Walt Disney Pictures 490 t Columbia/The Kobal Collection cl ITC/Universal/The Kobal Collection cr Columbia/The Kobal Collection bl Universal/The Kobal Collection br 20th Century Fox/The Kobal Collection 491 t Universal/Playtone/The Kobal Collection b Film 4/Pathe/The Kobal Collection 492 (1) Columbia Pictures Corporation/Rastar Productions (2) Chenault Productions/20th Century Fox Film Corporation (3) Paramount Pictures (4) Rastar Pictures/Tom Ward Enterprises (5) Barwood Films/First Artists (6) Warner Bros./Saticoy Productions (7) Columbia Pictures Corporation/Rastar Productions/Tom Ward Enterprises (8) TriStar Pictures/Japan Satellite Broadcasting (JBS)/IndieProd Company 493 (1) Barwood Films/First Artists/Winters Hollywood Entertainment Holdings Corporation (2) First Artists/Barwood Films (3) Artists/Barwood Films (4) Warner Bros./Barwood Films (5) Columbia Pictures Corporation/ Barwood Films/Longfellow Pictures (6) TriStar Pictures/Phoenix Pictures/Barwood Films (7) Phoenix Pictures/DreamWorks SKG/Tribeca Productions/Everyman Pictures (8) Paramount Pictures/Skydance Productions/Michaels-Goldwyn 494 (1) Aspen Productions (I)/Ingo Preminger Productions/20th Century Fox Film Corporation (2) Warner Bros./Gus Productions (3) Casey Productions/Eldorado Films (4) Productions/Produzioni Europee Associati (5) TriStar Pictures/Phoenix Pictures/Barwood Films (6) Warner Bros./Canal+/Regency Enterprises (7) Focus Features/Universal Pictures/StudioCanal/Working Title Films/Scion Films (8) Lionsgate/Color Force 495 (1) Mack Sennett Comedies (2) Paramount Pictures (3) Famous Players-Lasky Corporation (4) Gloria Swanson Pictures (5) Gloria Productions (6) Gloria Swanson Pictures (7) Warner Bros./Grandon Productions Ltd. (8) Paramount Pictures 496 (1) Svensk Filmindustri (2) Svensk Filmindustri (3) George Stevens Productions (4) Svensk Filmindustri (5) Svensk Filmindustri (6) Warner Bros./Warner Bros./Hoya Productions (7) Wildwood Enterprises/ Dino De Laurentiis Company (8) Starling Films/Dino De Laurentiis Company 497 (1) TaliaFilm II Productions/Woodcote/PSO International (2) Orion Pictures/Jack Rollins & Charles H. Joffe Productions (3) Per Holst Filmproduktion/ Svensk Filmindustri/Odyssey Entertainment (4) Columbia Pictures Corporation/Parkes/Lasker productions (5) SVT Drama/Danmarks Radio/Yleisradio/La Sept Cinéma/Zweites Deutsches Fernsehen/Channel Four Films/RAI Radiotelevisione Italiana/Norsk Rikskringkasting/Rikisútvarpið-Sjónvarp RÚV/Focus Features International (6) 20th Century Fox Film Corporation/DreamWorks SKG/Zanuck Company/Blue Tulip Productions/Ronald Shusett/ Gary Goldman/Amblin Entertainment (7) Pathé Renn Productions/France 3 Cinéma/The Kennedy/Marshall Company/C.R.R.A.V. Nord Pas de Calais/Région Nord-Pas-de-Calais/Canal+/CinéCinéma/Banque Populaire images 7 (8) Warner Bros./Scott Rudin Productions/Paramount Pictures (9) Shochiku Company (2) Shochiku Company/Shôchiku Eiga (3) Shôchiku Eiga (4) Fox Productions/Shintoho Film Distribution Committee (5) Daiei Studios (6) Daiei Studios (7) Shochiku Company (8) Hoyu-za Film Production Company Ltd./O&R Productions/Toho Company 499 (1) Agat Films & Cie/Arte France Cinéma/Tabo Tabo Films/Canal+/Sofinergie 4/Centre National de la Cinématographie (2) Claudie Ossard Productions/Union Générale Cinématographique/Victoires Productions/Tapioca Films/France 3 Cinéma/MMC Independent/Sofica Sofinergie 5/Filmstiftung Nordrhein-Westfalen/Canal+ (3) BBC Films/Celador Films/Jonescompany Productions (4) Columbia Pictures Corporation/Imagine Entertainment/Skylark Productions/Government of Malta (5) Les Films Pelléas/France 2 Cinéma/Tovo Films/France 3 Cinéma/KS2 Productions/ Canal+/TPS Star/Wild Bunch/Région Provence-Alpes-Côte d'Azur/Centre National du Cinéma et de l'Image Animée (6) Haut et Court/Cineb/Warner Bros./France 2 Cinéma/Canal+/CinéCinéma /France 2/Films Distribution/ Cofinova 5/Banque Populaire images 9/Scope Pictures/Le Tax Shelter du Gouvernement Fédéral de Belgique/Soficapital/SCOPE Invest (7) Les films du 24/France 3 Cinéma/TF1 Droits Audiovisuels/Canal+/Ciné+/France Télévision/ Sofica UGC 1/Soficinéma 8/La Banque Postale Images 5/Cofinova 7/Région Aquitaine/Centre National de la Cinématographie/Procirep/Cool Industrie/LBPI 5 (8) Brio Films/StudioCanal/Scope Pictures/France 2 Cinéma/ Hérodiade/Radio Télévision Belge Francophone/Belgacom/Cinémage 6/France Télévisions/Cinéimage 7/La Banque Postale Images 5/Sofica Manon 2/Anton Capital Entertainment/Canal+/Ciné+/France Télévisions/Centre National de la Cinématographie/Eurimages/Région Ile-de-France /Media Programme of the European Community/SCOPE Invest/Angoa-Agicoa/Procirep/Fédération Wallonie-Bruxelles/Le Tax Shelter du Gouvernement Fédéral de Belgique 500 (1) Paramount Pictures (2) Fox Film Corporation (3) 20th Century Fox Film Corporation (4) 20th Century Fox Film Corporation (5) 20th Century Fox Film Corporation (6) 20th Century Fox Film Corporation (7) 20th Century Fox Film Corporation (8) Argosy Pictures 501 (1) Merchant Ivory Productions/Sumitomo Corporation/Imagica/Cinema Ten/Japan Satellite Broadcasting Idle Productions/Film Four International (2) American Playhouse Theatrical Productions (3) Merchant Ivory Productions/Columbia Pictures Corporation (4) Hell's Kitchen Films/Universal Pictures (5) Columbia Pictures Corporation/Mirage Enterprises (6) Universal Pictures/StudioCanal/Working Title Films/DNA Films (7) BBC Films/Finola Dwyer Productions/Wildgaze Films/Endgame Entertainment/An Education Distribution (8) Walt Disney Pictures/Ruby Films/Essential Media & Entertainment/BBC Films/Hopscotch Features 502 (1) Fox Film Corporation (2) Columbia Pictures Corporation (3) Columbia Pictures Corporation (4) Columbia Pictures Corporation (5) Columbia Pictures Corporation (6) Columbia Pictures Corporation (7) Columbia Pictures Corporation (8) Columbia Pictures Corporation/Normandy Productions 503 (1) Lorimar Film Entertainment/NFH Productions (2) Walras & Associates (3) New Line Cinema/Fourth Vision (4) Miramax/A Band Apart/ Jersey Films (5) Miramax/Woods Entertainment (6) Columbia Pictures Corporation/Jersey Films (7) Miramax/A Band Apart/Super Cool ManChu (8) Zentropa Entertainments/Zentropa International Köln/Heimatfilm/Film i Väst /Slot Machine /Caviar Films/Concorde Filmverleih/Artificial Eye/Les Films du Losange/European Film Bonds/Caviar 504 (1) First National Pictures (2) Columbia Pictures/Fox Film (3) New Line Cinema (4) MGM (5) MGM (6) MGM (7) MGM (8) Liberty Films (II) 505 (1) MGM (2) MGM/Loew's (3) MGM (4) MGM (5) Leland Hayward Productions/Warner Bros. (6) Stanley Kramer Productions (7) Roxlom Films Inc. (8) Columbia Pictures Corporation 506 (1) Robert Stigwood Organization (2) Paramount Pictures/Robert Stigwood Organization/Allan Carr Production (3) Cinema 77/Gecko Productions/Filmways Pictures/Viscount Associates (4) TriStar Pictures/Management Company Entertainment Group/Krane Entertainment (5) Miramax/A Band Apart/Jersey Films (6) MGM/Jersey Films (7) Permut Presentations/Touchstone Pictures/Paramount Pictures/Douglas/Reuther Productions/WCG Entertainment Productions/Krane Entertainment (8) New Line Cinema/Ingenious Film Partners/Zadan/Meron Productions 507 (1) The Ladd Company (2) 20th Century Fox Film Corporation/El Corazon Producciones S.A./Nina Saxon Film Design/SLM Production Group (3) New World Pictures/China Blue Productions/Planet Productions (4) ABC Motion Pictures (5) TriStar Pictures/Rastar Pictures/Zoetrope Studios/Delphi V Productions (6) 20th Century Fox Film Corporation/Gracie Films (7) Polar Entertainment Corporation (8) American Zoetrope/Eternity Pictures/Muse Productions/Virgin Suicides LLC 508 (1) MGM (2) MGM (3) MGM (4) MGM (5) MGM (6) 20th Century Fox Film Corporation/Jerry Wald Productions (7) Universal International Pictures (8) Universal Pictures/Ross Hunter Productions (9) Warner Bros. 509 (1) Svensk Filmindustri (2) Svensk Filmindustri (3) Svensk Filmindustri (4) Paramount/Svenska Filminstitutet (5) Joseph E. Levine Productions/Personafilm/Filmédis/Incorporated Television Company/Suede Film (7) Clemi Cinematografica A2/Producteurs Associés/Président Films/Sorofilms (8) Danmarks Radio (DR)/Network Movie Film-und Fernsehproduktion/Nordisk Film- & TV-Fond/Nordiska TV-Samarbetsfonden/Norsk Rikskringkasting/RAI Radiotelevisione Italiana/SVT Filmkultur/Liberation Yleisradio/Zweites Deutsches Fernsehen/ Österreichischer Rundfunk 510 (1) Metro Pictures (2) Nazimova Productions (3) Metro Pictures (4) Paramount Pictures (5) Paramount Pictures/Famous Players-Lasky Corporation (6) Art Finance Corporation (7) Feature Productions (8) Famous Players-Lasky Corporation 511 (1) Del Duca Films/Antares Produzione Cinematografica (2) Nouvelles Éditions de Films (3) Movida Films/Les Films Odéon/Filmsonor (4) Les Productions Montaigne (5) Les Productions Fox Europa/Les Films du Siècle (6) Les Films Corona/Fono Roma (7) Produzione Europee Associati (8) Les Films Ariane/TF1 Films Production 512 (1) Cino del Duca/Productions Cinematographique Europee (P.C.E.)/Société Cinématographique Lyre (2) Nepi Film/Silver Films/Softedip (3) Cineriz/Interopa Film/Paris Film (4) Film Duemila/Federiz/Francoriz Production (5) Modesty Blaise Ltd./20th Century-Fox Productions (6) Cinematografica Lombarda/O.C.F./Neue Emelka (7) Komika Film/Gaumont (8) Jolly Film/Constantin Film Produktion/Ocean Films (2) Polifilm/Anouchka Films/CCC Filmkunst (3) Universal Films S.p.a. (4) Euro International Film/Les Films Corona/Selenia Cinematografica (5) Verona Produzione/Vides Cinematografica (6) Rai 2/Vides Cinematografica (7) Yarno Cinematografica (8) Italmedia Film/Les Films Ariane/France 3 Cinéma/Soprofilms/FOCINE/Rai 2 514 (1) Columbia Pictures Corporation/Robert M. Weitman Productions (2) Jack Rollins & Charles H. Joffe Productions (3) EMI Films/Universal Pictures (4) Partisan Productions (5) Reteitalia/Scena International/Caminito/The Rank Organisation (6) Miramax/A Band Apart/Jersey Films (7) Fast Films/Guild/October Films (8) Opening Night Productions/Concept Entertainment/Union Films Spring Pictures/RKO Pictures 515 (1) Universal Pictures/The Weinstein Company/A Band Apart/Studio Babelsberg/Visiona Romantica (2) Warner Bros./Heyday Films/Wild Bunch (4) Fox 2000 Pictures/3 Arts Entertainment/Flashpoint Entertainment/ Produktion/SPI Film Studio/Versátil Cinema/Zanagar Films/France 2 Cinéma/Canal+/CinéCinéma/France Télévisions/Polski Instytut Sztuki Filmowej/Wild Bunch (4) Fox 2000 Pictures/3 Arts Entertainment/Flashpoint Entertainment/ Dune Entertainment/Ingenious Media/Big Screen Productions/Impact Pictures/Nouvelles Éditions de films/Studio Babelsberg (6) The Weinstein Company/Columbia Pictures (7) Voltage Pictures/ Zanuck Independent/Zephyr Films/MediaPro Pictures/Le Pacte/Wild Side Films/Picture Perfect Corporation/Film Capital Europe Funds (8) The Weinstein Company/Silverwood Films/Tim Burton Productions/Electric City Entertainment 516 (1) First City/Herndale/RKO Pictures (2) Universal Pictures/Marble Arch Productions (3) TriStar Pictures/Freddie Fields Productions (4) Universal Pictures/40 Acres & A Mule Filmworks (5) Largo International N.V./JVC Entertainment Networks/40 Acres & A Mule Filmworks (6) Warner Bros. (7) TriStar Pictures/Clinica Estetico (8) Hollywood Pictures/Don Simpson/Jerry Bruckheimer Films 517 (1) TriStar Pictures/Clinica Estetico/Mundy Lane Entertainment (2) Azoff Entertainment/Beacon Communications/Universal Pictures (3) Warner Bros./Village Roadshow Pictures/NPV Entertainment/Outlaw Productions (I) /WV Films II (4) Universal Pictures/Imagine Entertainment/40 Acres & A Mule Filmworks/GH Two (5) Universal Pictures/Imagine Entertainment/Relativity Media/Scott Free Productions (6) Harpo Films/Marshall Production/The Weinstein Company (7) 40th Century Fox Film Corporation/Prospect Park/Scott Free Productions (8) Paramount Pictures/ImageMovers/Parkes+MacDonald Image Nation 518 (1) MGM (2) Walter Wanger Productions (3) Walter Wanger Productions/Argosy Pictures (4) Universal Pictures (5) Universal Pictures/Frank Lloyd Productions/Charles K. Feldman Group (6) MGM/Loew's (7) Argosy Pictures (8) Charles K. Feldman Group/Monterey Productions 519 (1) Republic Pictures (I) (2) Argosy Pictures (3) Republic Pictures (I)/Argosy Pictures (4) Warner Bros. (5) C.V. Whitney Pictures (6) Paramount Pictures/John Ford Productions (6) MGM/Cinerama Productions Corp (7) Otto Preminger Films (8) Paramount Pictures/ Skydance Productions/Scott Rudin Productions/Mike Zoss Productions 520 (1) 20th Century Fox Film Corporation (2) Paramount Pictures (3) Warner Brothers/Seven Arts (4) Columbia Pictures Corporation/Delphi IV Productions Films (5) Paramount Pictures/Skydance Productions/Mike Zoss Productions/Mike Zoss Productions (6) 20th Century Fox Film Corporation (7) Paramount Pictures (8) 20th Century Fox Film Corporation 521 (1) Morgan Creek Productions/20th Century Fox Film Corporation (2) Warner Bros./Malpaso Productions (3) Cinergi Pictures Entertainment/Hollywood Pictures (4) Warner Bros./Tig Productions/Kasdan Pictures/Paragon Entertainment Corporation (5) UK Film Council/Surefire Film Productions (6) Autonomous/Jackie O Productions/Pictures in Paradise/Pacific Film and Television Commission/Film Consortium/National Lottery through UK Film Council (6) Paramount Vantage/Miramax/Scott Rudin Productions/Mike Zoss Productions (7) Skydance Productions/Scott Rudin Productions/Mike Zoss Productions (8) Di Bonaventura Pictures 522 (1) Brandywine Productions/20th Century Fox Productions (2) McElroy & McElroy/MGM (3) Black Rhino Productions/Delphi Films (4) 20th Century Fox Film Corporation/Brandywine Productions/SLM Production Group (5) 20th Century Fox Film Corporation (6) Universal Pictures/Warner Bros./The Guber-Peters Company (7) Fox Searchlight Pictures/Good Machine/Canal+ Droits Audiovisuels (8) 20th Century Fox Film Corporation/Dune Entertainment/Ingenious Film Partners/Lightstorm Entertainment 523 (1) Paramount Pictures (2) MGM (3) MGM (4) MGM (5) Pimp-Thomas Productions (6) Esskay Pictures Corporation (7) The Katzman Corporation (8) Clover Productions 524 (1) RKO Radio Pictures/Mercury Productions (2) 20th Century Fox Film Corporation (3) International Pictures (I)/The Haig Corporation (4) Columbia Pictures Corporation/Mercury Productions (5) Mercury Productions (6) Carol Reed's Production/London Film Productions (7) Mercury Productions/Les Films Marceau (8) Filmonza/Cervantes Films/Sevilla Films/Mercury Productions/Bavaria Film 525 (1) Touchstone Pictures/ Wald Productions (2) Universal International Pictures (UI) (4) Paris-Europa Productions/Hisa-Film/Finanziaria Cinematografica Italiana (FICIT) (5) Alpine Films/Internacional Films (6) Highland Films (7) Paramount Pictures/Filmways Productions (8) BBS Productions/Columbia Pictures Corporation/The Rainbow Film Company/ 526 (1) Paramount Pictures (2) Paramount Pictures (3) Paramount Pictures (4) Paramount Pictures (5) Emanuel Cohen Productions (6) Paramount Pictures (7) Briggs and Sullivan 527 (1) Touchstone Pictures/Silver Screen Partners II (2) Touchstone Pictures/Silver Screen Partners III (3) The Malpaso Company/Warner Bros. (4) Palace Pictures/Channel Four Films/Eurotrustees/Nippon Film Development and Finance/British Screen Productions (5) Pandora Cinema/Arbeitsgemeinschaft der öffentlich-rechtlichen Rundfunkanstalten der Bundesrepublik Deutschland/Degeto Film/Playwood Productions/Bac Films/Canal+/JVC Entertainment Networks (6) Columbia Pictures Corporation/Hoffland/Polone/Indelible Pictures (7) Fox Searchlight Pictures/The Alamo Company (8) Film Council/Scottish Screen/Cowboy Films/Slate Films/Tatfilm (8) Follow Through Productions/Salamander Pictures/AI-Film/Laura Ziskin Productions/Lee Daniels Entertainment/Pam Williams Productions/Windy Hill Pictures 528 (1) 20th Century Fox Film Corporation (2) 20th Century Fox Film Corporation (3) 20th Century Fox Film Corporation (4) Paramount Pictures/Walt Disney Productions (5) Touchstone Pictures/Silver Screen Partners III (6) TriStar Pictures/Silver Screen Partners IV (8) Columbia Pictures Corporation Pictures/Bedford Productions Ltd. (8) MGM 529 (1) Paramount Pictures/Walt Disney Feature Animation (6) Blue Wolf/20th Century Fox Film Corporation (8) Be Gentlemen Limited Partnership/Lawrence Bender Productions/Miramax (8) Fox Searchlight Pictures/Catch 23 Entertainment/Killer Films/Laughlin Park Pictures/Madjak Films (2) Douglas Fairbanks Pictures (2) Toho Company (3) MGM (4) Eon Productions/Danjaq (5) Fox Productions (6) Paramount Pictures/ Lucasfilm (7) Paramount Pictures/Eddie Murphy Productions (8) Cannon Group/Golan-Globus Productions/Warner Bros. 531 (1) Amercent Films/American Entertainment Partners L.P./Davis Entertainment/Lawrence Gordon Productions/Silver Pictures/20th Century Fox Film Corporation (2) Warner Bros./Silver Pictures (3) 20th Century Fox Film Corporation/Gordon Company/Silver Pictures (4) Largo Entertainment/JVC Entertainment Networks (5) United Seven Combines/Venus Movies (6) Paramount Pictures/Cruise/Wagner Productions (7) Forge/New Line Cinema (8) Lakeshore Entertainment/Lions Gate Films/Radical Media/GreeneStreet Films 532 (1) TriStar Pictures/ Permut Presentations/Delphi V Productions/Prmut Presentations (2) 20th Century Fox Film Corporation/Gordon Company/Silver Pictures (3) 20th Century Fox Film Corporation/New Visions Pictures (7) Touchstone Pictures/Blinding Edge Pictures/Barry Mendel Productions (8) Endgame Entertainment/JVC Entertainment/FilmDistrict/Ram Bergman Productions (3) Be Gentlemen Limited Partnership/Lawrence Bender Productions/Miramax (6) American Playhouse/ Cinecom Pictures/Cinéfudes Films (3) Harpo Productions/King Phoenix Entertainment (4) LOMCO Productions (5) Harpo Films (6) Harpo Films/Clinica Estetico/Touchstone Pictures (7) Follow Through Productions/Salamander Pictures/AI-Film/Laura Ziskin Productions/Lee Daniels Entertainment/Pam Williams Productions/Windy Hill Pictures (8) Cloud Eight Films/Celador Films/Harpo/Pathé/Plan B Entertainment 534 (1) WingNut Films/New Zealand Film Commission/Fontana Productions (2) Lee Daniels Entertainment/Lightstorm Entertainment (3) British Broadcasting Corporation/PolyGram Filmed Entertainment/Revolution Films (4) Castle Rock Entertainment/Turner Pictures (I)/Fishmonger Films (5) 20th Century Fox Film Corporation/Paramount Pictures/Lightstorm Entertainment (6) Manhattan Pictures International/Intermedia Films/Senator Film Produktion/Meesperson Film CV/Jagged Films/ Broadway Video/Multimedia Pictures BV (7) British Broadcasting Corporation/Fox Iris Productions/Intermedia Films/Mirage Enterprises/Miramax (8) Focus Features/Anonymous Content/This Is That Productions 535 (1) Miramax/ FilmColony (2) New Line Cinema/Bona Fide Productions/Standard Film Company (3) The Weinstein Company/Mirage Enterprises/Studio Babelsberg/Filmförderungsanstalt/Deutsche Filmförderfonds/Medienboard Berlin-Brandenburg/Mitteldeutsche Medienförderung/Filmstiftung Nordrhein-Westfalen (4) DreamWorks SKG/BBC Films/Evamere Entertainment/Neal Street Productions/Scott Rudin Productions (5) SBS Productions (6) Participant Media/Imagenation Abu Dhabi FZ/Double Feature Films/Regency Enterprises (7) Indian Paintbrush/Mr. Mudd/Right of Way Films (8) Summit Entertainment/Red Wagon Entertainment 536 (1) Wingnut/Fontana/The Kobal Collection tr Columbia/The Kobal Collection b 20th Century Fox/Paramount/The Kobal Collection 537 tr Focus Features/The Kobal Collection cl Film Colony/The Kobal Collection cr Weinstein Company. The/The Kobal Collection bl SBS Productions/The Kobal Collection br Indian Paintbrush/The Kobal Collection 538 (1) 20th Century Fox Film Corporation (2) Warner Bros. (3) Warner Bros./Newton Productions/NBI Productions (4) Paramount Pictures/Seven Arts Pictures (5) Columbia Pictures Corporation/Frankovich Productions 539 (1) Paramount Famous Lasky Corporation (2) Paramount Pictures (3) Columbia Pictures Corporation (4) RKO Radio Pictures (5) Warner Bros./The Vitaphone Corporation (6) RKO Radio Pictures (7) MGM (8) Gaumont British Picture Corporation 540 (1) D & B Films Co. Ltd. (2) Golden Harvest Company/Golden Way Films Ltd. (3) Fuji Television Network/Golden Harvest Company/Pony Canyon (4) Danjaq/Eon Productions/MGM/United Artists (5) Asia Union Film & Entertainment Ltd./China Film Co-Production Corporation/Columbia Pictures Film Production Asia/Edko Films/Good Machine/Sony Pictures Classics/United China Vision/Zoom Hunt International Productions (6) Columbia Pictures Corporation/DreamWorks SKG/Spyglass Entertainment/Amblin Entertainment/Red Wagon Entertainment (7) Beijing Gallop Horse Film & TV Production/Media Asia Films/Zhejiang Dongyang Degen Entertainment Venture Investment/Lumiere Motion Picture Company/Beijing Heguchuan TV & Film/Lion Rock Productions/Stellar Entertainment (8) EuropaCorp/Left Bank Pictures/France 2 Cinéma/Canal+/France Télévision/Siam Movies 541 (1) D & B Films Co. Ltd. (2) Film Workshop/Golden Princess Film Production (3) Win's Movie Productions Ltd. (4) Golden Princess Film Production Limited/Milestone Pictures/Pioneer LDC (5) Columbia Pictures Corporation/Britstein-Grey Entertainment/WCG Entertainment Productions (6) Fox 2000 Pictures/Lawrence Bender Productions (7) Asia Union Film & Entertainment Ltd./China Film Co-Production Corporation (8) Walt Disney Pictures/Jerry Bruckheimer Productions/Second Mate Productions 542 (1) TriStar Pictures/Amblin Entertainment/David Foster Productions/Global Entertainment Productions GmbH & Company Medien KG/Zorro Productions (2) 20th Century Fox Film Corporation/Regency Enterprises/Fountainbridge Films/Taurus Film (3) The Bedford Falls Company/Compulsion Inc./Initial Entertainment Group/USA Films/Splendid Medien AG (4) Miramax/Producers Circle/Storyline Entertainment/Kalis Productions GmbH & Co. KG (5) Universal Pictures/Imagine Entertainment/Alphaville Films/Mike Zoss Productions (6) Warner Bros. /Village Roadshow Pictures/Jerry Weintraub Productions/Section Eight/WV Films III (7) Castle Rock Entertainment/Storefront Pictures/Village Roadshow Pictures/WV Films III/Warner Bros. (8) Endgame Entertainment/FilmNation Entertainment/Di Bonaventura Pictures 543 (1) Columbia Pictures Film Production Asia/Guangxi Film Studio (2) Asia Union Film & Entertainment Ltd./China Film Co-Production Corporation/Columbia Pictures Film Production Asia/Edko Films/Good Machine/Sony Pictures Classics/United China Vision/Zoom Hunt International Productions (3) New Line Cinema/Roger Birnbaum Productions/Salon Films (4) Beijing New Picture Film Co./China Film Co-Production Corporation/Edko Films/Elite Group Enterprises/Zhang Yimou Studio (5) Jet Tone Films/Shanghai Film Group/Orly Films/Paradis Films/ Classic/Precious Yield/Arte France Cinéma 3 Cinéma/ZDF/Arte (6) Jingxue Jimusyo Co./Dentsu/Eisei Gekijo/Geneon Entertainment/Nippon Herald Films/Shochiku Company (7) CJ Entertainment/China Film Group/ Perfect World (Beijing) Co./Sophie Production (8) Block 2 Pictures/Jet Tone Films/Sil-Metropole Organisation/Bona International Film Group

Award symbols: Academy Award® ©A.M.P.A.S.®; Golden Globe ® © Hollywood Foreign Press Association; BAFTA ® British Academy of Film and Television Arts; Cannes Film Festival © Festival de Cannes; Berlin Film Festival © Berlinale; Venice Film Festival © la Biennale di Venezia; Goya® ® Academia de las Artes y las Ciencias Cinematográficas de España; Golden Horse Film Festival © Taipei Golden Horse Film Festival Executive Committee